To B[...]
Hoping [...]
be needing this too
soon!
   Merry Christmas 1988.
   Lots of love,
      Brian & Lucille
         xxx

# THE
AUSTRALIAN
LITTLE OXFORD
DICTIONARY

# THE AUSTRALIAN LITTLE OXFORD DICTIONARY

Edited by
GEORGE TURNER

Based on
THE LITTLE OXFORD DICTIONARY
OF CURRENT ENGLISH

MELBOURNE
OXFORD UNIVERSITY PRESS
1987

*Oxford University Press*

*Melbourne Oxford New York Toronto
Delhi Bombay Calcutta Madras Karachi
Petaling Jaya Singapore Hong Kong Tokyo
Nairobi Dar es Salaam Cape Town
Auckland*

*and associated companies in
Beirut Berlin Ibadan Nicosia*

*Oxford is a trade mark of Oxford University Press*

© *Oxford University Press 1969, 1980, 1986*

*First edition 1930
Sixth edition 1986*

*First Australian edition 1987
Reprinted 1988*

*This book is copyright. Apart from any fair dealing
for the purposes of private study, research, criticism or review,
as permitted under the Copyright Act, no part may be reproduced
by any process without written permission.
Inquiries should be made to the publishers.*

*National Library of Australia Cataloguing in Publication Data*

*The Australian Little Oxford dictionary.*

*ISBN 0 19 554734 9.*

*1. English language—Dictionaries. 2. English
language—Australia. I. Turner, G. W. (George
William), 1921- . II. Title: The Little Oxford
dictionary of current English.
423*

*Printed in Australia by
The Book Printer, Victoria
Published by Oxford University Press,
253 Normanby Road,
South Melbourne, Australia*

# Contents

| | |
|---|---:|
| Preface to the Australian Edition | vii |
| Introduction | ix |
| Pronunciation | xi |
| Abbreviations used in the Dictionary | xii |
| Note on proprietary terms | xiv |
| DICTIONARY | 1 |
| Appendices | |
| I. Countries of the world and related adjectives | 668 |
| II. The metric system of weights and measures | 673 |

# Preface to the Australian Edition

The *Australian Little Oxford Dictionary* is closely based on *The Little Oxford Dictionary*, sixth edition, edited by Julia Swannell, who has given valuable assistance at every stage of its Australianization.

All entries have been reconsidered with Australian relevance in mind and many Australian items have been added. The pronunciation has been entirely revised to record educated Australian usage.

January 1987                                                                                           G. W. T.

# Introduction

**throw** /θrəʊ/ **1** *v.* (*past* **threw**; *p.p.* **thrown**) release (thing) after imparting motion, propel through space, send forth or dismiss esp. with some violence; compel to be in specified condition; project (rays, light, etc.); cast (shadow); bring to the ground; *colloq.* disconcert; put (clothes etc.) carelessly or hastily *on* or *off* etc.; cause (dice) to fall on table etc., obtain (specified number) thus; cause to pass or extend suddenly to another state or position; move (switch or lever) to on position; shape (pottery) on wheel; have (fit, tantrum, etc.); *colloq.* give (a party). **2** *n.* act of throwing; distance a missile is or may be thrown; being thrown in wrestling. **3 throw away** part with as unwanted, lose by neglect, waste, fail to make use of; **throw-away** (thing) to be thrown away after (one) use, deliberately under-emphasized; **throw back** (usu. in *pass.*) compel to rely *on*; **throwback** reversion to ancestral character, instance of this; **throw in** add as makeweight, interpose (word, remark), throw (football) from edge of pitch where it has gone out of play; **throw off** discard, contrive to get rid of, write or utter in offhand manner; **throw out** put out forcibly or suddenly, reject, confuse or distract; **throw over** desert, abandon; **throw up** abandon, resign from, vomit, erect, bring to notice.

1. The headword appears in bold: **throw**.

2. A guide to pronunciation is given, when necessary, in IPA (see page xi): /θrəʊ/.

3. The part of speech is given in italics: *v.* (and later *n.*). It is preceded by a bold number (**1**, **2**) if the headword exists as more than one part of speech.

4. Inflexional forms such as irregularly-formed past tenses are given in bold: (*past* **threw**; *p.p.* **thrown**). Irregularly-formed present participles (for example **lying** at the entry for **lie**¹) and comparatives and superlatives of adjectives and adverbs (for example **better** and **best** at the entry for **good**) are given in the same way.

5. Labels to indicate that a word or sense is restricted to a particular level of formality or to a particular subject are given in italics: *colloq.*, *sl.*, *Law*, *Crick.*, etc.

6. Round brackets () are used to enclose words that are explanatory or optional; for example 'release (thing) after imparting motion', or 'project (rays, light, etc.)', indicating the type of noun that often appears as the object of this verb; '**throw-away** (thing) to be thrown away', indicating that 'throw-away' can be an adjective meaning 'to be thrown away' *or* a noun meaning 'a thing to be thrown away'.

7. Words such as prepositions or adverbs which are commonly used with the headword in any particular sense are given in italic. For example 'put (clothes etc.) hastily *on* or *off* etc.' indicates that the usual construction would be 'to throw one's clothes on' or 'to throw one's clothes off' or any similar phrase.

8. Phrases and combinations involving the headword are listed together in strict alphabetical order, followed by any derivatives of obvious meaning, which are included without definition:

> **hole 1** *n.* cavity in solid body; opening through or sunken place on surface; burrow; *colloq.* small or gloomy place; *sl.* awkward situation; cavity into which ball must be got in some games, *Golf* section of course from tee to hole. **2** *v.* make hole(s) in; hit golf-ball into hole. **3 hole-and-corner** underhand; **hole up** *sl.* hide oneself. **4 holey** *a.*

9. When a word normally written with a lower-case initial letter also has a sense in which it is written with a capital letter, or vice versa, this is indicated by the word being repeated with the capital (or lower case) initial letter:

> **Apostle** /ə'pɒs(ə)l/ *n.* any of twelve sent forth by Christ to preach gospel; **apostle** leader of reform.

10. Headwords which are foreign and not fully naturalized in English are given in bold italics, and an indication of the language or origin is given in square brackets at the end of the entry:

> ***métier*** /'metjeɪ/ *n.* one's trade or profession; one's forte. [F]

11. Space has been saved by not listing obvious and regularly-formed derivatives such as agent-nouns in *-er* (for example *player*), nouns in *-ness* (for example *kindness*), or adverbs in *-ly* (for example *bravely*).

# Pronunciation

Guidance on pronunciation follows the system of the International Phonetic Alphabet (IPA). Only Educated Australian pronunciation is given. Where more than one permissible pronunciation exists, constraints of space have often compelled the omission of any but a preferred form.

## International Phonetic Alphabet

### Consonants

The following consonants have their usual English sound-values: b, d, f, h, k, l, m, n, p, r, s, t, v, w, z.

| | | |
|---|---|---|
| g as in go | ʃ as in ship | tʃ as in chin |
| ŋ as in sing | ʒ as in vision | dʒ as in jam |
| θ as in thin | j as in yet | |
| ð as in then | x (Scots etc.) as in loch | |

### Vowels

| | | |
|---|---|---|
| æ as in fat | ʊ as in book | eɪ as in fate |
| ɑ: as in cart | u: as in boot | eə(r) as in fare |
| e as in met | ɜ: as in fur | ɪə(r) as in fear |
| ɪ as in bit | ə as in ago, taker | ɔɪ as in boil |
| i: as in meet | aɪ as in bite | ʊə(r) as in tour |
| ɒ as in got | aʊ as in brow | əʊ as in goat |
| ɔ: as in port | aɪə(r) as in fire | |
| ʌ as in dug | aʊə(r) as in sour | |

Stress is indicated by ˈ preceding the relevant syllable.

˜ over a vowel indicates nasalization as in French *ancien régime* (ãsɪæ̃ reɪˈʒi:m)

# Abbreviations used in the Dictionary

Abbreviations that are in general use appear in the dictionary itself.

| | | | |
|---|---|---|---|
| a. | adjective | compar. | comparative |
| abbr(s). | abbreviation(s) | conj. | conjunction |
| abs. | absolute | Crick. | cricket |
| adj(s). | adjective(s) | derog. | derogatory |
| adv(s). | adverb(s) | dial. | dialect |
| Aeron. | aeronautics | Eccl. | ecclesiastical |
| Afr. | African | Econ. | economics |
| Alg. | algebra | Electr. | electricity |
| Amer. | America(n) | emphat. | emphatic |
| Anat. | anatomy | Engl. | English |
| ant. | antiquities | erron. | erroneous |
| approx. | approximately | esp. | especialy |
| arch. | archaic | euphem. | euphemistic |
| Archit. | architecture | Eur. | Europe(an) |
| Astrol. | astrology | exc. | except |
| Astron. | astronomy | expr. | expressing |
| attrib. | attributive(ly) | F | French |
| Aus. | Australian | fem. | feminine |
| aux. | auxiliary | fig. | figurative |
| Bibl. | biblical | Footb. | football |
| Biol. | biology | freq. | frequently |
| Bot. | botany | fut. | future |
| c. | century | G | German |
| C.Amer. | Central America(n) | Geog. | geography |
| | | Geol. | geology |
| Can. | Canadian | Geom. | geometry |
| cc. | centuries | Gk | Greek |
| Ch. | Church | Gmc | Germanic |
| Chem. | chemistry | Gram. | grammar |
| Cinemat. | cinematography | Her. | heraldry |
| collect. | collective(ly) | Hist. | history |
| colloq. | colloquial | imper. | imperative |
| comb. | combination | impers. | impersonal |
| Commerc. | commercial | Ind. | Indian |

# ABBREVIATIONS

| | | | |
|---|---|---|---|
| inf. | infinitive | poet. | poetical |
| int. | interjection | Polit. | political |
| interrog. | interrogative | pop. | popularly, not technically |
| intr. | intransitive | | |
| Ir. | Irish | poss. | possessive (case) |
| iron. | ironical | p.p. | past participle |
| It. | Italian | pr. | pronounced |
| joc. | jocular | pred. | predicative |
| L | Latin | pref. | prefix |
| Math. | mathematics | prep. | preposition |
| Mech. | mechanics | pres. | present (tense) |
| Med. | medicine | Print. | printing |
| Metaphys. | metaphysics | pron(s). | pronoun(s) |
| Meteor. | meteorology | Psych. | psychology |
| Mil. | military | refl. | reflexive |
| Mus. | music | rel. | relative |
| Myth. | mythology | Rom. | Roman |
| n. | noun | Sc. | Scottish |
| Naut. | nautical | sing. | singular |
| neg. | negative | sl. | slang |
| ns. | nouns | Sp. | Spanish |
| obj. | objective (case) | St. Exch. | Stock Exchange |
| occas. | occasionally | subj. | subjective (case) |
| opp. | opposed to | superl. | superlative |
| orig. | originally | Theatr. | theatre |
| **P** | proprietary term (see below) | Theol. | theology |
| | | trans. | transitive |
| Parl. | parliament(ary) | transf. | transferred |
| partic. | (esp. present) participle | univ. | university |
| | | usu. | usually |
| pass. | passive | v. | verb |
| pers. | person(al) | vbl. | verbal |
| Philos. | philosophical | vbs. | verbs |
| Phon. | phonetics | v.i. | verb intransitive |
| Photog. | photography | v.t. | verb transitive |
| Phys. | physics | vulg. | vulgar |
| Physiol. | physiology | Zool. | zoology |
| pl. | plural | | |

# Note on proprietary terms

This dictionary includes some words which are, or are asserted to be, proprietary names or trade marks. Their inclusion does not imply that they have acquired for legal purposes a non-proprietary or general significance, nor is any other judgement implied concerning their legal status. In cases where the editor has some evidence that a word is used as a proprietary name or trade mark this is indicated by the letter **P**, but no judgement concerning the legal status of such words is made or implied thereby.

# A

**a, an,** /ə, ən; *emphat.* eɪ, æn/ *a.* one, some, any, to or for each.

**A** *abbr.* ampere(s); Australian.

**AA** *abbr.* anti-aircraft; Automobile Association; Alcoholics Anonymous.

**aback** /ə'bæk/ *adv.* backwards, behind; **taken aback** disconcerted, surprised.

**abacus** /'æbəkəs/ *n.* (*pl.* **-cuses**) frame with wires along which beads are slid for calculating.

**abaft** /ə'bɑːft/ **1** *adv. Naut.* in or towards stern of ship. **2** *prep.* behind.

**abalone** /æbə'ləʊnɪ/ *n.* an edible mollusc.

**abandon** /ə'bænd(ə)n/ **1** *v.t.* give up, forsake. **2** *n.* reckless freedom.

**abandoned** *a.* forsaken; profligate.

**abandonment** *n.* reckless freedom.

**abase** /ə'beɪs/ *v.t.* humiliate; degrade. **abasement** *n.*

**abashed** /ə'bæʃt/ *a.* embarrassed; disconcerted.

**abate** /ə'beɪt/ *v.* make or become less; diminish. **abatement** *n.*

**abattoir** /'æbətwɑː(r)/ *n.* slaughterhouse.

**abbess** /'æbes/ *n.* female head of abbey of nuns.

**abbey** /'æbɪ/ *n.* building occupied by community of monks or nuns; such community; church or house that was formerly abbey.

**abbot** /'æbət/ *n.* head of abbey of monks.

**abbreviate** /ə'briːvɪeɪt/ *v.t.* shorten. **abbreviation** *n.*

**ABC** /eɪbiː'siː/ **1** *abbr.* Australian Broadcasting Corporation. **2** *n.* alphabet; rudiments of subject; alphabetical guide.

**abdicate** /'æbdəkeɪt/ *v.* renounce or resign from (throne etc.); renounce throne. **abdication** *n.*

**abdomen** /'æbdəmən/ *n.* belly; hinder part of insect etc. **abdominal** /-'dɒm-/ *a.*

**abduct** /æb'dʌkt/ *v.t.* carry off (person) illegally by force or fraud. **abduction** *n.*; **abductor** *n.*

**aberrant** /æ'berənt/ *a.* showing aberration. **aberrance** *n.*

**aberration** /æbə'reɪʃ(ə)n/ *n.* departure from normal type or accepted standard; deviation from biological type; distortion.

**abet** /ə'bet/ *v.t.* encourage or assist (offender or offence). **abetter**, (in *Law*) **abettor**, *n.*

**abeyance** /ə'beɪəns/ *n.* temporary disuse; suspension.

**abhor** /əb'hɔː(r)/ *v.t.* regard with disgust and hatred.

**abhorrence** /əb'hɒrəns/ *n.* disgust, hatred.

**abhorrent** *a.* disgusting *to*.

**abide** /ə'baɪd/ *v.* (*past* & *p.p.* **abode** or **abided**) tolerate; *arch.* remain, continue. **abide by** act upon, remain faithful to.

**abiding** /ə'baɪdɪŋ/ *a.* permanent.

**ability** /ə'bɪlətɪ/ *n.* sufficient power or being able (*to do*); cleverness; talent.

**abject** /'æbdʒekt/ *a.* degraded; craven. **abjection** *n.*

**abjure** /əb'dʒʊə(r)/ *v.t.* renounce on oath. **abjuration** *n.*

**ablaze** /ə'bleɪz/ *pred.a.* on fire; glittering; excited.

**able** /'eɪb(ə)l/ *a.* having power (*to do*); talented. **able-bodied** healthy, fit; **able rating, seaman,** one fit for all duties. **ably** *adv.*

**ablution** /ə'bluːʃ(ə)n/ *n.* usu. in *pl.* ceremonial washing of hands etc.; *colloq.* washing onself, place for this.

**ably**: see **able**.

**abnegate** /'æbnəgeɪt/ *v.t.* give up, renounce. **abnegation** *n.*

**abnormal** /æb'nɔːm(ə)l/ *a.* exceptional; deviating from its type. **abnormality** *n.*

**aboard** /ə'bɔːd/ *adv.* & *prep.* on board.

**abode**[1] *n. arch.* dwelling-place.

**abode**[2] *past* & *p.p.* of **abide**.

**abolish** /ə'bɒlɪʃ/ *v.t.* end existence of. **abolition** /æbə'lɪʃ(ə)n/ *n.*

**abolitionist** /æbə'lɪʃənɪst/ *n.* person who favours abolition (esp. of capital punishment).

**A-bomb** /'eɪbɒm/ *n.* atomic bomb.

**abominable** /ə'bɒmənəb(ə)l/ *a.* detestable, loathsome. **Abominable Snowman** yeti.

**abominate** /ə'bɒməneɪt/ *v.t.* detest, loathe.

**abomination** /əbɒməˈneɪʃ(ə)n/ n. loathing or disgust; object etc. deserving this.

**aboriginal** /æbəˈrɪdʒən(ə)l/ 1 a. indigenous; of the Australian Aborigines. 2 n. aboriginal inhabitant, esp. (**Aboriginal**) of Australia.

**aborigines** /æbəˈrɪdʒəniːz/ n.pl. aboriginal inhabitants, esp. (**Aborigines**) of Australia.

**abort** /əˈbɔːt/ v. cause or undergo abortion; (cause to) remain undeveloped; bring or come to premature end.

**abortion** /əˈbɔːʃ(ə)n/ n. natural or (esp.) induced premature expulsion of foetus, esp. in first 28 weeks of pregnancy; stunted or misshapen creature. **abortionist** n.

**abortive** /əˈbɔːtɪv/ a. producing abortion; unsuccessful.

**abound** /əˈbaʊnd/ v.i. be plentiful; be rich in; teem with.

**about** /əˈbaʊt/ 1 prep. pertaining to; in connection with; on subject of; surrounding; somewhere near; here and there. 2 adv. approximately; here and there; on the move, in action; all around; facing in opposite direction. 3 **about turn** turn made so as to face in opposite direction, reversal of policy etc.; **be about to** intend to (do something).

**above** /əˈbʌv/ 1 prep. over, higher than; more than; of higher rank, importance, etc. than; out of reach of, too good for. 2 adv. at or to higher point; overhead; in addition; further back in book etc. 3 **above-board** without concealment.

**abracadabra** /æbrəkəˈdæbrə/ n. magic formula, spell; gibberish.

**abrade** /əˈbreɪd/ v.t. scrape or wear away by rubbing.

**abrasion** /əˈbreɪʒ(ə)n/ n. rubbing or scraping away; area of damage made thus.

**abrasive** /əˈbreɪsɪv/ 1 a. capable of rubbing or grinding down; harsh and offensive in manner. 2 n. abrasive substance.

**abreast** /əˈbrest/ adv. side by side and facing same way. **abreast of** up to date with.

**abridge** /əˈbrɪdʒ/ v.t. condense, shorten. **abridgement** n.

**abroad** /əˈbrɔːd/ adv. in or to a foreign country; at large, over a wide area.

**abrogate** /ˈæbrəgeɪt/ v.t. repeal, cancel. **abrogation** n.

**abrupt** /əˈbrʌpt/ a. sudden, hasty; disjointed; steep.

**abscess** /ˈæbses/ n. swollen area of body in which pus gathers.

**abscond** /æbˈskɒnd/ v.i. go away secretly; flee from law.

**abseil** /ˈæbseɪl/ 1 n. descent of rockface by using doubled rope fixed at higher point. 2 v.i. make abseil.

**absence** /ˈæbsəns/ n. being away; non-existence or lack of. **absence of mind** inattentiveness.

**absent** 1 /ˈæbsənt/ a. not present, not existing. 2 /æbˈsent/ v.refl. **absent oneself** go or keep away. 3 **absent-minded** forgetful, inattentive.

**absentee** /æbsənˈtiː/ n. person not present, esp. at work or on his property.

**absenteeism** /æbsənˈtiːɪz(ə)m/ n. practice of absenting oneself from work esp. illicitly.

**absinthe** /ˈæbsɪnθ/ n. liqueur orig. flavoured with wormwood.

**absolute** /ˈæbsəluːt/ a. complete, perfect; unrestricted; independent; despotic; not relative; out of (ordinary) grammatical relation. **absolute majority** one over all rivals combined; **absolute temperature** one measured from absolute zero; **absolute zero** lowest possible temperature (-273°C).

**absolutely** adv. completely, without restrictions; colloq. quite so, yes.

**absolution** /æbsəˈluːʃ(ə)n/ n. formal forgiveness of sins.

**absolutism** /ˈæbsəluːtɪz(ə)m/ n. principle of government with unlimited powers. **absolutist** n. & a.

**absolve** /əbˈzɒlv/ v.t. set or pronounce free of blame or obligation.

**absorb** /əbˈsɔːb/ v.t. swallow up; assimilate; suck in; deal with easily, reduce intensity of; engross attention or interest of.

**absorbent** /əbˈsɔːbənt/ a. having tendency to absorb. **absorbency** n.

**absorption** /əbˈsɔːpʃ(ə)n/ n. absorbing, being absorbed. **absorptive** a.

**abstain** /əbˈsteɪn/ v.i. refrain, esp. from alcohol; decline to use one's vote.

**abstemious** /æbˈstiːmɪəs/ a. sparing or moderate, esp. in eating and drinking.

**abstention** /əbˈstenʃ(ə)n/ n. abstaining, esp. not using one's vote.

**abstinence** /ˈæbstənəns/ n. abstaining from an indulgence, esp. food or alcohol. **abstinent** a.

**abstract 1** /ˈæbstrækt/ a. to do with or existing in theory rather than practice, not concrete; (of painting etc.) not representational. **2** /əbˈstrækt/ v.t. remove; summarize. **3** /ˈæbstrækt/ n. summary; abstract idea or painting etc. **4 abstraction** n.

**abstracted** a. inattentive.

**abstruse** /æbˈstruːs/ a. hard to understand; profound.

**absurd** /əbˈsɜːd/ a. wildly inappropriate; ridiculous. **absurdity** n.

**abundance** /əˈbʌnd(ə)ns/ n. quantity more than enough; plenty; wealth. **abundant** a. plentiful; rich.

**abuse 1** /əˈbjuːz/ v.t. make bad use of; maltreat; attack verbally. **2** /əˈbjuːs/ n. misuse; corrupt practice; offensive language.

**abusive** /əˈbjuːsɪv/ a. using insulting language; insulting.

**abut** /əˈbʌt/ v. adjoin, border *on*; touch or lean *on* or *against*.

**abysmal** /əˈbɪzm(ə)l/ a. very bad.

**abyss** /əˈbɪs/ n. bottomless or deep chasm.

**AC** abbr. alternating current; Companion of the Order of Australia.

**a/c** abbr. account.

**acacia** /əˈkeɪʃə/ n. tree with yellow or white flowers; *Aus.* wattle.

**academic** /ækəˈdemɪk/ **1** a. scholarly; to do with learning; not of practical relevance. **2** n. member of scholarly institution. **3 academically** adv.

**academician** /əkædəˈmɪʃ(ə)n/ n. member of an Academy.

**academy** /əˈkædəmɪ/ n. place of study; place of special training; *Sc.* secondary school; **Academy** society for cultivating art and learning etc.

**acanthus** /əˈkænθəs/ n. herbaceous plant with prickly leaves.

**accede** /əkˈsiːd/ v.i. take office; come *to* throne; join party; assent *to*.

**accelerate** /əkˈseləreɪt/ v. make or become quicker; (cause to) happen earlier. **acceleration** n.

**accelerator** /əkˈseləreɪtə(r)/ n. device for increasing speed, esp. pedal that controls speed of motor vehicle; *Phys.* apparatus for producing fast charged particles.

**accent 1** /ˈæksənt/ n. prominence given to syllable by stress or pitch; local or national mode of pronunciation; mark indicating stress, vowel quality, etc.; emphasis. **2** /ækˈsent/ v.t. pronounce with accent; write accents on; emphasize.

**accentuate** /ækˈsentjueɪt/ v.t. emphasize, make prominent. **accentuation** n.

**accept** /əkˈsept/ v. consent to receive; answer affirmatively (invitation etc.); regard with favour; receive as valid or suitable. **acceptance** n.

**acceptable** /əkˈseptəb(ə)l/ a. worth accepting, welcome; tolerable. **acceptability** n.

**access** /ˈækses/ **1** n. means of admission, approach; attack, outburst, esp. *of* emotion. **2** v.t. obtain (data) from computer etc.

**accessible** /əkˈsesəb(ə)l/ a. able to be reached or obtained or understood. **accessibility** n.

**accession** /əkˈseʃ(ə)n/ n. acceding esp. *to* throne; thing added.

**accessory** /əkˈsesərɪ/ **1** n. additional or extra thing, (esp. in *pl.*) thing serving as accompaniment; person who helps in or is privy *to* illegal act. **2** a. additional, extra.

**accidence** /ˈæksəd(ə)ns/ n. part of grammar dealing with inflexions.

**accident** /ˈæksəd(ə)nt/ n. event without apparent cause; unexpected event; unintentional act; unfortunate esp. harmful event.

**accidental** /æksəˈdent(ə)l/ **1** a. happening or done by accident. **2** n. *Mus.* sharp, flat, or natural attached to single note and not in key signature.

**acclaim** /əˈkleɪm/ **1** v.t. welcome loudly; hail. **2** n. shout of applause, welcome, etc.

**acclamation** /ækləˈmeɪʃ(ə)n/ n. loud and eager assent.

**acclimatize** /əˈklaɪmətaɪz/ v. accustom or become accustomed to new climate or conditions. **acclimatization** n.

**acclivity** /əˈklɪvɪtɪ/ n. upward slope.

**accolade** /ˈækəleɪd/ n. bestowal of praise; sign at bestowal of knighthood.

**accommodate** /əˈkɒmədeɪt/ v.t. provide lodging for; do favour to; supply *with*; adapt, harmonize, reconcile.

**accommodating** *a*. obliging.

**accommodation** /əkɒməˈdeɪʃ(ə)n/ *n*. lodging; adaptation, adjustment; convenient arrangement. **accommodation address** one used on letters to person without permanent address.

**accompaniment** /əˈkʌmpənəmənt/ *n*. instrumental or orchestral part supporting singer(s) or solo instrument etc.; accompanying thing.

**accompanist** /əˈkʌmpənəst/ *n. Mus.* person who plays accompaniment.

**accompany** /əˈkʌmpəni/ *v.t.* go with, escort, attend; be done or found with; supplement; *Mus.* play accompaniment for.

**accomplice** /əˈkʌmpləs/ *n*. partner in crime.

**accomplish** /əˈkʌmplɪʃ/ *v.t.* perform, carry out; succeed in doing.

**accomplished** *a*. clever; skilled.

**accomplishment** *n*. skill; socially useful ability; completion; thing achieved.

**accord** /əˈkɔːd/ 1 *v.* be consistent *with*; grant, give. 2 *n.* harmony; consent. **3 of one's own accord** without being requested.

**accordance** /əˈkɔːd(ə)ns/ *n*. harmony, agreement. **accordant** *a*.

**according** *adv*. **according as** in proportion as; **according to** in manner consistent with, as stated by.

**accordingly** *adv*. as the (stated) circumstances suggest; therefore.

**accordion** /əˈkɔːdiːən/ *n*. portable musical instrument with bellows, metal reeds, and keyboard.

**accost** /əˈkɒst/ *v.t.* approach and speak to; (of prostitute) solicit.

**account** /əˈkaʊnt/ 1 *n*. statement of money etc. received and expended; business relationship esp. with bank or firm granting credit; narration; explanation; importance; reckoning. 2 *v*. regard as. 3 **account for** give reckoning of, answer for, explain; **on account** to be paid for later, in part payment; **on account of** because of.

**accountable** *a*. responsible; explicable. **accountability** *n*.

**accountant** /əˈkaʊnt(ə)nt/ *n*. person who keeps or inspects accounts. **accountancy** *n*.

**accoutrements** /əˈkuːtrəmənts/ *n.pl.* equipment, trappings.

**accredit** /əˈkredɪt/ *v.t.* attribute (*to*); credit (*with*); send (ambassador etc.) with credentials *to* person etc.; gain belief or influence for.

**accredited** *a*. holding credentials.

**accretion** /əˈkriːʃ(ə)n/ *n*. growth by accumulation or organic enlargement; the resulting whole; (adhesion of) extraneous matter added.

**accrue** /əˈkruː/ *v.i.* come as natural increase or advantage, esp. financial.

**accumulate** /əˈkjuːmjəleɪt/ *v*. heap up, bring together; get more and more of; produce or acquire thus; become numerous, go on increasing. **accumulation** *n*.; **accumulative** *a*.

**accumulator** /əˈkjuːmjəleɪtə(r)/ *n*. rechargeable electric cell; storage register in computer.

**accurate** /ˈækjərət/ *a*. precise, exact, correct. **accuracy** *n*.

**accursed** /əˈkɜːsəd/ *a*. lying under a curse; *colloq*. detestable, annoying.

**accusative** /əˈkjuːzətɪv/ *Gram*. 1 *n*. case expressing object of action. 2 *a*. of or in an accusative.

**accuse** /əˈkjuːz/ *v.t.* indict, charge; lay blame on. **accusation** /ækjʊˈzeɪʃən/ *n*.; **accusatory** /əˈkjuːzətəri/ *a*.

**accustom** /əˈkʌstəm/ *v.t.* make used *to*.

**accustomed** *a*. used *to*; customary.

**ace** *n*. playing-card with single spot; person who excels at something; *Tennis* service that opponent cannot return.

**acerbic** /əˈsɜːbɪk/ *a*. harsh and sharp, esp. of speech, temper, etc. **acerbity** *n*.

**acetate** /ˈæsəteɪt/ *n*. compound of acetic acid, esp. cellulose acetate used for textile fibre etc.

**acetic** /əˈsiːtɪk/ *a*. of vinegar. **acetic acid** essential ingredient of vinegar.

**acetone** /ˈæsətəʊn/ *n*. colourless volatile solvent of organic compounds.

**acetylene** /əˈsetɪliːn/ *n*. colourless gas burning with bright flame.

**ache** /eɪk/ 1 *n*. continuous or prolonged pain or longing. 2 *v.i.* suffer ache.

**achieve** /əˈtʃiːv/ *v.t.* reach or attain by effort; accomplish, perform. **achievement** *n*.

**Achilles** /əˈkɪliːz/ *n*. **Achilles' heel** vulnerable point; **Achilles' tendon** tendon attaching calf muscles to heel.

**achromatic** /ækrəʊˈmætɪk/ *a*. free

## achy / actionable

from colour; transmitting light without separating it into constituent colours. **achromatically** *adv.*

**achy** /ˈeɪkiː/ *a.* suffering aches.

**acid** /ˈæsəd/ 1 *n. Chem.* any of a class of substances that neutralize alkalis, and of which most contain hydrogen and are sour; *sl.* drug LSD. 2 *a.* sour; biting, severe. 3 **acid drop** sharp-tasting boiled sweet; **acid rain** rain containing acid formed from industrial waste in atmosphere; **acid test** severe or conclusive test; **put the acid on** *Aus. sl.* put pressure on (person) for loan etc. 4 **acidic** /-ˈsɪd-/ *a.*; **acidify** /-ˈsɪd-/ *v.t.*; **acidity** /-ˈsɪd-/ *n.*

**acidulate** /əˈsɪdjʊleɪt/ *v.t.* make acidulous.

**acidulous** /əˈsɪdjʊləs/ *a.* somewhat acid.

**acknowledge** /əkˈnɒlɪdʒ/ *v.t.* agree to truth of; admit; report receipt of (letter etc.); express appreciation of (service etc.); show that one has noticed.

**acknowledgement** *n.* acknowledging; thing given or done in return for service etc.

**acme** /ˈækmɪ/ *n.* highest point.

**acne** /ˈæknɪ/ *n.* skin eruption with red pimples esp. on face.

**acolyte** /ˈækəlaɪt/ *n.* person assisting priest in service etc.; assistant.

**aconite** /ˈækənaɪt/ *n.* poisonous plant with yellow or blue flowers.

**acorn** /ˈeɪkɔːn/ *n.* fruit of oak.

**acoustic** /əˈkuːstɪk/ *a.* of sound or sense of hearing; (of guitar etc.) not electric.

**acoustics** *n.pl.* acoustical properties (of room etc.); (as *sing.*) science of sound. **acoustical** *a.*; **acoustically** *adv.*

**acquaint** /əˈkweɪnt/ *v.t.* make aware or familiar. **be acquainted with** know.

**acquaintance** /əˈkweɪntəns/ *n.* being acquainted (with); person one knows slightly. **acquaintanceship** *n.*

**acquiesce** /ækwiˈes/ *v.i.* agree, esp. tacitly; not object. **acquiescence** *n.*; **acquiescent** *a.*

**acquire** /əˈkwaɪə(r)/ *v.t.* gain, come to have. **acquirement** *n.*

**acquisition** /ækwəˈzɪʃ(ə)n/ *n.* (esp. useful) thing acquired.

**acquisitive** /əˈkwɪzətɪv/ *a.* keen to acquire things.

**acquit** /əˈkwɪt/ *v.t.* declare not guilty, clear of blame etc. **acquit oneself** perform, conduct oneself.

**acquittal** /əˈkwɪt(ə)l/ *n.* deliverance from charge by verdict etc.

**acre** /ˈeɪkə(r)/ *n.* measure of land, 4840 sq. yards, 0.405 ha.; piece of land, field.

**acreage** /ˈeɪkərɪdʒ/ *n.* number of acres.

**acrid** /ˈækrɪd/ *a.* bitterly pungent; bitter in temper etc. **acridity** /-ˈkrɪd-/ *n.*

**acrimonious** /ækrɪˈməʊnɪəs/ *a.* bitter in manner or temper. **acrimony** /ˈækrɪmənɪ/ *n.*

**acrobat** /ˈækrəbæt/ *n.* performer of acrobatics. **acrobatic** *a.*

**acrobatics** /ækrəˈbætɪks/ *n.pl.* spectacular gymnastic feats.

**acronym** /ˈækrənɪm/ *n.* word made from initial letters of other words.

**acropolis** /əˈkrɒpəlɪs/ *n.* citadel or elevated part of ancient Greek city, esp. Athens.

**across** /əˈkrɒs/ 1 *prep.* from side to side of; to or on other side of; forming a cross with. 2 *adv.* from side to side; to or on other side. 3 **across the board** applying to all.

**acrostic** /əˈkrɒstɪk/ *n.* poem etc. in which first or first and last letters of lines form word(s).

**acrylic** /əˈkrɪlɪk/ 1 *a.* of material made with synthetic substance derived from acrylic acid. 2 *n.* acrylic fibre or paint etc. 3 **acrylic acid** colourless organic acid.

**ACT** *abbr.* Australian Capital Territory.

**act** 1 *n.* thing done, deed; process of doing; performance, pretence; item in variety etc. performance; main division of play; decree of legislative body. 2 *v.* perform functions or actions, behave; be actor; play part of; serve *as*.

**actinism** /ˈæktɪnɪz(ə)m/ *n.* property of short-wave radiation that produces chemical changes, as in photography. **actinic** /ækˈtɪnɪk/ *a.*

**action** /ˈækʃ(ə)n/ *n.* process of doing or performing; exertion of energy or influence; thing done; series of events in drama; battle; mechanism of instrument; mode or style of movement of horse or player etc.; legal process. **action replay** immediate repeat of section of broadcast sports event.

**actionable** *a.* providing grounds for legal action.

# activate

**activate** /'æktəveɪt/ *v.t.* make active; make radioactive. **activation** *n*.

**active** /'æktɪv/ *a.* consisting in or marked by action; energetic, diligent; working, operative. **active voice** *Gram.* all forms of verbs attributing action of verb to person etc. whence it proceeds.

**activism** /'æktɪvɪz(ə)m/ *n.* vigorous action in politics etc. **activist** *n*.

**activity** /æk'tɪvɪtɪ:/ *n.* being active; sphere or kind of operation.

**actor** /'æktə(r)/ *n.* performer in play or film etc. **actress** *n*.

**ACTU** *abbr.* Australian Council of Trade Unions.

**actual** /'æktʃuːəl/ *a.* existing, real; present, current. **actuality** /-'æl-/ *n*.

**actually** *adv.* in actual fact, really.

**actuary** /'æktʃuːərɪ/ *n.* person who calculates insurance risks and premiums. **actuarial** /-'eər-/ *a*.

**actuate** /'æktʃuːeɪt/ *v.t.* communicate motion to; cause to function or act. **actuation** *n*.

**acuity** /ə'kjuːɪtɪ:/ *n.* sharpness, acuteness.

**acumen** /'ækjəmen/ *n.* keen perception, insight.

**acupuncture** /'ækjəpʌŋktʃə(r)/ *n.* pricking of body tissues with needles as medical treatment.

**acute** /ə'kjuːt/ *a.* keen, penetrating, clever, perceptive; (of disease) coming sharply to crisis, not chronic; (of difficulty etc.) serious, critical; (of angle) less than right angle. **acute accent** ( ´ ) over vowels.

**ad** *n. colloq.* advertisement.

**AD** *abbr.* of the Christian era (*anno Domini*); Dame of the Order of Australia, Australian Democrats.

**adage** /'ædɪdʒ/ *n.* proverb, maxim.

**adagio** /ə'dɑːʒɪəʊ/ *Mus.* 1 *adv.* in slow time. 2 *n.* (*pl.* **-ios**) passage to be played thus.

**adamant** /'ædəmənt/ *a.* stubbornly resolute.

**Adam's apple** /'ædəm/ cartilaginous projection at front of neck.

**adapt** /ə'dæpt/ *v.t.* fit, adjust; make suitable; modify, alter. **adaptation** *n*.

**adaptable** /ə'dæptəb(ə)l/ *a.* able to be adapted; able to adapt oneself to new surroundings etc. **adaptability** *n*.

**adaptor** /ə'dæptə(r)/ *n.* device for making things compatible; *Electr.* device for connecting several plugs to one socket.

**add** *v.* join as increase or supplement; unite numbers to get their total; say further. **add up** find sum of, amount *to*.

**addendum** /ə'dendəm/ *n.* (*pl.* **-da**) thing to be added; in *pl.* appendix to book etc.

**adder** /'ædə(r)/ *n.* small venomous Eur. and Asian snake.

**addict** /'ædɪkt/ *n.* person addicted to drug etc.; enthusiastic devotee.

**addicted** /ə'dɪktɪd/ *a.* given over habitually *to* (drug etc.); devoted *to*.

**addiction** /ə'dɪkʃ(ə)n/ *n.* condition of being addicted.

**addictive** /ə'dɪktɪv/ *a.* causing addiction.

**addition** /ə'dɪʃ(ə)n/ *n.* adding; thing added. **in addition** as something added (*to*).

**additional** /ə'dɪʃən(ə)l/ *a.* added, extra.

**additive** /'ædətɪv/ *n.* substance added to another to impart specific qualities.

**addle** /'æd(ə)l/ *v.t.* muddle, confuse.

**addled** /'æd(ə)ld/ *a.* (of egg) rotten, producing no chick; muddled, confused.

**address** /ə'dres/ 1 *n.* place where person lives or firm etc. is situated; particulars of this esp. for postal purposes; speech delivered to an audience. 2 *v.t.* write postal directions on (envelope etc.); direct in speech or writing; speak or write to; apply (*oneself*).

**addressee** /ædre'siː/ *n.* person to whom letter etc. is addressed.

**adduce** /ə'djuːs/ *v.t.* cite as proof or instance. **adducible** *a*.

**adenoids** /'ædənɔɪdz/ *n.pl.* enlarged tissue at back of nose, often hindering breathing.

**adept** /ə'dept/ 1 *a.* thoroughly proficient. 2 *n.* adept person.

**adequate** /'ædəkwət/ *a.* satisfactory in quantity or quality (*to* need). **adequacy** *n*.

**adhere** /əd'hɪə(r)/ *v.i.* stick fast; give support or allegiance *to*. **adherence** *n*.; **adherent** *n.* & *a*.

**adhesion** /əd'hiːʒ(ə)n/ *n.* adhering, sticking.

**adhesive** /əd'hiːsɪv/ 1 *a.* sticking, sticky. 2 *n.* adhesive substance.

**ad hoc** /æd 'hɒk/ for this purpose. [L]

**adieu** /əˈdjuː/ int. & n. (pl. **adieus**) goodbye.

**ad infinitum** /æd ɪnfɪˈnaɪtəm/ for ever. [L]

**adipose** /ˈædəpəʊz/ a. of fat, fatty. **adiposity** /-ˈpɒs-/ n.

**adjacent** /əˈdʒeɪsənt/ a. lying near; next (to). **adjacency** n.

**adjective** /ˈædʒəktɪv/ n. word indicating attribute, added to noun to describe thing etc. **adjectival** /-ˈtaɪv-/ a.

**adjoin** /əˈdʒɔɪn/ v.t. be next to and joined with.

**adjourn** /əˈdʒɜːn/ v. postpone, break off; suspend proceedings; move to another place. **adjournment** n.

**adjudge** /əˈdʒʌdʒ/ v. pronounce judgement on; pronounce or award judicially. **adjudgement** n.

**adjudicate** /əˈdʒuːdəkeɪt/ v. act as judge and give decision; adjudge. **adjudication** n.; **adjudicator** n.

**adjunct** /ˈædʒʌŋkt/ n. thing subordinate or incidental to another.

**adjure** /əˈdʒʊə(r)/ v.t. charge or request solemnly or earnestly. **adjuration** n.

**adjust** /əˈdʒʌst/ v. arrange, put in order; regulate; harmonize; adapt. **adjustment** n.

**adjutant** /ˈædʒət(ə)nt/ n. army officer assisting superior in administrative duties.

**ad lib** /æd ˈlɪb/ to desired extent; colloq. improvise(d).

**administer** /ədˈmɪnɪstə(r)/ v.t. manage (affairs etc.); formally give out; apply, give.

**administrate** /ədˈmɪnɪstreɪt/ v. act as administrator (of).

**administration** /ədmɪnəˈstreɪʃ(ə)n/ n. administering; esp. of public affairs; the Government.

**administrative** /ədˈmɪnɪstrətɪv/ a. of management of affairs.

**administrator** /ədˈmɪnɪstreɪtə(r)/ n. person who manages affairs of organization, institution, etc.

**admirable** /ˈædmərəb(ə)l/ a. worthy of admiration; excellent.

**admiral** /ˈædmər(ə)l/ n. commander-in-chief of navy; naval officer commanding fleet or squadron. **Australian**, **red**, **white**, **admiral**, kinds of butterfly.

**Admiralty** /ˈædmərəltiː/ n. UK (also Admiralty Board) department formerly administering Royal Navy.

**admire** /ədˈmaɪə(r)/ v.t. regard with approval, respect, or satisfaction; express admiration of. **admiration** n.

**admirer** n. woman's suitor; devotee of able or famous person.

**admissible** /ədˈmɪsəb(ə)l/ a. worthy of being accepted or considered. **admissibility** n.

**admission** /ədˈmɪʃ(ə)n/ n. acknowledgement (of error etc.); admitting, being admitted.

**admit** /ədˈmɪt/ v. recognize as true; acknowledge, confess to; let in, allow entrance of; have room for. **admit of** allow as possible. **admittance** n.

**admittedly** /ədˈmɪtədliː/ adv. as acknowledged fact.

**admixture** /ədˈmɪkstʃə(r)/ n. thing added, esp. minor ingredient; adding of this.

**admonish** /ədˈmɒnɪʃ/ v.t. reprove, urge, warn, remind.

**admonition** /ædməˈnɪʃ(ə)n/ n. reproof; warning. **admonitory** /-ˈmɒn-/ a.

**ad nauseam** /æd ˈnɔːziːæm/ to sickening extent. [L]

**ado** /əˈduː/ n. fuss; difficulty.

**adobe** /əˈdəʊbiː/ or əˈdəʊb/ n. unburnt sun-dried brick.

**adolescent** /ædəˈlesənt/ 1 a. between childhood and adulthood. 2 n. adolescent person. 3 **adolescence** n.

**adopt** /əˈdɒpt/ v.t. take into relationship, esp. as one's own child; take over; accept; take up, choose. **adoption** n.

**adoptive** /əˈdɒptɪv/ a. due to adoption.

**adorable** /əˈdɔːrəb(ə)l/ a. worthy of love; colloq. charming, delightful.

**adore** /əˈdɔː(r)/ v.t. regard with deep respect and affection; worship; colloq. like very much. **adoration** n.

**adorn** /əˈdɔːn/ v.t. add beauty to, be ornament to; furnish with ornaments. **adornment** n.

**adrenal** /əˈdriːn(ə)l/ a. close to kidneys. **adrenal gland** each of two ductless glands above the kidneys.

**adrenalin** /əˈdrenəlɪn/ n. hormone secreted by adrenal glands, stimulating circulation and muscular activity.

**adrift** /əˈdrɪft/ adv. & pred.a. drifting; at mercy of circumstances; colloq. unfastened.

**adroit** /ə'drɔɪt/ *a.* dextrous, skilful.

**adulation** /ædjə'leɪʃ(ə)n/ *n.* obsequious flattery. **adulatory** *a.*

**adult** /'ædʌlt/ **1** *a.* grown up, mature. **2** *n.* adult person. **3** adulthood *n.*

**adulterate** /ə'dʌltəreɪt/ *v.t.* debase (esp. food) by admixture of other substances. **adulteration** *n.*

**adultery** /ə'dʌltərɪ/ *n.* voluntary sexual intercourse of married person other than with spouse. **adulterer** *n.*; **adulteress** *n.*; **adulterous** *a.*

**adumbrate** /'ædʌmbreɪt/ *v.t.* indicate faintly; represent in outline; foreshadow. **adumbration** *n.*

**advance** /əd'vɑːns or əd'væns/ **1** *v.* come or go forward; progress; put forward; help on; make (claim etc.); bring (event) to earlier date; lend (money); raise (price). **2** *n.* going forward; progress; loan; payment beforehand; in *pl.* amorous approaches; rise in price. **3** *a.* done etc. beforehand. **4 in advance** ahead, beforehand. **5 advancement** *n.*

**advanced** *a.* ahead of times, others, etc.; far on in progress.

**advantage** /əd'vɑːntɪdʒ or əd'væntɪdʒ/ **1** *n.* favourable circumstance; superiority; *Tennis* next point won after deuce. **2** *v.t.* be advantage to; help, profit. **3 take advantage of** use or exploit for personal benefit. **4 advantageous** /-'teɪdʒ-/ *a.*

**Advent** /'ædvent/ *n.* season before Christmas; coming of Christ; **advent** important arrival.

**Adventist** *n.* member of sect believing in imminent second coming of Christ.

**adventitious** /ædven'tɪʃəs/ *a.* accidental, casual.

**adventure** /əd'ventʃə(r)/ **1** *n.* unusual and exciting experience; daring enterprise. **2** *v.i.* dare, venture.

**adventurer** *n.* person who seeks adventures; person ready to take risks for personal gain. **adventuress** *n.*

**adventurous** /əd'ventʃərəs/ *a.* venturesome, enterprising.

**adverb** /'ædvɜːb/ *n.* word expressing manner or degree or circumstance etc. and used to modify adjective or verb or other adverb. **adverbial** *a.*

**adversary** /'ædvəsərɪ/ *n.* opponent; enemy. **adversarial** /-'seərɪ:(ə)l/ *a.*

**adverse** /'ædvɜːs/ *a.* unfavourable; harmful.

**adversity** /əd'vɜːsətɪ/ *n.* trouble; misfortune.

**advert**[1] /'ædvɜːt/ *n. colloq.* advertisement.

**advert**[2] /əd'vɜːt/ *v.i.* refer or allude *to*.

**advertise** /'ædvətaɪz/ *v.* proclaim merits of, esp. to encourage sales; make generally or publicly known; ask *for* by notice in newspaper etc. **advertisement** /əd'vɜːtɪsmənt/ *n.*

**advice** /əd'vaɪs/ *n.* opinion given as to action; information; notice of transaction.

**advisable** /əd'vaɪzəb(ə)l/ *a.* to be recommended; expedient. **advisability** *n.*

**advise** /əd'vaɪz/ *v.* give advice (to); recommend; inform.

**advisedly** /əd'vaɪzədlɪ/ *adv.* deliberately.

**adviser** /əd'vaɪzə(r)/ *n.* person who advises, esp. officially.

**advisory** /əd'vaɪzərɪ/ *a.* giving advice.

**advocacy** /'ædvəkəsɪ/ *n.* pleading in support *of*; advocate's function.

**advocate 1** /'ædvəkət/ *n.* person who speaks in favour of policy etc.; person who pleads for another, esp. in law courts. **2** /'ædvəkeɪt/ *v.t.* support or plead for (policy etc.).

**adze** /ædz/ *n.* kind of axe with arched blade at right angles to handle.

**aegis** /'iːdʒɪs/ *n.* (*pl.* **-ises**) protection; sponsorship.

**aeolian** /iː'əʊlɪən/ *a.* wind-borne. **aeolian harp** stringed instrument producing musical sounds on exposure to wind.

**aeon** /'iːɒn/ *n.* long or indefinite period of time; an age.

**aerate** /'eəreɪt/ *v.t.* charge with carbon dioxide; expose to action of air. **aeration** *n.*

**aerial** /'eərɪəl/ **1** *n.* wire or rod transmitting or receiving radio waves. **2** *a.* from the air; existing in the air; like air.

**aerie** var. of **eyrie**.

**aero-** *in comb.* of air or aircraft.

**aerobatics** /eərə'bætɪks/ *n.pl.* feats of expert and spectacular flying.

**aerobics** /eə'rəʊbɪks/ *n.pl.* vigorous exercises designed to increase oxygen intake.

**aerodrome** /'eərədrəʊm/ *n.* airfield.

**aerodynamics** /eərəʊdaɪ'næmɪks/

**aerofoil** /ˈeərəfɔɪl/ *n.* aircraft wing, fin, or tailplane, designed to give lift in flight.

**aeronautics** /ˌeərəʊˈnɔːtɪks/ *n.pl.* usu. treated as *sing.* science or practice of aerial navigation. **aeronautical** *a.*

**aeroplane** /ˈeərəpleɪn/ *n.* mechanically driven heavier-than-air aircraft with wings.

**aerosol** /ˈeərəsɒl/ *n.* system of minute particles suspended in gas; device for producing fine spray of substance packed under pressure.

**aerospace** /ˈeərəʊspeɪs/ *n.* technology of aviation in earth's atmosphere and outer space.

**aesthete** /ˈiːsθiːt/ *n.* appreciator of beauty in art etc.

**aesthetic** /iːsˈθetɪk/ *a.* concerned with or capable of appreciation of beauty. **aestheticism** *n.*

**aetiology** /ˌiːtɪˈɒlədʒɪ/ *n.* study of causation or of causes of disease. **aetiological** *a.*

**afar** /əˈfɑː(r)/ *adv.* at or to a distance. **from afar** from a distance.

**affable** /ˈæfəb(ə)l/ *a.* easy to approach and talk to; courteous. **affability** *n.*

**affair** /əˈfeə(r)/ *n.* matter, concern; love-affair; *colloq.* thing or event; in *pl.* business.

**affect** /əˈfekt/ *v.t.* produce effect on; (of disease) attack; move, touch; pretend to have or feel or *to do.*

**affectation** /ˌæfekˈteɪʃ(ə)n/ *n.* artificial manner; pretentious display.

**affected** *a.* full of affectation.

**affection** /əˈfekʃ(ə)n/ *n.* goodwill, fond feeling; disease.

**affectionate** /əˈfekʃənət/ *a.* loving.

**affiance** /əˈfaɪəns/ *v.t.* promise in marriage.

**affidavit** /ˌæfəˈdeɪvət/ *n.* written statement on oath.

**affiliate** /əˈfɪlɪeɪt/ *v.* adopt or attach or connect as member or branch (*to* or *with*).

**affiliation** *n.* affiliating or being affiliated. **affiliation order** one compelling putative father of illegitimate child to help support it.

**affinity** /əˈfɪnətɪ/ *n.* attraction; relationship, resemblance; *Chem.* tendency of substances to combine with others.

**affirm** /əˈfɜːm/ *v.* state as fact; make affirmation.

**affirmation** /ˌæfəˈmeɪʃ(ə)n/ *n.* affirming; solemn declaration in place of oath.

**affirmative** /əˈfɜːmətɪv/ **1** *a.* affirming, answering that a thing is so. **2** *n.* that which affirms.

**affix 1** /əˈfɪks/ *v.t.* attach, fasten; add in writing. **2** /ˈæfɪks/ *n.* thing affixed; prefix or suffix.

**afflict** /əˈflɪkt/ *v.t.* distress physically or mentally.

**affliction** *n.* distress, suffering; cause of this.

**affluence** /ˈæfluəns/ *n.* wealth, abundance.

**affluent** /ˈæfluənt/ **1** *a.* rich; abundant. **2** *n.* tributary stream.

**afford** /əˈfɔːd/ *v.t.* have enough money for; manage to spare (time etc.); provide; be in a position *to.*

**afforest** /əˈfɒrəst/ *v.t.* convert into forest; plant with trees. **afforestation** *n.*

**affray** /əˈfreɪ/ *n.* breach of peace by fighting or rioting in public.

**affront** /əˈfrʌnt/ **1** *n.* open insult. **2** *v.t.* insult openly.

**Afghan** /ˈæfɡæn/ **1** *n.* native or language of Afghanistan; *Aus. hist.* camel-driver from NW India. **2** *a.* of Afghanistan. **3 Afghan hound** large dog with long silky hair.

**afield** /əˈfiːld/ *adv.* away from home; at or to a distance.

**afire** /əˈfaɪə(r)/ *adv. & pred.a.* on fire.

**aflame** /əˈfleɪm/ *adv. & pred.a.* in flames; very excited.

**afloat** *adv. & pred.a.* floating; at sea; out of debt.

**afoot** /əˈfʊt/ *adv. & pred.a.* progressing; in operation.

**afore** /əˈfɔː(r)/ *adv. & prep.* before. **aforementioned, -said,** previously mentioned; **aforethought** premeditated.

**a fortiori** /eɪ fɔːtɪˈɔːraɪ/ with stronger reason. [L]

**afraid** /əˈfreɪd/ *pred.a.* frightened, alarmed; *colloq.* politely regretful.

**afresh** /əˈfreʃ/ *adv.* with fresh start.

**African** /ˈæfrɪkən/ **1** *n.* native (esp. dark-skinned) or inhabitant of Africa. **2** *a.* of Africa.

**Afrikaans** /æfrɪˈkɑːns/ *n.* language derived from Dutch, used in S. Africa.

**Afrikaner** /æfrɪˈkɑːnə(r)/ *n.* Afrikaans-speaking white person in S. Africa.

**Afro** /ˈæfrəʊ/ *a.* (of hair) long and bushy, as grown by some Blacks.

**aft** /ɑːft/ *adv.* in, near to, or towards, stern of ship or tail of aircraft.

**after** /ˈɑːftə(r)/ **1** *prep.* following in time; behind; in pursuit or quest of; about, concerning; according to; in allusion to or imitation of; despite. **2** *conj.* after time when. **3** *adv.* later; behind. **4** *a.* later, hinder. **5 afterbirth** placenta etc. discharged after childbirth; **after-care** attention after leaving hospital, prison, etc; **after-effect** effect after interval or after primary effect; **afterlife** life after death; **aftershave** lotion applied after shaving; **afterthought** thing thought of or added later.

**aftermath** /ˈɑːftəmæθ or -mɑːθ/ *n.* consequences; after-effects.

**aftermost** /ˈɑːftəməʊst/ *a.* furthest aft.

**afternoon** /ɑːftəˈnuːn/ *n.* time between midday and evening.

**afterwards** /ˈɑːftəwədz/ *adv.* later, subsequently.

**again** /əˈgeɪn/ *adv.* another time, once more; further, besides; on the other hand.

**against** /əˈgeɪnst or əˈgenst/ *prep.* in opposition to; into collision or in contact with; in contrast to; in anticipation of; as compensating factor to, in return for.

**agape** /əˈgeɪp/ *adv.* & *pred.a.* gaping.

**agate** /ˈægət/ *n.* kind of hard semi-precious stone with streaked colouring.

**agave** /əˈgeɪvi/ *n.* a spiny-leaved plant.

**age 1** *n.* length of past life or existence; *colloq.* (esp. in *pl.*) a long time; historical period; old age. **2** *v.* (*partic.* **ageing**) (cause to) grow old or show signs of age. **3 come of age** reach legal majority.

**aged** *a.* /eɪdʒd/ of the age of; /ˈeɪdʒɪd/ old.

**ageism** /ˈeɪdʒɪz(ə)m/ *n.* prejudice or discrimination against people because of their age.

**ageless** /ˈeɪdʒləs/ *a.* never growing or appearing old.

**agency** /ˈeɪdʒənsɪ/ *n.* business or establishment of agent; active operation, action; intervening action.

**agenda** /əˈdʒendə/ *n.* (*pl.* **-das**) list of items of business to be considered at meeting.

**agent** /ˈeɪdʒənt/ *n.* person acting for another in business, politics, etc.; person or thing producing effect.

**agent provocateur** /aːʒɑ̃ prəvɒkəˈtɜː/ (*pl.* **-ts -rs** *pr.* same) person employed to detect suspected offenders by tempting them to overt action. [F]

**agglomerate** /əˈglɒməreɪt/ *v.* collect into mass. **agglomeration** *n.*

**agglutinate** /əˈgluːtɪneɪt/ *v.* stick together as with glue; join (words) into compounds. **agglutination** *n.*; **agglutinative** *a.*

**aggrandize** /əˈgrændaɪz/ *v.t.* increase power, rank, or wealth of; make seem greater. **aggrandizement** /-dɪz-/ *n.*

**aggravate** /ˈægrəveɪt/ *v.t.* increase seriousness of; *colloq.* annoy. **aggravation** *n.*

**aggregate 1** /ˈægrəgət/ *n.* sum total; gravel, broken stone, etc., used in making concrete. **2** /ˈægrəgət/ *a.* collected, total. **3** /ˈægrəgeɪt/ *v.* collect together, unite; *colloq.* amount to. **4 aggregation** *n.*

**aggression** /əˈgreʃ(ə)n/ *n.* unprovoked attack; hostile act or feeling. **aggressor** *n.*

**aggressive** /əˈgresɪv/ *a.* given to aggression; forceful, self-assertive; hostile.

**aggrieved** /əˈgriːvd/ *a.* having grievance.

**aggro** /ˈægrəʊ/ *n. sl.* deliberate trouble-making.

**aghast** /əˈgɑːst/ *a.* amazed and horrified.

**agile** /ˈædʒaɪl/ *a.* quick-moving; nimble. **agility** /əˈdʒɪlətɪ/ *n.*

**agitate** /ˈædʒəteɪt/ *v.* disturb, excite; stir up disquiet and unrest; shake about. **agitation** *n.*; **agitator** *n.*

**AGM** *abbr.* annual general meeting.

**agnail** /ˈægneɪl/ *n.* torn skin at root of finger-nail; resulting soreness.

**agnostic** /ægˈnɒstɪk/ *n.* person who believes that nothing is or can be known of existence of God or any but material phenomena. **agnosticism** *n.*

**ago** /əˈgəʊ/ *adv.* in the past.

**agog** /əˈgɒg/ *adv.* & *pred.a.* eager, expectant.

**agonize** /ˈægənaɪz/ v. undergo mental anguish; suffer agony; cause agony to.

**agony** /ˈægəni:/ n. intense physical or mental suffering; severe struggle. **agony column** colloq. personal column.

**agoraphobia** /ˌægərəˈfəʊbɪə/ n. morbid dread of open spaces.

**agrarian** /əˈgreərɪən/ 1 a. relating to land or its cultivation. 2 n. advocate of redistribution of landed property. **agrarianism** n.

**agree** /əˈgri:/ v. hold similar opinion; consent; be or become in harmony (*with*); approve as correct; reach agreement about. **agree with** suit, be compatible with.

**agreeable** a. pleasing; willing to agree.

**agreement** n. sharing of opinion; mutual understanding; contract, promise.

**agriculture** /ˈægrɪkʌltʃə(r)/ n. cultivation of the soil and rearing of animals. **agricultural** a.; **agriculturalist** n.

**agronomy** /əˈgrɒnəmi:/ n. soil management and crop production.

**aground** /əˈgraʊnd/ adv. on or to bottom of shallow water.

**ague** /ˈeɪgju:/ n. malarial fever with cold, hot, and sweating stages; fit of shivering.

**ah** /ɑ:/ int. expr. surprise, admiration, sorrow, entreaty, etc.

**aha** /əˈhɑ:/ int. expr. surprise, triumph, mockery, irony, etc.

**ahead** /əˈhed/ adv. in advance, in front; forward.

**ahoy** /əˈhɔɪ/ int. Naut. used in hailing.

**aid** 1 n. help; person who or that which helps. 2 v. help, assist, promote. 3 **in aid of** in support of, colloq. for purpose of.

**aide** /eɪd/ n. aide-de-camp; assistant.

**aide-de-camp** /ˌeɪd də ˈkɑ̃/ n. (pl. *aides-pr.* same) officer assisting senior officer.

**AIDS** abbr. acquired immune deficiency syndrome.

**aikido** /aɪˈki:dəʊ/ n. Japanese form of self-defence.

**ail** v. trouble or afflict in body or mind; be in poor condition.

**aileron** /ˈeɪlərɒn/ n. hinged flap on aircraft wing controlling lateral balance.

**ailment** /ˈeɪlmənt/ n. illness, esp. minor one.

**aim** 1 v. direct or point (*at*); take aim; direct one's ambition etc. 2 n. object aimed at, purpose; aiming; directing of weapon, missile, etc. at object. 3 **take aim** direct weapon at object.

**aimless** /ˈeɪmləs/ a. purposeless.

**air** 1 n. gaseous mixture, chiefly of oxygen and nitrogen, enveloping earth; atmosphere; open space; atmosphere as place where aircraft operate; appearance, manner; in *pl*. affected manner; melody. 2 v.t. expose to air, ventilate; make known, show off. 3 **air-bed** inflated mattress; **airborne** transported by air, (of aircraft) in the air after taking off; **air-brick** brick perforated for ventilation; **airbus** short-range aircraft operating like bus; **air commodore** RAAF officer next below Air Vice-Marshal; **air-conditioning** regulation of humidity and temperature in building, apparatus for this; **airfield** area with runway(s) for aircraft; **air force** branch of armed forces fighting in the air; **airgun** gun using compressed air as propelling force; **air-hostess** stewardess in aircraft; **airlift** transport of supplies etc. by air esp. in emergency, (v.t.) transport thus; **airline** public air transport system or company; **airliner** large passenger aircraft; **airlock** stoppage of flow by air-bubble in pipe etc., compartment providing access to pressurized chamber; **airmail** mail carried by air; **airman** pilot or member of crew of aircraft; **Air (Vice-) Marshal** high rank in RAAF; **airplane** *US* aeroplane; **airport** airfield with facilities for passengers and goods; **air raid** attack by aircraft; **airship** flying machine lighter than air; **airspace** air above country and subject to its jurisdiction; **air speed** aircraft's speed relative to air through which it is moving; **airstrip** strip of ground for take-off and landing of aircraft; **air terminal** place in town with transport to and from airport; **airway** regular route of aircraft; **by air** in or by aircraft; **on the air** (being) broadcast.

**aircraft** /ˈeəkrɑ:ft/ n. (pl. same) aeroplane, helicopter. **aircraft-carrier** ship that carries and acts as base for aircraft; **aircraftman, -woman**, lowest rank in RAAF.

**Airedale** /ˈeədeɪl/ n. terrier of large rough-coated breed.
**airless** /ˈeələs/ a. stuffy; still, calm.
**airtight** a. impermeable to air.
**airworthy** a. (of aircraft) fit to fly. **airworthiness** n.
**airy** /ˈeəri/ a. well-ventilated; light as air; insubstantial; flippant.
**aisle** /aɪl/ n. side part of church divided by pillars from nave; passage between rows of pews, seats in theatre, etc.
**aitchbone** /ˈeɪtʃbəʊn/ n. rump-bone of animal; cut of beef lying over this.
**ajar** /əˈdʒɑː(r)/ adv. (of door etc.) slightly open.
**AK** abbr. Knight of the Order of Australia.
**akimbo** /əˈkɪmbəʊ/ adv. (of arms) with hands on hips and elbows out.
**akin** /əˈkɪn/ pred.a. similar; related.
**alabaster** /ˈæləbɑːstə(r)/ 1 n. translucent sus. white form of gypsum. 2 a. of alabaster; resembling it in whiteness or smoothness.
**à la carte** /ɑː lɑː ˈkɑːt/ ordered as separate items from menu.
**alacrity** /əˈlækrəti/ n. briskness, readiness.
**à la mode** /ɑː lɑː ˈməʊd/ in the fashion, fashionable.
**alarm** /əˈlɑːm/ 1 n. warning, warning sound or device; frightened expectation of danger etc.; alarm clock. 2 v.t. disturb, frighten; arouse to sense of danger etc. 3 **alarm clock** clock with device that rings at set time.
**alarmist** /əˈlɑːmɪst/ n. person spreading unnecessary alarm.
**alas** /əˈlæs/ int. expr. grief.
**alb** n. white vestment reaching to feet, worn by priests etc.
**albacore** /ˈælbəkɔː(r)/ n. large kind of tunny.
**albatross** /ˈælbətrɒs/ n. long-winged sea bird related to petrel.
**albeit** /ɔːlˈbiːɪt/ conj. although.
**albino** /ælˈbiːnəʊ/ n. (pl. -nos) person or animal lacking colouring pigment in skin and hair. **albinism** /ˈæl-/ n.
**album** /ˈælbəm/ n. blank book for photographs etc.; long-playing gramophone record with several items.
**albumen** /ˈælbjəmən/ n. white of egg.
**albumin** /ˈælbjəmən/ n. water-soluble protein found in egg-white, milk, blood, etc.

**alchemy** /ˈælkəmi:/ n. medieval chemistry, esp. seeking transmutation of base metals into gold. **alchemical** /-ˈkem-/ a.; **alchemist** n.
**alcheringa** /æltʃəˈrɪŋgə/ n. Abor. Myth. golden age.
**alcohol** /ˈælkəhɒl/ n. colourless volatile liquid, intoxicant present in wine, beer, spirits, etc., also used as solvent and fuel; liquor containing this; Chem. compound of this type.
**alcoholic** /ælkəˈhɒlɪk/ 1 a. of or like or containing or caused by alcohol. 2 n. person suffering from alcoholism.
**alcoholism** /ˈælkəhɒlɪz(ə)m/ n. continual heavy drinking of alcohol; diseased condition resulting from this.
**alcove** /ˈælkəʊv/ n. recess in wall of room, garden, etc.
**alder** /ˈɔːldə(r)/ n. tree related to birch; similar but unrelated Aus. tree.
**alderman** /ˈɔːldəmən/ n. (pl. -men) urban representative in some parts of Australia; UK chiefly hist. civic dignitary next in rank to mayor. **aldermanic** /-ˈmæn-/ a.
**ale** n. beer.
**alert** /əˈlɜːt/ 1 a. watchful. 2 n. alarm call; state or period of special vigilance. 3 v.t. make alert to; warn. 4 **on the alert** watchful, looking out for danger etc.
**alfalfa** /ælˈfælfə/ n. clover-like plant used for fodder.
**alfresco** /ælˈfreskəʊ/ a. & adv. in the open air.
**alga** /ˈælgə/ n. (pl. -gae /-dʒiː/) non-flowering stemless plant, e.g. seaweed or plankton.
**algebra** /ˈældʒəbrə/ n. study of properties of numbers using general symbols. **algebraic** /-ˈbreɪk/ a.
**ALGOL** n. mathematically-based computer language.
**algorithm** /ˈælgərɪðəm/ n. process or rules for (esp. machine) calculation etc.
**alias** /ˈeɪliəs/ 1 adv. called at other times. 2 n. assumed name.
**alibi** /ˈæləbaɪ/ n. (pl. -bis) plea that one was elsewhere.
**alien** /ˈeɪliən/ 1 n. non-naturalized foreigner; a being from another world. 2 a. foreign; not one's own; of a different kind; unfamiliar.
**alienate** /ˈeɪliəneɪt/ v.t. estrange; transfer ownership of. **alienation** n.

# alight — allspice

**alight**[1] /ə'laɪt/ *pred.a.* on fire; lighted up.

**alight**[2] /ə'laɪt/ *v.i.* get down or off *from*; settle, come to earth.

**align** /ə'laɪn/ *v.t.* place in or bring into line; ally (country, *oneself*, etc.) with party or cause. **alignment** *n.*

**alike** /ə'laɪk/ **1** *pred.a.* similar, like. **2** *adv.* in like manner.

**alimentary** /ælɪ'mentəri:/ *a.* concerning nutrition; nourishing. **alimentary canal** channel through which food passes during digestion.

**alimony** /'ælɪməni:/ *n.* allowance paid by man to his divorced or separated wife, maintenance.

**alive** *pred.a.* living; lively, active; responsive *to*; abounding in.

**alkali** /'ælkəlaɪ/ *n.* (*pl.* **-lis**) any of a class of compounds that neutralize acids and form caustic or corrosive solutions in water. **alkaline** *a.*; **alkalinity** /-'lɪn-/ *n.*

**alkaloid** /'ælkələɪd/ *n.* any of a class of vegetable bases often used as drugs.

**alkie** /'ælki:/ *n. Aus. sl.* alcoholic.

**all** /ɔːl/ **1** *a.* whole amount, number, or extent *of*. **2** *n.* all persons concerned; everything; the whole *of*. **3** *adv.* entirely, quite. **4 all along** from the beginning; **all but** very nearly; **all-clear** signal that danger or difficulty is over; **all fours** hands and knees; **all in** exhausted; **all-in** *attrib.* inclusive of all; **all in** everything considered; **all out** involving all one's strength etc.; **all over** completely finished, over one's whole body; **all right** satisfactory, safe and sound, in good condition, satisfactorily, as desired, I consent; **all round** in all respects, for each person; **all-round** (of person) versatile; **all-rounder** versatile person; **All Saints Day** 1 Nov.; **all the same** nevertheless; **all there** *colloq.* mentally alert; **in all** in total, altogether.

**Allah** /'ælə/ *n.* Muslim name of God.

**allay** /ə'leɪ/ *v.t.* (past & p.p. **allayed**) alleviate, lessen.

**allege** /ə'ledʒ/ *v.t.* state as fact, esp. without proof. **allegation** /-'geɪʃ-/ *n.*; **allegedly** /ə'ledʒɪdli/ *adv.*

**allegiance** /ə'liːdʒəns/ *n.* duty of subject to sovereign or government; loyalty.

**allegorize** /'æləgəraɪz/ *v.t.* treat as or by means of an allegory. **allegorist** *n.*

**allegory** /'æləgəri:/ *n.* narrative symbolizing another esp. abstract meaning. **allegorical** /-'gɒrə-/ *a.*

**allegro** /ə'legrəʊ/ *Mus.* **1** *adv.* in lively tempo. **2** *n.* (*pl.* **-os**) passage to be played this way.

**alleluia** /ælə'luːjə/ **1** *int.* God be praised. **2** *n.* (*pl.* **-as**) song of praise to God.

**allergenic** /ælə'dʒenɪk/ *a.* causing allergic reaction.

**allergic** /ə'lɜːdʒɪk/ *a.* having an allergy *to*; caused by allergy.

**allergy** /'ælədʒi:/ *n.* condition of reacting adversely to certain foods or pollen etc.; *colloq.* antipathy.

**alleviate** /ə'liːvɪeɪt/ *v.t.* lessen or make less severe (pain, evil). **alleviation** *n.*; **alleviatory** /ə'liːv-/ *a.*

**alley** /'æli:/ *n.* narrow passage or street; channel for balls in bowling or skittles etc.

**alliance** /ə'laɪəns/ *n.* union or agreement to co-operate, esp of States by treaty or families by marriage.

**allied** /'ælaɪd/ *a.* having similar origin or character *to*.

**alligator** /'ælɪɡeɪtə(r)/ *n.* Amer. or Chinese reptile of crocodile family; *Aus. colloq.* crocodile.

**alliteration** /əlɪtə'reɪʃ(ə)n/ *n.* recurrence of same initial letter or sound in several words of a phrase. **alliterate** *v.*; **alliterative** *a.*

**allocate** /'æləkeɪt/ *v.t.* assign (*to*). **allocation.** *n.*

**allot** /ə'lɒt/ *v.t.* distribute officially; apportion (*to*).

**allotment** /ə'lɒtmənt/ *n.* share; *UK* small plot of land let out for cultivation; something allotted.

**allow** /ə'laʊ/ *v.* permit; let happen; assign fixed sum to, esp. regularly; provide or set aside for a purpose. **allow for** take into consideration.

**allowance** /ə'laʊəns/ *n.* sum or quantity allowed; deduction or discount. **make allowances for** judge leniently.

**alloy 1** /'ælɔɪ/ *n.* mixture of metals; inferior metal mixed esp. with gold or silver. **2** /ə'lɔɪ/ *v.t.* mix (metals); debase by admixture; spoil (pleasure).

**allspice** /'ɔːlspaɪs/ *n.* aromatic spice got

**allude** /ə'luːd/ *v.i.* make indirect or passing reference *to*.

**allure** /ə'ljʊə(r)/ 1 *v.t.* entice, tempt, charm. 2 *n.* charm, attractiveness. 3 **allurement** *n.*

**allusion** /ə'luːʒ(ə)n/ *n.* indirect or passing reference. **allusive** /-sɪv/ *a.*

**alluvium** /ə'luːvɪəm/ *n.* (*pl.* -**via**) deposit left by flood, esp. in river valley. **alluvial** *a.*

**ally** 1 /'ælaɪ/ *n.* State or person formally co-operating or united with another for special purpose. 2 /ə'laɪ/ *v.t.* combine or unite in alliance.

**almanac** /'ɔːlmənæk/ *n.* calendar of months and days, usu with astronomical data.

**almighty** /ɔːl'maɪtɪ/ *a.* infinitely powerful; *colloq.* very great. **the Almighty** God.

**almond** /'ɑːmənd/ *n.* edible kernel of fruit related to plum; tree bearing it.

**almoner** /'ɑːmənə(r)/ *n.* social worker attached to a hospital.

**almost** /'ɔːlməʊst/ *adv.* very nearly, all but.

**alms** /ɑːmz/ *n.* donation of money or food given to the poor. **almshouse** house founded by charity for the poor.

**aloe** /'æləʊ/ *n.* plant with erect spikes of flowers and bitter juice; in *pl.* purgative drug from aloe juice.

**aloft** *adv.* high up, overhead.

**alone** 1 *pred.a.* by oneself or itself; without company, assistance, or addition. 2 *adv.* only, exclusively.

**along** 1 *adv.* onward, into more advanced state; in company, in addition; beside or through part or whole of thing's length. 2 *prep.* beside or through part or whole of the length of. 3 **alongside** close to side (of); **along with** in addition to.

**aloof** /ə'luːf/ 1 *a.* unconcerned, lacking in sympathy. *f.* 2 *adv.* away, apart.

**aloud** /ə'laʊd/ *adv.* in a normal voice so as to be audible.

**ALP** *abbr.* Australian Labor Party.

**alp** *n.* mountain-peak, esp. in *pl.* (**the Alps**) those in Switzerland and adjacent countries or (**Australian Alps**) in SE Australia or (**Southern Alps**) NZ.

**alpaca** /æl'pækə/ *n.* (*pl.* -**as**) llama with long wool; its wool; fabric made from it.

**alpha** /'ælfə/ *n.* (*pl.* -**as**) first letter of Greek alphabet ($A$, $α$). **Alpha and Omega** beginning and end; **alpha particle** helium nucleus emitted by radioactive substance.

**alphabet** /'ælfəbet/ *n.* set of letters used in a language; symbols or signs for this. **alphabetical** /-'bet-/ *a.*

**alphanumeric** /ælfənjuː'merɪk/ *a.* of or denoting or using the set of symbols consisting of the letters of the alphabet and the digits 0-9.

**Alpine** /'ælpaɪn/ 1 *a.* of the Alps or other high mountains. 2 *n.* plant suited to mountain regions.

**already** /ɔːl'redɪ/ *adv.* before the time in question; as early as this.

**alright** *incorrect* □ See **all.**

**Alsatian** /æl'seɪʃ(ə)n/ *n.* large dog of a breed of wolfhound.

**also** /'ɔːlsəʊ/ *adv.* in addition, besides. **also-ran** loser in race, undistinguished person.

**altar** /'ɔːltə(r)/ *n.* flat-topped block for offerings to deity; table used for Communion service.

**alter** /'ɔːltə(r)/ *v.* change in character, position, size, shape, etc. **alteration** *n.*

**altercation** /ɔːltə'keɪʃ(ə)n/ *n.* dispute, wrangle. **altercate** *v.i.*

**alternate** 1 /ɔːl'tɜːnət/ *a.* (of things of two kinds) occurring each after one of the other kind; (with *pl.*, of one class of thing) every other. 2 /'ɔːltəneɪt/ *v.* arrange or occur alternately; consist of alternate things. 3 **alternating current** electric current reversing direction at regular intervals. 4 **alternation** *n.*

**alternative** /ɔːl'tɜːnətɪv/ 1 *a.* available in place of something else. 2 *n.* choice available in place of another; one of two or more possibilities.

**alternator** /'ɔːltəneɪtə(r)/ *n.* dynamo producing alternating current.

**although** /ɔːl'ðəʊ/ *conj.* though.

**altimeter** /'æltɪmiːtə(r)/ *n.* instrument measuring altitude.

**altitude** /'æltɪtjuːd/ *n.* height, esp. of object above sea-level or star above horizon.

**alto** /'æltəʊ/ *n.* (*pl.* -**os**) low singing voice of woman or boy; highest adult

## altogether — amendment

male singing voice; singer with alto voice; music for alto voice.

**altogether** /ɔːltəˈɡeðə(r)/ *adv.* totally; on the whole.

**altruism** /ˈæltruːɪz(ə)m/ *n.* regard for others as principle of action. **altruist** *n.*; **altruistic** *a.*

**alum** /ˈæləm/ *n.* double sulphate of aluminium and another element, esp. potassium.

**alumina** /əˈluːmɪnə/ *n.* aluminium oxide, e.g. corundum.

**aluminium** /æljəˈmɪnɪəm/ *n.* a light silvery metallic element.

**alumnus** /əˈlʌmnəs/ *n.* (*pl.* **-ni** /-naɪ/) esp. *US* former pupil or student of a school or university etc.

**always** /ˈɔːlweɪz/ *adv.* at all times; on all occasions; whatever the circumstances.

**am** 1st person sing. of **be**.

**AM** *abbr.* Member of the Order of Australia.

**a.m.** *abbr.* before noon (*ante meridiem*).

**AMA** *abbr.* Australian Medical Association.

**amalgam** /əˈmælɡəm/ *n.* mixture, blend; alloy of any metal with mercury.

**amalgamate** /əˈmælɡəmeɪt/ *v.* mix; unite, combine. **amalgamation** *n.*

**amanuensis** /əmænjuˈensəs/ *n.* (*pl.* **-ses** /-siːz/) person who writes from dictation.

**amaranth** /ˈæmərænθ/ *n.* kind of plant with coloured foliage; imaginary unfading flower. **amaranthine** /-θaɪn/ *a.*

**amaryllis** /æməˈrɪləs/ *n.* plant with lily-like flowers.

**amass** /əˈmæs/ *v.t.* heap together, accumulate.

**amateur** /ˈæmətə(r)/ *n.* one who engages in a sport or interest etc. as a pastime not a profession.

**amateurish** /ˈæmətərɪʃ/ *a.* suggestive of an amateur, unskilled.

**amatory** /ˈæmətərɪ/ *a.* of or showing (esp. sexual) love.

**amaze** *v.t.* fill with surprise or wonder. **amazement** *n.*

**amazon** /ˈæməzən/ *n.* strong or athletic woman; (**Amazon**) one of a mythical race of female warriors. **amazonian** /-ˈzəʊn-/ *a.*

**ambassador** /æmˈbæsədə(r)/ *n.* diplomat sent by sovereign or State as permanent representative or on mission to another; official messenger. **ambassadorial** /-ˈdɔːr-/ *a.*

**amber** **1** *n.* yellow translucent fossil resin; colour of this; yellow traffic-light denoting caution. **2** *a.* made of or coloured like amber.

**ambergris** /ˈæmbəɡrɪs/ *n.* waxlike substance from intestines of sperm whale, used in perfumery.

**ambidextrous** /æmbɪˈdekstrəs/ *a.* able to use either hand equally well.

**ambience** /ˈæmbɪəns/ *n.* surroundings.

**ambient** /ˈæmbɪənt/ *a.* surrounding.

**ambiguous** /æmˈbɪɡjʊəs/ *a.* having more than one possible meaning; doubtful, uncertain. **ambiguity** /-ˈɡjuː-/ *n.*

**ambit** *n.* scope, bounds.

**ambition** /æmˈbɪʃ(ə)n/ *n.* desire for advancement; desire for specific attainment; object of this.

**ambitious** /æmˈbɪʃəs/ *a.* full of ambition; of high aspiration.

**ambivalent** /æmˈbɪvələnt/ *a.* having mixed feelings towards person or thing. **ambivalence** *n.*

**amble** /ˈæmb(ə)l/ **1** *v.i.* walk at a leisurely pace. **2** *n.* leisurely pace.

**ambrosia** /æmˈbrəʊʒə/ *n.* food of the gods in classical myth; thing delicious to taste or smell. **ambrosial** *a.*

**ambulance** /ˈæmbjələns/ *n.* vehicle for conveying sick or injured to hospital; mobile hospital serving army.

**ambulatory** /ˈæmbjələtərɪ/ *a.* of or for walking.

**ambuscade** /æmbəsˈkeɪd/ *n.* & *v.t.* ambush.

**ambush** /ˈæmbʊʃ/ **1** *n.* surprise attack by persons lying concealed; act or place of concealment for this. **2** *v.t.* attack from ambush; lie in wait for.

**ameliorate** /əˈmiːlɪəreɪt/ *v.* make or become better. **amelioration** *n.*

**amen** /ɑːˈmen or eɪ-/ *int.* so be it (esp. at end of prayer).

**amenable** /əˈmiːnəb(ə)l/ *a.* willing to be influenced or persuaded; answerable (*to* law etc.).

**amend** /əˈmend/ *v.t.* correct error in; make minor alterations in.

**amendment** *n.* minor alteration or addition in document etc.; article added to US constitution.

**amends** *n.* **make amends** give compensation *for.*

**amenity** /əˈmiːnəti:/ *n.* pleasant or useful feature or facility; pleasantness of a place.

**American** /əˈmerɪkən/ **1** *a.* of America, esp. the United States. **2** *n.* citizen of US; native of America; English as spoken in US. **3 Americanize** *v.t.*

**Americanism** /əˈmerɪkənɪz(ə)m/ *n.* word or phrase peculiar to or originating in US.

**amethyst** /ˈæməθɪst/ *n.* a precious stone, purple or violet quartz.

**amiable** /ˈeɪmɪəb(ə)l/ *a.* friendly and pleasant in temperament, likeable. **amiability** *n.*

**amicable** /ˈæmɪkəb(ə)l/ *a.* friendly. **amicability** *n.*

**amid** /əˈmɪd/ *prep.* in the middle of.

**amidships** /əˈmɪdʃɪps/ *adv.* in or to the middle of ship.

**amidst** var. of **amid**.

**amino** /əˈmiːnəʊ/ *a.* **amino acid** organic acid found in proteins.

**amiss 1** *pred.a.* out of order, wrong. **2** *adv.* wrongly, inappropriately. **3 take amiss** be offended by.

**amity** /ˈæmɪti:/ *n.* friendship.

**ammeter** /ˈæmətə(r)/ *n.* instrument for measuring electric current.

**ammo** /ˈæməʊ/ *n. sl.* ammunition.

**ammonia** /əˈməʊnɪə/ *n.* pungent gas with strong alkaline reaction; solution of this in water. **ammoniac** *a.*

**ammonite** /ˈæmənaɪt/ *n.* coil-shaped fossil shell.

**ammunition** /æmjəˈnɪʃ(ə)n/ *n.* military projectiles (bullets, shells, etc.) and propellants; points used to advantage in argument.

**amnesia** /æmˈniːzjə/ *n.* loss of memory. **amnesiac** *a.* & *n.*

**amnesty** /ˈæmnəsti:/ *n.* general pardon, esp. for political offences.

**amnion** /ˈæmnɪɒn/ *n.* (*pl.* **-nia**) membrane enclosing foetus. **amniotic** *a.*

**amoeba** /əˈmiːbə/ *n.* (*pl.* **-bas**) microscopic one-celled aquatic organism.

**amok** /əˈmɒk/ *adv.* **run amok** run about wildly in violent rage.

**among** /əˈmʌŋ/ *prep.* (also **amongst**) surrounded by; in the category or number of; from the joint resources of; between.

**amoral** /eɪˈmɒr(ə)l/ *a.* not based on moral standards; having no moral principles.

**amorous** /ˈæmərəs/ *a.* showing or feeling sexual love.

**amorphous** /əˈmɔːfəs/ *a.* shapeless; ill organized; *Min.* & *Chem.* uncrystallized.

**amount 1** *n.* total number, size, value, extent, etc. **2** *v.i.* be equivalent in number, size, etc. *to.*

**amour** /əˈmʊə(r)/ *n.* love-affair, esp. secret one.

**amour propre** /æmʊə ˈprɒpr/ self-respect. [F]

**amp** *n.* ampere; *colloq.* amplifier.

**ampere** /ˈæmpeə(r)/ *n.* unit of electric current.

**ampersand** /ˈæmpəsænd/ *n.* the sign & ( = 'and').

**amphetamine** /æmˈfetəmiːn/ *n.* synthetic stimulant drug.

**amphibian** /æmˈfɪbɪən/ *n.* amphibious animal or vehicle.

**amphibious** /æmˈfɪbɪəs/ *a.* able to live on land and in water; (of vehicle etc.) able to operate on land and on water; involving military forces landed from the sea.

**amphitheatre** /ˈæmfɪθɪətə(r)/ *n.* unroofed oval or circular building with tiers of seats surrounding central space.

**amphora** /ˈæmfərə/ *n.* (*pl.* **-rae** /-riː/) Greek or Roman two-handled jar.

**ample** /ˈæmp(ə)l/ *a.* abundant, extensive; enough or more than enough. **amply** *adv.*

**amplifier** /ˈæmpləfaɪə(r)/ *n.* apparatus for amplifying sounds or electrical signals.

**amplify** /ˈæmpləfaɪ/ *v.t.* increase strength of (sound or electrical signal); add details to (story etc.). **amplification** *n.*

**amplitude** /ˈæmplɪtjuːd/ *n.* spaciousness; maximum departure from average of oscillation, alternating current, etc.

**ampoule** /ˈæmpuːl/ *n.* small sealed vessel holding solution for injection.

**amputate** /ˈæmpjəteɪt/ *v.t.* cut off (diseased or injured limb). **amputation** *n.*

**amuck** var. of **amok**.

**amulet** /ˈæmjəlɛt/ *n.* thing worn as charm against evil.

# amuse

**amuse** /ə'mju:z/ *v.t.* cause (person) to laugh or smile; interest or occupy. **amusing** *a.*
**amusement** *n.* being amused; thing that amuses.
**an** see **a**.
**anabranch** /'ænəbrɑ:ntʃ/ *n.* branch stream that leaves river and rejoins it.
**anachronism** /ə'nækrənɪz(ə)m/ *n.* attribution of thing to period to which it does not belong; thing thus attributed; person or thing not suited to the period. **anachronistic** *a.*
**anaconda** /ænə'kɒndə/ *n.* large tropical S. Amer. snake.
**anaemia** /ə'ni:mɪə/ *n.* deficiency of red cells or their haemoglobin in the blood.
**anaemic** /ə'ni:mɪk/ *a.* suffering from anaemia; pale, lacking vitality.
**anaesthesia** /ænəs'θi:zjə/ *n.* artificially induced insensibility to pain.
**anaesthetic** /ænəs'θetɪk/ 1 *n.* drug, gas, etc., producing anaesthesia. 2 *a.* producing anaesthesia.
**anaesthetist** /ə'ni:sθətɪst/ *n.* one who administers anaesthetics.
**anaesthetize** /ə'ni:sθətaɪz/ *v.t.* administer anaesthetics to.
**anagram** /'ænəgræm/ *n.* word or phrase formed by transposing letters of another. **anagrammatic** /-'mæt-/ *a.*
**anal** /'eɪn(ə)l/ *a.* of the anus.
**analgesia** /ænæl'dʒi:zjə/ *n.* absence or relief of pain.
**analgesic** /ænæl'dʒi:sɪk/ 1 *n.* pain-killing drug. 2 *a.* pain-killing.
**analogous** /ə'næləgəs/ *a.* partially similar or parallel *to*.
**analogue** /'ænəlɒg/ *n.* analogous thing.
**analogue computer** one that uses physical quantities e.g. length or voltage to represent numbers.
**analogy** /ə'nælədʒi:/ *n.* correspondence, similarity; reasoning from parallel cases. **analogical** /-'lɒdʒ-/ *a.*
**analyse** /'ænəlaɪz/ *v.t.* perform analysis on.
**analysis** /ə'næləsɪs/ *n.* (*pl.* -ses /-si:z/) detailed examination; ascertaining of elements or structure of substance etc.; psychoanalysis.
**analyst** /'ænəlɪst/ *n.* one who analyses.
**analytical** /ænə'lɪtɪk(ə)l/ *a.* of or using analysis.
**anarchism** /'ænəkɪz(ə)m/ *n.* belief that government and law should be abolished. **anarchist** *n.*; **anarchistic** *a.*
**anarchy** /'ænəki:/ *n.* disorder, esp. political; lack of government. **anarchic** /ə'nɑ:kɪk/ *a.*
**anathema** /ə'næθəmə/ *n.* detested thing; curse of God or Church.
**anathematize** /ə'næθəmətaɪz/ *v.t.* curse.
**anatomy** /ə'nætəmɪ/ *n.* science of bodily structure; structure of animal or plant. **anatomical** /ænə'tɒmɪk(ə)l/ *a.*
**ancestor** /'ænsəstə(r)/ *n.* any person from whom one's father or mother is descended. **ancestress** *n.*
**ancestral** /æn'sestr(ə)l/ *a.* inherited from ancestors.
**ancestry** /'ænsəstrɪ:/ *n.* one's ancestors; ancient descent.
**anchor** /'æŋkə(r)/ *n.* 1 heavy metal structure used to moor ship to sea-bottom etc. or balloon etc. to ground. 2 *v.* secure (ship) with anchor; fix firmly; cast anchor. 3 **anchor man** person who co-ordinates activities, esp. compère in broadcast.
**anchorage** /'æŋkərɪdʒ/ *n.* place for anchoring; lying at anchor.
**anchorite** /'æŋkəraɪt/ *n.* hermit, recluse.
**anchovy** /'æntʃəvi:/ *n.* small pungent-flavoured fish of herring family.
**ancien régime** /ɑ̃sjæ̃ reɪ'ʒi:m/ political and social system formerly in being, esp. in France before Revolution.
**ancient** /'eɪnʃənt/ *a.* of times long past; old.
**ancillary** /æn'sɪlərɪ/ *a.* subsidiary, auxiliary.
**and** *conj.* connecting words, clauses, and sentences.
**andante** /æn'dæntɪ:/ *Mus.* 1 *adv.* in moderately slow time. 2 *n.* passage to be played thus.
**andiron** /'ændaɪən/ *n.* stand for supporting logs in hearth.
**androgynous** /æn'drɒdʒənəs/ *a.* hermaphrodite.
**anecdote** /'ænɪkdəʊt/ *n.* narrative of amusing or interesting incident. **anecdotal** *a.*
**anemometer** /ænɪ'mɒmətə(r)/ *n.* instrument for measuring force of wind.
**anemone** /ə'nemənɪ:/ *n.* plant akin to buttercup. **sea anemome** polyp with petal-like tentacles.

**aneroid** /'ænərɔɪd/ a. (of barometer) that measures air-pressure by its action on lid of metal box containing vacuum.

**aneurysm** /'ænjʊərɪz(ə)m/ (also **aneurism**) n. excessive enlargement of artery.

**anew** /ə'nju:/ adv. again; in a different way.

**angel** /'eɪmdʒ(ə)l/ n. attendant or messenger of God; kind or innocent person.

**angel cake** very light sponge cake. **angelic** /æn'dʒelɪk/ a.

**angelica** /æn'dʒelɪkə/ n. an aromatic plant; its candied stalks.

**angelus** /'ændʒələs/ n. RC Ch. devotional exercise said at morning, noon, and sunset; bell rung for this.

**anger** /'æŋgə(r)/ 1 n. extreme displeasure. 2 v.t. make angry.

**angina** /æn'dʒaɪnə/ n. (in full **angina pectoris**) pain in chest brought on by exertion, owing to poor blood supply to heart.

**angle**[1] /'æŋg(ə)l/ 1 n. space between two meeting lines or surfaces; inclination of two lines to each other; corner; *colloq.* point of view. 2 v.t. move or place obliquely; *colloq.* present (news etc.) from particular point of view.

**angle**[2] /'æŋg(ə)l/ v.i. fish with line and hook. **angler** n.

**Anglican** /'æŋglɪkən/ 1 a. of Church of England or Anglican Church of Australia. 2 n. member of Anglican Church. 3 **Anglicanism** n.

**Anglicism** /'æŋglɪsɪz(ə)m/ n. English idiom.

**Anglicize** /'æŋglɪsaɪz/ v.t. make English in form or character.

**Anglo-** /'æŋgləʊ/ *in comb.* English, British.

**Anglo-Catholic** 1 a. of section of Church of England that insists on its accordance with Catholic doctrine. 2 n. adherent of Anglo-Catholic belief.

**Anglo-Indian** 1 a. of England and India; of British descent but having lived long in India. 2 n. Anglo-Indian person.

**Anglophile** /'æŋgləʊfaɪl/ n. person well-disposed towards the English.

**Anglo-Saxon** 1 a. of English Saxons before Norman Conquest; of English descent. 2 n. Anglo-Saxon person or language.

**angora** /æŋ'gɔ:rə/ n. fabric made from hair of angora goat or rabbit. **angora cat, goat, rabbit**, long-haired varieties.

**angostura** /æŋgə'stjʊərə/ n. aromatic bitter bark of S. Amer tree.

**angry** /'æŋgrɪ/ a. feeling or showing anger; (of wound etc.) inflamed, painful.

**angstrom** /'æŋstrəm/ n. unit of wavelength measurement.

**anguish** /'æŋgwɪʃ/ n. severe mental or bodily pain. **anguished** a.

**angular** /'æŋgjələ(r)/ a. having sharp corners; lacking plumpness or smoothness. **angular distance** distance between two points in terms of the angle they make with a third. **angularity** /-'lær-/ n.

**anhydrous** /æn'haɪdrəs/ a. *Chem.* without water of crystallization.

**aniline** /'ænɪli:n/ n. oily liquid got from coal tar and used in dye-making.

**animadvert** /ænəmæd'vɜ:t/ v.i. pass criticism or censure (on). **animadversion** n.

**animal** /'ænəm(ə)l/ 1 n. living being having sensation and usu. ability to move; (esp.) other animal than man. 2 a. of or like animal; carnal.

**animalcule** /ænə'mælkju:l/ n. microscopic animal.

**animality** /ænə'mælətɪ/ n. the animal world; animal behaviour.

**animate** 1 /'ænəmət/ a. having life, lively. 2 /'ænəmeɪt/ v.t. enliven; give life to.

**animated** a. spirited, lively; (of film) characterized by animation.

**animation** /ænə'meɪʃ(ə)n/ n. liveliness, ardour; being alive; technique of film-making by photographing successive drawings or positions of puppets etc. to create illusion of movement.

**animator** /'ænəmeɪtə(r)/ n. artist who prepares animated films.

**animism** /'ænəmɪz(ə)m/ n. attribution of soul to inanimate objects and natural phenomena. **animist** n.; **animistic** a.

**animosity** /ænə'mɒsətɪ/ n. hostility.

**animus** /'ænəməs/ n. animosity shown in speech or action.

**anion** /'ænaɪən/ n. negatively charged ion. **anionic** /ænaɪ'ɒnɪk/ a.

**anise** /'ænɪs/ n. plant with aromatic seeds.

**aniseed** /'ænəsi:d/ n. seed of anise.

**ankle** /'æŋk(ə)l/ *n.* joint connecting foot with leg.

**anklet** /'æŋklət/ *n.* ornament worn round ankle.

**ankylosis** /æŋkə'ləusəs/ *n.* stiffening of joint by uniting of bones.

**annals** /'æn(ə)lz/ *n.pl.* narrative of events year by year; historical records. **annalist** *n.*

**anneal** /ə'ni:l/ *v.t.* heat (metal, glass) and allow to cool slowly, esp. to toughen.

**annelid** /'ænəlɪd/ *n.* worm made of segments, e.g. earth-worm.

**annex** /æ'neks/ *v.t.* add or append as subordinate part; take possession of. **annexation** *n.*

**annexe** /'æneks/ *n.* supplementary building.

**annihilate** /ə'naɪəleɪt/ *v.t.* destroy utterly. **annihilation** *n.*

**anniversary** /ænə'vɜ:sərɪ/ *n.* yearly return of date; celebration of this.

**Anno Domini** /ænəʊ 'dɒmɪnaɪ/ in the year of the Christian era; *colloq.* advancing age.

**annotate** /'ænəʊteɪt/ *v.t.* add explanatory notes to (book etc.). **annotation** *n.*

**announce** /ə'naʊns/ *v.t.* make publicly known; make known the approach of. **announcement** *n.*

**announcer** /ə'naʊnsə(r)/ *n.* person who announces, esp. in broadcasting.

**annoy** /ə'nɔɪ/ *v.t.* cause slight anger or mental distress to; molest. **annoyance** *n.*

**annual** /'ænjuəl/ **1** *a.* reckoned by year; recurring yearly. **2** *n.* book etc. published yearly; plant living only one year.

**annuity** /ə'nju:ətɪ/ *n.* yearly grant or allowance; investment entitling one to fixed annual sum.

**annul** /ə'nʌl/ *v.t.* declare invalid; abolish, cancel. **annulment** *n.*

**annular** /'ænjələ(r)/ *a.* ring-shaped.

**annulate** /'ænjələt/ *a.* marked with or formed of rings.

**annunciation** /ənʌnsɪ:'eɪʃ(ə)n/ *n.* announcement, esp. (**Annunciation**) that of the Incarnation made by Gabriel to Mary.

**anode** /'ænəʊd/ *n.* positive electrode or terminal.

**anodyne** /'ænəʊdaɪn/ **1** *a.* pain-killing; soothing. **2** *n.* anodyne drug, circumstance, etc.

**anoint** /ə'nɔɪnt/ *v.t.* apply ointment or oil to esp. as religious ceremony.

**anomalous** /ə'nɒmələs/ *a.* irregular, abnormal.

**anomaly** /ə'nɒməlɪ/ *n.* anomalous thing

**anon** /ə'nɒn/ *adv. arch.* soon, presently.

**anon.** *abbr.* anonymous.

**anonymous** /ə'nɒnəməs/ *a.* of unknown name or authorship; featureless. **anonymity** (/-'nɪm-/) *n.*

**anorak** /'ænəræk/ *n.* weatherproof jacket esp. with hood.

**anorexia** /ænə'reksɪə/ *n.* lack of appetite for food, esp. (in full **anorexia nervosa**) as chronic illness.

**another** /ə'nʌðə(r)/ **1** *a.* additional; one more; a different. **2** *n.* an additional or other or different person or thing.

**answer** /'ɑ:nsə(r) *or* 'æn-/ **1** *n.* thing said, written, or done to deal with question, accusation, etc.; solution to problem. **2** *v.* make an answer (to); act in response to; be satisfactory (*for*); be responsible *for* or *to*; correspond *to* description.

**answerable** /'ɑ:nsərəb(ə)l *or* 'æn-/ *a.* responsible (*for, to*); that can be answered.

**ant** *n.* small sou. wingless insect living in complex social group. **ant-eater** echidna, numbat; **anthill** mound over ants' nest.

**antacid** /æn'tæsəd/ *n.* & *a.* preventive or corrective of acidity.

**antagonism** /æn'tægənɪz(ə)m/ *n.* active opposition. **antagonistic** *a.*

**antagonist** /æn'tægənəst/ *n.* opponent.

**antagonize** /æn'tægənaɪz/ *v.t.* evoke hostility in.

**Antarctic** /æn'tɑ:ktɪk/ *a.* of south polar region.

**ante** /'æntɪ/ *n.* stake put up by poker player before drawing new cards.

**ante-** /'æntɪ/ *in comb.* before.

**antecedent** /æntə'si:d(ə)nt/ **1** *n.* preceding event or circumstance; *Gram.* noun, clause, etc., to which following adverb or pronoun refers; in *pl.* person's past history. **2** *a.* previous (*to*). **3** **antecedence** *n.*

**antechamber** /'æntɪ:tʃeɪmbə(r)/ *n.* ante-room.

**antedate** /ˈæntiːdeɪt/ v.t. precede in time; give earlier than true date to.

**antediluvian** /ˌæntidəˈluːviən/ a. before the Flood; colloq. very old.

**antelope** /ˈæntələʊp/ n. swift-running deer-like animal.

**antenatal** /ˌæntiˈneɪtəl/ a. before birth; relating to pregnancy.

**antenna** /ænˈtenə/ n. (pl. **-tennae** /-ˈtenɪ/) one of pair of sensory organs on head of insect or crustacean; feeler; (pl. **-tennas**) radio aerial.

**anterior** /ænˈtɪərɪə(r)/ a. nearer the front; prior (to).

**ante-room** /ˈæntiːruːm/ n. small room leading to more important one.

**anthem** /ˈænθəm/ n. choral composition for church use; song of praise, esp. for nation.

**anther** /ˈænθə(r)/ n. part of stamen containing pollen.

**anthology** /ænˈθɒlədʒi/ n. collection of passages from literature, esp. poems.

**anthracite** /ˈænθrəsaɪt/ n. hard kind of coal. **anthracitic** /-ˈsɪt-/ a.

**anthrax** /ˈænθræks/ n. disease of sheep and cattle, transmissible to humans.

**anthropoid** /ˈænθrəpɔɪd/ 1 a. manlike in form. 2 n. anthropoid ape.

**anthropology** /ˌænθrəˈpɒlədʒi/ n. study of mankind, esp. societies and customs. **anthropological** a.; **anthropologist** n.

**anthropomorphism** /ˌænθrəpəʊˈmɔːfɪz(ə)m/ n. attributing of human form or personality to god, animal, or thing. **anthropomorphic** a.

**anthropomorphous** /ˌænθrəpəʊˈmɔːfəs/ a. of human form.

**anti-** in comb. opposed to; retarding or preventing; of opposing kind.

**anti-aircraft** a. for defence against hostile aircraft.

**antibiotic** /ˌæntibaɪˈɒtɪk/ 1 n. substance capable of destroying or injuring bacteria etc. 2 a. functioning as antibiotic.

**antibody** /ˈæntibɒdi/ n. protein produced in reaction to antigens in body.

**antic** n. (usu. in pl.) foolish behaviour.

**anticipate** /ænˈtɪsɪpeɪt/ v.t. deal with or use before due time; forestall. **anticipation** n.; **anticipatory** a.

**anticlimax** /-ˈklaɪmæks/ n. lame conclusion to anything promising climax.

**anticlockwise** /-ˈklɒkwaɪz/ adv. & a. moving in curve opposite in direction to hands of clock.

**anticyclone** /-ˈsaɪkləʊn/ n. system of winds rotating outwards from area of high barometric pressure, producing fine weather.

**antidote** /ˈæntidəʊt/ n. medicine used to counteract poison.

**antifreeze** /ˈæntifriːz/ n. substance added to water (esp. in radiator of motor vehicle) to lower its freezing-point.

**antigen** /ˈæntɪdʒ(ə)n/ n. foreign substance that causes body to produce antibodies.

**anti-hero** n. (pl. **-oes**) central character in story etc. who lacks conventional heroic qualities.

**antihistamine** /-ˈhɪstəmiːn/ n. substance that counteracts effect of histamine.

**antimacassar** /-məˈkæsə(r)/ n. protective covering for chair-back.

**antimony** /ˈæntɪməni/ n. brittle bluish-white metallic element.

**antipathy** /ænˈtɪpəθi/ n. strong or deep-seated aversion. **antipathetic** /-ˈθet-/ a.

**antiperspirant** /-ˈpɜːspərənt/ a. substance that inhibits perspiration.

**antiphon** /ˈæntɪf(ə)n/ n. hymn sung antiphonally.

**antiphonal** /ænˈtɪfən(ə)l/ a. sung alternately by two bodies of singers.

**antipodes** /ænˈtɪpədiːz/ n.pl. region of the earth diametrically opposite, esp. to Europe, hence esp. Australia and NZ. **antipodean** /-ˈdiːən/ a. & n.

**antipyretic** /-paɪˈretɪk/ 1 a. that counteracts fever. 2 n. antipyretic drug.

**antiquarian** /ˌæntɪˈkweərɪən/ 1 a. of or dealing in rare books. 2 n. antiquary.

**antiquary** /ˈæntɪkwəri/ n. student or collector of antiques or antiquities.

**antiquated** /ˈæntɪkweɪtɪd/ a. old-fashioned, out of date.

**antique** /ænˈtiːk/ 1 n. object, esp. furniture etc., of considerable age. 2 a. of or existing since old times; old-fashioned.

**antiquity** /ænˈtɪkwəti/ n. ancient times, esp. before Middle Ages; in pl. remains from ancient times.

**antirrhinum** /ˌæntɪˈraɪnəm/ n. snapdragon.

**antiscorbutic** /-skɔːˈbjuːtɪk/ a. that prevents or cures scurvy.

**anti-Semitic** /-sə'mıtık/ *a.* hostile to Jews. **anti-Semite** /-'si:maıt/ *n.*; **anti-Semitism** /-'sem-/ *n.*

**antiseptic** /-'septɪk/ 1 *a.* that counteracts sepsis by destroying bacteria. 2 *n.* antiseptic substance.

**antisocial** /-'səʊʃ(ə)l/ *a.* not sociable; opposed or harmful to existing social order.

**antistatic** /-'stætɪk/ *a.* that counteracts effect of static electricity.

**antithesis** /æn'tɪθəsəs/ *n.* (*pl.* **-ses** /-si:z/) direct opposite; contrast; contrast of ideas marked by parallelism of contrasted words. **antithetical** /-'θet-/ *a.*

**antitoxin** /-'tɒksɪn/ *n.* antibody that counteracts a toxin.

**antitrades** /-'treɪdz/ *n.* winds blowing above and in opposite direction to trade winds.

**antler** /'æntlə(r)/ *n.* branched horn of deer.

**antonym** /'æntənɪm/ *n.* word opposite in meaning to another.

**ANU** *abbr.* Australian National University.

**anus** /'eɪnəs/ *n.* excretory opening at end of alimentary canal in mammals.

**anvil** *n.* block on which smith works metal.

**anxiety** /æŋ'zaɪətɪ/ *n.* troubled state of mind; eagerness.

**anxious** /'æŋkʃəs/ *a.* troubled; uneasy in mind; eagerly wanting *to* do.

**any** /'enɪ/ 1 *a.* one or some, no matter which. 2 *pron.* any one; any number or amount. 3 *adv.* at all, in some degree. 4 *anybody* any person, person of importance; **anyhow** anyway, at random; **anyone** anybody; **anything** any thing, a thing of any kind; **anyway** in any way, in any case; **anywhere** (in or to) any place.

**ANZAAS** *abbr.* Australian and New Zealand Association for the Advancement of Science.

**Anzac** /'ænzæk/ *n.* soldier in Aus. and NZ Army Corps (1914-18). **Anzac biscuit** kind of sweet oat biscuit; **Anzac Day** 25 Apr.

**ANZUS** *abbr.* (also **Anzus**) alliance of Australia, NZ, and US for Pacific defence.

**AO** *abbr.* Officer of the Order of Australia.

**aorist** /'eərəst/ *n.* *Gram.* past tense denoting occurrence without reference to continuance, completion, etc.

**aorta** /eɪ'ɔ:tə/ *n.* main artery carrying blood from left ventricle of heart.

**AP** *abbr.* Australia Party.

**apace** /ə'peɪs/ *adv.* swiftly.

**apart** /ə'pɑ:t/ *adv.* separately; into pieces; at or to a distance.

**apartheid** /ə'pɑ:theɪt/ *n.* racial segregation, esp. in S. Africa.

**apartment** /ə'pɑ:tmənt/ *n.* flat (*US*); in *pl.* set of rooms; single room.

**apathy** /'æpəθɪ/ *n.* lack of interest, indifference; insensibility. **apathetic** /-'θet-/ *a.*

**ape** 1 *n.* tailless monkey; imitator. 2 *v.t.* imitate.

**aperient** /ə'pɪərɪənt/ *a.* & *n.* laxative.

**aperitif** /əpərə'ti:f/ *n.* alcoholic drink as appetizer before meal.

**aperture** /'æpətjʊə(r)/ *n.* opening, gap.

**apex** /'eɪpeks/ *n.* (*pl.* **apexes**) highest point, pointed end.

**aphasia** /ə'feɪzjə/ *n.* loss of ability to speak or of understanding of speech. **aphasic** *a.*

**aphelion** /æ'fi:lɪən/ *n.* (*pl.* **-lia**) point of orbit farthest from sun.

**aphid** /'eɪfəd/ *n.* small insect infesting plants.

**aphis** /'eɪfəs/ *n.* (*pl.* **aphides** /'eɪfədi:z/) aphid.

**aphorism** /'æfərɪz(ə)m/ *n.* short pithy maxim. **aphoristic** *a.*

**aphrodisiac** /æfrə'dɪzɪæk/ 1 *a.* arousing sexual desire. 2 *n.* aphrodisiac substance.

**apiary** /'eɪpɪərɪ/ *n.* place where bees are kept. **apiarist** *n.*

**apiculture** /'eɪpəkʌltʃə(r)/ *n.* beekeeping.

**apiece** /ə'pi:s/ *adv.* for each one.

**aplomb** /ə'plɒm/ *n.* self-confidence.

**apocalypse** /ə'pɒkəlɪps/ *n.* revelation, esp. of the future of the world. **apocalyptic** *a.*

**Apocrypha** /ə'pɒkrəfə/ *n.pl.* OT books not in Hebrew Bible and not considered genuine.

**apocryphal** /ə'pɒkrəf(ə)l/ *a.* of doubtful authenticity.

**apogee** /'æpədʒi:/ *n.* highest point; point in orbit of moon farthest from earth.

**apologetic** /əpɒlə'dʒetɪk/ *a.* making

# apologia

**apology**, expressing regret; of nature of apology.

**apologia** /æpəˈləʊdʒə/ n. written defence of conduct or opinions.

**apologist** /əˈpɒlədʒɪst/ n. one who defends by argument.

**apologize** /əˈpɒlədʒaɪz/ v.i. make apology.

**apology** /əˈpɒlədʒi/ n. regretful acknowledgement of offence; explanation.

**apophthegm** /ˈæpəθem/ n. terse or pithy saying.

**apoplexy** /ˈæpəpleksi/ n. sudden inability to feel and move, caused by blockage or rupture of artery in brain. **apoplectic** a.

**apostasy** /əˈpɒstəsi/ n. abandonment of belief or religious faith etc.

**apostate** n. person who renounces former belief. **apostatize** /-ˈpɒs-/ v.i.

**a posteriori** /eɪ pɒsterɪˈɔːraɪ/ from effects to causes; involving reasoning thus.

**Apostle** /əˈpɒs(ə)l/ n. any of twelve sent forth by Christ to preach gospel; **apostle** leader of reform. **apostle-bird** Aus. grey mudnest-building bird.

**apostolic** /æpəsˈtɒlɪk/ a. of Apostles; of the Pope.

**apostrophe** /əˈpɒstrəfi/ n. sign (') showing omission of letter(s) or number(s), or denoting possessive case.

**apostrophize** /əˈpɒstrəfaɪz/ v.t. address (esp. absent person or thing.)

**apothecary** /əˈpɒθəkəri/ n. arch. druggist.

**apotheosis** /əpɒθiˈəʊsəs/ n. (pl. -ses /-siːz/) deification; deified ideal; highest development of a thing.

**appal** /əˈpɔːl/ v.t. dismay, shock.

**apparatus** /æpəˈreɪtəs/ n. equipment for scientific or other work.

**apparel** /əˈpær(ə)l/ n. arch. clothing. **apparelled** a.

**apparent** /əˈpærənt/ a. readily visible or perceivable; seeming.

**apparition** /æpəˈrɪʃ(ə)n/ n. appearance, esp. of startling kind; ghost.

**appeal** /əˈpiːl/ 1 v.i. make earnest request; be attractive to; call attention to as support; apply to higher court, tribunal, etc., for revision of lower court's decision; Crick. ask umpire to declare batsman out. 2 n. act or right of appealing; request for aid; feature or quality that appeals.

**appear** /əˈpɪə(r)/ v.i. become or be visible; give certain impression, seem; present oneself; be published.

**appearance** /əˈpɪərəns/ n. appearing, outward aspect; in pl. outward show of prosperity or good behaviour etc.

**appease** /əˈpiːz/ v.t. make calm or quiet, esp. conciliate (aggressor) with concessions; satisfy. **appeasement** n.

**appellant** /əˈpelənt/ n. person who appeals to higher court.

**appellate** /əˈpelət/ a. Law (of court) concerned with appeals.

**appellation** /æpəˈleɪʃ(ə)n/ n. name, title.

**append** /əˈpend/ v.t. attach, affix; add.

**appendage** /əˈpendɪdʒ/ n. thing attached; addition.

**appendectomy** /əpenˈdektəmi/ n. (also **appendicectomy** /-dɪˈsek-/) surgical removal of appendix.

**appendicitis** /əpendəˈsaɪtəs/ n. inflammation of the appendix.

**appendix** /əˈpendɪks/ n. (pl. **-dices** /-dɪsiːz/ or **-dixes**) subsidiary matter at end of book etc.; outgrowth of tissue attached to intestine.

**appertain** /æpəˈteɪn/ v.i. belong or relate to.

**appetite** /ˈæpətaɪt/ n. desire, inclination (for food, pleasure, etc.); one's relish for food.

**appetizer** /ˈæpətaɪzə(r)/ n. thing eaten or drunk to stimulate appetite.

**appetizing** /ˈæpətaɪzɪŋ/ a. (esp. of food) stimulating appetite.

**applaud** /əˈplɔːd/ v. express approval (of), esp. by clapping; commend.

**applause** /əˈplɔːz/ n. loud approbation, esp.by clapping.

**apple** /ˈæp(ə)l/ n. rounded firm fleshy fruit. **apple-berry** kind of slender Aus. vine, its fruit; **apple-box, -gum, -tree**, kinds of eucalyptus; **Apple Isle** Aus. colloq. Tasmania; **apple of one's eye** cherished person or thing; **apple-pie bed** bed with sheets so folded that one cannot stretch out one's legs; **apple-pie order** extreme neatness; **she's apples** Aus. sl. everything's fine.

**appliance** /əˈplaɪəns/ n. device or equipment for specific task.

**applicable** /ˈæplɪkəb(ə)l/ a. that may be applied (to). **applicability** n.

**applicant** /'æpləkənt/ n. person who applies for job etc.

**application** /æplə'keɪʃ(ə)n/ n. applying; thing applied; request; diligence; relevance.

**applicator** /'æpləkeɪtə(r)/ n. device for applying substance etc.

**appliqué** /æ'pliːkeɪ/ 1 n. ornamental work in which fabric is cut out and attached to surface of other fabric. 2 v.t. (past & p.p. -quéd; partic. -quéing) decorate with appliqué.

**apply** /ə'plaɪ/ v. make formal request; put close (to) or in contact; administer (remedy); devote or direct to; be relevant or use as relevant (to).

**appoint** /ə'pɔɪnt/ v.t. assign job or office to; fix (time etc.); equip, furnish.

**appointment** n. appointing, esp. of time and place for meeting; job or office assigned to person; in pl. equipment or fittings.

**apportion** /ə'pɔːʃ(ə)n/ v.t. portion out; assign as share. **apportionment** n.

**apposite** /'æpəzɪt/ a. well-expressed, appropriate.

**apposition** /æpə'zɪʃ(ə)n/ n. juxtaposition, esp. Gram. placing of word etc. syntactically parallel to another.

**appraise** /ə'preɪz/ v.t. estimate value or quality of. **appraisal** n.

**appreciable** /ə'priːʃəb(ə)l/ a. significant; considerable.

**appreciate** /ə'priːʃɪeɪt/ v. set high value on; be grateful for; estimate rightly; rise in value. **appreciation** n.; **appreciative** /-'priːʃ-/ a.

**apprehend** /æprə'hend/ v.t. seize, arrest; understand.

**apprehension** /æprə'henʃ(ə)n/ n. fearful anticipation; arrest; understanding.

**apprehensive** /æprə'hensɪv/ a. uneasy, anticipating with fear.

**apprentice** /ə'prentɪs/ 1 n. learner of craft bound to employer for specified term. 2 v.t. bind as apprentice. 3 **apprenticeship** n.

**apprise** /ə'praɪz/ v.t. inform of.

**approach** /ə'prəʊtʃ/ 1 v. come nearer (to) in space or time; be similar to; approximate to; set about. 2 n. act or means of approaching; approximation; final part of aircraft's flight before landing.

**approachable** /ə'prəʊtʃəb(ə)l/ a. that can be approached; friendly.

**approbation** /æprə'beɪʃ(ə)n/ n. approval, consent. **approbatory** a.

**appropriate** 1 /ə'prəʊprɪət/ a. suitable, proper. 2 /ə'prəʊprɪeɪt/ v.t. take possession of; devote (fund etc. to purpose). 3 **appropriation** n.; **appropriator** n.

**approval** /ə'pruːv(ə)l/ n. approving; **on approval** returnable to supplier if not satisfactory.

**approve** /ə'pruːv/ v. confirm, give assent to; pronounce good, have favourable opinion of.

**approximate** 1 /ə'prɒksəmət/ a. fairly correct; near to the actual. 2 /ə'prɒksɪmeɪt/ v. be or make near (to). 3 **approximation** n.

**appurtenances** /ə'pɜːtənənsəz/ n.pl. accessories; belongings.

**Apr.** abbr. April.

**après-ski** /æpreɪ'skiː/ done or worn after day's skiing at resort. [F]

**apricot** /'eɪprɪkɒt/ n. orange-pink stone-fruit.

**April** /eɪprəl/ n. fourth month of year. **April fool** victim of hoax on 1 April (**April Fools' Day**).

**a priori** /eɪ praɪ'ɔːraɪ/ from cause to effect; involving reasoning thus; assumed without investigation.

**apron** /'eɪprən/ n. garment worn in front of body to protect clothes; area on airfield used for manœuvring and loading aircraft; extension of stage in front of curtain.

**apropos** /'æprəpəʊ/ 1 a. to the point or purpose. 2 adv. incidentally. 3 **apropos of** in connection with.

**apse** /æps/ n. arched or domed recess esp. at end of church.

**apsidal** /'æpsəd(ə)l/ a. of the form or shape of an apse; of apsides.

**apsis** n. (pl. **apsides** /æp'saɪdiːz/) aphelion or perihelion of planet, apogee or perigee of moon.

**apt** a. suitable, appropriate; having a tendency (to); quick-witted.

**apteryx** /'æptərɪks/ n. kiwi.

**aptitude** /'æptɪtjuːd/ n. talent; ability, esp. in particular skill.

**aqualung** /'ækwəlʌŋ/ n. portable underwater breathing apparatus.

**aquamarine** /'ækwəməriːn/ n. bluish-green beryl; colour of this.

# aquaplane

**aquaplane** /'ækwəpleɪn/ 1 *n.* board for riding on water, pulled by speedboat. 2 *v.i.* ride on aquaplane; (of vehicle) glide uncontrollably on wet surface of road.

**aquarelle** /ækwə'rel/ *n.* painting in transparent water-colours.

**aquarium** /ə'kweəriːəm/ *n.* (*pl.* **-iums**) tank for keeping fish and other aquatic life; building with such tanks.

**Aquarius** /ə'kweəriːəs/ *n.* eleventh sign of zodiac.

**aquatic** /ə'kwɒtɪk/ *a.* living in or near water; done in or on water.

**aquatint** /'ækwətɪnt/ *n.* print produced from copper plate engraved with nitric acid.

**aqueduct** /'ækwədʌkt/ *n.* artificial channel, esp. raised structure across valley for conveying water.

**aqueous** /'eɪkwiːəs/ *a.* of or like water, produced by action of water.

**aquiline** /'ækwɪlaɪn/ *a.* of or like an eagle; (of nose) hooked like eagle's beak.

**Arab** /'ærəb/ 1 *n.* member of Semitic people orig. inhabiting Saudi Arabia, now Middle East generally. 2 *a.* of Arabia or Arabs.

**arabesque** /ærə'besk/ *n.* decoration with intertwined leaves, scrollwork, etc.; ballet dancer's pose on one foot with other leg extended behind.

**Arabian** /ə'reɪbiːən/ 1 *a.* of Arabia. 2 *n.* an Arab.

**Arabic** /'ærəbɪk/ 1 *n.* language of Arabs. 2 *a.* of the Arabs or their language. 3 **Arabic numerals** 1, 2, 3, etc., (opp. Roman numerals).

**arable** *a.* fit for ploughing and growing crops.

**arachnid** /ə'ræknɪd/ *n.* any of class comprising spiders, scorpions, etc.

**Aramaic** /ærə'meɪɪk/ 1 *n.* language of Syria at time of Christ. 2 *a.* of or in Aramaic.

**Aranda** /'ɑːrəndə/ *n.* Abor. people of Central Australia; their language.

**arbiter** /'ɑːbɪtə(r)/ *n.* judge; person with influence over or control of.

**arbitrary** /'ɑːbɪtrəri/ *a.* based on random choice or whim; capricious, despotic.

**arbitrate** /'ɑːbɪtreɪt/ *v.* determine; settle dispute.

**arbitration** /ɑːbɪ'treɪʃ(ə)n/ *n.* arbitrating; result of this. **Arbitration Court**

# archdiocese

Aus. & NZ tribunal resolving industrial disputes etc.

**arbitrator** /'ɑːbɪtreɪtə(r)/ *n.* person appointed by parties involved to settle dispute.

**Arbor Day** /'ɑːbə(r)/ day set apart annually for public planting of trees.

**arboreal** /ɑː'bɔːriːəl/ *a.* of or living in trees.

**arborescent** /ɑːbə'res(ə)nt/ *a.* tree-like in growth or form. **arborescence** *n.*

**arboretum** /ɑːbə'riːtəm/ *n.* (*pl.* **-ta**) tree-garden.

**arboriculture** /'ɑːbərəkʌltʃə(r)/ *n.* cultivation of trees or shrubs. **arboricultural** *a.*

**arbour** /'ɑːbə(r)/ *n.* shady retreat enclosed by trees or climbing plants.

**arc** *n.* part of circumference of circle or other curve; large luminous flow of electric current through gas. **arc lamp** one using electric arc.

**arcade** /ɑː'keɪd/ *n.* covered walk esp. lined with shops; series of arches supporting or along wall.

**Arcadian** /ɑː'keɪdiːən/ *a.* ideally rustic.

**arcane** /ɑː'keɪn/ *a.* mysterious, secret.

**arch**[1] 1 *n.* curved structure supporting bridge, floor, etc.; archlike curvature. 2 *v.* form arch; provide with or form into arch.

**arch**[2] *a.* consciously or affectedly playful.

**archaeology** /ɑːkiː'ɒlədʒi/ *n.* study of ancient peoples esp. by excavation of physical remains. **archaeological** *a.*, **archaeologist** *n.*

**archaic** /ɑː'keɪɪk/ *a.* of early period in culture; antiquated; (of word) no longer in ordinary use.

**archaism** /'ɑːkeɪɪz(ə)m/ *n.* archaic word etc.; use of the archaic. **archaistic** *a.*

**archangel** /'ɑːkeɪndʒ(ə)l/ *n.* angel of highest rank. **archangelic** /-'dʒel-/ *a.*

**archbishop** /ɑːtʃ'bɪʃəp/ *n.* chief bishop.

**archbishopric** *n.* office or diocese of archbishop.

**archdeacon** /ɑːtʃ'diːkən/ *n.* church dignitary next below bishop.

**archdeaconry** *n.* office or residence of archdeacon.

**archdiocese** /ɑːtʃ'daɪəsəs/ *n.* archbishop's diocese. **archdiocesan** /-daɪ'ɒsɪz(ə)n/ *a.*

**archduke** /ˌɑːtʃˈdjuːk/ n. hist. title of son of Emperor of Austria.

**archer** /ˈɑːtʃə(r)/ n. person who shoots with bow and arrows.

**archery** /ˈɑːtʃərɪ/ n. use of bow and arrows.

**archetype** /ˈɑːkətaɪp/ n. original model, typical specimen. **archetypal** a.

**archipelago** /ˌɑːkəˈpeləɡəʊ/ n. (pl. -gos) sea with many islands; group of islands.

**architect** /ˈɑːkətekt/ n. designer of buildings, ships, etc.

**architectonic** /ˌɑːkətekˈtɒnɪk/ a. of architecture; of systematization of knowledge.

**architecture** /ˈɑːkətektʃə(r)/ n. art or science of building; style of building. **architectural** a.

**architrave** /ˈɑːkətreɪv/ n. moulded frame round doorway or window.

**archive** /ˈɑːkaɪv/ n. (freq. in pl.) collection of documents or records; place where these are kept. **archival** a.

**archivist** /ˈɑːkəvɪst/ n. keeper of archives.

**archway** /ˈɑːtʃweɪ/ n. arched entrance or passage.

**Arctic** /ˈɑːktɪk/ a. of north polar regions.

**ardent** /ˈɑːd(ə)nt/ a. eager, enthusiastic, fervent; burning. **ardency** n.

**ardour** /ˈɑːdə(r)/ n. zeal, enthusiasm.

**arduous** /ˈɑːdjuːəs/ a. hard to accomplish; strenuous.

**are**[1]: see **be**.

**are**[2] /ɑː(r)/ n. metric unit of measure, 100 square metres.

**area** /ˈeərɪə/ n. region; space set aside for a purpose; extent or measure of surface; scope, range; space in front of house basement. **area school** Aus. combined primary and secondary school in rural area.

**areca** /ˈærəkə/ n. kind of palm-tree. **areca nut** astringent seed of areca.

**arena** /əˈriːnə/ n. centre of amphitheatre; scene of conflict; sphere of action.

**aren't**: see **be**.

**arête** /æˈreɪt/ n. sharp mountain ridge.

**argon** /ˈɑːɡɒn/ n. inert gaseous element.

**argosy** /ˈɑːɡəsɪ/ n. hist. large merchant-ship.

**argot** /ˈɑːɡəʊ/ n. jargon, orig. esp. of thieves.

**argue** /ˈɑːɡjuː/ v. exchange views, esp. heatedly; maintain by reasoning (that); reason; prove, indicate. **arguable** a.

**argument** /ˈɑːɡjəm(ə)nt/ n. (esp. heated) exchange of views; reason advanced; reasoning; summary in book etc. **argumentation** n.

**argumentative** /ˌɑːɡjəˈmentətɪv/ a. fond of arguing.

**aria** /ˈɑːrɪə/ n. song for one voice in opera, oratorio, etc.

**arid** /ˈærɪd/ n. dry, parched. **aridity** n.

**Aries** /ˈeəriːz/ n. first sign of zodiac.

**aright** /əˈraɪt/ adv. rightly.

**arise** /əˈraɪz/ v.i. (past **arose**; p.p. **arisen** /əˈrɪz(ə)n/) originate, result; present itself; rise.

**aristocracy** /ˌærəsˈtɒkrəsɪ/ n. supremacy of privileged order; the nobility.

**aristocrat** /ˈærəstəkræt/ n. member of aristocracy.

**aristocratic** /ˌærəstəˈkrætɪk/ a. of the aristocracy; grand, distinguished.

**Aristotelian** /ˌærəstəˈtiːlɪən/ a. of Aristotle.

**arithmetic 1** /əˈrɪθmətɪk/ n. science of numbers; computation, use of numbers. **2** /ˌærɪθˈmetɪk/ a. of arithmetic. **3 arithmetical** /-ˈmet-/ a.; **arithmetician** /-ˈtɪʃ-/ n.

**ark** n. covered floating wooden vessel in which Noah was saved in Flood; **Ark of the Covenant** wooden chest containing tables of Jewish law.

**arm**[1] n. upper limb of human body; sleeve; raised side part of chair; branch; armlike thing. **arm-chair** chair with arms; **armpit** hollow under arm at shoulder.

**arm**[2] **1** n. (usu. in pl.) weapon; branch of military forces; in pl. heraldic devices. **2** v. equip with arms; equip oneself with arms; provide with.

**Armada** /ɑːˈmɑːdə/ n. Spanish fleet sent against England in 1588.

**armadillo** /ˌɑːməˈdɪləʊ/ n. (pl. -os) S. Amer. burrowing mammal with body cased in bony plates.

**Armageddon** /ˌɑːməˈɡed(ə)n/ n. scene of supreme battle at end of world.

**armament** /ˈɑːməmənt/ n. military weapon etc.; equipping for war.

**armature** /ˈɑːmətʃə(r)/ n. wire-wound

**armistice**      26      **artful**

core of dynamo or electric motor; bar of soft iron placed in contact with poles of magnet; internal framework on which sculpture is constructed.

**armistice** /'ɑ:məstəs/ *n.* stopping of hostilities; short truce.

**armlet** /'ɑ:mlət/ *n.* band worn round arm.

**armorial** /ɑ:'mɔ:riːəl/ *a.* of heraldic arms.

**armour** /'ɑ:mə(r)/ *n.* defensive covering formerly worn in fighting; metal plates etc. protecting ship, car, tank, etc.; armoured vehicles etc.

**armoured** /'ɑ:məd/ *a.* furnished with armour; equipped with armoured vehicles.

**armourer** /'ɑ:mərə(r)/ *n.* maker of arms or armour; official in charge of arms.

**armoury** /'ɑ:məri/ *n.* arsenal.

**army** /'ɑ:mi/ *n.* organized force armed for fighting on land; vast number; organized body.

**arnica** /'ɑ:nɪkə/ *n.* kind of plant with yellow flowers; medicine made from it.

**aroma** /ə'rəʊmə/ *n.* fragrance, sweet smell; subtle quality. **aromatic** /ærə'mætɪk/ *a.*

**arose** *past of* **arise**.

**around** /ə'raʊnd/ **1** *adv.* on every side; round; all round; *colloq.* near at hand. **2** *prep.* round; on or along the circuit of; on every side of; about.

**arouse** /ə'raʊz/ *v.t.* awake from sleep; stir into activity.

**arpeggio** /ɑ:'pedʒɪəʊ/ *n.* (*pl.* **-os**) sounding of notes of chord in rapid succession; chord so sounded.

**arrack** /'ærək/ *n.* alcoholic spirit made esp. from rice.

**arraign** /ə'reɪn/ *v.t.* indict, accuse; find fault with. **arraignment** *n.*

**arrange** /ə'reɪndʒ/ *v.* put in order; plan or provide for; give instructions; agree (*with* person) about procedure for; *Mus.* adapt (composition). **arrangement** *n.*

**arrant** /'ærənt/ *a.* downright, unmitigated.

**arras** /'ærəs/ *n.* tapestry wall hanging.

**array** /ə'reɪ/ **1** *n.* imposing series; ordered arrangement, esp. of troops; *Math.* an arrangement of numbers in rows and columns; arrangement of data in computer such that program can access items by means of a key. **2** *v.t.* set in order; marshal (forces).

**arrears** /ə'rɪəz/ *n.pl.* outstanding debts; what remains not done; **in arrears** behindhand.

**arrest** /ə'rest/ **1** *v.t.* seize by authority; stop; catch attention of. **2** *n.* legal arresting of offender; stoppage.

**arrive** /ə'raɪv/ *v.i.* come to destination; establish one's position; *colloq.* be born, come. **arrival** *n.*

**arrogant** /'ærəgənt/ *a.* aggressively haughty; presumptuous. **arrogance** *n.*

**arrogate** /'ærəgeɪt/ *v.t.* claim without right. **arrogation** *n.*

**arrow** /'ærəʊ/ *n.* pointed missile shot from bow; representation of (head of) arrow, esp. to show direction.

**arrowroot** /'ærəʊru:t/ *n.* nutritious starch got from W. Ind. plant.

**arse** /ɑ:s/ *n. vulg.* buttocks.

**arsenal** /'ɑ:sən(ə)l/ *n.* place for storage or manufacture of weapons and ammunition.

**arsenic** /'ɑ:sənɪk/ *n.* brittle steel-grey chemical element; its violently poisonous trioxide. **arsenical** /-'sen-/ *a.*

**arson** /'ɑ:sən/ *n.* criminal and deliberate act of setting on fire house or other property. **arsonist** *n.*

**art** *n.* human creative skill or its application; branch of creative activity concerned with imitative and imaginative designs, e.g. painting; fine arts; thing in which skill can be exercised; in *pl.*, certain branches of learning (esp. languages, literature, history, etc.) as distinct from sciences; knack; cunning. **art union** *Aus. & NZ* lottery.

**artefact** /'ɑ:təfækt/ *n.* man-made object.

**arterial** /ɑ:'tɪərɪəl/ *a.* of or like an artery. **arterial road** important main road.

**arteriosclerosis** /ɑ:tɪərɪəʊsklɪə'rəʊsəs/ *n.* hardening of walls of arteries.

**artery** /'ɑ:təri/ *n.* muscular-walled blood-vessel conveying blood from heart; important channel of supplies etc.

**artesian well** /ɑ:'ti:ʒ(ə)n/ well in which water rises to surface by natural pressure through vertically-drilled hole.

**artful** /'ɑ:tfəl/ *a.* sly, crafty.

**arthritis** /ɑːˈθraɪtɪs/ n. inflammation of joint. **arthritic** /-ˈrɪt-/ a.

**arthropod** /ˈɑːθrəpɒd/ n. animal with segmented body and jointed limbs, e.g. insect or crustacean.

**artichoke** /ˈɑːtɪtʃəʊk/ n. plant allied to thistle with partly edible flowers; Jerusalem artichoke.

**article** /ˈɑːtɪk(ə)l/ 1 n. particular item or commodity; short self-contained piece of writing in newspaper etc.; clause of agreement etc. 2 v.t. bind by articles of apprenticeship. 3 **definite article** 'the'; **indefinite article** 'a, an'.

**articular** /ɑːˈtɪkjələ(r)/ a. of joints.

**articulate** 1 /ɑːˈtɪkjələt/ a. expressing oneself fluently and coherently; (of speech) in which separate sounds and words are clear; having joints. 2 /ɑːˈtɪkjəleɪt/ v. speak distinctly; express clearly; connect with joints. 3 **articulation** n.

**artifice** /ˈɑːtɪfɪs/ n. trick; cunning; skill.

**artificer** /ɑːˈtɪfɪsə(r)/ n. craftsman.

**artificial** /ɑːtəˈfɪʃ(ə)l/ a. produced by art, man-made; not natural or real. **artificial insemination** injection of semen into uterus other than by sexual intercourse; **artificial respiration** manual or mechanical stimulation of breathing. **artificiality** n.

**artillery** /ɑːˈtɪlərɪ/ n. large guns used in fighting on land; branch of army using these. **artilleryman** n.

**artisan** /ɑːtəˈzæn or ˈɑːtəzæn/ n. skilled workman or craftsman.

**artist** /ˈɑːtɪst/ n. person who practises fine art, esp. painting; highly gifted practiser of any craft; artiste; Aus. person given to specified activity. **artistic** a.; **artistry** n.

**artiste** /ɑːˈtiːst/ n. professional singer, dancer, etc.

**artless** /ˈɑːtləs/ a. guileless, ingenuous; not resulting from art; clumsy.

**arty** /ˈɑːtɪ/ a. pretentiously or quaintly artistic.

**arum** /ˈeərəm/ n. kind of plant with small flowers enclosed in bracts.

**Arunta** var. of **Aranda**.

**arvo** /ˈɑːvəʊ/ n. (pl. **-vos**) Aus. sl. afternoon.

**Aryan** /ˈeərɪən/ 1 n. speaker of parent language of Indo-European family; incorrect (esp. in Nazi Germany) non-Jewish Caucasian. 2 a. of Indo-European family of languages.

**as** /æz/ 1 adv. & conj. in the same degree; in the manner in which; in the form or function of; while; when; since, seeing that. 2 rel. pron. that, who, which.

**asafoetida** /æsəˈfiːtɪdə/ n. resinous gum with strong smell.

**asbestos** /æsˈbestəs/ n. a fibrous silicate mineral; fire-resistant substance made from this.

**asbestosis** /æsbesˈtəʊsəs/ n. lung disease caused by inhaling asbestos particles.

**ascend** /əˈsend/ v. go or come up; rise, mount, climb.

**ascendancy** /əˈsendənsɪ/ n. dominant control over.

**ascendant** /əˈsend(ə)nt/ a. rising; gaining favour or control; rising towards zenith; Astrol. (of sign) just above eastern horizon. **in the ascendant** at or near peak of one's fortunes.

**ascension** /əˈsenʃ(ə)n/ n. ascent, esp. (**Ascension**) of Christ into Heaven.

**ascent** /əˈsent/ n. ascending, rising; upward path or slope.

**ascertain** /æsəˈteɪn/ v.t. find out. **ascertainment** n.

**ascetic** /əˈsetɪk/ 1 a. severely abstinent, severe in self-discipline. 2 n. ascetic person. 3 **asceticism** n.

**ascorbic acid** /əˈskɔːbɪk/ vitamin C.

**ascribe** /əˈskraɪb/ v.t. regard (thing or circumstance) as belonging to; attribute. **ascription** n.

**asdic** /ˈæzdɪk/ n. earlier form of sonar.

**asepsis** /eɪˈsepsəs/ n. absence of sepsis or harmful bacteria; aseptic method in surgery.

**aseptic** /eɪˈseptɪk/ a. free from sepsis; surgically sterile; securing absence of septic matter; sterilized.

**asexual** /eɪˈseksjʊəl/ a. without sex; without sexuality; (of reproduction) not involving fusion of gametes.

**ash**[1] n. (freq. in pl.) powdery residue left after combustion of a substance; in pl. remains of human body after cremation; **the Ashes** symbol of victory in Anglo-Australian test cricket. **ashtray** receptacle for tobacco ash; **Ash Wednesday** first day of Lent, Aus. day of devastating bushfires in 1980 and esp. 1983.

**ash²** /n./ forest tree with silver-grey bark; its wood; any of several similar but unrelated Aus. trees.

**ashamed** /ə'ʃeɪmd/ *a.* feeling or affected by shame.

**ashen** /'æʃ(ə)n/ *a.* of ashes; pale as ashes.

**ashlar** /'æʃlə(r)/ *n.* (masonry made of) square-cut stones.

**ashore** /ə'ʃɔː(r)/ *adv.* to or on shore.

**ashram** /'æʃræm/ *n.* orig. in India, retreat for religious meditation.

**ashy** /'æʃiː/ *a.* ashen; covered with ash.

**Asian** /'eɪʃ(ə)n/ 1 *a.* of Asia or its peoples or languages. 2 *n.* native of Asia.

**Asiatic** /eɪzɪ'ætɪk/ *a.* & *n.* Asian (usu. with geogr. reference).

**aside** /ə'saɪd/ 1 *adv.* to or on one side, away, apart. 2 *n.* words spoken aside, esp. by actors.

**asinine** /'æsənaɪn/ *a.* like an ass; stupid.

**ASIO** *abbr.* Australian Security Intelligence Organization.

**ask** /ɑːsk/ *v.* call for answer to or about; seek to obtain from another person; make request (for); invite.

**askance** /ə'skæns/ *adv.* sideways; **look askance at** view suspiciously.

**askew** /ə'skjuː/ *adv.* crookedly; out of true position.

**aslant** /ə'slɑːnt/ 1 *adv.* on a slant. 2 *prep.* obliquely across.

**asleep** /ə'sliːp/ 1 *pred.a.* sleeping; *colloq.* inattentive; (of limb) numb. 2 *adv.* into state of sleep.

**asp** *n.* small venomous snake.

**asparagus** /əs'pærəgəs/ *n.* plant with feathery leaves; its edible young shoots.

**aspect** /'æspekt/ *n.* way thing presents itself to eye or mind; direction in which thing faces; side facing in specified direction; *Astrol.* relative position of planets.

**aspen** /'æspən/ *n.* kind of poplar with fluttering leaves.

**asperity** /æs'perətiː/ *n.* harshness; roughness.

**aspersion** /əs'pɜːʃ(ə)n/ *n.* damaging or derogatory remark; **cast aspersions on** defame.

**asphalt** /'æsfælt/ 1 *n.* tarlike bitumen made from petroleum; mixture of this with sand etc. for surfacing roads etc. 2 *v.t.* surface with asphalt.

**asphodel** /'æsfədel/ *n.* kind of lily; *poet.* immortal flower in Elysium.

**asphyxia** /æs'fɪksɪə/ *n.* condition caused by lack of oxygen in blood; suffocation.

**asphyxiate** /əs'fɪksɪeɪt/ *v.t.* suffocate. **asphyxiation** *n.*

**aspic** /'æspɪk/ *n.* clear meat jelly.

**aspidistra** /æspə'dɪstrə/ *n.* houseplant with broad tapering leaves.

**aspirant** /'æspərənt/ 1 *n.* person who aspires. 2 *a.* aspiring.

**aspirate** 1 /'æspəreɪt/ *v.t.* pronounce with *h*. 2 /'æspɪrət/ *n.* sound of *h*; consonant blended with this.

**aspiration** /æspə'reɪʃ(ə)n/ *n.* desire, ambition; aspirating.

**aspire** /ə'spaɪə(r)/ *v.i.* feel earnest desire or ambition; seek *after*.

**aspirin** /'æsprən/ *n.* white powder used to relieve pain and reduce fever; tablet of this.

**ass** *n.* four-legged animal with long ears, related to horse; stupid person.

**assail** /ə'seɪl/ *v.t.* attack; pester. **assailant** *n.*

**assassin** /ə'sæsɪn/ *n.* killer, esp. of important person for political motives.

**assassinate** /ə'sæsɪneɪt/ *v.t.* kill (esp. political etc. leader) by treacherous violence. **assassination** *n.*

**assault** /ə'sɔːlt/ 1 *n.* sudden violent attack; *euphem.* rape; unlawful personal attack. 2 *v.t.* make assault upon. 3 **assault course** series of obstacles to be climbed over or under etc. as part of military training.

**assay** /ə'seɪ/ 1 *n.* test of metal or ore for quality. 2 *v.t.* make assay of; *arch.* attempt.

**assegai** /'æsəgaɪ/ *n.* throwing-spear of S. Afr. peoples.

**assemblage** /ə'semblɪdʒ/ *n.* collection, group.

**assemble** /ə'semb(ə)l/ *v.* fit together parts of (machine etc.); bring or come together.

**assembly** /ə'sembliː/ *n.* assembling; collection of persons, esp. of deliberative body; fitting together of components. **assembly line** sequence of machines, workers, etc., assembling product.

**assent** /ə'sent/ 1 *n.* consent, approval. 2 *v.i.* agree *to*.

**assert** /ə'sɜːt/ *v.t.* declare; maintain claim to. **assert oneself** insist on one's rights.

**assertion** /ə'sɜːʃ(ə)n/ *n.* declaration; forthright statement.

**assertive** /ə'sɜːtɪv/ *a.* asserting oneself; forthright, positive.

**assess** /ə'ses/ *v.t.* estimate magnitude or value or quality of; fix amount of (fine, tax, etc.). **assessment** *n.*

**assessor** *n.* one who assesses taxes etc.; adviser to judge in court.

**asset** /'æset/ *n.* possession having value; (often in *pl.*) property available to meet debts; useful quality or person.

**asseverate** /ə'sevəreɪt/ *v.t.* declare solemnly. **asseveration** *n.*

**assiduous** /ə'sɪdjʊəs/ *a.* persevering, diligent. **assiduity** /æsɪ'djuːɪtɪ/ *n.*

**assign** /ə'saɪn/ *v.t.* allot; appoint, ascribe; make over formally; *Aus. hist.* allocate (convict) to settler as unpaid servant.

**assignation** /æsɪg'neɪʃ(ə)n/ *n.* appointment, esp. of lovers; assigning.

**assignee** /əsaɪ'niː/ *n.* person to whom property or right is legally transferred; *Aus. hist.* assigned convict.

**assignment** /ə'saɪnmənt/ *n.* task assigned.

**assimilate** /ə'sɪməleɪt/ *v.* absorb, be absorbed, into system; make or become like. **assimilable** *a.*; **assimilation** *n.*; **assimilative** *a.*

**assist** /ə'sɪst/ *v.* help; take part *in*; be present *at*. **assistance** *n.*

**assistant** /ə'sɪst(ə)nt/ *n.* helper; subordinate worker, esp. serving customers in shop.

**assizes** /ə'saɪzəz/ *n.* *UK hist.* periodical session for administration of civil and criminal justice.

**Assoc.** *abbr.* Association.

**associate** 1 /ə'səʊʃɪeɪt/ *v.* connect; join, combine; have frequent dealings (*with*). 2 /ə'səʊʃɪət/ *n.* subordinate member of society etc.; partner or colleague. 3 /ə'səʊʃɪət/ *a.* joined, allied.

**association** /əsəʊsɪ'eɪʃ(ə)n/ *n.* body of persons organized for joint purpose; connection of ideas; companionship. **Association football** kind played with round ball which may be handled only by goalkeeper, *Aus.* (also) Australian Rules competition run by an Association.

**assonance** /'æsənəns/ *n.* resemblance of sound between two syllables; rhyme depending on similarity of vowel-sounds only. **assonant** *a.*

**assort** /ə'sɔːt/ *v.* arrange in sorts; suit, harmonize (*with*).

**assorted** *a.* of various sorts put together.

**assortment** *n.* set composed of several sorts.

**assuage** /ə'sweɪdʒ/ *v.t.* soothe, allay.

**assume** /ə'sjuːm/ *v.t.* take to be true; take upon oneself; simulate.

**assumption** /ə'sʌmpʃ(ə)n/ *n.* assuming, thing assumed. **the Assumption** taking of Virgin Mary bodily into heaven.

**assurance** /ə'ʃʊərəns/ or -'ʃɔːr-/ *n.* declaration; self-confidence; impudence; insurance, esp. of life.

**assure** /ə'ʃʊə(r)/ or əʃɔː(r)/ *v.t.* make (person) sure (*of*); tell (person) confidently; ensure happening etc. of; insure (esp. life).

**assuredly** /ə'ʃʊərədlɪ/ or -'ʃɔːr-/ *adv.* certainly.

**aster** /'æstə(r)/ *n.* garden plant with bright daisy-like flowers.

**asterisk** /'æstərɪsk/ *n.* star-shaped symbol (\*) used esp. as mark of reference.

**astern** /ə'stɜːn/ *adv.* in or to rear of ship or aircraft; behind; backwards.

**asteroid** /'æstərɔɪd/ *n.* any of numerous small planets between orbits of Mars and Jupiter.

**asthma** /'æsmə/ *n.* disorder marked by difficulty in breathing. **asthmatic** /-'mæt-/ *a.* & *n.*

**astigmatism** /ə'stɪgmətɪz(ə)m/ *n.* defect in eye or lens in which light rays from a point produce a line image. **astigmatic** /-'mæt-/ *a.*

**astir** /ə'stɜː(r)/ *adv.* & *pred.a.* in motion; out of bed.

**astonish** /ə'stɒnɪʃ/ *v.t.* amaze, surprise. **astonishment** *n.*

**astound** /ə'staʊnd/ *v.t.* shock with surprise.

**astrakhan** /æstrə'kæn/ *n.* dark curly fleece of Astrakhan lamb; imitation of this.

**astral** /'æstr(ə)l/ *a.* of or connected with stars.

**astray** /əˈstreɪ/ *adv.* out of right way.

**astride** /əˈstraɪd/ **1** *adv.* with one leg on each side (*of*). **2** *prep.* astride of.

**astringent** /əˈstrɪndʒ(ə)nt/ **1** *a.* that causes contraction of body tissue; austere, severe. **2** *n.* astringent substance. **3 astringency** *n.*

**astrolabe** /ˈæstrəleɪb/ *n.* instrument for measuring altitudes of stars etc.

**astrologer** /əˈstrɒlədʒə(r)/ *n.* person who practises astrology.

**astrology** /əˈstrɒlədʒi/ *n.* study of influence of movements of stars etc. on human affairs. **astrological** *a.*

**astronaut** /ˈæstrənɔːt/ *n.* space traveller. **astronautical** *a.*

**astronautics** /æstrəˈnɔːtɪks/ *n.pl.* usu. treated as *sing.* science of space travel.

**astronomer** /əˈstrɒnəmə(r)/ *n.* person who practises astronomy.

**astronomical** /æstrəˈnɒmɪk(ə)l/ *a.* (of number etc.) very big or high; of or concerned with astronomy.

**astronomy** /əˈstrɒnəmi/ *n.* science of heavenly bodies.

**astrophysics** /æstrəʊˈfɪzɪks/ *n.* study of physics and chemistry of heavenly bodies. **astrophysical** *a.*; **astrophysicist** *n.*

**astute** /əˈstjuːt/ *a.* shrewd; crafty.

**asunder** /əˈsʌndə(r)/ *adv.* apart, in pieces.

**asylum** /əˈsaɪləm/ *n.* place of refuge or safety; (in full **political asylum**) protection given by State to political refugee from another country; *hist.* mental institution.

**asymmetry** /æˈsɪmətri/ *n.* lack of symmetry. **asymmetrical** /æsəˈmet-/ *a.*

**at** /æt/ *prep.* expr. position or state of activity or point in time or on a scale, or motion or aim towards. **at all** in any way, to any extent; **at that** moreover.

**atavism** /ˈætəvɪz(ə)m/ *n.* resemblance to remote ancestors; reversion to earlier type. **atavistic** *a.*

**ate** *past* of **eat**.

**atelier** /əˈteljeɪ/ *n.* workshop; artist's studio.

**atheism** /ˈeɪθiːɪz(ə)m/ *n.* belief that no God exists. **atheist** *n.*; **atheistic** *a.*

**atherosclerosis** /æθərəʊskliəˈrəʊsəs/ *n.* formation of fatty deposits in the arteries.

**athlete** /ˈæθliːt/ *n.* person who competes or excels in physical exercises. **athlete's foot** fungous disease of foot.

**athletic** /æθˈletɪk/ *a.* of athletes; physically powerful. **athleticism** *n.*

**athletics** *n.pl.* (occas. treated as *sing.*) sports such as running, jumping, etc.

**atlas** /ˈætləs/ *n.* book of maps.

**atmosphere** /ˈætməsfɪə(r)/ *n.* mixture of gases surrounding earth or heavenly body; mental or moral environment; tone, mood, etc., conveyed by place, book, etc.; air in room etc. **atmospheric** /-ˈfer-/ *a.*

**atmospherics** /ætməsˈferɪks/ *n.pl.* electrical disturbance in atmosphere; interference with telecommunications caused by this.

**atoll** /ˈætɒl/ *n.* ring-shaped coral reef enclosing lagoon.

**atom** /ˈætəm/ *n.* smallest particle of chemical element that can take part in chemical reaction; this as source of atomic energy; minute portion or thing. **atom bomb** atomic bomb.

**atomic** /əˈtɒmɪk/ *a.* of atom(s); using or concerned with atomic energy or atomic bombs. **atomic bomb** bomb whose power comes from release of nuclear energy; **atomic energy** nuclear energy; **atomic number** number of unit positive charges carried by nucleus of atom; **atomic weight** ratio between mass of one atom of element and 1/12 weight of atom of isotope carbon 12.

**atomize** /ˈætəmaɪz/ *v.t.* reduce to atoms; reduce (liquid) to fine spray. **atomization** *n.*; **atomizer** *n.*

**atonal** /eɪˈtəʊn(ə)l/ *a. Mus.* not written in any key. **atonality** /-ˈnæl-/ *n.*

**atone** /əˈtəʊn/ *v.t.* make amends (*for* wrong). **atonement** *n.*

**atrium** /ˈeɪtrɪəm/ *n.* (*pl.* **-tria** or **-triums**) either of two upper cavities of heart.

**atrocious** /əˈtrəʊʃəs/ *a.* very bad; extremely wicked.

**atrocity** /əˈtrɒsəti/ *n.* wicked or cruel act.

**atrophy** /ˈætrəfi/ **1** *n.* wasting away for lack of nourishment or use. **2** *v.* cause atrophy in; suffer atrophy.

**atropine** /ˈætrəpən/ *n.* poisonous alkaloid got from deadly nightshade.

**attach** /əˈtætʃ/ *v.* fasten, join; ac-

# attaché — au fait

**attaché** /ə'tæʃeɪ/ n. person attached to ambassador's staff. **attaché case** small rectangular case for carrying documents etc.

**attachment** /ə'tætʃmənt/ n. attaching, thing attached, esp. device; affection, devotion.

**attack** /ə'tæk/ 1 v. make attack (on); act harmfully on; (in sport) try to score against. 2 n. violent attempt to hurt or defeat; adverse criticism; onset.

**attain** /ə'teɪn/ v. gain, accomplish; reach; come to (goal etc.).

**attainment** n. attaining; (usu. in pl.) skills, achievements.

**attar** /'ætɑ:(r)/ n. fragrant oil esp. made from rose-petals.

**attempt** /ə'tempt/ 1 v.t. try; try to accomplish or conquer. 2 n. attempting; endeavour.

**attend** /ə'tend/ v. be present at; go regularly to; apply mind or oneself (to); accompany, wait on.

**attendance** /ə'tend(ə)ns/ n. attending; number of persons present.

**attendant** /ə'tend(ə)nt/ 1 n. person attending, esp. to provide service. 2 a. waiting on; accompanying.

**attention** /ə'tenʃ(ə)n/ n. act or faculty of applying one's mind; consideration, care; Mil. erect attitude of readiness; in pl. formal courtesies.

**attentive** /ə'tentɪv/ a. giving or paying attention (to).

**attenuate** /ə'tenju:eɪt/ v.t. make slender or thin; reduce in force or value. **attenuation** n.

**attest** /ə'test/ v. act as evidence of; certify validity of; bear witness to. **attestation** n.

**attic**[1] /'ætɪk/ n. room or space in storey immediately under roof.

**Attic**[2] /'ætɪk/ a. of Athens or Attica.

**attire** /ə'taɪə(r)/ n. dress, esp. formal.

**attitude** /'ætɪtju:d/ n. way of regarding things; disposition or reaction (to person or thing); posture of body.

**attitudinize** /ætɪ'tju:dənaɪz/ v.i. adopt attitudes; show affectation.

**attorney** /ə'tɜ:nɪ/ n. person appointed to act for another in business or legal affairs; US qualified lawyer. **Attorney-General** chief legal officer of government.

**attract** /ə'trækt/ v.t. draw to itself or oneself; arouse interest or pleasure in.

**attraction** /ə'trækʃ(ə)n/ n. attracting, thing that attracts; charm, inducement.

**attractive** /ə'træktɪv/ a. inviting, pleasing.

**attribute** 1 /ə'trɪbju:t/ v.t. regard as belonging or appropriate to. 2 /'ætrɪbju:t/ n. quality ascribed to person or thing; characteristic quality; object regularly associated with person etc. 3 **attribute** to consider to be caused by. 4 **attribution** /ætrɪ'bju:ʃ(ə)n/ n.

**attributive** /ə'trɪbjətɪv/ a. expressing an attribute; (of adj.) coming before noun it qualifies.

**attrition** /ə'trɪʃ(ə)n/ n. gradual wearing down; friction; abrasion.

**attune** /ə'tju:n/ v.t. adapt; tune; bring into musical accord.

**atypical** /eɪ'tɪpɪk(ə)l/ a. not belonging to any type.

**aubergine** /'əʊbədʒi:n/ n. egg-plant; fruit of this.

**aubrietia** /ɔ:'bri:ʃə/ n. spring-flowering dwarf perennial rock-plant.

**auburn** /'ɔ:bən/ a. reddish-brown.

**auction** /'ɔ:kʃ(ə)n/ 1 n. sale in which each article is sold to highest bidder. 2 v.t. sell by auction.

**auctioneer** /ɔ:kʃə'nɪə(r)/ n. person who conducts auctions.

**audacious** /ɔ:'deɪʃəs/ a. daring, bold; impudent. **audacity** /-'dæs-/ n.

**audible** /'ɔ:dəb(ə)l/ a. that can be heard. **audibility** n.

**audience** /'ɔ:dɪəns/ n. group of listeners or spectators; formal interview.

**audio** /'ɔ:dɪəʊ/ n. (reproduction of) sound. **audio typist** one who types directly from recording; **audio-visual** using both sight and sound.

**audit** /'ɔ:dɪt/ 1 n. official examination of accounts. 2 v.t. conduct audit of.

**audition** /ɔ:'dɪʃ(ə)n/ 1 n. trial hearing of actor, singer, etc. 2 v. give audition to; hold auditions; be auditioned.

**auditor** /'ɔ:dətə(r)/ n. person who audits accounts.

**auditorium** /ɔ:də'tɔ:rɪəm/ n. (pl. -iums) part of theatre etc. occupied by audience.

**auditory** /'ɔ:dətərɪ/ a. of hearing.

**au fait** /əʊ 'feɪ/ well acquainted with. [F]

**Aug.** *abbr.* August.

**auger** /'ɔːgə(r)/ *n.* tool for boring holes in wood.

**aught** /ɔːt/ *n. arch.* anything.

**augment** /ɔːg'ment/ *v.t.* make greater, increase. **augmentation** *n.*

**augmented** *a. Mus.* (of interval) increased by semitone.

**augur** /'ɔːgə(r)/ 1 *n.* Roman religious official who foretold events by observing omens; soothsayer. 2 *v.* portend; serve as omen for.

**augury** /'ɔːgjəri/ *n.* divination; omen.

**august**[1] /ɔː'gʌst/ *a.* venerable, imposing.

**August**[2] /'ɔːgəst/ *n.* eighth month of year.

**auk** /ɔːk/ *n.* Northern sea-bird with small narrow wings.

**aunt** /ɑːnt/ *n.* parent's sister or sister-in-law. **Aunt Sally** (figure used as target in) throwing game, target of general abuse.

**aunty** /'ɑːnti/ *n.* (also **auntie**) *colloq.* aunt.

**au pair** /əʊ 'peə(r)/ young woman usu. from abroad who helps with housework in return for room and board.

**aura** /'ɔːrə/ *n.* atmosphere diffused by or attending person etc.; subtle emanation.

**aural** /'ɔːr(ə)l/ *a.* of ear or hearing.

**aureola** /'ɔːriːəʊlə/ *n.* (also **aureole**) halo.

*au revoir* /əʊ rə'vwɑː(r)/ (good-bye) till we meet again. [F]

**auricle** /'ɔːrɪk(ə)l/ *n.* external part of ear; atrium of heart.

**auricular** /ɔː'rɪkjələ(r)/ *a.* pertaining to ear. **auricular confession** confession made privately to priest.

**auriferous** /ɔː'rɪfərəs/ *a.* yielding gold.

**aurora** /ɔː'rɔːrə/ *n.* luminous electrical radiation from northern (**aurora borealis** /bɔːriː'eɪləs/) or southern (**aurora australis** /ɒ'streɪləs/) magnetic pole.

**auscultation** /ɒskəl'teɪʃ(ə)n/ *n.* listening to sound of heart etc. for diagnosis.

**auspice** /'ɔːspəs/ *n.* omen; in *pl.* patronage.

**auspicious** /ɔː'spɪʃəs/ *a.* promising; favourable.

**Aussat** /'ɒsæt/ *n.* Aus. government-sponsored communications satellite.

**Aussie** /'ɒziː/ *n.* & *a. colloq.* Australian.

**austere** /ɒ'stɪə(r)/ *a.* severely simple; stern; morally strict. **austerity** /-'ter-/ *n.*

**austral** /'ɒstr(ə)l/ *a.* southern.

**Australasian** /ɒstrə'leɪʒ(ə)n/ *a.* of Australia and S.W. Pacific Islands.

**Australian** /ɒ'streɪljən/ 1 *a.* of Australia. 2 *n.* native or inhabitant of Australia. 3 **Australian cattle dog** blue heeler; **Australian crawl** overarm swimming stroke; **Australian Rules** football game played with oval ball by teams of 18, Australian National Football; **Australian salute** *Aus. sl.* movement to brush away flies; **Australian silky terrier** Sydney silky; **Australian terrier** dog of small sturdy breed.

**Australianism** /ɒs'treɪljənɪz(ə)m/ *n.* word or usage peculiar to or originating in Australia.

**australite** /'ɒstrəlaɪt/ *n.* small piece of dark metallic glass found in Australia.

**Australorp** /'ɒstrəlɔːp/ *n.* Aus. breed of Orpington fowl.

**autarchy** /'ɔːtɑːkɪ/ *n.* absolute sovereignty.

**autarky** /'ɔːtɑːkɪ/ *n.* self-sufficiency.

**authentic** /ɔː'θentɪk/ *a.* of undisputed origin, genuine; trustworthy. **authentically** *adv.*; **authenticity** /-'tɪs-/ *n.*

**authenticate** /ɔː'θentɪkeɪt/ *v.t.* establish truth, authorship, or validity of. **authentication** *n.*

**author** /'ɔːθə(r)/ *n.* writer of book etc.; originator. **authoress** *n.*; **authorship** *n.*

**authoritarian** /ɔːθɒrə'teərɪən/ 1 *a.* favouring unqualified obedience to authority. 2 *n.* authoritarian person.

**authoritative** /ɔː'θɒrətətɪv/ *a.* having or claiming authority.

**authority** /ɔː'θɒrətɪ/ *n.* power or right to enforce obedience; person or body having this; delegated power; personal influence; (book etc. referred to for) conclusive opinion or statement; expert.

**authorize** /'ɔːθəraɪz/ *v.t.* give authority to; recognize officially. **Authorized Version** English translation (1611) of Bible. **authorization** *n.*

**autism** /'ɔːtɪz(ə)m/ *n.* mental condition esp. in children preventing proper response to environment. **autistic** *a.*

**autobiography** /ɔːtəʊbaɪ'ɒgrəfɪ/ *n.*

## autochthonous          awake

story of one's own life. **autobiographer** *n.*; **autobiographical** *a.*
**autochthonous** /ɔː'tɒkθənəs/ *a.* indigenous; aboriginal.
**autocracy** /ɔː'tɒkrəsi/ *n.* absolute government by one person.
**autocrat** /'ɔːtəkræt/ *n.* absolute ruler. **autocratic** *a.*
**autograph** /'ɔːtəgrɑːf or 'ɔːtəgræf/ 1 *n.* person's own handwriting, esp. signature. 2 *v.t.* sign or write on in one's own hand.
**automate** /'ɔːtəmeɪt/ *v.t.* subject to or operate by automation.
**automatic** /ɔːtə'mætɪk/ 1 *a.* working of itself, without direct human involvement; done without thought or from habit; occurring as a necessary consequence; (of firearm) having mechanism for continuous loading and firing. 2 *n.* automatic gun etc.; vehicle with automatic transmission. 3 **automatic transmission** system in motor vehicle for automatic change of gears. 4 **automatically** *adv.*
**automation** /ɔːtə'meɪʃ(ə)n/ *n.* use of automatic equipment to save mental or manual labour.
**automaton** /ɔː'tɒmət(ə)n/ *n.* (*pl.* **-ta** or **-tons**) machine responding to automatic control.
**automobile** /'ɔːtəməbiːl/ *n.* US motor car.
**automotive** /ɔːtə'məʊtɪv/ *a.* concerned with motor vehicles.
**autonomous** /ɔː'tɒnəməs/ *a.* self-governing. **autonomy** *n.*
**autopsy** /'ɔːtɒpsi/ *n.* post-mortem examination.
**auto-suggestion** /ɔːtəʊsə'dʒestʃ(ə)n/ *n.* hypnotic or subconscious suggestion proceeding from subject himself.
**autumn** /'ɔːtəm/ *n.* season of year between summer and winter. **autumnal** /-'tʌmn(ə)l/ *a.*
**auxiliary** /ɔːk'zɪliəri/ 1 *a.* giving help, additional, subsidiary. 2 *n.* auxiliary person or thing; in *pl.* foreign or allied troops in service of nation at war; verb used in forming tenses etc. of other verbs.
**avail** /ə'veɪl/ 1 *v.* be of use or help (to). 2 *n.* use, profit. 3 **avail oneself of** use, profit by.
**available** /ə'veɪləb(ə)l/ *a.* capable of being used; at one's disposal. **availability** *n.*
**avalanche** /'ævəlɑːnʃ or 'ævəlæntʃ/ *n.* mass of snow, earth, and ice falling down mountain; sudden onrush.
**avant-garde** /ævɑ̃'gɑːd/ 1 *n.* group of innovators in art and music and literature. 2 *a.* new, progressive.
**avarice** /'ævərɪs/ *n.* greed for gain. **avaricious** *a.*
**avatar** /'ævətɑː(r)/ *n. Hindu Myth.* descent of god to earth in bodily form.
**avenge** /ə'vendʒ/ *v.t.* inflict retribution on behalf of; exact retribution for.
**avenue** /'ævənjuː/ *n.* road or path, usu. bordered by trees etc.; way of approach.
**aver** /ə'vɜː(r)/ *v.t.* assert, affirm.
**average** /'ævərɪdʒ/ 1 *n.* usual amount or extent or rate; number obtained by dividing total of given numbers by how many there are. 2 *a.* usual, ordinary; estimated by average. 3 *v.* amount on average to; do etc. on average; estimate average of. 4 **on average** as an average rate etc.
**averse** /ə'vɜːs/ *a.* opposed, disinclined, unwilling.
**aversion** /ə'vɜːʃ(ə)n/ *n.* dislike or antipathy; object of dislike.
**avert** /ə'vɜːt/ *v.t.* prevent; turn away.
**aviary** /'eɪvɪəri/ *n.* large cage or building for keeping birds.
**aviation** /eɪvɪ'eɪʃ(ə)n/ *n.* flying in aircraft.
**aviator** /'eɪvɪeɪtə(r)/ *n.* person who flies aircraft.
**avid** /'ævɪd/ *a.* eager; greedy. **avidity** *n.*
**avocado** /ævə'kɑːdəʊ/ *n.* (*pl.* **-dos**) pear-shaped tropical fruit.
**avocation** /ævə'keɪʃ(ə)n/ *n.* secondary activity; *colloq.* one's occupation.
**avocet** /'ævəset/ *n.* wading bird with long upturned bill.
**avoid** /ə'vɔɪd/ *v.t.* keep away or refrain from; escape from. **avoidance** *n.*
**avoirdupois** /ævədjə'pɔɪz/ *n.* system of weights based on pound of 16 ounces.
**avow** /ə'vaʊ/ *v.t.* declare; confess. **avowal** *n.*; **avowedly** *adv.*
**avuncular** /ə'vʌŋkjələ(r)/ *a.* of or like an uncle.
**await** /ə'weɪt/ *v.t.* wait for.
**awake** /ə'weɪk/ 1 *v.* (*past* **awoke**; *p.p.* **awoken**) rouse from sleep; cease to

sleep; become active. 2 *pred.a.* not asleep; alert.
**awaken** /əˈweɪk(ə)n/ *v.* awake, draw attention of (person *to*).
**award** /əˈwɔːd/ 1 *v.t.* order to be given as payment, penalty, or prize. 2 *n.* judicial decision; thing awarded. 3 **award wage** *Aus. & NZ* minimum weekly wage fixed by industrial court.
**aware** /əˈweə(r)/ *a.* conscious, having knowledge (*of*).
**awash** /əˈwɒʃ/ *pred.a.* at or near surface of water; covered or flooded by water.
**away** 1 *adv.* to or at distance; into non-existence; constantly, continuously. 2 *a.* (of match etc.) played on opponent's ground.
**awe** /ɔː/ 1 *n.* admiration mixed with reverential fear. 2 *v.t.* inspire with awe. 3 **awestruck** struck with awe.
**aweigh** /əˈweɪ/ *adv.* (of anchor) just lifted from sea bottom.
**awesome** /ˈɔːsəm/ *a.* inspiring awe.
**awful** /ˈɔːfəl/ *a.* inspiring awe; *colloq.* very bad; notable in its kind.
**awfully** *adv. colloq.* very.
**awhile** /əˈwaɪl/ *adv.* for a short time.
**awkward** /ˈɔːkwəd/ *a.* difficult to use; clumsy; embarrassing, embarrassed; hard to deal with.
**awl** /ɔːl/ *n.* small tool for pricking holes, esp. in leather.
**awning** /ˈɔːnɪŋ/ *n.* fabric roof, shelter.
**awoke(n)** *past* & *p.p.* of **awake**.
**AWOL** /ˈeɪwɒl/ *abbr.* absent without leave.
**awry** /əˈraɪ/ *adv.* crookedly; amiss.
**axe** /æks/ 1 *n.* chopping-tool. 2 *v.t.* cut down (costs, services, etc.); remove.
**axeman** /ˈæksmən/ *n.* (*pl.* **-men**) person skilled with axe. **axemanship** *n.*
**axial** /ˈæksiːəl/ *a.* of, forming, or placed around axis.
**axiom** /ˈæksiːəm/ *n.* established principle; self-evident truth. **axiomatic** *a.*
**axis** /ˈæksəs/ *n.* (*pl.* **axes** /-iːz/) imaginary line about which object rotates; line dividing regular figure symmetrically; reference line for measurement of co-ordinates etc.
**axle** /ˈæks(ə)l/ *n.* spindle on or with which wheel revolves; rod connecting pair of wheels.
**ayatollah** /aɪəˈtɒlə/ *n.* religious leader in Iran.
**aye**[1] /aɪ/ 1 *adv. arch.* yes. 2 *n.* affirmative answer or vote.
**aye**[2] /aɪ/ *adv. arch.* always.
**azalea** /əˈzeɪliːə/ *n.* flowering shrubby plant.
**azimuth** /ˈæzəməθ/ *n.* arc along horizon from N. or S. meridian to meridian through given point.
**azure** /ˈeɪʒə(r)/ 1 *a.* sky-blue. 2 *n.* sky-blue colour; clear sky.

# B

**B** *abbr.* black (pencil lead).

**b.** *abbr.* born.

**BA** *abbr.* Bachelor of Arts.

**baa** /bɑː/ *n. & v.i.* (*past & p.p.* **baaed** or **baa'd**) bleat.

**baba** /ˈbɑːbɑː/ *n.* (*pl.* **babas**) sponge-cake soaked in rum syrup.

**babble** /ˈbæb(ə)l/ 1 *v.* make incoherent sounds, talk inarticulately, say incoherently, divulge foolishly; (of stream) murmur. 2 *n.* idle talk; murmur of water etc.

**babe** *n.* baby.

**babel** /ˈbeɪb(ə)l/ *n.* confused noise esp. of voices; scene of confusion.

**baboon** /bəˈbuːn/ *n.* large kind of monkey.

**baby** /ˈbeɪbi/ *n.* very young child; childish person; youngest member of family etc.; thing small of its kind; young or small animal. **baby grand** small grand piano; **baby-sit** act as **baby-sitter**, person looking after child while parents are out.

**baccarat** /ˈbækərɑː/ *n.* gambling card-game.

**Bacchanalia** /bækəˈneɪlɪə/ *n.pl.* festival of Bacchus, Roman god of wine. **Bacchanalian** *a.*

**bach** /bætʃ/ *v.i.* Aus. & NZ (of man) do one's own cooking and housekeeping.

**bachelor** /ˈbætʃələ(r)/ *n.* unmarried man; person who has taken university first degree. **bachelor girl** *colloq.* young unmarried woman living independently.

**bacillus** /bəˈsɪləs/ *n.* (*pl.* **-illi** /-ˈɪlaɪ/) rod-shaped bacterium. **bacillary** *a.*

**back** 1 *n.* rear surface of human body from shoulders to hips; upper surface of animal's body; side or part at rear or normally away from spectator or direction of motion; part of garment covering back; defensive player in football etc. 2 *a.* situated behind or away from front; overdue; reversed. 3 *adv.* to rear; away from front; in or into the past or an earlier or normal position or condition; in return; at a distance. 4 *v.* help with money or moral support; cause to move backwards; go backwards; bet on; provide with or serve as back or support or backing to. 5 **back-bencher** MP without senior office; **backbite** speak badly of; **backblocks** *Aus. & NZ* land in remote interior; **backbone** spine, main support, firmness of character; **backchat** impudent repartee; **backcloth** painted cloth at back of stage or scene; **back country** land away from settled districts; **back-date** put earlier date to, make retrospectively valid; **back door** *fig.* secret or ingenious means of gaining objective; **back down** abandon claim etc.; **backdrop** backcloth; **backfire** (of engine or vehicle) undergo premature explosion in cylinder or exhaust-pipe, (of plan etc.) have opposite of intended effect; **backhand** stroke esp. in tennis with back of hand towards opponent; **back-handed** indirect, ambiguous; **back-hander** blow with back of hand, *sl.* bribe; **backlash** excessive or violent reaction; **backlog** arrears (of work etc.); **back number** old issue of magazine etc., *sl.* out-of-date person or thing; **back out** withdraw; **backpack** rucksack; **back-pedal** *fig.* reverse previous action or opinion; **back room** *fig.* place where (esp. secret) work goes on; **back seat** *fig.* inferior position or status; **backside** *colloq.* buttocks; **backslide** relapse into error or bad ways; **backstage** behind the scenes; **backstairs** *fig.* = *back door*; **backstroke** stroke made by swimmer lying on back; **backtrack** find way back by route by which one came, *fig.* = *back-pedal*; **back up** support by subordinate action; **back-up** such support; **back up for** *Aus. sl.* go back for more food or money etc.; **backwash** motion of receding wave, repercussions; **backwater** place remote from centre of activity or thought, stagnant water fed from stream; **back woods** remote uncleared forest land.

**backgammon** /ˈbækɡæmən/ *n.* game played on double board with draughts moved according to throw of dice.

**background** /ˈbækɡraʊnd/ *n.* back part of scene etc.; inconspicuous or obscure position; person's education or social circumstances etc.; explanatory information etc.

# backing — balance

**backing** *n.* help or support; material used to form thing's back or support; musical accompaniment.

**backward** *a.* directed backwards; slow in learning; shy.

**backwards** *adv.* away from one's front; back foremost; in reverse of usual way; back towards starting-point.

**bacon** /ˈbeɪk(ə)n/ *n.* cured meat from back and sides of pig.

**bacteriology** /bæktɪəriˈɒlədʒi/ *n.* science of bacteria. **bacteriological** *a.*

**bacterium** /bækˈtɪəriəm/ *n.* (*pl.* -ria) single-celled micro-organism. **bacterial** *a.*

**bad** *a.* (*compar.* **worse**; *superl.* **worst**) inferior; defective; unpleasant; harmful; serious, severe; wicked; naughty; decayed; ill, injured; incorrect, not valid.

**bade** *past* of **bid**.

**badge** *n.* small flat emblem fixed to clothing etc. as sign of office, membership, etc. or bearing slogan etc.

**badger** /ˈbædʒə(r)/ **1** *n.* Eur. and N. Amer. nocturnal burrowing mammal with black and white stripes along muzzle. **2** *v.t.* pester.

**badinage** /ˈbædɪnɑːʒ/ *n.* banter. [F]

**badly** *adv.* (*compar.* **worse**; *superl.* **worst**) in a bad manner; very much; severely.

**badminton** /ˈbædmɪnt(ə)n/ *n.* game played with rackets and shuttlecocks.

**baffle** /ˈbæf(ə)l/ **1** *v.t.* perplex, frustrate. **2** *n.* plate etc. hindering or regulating passage of fluid or sound. **3 bafflement** *n.*

**bag 1** *n.* receptacle of flexible material with opening usu. at top; in *pl. colloq.* large amount; sac in animal body; amount of game shot by sportsman. **2** *v.* secure, take possession of; bulge, hang loosely; put in bag.

**bagatelle** /bægəˈtel/ *n.* game like billiards played with small balls on inclined board; a mere trifle.

**baggage** /ˈbægɪdʒ/ *n.* luggage; portable equipment of army.

**baggy** *a.* hanging loosely.

**bagpipes** /ˈbægpaɪps/ *n.pl.* musical instrument with wind-bag for pumping air through set of reed-pipes. **bagpiper** *n.*

**bail**[1] **1** *n.* security given for released prisoner's return for trial; person(s) pledging thus. **2** *v.t.* (often with *out*) give bail for (person in prison) and secure release of.

**bail**[2] **1** *n.* *Crick.* one of two cross-pieces resting on stumps; *Aus.* & *NZ* framework for securing cow's head in milking-shed. **2** *v.* (with *up*) *Aus.* & *NZ* fasten cow's head in bail; corner (person or animal); stop and disarm (traveller); (of animal) go into bail; surrender.

**bail**[3] *v.* scoop water out of (boat etc.). **bail out** make emergency parachute jump from aircraft.

**bailey** /ˈbeɪli/ *n.* outer wall of castle; court enclosed by this.

**bailiff** /ˈbeɪlɪf/ *n.* sheriff's officer who executes writs, performs distraints, etc.; landlord's agent or steward.

**bairn** /beən/ *n.* *Sc.* child.

**bait 1** *v.t.* torment (chained animal); harrass (person); put bait on or in (fish-hook, trap, etc.). **2** *n.* food to entice prey; allurement.

**baize** /beɪz/ *n.* coarse woollen usu. green fabric used for coverings etc.

**bake** *v.* cook by dry heat esp. in oven; harden by heat; be or become baked; *colloq.* be hot. **baking-powder**, mixture of chemicals used as raising agent in cooking.

**bakelite** /ˈbeɪkəlaɪt/ *n.* kind of plastic.

**baker** /ˈbeɪkə(r)/ *n.* professional bread-maker. **baker's dozen** thirteen.

**bakery** /ˈbeɪkəri/ *n.* place where bread is made or sold.

**baksheesh** /bækˈʃiːʃ/ *n.* gratuity; tip; alms.

**Balaclava** /bæləˈklɑːvə/ *n.* (in full **balaclava helmet**) woollen covering for head and neck.

**balalaika** /bæləˈlaɪkə/ *n.* Russian triangular-bodied guitar-like musical instrument.

**balance** /ˈbæləns/ **1** *n.* weighing apparatus; regulating gear of clock etc.; even distribution of weight or amount, stability of body or mind; preponderating weight or amount; difference between credits and debits; remainder. **2** *v.* offset or compare; equal or neutralize; bring or come into or keep in equilibrium; equalize debits and credits of account, have debits and credits equal. **3 balance of payments** difference between payments into and out of a country; **balance of power** position in which

# balcony — band

no country, party, etc., predominates, power held by small group when larger groups are of equal strength; **balance of trade** difference between exports and imports; **balance-sheet** statement of assets and liabilities.

**balcony** /ˈbælkəni/ *n.* outside balustraded or railed platform with access from upper-floor window; upper tier of seats in public building, theatre, cinema, etc.

**bald** /bɔːld/ *a.* with scalp wholly or partly hairless; without fur, feathers, etc.; with surface worn away; direct; dull.

**balderdash** /ˈbɔːldədæʃ/ *n.* nonsense.

**balding** /ˈbɔːldɪŋ/ *a.* becoming bald.

**bale**[1] *n.* bundle or package of merchandise, hay, etc. 2 *v.t.* make up into bales.

**bale**[2] var. of **bail**[3].

**baleful** /ˈbeɪlfəl/ *a.* pernicious, destructive; malignant.

**balk** /bɔːlk/ 1 *v.* thwart, hinder, disappoint; refuse, hesitate (*at*). 2 *n.* hindrance, stumbling-block.

**ball**[1] /bɔːl/ *n.* solid or hollow sphere, esp. one used in games; material gathered or wound into round mass; rounded part of foot or hand at base of big toe or thumb; missile for cannon etc.; delivery of ball in a game; in *pl.*, *vulg.* testicles; nonsense, muddle. **ball-bearing** bearing using small metal balls to avoid friction, one such ball; **ballcock** valve in cistern etc. opened or shut by falling or rising of floating ball; **ballpoint (pen)** pen whose writing-point is a small ball.

**ball**[2] /bɔːl/ *n.* formal social gathering for dancing; *sl.* enjoyable time.

**ballad** /ˈbæləd/ *n.* simple or sentimental song; (esp. traditional) narrative poem in short stanzas. **balladry** *n.*

**ballast** /ˈbæləst/ 1 *n.* heavy material carried in ship's hold for stability or in balloon for control of height; coarse stone etc. as bed of road or railway. 2 *v.t.* furnish with ballast.

**ballerina** /bæləˈriːnə/ *n.* female ballet-dancer esp. taking leading role.

**ballet** /ˈbæleɪ/ *n.* theatrical performance of dancing and mime to music.

**ballistic** /bəˈlɪstɪk/ *a.* of projectiles. **ballistic missile** one that moves under gravity after being initially powered and guided.

**ballistics** *n.pl.* (usu. treated as *sing.*) science of projectiles and firearms.

**balloon** /bəˈluːn/ *n.* small inflated rubber bag as toy; large round bag inflated with gas or hot air so as to rise in air, esp. one with basket etc. below for carrying persons; outline containing words or thoughts of character in strip cartoon. **balloonist** *n.*

**ballot** /ˈbælət/ 1 *n.* voting in writing and usu. secret; votes recorded in ballot. 2 *v.* hold ballot among; vote by ballot. 3 **ballot-box** container for **ballot-papers**, slips for marking votes.

**ballroom** /ˈbɔːlruːm/ large room for dancing. **ballroom dancing** formal kind done in pairs.

**bally** /ˈbæli/ *a.* & *adv. sl.* mild or joc. euphem. for **bloody**.

**ballyhoo** /bæliˈhuː/ *n. sl.* vulgar or misleading publicity.

**balm** /bɑːm/ *n.* fragrant exudation from some trees; ointment; healing or soothing influence; kind of aromatic herb.

**balmy** /ˈbɑːmi/ *a.* fragrant, mild, soothing; *sl.* crazy.

**balsa** /ˈbɒlsə/ *n.* lightweight wood from tropical Amer. tree, used for making models.

**balsam** /ˈbɔːlsəm/ *n.* balm from trees; ointment; tree yielding balsam; a flowering plant.

**baluster** /ˈbæləstə(r)/ *n.* one of series of short pillars, usu. with curving outline; rail.

**balustrade** /bæləˈstreɪd/ *n.* railing supported by balusters esp. on balcony etc.

**bamboo** /bæmˈbuː/ *n.* tropical giant grass; its hollow jointed stem(s).

**bamboozle** /bæmˈbuːz(ə)l/ *v.t.* hoax, mystify; cheat.

**ban** 1 *v.t.* prohibit, forbid, esp. formally. 2 *n.* formal or authoritative prohibition.

**banal** /bəˈnɑːl/ *a.* commonplace, trite. **banality** /-ˈnæl-/ *n.*

**banana** /bəˈnɑːnə/ *n.* long curved yellow tropical fruit; tree bearing it. **Bananaland** *Aus. sl.* Queensland.

**band**[1] *n.* flat strip of thin material; hoop of iron, rubber, etc.; stripe of colour etc.; body of musicians; group of

# bandage

persons; range of wavelengths; division of gramophone record. 2 *v.t.* unite, form into league; put band on; in *p.p.* striped. 3 **bandbox** box for hats etc.; **bandmaster** conductor of musical band; **bandsman** member of musical band; **bandstand** platform for musicians, esp. outdoors.

**bandage** /'bændɪdʒ/ 1 *n.* strip of material for binding up wound etc. 2 *v.t.* tie up with bandage.

**bandanna** /bæn'dænə/ *n.* large handkerchief with spots or other pattern.

**bandeau** /'bændəʊ/ *n.* (*pl.* **-deaux** /-dəʊz/) band worn round head.

**bandicoot** /'bændiku:t/ *n.* ratlike Aus. marsupial.

**bandit** /'bændɪt/ *n.* outlaw; brigand. **banditry** *n.*

**bandoleer** /bændə'lɪə(r)/ (also **bandolier**) *n.* shoulder-belt with loops for ammunition.

**bandwagon** /'bændwægən/ *n.* wagon carrying musical band esp. in parade; **climb** etc. **on the bandwagon** join in popular or successful cause.

**bandy**¹ /'bændi:/ *v.t.* exchange (words etc. *with*).

**bandy**² /'bændi:/ *a.* (of legs) curved wide apart at knees. **bandy-legged** *a.*

**bane** *n.* cause of ruin or trouble. **baneful** *a.*

**bang** 1 *v.* strike or shut noisily; make or cause to make sound as of blow or explosion. 2 *n.* sound of blow or explosion; sharp blow. 3 *adv.* with bang, abruptly; *colloq.* exactly. 4 **bang on** *sl.* exactly right.

**bangle** /'bæŋg(ə)l/ *n.* rigid ring as bracelet or anklet.

**bangtail** /'bæŋteɪl/ *n.* Aus. cow or horse with tail cut straight across. **bangtail muster** round-up of cattle for counting by cutting off and counting tail tufts.

**banian** /'bæniən/ *n.* Indian fig-tree whose branches take root in ground.

**banish** /'bænɪʃ/ *v.t.* condemn to exile; dismiss from one's presence or mind. **banishment** *n.*

**banister** /'bænɪstə(r)/ *n.* (usu. in *pl.*) stair rail and supporting uprights; these uprights.

**banjo** /'bændʒəʊ/ *n.* (*pl.* **-jos**) musical instrument like guitar with circular body. **banjoist** /-dʒəʊəst/ *n.*

# baptism

**bank**¹ 1 *n.* establishment where money is deposited in accounts, lent, etc.; storage place; pool of money in gambling-game. 2 *v.* deposit (money) at bank; keep money *at* or *with* bank; count or rely *on*. **bank card** credit card issued by a bank; **bank holiday** public holiday when banks are closed; **banknote** promissory note from central bank payable on demand, serving as money.

**bank**² 1 *n.* sloping ground on each side of river; raised shelf of ground, esp. in sea; mass of cloud etc. 2 *v.* provide with or form with bank or slope; (freq. with *up*) heap or rise in banks, pack (fire) tightly for slow burning; incline (aircraft) laterally for turning; (of aircraft) incline thus.

**bank**³ *n.* row of lights, switches, organ keys, etc.; tier (of oars).

**banker**¹ *n.* owner or manager of bank; keeper of bank in gambling-game.

**banker**² *n.* Aus. flooded river almost overflowing.

**bankrupt** /'bæŋkrʌpt/ 1 *a.* insolvent; bereft (*of* quality etc.). 2 *n.* insolvent person. 3 *v.t.* make bankrupt. 4 **bankruptcy** *n.*

**banksia** /'bæŋksɪə/ *n.* Aus. evergreen shrub with yellowish flowers.

**banner** /'bænə(r)/ *n.* cloth, board, etc., carrying design or slogan, held high at rallies etc.; flag.

**bannister** var. of **banister**.

**banns** *n.pl.* public announcement of intended marriage read in church.

**banquet** /'bæŋkwət/ 1 *n.* elaborate formal dinner. 2 *v.* give banquet for; attend banquet.

**banquette** /bæŋ'ket/ *n.* long upholstered seat attached to wall.

**banshee** /'bænʃi:/ *n.* spirit whose wail is said to portend death in a house.

**bantam** /'bæntəm/ *n.* small variety of fowl; small but assertive person. **bantamweight** boxing-weight (up to 54 kg.).

**banter** /'bæntə(r)/ 1 *n.* gentle ridicule. 2 *v.* make good-humoured fun of; jest.

**banyan** var. of **banian**.

**baobab** /'beɪəbæb/ *n.* African tree with extremely thick stem and edible fruit.

**bap** *n.* round flat soft bread roll.

**baptism** /'bæptɪz(ə)m/ *n.* religious rite of immersing in or sprinkling with water in sign of admission to Christian

**Baptist** Church, usu. with name-giving; giving of name. **baptismal** *a*.

**Baptist** /'bæptɪst/ *n*. member of non-conformist Church practising adult baptism by immersion.

**baptize** /bæp'taɪz/ *v.t.* administer baptism to, christen; give name to.

**bar**[1] **1** *n*. long piece of rigid material, esp. used to confine or obstruct; oblong piece (*of* chocolate, soap, etc.); (room containing) counter at which alcoholic drinks are served; counter for particular service; barrier; place where prisoner stands in lawcourt; **(the bar)** barristers, their profession; *Mus*. vertical line dividing piece into sections of equal time value, such section; broad line or band; strip of silver below clasp of medal as extra distinction. **2** *v.t.* fasten with bars; keep *in* or *out* thus; obstruct; prevent; exclude. **3** *prep*. except, excluding. **4 barmaid, -man, -tender**, attendant at bar in public house etc; **not have a bar of** *Aus. sl.* have nothing to do with.

**bar**[2] *n*. unit of atmospheric pressure.

**barathea** /bærə'θiːə/ *n*. fine wool cloth.

**barb 1** *n*. back-curved point of arrow, fish-hook, etc.; *fig*. wounding remark. **2** *v.t.* furnish with barb. **3 barbed wire** wire with twisted wire spikes along length, for fences.

**barbarian** /bɑː'beərɪən/ **1** *a*. primitive; uncultured; very coarse or cruel. **2** *n*. such person.

**barbaric** /bɑː'bærɪk/ *a*. primitive; very coarse or cruel.

**barbarism** /'bɑːbərɪz(ə)m/ *n*. coarse or uncultured state; (use of) unacceptable word or expression in language.

**barbarity** /bɑː'bærətɪ/ *n*. savage cruelty.

**barbarous** /'bɑːbərəs/ *a*. uncivilized, cruel.

**barbecue** /'bɑːbəkjuː/ **1** *n*. metal frame for cooking meat esp. above open fire; meat thus cooked; open-air party at which such food is served. **2** *v.t.* cook on barbecue.

**barber** /'bɑːbə(r)/ *n*. person who cuts men's hair and shaves or trims beards.

**barbican** /'bɑːbɪk(ə)n/ *n*. outer defence to city or castle, esp. double tower over gate and bridge.

**barbie** /'bɑːbɪ/ *n. Aus. colloq.* barbecue.

**barbiturate** /bɑː'bɪtjərət/ *n*. sedative derived from an organic (**barbituric**) acid.

**bard** *n*. poet; Celtic poet. **bardic** *a*.

**bardie** /'bɑːdɪ/ *n. Aus.* edible wood-boring grub.

**bare** /beə(r)/ **1** *a*. unclothed, uncovered; exposed; unadorned, plain; scanty; only just sufficient. **2** *v.t.* uncover, reveal. **bareback** on unsaddled horse; **barefaced** shameless, impudent; **barefoot** with bare feet; **bareheaded** without a hat.

**barely** /'beəlɪ/ *adv*. scarcely, only just.

**bargain** /'bɑːgɪn/ **1** *n*. agreement on terms of transaction; thing acquired on terms advantageous to the buyer. **2** *v.i.* discuss terms of transaction; be prepared *for*.

**barge** /bɑːdʒ/ **1** *n*. flat-bottomed freight-boat for canal or river; ornamental vessel for state occasions. **2** *v.i.* lurch or rush heavily. **3 barge in** interrupt.

**bargee** /bɑː'dʒiː/ *n*. person in charge of barge.

**baritone** /'bærətəʊn/ *n*. adult male voice between tenor and bass; singer with baritone voice; music for baritone voice.

**barium** /'beərɪəm/ *n*. white metallic element. **barium meal** barium compound swallowed before radiography of digestive tract.

**bark**[1] **1** *n*. tough outer skin of tree trunk and branches. **2** *v.t.* graze (shin etc.); strip bark from.

**bark**[2] **1** *v*. (of dog etc.) utter sharp explosive cry; speak or utter petulantly or imperiously. **2** *n*. sound of barking.

**barker** *n*. tout at auction or side-show.

**barley** /'bɑːlɪ/ *n*. cereal used as food and in preparation of malt; (also **barleycorn**) its grain. **barley-sugar** hard sweet made of boiled sugar; **barley-water** drink made from water and boiled barley.

**barm** *n*. froth on fermenting malt liquor, yeast.

**bar mitzvah** /bɑː 'mɪtsvə/ religious initiation for Jewish boy of 13.

**barmy** /'bɑːmɪ/ *a. sl.* crazy.

**barn** *n*. roofed building for storing grain etc. **barn dance** social gathering for country dancing **barn owl** brown and white kind of owl.

**barnacle** /'bɑːnək(ə)l/ *n*. marine shellfish which clings to rocks and ships'

**barney** /'bɑːniː/ *colloq*. 1. *n*. argument, quarrel. 2 *v.i.* having barney.

**barometer** /bə'rɒmətə(r)/ *n*. instrument measuring atmospheric pressure and used to forecast weather. **barometric** *a*.

**baron** /'bærən/ *n*. member of lowest order of British or foreign nobility; powerful or influential person.

**baroness** /'bærənɪs/ *n*. baron's wife or widow; woman holding own rank of baron.

**baronet** /'bærənɪt/ *n*. member of lowest British hereditary titled order. **baronetcy** *n*.

**baronial** /bə'rəʊnɪəl/ *a*. of or befitting a baron.

**barony** /'bærənɪ/ *n*. baron's rank or domain.

**baroque** /bə'rɒk/ 1 *a*. ornate and exuberant in style, esp. of 17th–18th-c. European architecture and music. 2 *n*. baroque style.

**barrack**[1] /'bærək/ *n*. usu. in *pl*. permanent building for housing soldiers; large building of severely plain appearance.

**barrack**[2] /'bærək/ *v*. shout or jeer (at). **barrack for** *Aus*. support, cheer on.

**barracouta** /bærə'kuːtə/ *n*. long narrow edible Aus. fish.

**barracuda** /bærə'kuːdə/ *n*. large voracious W. Ind. sea-fish.

**barrage** /'bærɑːʒ/ *n*. artillery bombardment to keep enemy pinned down; rapid succession of questions etc.; artificial barrier in river etc.

**barramundi** /bærə'mʌndɪ/ *n*. edible Aus. freshwater fish of perch kind.

**barrel** /'bær(ə)l/ 1 *n*. cylindrical wooden or metal vessel; contents or capacity of this; tube forming part of thing, esp. gun or pen. 2 *v.t.* (*past & p.p.* **barrelled**) put in barrels. 3 **barrel-organ** musical instrument with pin-studded cylinder acting on pipes or keys.

**barren** /'bær(ə)n/ *a*. unable to bear young; unable to produce fruit or vegetation; unprofitable, dull. **barrenness** *n*.

**barricade** /bærɪ'keɪd/ 1 *n*. barrier, esp. hastily improvised one across street. 2 *v.t.* block or defend with barricade.

**barrier** /'bærɪə(r)/ *n*. fence or other obstacle barring advance or access; obstacle or circumstance etc. that keeps apart. **barrier cream** cream used to protect skin from damage or infection; **barrier reef** coral reef separated from land by channel.

**barrister** /'bærɪstə(r)/ *n*. lawyer entitled to practise as advocate in higher courts.

**barrow**[1] /'bærəʊ/ *n*. two-wheeled handcart; wheelbarrow.

**barrow**[2] /'bærəʊ/ *n*. mound over prehistoric burial-place.

**barter** /'bɑːtə(r)/ 1 *v.t.* exchange goods, rights, etc., for something other than money. 2 *n*. trade by exchange.

**basal** /'beɪs(ə)l/ *a*. of, at, or forming base; fundamental.

**basalt** /'bæsɔːlt/ *n*. dark-coloured rock of volcanic origin. **basaltic** *a*.

**base**[1] 1 *n*. what a thing rests or depends on, foundation; principle, starting-point; place from which operation or activity is directed; main ingredient; *Math*. number in terms of which other numbers are expressed; *Chem*. substance capable of combining with acid to form salt. 2 *v.t.* found or rest *on*; establish.

**base**[2] *a*. lacking moral worth, cowardly; despicable; menial; debased, not pure; of low value.

**baseball** /'beɪsbɔːl/ *n*. game played esp. in US with bat and ball and circuit of four bases.

**baseless** /'beɪslɪs/ *a*. unfounded.

**basement** /'beɪsmənt/ *n*. lowest floor of building, usu. below ground level.

**bash** 1 *v.t.* strike bluntly and with great force. 2 *n*. heavy blow; *sl*. attempt.

**bashful** /'bæʃfʊl/ *a*. shy; self-conscious.

**basic** /'beɪsɪk or 'bæsɪk/ *a*. serving as base; fundamental; simplest, lowest in level; of a chemical base. **basic wage** *Aus*. statutory minimum wage. **basically** *adv*.

**basil** /'bæzəl/ *n*. an aromatic herb.

**basilica** /bə'sɪlɪkə/ *n*. oblong hall with double colonnade and apse; such building used as church.

**basilisk** /'bæzəlɪsk/ mythical reptile with lethal breath or look; tropical crested lizard.

**basin** /'beɪs(ə)n/ *n*. round vessel with sloping or curving sides for holding water etc.; hollow depression; tract drained by river; land-locked harbour.

**basis** /ˈbeɪsəs/ *n.* (*pl.* **bases** /-siːz/) foundation; main ingredient or principle; starting-point for discussion etc.

**bask** /bɑːsk/ *v.i.* lie or sit etc. comfortably warming oneself (*in* sun, firelight, popularity).

**basket** /ˈbɑːskət/ *n.* container made of plaited or woven canes or wire etc.; amount held by basket. **basket-ball** team game in which goals are scored by tossing ball into net fixed high at opponent's end.

**bas-relief** /ˈbæsrɪliːf/ *n.* carving or sculpture projecting only slightly from background.

**bass**[1] /beɪs/ 1 *n.* lowest adult male voice; singer with bass voice; music for bass voice; *colloq.* double bass, bass guitar. 2 *a.* lowest in pitch; deep-sounding.

**bass**[2] /bæs/ *n.* kind of fish of perch family, including common perch.

**bass**[3] /bæs/ *n.* inner bark of lime tree; other similar fibre.

**basset** /ˈbæsɪt/ *n.* (in full **basset-hound**) short-legged hunting-dog.

**bassoon** /bəˈsuːn/ *n.* bass woodwind instrument of oboe family.

**bast** /bæst/ *var. of* **bass**[3].

**bastard** /ˈbɑːstəd/ 1 *n.* person born of unmarried parents; *colloq.* person regarded with dislike or pity. 2 *a.* illegitimate by birth; spurious; hybrid. 3 **bastardy** *n.*

**bastardize** /ˈbæstədaɪz/ *v.t.* declare bastard.

**baste**[1] /beɪst/ *v.t.* sew together with long loose stitches, tack.

**baste**[2] /beɪst/ *v.t.* moisten (roasting meat etc.) with fat etc.; beat, thrash.

**bastinado** /bæstəˈneɪdəʊ/ 1 *n.* (*pl.* -**dos**) caning on soles of feet. 2 *v.t.* cane thus.

**bastion** /ˈbæstɪən/ *n.* a projection from fortification; *fig.* thing regarded as protecting.

**bat**[1] 1 *n.* implement with handle for striking ball in various games; Batsman. 2 *v.* use bat; strike (as) with bat; have turn at batting. 3 **batsman** person who bats, esp. at cricket.

**bat**[2] *n.* small nocturnal mouselike winged mammal.

**bat**[3] *v.t.* **not bat an eyelid** *colloq.* show no reaction.

**batch**[1] *n.* group or collection or set; loaves baked at one time.

**batch**[2] *var. of* **bach**.

**bated** /ˈbeɪtəd/ *a.* **with bated breath** anxiously.

**bath** /bɑːθ/ 1 *n.* immersion in water etc. for cleansing; water etc. or vessel for bathing in; (usu. in *pl.*) building for bathing or swimming. 2 *v.* wash in bath. 3 **bath salts** additive for scenting and softening bath water.

**bathe** /beɪð/ 1 *v.* immerse in or treat with liquid; lie immersed in water etc., esp. to swim or wash; (of sunlight etc.) envelop. 2 *n.* instance of bathing. 3 **bathing-suit** garment worn for swimming.

**bathers** /ˈbeɪðəz/ *n.pl.Aus.* bathing-suit.

**bathos** /ˈbeɪθɒs/ *n.* fall from sublime to commonplace; anticlimax. **bathetic** /bəˈθetɪk/ *a.*

**Bathurst bur** /ˈbæθɜːst/ Aus. plant with burs that infest sheep's wool; one of these burs.

**bathyscaphe** /ˈbæθɪskeɪf/, **bathysphere** /-sfɪə(r)/ *ns.* vessel for deep-sea diving and observation.

**batik** /bəˈtiːk/ *n.* method of printing coloured designs on textiles by waxing parts not to be dyed.

**batiste** /bəˈtiːst/ *n.* fine light cotton or linen fabric.

**batman** /ˈbætmən/ *n.* (*pl.* -**men**) member of army etc. acting as officer's servant.

**baton** /ˈbæt(ə)n/ *n.* thin stick used by conductor for beating time; short stick carried in relay race; staff of office.

**batrachian** /bəˈtreɪkɪən/ 1 *a.* of amphibians that discard gills and tail, e.g. frog and toad. 2 *n.* such animal.

**battalion** /bəˈtæljən/ *n.* large body of men in battle array; infantry unit forming part of regiment or brigade.

**batten**[1] /ˈbæt(ə)n/ 1 *n.* long narrow piece of squared timber used in joining and fixing; strip of wood esp. to secure hatchway tarpaulin. 2 *v.t.* strengthen or fasten with battens.

**batten**[2] /ˈbæt(ə)n/ *v.i.* feed, grow fat, *on*.

**batter** /ˈbætə(r)/ 1 *v.* strike repeatedly so as to bruise or break. 2 *n.* mixture of flour and eggs beaten up with liquid

**battery** /ˈbætəri/ *n.* portable container of cell or cells for supplying electricity; series of cages etc. for poultry or cattle; set of connected or similar instruments etc.; *Mil.* emplacement for heavy guns; *Law* physical violence inflicted on person.

**battle** /ˈbæt(ə)l/ 1 *n.* combat, esp. of organized forces; contest. 2 *v.i.* struggle *with*, *for*, etc. 3 **battleaxe** medieval weapon, *colloq.* domineering middle-aged woman; **battle-cruiser** heavy-gunned ship of higher speed and lighter armour than battleship; **battledress** soldier's etc. everyday uniform; **battlefield** scene of battle; **battleship** most heavily armed and armoured warship.

**battlement** /ˈbæt(ə)lmənt/ *n.* usu. in *pl.* parapet with gaps at intervals at top of wall.

**battler** /ˈbætlə(r)/ *n. Aus.* person who struggles against adversity; *Aus. hist.* swagman.

**bauble** /ˈbɔːb(ə)l/ *n.* showy trinket.

**baulk** var. of **balk**.

**bauxite** /ˈbɔːksaɪt/ *n.* earthy mineral, chief source of aluminium.

**bawd** *n.* woman keeper of brothel.

**bawdy** /ˈbɔːdi/ 1 *a.* humorously indecent. 2 *n.* bawdy talk or writing. 3 **bawdy-house** brothel.

**bawl** *v.* shout or weep noisily. **bawl out** *colloq.* reprimand severely.

**bay**[1] *n.* broad inlet of sea where land curves inward.

**bay**[2] *n.* section of wall between buttresses etc.; recess; projecting window-space; compartment, allotted area. **bay window** window projecting from line of wall.

**bay**[3] 1 *v.* bark loudly (at). 2 *n.* bark of large dog, esp. chorus of pursuing hounds. 3 **at bay** unable to escape; **keep at bay** ward off.

**bay**[4] *n.* kind of laurel with deep-green leaves; in *pl.* conqueror's or poet's bay wreath, fame. **bay-leaf** leaf of bay tree used for flavouring.

**bay**[5] 1 *a.* reddish-brown (esp. of horse). 2 *n.* bay horse.

**bayonet** /ˈbeɪənet/ 1 *n.* stabbing-blade attachable to rifle. 2 *v.t.* stab with bayonet. 3 **bayonet fitting** connecting-part engaged by pushing and twisting.

**bazaar** /bəˈzɑː(r)/ *n.* Oriental market; sale of fancy goods etc. esp. for charity.

**BBC** *abbr.* British Broadcasting Corporation.

**BC** *abbr.* before Christ; British Columbia.

**be** 1 *v.i.* (*pres.* **am**, **are**, **is**, *pl.* **are**; *past* **was**, **were**, **was**, *pl.* **were**; *part.* **being**; *p.p.* **been**) exist, live; occur; remain, continue; have specified state or quality. 2 *v.aux.* with *p.p.* of *v.t.* forming passive, with *pres. part.* forming continuous tenses, with *inf.* expr. duty, intention, possibility, etc.

**beach** /biːtʃ/ 1 *n.* sandy or pebbly shore of sea, lake, etc. 2 *v.t.* run or haul up on shore. 3 **beachcomber** /-kəʊmə(r)/ vagrant living by beach; **beach-head** fortified position set up on beach by landing forces.

**beacon** /ˈbiːkən/ *n.* signal-fire on hill or pole; signal; signal-station.

**bead** 1 *n.* small ball pierced for threading with others; drop of liquid; small knob in front sight of gun; narrow moulding. 2 *v.t.* furnish or ornament with bead(s) or beading; string together.

**beading** /ˈbiːdɪŋ/ *n.* bead moulding.

**beadle** /ˈbiːd(ə)l/ *n. UK* ceremonial officer of church, college, etc.

**beady** /ˈbiːdi/ *a.* (of eyes) small and bright.

**beagle** /ˈbiːɡ(ə)l/ *n.* small hound used for hunting hares.

**beak** *n.* bird's horny projecting jaws; hooked nose; *hist.* prow of warship; *sl.* magistrate.

**beaker** /ˈbiːkə(r)/ *n.* small relatively tall cup for drinking; lipped glass for scientific experiments.

**beam** 1 *n.* long piece of squared timber used in house-building etc.; ray of light or radiation; this as guide to aircraft or missile; radiance; bright smile; crossbar of balance; in *pl.* horizontal crosstimbers of ship. 2 *v.* emit (light, radio waves, etc.); shine; smile radiantly.

**bean** *n.* leguminous plant with kidney-shaped seeds in long pods; seed of this or of coffee or other plant.

**bear**[1] /beə(r)/ *n.* heavy thick-furred mammal; rough surly person; *Stock Exch.* person who sells for future delivery hoping to buy cheaper before then. **bear-garden** noisy or rowdy scene; **bear-hug** powerful embrace; **bearskin** guardsman's tall furry cap.

**bear²** /beə(r)/ v. (*past* **bore**; *p.p.* **borne** or **born**) carry; show; produce, yield; give birth to; sustain; endure, tolerate.

**bearable** /'beərəb(ə)l/ a. endurable.

**beard** /bɪəd/ 1 n. hair growing on lower part of face; part on animal (esp. goat) resembling beard. 2 v.t. oppose, defy. 3 **bearded** a.

**bearer** /'beərə(r)/ n. carrier of message, cheque, etc.; carrier of coffin, or of equipment on safari.

**bearing** /'beərɪŋ/ n. outward behaviour, posture; relation, relevance; part of machine supporting rotating part; direction; in *pl.* relative position; heraldic device or design.

**beast** /biːst/ n. animal, usu. four-footed and wild; brutal person; disliked person or thing.

**beastly** /'biːstlɪ/ a. like a beast; *colloq.* unpleasant.

**beat** 1 v. ((*past* **beat**, *p.p.* **beaten**) strike repeatedly or persistently; inflict blows on; overcome, surpass; exhaust, perplex; forestall; drive or alter or shape by blows; stir vigorously; pulsate; move up and down; mark (time of music) with baton, foot, etc. 2 n. main accent in music or verse; strongly marked rhythm of popular music etc.; stroke on drum; movement of conductor's baton; throbbing; policeman's etc. appointed course; one's habitual round.

**beater** /'biːtə(r)/ n. whisk; implement for beating carpet; person who rouses game at a shoot.

**beatific** /biːə'tɪfɪk/ a. making blessed; *colloq.* blissful.

**beatify** /biː'ætɪfaɪ/ v.t. make happy; *RC Ch.* pronounce to be in heaven as first step to canonization. **beatification** n.

**beatitude** /biː'ætɪtjuːd/ n. blessedness; in *pl. the* blessings in Matt. 5: 3-11.

**beau** /bəʊ/ n. (*pl.* **beaux** /bəʊz/) dandy; ladies' man; suitor.

**Beaufort scale** /'bəʊfət/ scale of wind speeds.

**Beaujolais** /'bəʊʒəleɪ/ n. red or white wine from Beaujolais district of France.

**beaut** /bjuːt/ a. *Aus. sl.* excellent.

**beauteous** /'bjuːtɪəs/ a. *poet.* beautiful.

**beautician** /bjuː'tɪʃ(ə)n/ n. specialist in beauty treatment.

**beautiful** /'bjuːtəfəl/ a. having beauty; excellent.

**beautify** /'bjuːtɪfaɪ/ v.t. make beautiful, adorn. **beautification** n.

**beauty** /'bjuːtɪ/ n. combination of qualities that delights the sight or other senses or the mind; person or thing having this. **beauty queen** woman judged most beautiful in contest; **beauty spot** beautiful locality.

**beaver** 1 n. amphibious broad-tailed soft-furred rodent; its fur; hat of this. 2 v. **beaver away** work hard *at.*

**becalm** /bɪ'kɑːm/ v.t. deprive (ship etc.) of wind.

**because** /bɪ'kɒz/ conj. for the reason that. **because of** by reason of.

**beck** n. **at person's beck and call** subject to his constant orders.

**beckon** /'bek(ə)n/ v. summon by mute signal; signal thus.

**become** /bɪ'kʌm/ v. (*past* **became**; *p.p.* **become**) come to be, begin to be; suit, look well on. **become of** happen to.

**becomingly** /bɪ'kʌmɪŋlɪ/ adv. suitably, gracefully.

**bed** 1 n. thing to sleep or rest on, esp. piece of furniture with mattress and coverings; garden plot for plants; bottom of sea, river, etc.; flat base on which thing rests; stratum. 2 v.t. put or go to bed; plant in bed; fix firmly. 3 **bedclothes** sheets, blankets, etc.; **bedpan** pan for use as toilet by invalid in bed; **bedridden** confined to bed by infirmity; **bedrock** solid rock under alluvial deposits etc., *fig.* foundation, bottom; **bedroom** room for sleeping in; **bed-sitting-room, bed-sitter**, combined bedroom and sitting-room; **bedsore** one developed by lying in bed; **bedspread** coverlet; **bedstead** framework of bed; **bed-time** hour for going to bed.

**bedaub** /bɪ'dɔːb/ v.t. smear with paint etc.

**bedding** /'bedɪŋ/ n. mattress and bedclothes; litter for cattle etc.

**bedeck** /bɪ'dek/ v.t. adorn, decorate.

**bedevil** /bɪ'dev(ə)l/ v.t. (**bedevilled**) trouble, confuse, torment. **bedevilment** n.

**bedlam** /'bedləm/ n. scene of confusion or uproar.

**bedouin** /ˈbeduːən/ n. (pl. same) nomadic Arab of the desert.

**bedraggled** /bəˈdræɡ(ə)ld/ a. dishevelled, untidy.

**bee** n. four-winged stinging social insect producing wax and honey; busy worker; meeting for combined work or amusement. **beehive** hive; **beeline** straight line between two places; **beeswax** wax secreted by bees for honeycomb.

**beech** /biːtʃ/ n. smooth-barked glossy-leaved tree; its wood; any of various similar but unrelated Aus. trees. **beechmast** fruit of beech.

**beef** 1 n. meat of ox, bull, or cow; (pl. **beeves**) beef animal; sl. (pl. **beefs**) protest. 2 v.i. sl. complain. **beefburger** hamburger; **beefeater** warder in Tower of London; **beefroad** Aus. outback road for transporting cattle. **beef tea** stewed beef juice for invalids; **beefwood** any of several Aus. trees with red wood, esp. casuarina.

**beefy** /ˈbiːfi/ a. like beef; solid, muscular.

**been** p.p. of **be**.

**beep** 1 n. short high-pitched sound. 2 v.i. emit beep.

**beer** /bɪə(r)/ n. alcoholic liquor made from fermented malt etc. flavoured esp. with hops.

**beery** /ˈbɪəri/ a. of beer; showing influence of beer.

**beeswing** /ˈbiːzwɪŋ/ n. filmy scales of tartar on old port wine etc.

**beet** n. kind of plant with succulent root used for salads etc. and sugar-making.

**beetle**¹ /ˈbiːt(ə)l/ n. insect with hard outer wings.

**beetle**² /ˈbiːt(ə)l/ n. heavy-headed tool for ramming or crushing etc.

**beetle**³ /ˈbiːt(ə)l/ 1 a. projecting, shaggy, scowling. 2 v.i. overhang.

**beetroot** /ˈbiːtruːt/ n. crimson root of garden beet, used as vegetable.

**befall** /bəˈfɔːl/ v. (past **befell** /-ˈfɔːl/; p.p. **befallen** /-ˈfɔːlən/) happen, happen to.

**befit** /bəˈfɪt/ v.t. be suited to.

**befog** /bɪˈfɒɡ/ v.t. envelop in fog; obscure.

**before** /bəˈfɔː(r)/ 1 prep. in front of, ahead of; in presence of; earlier than. 2 adv. ahead, in front; previously, already; in the past. 3 conj. sooner than; rather than.

**beforehand** /bəˈfɔːhænd/ adv. in anticipation, in readiness, before time.

**befriend** /bəˈfrend/ v.t. act as friend to; help.

**befuddle** /bəˈfʌd(ə)l/ v.t. make drunk; confuse.

**beg** v. ask for as gift; ask earnestly, entreat; live by seeking charity; ask formally. **beg the question** assume truth of thing to be proved; **go begging** be unwanted.

**began** past of **begin**.

**beget** /bəˈɡet/ v.t. (past **begot**, arch. **begat**; p.p. **begotten**) be the father of; give rise to.

**beggar** /ˈbeɡə(r)/ 1 n. person who begs or lives by begging; poor person; colloq. person, fellow. 2 v.t. reduce to poverty. 3 **beggary** n.

**beggarly** /ˈbeɡəli/ a. poor, needy; mean.

**begin** /bəˈɡɪn/ v. (past **began**; p.p. **begun**) perform first part of; come to do thing; take first step; start, come into being.

**beginner** n. learner.

**beginning** n. first part; time at which thing begins; source, origin.

**begone** /bɪˈɡɒn/ int. go away at once!

**begonia** /bɪˈɡəʊnɪə/ n. plant with ornamental foliage and bright flowers.

**begot** past of **beget**.

**begotten** p.p. of **beget**.

**begrudge** /bəˈɡrʌdʒ/ v.t. grudge; feel or show resentment at or envy of.

**beguile** /bəˈɡaɪl/ v.t. (partic. **beguiling**) charm or divert; delude, cheat. **beguilement** n.

**beguine** /bəˈɡiːn/ n. a W. Ind. dance; its music or rhythm.

**begum** /ˈbeɪɡəm/ n. title of married woman in India and Pakistan.

**begun** p.p. of **begin**.

**behalf** /bəˈhɑːf/ n. **on behalf of**, **on one's behalf**, in the interests of, as representative of.

**behave** /bəˈheɪv/ v. conduct oneself or act in specified manner; show good manners; work well (or in specified manner).

**behaviour** /bəˈheɪvjə(r)/ n. manners, conduct, way of behaving. **behavioural** a.

**behaviourism** /bəˈheɪvjərɪz(ə)m/ n. study of human actions by analysis of

**behead** /bə'hed/ *v.t.* cut head from; execute thus.

**beheld** *past* & *p.p.* of **behold**.

**behest** /bə'hest/ *n.* command, request.

**behind** /bə'haɪnd/ **1** *adv.* & *prep.* in or to rear (of); hidden by, on farther side (of); in arrears (*with*); in support of. **2** *n. colloq.* buttocks; *Aus. Rules Footb.* point scored by sending ball over line between goal-post and outer post. **3 behindhand** in arrears, behind time, too late; **behind time** unpunctual.

**behold** /bə'həʊld/ *v.t.* (*past* & *p.p.* **beheld**) look at; take notice, observe.

**beholden** /bə'həʊld(ə)n/ *pred.a.* under obligation (*to*).

**behove** /bə'həʊv/ *v.t.* be incumbent on; befit.

**beige** /beɪʒ/ **1** *a.* of sandy fawn colour. **2** *n.* this colour.

**being** /'biːɪŋ/ *n.* existence; constitution, nature; existing person etc.

**belabour** /bə'leɪbə(r)/ *v.t.* attack physically or verbally.

**belah** /'biːlə/ *n.* (also **belar**) *n. Aus.* kind of casuarina; its wood.

**belated** /bə'leɪtəd/ *a.* coming late or too late.

**bel canto** /bel 'kæntəʊ/ singing marked by full rich tone.

**belch** /beltʃ/ **1** *v.* emit wind from stomach through mouth; (of volcano, gun, etc.) emit (fire, smoke, etc.) **2** *n.* act of belching.

**beleaguer** /bə'liːgə(r)/ *v.t.* besiege.

**belfry** /'belfri/ *n.* bell-tower; space for bells in church tower.

**belie** /bə'laɪ/ *v.t.* fail to confirm, fulfil, or justify; give false notion of.

**belief** /bə'liːf/ *n.* act of believing; what one believes; trust, confidence; acceptance as true.

**believe** /bə'liːv/ *v.* accept as true; think; have faith or confidence in; trust word of; have religious faith. **believer** *n.*

**belittle** /bə'lɪt(ə)l/ *v.t.* disparage.

**bell 1** *n.* hollow esp. cup-shaped metal body sounding esp. musical sound when struck; sound of bell; bell-shaped thing. **2** *v.t.* provide with bell. **3 bellbird** any of several Aus. birds with clear note; **bell-bottomed** (of trousers) widening below knee; **bell magpie** *Aus.* currawong; **bell-pull** cord attached to wire to sound bell; **bell-push** button to operate electric bell; **bell-tent** conical tent; **bell-wether** leading sheep of flock.

**belladonna** /belə'dɒnə/ *n.* deadly nightshade; drug obtained from this.

**belle** /bel/ *n.* handsome woman; reigning beauty.

***belles-lettres*** /bel 'letr/ *n.pl.* writings or studies of purely literary kind. [F]

**bellicose** /'belɪkəʊs/ *a.* eager to fight. **bellicosity** /-'kɒs-/ *n.*

**belligerent** /bə'lɪdʒər(ə)nt/ **1** *a.* engaged in war; given to constant fighting; pugnacious. **2** *n.* belligerent person or nation. **belligerency** *n.*

**bellow** /'beləʊ/ **1** *v.* roar like bull. **2** *n.* bellowing sound.

**bellows** /'beləʊz/ *n.pl.* device for driving air into fire, organ, etc.; expandable part of camera etc.

**belly** /'beli:/ **1** *n.* cavity of body containing stomach, bowels, etc.; stomach; front of body from waist to groin; cavity or bulging part of anything. **2** *v.* swell out. **3 belly-dance** dance by woman with voluptuous movements of belly; **belly-laugh** loud unrestrained laugh.

**belong** /bə'lɒŋ/ *v.i.* be proper to or connected *with*; be rightly placed or classified. **belong to** be property of or member of.

**belongings** /bə'lɒŋɪŋz/ *n.pl.* person's movable property or luggage.

**beloved** /bə'lʌvəd/ **1** *a.* loved. **2** *n.* beloved person.

**below** /bə'ləʊ/ **1** *prep.* under; lower than; less than; of lower rank or importance etc. than; unworthy of. **2** *adv.* at or to lower point or level; further on in book etc.

**belt 1** *n.* strip of leather etc. worn round waist or across chest; encircling strip of colour etc.; zone or district; looped strip connecting pulleys etc. **2** *v.* put belt round; thrash; *sl.* move rapidly.

**bemoan** /bə'məʊn/ *v.t.* lament, complain of.

**bemuse** /bə'mjuːz/ *v.t.* stupefy; make (person) confused.

**bench** *n.* long seat of wood or stone; carpenter's or laboratory table; lawcourt; judge's or magistrate's seat; seat for particular group in Parliament. **bench-mark** standard or point of reference; surveyor's mark at point in line of levels.

**bend** 1 *v.* (*past* & *p.p.* **bent**) force into curve or angle; be altered in this way; incline from vertical; bow, stoop; (force to) submit. 2 *n.* bending, curve; bent part of thing; in *pl.* symptoms due to too rapid decompression under water.

**beneath** /bɪˈniːθ/ *adv.* & *prep.* below, under; not worthy of.

**Benedictine** /benəˈdɪktiːn/ 1 *n.* monk or nun of Order of St Benedict; (**P**) kind of liqueur. 2 *a.* of St Benedict or his order.

**benediction** /benəˈdɪkʃ(ə)n/ *n.* utterance of blessing. **benedictory** *a.*

**benefaction** /benəˈfækʃ(ə)n/ *n.* charitable gift; doing good.

**benefactor** /ˈbenəfæktə(r)/ *n.* person who has given financial or other help. **benefactress** *n.*

**benefice** /ˈbenəfəs/ *n.* living from a church office.

**beneficent** /bəˈnefəs(ə)nt/ *a.* doing good; actively kind. **beneficence** *n.*

**beneficial** /benəˈfɪʃ(ə)l/ *a.* advantageous.

**beneficiary** /benəˈfɪʃəri/ *n.* receiver of benefits; holder of church living.

**benefit** /ˈbenəfət/ 1 *n.* advantage, profit; payment made under insurance or social security; performance or game etc. of which proceeds go to particular player or charity. 2 *v.* do good to; receive benefit. 3 **benefit of the doubt** assumption of innocence rather than guilt.

**benevolent** /bəˈnevəl(ə)nt/ *a.* wishing to do good; charitable; kind and helpful. **benevolence** *n.*

**benighted** /bəˈnaɪtɪd/ *a.* in darkness; intellectually or morally ignorant.

**benign** /bəˈnaɪn/ *a.* kindly, gentle; favourable; salutary; *Med.* mild, not malignant. **benignity** /-ˈnɪg-/ *n.*

**benignant** /bəˈnɪgnənt/ *a.* kindly; beneficial. **benignancy** *n.*

**bent** 1 *past* & *p.p.* of **bend**. 2 *a.* curved or having angle; *sl.* dishonest, illicit. 3 *n.* inclination, bias. 4 **bent on** determined on.

**benthos** /ˈbenθɒs/ *n.* flora and fauna of sea bottom. **benthic** *a.*

**benumb** /bəˈnʌm/ *v.t.* make numb; deaden; paralyse.

**benzene** /ˈbenziːn/ *n.* substance got from coal tar and used as solvent.

**benzine** /ˈbenziːn/ *n.* spirit obtained from petroleum and used as cleaning agent.

**benzoin** /ˈbenzəʊɪn/ *n.* aromatic resin of E. Asian tree. **benzoic** *a.*

**bequeath** /bəˈkwiːð/ *v.t.* leave by will; transmit to posterity.

**bequest** /bəˈkwest/ *n.* thing bequeathed.

**berate** /bəˈreɪt/ *v.t.* scold.

**bereave** /bəˈriːv/ *v.t.* leave desolate; deprive *of* near relative. **bereavement** *n.*

**bereft** /bəˈreft/ *a.* deprived (*of*).

**beret** /ˈbereɪ/ *n.* round flat felt or cloth cap.

**berg** *n.* iceberg.

**bergamot** /ˈbɜːgəmɒt/ *n.* a citrus tree; perfume from its fruit; an aromatic herb.

**beriberi** /beriˈberi/ *n.* disease caused by deficiency of vitamin B.

**berley** /ˈbɜːli/ *n. Aus.* ground-bait for fish; *Aus. sl.* nonsense.

**Bermuda shorts** /bəˈmjuːdə/ knee-length shorts.

**berry** /ˈberi/ *n.* any small round juicy stoneless fruit. **berried** *a.*

**berserk** /bəˈsɜːk/ *pred.a.* wild, frenzied.

**berth** /bɜːθ/ 1 *n.* sleeping-place; ship's place at wharf; sea-room; situation, appointment. 2 *v.t.* moor (ship) in berth; provide sleeping-berth for.

**beryl** /ˈber(ə)l/ *n.* kind of (esp. green) precious stone; mineral species including this and emerald.

**beryllium** /bəˈrɪliəm/ *n.* very light white metallic element.

**beseech** /bəˈsiːtʃ/ *v.t.* (*past* & *p.p.* **-sought** /-ˈsɔːt/) entreat; ask earnestly for.

**beset** /bəˈset/ *v.t.* (*past* & *p.p.* **beset**) attack or harass persistently.

**beside** /bəˈsaɪd/ *prep.* at side of, close to; compared with; irrelevant to. **beside oneself** frantic with anger or worry etc.

**besides** 1 *prep.* in addition to; apart from. 2 *adv.* also, as well.

**besiege** /bəˈsiːdʒ/ *v.t.* lay siege to; crowd round; assail with requests.

**besmirch** /bəˈsmɜːtʃ/ *v.t.* soil, dishonour.

**besom** /ˈbiːz(ə)m/ *n.* long-handled broom made of twigs.

**besot** /bəˈsɒt/ *v.t.* (*past* & *p.p.* **besotted**) stupefy; infatuate.

**besought** *past* & *p.p.* of **beseech**.

**bespatter** /bɪˈspætə(r)/ *v.t.* spatter all over; cover with abuse.

**bespeak** /bɪˈspiːk/ *v.t.* (*past* **-spoke**; *p.p.* **-spoken**) engaged beforehand; order (goods); be evidence of.

**bespoke** /bɪˈspəʊk/ *a.* ordered in advance; made to order.

**best 1** *a.* (*superl.* of **good**) of most excellent kind. **2** *adv.* (*superl.* of **well**) in best manner; to greatest degree. **3** *n.* that which is best. **4** *v.t. colloq.* defeat, outwit. **5 best man** bridegroom's chief attendant at wedding; **best-seller** book with large sale, author of such book.

**bestial** /ˈbestɪəl/ *a.* of or like beasts; brutish. **bestiality** *n.*; **bestially** *adv.*

**bestiary** /ˈbestɪəri/ *n.* medieval treatise on beasts.

**bestir** /bɪˈstɜː(r)/ *v.t.* exert or rouse (*oneself*).

**bestow** /bɪˈstəʊ/ *v.t.* confer as gift. **bestowal** *n.*

**bestrew** /bɪˈstruː/ *v.t.* (*p.p.* **-strewed** or **-strewn**) strew; lie scattered over.

**bestride** /bɪˈstraɪd/ *v.t.* (*past* **-strode**; *p.p.* **-stridden**) sit astride on; stand astride over.

**bet 1** *v.* (*past* & *p.p.* **bet** *or* **betted**) risk one's money etc. against another's on result of event. **2** *n.* such arrangement; sum of money bet.

**beta** /ˈbiːtə/ *n.* second letter of Greek alphabet (*B*, *β*). **beta particle** fast-moving electron emitted by radioactive substance.

**betake** /bɪˈteɪk/ *v.refl.* (*past* **-took**; *p.p.* **-taken**) go (*to*).

**betatron** /ˈbiːtətrɒn/ *n.* apparatus for accelerating electrons.

**betel** /ˈbiːt(ə)l/ *n.* tropical Asian plant whose leaf is chewed with betel-nut. **betel-nut** areca nut.

***bête noire*** /beɪt ˈnwɑː(r)/ *n.* particularly disliked person or thing. [F]

**bethink** /bɪˈθɪŋk/ *v.refl.* (*past* & *p.p.* **-thought** /-ˈθɔːt/) reflect, stop to think; be reminded.

**betide** /bɪˈtaɪd/ *v.* happen; happen to.

**betimes** /bɪˈtaɪmz/ *adv.* in good time, early.

**betoken** /bɪˈtəʊkən/ *v.t.* be sign of.

**betook** *past* of **betake**.

**betray** /bɪˈtreɪ/ *v.t.* be disloyal to; give up or reveal treacherously; reveal involuntarily; be evidence of. **betrayal** *n.*

**betroth** /bɪˈtrəʊð/ *v.t.* bind with promise to marry. **betrothal** *n.*

**better** /ˈbetə(r)/ **1** *a.* (*compar.* of **good**) having good qualities in higher degree; partly or fully recovered from illness. **2** *adv.* (*compar.* of **well**) in better manner; to greater degree. **3** *n.* better thing or person. **4** *v.* improve (*upon*); surpass. **5 get the better of** defeat, outwit.

**betterment** /ˈbetəmənt/ *n.* improvement.

**bettong** /ˈbetɒŋ/ *n.* short-nosed rat-kangaroo.

**between** /bɪˈtwiːn/ **1** *prep.* in or into space or interval; to and from; in shares among; (*choose* etc.) one or other of. **2** *adv.* between two or more points; between two extremes. **3 in between** intermediately in position.

**betwixt** /bɪˈtwɪkst/ *prep.* & *adv.* between.

**bevel** /ˈbev(ə)l/ **1** *n.* tool for making angles in carpentry and stonework; slope from horizontal or vertical; sloping edge or surface. **2** *v.* (*past* & *p.p.* **bevelled**) impart bevel to, slant.

**beverage** /ˈbevərɪdʒ/ *n.* drink.

**bevy** /ˈbevi/ *n.* company or flock.

**bewail** /bɪˈweɪl/ *v.t.* wail over; mourn for.

**beware** /bɪˈweə(r)/ *v.* take heed, be cautious (of).

**bewilder** /bɪˈwɪldə(r)/ *v.t.* perplex, confuse. **bewilderment** *n.*

**bewitch** /bɪˈwɪtʃ/ *v.t.* enchant, greatly delight; cast spell on.

**beyond** /bɪˈjɒnd/ **1** *adv.* at or to further side, further on. **2** *prep.* at or to further side of; outside the range of; more than; further on. **3** *n.* the future life. **4 back of beyond** very remote place.

**bezel** /ˈbez(ə)l/ *n.* sloped edge of chisel etc.; oblique face of cut gem; groove holding watch-glass or gem.

**bezique** /bəˈziːk/ *n.* card-game for two.

**biannual** /baɪˈænjʊəl/ *a.* occurring etc. twice a year.

**bias** /ˈbaɪəs/ **1** *n.* predisposition, prejudice; distortion of statistical results; (in bowls) bowl's curved course due to its lopsided form; diagonal across fabric. **2** *v.t.* (*past* & *p.p.* **biased**) give bias to; prejudice.

# bib      48      bilk

**bib** *n.* cloth put under child's chin while eating; apron top.

**Bible** /ˈbaɪb(ə)l/ *n.* Christian scriptures; copy of these; any authoritative book. **biblical** /ˈbɪb-/ *a.*

**bibliography** /bɪbliˈɒɡrəfi/ *n.* list of books of any author, subject, etc.; history of books, their editions, etc. **bibliographer** *n.*; **bibliographic(al)** *a.*

**bibliophile** /ˈbɪbliəfaɪl/ *n.* collector of books, book-lover.

**bibulous** /ˈbɪbjələs/ *a.* fond of or addicted to alcoholic drink.

**bicameral** /baɪˈkæmər(ə)l/ *a.* having two legislative chambers.

**bicarbonate** /baɪˈkɑːbənɪt/ *n.* carbonate containing double proportion of carbon dioxide. **bicarbonate of soda** compound used in cooking and medicine.

**bicentenary** /baɪsenˈtiːnəri/ *n.* 200th anniversary.

**bicentennial** /baɪsenˈteniəl/ 1 *a.* lasting or occurring every 200 years. 2 *n.* bicentenary.

**biceps** /ˈbaɪseps/ *n.* muscle with double head or attachment, esp. that at front of upper arm.

**bicker** /ˈbɪkə(r)/ *v.i.* quarrel, wrangle.

**bicuspid** /baɪˈkʌspɪd/ 1 *a.* having two cusps. 2 *n.* bicuspid tooth.

**bicycle** /ˈbaɪsɪk(ə)l/ 1 *n.* two-wheeled pedal-driven vehicle. 2 *v.i.* ride bicycle. 3 **bicyclist** *n.*

**bid** 1 *v.* (*past* & *p.p.* bid) offer (price); make bid; (also *past* bade /bæd/; *p.p.* bidden) command, invite; salute with *welcome* etc. 2 *n.* offer of price; *Bridge* statement of number of tricks player hopes to make.

**biddable** /ˈbɪdəb(ə)l/ *a.* obedient, docile.

**bidding** /ˈbɪdɪŋ/ *n.* command, invitation.

**bide** *v.t.* await (one's *time*).

**bidet** /ˈbiːdeɪ/ *n.* low washbasin that one can sit astride on.

**biennial** /baɪˈeniəl/ 1 *a.* lasting or recurring every two years. 2 *n.* plant that flowers, fruits, and dies in second year.

**bier** /bɪə(r)/ *n.* movable stand on which coffin or corpse rests.

**biff** *sl.* 1 *n.* smart blow. 2 *v.t.* strike.

**bifid** /ˈbɪfɪd/ *a.* divided by cleft into two parts.

**bifocal** /baɪˈfəʊk(ə)l/ 1 *a.* (of spectacle-lenses) with two segments of different focal lengths. 2 *n.* in *pl.* bifocal spectacles.

**bifurcate** /ˈbaɪfəkeɪt/ *v.* divide into two branches; fork. **bifurcation** *n.*

**big** 1 *a.* large; grown up; important; boastful; *colloq.* ambitious. 2 *adv. colloq.* in a big manner; with great effect. 3 **Big Brother** seemingly benevolent dictator; **big business** large-scale commerce; **big end** end of connecting-rod in engine encircling crank-pin; **bighead** *colloq.* conceited person; **bignote** *Aus. sl.* exaggerate one's own importance; **big shot** *colloq.* important person; **big smoke** *Aus. colloq.* city; **big time** *sl.* highest rank among entertainers; **big top** main tent at circus; **bigwig** important person.

**bigamy** /ˈbɪɡəmi/ *n.* crime of making second marriage while first is still valid. **bigamist** *n.*; **bigamous** *a.*

**bight** /baɪt/ *n.* loop of rope; recess of coast, bay.

**bigot** /ˈbɪɡət/ *n.* obstinate and intolerant adherent of creed or view. **bigoted** *a.*; **bigotry** *n.*

*bijou* /ˈbiːʒuː/ 1 *n.* (*pl.* **-oux** *pr.* same) jewel, trinket. 2 *a.* small and elegant.

**bike** /baɪk/ *n. colloq.* bicycle; motor cycle. **get off one's bike** *Aus. sl.* show anger.

**bikie** /ˈbaɪki/ *n. Aus.* & *NZ sl.* young motor cyclist, esp. in gang.

**bikini** /bɪˈkiːni/ *n.* woman's brief two-piece bathing-suit.

**bilateral** /baɪˈlætər(ə)l/ *a.* of or on or with two sides; between two parties.

**bilberry** /ˈbɪlbəri/ *n.* N. European heathland shrub; its small dark-blue berry.

**bilby** /ˈbɪlbi/ *n. Aus.* nocturnal burrowing marsupial.

**bile** *n.* bitter fluid secreted by liver to aid digestion; bad temper, peevishness.

**bilge** /bɪldʒ/ *n.* nearly flat part of ship's bottom; (also **bilge-water**) foul water in bilge; *sl.* nonsense, rubbish.

**bilharzia** /bɪlˈhɑːtsɪə/ *n.* disease caused by tropical parasitic flatworm.

**biliary** /ˈbɪljəri/ *a.* of bile.

**bilingual** /baɪˈlɪŋɡw(ə)l/ *a.* of or in or speaking two languages.

**bilious** /ˈbɪljəs/ *a.* affected by disorder of the bile; bad-tempered.

**bilk** *v.t.* evade payment of, cheat.

**bill**¹ 1 *n.* statement of charges for goods, work done, etc.; draft of proposed law; poster; *Law* written statement of case; programme of entertainment; *US* banknote. 2 *v.t.* anounce, put in programme; advertise *as*; send statement of charges to. **3 bill of exchange** written order to pay sum on given date; **bill of fare** menu; **bill of health** certificate regarding infectious disease on ship or in port at time of sailing; **billposter**, **billsticker**, person who pastes up advertisements on hoardings etc.

**bill**² 1 *n.* beak (of bird); narrow promontory. 2 *v.i.* (of doves etc.) stroke bill with bill. 3 **bill and coo** exchange caresses.

**bill**³ *n. hist.* weapon with hook-shaped blade.

**billabong** /ˈbɪləbɒŋ/ *n. Aus.* branch of river forming backwater.

**billboard** /ˈbɪlbɔːd/ *n.* large outdoor board for advertisements.

**billet**¹ /ˈbɪlɪt/ 1 *n.* place where soldier etc. is lodged; appointment, job. 2 *v.t.* allocate lodging to by billet.

**billet**² /ˈbɪlɪt/ *n.* thick piece of firewood; small metal bar.

**billet-doux** /ˈbɪleɪˈduː/ *n.* (*pl.* **billets-doux** /ˈbɪleɪˈduːz/) love-letter.

**billhook** /ˈbɪlhʊk/ concave-edged pruning-instrument.

**billiards** /ˈbɪljədz/ *n.* game played with cues and 3 balls on cloth-covered table.

**billion** /ˈbɪljən/ *n.* million millions; (esp. *US*) thousand millions.

**billow** /ˈbɪləʊ/ 1 *n.* large wave. 2 *v.i.* rise or move in billows. 3 **billowy** *a.*

**billy** /ˈbɪlɪ/ *n.* (in full **billycan**) tin can serving as kettle etc. in camping.

**billy-cart** *n. Aus.* child's simple 4-wheeled cart.

**billy-goat** *n.* male goat.

**bin** *n.* large box-shaped container for storage; receptacle for refuse.

**binary** /ˈbaɪnərɪ/ *a.* consisting of two parts, dual; of arithmetical system using 2 as base. **binary digit** either of two used in binary system.

**bind** /baɪnd/ *v.t.* (*past & p.p.* **bound** /baʊnd/) tie or fasten or hold together; restrain; fasten *round* etc.; fasten (sheets or book) into cover; be obligatory on; impose constraint or duty on; edge with braid etc.

**binder** /ˈbaɪndə(r)/ *n.* loose cover for papers; bookbinder; sheaf-binding machine.

**bindery** /ˈbaɪndərɪ/ *n.* bookbinder's workshop.

**bindi-eye** /ˈbɪndɪaɪ/ *n. Aus.* small perennial herb with burlike fruit.

**binding** /ˈbaɪndɪŋ/ 1 *n.* book-cover; braid etc. for edging. 2 *a.* obligatory (*on*).

**bindweed** /ˈbaɪndwiːd/ *n.* convolvulus.

**bine** *n.* stem of climbing plant, esp. hop; flexible shoot.

**binge** /bɪndʒ/ *n. sl.* drinking-bout, spree.

**bingo** /ˈbɪŋɡəʊ/ *n.* gambling game similar to lotto.

**binnacle** /ˈbɪnək(ə)l/ *n.* case for ship's compass.

**binocular** /bəˈnɒkjələ(r)/ 1 *n.* in *pl.* instrument with lens for each eye, for viewing distant objects. 2 *a.* for two eyes.

**binomial** /baɪˈnəʊmɪəl/ 1 *n.* algebraic expression of sum or difference of two terms. 2 *a.* consisting of two terms.

**biochemistry** /baɪəʊˈkemɪstrɪ/ *n.* chemistry of living organisms.

**biodegradable** /baɪəʊdəˈɡreɪdəb(ə)l/ *a.* capable of being decomposed by bacteria.

**biography** /baɪˈɒɡrəfɪ/ *n.* written life of person. **biographer** *n.*; **biographical** /-ˈɡræf-/ *a.*

**biological** /baɪəˈlɒdʒək(ə)l/ *a.* of biology; of plants and animals. **biological warfare** use of bacteria etc. to spread disease among enemy.

**biology** /baɪˈɒlədʒɪ/ *n.* science dealing with origin, forms, and behaviour of plants and animals. **biologist** *n.*

**bionic** /baɪˈɒnɪk/ *a.* having electronically-operated body-parts.

**bipartite** /baɪˈpɑːtaɪt/ *a.* consisting of two parts; in which two parties are concerned.

**biped** /ˈbaɪped/ 1 *n.* two-footed animal. 2 *a.* two-footed.

**biplane** /ˈbaɪpleɪn/ *n.* aeroplane with two pairs of wings one above the other.

**birch** /bɜːtʃ/ 1 *n.* smooth-barked forest tree; bundle of birch twigs used for flogging. 2 *v.t.* flog with birch.

**bird** /bɜːd/ *n.* feathered vertebrate with two wings and two feet; *sl.* young woman. **birdlime** sticky stuff spread to catch birds; **bird of passage** mi-

**biretta**   50   **black**

gratory bird, person who travels habitually; **birdseed** seeds as food for caged birds; **bird's-eye view** general view from above; **bird table** platform on which food for wild birds is placed.

**biretta** /bɪˈretə/ *n.* square cap of (esp. RC) priest.

**Biro** /ˈbaɪrəʊ/ *n.* (**P**) (*pl.* **-ros**) kind of ball-point pen.

**birth** /bɜːθ/ *n.* emergence of young from mother's body; origin, beginning; inherited position. **birth-control** prevention of undesired pregnancy; **birthday** anniversary of birth; **birthmark** unusual mark on body from birth; **birth-rate** number of births per thousand of population per year; **birthright** rights belonging to one by birth; **give birth to** produce (young).

**biscuit** /ˈbɪskət/ *n.* flat thin unleavened cake, usu. dry and crisp and often sweetened; porcelain etc. after first firing and before glazing; light-brown colour.

**bisect** /baɪˈsekt/ *v.t.* divide into two (usu. equal) parts. **bisection** *n.*; **bisector** *n.*

**bisexual** /baɪˈseksjuːəl/ *a.* sexually attracted to members of both sexes; having both sexes in one individual. **bisexuality** *n.*

**bishop** /ˈbɪʃəp/ *n.* senior clergyman in charge of diocese; mitre-shaped piece in chess.

**bishopric** /ˈbɪʃəprɪk/ *n.* office or diocese of bishop.

**bismuth** /ˈbɪzməθ/ *n.* reddish-white brittle metallic element; compound of it used medicinally.

**bison** /ˈbaɪs(ə)n/ *n.* wild ox; buffalo.

**bisque**[1] /bɪsk/ *n.* advantage of one free point or stroke awarded to player in certain games.

**bisque**[2] /bɪsk/ *n.* unglazed white china for statuettes.

**bistre** /ˈbɪstə(r)/ *n.* brown pigment made from soot; colour of this.

**bistro** /ˈbɪstrəʊ/ *n.* (*pl.* **-os**) small bar or restaurant.

**bit**[1] *n.* small piece or amount; short time or distance; mouthpiece of bridle; cutting part of tool etc.

**bit**[2] *n.* *Computers* unit of information expressed as choice between two possibilities, binary digit.

**bit**[3] *past* of **bite**.

**bitch** /bɪtʃ/ **1** *n.* female dog, fox, or wolf; abusive term for woman. **2** *v.* be spiteful; grumble. **3 bitchy** *a.*

**bite** **1** *v.* (*past* **bit**; *p.p.* **bitten**) nip or cut into or off with teeth; sting; penetrate, grip; have desired effect; be sharp; accept bait; *Aus. sl.* cadge or borrow from. **2** *n.* act of biting; wound so made; small amount to eat; incisiveness.

**bitten** *p.p.* of **bite**.

**bitter** /ˈbɪtə(r)/ **1** *a.* having sharp pungent taste, not sweet; showing or feeling resentment; harsh, biting, virulent. **2** *n.* in *pl.* liquor with bitter flavour, esp. of wormwood.

**bittern** /ˈbɪt(ə)n/ *n.* marsh bird allied to heron.

**bitumen** /ˈbɪtjəmən/ *n.* mixture of tarlike substances derived from petroleum; *Aus.* tarred road. **bituminous** /-ˈtjuːmən-/ *a.*

**bivalve** /ˈbaɪvælv/ **1** *a.* having two valves or (of shellfish) a hinged double shell. **2** *n.* bivalve shellfish.

**bivouac** /ˈbɪvuːæk/ **1** *n.* temporary encampment without tents. **2** *v.i.* make open camp.

**bizarre** /bɪˈzɑː(r)/ *a.* strange in appearance or effect; grotesque.

**blab** *v.* talk or tell foolishly or indiscreetly.

**black** **1** *a.* colourless from absence or complete absorption of light; very darkcoloured; dark-skinned; **Black** of Negroes or Aboriginals; dusky, gloomy; sinister, wicked; sullen; declared untouchable by workers in dispute. **2** *n.* black colour, paint, clothes, etc.; (player using) darker pieces in chess etc.; credit side of account; **Black** Negro. **3** *v.t.* make black; polish with blacking; declare (goods etc.) 'black'. **4 beyond the black stump** *Aus.* very far away; **black and blue** badly bruised; **black and white** not in colour, comprising only opposite extremes, *in* print; **black art** magic; **blackball** exclude from club, society, etc.; **black bean** *Aus.* hardwood tree, its wood; **blackbeetle** common cockroach; **black belt** (holder of) badge of proficiency in judo; **black box** flight-recorder in aircraft; **blackboy** *Aus.* tree with black trunk and head of grass-like leaves; **blackbutt** *Aus.* eucalyptus with blackish bark; **black coffee** coffee without milk or cream; **black comedy** comedy presenting tragedy in comic terms; **black eye** bruised skin round eye; **blackfish** any of several basslike Aus. fish; **blackfly** kind of aphid; **blackhead** black-topped pimple; **black hole** *Astron.* region from which matter and radiation cannot escape; **black ice** thin hard transparent ice; **blackjack** *US* short heavy club with pliable shaft; **blacklead** graphite; **blackleg** person who refuses to join strike or trade union; **black magic** magic involving invocation of devils; **Black Maria** police vehicle for transporting prisoners; **black market** illicit traffic in officially controlled or scarce commodities; **black mass** travesty of mass in worship of Satan; **black out** obscure (windows etc.) to prevent light entering or escaping, undergo blackout; **black-out** being blacked out, temporary esp. sudden or momentary loss of vision or consciousness; **black pudding** sausage of blood, suet, etc.; **Black Rod** ceremonial officer of upper house of parliament; **black sheep** scoundrel, disreputable member of; **blackshirt** Fascist; **black spot** place of danger or difficulty; **blackthorn** thorny shrub bearing white flowers and sloes, Aus. shrub with sprays of white flowers; **black tracker** *Aus.* Abor. tracker employed by police; **black velvet** mixture of stout and champagne; **black wattle** *Aus.* acacia with dark bark; **black widow** Amer. spider of which female devours mate; **blackwood** *Aus.* tall kind of acacia, its valuable dark wood.

**blackberry** /ˈblækbəri/ *n.* dark edible fruit of bramble.

**blackbird** /ˈblækbɜːd/ *n.* European song-bird.

**blackboard** /ˈblækbɔːd/ *n.* board for chalking on in classroom etc.

**blackcurrant** /blækˈkʌrənt/ *n.* small black fruit; shrub on which it grows.

**blacken** /ˈblækən/ *v.* make or become black; slander.

**blackguard** /ˈblægɑːd/ 1 *n.* villain, scoundrel. 2 *v.t.* abuse scurrilously. 3 **blackguardly** *a.*

**blacking** /ˈblækɪŋ/ *n.* black polish for boots.

**blacklist** /ˈblæklɪst/ 1 *n.* list of persons etc. in disfavour. 2 *v.t.* put on blacklist.

**blackmail** /ˈblækmeɪl/ 1 *n.* extortion by threats or pressure. 2 *v.t.* extort money from thus.

**blacksmith** /ˈblæksmɪθ/ *n.* smith working in iron.

**bladder** /ˈblædə(r)/ *n.* sac in human or other animal body, esp. that holding urine; inflated thing.

**blade** *n.* cutting-part of knife etc.; flat part of oar or spade or propeller etc.; flat narrow leaf of grass and cereals; flat bone of shoulder.

**blame** 1 *v.t.* find fault with; fix blame on. 2 *n.* censure; responsibility for bad result. 3 **blameworthy** deserving blame.

**blameless** /ˈbleɪmləs/ *a.* innocent.

**blanch** /blɑːntʃ *or* blæntʃ/ *v.* make white by peeling or by depriving (plant) of light; immerse briefly in boiling water; make or grow pale.

**blancmange** /bləˈmɒnʒ/ *n.* opaque jelly of sweet flavoured cornflour and milk.

**bland** *a.* insipid, tasteless; mild, gentle, suave.

**blandishment** /ˈblændɪʃmənt/ *n.* usu. in *pl.* flattering attention; cajolery.

**blank** 1 *a.* not written or printed on; (of form etc.) not filled in; without interest, result, or expression etc. 2 *n.* space to be filled up in document etc.; empty surface; dash written in place of word; blank cartridge. 3 **blank cartridge** one without bullet; **blank cheque** one with amount left for payee to fill in; **blank verse** unrhymed verse, esp. iambic pentameters.

**blanket** /ˈblæŋkɪt/ 1 *n.* large woollen sheet as bed-covering etc.; thick covering layer. 2 *a.* general, covering all cases or classes. 3 *v.t.* (*past & p.p.* **blanketed**) cover (as) with blanket.

**blare** /bleə(r)/ 1 *v.* make sound of trumpet; utter or sound loudly. 2 *n.* blaring sound.

**blarney** /ˈblɑːnɪ/ 1 *n.* empty or flattering talk. 2 *v.* flatter, use blarney.

**blasé** /ˈblɑːzeɪ/ *a.* bored or indifferent, esp. through familiarity.

**blaspheme** /blæsˈfiːm/ *v.* speak profanely of; talk impiously.

**blasphemy** /ˈblæsfəmɪ/ *n.* impious speech, profanity. **blasphemous** *a.*

**blast** /blɑːst/ 1 *n.* explosion; destructive wave of air from this; strong gust;

sound of wind instrument or car horn or whistle etc.; severe criticism or reprimand. 2 *v.t.* blow up with explosive; make explosive sound; blight; *colloq.* criticise forcibly. 3 *int.* damn. 4 **blast-furnace** one for smelting with compressed hot air driven in; **blast off** (of rocket) take off from launching-pad; **blast-off** *n.*

**blatant** /'bleɪt(ə)nt/ *a.* flagrant, unashamed.

**blather** /'blæðə(r)/ 1 *v.i.* chatter foolishly. 2 *n.* foolish talk.

**blaze**[1] 1 *n.* bright flame or fire; violent outburst of passion; bright display or light. 2 *v.i.* flame; burn with excitement etc.

**blaze**[2] 1 *n.* white mark on face of horse or chipped in bark of tree. 2 *v.t.* mark (tree, path) with blaze(s).

**blaze**[3] *v.t.* proclaim (*abroad, forth*).

**blazer** /'bleɪzə(r)/ *n.* light jacket esp. with colours of a school, team, etc.

**blazon** /'bleɪz(ə)n/ 1 *n.* heraldic shield, coat of arms, etc. 2 *v.t.* proclaim; inscribe ornamentally; describe or paint (coat of arms). 3 **blazonry** *n.*

**bleach** /bliːtʃ/ 1 *v.* make or become white or pale in sunlight or by chemical process. 2 *n.* bleaching process or substance.

**bleak** *a.* dreary; bare; chilly.

**bleary** /'blɪərɪ/ *a.* dim-sighted, blurred.

**bleat** 1 *v.* utter cry of sheep or goat etc.; speak foolishly or plaintively. 2 *n.* bleating cry.

**bleed** *v.* (*past & p.p.* **bled**) emit blood; draw blood from; emit or draw off other fluid; *colloq.* extort money from.

**bleep** 1 *v.* emit intermittent high-pitched sound; summon by bleep. 2 *n.* such sound.

**blemish** /'blemɪʃ/ 1 *v.t.* spoil beauty of, mar. 2 *n.* flaw, defect, stain.

**blench** /blentʃ/ *v.i.* flinch, quail.

**blend** 1 *v.* mix (various sorts) into required sort; mingle intimately; become one. 2 *n.* blending, mixture.

**blende** /blend/ *n.* native zinc sulphide.

**blenny** /'blenɪ/ *n.* spiny-finned seafish.

**bless** *v.t.* invoke divine favour on; consecrate; thank; make happy.

**blessed** /'blesɪd/ *attrib.a.* holy; *RC Ch.* beatified; *euphem.* cursed.

**blessing** /'blesɪŋ/ *n.* invocation of divine favour; grace at meals; benefit or advantage.

**blether** var. of **blather**.

**blew** *past* of **blow**.

**blight** /blaɪt/ 1 *n.* disease of plants caused esp. by insects; such insect; obscure malignant influence. 2 *v.t.* affect with blight, destroy; spoil.

**blighter** /'blaɪtə(r)/ *n. sl.* annoying person.

**blimey** /'blaɪmɪ/ *int.* expr. surprise.

**blimp** *n.* small non-rigid airship.

**blind** /blaɪnd/ 1 *a.* without sight; without adequate knowledge or information or foresight; reckless; not governed by purpose; concealed; closed at one end. 2 *v.* deprive of sight or judgement; deceive. 3 *n.* obstruction to sight or light; screen for window; misleading thing. 4 **blind date** social engagement between man and woman who have not met before; **blind Freddie** *Aus. sl.* the least perceptive person; **blind-man's buff** game in which blindfold player tries to catch others; **blind spot** spot on retina insensitive to light, area where vision or judgement fails; **blindworm** slow-worm; **turn a blind eye to** pretend not to notice.

**blindfold** /'blaɪndfəʊld/ 1 *a. & adv.* with eyes covered; without care and attention. 2 *n.* covering for eyes to prevent person seeing. 3 *v.t.* cover eyes of (person) with blindfold.

**blink** 1 *v.* move eyelids; look with eyes opening and shutting; shut eyes for a moment; cast sudden or momentary light; ignore or shirk (facts). 2 *n.* blinking movement; momentary gleam. 3 **on the blink** *sl.* (of machine etc.) out of order.

**blinker** /'blɪŋkə(r)/ *n.* usu. in *pl.* screen on bridle preventing horse from seeing sideways.

**blinking** /'blɪŋkɪŋ/ *a. & adv. sl.* expr. mild annoyance.

**blip** *n.* small spot or image on radar-screen.

**bliss** *n.* perfect joy; being in heaven. **blissful** *a.*; **blissfully** *adv.*

**blister** /'blɪstə(r)/ 1 *n.* small bubble on skin filled with watery fluid; any swelling resembling this. 2 *v.* raise blister on; become covered with blisters.

**blithe** /blaɪð/ *a.* joyous, gay; carefree, casual.

## blithering

**blithering** /ˈblɪðərɪŋ/ *a. colloq.* utter, hopeless; talking senselessly.
**blitz** /blɪts/ 1 *n.* intensive (esp. aerial) attack. 2 *v.t.* damage or destroy in blitz.
**blizzard** /ˈblɪzəd/ *n.* severe snowstorm.
**bloat** *v.* inflate, swell.
**bloater** /ˈbləʊtə(r)/ *n.* herring cured by salting and smoking.
**blob** *n.* small drop or spot.
**bloc** *n.* combination of countries, parties, or groups sharing some common purpose.
**block** 1 *n.* large solid piece of hard material; large building, esp. when subdivided; group of buildings surrounded by usu. four streets; *Aus.* area of land divided for settlement; *Aus.* plot of land for residential building; *Aus.* wooden support for house in Queensland; obstruction; large quantity as a unit; piece of wood or metal engraved for printing. 2 *v.t.* obstruct; stop (cricket ball) with bat. 3 **blockhead** stupid person; **block letter** separate capital letter; **block vote** vote proportional in size to number of persons voter represents; **do one's block** *Aus. sl.* become angry. **mental block** mental inability due to subconscious factors.
**blockade** /blɒˈkeɪd/ 1 *n.* surrounding or blocking of place by hostile forces. 2 *v.t.* subject to blockade.
**blockage** /ˈblɒkɪdʒ/ *n.* obstruction; blocked-up state.
**bloke** *n. sl.* man, fellow.
**blond** (of woman usu. **blonde**) 1 *a.* fair-haired; (of hair) light-coloured. 2 *n.* fair-haired person.
**blood** /blʌd/ 1 *n.* liquid, usu. red, circulating in arteries and veins of animals; murder, bloodshed; race, descent; relationship. 2 *v.t.* give first taste of blood to (hound); initiate (person). 3 **blood bank** reserve of blood for transfusion; **blood-bath** massacre; **blood count** count of red corpuscles in blood; **blood-curdling** horrifying; **blood donor** giver of blood for transfusion; **blood group** any of types of human blood; **bloodhound** large keen-scented dog used for tracking; **blood-letting** surgical removal of blood; **blood orange** one with red-streaked pulp; **blood-poisoning** poisoning due to harmful bacteria in blood; **blood pressure** force exerted by blood in arteries; **blood-relation** one related by common descent; **bloodshed** killing or wounding of people; **bloodshot** (of eyeball) tinged with blood; **blood sport** one involving killing of animals; **bloodstream** circulating blood; **bloodsucker** leech, extortioner; **bloodthirsty** eager for bloodshed; **blood-vessel** vein, artery, or capillary conveying blood; **bloodwood** Aus. eucalypt with red sap.
**bloodless** /ˈblʌdləs/ *a.* without blood or bloodshed; unemotional; pale.
**bloody** /ˈblʌdɪ/ 1 *a.* of or like blood; blood-stained, running with blood; involving bloodshed, cruel; *sl.* expr. annoyance. 2 *adv. sl.* extremely. 3 *v.t.* make bloody. 4 **bloody-minded** *colloq.* deliberately unco-operative.
**bloom** /bluːm/ 1 *n.* flower; flowering state; prime; freshness; powdery deposit on fruit etc. 2 *v.i.* bear blooms; be in flower; flourish.
**bloomer** /ˈbluːmə(r)/ *n. sl.* blunder.
**bloomers** /ˈbluːməz/ *n.pl.* loose knee-length trousers formerly worn by women; *colloq.* knickers.
**blooming** /ˈbluːmɪŋ/ *a. & adv.* in bloom; *sl.* expr. mild annoyance.
**blossom** /ˈblɒsəm/ 1 *n.* flower; mass of flowers on tree. 2 *v.i.* come into flower; thrive.
**blot** 1 *n.* spot of ink etc.; blemish; disgraceful act. 2 *v.t.* make blot on; stain; dry with blotting-paper. 3 **blot out** obliterate.
**blotch** *n.* inflamed patch on skin; dab of ink etc. **blotchy** *a.*
**blotter** /ˈblɒtə(r)/ *n.* device for holding blotting-paper.
**blotting-paper** /ˈblɒtɪŋ/ *n.* absorbent paper for drying wet ink.
**blouse** /blaʊz/ *n.* garment like shirt, worn by women; jacket forming part of military uniform.
**blow**[1] /bləʊ/ 1 *v.* (*past* **blew** /bluː/; *p.p.* **blown**) send directed air-current from mouth; move as wind does; puff, pant; sound (wind instrument); clear (nose) by sudden forceful breath; make or shape or work by blowing; break or burst suddenly; cause (fuse) to break; *Aus. sl.* boast; *sl.* (*p.p.* **blowed**) curse, confound, squander. 2 *n.* blowing; inhaling of fresh air; *Aus. colloq.* brief rest; 3 **blow-dry** use hand-held drier

**blow**

on (washed) hair; **blowfly** bluebottle; **blow in** break or drive inwards by explosion; **blow-in** Aus. newcomer; **blowlamp** apparatus for directing intensely hot flame on limited area; **blow out** extinguish by blowing, send outwards by blowing; **blow-out** burst in pneumatic tyre, sl. large meal; **blowpipe** tube from which dart or arrow is projected by blowing; **blow up** shatter or be shattered by explosion, inflate, enlarge (photograph), colloq. reprove.

**blow**² /bləʊ/ n. hard stroke with fist or weapon; disaster, shock; Aus. stroke of shears in shearing; Aus. outcrop of mineral.

**blower** /'bləʊə(r)/ n. device for blowing; colloq. telephone.

**blowie** /'bləʊi/ n. Aus. colloq. blowfly.

**blowy** /'bləʊi/ a. windy.

**blowzy** /'blaʊzi/ a. coarse-looking, red-faced; dishevelled.

**blub** v.i. sl. weep.

**blubber** /'blʌbə(r)/ 1 n. whale fat. 2 v.i. sob, weep noisily. 3 a. swollen, protruding.

**bludge** Aus. sl. 1 v. shirk responsibility or hard work; scrounge, impose on. 2 n. easy job; period of loafing. 3 **bludger** n.

**bludgeon** /'blʌdʒ(ə)n/ 1 n. heavy stick. 2 v.t. beat with bludgeon; coerce.

**blue** /bluː/ 1 a. coloured like clear sky or deep sea; sad, depressed; indecent. 2 n. blue colour, paint, clothes, etc.; person who has represented university at sport; in pl. melancholy, kind of melancholy music of Amer. Black origin; Aus. sl. argument or fight, summons, mistake, red-haired person. 3 v.t. make blue; sl. squander. 4 **blue baby** one with congenital heart defect; **bluebell** wild hyacinth, harebell, Aus. flower resembling harebell; **blue blood** noble birth; **bluebottle** large buzzing fly, Aus. Portuguese man of war; **bluebush** Aus. kind of saltbush; **blue cheese** cheese with veins of blue fungus; **blue-collar** of manual work; **blue-eyed boy** colloq. favourite; **blue flyer** Aus. female of red kangaroo; **blue-gum** Aus. eucalypt with bluish bark; **blue heeler** Aus. speckled dark-coloured cattle-dog; **blue-pencil** correct or edit, censor; **Blue Peter** blue flag with central white square hoisted before sailing; **blue pointer** Aus. kind of shark with pointed snout; **blueprint** photographic print on blue paper of plans for building etc., fig. detailed plan; **blue ribbon** high honour; **bluestocking** intellectual woman; **bluestone** Aus. basalt or brownish stone used in building; **blue-tongue** Aus. lizard with blue tongue, sl. rouseabout.

**bluey** /'bluːi/ n. Aus. swag; colloq. red-haired person; cattle-dog; sl. summons.

**bluff**¹ 1 v. make pretence of strength to gain advantage etc.; deceive thus. 2 n. act of bluffing.

**bluff**² 1 a. with steep or vertical broad front; blunt, frank, hearty. 2 n. bluff headland.

**blunder** /'blʌndə(r)/ 1 v.i. make serious-mistake; move about clumsily. 2 n. stupid or careless mistake.

**blunderbuss** /'blʌndəbʌs/ n. disused kind of short gun with large bore.

**blunt** 1 a. without sharp edge or point; dull, not sensitive; plain-spoken. 2 v.t. make blunt.

**blur** 1 v.t. make or become less distinct; smear. 2 n. thing seen or heard indistinctly.

**blurb** n. publisher's commendation of book, printed on its jacket etc.

**blurt** v.t. (usu. with out) utter abruptly or tactlessly.

**blush** 1 v.i. be or become red (as) with shame or other emotion; be ashamed. 2 n. blushing; pink tinge.

**bluster** /'blʌstə(r)/ 1 v. storm boisterously. 2 n. noisy self-assertive talk, threats. 3 **blustery** a.

**BMX** abbr. bicycle moto-cross.

**BO** abbr. body odour.

**boa** /'bəʊə/ n. large S. Amer. snake that kills its prey by crushing it; woman's long throat-wrap of fur or feather. **boa constrictor** Brazilian boa, python.

**boar** /bɔː(r)/ n. male wild pig; uncastrated male pig.

**board** /bɔːd/ 1 n. thin piece of sawn timber; material resembling this; wooden or cardboard etc. slab used in games or for posting notices etc.; thick stiff card; provision of meals; directors of company; council-table; committee; in pl. the stage; Aus. part of floor of shearing-shed where shearers work; committee. 2 v.t. go on board (ship etc.); cover with boards; provide or receive meals at

**boarder** / **bold**

fixed rate. **3 boarding-house** house providing board and lodging; **boarding-school** one providing board and lodging for pupils; **boardroom** meeting-place of board of directors; **boardsailing** *Aus.* using a sailboard; **on board** on or into ship or train or aircraft etc.

**boarder** /'bɔːdə(r)/ *n.* pupil who boards at boarding-school.

**boast 1** *v.* declare one's achievements etc. with pride; own with pride. **2** *n.* excessively proud statement; thing one is proud of. **3 boastful** *a.*

**boat 1** *n.* small open oared or engined or sailing vessel; (small) ship; boat-shaped utensil for sauce etc. **2** *v.i.* go in boat esp. for pleasure. **3 boat-hook** long pole with hook and spike; **boathouse** shed at water's edge for boats; **boatman** one who hires out or provides transport by boats.

**boater** /'bəʊtə(r)/ *n.* hard flat straw hat.

**boatswain** /'bəʊs(ə)n/ *n.* ship's officer in charge of crew and sails etc.

**bob**[1] **1** *v.* move up and down, rebound; cut (hair) short. **2** *n.* bobbing movement, curtsey; bobbed hair; horse's docked tail; weight on pendulum etc. **3 bobtail** docked tail, horse or dog with this.

**bob**[2] *n.* (*pl.* same) *sl.* shilling, 10c.

**bobbin** /'bɒbɪn/ *n.* cylinder for holding thread etc., reel, spool.

**bobble** /'bɒb(ə)l/ *n.* small woolly ball as ornament or trimming.

**bobby** /'bɒbɪ/ *n. UK sl.* uniformed policeman.

**bob-sled** /'bɒbsled/ (also **bob-sleigh**) *n.* sledge with two sets of runners.

**bode** *v.* portend, foretell.

**bodice** /'bɒdɪs/ *n.* upper part of woman's dress down to waist; undergarment for same part of body.

**bodiless** /'bɒdɪləs/ *a.* lacking (a) body.

**bodily** /'bɒdɪlɪ/ **1** *a.* of or affecting human body. **2** *adv.* as a whole, in a body.

**bodkin** /'bɒdkɪn/ *n.* blunt thick needle for drawing tape etc. through hem.

**body** /'bɒdɪ/ *n.* material part of man or animal alive or dead; trunk apart from head and limbs; main part; group of persons regarded as a unit; *colloq.* person; piece of matter; solidity, substantial characteristic or flavour. **body-guard** escort or personal guard; **body politic** State; **body stocking** woman's undergarment covering trunk and legs; **bodywork** structure of vehicle body.

**Boer** /'bəʊə(r) *or* bɔː(r)/ *n.* Dutch-descended S. African.

**boffin** /'bɒfɪn/ *n. colloq.* person engaged in scientific or technical research.

**bog 1** *n.* wet spongy ground, morass; *sl.* lavatory. **2** *v.t.* trap or submerge in bog. **3 bogged down** unable to move or make progress.

**bogey**[1] /'bəʊgɪ/ *n.* par or one more than par on a hole in golf.

**bogey**[2] /'bəʊgɪ/ *Aus.* **1** *n.* a bathe or swim; place for this. **2** *v.i.* bathe or swim.

**boggle** /'bɒg(ə)l/ *v.i.* be startled or baffled; hesitate, demur (*at*).

**boggy** /'bɒgɪ/ *a.* marshy, spongy.

**bogie**[1] /'bəʊgɪ/ *n.* wheeled under-carriage pivoted below locomotive etc.

**bogie**[2] var. of **bogey**[2].

**bogong** /'bəʊgɒŋ/ *n. Aus.* dark-coloured moth eaten by Aboriginals.

**bogus** /'bəʊgəs/ *a.* sham, spurious.

**bogy**[1] /'bəʊgɪ/ *n.* evil spirit, goblin; awkward thing or circumstance.

**bogy**[2] *var.* of **bogey**[2].

**Bohemian** /bə'hiːmɪən/ **1** *a.* socially unconventional; of Bohemia. **2** *n.* such person, esp. artist or writer. **3 Bohemianism** *n.*

**boil**[1] *v.* (of liquid or its vessel) bubble up with heat, reach temperature at which liquid turns to vapour; bring to boiling-point; subject to heat of boiling water, cook thus; be agitated like boiling water. **2** *n.* boiling heat. **3 boiled sweet** one made of boiled sugar; **boiling (hot)** *colloq.* very hot; **boiling-point** temperature at which liquid boils.

**boil**[2] *n.* inflamed pus-filled swelling under skin.

**boiler** /'bɔɪlə(r)/ *n.* fuel-burning apparatus for heating hot-water supply; tank for heating water or turning it into steam; vessel for boiling things in. **boiler suit** one-piece garment combining overalls and shirt.

**boisterous** /'bɔɪstərəs/ *a.* noisily cheerful; violent, rough.

**bold** /bəʊld/ *a.* confident; adventurous;

**bole** *n.* stem or trunk of tree.

**bolero** /bə'leərəʊ/ *n.* (*pl.* **-ros**) a Spanish dance; (also /'bɒlərəʊ/) woman's short jacket without fastenings.

**boll** /bəʊl/ *n.* round seed-vessel of cotton, flax, etc.

**bollard** /'bɒləd/ *n.* short thick post in street etc.; post on ship or quay for securing ropes to.

**boloney** /bə'ləʊni/ *n. sl.* nonsense.

**Bolshie** /'bɒlʃi:/ *sl.* 1 *a.* rebellious or unco-operative. 2 *n.* such person.

**bolster** /'bəʊlstə(r)/ 1 *n.* long stuffed pillow. 2 *v.* support with bolster, prop *up*.

**bolt**[1] /bəʊlt/ 1 *n.* door-fastening of metal bar and socket; headed metal pin secured with rivet or nut; act of bolting; discharge of lightning; short heavy crossbow arrow. 2 *v.* fasten with bolt; gulp down unchewed; dart off, run away; (of horse) escape from control; run to seed. 3 **bolt-hole** means of escape; **bolt upright** erect.

**bolt**[2] /bəʊlt/ *v.t.* sift.

**bomb** /bɒm/ 1 *n.* high explosive or incendiary material or smoke etc. in container for release on impact or by time mechanism; *the* atomic bomb; *Aus. sl.* old car. 2 *v.t.* attack with bombs; throw or drop bombs on; *sl.* travel fast. 3 **bombshell** cause of great surprise or disappointment.

**bombard** /bɒm'bɑ:d/ *v.t.* attack with heavy guns; assail with abuse etc.; subject to stream of high-speed particles. **bombardment** *n.*

**bombardier** /bɒmbə'dɪə(r)/ *n.* artillery NCO below sergeant; *US* airman who releases bombs from aircraft.

**bombast** /'bɒmbæst/ *n.* pompous or extravagant language. **bombastic** *a.*

**bombazine** /'bɒmbəzi:n/ *n.* twilled worsted dress-material.

**bomber** /'bɒmə(r)/ *n.* aircraft used for bombing; person who throws or plants bombs.

**bombora** /bɒm'bɔ:rə/ *n. Aus.* submerged reef; dangerous water over reef.

**bona fide** /bəʊnə 'faɪdɪ/ in good faith, genuine.

**bonanza** /bə'nænzə/ *n.* source of great wealth; rich mine.

**bon-bon** *n.* sweet.

**bond**[1] 1 *n.* thing or force that unites or (usu. in *pl.*) restrains; binding agreement; document binding person to pay or repay money; adhesion; *Chem.* linkage of atoms in molecule. 2 *v.t.* bind or connect together; put in bond. 3 **bond paper** high-quality writing-paper; **in bond** stored by Customs until duty is paid.

**bondage** /'bɒndɪdʒ/ *n.* slavery; confinement, subjection to constraint.

**bondman** /'bɒndmən/ (also **bondsman**) *n.* serf or slave.

**bone** 1 *n.* any of separate parts of vertebrate skeleton; in *pl.* skeleton, mortal remains; substance of which these consist; thing made of this. 2 *v.t.* remove bones from. 3 **bone china** fine semitranslucent earthenware; **bone-dry** quite dry; **bonehead** *sl.* stupid person; **bone idle** completely idle; **bone-meal** crushed bone as fertilizer; **boneshaker** jolting vehicle; **point the bone at** *Aus.* cast fatal spell on.

**bonfire** /'bɒnfaɪə(r)/ *n.* open-air fire.

**bongo** /'bɒŋgəʊ/ *n.* (*pl.* **-gos** or **-goes**) one of pair of small drums played with fingers.

**bonhomie** /bɒnɒ'mi:/ *n.* geniality. [F]

**bonnet** /'bɒnət/ *n.* woman's or child's outdoor head-dress with strings; *Sc.* man's round cap; hinged cover over engine of motor vehicle.

**bonny** /'bɒni/ *a.* comely, healthy-looking.

**bonsai** /'bɒnsaɪ/ *n.* dwarf tree or shrub; art of growing these.

**bonus** /'bəʊnəs/ *n.* something extra, esp. addition to dividends or wages.

**bony** /'bəʊni/ *a.* of or like bone; thin with prominent bones.

**bonzer** /'bɒnzə(r)/ *a. Aus. hist. sl.* excellent.

**boo** 1 *int.* expr. disapproval or contempt. 2 *n.* the sound *boo*. 3 *v.* utter boos (at).

**boob** *sl.* 1 *n.* silly mistake; woman's breast. 2 *v.i.* make mistake.

**boobook** /'bu:bʊk/ *n.* medium-sized brown Aus. owl.

**booby** /'bu:bi/ *n.* silly or awkward person. **booby prize** small prize for last competitor in contest; **booby trap** disguised exploding device triggered by unknowing victim, device to trick un-

# book | bore

**suspecting person, (*v.t.*) set booby trap in.

**book** /bʊk/ 1 *n*. sheets of paper, written or printed on or blank, fastened together usu. hingewise in cover; literary composition that would fill such sheets; set of tickets, stamps, matches, cheques, etc., bound up together; main division of literary work or Bible; in *pl*. society's records, trader's accounts; *colloq*. magazine; record of bets made; libretto. 2 *v*. enter in book or list; bring charge against; secure (seat etc.) in advance; obtain ticket for journey etc.; make reservation. 3 **bookcase** cabinet containing shelves for books; **book-ends** pair of props to support row of books; **bookkeeper** person who keeps accounts of business etc.; **bookmaker** person whose business is taking bets; **bookmark** strip of card or leather etc. for marking place in book; **bookplate** label in book with owner's name; **book token** voucher exchangeable for books of given value; **bookworm** person devoted to reading, larva that eats through books.

**bookie** /ˈbʊki/ *n*. *colloq*. bookmaker.

**bookish** /ˈbʊkɪʃ/ *a*. fond of reading; getting knowledge from books only.

**booklet** /ˈbʊklət/ *n*. small usu. paper-covered book.

**boom**[1] /buːm/ 1 *n*. deep resonant sound. 2 *v*. emit or utter with boom.

**boom**[2] /buːm/ 1 *n*. sudden activity in commerce etc. 2 *v.i.* be prosperous or very successful.

**boom**[3] /buːm/ *n*. long pole with one fixed end to support sail-foot, camera, microphone, etc.; barrier across harbour etc.

**boomer** /ˈbuːmə(r)/ *n*. *Aus*. large male kangaroo; *sl*. anything large of its kind.

**boomerang** /ˈbuːməræŋ/ 1 *n*. Australian missile of curved wood that can be so thrown as to return to thrower. 2 *v.i.* (of scheme) recoil on originator.

**boon**[1] /buːn/ *n*. advantage or benefit; blessing.

**boon**[2] /buːn/ *a*. convivial, jolly.

**boor** /bʊə(r)/ *n*. uncouth or ill-mannered person. **boorish** *a*.

**boost** /buːst/ 1 *v.t.* increase strength or reputation of; *colloq*. push from below, increase, assist. 2 *n*. act or effect of boosting.

**booster** *n*. device for increasing power or signal; auxiliary engine or rocket for initial acceleration; dose increasing effect of earlier one.

**boot** /buːt/ 1 *n*. outer foot-covering reaching above ankle; luggage compartment of motor car etc.; *sl*. dismissal. 2 *v.t.* kick; *Computers* bootstrap. 3 **boots and all** *Aus*. *sl*. with no holds barred, whole heartedly.

**bootee** /buːˈtiː/ *n*. infant's woollen boot; woman's short lined boot.

**booth** /buːð/ *n*. temporary structure of canvas or wood; enclosure for public telephone etc. or for voting.

**bootleg** /ˈbuːtleg/ *a*. smuggled, illicit. **bootlegger** *n*.

**bootstrap** /ˈbuːtstræp/ 1 *n*. in *pl*. unaided effort. 2 *v.t.* load operating system etc. into (computer), esp. from disc etc.

**booty** /ˈbuːti/ *n*. plunder gained esp. in war; prize.

**booze** /buːz/ *colloq*. 1 *n*. alcoholic drink; drinking of it. 2 *v.i.* drink liquor, esp. excessively. 3 **boozy** *a*.

**boozer** /ˈbuːzə(r)/ *n*. *colloq*. hard drinker; public house.

**bora** /ˈbɔːrə/ *n*. *Aus*. Abor. boy's initiation rite.

**boracic** /bəˈræsɪk/ *a*. of borax. **boracic acid** boric acid.

**borage** /ˈbɒrɪdʒ/ *n*. blue-flowered plant used in salads etc.

**borak** /ˈbɔːræk/ *n*. *Aus*. *sl*. **poke borak at** make fun of.

**borax** /ˈbɔːræks/ *n*. salt of boric acid used as antiseptic.

**border** /ˈbɔːdə(r)/ 1 *n*. side, edge, boundary, or part near it; frontier; distinct edging round anything. 2 *v*. put or be border to; adjoin. 3 **borderline** boundary between areas or classes, (*a*.) on borderline.

**bore**[1] 1 *v*. make (hole), esp. with revolving tool; drill (shaft of well); make hole (in) thus. 2 *n*. hollow of gun-barrel or cylinder; diameter of this; deep narrow hole made to find water etc; *Aus*. artesian well, water-hole for cattle.

**bore**[2] 1 *v.t.* weary by tedious talk or dullness. 2 *n*. tiresome person or thing; nuisance.

**bore**[3] *n.* tide-wave of exceptional height rushing up estuary.

**bore**[4] *past of* **bear**[1].

**boredom** /'bɔːdəm/ *n.* being bored (**bore**[5]).

**boree** /'bɔːriː/ *n. Aus.* myall; kind of wattle.

**boric acid** /'bɔrɪk/ acid used as mild antiseptic.

**born** *a.* existing as a result of birth; being (specified thing) by nature; destined *to be*.

**boron** /'bɔːrɒn/ *n.* a non-metallic element.

**boronia** /bə'rəʊniːə/ *n.* sweet-scented Aus. shrub.

**borough** /'bʌrə/ *n. UK hist.* town with municipal corporation; category of urban area in Victoria.

**borrow** /'bɒrəʊ/ *v.* get temporary use of (something to be returned); adopt or use as one's own (idea, word, etc.).

**Borstal** /'bɔːst(ə)l/ *n.* institution to which young offenders were formerly sent for reformative training.

**bortsch** /bɔːtʃ/ *n.* Russian beetroot soup.

**borzoi** /'bɔːzɔɪ/ *n.* Russian wolf-hound.

**bosey** var. of **bosie**.

**bosh** *n.* nonsense, rubbish.

**bosie** /'bəʊziː/ *n. Aus. Crick.* googly.

**bosom** /'bʊz(ə)m/ *n.* person's breast; enclosure formed by breast and arms; enfolding relationship; part of dress covering breast. **bosom friend** intimate friend.

**boss**[1] **1** *n.* employer or manager, supervisor. **2** *v.t.* be boss of, control. **boss about** continually give orders to.

**boss**[2] *n.* protuberance, round knob or stud.

**boss**[3] *a. sl.* **boss-eyed** cross-eyed, crooked; **boss shot** failure, bungle.

**bossy** /'bɒsiː/ *a.* domineering. **bossiness** *n.*

**bot** *Aus. sl.* **1** *n.* cadger. **2** *v.* scrounge *on.* **3 on the bot** cadging.

**bo'sun** /'bəʊs(ə)n/ *n.* boatswain.

**botany** /'bɒtəniː/ *n.* science of plants. **botanical** (/·'tæn·/-) *a.*; **botanist** *n.*

**botch** **1** *v.t.* bungle; patch clumsily. **2** *n.* botched work, bungle.

**both** /bəʊθ/ **1** *a.* & *pron.* the two (not only one). **2** *adv.* with equal truth in two cases.

**bother** /'bɒðə(r)/ *v.* **1** give trouble to, worry; take trouble. **2** *n.* person or thing that bothers; nuisance. **3** *int.* of impatience. **4 bothersome** *a.*

**bottle** /'bɒt(ə)l/ **1** *n.* narrow-necked usu. glass vessel for storing liquid; liquid in bottle. **2** *v.t.* put into bottles; preserve (fruit etc.) in jars. **3 bottle-brush** Aus. shrub with cylindrical flower-spikes; **bottle-green** dark green; **bottle-neck** point at which flow of traffic or production etc. is constricted, narrow place; **bottle-oh** *Aus.* collector of empty bottles; **bottle-party** one to which each guest contributes a bottle of drink; **bottle up** restrain (feelings etc.).

**bottler** /'bɒtlə(r)/ *n. Aus. sl.* excellent person or thing.

**bottom** /'bɒtəm/ *n.* **1** lowest point or part; buttocks; less honourable end of table, class, etc.; ground under water of sea etc.; bottom of ship's hull, ship; basis; essential nature. **2** *a.* lowest, last. **3** *v.* provide with bottom; touch bottom (of); *Aus.* reach gold or bedrock in mine; find extent of.

**bottomless** /'bɒtəmləs/ *a.* without bottom; inexhaustible.

**botulism** /'bɒtjʊlɪz(ə)m/ *n.* food-poisoning caused by bacillus in inadequately preserved food.

**bouclé** /'buːkleɪ/ *n.* yarn with looped or curled strands.

**boudoir** /'buːdwɑː(r)/ *n.* woman's private room.

**bougainvillaea** /buːgən'vɪliːə/ *n.* tropical plant with large coloured bracts.

**bough** /baʊ/ *n.* branch of tree.

**bought** /bɔːt/ *past* & *p.p. of* **buy**.

***bouillon*** /'buːjɔ̃/ *n.* broth. [F]

**boulder** /'bəʊldə(r)/ *n.* large stone worn smooth by weather or water.

**boulevard** /'buːləvɑːd/ *n.* broad tree-lined street.

**boult** var. of **bolt**[2].

**bounce** /baʊns/ **1** *v.* rebound; cause to rebound; *sl.* (of cheque) be returned by bank when there are no funds to meet it; rush noisily. **2** *n.* rebound; boast, swagger; *colloq.* energy. **3 bouncy** *a.*

**bouncer** *n. sl.* person employed to eject troublesome people from night-club etc.

**bouncing** *a.* big and healthy.

**bound**[1] /baʊnd/ **1** *v.i.* spring, leap; (of

**bound** ... ball etc.) recoil from wall or ground. 2 *n.* springy upward or forward movement; recoil of ball etc.

**bound²** /baʊnd/ 1 *n.* usu. in *pl.* limit of territory, limitation, restriction. 2 *v.t.* set bounds to; be boundary of. 3 **out of bounds** beyond permitted area.

**bound³** /baʊnd/ *a.* ready to start or having started (*for*).

**bound⁴** /baʊnd/ *a.* (*past & p.p.* of **bind**) required by duty; certain *to* do. **bound up** closely associated *with*.

**boundary** /ˈbaʊndəri/ *n.* line etc. indicating bounds or limits; *Crick.* hit to limit of field, runs scored for this.

**bounteous** /ˈbaʊntiəs/ *a.* freely bestowed.

**bountiful** /ˈbaʊntəfʊl/ *a.* generous.

**bounty** /ˈbaʊnti/ *n.* generosity in giving; gift; official reward.

**bouquet** /bʊˈkeɪ/ *n.* bunch of flowers; perfume of wine; *fig.* praise. **bouquet garni** (/ˈɡɑːniː/) bunch of herbs for flavouring.

**bourbon** /ˈbɜːbən/ *n. US* whisky distilled from maize and rye.

**bourgeois** /ˈbʊəʒwɑː/ 1 *a.* of middle class; conventional; materialist. 2 *n.* bourgeois person.

**bourgeoisie** /bʊəʒwɑːˈziː/ *n.* bourgeois class.

**bourse** /bʊəs/ *n.* money-market, esp. **Bourse** stock exchange in Paris.

**bout** /baʊt/ *n.* spell or turn or fit of work, illness, etc.; match at wrestling or boxing.

**boutique** /buːˈtiːk/ *n.* small shop selling fashionable clothes etc.

**bouzouki** /bəˈzuːki/ *n.* Greek instrument like mandoline.

**bovine** /ˈbəʊvaɪn/ *a.* of oxen; dull, inert.

**bow¹** /bəʊ/ 1 *n.* shallow curve or bend; weapon for shooting arrows; rod with horsehair stretched from end to end for playing violin etc.; ornamental knot with two loops, ribbon etc. so tied. 2 *v.t.* use bow on (violin etc.). 3 **bow-legged** having bandy legs; **bow-tie** necktie for tying in double loop; **bow-window** curved bay window.

**bow²** /baʊ/ 1 *v.* bend or kneel in sign of submission or reverence or greeting or assent; incline head in salutation. 2 *n.* bowing of head or body.

**bow³** /baʊ/ *n.* fore-end of boat or ship; rower nearest bow.

**bowdlerize** /ˈbaʊdləraɪz/ *v.t.* expurgate. **bowdlerization** *n.*

**bowel** /ˈbaʊəl/ *n.* intestine; in *pl.* innermost parts.

**bower** /ˈbaʊə(r)/ *n.* arbour, summerhouse, leafy nook. **bower-bird** Aus. bird that adorns its run with shells etc. **bowery** *a.*

**bowie knife** /ˈbəʊi:/ hunting-knife with long curved blade.

**bowl¹** /bəʊl/ *n.* hollow dish esp. for food or liquid; hollow part of tobacco-pipe, spoon, etc.

**bowl²** /bəʊl/ 1 *n.* hard heavy ball made with bias to run in curve; in *pl.* game with these on grass. 2 *v.* play bowls; roll (ball); *Crick.* deliver ball, put (batsman) out by knocking off bails with bowled ball; go along by rolling or on wheels. 3 **bowling-alley** long enclosure for playing skittles or bowling; **bowling-green** lawn for playing bowls.

**bowler¹** /ˈbəʊlə(r)/ *n. Crick.* player who bowls.

**bowler²** /ˈbəʊlə(r)/ *n.* hard felt hat with rounded crown.

**bowsprit** /ˈbaʊsprɪt/ *n.* spar running forward from ship's bow.

**bowyang** /ˈbəʊjæŋ/ *n. Aus.* string or strap worn round trouser-leg below knee.

**box¹** *n.* container, usu. with flat sides and of firm material; quantity contained in this; separate compartment in theatre or stable etc.; enclosed area or space; witness-box; telephone-box; receptacle at newspaper office for replies to advertisement; *colloq. the* television; coachman's seat. 2 *v.* put in or provide with box. 3 **box girder** girder with square cross-section; **box-office** office for booking seats at theatre etc.; **box-pleat** two parallel pleats forming raised band.

**box²** 1 *v.* fight with fists, usu. in padded gloves, as sport; slap (person's ears). 2 *n.* slap on ear.

**box³** *n.* kind of evergreen shrub with small dark-green leaves; its wood; *Aus.* any of various kinds of eucalyptus.

**boxer** *n.* fighter using fists; smooth-coated dog of bulldog type.

**boxing** *n.* fighting with fists. **boxing-glove** padded kind worn in this.

**Boxing Day** first weekday after Christmas Day.

**boy** *n.* male child, young man; male servant, attendant, etc. **boy-friend** girl's or woman's regular male companion. **boyhood** *n.*; **boyish** *a.*

**boycott** /'bɔɪkɒt/ 1 *v.t.* refuse social or commercial relations with by common consent; refuse to handle (goods). 2 *n.* such refusal.

**bra** /brɑː/ *n.* brassière.

**brace** 1 *n.* thing that clamps or fastens tightly; in *pl.* straps supporting trousers from shoulders; wire device for straightening teeth; pair. 2 *v.t.* fasten tightly; strengthen, make taut; invigorate.

**bracelet** /'breɪslət/ *n.* ornamental band or chain worn on arm or wrist; in *pl.*, *sl.* handcuffs.

**bracken** /'brækən/ *n.* coarse hardy fern; mass of this.

**bracket** /'brækət/ 1 *n.* projection from wall serving as support; angular support for something fastened to wall; mark used in pairs (), [], {}, for enclosing words or figures; group classified as similar or falling between limits. 2 *v.t.* enclose in brackets; group in same category.

**brackish** /'brækɪʃ/ *a.* (of water) slightly salt.

**bract** *n. Bot.* leaf or scale below calyx.

**brad** *n.* thin flat nail.

**bradawl** /'brædɔːl/ *n.* small boring-tool.

**brae** /breɪ/ *n. Sc.* hillside.

**brag** 1 *v.* talk boastfully, boast. 2 *n.* boastful statement or talk; card-game like poker.

**braggart** /'brægət/ *n.* person given to bragging.

**Brahma** /'brɑːmə/ *n.* supreme Hindu deity.

**brahmin** /'brɑːmɪn/ *n.* member of Hindu priestly caste.

**braid** 1 *n.* silk, thread, wire, etc. woven into band for trimming etc; plaited tress of hair. 2 *v.t.* trim with braid; form into braid.

**Braille** /breɪl/ *n.* system of writing or printing for the blind formed by raised points interpreted by touch.

**brain** *n.* organ of convoluted nervous tissue in skull of vertebrates; centre of sensation or thought; in *sing.* or *pl.* (source of) intellectual power. 2 *v.t.* dash out brains of. 3 **brain-child** *colloq.* product of thought; **brainstorm** violent mental disturbance; **brains trust** group of experts giving impromptu answers to questions; **brainwash** systematically replace established ideas in person's mind by new ones; **brainwave** bright idea.

**brainy** /'breɪnɪ/ *a.* intellectually clever.

**braise** /breɪz/ *v.t.* stew (esp. meat) slowly in closed container with small amount of liquid.

**brake**¹ 1 *n.* apparatus for checking motion of wheel or vehicle. 2 *v.* apply brake; retard with brake.

**brake**² *n.* thicket, brushwood.

**bramble** /'bræmb(ə)l/ *n.* wild prickly shrub with long trailing shoots, blackberry.

**bran** *n.* husks separated from flour after grinding. **bran-tub** lucky dip with prizes hidden in bran.

**branch** /brɑːntʃ or bræntʃ/ 1 *n.* limb growing from stem or bough of tree; lateral extension or subdivision of river, railway, family, etc.; local establishment of business etc. 2 *v.i.* put *out* branches; divide, diverge, strike *off*, *out*, etc. in new path.

**brand** 1 *n.* goods of particular name or trade mark; permanent mark deliberately made with hot iron, iron stamp for this; stigma; piece of burning or smouldering wood; torch. 2 *v.t.* label with trade mark; stigmatize; stamp with hot iron; impress indelibly. 3 **brand-new** completely or obviously new.

**brandish** /'brændɪʃ/ *v.t.* wave or flourish.

**brandy** /'brændɪ/ *n.* strong spirit distilled from wine or fermented fruit-juice. **brandy-snap** crisp usu. rolled-up gingerbread wafer.

**brash** *a.* vulgarly assertive; impudent.

**brass** /brɑːs/ 1 *n.* dark yellow alloy of copper and zinc; brass objects; brass wind-instruments; memorial tablet of brass; brass ornament worn by horse; *colloq.* effrontery; *sl.* money. 2 *a.* made of brass. 3 **brass band** band of musicians with brass instruments; **brass hat** *colloq.* high-ranking officer; **brass-rubbing** reproducing design from sepulchral brass on paper by rub-

**brasserie** /'bræsəri/ *n.* restaurant, orig. one serving beer with food.

**brassica** /'bræsɪkə/ *n.* plant of family including cabbage.

**brassière** /'bræsɪeə(r)/ *n.* undergarment worn by women to support breasts.

**brassy** /'brɑːsɪ/ *a.* impudent; showy; loud and blaring; of or like brass.

**brat** *n. derog.* child.

**bravado** /brə'vɑːdəʊ/ *n.* show of boldness.

**brave 1** *a.* able to face and endure danger or pain; splendid, spectacular. **2** *v.* defy, encounter bravely. **3** *n.* N. Amer. Indian warrior. **4 bravery** *n.*

**bravo**[1] /'brɑːvəʊ/ *int. & n.* (*pl.* **-vos**) cry of approval.

**bravo**[2] /'brɑːvəʊ/ *n.* (*pl.* **-voes**) hired ruffian or killer.

**bravura** /brə'vjʊərə/ *n.* brilliant or ambitious performance; music requiring brilliant technique.

**brawl 1** *n.* noisy quarrel. **2** *v.i.* engage in brawl; (of stream) flow noisily.

**brawn** *n.* muscle, muscular strength; pressed jellied meat made esp. from pig's head.

**brawny** /'brɔːnɪ/ *a.* muscular.

**bray 1** *n.* loud strident cry of donkey; harsh sound. **2** *v.* emit bray; utter harshly.

**braze** *v.t.* solder with alloy of brass.

**brazen** /'breɪz(ə)n/ **1** *a.* shameless; of or like brass. **2** *v.t.* **brazen out** face or undergo shamelessly.

**brazier** /'breɪzɪə(r)/ *n.* portable pan or stand for holding burning coals.

**Brazil nut** /brə'zɪl/ large three-sided nut from S. Amer. tree.

**breach** /briːtʃ/ **1** *n.* breaking or neglect of rule, duty, promise, etc.; breaking off of relations, quarrel; gap. **2** *v.t.* break, make gap in.

**bread** /bred/ *n.* food of baked dough of flour usu. leavened with yeast; *sl.* money. **breadcrumbs** bread crumbled for use in cooking; **breadline** subsistence level; **bread-winner** person whose work supports a family.

**breadth** /bredθ/ *n.* broadness, distance from side to side; freedom from mental limitations or prejudices.

**break** /breɪk/ **1** *v.* (*past* **broke**; *p.p.* **broken**) divide or split or separate otherwise than by cutting; make or become inoperative; fall to pieces, shatter; break bone in (limb etc.); interrupt, pause; fail to observe or keep; make or become weak, destroy; tame, subdue; reveal or be revealed; come, produce, change, etc., with suddenness or violence; (of voice) change in quality at manhood or with emotion; escape, emerge from; (of ball) change direction after touching ground. **2** *n.* breaking; point where thing is broken; gap; pause in work etc.; sudden dash; a chance; points scored in one sequence at billiards etc. **3 break away** make or become free or separate; **break down** fail or collapse, itemize, analyse; **breakdown** collapse, failure of health or mental power or mechanical action, analysis; **break even** emerge with neither gain nor loss; **break in** intrude forcibly esp. as thief, interrupt, accustom to habit, *Aus.* bring (land) into production; **breakneck** (of speed) dangerously fast; **break off** detach by breaking, bring to an end, cease talking etc.; **break open** open forcibly; **break out** escape, exclaim, become covered in (rash etc.); **breakthrough** major advance in knowledge etc.; **break up** break into pieces, disband, part; **breakup** disintegration, collapse; **breakwater** object breaking force of waves; **break wind** emit wind through anus; **breakwind** *Aus.* wind-break.

**breakable** /'breɪkəb(ə)l/ *a.* easily broken.

**breakage** /'breɪkɪdʒ/ *n.* breaking, broken thing.

**breaker** /'breɪkə(r)/ *n.* heavy wave breaking on coast or over reef.

**breakfast** /'brekfəst/ **1** *n.* first meal of day. **2** *v.i.* have breakfast.

**bream** *n.* yellowish freshwater fish; similar sea-fish; /brɪm/ *Aus.* edible seafish.

**breast** /brest/ **1** *n.* either of two milk-secreting organs on upper front of woman's body; upper front of body; seat of emotions. **2** *v.t.* face up to; contend with; reach top of (hill). **3 breastbone** that connecting ribs in front; **breast-feed** feed (baby) from breast, not from bottle; **breastplate** armour covering breast; **breast-stroke** stroke made

**breath** while swimming on breast by extending arms forward and sweeping them back.

**breath** /breθ/ *n.* air as used by lungs; breathing; breath as perceived by senses; one respiration; slight movement of air. **breathtaking** spectacular, very exciting; **breath test** test of breath to determine level of alcohol in blood.

**breathalyser** /'breθəlaɪzə(r)/ *n.* device for measuring alcohol in breath.

**breathe** /briːð/ *v.* take air into lungs and send it out again; perform comparable function; live; take breath, pause; send up or take in (as) with measured air; utter or speak softly. **breathing-space** time to breathe, pause.

**breather** /'briːðə(r)/ *n.* short spell of rest.

**breathless** /'breθləs/ *a.* panting, out of breath; unstirred by wind.

**bred** *past & p.p.* of **breed**.

**breech** /briːtʃ/ *n.* back part of gun or gun-barrel; in *pl.* short trousers fastened below knee. **breech birth** birth in which baby's buttocks emerge first.

**breed** 1 *v.* (*past & p.p.* **bred**) produce offspring; propagate; raise (cattle etc.); yield, result in; train, bring up; arise, spread; *Phys.* create (fissile material) by nuclear reaction. 2 *n.* stock of animals within species; race, lineage; sort, kind. 3 **breeder reactor** nuclear reactor that can create more fissile material than it consumes.

**breeding** *n.* result or qualities of upbringing.

**breeze**[1] 1 *n.* gentle wind. 2 *v.i. colloq.* move in lively or offhand manner.

**breeze**[2] *n.* small cinders used to make **breeze blocks**, lightweight building blocks.

**breezy** /'briːzi/ *a.* pleasantly windy.

**Bren** *n.* lightweight quick-firing machine-gun.

**brethren** /'breðrən/ *n.pl. arch.* brothers, esp. (fellow-)members of religious order etc.

**Breton** /'bret(ə)n/ *n.* native or language of Brittany. 2 *a.* of Brittany.

**breve** /briːv/ *n.* mark (˘) over short or unstressed vowel; *Mus.* note equal to two semibreves.

**breviary** /'briːvjəri/ *n.* book containing RC Divine Office for each day.

**brevity** /'brevɪti/ *n.* conciseness, shortness.

**brew** 1 *v.* make (beer etc.) by infusion, boiling, and fermenting; make (tea etc.) by infusion or mixture; undergo these processes; *fig.* be forming. 2 *n.* amount brewed; liquor brewed.

**brewery** /'bruːəri/ *n.* place where beer is brewed commercially.

**briar**[1,2] var. of **brier**[1,2].

**bribe** 1 *n.* inducement offered to procure esp. dishonest or illegal service to giver. 2 *v.t.* persuade by offering bribe. 3 **bribery** *n.*

**bric-à-brac** /'brɪkəbræk/ *n.* miscellaneous old ornaments, furniture, etc.

**brick** 1 *n.* small rectangular block of baked clay, used in building; toy building-block; brick-shaped block of anything. 2 *a.* made of bricks. 3 *v.t.* block *up* with brickwork. 4 **brickbat** piece of brick esp. as missile; **bricklayer** person who builds with bricks; **brick veneer** *Aus.* brick exterior on timber-frame house; **brickwork** structure or building in brick.

**bridal** /'braɪd(ə)l/ *a.* of bride or wedding.

**bride** *n.* woman on her wedding day or shortly before or after it. **bridegroom** man on wedding day or shortly before or after it; **bridesmaid** unmarried woman or girl attending bride.

**bridge**[1] *n.* structure carrying way over road, railway, river, etc.; upper bony part of nose; prop under strings of violin etc.; raised platform from which ship is directed; false tooth or teeth connected to real teeth on each side. 2 *v.t.* be or make bridge over; join, connect. 3 **bridgehead** position held on far side of river etc. facing enemy; **bridging finance** loan to cover interval between buying one house and selling another.

**bridge**[2] *n.* card-game developed from whist.

**bridle** /'braɪd(ə)l/ 1 *n.* gear to control horse etc.; restraint. 2 *v.* put bridle on, control, curb; express resentment, esp. by throwing up head and drawing in chin. 3 **bridle-path** path suitable for horse-riding.

**brief** /briːf/ 1 *a.* of short duration; concise. 2 *n.* solicitor's summary of case for guidance of barrister; in *pl.* very short knickers or pants. 3 *v.t.* give instruc-

# briefcase     briefcase

tions, necessary information, etc. to; give legal brief to (counsel).
**briefcase** /'bri:fkeɪs/ *n*. flat case for documents etc.
**brier**[1] /braɪə(r)/ *n*. wild-rose bush. **brier-rose** wild rose.
**brier**[2] /braɪə(r)/ *n*. shrub with root used for tobacco-pipes; pipe made from this.
**brig**[1] *n. Sc.* bridge.
**brig**[2] *n*. two-masted square-rigged vessel.
**brigade** /brə'geɪd/ *n*. military sub-unit of division; organized band of workers etc.
**brigadier** /brɪgə'dɪə(r)/ *n*. army officer next below major-general.
**brigalow** /'brɪgələʊ/ *n. Aus.* kind of acacia forming dense scrub.
**brigand** /'brɪgənd/ *n*. member of robber gang. **brigandage** *n*.
**bright** /braɪt/ *a*. emitting or reflecting much light, shining; vivid, conspicuous; intelligent, talented; cheerful, vivacious.
**brighten** /'braɪt(ə)n/ *n*. make or become bright.
**brilliant** /'brɪljənt/ **1** *a*. bright, sparkling; highly talented; distinguished. **2** *n*. diamond of finest quality. **3 brilliance** *n*.
**brilliantine** /'brɪljənti:n/ *n*. cosmetic for making hair glossy.
**brim 1** *n*. edge of cup, hollow, channel, etc.; projecting edge of hat. **2** *v*. fill or be full to brim.
**brimstone** /'brɪmstəʊn/ *n. arch.* sulphur.
**brindled** /'brɪnd(ə)ld/ *a*. brown with streaks of other colour.
**brine 1** *n*. salt water; sea-water. **2** *v.t.* soak in brine.
**bring** *v.t.* (*past* & *p.p.* **brought** /brɔːt/) come with or convey; cause to be present; cause, result in; be sold for; prefer (charge); initiate (legal action). **bring about** cause to happen; **bring down** cause to fall; **bring forward** draw attention to, move to earlier time or date; **bring in** introduce, produce as profit, pronounce (verdict); **bring off** succeed in; **bring round** restore to consciousness, win over; **bring to bear** apply; **bring up** educate, rear, draw attention to, vomit.
**brink** *n*. edge of precipice etc.; furthest point before something dangerous etc. is encountered. **brinkmanship** policy of pursuing dangerous course to brink of catastrophe.
**briny** /'braɪnɪ/ *a*. of brine or sea, salt. **the briny** *sl*. the sea.
**briquette** /brɪ'ket/ *n*. block of compressed coal-dust.
**brisk** *a*. active, lively, quick.
**brisket** /'brɪskɪt/ *n*. animal's breast, esp. that of beef animal as joint of meat.
**bristle** /'brɪs(ə)l/ **1** *n*. short stiff hair; bristle of pig etc. used in brushes etc. **2** *v*. show temper; (of hair etc.) stand up; cause to bristle; be thickly set (*with* obstacles etc.).
**Britannia** /brɪ'tænɪə/ *n*. Britain personified. **Britannia metal** silvery alloy.
**Britannic** /brɪ'tænɪk/ *a*. of Britain.
**British** /'brɪtɪʃ/ **1** *a*. of Britain. **2** *n.pl. the* British people
**Briton** /'brɪt(ə)n/ *n*. one of people in S. Britain before Roman conquest; native of Great Britain.
**brittle** /'brɪt(ə)l/ *a*. apt to break, fragile.
**broach** /brəʊtʃ/ *v.t.* raise (subject) for discussion; pierce or begin drawing liquor from (cask); open and start using.
**broad** /brɔːd/ **1** *a*. large across, extensive; of specified breadth; (of accent) marked, strong; tolerant; comprehensive; coarse; full, clear. **2** *n*. broad part; *US sl.* woman. **3 broad bean** variety of bean with large flat seeds, one of these seeds; **broadcloth** fine twilled or plain-woven cloth; **broadloom** (carpet) woven in broad width; **broadsheet** large sheet of paper printed on one side only.
**broadcast** /'brɔːdkɑːst/ **1** *v*. (*past* & *p.p.* **-cast**) transmit (news, musical performance, etc.) by radio or television; speak or perform thus; disseminate widely; sow (seed) by scattering freely. **2** *n*. transmission by radio or television. **3** *a*. transmitted by broadcasting; scattered widely.
**broaden** /'brɔːd(ə)n/ *v*. make or become broader.
**broadside** /'brɔːdsaɪd/ *n*. firing of all guns on one side of ship; fierce verbal attack; ship's side above water. **broadside on** sideways on.

# brocade · browse

**brocade** /brəˈkeɪd/ n. kind of fabric with raised patterns woven in.

**broccoli** /ˈbrɒkəli/ n. hardy variety of cauliflower with greenish flower-head.

**brochure** /ˈbrəʊʃʊə(r)/ n. booklet, pamphlet, esp. containing information etc.

**broderie anglaise** /ˌbrəʊdəriː ˈɑ̃ɡleɪz/ openwork embroidery on fine cotton etc. fabric.

**brogue** /brəʊɡ/ n. strong shoe for sports and country wear; rough shoe of untanned leather; marked local esp. Irish accent.

**broil** v. cook on fire or gridiron; make or be very hot.

**broiler** /ˈbrɔɪlə(r)/ n. young chicken raised for broiling.

**broke** 1 past of **break**. 2 a. colloq. having no money, bankrupt.

**broken** /ˈbrəʊkən/ 1 p.p. of **break**. 2 a. that has been broken; (of language) spoken imperfectly; interrupted. 3 **broken-hearted** crushed by grief; **broken home** one where parents are separated or divorced.

**broker** /ˈbrəʊkə(r)/ n. middleman, agent; pawnbroker; stockbroker; appraiser and seller of distrained goods. **broking** n.

**brokerage** /ˈbrəʊkərɪdʒ/ n. broker's fee or commission.

**brolga** /ˈbrɒlɡə/ n. Aus. large grey crane with red and green head.

**brolly** /ˈbrɒli/ n. colloq. umbrella.

**bromide** /ˈbrəʊmaɪd/ n. compound of bromine esp. used as sedative; trite remark.

**bromine** /ˈbrəʊmiːn/ n. poisonous liquid non-metallic element with rank smell.

**bronchial** /ˈbrɒŋkɪəl/ a. of two main divisions of windpipe or smaller tubes into which they divide.

**bronchitis** /brɒŋˈkaɪtɪs/ n. inflammation of bronchial mucous membrane.

**bronco** /ˈbrɒŋkəʊ/ n. (pl. -coes) wild or half-tamed horse of western US

**brontosaurus** /ˌbrɒntəˈsɔːrəs/ n. large plant-eating dinosaur.

**bronze** /brɒnz/ 1 n. brown alloy of copper and tin; its colour; work of art or medal in it. 2 a. made of or coloured like bronze. 3 v. give bronzelike surface to; make or grow brown; tan. 4 **Bronze Age** stage of culture when tools were of bronze; **bronze medal** medal given usu. as third prize; **bronze-wing** Aus. pigeon with bronze patches on wings.

**brooch** /brəʊtʃ/ n. ornamental hinged pin.

**brood** /bruːd/ 1 n. bird's or other animal's young produced at one hatch or birth; joc. children of a family. 2 v. worry or ponder resentfully; (of hen) sit on eggs.

**broody** /ˈbruːdi/ a. (of hen) wanting to incubate eggs; fig. depressed.

**brook**[1] /brʊk/ n. UK small stream.

**brook**[2] /brʊk/ v.t. tolerate; allow.

**broom** /bruːm/ n. long-handled sweeping-brush; yellow-flowered shrub.

**broomstick** /ˈbruːmstɪk/ n. broom-handle.

**Bros.** abbr. Brothers.

**broth** /brɒθ/ n. thin meat or fish soup.

**brothel** /ˈbrɒθ(ə)l/ n. house of prostitution.

**brother** /ˈbrʌðə(r)/ n. son of same parents; close man friend, equal; member of religious order, esp. monk; (pl. **brethren**) man who is fellow member of religious society etc. **brother-in-law** wife's or husband's brother, sister's husband. **brotherly** a.

**brotherhood** /ˈbrʌðəhʊd/ n. relationship (as) between brothers; (members of) association for mutual help etc.

**brought** past & p.p. of **bring**.

**brow** /braʊ/ n. eyebrow (usu. in pl.); forehead; summit of pass or hill; edge of cliff etc.

**browbeat** /ˈbraʊbiːt/ v.t. bully with looks and words.

**brown** /braʊn/ 1 a. of colour produced by mixing red, yellow, and black pigments; dark-skinned; tanned. 2 n. brown colour, paint, clothes, etc. 3 v. make or become brown. 4 **brown bomber** Aus. sl. traffic warden; **brown bread** bread made of wholemeal flour or resembling such bread; **browned off** sl. bored, fed up; **brown snake** poisonous Aus. snake; **brown sugar** partially refined kind; **brown top** Aus. kind of pasture grass.

**Brownie** /ˈbraʊni/ n. junior Guide; **brownie** benevolent sprite in folklore, haunting house; Aus. sweet currant bread.

**browse** /braʊz/ 1 v. read or look around desultorily; feed on leaves and young shoots. 2 n. browsing.

**bruise** /bruːz/ 1 *n*. injury caused by blow or pressure and discolouring but not breaking skin. 2 *v*. inflict bruise on; be susceptible to bruises.

**bruiser** /'bruːzə(r)/ *n*. tough brutal person.

**bruit** /bruːt/ *v.t. arch*. spread *about, abroad*.

**brumby** /'brʌmbɪ/ *n. Aus*. wild or unbroken horse.

**brunette** /bruː'net/ *n*. woman with dark hair.

**brunt** *n*. chief impact *of* attack etc.

**brush** 1 *n*. cleaning or hairdressing or painting implement of bristles etc. set in holder; application of brush; *Aus*. thicket or forest; skirmish; fox's tail; brushlike carbon or metal piece serving as electrical contact. 2 *v*. use brush on; touch lightly, graze in passing. 3 **brush-off** dismissal, rebuff; **brush turkey** large mound-building Aus. bird; **brush up** clean up or smarten, renew acquaintance with (subject); **brush wallaby** large long-tailed kind; **brushwood** cut or broken twigs etc., undergrowth; thicket; **brushwork** painter's way of using brush.

**brusque** /brʊsk/ *a*. blunt, off-hand.

**Brussels sprouts** /'brʌs(ə)lz/ edible buds of kind of cabbage.

**brutal** /'bruːt(ə)l/ *a*. savagely cruel; coarse; mercilessly frank. **brutality** /-'tæl-/ *n*.; **brutalize** *v.t*.

**brute** 1 *n*. animal other than man; cruel person; *colloq*. unpleasant person. 2 *a*. unable to reason; stupid; unthinking. 3 **brutish** *a*.

**bryony** /'braɪənɪ/ *n*. climbing hedge plant.

**B.Sc.** *abbr*. Bachelor of Science.

**Bt.** *abbr*. Baronet.

**bubble** /'bʌb(ə)l/ 1 *n*. globular film of liquid enclosing air or gas; air-filled cavity in glass etc.; transparent dome cavity; visionary project. 2 *v.i*. send up or rise in bubbles, boil; make sound of bubbles. 3 **bubble-and-squeak** cooked potatoes and cabbage fried together; **bubble bath** additive to make bathwater bubbly; **bubble car** small car with transparent dome; **bubble gum** chewing-gum that can be blown into large bubbles.

**bubbly** /'bʌblɪ/ 1 *a*. full of bubbles. 2 *n. sl*. champagne.

**bubonic** /bjuː'bɒnɪk/ *a*. (of plague) marked by swellings esp. in groin and armpits.

**buccaneer** /bʌkə'nɪə(r)/ *n*. pirate, adventurer. **buccaneering** *a*. & *n*.

**buck**[1] 1 *n*. male deer, hare, or rabbit; *attrib. sl*. male. 2 *v*. (of horse) jump vertically with back arched, throw (rider) thus. 3 **buckshot** coarse shot; **bucktooth** projecting tooth; **buck up** hurry up, cheer up.

**buck**[2] *n*. small object placed before dealer at poker. **pass the buck** shift responsibility (*to*).

**buck**[3] *n*. US & Aus. *sl*. dollar.

**bucket** /'bʌkɪt/ 1 *n*. round open container with handle, for carrying or holding water etc.; amount contained in this; compartment in water-wheel or dredger or grain-elevator. 2 *v.i*. move jerkily or bumpily. 3 **bucket seat** one with rounded back, to fit one person; **bucket-shop** agency dealing in cheap airline tickets, unregistered broking agency; **kick the bucket** die.

**buckle** /'bʌk(ə)l/ 1 *n*. metal rim with usu. hinged pin for securing strap or belt etc. 2 *v*. fasten with buckle; (cause to) crumple under pressure. 3 **buckle down** make determined start.

**buckler** /'bʌklə(r)/ *n*. small round shield.

**Buckley's** /'bʌkliːz/ *n. Aus. colloq*. little or no chance.

**buckram** /'bʌkrəm/ *n*. coarse linen or cloth stiffened with paste etc.

**buckshee** /bʌk'ʃiː/ *a*. & *adv. sl*. free, gratis.

**buckwheat** /'bʌkwiːt/ *n*. a cereal plant.

**bucolic** /bjuː'kɒlɪk/ *a*. of shepherds, rustic, pastoral.

**bud** 1 *n*. projection from which branch or leaf-cluster or flower develops; flower or leaf not fully open; asexual growth separating from organism as new animal. 2 *v*. put forth buds, sprout as bud; begin to grow or develop; graft bud of (plant) on another plant.

**Buddhism** /'bʊdɪz(ə)m/ *n*. Asian religion founded by Gautama Buddha. **Buddhist** *a*. & *n*.

**buddleia** /'bʌdlɪə/ *n*. shrub with usu. purple or yellow flowers.

**buddy** /'bʌdɪ/ *n. colloq*. friend; mate.

**budge** *v*. move in slightest degree.

**budgerigar** /ˈbʌdʒəriːgɑː(r)/ n. kind of Aus. parakeet often kept as caged bird.

**budget** /ˈbʌdʒət/ 1 n. annual estimate of country's revenue and expenditure; similar estimate for person or group; amount of money required or available. 2 v. allow or arrange *for* in budget. 3 **budgetary** a.

**buff** 1 n. velvety dull-yellow leather; colour of this; *sl.* the skin; *colloq.* enthusiast. 2 a. buff-coloured. 3 v.t. polish; make velvety like buff.

**buffalo** /ˈbʌfələʊ/ n. (pl. **-loes**) any of various kinds of ox; Amer. bison.

**buffer**[1] /ˈbʌfə(r)/ n. apparatus for deadening impact esp. of railway vehicles. **buffer state** minor one between two great ones, regarded as reducing danger of quarrels.

**buffer**[2] /ˈbʌfə(r)/ n. *sl.* old or incompetent fellow.

**buffet**[1] /ˈbʊfeɪ/ n. place where light meals may be bought and eaten; provision of food where guests serve themselves; sideboard. **buffet car** railway coach in which refreshments are served.

**buffet**[2] /ˈbʌfət/ 1 n. blow with hand; shock. 2 v.t. deal blows to, knock about.

**buffoon** /bəˈfuːn/ n. silly or ludicrous person; jester. **buffoonery** n.

**bug** 1 n. flat evil-smelling blood-sucking insect infesting beds etc.; *US* any small insect; *colloq.* virus, infection; concealed microphone; defect in machine or computer program etc. 2 v.t. conceal microphone in; *sl.* annoy.

**bugbear** /ˈbʌɡbeə(r)/ n. cause of annoyance; object of baseless fear.

**bugger** /ˈbʌɡə(r)/ 1 n. sodomite; *vulg.* unpleasant person or thing. 2 v. commit sodomy with; *vulg.* damn, mess *about* or *up*, clear *off.* 3 **buggery** n.

**buggy** /ˈbʌɡi/ n. light horse-drawn vehicle for one or two persons; small sturdy motor vehicle.

**bugle**[1] /ˈbjuːɡ(ə)l/ 1 n. brass instrument like small trumpet. 2 v.i. sound bugle. 3 **bugler** n.

**bugle**[2] /ˈbjuːɡ(ə)l/ n. creeping plant with usu. blue flowers.

**bugong** /ˈbjuːɡɒŋ/ var. of **bogong**.

**build** /bɪld/ 1 v. (*past* & *p.p.* **built**) construct by putting parts or material together; develop or establish. 2 n. style of construction; proportions of human body. 3 **build up** gradually establish or be established; **build-up** favourable description in advance, gradual approach to climax.

**builder** /ˈbɪldə(r)/ n. contractor who builds houses etc.

**building** /ˈbɪldɪŋ/ n. house or other structure with roof and walls. **building society** society of investors that lends money on mortgage to those buying houses.

**built** *past* & *p.p.* of **build**. **built-in** forming integral part of structure etc.; **built-up** increased in height or thickness etc., covered with buildings.

**bulb** n. globular base of stem of some plants; electric lamp filament, its glass container; object or part shaped like bulb.

**bulbous** /ˈbʌlbəs/ a. bulb-shaped, having bulb or bulbs; swollen.

**bulge** /bʌldʒ/ 1 n. irregular swelling-out of surface or line; *colloq.* temporary increase in numbers or volume. 2 v.i. form or show bulge. 3 **bulgy** a.

**bulk** 1 n. size, magnitude, esp. when great; *the* greater part *of*; large quantity. 2 v. increase size or thickness of; seem in terms of size or importance. 3 **bulk buying** buying in large amounts; **bulkhead** upright partition between compartments in ship, aircraft, vehicle, etc.

**bulky** /ˈbʌlkɪ/ a. large, unwieldy.

**bull**[1] /bʊl/ n. uncastrated male ox; male whale or elephant etc.; bull's-eye of target; *Stock Exch.* person who buys hoping to sell at higher price later. **bull ant** Aus. bulldog ant; **bull artist** Aus. *sl.* boastful know-all; **bull-bar** Aus. grid fixed to front of vehicle to prevent damage in case of collision with animals; **bulldog** dog of sturdy powerful large-headed breed, tenacious and courageous person; **bulldog ant** large Aus. ant with vicious sting; **bulldog clip** strong sprung clip for papers etc. **bulldoze** clear with bulldozer, *colloq.* make one's way forcibly, intimidate; **bulldozer** powerful tractor with broad vertical blade for clearing ground; **bulldust** Aus. fine dust on outback roads, *sl.* nonsense; **bullfight** Spanish etc. sport of baiting bulls as public spectacle; **bullfinch** small song-bird with strong beak and fine plumage; **bull-**

**bull**     **bunting**

**frog** large Aus. or Amer. frog with loud bellow; **bullring** arena for bullfight; **bull's-eye** centre of target; **bull-terrier** cross between bulldog and terrier.

**bull²** /bʊl/ *n.* Papal edict.

**bull³** /bʊl/ *n.* absurdly illogical statement; *sl.* unnecessary routine tasks.

**Bullamakanka** /bʊləmə'kæŋkə/ *n.* Aus. imaginary remote town.

**bullet** /'bʊlɪt/ *n.* missile, usu. round or cylindrical with pointed end, fired from rifle or revolver, etc.

**bulletin** /'bʊlɪtɪn/ *n.* short official statement or broadcast report of news etc.

**bullion** /'bʊljən/ *n.* gold or silver in lump or valued by weight.

**bullock** /'bʊlək/ *n.* castrated bull.

**bullocky** /'bʊləki/ *n.* Aus. bullock-driver. **bullocky's joy** *sl.* treacle.

**bully¹** /'bʊli/ 1 *n.* person using strength or power to coerce others by fear. 2 *v.* persecute or oppress by force or threats. 3 *int. sl.* very good.

**bully²** /'bʊli/ 1 *n.* putting ball into play in hockey. 2 *v.* **bully off** start play thus.

**bully³** /'bʊli/ *n.* (in full **bully beef**) corned beef.

**buln-buln** /'bʊlnbʊln/ *n.* Aus. lyrebird.

**bulrush** /'bʊlrʌʃ/ *n.* tall rush, esp. reed-mace; *Bibl.* papyrus.

**bulwark** /'bʊlwək/ *n.* earthwork or other material defence; person or principle that protects; usu. in *pl.* ship's side above deck.

**bum¹** *n. sl.* buttocks.

**bum²** *colloq.* 1 *v.* loaf, wander *around*; cadge. 2 *n.* loafer, dissolute person. 3 *a.* worthless, of poor quality.

**bumble** /'bʌmb(ə)l/ *v.i.* blunder; act ineptly; make buzz. **bumble-bee** large loud-humming bee.

**bump** 1 *n.* dull-sounding blow or collision; swelling caused by it; rounded swelling or lump on a surface; uneven patch on road etc.; prominence on skull, thought to indicate mental faculty. 2 *v.* come or strike with a bump against; hurt thus; move *along* etc. with bumps. 3 **bump into** *colloq.* meet by chance; **bump off** *sl.* murder. 4 **bumpily** *adv.* **bumpy** *a.*

**bumper** /'bʌmpə(r)/ 1 *n.* unusually large or fine example; metal etc. bar on motor vehicle to reduce damage in collisions; brim-full glass. 2 *a.* unusually large or abundant.

**bumpkin** /'bʌmpkɪn/ *n.* rustic or awkward person.

**bumptious** /'bʌmpʃəs/ *a.* self-assertive, conceited.

**bun** *n.* small soft sweet cake often with dried fruit; small coil of hair at back of head.

**bunch** 1 *n.* cluster of things growing or fastened together; lot; *sl.* gang, group. 2 *v.i.* arrange in bunch(es); gather in folds; come or cling or crowd together. 3 **bunchy** *a.*

**bundle** /'bʌnd(ə)l/ 1 *n.* collection of things tied or fastened together; *sl.* large amount of money. 2 *v.* tie in bundle; throw confusedly *in(to)* receptacle; go or send unceremoniously *away* or *out* etc. 3 **drop one's bundle** Aus. give up hope, admit failure.

**bung¹** 1 *n.* stopper, esp. large cork stopping hole in cask. 2 *v.t.* stop with bung; stop *up*; *sl.* throw.

**bung²** *a.* Aus. *sl.* dead; bankrupt; useless. **go bung** die, fail, go bankrupt.

**bungalow** /'bʌŋgələʊ/ *n.* one-storeyed house.

**bunger** /'bʌŋə(r)/ *n.* Aus. *sl.* cracker, firework.

**bungle** /'bʌŋg(ə)l/ *v.* mismanage, fail to accomplish; work awkwardly. 2 *n.* bungled work or attempt.

**bunion** /'bʌnjən/ *n.* swelling on side of big toe.

**bunk¹** *n.* shelflike bed against wall. **bunk-bed** two or more bunks one above the other.

**bunk²** *sl.* **do a bunk** run away.

**bunk³** *n. sl.* nonsense, humbug.

**bunker** /'bʌŋkə(r)/ 1 *n.* container for fuel; reinforced underground shelter; sand-pit or hollow as hazard on golf-course. 2 *v.* fill fuel bunkers of (ship etc.).

**bunkum** /'bʌŋkəm/ *n.* nonsense, humbug.

**bunny** /'bʌni/ *n.* childish name for rabbit.

**Bunsen burner** /'bʌns(ə)n/ gas-burner burning mixed air and gas, giving great heat.

**bunting** /'bʌntɪŋ/ *n.* flags and other decorations; loosely-woven fabric used for these.

**bunyip** /ˈbʌnjɪp/ *n. Aus.* fabulous monster of swamps and lagoons.

**buoy** /bɔɪ/ 1 *n.* anchored float as navigational mark etc.; lifebuoy. 2 *v.t.* mark with buoy(s). 3 **buoy up** keep afloat, sustain.

**buoyant** /ˈbɔɪənt/ *a.* apt to float, light; cheerful. **buoyancy** *n.*

**bur** *n.* clinging seed-vessel or other part of plant, plant producing burs; person hard to shake off.

**burble** /ˈbɜːb(ə)l/ *v.i.* make murmuring noise; speak lengthily.

**burden** /ˈbɜːd(ə)n/ 1 *n.* thing carried, load; weight of duty or sorrow etc.; obligatory expense; ship's carrying-capacity; refrain of song; theme. 2 *v.t.* load, encumber, oppress. 3 **beast of burden** animal used for carrying or pulling loads; **burden of proof** obligation to prove one's case. 4 **burdensome** *a.*

**burdock** /ˈbɜːdɒk/ *n.* plant with prickly flowers and docklike leaves.

**bureau** /ˈbjʊərəʊ/ *n.* (*pl.* -**reaux** *or* -**reaus** /-rəʊz/) writing-desk with drawers; *US* chest of drawers; office or department for transacting specific business; government department.

**bureaucracy** /bjʊəˈrɒkrəsɪ/ *n.* government by central administration; officialism; set of dominant officials.

**bureaucrat** /ˈbjʊərəkræt/ *n.* official in bureaucracy. **bureaucratic** *a.*

**burgeon** /ˈbɜːdʒən/ *v.i.* begin to grow rapidly, flourish.

**burger** /ˈbɜːgə(r)/ *n. colloq.* hamburger; food resembling hamburger.

**burgh** /ˈbʌrə/ *n.* Scottish borough.

**burgher** /ˈbɜːgə(r)/ *n.* citizen esp. of foreign town.

**burglar** /ˈbɜːglə(r)/ *n.* person who commits burglary. **burglarious** /-ˈgleər-/ *a.*

**burglary** /ˈbɜːglərɪ/ *n.* illegal entry into building to commit theft.

**burgle** /ˈbɜːg(ə)l/ *v.* commit burglary (on).

**burgomaster** /ˈbɜːgəmɑːstə(r)/ *n.* Dutch or Flemish mayor.

**burgundy** /ˈbɜːgəndɪ/ *n.* red or white wine produced in Burgundy; similar wine from elsewhere.

**burial** /ˈberɪəl/ *n.* burying, esp. of dead body; funeral.

**burlesque** /bɜːˈlesk/ 1 *n.* dramatic or literary parody; *US* broadly humorous variety show. 2 *a.* of derisively imitative kind. 3 *v.t.* make or give burlesque of, travesty.

**burley** var. of **berley**.

**burly** /ˈbɜːlɪ/ *a.* of stout sturdy build.

**burn**[1] 1 *v.* (*past & p.p.* **burnt** *or* **burned**) (cause to) be consumed by fire; blaze or glow with fire; (cause to) be injured or damaged by fire, sun, or great heat; brand; give or feel sensation or pain (as) of heat. 2 *n.* sore or mark made by burning. 3 **burnt offering** sacrifice offered by burning.

**burn**[2] *n. Sc.* brook, stream.

**burner** /ˈbɜːnə(r)/ *n.* part of lamp or cooker etc. that emits and shapes flame.

**burnish** /ˈbɜːnɪʃ/ *v.t.* polish by rubbing.

**burnous** /bɜːˈnuːs/ *n.* Arab or Moorish hooded cloak.

**burnt** *past & p.p.* of **burn**.

**burp** *n. & v.i. colloq.* belch.

**burr**[1] *n.* rough sounding of *r*; rough edge left by cutting metal etc.

**burr**[2] var. of **bur**.

**burrow** /ˈbʌrəʊ/ 1 *n.* hole excavated by animal as dwelling. 2 *v.* make or live in burrow; excavate; investigate or search *into*.

**bursar** /ˈbɜːsə(r)/ *n.* treasurer of college etc.; holder of bursary. **bursarial** (/-ˈseər-/) *a.*

**bursary** /ˈbɜːsərɪ/ *n.* scholarship or grant awarded to student; bursar's office.

**burst** 1 *v.* (*past & p.p.* **burst**) fly violently apart or give way suddenly, explode; rush, move, speak, be spoken, etc. suddenly or violently. 2 *n.* bursting, explosion, outbreak; spurt.

**bury** /ˈberɪ/ *v.t.* place (dead body) in the earth or tomb or sea, celebrate burial rites over; put underground, hide in earth; consign to obscurity; involve (oneself) deeply.

**bus** /bʌs/ 1 *n.* (*pl.* **buses**, *US* **busses**) large public passenger-carrying vehicle usu. plying on fixed route. 2 *v.* (*past & p.p.* **bused**, *US* **bussed**) go by bus; *US* transport by bus (esp. to counteract racial segregation). 3 **busman** bus-driver; **busman's holiday** leisure spent in same occupation as working hours; **bus-shelter** roadside shelter for persons awaiting bus; **bus-stop** regular stopping-place of bus.

**busby** /'bʌzbi:/ *n.* tall fur cap worn by hussars etc.

**bush**[1] /buʃ/ *n.* shrub, clump of shrubs; clump of hair or fur; *Aus.* etc. woodland, untilled land; **bush-baby** small Afr. tree-climbing lemur; **bush-baptist** *Aus. sl.* member of no established religion; **bush carpenter** *Aus.* untrained one; **bushfire** forest or scrub fire; **Bushman** aboriginal or language of a S.Afr. people; **bushman** dweller or traveller in Aus. bush; **bush telegraph** rapid spreading of information, rumour, etc; **go bush** *Aus.* leave the city or one's usual surroundings.

**bush**[2] /buʃ/ *n.* metal lining of axle-hole etc.; electrically insulating sleeve.

**bushed** /buʃt/ *a. Aus.* lost, bewildered; *US colloq.* tired out.

**bushel** /'buʃ(ə)l/ *n.* measure of capacity for corn, fruit, etc. (8 gals., c. 36.4l.)

**bushy** /'buʃi:/ 1 *n. Aus.* bush-dweller. 2 *a.* growing thickly or like bush; having many bushes.

**business** /'bɪznəs/ *n.* one's occupation or affairs; one's province or duty; serious work; thing(s) needing dealing with; buying and selling, trade; commercial firm; action on theatre stage. **business-like** practical, systematic; **business man** (or **woman**) man (or woman) engaged in trade or commerce.

**busker** /'bʌskə(r)/ *n.* street musician; itinerant entertainer.

**bust**[1] *colloq.* 1 *v.* (past & p.p. **bust** or **busted**) burst, break; arrest. 2 *a.* burst, broken; bankrupt. 3 *n.* sudden failure, drinking-bout; arrest. 4 **bust-up** quarrel; explosion; collapse.

**bust**[2] *n.* sculptured representation of head, shoulders, and chest; upper front or circumference of (woman's) body.

**bustard** /'bʌstəd/ *n.* large swift-running bird.

**buster** /'bʌstə(r)/ *n. Aus.* strong gale; fall, mishap.

**bustle**[1] /'bʌs(ə)l/ 1 *v.* make show of activity, hurry *about*; make (person) hurry. 2 *n.* excited activity.

**bustle**[2] /'bʌs(ə)l/ *n. hist.* pad or framework used to puff out back of woman's skirt.

**busy** /'bɪzi:/ 1 *a.* working with concentrated attention, fully employed; full of activity; fussy, meddlesome. 2 *v.t.* occupy, keep busy. 3 **busybody** meddlesome person.

**but** 1 *conj.* however; on the other hand; otherwise than. 2 *prep.* except, apart from. 3 *adv.* only; *Aus.* however. 4 *pron.* who not.

**butane** /'bju:teɪn/ *n.* hydrocarbon of paraffin series used in liquefied form as fuel.

**butch** /butʃ/ *a. sl.* masculine, tough-looking.

**butcher** /'butʃə(r)/ 1 *n.* person who sells meat; slaughterer of animals for food; person who causes people to be killed needlessly or brutally. 2 *v.* slaughter or cut up (animal); kill or destroy wantonly or cruelly; make a mess of. 3 **butchery** *n.*

**butler** /'bʌtlə(r)/ *n.* chief manservant of household in charge of wine-cellar and plate.

**butt**[1] 1 *v.* push with head; meet end to end; 2 *n.* (violent) push or blow with head or horns. 3 **butt in** intervene, meddle.

**butt**[2] *n.* object of ridicule etc., person habitually ridiculed or teased; mound behind target; in *pl.* shooting-range.

**butt**[3] *n.* thicker end esp. of tool or weapon; remnant of smoked cigarette etc.

**butt**[4] *n.* large cask.

**butter** /'bʌtə(r)/ 1 *n.* yellow fatty food-substance made from cream; substance of similar texture. 2 *v.t.* spread, cook, etc., with butter. 3 **butter bean** dried large flat white kind; **butter-bush** silver-barked Aus. tree; **buttercup** a yellow-flowered plant; **butter-fingers** person likely to drop things; **butter-fish** any of several Aus. fish with slippery coating of mucus; **buttermilk** liquid left after butter-making; **butter muslin** thin loosely-woven cloth; **butterscotch** sweet made of butter and sugar; **butter up** flatter.

**butterfly** /'bʌtəflaɪ/ *n.* insect with large often showy wings, active by day; in *pl.* nervous sensation in stomach. **butterfly nut** *Mech.* nut with projections turned with finger and thumb; **butterfly stroke** method of swimming with both arms lifted at same time.

**buttery**[1] /'bʌtəri:/ *a.* like or containing butter.

**buttery**[2] /'bʌtəri/ *n.* place in college etc. where provisions are kept.

**buttock** /ˈbʌtək/ n. either protuberance on lower rear part of human body; corresponding part of animal.

**button** /ˈbʌt(ə)n/ 1 n. disc or knob sewn to garment etc. as fastening or for ornament; small rounded object; knob etc. pressed to operate electrical device. 2 v. fasten with buttons. 3 **button mushroom** small unopened mushroom.

**buttonhole** /ˈbʌtənhəʊl/ 1 n. slit to receive fastening button, flower(s) worn in coat-lapel buttonhole. 2 v. seize or detain (reluctant listener).

**buttress** /ˈbʌtrəs/ 1 n. support built against wall etc. 2 v.t. support or strengthen.

**buxom** /ˈbʌksəm/ a. plump, large and shapely.

**buy** /baɪ/ 1 v.t. (past & p.p. **bought** /bɔːt/) obtain in exchange for money or other consideration; gain (over) by bribery; sl. accept, believe. 2 n. purchase. 3 **buy into** Aus. sl. become involved in.

**buyer** /ˈbaɪə(r)/ n. person who buys, esp. stock for large shop etc. **buyer's market** time when goods are plentiful and prices low.

**buzz** 1 v. make humming sound of bee; be filled with activity etc.; interfere with (aircraft) by flying close. 2 n. humming sound; confused low sound; sound of buzzer.

**buzzard** /ˈbʌzəd/ n. kind of predatory hawk.

**buzzer** /ˈbʌzə(r)/ n. electric machine producing buzzing sound as signal.

**by** /baɪ/ 1 adv. near at hand; aside, in reserve; past. 2 prep. near, beside, along, via, past; through action, agency, means, or instrumentality of; as soon as, not later than; in accordance with; to extent of. 3 **by and by** before long, the future; **by-election** election of MP in single constituency; **bypath** secluded path; **by-play** subsidiary action in play; **by-product** substance etc. produced incidentally in making of something else; **by-road** minor road; **by the by, by the way,** incidentally; **byway** by-road or bypath; **byword** person or thing cited as notable example, proverb.

**bye** /baɪ/ n. Crick. run made from ball that passes batsman without being hit; (in tournament) position of competitor left without opponent in round.

**bye-bye** int. colloq. goodbye.

**bygone** /ˈbaɪɡɒn/ 1 a. past, departed. 2 n. in pl. past offences.

**by-law** /ˈbaɪlɔː/ n. regulation made by local authority etc.

**byline** /ˈbaɪlaɪn/ n. line in newspaper etc. naming writer of article etc.

**BYO(G)** abbr. Aus. & NZ bring your own (grog).

**bypass** /ˈbaɪpɑːs/ 1 n. road round town or its centre as alternative route for through traffic. 2 v. (past & p.p. **-passed**) avoid; provide with bypass.

**byre** /ˈbaɪə(r)/ n. UK cow-shed.

**bystander** /ˈbaɪstændə(r)/ n. person who stands by but does not take part.

**Byzantine** /baɪˈzæntaɪn/ a. of Byzantium or E. Roman Empire; of architectural etc. style developed in Eastern Empire; complicated, underhand.

# C

**C, c,** Roman numeral 100.

**C** *abbr.* centigrade; Celsius.

**c.** *abbr.* cent; century; chapter.

**c.** *abbr. circa.*

**cab** *n.* taxi, *hist.* hackney carriage; compartment for driver of train, lorry, crane, etc.

**cabal** /kə'bæl/ *n.* secret intrigue; political clique.

**cabaret** /'kæbəreɪ/ *n.* entertainment in restaurant etc. while guests are at table; such restaurant etc.

**cabbage** /'kæbɪdʒ/ *n.* green vegetable with leaves forming round heart or head; *colloq.* person without ambition or interests. **cabbage-tree** Aus. palm with fan-shaped leaves; **cabbage-tree hat** hat made from its leaves; **cabbage white** white butterfly.

**cabby** /'kæbɪ/ *n. colloq.* taxi-driver.

**caber** /'keɪbə(r)/ *n.* tree-trunk used in Sc. sport of **tossing the caber**.

**cabin** /'kæbɪn/ *n.* small dwelling or shelter esp. of wood; room or compartment in ship, aircraft, etc. **cabin-boy** ship's waiter; **cabin cruiser** large motor-boat with cabin.

**cabinet** /'kæbənət/ *n.* case or cupboard with drawers, shelves, or compartments; wooden etc. container for radio, television, etc.; **Cabinet** group of ministers controlling Government policy. **cabinet-maker** skilled joiner.

**cable** /'keɪb(ə)l/ **1** *n.* encased group of insulated wires for transmitting electricity or telegraph messages; anchor chain of ship; thick rope of wire or hemp; cablegram. **2** *v.* send (message), communicate, by undersea cable. **3 cable-car** car mounted on endless cable and drawn up and down mountainside etc.; **cablegram** message sent by undersea cable; **cable-stitch** knitting stitch resembling twisted rope; **cable television** transmission of television programmes by cable to subscribers.

**caboodle** /kə'bu:d(ə)l/ *n. sl.* **the whole caboodle** the whole lot.

**caboose** /kə'bu:s/ *n.* kitchen on ship's deck; *US* guard's van on goods train.

**cacao** /kə'ka:əʊ/ *n.* seed from which cocoa and chocolate are made; tree producing it.

**cachalot** /'kæʃəlɒt/ *n.* sperm whale.

**cache** /kæʃ/ **1** *n.* place for hiding or storing treasure or supplies; things so hidden. **2** *v.t.* place in cache.

**cachet** /'kæʃeɪ/ *n.* distinctive stamp; mark of authenticity; prestige; flat capsule for medicine.

**cack-handed** *a. colloq.* clumsy, awkward; left-handed.

**cackle** /'kæk(ə)l/ **1** *n.* clucking of hen; noisy inconsequential talk; loud silly laughter. **2** *v.* emit cackle; utter or express with cackle.

**cacophony** /kə'kɒfənɪ/ *n.* harsh discordant sound. **cacophonous** *a.*

**cactus** /'kæktəs/ *n.* (*pl.* **-ti** /-taɪ/ or **-tuses**) plant with thick fleshy stem, usu. with spines but no leaves.

**cad** *n.* person (esp. man) who behaves dishonourably. **caddish** *a.*

**cadaver** /kə'deɪvə(r)/ *n.* corpse. **cadaverous** /-'dæv-/ *a.*

**caddie** /'kædɪ/ **1** *n.* golfer's attendant carrying clubs etc. **2** *v.i.* act as caddie.

**caddis** /'kædɪs/ *n.* **caddis-fly** four-winged insect living near water; **caddis-worm** larva of caddis-fly.

**caddy**[1] /'kædɪ/ *n.* small box for holding tea.

**caddy**[2] var. of **caddie**.

**cadence** /'keɪd(ə)ns/ *n.* fall of the voice, esp. at end of phrase; tonal inflexion; movement of sound; close of musical phrase.

**cadenza** /kə'denzə/ *n. Mus.* elaborate improvisation by soloist near end of concerto movement.

**cadet** /kə'det/ *n.* young trainee in armed services or police force.

**cadge** *v.* get or seek by begging; be beggar.

**cadi** /'ka:dɪ/ *n.* judge in Muslim country.

**cadmium** /'kædmɪəm/ *n.* soft bluish-white metallic element.

**cadre** /'ka:də(r)/ *n.* basic unit, esp. of servicemen; politically active group in Communist countries.

**caecum** /'si:kəm/ *n.* (*pl.* **-ca**) *Biol.* tube with closed end forming first part of large intestine.

**Caesarean** /sɪˈzeərɪən/ a. (of birth) effected by cutting into womb through wall of abdomen.

**caesura** /sɪˈzjʊərə/ n. pause in verse line.

**café** /ˈkæfeɪ/ n. coffee-house or restaurant.

**cafeteria** /kæfəˈtɪərɪːə/ n. self-service restaurant.

**caffeine** /ˈkæfiːn/ n. alkaloid stimulant found in coffee and tea plants.

**caftan** /ˈkæftæn/ n. long usu. belted tunic worn by men in Near East; woman's long loose dress.

**cage** 1 n. structure of wire or bars, esp. for confining animals; open framework, mineshaft lift-frame, etc. 2 v.t. confine in cage.

**cagey** /ˈkeɪdʒɪ/ a. sl. cautious and uncommunicative; wary.

**cahoots** /kəˈhuːts/ n. sl. **in cahoots** in league or partnership.

**caiman** var. of **cayman**.

**cairn** /keən/ n. pyramid of rough stones. **cairn terrier** small short-legged shaggy-haired terrier.

**cairngorm** /ˈkeəŋɡɔːm/ n. yellow or wine-coloured gem-stone.

**caisson** /ˈkeɪsɒn/ n. watertight chamber in which underwater construction work can be done.

**cajole** /kəˈdʒəʊl/ v.t. persuade or soothe by flattery or deceit. **cajolery** n.

**cake** 1 n. mixture of flour, butter, eggs, sugar, etc., baked in oven; flattish compact mass. 2 v. form into cohesive mass, harden.

**calabash** /ˈkæləbæʃ/ n. gourd or hard-shelled fruit of tropical Amer. tree; bowl or pipe made from gourd.

**calamine** /ˈkæləmaɪn/ n. pink powder, chiefly zinc carbonate or oxide, used esp. in skin lotion.

**calamity** /kəˈlæmətɪ/ n. grave disaster. **calamitous** a.

**calcareous** /kælˈkeərɪəs/ a. of or containing limestone.

**calceolaria** /kælsɪəˈleərɪːə/ n. plant with slipper-shaped flower.

**calcify** /ˈkælsəfaɪ/ v. harden by deposit of calcium salts. **calcification** n.

**calcine** /ˈkælsaɪn/ v. reduce or be reduced to quicklime or powder by burning or roasting. **calcination** n.

**calcium** /ˈkælsɪəm/ n. light silver-white malleable metallic element.

**calculate** /ˈkælkjəleɪt/ v. compute by figures, ascertain by exact reckoning; plan deliberately; *US colloq.* suppose, believe. **calculation** n.

**calculated** a. done with awareness of likely consequences; designed *to* do.

**calculator** n. device, esp. small electronic one, used for making calculations.

**calculus** /ˈkælkjələs/ n. (pl. **-li** /-laɪ/ or **-luses**) *Math.* particular method of calculation; *Med.* stone or concretion in some part of body.

**caldron** var. of **cauldron**.

**Caledonian** /kælɪˈdəʊnɪən/ 1 a. of Scotland. 2 n. Scotsman or Scotswoman.

**calendar** /ˈkæləndə(r)/ n. system fixing year's beginning, length, etc.; chart showing days, weeks, and months of particular year; adjustable device showing day's date etc.; list of special dates or events.

**calends** /ˈkæləndz/ n.pl. first of month in ancient Roman calendar.

**calf**[1] /kɑːf/ n. (pl. **calves** /kɑːvz/) young of cow, elephant, whale, etc.; calf-leather. **calf-love** immature romantic affection.

**calf**[2] /kɑːf/ n. (pl. **calves** /kɑːvz/) fleshy hind part of human leg below knee.

**calibrate** /ˈkælɪbreɪt/ v.t. determine or correct graduations of (gauge); find calibre of. **calibration** n.

**calibre** /ˈkælɪbə(r)/ n. internal diameter of gun or tube; diameter of bullet or shell; degree of merit or importance.

**calico** /ˈkælɪkəʊ/ 1 n. (pl. **-oes**) cotton cloth, esp. plain white kind; *US* printed cotton cloth. 2 a. of calico; *US* multicoloured.

**caliph** /ˈkælɪf/ n. chief civil and religious ruler in Muslim countries.

**calk** *US* var. of **caulk**.

**call** /kɔːl/ 1 v. cry, shout, speak loudly; summon; order to take place; invite; name, describe, or regard as; communicate (with) by radio or telephone; *Aus.* describe (horse-race) for broadcasting; make brief visit; utter characteristic sound. 2 n. shout; summons; telephone conversation; signal on bugle etc.; short visit; need, occasion; bird's cry. 3 **call-box** telephone-box; **call-girl** prostitute who accepts appointments by tele-

## calligraphy / camp

phone; **call in** withdraw from circulation, seek advice or help from, make brief visit; **call off** cancel, abandon; **call-sign** one which indicates identity of radio transmitter; **call up** summon (esp. to do military service), ring up; **call-up** summons to do military service. 4 **caller** n.

**calligraphy** /kəˈlɪgrəfi:/ n. handwriting; art of fine handwriting. **calligraphic** /kælɪˈgræfɪk/ a.

**calling** /ˈkɔːlɪŋ/ n. profession, occupation.

**calliper** /ˈkælɪpə(r)/ n. **calliper compasses** or **callipers** pair of hinged arms for measuring diameters; metal support for weak or injured leg.

**callisthenics** /kæləsˈθenɪks/ n.pl. exercises to develop strength and grace.

**callop** /ˈkæləp/ n. Aus. golden perch.

**callosity** /kəˈlɒsəti:/ n. hardness of skin, callus.

**callous** /ˈkæləs/ a. unfeeling, unsympathetic; (of skin) hardened.

**callow** /ˈkæləʊ/ a. raw, inexperienced.

**callus** /ˈkæləs/ n. thickened part of skin or soft tissue.

**calm** /kɑːm/ 1 a. tranquil, windless, not agitated; confident. 2 n. calm condition or period. 3 v. make or become calm, pacify.

**calomel** /ˈkæləmel/ n. a purgative compound of mercury.

**calorie** /ˈkæləri:/ n. unit of heat, amount required to raise temperature of one kg. (**large calorie**) or one g. (**small calorie**) of water 1°C; large calorie as unit of energy value of foods.

**calorific** /kæləˈrɪfɪk/ a. heat-producing.

**calumniate** /kəˈlʌmnɪeɪt/ v.t. slander. **calumniation** n.

**calumny** /ˈkæləmni:/ n. malicious misrepresentation, slander. **calumnious** /-ˈlʌm-/ a.

**Calvary** /ˈkælvəri:/ n. place or representation of Crucifixion.

**calve** /kɑːv/ v.i. give birth to calf.

**calves** pl. of **calf**[1,2].

**Calvinism** /ˈkælvɪnɪz(ə)m/ n. Calvin's theology, esp. his doctrine of predestination. **Calvinist** n.; **Calvinistic** a.

**calx** n. (pl. **calces** /ˈkælsiːz/) friable residue left after burning of metal or mineral.

**calpyso** /kəˈlɪpsəʊ/ n. (pl. **-sos**) W. Ind. song, usu. with improvised topical words.

**calyx** /ˈkeɪlɪks/ n. (pl. **-lyces** /-lɪsiːz/ or **-lyxes**) whorl of leaves forming outer case of bud.

**cam** n. projecting part of wheel etc. in machinery, shaped to convert circular into reciprocal or variable motion.

**camaraderie** /kæməˈrɑːdəri:/ n. comradeship; mutual trust and friendship.

**camber** /ˈkæmbə(r)/ 1 n. convex or arched shape of road or deck etc. 2 v.t. construct with camber.

**cambric** /ˈkeɪmbrɪk/ n. fine linen or cotton cloth.

**came** past of **come**.

**camel** /ˈkæm(ə)l/ n. large four-legged animal with one hump or two, used as beast of burden in arid regions; fawn colour.

**camellia** /kəˈmiːlɪə/ n. evergreen flowering shrub.

**Camembert** /ˈkæməmbeə(r)/ n. a kind of rich soft white cheese.

**cameo** /ˈkæmɪəʊ/ n. (pl. **-os**) onyx or similar stone carved in relief; short literary sketch or acted scene.

**camera** /ˈkæmərə/ n. apparatus for taking photographs or film or television pictures. **cameraman** operator of esp. film or television camera; **in camera** in private.

**camomile** /ˈkæməmaɪl/ n. aromatic herb with flowers used to make medicinal tea.

**camouflage** /ˈkæməflɑːʒ/ 1 n. disguising of guns, ships, etc., by obscuring with splashes of various colours, foliage, etc.; means of disguise or evasion. 2 v.t. hide (as) by camouflage.

**camp**[1] 1 n. place where troops etc. are lodged or trained; fortified site; accommodation of tents, huts, etc. for temporary holiday-makers, nomads, explorers, etc.; Aus. place where livestock rest. 2 v. live in camp; make camp. 3 **camp-bed** portable folding bed; **camp-follower** civilian worker in military camp; **camp out** lodge in open air or in temporary quarters; **camp oven** Aus. metal pot or box for cooking over open fire; **campsite** place for camping.

**camp**[2] 1 a. affected; effeminate; homosexual; exaggerated for effect. 2 n. camp

## campaign

behaviour. 3 *v.* behave or do in camp way.

**campaign** /kæm'peɪn/ 1 *n.* organized course of action in politics etc.; series of military operations. 2 *v.i.* take part in campaign.

**campanile** /kæmpə'niːliː/ *n.* detached bell-tower.

**campanology** /kæmpə'nɒlədʒiː/ *n.* study of bells; bell-ringing. **campanologist** *n.*

**campanula** /kæm'pænjələ/ *n.* plant with bell-shaped flowers.

**camphor** /'kæmfə(r)/ *n.* crystalline bitter substance used in medicine and to repel insects.

**camphorate** /'kæmfəreɪt/ *v.t.* impregnate with camphor.

**campus** /'kæmpəs/ *n.* grounds of university or college.

**camshaft** /'kæmʃɑːft/ *n.* shaft carrying cams.

**can**[1] *v.aux.* (*neg.* **cannot, can't** /kɑːnt/; *past* **could** /kʊd/, *neg.* **could not, couldn't** /'kʊd(ə)nt/) be able to; have the right to; *colloq.* be permitted to.

**can**[2] 1 *n.* metal vessel for liquids; tin plate container in which food etc. is sealed for preserving. 2 *v.t.* preserve (food etc.) in can. 3 **canned music** music recorded for reproduction; **carry the can** bear responsibility.

**Canadian** /kə'neɪdɪən/ 1 *a.* of Canada. 2 *n.* native or inhabitant of Canada.

**canal** /kə'næl/ *n.* artificial waterway for inland navigation or irrigation; duct; tubular passage in plant or animal.

**canalize** /'kænəlaɪz/ *v.t.* convert (river) into canal; give desired direction to.

**canapé** /'kænəpeɪ/ *n.* piece of bread, toast, etc., with small savoury on top.

**canard** /kæ'nɑːd/ *n.* unfounded rumour.

**canary** /kə'neərɪ/ *n.* small songbird with yellow plumage.

**canasta** /kə'næstə/ *n.* card-game resembling rummy.

**cancan** /'kænkæn/ *n.* high-kicking dance.

**cancel** /'kæns(ə)l/ *v.* (*past* & *p.p.* **cancelled**) withdraw, revoke, discontinue; obliterate, delete; mark (ticket, stamp, etc.) to invalidate it; annul; neutralize, counterbalance; *Math.* strike out (equal factor) on each side of equation etc.

**cancel out** neutralize (each other). **cancellation** *n.*

**cancer** /'kænsə(r)/ *n.* malignant tumour, disease featuring this; *fig.* corruption; **Cancer** fourth sign of zodiac. **cancerous** *a.*

**candelabrum** /kændə'lɑːbrəm/ *n.* (*pl.* **-bra**) large usu. branched candlestick.

**candid** /'kændɪd/ *a.* frank, not hiding one's thoughts; informal, of photograph taken usu. without subject's knowledge.

**candidate** /'kændɪdeɪt/ *n.* person who seeks, or is nominated for, election, office, position, etc.; person who sits examination etc. **candidacy** *n.*; **candidature** *n.*

**candle** /'kænd(ə)l/ *n.* cylinder of wax, tallow, etc. enclosing wick, for burning to give light. **candlepower** unit of luminous intensity; **candlestick** holder for candle(s); **candlewick** thick soft yarn, material with raised tufted pattern in this.

**candour** /'kændə(r)/ *n.* candidness.

**candy** /'kændɪ/ 1 *n.* sugar crystallized by repeated boiling and evaporation; *US* sweets, a sweet. 2 *v.* preserve (fruit etc.) by impregnating with sugar. 3 **candy-floss** mass of fluffy spun sugar; **candy-striped** patterned in alternate white and esp. pink stripes

**candytuft** /'kændɪtʌft/ *n.* garden plant with flowers in flat clusters.

**cane** 1 *n.* hollow jointed stem of giant reed or grass, or of slender palm, used for wickerwork or as walking-stick, instrument of punishment, etc.; sugarcane; stem of raspberry etc. 2 *v.t.* beat with cane; weave cane into (chair etc.). 3 **cane toad** large destructive toad introduced into Queensland.

**canine** /'keɪnaɪn/ 1 *a.* of a dog or dogs. 2 *n.* dog; canine tooth. 3 **canine tooth** tooth between incisors and molars.

**canister** /'kænɪstə(r)/ *n.* small usu. metal box for tea etc.; cylinder of shot or tear-gas.

**canker** /'kæŋkə(r)/ 1 *n.* disease of plants and trees; ulcerous disease of animals; *fig.* corrupting influence. 2 *v.t.* consume with canker; corrupt. 3 **cankerous** *a.*

**cannabis** /'kænəbɪs/ *n.* hemp plant; preparation of parts of it used as intoxi-

cant. **cannabis resin** sticky product of this plant.
**cannibal** /'kænəb(ə)l/ 1 *n*. person or animal that eats its own species. 2 *a*. of or having this habit. 3 **cannibalism** *n*.; **cannibalistic** *a*.
**cannibalize** /'kænəbəlaɪz/ *v.t.* use (machine etc.) as spare parts for others.
**cannon** /'kænən/ 1 *n. hist.* large gun; *Billiards* hitting of two balls successively by player's ball. 2 *v.i.* make cannon at billiards; collide heavily *against*, *into*, etc. 3 **cannon-ball** large metal ball fired by cannon.
**cannonade** /kænə'neɪd/ 1 *n*. continuous gunfire. 2 *v*. bombard with cannon.
**cannot** see **can**[1].
**canny** /'kænɪ/ *a*. shrewd, thrifty, circumspect.
**canoe** /kə'nu:/ 1 *n*. light boat propelled with paddle(s). 2 *v.i.* (*partic.* **canoeing**) go in or paddle canoe. 3 **canoeist** *n*.
**canon** /'kænən/ *n*. general law, rule, or principle; criterion; church decree; member of cathedral chapter; body of (esp. sacred) writings etc. accepted as genuine; *Mus.* piece with different parts taking up same theme successively.
**canonical** /kə'nɒnɪk(ə)l/ *a*. according to or ordered by canon law; included in canon of Scripture; authoritative or accepted; of cathedral canon or chapter.
**canonize** /'kænənaɪz/ *v.t.* declare officially to be a saint. **canonization** *n*.
**canopy** /'kænəpɪ/ 1 *n*. covering hung or held up over throne, bed, person, etc.; *fig.* sky or overhanging shelter; uppermost layer of forest foliage; rooflike projection. 2 *v.t.* supply or be canopy to.
**cant**[1] 1 *n*. insincere pious or moral talk; language peculiar to one class of people; jargon. 2 *v.i.* use cant.
**cant**[2] 1 *n*. slanting surface, bevel; oblique push or jerk; tilted position. 2 *v*. push or jerk or hold out of level.
**can't** see **can**[1].
**cantaloup** /'kæntəlu:p/ *n*. small round ribbed melon.
**cantankerous** /kæn'tæŋkərəs/ *a*. bad-tempered, quarrelsome.
**cantata** /kæn'tɑ:tə/ *n*. choral work like oratorio but usu. shorter.
**canteen** /kæn'ti:n/ *n*. restaurant for employees in factory, office, etc.; school shop selling lunches; shop for provisions or liquor in barracks or camp; case or chest containing set of cutlery; soldier's or camper's water-flask.
**canter** /'kæntə(r)/ 1 *n*. easy gallop. 2 *v*. go at a canter.
**canticle** /'kæntɪk(ə)l/ *n*. song or chant on biblical text.
**cantilever** /'kæntɪli:və(r)/ *n*. beam, bracket, etc., projecting from wall to support balcony etc.; beam or girder fixed at one end only. **cantilever bridge** one in which cantilevers project from piers and are connected by girders.
**canto** /'kæntəʊ/ *n*. (*pl.* -tos) division of long poem.
**canton** 1 /'kæntɒn/ *n*. subdivision of country, esp. Switzerland.
**cantor** /'kæntɔ:(r)/ *n*. precentor in synagogue.
**canvas** /'kænvəs/ *n*. strong coarse cloth used for sails and tents and as surface for oil-painting, etc.; a painting.
**canvass** /'kænvəs/ 1 *v*. solicit votes (from), ascertain opinions of; solicit custom of; propose (idea etc.). 2 *n*. canvassing.
**canyon** /'kænjən/ *n*. deep gorge cut by river.
**cap** 1 *n*. soft brimless head-covering, freq. with peak; nurse's or woman servant's indoor head-dress; cap awarded as sign of membership of sports team; academic mortar-board; cover resembling cap, or designed to close, seal or protect something; explosive device esp. of paper for toy pistol; contraceptive diaphragm. 2 *v.t.* put cap on; cover top or end of; award sports cap to; lie on top of, surpass.
**capable** /'keɪpəb(ə)l/ *a*. able, competent. **capable of** having ability, fitness, or necessary quality for, susceptible of or admitting of. **capability** *n*.; **capably** *adv*.
**capacious** /kə'peɪʃəs/ *a*. roomy, able to hold much.
**capacitance** /kə'pæsɪt(ə)ns/ *n*. ability of apparatus to store electric charge.
**capacitor** /kə'pæsɪtə(r)/ *n*. *Electr.* device able to store electric charge.
**capacity** /kə'pæsɪtɪ/ *n*. power of containing, producing, etc.; maximum amount that can be contained, pro-

duced, etc.; mental power; function or character.
**caparison** /kə'pærəs(ə)n/ 1 *n.* harness, trappings; finery. 2 *v.t.* adorn.
**cape**[1] *n.* sleeveless cloak.
**cape**[2] *n.* headland, promontory; **the Cape** Cape of Good Hope. **capeweed** common yellow-flowered weed.
**caper**[1] /'keɪpə(r)/ 1 *v.i.* move playfully. 2 *n.* playful jump or leap; *sl.* activity, occupation.
**caper**[2] /'keɪpə(r)/ *n.* bramble-like shrub; in *pl.* its pickled flower-buds.
**capillary** /kə'pɪləri/ 1 *a.* of hair; of hairlike fineness. 2 *n.* capillary tube, blood-vessel, etc. 3 **capillary attraction** tendency of liquid to be drawn up in capillary tube.
**capital** /'kæpɪt(ə)l/ 1 *n.* most important town or city of a country or region; money etc. with which company starts business; accumulated wealth; capital letter; head of column or pillar. 2 *a.* most important; *colloq.* excellent; involving punishment by death; (of letters of alphabet) large in size and form, such as begin sentence and name. 3 **capital gain** profit from sale of investments or property.
**capitalism** /'kæpɪtəlɪz(ə)m/ *n.* economic system with ownership and control of capital in private hands.
**capitalist** /'kæpɪtəlɪst/ 1 *n.* person using or possessing capital. 2 *a.* of or favouring capitalism. 3 **capitalistic** *a.*
**capitalize** /'kæpɪtəlaɪz/ *v.* convert into or provide with capital; write (letter of alphabet) as capital, begin (word) with capital letter. **capitalize on** use to one's advantage. **capitalization** *n.*
**capitulate** /kə'pɪtjʊleɪt/ *v.i.* surrender esp. on stated conditions. **capitulation** *n.*
**capon** /'keɪpən/ *n.* castrated cock.
**caprice** /kə'priːs/ *n.* unaccountable change of mind or conduct; work of lively fancy.
**capricious** /kə'prɪʃəs/ *a.* liable to caprice, unpredictable.
**Capricorn** /'kæprɪkɔːn/ *n.* tenth sign of zodiac.
**capsicum** /'kæpsɪkəm/ *n.* tropical plant with hot-flavoured seeds; its edible fleshy seed-pod.
**capsize** /kæp'saɪz/ *v.* overturn, esp. on water.
**capstan** /'kæpst(ə)n/ *n.* thick revolving cylinder round which cable or rope is wound; revolving spindle carrying spool on tape recorder. **capstan lathe** one with tools mounted on capstan-like holder.
**capsule** /'kæpsjuːl/ *n.* small soluble case enclosing dose of medicine; detachable nose-cone of rocket etc. or compartment of spacecraft; enclosing membrane; plant's seed-case.
**captain** /'kæptɪn/ 1 *n.* chief, leader; naval officer next below commodore; master of merchant ship; army officer next below major; pilot of civil aircraft; leader of side at games. 2 *v.t.* be captain of. 3 **captaincy** *n.*
**caption** /'kæpʃ(ə)n/ 1 *n.* heading of chapter, article, etc.; wording on cinema or televison screen, or appended to illustration or cartoon. 2 *v.t.* provide with caption.
**captious** /'kæpʃəs/ *a.* fond of finding fault, quibbling, etc.
**captivate** /'kæptɪveɪt/ *v.t.* fascinate, charm. **captivation** *n.*
**captive** /'kæptɪv/ 1 *n.* person or animal taken prisoner or confined. 2 *a.* taken prisoner; in confinement; unable to escape. **captivity** *n.*
**captor** /'kæptə(r)/ *n.* one who captures.
**capture** /'kæptʃə(r)/ 1 *v.t.* take prisoner; seize; portray in permanent form. 2 *n.* act of capturing; thing or person captured.
**Capuchin** /'kæpjʊtʃən/ *n.* friar of branch of Franciscans; **capuchin** *Amer.* monkey with hair like black hood.
**car** *n.* wheeled vehicle; motor car; railway carriage of specified type; *US* any railway carriage or van. **car-park** area for parking cars; **carport** roofed opensided shelter for car; **car-sick** affected by nausea through motion of car.
**carafe** /kə'ræf/ *n.* glass container for water or wine.
**caramel** /'kærəmel/ *n.* brown substance got by heating sugar or syrup; soft toffee made with this.
**carapace** /'kærəpeɪs/ *n.* upper shell of tortoise or crustacean.
**carat** /'kærət/ *n.* unit of weight for precious stones; unit of purity of gold.
**caravan** /'kærəvæn/ *n.* vehicle equipped for living in and usu. towed by

# caravanserai / careless

**motor vehicle; company travelling together esp. across desert.

**caravanserai** /ˌkærəˈvænsəraɪ/ n. Eastern inn with central courtyard.

**caravel** /ˈkærəvel/ n. hist. small light fast ship.

**caraway** /ˈkærəweɪ/ n. plant with small aromatic fruit (**caraway-seed**) used in cakes etc.

**carbide** /ˈkɑːbaɪd/ n. compound of carbon with metal.

**carbine** /ˈkɑːbaɪn/ n. kind of short rifle.

**carbohydrate** /ˌkɑːbəʊˈhaɪdreɪt/ n. energy-producing compound of carbon, hydrogen, and oxygen.

**carbolic** /kɑːˈbɒlɪk/ n. (in full **carbolic acid**) kind of disinfectant and antiseptic; **carbolic soap** soap containing this.

**carbon** /ˈkɑːbən/ n. non-metallic element occurring as diamond, graphite, charcoal, etc. and in all organic compounds; carbon paper, carbon copy; carbon rod used in arc-lamp. **carbon copy** copy made with carbon paper; **carbon dating** determination of age of object etc. from decay of radio-carbon in it; **carbon dioxide** gas formed by burning carbon or by breathing; **carbon monoxide** poisonous gas formed by burning carbon incompletely; **carbon paper** thin carbon-coated paper for making copy as thing is typed or written.

**carbonate** /ˈkɑːbəneɪt/ 1 n. salt of carbonic acid. 2 v.t. impregnate with carbon dioxide.

**carbonic** /kɑːˈbɒnɪk/ a. of carbon. **carbonic acid** weak acid formed from carbon dioxide and water.

**carboniferous** /ˌkɑːbəˈnɪfərəs/ a. producing coal.

**carbonize** /ˈkɑːbənaɪz/ v.t. reduce to charcoal or coke by burning; coat with carbon. **carbonization** n.

**Carborundum** /ˌkɑːbəˈrʌndəm/ n. (P) compound of carbon and silicon used as abrasive etc.

**carboy** /ˈkɑːbɔɪ/ n. large globular glass bottle.

**carbuncle** /ˈkɑːbʌŋk(ə)l/ n. severe abscess in the skin; bright red jewel.

**carburettor** /ˈkɑːbjəretə(r)/ n. apparatus mixing air with petrol vapour in internal-combustion engine.

**carcass** /ˈkɑːkəs/ (also **carcase**) n. dead body of animal or bird or (*derog.*) person; framework, worthless remains.

**carcinogen** /ˈkɑːsɪnədʒ(ə)n/ n. substance that produces cancer. **carcinogenic** /-ˈdʒen-/ a.

**card**[1] n. thick paper or thin pasteboard; piece of this for writing or printing on, esp. to send greetings, to identify person, or to record information; playing-card; in pl. card-playing; in pl. colloq. employee's documents; sl. eccentric person. **card-carrying** having valid membership (esp. of political party); **card index** one with each item on separate card; **card-sharp** swindler at card-games; **card vote** block vote.

**card**[2] 1 n. toothed instrument or wire brush etc. for combing wool etc. 2 v.t. treat with card.

**cardamom** /ˈkɑːdəməm/ n. E. Ind. spice from seeds of aromatic plant.

**cardboard** /ˈkɑːdbɔːd/ n. stiff paper or pasteboard.

**cardiac** /ˈkɑːdɪæk/ a. of the heart.

**cardigan** /ˈkɑːdɪɡən/ n. knitted jacket with buttons down front.

**cardinal** /ˈkɑːdɪn(ə)l/ 1 a. chief, fundamental; of deep scarlet. 2 n. one of leading officials of RC Church, who elect Pope. 3 **cardinal numbers** those representing quantity 1, 2, 3, etc. (cf. **ordinal**).

**cardiogram** /ˈkɑːdɪəɡræm/ n. record of heart movements.

**cardio-vascular** /ˌkɑːdɪəʊˈvæskjələ(r)/ a. of heart and blood-vessels.

**care** /keə(r)/ 1 n. anxiety, concern; serious attention; caution; task, charge, protection. 2 v.i. feel concern or interest or affection. 3 **in care** (of child) under supervision of local authority etc.

**careen** /kəˈriːn/ v. turn (ship) on side for repair; tilt, lean over.

**career** /kəˈrɪə(r)/ 1 n. course through life, esp. in a profession; profession or occupation; swift course. 2 v.i. move or swerve about wildly.

**careerist** /kəˈrɪərɪst/ n. person predominantly concerned with personal advancement.

**carefree** /ˈkeəfriː/ a. free from anxiety or responsibility.

**careful** /ˈkeəf(ə)l/ a. painstaking; cautious; done with care and attention.

**careless** /ˈkeələs/ a. lacking care or

attention; unthinking, insensitive; light-hearted.
**caress** /kə'res/ 1 *v.t.* touch lovingly, kiss. 2 *n.* loving touch, kiss.
**caret** /'kærət/ *n.* omission-mark.
**caretaker** /'keəteɪkə(r)/ *n.* person in charge of maintenance etc. of house, building, etc.; *attrib.* taking temporary control.
**careworn** /'keəwɔːn/ *a.* fatigued by trouble and anxiety.
**cargo** /'kɑːgəʊ/ *n.* (*pl.* **-goes**) goods carried by ship, aircraft, etc.
**Caribbean** /kærə'biːən/ *a.* of the West Indies.
**caribou** /'kærəbuː/ *n.* N. Amer. reindeer.
**caricature** /'kærəkətjʊə(r)/ 1 *n.* grotesque or ludicrously exaggerated representation. 2 *v.t.* make or give caricature of. 3 **caricaturist** *n.*
**caries** /'keəriːz/ *n.* (*pl.* same) decay of tooth or bone.
**carillon** /kə'rɪljən/ *n.* set of bells sounded mechanically or from keyboard; tune played on this.
**Carmelite** /'kɑːməlaɪt/ 1 *n.* member of ascetic order of friars or of nuns. 2 *a.* of Carmelites.
**carminative** /'kɑːmənətɪv/ 1 *a.* curing flatulence. 2 *n.* carminative drug.
**carmine** /'kɑːmaɪn/ 1 *a.* of vivid crimson colour. 2 *n.* this colour.
**carnage** /'kɑːnɪdʒ/ *n.* great slaughter.
**carnal** /'kɑːn(ə)l/ *a.* worldly; sensual; sexual. **carnality** *n.*
**carnation** /kɑː'neɪʃ(ə)n/ 1 *n.* cultivated clove-scented pink; rosy pink colour. 2 *a.* of this colour.
**carnelian** var. of **cornelian**².
**carnival** /'kɑːnəv(ə)l/ *n.* festival or festivities, esp. preceding Lent; riotous revelry; *Aus.* series of sporting events.
**carnivore** /'kɑːnəvɔː(r)/ *n.* animal or plant that feeds on flesh. **carnivorous** /-'nɪv-/ *a.*
**carol** /'kær(ə)l/ 1 *n.* joyous song, esp. Christmas hymn. 2 *v.i.* (*past* & *p.p.* **carolled**) sing joyfully.
**carotid** /kə'rɒtəd/ 1 *a.* of two main arteries carrying blood to head. 2 *n.* carotid artery.
**carouse** /kə'raʊz/ 1 *v.i.* have noisy drinking-party. 2 *n.* such party. 3 **carousal** *n.*
**carp**¹ *n.* a freshwater fish.

**carp**² *v.i.* find fault, complain.
**carpal** /'kɑːp(ə)l/ *a.* of the wrist-bone.
**carpel** /'kɑːp(ə)l/ *n. Bot.* unit of compound pistil.
**carpenter** /'kɑːpəntə(r)/ 1 *n.* craftsman in woodwork. 2 *v.* do, make by, carpenter's work. 3 **carpentry** *n.*
**carpet** /'kɑːpət/ 1 *n.* textile fabric for covering floors etc.; ground covering of grass, flowers, etc. 2 *v.t.* cover (as) with carpet. 3 **carpet-bag** travelling-bag orig. made of carpet material; **carpet-bagger** political candidate etc. without local connections; **carpet shark** *Aus.* wobbegong; **carpet slipper** one of kind with uppers made orig. of carpet-like material; **carpet snake** large Aus. non-venomous snake.
**carpus** /'kɑːpəs/ *n.* (*pl.* **-pi** /-paɪ/) one of small bones connecting hand and forearm.
**carriage** /'kærɪdʒ/ *n.* wheeled passenger vehicle esp. drawn by horse(s); railway coach; conveying of goods etc.; cost of this; carrying; bearing, deportment; sliding etc. part of machine shifting position of other parts; gun-carriage.
**carriageway** part of road used by vehicles.
**carrier** /'kærɪə(r)/ *n.* person or thing that carries; person or company conveying goods or passengers for payment; carrier-bag; part of bicycle etc. for carrying luggage etc.; person or animal that transmits disease without suffering from it; aircraft-carrier. **carrier bag** large paper or plastic bag with handles; **carrier pigeon** homing pigeon used for carrying messages etc.; **carrier wave** high-frequency electromagnetic wave used to convey signal.
**carrion** /'kærɪən/ *n.* dead flesh; garbage, filth.
**carrot** /'kærət/ *n.* plant with tapering orange-red sweet fleshy edible root; this root; *fig.* means of enticement. **carroty** *a.*
**carry** /'kærɪ/ *v.* support or hold up, esp. while moving; convey; have with one, possess; take (process etc.) to specified point; involve, imply; transfer (figure) to column of higher value; (of sound) be heard at a distance; win victory or acceptance for; capture. **carry away** remove, inspire, deprive of self-control; **carry-cot** portable cot

**cart** for baby; **carry forward** transfer (figure) to new page or account; **carry off** remove by force, win, render acceptable or passable; **carry on** continue, *colloq.* behave excitedly, flirt; **carry out** put into practice; **carry through** complete, bring safely out of difficulties.

**cart 1** *n.* strong two- or four-wheeled vehicle for carrying heavy goods etc.; light vehicle for pulling or pushing by hand. **2** *v.t.* carry in cart; *sl.* carry (esp. cumbersome thing) with difficulty. **3 cart-horse** horse of heavy build; **cartwheel** wheel of cart, sideways somersault with arms and legs extended.

*carte blanche* /kɑːt 'blɑ̃ʃ/ full discretionary power. [F]

**cartel** /kɑː'tel/ *n.* manufacturers' or producers' union to control prices etc.

**Carthusian** /kɑː'θjuːzjən/ **1** *n.* monk of comtemplative order founded by St Bruno. **2** *a.* of the Carthusians.

**cartilage** /'kɑːtəlɪdʒ/ *n.* tough flexible tissue in vertebrates; structure of this. **cartilaginous** /-'lædʒ-/ *a.*

**cartography** /kɑː'tɒɡrəfɪ/ *n.* map-drawing. **cartographer** *n.*; **cartographic** *a.*

**carton** /'kɑːt(ə)n/ *n.* light cardboard etc. box for goods.

**cartoon** /kɑː'tuːn/ *n.* humorous esp. topical drawing in newspaper etc., sequence of these; film made by photographing series of drawings; full-size drawing as sketch for work of art. **cartoonist** *n.*

**cartouche** /kɑː'tuːʃ/ *n.* scroll-like ornament; oval enclosing name of ancient Egyptian king.

**cartridge** /'kɑːtrɪdʒ/ *n.* case containing charge of explosive, with bullet or shot if for small arms; spool of film, magnetic tape, etc., in container; removable pick-up head of record-player; ink-container for insertion in pen. **cartridge paper** thick rough kind for drawing etc.

**carve** *v.* cut, make by cutting; cover or adorn with carved figures etc.; cut up meat at or for table. **carve out** take from larger whole; **carve up** subdivide. **carver** *n.*

**carvel** /'kɑːv(ə)l/ var. of **caravel**. **carvel-built** (of boat) with planks flush with side.

**carving** /'kɑːvɪŋ/ *n.* carved object, esp. as work of art.

**cascade** /kæs'keɪd/ **1** *n.* waterfall esp. one in series. **2** *v.i.* fall in or like cascade.

**case**[1] /keɪs/ *n.* instance of thing's occurring; hypothetical or actual situation; instance or condition of person receiving medical treatment; person being treated; crime etc. investigated by detective or police; *Law* suit or cause for trial; sum of arguments presented on one side; *Gram.* (relation expressed by) inflected form of noun etc. **case-law** law as settled by decided cases; **casework** social work concerned with individual cases; **in any case** whatever the fact is; **in case** in event (of); **is (not) the case** is (not) so.

**case**[2] /keɪs/ **1** *n.* container or covering serving to enclose or contain something. **2** *v.t.* enclose in case; surround (*with*); *sl.* inspect or examine closely, esp. for criminal purpose. **3 case-harden** harden surface of (esp. steel), *fig.* make callous.

**casement** /'keɪsmənt/ *n.* part of window hinged to open like door.

**cash 1** *n.* money in form of coin or banknotes; money paid in full at time of purchase. **2** *v.t.* give or obtain cash for. **3 cash and carry** store selling goods which are paid for in cash and removed by buyer, this method of trading; **cash crop** crop produced for sale; **cash flow** movement of money into and out of a business etc.; **cash in** obtain cash for, *fig.* profit; **cash register** till recording amount of each sale.

**cashew** /'kæʃuː/ *n.* kidney-shaped edible nut; tropical tree bearing it.

**cashier**[1] /kæ'ʃɪə(r)/ *n.* person in charge of cash in bank or other business firm.

**cashier**[2] /kæ'ʃɪə(r)/ *v.t.* dismiss from service.

**cashmere** /kæʃ'mɪə(r)/ *n.* fine soft material of wool of goats of Kashmir etc.

**casing** /'keɪsɪŋ/ *n.* enclosing material or framework etc.

**casino** /kə'siːnəʊ/ *n.* (*pl.* **-nos**) public building for gambling.

**cask** /kɑːsk/ *n.* barrel, esp. for alcoholic liquor; *Aus.* plastic-lined cardboard container for wine.

**casket** /'kɑːskət/ n. small box for holding valuables; *US* coffin.

**cassava** /kə'sɑːvə/ n. W. Ind. plant; starch or flour obtained from its roots.

**casserole** /'kæsərəʊl/ 1 n. covered dish in which food is cooked and served; food thus prepared. 2 v.t. cook in casserole.

**cassette** /kə'set/ n. small sealed case containing magnetic tape or film, ready for insertion.

**cassia** /'kæsɪə/ n. kind of cinnamon; plant yielding senna.

**cassock** /'kæsək/ n. long close usu. black tunic worn by clergy and choristers etc.

**cassowary** /'kæsəwərɪ/ n. large flightless bird related to emu.

**cast** /kɑːst/ 1 v. (*past* & *p.p.* **cast**) throw, emit; cause to fall, direct; shed or lose; record or register (vote); shape (molten metal or plastic material) in mould; make (product) thus; assign (actor) *as* character; allocate roles in (play, film, etc.); add *up*; calculate (horoscope). 2 n. throwing of missile, dice, fishing-line, etc.; (thing made in) mould for molten metal etc.; moulded mass of solidified material; set of actors in play etc.; tinge of colour; slight squint; form, type, or quality; worm-cast. 3 **cast about, around, for** try to find or think of; **cast down** depress; **cast iron** hard alloy of iron, carbon, and silicon, cast in mould; **cast-iron** of cast iron, *fig.* hard, unshakeable; **cast off** abandon, *Knitting* pass (stitch) over next and drop from needle, cast off stitches of; **cast-off** *a.* & *n.* abandoned or discarded (thing, esp. garment); **cast on** *Knitting* make first row of loops on needle.

**castanet** /kæstə'net/ n. one of pair of small concave wooden or ivory shells held in palm of hand and clicked or rattled in time with dancing.

**castaway** /'kɑːstəweɪ/ 1 n. shipwrecked person. 2 a. shipwrecked.

**caste** /kɑːst/ n. Hindu hereditary class with members having no social contact with other classes; exclusive social class.

**castellated** /'kæstəleɪtɪd/ a. built with battlements.

**caster** var. of **castor**[1].

**castigate** /'kæstɪgeɪt/ v.t. punish, chastise. **castigation** n.

**castle** /'kɑːs(ə)l/ 1 n. building designed to serve as both residence and fortress; *Chess* rook. 2 v.i. *Chess* make combined move of king and rook.

**castor**[1] /'kɑːstə(r)/ n. small swivelled wheel enabling heavy furniture to be moved; vessel with perforated top for sprinkling sugar etc. **castor sugar** finely granulated white sugar.

**castor**[2] /'kɑːstə(r)/ n. substance from beaver used in perfumery etc.

**castor oil** /'kɑːstə(r)/ vegetable oil used as purgative and lubricant.

**castrate** /kæs'treɪt/ v.t. remove testicles of, geld. **castration** n.

**casual** /'kæʒjʊəl/ 1 a. due to chance; not regular or permanent; careless, unconcerned; not ceremonious; (of clothes etc.) informal. 2 n. casual worker; in *pl.* casual clothes or shoes.

**casualty** /'kæʒjʊəltɪ/ n. person killed or injured in war, accident, etc.; casualty ward; accident. **casualty department, ward**, one for treatment of accidental injuries etc.

**casuarina** /kæzjʊə'riːnə/ n. quick-growing Aus. tree with jointed leafless branches.

**casuist** /'kæzjʊəst/ n. theologian etc. who studies and resolves cases of conscience etc.; sophist, quibbler. **casuistic** *a.*; **casuistry** n.

**cat** n. small furry domestic quadruped; any wild feline or catlike animal; spiteful or malicious woman; *sl.* person, esp. jazz fan; cat-o'-nine-tails. **cat burglar** one who enters by climbing wall to upper storey; **catcall** (make) shrill whistle of disapproval; **catfish** fish with whisker-like filaments round mouth; **catnap** (have) short sleep; **cat-o'-nine-tails** whip of nine knotted cords; **cat's-cradle** child's game with string; **Cat's-eye** (P) reflector stud on road etc.; **cat's-paw** person used as tool by another; **catsuit** close-fitting garment with trouser legs, that covers body from neck to feet; **catwalk** narrow footway.

**catachresis** /kætə'kriːsɪs/ n. (*pl* **-ses** /-siːz/) incorrect use of words. **catachrestic** (/-'krɪs-/) *a.*

**cataclysm** /'kætəklɪz(ə)m/ n. violent event; political or social upheaval. **cataclysmic** *a.*

**catacomb** /ˈkætəkuːm/ *n.* underground gallery for burials.

**catafalque** /ˈkætəfælk/ *n.* structure for display or conveying of coffin at funeral.

**catalepsy** /ˈkætəlepsi/ *n.* seizure or trance with rigidity of body. **cataleptic** *a. & n.*

**catalogue** /ˈkætəlɒg/ 1 *n.* complete list, usu. in alphabetical or other systematic order. 2 *v.t.* make catalogue of; enter in catalogue.

**catalysis** /kəˈtæləsəs/ *n.* (*pl.* **-ses** /-siːz/) *n. Chem.* effect of substance that aids chemical change without itself changing.

**catalyst** /ˈkætələst/ *n.* substance causing catalysis; person or thing that precipitates a change. **catalytic** (/-ˈlɪt-/) *a.*

**catamaran** /ˌkætəməˈræn/ *n.* boat or raft with two hulls side by side.

**catamite** /ˈkætəmaɪt/ *n.* passive partner in male homosexual practices, esp. boy.

**catapult** /ˈkætəpʌlt/ 1 *n.* forked stick with elastic for shooting stones; *hist.* military machine for hurling stones etc.; mechanical device for launching glider etc. 2 *v.* launch with catapult; fling forcibly; leap or be hurled forcibly.

**cataract** /ˈkætərækt/ *n.* waterfall, downpour; progressive opacity of eye-lens.

**catarrh** /kəˈtɑː(r)/ *n.* inflammation of mucous membrane; watery discharge in nose or throat due to this. **catarrhal** *a.*

**catastrophe** /kəˈtæstrəfi/ *n.* great usu. sudden disaster; disastrous event. **catastrophic** /-ˈstrɒf-/ *a.*

**catch** /kætʃ/ 1 *v.* (*past & p.p.* **caught** /kɔːt/) capture, lay hold of, seize; detect or surprise; trick; receive and hold (moving thing) in hand etc.; *Crick.* dismiss (batsman) by catching ball directly from bat; get by infection etc.; apprehend; be in time for (train etc.); reach or overtake; check or be checked suddenly; become entangled. 2 *n.* act of catching; *Crick.* chance or act of catching ball; thing or person caught or worth catching; question etc. intended to trick; unexpected difficulty or disadvantage; device for fastening door or window etc.; musical round. 3 **catch crop** one grown between two staple crops; **catch fire** begin to burn; **catch on** *colloq.* become popular, understand what is meant; **catch out** detect in mistake etc., *Crick.* catch; **catchpenny** intended merely to sell quickly; **catch-phrase** one in frequent current use; **catch up** reach (person etc. ahead), make up arrears; **catchword** word or phrase in frequent current use, word so placed as to draw attention.

**catching** /ˈkætʃɪŋ/ *a. colloq.* infectious.

**catchment area** /ˈkætʃmənt/ area from which rainfall flows into river etc., area served by school or hospital etc.

**catchy** /ˈkætʃi/ *a.* (of tune) easily remembered, attractive.

**catechism** /ˈkætəkɪz(ə)m/ *n.* summary of principles of a religion in form of questions and answers; series of questions.

**catechize** /ˈkætəkaɪz/ *v.t.* instruct by question and answer; put questions to.

**catechumen** /ˌkætəˈkjuːmən/ *n.* person being instructed before baptism.

**categorical** /ˌkætəˈgɒrək(ə)l/ *a.* unconditional, absolute, explicit. **categorically** *adv.*

**categorize** /ˈkætəgəraɪz/ *v.t.* place in category. **categorization** *n.*

**category** /ˈkætəgəri/ *n.* class or division (of ideas or things).

**cater** /ˈkeɪtə(r)/ *v.i.* supply food; provide what is required *for.*

**caterpillar** /ˈkætəpɪlə(r)/ *n.* larva of butterfly or moth; **Caterpillar track** (P) articulated steel band with treads passing round wheels of vehicle to be used on rough ground.

**caterwaul** /ˈkætəwɔːl/ *v.i.* scream like cat.

**catgut** /ˈkætgʌt/ *n.* thread made from dried intestines of sheep etc. used for strings of musical instruments etc.

**catharsis** /kəˈθɑːsəs/ *n.* (*pl.* **-ses** /-siːz/) purgation; emotional release in drama or art.

**cathartic** /kəˈθɑːtɪk/ 1 *a.* effecting catharsis; purgative. 2 *n.* cathartic drug.

**cathedral** /kəˈθiːdr(ə)l/ *n.* principal church of diocese.

**Catherine wheel** /ˈkæθərən/ rotating firework.

**catheter** /ˈkæθətə(r)/ *n.* tube inserted

**cathode** /'kæθəʊd/ *n*. negative electrode or terminal. **cathode ray** beam of electrons from cathode of high-vacuum tube; **cathode-ray tube** vacuum tube in which cathode rays produce luminous image on fluorescent screen.

**catheterize** *v.t.*

**catholic** /'kæθəlɪk/ **1** *a*. universal, all-embracing; broad-minded; Roman Catholic; **Catholic** including all Christians or all of Western Church. **2** *n*. **Catholic** Roman Catholic. **3 catholicism** /-'θɒl-/ *n*. **catholicity** /-'lɪs-/ *n*.

**cation** /'kætaɪən/ *n*. positively charged ion. **cationic** *a*.

**catkin** /'kætkɪn/ *n*. hanging flower of willow, hazel, etc.

**catmint** /'kætmɪnt/ *n*. aromatic plant with blue flowers.

**catnip** /'kætnɪp/ *n*. catmint.

**cattle** /'kæt(ə)l/ *n.pl*. livestock, esp. oxen. **cattle-dog** *Aus*. dog trained for droving cattle; **cattle-grid, -pit, -ramp, -stop** grid covering ditch, allowing vehicles to pass over but not livestock.

**catty** /'kæti/ *a*. catlike; spiteful.

**caucus** /'kɔːkəs/ *n. Aus*. committee of parliamentary members of political party, meeting of this; *UK & US* local political party committee.

**caudal** /'kɔːd(ə)l/ *a*. of or at or like tail.

**caudate** /'kɔːdeɪt/ *a*. tailed.

**caught** past & p.p. of **catch**.

**caul** /kɔːl/ *n*. membrane enclosing foetus; part of this sometimes found on child's head at birth.

**cauldron** /'kɔːldrən/ *n*. large vessel for boiling things in.

**cauliflower** /'kɒlɪflaʊə(r)/ *n*. kind of cabbage with edible white flower-head.

**caulk** /kɔːk/ *v.t.* stop up (ship's seams) with oakum and pitch.

**causal** /'kɔːz(ə)l/ *a*. relating to cause and effect. **causality** *n*.

**causation** /kɔːˈzeɪʃ(ə)n/ *n*. causing, causality.

**cause** /kɔːz/ **1** *n*. what produces effect; reason or motive for action; justification; principle or belief advocated or upheld; matter about which person goes to law. **2** *v.t.* be cause of; produce, make (*to* do etc.).

*cause célèbre* /kəʊz seˈlebr/ (*pl. causes célèbres pr*. same) lawsuit that excites much interest. [F]

**causeway** /'kɔːzweɪ/ *n*. raised road across low or wet ground; raised footway at side of road.

**caustic** /'kɔːstɪk/ **1** *a*. that burns or corrodes; sarcastic, biting. **2** *n*. caustic substance. **3 caustic soda** sodium hydroxide. **4 causticity** *n*.

**cauterize** /'kɔːtəraɪz/ *v.t.* burn (tissue) with caustic substance or hot iron, esp. to destroy infection. **cauterization** *n*.

**caution** /'kɔːʃ(ə)n/ **1** *n*. avoidance of rashness, attention to safety; warning; *sl.* surprising or amusing person or thing. **2** *v.t.* warn, admonish.

**cautionary** /'kɔːʃənərɪ/ *a*. that warns.

**cautious** /'kɔːʃəs/ *a*. having or showing caution.

**cavalcade** /kævəlˈkeɪd/ *n*. company of riders, cars, etc.

**cavalier** /kævəˈlɪə(r)/ **1** *n*. courtly gentleman or soldier; *arch*. horseman; **Cavalier** *hist*. supporter of Charles I in English Civil War. **2** *a*. offhand, curt, discourteous.

**cavalry** /'kævəlrɪ/ *n*. (usu. treated as *pl*.) soldiers on horseback or in armoured vehicles.

**cave 1** *n*. large hollow in side of hill, cliff, etc. or underground. **2** *v*. explore caves. **3 cave in** (cause to) subside or fall in, yield to pressure, submit.

**caveat** /'kævɪæt/ *n*. warning, proviso.

**cavern** /'kæv(ə)n/ *n*. cave, esp. large or dark one.

**cavernous** /'kævənəs/ *a*. full of caverns; huge or deep as cavern.

**caviare** /kævɪˈɑː(r)/ *n*. pickled sturgeon-roe.

**cavil** /'kævəl/ **1** *v.i.* take exception *at*, find fault. **2** *n*. petty objection.

**cavity** /'kævɪtɪ/ *n*. hollow within solid body. **cavity wall** double wall with internal cavity.

**cavort** /kəˈvɔːt/ *v.i.* prance.

**caw 1** *n*. cry of rook etc. **2** *v.i.* utter caw.

**cayenne** /keɪˈen/ *n*. (in full **cayenne pepper**) hot red pepper from capsicum.

**cayman** /'keɪmən/ *n*. S. Amer. alligator.

**CBE** *abbr*. Commander of the Order of the British Empire.

**cc** *abbr*. cubic centimetre(s).

**CD** *abbr*. Corps Diplomatique; compact disc.

**cease** /siːs/ 1 *v.* end; stop; come or bring to an end. 2 *n.* **without cease** not ceasing. 3 **cease-fire** halt in hostilities.

**ceaseless** /ˈsiːsləs/ *a.* without end.

**cedar** /ˈsiːdə(r)/ *n.* evergreen coniferous tree; its fragrant fine-grained wood; any of various similar Aus. trees.

**cede** /siːd/ *v.t.* give up one's rights to or possession of.

**cedilla** /səˈdɪlə/ *n.* mark written under c (ç) to show that it is sibilant.

**ceiling** /ˈsiːlɪŋ/ *n.* upper interior surface of room or other compartment; material forming this; upper limit; maximum altitude of aircraft.

**celandine** /ˈseləndaɪn/ *n.* a yellow-flowered wild plant.

**celebrant** /ˈselɪbrənt/ *n.* officiating priest at Eucharist.

**celebrate** /ˈselɪbreɪt/ *v.* mark (event or festival) with festivities; perform (rite or ceremony); honour or praise publicly; engage in festivities after success etc. **celebration** *n.*

**celebrated** /ˈselɪbreɪtɪd/ *a.* famous.

**celebrity** /səˈlebrətɪ/ *n.* well-known person; fame.

**celeriac** /sɪˈlerɪæk/ *n.* variety of celery with edible turnip-like root.

**celerity** /sɪˈlerətɪ/ *n. arch.* swiftness.

**celery** /ˈselərɪ/ *n.* plant of which stems are used as salad and vegetable.

**celesta** /sɪˈlestə/ *n.* keyboard musical instrument with metal plates struck with hammers.

**celestial** /sɪˈlestɪəl/ *a.* of sky or heavenly bodies; heavenly, divinely good or beautiful etc.

**celibate** /ˈselɪbət/ 1 *a.* unmarried, esp. for religious reasons; abstaining from sexual relations. 2 *n.* unmarried person. 3 **celibacy** *n.*

**cell** /sel/ *n.* small room esp. in monastery or prison; cavity or compartment in honeycomb etc.; *Biol.* unit of structure of organic matter; portion of protoplasm usu. enclosed in membrane; group as nucleus of political activity; vessel containing electrodes for current-generation or electrolysis.

**cellar** /ˈselə(r)/ *n.* underground room for storage etc.; wine-cellar, stock of wines.

**cello** /ˈtʃeləʊ/ *n.* (*pl.* -**os**) bass instrument like large violin, held upright on floor by seated player. **cellist** *n.*

**Cellophane** /ˈseləfeɪn/ *n.* (**P**) tough glossy transparent wrapping-material.

**cellular** /ˈseljələ(r)/ *a.* of or having or consisting of cells; porous, of open texture. **cellularity** *n.*

**celluloid** /ˈseljəlɔɪd/ *n.* plastic made from cellulose nitrate and camphor.

**cellulose** /ˈseljələʊs/ *n.* main chief constituent of cell-walls of plants; derivative of this used in making rayon, plastics, glossy paints, etc.

**Celsius** /ˈselsɪəs/ *a.* Centigrade.

**Celt** /kelt/ *n.* member of one of ancient peoples of W. Europe or of peoples speaking languages related to those of ancient Gauls.

**Celtic** /ˈkeltɪk/ 1 *a.* of the Celts. 2 *n.* group of languages spoken by Celtic peoples.

**cement** /səˈment/ 1 *n.* substance of lime and clay that sets like stone after mixing with water; adhesive material. 2 *v.t.* apply cement to; unite firmly; substance for filling cavities in teeth.

**cemetery** /ˈsemətərɪ/ *n.* burial ground, esp. one not in churchyard.

**cenotaph** /ˈsenətɑːf/ *n.* monument to person(s) whose remains are elsewhere.

**censer** /ˈsensə(r)/ *n.* incense-burning vessel.

**censor** /ˈsensə(r)/ 1 *n.* official with power to suppress whole or parts of books, plays, films, news, letters, etc. on grounds of obscenity, threat to security, etc. 2 *v.t.* act as censor of; make deletions or changes in. 3 **censorial** *a.*; **censorship** *n.*

**censorious** /senˈsɔːrɪəs/ *a.* severely critical.

**censure** /ˈsenʃə(r)/ 1 *n.* expression of disapproval or blame. 2 *v.t.* criticize harshly; reprove.

**census** /ˈsensəs/ *n.* official count of population.

**cent** /sent/ *n.* hundredth part of dollar or other metric unit of currency.

**centaur** /ˈsentɔː(r)/ *n. Gk. Myth.* creature with head, arms, and trunk of man joined to body and legs of horse.

**centenarian** /sentəˈneərɪən/ 1 *n.* person 100 or more years old. 2 *a.* of 100 years.

**centenary** /senˈtiːnərɪ/ 1 *n.* 100th anniversary. 2 *a.* of 100 years; of a centenary.

**centennial** /sen'teniːəl/ 1 *a.* lasting for or occurring every 100 years. 2 *n.* centenary.

**centigrade** /'sentəgreɪd/ *a.* pertaining to scale of temperature on which water freezes at 0° and boils at 100°.

**centigram** /'sentəgræm/ *n.* hundredth part of gram.

**centilitre** /'sentəliːtə(r)/ *n.* hundredth part of litre.

**centime** /'sɑ̃tiːm/ *n.* hundredth part of franc.

**centimetre** /'sentəmiːtə(r)/ *n.* hundredth part of metre.

**centipede** /'sentəpiːd/ *n.* small crawling creature with long body and many legs.

**central** /'sentr(ə)l/ *a.* of, in, at, etc. centre; leading, principal. **central bank** national bank issuing currency etc.; **central heating** heating of building from central source. **centrally** *adv.*

**centralize** /'sentrəlaɪz/ *v.t.* concentrate (administration etc.) at single centre; subject (State etc.) to this system. **centralization** *n.*

**centre** /'sentə(r)/ 1 *n.* middle point or part; place or group of buildings forming central point in district etc. or main area for activity etc.; point of concentration or dispersion; political party holding moderate opinions. 2 *v.* concentrate or be concentrated *in, on, at,* etc.; place in centre. 3 **the Centre** *Aus.* Central Australia; **centre-forward, centre-half,** *Footb.* etc. middle player in forward, half-back, line; **centre of gravity** point about which the mass of an object is evenly distributed; **centre-piece** ornament for middle of table, main item; **centre spread** two facing middle pages of magazine etc.

**centrifugal** /sen'trɪfjʊg(ə)l/ *a.* moving or tending to move from centre. **centrifugal force** force with which body revolving round centre seems to tend from it. **centrifugally** *adv.*

**centrifuge** /'sentrəfjuːdʒ/ *n.* machine using centrifugal force for separating e.g. cream from milk.

**centripetal** /sen'trɪpɪt(ə)l/ *a.* moving or tending to move towards centre.

**centrist** /'sentrɪst/ *n.* person, party, etc. holding moderate views. **centrism** *n.*

**centurion** /sen'tjʊəriːən/ *n.* commander of century in ancient Roman army.

**century** /'sentjəriː/ *n.* 100 years; *Crick.* 100 runs in one batsman's innings; company in ancient Roman army.

**cephalic** /sɪ'fælɪk/ *a.* of or in head.

**cephalopod** /'sefələpɒd/ *n.* mollusc with tentacles attached to head, e.g. octopus.

**ceramic** /sə'ræmɪk/ 1 *a.* of pottery, porcelain or other items of baked clay. 2 *n.* pottery etc. article.

**ceramics** *n.pl.* pottery collectively; (usu. treated as *sing.*) ceramic art.

**cereal** /'sɪəriːəl/ 1 *a.* of edible grain. 2 *n.* any kind of grain used as food; breakfast food made from cereal.

**cerebellum** /serə'beləm/ *n.* smaller part of brain.

**cerebral** /'serəbr(ə)l/ *a.* of brain; intellectual.

**cerebration** /serə'breɪʃ(ə)n/ *n.* working of brain.

**cerebro-spinal** /serəbrəʊ'spaɪn(ə)l/ *a.* of brain and spinal cord.

**cerebrum** /'serəbrəm/ *n.* principal part of brain.

**ceremonial** /serə'məʊniːəl/ 1 *a.* with or of ceremony, formal. 2 *n.* system of rites or ceremonies.

**ceremonious** /serə'məʊniːəs/ *a.* fond of or characterized by ceremony, formal.

**ceremony** /'serəməniː/ *n.* piece of formal procedure; religious rite; observance of formalities; punctilious behaviour; **stand (up)on ceremony** insist on formalities.

**cerise** /sə'riːz/ *n.* & *a.* light clear red.

**cert** /sɜːt/ *n. sl.* event or result certain to happen; horse sure to win.

**certain** /'sɜːt(ə)n/ *a.* settled, unfailing, unerring; reliable; indisputable; convinced, sure; particular but not named; some.

**certainly** /'sɜːtənliː/ *adv.* no doubt, yes, I admit it.

**certainty** /'sɜːtəntiː/ *n.* undoubted fact; absolute conviction.

**certificate** 1 /sə'tɪfəkət/ *n.* document formally attesting fact. 2 /sə'tɪfəkeɪt/ *v.t.* furnish with certificate. 3 **certification** *n.*

**certify** /'sɜːtəfaɪ/ *v.t.* declare by certificate, make formal statement of; officially declare insane. **certifiable** *a.*

# certitude

**certitude** /'sɜ:tɪtju:d/ n. feeling certain.

**cerulean** /sə'ru:lɪən/ a. sky-blue.

**cervical** /sə'vaɪk(ə)l/ a. of cervix. **cervical smear** smear taken from cervix to test for cancer.

**cervix** /'sɜ:vɪks/ n. (pl. **-vices** /-vəsi:z/) Anat. neck; neck-like structure, esp. neck of womb.

**cessation** /se'seɪʃ(ə)n/ n. ceasing.

**cession** /'seʃ(ə)n/ n. ceding.

**cesspit** /'sespɪt/ n. pit for liquid waste or sewage.

**cesspool** /'sespu:l/ n. cesspit.

**cetacean** /sɪ'teɪʃ(ə)n/ 1 n. member of order of mammals including whales. 2 a. of cetaceans.

**cf.** abbr. compare.

**cg.** abbr. centigram(s).

**CH** abbr. Companion of Honour.

**Chablis** /'ʃæbli:/ n. kind of dry white wine.

**chaconne** /ʃæ'kɒn/ n. piece of music on ground bass; dance to this.

**chafe** /tʃeɪf/ 1 v. rub (skin etc.) to restore warmth; make or become sore by rubbing; irritate; show irritation, fret. 2 n. sore caused by rubbing.

**chafer** /'tʃeɪfə(r)/ n. large slow-moving beetle.

**chaff** /tʃɑ:f/ 1 n. separated grain-husks; chopped hay or straw; worthless stuff; good-humoured teasing. 2 v.t. banter, tease.

**chaffer** /'tʃæfə(r)/ v.i. bargain, haggle.

**chaffinch** /'tʃæfɪntʃ/ n. a common European finch.

**chafing-dish** /'tʃeɪfɪŋ/ n. vessel in which food is cooked or kept warm at table.

**chagrin** /'ʃægrɪn/ 1 n. acute vexation or mortification. 2 v.t. affect with this.

**chain** 1 n. series of links; sequence, connected series (of proof, events, mountains, etc.); in pl. fetters, restraining force; measure of length (66 ft.). 2 v.t. secure with chain. 3 **chain-gang** convicts chained together at work etc.; **chain-mail** armour made from interlaced rings; **chain reaction** reaction forming products which themselves cause further reactions, fig. series of events each due to previous one; **chain-saw** one with teeth on loop of chain; **chain-smoke** smoke continuously, esp. by lighting next cigarette etc. from previous one; **chain store** one of series of shops owned by one firm and selling same class of goods.

**chair** 1 n. movable backed seat for one; seat of authority; (office of) chairman; professorship; sedan-chair. 2 v.t. install in chair of authority; conduct (meeting) as chairman; carry aloft in honour. 3 **chair-lift** series of chairs on loop of cable for carrying passengers up mountain etc.; **chairman**, **chairperson**, **chairwoman**, person who presides over meeting or board or committee.

**chaise** /ʃeɪz/ n. light open carriage for one or two persons.

*chaise longue* /ʃeɪz 'lɒŋg/ kind of chair with seat long enough to support sitter's legs.

**chalcedony** /tʃæl'sedəni:/ n. precious stone of quartz kind.

**chalet** /'ʃæleɪ/ n. Swiss hut or cottage; small villa; small cabin in holiday camp etc.

**chalice** /'tʃælɪs/ n. goblet; cup used in Eucharist.

**chalk** /tʃɔ:k/ 1 n. white soft limestone; this or similar white or coloured substance used for drawing, writing on blackboard, etc. 2 v. mark, draw, write, rub, etc. with chalk. 3 **chalky** a.

**challenge** /'tʃæləndʒ/ 1 n. call to take part in contest etc. or to prove or justify something; demanding or difficult task; calling to respond, esp. sentry's call for password etc. 2 v.t. call to respond; take exception to; dispute; summon to contest.

**chamber** /'tʃeɪmbə(r)/ n. assembly hall, the council etc. that meets in it; one of the houses of a parliament or its debating-room; judge's room for hearing cases not needing to be taken in court; cavity or compartment in body, machinery, etc., esp. part of gun that contains charge; room, esp. bedroom. **chambermaid** woman employed to clean bedrooms in hotel etc.; **chamber music** music for small group of instruments; **chamber-pot** vessel for urine etc. used in bedroom.

**chamberlain** /'tʃeɪmbələn/ n. officer managing royal or noble household; treasurer of corporation etc.

**chameleon** /kə'mi:lɪən/ n. lizard able to change colour to suit surroundings.

## chamfer

**chamfer** /'tʃæmfə(r)/ 1 *v.t.* bevel symmetrically. 2 *n.* surface so made.
**chamois** /'ʃæmwa:/ *n.* small mountain antelope; (/'ʃæmi:/) soft leather from sheep, goats, etc.
**champ**¹ 1 *v.* munch or bite noisily or vigorously. 2 *n.* noise of champing. 3 **champ at the bit** *fig.* show impatience.
**champ**² *n. sl.* champion.
**champagne** /ʃæm'peɪn/ *n.* white sparkling wine from Champagne in France.
**champion** /'tʃæmpɪən/ 1 *n.* person or thing that has defeated all competitors; person who fights for another or for cause. 2 *a.* that is a champion; *colloq.* first-class. 3 *v.t.* support cause of, defend.
**championship** *n.* contest to decide champion in sport etc.; position of this.
**chance** /tʃa:ns or tʃæns/ 1 *n.* way things happen; absence of design or discoverable cause; opportunity, possibility. 2 *a.* due to chance. 3 *v.* happen; risk.
**chancel** /tʃa:ns(ə)l or tʃæns(ə)l/ *n.* part of church near altar.
**chancellery** /'tʃa:nsələri or 'tʃæns-/ *n.* chancellor's department or staff or residence; office attached to embassy.
**chancellor** /'tʃa:nsələ(r) or 'tʃæns-/ *n.* (in UK, Germany, etc.) State or law official; non-resident head of university.
**Chancery** /'tʃa:nsəri/ *n. UK* division of High Court of Justice.
**chancy** /'tʃa:nsi: or 'tʃænsi:/ *a.* risky.
**chandelier** /ʃændə'lɪə(r)/ *n.* branched hanging support for lights.
**chandler** /'tʃa:ndlə(r) or 'tʃændlə(r)/ *n.* dealer in supplies for ships; dealer in candles. **chandlery** *n.*
**change** /tʃeɪndʒ/ 1 *n.* making or becoming different; substitution of one for another; variation; money in small coins; money returned as balance of that tendered in payment; one of different orders in which bells can be rung. 2 *v.* make or become different; alter; take or use another instead of; interchange, exchange; put on other clothes; give or get money change for; put fresh clothes, coverings, etc., on. 3 **change hands** pass to different owner. 4 **changeful** *a.*; **changeless** *a.*

## chapter

**changeable** /'tʃeɪndʒəb(ə)l/ *a.* liable to change; inconstant. **changeability** *n.*
**changeling** /'tʃeɪndʒlɪŋ/ *n.* child believed to have been substituted for another child.
**channel** /'tʃæn(ə)l/ 1 *n.* bed in which water runs; navigable part of waterway; piece of water connecting two seas; passage for liquid; groove; medium of communication, agency; narrow band of frequencies used for radio and esp. television transmission; path for transmitted electrical signal or data. 2 *v.* form channels in; guide, direct.
**chant** /tʃa:nt or tʃænt/ 1 *n.* song; melody for reciting unmetrical texts. 2 *v.* sing; intone, sing to chant; utter rhythmically.
**chanter** /'tʃa:ntə(r) or 'tʃæntə(r)/ *n.* melody-pipe of bagpipes.
**chantry** /'tʃa:ntri: or 'tʃæntri:/ *n.* endowment for singing of masses for founder's soul; chapel or priests so endowed.
**chaos** /'keɪɒs/ *n.* utter confusion; formless primordial matter. **chaotic** /keɪ'ɒtɪk/ *a.*
**chap**¹ *n. colloq.* fellow; boy.
**chap**² 1 *v.* (of skin etc.) develop cracks or soreness; (of wind etc.) cause this. 2 *n.* crack in skin etc.
**chap**³ *n.* lower jaw or half of cheek, esp. of pig as food.
**chaparral** /ʃæpə'ræl/ *n. US* dense tangled brushwood.
**chapel** /'tʃæp(ə)l/ *n.* place of worship attached to institution or private house; separate part of cathedral or church with its own altar; place of worship of Nonconformist bodies; association or meeting of workers in printing-office.
**chaperon** /'ʃæpərəʊn/ 1 *n.* older woman in charge of young unmarried woman on certain social occasions. 2 *v.t.* act as chaperon to. 3 **chaperonage** *n.*
**chaplain** /'tʃæplən/ *n.* clergyman of institution, private chapel, ship, regiment, etc. **chaplaincy** *n.*
**chaplet** /'tʃæplɪt/ *n.* wreath or circlet for head; string of beads, short rosary.
**chapter** /'tʃæptə(r)/ *n.* division of book; period of time; canons of cathedral etc.; meeting of these.

**char**¹ v. scorch or blacken with fire; burn to charcoal.

**char**² 1 n. charwoman. 2 v.t. work as charwoman.

**character** /'kærəktə(r)/ n. distinguishing quality or qualities; mental or moral qualities; reputation; odd or eccentric person; person in novel, play, etc.; letter, sign; testimonial.

**characteristic** /kærəktə'rıstık/ 1 a. typical or distinctive. 2 n. characteristic feature or quality.

**characterize** /'kærəktəraız/ v.t. describe *as*; be characteristic of. **characterization** n.

**charade** /ʃə'rɑːd/ n. game of guessing word from acted clues; absurd pretence.

**charcoal** /'tʃɑːkəʊl/ n. black porous residue of partly burnt wood etc.

**chard** n. kind of beet with edible leaves and stalks.

**charge** 1 n. price; expense; accusation; exhortation; task, duty; care, custody; thing or person entrusted; appropriate quantity of material to put into receptacle, mechanism, etc. at one time, esp. of explosive for gun; quantity of electricity carried by body. 2 v. ask (amount) as price; ask (person) for amount as price; make debit cost of to; make accusation *that*; instruct or urge; entrust *with*; attack or rush impetuously; load or fill with charge of explosive etc.; fill (*with*). 3 **charge-sheet** record of charges made at police station; **charge with** accuse of; **in charge** having command.

**chargeable** /'tʃɑːdʒəb(ə)l/ a. capable of being charged *to* particular account.

**chargé d'affaires** /ʃɑːʒeɪ dæ'feə/ (*pl.* **-gés** *pr.* same) ambassador's deputy; ambassador to minor government.

**charger** /'tʃɑːdʒə(r)/ n. cavalry-horse; apparatus for charging battery.

**chariot** /'tʃærɪət/ n. *hist.* two-wheeled vehicle used in ancient fighting and racing.

**charioteer** /tʃærɪə'tɪə(r)/ n. chariot-driver.

**charisma** /kə'rɪzmə/ n. capacity to inspire followers or disciples with devotion and enthusiasm; divine gift or talent. **charismatic** /kærɪz'mætɪk/ a.

**charitable** /'tʃærɪtəb(ə)l/ a. having or marked by charity; of or connected with charity.

**charity** /'tʃærɪtɪ/ n. giving voluntarily to those in need or distress; leniency in judging others; institution or organization for helping those in need, help so given; love of fellow men.

**charlatan** /'ʃɑːlət(ə)n/ n. person falsely claiming knowledge or skill. **charlatanism** n.

**charlock** /'tʃɑːlɒk/ n. field mustard.

**charlotte** /'ʃɑːlət/ n. pudding of cooked fruit under bread-crumbs etc.

**charm** 1 n. power of giving delight; usu. in *pl.* quality or feature that arouses admiration, fascination, attractiveness; speech or action or object supposedly having occult power. 2 v.t. delight, captivate; influence or protect by magic.

**charming** /'tʃɑːmɪŋ/ a. delightful.

**charnel-house** /'tʃɑːn(ə)l/ n. place containing corpses or bones.

**chart** 1 n. map esp. for sea or air navigation or showing weather conditions etc.; sheet of information in form of tables or diagrams; list of currently most popular gramophone records. 2 v.t. make chart of.

**charter** /'tʃɑːtə(r)/ 1 n. written grant of rights esp. by sovereign or legislature; written description of organization's functions etc. 2 v.t. grant charter to; hire (aircraft etc.) for one's own use. 3 **charter flight** flight by chartered aircraft.

**chartered** a. having royal charter; belonging to chartered body.

**Chartism** /'tʃɑːtɪz(ə)m/ n. UK working-class reform movement of 1837–48. **Chartist** n.

**chartreuse** /ʃɑː'trɜːz/ n. green or yellow brandy liqueur.

**charwoman** /'tʃɑːwʊmən/ n. (*pl.* **-women** /-wɪmən/) woman hired by day or hour for housework.

**chary** /'tʃeərɪ/ a. cautious; sparing *of*.

**chase**¹ /tʃeɪs/ 1 v. pursue, drive; hurry; *colloq.* try to attain. 2 n. pursuit; unenclosed parkland.

**chase**² /tʃeɪs/ v.t. emboss or engrave (metal).

**chaser** n. horse for steeplechasing; *colloq.* drink taken after another of different kind.

**chasm** /kæz(ə)m/ *n.* deep cleft, gulf, fissure; wide difference.

**chassis** /'ʃæsi:/ *n.* base-frame of motor-car, carriage, etc.

**chaste** /tʃeɪst/ *a.* abstaining from extramarital or from all sexual intercourse; pure in taste or style, unadorned.

**chasten** /'tʃeɪs(ə)n/ *v.t.* discipline by inflicting suffering, restrain.

**chastise** /tʃæs'taɪz/ *v.t.* punish, beat. **chastisement** *n.*

**chastity** /'tʃæstəti/ *n.* being chaste.

**chasuble** /'tʃæzjəb(ə)l/ *n.* sleeveless vestment worn by celebrant of Mass or Eucharist.

**chat** 1 *v.i.* talk in light familiar way. 2 *n.* informal talk.

**chateau** /'ʃætəʊ/ *n.* (*pl.* -teaux /-təʊz/) large French country-house.

**chatelaine** /'ʃætəleɪn/ *n.* mistress of country house.

**chattel** /'tʃæt(ə)l/ *n.* usu. in *pl.* movable possession.

**chatter** /'tʃætə(r)/ 1 *v.* talk fast, incessantly, or foolishly. 2 *n.* such talk.

**chatty** /'tʃæti/ *a.* fond of or resembling chat.

**chauffeur** /'ʃəʊfə(r)/ *n.* person employed to drive private or hired car.

**chauvinism** /'ʃəʊvɪnɪz(ə)m/ *n.* exaggerated patriotism; excessive or prejudiced support or loyalty for something. **chauvinist** *n.*; **chauvinistic** *a.*

**cheap** *a.* low in price; charging low prices; easily got; of little account.

**cheapen** /'tʃi:pən/ *v.* make or become cheap; degrade.

**cheapjack** /'tʃi:pdʒæk/ *a.* shoddy.

**cheat** 1 *v.* trick, deceive; deprive *of* by deceit; act fraudulently. 2 *n.* swindler; unfair player; deception.

**check** 1 *n.* sudden stopping or slowing of motion; pause; rebuff; restraint; means of testing or ensuring accuracy etc.; pattern of cross-lines forming squares; fabric so patterned; *US* cheque; *US* counter used in games; token of identification; (announcement of) exposure of chess king to attack. 2 *v.* stop or slow motion of, restrain; test, examine, verify; *US* agree on comparison; threaten (opponent's king) at chess. 3 **check in** register at hotel or airport or workplace etc.; **check out** leave hotel or airport etc. with formalities; **check-out** pay-desk in supermarket etc.; **check-up** careful (esp. medical) examination.

**checked** *a.* having a check pattern.

**checker** var. of **chequer**.

**checkmate** /'tʃekmeɪt/ 1 *n.* check at chess from which there is no escape; final defeat. 2 *v.t.* put into checkmate; frustrate.

**cheddar** /'tʃedə(r)/ *n.* kind of firm smooth cheese.

**cheek** 1 *n.* side of face below eye; impertinent speech, effrontery; *sl.* buttocks. 2 *v.t.* address impudently.

**cheeky** /'tʃi:ki/ *a.* impertinent, saucy.

**cheep** 1 *n.* shrill feeble note as of young bird. 2 *v.i.* make such cry.

**cheer** 1 *n.* shout of encouragement or applause; *arch.* mood, disposition. 2 *v.* urge *on* by shouts etc.; applaud; shout for joy; comfort, gladden. 3 **cheer up** make or become happier.

**cheerful** /'tʃɪəfəl/ *a.* in good spirits; bright, pleasant; not reluctant. **cheerfully** *adv.*

**cheerio** /tʃɪərɪ'əʊ/ *n.* (*pl.* **-rios**) *Aus.* & *NZ* small cocktail sausage.

**cheerless** /'tʃɪəlɪs/ *a.* gloomy, dreary.

**cheery** /'tʃɪəri/ *a.* lively, genial.

**cheese** /tʃi:z/ *n.* food made from pressed curds; cake etc. of this within rind; thick conserve of fruit. **cheeseburger** hamburger with cheese in or on it; **cheesecake** tart filled with sweetened curds, *sl.* display of shapely female body in advertisement etc.; **cheesecloth** loosely-woven cotton fabric; **cheesed off** *sl.* bored, fed up; **cheese-paring** stingy, stinginess; **cheesewood** Aus. tree with hard yellowish wood, its wood. **cheesy** *a.*

**cheetah** /'tʃi:tə/ *n.* swift-running spotted feline resembling leopard.

**chef** /ʃef/ *n.* cook, esp. head cook, in hotel etc.

**chemical** /'kemɪk(ə)l/ 1 *a.* of, made by, or employing chemistry. 2 *n.* substance obtained by or used in chemistry. 3 **chemical warfare** warfare involving use of poison gas or other chemicals. 4 **chemically** *adv.*

**chemise** /ʃə'mi:z/ *n.* woman's loose-fitting undergarment or dress.

**chemist** /'kemɪst/ *n.* dealer in medical drugs; person skilled in chemistry.

**chemistry** /'kemɪstri/ *n.* science of

## chenille

elements and their laws of combination and change.

**chenille** /ʃəˈniːl/ n. tufted velvety yarn; fabric made of this.

**cheque** /tʃek/ n. written order to bank to pay sum of money; printed form for this. **cheque-book** book of forms for writing cheques.

**chequer** /ˈtʃekə(r)/ 1 n. (often in pl.) pattern of squares often alternately coloured; US in pl. game of draughts. 2 v.t. mark with chequers, variegate; break uniformity of; (in p.p.) with varied fortunes.

**cherish** /ˈtʃerɪʃ/ v.t. tend lovingly; hold dear; cling to.

**cheroot** /ʃəˈruːt/ n. kind of cigar made with both ends open.

**cherry** /ˈtʃeri/ 1 n. small stone-fruit, tree bearing it, wood of this; light red. 2 a. of light red colour.

**cherub** /ˈtʃerəb/ n. (pl. **cherubim** or **cherubs**) angelic being; beautiful child. **cherubic** /-ˈruːb-/ a.

**chervil** /ˈtʃɜːvəl/ n. garden herb with aniseed flavour.

**chess** n. game for two players with 32 **chessmen** on chequered **chessboard** of 64 squares.

**chest** n. large box, esp. for storage or transport; part of body enclosed by ribs, front surface of body from neck to waist; small cabinet for medicines etc. **chest of drawers** piece of furniture with set of drawers in frame.

**chesterfield** /ˈtʃestəfiːld/ n. sofa with padded seat, back, and ends.

**chestnut** /ˈtʃesnʌt/ n. glossy hard brown edible nut (**sweet chestnut**); horse-chestnut; deep reddish-brown; horse of this colour; stale anecdote. 2 a. chestnut-coloured.

**chesty** /ˈtʃesti/ a. colloq. inclined to or symptomatic of chest disease. **chestily** adv. **chestiness** n.

**cheval-glass** /ʃəˈvælɡlɑːs/ n. tall mirror swung on upright frame.

**chevalier** /ʃevəˈlɪə(r)/ n. member of certain orders of knighthood etc.

**chevron** /ˈʃevrən/ n. V-shaped mark of rank or long service on uniform sleeve.

**chew** 1 v. work (food etc.) between teeth; crush or indent thus; meditate *on*; ruminate *over*. 2 n. act of chewing; thing for chewing. 3 **chewing-gum** flavoured gum for prolonged chewing.

## chihuahua

**chewy** /ˈtʃuːi/ a. suitable for or requiring chewing.

**chez** /ʃeɪ/ prep. at the house or home of. [F]

**chiack** /ˈtʃaɪæk/ Aus. sl. 1. v.t. jeer at, tease. 2 n. jeering, cheek.

**Chianti** /kiˈænti:/ n. dry usu. red Italian wine.

**chiaroscuro** /kiɑːrəˈskʊərəʊ/ n. treatment of light and shade in painting; use of contrast in literature etc.

**chic** /ʃiːk/ 1 n. stylishness, elegance, in dress. 2 a. stylish, elegant.

**chicane** /ʃɪˈkeɪn/ 1 v. use chicanery, cheat. 2 n. chicanery; artificial barrier or obstacle on motor-racing course.

**chicanery** /ʃɪˈkeɪnəri/ n. trickery; clever but misleading talk; deception.

**chick** n. young bird; sl. young woman.

**chicken** /ˈtʃɪkən/ 1 n. young bird, esp. of domestic fowl; flesh of domestic fowl as food; youthful person. 2 a. cowardly. 3 v.i. (usu. with *out*) sl. withdraw through cowardice. 4 **chicken-feed** food for poultry, colloq. insignificant amount esp. of money. **chicken-pox** infectious disease with rash of small blisters.

**chick-pea** /ˈtʃɪkpiː/ n. dwarf pea with knobby yellow seeds.

**chickweed** /ˈtʃɪkwiːd/ n. a small weed.

**chicle** /ˈtʃɪk(ə)l/ n. juice of tropical S. Amer. tree, chiefly used in chewing-gum.

**chicory** /ˈtʃɪkəri/ n. salad plant; its root, roasted and ground and used with or instead of coffee.

**chide** v. (past **chid** or **chided**; p.p. **chidden** or **chid**) rebuke, scold.

**chief** /tʃiːf/ 1 n. leader or ruler; head of tribe or clan; head of department etc. 2 a. first in importance or influence; prominent, leading.

**chiefly** /ˈtʃiːfli/ adv. above all; mainly but not exclusively.

**chieftain** /ˈtʃiːftən/ n. chief of clan, tribe, or other group. **chieftaincy** n.

**chiffon** /ˈʃɪfɒn/ n. diaphanous silky fabric.

**chigger** /ˈtʃɪɡə(r)/ n. var. of **chigoe**.

**chignon** /ˈʃiːnjɔ̃/ n. large coil or plait etc. of hair at back of head.

**chigoe** /ˈtʃɪɡəʊ/ n. tropical flea that burrows into skin.

**chihuahua** /tʃəˈwɑːwə/ n. tiny short-haired orig. Mexican dog.

**chilblain** /'tʃɪlbleɪn/ n. itching swelling on hand or foot etc. caused by exposure to cold.

**child** /tʃaɪld/ n. (pl. **children** /'tʃɪldrən/) young human being; one's son or daughter; descendant, follower, or product (of). **childbirth** process of giving birth to child; **child's play** easy task.

**childhood** /'tʃaɪldhʊd/ n. state or period of being a child.

**childish** /'tʃaɪldɪʃ/ a. of or like child; immature, silly.

**childlike** /'tʃaɪldlaɪk/ a. innocent, frank, etc., like child.

**chili** var. of **chilli**.

**chill** 1 n. cold sensation; feverish cold; unpleasant coldness of air etc.; depressing influence. 2 a. chilly. 3 v. make or become cold; depress, dispirit; preserve (food) at low temperature without freezing.

**chilli** /'tʃɪli:/ n. hot-tasting pod of kind of capsicum.

**chilly** /'tʃɪli/ a. rather cold; sensitive to cold; cold-mannered.

**chime** 1 n. set of attuned bells; sounds made by this. 2 v. (of bells) ring; show (hour) by chiming; be in agreement; join in.

**chimera** /kaɪ'mɪərə/ n. bogy; wild impossible scheme or fancy. **chimerical** /kɪ'merɪk(ə)l/ a.

**chimney** /'tʃɪmni:/ n. structure by which smoke or steam is carried off; part of this above roof; glass tube protecting lamp-flame. **chimney-breast** projecting wall round chimney; **chimney-pot** pipe at top of chimney; **chimney-sweep** person who clears chimneys of soot.

**chimpanzee** /tʃɪmpæn'zi:/ n. manlike African ape.

**chin** n. front of lower jaw. **chin-wag** n. & v.i. sl. talk.

**china** /'tʃaɪnə/ n. fine semi-transparent or white earthenware, porcelain; things made of this. **china clay** kaolin.

**Chinaman** /'tʃaɪnəmən/ n. (pl. **-men**) arch. a Chinese.

**chinchilla** /tʃɪn'tʃɪlə/ n. small S. Amer. rodent; its soft grey fur; breed of domestic cat or rabbit.

**chine** 1 v.t. cut or slit along or across chine. 2 n. backbone; joint of meat from backbone; hill-ridge.

**Chinese** /tʃaɪ'ni:z/ 1 n. native or language of China; person of Chinese descent. 2 a. of China. 3 **Chinese lantern** collapsible lantern of coloured paper, plant with inflated orange calyx.

**chink**[1] n. narrow opening.

**chink**[2] 1 n. sound as of glasses or coins striking together. 2 v. (cause to) make chink.

**chintz** n. colour-printed usu. glazed cotton cloth.

**chip** 1 v. cut or break (off) at surface or edge; shape thus; suffer chipping; cut (potato) into chips. 2 n. piece chipped off; chipped place; long slender piece of potato fried; US in pl. potato crisps; counter used in game of chance; microchip. 3 **chipboard** board made of compressed wood chips; **chip-heater** Aus. domestic water-heater that burns chips of wood.

**chipmunk** /'tʃɪpmʌŋk/ n. N. Amer. striped animal like squirrel.

**chipolata** /tʃɪpə'lɑ:tə/ n. kind of thin sausage.

**chiropody** /kə'rɒpədi:/ n. treatment of feet and their ailments. **chiropodist** n.

**chiropractic** /kaɪərə'præktɪk/ n. treatment of physical disorders by manipulation of spinal column. **chiropractor** n.

**chirp** 1 n. short sharp thin note as of small bird. 2 v. emit chirp(s); express thus; talk merrily.

**chirpy** /'tʃɜ:pi/ a. cheerful.

**chirrup** /'tʃɪrəp/ 1 n. series of chirps. 2 v.i. emit chirrup.

**chisel** /'tʃɪz(ə)l/ 1 n. tool with bevelled sharp end for shaping wood, stone, or metal. 2 v.t (past & p.p. **chiselled**) cut or shape with chisel; sl. defraud.

**chit**[1] n. young child, little woman.

**chit**[2] n. written note.

**chit-chat** n. light conversation, gossip.

**chitterlings** /'tʃɪtəlɪŋz/ n.pl. smaller intestines of pig etc. as food.

**chivalry** /'ʃɪvəlri/ n. courtesy and honour, esp. shown to those weaker; medieval knightly system. **chivalrous** a.

**chive** n. herb related to onion.

**chivvy** /'tʃɪvi:/ v.t. colloq. chase, harry.

**chloral** /'klɔ:r(ə)l/ n. compound used as sedative and analgesic.

**chloride** /'klɔ:raɪd/ n. compound of chlorine with metal.

**chlorinate** /'klɔ:rəneɪt/ v.t. impregnate

**chlorine** / **chough**

or disinfect (water etc.) with chlorine. **chlorination** *n.*

**chlorine** /ˈklɔːriːn/ *n.* heavy yellowish-green gas with irritating smell and powerful bleaching and disinfecting properties.

**chloroform** /ˈklɒrəfɔːm/ 1 *n.* thin colourless liquid whose inhaled vapour produces unconsciousness. 2 *v.t.* render unconscious with this.

**chlorophyll** /ˈklɒrəfɪl/ *n.* colouring matter of green parts of plants.

**choc** *n. colloq.* chocolate. **choc-ice** bar of ice cream enclosed in chocolate.

**chock** 1 *n.* block of wood, wedge. 2 *v.t.* make fast or wedge with chocks. 3 **chock-a-block** jammed together, crammed *with*; **chock-full** crammed full (*of*).

**chocolate** /ˈtʃɒkələt/ 1 *n.* edible substance made as paste or powder or solid block etc., from ground cacao seeds; sweet made of or covered with this; hot drink made from chocolate; dark brown colour. 2 *a.* flavoured with chocolate; chocolate-coloured.

**choice** 1 *n.* act or power of choosing; variety to choose from; thing or person chosen. 2 *a.* of special quality.

**choir** /kwaɪə(r)/ *n.* group of trained singers; chancel in large church. **choirboy** boy singer in church choir.

**choke** 1 *v.* stop breath of, suffocate; suffer such stoppage; block up. 2 *n.* valve in petrol engine controlling inflow of air; *Electr.* device for smoothing variations of current.

**choker** /ˈtʃəʊkə(r)/ *n.* high collar; close-fitting necklace.

**choko** /ˈtʃəʊkəʊ/ *n. Aus.* succulent cucumber-like vegetable.

**choler** /ˈkɒlə(r)/ *n. arch.* anger, irascibility.

**cholera** /ˈkɒlərə/ *n.* infectious, often fatal, bacterial disease with severe intestinal symptoms.

**choleric** /ˈkɒlərɪk/ *a.* easily angered.

**cholesterol** /kəˈlestərɒl/ *n.* steroid alcohol present in human tissues.

**chook** /tʃʊk/ *n. Aus. & NZ colloq.* domestic fowl.

**choose** /tʃuːz/ *v.* (*past* **chose**; *p.p.* **chosen**) select out of greater number; decide or think fit to do; make choice (*between* or *from*).

**chop**¹ 1 *v.* cut with axe or heavy edgewise tool; mince; make chopping blow (*at*); strike (ball) with heavy edgewise blow. 2 *n.* chopping stroke; thick slice of meat usu. including rib; *Aus.* wood-chopping contest. 3 **chop up** cut into small pieces; **in for one's chop** *Aus. sl.* making the most of one's opportunities.

**chop**² *n.* usu. in *pl.* jaw of animal or person.

**chop**³ *v.i.* **chop and change** vacillate.

**chop**⁴ *n. Aus. sl.* **not much chop** not much good.

**chopper** /ˈtʃɒpə(r)/ *n.* large-bladed short axe; cleaver; *colloq.* helicopter.

**choppy** /ˈtʃɒpɪ/ *a.* (of water) breaking in short waves.

**chopstick** /ˈtʃɒpstɪk/ *n.* one of pair of sticks held in one hand used in some Asian countries to lift food to mouth.

**chop-suey** /tʃɒpˈsuːɪ/ *n.* Chinese dish of meat or fish fried with various vegetables.

**choral** /ˈkɔːr(ə)l/ *a.* of or for or sung by choir; of or with chorus.

**chorale** /kəˈrɑːl/ *n.* simple tune or hymn usu. sung in unison; group of singers.

**chord**¹ /kɔːd/ *n. Mus.* combination of notes sounded together.

**chord**² /kɔːd/ *n. Math.* straight line joining ends of arc; string of harp etc.

**chore** *n.* routine or tedious task; odd job.

**choreography** /kɒrɪˈɒɡrəfɪ/ *n.* design or arrangement of ballet or stage-dance. **choreograph** /ˈkɒr-/ *v.*; **choreographer** *n.*; **choreographic** /-ˈɡræf-/ *a.*

**chorister** /ˈkɒrɪstə(r)/ *n.* member of choir; choir-boy.

**chortle** /ˈtʃɔːt(ə)l/ *v.i. sl.* chuckle loudly.

**chorus** /ˈkɔːrəs/ 1 *n.* group of singers, choir; such group singing and dancing in opera, musical comedy, etc.; refrain of song; thing sung or said by several people at once; group of dancers and singers in ancient Greek plays and religious rites, any of its utterances. 2 *v.* speak or say or sing in chorus. 3 **in chorus** with all singing or speaking in unison.

**chose** *past* of **choose**.

**chosen** *p.p.* of **choose**.

**chough** /tʃʌf/ *n. Aus.* bird resembling magpie; *UK* red-legged crow.

## chou moellier

**chou' moellier** /tʃaʊ 'mɒliːə/, *Aus.* & *NZ* kind of kale grown as fodder.

**chow** *n.* Chinese breed of dog; *sl.* food.

**chowder** /'tʃaʊdə(r)/ *n.* soup or stew esp. of fish with bacon and onions etc.

**chow mein** /tʃaʊ 'meɪn/ *n.* Chinese dish of fried noodles usu. with shredded meat and vegetables.

**chrism** /'krɪz(ə)m/ *n.* consecrated oil.

**christen** /'krɪsən/ *v.t.* baptize and give name to; name.

**Christendom** /'krɪsəndəm/ *n.* Christians, Christian countries.

**Christian** /'krɪstʃ(ə)n/ 1 *a.* of Christ or his teaching; believing in or professing or belonging to Christian religion; charitable, kind. 2 *n.* adherent of Christianity. 3 **Christian era** era counted from birth of Christ; **Christian name** name given at christening, personal name; **Christian Science** system by which Christian faith is alleged to overcome disease without medical treatment; **Christian Scientist** adherent of this. 4 **Christianize** *v.t.*

**Christianity** /krɪsti:'ænəti:/ *n.* Christian faith or quality or character.

**Christmas** /'krɪsməs/ *n.* festival of Christ's birth celebrated on 25 Dec. **Christmas-box** small present or tip given at Christmas; **Christmas bush** *Aus.* any of several shrubs or trees flowering at Christmas; **Christmas card** card sent as Christmas greeting; **Christmas Day** 25 Dec.; **Christmas Eve** 24 Dec.; **Christmas pudding** rich boiled pudding with dried fruit; **Christmas rose** white-flowered winter-flowering hellebore; **Christmas tree** evergreen tree decorated with lights etc. at Christmas, *Aus.* Christmas bush. **Christmassy** *a.*

**chromatic** /krə'mætɪk/ *a.* of colour, in colours; *Mus.* of or having notes not belonging to prevailing key. **chromatic scale** one that proceeds by semitones. **chromatically** *adv.*

**chrome** /krəʊm/ *n.* chromium; yellow pigment got from compound of chromium.

**chromium** /'krəʊmiːəm/ *n.* metallic element used esp. in electroplating and making of stainless steel alloys.

**chromosome** /'krəʊməsəʊm/ *n. Biol.*

## church

structure occurring in pairs in cell-nucleus, carrying genes.

**chronic** /'krɒnɪk/ *a.* (of disease) lingering, long-lasting; (of patient) having chronic illness; *colloq.* bad, intense, severe.

**chronicle** /'krɒnɪk(ə)l/ 1 *n.* record of events in order of occurrence. 2 *v.t.* enter or record in chronicle.

**chronological** /krɒnə'lɒdʒɪk(ə)l/ *a.* according to order of occurrence.

**chronology** /krə'nɒlədʒiː/ *n.* science of computing dates; arrangement of events with dates.

**chronometer** /krə'nɒmətə(r)/ *n.* time-measuring instrument, esp. one unaffected by temperature changes.

**chrysalis** /'krɪsəlɪs/ *n.* pupa, esp. quiescent one of butterfly or moth; case enclosing it.

**chrysanthemum** /krə'sænθəməm/ *n.* garden plant flowering in autumn.

**chubby** /'tʃʌbiː/ *a.* plump, round-faced.

**chuck**[1] 1 *v.* fling or throw in careless manner. 2 *n.* act of chucking. 3 **the chuck** *sl.* dismissal; **chuck it** *sl.* stop; **chuck off at** *Aus. sl.* ridicule; **chuck out** expel; **chuck person under the chin** give him playful or affectionate touch there; **chuck up** abandon.

**chuck**[2] 1 *n.* part of lathe holding work; cut of beef from neck to ribs. 2 *v.t.* fix in chuck.

**chuckle** /'tʃʌk(ə)l/ 1 *n.* quiet or suppressed laugh. 2 *v.i.* emit chuckle.

**chuffed** /tʃʌft/ *a. sl.* pleased; displeased.

**chug** *v.i.* make intermittent explosive sound; progress with this.

**chukker** /'tʃʌkə(r)/ *n.* period of play in game of polo.

**chum** 1 *n. colloq.* close friend. 2 *v.i.* strike *up* friendship. 3 **chummy** *a.*

**chump** *n.* lump of wood; thick end of loin of lamb or mutton; *colloq.* foolish person.

**chunder** /'tʃʌndə(r)/ *n.* & *v.i. Aus. sl.* vomit.

**chunk** *n.* lump cut or broken off.

**chunky** /'tʃʌŋkiː/ *a.* consisting of or resembling chunks; small and sturdy.

**chunter** /'tʃʌntə(r)/ *v.i. colloq.* mutter, talk at length.

**church** *n.* building for public Christian worship; public worship; **Church** collective body of Christians, organized

Christian society; *the* clerical profession. **churchgoer** person who goes to church; **churchman** member of clergy or church; **churchwarden** elected lay representative of parish, long clay pipe; **churchyard** enclosed ground round church, esp. used for burials.

**churinga** /tʃəˈrɪŋgə/ *n. Aus.* sacred object; amulet.

**churl** *n.* bad-mannered, surly, or stingy person. **churlish** *a.*

**churn 1** *n.* butter-making vessel; large milk can. **2** *v.* agitate (milk) in churn; make (butter) in churn; stir *up* or agitate violently. **3 churn out** produce in quantity without quality.

**chute** /ʃuːt/ *n.* slide for conveying things to lower level; *colloq.* parachute. **up the chute** (*Aus. sl.*) quite wrong, confused.

**chutty** /ˈtʃʌtiː/ *n. Aus. sl.* chewing-gum.

**chutney** /ˈtʃʌtnɪ/ *n.* relish made of fruits and vinegar and spices etc.

**chyack** var. of **chiack**.

**chyle** /tʃaɪl/ *n.* milky fluid into which chyme is converted.

**chyme** /tʃaɪm/ *n.* pulp into which gastric secretion converts food.

**ciao** /tʃaʊ/ *int. colloq.* goodbye; hello.

**cicada** /sɪˈkɑːdə or səˈkeɪdə/ *n.* winged chirping insect.

**cicatrice** /ˈsɪkətrəs/ *n.* scar of healed wound.

**CID** *abbr.* Criminal Investigation Department.

**cider** /ˈsaɪdə(r)/ *n.* drink made from fermented apple-juice.

**cigar** /sɪˈgɑː(r)/ *n.* roll of tobacco-leaf for smoking.

**cigarette** /sɪgəˈret/ *n.* finely-cut tobacco etc. rolled in paper for smoking.

**cilium** /ˈsɪlɪəm/ *n.* (*pl.* **-lia**) eyelash; similar fringe on leaf or insect's wing etc.; hairlike vibrating organ on animal or vegetable tissue. **ciliary** *a.*

**cinch** /sɪntʃ/ *n. sl.* sure or easy thing; certainty.

**cinchona** /sɪŋˈkəʊnə/ *n.* S. Amer. evergreen tree; its bark which yields quinine.

**cincture** /ˈsɪŋktʃə(r)/ *n.* girdle, belt, border.

**cinder** /ˈsɪndə(r)/ *n.* residue of coal etc. after burning.

**Cinderella** /sɪndəˈrelə/ *n.* neglected or despised member of group etc.

**cine-** /smi:/ *in comb.* cinematographic.

**cine-camera** *n.* motion-picture camera.

**cinema** /ˈsɪnəmə/ *n.* theatre where motion-picture films are shown; production of these as art or industry. **cinematic** *a.*

**cinematograph** /sɪnəˈmætəgrɑːf/ *n.* apparatus for making or projecting motion-picture films. **cinematographic** *a.*; **cinematography** *n.*

**cineraria** /sɪnəˈreərɪə/ *n.* kind of flowering plant with downy leaves.

**cinerary** /ˈsɪnərərɪ/ *a.* of ashes (esp. of urn holding cremated ashes).

**cinnabar** /ˈsɪnəbɑː(r)/ *n.* red mercuric sulphide; vermilion.

**cinnamon** /ˈsɪnəmən/ *n.* spice from aromatic inner bark of SE Asian tree; this tree; yellowish-brown.

**cinquefoil** /ˈsɪŋkfɔɪl/ *n.* plant with compound leaf of 5 leaflets.

**cipher** /ˈsaɪfə(r)/ **1** *n.* secret or disguised writing, key to this; arithmetical symbol 0; person or thing of no importance; monogram. **2** *v.t.* write in cipher.

**circa** /ˈsɜːkə/ *prep.* about. [L]

**circle** /ˈsɜːk(ə)l/ **1** *n.* perfectly round plane figure; roundish enclosure, ring; curved upper tier of seats in theatre etc.; set or restricted group of people; persons grouped round centre of interest; period or cycle. **2** *v.* move in circle (*round*).

**circlet** /ˈsɜːklət/ *n.* small circle; circular band esp. as ornament.

**circuit** /ˈsɜːkɪt/ *n.* line or course or distance enclosing an area; path of electric current, apparatus through which current passes; judge's itinerary through district, such a district; chain of theatres or cinemas etc. under single management; motor-racing track; sequence of sporting events.

**circuitous** /səˈkjuːɪtəs/ *a.* roundabout, indirect.

**circuitry** /ˈsɜːkɪtrɪ/ *n.* system of electric circuits.

**circular** /ˈsɜːkjələ(r)/ **1** *a.* having form of or moving in circle; (of letter, notice) addressed to circle of persons, customers, etc. **2** *n.* circular letter or notice. **3 circular saw** rotating toothed disc for sawing wood etc. **4 circularity** *n.*

**circularize** /'sɜːkjələraɪz/ *v.t.* send circular to.

**circulate** /'sɜːkjəleɪt/ *v.* be or put in circulation; send particulars to (several people).

**circulation** /sɜːkjə'leɪʃ(ə)n/ *n.* movement from and back to starting-point, esp. movement of blood from and back to heart; transmission, distribution; number of copies of newspaper etc. sold. **circulatory** *a.*

**circumcise** /'sɜːkəmsaɪz/ *v.t.* cut off foreskin of (male person) as religious rite or surgical operation. **circumcision** /-'sɪʒ(ə)n/ *n.*

**circumference** /sə'kʌmfərəns/ *n.* line enclosing circle; distance round thing.

**circumflex** /'sɜːkəmfleks/ *n.* (in full **circumflex accent**) mark ( ˆ ) over vowel to indicate contraction or length etc.

**circumlocution** /sɜːkəmlə'kjuːʃ(ə)n/ *n.* use of many words where a few would do; evasive speech. **circumlocutory** *a.*

**circumnavigate** /sɜːkəm'nævəgeɪt/ *v.t.* sail round. **circumnavigation** *n.*; **circumnavigator** *n.*

**circumscribe** /'sɜːkəmskraɪb/ *v.t.* enclose or outline; mark or lay down limits of; confine, restrict. **circumscription** *n.*

**circumspect** /'sɜːkəmspekt/ *a.* wary, taking everything into account. **circumspection** *n.*

**circumstance** /'sɜːkəmstæns/ *n.* occurrence, fact, detail, esp. in *pl.* connected with or affecting an event etc.; in *pl.* financial condition; ceremony, fuss.

**circumstantial** /sɜːkəm'stænʃ(ə)l/ *a.* (of account, story) detailed; (of evidence) tending to establish a conclusion by reasonable inference.

**circumvent** /sɜːkəm'vent/ *v.t.* evade, outwit.

**circus** /'sɜːkəs/ *n.* travelling show of performing animals and acrobats and clowns etc.; group of persons performing in sports etc.; open space in town with streets converging on it; *hist.* arena for sports and games.

**cirrhosis** /sə'rəʊsɪs/ *n.* chronic progressive disease of liver.

**cirriped** /'sɪrəped/ *n.* marine crustacean in valved shell, e.g. barnacle.

**cirrus** /'sɪrəs/ *n.* (*pl.* **cirri** /-raɪ/) white wispy cloud.

**Cistercian** /sɪs'tɜːʃ(ə)n/ **1** *n.* monk or nun of strict Benedictine order. **2** *a.* of the Cistercians.

**cistern** /'sɪst(ə)n/ *n.* tank for water esp. supplying taps or as part of flushing lavatory; underground reservoir.

**cistus** /'sɪstəs/ *n.* flowering shrub with white or red flowers.

**citadel** /'sɪtəd(ə)l/ *n.* fortress protecting or dominating city.

**citation** /saɪ'teɪʃ(ə)n/ *n.* citing or passage cited; description of reasons for award.

**cite** *v.t.* adduce as instance; quote in support; summon at law.

**citizen** /'sɪtɪz(ə)n/ *n.* native or inhabitant *of* State; inhabitant of a city. **citizen's band** system of local intercommunication by radio. **citizenship** *n.*

**citrate** /'sɪtreɪt/ *n.* salt of citric acid.

**citric** /'sɪtrɪk/ *a.* **citric acid** sharp-tasting acid found in juice of lemon, orange, etc.

**citron** /'sɪtrən/ *n.* fruit of kind but larger; tree bearing it.

**citronella** /sɪtrə'nelə/ *n.* a fragrant oil; grass from S. Asia yielding it.

**citrus** /'sɪtrəs/ *n.* tree of group including orange, lemon, etc.; fruit of such tree.

**city** /'sɪtɪ/ *n.* important town; *Aus.* town qualified by population for city status; *UK* town created city by charter, esp. as containing cathedral; **the City** part of London governed by Lord Mayor and Corporation, business quarter of this, commercial circles.

**civet** /'sɪvət/ *n.* strong musky perfume got from **civet cat** a catlike animal of Central Africa.

**civic** /'sɪvɪk/ *a.* of city or citizenship.

**civics** *n.pl.* treated as *sing.* study of civic rights and duties.

**civil** /'sɪvəl/ *a.* of or belonging to citizens; non-military; polite, obliging; *Law* concerning private rights and not criminal offences. **civil defence** organization for protecting civilians in case of enemy action; **civil engineer** one who designs or maintains works of public utility; **civil marriage** one solemnized without religious ceremony; **Civil Servant** Public Servant; **Civil Service** Public Service; **civil war** one between sections of one State.

**civilian** /sə'vɪliːən/ 1 *n.* person not in or of armed forces. 2 *a.* of or for civilians

**civility** /sə'vɪlɪtiː/ *n.* politeness; act of politeness.

**civilization** /sɪvəlaɪ'zeɪʃ(ə)n/ *n.* advanced stage of social development; civilized conditions or society; making or becoming civlized.

**civilize** /'sɪvəlaɪz/ *v.t.* bring out of barbarism; enlighten, refine.

**cl.** *abbr.* centilitre(s).

**clack** 1 *v.i.* make sharp sound of boards struck together. 2 *n.* such sound; chatter.

**clad** *a.* clothed; provided with cladding.

**cladding** /'klædɪŋ/ *n.* protective covering or coating.

**claim** 1 *v.t.* demand as one's due; represent oneself as having; assert; deserve. 2 *n.* demand; right or title (*to*); assertion; thing (esp. land) claimed.

**claimant** /'kleɪmənt/ *n.* person making claim, esp. in lawsuit.

**clairvoyance** /kleə'vɔɪəns/ *n.* supposed faculty of seeing mentally things or events in the future or out of sight. **clairvoyant** *n.* & *a.*

**clam** 1 *n.* edible bivalve mollusc. 2 *v.i.* **clam up** become reticent.

**clamber** /'klæmbə(r)/ *v.i.* climb with help of hands or with difficulty.

**clammy** /'klæmɪ/ *a.* damp and sticky.

**clamour** /'klæmə(r)/ 1 *n.* shouting, confused noise; loud protest or demand. 2 *v.* make clamour, shout or assert. 3 **clamorous** *a.*

**clamp**[1] 1 *n.* device, esp. brace or band of iron etc., for strengthening or holding things together. 2 *v.t.* strengthen or fasten with clamp. 3 **clamp down on** become stricter about.

**clamp**[2] *n.* mound of potatoes etc. stored under straw and earth.

**clan** *n.* group of families with common ancestor, esp. in Scotland; family holding together; group with common interest. **clannish** *a.*; **clansman** *n.*

**clandestine** /klæn'destɪn/ *a.* surreptitious, secret.

**clang** 1 *n.* loud resonant metallic sound. 2 *v.i.* make clang.

**clangour** /'klæŋgə(r)/ *n.* continued clanging. **clangorous** *a.*

**clank** 1 *n.* sound as of heavy pieces of metal struck together. 2 *v.* (cause to) make clank.

**clap**[1] 1 *v.* strike palms of hands loudly together, applaud; put or place with vigour or determination; flap (wings) audibly. 2 *n.* sound or act of clapping; explosive noise, esp. of thunder; slap. 3 **clap eyes on** *colloq.* see.

**clap**[2] *n. vulg.* gonorrhoea.

**clapper** /'klæpə(r)/ *n.* tongue or striker of bell. **clapper-board** device in film-making for making sharp noise for synchronization of picture and sound.

**claptrap** /'klæptræp/ *n.* insincere or pretentious language; nonsense.

**claque** /klæk/ *n.* hired group of applauders in theatre.

**claret** /'klærət/ *n.* red Bordeaux wine.

**clarify** /'klærɪfaɪ/ *v.* make or become clear; free from obscurity or impurities. **clarification** *n.*

**clarinet** /klærə'net/ *n.* wood-wind musical instrument with single reed.

**clarion** /'klærɪən/ *n.* rousing sound, call to action.

**clarity** /'klærətiː/ *n.* clearness.

**clash** 1 *n.* loud jarring sound as of metal objects being struck together; collision, conflict; discord of colours etc. 2 *v.* (cause to) make clash; coincide awkwardly; be at variance with.

**clasp** /klɑːsp/ 1 *n.* device with interlocking parts for fastening; grip of arms or hand, embrace, handshake; bar on medal-ribbon. 2 *v.* fasten with clasp; grasp, embrace. 3 **clasp-knife** large folding knife.

**class** /klɑːs/ 1 *n.* division or order of society; any set of persons or things grouped together or differentiated from others; set of students taught together; their time of meeting; their course of instruction. 2 *v.t.* place in a class. 3 **classroom** room where class of students is taught.

**classic** /'klæsɪk/ 1 *a.* of acknowledged excellence; important; typical; of ancient Greek or Latin culture etc.; resembling this esp. in restraint and harmony; having historic associations. 2 *n.* classic writer, work, example, etc.; in *pl.* study of ancient Greek and Latin.

**classical** /'klæsɪk(ə)l/ *a.* of ancient

**classicism** /'klæsəsız(ə)m/ n. following of classic style; classical scholarship. **classicist** n.

**classify** /'klæsəfaɪ/ v.t. arrange in classes; class; designate as officially secret. **classification** n.; **classificatory** a.

**classy** /'klɑːsiː/ a. sl. superior. **classiness** n.

**clatter** /'klætə(r)/ 1 n. sound as of hard objects struck together or falling; noisy talk. 2 v. make clatter; fall etc. with clatter.

**clause** /klɔːz/ n. single statement in treaty or law or contract etc.; *Gram.* distinct part of sentence, including subject and predicate.

**claustrophobia** /ˌklɔːstrəˈfəʊbɪə/ n. morbid dread of confined places.

**claustrophobic** /ˌklɔːstrəˈfəʊbɪk/ a. suffering from or inducing claustrophobia.

**clavichord** /'klævɪkɔːd/ n. earliest stringed keyboard instrument.

**clavicle** /'klævɪk(ə)l/ n. collarbone.

**claw** 1 n. pointed nail of animal's or bird's foot; foot armed with claws; pincers of shellfish; device for grappling, holding, etc. 2 v. scratch or maul or pull with claws or fingernails.

**clay** n. stiff sticky earth, used esp. for bricks, pottery, etc. **clay-pan** *Aus.* natural hollow in clay soil retaining water after rain; **clay pigeon** breakable disc thrown into air as target for shooting. **clayey** a.

**clean** 1 a. free from dirt; unsoiled; preserving what is regarded as original state; free from obscenity or indecency; clear-cut; attentive to cleaness. 2 adv. completely; simply; in a clean manner. 3 v. make or become clean. 4 n. process of cleaning. 5 **clean-cut** sharply outlined; **clean out** clean thoroughly, empty or deprive (esp. sl. of money); **clean-shaven** without beard or moustache; **cleanskin** *Aus.* unbranded animal; **clean up** sl. acquire as profit, make profit.

**cleanly**[1] /'kliːnlɪ/ adv. in clean manner.

**cleanly**[2] /'klenlɪ/ a. habitually clean; attentive to cleanness. **cleanliness** n.

**cleanse** /klenz/ v.t. make clean or pure.

**clear** 1 a. not clouded; transparent; readily perceived or understood; able to discern readily; unobstructed, open; net, complete; unhampered, free (*of*). 2 adv. clearly; completely; apart. 3 v. make or become clear; free from or of obstruction, suspicion, etc.; show or declare innocent *of*; pass over or by without touching; make (sum) as net gain; pass (cheque) through clearing-house. 4 **clear-cut** sharply defined; **clear off** get rid off, *colloq.* go away; **clear out** empty, remove, *colloq.* go away; **clearskin** *Aus.* unbranded animal; **clearway** n. road where vehicles may not stop on carriageway.

**clearance** /'klɪərəns/ n. removal of obstructions etc.; space allowed for passing of two objects; permission to proceed; clearing (esp. of cheques etc.). **clearance sale** sale to dispose of surplus stock.

**clearing** /'klɪərɪŋ/ n. piece of land in forest cleared esp. for cultivation. **clearing-house** bankers' institution where cheques etc. are exchanged, agency for collecting and distributing information etc.

**cleat** n. projecting piece to provide footing or for fastening ropes to.

**cleavage** /'kliːvɪdʒ/ n. hollow between woman's breasts; way in which thing tends to split.

**cleave**[1] v. (past **clove** or **cleft**; p.p. **cloven** or **cleft**) split, divide; break or come apart.

**cleave**[2] v.i. (past & p.p. **cleaved**) stick fast; adhere *to*.

**cleaver** /'kliːvə(r)/ n. heavy chopping-tool used by butchers etc.

**clef** n. *Mus.* symbol showing pitch of staff.

**cleft**[1] past & p.p. of **cleave**[1]. **cleft palate** congenital split in roof of mouth; **in a cleft stick** in a difficult position.

**cleft**[2] n. fissure, split.

**clematis** /'klemətəs/ n. cultivated climbing flowering plant.

**clement** /'klemənt/ a. mild, merciful. **clemency** n.

**clementine** /'klemənˌtaɪn/ n. kind of small orange.

**clench** 1 v. close tightly, grasp firmly;

**clergy** /'klɜːdʒi/ *n.* (usu. treated as *pl.*) all persons ordained as priests or ministers.

**clergyman** /'klɜːdʒimən/ *n.* (*pl* -men) member of clergy.

**cleric** /'klerɪk/ *n.* clergyman.

**clerical** /'klerɪk(ə)l/ *a.* of clergy or clergyman; of or done by clerks.

**clerihew** /'klerəhjuː/ *n.* witty or humorous 4-line verse on (usu.) biographical subject.

**clerk** /klɑːk/ 1 *n.* person employed to keep records, accounts etc., attend to correspondence etc.; record-keeper or agent of council, court, etc.; lay officer of parish church etc. 2 *v.i.* work as clerk.

**clever** /'klevə(r)/ *a.* skilful, talented, quick to learn and understand; ingenious.

**clew** 1 *n.* lower corner of sail; *arch.* ball of thread or yarn. 2 *v.t. Naut.* haul *up* or let *down* (sail).

**cliché** /'kliːʃeɪ/ *n.* hackneyed phrase or opinion.

**click** 1 *n.* slight sharp sound as of switch being operated. 2 *v.* make click; *sl.* be successful or understood, become friendly *with* person.

**client** /'klaɪənt/ *n.* person using services of lawyer or other professional person; customer.

**clientele** /kliːɒn'tel/ *n.* clients collectively; customers.

**cliff** *n.* steep rock-face, esp. on coast.

**cliff-hanger** story etc. with strong element of suspense.

**climacteric** /klaɪ'mæktərɪk/ *n.* period of life when physical powers being to decline.

**climate** /'klaɪmət/ *n.* prevailing weather conditons of an area; region with certain weather conditions; prevailing trend of opinion etc. **climatic** /-'mæt-/ *a.*; **climatically** *adv.*

**climax** /'klaɪmæks/ 1 *n.* event or point of greatest intensity or interest, culmination. 2 *v.* reach or bring to a climax.

**climb** /klaɪm/ 1 *v.* ascend, mount, go *up*; (of plant) grow up wall etc. by clinging etc.; rise in social rank. 2 *n.* action of climbing; place to be climbed.

**climber** /'klaɪmə(r)/ *n.* mountaineer; climbing plant; person climbing socially.

**clime** *n.* region; climate.

**clinah** /'klaɪnə/ *n. Aus. arch.* girlfriend.

**clinch** *v.* confirm or settle; settle conclusively; (of boxer) come too close to opponent for full-arm blow; secure (nail or rivet) by driving point sideways when through. 2 *n.* clinching, resulting state or position; *colloq.* embrace.

**cliner** var. of **clinah**.

**cling** *v.i.* (*past* & *p.p.* **clung**) maintain grasp, keep hold, adhere closely.

**clinic** /'klɪnɪk/ *n.* private or specialized hospital; place or occasion for giving medical treatment or advice; teaching of medicine at hospital bedside.

**clinical** /'klɪnɪk(ə)l/ *a.* of or for the treatment of patients; *fig.* objective, coldly detached.

**clink**[1] 1 *n.* sharp ringing sound. 2 *v.* (cause to) make clink.

**clink**[2] *n. sl.* prison.

**clinker** /'klɪŋkə(r)/ *n.* mass of slag or lava; stony residue from burnt coal.

**clinker-built** *a.* (of boat) with external planks overlapping downwards.

**clip**[1] *n.* device for attaching something or holding things together; set of cartridges for firearm, held together at base. 2 *v.t.* fix with clip; grip tightly. 3 **clipboard** board with spring clip for holding papers etc.

**clip**[2] 1 *v.* cut with shears or scissors; *colloq.* hit sharply; remove small piece from (bus etc. ticket) to show it has been used; cut short. 2 *n.* clipping; *colloq.* sharp blow; yield of wool; extract from motion-picture film.

**clipper** /'klɪpə(r)/ *n.* fast sailing-ship; usu. in *pl.*, instrument for clipping.

**clippie** /'klɪpiː/ *n. Aus. sl.* bus conductress woman who clips tickets on train.

**clipping** /'klɪpɪŋ/ *n.* piece clipped off; newspaper cutting.

**clique** /kliːk/ *n.* exclusive set of associates. **cliquish** *a.*; **cliquy** *a.*

**clitoris** /'klɪtərəs/ *n.* small erectile part of female genitals.

**cloak** 1 *n.* loose usu. sleeveless outdoor garment; covering; pretext. 2 *v.* cover with cloak; conceal, disguise. 3 **cloakroom** room for temporary deposit of clothes or luggage, *euphem.* lavatory.

**clobber**[1] /'klɒbə(r)/ *sl. n.* clothing, personal belongings.

**clobber²** /ˈklɒbə(r)/ v.t. sl. hit repeatedly; defeat; criticize severely.

**cloche** /klɒʃ/ n. small translucent cover for outdoor plants; woman's close-fitting bell-shaped hat.

**clock¹** 1 n. instrument measuring time and indicating it on dial or by displayed figures; clocklike device showing readings on dial; seed-head of dandelion. 2 v.t. time (race etc.) by stop-watch. 3 **clock in** or **on**, or **out** or **off**, register time of arrival or departure by automatic clock; **clock (up)** attain or register (time, speed, distance, etc.); **clockwise** moving in a curve corresponding in direction to hands of clock; **clockwork** mechanism with coiled springs etc. on clock principle (**like clockwork** with mechanical precision).

**clock²** n. ornamental pattern on side of stocking or sock.

**clod** n. lump of earth or clay.

**clog** 1 n. wooden-soled shoe; arch. encumbrance. 2 v. impede; (cause to) become obstructed; choke up.

**cloister** /ˈklɔɪstə(r)/ 1 n. covered walk esp. in convent, college, or cathedral; monastic house or life. 2 v.t. seclude in convent.

**clone** 1 n. group of organisms produced asexually from one ancestor; one such organism. 2 v. propagate as clone.

**close¹** /kləʊs/ 1 a. near together; dense, compact; nearly equal; rigorous; shut; secret; niggardly; stifling. 2 adv. closely. 3 n. enclosed place; street closed at one end; precinct of cathedral. 4 **close harmony** singing of parts within an octave or a twelfth; **close season** time when killing of game etc. is illegal; **close shave** narrow escape; **close-up** photograph etc. taken at short range.

**close²** /kləʊz/ 1 v. shut, block up; bring or come to an end; end day's business; bring or come closer or into contact etc; make (electric circuit) continuous. 2 n. conclusion, end. 3 **closed-circuit** (of television) transmitted by wires for restricted number of receivers; **closed shop** business etc. where employees must belong to agreed trade union.

**closet** /ˈklɒzɪt/ 1 n. small cupboard or room; water-closet. 2 v.t. shut away esp. in private consultation etc.

**closure** /ˈkləʊʒə(r)/ 1 n. closing, closed state; closing of debate. 2 v.t. apply closure to.

**clot** 1 n. semi-solid lump formed from liquid, esp. blood; sl. stupid person. 2 v. form into clots. 3 **clotted cream** thick cream formed by slow scalding.

**cloth** /klɒθ/ n. woven or felted material; piece of this; **the** clergy.

**clothe** /kləʊð/ v.t. (past & p.p. **clothed** or **clad**) put clothes upon; provide with clothes; cover as with clothes.

**clothes** /kləʊðz/ n.pl. things worn to cover body and limbs; bedclothes.

**clothier** /ˈkləʊðɪːə(r)/ n. dealer in cloth and men's clothes.

**clothing** /ˈkləʊðɪŋ/ n. clothes.

**cloud** /klaʊd/ 1 n. visible mass of condensed watery vapour floating in air; mass of dust, smoke, etc.; great number (of birds, insects, etc.) moving together; state of gloom, trouble or suspicion. 2 v. cover or darken with clouds; become overcast or gloomy. 3 **cloudburst** sudden violent rainstorm.

**cloudy** /ˈklaʊdɪ/ a. covered with clouds; not transparent, unclear.

**clout** /klaʊt/ 1 n. heavy blow; colloq. power of effective action; influence; piece of cloth or clothing. 2 v.t. hit hard.

**clove¹** n. dried bud of tropical tree, used as spice.

**clove²** n. one segment of bulb of garlic etc.

**clove³** past of **cleave¹**.

**clove hitch** knot for fastening rope round pole etc.

**cloven** /ˈkləʊv(ə)n/ p.p. of **cleave¹**. **cloven hoof** one that is divided, as of oxen or sheep.

**clover** /ˈkləʊvə(r)/ n. kind of trefoil used as fodder; **in clover** in ease and luxury.

**clown** /klaʊn/ 1 n. comic entertainer esp. in circus; person acting like clown. 2 v.i. behave like clown. 3 **clownish** a.

**cloy** v.t. satiate or weary by richness, sweetness, etc.

**club** 1 n. heavy stick used as weapon; stick with head, used in golf etc.; playing-card of suit marked with black trefoils; body of persons associated for social, sporting, etc. purposes; premises of this. 2 v. strike with club; combine together or with esp. in making up sum of money. 3 **club-foot** congenitally

**cluck**                      **cobble**

deformed foot; **clubhouse** premises used by club; **club-root** disease of cabbages etc.; **club sandwich** one with two layers of filling between three slices of bread or toast.

**cluck** 1 *n.* guttural cry like that of hen. 2 *v.i.* make clucks.

**clue** 1 *n.* guiding or suggestive fact; piece of evidence used in detection of crime; word(s) used to indicate word(s) for insertion in crossword. 2 *v.* **clue in** or **up** *sl.* inform.

**clump** 1 *n.* cluster *of* trees or plants etc. 2 *v.* form clump; arrange in clump; tread heavily.

**clumsy** /'klʌmzi/ *a.* awkward in movement or shape; difficult to handle or use; tactless.

**clung** past & *p.p.* of **cling**.

**cluster** /'klʌstə(r)/ 1 *n.* close group or bunch of similar things. 2 *v.* be in or form into cluster; gather *round*.

**clutch**[1] 1 *v.* seize eagerly; grasp tightly; snatch *at*. 2 *n.* tight or (in *pl.*) cruel grasp; (in motor vehicle) device for connecting engine to transmission, pedal operating this.

**clutch**[2] *n.* set of eggs; brood of chickens.

**clutter** /'klʌtə(r)/ 1 *n.* crowded untidy collection of things. 2 *v.t.* fill with clutter, crowd untidily.

**cm** *abbr.* centimetre(s).

**CND** *abbr.* Campaign for Nuclear Disarmament.

**c/o** *abbr.* care of.

**CO** *abbr.* Commanding Officer.

**Co.** *abbr.* company; county.

**coach** 1 *n.* single-decker bus usu. for longer journeys; railway carriage; closed horse-drawn carriage; tutor or trainer. 2 *v.t.* instruct or train. 3 **coachman** driver of horse-carriage; **coachwood** Aus. tree yielding aromatic wood used in cabinet-making, this wood; **coachwork** bodywork of road or railway vehicle.

**coagulant** /kəʊ'ægjələnt/ *n.* substance that causes coagulation.

**coagulate** /kəʊ'ægjəleɪt/ *v.* change from liquid to semisolid state; clot, curdle. **coagulation** *n.*

**coal** *n.* hard black mineral used as fuel etc.; piece of this. **coal-face** exposed surface of coal in mine; **coalfield** area yielding coal; **coal gas** mixed gases extracted from coal and used for heating, cooking, etc.; **coal-scuttle** receptacle for coal to supply domestic fire; **coal tar** tar extracted from coal.

**coalesce** /kəʊə'les/ *v.t.* come together and form one mass etc. **coalescence** *n.*; **coalescent** *a.*

**coalition** /kəʊə'lɪʃ(ə)n/ *n.* fusion into one whole; temporary alliance of political parties.

**coaming** /'kəʊmɪŋ/ *n.* raised border round ship's hatches etc.

**coarse** /kɔːs/ *a.* rough, loose, or large in texture etc.; lacking delicacy, unrefined; inferior, common; vulgar, obscene.

**coarsen** /'kɔːs(ə)n/ *v.* make or become coarse.

**coast** 1 *n.* border of land near sea; sea-shore. 2 *v.i.* ride or move (usu. downhill) without use of power; sail along coast; *fig.* make progress without exertion. 3 **coastguard** (one of) body of men employed to keep watch on coasts, prevent smuggling, etc.; **coastline** line of sea-shore esp. with regard to its shape. 4 **coastal** *a.*

**coaster** /'kəʊstə(r)/ *n.* coasting vessel; tray or mat for bottle or glass.

**coat** 1 *n.* sleeved outer garment, overcoat, jacket; animal's hair or fur; layer of paint etc. 2 *v.t.* cover *with* coat or layer, form covering to. 3 **coat of arms** heraldic bearings or shield; **coathanger** shaped piece of wood, wire, etc. from which clothes may be hung in normal shape.

**coating** /'kəʊtɪŋ/ *n.* covering of paint, chocolate, etc; cloth for coats.

**coax** *v.t.* persuade gradually or by flattery; manipulate gently.

**coaxial** /kəʊ'æksɪəl/ *a.* having common axis; (of electric cable etc.) transmitting by means of two concentric conductors separated by insulator.

**cob** *n.* roundish lump; corn-cob; stout short-legged riding-horse; male swan; large hazel nut; roundish loaf.

**cobalt** /'kəʊbɔːlt/ *n.* silvery-white metallic element; deep-blue pigment made from it.

**cobber** /'kɒbə(r)/ *n.* Aus. & NZ *colloq.* companion, friend.

**cobble**[1] /'kɒb(ə)l/ 1 *n.* rounded stone used for paving. 2 *v.t.* pave with cobbles.

**cobble**² /ˈkɒb(ə)l/ v.t. mend or patch (esp. shoes); put together roughly.

**cobbler** /ˈkɒblə(r)/ n. mender of shoes.

**COBOL** /ˈkəʊbɒl/ n. computer language designed for use in business operations.

**cobra** /ˈkəʊbrə/ n. venomous hooded snake.

**cobweb** /ˈkɒbweb/ n. spider's network or thread. **cobwebby** a.

**coca** /ˈkəʊkə/ n. S. Amer. shrub; its leaves chewed as stimulant.

**cocaine** /kəʊˈkeɪn/ n. drug from coca used as local anaesthetic and as stimulant.

**coccyx** /ˈkɒksɪks/ n. bone at base of spinal column.

**cochineal** /kɒtʃəˈniːl/ n. scarlet dye; insects whose dried bodies yield this.

**cock**¹ **1** n. male bird, esp. of domestic fowl; *vulg.* penis; lever in gun raised to be released by trigger; tap or valve controlling flow. **2** v.t. put in noticeably upright position; turn or move (eye or ear) attentively, knowingly, etc.; raise cock of (gun). **3 cock-a-hoop** exultant; **cock-crow** dawn; **cocked hat** triangular brimless hat pointed at front, back, and top, three-cornered hat; **cock-eyed** *sl.* crooked, askew, absurd.

**cock**² n. small conical heap of hay.

**cockade** /kɒˈkeɪd/ n. rosette etc. worn in hat.

**cockatiel** /kɒkəˈtiːl/ n. small delicately-coloured cockatoo.

**cockatoo** /kɒkəˈtuː/ n. crested parrot; *Aus.* cocky, small farmer; *Aus. sl.* lookout to protect illegal activity. **cockatoo fence** *Aus.* rough fence of logs and saplings.

**cockchafer** /ˈkɒktʃeɪfə(r)/ n. large pale-brown beetle.

**cocker** /ˈkɒkə(r)/ n. breed of spaniel.

**cockerel** /ˈkɒkər(ə)l/ n. young cock.

**cockle** /ˈkɒk(ə)l/ **1** n. edible bivalve shellfish; its shell; pucker or wrinkle. **2** v. make or become puckered. **3 cockles of the heart** innermost feelings.

**cockney** /ˈkɒknɪ/ **1** n. native of London, esp. East End; cockney dialect. **2** a. of cockneys.

**cockpit** /ˈkɒkpɪt/ n. site of battle(s); place for pilot etc. in aircraft or spacecraft or for driver in racing car; arena of war etc.

**cockroach** /ˈkɒkrəʊtʃ/ n. dark-brown insect infesting esp. kitchens.

**cockscomb** /ˈkɒkskəʊm/ n. cock's crest.

**cocksure** /ˈkɒkʃʊə(r)/ a. quite convinced; dogmatic, confident.

**cocktail** /ˈkɒkteɪl/ n. drink of spirits with bitters etc.; appetizer containing shellfish; finely-chopped fruit salad. **cocktail stick** small pointed stick.

**cocky**¹ /ˈkɒkɪ/ a. conceited, arrogant.

**cocky**² n. *Aus. colloq.* small farmer.

**coco** /ˈkəʊkəʊ/ n. (*pl.* **-cos**) a tropical palm-tree.

**cocoa** /ˈkəʊkəʊ/ n. powder of crushed cacao seeds, drink made from this.

**coconut** /ˈkəʊkənʌt/ n. large brown seed of coco, with edible white lining enclosing whitish liquid (**coconut milk**). **coconut matting** matting made from fibre of coconut husks; **coconut shy** fairground side-show where balls are thrown to dislodge coconuts.

**cocoon** /kəˈkuːn/ **1** n. silky case spun by larva (esp. of silkworm) to protect it as pupa; protective covering. **2** v.t. wrap (as) in cocoon.

**cocotte** /kəˈkɒt/ n. small fireproof dish for cooking and serving food.

**cod**¹ n. large N. hemisphere sea fish; similar Aus. fish. **cod-liver oil** medicinal oil rich in vitamins.

**cod**² n. & v. hoax, parody.

**COD** *abbr.* cash on delivery.

**coddle** /ˈkɒd(ə)l/ v. treat as an invalid; pamper; cook gently in water just below boiling-point.

**code 1** n. system of signals or of symbols etc. used for brevity, secrecy, or machine processing of information; systematic set of laws etc.; standard of moral behaviour. **2** v.t. put into code.

**codeine** /ˈkəʊdiːn/ n. alkaloid got from opium, used as pain-killer and sedative.

**codex** /ˈkəʊdeks/ n. (*pl.* **codices** /ˈkəʊdɪsiːz/) manuscript volume esp. of ancient texts.

**codger** /ˈkɒdʒə(r)/ n. *sl.* fellow.

**codicil** /ˈkəʊdəsɪl/ n. supplement modifying or revoking will etc.

**codify** /ˈkəʊdəfaɪ/ v.t. arrange (laws etc.) into code. **codification** n.

**codling**¹ /ˈkɒdlɪŋ/ n. (also **codlin**) variety of apple; moth whose larva feeds on apples.

**codling²** /ˈkɒdlɪŋ/ n. small cod.

**coeducation** /ˌkəʊedjəˈkeɪʃ(ə)n/ n. education of both sexes together. **coeducational** a.

**coefficient** /ˌkəʊəˈfɪʃ(ə)nt/ n. Math. quantity placed before and multiplying another; Phys. multiplier or factor by which a property is measured.

**coequal** /kəʊˈiːkw(ə)l/ n. & a. equal.

**coerce** /kəʊˈɜːs/ v.t. impel or force into obedience. **coercive** a.; **coercion** n.

**coeval** /kəʊˈiːv(ə)l/ 1 a. having same age, existing at same epoch. 2 n. coeval person.

**coexist** /ˌkəʊəɡˈzɪst/ v.i. exist together (with).

**coexistence** /ˌkəʊəɡˈzɪst(ə)ns/ n. coexisting, esp. peaceful existence with nations professing different ideologies etc. **coexistent** a.

**coextensive** /ˌkəʊəkˈstensɪv/ a. extending over same space or time.

**C. of E.** abbr. Church of England.

**coffee** /ˈkɒfi:/ n. drink made from roasted and ground seeds of a tropical shrub; a cup of this; the seeds or shrub; pale brown colour. **coffee-bar** café selling coffee and other refreshments; **coffee-bean** seed of coffee; **coffee-grounds** sediment of coffee after infusion; **coffee-mill** small machine for grinding coffee-beans; **coffee-table** small low table; **coffee-table book** large illustrated book.

**coffer** /ˈkɒfə(r)/ n. box esp. for valuables; in pl. funds or treasury; sunk panel in ceiling etc.

**coffin** /ˈkɒfɪn/ n. chest in which corpse is buried or cremated.

**cog** n. one of series of projections on wheel etc. transferring motion by engaging with another series.

**cogent** /ˈkəʊdʒ(ə)nt/ a. convincing, compelling. **cogency** n.

**cogitate** /ˈkɒdʒɪteɪt/ v. ponder, meditate. **cogitation** n.

**cognac** /ˈkɒnjæk/ n. French brandy.

**cognate** /ˈkɒɡneɪt/ 1 a. descended from same ancestor or root or origin. 2 n. cognate word or person.

**cognition** /kɒɡˈnɪʃ(ə)n/ n. knowing or perceiving or conceiving; notion. **cognitive** a.

**cognizance** /ˈkɒɡnəz(ə)ns/ n. being aware, notice; distinctive device or mark.

**cognizant** /ˈkɒɡnəz(ə)nt/ a. having knowledge or taking note of.

**cognomen** /kɒɡˈnəʊmən/ n. nickname, surname.

**cohabit** /kəʊˈhæbɪt/ v.i. live together as husband and wife. **cohabitation** n.

**cohere** /kəʊˈhɪə(r)/ v.i. stick together, remain united; be logical or consistent.

**coherent** /kəʊˈhɪərənt/ a. sticking together; consistent, easily understood. **coherence** n.

**cohesion** /kəʊˈhiːʒ(ə)n/ n. force with which parts cohere; tendency to cohere. **cohesive** a.

**cohort** /ˈkəʊhɔːt/ n. tenth part of Roman legion; persons banded together.

**coif** /kɔɪf/ n. hist. kind of close-fitting cap.

**coiffeur** /kwæˈfɜː(r)/ n. (fem. **coiffeuse** /-ˈfɜːz/) n. hairdresser. [F]

**coiffure** /kwæˈfjʊə(r)/ n. hair style. [F]

**coign** /kɔɪn/ n. **coign of vantage** place affording good view.

**coil** 1 v. arrange or be arranged in concentric rings; move sinuously. 2 n. coiled length of rope etc.; coiled arrangement; flexible loop as contraceptive device in womb; coiled wire for passage of electric current.

**coin** 1 n. piece of stamped metal money; coins collectively. 2 v.t. make (money) by stamping metal; make (metal) into money; invent (new word etc.).

**coinage** /ˈkɔɪnɪdʒ/ n. coining; coins; system of coins in use; invention of new word, word so invented.

**coincide** /ˌkəʊɪnˈsaɪd/ v.i. occur at same time; agree or be identical with.

**coincidence** /kəʊˈɪnsɪd(ə)ns/ n. remarkable concurrence of events without apparent causal connection. **coincident** a.

**coincidental** /kəʊˌɪnsɪˈdent(ə)l/ a. occurring by or in the nature of a coincidence.

**coir** /ˈkɔɪə(r)/ n. fibre of coconut husk used for ropes and matting etc.

**coition** /kəʊˈɪʃ(ə)n/ n. sexual intercourse.

**coitus** /ˈkəʊɪtəs/ n. coition.

**coke¹** 1 n. solid substance left after gases have been extracted from coal. 2 v. convert into coke.

**coke²** n. sl. cocaine.

**col** *n.* depression in summit-line of mountain-chain.

**cola** /'kəʊlə/ *n.* W. Afr. tree with seed producing extract used as tonic etc.; carbonated drink flavoured with this.

**colander** /'kʌləndə(r)/ *n.* perforated vessel used as strainer in cookery.

**cold** /kəʊld/ **1** *a.* of or at low temperature; not heated; having lost heat; feeling or suggesting cold; *sl.* unconscious; lacking ardour or affection or geniality; depressing, dispiriting; (of huntingscent) faint. **2** *n.* prevalence of low temperature; cold condition; catarrh of nose or throat or both. **3 cold-blooded** having blood temperature varying with that of environment, *fig.* callous; **cold cream** ointment for cleansing and softening the skin; **cold feet** fear, reluctance; **cold shoulder** deliberately unfriendly treatment; **cold storage** storage in refrigerator, *fig.* state of abeyance; **cold war** hostility between nations without actual fighting.

**coleopterous** /kɒli:'ɒptərəs/ *a.* of the order of insects with front wings forming hard sheaths for hind pair.

**coleslaw** /'kəʊlslɔ:/ *n.* salad of sliced raw white cabbage etc.

**colic** /'kɒlɪk/ *n.* griping belly-pain.

**colitis** /kə'laɪtəs/ *n.* inflammation of colon.

**collaborate** /kə'læbəreɪt/ *v.i.* work jointly (*with*). **collaboration** *n.*; **collaborator** *n.*

**collage** /'kɒlɑ:ʒ/ *n.* picture made by gluing pieces of paper or other items on to backing; art of making these.

**collapse** /kə'læps/ **1** *n.* tumbling down or falling to ruin; physical or mental breakdown. **2** *v.* (cause to) suffer collapse; fold up. **3 collapsible** *a.*

**collar** /'kɒlə(r)/ **1** *n.* neckband, upright or turned over, of coat, shirt, dress, etc.; leather band round animal's neck; collar-shaped piece in machine etc. **2** *v.t.* seize by collar; lay hold of; *sl.* take, esp. without permission. **3 collar-bone** bone joining breastbone and shoulderblade.

**collate** /kə'leɪt/ *v.* compare in detail; collect and put in order. **collator** *n.*

**collateral** /kə'lætər(ə)l/ **1** *a.* side by side; additional but subordinate; connected but aside from main subject; descended from same stock but by different line. **2** *n.* collateral person or security. **3 collateral security** property pledged as guarantee for repayment of money.

**collation** /kə'leɪʃ(ə)n/ *n.* collating; light meal.

**colleague** /'kɒli:g/ *n.* associate in office etc.; member of same profession etc.

**collect**[1] /kə'lekt/ *v.* bring or come together; assemble, accumulate, amass; seek and obtain (books, stamps, etc.) for addition to others; get (contributions, taxes, etc.) from a number of people; call for, fetch; concentrate (one's thoughts etc.).

**collect**[2] /'kɒlekt/ *n.* short prayer of Anglican or RC Church.

**collected** kə'lektəd/ *a.* not perturbed or distracted.

**collection** /kə'lekʃ(ə)n/ *n.* collecting; things collected; money collected, esp. in meeting or church service etc.

**collective** /kə'lektɪv/ **1** *a.* representing or including many; taken as a whole, aggregate, common; owned or worked in common. **2** *n.* collective farm or other enterprise; collective noun. **3 collective bargaining** negotiation of wages etc. by organized body of employees; **collective farm** jointly-operated amalgamation of several smallholdings; **collective noun** singular noun denoting group of individuals. **4 collectivize** *v.t.*

**collectivism** /kə'lektəvɪz(ə)m/ *n.* theory or practise of collective ownership of land and means of production. **collectivist** *n.* & *a.*

**collector** /kə'lektə(r)/ *n.* person who collects things of interest; person who collects money due.

**colleen** /'kɒli:n/ *n. Ir.* girl.

**college** /'kɒlɪdʒ/ *n.* establishment for higher or professional education; body of teachers and students within a university, their premises; small university, school; organized body of persons with shared functions and privileges.

**collegian** /kə'li:dʒ(ə)n/ *n.* member of college.

**collegiate** /kə'li:dʒət/ *a.* of or constituted as a college, corporate.

**collide** /kə'laɪd/ *v.i.* come into collision.

**collie** /'kɒli/ *n.* sheep-dog of orig. Scottish breed.

**collier** /ˈkɒliːə(r)/ n. coal-miner; coal-ship, member of its crew.

**colliery** /ˈkɒliːəriː/ n. coal-mine.

**collision** /kəˈlɪʒ(ə)n/ n. violent striking of moving body against another or against fixed object; clashing of opposed interests etc.

**collocate** /ˈkɒləkeɪt/ v.t. place (esp. words) together; arrange. **collocation** n.

**colloid** /ˈkɒlɔɪd/ n. gluey substance; substance in non-crystalline state, with very large molecules. **colloidal** a.

**colloquial** /kəˈləʊkwiːəl/ a. belonging or proper to ordinary conversation, not formal or literary.

**colloquialism** /kəˈləʊkwiːəlɪz(ə)m/ n. colloquial word or phrase; use of these.

**colloquy** /ˈkɒləkwiː/ n. talk, dialogue.

**collusion** /kəˈluːʒ(ə)n/ n. secret agreement or co-operation esp. for fraud or deceit.

**collywobbles** /ˈkɒliːwɒb(ə)lz/ n.pl. colloq. ache or rumbling in stomach; apprehensive feeling.

**cologne** /kəˈləʊn/ n. eau-de-Cologne.

**colon**[1] /ˈkəʊlən/ n. punctuation-mark (:).

**colon**[2] /ˈkəʊlən/ n. lower and greater part of large intestine. **colonic** /-ˈlɒn-/ a.

**colonel** /ˈkɜːn(ə)l/ n. officer commanding regiment next in rank below brigadier. **colonelcy** n.

**colonial** /kəˈləʊniːəl/ 1 a. of a colony or colonies. 2 n. inhabitant of colony. 3 **colonial goose** Aus. & NZ stuffed leg of mutton; **colonial oven** Aus. oven heated above and below; **my colonial oath** Aus. sl. yes, emphatically.

**colonialism** /kəˈləʊniːəlɪz(ə)m/ n. policy of having colonies.

**colonist** /ˈkɒlənəst/ n. settler in or inhabitant of colony.

**colonize** /ˈkɒlənaɪz/ v. establish colony (in); join colony. **colonization** n.

**colonnade** /kɒləˈneɪd/ n. row of columns supporting entablature or roof.

**colony** /ˈkɒləniː/ n. settlement or settlers in new territory remaining subject to parent State; persons of one nationality or occupation etc. forming community in town etc.; group of animals that live close together.

**colophon** /ˈkɒləf(ə)n/ n. tail-piece in book.

**Colorado beetle** /kɒləˈrɑːdəʊ/ small beetle with larva destructive to potato.

**coloration** /kʌləˈreɪʃ(ə)n/ n. colouring, arrangement of colours.

**coloratura** /kɒlərəˈtjʊərə/ n. elaborate ornamentation in vocal music; soprano singer of such music.

**colossal** /kəˈlɒs(ə)l/ a. gigantic, huge; colloq. splendid, glorious.

**colossus** /kəˈlɒsəs/ n. (pl. -lossi /-ˈlɒsaɪ/ or -lossuses) statue of more than life size; gigantic person or personified empire.

**colour** /ˈkʌlə(r)/ 1 n. one, or any mixture, of the constituents into which light can be separated as in spectrum or rainbow; use of all colours as in photography; colouring substance, esp. paint; skin pigmentation, esp. when dark; ruddiness of face; appearance or aspect; flag of regiment or ship etc.; coloured ribbon, rosette, dress, etc. worn as symbol of school or club or party etc. 2 v. give colour to, paint, stain, dye; blush. 3 **colour-blind** unable to distinguish certain colours; **colour-fast** dyed in colours that will not fade or run.

**coloured** /ˈkʌləd/ 1 a. having colour; wholly or partly of non-white descent; **Coloured** S. Afr. of mixed white and non-white descent. 2 n. coloured person.

**colourful** /ˈkʌləfʊl/ a. full of colour or interest.

**colouring** /ˈkʌlərɪŋ/ n. arrangement of colours; substance giving colour; facial complexion.

**colourless** /ˈkʌləlǝs/ a. lacking colour or vividness.

**colt** /kəʊlt/ n. young male horse; inexperienced person.

**columbine** /ˈkɒləmbaɪn/ n. garden flower with pointed projections on its petals.

**column** /ˈkɒləm/ n. round pillar, esp. one with base and capital; column-shaped thing; vertical division of printed page; part of newspaper devoted to particular subject or by one writer; narrow-fronted deep arrangement of troops, vehicles, etc.

**columnist** /ˈkɒləmnəst/ n. journalist who contributes regularly to a newspaper.

**coma** /ˈkəʊmə/ n. prolonged deep unconsciousness.

**comatose** /ˈkəʊmətəʊz/ a. in coma; very sleepy.

**comb** /kəʊm/ 1 n. toothed strip of rigid material for tidying and arranging hair; thing of similar shape or function, esp. for dressing wool; red fleshy crest of cock etc.; honeycomb. 2 v.t. draw comb through (hair), dress (wool etc.) with comb; search thoroughly.

**combat** /ˈkɒmbæt/ 1 n. fight, struggle. 2 v. do battle; contend with, oppose.

**combatant** /ˈkɒmbət(ə)nt/ 1 a. fighting. 2 n. fighter.

**combative** /ˈkɒmbətɪv/ a. pugnacious.

**combe** var. of **coomb**.

**combination** /kɒmbɪˈneɪʃ(ə)n/ n. combining; combined state; combined set of persons or things; sequence of numbers etc. used to open **combination lock**; motor cycle with side-car attached; in pl. single undergarment for body and legs.

**combine** 1 /kəmˈbaɪn/ v. join together; unite; form into chemical compound; co-operate. 2 /ˈkɒmbaɪn/ n. combination of persons or firms acting together in business. 3 **combine harvester** combined reaping and threshing machine.

**combustible** /kəmˈbʌstəb(ə)l/ 1 a. capable of or used for burning. 2 n. combustible thing. 3 **combustibility** n.

**combustion** /kəmˈbʌstʃ(ə)n/ n. burning; consumption by fire.

**come** /kʌm/ v.i. (past **came**; p.p. **come**) move or be brought towards, or reach, a place, time, situation, or result; be available; occur; become; traverse; colloq. behave like. **come about** happen; **come across** meet or find; **come at** Aus. colloq. accept; **come-back** colloq. retort or retaliation; **come by** obtain; **come clean** colloq. confess; **comedown** downfall, degradation; **come down with** begin to suffer from (disease); **come in for** receive; **come of** be result of, be descended from; **come off** succeed, occur, fare; **come out** appear, go on strike, be satisfactorily visible in photograph, be solved, make début; **come round** recover normal state, esp. of consciousness; **come to** revive, recover; **come to light with** Aus. colloq. produce or provide; **come true** be realized in fact; **come up** be mentioned or discussed; **come up against** be faced with or opposed to; **come up to** reach, be equal to; **come-uppance** US sl. one's deserts (for misbehaviour etc.); **come up with** produce (idea etc.); **come what may** whatever happens.

**comedian** /kəˈmiːdɪən/ n. humorous performer; actor in comedy.

**comedienne** /kəmiːdɪˈen/ n. woman comedian.

**comedy** /ˈkɒmədɪ/ n. stage-play or film of light amusing character; humorous genre of drama etc.; humour; amusing aspects of life.

**comely** /ˈkʌmlɪ/ a. pleasant to look at.

**comestibles** /kəˈmestəb(ə)lz/ n.pl. things to eat.

**comet** /ˈkɒmɪt/ n. heavenly body with starlike nucleus and luminous 'tail', moving in path about sun.

**comfit** /ˈkʌmfɪt/ n. sweet consisting of nut etc. in sugar.

**comfort** /ˈkʌmfət/ 1 n. physical or mental well-being; relief from trouble or hardship; consolation; in pl. things that make life comfortable. 2 v. bring comfort to; make comfortable.

**comfortable** /ˈkʌmfətəb(ə)l/ a. at ease in body or mind; promoting comfort.

**comforter** /ˈkʌmfətə(r)/ n. person who comforts; baby's dummy; woollen scarf.

**comfy** /ˈkʌmfɪ/ a. colloq. comfortable.

**comic** /ˈkɒmɪk/ 1 a. of or like comedy; designed to amuse; funny. 2 n. comedian; comic paper, esp. periodical with narrative mainly in pictures. 3 **comic strip** sequence of drawings telling comic or serial story in newspaper etc.

**comical** /ˈkɒmɪk(ə)l/ a. laughable. **comicality** n.

**comity** /ˈkɒmɪtɪ/ n. courtesy. **comity of nations** friendly recognition of each other's law and customs.

**comma** /ˈkɒmə/ n. punctuation-mark (,).

**command** /kəˈmɑːnd or kəˈmænd/ 1 v. order, issue orders; have authority over or control of; have at one's disposal; deserve and get; look down over; dominate. 2 n. order given; description of, or signal initiating, operation in computer; exercise or tenure of authority; control, mastery; forces or dis-

**commandant** /kɒmən'dænt/ n. commander of military force.

**commandeer** /kɒmən'dɪə(r)/ v.t. seize for military purposes; take arbitrarily.

**commander** /kə'mɑ:ndə(r) or kə'mændə/ n. person who commands, esp. naval officer ranking next below captain. **commander-in-chief** supreme commander esp. of nation's forces.

**commanding** /kə'mɑ:ndɪŋ or kə'mændɪŋ/ a. in command; exalted or impressive; dominant.

**commandment** /kə'mɑ:ndmənt or kə'mændmənt/ n. divine command.

**commando** /kə'mɑ:ndəʊ or kə'mændəʊ/ n. (pl. **-dos**) body of specially-trained shock troops; member of this.

**commemorate** /kə'meməreɪt/ v.t. keep in memory by celebration or ceremony; be memorial of. **commemoration** n.; **commemorative** a.

**commence** /kə'mens/ v. begin, start.

**commencement** /kə'mensmənt/ n. beginning; US graduation ceremony.

**commend** /kə'mend/ v.t. praise; recommend; entrust. **commendation** n.

**commendable** /kə'mendəb(ə)l/ a. praiseworthy.

**commensurable** /kə'menʃərəb(ə)l/ a. measurable by same standard. **commensurability** n.

**commensurate** /kə'menʃərət/ a. coextensive; proportionate.

**comment** /'kɒment/ 1 n. explanatory note; remark, opinion. 2 v. make comment(s) *on, upon, that*.

**commentary** /'kɒməntəri/ n. series of comments on book or performance etc.

**commentator** /'kɒmənteɪtə(r)/ n. writer or speaker of commentary; person who comments on current events. **commentate** v.

**commerce** /'kɒmɜ:s/ n. buying and selling; all forms of trading.

**commercial** /kə'mɜ:ʃ(ə)l/ 1 a. of, in, or for, commerce; done primarily for financial profit; (of broadcasting) financed by revenue from advertising. 2 n. broadcast advertisement. 3 **commercial traveller** representative sent out to obtain orders for firm's products.

**commingle** /kə'mɪŋg(ə)l/ v. mix, unite.

**comminute** /'kɒmɪnju:t/ v.t. reduce to small fragments or portions. **comminution** n.

**commiserate** /kə'mɪzəreɪt/ v. have or express sympathy *with*. **commiseration** n.; **commiserative** a.

**commissar** /'kɒmɪsɑ:(r)/ n. hist. head of government department in USSR.

**commissariat** /kɒmɪ'seərɪət/ n. department responsible for supply of food etc. for army; food supplied.

**commissary** /'kɒmɪsəri/ n. deputy, delegate. **commissarial** /-'seər-/ a.

**commission** /kə'mɪʃ(ə)n/ 1 n. task given to person to perform; body of persons constituted to perform certain duties; warrant conferring authority, esp. that of officer in armed forces above a certain rank; pay or percentage received by agent; committing. 2 v.t. empower by commission; commit task to (person); give (officer) command of ship; prepare (ship) for active service. 3 **in commission** (of warship) ready for active service; **out of commission** not in service, not in working order.

**commissionaire** /kəmɪʃə'neə(r)/ n. uniformed attendant at door of theatre, office, etc.

**commissioner** /kə'mɪʃənə(r)/ n. member of commission; official representing government in a district etc.; person who has been commissioned.

**commit** /kə'mɪt/ v.t. be doer of (crime etc.); entrust, consign; send (person) to prison; involve in course of action; pledge or dedicate *oneself*.

**commitment** /kə'mɪtmənt/ n. undertaking or pledge that restricts freedom of action; dedication to or involvement with a particular action, cause, etc.

**committal** /kə'mɪt(ə)l/ n. action of committing.

**committee** /kə'mɪti:/ n. group of persons appointed usu. out of larger body to attend to particular business.

**commode** /kə'məʊd/ n. chamber-pot mounted in chair or box with cover; chest of drawers.

**commodious** /kə'məʊdɪəs/ a. roomy.

**commodity** /kə'mɒdɪti/ n. article of trade esp. product as opp. service.

**commodore** /'kɒmədɔ:(r)/ n. naval officer next below rear-admiral; com-

**common** /'kɒmən/ 1 *a.* shared by all; of or belonging to the whole community; occurring often; ordinary, of the most familiar or numerous kind; of inferior quality, vulgar; *Gram.* (of noun) applicable to any one of a class, (of gender) applicable to individuals of either sex. 2 *n. UK* land belonging to community, esp. unenclosed waste land. 3 **common ground** basis for argument accepted by both sides; **common law** unwritten law of England based on custom and precedent; **common-law husband, wife,** one recognized by common law without formal marriage; **Common Market** European Economic Community; **common or garden** *colloq.* ordinary; **common-room** room for social use of students or teachers at college etc.; **common sense** good practical sense esp. in everyday matters; **common time** *Mus.* four crotchets in a bar; **in common** shared by several, in joint use.

**commonalty** /'kɒmənəlti:/ *n.* general community, common people.

**commoner** /'kɒmənə(r)/ *n.* person below rank of peer.

**commonly** /'kɒmənli:/ *adv.* usually, frequently.

**commonplace** /'kɒmənpleɪs/ 1 *n.* event, topic, etc. that is ordinary or usual; trite remark. 2 *a.* lacking originality or individuality.

**commons** /'kɒmənz/ *n.pl. UK* common people; **(House of) Commons** lower house of British Parliament.

**commonwealth** /'kɒmənwelθ/ *n.* independent community. **the Commonwealth** the federated States of Australia, Australia central government; **the (British) Commonwealth** association of UK with various independent States and dependencies.

**commotion** /kə'məʊʃ(ə)n/ *n.* noisy disturbance.

**communal** /'kɒmjʊn(ə)l/ *a.* shared between members of group or community. **communally** *adv.*

**commune**¹ /'kɒmju:n/ *n.* group of people, not all of one family, sharing living accommodation and goods; small territorial administrative district.

**commune**² /kə'mju:n/ *v.i.* communicate spiritually or feel in close touch (*with*).

**communicant** /kə'mju:nɪkənt/ *n.* receiver of Holy Communion; person who imparts information.

**communicate** /kə'mju:nɪkeɪt/ *v.* impart *to,* have social dealings *with;* convey information; receive Holy Communion.

**communication** /kəmju:nɪ'keɪʃ(ə)n/ *n.* imparting or exchange of information; letter, message, etc.; social dealings; connection or means of access; in *pl.* science and practice of transmitting information. **communication cord** cord or chain for pulling by passenger to stop train in emergency.

**communicative** /kə'mju:nɪkətɪv/ *a.* ready and willing to talk.

**communion** /kə'mju:nɪən/ *n.* communing; fellowship; body of Christians of same denomination; **(Holy) Communion** Eucharist.

**communiqué** /kə'mju:nɪkeɪ/ *n.* official communication, esp. report.

**communism** /'kɒmjənɪz(ə)m/ *n.* social system based on common ownership of property, means of production, etc.; **Communism** movement or political party advocating communism. **communist** *n.* & *a.;* **communistic** *a.*

**community** /kə'mju:nəti:/ *n.* group of people etc. living in same locality or having same religion, race, profession, interests, etc.; commune; joint ownership. **community centre** place providing social, recreational, and educational facilities for a neighbourhood; **community singing** singing in chorus by large gathering of people.

**commute** /kə'mju:t/ *v.* travel regularly by train or bus or car to work at a distance from home; exchange, interchange; change (punishment *to* another less severe).

**commuter** *n.* person who commutes to and from work.

**compact**¹ 1 /kəm'pækt/ *a.* closely or neatly packed together; occupying small space. 2 /kəm'pækt/ *v.t.* make compact. 3 /'kɒmpækt/ *n.* small flat case for face-powder etc. 4 **compact disc** small disc from which sound is reproduced by laser action.

**compact**² /'kɒmpækt/ *n.* agreement or contract.

**companion** /kəm'pænjən/ *n.* one who accompanies or associates with another; woman paid to live with another; handbook or reference-book; thing that matches another; member of some orders of distinction. **companionway** staircase from deck of ship to cabins etc.

**companionable** /kəm'pænjənəb(ə)l/ *a.* sociable, agreeable as companion.

**companionship** /kəm'pænjənʃɪp/ *n.* state of being companions.

**company** /'kʌmpəni:/ *n.* being with another or others; number of people assembled; guests; body of persons combined for commercial or other purpose; group of actors etc.; subdivision of infantry battalion. **ship's company** entire crew.

**comparable** /'kɒmpərəb(ə)l/ *a.* that can be compared (*with*, *to*).

**comparative** /kəm'pærətɪv/ 1 *a.* of or involving comparison; perceptible or estimated by comparison; considered in relation to each other; *Gram.* expressing a higher degree of a quality. 2 *n. Gram.* comparative degree or form.

**compare** /kəm'peə(r)/ 1 *v.* estimate similarity of; liken *to*; bear comparison (*with*). 2 *n.* comparison. 3 **compare notes** exchange information or ideas.

**comparison** /kəm'pærəs(ə)n/ *n.* comparing. **bear comparison** be able to be compared favourably *with*; **degrees of comparison** *Gram.* positive, comparative, and superlative of adjectives and adverbs.

**compartment** /kəm'pɑ:tmənt/ *n.* division or space partitioned off, esp. in railway-carriage.

**compass** /'kʌmpəs/ *n.* instrument showing direction of magnetic north and bearings from it; (usu. in *pl.*) V-shaped hinged instrument for drawing circles and taking measurements; circumference, area, extent, scope, range.

**compassion** /kəm'pæʃ(ə)n/ *n.* pity.

**compassionate** /kəm'pæʃənət/ *a.* sympathetic, showing compassion; granted out of compassion.

**compatible** /kəm'pætəb(ə)l/ *a.* able to coexist (*with*); (of equipment) able to be used in combination. **compatibility** *n.*

**compatriot** /kəm'pætrɪət/ *n.* person from same country.

**compeer** /kɒm'pɪə(r)/ *n.* equal; comrade.

**compel** /kəm'pel/ *v.t.* force or constrain; bring about irresistibly.

**compelling** /kəm'pelɪŋ/ *a.* rousing strong interest.

**compendious** /kəm'pendɪəs/ *a.* comprehensive but brief.

**compendium** /kəm'pendɪəm/ *n.* (*pl.* **-dia** or **-diums**), summary; collection of table-games etc.

**compensate** /'kɒmpənseɪt/ *v.* recompense, make amends for; counterbalance.

**compensation** /kɒmpən'seɪʃ(ə)n/ *n.* compensating, thing (esp. money) that compensates. **compensatory** *a.*

**compère** /'kɒmpeə(r)/ 1 *n.* person who introduces performers in variety entertainment etc. 2 *v.t.* act as compère to.

**compete** /kəm'pi:t/ *v.* take part in contest, race, examination, etc.; strive *with* or *against* others.

**competence** /'kɒmpɪt(ə)ns/ *n.* being competent; ability; comfortably adequate income.

**competent** /'kɒmpɪt(ə)nt/ *a.* having adequate ability, knowledge, or authority; adequate, effective.

**competition** /kɒmpə'tɪʃ(ə)n/ *n.* event in which persons compete; competing; those competing with one.

**competitive** /kəm'petətɪv/ *a.* of, enjoying, or involving competition; (of prices etc.) comparable with those of rivals.

**competitor** /kəm'petɪtə(r)/ *n.* one who competes; rival, esp. in trade.

**compile** /kəm'paɪl/ *v.t.* collect together (facts, quotations, etc.); make (book) thus. **compilation** /-pɪl-/*n.*

**complacent** /kəm'pleɪs(ə)nt/ *a.* self-satisfied; calmly content. **complacency** *n.*

**complain** /kəm'pleɪn/ *v.i.* express dissatisfaction. **complain of** say that one is suffering from.

**complaint** /kəm'pleɪnt/ *n.* statement that one is aggrieved or dissatisfied; formal protest; illness.

**complaisant** /kəm'pleɪz(ə)nt/ *a.* inclined to please or defer to others; acquiescent. **complaisance** *n.*

**complement** 1 /'kɒmplɪmənt/ *n.* something which completes whole; full

**complete** /kəm'pli:t/ 1 *a.* having all its parts; finished; total. 2 *v.t.* make complete, finish; fill in (form etc.) 3 **completion** *n.*

**complex** /'kɒmpleks/ 1 *a.* consisting of several parts; complicated. 2 *n.* complex whole; group of usu. repressed ideas etc. causing abnormal mental state. 3 **complexity** *n.*

**complexion** /kəm'plekʃ(ə)n/ *n.* natural colour and texture of skin, esp. of face; character.

**compliance** /kəm'plaɪəns/ *n.* acting in accordance with request or command etc.

**compliant** /kəm'plaɪənt/ *a.* ready to comply.

**complicate** /'kɒmplɪkeɪt/ *v.t.* (esp. in *p.p.*) make complex, confused, or difficult.

**complication** /kɒmplɪ'keɪʃ(ə)n/ *n.* complicated state; complicating circumstance.

**complicity** /kəm'plɪsəti:/ *n.* involvement in wrongdoing.

**compliment** 1 /'kɒmpləmənt/ *n.* expression or implication of praise; in *pl.* formal greetings. 2 /'kɒmpləment/ *v.t.* pay compliment to.

**complimentary** /kɒmplə'mentəri:/ *a.* expressing or conveying compliment; given free of charge.

**comply** /kəm'plaɪ/ *v.i.* act in accordance (*with*).

**compo** /'kɒmpəʊ/ *n. Aus. sl.* compensation, esp. for an injury.

**component** /kəˈpəʊnənt/ 1 *a.* being one of the parts of a whole. 2 *n.* component part.

**comport** /kəm'pɔːt/ *v.* behave or conduct (one*self*); agree or accord *with*.

**compose** /kəm'pəʊz/ *v.t.* create in music or writing; make up, constitute; set up (type); set in type; arrange artistically or for specified purpose; make calm.

**composed** /kəm'pəʊzd/ *a.* calm, self-possessed

**composer** /kəm'pəʊzə(r)/ *n.* person who composes, esp. music.

**composite** /'kɒmpəzət/ 1 *a.* made up of various parts or materials; (of plant) having head of many flowers forming one bloom. 2 *n.* composite thing or plant.

**composition** /kɒmpə'zɪʃ(ə)n/ *n.* composing; thing composed; constitution of substance; compound artificial substance.

**compositor** /kəm'pɒzɪtə(r)/ *n.* person who sets up type for printing.

**compost** /'kɒmpɒst/ *n.* prepared mixture, esp. of rotted organic matter, for horticultural use.

**composure** /kəm'pəʊʒə(r)/ *n.* calmness.

**compote** /'kɒmpəʊt/ *n.* fruit in syrup.

**compound**[1] 1 /'kɒmpaʊnd/ *n.* thing made up of two or more parts or ingredients; substance consisting of two or more elements chemically united. 2 /kəm'paʊnd/ *v.* mix or combine (ingredients etc.), make up (whole); complicate; condone (offence etc.) for personal gain; settle (matter) by mutual concession; come to terms. 3 /'kɒmpaʊnd/ *a.* made up of two or more parts or ingredients; combined, collective. 4 **compound fracture** one complicated by skin wound; **compound interest** interest paid on principal and accumulated interest.

**compound**[2] /'kɒmpaʊnd/ *n.* enclosure, fenced-in space.

**comprehend** /kɒmprɪ'hend/ *v.t.* grasp mentally; include.

**comprehensible** /kɒmprɪ'hensəb(ə)l/ *a.* that can be understood.

**comprehension** /kɒmprɪ'henʃ(ə)n/ *n.* understanding; inclusion.

**comprehensive** /kɒmprɪ'hensɪv/ 1 *a.* including much or all; of wide scope; *UK* (of secondary school) providing education for children of all abilities. 2 *n. UK* comprehensive school.

**compress** 1 /kəm'pres/ *v.* squeeze together, bring into smaller space. 2 /'kɒmpres/ *n.* pad or cloth pressed on to part of body to stop bleeding or relieve inflammation etc.

**compression** /kəm'preʃ(ə)n/ *n.* compressing; reduction in volume of fuel mixture in internal-combustion engine before ignition.

**compressor** /kəm'presə(r)/ *n.*

**comprise** /kəmˈpraɪz/ v.t. have or include as constituent parts; consist of.

**compromise** /ˈkɒmprəmaɪz/ 1 n. agreement reached by mutual concession. 2 v. settle (dispute) or modify (principles etc.) by compromise; bring under suspicion or into danger; make compromise.

**comptroller** /kənˈtrəʊlə(r)/ n. controller.

**compulsion** /kəmˈpʌlʃ(ə)n/ n. act of compelling; irresistible urge. **under compulsion** because one is compelled.

**compulsive** /kəmˈpʌlsɪv/ a. resulting or acting (as if) from compulsion; irresistible.

**compulsory** /kəmˈpʌlsərɪ/ a. that must be done; required by the rules etc. **compulsorily** adv.

**compunction** /kəmˈpʌŋkʃ(ə)n/ n. pricking of conscience.

**compute** /kəmˈpjuːt/ v. reckon, calculate; use computer. **computation** n.

**computer** /kəmˈpjuːtə(r)/ n. electronic apparatus for analysing or storing data, making calculations, or controlling operations.

**computerize** /kəmˈpjuːtəraɪz/ v.t. equip with or perform by or produce by computer. **computerization** n.

**comrade** /ˈkɒmreɪd/ n. associate or companion in some activity; fellow socialist or communist, etc. **comradeship** n.

**con**[1] sl. 1 v.t. persuade, swindle. 2 n. confidence trick.

**con**[2] v.t. arch. study, learn by heart.

**con**[3] v.t. direct steering of (ship).

**concatenate** /kɒnˈkætəneɪt/ v.t. link together; form sequence of. **concatenation** n.

**concave** /kɒnˈkeɪv/ a. curved like interior of circle or sphere. **concavity** /-ˈkæv-/ n.

**conceal** /kənˈsiːl/ v.t. hide or keep secret. **concealment** n.

**concede** /kənˈsiːd/ v.t. admit to be true; grant; admit defeat in (contest etc.).

**conceit** /kənˈsiːt/ n. personal vanity; fanciful notion, far-fetched comparison.

**conceited** /kənˈsiːtɪd/ a. having too high an opinion of oneself.

**conceive** /kənˈsiːv/ v. become pregnant; form in mind; imagine, think (of). **conceivable** a.

**concentrate** /ˈkɒnsəntreɪt/ 1 v. employ one's full thoughts or efforts (on); bring together at or on one point; increase strength of (liquid etc.) by removing water. 2 n. concentrated substance.

**concentration** /kɒnsənˈtreɪʃ(ə)n/ n. concentrating or being concentrated; amount or strength of substance in mixture; mental faculty of exclusive attention. **concentration camp** place for detention of political prisoners etc.

**concentric** /kənˈsentrɪk/ a. having the same centre. **concentricity** n.

**concept** /ˈkɒnsept/ n. generalized idea or notion.

**conception** /kənˈsepʃ(ə)n/ n. conceiving, being conceived; thing conceived; idea.

**conceptual** /kənˈseptjuːəl/ a. of mental concepts. **conceptually** adv.

**conceptualize** /kənˈseptjuːəlaɪz/ v.t. form concept or idea of.

**concern** /kənˈsɜːn/ 1 v.t. be relevant or important to; affect; relate to; interest (oneself). 2 n. thing of interest or importance to one; solicitude, anxiety; firm or enterprise; in pl. one's affairs.

**concerned** /kənˈsɜːnd/ a. anxious or troubled; involved or interested.

**concerning** /kənˈsɜːnɪŋ/ prep. about.

**concert** /ˈkɒnsət/ n. live musical entertainment; combination of voices etc.; agreement, union.

**concerted** /kənˈsɜːtɪd/ a. effected by mutual agreement; done in co-operation.

**concertina** /kɒnsəˈtiːnə/ 1 n. portable musical instrument consisting of reeds sounded by bellows worked by the player's hands. 2 v. compress or collapse in folds like those of concertina.

**concerto** /kənˈtʃɜːtəʊ/ n. (pl. **-tos**) musical piece for solo instrument and orchestra.

**concession** /kənˈseʃ(ə)n/ n. conceding, thing conceded; right to use land, sell goods, etc.; reduction in price for certain category of person.

**concessionaire** /kənseʃəˈneə(r)/ n. holder of concession.

**concessive** /kənˈsesɪv/ a. Gram. expressing concession.

**conch** /kɒntʃ/ n. spiral shell of certain

**conchology** /kɒŋˈkɒlədʒiː/ n. study of shells and shellfish.

**conciliate** /kənˈsɪliːeɪt/ v.t. win over from anger or hostility; reconcile. **conciliation** n.; **conciliatory** a.

**concise** /kənˈsaɪs/ a. brief, condensed.

**conclave** /ˈkɒŋkleɪv/ n. private meeting; assembly or meeting-place of cardinals for papal election.

**conclude** /kənˈkluːd/ v. bring or come to end; settle finally; draw conclusion.

**conclusion** /kənˈkluːʒ(ə)n/ n. ending; judgement reached by reasoning; settling of peace etc.

**conclusive** /kənˈkluːsɪv/ a. decisive, convincing.

**concoct** /kənˈkɒkt/ v.t. prepare, esp. by mixing; invent or devise. **concoction** n.

**concomitant** /kənˈkɒmət(ə)nt/ 1 a. accompanying. 2 n. accompanying thing. 3 **concomitance** n.

**concord** /ˈkɒŋkɔːd/ n. agreement, harmony; Mus. chord satisfactory in itself; Gram. agreement between words in gender, number, etc. **concordant** a.

**concordance** /kənˈkɔːd(ə)ns/ n. agreement; index of words used by author in book, esp. Bible.

**concordat** /kənˈkɔːdæt/ n. official agreement between Church and State.

**concourse** /ˈkɒŋkɔːs/ n. crowd; open central area in large public building, railway station, etc.

**concrete** /ˈkɒŋkriːt/ 1 n. mixture of cement and gravel etc., used in building etc. 2 a. existing in material form, real, definite; not abstract; made of concrete. 3 v. cover with or embed in concrete; /kənˈkriːt/ form into mass, solidify.

**concretion** /kənˈkriːʃ(ə)n/ n. hard solid mass; forming of this by coalescence.

**concubine** /ˈkɒŋkjʊbaɪn/ n. woman who cohabits with man without marriage; (among polygamous peoples) secondary wife. **concubinage** /-ˈkjuː-bɪnɪdʒ/ n.

**concupiscence** /kənˈkjuːpəs(ə)ns/ n. sexual desire. **concupiscent** a.

**concur** /kənˈkɜː(r)/ v.i. (past & p.p. **concurred**) agree; coincide.

**concurrent** /kənˈkʌrənt/ a. existing or acting together or at the same time. **concurrence** n.

**concuss** /kənˈkʌs/ v.t. subject to concussion.

**concussion** /kənˈkʌʃ(ə)n/ n. temporary unconsciousness or incapacity due to injury to head; violent shaking.

**condemn** /kənˈdem/ v.t. give judicial decision against; sentence (to); doom to; pronounce unfit for use etc. **condemnation** n.; **condemnatory** a.

**condensation** /kɒndenˈseɪʃ(ə)n/ n. condensing; condensed material.

**condense** /kənˈdens/ v. make denser or briefer; compress; change or be changed from gas or vapour to liquid.

**condescend** /kɒndəˈsend/ v.i. consent to do something less dignified than is fitting or customary.

**condescending** /kɒndəˈsendɪŋ/ a. patronizing.

**condescension** /kɒndəˈsenʃ(ə)n/ n. condescending manner or act.

**condign** /kənˈdaɪn/ a. adequate, fitting.

**condiment** /ˈkɒndəmənt/ n. seasoning or relish for use with food.

**condition** /kənˈdɪʃ(ə)n/ 1 n. thing necessary for something else to be possible; state of being, state of physical fitness or fitness for use; ailment or abnormality; in pl. circumstances. 2 v.t. bring into desired condition; teach, accustom; govern, determine; be essential to.

**conditional** /kənˈdɪʃən(ə)l/ a. dependent (on), not absolute; Gram. expressing condition.

**condole** /kənˈdəʊl/ v.i. express sympathy in sorrow. **condolence** n.

**condom** /ˈkɒndəm/ n. contraceptive sheath.

**condominium** /kɒndəˈmɪnɪəm/ n. joint control of State by other States; US building in which flats are individually owned.

**condone** /kənˈdəʊn/ v.t. forgive, overlook. **condonation** n.

**condor** /ˈkɒndɔː(r)/ n. large S. Amer. vulture.

**conduce** /kənˈdjuːs/ v.i. lead or contribute to. **conducive** a.

**conduct** 1 /ˈkɒndʌkt/ n. behaviour, manner of conducting oneself, business, etc. 2 /kənˈdʌkt/ v.t. lead, escort; control, manage; be conductor of (or-

**conduction** /kənˈdʌkʃ(ə)n/ n. conducting of heat, electricity, etc.

**conductive** /kənˈdʌktɪv/ a. having property of conducting heat or electricity. **conductivity** /-ˈtɪv-/ n.

**conductor** /kənˈdʌktə(r)/ n. director of orchestra, choir, etc.; person who collects fares on bus etc.; substance that conducts heat or electricity. **conductress** n.

**conduit** /ˈkɒndɪt/ n. channel or pipe for conveying liquid or protecting insulated cable.

**cone** n. solid figure with usu. circular base and tapering to a point; cone-shaped object; dry fruit of pine or fir; ice-cream cornet.

**coney** var. of **cony**.

**confab** /ˈkɒnfæb/ n. colloq. confabulation.

**confabulate** /kənˈfæbjuːleɪt/ v.i. talk together. **confabulation** n.

**confection** /kənˈfekʃ(ə)n/ n. mixture; delicacy, esp. made of sweet ingredients.

**confectioner** /kənˈfekʃənə(r)/ n. dealer in sweets or pastries etc. **confectionery** n.

**confederacy** /kənˈfedərəsɪ:/ n. alliance or league esp. of confederate States.

**confederate 1** /kənˈfedərət/ a. allied. **2** /kənˈfedərət/ n. ally; accomplice. **3** /kənˈfedəreɪt/ v.t. bring or come into alliance. **4 Confederate States** those which seceded from US in 1860-1.

**confederation** /kənfedəˈreɪʃ(ə)n/ n. union or alliance of States or organizations.

**confer** /kənˈfɜː(r)/ v. (past & p.p. **conferred**) bestow; meet for discussion.

**conference** /ˈkɒnfər(ə)ns/ n. consultation; meeting (esp. regular) for discussion etc.

**conferment** /kənˈfɜːmənt/ n. conferring of honour etc.

**confess** /kənˈfes/ v. acknowledge, admit; declare one's sins, esp. to priest; (of priest) hear confession.

**confessedly** /kənˈfesɪdlɪ:/ adv. by personal or general admission.

**confession** /kənˈfeʃ(ə)n/ n. confessing; thing confessed; statement of principles etc.

**confessional** /kənˈfeʃən(ə)l/ **1** n. enclosed place where priest hears confession. **2** a. of confession.

**confessor** /kənˈfesə(r)/ n. priest who hears confession.

**confetti** /kənˈfetɪ:/ n. small bits of coloured paper thrown by wedding guests at bride and bridegroom.

**confidant** /ˈkɒnfɪdænt/ n. (fem. **confidante** pr. same) person to whom one confides knowledge of one's private affairs.

**confide** /kənˈfaɪd/ v. tell (secret) or entrust (task) to. **confide in** talk confidentially to.

**confidence** /ˈkɒnfɪd(ə)ns/ n. firm trust; assured expectation; self-reliance; boldness; something told confidentially. **confidence trick** swindle in which victim is persuaded to trust swindler in some way; **in confidence** as a secret; **in person's confidence** trusted with his secrets.

**confident** /ˈkɒnfɪd(ə)nt/ a. feeling or showing confidence.

**confidential** /kɒnfɪˈdenʃ(ə)l/ a. spoken or written in confidence; entrusted with secrets; inclined to confide. **confidentially** a.; **confidentiality** n.

**configuration** /kənfɪgəˈreɪʃ(ə)n/ n. manner of arrangement, shape, outline.

**confine 1** /kənˈfaɪn/ v.t. keep or restrict within certain limits; imprison. **2** /ˈkɒnfaɪn/ n. (usu. in pl.) boundary. **3 be confined** be in childbirth.

**confinement** /kənˈfaɪnmənt/ n. confining, being confined; childbirth.

**confirm** /kənˈfɜːm/ v.t. provide support for truth or correctness of; establish more firmly; formally make definite; administer confirmation to.

**confirmation** /kɒnfəˈmeɪʃ(ə)n/ n. corroborative circumstance or statement; rite confirming baptized person as member of Christian Church.

**confiscate** /ˈkɒnfɪskeɪt/ v.t. take or seize by authority. **confiscation** n.

**conflagration** /kɒnfləˈgreɪʃ(ə)n/ n. great and destructive fire.

**conflate** /kənˈfleɪt/ v.t. fuse together, blend.

**conflict 1** /ˈkɒnflɪkt/ n. fight, struggle; opposition; clashing. **2** /kənˈflɪkt/ v.i. struggle; clash, be incompatible with.

**confluent** /'kɒnflu:ənt/ **1** *a.* merging into one. **2** *n.* one of confluent streams etc. **3 confluence** *n.*

**conform** /kən'fɔ:m/ *v.* (cause to) fit or be suitable; comply with rules or general custom.

**conformable** /kən'fɔ:məb(ə)l/ *a.* adapted or corresponding (*to*), consistent *with*.

**conformation** /kɒnfɔ:'meɪʃ(ə)n/ *n.* thing's structure.

**conformist** /kən'fɔ:məst/ *n.* person who conforms to an established practice. **conformism** *n.*

**conformity** /kən'fɔ:məti/ *n.* conforming with established practice; suitability.

**confound** /kən'faʊnd/ *v.t.* baffle; confuse; overthrow or defeat; (as mild oath) damn.

**confront** /kən'frʌnt/ *v.t.* meet or stand facing, esp. in hostility or defiance; (of problem etc.) present itself to; bring face to face *with*. **confrontation** *n.*

**confuse** /kən'fju:z/ *v.t.* throw into disorder; bewilder; mix up; make obscure. **confusion** *n.*

**confute** /kən'fju:t/ *v.t.* prove to be false or wrong. **confutation** *n.*

**conga** /'kɒŋɡə/ *n.* Latin-Amer. dance usu. performed in single file.

**congeal** /kən'dʒi:l/ *v.* solidify by cooling; stiffen, coagulate. **congelation** *n.*

**congenial** /kən'dʒi:nɪəl/ *a.* having sympathetic nature, similar interests, etc.; suited or agreeable *to*. **congeniality** *a.*

**congenital** /kən'dʒenɪt(ə)l/ *a.* existing or as such from birth.

**conger** /'kɒŋɡə(r)/ *n.* large sea eel.

**congeries** /kən'dʒɪəri:z/ *n.* (*pl.* same) disorderly collection; mass, heap.

**congest** /kən'dʒest/ *v.t.* affect with congestion.

**congestion** /kən'dʒestʃ(ə)n/ *n.* abnormal accumulation or obstruction, esp. of traffic etc. or mucus in nose etc.

**conglomerate 1** /kən'ɡlɒmərət/ *a.* gathered into a rounded mass. **2** /kən'ɡlɒmərət/ *n.* conglomerate mass; business etc. corporation formed by merging separate firms. **3** /kən'ɡlɒməreɪt/ *v.* collect into coherent mass. **4 conglomeration** *n.*

**congratulate** /kən'ɡrætjʊleɪt/ *v.t.* express pleasure at happiness or excellence or good fortune of. **congratulatory** *a.*

**congratulation** /kənɡrætjə'leɪʃ(ə)n/ *n.* congratulating, (usu. in *pl.*) expression of this.

**congregate** /'kɒŋɡrəɡeɪt/ *v.* collect or gather in crowd.

**congregation** /kɒŋɡrə'ɡeɪʃ(ə)n/ *n.* assembly of people, esp. for religious worship; group of persons regularly attending at particular church etc.

**congregational** /kɒŋɡrə'ɡeɪʃən(ə)l/ *a.* of congregation; **Congregational** of or adhering to Congregationalism.

**Congregationalism** /kɒŋɡrə'ɡeɪʃənəlɪz(ə)m/ *n.* system of ecclesiastical organization whereby individual churches are self-governing. **Congregationalist** *n.*

**congress** /'kɒŋɡres/ *n.* formal meeting of delegates for discussion; **Congress** national legislative body of US etc. **congressional** *a.*

**congruent** /'kɒŋɡru:ənt/ *a.* suitable, agreeing (*with*); (of geometrical figures) coinciding exactly when superimposed. **congruence** *n.*

**conic** /'kɒnɪk/ *a.* of cone. **conic section** *Math.* figure formed by intersection of cone and plane.

**conical** /'kɒnɪk(ə)l/ *a.* cone-shaped.

**conifer** /'kɒnɪfə(r)/ *n.* cone-bearing tree. **coniferous** /kə'nɪfərəs/ *a.*

**conjectural** /kən'dʒektʃərəl/ *a.* involving conjecture.

**conjecture** /kən'dʒektʃə(r)/ **1** *n.* guessing, guess. **2** *v.* make conjecture, guess.

**conjoin** /kən'dʒɔɪn/ *v.* join, combine.

**conjoint** /kən'dʒɔɪnt/ *a.* associated, conjoined.

**conjugal** /'kɒndʒəɡ(ə)l/ *a.* of marriage; between husband and wife.

**conjugate 1** /'kɒndʒəɡeɪt/ *v.* give the different forms of (verb); unite, become fused. **2** /'kɒndʒəɡət/ *a.* joined together; coupled, fused.

**conjugation** /kɒndʒə'ɡeɪʃ(ə)n/ *n.* *Gram.* (system of) verbal inflexion.

**conjunct** /kən'dʒʌŋkt/ *a.* joined, combined, associated.

**conjunction** /kən'dʒʌŋkʃ(ə)n/ *n.* joining, connection; *Gram.* word used to connect clauses, phrases, words, etc.; combination of events or circumstances.

**conjunctiva** /kɒndʒʌŋk'taɪvə/ n. mucous membrane lining inner eyelid.

**conjunctive** /kən'dʒʌŋktɪv/ a. joining, uniting; *Gram.* of nature of a conjunction.

**conjunctivitis** /kəndʒʌŋktə'vaɪtəs/ n. inflammation of conjunctiva.

**conjuncture** /kən'dʒʌŋktʃə(r)/ n. position of affairs at particular moment.

**conjure** /'kʌndʒə(r)/ v. perform deceptive tricks esp. by movement of hands; produce as if from nothing. **conjure up** evoke.

**conjuror** /'kʌndʒərə(r)/ n. (also **conjurer**) skilled performer of conjuring tricks.

**conk**[1] n. *sl.* nose.

**conk**[2] v.i. *sl.* **conk out** break down.

**connect** /kə'nekt/ v. join, be joined; associate mentally or practically (*with*); (of train, boat, etc.) arrive in time for passengers to catch another conveyance; put into communication by telephone; (usu. in *pass.*) unite or associate *with* others in relationship etc. **connecting-rod** rod between piston and crankpin etc. in engine. **connector** n.

**connection** /kə'nekʃ(ə)n/ n. being connected or related; association of ideas; connecting part; close associate, group of associates etc.; connecting train etc.

**connective** /kə'nektɪv/ a. serving to connect.

**conning-tower** /'kɒnɪŋtaʊə(r)/ n. raised structure of submarine containing periscope; pilot-house of warship.

**connive** /kə'naɪv/ v.i. **connive at** disregard or tacitly consent to (wrongdoing). **connivance** n.

**connoisseur** /kɒnə'sɜː(r)/ n. person with good taste and judgement (*of*, *in*).

**connote** /kə'nəʊt/ v.t. imply; mean; include in its meaning. **connotation** /kɒnə'teɪʃ(ə)n/ n.; **connotative** a.

**connubial** /kə'njuːbɪəl/ a. connected with marriage.

**conquer** /'kɒŋkə(r)/ v. overcome, defeat; be victor; subjugate. **conqueror** n.

**conquest** /'kɒŋkwest/ n. conquering, what is won by it; person whose affections have been won.

**consanguineous** /kɒnsæŋ'gwɪnɪəs/ a. descended from same ancestor; akin. **consanguinity** n.

**conscience** /'kɒnʃ(ə)ns/ n. moral sense of right and wrong, esp. as affecting person's behaviour. **conscience money** money paid to relieve conscience, esp. in respect of evaded payment etc.; **conscience-stricken** made uneasy by bad conscience.

**conscientious** /kɒnʃɪ'enʃəs/ a. obedient to conscience; scrupulous; assiduous. **conscientious objector** person who refuses to do military service on grounds of conscience.

**conscious** /'kɒnʃəs/ 1 a. awake and aware of one's surroundings etc.; aware (*of*), knowing; consciously performed or felt etc. 2 n. the conscious mind.

**consciousness** n. awareness; person's conscious thoughts and feelings as a whole.

**conscript** 1 /kən'skrɪpt/ v. summon for compulsory State (esp. military) service. 2 /'kɒnskrɪpt/ n. conscripted person. 3 **conscription** n.

**consecrate** /'kɒnsəkreɪt/ v.t. make or declare sacred (*to*); dedicate formally to religious purpose; devote *to*. **consecration** n.

**consecutive** /kən'sekjətɪv/ a. following continuously; proceeding in logical sequence.

**consensus** /kən'sensəs/ n. agreement in opinion; majority view.

**consent** /kən'sent/ 1 v.i. express willingness, give permission; agree *to*. 2 n. agreement, compliance; permission.

**consequence** /'kɒnsəkwəns/ n. that which follows from any cause or condition; importance.

**consequent** /'kɒnsəkwənt/ a. that results; following as consequence.

**consequential** /kɒnsə'kwenʃ(ə)l/ a. following as result or inference; self-important. **consequentiality** n.

**conservancy** /kən'sɜːvənsɪ/ n. board controlling river, port, etc. or concerned with conservation.

**conservation** /kɒnsə'veɪʃ(ə)n/ n. preservation, esp. of natural environment. **conservation of energy** *Phys.* principle that quantity of energy etc. of any closed system of bodies remains constant.

**conservationist** /kɒnsə'veɪʃənəst/ n. supporter or advocate of conservation.

**conservative** /kən'sɜːvətɪv/ 1 a. tend-

**conservatoire**      114      **consternation**

ing to conserve; averse to rapid change; (of estimate) purposely low. **2** *n.* conservative person; **3 Conservative Party** UK political party disposed to promote private enterprise. **4 conservatism** *n.*

**conservatoire** /kənˈsɜːvətwɑː(r)/ *n.* (usu. Continental) school of music or other arts. [F]

**conservatory** /kənˈsɜːvətəri:/ *n.* greenhouse for tender plants; (US) *conservatoire.*

**conserve** /kənˈsɜːv/ **1** *v.t.* preserve, keep from harm, decay, or loss. **2** *n.* fruit etc. preserved in sugar; jam.

**consider** /kənˈsɪdə(r)/ *v.* contemplate; deliberate thoughtfully; make allowance for, take into account; have the opinion *that*; show consideration for.

**considerable** /kənˈsɪdərəb(ə)l/ *a.* not negligible; of some importance or size.

**considerate** /kənˈsɪdərət/ *a.* thoughtful for feelings or rights of others.

**consideration** /kənsɪdəˈreɪʃ(ə)n/ *n.* careful thought; being considerate; fact or thing regarded as a reason; compensation.

**considering** /kənˈsɪdərɪŋ/ *prep.* in view of.

**consign** /kənˈsaɪn/ *v.t.* commit or deliver *to*; send (goods etc.) *to.*

**consignee** /kɒnsaɪˈniː/ *n.* person to whom goods are sent.

**consignor** /kənˈsaɪnə(r)/ *n.* person by whom goods are sent.

**consignment** /kənˈsaɪnmənt/ *n.* consigning, goods consigned.

**consist** /kənˈsɪst/ *v.i.* be composed *of*; have its essential features *in*; be consistent *with.*

**consistency** /kənˈsɪstənsi:/ *n.* degree of density, esp. of thick liquids; being consistent.

**consistent** /kənˈsɪst(ə)nt/ *a.* compatible; constant to same principles.

**consistory** /kənˈsɪstəri:/ *n.* council of cardinals.

**consolation** /kɒnsəˈleɪʃ(ə)n/ *n.* alleviation of grief or disappointment. **consolation prize** one given to competitor just failing to win main prizes. **consolatory** /kənˈsɒlətəri:/ *a.*

**console**[1] /kənˈsəʊl/ *v.t.* bring consolation to.

**console**[2] /ˈkɒnsəʊl/ *n.* bracket supporting a shelf etc.; cabinet with keys and stops of organ; panel for controls of electronic or mechanical equipment; cabinet for radio etc. equipment.

**consolidate** /kənˈsɒlədeɪt/ *v.* make or become strong or solid; combine (territories, companies, debts, etc.) into one whole. **consolidation** *n.*

**consols** /ˈkɒnsɒlz/ *n.pl.* UK Government securities.

**consommé** /kənˈsɒmeɪ/ *n.* clear soup.

**consonance** /ˈkɒnsənəns/ *n.* agreement or harmony.

**consonant** /ˈkɒnsənənt/ **1** *n.* speech sound that forms a syllable only in combination with vowel, letter representing this. **2** *a.* in agreement or harmony *with*; agreeable *to.* **3 consonantal** /-ˈnænt-/ *a.*

**consort**[1] /ˈkɒnsɔːt/ *n.* wife or husband; ship sailing with another. **2** /kənˈsɔːt/ *v.i.* associate or keep company (*with*); be in harmony.

**consort**[2] /ˈkɒnsɔːt/ *n. Mus.* group of players or instruments.

**consortium** /kənˈsɔːtiːəm/ *n.* (*pl.* -tia) association esp. of several business companies.

**conspectus** /kənˈspektəs/ *n.* general view; synopsis.

**conspicuous** /kənˈspɪkjuːəs/ *a.* clearly visible; attracting attention.

**conspiracy** /kənˈspɪrəsi:/ *n.* act of conspiring; unlawful combination or plot.

**conspirator** /kənˈspɪrətə(r)/ *n.* person who takes part in conspiracy. **conspiratorial** /-ˈtɔːr-/ *a.*

**conspire** /kənˈspaɪə(r)/ *v.i.* combine secretly for unlawful or harmful purpose; agree together.

**constable** /ˈkʌnstəb(ə)l/ *n.* policeman; policeman or policewoman of lowest rank; *hist.* principal officer of royal household. **Chief Constable** UK head of police force of county etc.

**constabulary** /kənˈstæbjələri:/ *n.* police force.

**constancy** /ˈkɒnstənsi:/ *n.* quality of being unchanging and dependable.

**constant** /ˈkɒnst(ə)nt/ **1** *a.* continuous; frequently occurring; having constancy. **2** *n. Math. & Phys.* unvarying quantity.

**constellation** /kɒnstəˈleɪʃ(ə)n/ *n.* group of fixed stars.

**consternation** /kɒnstəˈneɪʃ(ə)n/ *n.* amazement or dismay.

**constipate** /'kɒnstəpeɪt/ v.t. affect with constipation.

**constipation** /kɒnstɪ'peɪʃ(ə)n/ n. difficulty in evacuating bowels.

**constituency** /kən'stɪtjuːənsɪ/ n. UK body electing representative; area represented.

**constituent** /kən'stɪtjuːənt/ 1 a. making part of whole; appointing, electing. 2 n. constituent part; member of constituency.

**constitute** /'kɒnstɪtjuːt/ v.t. be essence or components of; appoint, make into; establish.

**constitution** /kɒnstɪ'tjuːʃ(ə)n/ n. composition; form in which State is organized; body of fundamental principles according to which State etc. is governed; condition of person's body as regards health, strength, etc.

**constitutional** /kɒnstə'tjuːʃən(ə)l/ 1 a. of or in harmony with or limited by the constitution. 2 n. walk taken as healthy exercise. 3 **constitutionality** n.

**constitutive** /'kɒnstətjuːtɪv/ a. able to form or appoint; constituent.

**constrain** /kən'streɪn/ v.t. compel, force; confine; in p.p. forced, embarrassed.

**constraint** /kən'streɪnt/ n. compulsion; restriction; emotional etc. self-control.

**constrict** /kən'strɪkt/ v.t. compress, make narrow or tight. **constriction** n.; **constrictive** a.

**constrictor** /kən'strɪktə(r)/ n. muscle that draws together a part; snake that kills by compressing.

**construct** 1 /kən'strʌkt/ v.t. fit together, frame, build; Geom. draw. 2 /'kɒnstrʌkt/ n. thing constructed, esp. by the mind. 3 **constructor** n.

**construction** /kən'strʌkʃ(ə)n/ n. constructing or thing constructed; syntactical connection; interpretation or explanation. **constructional** a.

**constructive** /kən'strʌktɪv/ a. of construction; positive, helpful.

**construe** /kən'struː/ v.t. interpret; combine grammatically with; translate word for word.

**consubstantial** /kɒnsəb'stænʃ(ə)l/ a. of one substance.

**consubstantiation** /kɒnsəbstænʃɪ'eɪʃ(ə)n/ n. doctrine of presence of body and blood of Christ together with bread and wine of Eucharist.

**consul** /'kɒns(ə)l/ n. official appointed by State to live in foreign town and protect subjects there and assist commerce; hist. either of two annually-elected magistrates in ancient Rome. **consular** a.

**consulate** /'kɒnsjələt/ n. position of consul; consul's official residence.

**consult** /kən'sʌlt/ v. seek information or advice from; take counsel (with); take into consideration.

**consultant** /kən'sʌlt(ə)nt/ n. person who gives expert advice in medicine, business, etc. **consultancy** n.

**consultation** /kɒnsəl'teɪʃ(ə)n/ n. consulting; meeting for consulting.

**consultative** /kən'sʌltətɪv/ a. of or for consultation.

**consume** /kən'sjuːm/ v.t. eat or drink; use up; destroy.

**consumer** /kən'sjuːmə(r)/ n. user of product or service.

**consumerism** /kən'sjuːmərɪz(ə)m/ n. protection or promotion of consumers' interests.

**consummate** 1 /kən'sʌmət/ a. complete, perfect; supremely skilled. 2 /'kɒnsəmeɪt/ v.t. complete (esp. marriage by sexual intercourse). 3 **consummation** n.

**consumption** /kən'sʌmpʃ(ə)n/ n. consuming; purchase and use of goods etc.; wasting disease, esp. pulmonary tuberculosis.

**consumptive** /kən'sʌmptɪv/ 1 a. tending to or affected with tuberculosis. 2 n. consumptive person.

**contact** /'kɒntækt/ 1 n. condition or state of touching, meeting, or communicating; person who is, or may be, contacted for information etc.; Med. person likely to carry contagion through being near infected person; Electr. connection for passage of current. 2 v.t. get in touch with. 3 **contact lens** small lens placed against eyeball to correct faulty vision.

**contagion** /kən'teɪdʒ(ə)n/ n. spreading of disease by contact; corrupting influence. **contagious** a.

**contain** /kən'teɪn/ v.t. have or hold or have the capacity for holding within itself; include; comprise; enclose, pre-

**container** /kən'teɪnə(r)/ n. vessel, box, etc. designed to contain particular things; large boxlike receptacle of standard design for transport of goods.

**containerize** /kən'teɪnəraɪz/ v.t. pack in or transport by container. **containerization** n.

**containment** /kən'teɪnmənt/ n. action or policy of preventing expansion of hostile nation etc.

**contaminate** /kən'tæmɪneɪt/ v.t. pollute, infect. **contamination** n.

**contemn** /kən'tem/ v.t. poet. despise; disregard.

**contemplate** /'kɒntəmpleɪt/ v.t. survey with eyes or mind; regard as possible; intend. **contemplation** n.

**contemplative** /kən'templətɪv/ a. of or given to (esp.) religious contemplation and prayer.

**contemporaneous** /kəntempə'reɪnɪəs/ a. existing or occurring at same time.

**contemporary** /kən'tempərəri/ 1 a. belonging to same time or of same age; modern in style or design. 2 n. contemporary person etc.

**contempt** /kən'tempt/ n. feeling that person or thing is inferior or worthless; condition of being held in contempt; disobedience, disrespect.

**contemptible** /kən'temptəb(ə)l/ a. deserving contempt.

**contemptuous** /kən'temptjʊəs/ a. feeling or showing contempt.

**contend** /kən'tend/ v.i. strive, struggle; compete; argue (*with*), maintain (*that*).

**content**[1] /'kɒntent/ n. what is contained, esp. in vessel or house or book etc. (usu. in *pl.*); capacity (of vessel); amount contained in thing; substance of book etc. as opposed to *form*.

**content**[2] /kən'tent/ 1 *pred.a.* satisifed (*with*; willing (*to do*). 2 v.t. make content; satisfy. 3 n. contented state, satisfaction. 4 **contentment** n.

**contention** /kən'tenʃ(ə)n/ n. strife, controversy, rivalry; point etc. contended for in argument etc.

**contentious** /kən'tenʃəs/ a. quarrelsome, likely to cause argument.

**contest** 1 /'kɒntest/ n. contending; a competition. 2 v.t. /kən'test/ dispute; contend or compete for.

**contestant** /kən'test(ə)nt/ n. person who takes part in contest.

**context** /'kɒntekst/ n. what precedes and follows word or passage. **contextual** a.

**contiguous** /kən'tɪgjʊəs/ a. next to; touching; in contact (*with*). **contiguity** /kɒntɪ'gjuːətɪ/ n.

**continent** /'kɒntɪnənt/ 1 n. one of the main continuous bodies of land of the earth. 2 a. exercising self-restraint; able to control one's excretions. 3 **the Continent** mainland of Europe. 4 **continence** n.

**continental** /kɒntɪ'nent(ə)l/ a. of or characteristic of continent; **Continental** characteristic of the Continent. **Continental breakfast** light breakfast of coffee and rolls etc.; **Continental quilt** duvet.

**contingency** /kən'tɪndʒənsɪ/ n. event that may or may not occur; unknown or unforeseen circumstance.

**contingent** /kən'tɪndʒ(ə)nt/ 1 a. conditional or dependent (*on*); that may or may not occur; incidental. 2 n. body of troops or ships etc. forming part of larger group.

**continual** /kən'tɪnjʊəl/ a. frequently recurring; always happening.

**continuance** /kən'tɪnjʊəns/ n. continuing in existence or operation; duration.

**continuation** /kəntɪnjʊ'eɪʃ(ə)n/ n. act of continuing; thing that continues something else.

**continue** /kən'tɪnjuː/ v. maintain; keep up; resume; prolong, remain.

**continuity** /kɒntɪ'njuːɪtɪ/ n. being continuous; logical sequence; detailed scenario of film; linkage between broadcast items.

**continuo** /kən'tɪnjʊəʊ/ n. (pl. **-nuos**) *Mus.* continuous bass accompaniment played usu. on keyboard instrument.

**continuous** /kən'tɪnjʊəs/ a. connected without break; uninterrupted.

**continuum** /kən'tɪnjʊəm/ n. (pl. **-nua**) thing of continuous structure.

**contort** /kən'tɔːt/ v.t. twist or force out of normal shape. **contortion** n.

**contortionist** /kən'tɔːʃənəst/ n. performer who can twist his body into unusual positions.

**contour** /'kɒntʊə(r)/ n. outline; line on map joining points at same altitude;

**contraband** /'kɒntrəbænd/ 1 *n.* smuggled goods; smuggling. 2 *a.* forbidden to be imported or exported.

**contraception** /kɒntrə'sepʃ(ə)n/ *n.* use of contraceptives.

**contraceptive** /kɒntrə'septɪv/ 1 *a.* preventive of pregnancy. 2 *n.* contraceptive device or drug.

**contract** 1 /'kɒntrækt/ *n.* written or spoken agreement esp. one enforceable by law; document recording it. 2 /kən'trækt/ *v.* make or become smaller; make contract; incur (disease, debt); form (habit etc.); draw together; shorten. 3 **contract bridge** type of bridge in which no tricks bid and won count towards game; **contract in, out**, elect to enter, not to enter, scheme etc.

**contractile** /kən'træktaɪl/ *a.* capable of or producing contraction.

**contraction** /kən'trækʃ(ə)n/ *n.* contracting; shrinking; diminution; shortened word.

**contractor** /kən'træktə(r)/ *n.* person who undertakes contract, esp. in building, engineering, etc.

**contractual** /kən'træktjʊəl/ *a.* of or in the nature of a contract.

**contradict** /kɒntrə'dɪkt/ *v.* deny; oppose verbally; be at variance with. **contradiction** *n.*; **contradictory** *a.*

**contradistinction** /kɒntrədəs'tɪŋkʃ(ə)n/ *n.* distinction by contrast.

**contralto** /kən'træltəʊ/ *n.* (*pl.* -tos) lowest female voice; singer with contralto voice; music for contralto voice.

**contraption** /kən'træpʃ(ə)n/ *n.* machine or device, esp. strange one.

**contrapuntal** /kɒntrə'pʌnt(ə)l/ *a.* of or in counterpoint.

**contrariwise** /kən'treərɪwaɪz/ *adv.* on the other hand; in the opposite way.

**contrary** /'kɒntrərɪ/ 1 *a.* opposed in nature or tendency or direction; *colloq.* /kən'treərɪ/ perverse, self-willed. 2 *n. the* opposite. 3 *adv.* in opposition (*to*).

**contrast** 1 /'kɒntra:st/ *n.* comparison showing striking differences; difference so revealed; thing or person having noticeably different qualities (*to*); degree of difference between tones in photograph or television picture. 2 /kən'tra:st/ *v.* make or show contrast between.

**contravene** /kɒntrə'vi:n/ *v.t.* infringe, conflict with. **contravention** *n.*

**contretemps** /'kɒntrətɑ̃/ *n.* unlucky accident; embarrassing occurrence.

**contribute** /kən'trɪbju:t/ *v.* give jointly with others (*to* common fund etc.); supply (article etc.) for publication with others. **contribute to** help to bring about. **contributor** *n.*

**contribution** /kɒntrɪ'bju:ʃ(ə)n/ *n.* contributing; thing contributed.

**contributory** /kən'trɪbjətərɪ/ *a.* that contributes, using contributions.

**contrite** /kən'traɪt/ *a.* penitent for one's sin. **contrition** /kən'trɪʃ(ə)n/ *n.*

**contrivance** /kən'traɪv(ə)ns/ *n.* something contrived, esp. a device or plan; act of contriving.

**contrive** /kən'traɪv/ *v.* devise, think out; plan, manage.

**control** /kən'trəʊl/ 1 *n.* power of directing or restraining; self-restraint; means of restraining or regulating; (usu. in *pl.*) device to operate machine, esp. car or aircraft etc.; place where something is controlled or verified; standard of comparison for checking results of experiment; personality said to direct actions etc. of spiritualist medium. 2 *v.t.* have control of; regulate; serve as control to; verify. 3 **in control** in charge (*of*); **out of control** unrestrained.

**controller** *n.* person or thing that controls; officer controlling expenditure.

**controversial** /kɒntrə'vɜ:ʃ(ə)l/ *a.* causing or subject to controversy.

**controversy** /'kɒntrəvɜ:sɪ/ *n.* dispute, argument.

**controvert** /kɒntrə'vɜ:t/ *v.t.* dispute truth of.

**contumacy** /'kɒntjəməsɪ/ *n.* stubborn disobedience. **contumacious** /-'meɪ-/ *a.*

**contumely** /'kɒntju:mlɪ/ *n.* insulting language or treatment. **contumelious** /-'mi:-/ *a.*

**contuse** /kən'tju:z/ *v.t.* bruise. **contusion** *n.*

**conundrum** /kə'nʌndrəm/ *n.* riddle.

**conurbation** /kɒnɜ:'beɪʃ(ə)n/ *n.* group of towns and suburbs united by expansion.

**convalesce** /kɒnvə'les/ *v.i.* recover health after illness.

**convalescent** /kɒnvə'les(ə)nt/ 1 *a.* re-

**convection** /kənˈvekʃ(ə)n/ n. transmission of heat by movement of heated substance.

**convector** /kənˈvektə(r)/ n. heating appliance that circulates warm air.

**convene** /kənˈviːn/ v. summon, assemble.

**convenience** /kənˈviːnɪəns/ n. quality of being convenient; freedom from difficulty or trouble; advantage; useful thing; public lavatory. **convenience food** manufactured food needing little further preparation.

**convenient** /kənˈviːnɪənt/ a. serving one's comfort or interests; available or occurring at suitable time or place; *colloq.* well situated for access.

**convent** /ˈkɒnv(ə)nt/ n. religious community, esp. of nuns; its house.

**convention** /kənˈvenʃ(ə)n/ n. assembly or conference; agreement or treaty; general agreement on social behaviour etc. by implicit consent of the majority; customary practice.

**conventional** /kənˈvenʃən(ə)l/ a. depending on or according with convention; attentive to social conventions; not spontaneous or sincere; (of weapon, power source, etc.) other than nuclear. **conventionalism** n.; **conventionality** n.

**converge** /kənˈvɜːdʒ/ v.i. come together or towards the same point. **converge on** approach from different directions. **convergence** n.; **convergent** a.

**conversant** /kənˈvɜːs(ə)nt/ a. well acquainted (*with* subject etc.).

**conversation** /kɒnvəˈseɪʃ(ə)n/ n. informal exchange of ideas etc. by spoken words; instance of this.

**conversational** /kɒnvəˈseɪʃən(ə)l/ a. of or in conversation; colloquial.

**conversationalist** /kɒnvəˈseɪʃənəlɪst/ n. person fond of or good at conversation.

**converse**[1] /kənˈvɜːs/ v.i. have conversation. 2 /ˈkɒnvɜːs/ n. *arch.* conversation.

**converse**[2] /ˈkɒnvɜːs/ 1 a. opposite, contrary, reversed. 2 n. converse statement or proposition.

**conversion** /kənˈvɜːʃ(ə)n/ n. converting or being converted.

**convert** 1 /kənˈvɜːt/ v.t. change (*into*); cause (person) to change beliefs or party etc.; change (money etc.) into different form or currency etc.; *Rugby footb.* kick goal from (try). 2 /ˈkɒnvɜːt/ n. person converted esp. to religious faith.

**convertible** /kənˈvɜːtəb(ə)l/ 1 a. that may be converted. 2 n. motor car with folding or detachable roof.

**convex** /ˈkɒnveks/ a. curved like outside of sphere or circle. **convexity** n.

**convey** /kənˈveɪ/ v.t. transport, carry; communicate (meaning etc.); transfer by deed or legal process; transmit.

**conveyance** /kənˈveɪəns/ n. conveying; vehicle, carriage; legal transfer of property, deed effecting this.

**conveyancing** /kənˈveɪənsɪŋ/ n. branch of law dealing with transfer of property.

**convict** 1 /kənˈvɪkt/ v.t. prove or declare guilty. 2 /ˈkɒnvɪkt/ n. sentenced criminal.

**conviction** /kənˈvɪkʃ(ə)n/ n. convicting or being convicted; firm belief.

**convince** /kənˈvɪns/ v.t. firmly persuade.

**convivial** /kənˈvɪvɪəl/ a. fond of company; sociable, lively. **conviviality** n.

**convocation** /kɒnvəˈkeɪʃ(ə)n/ n. convoking; provincial synod of Anglican clergy; legislative assembly of university.

**convoke** /kənˈvəʊk/ v.t. call together; summon to assembly.

**convoluted** /ˈkɒnvəluːtəd/ a. coiled, twisted; complex.

**convolution** /kɒnvəˈluːʃ(ə)n/ n. coiling, coil, twist.

**convolvulus** /kənˈvɒlvjʊləs/ n. twining plant, esp. bindweed.

**convoy** /ˈkɒnvɔɪ/ 1 v.t. escort as protection. 2 n. convoying; group of ships, vehicles, etc., travelling together.

**convulse** /kənˈvʌls/ v.t. affect with convulsions.

**convulsion** /kənˈvʌlʃ(ə)n/ n. violent irregular motions of limbs or body caused by momentary contraction of muscles; violent disturbance; in *pl.* uncontrollable laughter. **convulsive** a.

**cony** /ˈkəʊnɪ/ n. rabbit.

**coo** 1 n. soft murmuring sound as of doves. 2 v.i. emit coo.

**cooee** /ˈkuːiː/ 1 n. & *int.* sound used to attract attention esp. at a distance. 2

**cook**

*v.i.* emit cooee. **3 within cooee of** *Aus.* within hailing distance of, close to.

**cook** /kʊk/ **1** *v.* prepare food; prepare (food) by heating; undergo cooking; *colloq.* falsify (accounts etc.). **2** *n.* person who cooks esp. professionally or in specified way.

**cooker** /ˈkʊkə(r)/ *n.* appliance or vessel for cooking food; fruit etc. suitable for cooking.

**cookery** /ˈkʊkəri/ *n.* art of cooking. **cookery-book** book of recipes and instructions in cookery.

**cookie** /ˈkʊki/ *n. US* sweet biscuit.

**cool** /kuːl/ **1** *a.* of or at fairly low temperature; suggesting or achieving coolness; unperturbed, self-possessed; lacking zeal or cordiality. **2** *n.* coolness; cool place; *sl.* composure. **3** *v.* make or become cool. **4 cool one's heels** be kept waiting. **5 coolly** *adv.*

**coolabah** /ˈkuːləbɑː/ *n.* any of several kinds of eucalyptus usu. found near water.

**coolamon** /ˈkuːləmən/ *n. Aus.* wooden or bark dish for carrying water.

**coolant** /ˈkuːlənt/ *n.* cooling agent esp. fluid to remove heat from engine.

**cooler** /ˈkuːlə(r)/ *n.* vessel in which thing is cooled; *sl.* prison cell.

**coolgardie safe** /kuːlˈgɑːdi/, *Aus.* safe of water-cooled hessian for keeping perishable foods.

**coolibah** var. of **coolabah**.

**coolie** /ˈkuːli/ *n.* unskilled native labourer in Eastern countries.

**coomb** /kuːm/ *n. UK* valley on side of hill; steep valley.

**coon** /kuːn/ *n.* raccoon.

**coop** /kuːp/ **1** *n.* cage for keeping poultry. **2** *v.t.* keep (fowl) in coop; confine.

**co-op** /ˈkəʊɒp/ *n. colloq.* co-operative society or shop; co-operative.

**cooper** /ˈkuːpə(r)/ *n.* maker or repairer of casks and barrels.

**co-operate** /kəʊˈɒpəreɪt/ *v.i.* work or act together. **co-operation** *n.*

**co-operative** /kəʊˈɒpərətɪv/ **1** *a.* co-operating, willing to co-operate; jointly owned by and managed for use and profit of members of organized group. **2** *n.* co-operative association or enterprise. **3 co-operative society** trading etc. organization in which profits are shared among members esp. as dividend on purchases.

**co-opt** /kəʊˈɒpt/ *v.t.* elect into body by votes of existing members. **co-option** *n.*; **co-optive** *a.*

**co-ordinate 1** /kəʊˈɔːdənət/ *a.* equal in status. **2** /kəʊˈɔːdənət/ *n.* each of set of quantities used to fix position of point, line, or plane; in *pl.* items of women's clothing that can be worn together harmoniously. **3** /kəʊˈɔːdəneɪt/ *v.t.* make co-ordinate; bring into proper relation; cause to function together or in proper order. **4 co-ordination** *n.*; **co-ordinative** *a.*; **co-ordinator** *n.*

**coot** /kuːt/ *n.* a water-bird.

**cootamundra wattle** /kuːtəˈmʌndrə/, *Aus.* tree with feathery foliage and fluffy golden flowers.

**cop** *sl.* **1** *n.* policeman; capture. **2** *v.t.* catch. **3 cop-out** cowardly evasion.

**copal** /ˈkəʊp(ə)l/ *n.* kind of resin used for varnish.

**copartner** /kəʊˈpɑːtnə(r)/ *n.* partner, associate. **copartnership** *n.*

**cope**[1] *v.i.* deal effectively or contend *with*; *colloq.* manage successfully.

**cope**[2] **1** *n.* long cloak worn by priest in processions etc. **2** *v.t.* furnish with cope or coping.

**copeck** /ˈkəʊpek/ *n.* hundredth of rouble.

**copier** /ˈkɒpɪə(r)/ *n.* person or machine that copies (esp. documents).

**coping** /ˈkəʊpɪŋ/ *n.* top course of masonry or brickwork, usu. sloping. **coping-stone** stone used in coping.

**copious** /ˈkəʊpɪəs/ *a.* abundant, plentiful; producing much.

**copper**[1] /ˈkɒpə(r)/ **1** *n.* metal of brownish-pink colour; bronze coin. **2** *a.* made of or coloured like copper. **3** *v.t.* cover with copper. **4 copperplate** copper plate for engraving or etching, print taken from it, sloping rounded cursive handwriting.

**copper**[2] /ˈkɒpə(r)/ *n. sl.* policeman.

**coppice** /ˈkɒpɪs/ *n.* small wood of undergrowth and small trees.

**copula** /ˈkɒpjʊlə/ *n.* part of verb *be* connecting subject with predicate.

**copulate** /ˈkɒpjʊleɪt/ *v.i.* have sexual intercourse. **copulation** *n.*

**copy** /ˈkɒpi/ **1** *n.* thing made to look like another; specimen of book etc.; matter to be printed; material of newspaper article; text of advertisement. **2** *v.* make copy (of); imitate. **3 copy-book**

book containing models of handwriting etc. for learners to imitate; **copy-typist** typist working from copy; **copy-writer** writer of copy esp. for advertisements.

**copyist** /'kɒpi:əst/ *n.* person who makes copies; imitator.

**copyright** /'kɒpi:raɪt/ 1 *n.* exclusive right to print, publish, perform, etc., a work. 2 *a.* protected by copyright. 3 *v.t.* secure copyright for.

**coquette** /kə'ket/ 1 *n.* woman who flirts. 2 *v.i.* flirt. 3 **coquettish** *a.*; **coquetry** *n.*

**coracle** /'kɒrək(ə)l/ *n.* small boat made of wicker covered with waterproof material.

**coral** /'kɒr(ə)l/ 1 *n.* hard substance built up by marine polyps. 2 *a.* of coral, of red colour of coral. 3 **coral island** one formed by growth of coral. 4 **coralline** /-ləm/ *a.*

**cor anglais** /kɔːr 'ɑːgleɪ/ *n.* wood-wind instrument like oboe but lower in pitch.

**corbel** /'kɔːb(ə)l/ *n.* stone or timber projection from wall, acting as supporting bracket.

**cord** 1 *n.* thick string; piece of this; similar structure in body; ribbed cloth, esp. corduroy; in *pl.* corduroy trousers; electric flex or telephone wire. 2 *v.t.* secure with cords.

**cordial** /'kɔːdi:əl/ 1 *a.* heartfelt, sincere; warm, friendly. 2 *n.* fruit-flavoured drink. 3 **cordiality** *n.*

**cordite** /'kɔːdaɪt/ *n.* smokeless explosive.

**cordon** /'kɔːd(ə)n/ 1 *n.* line or circle of police etc.; ornamental cord or braid; fruit-tree trained to grow as single stem. 2 *v.t.* enclose or separate *off* with cordon of police etc.

**cordon bleu** /kɔːdɔ̃ 'bləː/ first-class cook.

**corduroy** /'kɔːdəɔɪ/ *n.* fabric with velvety ribs; in *pl.* corduroy trousers.

**core** 1 *n.* horny central part of certain fruits, containing seeds; centre or most important part of anything; region of fissile material in nuclear reactor; unit of structure in computer, storing one bit of data; inner strand of electric cable; piece of soft iron forming centre of magnet etc. 2 *v.t.* remove core from.

**corella** /kə'relə/ *n. Aus.* white long-billed cockatoo.

**coreopsis** /kɒri:'ɒpsəs/ *n.* plant with daisy-like usu. yellow flowers.

**co-respondent** /kəʊrə'spɒnd(ə)nt/ *n.* person charged with committing adultery with respondent in divorce case.

**corgi** /'kɔːgi:/ *n.* small Welsh breed of dog.

**coriander** /'kɒri:ændə(r)/ *n.* aromatic plant with fruit (**coriander seed**) used as flavouring.

**cork** 1 *n.* thick light tough elastic bark of **cork-oak**; piece of this as bottle-stopper, float, etc. 2 *v.t.* stop (*up*) (as) with cork; bottle *up* (feelings etc.).

**corkage** /'kɔːkɪdʒ/ *n.* charge made by restaurant etc. for serving wine etc.

**corked** /kɔːkt/ *a.* (of wine) spoiled by defective cork.

**corkscrew** /'kɔːkskruː/ 1 *n.* spiral steel device for extracting corks from bottles. 2 *v.* move spirally.

**corm** *n.* swollen underground stem in certain plants, e.g. crocus.

**cormorant** /'kɔːmərənt/ *n.* large voracious sea-bird.

**corn**[1] *n.* cereal before or after harvesting, esp. wheat or maize; grain or seed of cereal plant; *colloq.* something corny. **corn-cob** cylindrical centre of ear of maize (**corn on the cob** maize eaten in this form); **corncrake** bird with harsh grating cry; **corn dolly** figure made of plaited straw; **cornflakes** breakfast cereal of toasted flakes made from maize flour; **cornflour** fine-ground maize flour; **cornflower** blue-flowered plant growing in cornfields; **cornstalk** *Aus. arch.* an Australian, esp. native of NSW.

**corn**[2] *n.* horny tender place with hard centre, esp. on foot.

**cornea** /'kɔːni:ə/ *n.* transparent membrane covering iris and pupil of eyeball.

**corned** /kɔːnd/ *a.* preserved in salt or brine.

**cornel** /'kɔːn(ə)l/ *n.* a hard-wooded tree; cornelian cherry.

**cornelian** /kɔː'niːli:ən/ *n.* red dull variety of chalcedony.

**cornelian cherry** /kɔː'niːli:ən/ European berry-bearing tree.

**corner** /'kɔːnə(r)/ 1 *n.* place where converging sides, edges, streets, etc. meet; recess formed by meeting of two internal sides of room, box, etc.; difficult or inescapable position; remote or se-

**cluded** place; action or result of buying whole available stock of a commodity. **2** *v.* force into difficult or inescapable position; establish corner in (commodity); move round corner. **3 cornerstone** stone in projecting angle of wall, indispensable part or basis.

**cornet** /'kɔːnət/ *n.* brass musical instrument resembling trumpet; conical wafer for holding ice cream.

**cornice** /'kɔːnɪs/ *n.* horizontal moulding in relief, esp. along top of internal wall.

**Cornish** /'kɔːnɪʃ/ **1** *a.* of Cornwall. **2** *n.* Celtic language of Cornwall. **3 Cornish pasty** seasoned meat and vegetables baked in pastry.

**cornucopia** /kɔːnjəˈkəʊpiːə/ *n.* symbol of plenty.

**corny** /'kɔːnɪ/ *a. colloq.* old-fashioned; trite, sentimental.

**corolla** /kəˈrɒlə/ *n.* whorl of petals forming inner envelope of flower.

**corollary** /kəˈrɒlərɪ/ *n.* proposition that follows from one proved; natural consequence.

**corona** /kəˈrəʊnə/ *n.* (*pl.* **-nae** /-niː/) small circle of light round sun or moon, esp. that seen in total eclipse of sun.

**coronary** /'kɒrənərɪ/ **1** *a.* of the arteries supplying blood to the heart. **2** *n.* coronary artery or thrombosis. **3 coronary thrombosis** blockage of coronary artery by blood-clot.

**coronation** /kɒrəˈneɪʃ(ə)n/ *n.* ceremony of crowning sovereign.

**coroner** /'kɒrənə(r)/ *n.* officer holding inquest on deaths thought to be violent or accidental.

**coronet** /'kɒrənət/ *n.* small crown.

**corpora** *pl.* of **corpus**.

**corporal**[1] /'kɔːpər(ə)l/ *n.* non-commissioned army or air force officer next below sergeant.

**corporal**[2] /'kɔːpər(ə)l/ *a.* of human body. **corporal punishment** punishment by flogging etc. **corporality** *n.*

**corporate** /'kɔːpərət/ *a.* of or being or belonging to a corporation or group.

**corporation** /kɔːpəˈreɪʃ(ə)n/ *n.* body of persons authorized to act as individual; civic authorities.

**corporative** /'kɔːpərətɪv/ *a.* of corporation; (of State) organized in professional, industrial, etc. corporations.

**corporeal** /kɔːˈpɔːriːəl/ *a.* having body; material, tangible. **corporeality** *n.*

**corps** /kɔː(r)/ *n.* (*pl.* same /kɔːz/) military force; organized body.

**corpse** /kɔːps/ *n.* dead (usu. human) body.

**corpulent** /'kɔːpjələnt/ *a.* fleshy, bulky. **corpulence** *n.*

**corpus** /'kɔːpəs/ *n.* (*pl.* **corpora** /'kɔːpərə/) body of writings of particular kind; collection.

**corpuscle** /'kɔːpʌs(ə)l/ *n.* minute body or cell in organism, esp. (in *pl.*) red and white cells in blood of vertebrates. **corpuscular** /-'pʌs-/ *a.*

**corral** /kəˈrɑːl/ *US* **1** *n.* pen for horses, cattle, etc., or for capturing wild animals. **2** *v.t.* (*past* & *p.p.* **corralled**) put or keep in corral.

**correct** /kəˈrekt/ **1** *a.* true, accurate; proper, in accordance with taste, standards, etc. **2** *v.t.* set right; mark errors in; admonish; counteract; bring into accordance with standard. **3 corrector** *n.*

**correction** /kəˈrekʃ(ə)n/ *n.* correcting; thing substituted for what is wrong; *arch.* punishment.

**correctitude** /kəˈrektɪtjuːd/ *n.* consciously correct behaviour.

**corrective** /kəˈrektɪv/ **1** *a.* serving to correct. **2** *n.* corrective measure or thing.

**correlate** /'kɒrəleɪt/ **1** *v.* have or bring into mutual relation (*with*, *to*). **2** *n.* each of two related or complementary things. **3 correlation** *n.*

**correlative** /kəˈrelətɪv/ **1** *a.* having a mutual relation; *Gram.* corresponding and regularly used together. **2** *n.* correlative thing or word.

**correspond** /kɒrəˈspɒnd/ *v.i.* be analogous (*to*) or in agreement (*with*); communicate by interchange of letters.

**correspondence** /kɒrəˈspɒnd(ə)ns/ *n.* agreement or similarity; communication by letters; letters sent or received. **correspondence course** course of study conducted by post.

**correspondent** /kɒrəˈspɒnd(ə)nt/ *n.* person who writes letters to another; person employed by newspaper etc. to write regularly on particular subject.

**corridor** /'kɒrɪdɔː(r)/ *n.* passage or gallery with doors leading into many rooms etc.; passage in railway coach

**corrigendum** /kɒrə'dʒendəm/ n. (pl. -da) thing to be corrected, esp. in book.

**corrigible** /'kɒrədʒəb(ə)l/ a. that can be corrected.

**corroborate** /kə'rɒbəreɪt/ v.t. give support to, confirm. **corroboration** n.; **corroborative** a.; **corroboratory** a.

**corroboree** /kərɒbə'ri:/ n. Aboriginal singing and dancing.

**corrode** /kə'rəʊd/ v. wear away, esp. by chemical action; destroy gradually; decay.

**corrosion** /kə'rəʊʒ(ə)n/ n. corroding; corroded part or substance. **corrosive** a. & n.

**corrugate** /'kɒrəgeɪt/ v. bend into wavy ridges. **corrugation** n.

**corrupt** /kə'rʌpt/ 1 a. morally depraved; influenced by or using bribery. 2 v. make or become corrupt. 3 **corruptible** a.; **corruption** n.

**corsage** /kɔː'sɑːʒ/ n. US small bouquet worn by woman.

**corsair** /kɔː'seə(r)/ n. pirate ship; pirate.

**corset** /'kɔːsət/ n. tight-fitting supporting undergarment worn esp. by women.

**corslet** /'kɔːslət/ n. garment covering body; hist. coat of armour.

**cortège** /kɔː'teɪʒ/ n. procession, esp. for funeral.

**cortex** /'kɔːteks/ n. outer covering of some organs; outer grey matter of brain. **cortical** a.

**cortisone** /'kɔːtɪzəʊn/ n. hormone used medicinally against inflammation and allergy.

**corundum** /kə'rʌndəm/ n. crystallized native alumina used as abrasive.

**coruscate** /'kɒrəskeɪt/ v.i. sparkle, flash. **coruscation** n.

**corvette** /kɔː'vet/ n. small naval escort vessel.

**cos**[1] /kɒs/ n. crisp long-leaved lettuce.

**cos**[2] /kɒs/ abbr. cosine.

**cosh** colloq. 1 n. short heavy stick. 2 v.t. hit with cosh.

**cosine** /'kəʊsaɪn/ n. sine of complement of given angle.

**cosmetic** /kɒz'metɪk/ 1 a. designed to beautify hair or skin etc.; intended (only) to improve appearances. 2 n. cosmetic preparation. 3 **cosmetic surgery** undertaken to correct defects or alter features etc. 4 **cosmetically** adv.

**cosmic** /'kɒzmɪk/ a. of the cosmos. **cosmic rays** high-energy radiations originating in outer space.

**cosmogony** /kɒz'mɒgəni/ n. origin of universe; theory about this.

**cosmology** /kɒz'mɒlədʒi/ n. science or theory of the universe. **cosmological** a.; **cosmologist** n.

**cosmonaut** /'kɒzmənɔːt/ n. Russian astronaut.

**cosmopolitan** /kɒzmə'pɒlɪt(ə)n/ 1 a. of all parts of world; free from national limitations. 2 n. cosmopolitan person. 3 **cosmopolitanism** n.

**cosmos** /'kɒzmɒs/ n. universe as a well-ordered whole.

**Cossack** /'kɒsæk/ n. member of S. Russian people famous as horsemen.

**cosset** /'kɒsət/ v.t. pamper, pet.

**cost** 1 v.t. (past & p.p. **cost**) have as price; involve payment or sacrifice of; (past & p.p. **costed**) fix or estimate cost of. 2 n. what thing costs; in pl. legal expenses. 3 **cost-effective** effective in relation to its cost; **cost of living** cost of basic necessities of life.

**costal** /'kɒst(ə)l/ a. of ribs.

**coster(monger)** /'kɒstəmʌŋgə(r)/ n. person who sells fruit etc. from barrow.

**costive** /'kɒstɪv/ a. constipated.

**costly** /'kɒstli/ a. costing much, expensive. **costliness** n.

**costume** /'kɒstjuːm/ n. style of dress; set of outer clothes; garment(s) for particular activity; matching jacket and skirt; actor's clothes for part. **costume jewellery** jewellery made from artificial materials.

**costumier** /kɒs'tjuːmɪə(r)/ n. person who deals in or makes costumes.

**cosy** /'kəʊzi/ 1 a. snug, comfortable. 2 n. cloth etc. cover to retain warmth in teapot or boiled egg.

**cot**[1] n. small tall-sided bed for child etc.; small or light bed. **cot-death** unexplained death of sleeping baby.

**cot**[2] n. poet. small shelter, cote; small cottage.

**cote** n. shelter esp. for birds or animals.

**coterie** /'kəʊtəri/ n. set of persons with exclusive interests; select circle.

**cotoneaster** /kətəʊni'æstə(r)/ n.

**cottage** /'kɒtɪdʒ/ n. Aus. one-storey house; UK small house, esp. in the country. **cottage cheese** soft white cheese; **cottage hospital** one without resident medical staff; **cottage industry** one carried on at home; **cottage loaf** one with smaller mass of bread on top of larger; **cottage pie** shepherd's pie.

**cottager** /'kɒtədʒə(r)/ n. person who lives in cottage.

**cotter pin** /'kɒtə(r)/ bolt or wedge for securing parts of machinery.

**cotton** /'kɒt(ə)n/ 1 n. white downy fibrous substance covering seeds of certain plants; such a plant; thread or cloth made from this. 2 v.i. be drawn to. 3 **cottonbush** any of various Aus. shrubs with downy appearance; **cotton on (to)** sl. understand; **cottonwood** Aus. tree with downy leaves; **cotton wool** raw cotton, wadding made from this.

**cotyledon** /kɒtɪ'li:d(ə)n/ n. first leaf produced by plant embryo.

**couch** /kaʊtʃ/ 1 n. piece of furniture made for reclining on; sofa; arch. bed. 2 v. express in specified terms; place (as) on couch; (of animal) lie, esp. in lair.

**couchette** /ku:'ʃet/ n. railway carriage etc. with seats convertible into sleeping-berths; berth in this.

**couch-grass** /'ku:tʃgrɑ:s/ n. kind of grass with long creeping roots.

**cougar** /'ku:gə(r)/ n. US puma.

**cough** /kɒf/ 1 v. expel air from lungs violently and with characteristic noise. 2 n. act or sound of coughing; condition of respiratory organs causing coughing. 3 **cough mixture** medicine to relieve cough; **cough-sweet** medicated sweet to relieve cough; **cough up** sl. bring out or provide (money, information, etc.) reluctantly.

**could** past of **can**¹.

**coulomb** /'ku:lɒm/ n. unit of electric charge.

**coulter** /'kəʊltə(r)/ n. vertical blade in front of ploughshare.

**council** /'kaʊns(ə)l/ n. advisory, deliberative, or administrative body; local administrative body of county, city, town, etc.

**councillor** /'kaʊnsələ(r)/ n. member of council.

**counsel** /'kaʊns(ə)l/ 1 n. advice; consultation; legal adviser, esp. barrister; a group of these. 2 v.t. advise.

**counsellor** /'kaʊnsələ(r)/ n. adviser.

**count**¹ /kaʊnt/ 1 v. find number of esp. by assigning successive numerals; repeat numerals in order; include or be included in reckoning or consideration; consider to be. 2 n. counting, reckoning; total; Law each charge in an indictment. 3 **countdown** counting numbers backwards to zero, esp. before launching rocket etc.; **count on** rely on for help etc.; **count out** exclude; complete count of 10 seconds over (fallen boxer etc.).

**count**² /kaʊnt/ n. foreign nobleman equivalent in rank to earl.

**countenance** /'kaʊntənəns/ 1 n. face, esp. with respect to its expression; composure of face; moral support. 2 v.t. give approval to; connive at.

**counter**¹ /'kaʊntə(r)/ n. flat-topped fitment in bank or shop etc., at which customer is served or business transacted; similar structure in cafeteria etc.; small disc etc. used in scoring at cards etc.; token representing coin; device for counting things.

**counter**² /'kaʊntə(r)/ 1 v. oppose, contradict; meet or baffle by answering move etc. 2 adv. in opposite direction 3 a. opposite. 4 n. return blow, counter-move; curved part of ship's stern.

**counteract** /kaʊntə'rækt/ v.t. neutralize or hinder by contrary action. **counteraction** n.

**counter-attack** /'kaʊntərə'tæk/ v. & n. attack in reply to enemy's attack.

**counterbalance** /kaʊntə'bæləns/ 1 n. weight balancing another. 2 v.t. neutralize by contrary force or influence.

**counter-clockwise** /kaʊntə-'klɒkwaɪz/ adv. & a. anticlockwise.

**counter-espionage** /kaʊntə-'espɪənɑ:ʒ/ n. action against an enemy's spy system.

**counterfeit** /'kaʊntəfɪt/ 1 a. made in imitation; forged; not genuine. 2 n. counterfeit thing. 3 v.t. imitate; forge; simulate.

**counterfoil** /'kaʊntəfɔɪl/ n. part of cheque, receipt, etc. retained as record.

**counter-intelligence** /ˌkaʊntərɪnˈtelɪdʒ(ə)ns/ *n.* counter-espionage.

**countermand** /ˌkaʊntəˈmɑːnd or -ˈmænd/ *v.t.* revoke (order), recall by contrary order; cancel order for.

**countermarch** /ˈkaʊntəmɑːtʃ/ 1 *n.* march in opposite direction. 2 *v.* (cause to) march back.

**counterpane** /ˈkaʊntəpeɪn/ *n.* bedspread.

**counterpart** /ˈkaʊntəpɑːt/ *n.* duplicate; person or thing naturally complementary to another.

**counterpoint** /ˈkaʊntəpɔɪnt/ *n. Mus.* harmonious combination of simultaneous parts or voices in music; one part or voice added to another.

**counterpoise** /ˈkaʊntəpɔɪz/ 1 *n.* balancing of each other by two weights or forces; counterbalancing weight or force. 2 *v.t.* counterbalance; compensate for.

**counter-productive** /ˌkaʊntəprəˈdʌktɪv/ *a.* having the opposite of the desired effect.

**counter-revolution** /ˌkaʊntərevəˈluːʃ(ə)n/ *n.* revolution opposed to former one or reversing its effects.

**countersign** /ˈkaʊntəsaɪn/ 1 *v.* add confirming signature to. 2 *n.* word to be given in answer to sentry's challenge.

**countersink** /ˈkaʊntəsɪŋk/ *v.t.* (*past & p.p.* **-sunk**) shape (screw-hole) so that screw-head lies level with surface; provide (screw) with countersunk hole.

**counter-tenor** /ˈkaʊntətenə(r)/ *n.* male alto.

**countervail** /ˌkaʊntəˈveɪl/ *v.* counterbalance; avail against.

**countess** /ˈkaʊntɪs/ *n.* earl's or count's wife or widow; woman with own rank of earl or count.

**countless** /ˈkaʊntlɪs/ *a.* too many to count.

**countrified** /ˈkʌntrɪfaɪd/ *a.* rustic.

**country** /ˈkʌntrɪ/ *n.* nation's territory; State of which one is a member; land of a region with regard to its aspect etc.; open regions of fields etc. as opp. town; country-and-western. **country-and-western** *n.* rural or cowboy songs to guitar etc.; **country dance** rural or traditional dance; **countryman**, **country-woman**, member of same State or district as oneself, person living in rural parts; **country seat** *UK* country house with park; **countryside** rural areas generally.

**county** /ˈkaʊntɪ/ *n.* territorial division of UK, forming chief unit of local administration and justice; political and administrative division of State of US etc.; *UK* people, esp. gentry, of county. **county council** elective administrative body of county; **county town** town that is centre of county administration.

**coup** /kuː/ *n.* successful stroke or move; *coup d'état*.

**coup de grâce** /kuː də ˈgrɑːs/ finishing stroke. [F]

**coup d'état** /kuː deɪˈtɑː/ sudden overthrow of government esp. by force. [F]

**coupé** /ˈkuːpeɪ/ *n.* closed 2-door car with sloping back.

**couple** /ˈkʌp(ə)l/ 1 *n.* man and woman together, esp. married etc.; pair of partners in dance etc.; two things or a few. 2 *v.* link or fasten or associate together; copulate.

**couplet** /ˈkʌplət/ *n.* pair of successive lines of rhyming verse.

**coupling** /ˈkʌplɪŋ/ *n.* link connecting railway-carriages or parts of machine.

**coupon** /ˈkuːpɒn/ *n.* detachable ticket or form entitling holder to something.

**courage** /ˈkʌrɪdʒ/ *n.* readiness to face and capacity to endure danger; courageous mood. **courageous** /kəˈreɪdʒəs/ *a.*

**courgette** /kʊəˈʒet/ *n.* small vegetable marrow, zucchini.

**courier** /ˈkʊrɪə(r)/ *n.* special messenger; person employed to guide and assist group of tourists.

**course** /kɔːs/ 1 *n.* onward movement in space or time; direction of going; line of conduct or action; series or sequence; series of lectures or lessons etc.; each of successive parts of meal; golf-course, race-course, etc.; continuous line of masonry or bricks at one level of building. 2 *v.* use hounds in coursing; move or flow freely.

**courser** /ˈkɔːsə(r)/ *n.* swift horse.

**court** /kɔːt/ 1 *n.* space enclosed by wall or buildings; number of houses enclosing a yard; area within walls or marked boundaries used for some games; sovereign's residence, his establishment and retinue; body with judicial powers, tribunal; place in which court sits. 2 *v.t.* treat with flatterying or amorous attention; seek favour or love of; unwisely invite. 3 **court-card** playing-card that is king or queen or jack; **court martial** (*pl.* **courts martial**) judicial court of military officers; **court-martial** try by court martial; **court shoe** woman's light shoe with low-cut upper; **courtyard** space enclosed by walls or buildings; **pay court to** court (person) to win favour.

**courteous** /'kɜːtiːəs/ *a.* polite, considerate.

**courtesan** /kɔːtəˈzæn/ *n.* prostitute, esp. one whose clients are wealthy or upper-class.

**courtesy** /'kɜːtəsi/ *n.* courteous behaviour or act. **courtesy light** light in car switched on when door is opened.

**courtier** /'kɔːtliːə(r)/ *n.* companion of sovereign at court.

**courtly** /'kɔːtli/ *a.* polished or refined in manners. **courtliness** *n.*

**courtship** /'kɔːtʃɪp/ *n.* courting esp. of intended spouse or mate.

**cousin** /'kʌz(ə)n/ *n.* child of one's uncle or aunt. **cousinly** *a.*

**couture** /kuːˈtjʊə(r)/ *n.* design and making of fashionable garments.

**cove** 1 *n.* small bay or inlet of coast; sheltered recess; curved moulding at junction of ceiling and walls. 2 *v.t.* provide (room etc.) with cove.

**coven** /'kʌv(ə)n/ *n.* assembly of witches.

**covenant** /'kʌvənənt/ 1 *n.* agreement, *Law* sealed contract. 2 *v.* agree, esp. by legal covenant.

**Coventry** /'kɒvəntri/ *n.* **send to Coventry** refuse to associate with.

**cover** /'kʌvə(r)/ 1 *v.t.* be over whole top or front of; lie over or above; conceal or shield; enclose or include; (of sum) be large enough to meet (expense); protect by insurance; investigate or describe as reporter; have within range (of gun etc.). 2 *n.* thing that covers, wrapper; screen or pretence; shelter, protection; funds to meet liability or contingent loss; place laid for one person at meal. 3 **cover charge** service charge per person in restaurant; **cover-point** *Crick.* fielder standing behind point.

**coverage** /'kʌvərɪdʒ/ *n.* area or amount covered or reached; reporting of events in newspaper etc.

**coverlet** /'kʌvələt/ *n.* cover lying over other bedclothes.

**covert** /'kʌvət/ 1 *a.* secret, disguised; not open or explicit. 2 *n.* wood or thicket affording cover for game; in *pl.* feathers covering base of wing and tail feathers.

**covet** /'kʌvət/ *v.t.* envy another the possession of; long to possess.

**covetous** /'kʌvətəs/ *a.* avaricious, grasping.

**covey** /'kʌvi:/ *n.* brood of partridges etc.; family, set.

**cow**[1] /kaʊ/ *n.* fully-grown female of any bovine animal, esp. of domestic kind; female of elephant or rhinoceros or whale or seal etc.; *Aus. sl.* unpleasant thing or situation. **cowboy** *US* man in charge of grazing cattle on ranch, *colloq.* unscrupulous or reckless business man or workman; **cowherd** *UK* person who looks after cattle at pasture; **cowhide** cow's hide, leather or whip made of this; **cow-pat** roundish flat piece of cow-dung; **cowpox** disease of cows, source of smallpox vaccine.

**cow**[2] /kaʊ/ *v.t.* intimidate.

**coward** /'kaʊəd/ *n.* person having little or no bravery.

**cowardice** /'kaʊədɪs/ *n.* cowardly conduct.

**cowardly** /'kaʊədli/ *a.* of or like a coward.

**cower** /'kaʊə(r)/ *v.i.* crouch or shrink with fear or with cold.

**cowl** /kaʊl/ *n.* monk's hooded cloak; its hood; hood-shaped top of chimney or shaft.

**cowrie** /'kaʊri/ *n.* tropical mollusc with bright shell; its shell, used as money in some parts of Asia etc.

**cowslip** /'kaʊslɪp/ *n.* European yellow-flowered plant.

**cox** 1 *n.* coxswain. 2 *v.* act as cox (of).

**coxcomb** /'kɒkskəʊm/ *n.* conceited showy person; *hist.* medieval jester's cap.

**coxswain** /'kɒks(ə)n or 'kɒkswein/ *n.* steersman of (esp. rowing-)boat.

**coy** *a.* (affectedly) modest, shy.

**coyote** /kɔːˈəʊti/ *n.* N. Amer. prairie-wolf.

**coypu** /'kɔɪpu:/ *n.* aquatic beaver-like rodent orig. from S. Amer.

**cozen** /'kʌz(ə)n/ *v.* cheat; defraud.

**crab** 1 *n.* shellfish with ten legs; flesh of edible species of this; **crab-apple**;

**crabbed**

crab-louse. 2 v. *colloq*. criticize adversely; act so as to spoil. 3 **catch a crab** get oar jammed under water by faulty stroke; **crab-apple** wild appletree, sour fruit of this; **crab-hole** *Aus*. depression in ground attributed to action of land crabs, gilgai; **crab-louse** parasite infesting human body.

**crabbed** /kræbd/ *a*. crabby; (of handwriting) ill-formed and hard to decipher.

**crabby** /'kræbɪ/ *a*. perverse, morose, irritable.

**crack 1** *n*. sudden sharp noise; sharp blow; narrow opening; split or rift not extending far enough to break thing; *sl*. cutting or witty remark. 2 *v*. (cause to) make crack; suffer crack or partial break; (of voice) become dissonant as effect of emotion or age; tell (joke); open (bottle of wine etc.); break into (safe); find solution to (problem); give way, yield. 3 **crack-brained** crazy; **crack down on** take severe measures against; **crack hardy** or **hearty** *Aus*. put good face on, endure patiently; **crack of dawn** daybreak; **crackpot** *colloq*. eccentric or impractical person; **crack up** *colloq*. collapse under strain.

**cracked** /krækt/ *a*. *colloq*. crazy.

**cracker** /'krækə(r)/ *n*. explosive firework; small paper cylinder containing paper hat, etc., and exploding with crack when ends are pulled; thin crisp savoury biscuit; piece of horsehair etc. in end of whiplash. **cracker night** night (usu. 24 May) when fireworks are let off; **not worth a cracker** *Aus*. worthless.

**crackers** /'krækəz/ *pred.a*. *colloq*. crazy.

**crackle** /'kræk(ə)l/ 1 *n*. sound of repeated slight cracking. 2 *v.i*. emit crackle.

**crackling** /'kræklɪŋ/ *n*. crisp skin of roast pork.

**cracknel** /'krækn(ə)l/ *n*. light crisp biscuit.

**cradle** /'kreɪd(ə)l/ 1 *n*. infant's bed esp. on rockers; place regarded as origin of something; supporting framework or structure. 2 *v.t*. place in cradle; contain or shelter as in cradle.

**craft** /krɑːft/ *n*. skill, cunning; branch of skilled handiwork; (*pl*. same) boat, vessel, aircraft, or spacecraft.

**crash**

**craftsman** /'krɑːftsmən/ *n*. (*pl*. **-men**) person who practises a craft. **craftsmanship** *n*.

**crafty** /'krɑːftɪ/ *a*. cunning, artful; ingenious.

**crag** *n*. steep rugged rock. **craggy** *a*.

**cram** *v*. fill to excess; force (thing) *into*; study intensively for examination.

**cramp 1** *n*. sudden painful contraction of muscles from chill or strain etc. 2 *v.t*. affect with cramp; restrict, enclose too narrowly.

**cramped** /kræmpt/ *a*. (of space) too narrow; (of handwriting) small and difficult to read.

**crampon** /'kræmpɒn/ *n*. spiked iron plate fixed to boot for climbing etc. on ice.

**cranberry** /'krænbərɪ/ *n*. small dark-red acid berry; shrub bearing it.

**crane 1** *n*. machine for moving heavy weights; large wading bird. 2 *v*. stretch (one's neck) in order to see something. 3 **crane-fly** two-winged long-legged fly; **crane's-bill** kind of wild geranium.

**cranium** /'kreɪnɪəm/ *n*. (*pl*. **-nia**) bones enclosing brain, skull. **cranial** *a*.

**crank 1** *n*. part of axis bent at right angles for converting rotary into reciprocal motion and vice versa; eccentric person. 2 *v.t*. turn with crank. 3 **crankpin** pin attaching connecting-rod to crank; **crankshaft** shaft driven by crank; **crank up** start (motor engine) by turning crank.

**cranky** /'kræŋkɪ/ *a*. shaky; eccentric; ill-tempered.

**cranny** /'krænɪ/ *n*. chink, crevice.

**crap** *vulg*. 1 *n*. faeces; nonsense; rubbish. 2 *v.i*. defecate. 3 **crappy** *a*.

**crape** *n*. crêpe, usu. of black silk, esp. for mourning-dress.

**craps** *n*. US game of chance played with dice.

**crapulence** /'kræpjələns/ *n*. state following intemperate drinking or eating. **crapulent** *a*.; **crapulous** *a*.

**crash 1** *n*. sudden violent noise; violent fall or impact esp. with loud noise; sudden downfall or collapse; *attrib*. done rapidly or urgently. 2 *v*. (cause to) fall or collide with crash; make crash; (of aircraft or pilot) fall violently to land or sea; fail, esp. financially; gatecrash. 3 **crash barrier** barrier against car

**crass**   127   **credulous**

leaving road etc.; **crash-dive** (of submarine) dive hastily and steeply, (of aircraft) dive and crash; **crash-helmet** helmet worn to protect head in case of crash; **crash hot** *Aus. sl.* excellent. **crash-land** (of aircraft or pilot) make emergency landing.

**crass** *a.* grossly stupid; insensitive.

**crate 1** *n.* open-work case of wooden bars or basket-work etc. **2** *v.t.* pack in crate.

**crater** /ˈkreɪtə(r)/ *n.* mouth of volcano; bowl-shaped cavity.

**cravat** /krəˈvæt/ *n.* scarf, neck-tie.

**crave** *v.t.* greatly desire, long for; *arch* ask for.

**craven** /ˈkreɪv(ə)n/ **1** *a.* cowardly, abject. **2** *n.* craven person.

**craving** /ˈkreɪvɪŋ/ *n.* strong desire, longing.

**craw** *n.* crop of bird or insect.

**crawchie** /ˈkrɔːtʃiː/ *n. Aus. sl.* yabbie.

**crawfish** /ˈkrɔːfɪʃ/ *n.* crayfish.

**crawl 1** *v.i.* move slowly with body on or close to ground, or on hands and knees; go slowly; *colloq.* behave ingratiatingly *to.* **2** *n.* crawling motion; slow rate of motion; fast swimming-stroke.

**cray** *n. Aus.* crayfish.

**crayfish** /ˈkreɪfɪʃ/ *n.* lobster-like freshwater crustacean; large spiny sea-lobster.

**crayon** /ˈkreɪən/ **1** *n.* stick or pencil of coloured wax or other material for drawing. **2** *v.t.* draw or colour with crayons.

**craze 1** *n.* great but usu. temporary enthusiasm; object of this. **2** *v.t.* drive crazy.

**crazy** /ˈkreɪzi/ *a.* insane; outrageously foolish; madly eager; unsound, shaky. **crazy paving** paving made of irregular pieces.

**creak 1** *n.* harsh grating noise as of unoiled hinge. **2** *v.i.* emit creak. **3 creaky** *a.*

**cream 1** *n.* part of milk with high content of fat; yellowish-white colour of this; food or drink like or made with cream; creamlike preparation or ointment; *the* best part or pick *of.* **2** *v.* take cream from; work to creamy consistency; treat with cosmetic cream; form cream or scum. **3 cream cheese** soft rich cheese made of cream and unskimmed milk; **cream cracker** crisp unsweetened biscuit; **cream off** remove best part of; **cream of tartar** purified tartar used in medicine and cookery. **4 creamy** *a.*

**creamer** /ˈkriːmə(r)/ *n.* jug for cream.

**creamery** /ˈkriːməri/ *n.* place where dairy products are produced or sold.

**crease** /kriːs/ **1** *n.* line made by folding, wrinkle; *Crick.* line defining position of bowler or batsman. **2** *v.* make creases in, develop creases; *sl.* tire out.

**create** /kriːˈeɪt/ *v.* bring into existence; originate; invest with rank; *sl.* make fuss.

**creation** /kriːˈeɪʃ(ə)n/ *n.* creating; all created things; production of human mind.

**creative** /kriːˈeɪtɪv/ *a.* inventive, imaginative. **creativity** *n.*

**creator** /kriːˈeɪtə(r)/ *n.* one who creates; **the Creator** God.

**creature** /ˈkriːtʃə(r)/ *n.* created being, esp. animal; person, esp. one in subservient position.

**crèche** /kreʃ/ *n.* day-nursery for babies and young children.

**credence** /ˈkriːd(ə)ns/ *n.* belief, credit.

**credentials** /krəˈdenʃ(ə)lz/ *n.pl.* letters of recommendation (also *fig.*).

**credible** /ˈkredəb(ə)l/ *a.* believable; worthy of belief. **credibility** *n.*

**credit** /ˈkredɪt/ **1** *n.* belief, trust; good reputation; acknowledgement of merit or (usu. in *pl.*) of contributor's services to film or book etc.; allowing customers to take goods and defer payment; acknowledgement of payment by entry in account; sum at person's disposal in bank etc. or entered on credit side of account; *US* certificate of completion of course by student. **2** *v.t.* believe; enter on credit side of account; attribute (*to*). **3 credit card** card authorizing obtaining of goods on credit; **credit person with** ascribe to him; **give person credit for** acknowledge that he may have; **to one's credit** in one's favour.

**creditable** /ˈkredɪtəb(ə)l/ *a.* praiseworthy.

**creditor** /ˈkredɪtə(r)/ *n.* person or body to whom debt is owing.

**credo** /ˈkriːdəʊ/ *n.* (*pl.* **-dos**) creed.

**credulous** /ˈkredjələs/ *a.* too ready to believe. **credulity** *n.*

**creed** *n.* system of (esp. religious) belief; formal summary of Christian doctrine.

**creek** *n.* inlet on sea-coast or arm of river; small stream.

**creel** *n.* angler's fishing-basket.

**creep** 1 *v.i.* (*past & p.p.* **crept**) crawl; move stealthily or timidly or slowly; (of plant) grow along ground or up wall etc.; experience nervous shivering sensation; develop gradually. 2 *n.* spell of creeping; *sl.* unpleasant person; gradual change in shape of metal under stress. 3 **the creeps** *colloq.* creeping sensation.

**creeper** /'kriːpə(r)/ *n.* creeping or climbing plant.

**creepy** /'kriːpiː/ *a.* causing nervous revulsion or fear; having this feeling. **creepy-crawly** small creeping insect etc.

**cremate** /krə'meɪt/ *v.t.* burn (corpse) to ashes. **cremation** *n.*

**crematorium** /kreməˈtɔːrɪəm/ *n.* (*pl.* **-ria** or **-riums**) place where corpses are cremated.

**crematory** /'kremətəri/ 1 *a.* of cremation. 2 *n.* US crematorium.

**crenellated** /'krenəleɪtəd/ *a.* having battlements. **crenellation** *n.*

**Creole** /'kriːəʊl/ 1 *n.* descendant of European settlers in W. Indies or Central or S. America, or of French settlers in southern US; person of mixed European and Negro descent; language spoken by Creoles. 2 *a.* that is a Creole; **creole** of local origin or production.

**creosote** /'kriːəsəʊt/ *n.* oily wood-preservative distilled from wood-tar.

**crêpe** /kreɪp/ *n.* textile fabric with wrinkled surface; wrinkled sheet rubber used for shoe-soles etc.; **crêpe de Chine** /də ˈʃiːn/ fine silk crêpe; **crêpe paper** thin crinkled paper.

**crepitate** /'krepɪteɪt/ *v.i.* make crackling sound. **crepitation** *n.*

**crept** *past & p.p.* of **creep**.

**crepuscular** /krə'pʌskjələ(r)/ *a.* of twilight; (of animal) active etc. at twilight.

**crescendo** /krə'ʃendəʊ/ *Mus.* 1 *adv.* with gradually increasing volume. 2 *n.* (*pl.* **-dos**) passage to be performed thus.

**crescent** /'kres(ə)nt/ 1 *n.* waxing moon; figure with this outline esp. as emblem of Turkey or Islam; street of houses on curve. 2 *a.* increasing; crescent-shaped.

**cress** *n.* plant with pungent edible leaves.

**crest** 1 *n.* comb or tuft on animal's head; plume of helmet; top esp. of mountain; curl of foam on wave; heraldic device above shield or used separately. 2 *v.t.* reach top of; crown; serve as crest to. 3 **crestfallen** mortified, dejected.

**cretaceous** /krə'teɪʃəs/ *a.* chalky.

**cretin** /'kretən/ *n.* person with deformity and mental retardation caused by thyroid deficiency; *colloq.* stupid person. **cretinism** *n.*; **cretinous** *a.*

**cretonne** /kre'tɒn/ *n.* unglazed colour-printed cotton cloth.

**crevasse** /krə'væs/ *n.* deep open crack in ice of glacier.

**crevice** /'krevəs/ *n.* narrow opening, fissure.

**crew**¹ 1 *n.* body of persons engaged in particular piece of work, esp. manning ship or aircraft or spacecraft etc.; these other than the officers. 2 *v.* supply or act as (member of) crew (for). 3 **crew cut** man's hair cut short all over; **crew neck** round close-fitting neckline.

**crew**² *arch. past* of **crow**.

**crewel** /'kruːəl/ *n.* thin worsted yarn for embroidery. **crewel needle** blunt-ended embroidery needle.

**crib** 1 *n.* wooden framework for fodder; child's bed; model representing nativity scene at Bethlehem; *colloq.* cribbage; *colloq.* plagiarism; translation. 2 *v.* confine in small space; plagiarize, copy.

**cribbage** /'krɪbɪdʒ/ *n.* a card-game.

**crick** 1 *n.* sudden painful stiffness in neck or back. 2 *v.t.* cause crick in.

**cricket**¹ /'krɪkət/ *n.* open-air game played with ball, bats, and wickets between two teams of 11. **not cricket** *colloq.* unfair, infringing code of fair play. **cricketer** *n.*

**cricket**² /'krɪkət/ *n.* jumping chirping insect.

**cried** *past & p.p.* of **cry**.

**crier** /'kraɪə(r)/ *n.* officer who makes public announcements in judicial court or in streets of town etc.

**crikey** /'kraɪkiː/ *int. sl.* expressing astonishment.

**crime** *n.* act punishable by law; wicked act; such acts collectively.

**criminal** /'krɪmən(ə)l/ 1 *n.* person

**criminology**

guilty of crime. **2** *a.* of or involving or concerning crime. **3 criminality** *n.*

**criminology** /ˌkrɪmɪˈnɒlədʒi:/ *n.* study of crime. **criminologist** *n.*

**crimp** *v.t.* press into small folds; frill, corrugate.

**crimson** /ˈkrɪmz(ə)n/ *a. & n.* rich deep red.

**cringe** *v.i.* cower; behave obsequiously.

**crinkle** /ˈkrɪŋk(ə)l/ *n. & v.* wrinkle. **crinkly** *a.*

**crinoline** /ˈkrɪnəlɪn/ *n.* hooped petticoat used to make long skirt stand out; stiff fabric of horsehair etc.

**cripple** /ˈkrɪp(ə)l/ **1** *n.* lame person. **2** *v.t.* lame, disable; impair.

**crisis** /ˈkraɪsɪs/ *n.* (*pl.* **-ses** /-siːz/) decisive moment; time of acute danger or difficulty.

**crisp 1** *a.* hard but brittle; bracing, brisk; clear-cut; decisive; crackling; curly. **2** *n.* very thin slice of potato fried crisp. **3** *v.* make or become crisp. **4 crispy** *a.*

**criss-cross 1** *n.* pattern of crossing lines etc. **2** *a.* crossing, in crossing lines. **3** *adv.* crosswise. **4** *v.t.* mark with criss-cross lines.

**criterion** /kraɪˈtɪərɪən/ *n.* (*pl.* **-ria**) principle taken as standard in judging.

**critic** /ˈkrɪtɪk/ *n.* person who censures; person who reviews or judges merit of artistic etc. work.

**critical** /ˈkrɪtɪk(ə)l/ *a.* fault-finding; expressing criticism; of the nature of a crisis, decisive; marking transition from one state to another.

**criticism** /ˈkrɪtɪsɪz(ə)m/ *n.* finding fault, censure; work of a critic; critical article or remark etc.

**criticize** /ˈkrɪtɪsaɪz/ *v.* find fault (with); discuss critically.

**critique** /krɪˈtiːk/ *n.* critical essay.

**croak 1** *n.* deep hoarse note as of frog or raven. **2** *v.* utter or speak with croak; *sl.* kill, die.

**crochet** /ˈkrəʊʃeɪ/ **1** *n.* kind of handiwork done with thread and single hooked needle. **2** *v.* (*past & p.p.* **crocheted** /ˈkrəʊʃeɪd/) do crochet; make by crochet.

**crock**[1] *n.* worn-out or disabled or inefficient person or thing.

**crock**[2] *n.* earthenware jar; broken piece of earthenware.

**cross**

**crockery** /ˈkrɒkəri:/ *n.* earthenware etc. vessels and plates.

**crocodile** /ˈkrɒkədaɪl/ *n.* large amphibious reptile; *colloq.* line of schoolchildren etc. walking in pairs. **crocodile tears** insincere grief.

**crocus** /ˈkrəʊkəs/ *n.* (*pl.* **-cuses**) dwarf plant with corm and yellow or purple or white flowers.

**croft 1** *n.* small piece of arable land close to house; small agricultural holding esp. of crofter. **2** *v.i.* farm croft.

**crofter** /ˈkrɒftə(r)/ *n.* person who rents a smallholding, esp. joint tenant of divided farm in Scotland.

**croissant** /ˈkrwæsɑ̃/ *n.* rich crescent-shaped bread roll.

**cromlech** /ˈkrɒmlek/ *n.* dolmen; circle of upright stones.

**crone** *n.* withered old woman.

**cronk** *a. Aus. colloq.* unsound; fraudulent; sick.

**crony** /ˈkrəʊni:/ *n.* close friend.

**crook** /krʊk/ **1** *n.* hooked staff, esp. of shepherd or bishop; bend, curve; *colloq.* swindler, criminal. **2** *v.* bend, curve; **3** *a. Aus. & NZ sl.* sick, disabled; bad or inferior; unpleasant. **4 go crook** *Aus. sl.* lose one's temper.

**crooked** /ˈkrʊkəd/ *a.* not straight; bent, twisted; dishonest.

**croon** /kruːn/ **1** *v.* hum or sing in low subdued voice. **2** *n.* such singing.

**crop 1** *n.* produce of any cultivated plant or of land; group or amount produced at one time; thick end of whip; hair cut very short; pouch in bird's gullet as preliminary digesting-place. **2** *v.* cut off; (of animal) bite off or eat down; cut short; raise crop on; bear crop. **3 crop up** occur unexpectedly or by chance.

**cropper** /ˈkrɒpə(r)/ *n. sl.* **come a cropper** fall heavily.

**croquet** /ˈkrəʊkeɪ/ **1** *n.* lawn game with hoops, wooden balls, and mallets; croqueting. **2** *v.t.* drive away (player's ball) by striking one's own ball placed in contact with it.

**croquette** /krəʊˈket/ *n.* fried breaded ball of meat, potato, etc.

**crosier** /ˈkrəʊzɪə(r)/ *n.* hooked staff carried by bishop as symbol of office.

**cross 1** *n.* stake used for crucifixion usu. with transverse bar; representation of this as emblem of Christianity; cross-shaped thing; figure or mark etc. of two roughly equal lines etc. crossing near their centres; decoration indicating rank in some orders of knighthood or awarded for personal valour; intermixture of breeds, hybrid; mixture or compromise *between*; trial or annoyance. **2** *v.* go across (road, sea, etc.); cross road etc.; place crosswise; draw line(s) across; make sign of cross on or over; meet and pass; thwart; (cause to) interbreed; cross-fertilize (plants). **3** *a.* transverse; reaching from side to side; intersecting; reciprocal; out of temper, angry *with*. **4 be at cross purposes** talk without either party realizing that the other is talking of a different thing; **crossbar** horizontal bar esp. between uprights; **cross-bench** bench in Parliament for members not belonging to Government or official opposition party; **crossbow** bow fixed across wooden stock, with mechanism working string; **cross-bred** hybrid; **cross-breed** (produce) hybrid animal or plant; **cross-check** check by alternative method of verification; **cross-country** across fields etc., not following roads; **cross-examine** examine (esp. witness in lawcourt) minutely to check or extend previous testimony; **cross-examination** *n.*; **cross-eyed** having one or both eyes turned inwards; **cross-fertilize** fertilize (animal or plant) from a different individual; **crossfire** firing of guns in two crossing directions; **cross-grained** (of wood) with grain running irregularly, (of person) perverse, intractable; **cross-legged** with ankles crossed and knees apart; **cross off, out,** cancel, expunge; **cross-patch** *colloq.* bad-tempered person; **cross-ply** (of tyre) having fabric layers with cords lying crosswise; **cross-pollinate** pollinate (plant) from another; **cross-question** cross-examine; **cross-reference** reference to another passage in same book; **crossroad** (often in *pl.*) intersection of roads; **cross-section** transverse section, diagram etc. of thing as if cut through, representative sample; **cross-stitch** one formed of two stitches that cross; **crossword** puzzle in which words crossing each other vertically and horizontally have to be filled in from clues; **on the cross** diagonally, *Aus. sl.* dishonestly.

**crossing** /'krɒsɪŋ/ *n.* place where things (esp. roads) meet; part of street marked for pedestrians to cross by; travel across water.

**crosswise** /'krɒswaɪz/ *adv.* in shape or manner of cross.

**crotch** *n.* fork, esp. of human body where legs join trunk.

**crotchet** /'krɒtʃət/ *n. Mus.* black-headed note with stem, equal to half minim.

**crotchety** /'krɒtʃəti/ *a.* peevish.

**crouch** /kraʊtʃ/ **1** *v.i.* stand or lie with legs bent close to body. **2** *n.* this position.

**croup**[1] /kruːp/ *n.* laryngitis in children, with sharp cough.

**croup**[2] /kruːp/ *n.* rump, esp. of horse.

**croupier** /'kruːpɪə(r)/ *n.* person in charge of gaming-table.

**croûton** /'kruːtɒn/ *n.* small piece of fried or toasted bread. [F]

**crow** /krəʊ/ **1** *n.* any of various kinds of large black-plumaged bird; cock's cry; infant's crowing; crowbar. **2** *v.i.* (*past* crowed, *arch.* crew) utter cock's cry; (of infants) utter joyful sounds; exult. **3 crow's-foot** wrinkle at outer corner of eye; **crow's nest** barrel fixed at masthead as shelter for look-out man.

**crowbar** /'krəʊbɑː(r)/ *n.* bar of iron used as lever.

**crowd** /kraʊd/ **1** *n.* number of people or animals standing or moving close together without order; *colloq.* set, gang, large number of things. **2** *v.* collect in crowd; fill or cram (*with*); force way *into* or *through* etc. confined space etc. **3 crowd out** exclude by crowding.

**crown** /kraʊn/ **1** *n.* monarch's head-covering or circlet; *the* supreme governing power in monarchy; wreath for head, esp. as emblem of victory; top part of thing, esp. of head or hat etc.; visible part of tooth, artificial replacement for (part of) this; perfection, completion. **2** *v.t.* put crown on; make king or queen; be consummation or reward or finishing touch to; *sl.* hit on head. **3 crown jewels** sovereign's regalia; **Crown land** land belonging to government; **Crown Prince** male heir to

**crozier** *var.* of **crosier**.

**CRT** *abbr.* cathode-ray tube.

**cruces** *pl.* of **crux**.

**crucial** /ˈkruːʃ(ə)l/ *a.* decisive between two hypotheses; very important.

**crucible** /ˈkruːsəb(ə)l/ *n.* melting-pot for metals.

**cruciferous** /kruːˈsɪfərəs/ *a.* with four equal petals arranged crosswise.

**crucifix** /ˈkruːsəfɪks/ *n.* image of Christ on Cross.

**crucifixion** /kruːsəˈfɪkʃ(ə)n/ *n.* crucifying, esp. of Christ.

**cruciform** /ˈkruːsəfɔːm/ *a.* cross-shaped.

**crucify** /ˈkruːsəfaɪ/ *v.t.* put to death by fastening to a cross; persecute, torment.

**crude** 1 *a.* in natural or raw state; lacking finish, unpolished; rude, blunt. 2 *n.* natural mineral oil. 3 **crudity** *n.*

**cruel** /ˈkruːəl/ 1 *a.* indifferent to or taking pleasure in another's suffering; causing pain or suffering. 2 *v.t. Aus. sl.* spoil, destroy all chances of success with. 3 **cruelty** *n.*

**cruet** /ˈkruːət/ *n.* small stoppered bottle for condiments at table; stand holding cruets and mustard pot etc.

**cruise** /kruːz/ 1 *v.i.* sail about without precise destination, or calling at series of places; travel at **cruising speed**, economical travelling speed. 2 *n.* cruising voyage. 3 **cruise missile** one able to fly at low altitudes and guide itself by reference to features of region traversed.

**cruiser** *n.* warship faster and less heavily armoured than battleship. **cruiser-weight** light heavyweight.

**crumb** /krʌm/ 1 *n.* small fragment of bread *or of* food etc.; soft inner part of loaf. 2 *v.t.* coat with breadcrumbs; crumble (bread). 3 **crumby** *a.*

**crumble** /ˈkrʌmb(ə)l/ 1 *v.* break or fall into crumbs or fragments. 2 *n.* dish, esp. of cooked fruit, with crumbly topping. 3 **crumbly** *a.*

**crummy** /ˈkrʌmɪ/ *a. sl.* squalid, inferior.

**crumpet** /ˈkrʌmpət/ *n.* flat soft battercake eaten toasted; *sl.* sexually attractive woman or women.

**crumple** /ˈkrʌmp(ə)l/ *v.* crush or become crushed into creases; give way, collapse.

**crunch** 1 *v.* crush with teeth, esp. noisily; make or emit crunch. 2 *n.* crunching sound; *sl.* decisive event. 3 **crunchy** *a.*

**crupper** /ˈkrʌpə(r)/ *n.* strap looped under horse's tail from back of saddle.

**crusade** /kruːˈseɪd/ 1 *n.* campaign or movement against recognized evil; **Crusade** medieval Christian military expedition to recover Holy Land from Muslims. 2 *v.* take part in crusade.

**crush** 1 *v.* compress with violence so as to break or bruise or crumple; be liable to crumple; defeat utterly; discomfit. 2 *n.* act of crushing; crowded mass of people; drink made of juice of crushed fruit; *sl.* infatuation; *Aus. & NZ* funnel-shaped fenced passage for handling livestock.

**crust** 1 *n.* hard outer part of bread etc.; pastry covering pie; rocky outer part of earth; deposit on sides of wine-bottle; *Aus. & NZ colloq.* livelihood. 2 *v.* cover with or form into crust; become covered with crust.

**crustacean** /krʌsˈteɪʃ(ə)n/ 1 *n.* member of group of hard-shelled mainly aquatic animals. 2 *a.* of crustaceans.

**crusty** /ˈkrʌstɪ/ *a.* having a crisp crust; irritable, surly.

**crutch** 1 *n.* support for lame person usu. with cross-piece fitting under armpit; support; crotch. 2 *v.t. Aus.* immerse (sheep) in dip by means of crutch-shaped instrument; clip wool from hindquarters of (sheep).

**crux** *n.* (*pl.* **cruces** /ˈkruːsiːz/) decisive point, crucial element of problem.

**cry** /kraɪ/ 1 *v.* (*past & p.p.* **cried** /kraɪd/) make loud or shrill sound, esp. to express pain or grief or joy etc.; weep; utter loudly, exclaim. 2 *n.* loud inarticulate utterance of grief or fear or joy etc.; loud excited utterance; appeal; fit of weeping; watchword; call esp. of birds; yelping of hounds. 3 **cry-baby** person who weeps easily or without good reason; **cry down** disparage; **cry off** abandon undertaking; **cry up** praise; **a far cry** a long way; **in full cry** in full pursuit.

**crying** /ˈkraɪɪŋ/ *a.* (of injustice etc.) flagrant, demanding redress.

**cryogenics** /kraɪəʊˈdʒenɪks/ *n.* branch

**crypt**      132      **culture**

of physics dealing with very low temperatures.

**crypt** /krɪpt/ *n.* vault, esp. one below church used as burial-place.

**cryptic** /'krɪptɪk/ *a.* secret, mysterious; obscure in meaning.

**cryptogam** /'krɪptəgæm/ *n.* plant with no true flowers or seeds, e.g. fern or fungus. **cryptogamous** /-'tɒg-/ *a.*

**cryptogram** /'krɪptəgræm/ *n.* thing written in cipher.

**crystal** /'krɪst(ə)l/ 1 *n.* clear transparent colourless mineral; highly transparent glass; substance solidified in definite geometrical form. 2 *a.* made of or as clear as crystal.

**crystalline** /'krɪstəlaɪn/ *a.* of or like or clear as crystal.

**crystallize** /'krɪstəlaɪz/ *v.* form into crystals; become definite; preserve (fruit) in sugar. **crystallization** *n.*

**CSIRO** *abbr.* Commonwealth Scientific and Industrial Research Organization.

**cu.** *abbr.* cubic.

**cub** *n.* young of fox or bear or lion etc.; ill-mannered child or youth; *colloq.* inexperienced newspaper reporter; junior Scout.

**cubby-hole** /'kʌbɪhəʊl/ *n.* very small confined room, cupboard, etc.

**cube** /kju:b/ 1 *n.* solid contained by six equal squares; cube-shaped block; product of a number multiplied by its square. 2 *v.t.* find cube of; cut into small cubes. 3 **cube root** number which produces given number when cubed.

**cubic** /'kju:bɪk/ *a.* of three dimensions; involving cube of a quantity. **cubic metre** etc. volume of a cube whose edge is one metre etc.

**cubical** /'kju:bɪk(ə)l/ *a.* cube-shaped.

**cubicle** /'kju:bɪk(ə)l/ *n.* small separate sleeping-compartment; enclosed space screened for privacy.

**cubism** /'kju:bɪz(ə)m/ *n.* style in art in which objects are represented by juxtaposed geometrical figures. **cubist** *a.* & *n.*

**cubit** /'kju:bɪt/ *n.* ancient measure of length, equal to length of forearm.

**cuboid** /'kju:bɔɪd/ 1 *a.* like a cube; cube-shaped. 2 *n.* rectangular parallelepiped.

**cuckold** /'kʌkəʊld/ 1 *n.* husband of adulterous wife. 2 *v.t.* make cuckold of.

**cuckoo** /'kʊku:/ 1 *n.* migratory bird with characteristic cry. 2 *a. sl.* crazy. 3 **cuckoo-spit** froth exuded by larvae of certain insects.

**cucumber** /'kju:kʌmbə(r)/ *n.* long green fleshy fruit used in salads etc.; plant producing this.

**cud** *n.* half-digested food chewed by ruminant.

**cuddle** /'kʌd(ə)l/ 1 *v.* hug; lie close and snug; nestle. 2 *n.* hug, embrace.

**cudgel** /'kʌdʒ(ə)l/ 1 *n.* thick stick used as weapon. 2 *v.t.* beat with cudgel.

**cue**[1] /kju:/ 1 *n.* last words of actor's speech as signal for another to begin; signal, hint. 2 *v.t.* give cue to. 3 **cue in** insert cue for.

**cue**[2] /kju:/ 1 *n.* long tapered rod for striking ball in billiards etc. 2 *v.t.* strike with cue.

**cuff**[1] *n.* thicker end part of sleeve; separate band of material worn round wrist; in *pl. colloq.* handcuffs; **cuff-link** one of pair of fasteners for shirt cuffs; **off the cuff** extempore, without preparation.

**cuff**[2] *v.t.* strike with open hand. 2 *n.* cuffing blow.

**cuisine** /kwɪ'zi:n/ *n.* style of cooking.

**cul-de-sac** /'kʌldəsæk/ *n.* street, passage, etc., closed at one end.

**culinary** /'kʌlɪnərɪ/ *a.* of or for cooking.

**cull** 1 *v.t.* pick (flowers); select; select and kill (surplus animals etc.). 2 *n.* culling; what is culled.

**culminate** /'kʌlmɪneɪt/ *v.i.* reach highest point of development. **culmination** *n.*

**culpable** /'kʌlpəb(ə)l/ *a.* deserving blame. **culpability** *n.*

**culprit** /'kʌlprɪt/ *n.* person accused of or guilty of offence.

**cult** *n.* system of religious worship; devotion or homage to person or thing.

**cultivar** /'kʌltɪvɑ:(r)/ *n.* variety of plant produced by cultivation.

**cultivate** /'kʌltɪveɪt/ *v.t.* prepare and use (soil) for crops; raise, produce (plant etc.); improve, develop; pay attention to, cherish. **cultivation** *n.*

**cultivator** /'kʌltɪveɪtə(r)/ *n.* agricultural implement for breaking up ground etc.

**culture** /'kʌltʃə(r)/ 1 *n.* refined understanding of the arts and other intellectual achievement; customs and

**cultured** civilization of a particular time or people; improvement by care and training; cultivation of plants, rearing of bees or silkworms etc.; quantity of bacteria grown for study. 2 *v.t.* grow (bacteria) for study. 3 **cultural** *a.*

**cultured** /'kʌltʃəd/ *a.* exhibiting culture. **cultured pearl** one formed by oyster after insertion of foreign body into its shell.

**culvert** /'kʌlvət/ *n.* underground channel or conduit for water crossing road etc.

**cumber** /'kʌmbə(r)/ *v.t.* hamper, hinder; burden.

**cumbersome** /'kʌmbəsəm/ *a.* hampering; inconveniently large or heavy.

**cumin** /'kʌmɪn/ *n.* plant with aromatic seed.

**cummerbund** /'kʌməbʌnd/ *n.* waistsash.

**cumulative** /'kju:mjələtɪv/ *a.* increasing in force etc. by successive additions.

**cumulus** /'kju:mjələs/ *n.* (*pl.* **-li** /-laɪ/) cloud in heaped-up rounded masses.

**cuneiform** /'kju:nəfɔ:m/ 1 *a.* of or using writing composed of wedge-shaped marks. 2 *n.* cuneiform writing.

**cunjevoi** /'kʌndʒəvɔɪ/ *n. Aus.* kind of arum; sea-squirt used as bait.

**cunning** /'kʌnɪŋ/ 1 *a.* skilled in ingenuity or deceit; ingenious. 2 *n.* skill in deceit; craftiness.

**cup** 1 *n.* drinking-vessel, usu. with one side-handle; cupful; cup-shaped thing; wine or cider etc. with various flavourings; ornamental vessel as prize. 2 *v.t.* make cup-shaped.

**cupboard** /'kʌbəd/ *n.* recess or piece of furniture with door and (usu.) shelves, in which things may be stored.

**Cupid** /'kju:pɪd/ *n.* Roman god of love pictured as winged boy with bow.

**cupidity** /kju:'pɪdəti/ *n.* greed for gain.

**cupola** /'kju:pələ/ *n.* small dome; kind of furnace; ship's or fort's revolving gun-turret.

**cur** *n.* worthless or snappish dog; contemptible person.

**curaçao** /'kjʊərəsəʊ/ *n.* liqueur flavoured with orange-peel.

**curacy** /'kjʊərəsi/ *n.* curate's office.

**curare** /kjʊ'rɑ:ri/ *n.* vegetable poison that paralyses motor nerves.

**curate** /'kjʊərət/ *n.* assistant to parish priest.

**curative** /'kjʊərətɪv/ 1 *a.* tending to cure. 2 *n.* curative drug or measure.

**curator** /kjʊ'reɪtə(r)/ *n.* person in charge esp. of museum or library.

**curb** 1 *n.* check, restraint; chain or strap passing under horse's lower jaw; kerb. 2 *v.t.* restrain; apply curb to.

**curd** *n.* coagulated substance formed by action of acids on milk, made into cheese or eaten as food.

**curdle** /'kɜ:d(ə)l/ *v.* coagulate, form into curd.

**cure** /kjʊə(r)/ 1 *n.* thing that cures; restoration to health; course of treatment. 2 *v.t.* restore to health; remedy; relieve *of* disease etc.; preserve (meat etc. or skins).

**curé** /'kjʊəreɪ/ *n.* parish priest in France etc. [F]

**curette** /kjʊ'ret/ 1 *n.* surgeon's scraping-instrument. 2 *v.t* scrape with this. 3 **curettage** *n.*

**curfew** /'kɜ:fju:/ *n.* prohibition of being out of doors during specified hours.

**curie** /'kjʊəri:/ *n.* unit of radioactivity.

**curio** /'kjʊəriəʊ/ *n.* (*pl.* **-rios**) object prized for its rarity etc.

**curiosity** /kjʊəri'ɒsəti/ *n.* desire to know; tendency to pry; strange or rare thing.

**curious** /'kjʊəri:əs/ *a.* eager to learn; inquisitive; strange, surprising.

**curl** 1 *v.* bend or coil into spiral shape; move in curve; play at curling. 2 *n.* curled lock of hair; anything spiral or curved inwards. 3 **curly** *a.*

**curler** /'kɜ:lə(r)/ *n.* pin or clip etc. for curling the hair.

**curlew** /'kɜ:lju:/ *n.* long-billed wading bird with musical cry.

**curling** /'kɜ:lɪŋ/ *n.* game like bowls played on ice with large flattish stones.

**curmudgeon** /kɜ:'mʌdʒ(ə)n/ *n.* churlish or miserly person.

**currant** /'kʌrənt/ *n.* dried fruit of small seedless grape; any of various shrubs producing red or black or white berries; such a berry.

**currawong** /'kʌrəwɒŋ/ *n.* crow-like bird with resonant call.

**currency** /'kʌrənsi/ 1 *n.* money in use in a country or *Aus. arch.* locally; being current; prevalent. 2 *a. Aus. arch.* born in Australia.

**current** /'kʌrənt/ 1 *a.* belonging to present time; happening now; in general

## curriculum    134    cut

circulation or use. 2 *n.* body of water or air etc., moving in definite direction; general tendency or course; movement of electrically charged particles. 3 **current account** bank account that may be drawn on by cheque.

**curriculum** /kəˈrɪkjələm/ *n.* (*pl.* **-la**) course (of study). **curriculum vitae** /ˈviːtaɪ/ brief account of one's life.

**curry**¹ /ˈkʌrɪ/ 1 *n.* dish of meat etc. cooked with various spices and usu. served with rice. 2 *v.t.* make into or flavour like curry. 3 **curry paste**, **powder**, preparation of spices suitable for flavouring curry.

**curry**² /ˈkʌrɪ/ *v.t.* rub down or dress (horse etc.) with curry-comb; dress (leather). **curry-comb** metal brush for horses etc.

**curse** /kɜːs/ 1 *n.* invocation of destruction or punishment; profane oath; great evil, bane. 2 *v.* utter curse against; afflict *with*; utter curses. 3 **the curse** *colloq.* menstruation.

**cursed** /ˈkɜːsəd/ *a.* damned.

**cursive** /ˈkɜːsɪv/ 1 *a.* (of writing) done with joined characters. 2 *n.* cursive writing.

**cursor** /ˈkɜːsə(r)/ *n.* indicator on VDU screen showing particular position in displayed matter; transparent slide on slide-rule.

**cursory** /ˈkɜːsərɪ/ *a.* without attention to details; rapid, desultory.

**curt** *a.* noticeably or rudely brief.

**curtail** /kɜːˈteɪl/ *v.t.* cut down, shorten, reduce. **curtailment** *n.*

**curtain** /ˈkɜːt(ə)n/ 1 *n.* piece of cloth etc. hung up as screen esp. at window or between stage and auditorium; rise or fall of curtain in theatre; curtain-call; in *pl. sl.* the end. 2 *v.t.* provide or shut *off* with curtains. 3 **curtain-call** audience's summons to actor(s) to take bow after fall of curtain; **curtain-raiser** short opening theatre-piece, preliminary event.

**curtsy** /ˈkɜːtsɪ/ 1 *n.* woman's or girl's salutation made by bending knees. 2 *v.i.* make curtsy.

**curvaceous** /kɜːˈveɪʃəs/ *a. colloq.* having many curves (esp. of shapely female figure).

**curvature** /ˈkɜːvətʃə(r)/ *n.* curving; curved form.

**curve** 1 *n.* line or surface of which no part is straight; line showing diagrammatically a continuous variation of quantity or force etc. 2 *v.* bend or shape so as to form a curve.

**curvet** /kɜːˈvet/ 1 *n.* horse's frisky leap. 2 *v.i.* perform curvet.

**curvilinear** /kɜːvəˈlɪnɪə(r)/ *a.* of curved lines.

**cuscus** /ˈkʌskʌs/ *n. Aus.* spotted phalanger of Australia and New Guinea.

**cushion** /ˈkʊʃ(ə)n/ 1 *n.* bag filled with mass of soft material or air; means of protection against shock; elastic lining of billiard table's sides; body of air supporting hovercraft. 2 *v.t.* provide or protect with cushions; mitigate effects of.

**cushy** /ˈkʊʃɪ/ *a. colloq.* (of job etc.) easy, pleasant.

**cusp** *n.* point at which two curves meet.

**cuss** *colloq.* 1 *n.* curse; awkward person. 2 *v.* curse.

**cussed** /ˈkʌsəd/ *a.* awkward and stubborn.

**custard** /ˈkʌstəd/ *n.* dish or sauce made with milk and beaten eggs, usu. sweetened; sweet sauce made of milk and flavoured cornflour etc.

**custodian** /kʌsˈtəʊdɪən/ *n.* curator, guardian.

**custody** /ˈkʌstədɪ/ *n.* keeping, guardianship; imprisonment.

**custom** /ˈkʌstəm/ *n.* usual way of behaving or acting; established usage; business patronage; customers; in *pl.* duty levied on imports, government department dealing with this. **customhouse** office at which customs duties are levied; **custom-made** etc., made etc. to customer's order.

**customary** /ˈkʌstəmərɪ/ *a.* in accordance with custom; usual.

**customer** /ˈkʌstəmə(r)/ *n.* person entering shop etc. to buy; person who buys; *colloq.* person one has to deal with.

**cut** 1 *v.* (*past* & *p.p.* **cut**) divide or wound or penetrate with edged instrument; detach or trim or shape by cutting; cause pain to; reduce (prices, services, etc.); cross, intersect; divide (pack of cards); *Cinemat.* edit (film), stop cameras; end the acquaintance or ignore presence of; avoid or absent oneself from; hit (ball) with chopping motion;

**cutaneous** /kjuːˈteɪnɪəs/ a. of the skin.

**cute** /kjuːt/ a. colloq. clever, ingenious; US attractive.

**cuticle** /ˈkjuːtɪk(ə)l/ n. skin at base of finger-nail or toe-nail.

**cutlass** /ˈkʌtləs/ n. short broad-bladed curved sword.

**cutlery** /ˈkʌtlərɪ/ n. knives, forks, and spoons, for use at table.

**cutlet** /ˈkʌtlət/ n. neck-chop of mutton or lamb; small piece of veal etc. for frying; flat cake of minced meat etc.

**cutter** /ˈkʌtə(r)/ n. tailor etc. who cuts cloth; small fast sailing-ship; small boat carried by large ship.

**cutting** /ˈkʌtɪŋ/ 1 n. piece cut from newspaper etc.; piece cut from plant for replanting; excavation of high ground for railway, road, etc. 2 a. that cuts; wounding to feelings. 3 **cutting grass** Aus. any of various sedges with sharp-edged leaves.

**cuttlefish** /ˈkʌt(ə)lfɪʃ/ n. ten-armed sea mollusc that ejects black fluid when pursued.

**cutwater** /ˈkʌtwɔːtə(r)/ n. forward edge of ship's prow; wedge-shaped projection from bridge-pier.

**cwt.** abbr. hundredweight.

**cyanide** /ˈsaɪənaɪd/ n. highly poisonous substance used in extraction of gold and silver.

**cyanosis** /saɪəˈnəʊsɪs/ n. blue discoloration of skin.

**cybernetics** /saɪbəˈnetɪks/ n. science of control and communications in animals and machines.

**cyclamate** /ˈsɪkləmeɪt/ n. artificial sweetening agent.

**cyclamen** /ˈsɪkləmən or ˈsaɪkləmən/ n. plant with pinkish-purple or white flowers with reflexed petals.

**cycle** /ˈsaɪk(ə)l/ 1 n. recurrent period; period of thing's completion; recurring series; complete set or series; bicycle, tricycle, etc.; hertz. 2 v.i. ride bicycle etc.; move in cycles.

**cyclic** /ˈsaɪklɪk/ a. recurring in cycles; of or forming cycle or circle.

**cyclist** /ˈsaɪklɪst/ n. person who rides bicycle etc.

**cyclone** /ˈsaɪkləʊn/ n. system of winds rotating around low-pressure region; violent destructive form of this. **cyclonic** /-ˈklɒn-/ a.

**cyclostyle** /ˈsaɪkləstaɪl/ 1 n. apparatus for making copies of written document from stencil-plate. 2 v. reproduce thus.

**cyclotron** /ˈsaɪklətrɒn/ n. Phys. apparatus for acceleration of charged atomic particles revolving in magnetic field.

**cygnet** /ˈsɪgnət/ n. young swan.

**cylinder** /ˈsɪlɪndə(r)/ n. solid or hollow roller-shaped body; container for liquefied gas etc.; cylindrical part of machine, e.g. piston-chamber in engine. **cylindrical** /-ˈlɪn-/ a.

**cymbal** /ˈsɪmb(ə)l/ n. concave brass etc. plate struck with another or with stick etc. to make ringing sound.

**cynic** /ˈsɪnɪk/ n. person who has little faith in human sincerity and merit; **Cynic** philosopher of ancient Greek sect showing contempt for sophistication and luxury. **cynical** a.; **cynicism** /-sɪz(ə)m/ n.

**cynosure** /ˈsɪnəʃʊə(r)/ n. centre of attention or admiration.

**cypress** /ˈsaɪprəs/ n. coniferous tree with dark foliage, symbolic of mourning.

**cyst** /sɪst/ n. sac formed in body, containing morbid matter.
**cystic** /'sɪstɪk/ a. of the bladder; like a cyst.

**cystitis** /sɪs'taɪtəs/ n. inflammation of the bladder.
**czar** var. of **tsar**.

# D

**D, d,** Roman numeral 500.

**d.** *abbr.* daughter; departs; died; (former) pence or penny.

**dab**[1] *v.* press (surface) briefly with sponge etc. without rubbing; press (sponge etc. or colour) on surface thus; aim feeble blow (*at*); strike lightly. **2** *n.* dabbing or light blow; smear of paint etc.; in *pl. sl.* fingerprints.

**dab**[2] *n. & a. colloq.* adept. **dab hand** expert.

**dabble** /'dæb(ə)l/ *v.* take casual interest or part (*in*); wet slightly or partly; soil, splash; move (hand, foot, object) about in shallow water, mud, etc.

**dabchick** /'dæbtʃɪk/ *n.* little grebe.

**dacha** /'dætʃə/ *n.* Russian country cottage.

**dachshund** /'dækshʊnd/ *n.* small short-legged long-bodied dog.

**dad** *n. colloq.* father.

**daddy** /'dædi/ *n. colloq. & childish* father; *Aus. colloq.* the supreme instance of. **daddy-long-legs** crane-fly.

**dado** /'deɪdəʊ/ *n.* (*pl.* **-dos**) lower part of interior wall when of different material or colour.

**daffodil** /'dæfədɪl/ *n.* bulbous plant with trumpet-shaped yellow flowers.

**daft** /dɑːft/ *a.* foolish, wild, crazy.

**dag** *n. Aus. & NZ* (usu. in *pl.*) lock of wool clotted with dung about hinder parts of sheep; *sl.* remarkable or amusing person. **rattle your dags** *sl.* hurry up.

**dagger** /'dægə(r)/ *n.* short stabbing-weapon; obelus.

**daguerreotype** /də'gerəʊtaɪp/ *n.* early kind of photograph.

**dahlia** /'deɪlɪə/ *n.* garden plant with large brightly-coloured flowers.

**Dáil (Éireann)** /dɔɪl 'eərən/ *n.* lower house of Parliament in Republic of Ireland.

**daily** /'deɪlɪ/ **1** *a.* done or produced or occurring every (week)day. **2** *adv.* every day; constantly. **3** *n.* daily newspaper; *colloq.* charwoman.

**dainty** /'deɪntɪ/ **1** *a.* delicately pretty; choice; fastidious. **2** *n.* choice morsel, delicacy.

**daiquiri** /'dækəri/ *n.* cocktail of light rum and lime-juice etc.

**dairy** /'deərɪ/ *n.* place for keeping, processing, or selling milk and milk products. **dairy farm** one producing chiefly milk etc.; **dairymaid** woman employed in dairy; **dairyman** dealer in milk etc.

**dais** /'deɪəs/ *n.* low platform, esp. at end of room or hall.

**daisy** /'deɪzɪ/ *n.* wild or garden flower with yellow centre and usu. white rays. **daisy-chain** string of field daisies threaded together; **daisy-wheel** printing-head in form of spokes radiating from centre, with characters at ends, printer having this.

**dale** *n.* valley, esp. in N. England.

**dally** /'dælɪ/ *v.i.* waste time, delay; flirt (*with*). **dalliance** *n.*

**Dalmatian** /dæl'meɪʃ(ə)n/ *n.* native of Dalmatia in Yugoslavia; large white dark-spotted dog.

**dam**[1] **1** *n.* barrier restraining flow of water in stream etc; *Aus.* artificial pond with earth walls. **2** *v.t.* confine, block (*up*), or restrain (as) with dam.

**dam**[2] *n.* mother (usu. of animal).

**damage** /'dæmɪdʒ/ **1** *n.* harm; injury; loss; in *pl.* sum claimed or adjudged in compensation for loss or injury. **2** *v.t.* do harm to, injure.

**damask** /'dæməsk/ **1** *n.* fabric woven with pattern visible on both sides. **2** *a.* made of damask; velvety pink. **3 damask rose** old sweet-scented variety.

**dame** *n.* (title of) woman who has received order of knighthood (**Dame**); comic female pantomime character played by man; *arch.* or *US sl.* woman.

**damn** /dæm/ **1** *v.t.* curse; condemn, censure; condemn to hell. **2** *n.* uttered curse. **3 damn all** *sl.* nothing.

**damnable** /'dæmnəb(ə)l/ *a.* hateful; annoying.

**damnation** /dæm'neɪʃ(ə)n/ **1** *n.* eternal punishment in hell. **2** *int.* of annoyance.

**damned** /dæmd/ **1** *a.* damnable. **2** *adv.* extremely.

**damp** **1** *n.* moisture in air or on surface or diffused through solid. **2** *a.* slightly wet, moist. **3** *v.t.* make damp; stifle, dull, extinguish; discourage, depress;

**dampen** 138 **dart**

*Mus.* stop vibration of (string etc.). 4 **damp course** layer of damp-proof material in wall to keep damp from rising.

**dampen** /'dæmpən/ *v.* make or become damp.

**damper** /'dæmpə(r)/ *n.* device that reduces shock or noise; small pad to stop vibration of piano string; metal plate in flue controlling combustion; *Aus.* bread made of flour and water and cooked in hot ashes.

**damsel** /'dæmz(ə)l/ *n. arch.* young unmarried woman.

**damson** /'dæmz(ə)n/ *n.* small dark-purple plum; tree bearing it.

**dance** /dɑːns or dæns/ 1 *v.* move with rhythmical steps and gestures etc., usu. to music; jump about, move in a lively way. 2 *n.* piece of dancing; special form of this; dancing-party. 3 **dance attendance** wait (*on*) with assiduous attention.

**dandelion** /'dændɪlaɪən/ *n.* yellow-flowered wild plant.

**dander** /'dændə(r)/ *n. colloq.* temper, indignation.

**dandle** /'dænd(ə)l/ *v.t.* dance (child) on knee or in arms.

**dandruff** /'dændrʌf/ *n.* dead skin in small scales among hair.

**dandy** /'dændiː/ 1 *n.* man paying excessive attention to smartness in his dress etc. 2 *a. colloq.* splendid. 3 **dandy-brush** stiff brush for cleaning horses. 4 **dandyism** *n.*

**Dane** *n.* native of Denmark; *hist.* Norse invader of England in Anglo-Saxon period. **great dane** large powerful short-haired dog.

**danger** /'deɪndʒə(r)/ *n.* liability or exposure to harm; thing that causes peril. **danger-money** extra payment for dangerous work.

**dangerous** /'deɪndʒərəs/ *a.* involving or causing danger, unsafe.

**dangle** /'dæŋg(ə)l/ *v.* hang loosely; hold or carry swaying loosely; hold as temptation (*before*).

**Danish** /'deɪnɪʃ/ 1 *a.* of Denmark. 2 *n.* language of Denmark. 3 **Danish blue** white cheese with blue veins; **Danish pastry** kind of yeast cake with icing and nuts etc.

**dank** *a.* damp and cold.

**danthonia** /dæn'θəʊnɪə/ *n.* member of a genus of chiefly Aus. tufted perennial pasture grasses.

**daphne** /'dæfniː/ *n.* a flowering shrub.

**dapper** /'dæpə(r)/ *a.* neat, smart in appearance.

**dapple** /'dæp(ə)l/ *v.t.* mark with rounded spots or patches of colour or shadow. **dapple-grey** (of horse) grey with darker spots.

**Darby and Joan** devoted old married couple. **Darby and Joan club** social club for elderly people.

**dare** /deə(r)/ 1 *v.* venture, have courage or impudence, (to); defy, challenge. 2 *n.* challenge. 3 **daredevil** reckless (person); **I dare say** very likely, I am prepared to believe.

**daring** /'deərɪŋ/ 1 *n.* adventurous courage. 2 *a.* bold, fearless.

**dariole** /'dærɪəʊl/ *n.* savoury or sweet dish cooked and served in individual mould.

**dark** 1 *a.* with little or no light; of deep or sombre colour; brown-complexioned or dark-haired; gloomy; secret, mysterious. 2 *n.* absence of light; lack of knowledge; dark place. 3 **after dark** after nightfall; **Dark Ages** Middle Ages, esp. 5th-10th-c., *fig.* unenlightened period; **dark horse** little-known person who is unexpectedly successful; **dark-room** room with daylight excluded for photographic work; **in the dark** without information.

**darken** /'dɑːkən/ *v.* make or become dark.

**darkness** /'dɑːknəs/ *n.* state of being dark.

**darling**[1] /'dɑːlɪŋ/ 1 *n.* beloved person or animal. 2 *a.* loved, lovable.

**Darling**[2] /'dɑːlɪŋ/ *n.* **Darling pea** Aus. plant with flowers poisonous to sheep; **Darling shower** dust-storm.

**darn**[1] *v.t.* mend (esp. knitted fabric) by interweaving yarn with needle across hole. 2 *n.* place so mended.

**darn**[2] *n.* & *v.t. sl.* mild form of **damn**.

**darnel** /'dɑːn(ə)l/ *n.* grass growing as weed among corn.

**dart** 1 *n.* small pointed missile esp. used as weapon; in *pl.* treated as *sing.*, indoor game in which darts are thrown at target; sudden rapid movement; tapering stitched tuck in garment. 2 *v.* throw (missile); direct suddenly (glance, flash); move with sudden rapid motion.

# Darwinian 139 dazzle

**3 dartboard** circular target in game of darts.

**Darwinian** /dɑːˈwɪniːən/ *a.* of Darwin's doctrine of evolution of species. **Darwinism** *n.*; **Darwinist** *n.*

**Darwin stubby** /ˈdɑːwɪn/, beer bottle of 2 or 2.25 l capacity.

**dash 1** *v.* go with great haste or force; strike with violence so as to shatter; fling (*against* etc.); knock, drive, throw, thrust, (*away, off,* etc.); frustrate, daunt, dispirit; *sl.* (mild form of) damn. **2** *n.* rush, onset; (capacity for) vigorous action; showy appearance or behaviour; horizontal stroke in writing or printing; longer signal of two in Morse code; slight admixture; dashboard. **3 dashboard** surface beneath windscreen of motor vehicle, containing instruments and controls; **dash off** write (letter etc.) hurriedly.

**dashing** /ˈdæʃɪŋ/ *a.* spirited, showy.

**dastardly** /ˈdæstədli/ *a.* malicious and cowardly.

**data** /ˈdeɪtə/ *n.pl.* □ See **datum**. known facts or things used as basis for inference or reckoning; facts, information; material (to be) processed or stored etc. by computer. **data bank** large store of computer-processed information; **database** organized store of data held on computer; **data processing** performance of operations on data by computer.

**date¹ 1** *n.* day of month; statement in document etc. of time of composition or publication; period to which work of art etc. belongs; time at which thing happens or is to happen; *colloq.* social appointment; *US colloq.* person of opposite sex with whom one has social engagement. **2** *v.* mark with date; refer to its time; bear date; have origin *from*; be recognizable as of particular date; *colloq.* be or become out of date; *colloq.* make social appointment with. **3 dateline** line partly along meridian 180° from Greenwich east and west of which date differs, line in newspaper at top of dispatch etc. to show date and place of writing; **out of date** old-fashioned, obsolete; **to date** until now; **up to date** in accordance with modern standards or latest knowledge.

**date²** *n.* oblong stone-fruit; tree (**date-palm**) bearing this.

**dative** /ˈdeɪtɪv/ **1** *n. Gram.* case expressing indirect object of action of verb. **2** *a.* of or in the dative.

**datum** /ˈdeɪtəm/ *n.* (*pl.* **data**) fixed starting-point of scale etc.

**daub 1** *v.* coat or smear with clay etc.; paint crudely or unskilfully. **2** *n.* material for daubing walls etc.; smear of grease etc.; crude painting.

**daughter** /ˈdɔːtə(r)/ *n.* female child in relation to her parents; female descendant; female member of family etc. **daughter-in-law** son's wife.

**daunt** *v.t.* discourage, intimidate.

**dauntless** /ˈdɔːntləs/ *a.* not to be daunted, intrepid.

**dauphin** /ˈdɔːfɪn/ *n. hist.* title of eldest son of king of France.

**davenport** /ˈdævənpɔːt/ *n.* kind of writing-desk; *US* large sofa.

**davit** /ˈdævɪt/ *n.* one of pair of curved uprights for suspending or lowering ship's boat.

**daw** *n.* jackdaw.

**dawdle** /ˈdɔːd(ə)l/ *v.i.* loiter, be sluggish, idle.

**dawn 1** *n.* first light, daybreak; incipient gleam; beginning. **2** *v.i.* begin to be day, grow light, become evident. **3 dawn chorus** early-morning birdsong.

**day** *n.* time during which sun is above horizon; daylight; part of day allotted for work; period of 24 hours as unit of time; period; lifetime, period of prosperity; specified or appointed day. **daydream** (indulge in) fancy or reverie while awake; **daylight** light of day, dawn, visible interval (*between*); **daylight robbery** *colloq.* excessive charge or expense; **daylight saving** obtaining longer evening daylight in summer by making clocks show later time; **day nursery** one for children in daytime esp. while mothers work; **day release** system of allowing employees days off work for education; **day-return** ticket at reduced rate for journey both ways in one day; **day-school** one attended by pupils living at home; **daytime** time of daylight.

**daze 1** *v.t.* stupefy, bewilder. **2** *n.* dazed state.

**dazzle** /ˈdæz(ə)l/ **1** *v.t.* confuse sight of by excess of light or intricate motion etc.; impress or overpower (person) by brilliant display. **2** *n.* bright blinding light.

**dB** *abbr.* decibel(s).

**DC** *abbr.* direct current; District of Columbia.

**DDT** *abbr.* white chlorinated hydrocarbon used as an insecticide.

**deacon** /'di:kən/ *n.* clergyman of order below priest; layman dealing with secular affairs of church. **deaconess** *n. fem.*

**deactivate** /di:'æktəveɪt/ *v.t.* render inactive or less reactive.

**dead** /ded/ 1 *a.* no longer alive; numb; insensitive (*to*); not effective; extinct; inactive; inanimate; dull; not resonant; lacking activity; not transmitting sounds; out of play; abrupt; complete; exact; unqualified. 2 *adv.* absolutely, completely. 3 *n.* dead person(s); inactive or silent time. 4 **dead-and-alive** dull, spiritless; **dead beat** *a.* utterly exhausted; **dead-beat** penniless person; **dead end** closed end of passage etc.; **dead-end** having no prospects; **dead finish** *Aus.* any of various trees or shrubs forming a thicket, this thicket, *colloq.* limit of endurance or excellence etc.; **dead heat** race etc. in which winners finish exactly even; **dead letter** law etc. no longer observed, undelivered or unclaimed letter; **deadline** time-limit; **deadlock** state of affairs from which no progress is possible; **dead loss** useless person or thing; **dead man's handle** controlling handle on electric train etc. disconnecting power supply if released; **dead march** funeral march; **dead marine** empty bottle; **dead-pan** expressionless; **dead reckoning** estimation of position of ship etc. without taking observations; **dead shot** unerring marksman; **dead weight** inert mass; **dead wood** *fig.* useless person(s) or thing(s).

**deaden** /'ded(ə)n/ *v.* deprive of or lose vitality, force, etc.; make insensible (*to*).

**deadly** /'dedli/ 1 *a.* causing fatal injury or serious damage; intense; accurate; deathlike. 2 *adv.* as if dead; extremely. 3 **deadly nightshade** woody plant with poisonous black berries.

**deaf** /def/ *a.* wholly or partly without hearing; unresponsive (*to*). **deaf aid** hearing aid; **deaf-and-dumb alphabet** manual signs for communication with the deaf; **deaf mute** deaf and dumb person.

**deafen** /'def(ə)n/ *v.t.* be so loud as to deprive of hearing.

**deal**[1] 1 *v.* (*past* & *p.p.* dealt /delt/) distribute among several; distribute (cards) to players; assign as share; deliver (blow); behave in specified way (*with*). 2 *n.* dealing, turn to deal; business transaction, bargain; *colloq.* a large amount. 3 **deal in** be seller of; **deal with** do business with, take measures regarding, treat (subject).

**deal**[2] *n.* sawn fir or pine wood.

**dealer** /'di:lə(r)/ *n.* player dealing at cards; trader.

**dealings** /'di:lɪŋz/ *n.pl.* conduct or transactions.

**dean** *n.* head of cathedral chapter; fellow of college with disciplinary functions; head of university faculty.

**deanery** /'di:nərɪ/ *n.* dean's house or office; group of parishes presided over by rural dean.

**dear** 1 *a.* beloved (often *iron.* or as polite form esp. at beginning of letters); precious *to*; high-priced. 2 *n.* dear person. 3 *adv.* at high price. 4 *int.* (usu. **oh dear!** or **dear me!**) expressing surprise or distress etc.

**dearth** /dɜ:θ/ *n.* scarcity or lack, esp. of food.

**death** /deθ/ *n.* dying, end of life; being dead; cause of death; ceasing to be; destruction. **death adder** *Aus.* venomous snake; **death duty** tax levied on property after owner's death; **death-mask** cast taken from dead person's face; **death penalty** capital punishment; **death rate** yearly number of deaths per 1000 of population; **death toll** number of people killed in war or disaster etc.; **death-trap** unsafe place or vehicle etc.; **death-warrant** order for execution (also *fig.*); **death-watch (beetle)** small beetle whose larvae bore into wood with ticking sound.

**deathless** /'deθləs/ *a.* immortal.

**deathly** /'deθli/ *a.* & *adv.* deadly; like death.

**deb** *n. colloq.* débutante.

**débâcle** /deɪ'bɑ:k(ə)l/ *n.* utter collapse or downfall.

**debar** /dɪ'bɑ:(r)/ *v.t.* exclude *from*.

**debark** /di:'bɑ:k/ *v.* disembark. **debarkation** *n.*

**debase** /dɪˈbeɪs/ v.t. lower in character, quality, or value; depreciate (coin) by alloying etc.

**debatable** /dɪˈbeɪtəb(ə)l/ a. open to dispute.

**debate** /dɪˈbeɪt/ 1 v. discuss; hold formal argument esp. in legislature or public meeting; consider, ponder. 2 n. formal discussion; public argument.

**debauch** /dɪˈbɔːtʃ/ 1 v.t. corrupt morally; deprave or debase; in *p.p.* dissolute. 2 n. bout of sensual indulgence.

**debauchery** /dɪˈbɔːtʃəri/ n. excessive sensual indulgence.

**debenture** /dɪˈbentʃə(r)/ n. bond of company etc. acknowledging sum on which interest is due, esp. as prior charge on assets.

**debilitate** /dɪˈbɪlɪteɪt/ v.t. enfeeble.

**debility** /dɪˈbɪlɪti/ n. feebleness, weakness.

**debit** /ˈdebɪt/ 1 n. entry in account for sum owing. 2 v.t. enter (sum) on debit side of account *against* or *to*.

**debonair** /debəˈneə(r)/ a. carefree, self-assured.

**debouch** /dɪˈbaʊtʃ/ v.i. issue from ravine or woods etc. into open ground.

**debrief** /diːˈbriːf/ v.t. obtain report from, after completion of mission etc.

**debris** /ˈdebriː/ n. scattered fragments; wreckage.

**debt** /det/ n. money etc. owing; obligation; state of owing something.

**debtor** /ˈdetə(r)/ n. person in debt.

**debug** /diːˈbʌɡ/ v.t. remove hidden microphones from; correct operational defects in.

**debunk** /diːˈbʌŋk/ v.t. *colloq.* expose false claims or pretensions of.

**début** /ˈdeɪbjuː/ n. first appearance as performer or in society etc.

**débutante** /ˈdebjutɑːnt/ n. young woman making her social début.

**Dec.** *abbr.* December.

**deca-** /ˈdekə/ *in comb.* ten.

**decade** /ˈdekeɪd/ n. 10 years; set or series of 10.

**decadence** /ˈdekəd(ə)ns/ n. period of decline esp. of art or literature; decadent attitude or behaviour.

**decadent** a. declining; belonging to decadent age; self-indulgent.

**decaffeinate** /diːˈkæfəneɪt/ v.t. remove caffeine from.

**decagon** /ˈdekəɡən/ n. plane figure with 10 sides and angles. **decagonal** /-ˈkæɡ-/ a.

**decagram** /ˈdekəɡræm/ n. 10 grams.

**decalitre** /ˈdekəliːtə(r)/ n. 10 litres.

**Decalogue** /ˈdekəlɒɡ/ n. the Ten Commandments.

**decametre** /ˈdekəmiːtə(r)/ n. 10 metres.

**decamp** /diːˈkæmp/ v.i. break up or leave camp; take oneself off, go away suddenly.

**decant** /dɪˈkænt/ v.t. pour off (wine etc.) leaving sediment behind; move or transfer as if by pouring.

**decanter** /dɪˈkæntə(r)/ n. stoppered bottle into which wine or spirit is decanted.

**decapitate** /dɪˈkæpɪteɪt/ v.t. behead. **decapitation** n.

**decarbonize** /diːˈkɑːbənaɪz/ v.t. remove carbon deposit from (engine of car etc.).

**decathlon** /dɪˈkæθlən/ n. composite athletic contest of 10 events.

**decay** /dɪˈkeɪ/ 1 v. (cause to) rot, decompose; decline in quality or power or energy etc. 2 n. ruinous state; decline, loss of quality; decomposition.

**decease** /dɪˈsiːs/ n. *Law* death.

**deceased** /dɪˈsiːst/ 1 a. dead. 2 n. person who has died.

**deceit** /dɪˈsiːt/ n. concealing of truth in order to mislead; trick. **deceitful** a.

**deceive** /dɪˈsiːv/ v.t. persuade of what is false; mislead; use deceit.

**decelerate** /diːˈseləreɪt/ v. decrease speed (of). **deceleration** n.

**December** /dɪˈsembə(r)/ n. twelfth month of year.

**decency** /ˈdiːsənsi/ n. decent behaviour; recognized code of propriety; in *pl.* requirements of respectable behaviour.

**decennial** /dɪˈseniəl/ a. lasting 10 years; recurring every 10 years.

**decent** /ˈdiːs(ə)nt/ a. seemly; not immodest or obscene; respectable; passable; good enough; *colloq.* kind, obliging.

**decentralize** /diːˈsentrəlaɪz/ v.t. transfer from central to local authority; distribute among local centres.

**deception** /dɪˈsepʃ(ə)n/ n. deceiving or being deceived; thing that deceives.

**deceptive** /dɪˈseptɪv/ a. apt to mislead.

**deci-** /ˈdesɪ/ *in comb.* one-tenth.

**decibel** /ˈdesəbel/ n. unit used in comparison of intensities of sound.

**decide** /dəˈsaɪd/ v. bring or come to resolution or decision; settle by giving victory to one side; give judgement.

**decided** a. definite, unquestionable; positive in judgement.

**deciduous** /dəˈsɪdjuːəs/ a. (of plant) shedding leaves annually; periodically or normally shed.

**decigram** /ˈdesɪɡræm/ n. one-tenth of a gram.

**decilitre** /ˈdesɪliːtə(r)/ n. one-tenth of a litre.

**decimal** /ˈdesəm(ə)l/ **1** a. of tenths or 10; proceeding by tens; of decimal coinage. **2** n. decimal fraction. **3 decimal coinage** one using decimal system; **decimal fraction** one with power of 10 as denominator, esp. expressed as figures after decimal point; **decimal point** dot placed after unit figure in decimal notation; **decimal system** that in which each denomination or weight or measure etc. is worth 10 times the value of the one immediately below it.

**decimalize** /ˈdesəməlaɪz/ v.t. express as decimal; convert to decimal system. **decimalization** n.

**decimate** /ˈdesəmeɪt/ v.t. kill tenth or large proportion of. **decimation** n.

**decimetre** /ˈdesɪmiːtə(r)/ n. one-tenth of a metre.

**decipher** /dəˈsaɪfə(r)/ v.t. convert (text written in cipher or unfamiliar script) into understandable form; make out meaning of. **decipherment** n.

**decision** /dəˈsɪʒ(ə)n/ n. act of deciding; settlement; conclusion; resolve; tendency to decide firmly.

**decisive** /dəˈsaɪsɪv/ a. that decides issue; conclusive; positive.

**deck** **1** n. platform extending from side to side of (part of) ship or boat; floor of bus etc.; part of record player or tape recorder which moves or plays etc. record or tape; *US* pack (of cards). **2** v.t. array, adorn. **3 deck-chair** outdoor folding chair.

**declaim** /dəˈkleɪm/ v. speak or utter rhetorically; recite; deliver impassioned speech. **declamation** n.; **declamatory** a.

**declaration** /dekləˈreɪʃ(ə)n/ n. declaring; emphatic, deliberate, or formal statement. **declaratory** /-ˈklær-/ a.

**declare** /dəˈkleə(r)/ v. announce openly or formally; pronounce (person, thing) to be (something); acknowledge possession of (dutiable goods, income, etc.); *Crick.* choose to end one's side's innings before all wickets have fallen; *Cards* name trump suit.

**declassify** /diːˈklæsəfaɪ/ v.t. cease to designate as secret.

**declension** /dəˈklenʃ(ə)n/ n. *Gram.* list of inflexions for noun, adjective, etc.; class according to which noun etc. is declined; decline, deterioration.

**declination** /dekləˈneɪʃ(ə)n/ n. downward bend; angular distance N. or S. of celestial equator; deviation of compass needle from true N.

**decline** /dəˈklaɪn/ **1** v. deteriorate, lose strength or vigour; decrease; refuse; show downward tendency; *Gram.* inflect, state case forms of (noun etc.). **2** n. deterioration; decay.

**declivity** /dəˈklɪvɪtɪ/ n. downward slope.

**declutch** /diːˈklʌtʃ/ v.i. disengage clutch of motor vehicle.

**decoction** /dəˈkɒkʃ(ə)n/ n. extraction by boiling; liquid obtained thus.

**decode** /diːˈkəʊd/ v.t. convert (coded message) into understandable language.

**decoke** /diːˈkəʊk/ v.t. colloq. decarbonize.

*décolletage* /deɪkɒlˈtɑːʒ/ n. low-cut neckline of woman's dress. [F]

*décolleté* /deɪˈkɒləteɪ/ a. having low neckline. [F]

**decompose** /diːkəmˈpəʊz/ v. rot; separate into elements. **decomposition** n.

**decompress** /diːkəmˈpres/ v.t. relieve pressure on (person etc.) by means of an air-lock. **decompression** n.

**decongestant** /diːkənˈdʒest(ə)nt/ n. drug etc. that relieves congestion.

**decontaminate** /diːkənˈtæmɪneɪt/ v.t. remove (esp. radioactive) contamination from. **decontamination** n.

**décor** /ˈdeɪkɔː(r)/ n. furnishings and decoration of room, stage, etc.

**decorate** /ˈdekəreɪt/ v.t. adorn; paint and paper etc. (room etc.); invest with order or medal etc.

**decoration** /dekəˈreɪʃ(ə)n/ n. decorating; thing serving to decorate; medal etc.; in *pl.* flags etc. put up on festive occasion.

**decorative** /'dekərətɪv/ *a.* serving to decorate; *colloq.* pleasing to look at.

**decorator** /'dekəreɪtə(r)/ *n.* person who decorates houses etc. esp. professionally.

**decorous** /'dekərəs/ *a.* not offending against decency or seemliness.

**decorum** /də'kɔːrəm/ *n.* seemliness, propriety; etiquette.

**decoy** /'diːkɔɪ/ 1 *n.* thing or person used to lure animal or other person into trap; bait, enticement. 2 /də'kɔɪ/ *v.* lure by means of decoy.

**decrease** 1 /də'kriːs/ *v.* make or become smaller or fewer. 2 /'diːkriːs/ *n.* decreasing; amount by which thing decreases.

**decree** /də'kriː/ 1 *n.* authoritative order; judicial decision. 2 *v.* ordain by decree. 3 **decree nisi** /'naɪsaɪ/ order for divorce, remaining conditional for period.

**decrepit** /də'krepɪt/ *a.* weakened by age or hard use; dilapidated. **decrepitude** *n.*

**decretal** /də'kriːt(ə)l/ *n.* papal decree.

**decry** /də'kraɪ/ *v.t.* disparage.

**dedicate** /'dedɪkeɪt/ *v.t.* devote or give up (*to* God, person, purpose, etc.); put words in (book etc.) as compliment to friend or patron etc.; in *p.p.* devoted, having single-minded loyalty. **dedicatory** *a.*

**dedication** /dedɪ'keɪʃ(ə)n/ *n.* dedicating or being dedicated; words with which book is dedicated.

**deduce** /də'djuːs/ *v.t.* draw as logical conclusion. **deducible** *a.*

**deduct** /də'dʌkt/ *v.t.* take away; put aside; withhold.

**deductible** /də'dʌktəb(ə)l/ *a.* that may be deducted esp. from one's tax or taxable income.

**deduction** /də'dʌkʃ(ə)n/ *n.* deducting; amount deducted; inference from general to particular; thing deduced.

**deductive** /də'dʌktɪv/ *a.* of or reasoning by deduction.

**deed** *n.* thing consciously done; actual fact; performance; legal document. **deed poll** deed made and executed by one party only.

**deem** *v.t.* regard or consider or judge to be.

**deep** 1 *a.* going or situated far down or in; to or at specified depth; low-pitched; intense; profound, heartfelt; fully absorbed *in.* 2 *adv.* far down or in. 3 *n.* deep place; *the* sea. 4 **deep-freeze** freezer; **deep fry** fry with fat covering food; **deep-laid** secret and elaborate.

**deepen** /'diːpən/ *v.* make or become deep or deeper.

**deer** *n.* (*pl.* same) four-footed ruminant animal of which the male usu. has antlers. **deerstalker** cloth cap with peak in front and at back.

**deface** /də'feɪs/ *v.t.* spoil appearance of; make illegible. **defacement** *n.*

***de facto*** /deɪ 'fæktəʊ/ existing in fact, whether by right or not. [L]

**defalcate** /'diːfælkeɪt/ *v.i.* misappropriate money.

**defalcation** /diːfæl'keɪʃ(ə)n/ *n.* misappropriation of money; shortcoming.

**defame** /də'feɪm/ *v.t.* attack good name of. **defamation** /def-/ *n.*; **defamatory** /-'fæm-/ *a.*

**default** /də'fɔːlt/ 1 *n.* failure to act or appear or pay; option selected by computer program etc. unless given alternative instruction. 2 *v.i.* fail to meet obligations.

**defaulter** *n.* person who defaults, esp. soldier guilty of military offence.

**defeat** /də'fiːt/ 1 *v.t.* overcome in battle or other contest; frustrate, baffle. 2 *n.* defeating; being defeated.

**defeatism** /də'fiːtɪz(ə)m/ *n.* tendency to expect defeat. **defeatist** *n.* & *a.*

**defecate** /'diːfəkeɪt/ *v.i.* discharge faeces from bowels. **defecation** *n.*

**defect** 1 /'diːfekt/ *n.* failing, shortcoming; blemish. 2 /də'fekt/ *v.i.* desert, transfer allegiance to another country, party, etc. 3 **defection** *n.*; **defector** *n.*

**defective** /də'fektɪv/ *a.* incomplete, faulty; lacking, deficient.

**defence** /də'fens/ *n.* defending; means of resisting attack; justification; defendant's case or counsel; players in defending position in game; in *pl.* fortifications. **defenceless** *a.*

**defend** /də'fend/ *v.* ward off attack made on; protect; uphold by argument; *Law* conduct defence (of).

**defendant** /də'fend(ə)nt/ *n.* person accused or sued in court of law.

**defensible** /də'fensəb(ə)l/ *a.* able to be defended or justified.

**defensive** /də'fensɪv/ *a.* done or in-

# defer · dejection

tended for defence. **on the defensive** in attitude or position of defence.

**defer**[1] /dɪˈfɜː(r)/ v.t. put off, postpone. **deferment** n.

**defer**[2] /dɪˈfɜː(r)/ v.i. yield or make concessions *to*.

**deference** /ˈdefərəns/ n. respectful conduct; compliance with advice etc. of another. **in deference to** out of respect for.

**deferential** /defəˈrenʃ(ə)l/ a. showing deference.

**defiance** /dɪˈfaɪəns/ n. defying; open disobedience or disregard. **defiant** a.

**deficiency** /dɪˈfɪʃənsɪ/ n. lack or shortage; thing lacking; deficit. **deficiency disease** one caused by lack of essential element in diet.

**deficient** /dɪˈfɪʃ(ə)nt/ a. incomplete or insufficient in some essential respect.

**deficit** /ˈdefəsɪt/ n. amount by which total falls short of what is required; excess of liabilities over assets.

**defile**[1] /dɪˈfaɪl/ v.t. make dirty; pollute; profane. **defilement** n.

**defile**[2] /dɪˈfaɪl/ 1 n. narrow gorge or pass. 2 v.i. march in file.

**define** /dɪˈfaɪn/ v.t. state precise meaning of; describe scope of; outline; mark out (limits, boundary).

**definite** /ˈdefənət/ a. with exact limits; determinate, distinct, precise.

**definition** /defəˈnɪʃ(ə)n/ n. defining; statement of precise meaning; degree of distinctness.

**definitive** /dɪˈfɪnətɪv/ a. final, decisive, unconditional; most authoritative.

**deflate** /dɪˈfleɪt/ v. let air out of (tyre etc.); (cause to) lose confidence; apply deflation to (economy); pursue policy of deflation.

**deflation** /dɪˈfleɪʃ(ə)n/ n. deflating; reduction of amount of money in circulation to increase its value. **deflationary** a.

**deflect** /dɪˈflekt/ v. bend or turn aside from straight course. **deflection** n.

**deflower** /diːˈflaʊə(r)/ v.t. deprive of virginity; ravage; strip of flowers.

**defoliate** /diːˈfəʊlɪeɪt/ v.t. remove leaves from. **defoliant** n.; **defoliation** n.

**deform** /dɪˈfɔːm/ v.t. spoil appearance or shape of; put out of shape. **deformation** n.

**deformity** /dɪˈfɔːmətɪ/ n. deformed state; malformation.

**defraud** /dɪˈfrɔːd/ v.t. cheat by fraud.

**defray** /dɪˈfreɪ/ v.t. provide money to pay.

**defrost** /diːˈfrɒst/ v.t. remove frost or ice from; unfreeze.

**deft** a. dextrous, skilful.

**defunct** /dɪˈfʌŋkt/ a. no longer existing or in use; dead.

**defuse** /diːˈfjuːz/ v.t. remove fuse from (bomb etc.); reduce danger in (crisis etc.).

**defy** /dɪˈfaɪ/ v.t. resist openly; present insuperable obstacles to; challenge *to* do or prove something.

**degenerate 1** /dɪˈdʒenərət/ a. having lost qualities proper to race or kind, debased. **2** /dɪˈdʒenərət/ n. degenerate person etc. **3** /dɪˈdʒenəreɪt/ v.i. become degenerate. **4 degeneracy** n.; **degeneration** n.

**degrade** /dɪˈɡreɪd/ v.t. reduce to lower rank or simpler structure; bring into dishonour or contempt. **degradation** /deɡ-/ n.

**degrading** a. humiliating; lowering one's self-respect.

**degree** /dɪˈɡriː/ n. stage in ascending or descending scale; unit of angular measurement or in scale of temperature; academic rank conferred by university etc. for proficiency in specified subject(s).

**dehumanize** /diːˈhjuːmənaɪz/ v.t. remove human qualities from.

**dehydrate** /diːˈhaɪdreɪt/ v. remove water from; make dry; lose water. **dehydration** n.

**de-ice** /diːˈaɪs/ v.t. remove ice from; prevent formation of ice on.

**deify** /ˈdiːɪfaɪ/ v.t. make a god of, worship as a god. **deification** n.

**deign** /deɪn/ v.i. condescend *to*.

**deism** /ˈdiːɪz(ə)m/ n. belief in existence of a god without accepting revelation. **deist** n.; **deistic** a.

**deity** /ˈdiːɪtɪ/ n. divine status or nature; god.

**déjà vu** /deɪʒɑː ˈvuː/ illusion of having already experienced present situation. [F]

**deject** /dɪˈdʒekt/ v.t. make sad or gloomy.

**dejection** /dɪˈdʒekʃ(ə)n/ n. dejected mood.

**de jure** /di: 'dʒʊəri:/ rightful, by right. [L]

**delay** /də'leɪ/ 1 v. make or be late; hinder; postpone. 2 n. act or process of delaying; hindrance, time lost by delaying.

**delectable** /də'lektəb(ə)l/ a. delightful.

**delectation** /di:lek'teɪʃ(ə)n/ n. enjoyment.

**delegacy** /'deləgəsi:/ n. body of delegates.

**delegate** 1 /'deləgət/ n. person appointed as representative; member of deputation. 2 /'delegert/ v.t. appoint or send as representative; entrust (task) *to* representative.

**delegation** /delə'geɪʃ(ə)n/ n. delegating, delegacy.

**delete** /də'li:t/ v.t. strike out (word, passage, etc.). **deletion** n.

**deleterious** /delə'tɪəri:əs/ a. harmful.

**delft** n. kind of glazed earthenware.

**deli** /'deli:/ n. delicatessen; *Aus.* small shop open long hours, selling perishable goods and newspapers etc.

**deliberate** 1 /də'lɪbərət/ a. intentional, fully considered. 2 /də'lɪbəreɪt/ v. think carefully (about); take counsel.

**deliberation** /dəlɪbə'reɪʃ(ə)n/ n. careful consideration; careful slowness.

**deliberative** /də'lɪbərətɪv/ a. of or for deliberation.

**delicacy** /'deləkəsi:/ n. delicateness; sensitiveness; choice kind of food.

**delicate** /'deləkət/ a. fine in texture or construction; subtle, hard to discern; tender, easily harmed; requiring deftness or tact.

**delicatessen** /deləkə'tes(ə)n/ n. shop selling prepared foods and delicacies; such food.

**delicious** /də'lɪʃəs/ a. highly delightful esp. to taste or smell.

**delight** /də'laɪt/ 1 v. please greatly; take great pleasure *in*. 2 n. great pleasure; source of this. **delightful** a.

**delimit** /di:'lɪmɪt/ v.t. determine limits or boundaries of. **delimitation** n.

**delineate** /də'lɪni:eɪt/ v.t. portray by drawing or description. **delineation** n.; **delineator** n.

**delinquent** /də'lɪŋkwənt/ 1 a. committing an offence; failing in a duty. 2 n. offender. 3 **delinquency** n.

**deliquesce** /delɪ'kwes/ v.i. become liquid; dissolve in moisture from the air. **deliquescence** n.; **deliquescent** a.

**delirious** /də'lɪri:əs/ a. affected with delirium; raving; wildly excited.

**delirium** /də'lɪri:əm/ n. disordered state of mind; wildly excited mood.

**delirium tremens** /'tri:menz/ form of delirium with terrifying delusions due to prolonged drunkenness.

**deliver** /də'lɪvə(r)/ v.t. convey (letters, goods) to destination; transfer or hand over; utter (speech); launch, aim, (blow, ball, attack); rescue, save, set free; assist in giving birth or at birth of. **be delivered of** give birth to.

**deliverance** /də'lɪvərəns/ n. rescue, setting free.

**delivery** /də'lɪvəri:/ n. delivering or being delivered; periodical distribution of letters or goods; manner of delivering.

**dell** n. small wooded hollow.

**delphinium** /del'fɪni:əm/ n. garden plant with usu. blue flowers; larkspur.

**delta** /'deltə/ n. fourth letter of Greek alphabet (Δ, δ); triangular alluvial tract at mouth of river. **delta wing** triangular swept-back wing of aircraft.

**delude** /də'lu:d/ v.t. fool, deceive.

**deluge** /'delju:dʒ/ 1 n. flood; downpour; overwhelming rush. 2 v.t. flood, overwhelm.

**delusion** /də'lu:ʒ(ə)n/ n. false belief or impression; false hope. **delusive** a.

**de luxe** /də 'lʌks/ of superior kind; sumptuous.

**delve** v. make laborious research; search *in* or *among*; *arch.* dig.

**demagogue** /'deməgɒg/ n. political agitator appealing to emotions of mob. **demagogic** /-'gɒgɪk/ a.; **demagogy** /-gɒgi:/ n.

**demand** /də'mɑ:nd or də'mænd/ 1 n. request made as of right or peremptorily; urgent claim; desire of would-be purchasers for commodity. 2 v.t. make demand for; require.

**demarcation** /di:mɑ:'keɪʃ(ə)n/ n. marking of boundary or limits of anything.

**demean** /də'mi:n/ v.t. lower dignity of.

**demeanour** /də'mi:nə(r)/ n. bearing; outward behaviour.

**demented** /də'mentəd/ a. driven mad, crazy.

**dementia** /də'menʃə/ n. insanity with

**demerara** /deməˈreərə/ n. yellowish-brown raw cane sugar.

**demerit** /diːˈmerɪt/ n. fault, defect.

**demesne** /dəˈmiːn/ n. landed property, estate; possession (of land) as one's own.

**demigod** /ˈdemiɡɒd/ n. partly divine being; *fig.* godlike person.

**demijohn** /ˈdemidʒɒn/ n. large wicker-cased bottle.

**demilitarize** /diːˈmɪlɪtəraɪz/ v.t. remove military forces from.

**demi-monde** /ˈdemimɒnd/ n. women of doubtful repute in society; group behaving with doubtful legality etc. [F]

**demise** /dəˈmaɪz/ n. death (*lit.* or *fig.*).

**demisemiquaver** /demiˈsemikweɪvə(r)/ n. *Mus.* note equal to half semiquaver.

**demist** /diːˈmɪst/ v. clear mist from (windscreen etc.).

**demo** /ˈdeməʊ/ n. (*pl.* -mos) *colloq.* political etc. demonstration.

**demobilize** /diːˈməʊbəlaɪz/ v.t. release from military service. **demobilization** n.

**democracy** /dəˈmɒkrəsi/ n. government by all the people, usu. through elected representatives; equality of rights in society, group, etc.

**democrat** /ˈdeməkræt/ n. advocate of democracy; **Democrat** member of US Democratic Party.

**democratic** /deməˈkrætɪk/ a. of or practising etc. democracy. **democratically** adv.; **democratize** /-ˈmɒk-/ v.t.

**demography** /dəˈmɒɡrəfi/ n. statistical study of life in human communities. **demographic** a.

**demolish** /dɪˈmɒlɪʃ/ v.t. pull or throw down (building); destroy; refute. **demolition** /deməˈlɪʃ(ə)n/ n.

**demon** /ˈdiːmən/ n. devil; evil spirit; malignant or energetic person; *Aus. sl.* policeman, detective. **demonic** /-ˈmɒn-/ n.

**demoniac** /dəˈməʊniæk/ 1 a. possessed by evil spirit; of or like demon; frenzied. 2 n. demoniac person.

**demonology** /diːməˈnɒlədʒi/ n. study of beliefs about demons.

**demonstrable** /ˈdemənstrəb(ə)l/ a. capable of being shown or proved.

**demonstrate** /ˈdemənstreɪt/ v. show evidence of; describe and explain by help of specimens or experiments; prove truth or existence of; take part in public demonstration.

**demonstration** /demənˈstreɪʃ(ə)n/ n. demonstrating; show of feeling; collective expression of opinion e.g. by public meeting; show of armed force.

**demonstrative** /dəˈmɒnstrətɪv/ a. showing or proving; given to or marked by open expression of feelings; *Gram.* indicating person or thing referred to.

**demonstrator** /ˈdemənstreɪtə(r)/ n. person making or taking part in demonstration.

**demoralize** /diːˈmɒrəlaɪz/ v.t. weaken morale of. **demoralization** n.

**demote** /diːˈməʊt/ v.t. reduce to lower rank or grade.

**demur** /dəˈmɜː(r)/ 1 v.i. raise objection; be unwilling. 2 n. raising of objection.

**demure** /dəˈmjʊə(r)/ a. quiet and serious or affectedly so.

**den** n. wild beast's lair; resort of criminals etc.; person's small private room.

**denarius** /dəˈneəriəs/ n. (*pl.* **-rii** /-rɪaɪ/) ancient Roman silver coin.

**denary** /ˈdiːnəri/ a. of 10; decimal.

**denationalize** /diːˈnæʃnəlaɪz/ v.t. transfer (industry etc.) from national to private ownership. **denationalization** n.

**denature** /diːˈneɪtʃə(r)/ v.t. change properties of; make (alcohol) unfit for drinking.

**denial** /dəˈnaɪəl/ n. denying or refusing; contradiction.

**denier** /ˈdeniə(r)/ n. unit of weight for estimating fineness of yarn.

**denigrate** /ˈdenɪɡreɪt/ v.t. blacken, defame.

**denim** /ˈdenəm/ n. twilled cotton fabric; in *pl.* garment made of this.

**denizen** /ˈdenɪz(ə)n/ n. inhabitant or occupant (*of* place).

**denominate** /dəˈnɒmɪneɪt/ v.t. give name to, describe as, call.

**denomination** /dənɒmɪˈneɪʃ(ə)n/ n. name, designation; Church or religious sect; class of units in numbers, money, etc.

**denominational** /dənɒməˈneɪʃən(ə)l/ a. of a particular religious denomination.

**denominator** /dəˈnɒmɪneɪtə(r)/ n.

**denote**     147     **depositor**

number below line in vulgar fraction; divisor.
**denote** /dɪˈnəʊt/ *v.t.* be name for; be sign of; indicate; signify. **denotation** *n.*
**dénouement** /deɪˈnuːmɑ̃/ *n.* final resolution in play, novel, etc.
**denounce** /dɪˈnaʊns/ *v.t.* inform against; accuse publicly; speak violently against.
**dense** /dens/ *a.* closely compacted; crowded together; stupid. **density** *n.*
**dent 1** *n.* depression in surface (as) from blow. **2** *v.t.* make dent in.
**dental** /ˈdent(ə)l/ *a.* of tooth or teeth or dentistry; (of sound) made with tongue-tip against front teeth. **dental floss** fine strong thread used to clean between teeth; **dental surgeon** dentist.
**dentate** /ˈdenteɪt/ *a.* toothed, notched.
**dentifrice** /ˈdentɪfrəs/ *n.* powder or paste etc. for cleaning teeth.
**dentine** /ˈdentiːn/ *n.* hard dense tissue forming main part of tooth.
**dentist** /ˈdentɪst/ *n.* person who treats diseases etc. of teeth. **dentistry** *n.*
**dentition** /denˈtɪʃ(ə)n/ *n.* characteristic arrangement of teeth in species; teething.
**denture** /ˈdentʃə(r)/ *n.* set of artificial teeth.
**denude** /dɪˈnjuːd/ *v.t.* make naked or bare; strip *of*. **denudation** *n.*
**denunciation** /dɪnʌnsɪˈeɪʃ(ə)n/ *n.* denouncing; invective. **denunciatory** *a.*
**deny** /dɪˈnaɪ/ *v.t.* declare untrue or nonexistent; disavow; refuse. **deny oneself** be abstinent.
**deodorant** /diːˈəʊdərənt/**1** *a.* that removes or conceals odours. **2** *n.* deodorant substance.
**deodorize** /diːˈəʊdəraɪz/ *v.t.* destroy odour of. **deodorization** *n.*
**deoxyribonucleic acid** /diːˌɒksɪraɪbəʊnjuːˈkliːɪk/ substance in chromosomes storing genetic information.
**depart** /dɪˈpɑːt/ *v.* go away, leave; set out; diverge or deviate. **depart this life** die.
**departed** *a.* bygone, deceased.
**department** /dɪˈpɑːtmənt/ *n.* separate part of complex whole, esp. of business or of municipal or State administration; French administrative district. **department store** large shop selling variety of goods. **departmental** *a.*

**departure** /dɪˈpɑːtʃə(r)/ *n.* departing.
**depend** /dɪˈpend/ *v.i.* (usu. with *on* or *upon*) be controlled or determined by; be unable to do without.
**dependable** /dɪˈpendəb(ə)l/ *a.* that may be depended on.
**dependant** /dɪˈpend(ə)nt/ *n.* person who depends on another for support.
**dependence** /dɪˈpend(ə)ns/ *n.* depending, being dependent; reliance.
**dependency** /dɪˈpendənsɪ/ *n.* country etc. controlled by another.
**dependent** /dɪˈpend(ə)nt/ *a.* depending (*on*); unable to do without something; maintained at another's cost; *Gram.* in subordinate relation to another word.
**depict** /dɪˈpɪkt/ *v.t.* represent in picture or words. **depiction** *n.*
**depilate** /ˈdepɪleɪt/ *v.t.* remove hair from. **depilation** *n.*
**depilatory** /dɪˈpɪlətərɪ/ **1** *a.* that removes unwanted hair. **2** *n.* depilatory substance.
**deplete** /dɪˈpliːt/ *v.t.* empty out; reduce numbers or quantity of. **depletion** *n.*
**deplorable** /dɪˈplɔːrəb(ə)l/ *a.* lamentable; to be regretted; exceedingly bad.
**deplore** /dɪˈplɔː(r)/ *v.t.* find or call deplorable.
**deploy** /dɪˈplɔɪ/ *v.* spread out, put into or take up position, for most effective action etc. **deployment** *n.*
**deponent** /dɪˈpəʊnənt/ *n.* maker of legal deposition.
**depopulate** /diːˈpɒpjʊleɪt/ *v.t.* reduce population of. **depopulation** *n.*
**deport** /dɪˈpɔːt/ *v.t.* remove into exile; send out of the country; behave or conduct *oneself*. **deportation** *n.*
**deportment** /dɪˈpɔːtmənt/ *n.* behaviour, bearing.
**depose** /dɪˈpəʊz/ *v.* remove from office; dethrone; state *that*; testify *to*.
**deposit** /dɪˈpɒzɪt/ **1** *n.* thing stored for safe keeping; sum placed in bank; sum paid as pledge or first instalment; layer of accumulated matter. **2** *v.t.* entrust for keeping; pay as pledge; lay or set down; leave as deposit.
**depositary** /dɪˈpɒzɪtərɪ/ *n.* person to whom thing is entrusted.
**deposition** /dɪːpəˈzɪʃ(ə)n/ *n.* deposing; sworn evidence; giving of this.
**depositor** /dɪˈpɒzɪtə(r)/ *n.* person who deposits money or property etc.

**depository** /dɪˈpɒzətəri/ *n.* storehouse.

**depot** /ˈdepəʊ/ *n.* storehouse, esp. for military supplies; headquarters of regiment; place from which goods or vehicles etc. are dispatched.

**deprave** /dɪˈpreɪv/ *v.t.* corrupt morally; in *p.p.* wicked, dissolute.

**depravity** /dɪˈprævəti:/ *n.* wickedness; moral corruption.

**deprecate** /ˈdeprəkeɪt/ *v.* express disapproval of. **deprecation** *n.*; **deprecatory** *a.*

**depreciate** /dɪˈpriːʃɪeɪt/ *v.* lower in value; disparage.

**depreciation** /dɪpriːʃɪˈeɪʃ(ə)n/ *n.* depreciating; fall in value.

**depreciatory** /dɪˈpriːʃətəri/ *a.* disparaging.

**depredation** /deprəˈdeɪʃ(ə)n/ *n.* (usu. in *pl.*) plundering, destruction.

**depress** /dɪˈpres/ *v.t.* make despondent, deject; lower or reduce; affect with economic depression; push down.

**depressant** /dɪˈpres(ə)nt/ 1 *a.* causing depression. 2 *n.* depressant agent or influence.

**depression** /dɪˈpreʃ(ə)n/ *n.* state of extreme dejection; long period of financial and industrial slump; lowering of barometric pressure; sunken area in surface.

**depressive** /dɪˈpresɪv/ 1 *a.* characterized by or tending to depression. 2 *n.* person suffering from depression.

**deprivation** /deprəˈveɪʃ(ə)n/ *n.* depriving, being deprived; loss.

**deprive** /dɪˈpraɪv/ *v.t.* prevent from use or enjoyment of; strip of; in *p.p.*, (esp. of child) lacking normal home life etc.

**dept.** *abbr.* department.

**depth** *n.* deepness or measure of it; (usu. in *pl.*) deep or lowest or inmost part, middle (of night, winter, etc.). **depth-charge** bomb exploding under water; **in depth** thoroughly.

**deputation** /depjuːˈteɪʃ(ə)n/ *n.* body of persons sent to represent others.

**depute** /dɪˈpjuːt/ *v.t.* commit (task, authority) to another; appoint as substitute.

**deputize** /ˈdepjətaɪz/ *v.i.* act as deputy (*for*).

**deputy** /ˈdepjəti/ *n.* person appointed to act for another; parliamentary representative in some countries.

**derail** /diːˈreɪl/ *v.t.* cause (train etc.) to leave rails. **derailment** *n.*

**derange** /dɪˈreɪndʒ/ *v.t.* throw into confusion, disrupt; make insane. **derangement** *n.*

**Derby** /ˈdɑːbi/ *n.* annual horse-race at Epsom; similar race elsewhere; important sporting event.

**derelict** /ˈderəlɪkt/ 1 *a.* left ownerless (esp. of ship at sea or decrepit property); abandoned by society. 2 *n.* derelict property; socially forsaken person.

**dereliction** /derəˈlɪkʃ(ə)n/ *n.* neglect (*of* duty etc.); shortcoming.

**deride** /dɪˈraɪd/ *v.t.* scoff at. **derision** /-ˈrɪʒ-/ *n.*

**derisive** /dɪˈraɪsɪv/ *a.* mocking, ironical.

**derisory** /dɪˈraɪsəri/ *a.* showing derision; deserving derision.

**derivation** /derəˈveɪʃ(ə)n/ *n.* deriving; formation of word from its origin; tracing of this.

**derivative** /dɪˈrɪvətɪv/ 1 *a.* derived, from a source, not original. 2 *n.* derivative word or substance.

**derive** /dɪˈraɪv/ *v.* get or obtain (*from* source); have origin *from*; trace or assert origin and formation of (word etc.).

**dermatitis** /dɜːməˈtaɪtɪs/ *n.* inflammation of skin.

**dermatology** /dɜːməˈtɒlədʒi/ *n.* study of skin and its diseases. **dermatological** *a.*; **dermatologist** *n.*

**derogate** /ˈderəgeɪt/ *v.i.* detract *from.* **derogation** *n.*

**derogatory** /dɪˈrɒgətəri/ *a.* involving discredit or disparagement *to.*

**derrick** /ˈderɪk/ *n.* kind of hoisting apparatus; framework over deep borehole, esp. oil-well.

**derris** /ˈderɪs/ *n.* insecticide made from powdered root of tropical plant.

**derry** /ˈderi/ *n.* *Aus. colloq.* **have a derry on** be prejudiced against.

**derv** *n.* diesel fuel used in heavy road vehicles.

**dervish** /ˈdɜːvɪʃ/ *n.* member of Muslim religious order vowed to poverty and austerity.

**descant** 1 /ˈdeskænt/ *n.* melodic treble accompaniment to hymn-tune etc. 2 /dɪˈskænt/ *v.i.* talk lengthily *upon.* 3 **descant recorder** highest-pitched of standard kinds of recorder.

**descend** /dɪˈsend/ *v.* come or go down;

**descendant** /dɪˈsend(ə)nt/ n. person etc. descended from another.

**descended** /dɪˈsendəd/ a. having origin *from*.

**descent** /dɪˈsent/ n. act or way of descending; downward slope; lineage; sudden attack; decline, fall.

**describe** /dɪˈskraɪb/ v.t. set forth in words; list characteristics of; mark out, draw, or move in (specified line or curve etc.).

**description** /dɪˈskrɪpʃ(ə)n/ n. describing; verbal portrait; sort, kind, class.

**descriptive** /dɪˈskrɪptɪv/ a. serving or seeking to describe.

**descry** /dɪˈskraɪ/ v.t. catch sight of; succeed in discerning.

**desecrate** /ˈdesɪkreɪt/ v.t. violate sanctity of. **desecration** n.; **desecrator** n.

**desegregate** /diːˈsegrəgeɪt/ v.t. abolish racial segregation in.

**desert**¹ /dɪˈzɜːt/ v. abandon, forsake; cease to frequent; leave military service unlawfully. **desertion** n.

**desert**² /ˈdezət/ 1 n. uninhabited and barren esp. waterless region. 2 a. uninhabited, barren.

**desert**³ /dɪˈzɜːt/ n. deserving, being worthy of reward or punishment; in *pl.* deserved recompense.

**deserve** /dɪˈzɜːv/ v. be entitled to, esp. by conduct or qualities.

**deservedly** /dɪˈzɜːvɪdli/ adv. as deserved.

**deserving** /dɪˈzɜːvɪŋ/ a. worthy (*of*); worth rewarding or supporting.

**desiccate** /ˈdesɪkeɪt/ v.t. remove moisture from, dry. **desiccation** n.

**desideratum** /dɪzɪdəˈrɑːtəm/ n. (*pl.* -ta) something required or desired.

**design** /dɪˈzaɪn/ 1 n. sketch or plan etc. for future product; art of making these; scheme of lines or shapes forming a decoration; layout; established form of product; mental plan; purpose. 2 v. make design for; be designer for; intend.

**designate** 1 /ˈdezɪgneɪt/ v. specify; indicate as having some function; describe as; appoint to office. 2 a. /ˈdezɪgnət/ (placed after n.) appointed but not yet installed.

**designation** /dezɪgˈneɪʃ(ə)n/ n. designating; name or title.

**designedly** /dɪˈzaɪnɪdli/ adv. intentionally.

**designer** /dɪˈzaɪnə(r)/ n. person who makes designs for products, clothes, stage sets, etc.

**designing** /dɪˈzaɪnɪŋ/ a. crafty, scheming.

**desirable** /dɪˈzaɪərəb(ə)l/ a. worth having or wishing for; causing desire. **desirability** n.

**desire** /dɪˈzaɪə(r)/ 1 n. unsatisfied longing; feeling of potential pleasure in something; expression of this; request; thing desired; lust. 2 v.t. have desire for; ask for.

**desirous** /dɪˈzaɪərəs/ a. having desire; wishful.

**desist** /dɪˈzɪst/ v.i. cease (*from*).

**desk** n. piece of furniture with flat or sloping top for reading or writing etc. at; compartment for cashier or receptionist etc.; subdivision of (esp. newspaper) office.

**desolate** 1 /ˈdesələt/ a. left alone; uninhabited; dreary, forlorn. 2 /ˈdesəleɪt/ v.t. depopulate; devastate; make wretched. 3 **desolation** n.

**despair** /dɪˈspeə(r)/ 1 n. loss or absence of hope; thing that causes this. 2 v.i. lose all hope (*of*).

**despatch** var. of **dispatch**.

**desperado** /despəˈrɑːdəʊ/ n. (*pl.* -does) desperate or reckless criminal.

**desperate** /ˈdespərət/ a. leaving little or no room for hope; extremely dangerous or serious; reckless from despair.

**desperation** /despəˈreɪʃ(ə)n/ n. despair; reckless state of mind.

**despicable** /dɪˈspɪkəb(ə)l/ a. deserving to be despised; contemptible.

**despise** /dɪˈspaɪz/ v.t. regard with contempt.

**despite** /dɪˈspaɪt/ prep. in spite of.

**despoil** /dɪˈspɔɪl/ v.t. plunder, strip. **despoliation** n.

**despondent** /dɪˈspɒnd(ə)nt/ a. in low spirits, dejected. **despondency** n.

**despot** /ˈdespɒt/ n. absolute ruler; tyrant.

**despotic** /dɪˈspɒtɪk/ a. having unrestricted power, tyrannous.

**despotism** /ˈdespətɪz(ə)m/ n. rule by despot; country ruled by despot.

**dessert** /dɪˈzɜːt/ n. sweet course ending meal. **dessertspoon** spoon between teaspoon and tablespoon in size.

**destination** /destɪˈneɪʃ(ə)n/ n. place to which person or thing is going.

**destine** /ˈdestɪn/ v.t. settle or determine future of; set apart for purpose.

**destiny** /ˈdestɪni:/ n. what is destined to happen; fate; power that foreordains.

**destitute** /ˈdestɪtju:t/ a. in great need, esp. of food or shelter etc.; devoid of. **destitution** n.

**destroy** /dəˈstrɔɪ/ v.t. pull or break down; make useless; kill.

**destroyer** /dəˈstrɔɪə(r)/ n. small fast warship.

**destruct** /dəˈstrʌkt/ v.t. US bring about deliberate destruction of (one's own equipment etc.). **destructible** a.

**destruction** /dəˈstrʌkʃ(ə)n/ n. destroying or being destroyed.

**destructive** /dəˈstrʌktɪv/ a. causing destruction; tending to destroy; criticizing without amending.

**desuetude** /dəˈsju:ətju:d/ n. state of disuse.

**desultory** /ˈdezəltri/ a. going constantly from one thing to another, unmethodical.

**detach** /dəˈtætʃ/ v.t. unfasten and remove (from); send off on separate mission.

**detached** /dəˈtætʃt/ a. standing apart; separate, not joined to another; unemotional, impartial.

**detachment** /dəˈtætʃmənt/ n. detaching or being detached; lack of emotion or concern; party of soldiers etc. detached for special duty.

**detail** /ˈdi:teɪl/ **1** n. item, small or subordinate particular; dealing with things item by item; small detachment for special duty. **2** v.t. give particulars of, relate in detail; assign for special duty etc.

**detain** /dəˈteɪn/ v.t. keep in custody or under restraint; keep waiting, delay.

**detainee** /di:teɪˈni:/ n. person detained in custody usu. on political grounds.

**detect** /dəˈtekt/ v.t. discover, find out. **detection** n.; **detector** n.

**detective** /dəˈtektɪv/ n. person, esp. policeman, employed in investigating crime.

**détente** /deɪˈtɑ:t/ n. relaxing of strained diplomatic relations. [F]

**detention** /dəˈtenʃ(ə)n/ n. detaining; being detained. **detention centre** institution for brief detention of young offenders.

**deter** /dəˈtɜ:(r)/ v.t. discourage, hinder.

**detergent** /dəˈtɜ:dʒ(ə)nt/ **1** n. cleansing agent, esp. substance used with water for removing dirt etc. **2** a. cleansing.

**deteriorate** /dəˈtɪəriəreɪt/ v.i. become worse. **deterioration** n.

**determinant** /dəˈtɜ:mənənt/ n. decisive factor.

**determinate** /dəˈtɜ:mənət/ a. limited; of definite scope or nature.

**determination** /dətɜ:məˈneɪʃ(ə)n/ n. resolute purpose or conduct; determining; fixing of intention.

**determine** /dəˈtɜ:mən/ v. ascertain or fix with precision; settle, decide; be decisive factor in.

**determined** a. resolute.

**determinism** /dəˈtɜ:mənɪz(ə)m/ n. theory that action is determined by forces independent of will. **determinist** n.; **deterministic** a.

**deterrent** /dəˈterənt/ **1** a. serving to deter. **2** n. thing that deters, esp. nuclear weapon deterring attack by enemy country.

**detest** /dəˈtest/ v.t. hate, loathe. **detestation** n.

**detestable** /dəˈtestəb(ə)l/ a. hated, loathed.

**dethrone** /di:ˈθrəʊn/ v.t. remove (ruler) from throne. **dethronement** n.

**detonate** /ˈdetəneɪt/ v. (cause to) explode with loud report. **detonation** n.

**detonator** /ˈdetəneɪtə(r)/ n. device for detonating explosive.

**detour** /ˈdi:tʊə(r)/ n. divergence from direct or intended route; roundabout way.

**detract** /dəˈtrækt/ v. take away from. **detract from** reduce credit due to, depreciate. **detraction** n.; **detractor** n.

**detriment** /ˈdetrəmənt/ n. damage, harm; thing causing this. **detrimental** a.

**detritus** /dəˈtraɪtəs/ n. Geol. matter produced by erosion, e.g. gravel or rock debris.

**de trop** /də trəʊ/ not wanted; in the way. [F]

**deuce**[1] /dju:s/ n. two on dice or cards; Tennis state of score at which either side must gain two successive points or games to win.

**deuce**² /djuːs/ *n.* the Devil.

**deuterium** /djuːˈtɪərɪəm/ *n.* heavy isotope of hydrogen with mass about twice that of ordinary hydrogen.

**Deutschmark** /ˈdɔɪtʃmɑːk/ *n.* currency unit of Federal Republic of Germany.

**devalue** /diːˈvæljuː/ *v.t.* reduce value of, esp. currency relative to that of other currencies or gold. **devaluation** *n.*

**devastate** /ˈdevəsteɪt/ *v.t.* lay waste; cause great destruction to. **devastation** *n.*

**develop** /dəˈveləp/ *v.* make or become fuller or bigger or more elaborate or systematic; bring or come to active or visible state or to maturity; reveal or be revealed; begin to exhibit or suffer from; build on or make fuller use of (land); treat (photographic material) to make picture visible. **developing country** poor or primitive country developing better social and economic conditions.

**development** /dəˈveləpmənt/ *n.* developing or being developed; growth or evolution; stage of advancement, product; area of developed land. **developmental** *a.*

**deviant** /ˈdiːvɪənt/ **1** *a.* that deviates from normal behaviour. **2** *n.* deviant person or thing.

**deviate** /ˈdiːvɪeɪt/ *v.i.* turn aside (*from*); digress; diverge.

**deviation** /diːvɪˈeɪʃ(ə)n/ *n.* deviating, esp. divergence from standard or normal position etc.

**device** /dəˈvaɪs/ *n.* thing made or adapted for particular purpose; scheme, trick; emblematic or heraldic design. **left to one's own devices** without supervision or help.

**devil** /ˈdev(ə)l/ **1** *n.* personified spirit of evil, esp. *the* **Devil** supreme spirit of evil; cruel or malignant being; mischievously energetic or clever person. **2** *v.* cook with hot condiments. **3 devil-may-care** cheerful and reckless; **devil's advocate** person who tests proposition by arguing against it.

**devilish** /ˈdevəlɪʃ/ **1** *a.* of or like a devil; mischievous. **2** *adv. colloq.* very.

**devilment** /ˈdevəlmənt/ *n.* mischief; wild spirits.

**devilry** /ˈdevəlri/ *n.* wickedness; reckless mischief; black magic.

**devious** /ˈdiːvɪəs/ *a.* winding, circuitous; unscrupulous, insincere.

**devise** /dəˈvaɪz/ *v.t.* plan or think out; leave (real estate) by will.

**devoid** /dəˈvɔɪd/ *a.* **devoid of** quite lacking or free from.

**devolution** /diːvəˈluːʃ(ə)n/ *n.* delegation of power esp. from central to local or regional government.

**devolve** /dəˈvɒlv/ *v.* (of duties etc.) pass or be passed on to another; (of property) descend in succession.

**devon** /ˈdev(ə)n/ *n. Aus.* bland sausage usu. sliced and eaten cold.

**devote** /dəˈvəʊt/ *v.t.* apply or give over *to* particular activity or purpose.

**devoted** /dəˈvəʊtɪd/ *a.* showing devotion; very loyal or loving.

**devotee** /devəˈtiː/ *n.* person devoted to something, enthusiast; very pious person.

**devotion** /dəˈvəʊʃ(ə)n/ *n.* great love or loyalty; enthusiastic zeal; in *pl.* worship, prayers. **devotional** *a.*

**devour** /dəˈvaʊə(r)/ *v.t.* eat greedily or quickly; destroy or consume; take in greedily with eyes or ears.

**devout** /dəˈvaʊt/ *a.* earnestly religious; reverent; sincere.

**dew** *n.* atmospheric vapour condensed in droplets during night; beaded moisture resembling it. **dew-claw** rudimentary inner toe of some dogs; **dewdrop** drop of dew; **dew-point** temperature at which dew forms. **dewy** *a.*

**dewlap** /ˈdjuːlæp/ *n.* fold of loose skin hanging from throat esp. in cattle.

**dexterity** /dekˈsterəti/ *n.* dextrousness.

**dextrous** /ˈdekstrəs/ *a.* handling things neatly; skilful, clever.

**dg.** *abbr.* decigram.

**dharma** /ˈdɑːmə/ *n.* right behaviour; Buddhist truth; Hindu moral law.

**dhoti** /ˈdəʊtiː/ *n.* loin-cloth worn by male Hindus.

**dhow** /daʊ/ *n.* Arabian-Sea ship.

**diabetes** /daɪəˈbiːtiːz/ *n.* disease in which sugar and starch are not properly absorbed by the body.

**diabetic** /daɪəˈbetɪk/ **1** *a.* of or having diabetes; for diabetics. **2** *n.* diabetic person.

**diabolic** /daɪəˈbɒlɪk/ *a.* (also **diabol-**

**diabolism** /dɑɪˈæbəlɪz(ə)m/ n. devil-worship; sorcery.

**diaconal** /dɑɪˈækən(ə)l/ a. of a deacon.

**diaconate** /dɑɪˈækənət/ n. office of a deacon; body of deacons.

**diacritical** /dɑɪəˈkrɪtɪk(ə)l/ a. distinguishing; (of mark) indicating that written letter has particular sound.

**diadem** /ˈdɑɪədem/ n. crown.

**diaeresis** /dɑɪˈɪərəsəs/ n. (pl. -reses /-rəsiːz/ mark (¨) placed over vowel to show it is sounded separately.

**diagnose** /dɑɪəgˈnəʊz/ v.t. determine nature of or deduce presence of (disease).

**diagnosis** /dɑɪəgˈnəʊsəs/ n. (pl. -noses /-ˈnəʊsiːz/) identification of disease by means of symptoms etc.

**diagnostic** /dɑɪəgˈnɒstɪk/1 a. of or assisting diagnosis. 2 n. symptom.

**diagonal** /dɑɪˈægən(ə)l/ 1 a. crossing a straight sided figure from corner to corner, oblique. 2 n. straight line joining opposite corners of a thing.

**diagram** /ˈdɑɪəgræm/ n. drawing done to explain or illustrate statement or process etc. **diagrammatic** /-ˈmæ-/ a.

**dial** /ˈdɑɪəl/ 1 n. face of clock or watch; plate on which measurement is registered by pointer; numbered plate on telephone with movable disc for making call to selected number; device for selecting radio wavelength or television channel. 2 v. make telephone call by using dial; call (number) thus.

**dialect** /ˈdɑɪəlekt/ n. form of speech peculiar to particular region etc. **dialectal** a.

**dialectic** /dɑɪəˈlektɪk/ n. (often in pl.) art of investigating truth by logical discussion etc. **dialectical** a.

**dialogue** /ˈdɑɪəlɒg/ n. conversation, esp. as represented in play, novel, etc.; discussion between representatives of two groups.

**dialysis** /dɑɪˈæləsəs/ n. (pl. -ses /-siːz/) separation of particles by difference in their ability to pass through suitable membrane ; purification of blood thus.

**diamanté** /dɪəˈmɑ̃teɪ/ a. sparkling with powdered crystal etc.

**diameter** /dɑɪˈæmətə(r)/ n. straight line passing from side to side through centre of circle or sphere; transverse measurement.

**diametrical** /dɑɪəˈmetrɪk(ə)l/ a. of or along diameter; (of opposition etc.) direct, complete.

**diamond** /ˈdɑɪəmənd/ n. transparent usu. colourless very hard brilliant precious stone; rhombus; playing-card of suit marked with red rhombuses. **diamond-bird** Aus. pardalote; **diamondsnake** Aus. greenish-black carpet-snake with diamond-shaped markings; **diamond wedding** 60th or 75th anniversary of wedding.

**diapason** /dɑɪəˈpeɪz(ə)n/ n. entire compass of musical instrument or voice; organ-stop extending through whole compass.

**diaper** /ˈdɑɪəpə(r)/ n. linen or cotton fabric with small diamond pattern; baby's nappy.

**diaphanous** /dɑɪˈæfənəs/ a. (of fabric etc.) light and almost transparent.

**diaphragm** /ˈdɑɪəfræm/ n. muscular partition between thorax and abdomen in mammals; vibrating membrane etc. in acoustic instrument; device for varying aperture of camera lens; contraceptive cap fitting over cervix.

**diarist** /ˈdɑɪərəst/ n. keeper of diary.

**diarrhoea** /dɑɪəˈriːə/ n. excessive evacuation of too fluid faeces.

**diary** /ˈdɑɪəri/ n. daily record of events etc.; book for keeping this or noting future engagements etc.

**Diaspora** /dɑɪˈæspərə/ n. dispersion of the Jews; Jews thus dispersed.

**diastole** /dɑɪˈæstəliː/ n. dilatation of heart alternating with systole in pulse.

**diatomic** /dɑɪəˈtɒmɪk/ a. of two atoms.

**diatonic** /dɑɪəˈtɒnɪk/ a. Mus. (of scale) involving only notes proper to key without chromatic alteration.

**diatribe** /ˈdɑɪətrɑɪb/ n. bitter criticism or denunciation.

**dibble** /ˈdɪb(ə)l/ 1 n. (also **dibber**) garden tool for making holes to receive bulbs or plants. 2 v. plant (bulb etc.) thus.

**dice** 1 n. (pl. of **die**[2], often used as sing.) small cube marked on each face with 1-6 spots etc., used in games of chance; game played with dice. 2 v. gamble with dice; take risks; cut into small cubes; Aus. sl. reject, abandon.

**dicey** /ˈdɑɪsiː/ a. sl. risky, unreliable.

# dichotomy     diffident

**dichotomy** /daɪˈkɒtəmɪ/ *n.* division into two.

**dichromatic** /daɪkrəˈmætɪk/ *a.* of two colours.

**dick** *n. US sl.* detective.

**dickens** /ˈdɪkənz/ *n. colloq.* the Devil.

**dicker** /ˈdɪkə(r)/ *v.i.* haggle; hesitate.

**dicky** /ˈdɪkɪ/ 1 *n. colloq.* false shirt-front. 2 *a. sl.* shaky, unsound.

**dicotyledon** /daɪkɒtɪˈliːd(ə)n/ *n.* flowering plant with two cotyledons. **dicotyledonous** *a.*

**Dictaphone** /ˈdɪktəfəʊn/ *n.* (P) machine for recording and playing back dictated words.

**dictate** 1 /dɪkˈteɪt/ *v.* say aloud (matter to be written down); lay down authoritatively; give peremptory order. 2 /ˈdɪkteɪt/ *n.* (usu. in *pl.*) authoritative instruction esp. *of* conscience or reason etc. 3 **dictation** *n.*

**dictator** /dɪkˈteɪtə(r)/ *n.* absolute ruler of State; person with absolute authority. **dictatorship** *n.*

**dictatorial** /dɪktəˈtɔːrɪəl/ *a.* of a dictator; imperious, overbearing.

**diction** /ˈdɪkʃ(ə)n/ *n.* manner of enunciation; choice and use of words in speech or writing.

**dictionary** /ˈdɪkʃənərɪ/ *n.* book explaining, usu. in alphabetical order, words of a language, or giving their equivalents in another language; reference book of words and topics of subject arranged alphabetically.

**dictum** /ˈdɪktəm/ *n.* (*pl.* -ta) formal expression of opinion; maxim.

**did** *past* of **do**¹.

**didactic** /dəˈdæktɪk/ *a.* meant to instruct; having manner of authoritarian teacher. **didacticism** *n.*

**diddle** /ˈdɪd(ə)l/ *v.t. sl.* cheat, swindle.

**didgeridoo** /dɪdʒərɪˈduː/ *n.* Aus. Abor. musical instrument in form of long wooden tube.

**die**¹ *v.i.* (*partic.* **dying**) cease to live; cease to exist; fade away; (of fire) go out. **be dying for, to**, have great desire; **die down** become less loud or strong; **die-hard** conservative or stubborn person; **die (of) laughing** laugh to exhaustion; **die out** become extinct, cease to exist.

**die**² *n.* see **dice**; engraved stamp for impressing design etc. on softer metal.

**die-casting** process or product of making castings from metal moulds.

**dielectric** /daɪəˈlektrɪk/ 1 *a. Electr.* that does not conduct electricity. 2 *n.* dielectric substance usable for insulating.

**diesel** /ˈdiːz(ə)l/ *n.* internal-combustion engine in which fuel is ignited by heat of highly compressed air (in full **diesel engine**); fuel for or vehicle driven by diesel engine. **diesel-electric** driven by electric current from generator driven by diesel engine; **diesel oil** petroleum fraction used in diesel engines.

**diet**¹ /ˈdaɪət/ 1 *n.* one's habitual food; prescribed course of food. 2 *v.* keep to special diet. 3 **dietary** *a.*

**diet**² /ˈdaɪət/ *n.* conference, congress.

**dietetic** /daɪəˈtetɪk/ *a.* of diet and nutrition.

**dietetics** *n.pl.* scientific study of diet and nutrition.

**dietitian** /daɪəˈtɪʃ(ə)n/ *n.* (also -**ician**) expert in dietetics.

**differ** /ˈdɪfə(r)/ *v.i.* be unlike; be distinguishable; diverge in opinion.

**difference** /ˈdɪfrəns/ *n.* being different or unlike; point in which things differ; degree or amount of unlikeness; remainder after subtraction; disagreement.

**different** /ˈdɪfrənt/ *a.* unlike, of other nature, form or quality; separate, unusual.

**differential** /dɪfəˈrenʃ(ə)l/ 1 *a.* varying with circumstances; constituting or relating to specific difference(s); *Math.* relating to infinitesimal differences. 2 *n.* differential gear; difference between rates of interest etc. or between wage-rates. 3 **differential calculus** means of finding rates of change, maximum and minimum values, etc.; **differential gear** arrangement of gears enabling driving wheels to revolve at different speeds in rounding corners.

**differentiate** /dɪfəˈrenʃɪeɪt/ *v.* constitute difference between or of or in; discriminate; make or become different. **differentiation** *n.*

**difficult** /ˈdɪfɪk(ə)lt/ *a.* hard to do, deal with, or understand; troublesome.

**difficulty** /ˈdɪfɪkəltɪ/ *n.* being difficult; difficult point or situation; obstacle; in *pl.* trouble, esp. shortage of money.

**diffident** /ˈdɪfɪd(ə)nt/ *a.* lacking self-confidence. **diffidence** *n.*

**diffract** /dəˈfrækt/ v.t. break up (beam of light) into series of dark and light bands or coloured spectra. **diffraction** n.; **diffractive** a.

**diffuse 1** /dəˈfjuːz/ v. spread widely or thinly; (esp. of fluids) intermingle. **2** /dəˈfjuːs/ a. spread out; not concentrated; verbose, not concise. **3 diffusible** a.; **diffusive** a.; **diffusion** n.

**dig 1** v. (past & p.p. **dug**) turn up soil with spade etc. or with hands or claws etc.; excavate; thrust or plunge in or into; make search; prod, poke; sl. understand, admire. **2** n. piece of digging; archaeological excavation; thrust, poke; gibe; in pl. colloq. lodgings. **3 dig oneself in** prepare or occupy defensive position; **dig out, up**, get or find by digging.

**digest 1** /dəˈdʒest/ v.t. assimilate (food) in stomach and bowels; understand and assimilate mentally; summarize. **2** /ˈdaɪdʒest/ n. compendium, esp. of laws; periodical synopsis of current news etc. **3 digestible** a.

**digestion** /dəˈdʒestʃ(ə)n/ n. digesting; power of digesting food.

**digestive** /dəˈdʒestɪv/ a. of or promoting digestion.

**digger** /ˈdɪɡə(r)/ n. person or thing that digs; Aus. colloq. person who digs for gold; colloq. Australian, New Zealander; Aus. colloq. (as form of address) mate.

**digit** /ˈdɪdʒət/ n. any numeral from 0 to 9; finger or toe.

**digital** /ˈdɪdʒət(ə)l/ a. of digits. **digital clock** etc. one showing time by displayed digits, not by hands; **digital computer** one making calculations with data represented by digits; **digital recording** recording with sound-information represented in digits.

**digitalis** /dɪdʒəˈteɪləs/ n. heart stimulant drug made from foxglove.

**dignified** /ˈdɪɡnəfaɪd/ a. having or showing dignity.

**dignify** /ˈdɪɡnəfaɪ/ v.t. give dignity to.

**dignitary** /ˈdɪɡnətərɪ/ n. holder of high rank or office, esp. in Church.

**dignity** /ˈdɪɡnəti/ n. composed and serious manner or style; being worthy of respect; high rank or position.

**digraph** /ˈdaɪɡrɑːf/ n. group of two letters expressing single sound.

**digress** /daɪˈɡres/ v.i. diverge temporarily from main track, esp. in speech or writing. **digression** n.; **digressive** a.

**dike 1** n. long ridge of earth, embankment; channel or ditch; Aus. sl. urinal. **2** v.t. protect with dike(s).

**dilapidated** /dəˈlæpədeɪtəd/ a. in disrepair or decay.

**dilapidation** /dəlæpəˈdeɪʃ(ə)n/ n. state of bad repair; falling into decay.

**dilate** /daɪˈleɪt/ v. widen or expand; speak or write at length. **dilatation** n.; **dilation** n.

**dilatory** /ˈdɪlətəri/ a. tending or designed to cause delay.

**dilemma** /dəˈlemə/ n. position presenting choice between equally unwelcome possibilities.

**dilettante** /dɪləˈtæntɪ/ n. (pl. **-ti** /-tiː/ or **-tes**) person who dabbles in subject without serious study. **dilettantism** n.

**diligence** /ˈdɪlɪdʒ(ə)ns/ n. persistent effort or work. **diligent** a.

**dill**¹ n. herb with scented leaves and seeds. **dill pickle** pickled cucumber etc. flavoured with dill.

**dill**² n. Aus. sl. fool, simpleton.

**dilly** /ˈdɪli/ n. (in full **dilly-bag**) small bag, orig. of plaited grass or fibre.

**dilly-dally** /ˈdɪliːdæli/ v.i. colloq. dawdle, vacillate.

**dilute** /daɪˈljuːt/ **1** v.t. reduce in strength by addition of water etc.; make less forceful etc. **2** a. diluted. **3 dilution** n.

**diluvial** /daɪˈluːvɪəl/ a. of flood, esp. Flood in Genesis.

**dim 1** a. deficient in brightness or clearness; obscure; indistinct; colloq. stupid. **2** v. make or become dim.

**dime** n. US 10-cent coin.

**dimension** /daɪˈmenʃ(ə)n/ n. any of the three linear measurements, length, breadth, and depth; in pl. size or extent. **dimensional** a.

**diminish** /dəˈmɪnɪʃ/ v. make or become less; impair.

**diminuendo** /dəmɪnjuːˈendəʊ/ **1** adv. with decreasing volume of sound. **2** n. (pl. **-dos**) passage to be played thus.

**diminution** /dɪmɪnˈjuːʃ(ə)n/ n. diminishing.

**diminutive** /dəˈmɪnjətɪv/ **1** a. tiny, undersized; (of word etc.) denoting or implying smallness. **2** n. diminutive word.

**dimple** /'dɪmp(ə)l/ 1 *n.* small hollow, esp. in cheek or chin. 2 *v.* produce dimples in; show dimples.

**din** 1 *n.* continuous roar of confused noise. 2 *v.* make din. 3 **din into** teach or weary by constant repetition.

**dinar** /'di:nɑ:(r)/ *n.* currency unit in Yugoslavia and several Middle Eastern and N. African countries.

**dine** *v.* eat dinner; entertain to dinner. **dining-car** railway coach where meals are served; **dining-room** room in which meals are eaten.

**diner** /'daɪnə(r)/ *n.* person who dines; small dining-room; railway dining-car; *US* restaurant.

**dingbat** /'dɪŋbæt/ *n. Aus. sl.* an eccentric person. **give person the dingbats** give him feeling of nervous discomfort; **have the dingbats** be mad or eccentric.

**ding-dong** /'dɪŋdɒŋ/ 1 *n.* sound of alternating strokes as of two bells. 2 *a.* (of contest) in which each contestant alternately has advantage. 3 *adv.* with great energy.

**dinghy** /'dɪŋɡɪ/ *n.* small boat.

**dingle** /'dɪŋɡ(ə)l/ *n.* deep dell.

**dingo** /'dɪŋɡəʊ/ *n.* (*pl.* **-goes**) Aus. wild dog.

**dingy** /'dɪndʒɪ/ *a.* dull-coloured; drab; dirty-looking. **dinginess** *n.*

**dink** *v.t. Aus. sl.* carry (person) on bar of bicycle.

**dinkum** /'dɪŋkəm/ *a. Aus. sl.* genuine, real.

**dinky** /'dɪŋkɪ/ *a. colloq.* pretty, small and neat.

**dinky-die** /dɪŋkɪ'daɪ/ *a. Aus. colloq.* dinkum.

**dinner** /'dɪnə(r)/ *n.* chief meal of day; formal evening meal in honour of person or event. **dinner-jacket** man's short usu. black coat for evening wear.

**dinosaur** /'daɪnəsɔ:(r)/ *n.* extinct usu. large reptile.

**dint** 1 *n.* dent. 2 *v.t.* mark with dints. 3 **by dint of** by force or means of.

**diocese** /'daɪəsɪs/ *n.* district under bishop's pastoral care. **diocesan** /daɪ'ɒsɪz(ə)n/ *a.*

**diode** /'daɪəʊd/ *n.* thermionic valve with two electrodes; semiconductor rectifier having two terminals.

**dioxide** /daɪ'ɒksaɪd/ *n.* oxide with two atoms of oxygen to one of metal etc.

**dip** 1 *v.* put or let down into liquid, immerse; go under water and emerge quickly; go below any surface or level; lower for an instant and raise again; lower beam of (headlights); slope or extend downwards; put (hand etc.) *into* to take something out; look cursorily *into* book etc. 2 *n.* dipping; liquid into which thing is dipped; *colloq.* short bathe; downward slope; sauce etc. into which food is dipped before eating.

**Dip.** *abbr.* Diploma.

**diphtheria** /dɪf'θɪərɪə/ *n.* infectious disease with inflammation of mucous membrane esp. of throat.

**diphthong** /'dɪfθɒŋ/ *n.* union of two vowels in one syllable. **diphthongal** *a.*

**diploma** /dɪ'pləʊmə/ *n.* certificate of educational qualification; document conferring honour, privilege, or licence.

**diplomacy** /dɪ'pləʊməsɪ/ *n.* management of international relations; tact.

**diplomat** /'dɪpləmæt/ *n.* person engaged in diplomacy; tactful person.

**diplomatic** /dɪplə'mætɪk/ *a.* of or involved in diplomacy; tactful. **diplomatic bag** bag containing official mail from embassy etc.; **diplomatic immunity** exemption of diplomatic staff etc. abroad from arrest or taxation etc.

**diplomatist** /dɪ'pləʊmətɪst/ *n.* diplomat.

**dipper** /'dɪpə(r)/ *n.* thing that dips; kind of diving-bird.

**dipsomania** /dɪpsə'meɪnɪə/ *n.* abnormal craving for alcohol. **dipsomaniac** *n.* & *a.*

**dipterous** /'dɪptərəs/ *a.* two-winged.

**diptych** /'dɪptɪk/ *n.* pair of pictures or carvings on panels hinged together.

**dire** *a.* dreadful, ominous; urgent.

**direct** /daɪ'rekt/ 1 *a.* extending or moving in straight line or by shortest route, not crooked or oblique; straightforward, frank; without intermediaries. 2 *adv.* in a direct way or manner; by direct route. 3 *v.t.* control; guide; order; tell way *to* (place etc.); address (letter etc. to); send or point or utter etc. *to* or *at* or *towards* etc.; supervise acting etc. of (film, play, etc.). 4 **direct action** exertion of pressure on community by strikes etc. rather than by parliamentary means; **direct current** electric current flowing in one direction only;

**direct object** primary object of verbal action; **direct speech** words as actually spoken, not as modified in reporting; **direct tax** levied on income.

**direction** /dəˈrekʃ(ə)n/ n. directing; (usu. in pl.) orders or instructions; point to or from or along which person or thing looks or moves.

**directional** /dəˈrekʃən(ə)l/ a. of or indicating direction; *Radio* sending or receiving signals in one direction only.

**directive** /dəˈrektɪv/ 1 n. general instruction. 2 a. serving to direct.

**directly** /dəˈrektlɪ/ 1 adv. in direct manner; at once, without delay. 2 conj. as soon as.

**director** /dəˈrektə(r)/ n. person who directs, esp. member of board managing affairs of company etc.; person who directs film, play, etc. **directorial** a.; **directorship** n.

**directorate** /dəˈrektərət/ n. office of director; board of directors.

**directory** /dəˈrektərɪ/ n. book with list of telephone subscribers, inhabitants of town etc., members of profession, etc.

**dirge** n. song of mourning.

**dirigible** /ˈdɪrɪdʒəb(ə)l/ 1 a. that can be steered. 2 n. dirigible balloon or airship.

**dirk** n. long dagger.

**dirndl** /ˈdɜːnd(ə)l/ n. full gathered skirt with tight waistband.

**dirt** n. unclean matter that soils; earth; foul or malicious talk; excrement. **dirt cheap** extremely cheap; **dirt road** unmade road; **dirt-track** racing track with surface of earth or cinders etc.

**dirty** /ˈdɜːtɪ/ 1 a. soiled; unclean; sordid, obscene; mean, unfair; (of weather) rough; muddy-looking. 2 v. make or become dirty. 3 **dirty look** *colloq*. look of disapproval or disgust. 4 **dirtiness** n.

**disability** /dɪsəˈbɪlətɪ/ n. thing or lack that prevents one doing something; physical incapacity.

**disable** /dɪsˈeɪb(ə)l/ v.t. deprive of an ability; (esp. in p.p.) cripple, deprive of or reduce power of walking etc. **disablement** n.

**disabuse** /dɪsəˈbjuːz/ v.t. free of false idea; disillusion.

**disadvantage** /dɪsədˈvɑːntɪdʒ or -ˈvæn-/ n. unfavourable condition or circumstance. **disadvantageous** /dɪsædvɑːnˈteɪdʒəs or -ˈvæn-/ a.

**disadvantaged** a. in unfavourable conditions, esp. lacking normal social opportunities.

**disaffected** /dɪsəˈfektəd/ a. discontented; disloyal. **disaffection** n.

**disagree** /dɪsəˈɡriː/ v.i. hold different opinion; fail to agree; quarrel. **disagree with** have bad effect on. **disagreement** n.

**disagreeable** /dɪsəˈɡriːəb(ə)l/ a. unpleasant; bad-tempered.

**disallow** /dɪsəˈlaʊ/ v.t. reject; prohibit.

**disappear** /dɪsəˈpɪə(r)/ v.i. pass from sight or existence; cease to be visible. **disappearance** n.

**disappoint** /dɪsəˈpɔɪnt/ v.t. fail to fulfil desire or expectation of; frustrate. **disappointment** n.

**disapprobation** /dɪsæprəˈbeɪʃ(ə)n/ n. disapproval.

**disapprove** /dɪsəˈpruːv/ v. have or express unfavourable opinion (*of*). **disapproval** n.

**disarm** /dɪˈsɑːm/ v. deprive of weapons; abandon or reduce military establishment; pacify hostility or suspicions of. **disarmament** n.

**disarrange** /dɪsəˈreɪndʒ/ v.t. put into disorder; disorganize. **disarrangement** n.

**disarray** /dɪsəˈreɪ/ n. disorder, confusion.

**disaster** /dɪˈzɑːstə(r)/ n. sudden or great misfortune; complete failure. **disastrous** a.

**disavow** /dɪsəˈvaʊ/ v.t. say one does not know or have responsibility for or approve of. **disavowal** n.

**disband** /dɪsˈbænd/ v. break up, disperse.

**disbar** /dɪsˈbɑː(r)/ v.t. deprive of status of barrister. **disbarment** n.

**disbelieve** /dɪsbɪˈliːv/ v. refuse to believe; not believe (*in*). **disbelief** n.

**disburden** /dɪsˈbɜːd(ə)n/ v.t. relieve of burden.

**disburse** /dɪsˈbɜːs/ v.t. pay out (money). **disbursement** n.

**disc** n. round flat or apparently flat plate or surface or part; layer of cartilage between vertebrae; gramophone record; similar object used to store computer data etc. **disc brake** one using disc-shaped friction surfaces;

**disc jockey** presenter of broadcast programme featuring records of popular music.

**discard 1** /dɪsˈkɑːd/ *v.t.* cast aside, give up; reject as unwanted. **2** /ˈdɪskɑːd/ *n.* discarded thing.

**discern** /dɪˈsɜːn/ *v.t.* perceive clearly with mind or senses; make out. **discernment** *n.*

**discerning** /dɪˈsɜːnɪŋ/ *a.* having good judgement or insight.

**discharge** /dɪsˈtʃɑːdʒ/ **1** *v.* put forth, emit; send as missile; release, let go; dismiss; pay or perform (duty, debt); fire (gun etc.); relieve (bankrupt) of residual liability; relieve of cargo; unload. **2** *n.* (also /ˈdɪs-/) discharging or being discharged; matter or thing discharged.

**disciple** /dɪˈsaɪp(ə)l/ *n.* person who takes another as his teacher or leader.

**disciplinarian** /dɪsəpləˈneərɪən/ *n.* maintainer of strict discipline.

**disciplinary** /dɪsəˈplɪnərɪ/ *a.* of or enforcing discipline.

**discipline** /ˈdɪsəplən/ **1** *n.* mental or moral training; orderly behaviour maintained (as) among persons under control or command; chastisement; branch of instruction. **2** *v.t.* train to obedience and order; punish.

**disclaim** /dɪsˈkleɪm/ *v.t.* disown, deny.

**disclaimer** *n.* statement disclaiming something.

**disclose** /dɪsˈkləʊz/ *v.t.* expose to view; make known, reveal. **disclosure** *n.*

**disco** /ˈdɪskəʊ/ *n.* (*pl.* **-cos**) *colloq.* discothèque.

**discolour** /dɪsˈkʌlə(r)/ *v.* impair colour of; stain or become stained. **discoloration** *n.*

**discomfit** /dɪsˈkʌmfɪt/ *v.t.* disconcert; baffle. **discomfiture** *n.*

**discomfort** /dɪsˈkʌmfət/ *n.* uneasiness of body or mind.

**discompose** /dɪskəmˈpəʊz/ *v.t.* disturb composure of. **discomposure** *n.*

**disconcert** /dɪskənˈsɜːt/ *v.t.* disturb self-possession of; fluster.

**disconnect** /dɪskəˈnekt/ *v.t.* break connection of or between; put (electrical apparatus) out of action by disconnecting parts. **disconnection** *n.*

**disconnected** *a.* incoherent, having abrupt transitions.

**disconsolate** /dɪsˈkɒnsələt/ *a.* forlorn, unhappy; disappointed.

**discontent** /dɪskənˈtent/ **1** *n.* dissatisfaction; lack of contentment. **2** *v.t.* make dissatisfied.

**discontinue** /dɪskənˈtɪnjuː/ *v.t.* (cause to) cease; not go on with. **discontinuance** *n.*

**discontinuous** /dɪskənˈtɪnjuːəs/ *a.* lacking continuity; intermittent. **discontinuity** /-ˈnjuː-/ *n.*

**discord** /ˈdɪskɔːd/ *n.* disagreement, strife; harsh noise; lack of harmony. **discordance** *n.*; **discordant** *a.*

**discothèque** /ˈdɪskətek/ *n.* club etc. where records are played for dancing.

**discount 1** /ˈdɪskaʊnt/ *n.* deduction from nominal value or price or amount. **2** *v.t.* /dɪsˈkaʊnt/ disregard partly or wholly; deduct amount from (price etc.); give or get present value of (bill of exchange not yet due). **3 at a discount** below nominal or usual price, *fig.* depreciated.

**discountenance** /dɪsˈkaʊntənəns/ *v.t.* refuse to approve of; disconcert.

**discourage** /dɪsˈkʌrɪdʒ/ *v.t.* reduce confidence or spirits of; dissuade. **discouragement** *n.*

**discourse 1** /ˈdɪskɔːs/ *n.* talk or conversation; lecture or sermon or other exposition. **2** /dɪsˈkɔːs/ *v.i.* converse, speak or write at length.

**discourteous** /dɪsˈkɜːtɪəs/ *a.* rude, uncivil. **discourtesy** *n.*

**discover** /dɪsˈkʌvə(r)/ *v.t.* acquire knowledge or sight of by effort or chance; be first to do this in particular case.

**discovery** /dɪsˈkʌvərɪ/ *n.* discovering; thing discovered.

**discredit** /dɪsˈkredɪt/ **1** *v.t.* harm good reputation of; refuse to believe; cause to be disbelieved. **2** *n.* harm to reputation; cause of this; lack of credibility.

**discreditable** /dɪsˈkredɪtəb(ə)l/ *a.* bringing discredit, shameful.

**discreet** /dɪsˈkriːt/ *a.* prudent; cautious in speech or action; unobtrusive.

**discrepancy** /dɪsˈkrepənsɪ/ *n.* difference; inconsistency. **discrepant** *a.*

**discrete** /dɪsˈkriːt/ *a.* separate; distinct.

**discretion** /dɪsˈkreʃ(ə)n/ *n.* prudence; judgement; liberty of deciding as one thinks fit.

**discretionary** /dɪˈskreʃənəri/ *a.* left to discretion.

**discriminate** /dɪˈskrɪmɪneɪt/ *v.* make or see a distinction (*between*), esp. as a basis for unfair treatment. **discrimination** *n.*; **discriminatory** *a.*

**discursive** /dɪˈskɜːsɪv/ *a.* rambling, not sticking to main subject.

**discus** /ˈdɪskəs/ *n.* heavy disc thrown in athletic exercises.

**discuss** /dɪsˈkʌs/ *v.t.* examine by argument; debate; have argument about. **discussion** *n.*

**disdain** /dɪsˈdeɪn/ 1 *n.* scorn, contempt. 2 *v.t.* regard with disdain; think beneath oneself or one's notice. 3 **disdainful** *a.*

**disease** /dəˈziːz/ *n.* unhealthy condition; (specific) disorder or illness. **diseased** *a.* affected with disease; abnormal, disordered.

**disembark** /ˌdɪsəmˈbɑːk/ *v.* put or go ashore. **disembarkation** *n.*

**disembarrass** /ˌdɪsəmˈbærəs/ *v.t.* free from embarrassment; rid or relieve (*of*). **disembarrassment** *n.*

**disembody** /ˌdɪsəmˈbɒdi/ *v.t.* separate (soul, voice, etc.) from body.

**disembowel** /ˌdɪsəmˈbaʊəl/ or -tʃænt/ *v.t.* remove entrails of.

**disenchant** /ˌdɪsɪnˈtʃɑːnt/ or -ˈtʃænt/ *v.t.* free from enchantment; disillusion. **disenchantment** *n.*

**disencumber** /ˌdɪsɪnˈkʌmbə(r)/ *v.t.* disburden; free from encumbrance.

**disengage** /ˌdɪsɪnˈɡeɪdʒ/ *v.* detach; loosen; release from engagement; become detached. **disengagement** *n.*

**disengaged** *a.* at leisure; not occupied.

**disentangle** /ˌdɪsɪnˈtæŋɡ(ə)l/ *v.t.* free or become free of tangles or complications. **disentanglement** *n.*

**disestablish** /ˌdɪsɪˈstæblɪʃ/ *v.t.* deprive (Church) of State connection. **disestablishment** *n.*

**disfavour** /dɪsˈfeɪvə(r)/ *n.* dislike; disapproval.

**disfigure** /dɪsˈfɪɡə(r)/ *v.t.* spoil appearance of. **disfigurement** *n.*

**disfranchise** /dɪsˈfræntʃaɪz/ *v.t.* deprive of franchise. **disfranchisement** *n.*

**disgorge** /dɪsˈɡɔːdʒ/ *v.t.* eject from throat; pour forth.

**disgrace** /dɪsˈɡreɪs/ 1 *n.* loss of favour, downfall from position of honour; shame; cause of reproach. 2 *v.t.* bring shame or discredit on; dismiss from favour.

**disgraceful** /dɪsˈɡreɪsfəl/ *a.* causing disgrace; shameful.

**disgruntled** /dɪsˈɡrʌnt(ə)ld/ *a.* discontented.

**disguise** /dɪsˈɡaɪz/ 1 *v.t.* conceal identity of, make unrecognizable; conceal, cover up. 2 *n.* (use of) changed dress or appearance for concealment or deception; disguised condition.

**disgust** /dɪsˈɡʌst/ 1 *n.* loathing, strong aversion; indignation. 2 *v.t.* cause disgust in.

**disgusting** *a.* distasteful; repellent.

**dish** 1 *n.* shallow flat-bottomed container for holding food; food served in dish or prepared for table; dish-shaped receptacle or object or cavity; *colloq.* attractive person. 2 *v.* make concave; *colloq.* defeat completely. 3 **dish out** *sl.* distribute; **dish up** (prepare to) serve meal; **dish-water** water in which dirty dishes etc. have been washed.

**disharmony** /dɪsˈhɑːməni/ *n.* lack of harmony, discord.

**dishearten** /dɪsˈhɑːt(ə)n/ *v.t.* cause to lose courage or confidence. **disheartenment** *n.*

**dishevelled** /dəˈʃev(ə)ld/ *a.* ruffled, untidy.

**dishonest** /dɪˈsɒnəst/ *a.* not honest; fraudulent; insincere. **dishonesty** *n.*

**dishonour** /dɪˈsɒnə(r)/ 1 *v.t.* bring dishonour upon; treat without honour or respect; refuse to pay (cheque etc.). 2 *n.* state of shame or disgrace; cause of this.

**dishonourable** /dɪˈsɒnərəb(ə)l/ *a.* causing disgrace; ignominious.

**disillusion** /ˌdɪsəˈluːʒ(ə)n/ 1 *v.t.* free from illusion or mistaken belief. 2 *n.* being disillusioned. 3 **disillusionment** *n.*

**disincentive** /ˌdɪsɪnˈsentɪv/ *n.* thing that tends to discourage.

**disincline** /ˌdɪsɪnˈklaɪm/ *v.t.* make unwilling. **disinclination** *n.*

**disinfect** /ˌdɪsɪnˈfekt/ *v.t.* cleanse of infection; remove bacteria from. **disinfection** *n.*

**disinfectant** /ˌdɪsɪnˈfekt(ə)nt/ 1 *a.* having disinfecting qualities. 2 *n.* disinfectant substance.

**disinflation** /dɪsɪnˈfleɪʃ(ə)n/ n. reduction of inflation.

**disingenuous** /ˌdɪsɪnˈdʒenjuːəs/ a. insincere; not candid.

**disinherit** /ˌdɪsɪnˈherɪt/ v.t. deprive of right to inherit. **disinheritance** n.

**disintegrate** /dɪsˈɪntəgreɪt/ v. separate into component parts; deprive of or lose cohesion. **disintegration** n.

**disinter** /ˌdɪsɪnˈtɜː(r)/ v.t. dig up (esp. corpse) from ground. **disinterment** n.

**disinterested** /dɪsˈɪntərəstəd/ a. not influenced by involvement or advantage.

**disjoin** /dɪsˈdʒɔɪn/ v.t. separate, disunite.

**disjoint** /dɪsˈdʒɔɪnt/ v.t. separate at joints; dislocate.

**disjointed** a. disconnected, incoherent.

**disjunction** /dɪsˈdʒʌŋkʃ(ə)n/ n. disjoining, separation.

**disjunctive** /dɪsˈdʒʌŋktɪv/ a. involving separation or expressing alternative.

**disk** var. of **disc**.

**dislike** /dɪsˈlaɪk/ 1 n. feeling that thing etc. is unattractive, unpleasant, etc. 2 v.t. have dislike for.

**dislocate** /ˈdɪsləkeɪt/ v.t. disturb normal connection of; put out of order. **dislocation** n.

**dislodge** /dɪsˈlɒdʒ/ v.t. move from established position. **dislodgement** n.

**disloyal** /dɪsˈlɔɪəl/ a. unfaithful; lacking loyalty. **disloyalty** n.

**dismal** /ˈdɪzm(ə)l/ a. cheerless, dreary.

**dismantle** /dɪsˈmænt(ə)l/ v.t. pull down, take to pieces; deprive of defences, equipment, etc.

**dismay** /dɪsˈmeɪ/ 1 n. feeling of intense disappointment and discouragement. 2 v.t. affect with dismay.

**dismember** /dɪsˈmembə(r)/ v.t. remove limbs from; partition (country etc.). **dismemberment** n.

**dismiss** /dɪsˈmɪs/ v.t. send away, disband; allow to go; send away (esp. dishonourably); put out of one's thoughts; *Law* refuse further hearing to; *Crick.* put (batsman, side) out. **dismissal** n.; **dismissive** a.

**dismount** /dɪsˈmaʊnt/ v. (cause to) get off or down from cycle or horseback etc.; remove (thing) from mounting.

**disobedience** /ˌdɪsəˈbiːdɪəns/ n. disobeying; rebelliousness. **disobedient** a.

**disobey** /ˌdɪsəˈbeɪ/ v. fail or refuse to obey; disregard orders.

**disoblige** /ˌdɪsəˈblaɪdʒ/ v.t. refuse to consider convenience or wishes of. **disobliging** a.

**disorder** /dɪsˈɔːdə(r)/ 1 n. confusion; tumult, riot; bodily or mental ailment. 2 v.t. put into disorder, upset.

**disorderly** /dɪsˈɔːdəli:/ a. untidy; riotous.

**disorganize** /dɪsˈɔːgənaɪz/ v.t. upset order or system of; throw into confusion. **disorganization** n.

**disorientate** /dɪsˈɔːrɪənteɪt/ v.t. confuse (person) as to his bearings.

**disown** /dɪsˈəʊn/ v.t. refuse to recognize or acknowledge; repudiate.

**disparage** /dɪsˈpærɪdʒ/ v.t. speak slightingly of. **disparagement** n.

**disparate** /ˈdɪspərət/ a. essentially different, unrelated.

**disparity** /dɪsˈpærəti:/ n. inequality, difference.

**dispassionate** /dɪsˈpæʃənət/ a. free from emotion; impartial.

**dispatch** /dɪsˈpætʃ/ 1 v.t. send off; kill; get (business etc.) done promptly; eat quickly. 2 n. dispatching; rapidity; efficiency; official communication on State affairs. 3 **dispatch-box** case for dispatches and other papers; **dispatch-rider** motor-cyclist etc. carrying official messages.

**dispel** /dɪˈspel/ v.t. drive away; scatter.

**dispensary** /dɪˈspensəri:/ n. place where medicines etc. are dispensed.

**dispensation** /ˌdɪspenˈseɪʃ(ə)n/ n. distributing, dealing out; ordering or management, esp. of world by Providence; exemption from penalty or obligation.

**dispense** /dɪˈspens/ v. distribute; administer; make up (medicine) from prescription or formula. **dispense with** do without.

**dispenser** n. person who dispenses something; device that dispenses selected quantity at a time.

**disperse** /dɪˈspɜːs/ v. (make) go various ways, scatter; put in circulation; separate (light) into coloured constituents. **dispersal** n.; **dispersion** n.

**dispirit** /dɪˈspɪrɪt/ v.t. make despondent.

**displace** /dɪsˈpleɪs/ v.t. shift from pro-

# displacement — dissimulate

per position; oust, take the place of; remove from office. **displaced person** one who has had to leave his home country as result of war etc.

**displacement** /n./ displacing or being displaced; amount of fluid displaced by body floating or immersed in it.

**display** /dɪˈspleɪ/ 1 v.t. spread out to view; exhibit. 2 n. displaying; exhibition; ostentation.

**displease** /dɪsˈpliːz/ v.t. offend; make angry; be unpleasing to.

**displeasure** /dɪsˈpleʒə(r)/ n. disapproval, dissatisfaction, anger.

**disport** /dɪˈspɔːt/ v. arch. frolic, enjoy oneself.

**disposable** /dɪˈspəʊzəb(ə)l/ a. that can be disposed of; designed to be thrown away after one use.

**disposal** /dɪˈspəʊz(ə)l/ n. disposing (of). **at one's disposal** available.

**dispose** /dɪˈspəʊz/ v. place suitably or in order; incline (to); bring into certain state; determine course of events. **dispose of** get rid of, deal with, finish.

**disposition** /dɪspəˈzɪʃ(ə)n/ n. disposing or arrangement; temperament.

**dispossess** /dɪspəˈzes/ v.t. oust or dislodge. **dispossession** n.

**disproof** /dɪsˈpruːf/ n. disproving, refutation.

**disproportion** /dɪsprəˈpɔːʃ(ə)n/ n. lack of proportion.

**disproportionate** /dɪsprəˈpɔːʃənət/ a. relatively too large or too small.

**disprove** /dɪsˈpruːv/ v.t. prove to be false.

**disputable** /dɪˈspjuːtəb(ə)l/ a. open to question.

**disputant** /dɪˈspjuːt(ə)nt/ n. person involved in dispute.

**disputation** /dɪspjuˈteɪʃ(ə)n/ n. argument, debate; formal discussion of question.

**disputatious** /dɪspjuˈteɪʃəs/ a. fond of argument.

**dispute** /dɪˈspjuːt/ 1 v. hold debate; quarrel, controvert; contend; resist. 2 n. controversy, debate; quarrel; difference of opinion.

**disqualify** /dɪsˈkwɒlɪfaɪ/ v.t. make or pronounce unfit or ineligible. **disqualification** n.

**disquiet** /dɪsˈkwaɪət/ 1 n. uneasiness,

anxiety. 2 v.t. cause disquiet to. 3 **disquietude** n.

**disquisition** /dɪskwɪˈzɪʃ(ə)n/ n. long or elaborate treatise or discourse.

**disregard** /dɪsrəˈɡɑːd/ 1 v.t. ignore, be uninfluenced by. 2 n. neglect.

**disrepair** /dɪsrəˈpeə(r)/ n. bad condition due to lack of repairs.

**disreputable** /dɪsˈrepjətəb(ə)l/ a. having a bad reputation; not respectable.

**disrepute** /dɪsrəˈpjuːt/ n. lack of good repute; discredit.

**disrespect** /dɪsrəˈspekt/ n. lack of respect. **disrespectful** a.

**disrobe** /dɪsˈrəʊb/ v. undress.

**disrupt** /dɪsˈrʌpt/ v.t. shatter; separate forcibly; cause disturbance in. **disruption** n.; **disruptive** a.

**dissatisfaction** /dɪsætəsˈfækʃ(ə)n/ n. discontent.

**dissatisfy** /dɪsˈsætəsfaɪ/ v.t. fail to satisfy; make discontented.

**dissect** /dɪˈsekt/ v.t. cut in pieces, esp. to examine parts or structure; criticize in detail. **dissection** n.; **dissector** n.

**dissemble** /dɪˈsemb(ə)l/ v. conceal or disguise; be hypocritical.

**disseminate** /dɪˈsemənət/ v.t. scatter about, spread. **dissemination** n.; **disseminator** n.

**dissension** /dɪˈsenʃ(ə)n/ n. discord arising from difference in opinion.

**dissent** /dɪˈsent/ 1 v.i. disagree openly; think differently or express different opinion (from), esp. from established or orthodox church. 2 n. such difference of opinion; expression of this.

**dissenter** /dɪˈsentə(r)/ n. member of dissenting sect.

**dissentient** /dɪˈsenʃɪənt/ 1 a. not agreeing, dissenting. 2 n. dissentient person.

**dissertation** /dɪsəˈteɪʃ(ə)n/ n. detailed discourse, esp. as submitted for higher degree in university.

**disservice** /dɪsˈsɜːvəs/ n. harmful action.

**dissident** /ˈdɪsɪd(ə)nt/ 1 a. disagreeing, at variance. 2 n. person disagreeing or at variance, esp. with established government.

**dissimilar** /dɪˈsɪmələ(r)/ a. not similar. **dissimilarity** n.

**dissimulate** /dɪˈsɪmjəleɪt/ v. dissemble. **dissimulation** n.; **dissimulator** n.

**dissipate** /ˈdɪsəpeɪt/ v. dispel, disperse; squander or fritter away.

**dissipated** a. given to dissipation.

**dissipation** /dɪsəˈpeɪʃ(ə)n/ n. frivolous or dissolute way of life.

**dissociate** /dɪˈsəʊsɪeɪt/ v. disconnect or separate in thought or fact. **dissociation** n.

**dissolute** /ˈdɪsəluːt/ a. lax in morals, licentious.

**dissolution** /dɪsəˈluːʃ(ə)n/ n. dissolving or being dissolved; undoing or relaxing *of* bond or partnership etc.; dismissal or dispersal of assembly, esp. parliament.

**dissolve** /dɪˈzɒlv/ v. make or become liquid, esp. by immersion or dispersion in liquid; (cause to) vanish; dismiss or disperse (assembly); put an end to, annul.

**dissonant** /ˈdɪsənənt/ a. jarring, clashing, discordant. **dissonance** n.

**dissuade** /dɪˈsweɪd/ v.t. advise to refrain (*from*), persuade against. **dissuasion** n.; **dissuasive** a.

**distaff** /ˈdɪstɑːf/ n. cleft stick holding wool etc. used in spinning. **distaff side** female branch of family.

**distance** /ˈdɪst(ə)ns/ 1 n. length from one point to another; being far off; remoteness; distant point. 2 v.t. place or cause to seem far off; leave behind in race etc.

**distant** /ˈdɪst(ə)nt/ a. at considerable or specified distance; reserved, cool.

**distaste** /dɪsˈteɪst/ n. dislike; aversion.

**distasteful** /dɪsˈteɪstfəl/ a. causing distaste.

**distemper**[1] /dɪˈstempə(r)/ n. catarrhal disease of dogs etc.

**distemper**[2] /dɪˈstempə(r)/ 1 n. pigment used for painting on plaster etc. with powder colours mixed with size etc. 2 v.t. paint with distemper.

**distend** /dɪˈstend/ v. swell out by pressure from within. **distensible** a.; **distension** n.

**distich** /ˈdɪstɪk/ n. verse couplet.

**distil** /dɪˈstɪl/ v. subject to or undergo distillation; make or produce or extract or drive off etc. by distillation.

**distillation** /dɪstɪˈleɪʃ(ə)n/ n. vaporizing and subsequent condensation of substance to purify or decompose it; extracting of essence or making of whisky etc. thus.

**distiller** /dɪˈstɪlə(r)/ n. person who distils, esp. maker of alcoholic liquor.

**distillery** /dɪˈstɪləri/ n. factory etc. for distilling liquor.

**distinct** /dɪˈstɪŋkt/ a. separate, different in quality or kind; clearly perceptible, definite, positive.

**distinction** /dɪˈstɪŋkʃ(ə)n/ n. seeing or making a difference; difference seen or made; thing that differentiates; excellence; individuality; mark of honour.

**distinctive** /dɪˈstɪŋktɪv/ a. distinguishing, characteristic.

**distingué** /dɪˈstæŋgeɪ/ a. having distinguished air, manners, etc. [F]

**distinguish** /dɪˈstɪŋgwɪʃ/ v. observe or identify a difference in; draw distinctions between; characterize; make out by listening or looking etc.; make prominent or eminent.

**distinguished** a. eminent, having distinction.

**distort** /dɪˈstɔːt/ v.t. pull or twist out of shape; misrepresent. **distortion** n.

**distract** /dɪˈstrækt/ v.t. draw attention etc. away *from* or in different directions; bewilder.

**distraction** /dɪˈstrækʃ(ə)n/ n. distracting or being distracted; thing which distracts; interruption; amusement, relaxation; mental confusion.

**distrain** /dɪˈstreɪn/ v. levy distraint (on).

**distraint** /dɪˈstreɪnt/ n. seizure of goods as method of enforcing payment.

**distrait** /dɪˈstreɪ/ a. not paying attention; distraught. [F]

**distraught** /dɪˈstrɔːt/ a. much agitated in mind.

**distress** /dɪˈstres/ 1 n. mental pain; exhaustion; lack of money or necessaries; *Law* distraint. 2 v.t. subject to distress; make unhappy.

**distribute** /dɪˈstrɪbjuːt/ v.t. divide and give share of to each of number; spread about; put at different points; arrange, classify. **distribution** n.

**distributive** /dɪˈstrɪbjʊtɪv/ a. of or concerned with or effecting distribution; (of word etc.) referring to each individual of class, not collective.

**distributor** /dɪˈstrɪbjətə(r)/ n. agent who markets goods; device in internal combustion engine for passing current to each sparking-plug in turn.

**district** /ˈdɪstrɪkt/ n. region; administrative division; province; territory. **district attorney** *US* public prosecutor of district; **district nurse** nurse visiting patients in their homes.

**distrust** /dɪsˈtrʌst/ 1 *n.* lack of trust; suspicion. 2 *v.t.* have no confidence in. 3 **distrustful** *a.*

**disturb** /dəˈstɜːb/ *v.t.* break rest or quiet of; worry; disorganize; in *p.p.* emotionally or mentally unstable or abnormal.

**disturbance** /dəˈstɜːbəns/ *n.* disturbing; disturbed state, tumult, disorder.

**disunion** /dɪsˈjuːnɪən/ *n.* separation; lack of union.

**disunite** /dɪsjuːˈnaɪt/ *v.* separate; divide. **disunity** *n.*

**disuse** 1 /dɪsˈjuːz/ *v.t.* cease to use. 2 /dɪsˈjuːs/ *n.* disused state.

**disyllable** /dɪˈsɪləb(ə)l/ *n.* word or metrical foot of two syllables. **disyllabic** /-ˈlæb-/ *a.*

**ditch** 1 *n.* long narrow excavation esp. to hold or conduct water or serve as boundary. 2 *v.* make or repair ditches; provide with ditches; drive (vehicle) into ditch; *sl.* make forced landing, land (aircraft) on sea; *sl.* abandon, discard, defeat.

**dither** /ˈdɪðə(r)/ 1 *v.i.* be nervously hesitant; tremble, quiver. 2 *n.* nervous excitement or apprehension.

**dithyramb** /ˈdɪθɪræm/ *n.* Greek choric hymn, wild in character; passionate or inflated speech or writing. **dithyrambic** /-ˈræmbɪk/ *a.*

**ditto** /ˈdɪtəʊ/ *n.* the aforesaid, the same or a similar thing.

**ditty** /ˈdɪtɪ/ *n.* short simple song.

**diuretic** /daɪjʊˈretɪk/ 1 *a.* causing increased excretion of urine. 2 *n.* diuretic drug.

**diurnal** /daɪˈɜːn(ə)l/ *a.* in or of day; occupying one day.

**diva** /ˈdiːvə/ *n.* great woman singer.

**divan** /dɪˈvæn/ *n.* low couch or bed without back or ends.

**dive** 1 *v.i.* plunge, esp. head foremost, into water etc.; (of aircraft) descend steeply; (of submarine or diver) submerge; go down or out of sight suddenly; put one's hand *into*. 2 *n.* act of diving; *colloq.* disreputable place of resort. 3 **dive-bomb** drop bombs on from diving aircraft; **diving-board** sprung board for diving from.

**diver** /ˈdaɪvə(r)/ *n.* person who dives esp. person who works under water; diving bird.

**diverge** /daɪˈvɜːdʒ/ *v.i.* go in different directions from point or each other; go aside *from* track. **divergence** *n.*; **divergent** *a.*

**divers** /ˈdaɪvəz/ *a. arch.* various, several.

**diverse** /daɪˈvɜːs/ *a.* of differing kinds; varied.

**diversify** /daɪˈvɜːsəfaɪ/ *v.t.* make diverse; vary; spread (investment) over several enterprises.

**diversion** /daɪˈvɜːʃ(ə)n/ *n.* diverting; recreation, pastime; alternative route for traffic.

**diversity** /daɪˈvɜːsətɪ/ *n.* being diverse.

**divert** /daɪˈvɜːt/ *v.t.* turn in another direction; ward off; draw off attention of; entertain, amuse.

**divest** /daɪˈvest/ *v.t.* unclothe, strip; deprive or rid *of*.

**divide** /dɪˈvaɪd/ 1 *v.* separate *into* parts; split or break up; separate (one thing) *from* another; become or be able to be divided; mark out into parts or groups; cause to disagree, set at variance; distribute; share *with* others; find how many times number contains another, be contained exact number of times; part (legislative assembly) into two sets for voting, be thus parted. 2 *n.* watershed; dividing-line.

**dividend** /ˈdɪvɪdend/ *n.* number to be divided by another; sum payable as interest or profit or share.

**divider** /dɪˈvaɪdə(r)/ *n.* screen etc. dividing room; in *pl.* measuring compasses.

**divination** /dɪvəˈneɪʃ(ə)n/ *n.* divining the future; good guess.

**divine** /dɪˈvaɪn/ 1 *a.* of or from or like God or a god; sacred; *colloq.* excellent. 2 *n.* theologian. 3 *v.* discover by intuition or inspiration or guessing; foresee; conjecture; practise divination. 4 **divining-rod** dowser's forked twig.

**diviner** /dɪˈvaɪnə(r)/ *n.* expert in divination; dowser.

**divinity** /dɪˈvɪnətɪ/ *n.* being divine; god; theology.

**divisible** /dɪˈvɪzəb(ə)l/ *a.* that can be divided. **divisibility** *n.*

**division** /dɪˈvɪʒ(ə)n/ *n.* dividing or being divided; one of parts into which

**divisor** /dəˈvaɪzə(r)/ n. number by which another is to be divided.

**divorce** /dɪˈvɔːs/ 1 n. legal dissolution of marriage; separation, severance. 2 v.t. legally dissolve marriage between; end marriage with by divorce; detach, separate.

**divot** /ˈdɪvət/ n. Golf piece of turf dislodged by club-head in making stroke.

**divulge** /daɪˈvʌldʒ/ v.t. disclose (secret); make public.

**divvy** /ˈdɪvɪ/ colloq. 1 n. dividend. 2 v. **divvy (up)** share out.

**Dixie**[1] /ˈdɪksɪ/ n. Southern States of US. **Dixieland** Dixie, kind of jazz.

**dixie**[2] /ˈdɪksɪ/ n. large iron pot for making stew etc.

**DIY** abbr. do-it-yourself.

**dizzy** /ˈdɪzɪ/ 1 a. giddy, dazed, unsteady; causing dizziness. 2 v.t. make dizzy.

**DJ** abbr. disc jockey; dinner jacket.

**dl.** abbr. decilitre.

**D.Litt.** abbr. Doctor of Letters.

**dm.** abbr. decimetre.

**DNA** abbr. deoxyribonucleic acid.

**do** /duː/ 1 v. (past **did**; p.p. **done** /dʌn/; 3 sing. pres. **does** /dʌz/) perform, carry out; produce, make; act or proceed; fare; operate on, deal with; bestow, impart; solve; be suitable, suffice; colloq. provide or cater for (well etc.); sl. swindle; exhaust. 2 v. aux. used esp. in questions and negative or emphatic statements and commands; also as vbl. substitute to avoid repetition of verb just used. 3 n. colloq. entertainment, elaborate operation etc.; swindle, hoax. 4 **do away with** abolish, kill; **do down** get the better of, swindle; **do for** be sufficient for, colloq. destroy or ruin or kill, colloq. do housework for; **do in** sl. kill, colloq. exhaust; Aus. sl. spend completely; **do-it-yourself** (to be) done or made by amateur handyman; **do up** fasten, wrap up, restore, repair; **do with** use, need; **do without** forgo, complete one's task in the absence of.

**do.** abbr. ditto.

**dob** v.t. Aus. sl. **dob in** inform against.

**docile** /ˈdəʊsaɪl/ a. submissive, easily managed. **docility** /-ˈsɪl-/ n.

**dock**[1] 1 n. artificial enclosed body of water for loading and repairing of ships; (usu. in pl.) range of docks with wharves, warehouses, etc. 2 v. bring or come into dock; join (spacecraft) together in space, be thus joined. 3 **dockyard** area with docks and shipbuilding and repairing equipment.

**dock**[2] n. enclosure in criminal court for accused.

**dock**[3] n. coarse weed with broad leaves.

**dock**[4] v.t. cut short (tail); reduce or deduct (money etc.)

**docket** /ˈdɒkət/ 1 n. document recording payment of customs, nature of goods delivered, jobs done, etc. 2 v.t. label with docket.

**doctor** /ˈdɒktə(r)/ 1 n. qualified medical practitioner; holder of doctorate. 2 v.t. treat medically; castrate, spay; tamper with.

**doctoral** /ˈdɒktər(ə)l/ a. of the degree of doctor.

**doctorate** /ˈdɒktərət/ n. higher university degree in any faculty.

**doctrinaire** /dɒktrɪˈneə(r)/ a. applying principles pedantically.

**doctrine** /ˈdɒktrɪn/ n. what is taught; principal of religious or political etc. belief. **doctrinal** /-ˈtraɪn(ə)l/ a.

**document** /ˈdɒkjəmənt/ n. something written or inscribed etc. that furnishes evidence or information on any subject. 2 /ˈdɒkjəment/ v.t. prove by or provide with documents. 3 **documentation** n.

**documentary** /dɒkjəˈmentərɪ/ 1 a. consisting of documents; factual, based on real events. 2 n. documentary film.

**dodder** /ˈdɒdə(r)/ v.i. shake, totter, be feeble. **doddery** a.

**dodecagon** /dəʊˈdekəgən/ n. plane figure with 12 sides and angles.

**dodge** 1 v. move quickly to one side; evade by cunning or trickery. 2 n. quick side-movement; trick, clever expedient.

**dodgem** /ˈdɒdʒəm/ n. small electrically-powered car at fun-fair, in which driver bumps into similar cars in enclosure.

**dodo** /ˈdəʊdəʊ/ n. (pl. **-dos**) large extinct flightless bird.

**doe** n. female of fallow deer or hare or rabbit. **doeskin** leather made from doe's skin.

**does** see **do**.

**doff** v.t. take off (hat etc.).

**dog** 1 n. 4-legged carnivorous animal of many breeds wild and domesticated; male of this or of fox or wolf; colloq.

**doge** /dəʊdʒ/ n. hist. chief magistrate of Venice or Genoa.

**dogged** /'dɒgəd/ a. tenacious.

**dogger** /'dɒgə(r)/ n. Aus. dingo-hunter.

**doggerel** /'dɒgərəl/ n. poor or trivial verse.

**doggo** /'dɒgəʊ/ adv. sl. **lie doggo** wait motionless or hidden.

**doggy** /'dɒgi/ a. of or like dogs; devoted to dogs.

**dogma** /'dɒgmə/ n. principle, tenet; doctrinal system.

**dogmatic** /dɒg'mætɪk/ a. of dogma, doctrinal; authoritative, arrogant. **dogmatically** adv.; **dogmatism** n.

**dogmatize** /'dɒgmətaɪz/ v.i. make positive unsupported statements.

**doh** /dəʊ/ n. Mus. first note of scale in tonic sol-fa.

**doily** /'dɔɪli/ n. small ornamental mat placed on plate for cakes etc.

**doings** /'du:ɪŋz/ n.pl. activity, proceedings; sl. things needed.

**Dolby** /'dɒlbi/ n. (P) system used in tape-recoding to reduce unwanted sounds at high frequency.

**doldrums** /'dɒldrəmz/ n.pl. low spirits; equatorial ocean region of calms.

**dole** 1 n. charitable (esp. niggardly) gift of food etc. or money; colloq. benefit claimable by the unemployed from the State. 2 v.t. deal *out* sparingly. 3 **on the dole** receiving State benefit for the unemployed.

**doleful** /'dəʊlfəl/ a. dreary, dismal, melancholy.

**doll** 1 n. child's toy representing human figure; ventriloquist's dummy; sl. young woman. 2 v. dress *up* smartly.

**dollar** /'dɒlə(r)/ n. unit of currency in US and other countries.

**dollop** /'dɒləp/ n. colloq. clumsy or shapeless lump of food etc.

**dolly** /'dɒli/ n. pet-name for doll; movable platform for cine-camera etc.

**dolman sleeve** /'dɒlmən/ loose sleeve cut in one piece with body of garment.

**dolmen** /'dɒlmən/ n. megalithic structure of large flat stone laid on upright ones.

**dolomite** /'dɒləmaɪt/ n. mineral or rock of calcium magnesium carbonate.

**dolour** /'dɒlə(r)/ n. sorrow, distress. **dolorous** a.

**dolphin** /'dɒlfɪn/ n. porpoise-like sea mammal.

**dolt** /dəʊlt/ n. stupid person. **doltish** a.

**Dom** n. title prefixed to names of some RC dignitaries and Carthusian and Benedictine monks.

**domain** /də'meɪn/ n. lands held or ruled over; estate, realm; province, scope.

**dome** n. rounded vault as roof; dome-shaped thing.

**domed** /dəʊmd/ a. having dome(s); shaped like dome; rounded.

**domestic** /də'mestɪk/ 1 a. of home, household, of family affairs; of one's own country; fond of home life; (of animal) kept by or living with man. 2 n. household servant.

**domesticate** /də'mestɪkeɪt/ v.t. tame, bring (animal) under human control; make fond of home life. **domestication** n.

**domesticity** /dɒməs'tɪsəti:/ n. being domestic; home life or privacy.

**domicile** /'dɒməsaɪl/ n. place of permanent residence.

**domiciled** a. having domicile *at* or *in*.

**domiciliary** /dɒmə'sɪli:əri:/ a. of a dwelling place; (of visit) to person's home.

**dominant** /'dɒmənənt/ 1 a. dominat-

**dominate**

ing, ruling, prevailing. 2 *n. Mus.* 5th note of scale. 3 **dominance** *n.*

**dominate** /'dɒmɪneɪt/ *v.* have commanding influence over; overlook, occupy commanding position in. **domination** *n.*

**domineer** /dɒmə'nɪə(r)/ *v.i.* behave overbearingly.

**Dominican** /də'mɪnɪkən/ *n.* friar or nun of order founded by St. Dominic.

**dominion** /də'mɪnjən/ *n.* sovereignty or lordship; territory of sovereign or government; *hist.* title of self-governing territories of British Commonwealth.

**domino** /'dɒmɪnəʊ/ *n.* (*pl.* **-noes**) any of 28 oblong pieces marked with pips; in *pl.* game played with these; hooded cloak worn with half-mask to conceal identity.

**don**[1] *n. UK* head, fellow, or tutor of college esp. at Oxford or Cambridge; **Don** title of Spanish gentleman.

**don**[2] *v.t.* put on (garment).

**donate** /dəʊ'neɪt/ *v.t.* make donation of.

**donation** /dəʊ'neɪʃ(ə)n/ *n.* gift (esp. of money to fund or institution).

**done** 1 *p.p.* of do. 2 *a. colloq.* socially acceptable. 3 **done like a dinner** *Aus. sl.* defeated or outwitted.

**dong** *Aus. sl.* 1 *n.* heavy blow, punch. 2 *v.t.* hit, punch.

**donkey** /'dɒŋkɪ/ *n.* ass. **donkey's years** a long time; **donkey vote** *Aus. sl.* vote cast by elector(s) who record preferences unthinkingly from top to bottom of ballot paper; **donkey-work** drudgery.

**donna** /'dɒnə/ *n.* title of Italian or Spanish or Portuguese lady.

**donnish** /'dɒnɪʃ/ *a.* like a college don; pedantic.

**donor** /'dəʊnə(r)/ *n.* giver of gift; person or animal providing blood for transfusion, organ for transplantation, etc.

**don't** /dəʊnt/ 1 *v.* do not. 2 *n.* prohibition.

**doodle** /'duːd(ə)l/ 1 *v.i.* scrawl or draw absentmindedly. 2 *n.* such scrawl.

**doom** /duːm/ 1 *n.* fate, destiny; ruin, death. 2 *v.t.* condemn *to* misfortune etc. 3 **doomsday** Last Judgement.

**door** /dɔː(r)/ *n.* hinged or sliding barrier of wood etc. closing entrance to building or room or cupboard etc.; doorway. **doormat** mat for wiping shoes on, *fig.* feebly subservient person;

**dotterel**

**doorstep** step or area immediately outside esp. outer door; **doorstop** device for keeping door open; **door-to-door** (of selling etc.) done at each house in turn; **doorway** opening filled by door.

**dope** 1 *n.* thick liquid; varnish; *sl.* drug, esp. narcotic; *sl.* information; *sl.* stupid person. 2 *v.* drug; take drugs; apply dope to.

**dopey** /'dəʊpɪ/ *a.* slow-witted, stupid.

***doppelgänger*** /'dɒpəl,geŋə(r)/ *n.* wraith of living person. [G]

**Doppler effect** /'dɒplə(r)/ apparent change in pitch of sound or other waves when source or observer is moving.

**dormant** /'dɔːmənt/ *a.* lying inactive (as) in sleep; not acting or in use. **dormancy** *n.*

**dormer** *n.* /'dɔːmə(r)/ upright window set in sloping roof.

**dormitory** /'dɔːmətərɪ/ *n.* sleeping-room with several beds; (in full **dormitory town**) small town or suburb from which people travel to work in city.

**dormouse** /'dɔːmaʊs/ *n.* (*pl.* **-mice**) small hibernating rodent.

**dormy** /'dɔːmɪ/ *a. Golf* leading by as many holes as there are holes left to play.

**dorsal** /'dɔːs(ə)l/ *a.* of or on back.

**dory** /'dɔːrɪ/ *n.* edible sea-fish.

**dosage** /'dəʊsɪdʒ/ *n.* giving of dose; size of dose.

**dose** /dəʊs/ 1 *n.* amount of medicine etc. to be taken at one time; amount of radiation received by person etc. exposed to it. 2 *v.* give medicine to; treat *with*.

**doss** *v.i. sl.* sleep, esp. in doss-house. **doss down** sleep on makeshift bed; **doss-house** cheap lodging-house.

**dossier** /'dɒsɪə(r)/ *n.* set of documents relating to person or event.

**dot** *n.* 1 small spot, point; decimal point; shorter signal of two in Morse code. 2 *v.t.* mark or scatter with dot(s); scatter like dots; place dot over (letter *i* etc.); *sl.* hit. 3 **dotted line** line of dots for signature etc. on document; **on the dot** punctually.

**dotage** /'dəʊtɪdʒ/ *n.* feeble-minded senility.

**dotard** /'dəʊtəd/ *n.* person in his dotage.

**dote** *v.i.* be silly or infatuated. **dote on** be excessively fond of.

**dotterel** /'dɒtər(ə)l/ *n.* kind of plover.

**dottle** /ˈdɒt(ə)l/ n. tobacco left in pipe after smoking.

**dotty** /ˈdɒtiː/ a. colloq. eccentric, silly.

**double** /ˈdʌb(ə)l/ 1 a. consisting of or combining two things; multiplied by two; twice as much or many or large etc.; of extra size or strength etc.; having some part double; (of flower) having more than one circle of petals; deceitful. 2 adv. twice the amount; two together. 3 n. double quantity or thing; double measure of spirits etc.; twice the amount or quantity; person or thing mistakable for another; in pl. game between two pairs of players; *Racing* cumulative bet on two horses. 4 v. make or become double; increase twofold; fold over upon itself; become folded; play two parts in same play etc.; turn sharply; *Naut.* get round (headland). 5 **at the double** running; **double agent** one who spies for two rival countries etc; **double-bank** Aus. ride with another person on a bicycle or horse etc.; **double-barrelled** (of gun) having two barrels, (of surname) hyphened; **double-bass** lowest-pitched instrument of violin kind; **double bed** bed for two people; **double-breasted** (of garment) having fronts overlapping across body; **double chin** fold of flesh below chin; **double-cross** deceive or betray; **double-dealing** duplicity; **double-decker** (bus etc.) with two decks, (sandwich) of several layers; **double-dink** Aus. dink; **double Dutch** gibberish; **double eagle** figure of eagle with two heads; **double-edged** *fig.* damaging to user as well as opponent; **double figures** numbers from 10 to 99; **double gee** Aus. spiny emex; **double glazing** two sheets of glass in window to reduce heat loss etc.; **double pneumonia** pneumonia of both lungs; **double standard** rule etc. applied more strictly to some persons than to others; **double-stopping** sounding of two notes at once on stringed instrument; **double take** delayed reaction to situation etc. immediately after first reaction; **double-talk** verbal expression that is (usu. deliberately) ambiguous.

**double entendre** /duːbl ɑːnˈtɑːndr/ phrase capable of two meanings, one usu. indecent. [F]

**doublet** /ˈdʌblət/ n. one of a pair of similar things; *hist.* man's close-fitting jacket.

**doubloon** /dʌˈbluːn/ n. *hist.* Spanish gold coin.

**doubt** /daʊt/ 1 n. feeling of uncertainty; inclination to disbelieve; uncertain state. 2 v. be in doubt or uncertainty; call in question, mistrust. 3 **no doubt** certainly, admittedly.

**doubtful** /ˈdaʊtfəl/ a. feeling or causing doubt; uncertain.

**doubtless** /ˈdaʊtləs/ adv. certainly, admittedly.

**douche** /duːʃ/ 1 n. jet of liquid applied to body externally or internally. 2 v. administer douche to; take douche.

**dough** /dəʊ/ n. kneaded moistened flour; bread-paste; *sl.* money. **doughnut** small spongy cake of dough fried in deep fat. **doughy** a.

**doughty** /ˈdaʊtiː/ a. *arch.* valiant.

**dour** /ˈdʊə(r)/ a. grim, stubborn.

**douse** /daʊs/ v.t. drench; extinguish (light).

**dove** /dʌv/ n. pigeon; person advocating negotiation rather than violence; gentle or innocent person. **dovecote** pigeon-house; **dovetail** joint made with tenon shaped like dove's tail, (v.) fit together (as) with dovetails.

**dowager** /ˈdaʊədʒə(r)/ n. woman with title or property derived from her late husband.

**dowdy** /ˈdaʊdiː/ a. lacking smartness, ill dressed.

**dowel** /ˈdaʊəl/ n. headless pin fastening together two pieces of wood etc.

**dowelling** n. round wooden rods for cutting into dowels.

**dower** /ˈdaʊə(r)/ 1 n. widow's share for life of husband's estate; *arch.* dowry. 2 v.t. *arch.* give dowry to; endow *with* talent etc.

**down**[1] /daʊn/ 1 adv. towards or in lower place or state or number; from earlier to later time; on ground. 2 prep. downwards along or through or into; at lower part of. 3 a. directed downwards. 4 v.t. colloq. put or throw or knock or bring etc. down; swallow. 5 n. reverse of fortune. 6 **down and out** penniless, destitute; **downcast** dejected, (of eyes) looking down; **downfall** fall from prosperity or power, cause of this; **downgrade** lower in

**down** rank etc.; **down-hearted** despondent; **downhill** sloping down, declining, in descending direction, on a decline; **down in the mouth** down-hearted; **downpour** heavy fall of rain; **downright** plain, straightforward, blunt, thoroughly, quite; **downstairs** down the stairs; to or on or of lower floor of house etc.; **downstream** in direction of flow of stream etc., moving downstream; **down-to-earth** practical, realistic; **downtown** *US* central part of town or city; **downtrodden** oppressed; **down under** in Australia or NZ; **have a down on** *colloq*. dislike, be prejudiced against. **7 downward** *a*. & *adv*.; **downwards** *adv*.

**down²** /daʊn/ *n*. fine soft short hair or feathers or fluff.

**down³** /daʊn/ *n*. open high land; esp. in *pl*. chalk uplands of S. England etc. or Darling Downs in SE Qld.

**Down's syndrome** congenital mental deficiency with mongoloid appearance.

**downy** /ˈdaʊnɪ/ *a*. of or like or covered with down; *sl*. knowing, sly.

**dowry** /ˈdaʊərɪ/ *n*. property brought by bride to her husband.

**dowse** /daʊz/ *v.i.* search for hidden water or minerals with forked twig which dips suddenly when over right spot. **dowser** *n*.

**doxology** /dɒkˈsɒlədʒɪ/ *n*. formula of praise to God.

**doyen** /ˈdɔɪən/ *n*. (*fem.* **doyenne** /dɔɪˈen/) senior member *of* a body of colleagues.

**doz.** *abbr.* dozen.

**doze 1** *v.i.* sleep lightly, be half asleep. **2** *n*. short light sleep. **3 doze off** fall lightly asleep.

**dozen** /ˈdʌz(ə)n/ *n*. set of twelve.

**D.Phil.** *abbr.* Doctor of Philosophy.

**Dr** *abbr.* Doctor.

**drab 1** *a*. dull, monotonous; of dull brownish colour. **2** *n*. drab colour.

**drac** *a*. *Aus. sl.* (of a woman) slovenly, unattractive.

**drachm** /dræm/ *n*. apothecaries' weight (60 grains).

**drachma** /ˈdrækmə/ *n*. (*pl.* -**mas**) Greek currency unit.

**drack** var. of **drac**.

**Draconian** /drəˈkəʊnɪən/ *adj.* (of laws) rigorous, harsh.

**draft** /drɑːft/ **1** *n*. rough preliminary outline of scheme or speech or document etc.; order for drawing money; bill or cheque drawn; detachment of troops etc. from larger body; selection of this; *Aus. & NZ* group of sheep or cattle separated from herd; *US Mil.* conscription. **2** *v.t.* prepare draft of; select as draft; *Aus. & NZ* separate (sheep or cattle) from herd for some purpose; *US* conscript.

**draftsman** /ˈdrɑːftsmən/ *n*. (*pl.* -**men**) drafter of documents.

**drag 1** *v*. draw along with effort or difficulty; (allow to) trail or go heavily; search (river-bed etc.) with grapnels and nets etc. **2** *n*. obstruction to progress, retarding force; *colloq*. boring or dreary task or person etc.; apparatus for dredging etc.; *colloq*. pull at cigarette; *sl*. women's clothes worn by men. **3 drag race** acceleration race between cars over short distance.

**draggle** /ˈdræg(ə)l/ *v*. make dirty and wet by trailing; hang trailing.

**dragon** /ˈdrægən/ *n*. mythical monster like reptile, usu. with wings and claws and often breathing fire; fierce person.

**dragonfly** /ˈdrægənflaɪ/ *n*. long-bodied gauzy-winged insect.

**dragoon** /drəˈguːn/ **1** *n*. cavalryman; *hist*. mounted infantryman; fierce fellow. **2** *v.t.* force *into* course of action.

**dragster** /ˈdrægstə(r)/ *n*. low car or bicycle designed for speed.

**drain 1** *v*. draw off liquid from; draw off (liquid); flow or trickle away; dry or become dry; exhaust; drink (liquid); empty (glass etc.) **2** *n*. channel or pipe carrying off water or sewage etc.; constant outlet or expenditure. **3 draining-board** sloping board on which washed dishes etc. are left to drain.

**drainage** /ˈdreɪnɪdʒ/ *n*. draining; system of drains; what is drained off.

**drake** *n*. male duck.

**dram** *n*. small drink of spirits etc.; drachm.

**drama** /ˈdrɑːmə/ *n*. play for acting on stage or broadcasting; dramatic art; dramatic series of events.

**dramatic** /drəˈmætɪk/ *a*. of drama; forcible, theatrical; striking.

**dramatis personae** /ˈdræmətɪs pɜːˈsəʊnaɪ/ characters in a play.

**dramatist** /ˈdræmətɪst/ *n*. writer of plays.

**dramatize** /'dræmətaɪz/ v. convert into play; make dramatic; behave dramatically. **dramatization** n.

**drank** past of **drink**.

**drape** 1 v. cover or hang or adorn with cloth etc.; arrange or hang in graceful folds. 2 n. US curtain.

**draper** /'dreɪpə(r)/ n. retailer of textile fabrics.

**drapery** /'dreɪpərɪ/ n. cloth or textile fabrics; draper's trade; clothing or hangings disposed in folds.

**drastic** /'dræstɪk/ a. acting strongly or severely; vigorous; violent.

**drat** v.t. curse, bother.

**draught** /drɑːft/ n. current of air; traction; depth of water needed to float ship; drawing of liquor from cask etc.; single act of drinking; amount so drunk; in pl. game played with 12 uniform pieces on each side, on **draughtboard** like chess-board. **draught beer** beer drawn from cask, not bottled.

**draughtsman** /'drɑːftsmən/ n. (pl. -men) person who makes drawings; piece in game of draughts.

**draughty** /'drɑːftɪ/ a. liable to draughts of air.

**draw** /drɔː/ 1 v. (past **drew**; p.p. **drawn**) pull, drag, haul; protract, stretch; attract; derive, deduce, infer; inhale; extract; entice; induce; elicit; take from or out; pull into or out of position; make (picture) by making lines; describe in words; write out (bill, cheque, etc.); bring (game etc.) to undecided conclusion; (of ship) require (stated depth of water); draw lots; obtain by lot; search (cover) for game etc.; (of chimney, pipe, etc.) promote or allow draught of air; make one's way, come, move. 2 n. act of drawing; thing that draws custom or attention; drawing of lots, lottery; drawn game. 3 **draw back** withdraw; **drawback** thing that impairs satisfaction, disadvantage; **drawbridge** bridge hinged at one end for drawing up; **draw in** (of days etc.) become shorter; **draw out** prolong, induce to talk, (of days etc.) become longer; **draw-string** string that can be pulled to tighten mouth of bag or waist of garment etc.; **draw up** compose (document etc.), bring or come into regular order, come to a halt, make oneself stiffly erect.

**drawer** /drɔː(r)/ n. person who draws; (also /drɔː(r)/) receptacle sliding in and out of frame (**chest of drawers**) or of table etc.; in pl. undergarment worn next to body below waist.

**drawing** /'drɔːɪŋ/ n. art of representing by line with pencil etc.; picture etc. drawn thus. **drawing-board** board for stretching paper on while drawing is made; **drawing-pin** flat-headed pin for fastening paper to a surface.

**drawing-room** room for entertainment of company esp. in private house.

**drawl** 1 v. speak or utter with drawn-out vowel sounds. 2 n. drawling way of speaking.

**dray** n. low esp. brewer's cart for heavy loads.

**dread** /dred/ 1 v. be in great fear of; look forward to with terror. 2 n. great fear; awe. 3 a. dreaded, dreadful.

**dreadful** /'dredful/ a. terrible; colloq. troublesome; very bad.

**dream** /driːm/ 1 n. series of pictures or events in mind of sleeping person; day-dream; ideal; aspiration or ambition. 2 v. (past & p.p. **dreamt** /dremt/ or **dreamed**) experience dream; imagine as in dream; (esp. with neg.) think of as a possibility; fall into reverie. 3 **dreamtime** Aus. alcheringa.

**dreamy** /'driːmɪ/ a. dreamlike; given to day-dreaming, impractical, vague.

**dreary** /'drɪərɪ/ a. dismal, gloomy, dull.

**dredge¹** 1 n. apparatus for clearing out mud etc. or collecting oysters etc. from bottom of sea etc. 2 v. use dredge; clean or fetch up with dredge.

**dredge²** v.t. sprinkle with flour etc.

**dredger¹** /'dredʒə(r)/ n. dredge; boat with dredge.

**dredger²** /'dredʒə(r)/ n. container with perforated lid for sprinkling flour etc.

**dregs** n.pl. sediment, grounds; worst part.

**drench** 1 v.t. wet thoroughly; force (animal) to take dose of medicine. 2 n. dose for animal; thorough wetting.

**dress** 1 v. clothe, clothe oneself; arrange or adorn; put dressing on (wound etc.); prepare (food); apply manure to. 2 n. clothing, esp. visible part of it; woman's or girl's one-piece garment of bodice and skirt. 3 **dress-circle** first gallery in theatre; **dressmaker** person who

**dressage** /'dresɑː/ *n.* training of horse in obedience and deportment.

**dresser**¹ /'dresə(r)/ *n.* kitchen sideboard with shelves.

**dresser**² /'dresə(r)/ *n.* person who helps actor to dress for stage.

**dressing** /'dresɪŋ/ *n.* putting one's clothes on; sauce or seasoning etc. for food; ointment etc. applied to wound; manure. **dressing-down** scolding; **dressing-gown** loose robe worn while one is not fully dressed; **dressing-table** one with mirror etc. for use while dressing.

**dressy** /'dresɪ/ *a.* fond of smart dress.

**drew** *past* of **draw**.

**dribble** /'drɪb(ə)l/ 1 *v.* allow saliva to flow from the mouth; (let) flow in drops; *Footb.* etc. move ball forward with repeated touches of feet etc. 2 *n.* act or process of dribbling; dribbling flow.

**driblet** /'drɪblət/ *n.* small quantity.

**dried** *past & p.p.* of **dry**.

**drier** /'draɪə(r)/ *n.* machine for drying hair or laundry etc.

**drift** 1 *n.* being driven by current; slow movement or variation; snow etc. heaped by wind etc.; purpose, meaning, tenor; inaction; deviation due to current or wind etc. 2 *v.* be carried (as) by current; (of current) carry; heap or be heaped into drifts; move passively or casually or aimlessly. 3 **drift-net** large net allowed to drift with tide, for catching herring etc.; **driftwood** wood washed ashore by sea.

**drifter** /'drɪftə(r)/ *n.* aimless person; boat with drift-net.

**drill**¹ 1 *n.* tool or machine for boring holes; exercising of soldiers etc.; routine; *colloq.* recognized procedure. 2 *v.* bore (hole etc.); subject to or undergo drill; impart (knowledge etc.) by strict method.

**drill**² 1 *n.* small furrow for sowing seed in; machine for furrowing, sowing, and covering seed. 2 *v.t.* sow or plant in drills.

**drill**³ *n.* coarse twilled fabric.

**drill**⁴ *n.* kind of baboon.

**drink** 1 *v.* (*past* **drank**; *p.p.* **drunk**) swallow liquid; take *in* with eager delight; take alcoholic liquor, esp. to excess; absorb moisture. 2 *n.* liquid for drinking; glass or portion of this, esp. alcoholic; intoxicating liquor. 3 **the drink** *sl.* the sea; **drink to** toast, wish success to, by drinking.

**drip** 1 *v.* fall or let fall in drops; be so wet as to shed drops. 2 *n.* falling drop of liquid; liquid falling in drops; *colloq.* feeble person. 3 **drip-dry** (of fabric etc.) that needs no ironing after hanging up to dry; **drip-feed** feeding (esp. intravenously) by liquid a drop at a time.

**dripping** /'drɪpɪŋ/ *n.* fat melted from roasting meat.

**drive** 1 *v.* (*past* **drove**; *p.p.* **driven** /'drɪv(ə)n/); urge onwards by force; throw or cause to go in some direction; operate and direct course of (vehicle etc.); convey or be conveyed in vehicle; *Golf* strike ball from tee; chase (game etc.) from large area into small; impel or carry along; force, constrain. 2 *n.* excursion in vehicle; driveway; forcible blow at cricket etc.; energy; energetic campaign; transmission of power to machinery or wheels of motor vehicle etc.; social gathering to play card-games etc. 3 **drive at** seek, intend, mean; **drive-in** (bank, restaurant, etc.) that may be used without getting out of one's car; **driveway** road for vehicles, esp. private one leading to house; **driving-licence** licence permitting one to drive motor vehicle; **driving-test** official test of competence to drive motor vehicle; **driving-wheel** wheel communicating motive power in machinery.

**drivel** /'drɪv(ə)l/ 1 *n.* silly nonsense. 2 *v.i.* talk silly nonsense; run at mouth or nose.

**driver** /'draɪvə(r)/ *n.* person who drives; golf-club for driving from tee.

**drizzle** /'drɪz(ə)l/ 1 *n.* fine dense rain. 2 *v.i.* fall in fine dense rain.

**droll** /drəʊl/ *a.* amusing, odd, queer.

**drollery** /'drəʊlərɪ/ *n.* quaint humour.

**dromedary** /'drɒmədərɪ/ *n.* swift usu. one-humped camel bred for riding.

**drone** 1 *n.* male or non-worker bee; idler; bass-pipe of bagpipes or its continuous note. 2 *v.* make deep humming sound; talk or utter monotonously.

**drongo** /'drɒŋgəʊ/ *n. Aus.* (*pl.* **-gos**)

**drool** *v.* dribble; show unrestrained admiration (*over*).

**droop** /druːp/ *v.* bend or hang down; languish, lose heart. **2** *n.* drooping attitude.

**drop 1** *n.* small quantity of liquid such as falls or hangs or adheres to surface; thing in shape of drop, esp. sweet or pendant; in *pl.* liquid medicine to be measured in drops; minute quantity; act of dropping, fall, abrupt descent, distance dropped. **2** *v.* fall by force of gravity; allow to fall; leave hold of; fall or let fall or shed in drops; sink to ground; sink to lower level; lower (eyes etc.); allow oneself to fall *behind* etc.; break off acquaintance etc. with; cease, lapse; utter be uttered casually; come on or go casually *by* or in etc.; lose (money in transaction); omit; *Footb.* make (goal) by drop-kick. **3 drop-kick** kick at football made by dropping ball and kicking it as it touches ground; **drop off** fall asleep, decrease or depart gradually; **drop out** cease to appear or participate; **drop-out** person who drops out esp. of course of study or conventional society; **drop scone** one made by dropping spoonful of mixture on cooking surface; **drop-shot** *Tennis* shot dropping abruptly after clearing net.

**droplet** /ˈdrɒplət/ *n.* small drop of liquid.

**dropper** /ˈdrɒpə(r)/ *n.* device for releasing liquid in drops.

**droppings** /ˈdrɒpɪŋz/ *n.pl.* what falls or has fallen in drops; dung.

**dropsy** /ˈdrɒpsɪ/ *n.* disease with watery fluid collecting in body. **dropsical** *a.*

**dross** *n.* scum of molten metal; impurities; rubbish.

**drought** /draʊt/ *n.* abnormally prolonged spell of dry weather.

**drove**¹ *n.* moving herd or flock; crowd in motion.

**drove**² past of **drive**.

**drover** /ˈdrəʊvə(r)/ *n.* driver of or dealer in cattle.

**drown** /draʊn/ *v.* (cause to) suffocate by submersion; flood, drench; assuage (grief etc.) with drink; overpower (sound) by greater loudness.

**drowse** /draʊz/ *v.i.* be half asleep.

**drowsy** /ˈdraʊzɪ/ *a.* half asleep.

**drub** *v.t.* thrash, beat. **drubbing** *n.*

**drudge 1** *n.* person who does dull, laborious, or menial work. **2** *v.i.* work hard or laboriously. **3 drudgery** *n.*

**drug 1** *n.* medicinal substance, esp. pain-killer, stimulant, narcotic, etc. (**dangerous drug** one causing addiction). **2** *v.* add drug to (drink, food, etc.); administer drugs to; indulge in narcotics etc. **3 drug-store** *US* chemist's shop also selling miscellaneous articles, light refreshments, etc.

**drugget** /ˈdrʌɡət/ *n.* coarse woven fabric for floor covering etc.

**druggist** /ˈdrʌɡɪst/ *n.* pharmaceutical chemist.

**Druid** /ˈdruːɪd/ *n.* ancient Celtic priest; officer of a Gorsedd. **Druidical** *a.*; **Druidism** *n.*

**drum 1** *n.* musical instrument sounded by striking skin stretched over frame; sound (as) of this; its player; cylindrical structure or object; cylinder used for storage etc.; tympanum of ear; *Aus. sl.* reliable and usu. confidential (piece of) information; *Aus. sl.* swag. **2** *v.* play drum; tap or thump repeatedly; drive facts etc. *into* person by persistence; (of bird etc.) make loud noise with wings. **3 drum brake** kind in which shoes on vehicle press against drum on wheel; **drum major** leader of marching band; **drum majorette** female drum major; **drum out** dismiss with ignominy; **drumstick** stick for beating drum, lower joint of cooked fowl's leg; **drum up** produce or obtain by vigorous effort.

**drummer** /ˈdrʌmə(r)/ *n.* player of drum.

**drunk 1** *p.p.* of **drink**. **2** *a.* deprived of proper control of oneself by alcoholic liquor. **3** *n.* drunken person; *sl.* drinking-bout.

**drunkard** /ˈdrʌŋkəd/ *n.* person often drunk.

**drunken** /ˈdrʌŋkən/ *a.* drunk, often drunk; caused by or exhibiting drunkenness.

**drupe** *n.* stone-fruit.

**dry 1** *a.* without or deficient in moisture; without rain; not yielding or using liquid; thirsty; teetotal, prohibiting sale of alcoholic liquor; solid, not liquid; without butter etc.; (of wine etc.) free

**dryad** /'draɪæd/ n. nymph inhabiting tree.

**D.Sc.** abbr. Doctor of Science.

**DSC, DSM, DSO** abbrs. Distinguished Service Cross, Medal, Order.

**d.t.('s)** abbr. delirium tremens.

**dual** /'dju:əl/ 1 a. of two; twofold, double. 2 n. Gram. dual number or form. 3 **dual carriageway** road with dividing strip between traffic in opposite directions; **dual-control** (of vehicle etc.) that can be controlled by instructor as well as learner. 4 **duality** n.

**dub**[1] v.t. make (person) into knight; give title or nickname to.

**dub**[2] v.t. add sound effects etc. or new sound track, esp. in different language, to (film etc.).

**dubbin** /'dʌbɪn/ n. (also **dubbing**) grease for softening and waterproofing leather.

**dubiety** /dju:'baɪətɪ/ n. feeling of doubt.

**dubious** /'dju:bɪəs/ a. doubtful; of questionable or suspected character.

**ducal** /'dju:k(ə)l/ a. of or like duke.

**ducat** /'dʌkət/ n. gold coin formerly current in most European countries.

**duchess** /'dʌtʃəs/ n. duke's wife or widow; woman with own rank of duke.

**duchy** /'dʌtʃɪ/ n. duke's territory.

**duck**[1] 1 n. kind of swimming-bird; female of this; its flesh as food; Crick. batsman's score of 0; darling. 2 v. bob down esp. to avoid blow etc.; dip head under water and emerge; plunge (person) in or in water. 3 **duckbill** a platypus; **duck-boards** narrow path of wooden slats over muddy ground; **duckshove** Aus. & NZ gain unethical advantage, jump a queue; **duckweed** a plant that covers surface of still water.

**duck**[2] n. strong linen or cotton material; in pl. trousers of this.

**duckling** /'dʌklɪŋ/ n. young duck.

**duct** n. channel, tube; Anat. tube in body conveying secretions etc.

**ductile** /'dʌktaɪl/ a. capable of being drawn into wire; pliable; docile. **ductility** n.

**ductless** /'dʌktləs/ a. (of gland) secreting directly into bloodstream.

**dud** sl. 1 n. thing that fails to work, useless thing; in pl. clothes, rags. 2 a. defective, useless.

**dude** n. US sl. dandy; city man.

**dudgeon** /'dʌdʒ(ə)n/ n. resentment; state of wrath or indignation.

**due** 1 a. owing or payable as debt or obligation; merited, appropriate; to be ascribed or attributed to (cause etc.); under engagement to do something or arrive at certain time. 2 adv. exactly, directly. 3 n. what one owes; toll or fee legally demandable; what is owed to person.

**duel** /'dju:əl/ 1 n. fight with weapons between two persons; contest. 2 v.i. fight duel(s). 3 **duellist** n.

**duenna** /dju:'enə/ n. older woman acting as chaperon to girls.

**duet** /dju:'et/ n. musical composition for two performers.

**duff** 1 a. sl. useless, counterfeit. 2 n. boiled pudding. 3 v.t. Aus. sl. steal (cattle), esp. by altering brand.

**duffer** /'dʌfə(r)/ n. colloq. inefficient or stupid person; Aus. unproductive mine.

**duffle** /'dʌf(ə)l/ n. (also **duffel**) coarse woollen cloth. **duffle bag** cylindrical canvas bag closed by draw-string; **duffle coat** short heavy overcoat with toggle fastenings.

**dug**[1] past & p.p. of **dig**.

**dug**[2] n. udder, teat.

**dugite** /'du:gaɪt or 'dju:-/ n. brown snake of southern WA.

**dugong** /'du:gɒŋ/ n. Asian sea-mammal.

**dug-out** /'dʌgaʊt/ n. hollowed tree as canoe; roofed shelter esp. for troops in trenches.

**duke** /dju:k/ n. British peer of highest hereditary rank; sovereign ruling duchy or small State. **dukedom** n.

**dulcet** /'dʌlsət/ a. sweet-sounding.

**dulcimer** /'dʌlsəmə(r)/ n. musical instrument with metal strings struck by hammers held in hands.

**dull** 1 a. not bright; tedious; slow of understanding, stupid; listless, depressed. 2 v. make or become dull. **dully** /'dʌl-li:/ adv.

**dullard** /'dʌləd/ n. slow-witted person.

**duly** /'dju:li/ adv. in due time or manner; rightly, properly; sufficiently.

**dumb** /dʌm/ a. unable to speak; silent, taciturn; stupid, ignorant. **dumb-bell** short bar with weight at each end, used in pairs to exercise muscles; **dumb show** gestures instead of speech.

**dumbfound** /dʌm'faʊnd/ v.t. nonplus; make speechless with surprise.

**dumdum bullet** /'dʌmdʌm/ soft-nosed bullet that expands on impact.

**dummy** /'dʌmi/ 1 n. model of human form to hang clothes on or used by ventriloquist; imitation object, object serving to replace real or normal one; baby's rubber or plastic teat; stupid person; player or imaginary player in some card-games, whose cards are exposed and played by partner. 2 a. sham, imitation. 3 v.i. use feigned pass etc. in football. 4 **dummy run** trial attempt.

**dummying** n. Aus. hist. practice of buying land on behalf of person not entitled to do so.

**dump** 1 v.t. deposit as rubbish; put down firmly or clumsily; colloq. abandon; send (surplus goods) to foreign market at low price. 2 n. rubbish-heap; temporary depot of ammunition etc.; colloq. depressing place.

**dumper** n. Aus. wave that breaks suddenly and hurls surfer down with great force.

**dumpling** /'dʌmplɪŋ/ n. ball of dough boiled in stew or containing apple etc.

**dumps** n.pl. colloq. low spirits.

**dumpy** /'dʌmpi/ a. short and stout.

**dun**[1] 1 a. greyish-brown. 2 n. dun colour; dun horse.

**dun**[2] 1 v. ask persistently for payment of debt. 2 n. demand for payment.

**dunce** n. bad learner; dullard.

**dunderhead** /'dʌndəhed/ n. stupid person.

**dune** /dju:n/ n. mound of loose sand etc. formed by wind.

**dung** 1 n. excrement of animals; manure. 2 v.t. apply dung to (land). 3 **dunghill** heap of dung or refuse in farmyard.

**dungaree** /dʌŋgə'ri:/ n. strong coarse cotton cloth; in pl. overalls etc. of dungaree or similar material.

**dungeon** /'dʌndʒ(ə)n/ n. underground cell for prisoners.

**dunk** v. dip (bread etc.) into soup or beverage before eating it.

**dunny** /'dʌni/ n. Aus. sl. toilet, esp. outside one in unsewered area.

**duo** /'dju:əʊ/ n. (pl. -os) pair of performers; duet.

**duodecimal** /dju:əʊ'desɪm(ə)l/ a. of twelfths or 12; proceeding by twelves.

**duodenum** /dju:əʊ'di:nəm/ n. part of small intestine next to stomach. **duodenal** a.

**duologue** /'dju:əlɒg/ n. dialogue between two persons.

**dupe** /dju:p/ 1 n. victim of deception. 2 v.t. deceive and make use of.

**duple** /'dju:p(ə)l/ a. of two parts. **duple time** Mus. of two beats to bar.

**duplex** /'dju:pleks/ a. having two elements; twofold.

**duplicate** 1 /'dju:plɪkət/ a. exactly like thing already existing; doubled. 2 /'dju:plɪkət/ n. one of two things exactly alike. 3 /'dju:plɪkeɪt/ v.t. make exact copy of; repeat; double. 4 **duplication** n.

**duplicator** /'dju:plɪkeɪtə(r)/ n. machine for producing documents in multiple copies.

**duplicity** /dju:'plɪsəti/ n. deceitfulness.

**durable** /'djʊərəb(ə)l/ a. capable of lasting; resisting wear. **durability** n.

**durance** /'djʊərəns/ n. arch. imprisonment.

**duration** /djʊ'reɪʃ(ə)n/ n. time thing lasts.

**duress** /dju:'res/ n. use of force or threats esp. illegally.

**during** /'djʊərɪŋ/ prep. throughout or at point in duration of.

**dusk** n. darker stage of twilight.

**dusky** /'dʌski/ a. shadowy, dim; dark-coloured.

**dust** 1 n. light fine powder of earth or other matter; dead person's remains. 2 v. clear of dust; sprinkle with powder. 3 **dust bowl** area denuded of vegetation and reduced to desert; **dust-cover, -jacket**, book's paper wrapper; **dust-**

**duster** /ˈdʌstə(r)/ n. cloth for dusting.

**dusty** /ˈdʌsti/ a. covered with or full of or like dust.

**Dutch** 1 a. of the Netherlands. 2 n. Dutch language; *the* Dutch people. 3 **Dutch auction** sale in which price is reduced till purchaser is found; **Dutch barn** roof on poles over hay etc.; **Dutch courage** courage induced by drink; **Dutch treat** party or outing where each pays for his own share; **go Dutch** share expenses on outing. 4 **Dutchman** n.; **Dutchwoman** n.

**duteous** /ˈdjuːtɪəs/ a. dutiful.

**dutiable** /ˈdjuːtɪəb(ə)l/ a. liable to customs etc. duties.

**dutiful** /ˈdjuːtəfəl/ a. doing or observant of one's duty.

**duty** /ˈdjuːti/ n. moral or legal obligation; office or function; tax levied on article or transaction. **on, off, duty** actually engaged, not engaged, in one's regular work or some obligation.

**duvet** /ˈduːveɪ/ n. thick soft quilt used as bedclothes.

**dwarf** /dwɔːf/ 1 n. person or plant etc. much below ordinary size; small mythological being with magical powers. 2 a. of a kind very small in size. 3 v.t. stunt in growth; make look small by contrast.

**dwell** v.i. (past & p.p. **dwelt**) reside, live; keep attention fixed *on*; write or speak at length *on*.

**dwelling** /ˈdwelɪŋ/ n. residence, house.

**dwindle** /ˈdwɪnd(ə)l/ v.i. become gradually less or smaller; lose importance.

**dye** /daɪ/ 1 n. substance used to change colour of fabric or wood or hair etc.; colour produced by this. 2 v. (*partic.* **dyeing**) impregnate with dye; make (thing) specified colour; take dye.

**dying** *partic.* of **die**[1].

**dyke** var. of **dike**.

**dynamic** /daɪˈnæmɪk/ a. of motive force; of force in operation; of dynamics; potent, forceful. **dynamically** *adv.*

**dynamics** n.pl. (usu. treated as *sing.*) branch of mechanics that treats of motion and of action of forces.

**dynamism** /ˈdaɪnəmɪz(ə)m/ n. energizing or dynamic action or power.

**dynamite** /ˈdaɪnəmaɪt/ 1 n. high explosive of nitroglycerine mixed with absorbent substance. 2 *v.t.* blow up with this.

**dynamo** /ˈdaɪnəməʊ/ n. (*pl.* -mos) machine converting mechanical into electrical energy; energetic person.

**dynast** /ˈdɪnəst/ n. member of dynasty.

**dynasty** /ˈdɪnəsti/ n. line of hereditary rulers. **dynastic** /-ˈnæs-/ a.

**dyne** n. *Phys.* unit of force.

**dysentery** /ˈdɪsəntəri/ n. inflammation of bowels.

**dyslexia** /dɪsˈleksɪə/ n. abnormal difficulty in reading and spelling caused by a condition of the brain. **dyslexic** a.

**dyspepsia** /dɪsˈpepsɪə/ n. indigestion. **dyspeptic** a.

**dystrophy** /ˈdɪstrəfi/ n. defective nutrition. **muscular dystrophy** hereditary progressive weakening of muscles.

# E

**E.** *abbr.* east(ern).

**each 1** *a.* every one of two or more taken separately. **2** *pron.* each person or thing. **3 each way** (of bet) backing horse etc. to win or to be placed.

**eager** /'i:gə(r)/ *a.* full of keen desire; enthusiastically impatient.

**eagle** /'i:g(ə)l/ *n.* large bird of prey; figure of eagle esp. as symbol of US; *Golf* score of 2 under par for hole. **eagle eye** keen sight or watchfulness; **eagle-hawk** *n. Aus. colloq.* wedge-tailed eagle.

**ear**¹ /ɪə(r)/ *n.* organ of hearing, esp. external part; sense of hearing; attention; faculty of discriminating sound; ear-shaped thing. **earache** pain in inner ear; **ear-bash** *Aus. sl.* talk excessively to; **ear-drum** internal membrane of ear; **earmark** (*n.*) owner's mark on ear of sheep etc., (*v.t.*) mark (animal) thus, *fig.* assign (fund etc.) *for* some definite purpose; **earphone** device worn on ear to listen to radio or telephone communication; **ear-plug** device to protect ear from water, noise, etc., or to listen to radio etc. communication; **ear-ring** ornament worn on lobe of ear; **earshot** hearing-distance; **ear-trumpet** trumpet-shaped tube formerly used as hearing aid.

**ear**² /ɪə(r)/ *n.* seed-bearing head of cereal plant.

**earl** /ɜːl/ *n.* British nobleman ranking next below marquis. **Earl Marshal** officer of State with ceremonial duties. **earldom** *n.*

**early** /'ɜːlɪ/ *a. & adv.* before due, usual, or expected time, not far on in day, night, etc., or in development etc.

**earn** /ɜːn/ *v.t.* obtain as reward of work or merit; bring as income or interest.

**earnest**¹ /'ɜːnəst/ *a.* serious; showing intense feeling. **in earnest** serious(ly).

**earnest**² /'ɜːnəst/ *n.* money paid as instalment to confirm contract; foretaste.

**earnings** /'ɜːnɪŋz/ *n.pl.* money earned.

**earth** /ɜːθ/ **1** *n.* planet we live on; land and sea as opp. sky; dry land; ground; soil, mould; *Electr.* connection to earth as completion of circuit; hole of fox etc. **2** *v.t. Electr.* connect to earth; heap earth over (roots etc.). **3 earthwork** bank of earth in fortification; **earthworm** worm living in earth; **run to earth** find after long search.

**earthen** /'ɜːθ(ə)n/ *a.* made of earth or of baked clay. **earthenware** baked clay, vessels made of this.

**earthly** /'ɜːθlɪ/ *a.* of earth, terrestrial. **no earthly** *colloq.* absolutely no; **not an earthly** *sl.* no chance whatever.

**earthquake** /'ɜːθkweɪk/ *n.* convulsion of earth's surface.

**earthy** /'ɜːθɪ/ *a.* of or like earth or soil; grossly material.

**earwig** /'ɪəwɪg/ *n.* insect with pincers at tail end.

**ease** /iːz/ **1** *n.* freedom from pain or trouble or constraint; facility. **2** *v.* relieve from pain etc.; relax, slacken; cause to move by gentle force. **3 ease (off)** become less burdensome or severe.

**easel** /'iːz(ə)l/ *n.* frame to support painting or blackboard etc.

**easement** /'iːzmənt/ *n. Law* right of way over another's property.

**east** /iːst/ **1** *n.* point of horizon where sun rises; eastern part of world or country or town etc. **2** *a.* towards or at or near or facing east; coming from east. **3** *adv.* towards or at or near east. **4 East End** eastern part of London. **5 eastward** *adv.*, *a., & n.*; **eastwards** *adv.*

**Easter** /'iːstə(r)/ *n.* festival of Christ's resurrection. **Easter egg** artificial usu. chocolate egg as Easter gift.

**easterly** /'iːstəlɪ/ *a.* from or to east.

**eastern** /'iːst(ə)n/ *a.* of or in east. **Eastern Church** Orthodox Church; **Eastern States** *Aus.* the States to the east of WA or SA, esp. Victoria and NSW.

**easterner** /'iːstənə(r)/ *n.* inhabitant of east.

**easy** /'iːzɪ/ **1** *a.* not difficult; free from bodily or mental pain or worry etc.; free from embarrassment or strictness etc.; compliant. **2** *adv.* in comfortable fashion; gently. **3 easy chair** large comfortable chair; **easygoing** not fussy, content with things as they are; **take it easy** proceed gently, relax.

**eat** *v.* (*past* **ate** /et/; *p.p.* **eaten**) chew and swallow (food); consume food, have meal; destroy, consume.

# eatable — edge

**eatable** /'i:təb(ə)l/ 1 *a.* that may be eaten. 2 *n.* (usu. in *pl.*) food.

**eau-de-Cologne** /əʊdəkə'ləʊn/ *n.* perfume made orig. at Cologne.

**eaves** /i:vz/ *n.pl.* projecting lower edge of roof.

**eavesdrop** /'i:vzdrɒp/ *v.i.* listen secretly to private conversation.

**ebb** 1 *n.* outward movement of tide; decline, decay. 2 *v.i.* flow back; decline.

**ebonite** /'ebənaɪt/ *n.* vulcanized rubber.

**ebony** /'ebəni/ 1 *n.* hard heavy black wood. 2 *a.* made of or black as ebony.

**ebullient** /ə'bʌlɪənt/ *a.* exuberant; high-spirited. **ebullience** *n.*

**ebullition** /ebə'lɪʃ(ə)n/ *n.* boiling; outburst.

**eccentric** /ək'sentrɪk/ 1 *a.* odd or capricious in behaviour or appearance; not placed centrally, not having axis etc. placed centrally; not concentric; not circular. 2 *n.* eccentric person. 3 **eccentricity** /-'trɪs-/ *n.*

**ecclesiastic** /əkli:zi:'æstɪk/ *n.* clergyman.

**ecclesiastical** /əkli:zi:'æstək(ə)l/ *a.* of the Church or clergy.

**ECG** *abbr.* electrocardiogram.

**echelon** /'eʃəlɒn/ *n.* formation of troops in parallel divisions, each with its end clear of those ahead or behind; any similar formation; level or rank in organization.

**echidna** /ə'kɪdnə/ *n.* Aus. spiny egg-laying burrowing mammal that feeds on ants.

**echo** /'ekəʊ/ 1 *n.* (*pl.* **-oes**) repetition of sound by reflection of sound-waves; close imitation. 2 *v.* resound with echo; repeat, imitate; be repeated.

**éclair** /eɪ'kleə(r)/ *n.* finger-shaped cake filled with cream and iced.

**éclat** /eɪ'klɑ:/ *n.* brilliant success; prestige.

**eclectic** /ə'klektɪk/ *a.* selecting ideas or beliefs from various sources. 2 *n.* eclectic person.

**eclipse** /ə'klɪps/ 1 *n.* interception of light of sun or moon etc. by another body; loss of brilliance or splendour. 2 *v.t.* intercept light of; *fig.* outshine, surpass.

**ecliptic** /ə'klɪptɪk/ *n.* sun's apparent path among stars during year.

**eclogue** /'eklɒg/ *n.* short pastoral poem.

**ecology** /ə'kɒlədʒɪ/ *n.* study of organisms in relation to one another and their surroundings. **ecological** *a.*; **ecologist** *n.*

**economic** /i:kə'nɒmɪk/ *a.* of economics; maintained for profit; adequate to pay for expenses or costs; practical, utilitarian.

**economical** /i:kə'nɒmɪk(ə)l/ *a.* thrifty; saving, avoiding waste, (*of*).

**economics** /i:kə'nɒmɪks/ *n.pl.* treated as *sing.* science of production and distribution of wealth; application of this to particular subject. **economist** *n.*

**economize** /ə'kɒnəmaɪz/ *v.* make economies; reduce expenditure.

**economy** /ə'kɒnəmɪ/ *n.* management of concerns or resources of State or business or household; frugality, instance of this.

**ecru** /'eɪkru:/ *n.* light fawn colour.

**ecstasy** /'ekstəsɪ/ *n.* overwhelming feeling of joy; rapture. **ecstatic** /-'stæt-/ *a.*

**ECT** *abbr.* electroconvulsive therapy.

**ectoplasm** /'ektəplæz(ə)m/ *n.* viscous substance supposed to emanate from body of spiritualistic medium during trance.

**ecumenical** /i:kju:'menək(ə)l/ *a.* of or representing whole Christian world; seeking world-wide Christian unity; worldwide. **ecumenicalism** *n.* **ecumenism** *n.*

**eczema** /'ekzəmə/ *n.* kind of inflammation of skin.

**ed.** *abbr.* edited; edition; editor.

**eddy** /'edɪ/ 1 *n.* small whirlpool; smoke etc. moving like this. 2 *v.* move in eddies.

**edelweiss** /'eɪdəlvaɪs/ *n.* white-flowered Alpine plant.

**Eden** /'i:d(ə)n/ *n.* (in full **Garden of Eden**) abode of Adam and Eve; delightful place or state.

**edentate** /i:'denteɪt/ *a.* having few or no teeth.

**edge** 1 *n.* cutting side of blade; sharpness; effectiveness; crest of ridge, line where two surfaces meet abruptly; rim, narrow surface of thin or flat object; boundary, brink. 2 *v.* sharpen; give or form border to; advance esp. gradually and obliquely. 3 **edgeways**, **edgewise**, with edge foremost or uppermost; **have**

**edging** /'edʒɪŋ/ n. border, fringe.

**edgy** /'edʒi:/ a. irritable, on edge.

**edible** /'edəb(ə)l/ 1 a. fit to be eaten. 2 n. edible thing. 3 **edibility** n.

**edict** /'i:dɪkt/ n. order proclaimed by authority.

**edifice** /'edɪfəs/ n. building, esp. large imposing one.

**edify** /'edəfaɪ/ v.t. improve morally. **edification** n.

**edit** /'edɪt/ v.t. prepare for publication; act as editor of; cut and collate (films etc.) to make unified sequence; reword, modify.

**edition** /ə'dɪʃ(ə)n/ n. edited or published form of a book etc.; copies of book or newspaper etc. issued at one time.

**editor** /'edətə(r)/ n. person who edits; person who directs writing of newspaper or section of one; head of department of publishing house.

**editorial** /edə'tɔ:rɪəl/ 1 a. of an editor. 2 n. newspaper article written or sanctioned by editor.

**educate** /'edjəkeɪt/ v.t. train or instruct mentally and morally; provide schooling for. **educable** a.; **education** n.; **educator** n.; **educational** a.

**educationist** /edjə'keɪʃənɪst/ n. (also **educationalist**) expert in educational methods.

**educe** /ə'dju:s/ v.t. bring out, develop. **eduction** n.

**Edwardian** /ed'wɔ:dɪən/ 1 a. of or characteristic of reign (1901-10) of Edward VII. 2 n. person of this period.

**EEC** abbr. European Economic Community.

**EEG** abbr. electroencephalogram.

**eel** n. snakelike fish.

**eerie** /'ɪərɪ/ a. strange; weird.

**efface** /ə'feɪs/ v.t. rub or wipe out; surpass, eclipse; make one*self* inconspicuous. **effacement** n.

**effect** /ə'fekt/ n. result, consequence; efficacy; impression; in pl. property; in pl. sounds and visual features as accompaniment to play etc. 2 v.t. bring about; accomplish.

**effective** /ə'fektɪv/ a. having effect; impressive; actual; existing.

**effectual** /ə'fektjʊəl/ a. answering its purpose; valid.

**effeminate** /ə'femənət/ a. (of a man) unmanly, womanish. **effeminacy** n.

**effervesce** /efə'ves/ v.i. give off bubbles of gas. **effervescent** a.; **effervescence** n.

**effete** /ə'fi:t/ a. worn out; feeble.

**efficacious** /efə'keɪʃəs/ a. producing desired effect. **efficacy** /'efəkəsɪ:/ n.

**efficient** /ə'fɪʃ(ə)nt/ a. productive with minimum waste of effort; competent, capable; producing desired result. **efficiency** n.

**effigy** /'efədʒɪ:/ n. sculpture or model of person.

**effloresce** /eflə'res/ v.i. burst into flower. **efflorescence** n.; **efflorescent** a.

**effluence** /'eflʊəns/ n. flowing out (of liquid etc.); what flows out.

**effluent** /'eflʊənt/ 1 a. flowing out. 2 n. stream flowing from lake etc.; outflow from sewage tank or waste product of industrial process etc.

**effluvium** /ə'flu:vɪəm/ n. (pl. **-via**) outflow of substance, esp. unpleasant or harmful one.

**effort** /'efət/ n. exertion; vigorous attempt; force exerted; colloq. something accomplished.

**effrontery** /ə'frʌntərɪ/ n. impudence.

**effulgent** /ə'fʌldʒ(ə)nt/ a. bright, radiant. **effulgence** n.

**effuse** /ə'fju:z/ v.t. pour forth.

**effusion** /ə'fju:ʒ(ə)n/ n. outpouring.

**effusive** /ə'fju:sɪv/ a. demonstrative; gushing.

**eft** n. newt.

**EFTA** abbr. European Free Trade Association.

**e.g.** abbr. for example.

**egalitarian** /əgælɪ'teərɪən/ 1 a. of or advocating equal rights for all. 2 n. egalitarian person. 3 **egalitarianism** n.

**egg**[1] n. oval body produced by female of birds etc., containing germ of new individual, esp. that of domestic fowl for eating; ovum. **egghead** colloq. intellectual; **egg-plant** plant with oval usu. purple fruit, this fruit used as vegetable; **egg-timer** device for timing boiling of egg.

**egg**[2] v.t. urge (person) on.

**eglantine** /'eglәntaɪn/ n. sweet-brier.

**ego** /'i:gəʊ or 'e-/ n. the self; part of mind

**egocentric** /egəʊ'sentrɪk/ a. self-centred.

**egoism** /'egəʊɪz(ə)m/ n. systematic selfishness; egotism. **egoist** n.; **egoistic** a.

**egotism** /'egətɪz(ə)m/ n. practice of talking about oneself; self-conceit. **egotist** n.; **egotistic** a.

**egregious** /ə'gri:dʒəs/ a. shocking; *arch.* remarkable.

**egress** /'i:gres/ n. going out; way out.

**egret** /'i:gret/ n. kind of white heron.

**Egyptian** /ə'dʒɪpʃ(ə)n/ 1 a. of Egypt. 2 n. native of Egypt; language of ancient Egyptians.

**Egyptology** /i:dʒɪp'tɒlədʒi:/ n. study of Egyptian antiquities. **Egyptologist** n.

**eh** /eɪ/ int. expressing inquiry, surprise, etc.

**eider** /'aɪdə(r)/ n. northern species of duck. **eiderdown** quilt stuffed with down or other soft material.

**eight** /eɪt/ n. & a. one more than seven; 8-oared rowing-boat or its crew. **eightsome reel** lively Sc. dance for 8 persons. **eighth** /eɪtθ/ a. & n.

**eighteen** /eɪ'ti:n/ n. & a. one more than seventeen; Aus. rules team. **eighteenth** a. & n.

**eighty** /'eɪtɪ/ n. & a. eight times ten. **eightieth** /'eɪtɪəθ/ a. & n.

**eisteddfod** /aɪ'steðvɒd/ n. Welsh congress of bards; national or local gathering for musical and literary competition.

**either** /'aɪðə(r) or 'i:ðə(r)/ 1 pron. & a. one or other of two; each of two. 2 adv. introducing first alternative; (with *neg.* or *interrog.*) any more than the other.

**ejaculate** /ə'dʒækjʊleɪt/ v. utter suddenly, cry out; eject (fluid etc. esp. semen) from body. **ejaculation** n.; **ejaculatory** a.

**eject** /ə'dʒekt/ v.t. throw out, expel; emit. **ejection** n.

**ejector seat** device for ejection of pilot from aircraft etc. in emergency.

**eke** v.t. (with *out*) make (living) or support (existence) with difficulty; supply deficiencies of.

**elaborate** 1 /ə'læbərət/ a. minutely worked out; highly developed or complicated. 2 /ə'læbəreɪt/ v.t. work out or explain in detail. 3 **elaboration** n.; **elaborative** a.; **elaborator** n.

***élan*** /eɪ'lɑ̃/ n. vivacity, dash. [F]

**eland** /'i:lənd/ n. large Afr. antelope.

**elapse** /ə'læps/ v.i. (of time) pass by.

**elastic** /ə'læstɪk/ 1 a. able to resume normal bulk or shape after dilation etc.; buoyant; flexible; springy. 2 n. elastic cord or fabric usu. woven with strips of rubber. 3 **elasticity** n.

**elasticated** /ə'læstəkeɪtɪd/ a. (of fabric) made elastic by weaving with rubber thread.

**elate** /ə'leɪt/ v.t. raise spirits of, excite. **elation** n.

**elbow** /'elbəʊ/ 1 n. joint between forearm and upper arm; part of sleeve of garment covering elbow; elbow-shaped thing. 2 v.t. thrust, jostle. 3 **elbow-grease** *joc.* vigorous polishing, hard work; **elbow-room** sufficient space to move or work in.

**elder**[1] /'eldə(r)/ 1 a. of greater age; senior. 2 n. person of greater age; official in early Christian and some modern Churches.

**elder**[2] /'eldə(r)/ n. white-flowered black-berried tree or shrub.

**elderly** /'eldəli:/ a. growing old.

**eldest** /'eldəst/ a. first-born; oldest surviving.

**eldorado** /eldə'rɑ:dəʊ/ n. (pl. -dos) fictitious region rich in gold.

**eldritch** /'eldrɪtʃ/ a. Sc. weird, hideous.

**elect** /ə'lekt/ 1 v.t. choose by voting; choose, decide. 2 a. chosen; (placed after n.) chosen but not yet in office.

**election** /ə'lekʃ(ə)n/ n. electing, being elected; process of electing esp. MPs.

**electioneer** /əlekʃə'nɪə(r)/ v.i. take part in election campaign.

**elective** /ə'lektɪv/ a. chosen or appointed by election; entitled to elect; optional.

**elector** /ə'lektə(r)/ n. person entitled to vote in election. **electoral** a.

**electorate** /ə'lektərət/ n. body of electors electing a representative.

**electric** /ə'lektrɪk/ a. of, charged with, or worked by electricity; startling. **electric blanket** one heated by internal wires; **electric chair** chair used for electrocution of criminals; **electric eel** eel-like fish able to give electric shock; **electric shock** effect of sudden discharge of electricity through body of person etc.

**electrical** /əˈlektrɪk(ə)l/ *a.* of or concerned with electricity; electric.

**electrician** /əlekˈtrɪʃ(ə)n/ *n.* person who installs and maintains electrical equipment professionally.

**electricity** /əlekˈtrɪsəti:/ *n.* form of energy present in protons and electrons; supply of electricity; science of electricity.

**electrify** /əˈlektrəfaɪ/ *v.t.* charge with electricity; convert to electric working; startle, excite. **electrification** *n.*

**electro-** /əˈlektrəʊ/ *in comb.* of or caused by electricity.

**electrocardiogram** /əlektrəʊˈkɑːdɪəgræm/ *n.* record of voltage generated by heartbeats. **electrocardiograph** *n.* instrument for taking such records.

**electroconvulsive** /əlektrəʊkənˈvʌlsɪv/ *a.* (of therapy) making use of convulsive response to electric shocks.

**electrocute** /əˈlektrəkjuːt/ *v.t.* kill or execute by electric shock. **electrocution** *n.*

**electrode** /əˈlektrəʊd/ *n.* conductor through which electricity enters or leaves electrolyte or gas or vacuum etc.

**electroencephalogram** /əlektrəʊenˈsefələgræm/ *n.* record of electrical activity of brain; **electroencephalograph** *n.* instrument for taking such record.

**electrolysis** /əlekˈtrɒləsəs/ *n.* chemical decomposition by action of electric current; breaking up of tumours, hairroots, etc. thus.

**electrolyte** /əˈlektrəlaɪt/ *n.* solution able to conduct electric current; substance that can dissolve to produce this. **electrolytic** /-ˈlɪt-/ *a.*

**electromagnet** /əlektrəʊˈmægnət/ *n.* piece of material made into magnet by electric current through coil surrounding it.

**electromagnetism** /əlektrəʊˈmægnətɪz(ə)m/ *n.* magnetic forces produced by electricity; study of these.

**electron** /əˈlektrɒn/ *n.* stable elementary particle with indivisible charge of negative electricity, found in all atoms and acting as carrier of electricity in solids. **electron microscope** one with high magnification, using focused beam of electrons.

**electronic** /əlekˈtrɒnɪk/ *a.* of electrons or electronics.

**electronics** *n. pl.* treated as *sing.* branch of physics and technology dealing with behaviour of electrons in vacuum or gas or semiconductor etc.

**electroplate** /əˈlektrəʊpleɪt/ **1** *v.t.* coat with chromium or silver etc. by electrolysis. **2** *n.* objects so produced.

**elegant** /ˈeləgənt/ *a.* graceful, tasteful; of refined luxury. **elegance** *n.*

**elegiac** /eləˈdʒaɪək/ *a.* suited to elegies, mournful.

**elegy** /ˈelədʒi:/ *n.* song or poem of lamentation, esp. for dead.

**element** /ˈeləmənt/ *n.* component part; *Chem.* any of substances which cannot be resolved by chemical means into simpler substances; *arch.* one of **the four elements** (earth, water, air, fire) formerly supposed to make up all matter; *Electr.* wire that gives out heat in electric heater, cooker, etc.; in *pl.* rudiments, first principles; in *pl.* atmospheric agencies. **in one's element** in one's preferred surroundings.

**elemental** /eləˈment(ə)l/ *a.* of or like the elements or the powers of nature; basic, essential.

**elementary** /eləˈmentəri:/ *a.* dealing with the simplest facts of subject, rudimentary, simple; that cannot be decomposed. **elementary particle** *Phys.* any of several subatomic particles not known to consist of simpler ones.

**elephant** /ˈeləf(ə)nt/ *n.* largest living mammal, with trunk and ivory tusks.

**elephantiasis** /eləfənˈtaɪəsəs/ *n.* skin disease causing gross enlargement of limb etc.

**elephantine** /eləˈfæntaɪn/ *a.* of elephants; huge, clumsy, unwieldy.

**elevate** /ˈeləveɪt/ *v.t.* lift up, raise; in *p.p.* exalted.

**elevation** /eləˈveɪʃ(ə)n/ *n.* elevating, being elevated; height above given level; angle above horizontal; drawing showing one side of building.

**elevator** /ˈeləvertə(r)/ *n.* hoisting-machine; movable part of tailplane for changing aircraft's altitude; *US* lift.

**eleven** /əˈlev(ə)n/ *n.* & *a.* one more than ten; side of 11 persons at cricket etc. **eleventh** *a.* & *n.*

**elf** /elf/ n. (pl. **elves**) mythical dwarfish being; mischievous child. **elfish** a.

**elfin** /'elfən/ a. of elves, elflike.

**elicit** /ə'lɪsɪt/ v.t. (usu. fig.) draw out.

**elide** /ə'laɪd/ v.t. omit in pronunciation.

**eligible** /'elədʒəb(ə)l/ a. fit or entitled to be chosen etc. (for); desirable or suitable esp. for marriage. **eligibility** n.

**eliminate** /ə'lɪmɪneɪt/ v.t. remove, get rid of; expel, exclude. **elimination** n.; **eliminator** n.

**elision** /ə'lɪʒ(ə)n/ n. omission of vowel or syllable in pronunciation.

**élite** /eɪ'liːt/ n. select group or class; the choice part (of).

**élitism** /eɪ'liːtɪz(ə)m/ n. advocacy of or reliance on dominance by a select group. **élitist** n.

**elixir** /ə'lɪksɪə(r)/ n. alchemist's preparation designed to change metal into gold or prolong life indefinitely.

**Elizabethan** /əlɪzə'biːθ(ə)n/ 1 a. of time of Elizabeth I or II. 2 n. person of this time.

**elk** n. large species of deer.

**ell** n. hist. measure of length (45 in.).

**ellipse** /ə'lɪps/ n. regular oval.

**ellipsis** /ə'lɪpsəs/ n. (pl. **-ses** /-siːz/) omission of words needed to complete construction or sense.

**elliptical** /ə'lɪptɪk(ə)l/ a. of or like an ellipse or ellipsis.

**elm** n. tree with rough serrated leaves; its wood.

**elocution** /elə'kjuːʃ(ə)n/ n. style or art of expressive speaking. **elocutionary** a.; **elocutionist** n.

**elongate** /'iːlɒŋɡeɪt/ v.t. lengthen, extend, draw out. **elongation** n.

**elope** /ə'ləʊp/ v.i. run away to get secretly married. **elopement** n.

**eloquence** /'eləkwəns/ n. fluent and powerful use of language. **eloquent** a.

**else** /els/ adv. besides; instead; otherwise; if not. **elsewhere** in or to some other place.

**elucidate** /ə'luːsɪdeɪt/ v.t. throw light on, explain. **elucidation** n.; **elucidator** n.; **elucidatory** a.

**elude** /ə'ljuːd/ v.t. escape adroitly from; avoid; baffle.

**elusive** /ə'luːsɪv/ a. difficult to grasp or perceive or define.

**elver** /'elvə(r)/ n. young eel.

**elves** pl. of **elf**.

**Elysium** /ə'lɪzɪəm/ n. Gk. myth. abode of blessed after death; place of ideal happiness. **Elysian** a.

**em** n. Print. unit of measurement equal to space occupied by m.

**emaciate** /ə'meɪsɪeɪt/ v.t. make thin or feeble. **emaciation** n.

**emanate** /'eməneɪt/ v.i. (cause to) originate or proceed from. **emanation** n.

**emancipate** /ə'mænsɪpeɪt/ v.t. set free from legal or social or political or moral restraint. **emancipation** n.; **emancipator** n.

**emasculate** 1 /ə'mæskjʊleɪt/ v.t. castrate; enfeeble. 2 /ə'mæskjʊlət/ a. castrated; effeminate. 3 **emasculation** n.; **emasculatory** a.

**embalm** /em'bɑːm/ v.t. preserve (corpse) from decay; preserve from oblivion; make fragrant. **embalmment** n.

**embankment** /em'bæŋkmənt/ n. mound of earth, or stone structure etc., confining river, or carrying road or railway.

**embargo** /em'bɑːɡəʊ/ n. (pl. **-goes**) order forbidding ships to enter or leave port; suspension of commerce; stoppage, prohibition.

**embark** /em'bɑːk/ v. put or go on board ship; enter on (course etc.).

**embarkation** /embɑː'keɪʃ(ə)n/ n. embarking on ship.

**embarrass** /em'bærəs/ v.t. make (person) feel awkward or ashamed; encumber. **embarrassment** n.

**embassy** /'embəsɪ/ n. ambassador's function or office or residence; deputation.

**embattle** /em'bæt(ə)l/ v.t. set in battle array; furnish with battlements.

**embed** /em'bed/ v.t. fix in surrounding mass.

**embellish** /em'belɪʃ/ v.t. beautify, adorn; make fictitious additions to. **embellishment** n.

**ember** /'embə(r)/ n. (usu. in pl.) small piece of fuel in dying fire.

**ember day** /'embə(r)/ any of appointed days of fasting and prayer in each of four seasons.

**embezzle** /em'bez(ə)l/ v.t. divert (money) fraudulently to one's own use. **embezzlement** n.

**embitter** /em'bɪtə(r)/ v.t. arouse bitter

feelings in, make bitter. **embitterment** n.

**emblazon** /em'bleɪz(ə)n/ v.t. blazon.

**emblem** /'embləm/ n. symbol; distinctive badge. **emblematic** a.

**embody** /em'bɒdi:/ v.t. give concrete form to; be an expression of; include, comprise. **embodiment** n.

**embolden** /em'bəʊld(ə)n/ v.t. encourage.

**embolism** /'embəlɪz(ə)m/ n. obstruction of artery etc. by blood-clot etc.

**emboss** /em'bɒs/ v.t. carve or decorate with design in relief. **embossment** n.

**embrace** /em'breɪs/ 1 v.t. hold closely in arms, enclose; accept, adopt; include. 2 n. holding in arms, clasp.

**embrasure** /em'breɪʒə(r)/ n. bevelling of wall at sides of window etc.; opening in parapet for gun.

**embrocation** /embrə'keɪʃ(ə)n/ n. liquid for rubbing on body to relieve muscular pain.

**embroider** /em'brɔɪdə(r)/ v.t. ornament with needlework; embellish. **embroidery** n.

**embroil** /em'brɔɪl/ v.t. bring into confusion; involve in hostility.

**embryo** /'embrɪəʊ/ n. (pl. -os) unborn or unhatched offspring; thing in rudimentary stage. **embryonic** /-'ɒn-/ a.

**emend** /ə'mend/ v.t. correct, remove errors from (text of book etc.). **emendation** n.; **emendatory** a.

**emerald** /'emər(ə)ld/ n. bright-green precious stone; colour of emerald.

**emerge** /ə'mɜːdʒ/ v.i. come up or out into view or notice (from); come out.

**emergency** /ə'mɜːdʒənsi/ n. sudden state of danger or conflict etc., requiring immediate action.

**emergent** /ə'mɜːdʒ(ə)nt/ a. emerging; (of nation) newly independent. **emergence** n.

**emeritus** /ə'merətəs/ a. retired and holding honorary title.

**emery** /'emərɪ/ n. coarse corundum for polishing metal etc.

**emetic** /ə'metɪk/ 1 a. that causes vomiting. 2 n. emetic medicine.

**emigrate** /'emɪgreɪt/ v.i. go to settle in another country. **emigrant** a. & n.; **emigration** n.

**émigré** /'emɪgreɪ/ n. emigrant, esp. political exile. [F]

**eminence** /'emɪnəns/ n. recognized superiority; rising ground; **Eminence** cardinal's title of honour.

**eminent** /'emɪnənt/ a. distinguished, notable.

**eminently** adv. particularly; notably.

**emir** /e'mɪə(r)/ n. title of various Muslim rulers.

**emirate** /'emɪərət/ n. position, reign, or domain of emir.

**emissary** /'emɪsərɪ/ n. person sent on special diplomatic mission.

**emission** /ə'mɪʃ(ə)n/ n. emitting; what is emitted. **emissive** a.

**emit** /ə'mɪt/ v.t. give out, send forth.

**emollient** /ə'mɒlɪənt/ 1 a. softening; soothing. 2 n. emollient substance.

**emolument** /ə'mɒljəmənt/ a. profit from employment; salary.

**emotion** /ə'məʊʃ(ə)n/ n. strong mental or instinctive feeling such as love or fear.

**emotional** /ə'məʊʃən(ə)l/ a. of or expressing emotion(s); liable to excessive emotion. **emotionalism** n.

**emotive** /ə'məʊtɪv/ a. of or tending to excite emotion.

**empanel** /em'pæn(ə)l/ v.t. enter (jury) on panel.

**empathy** /'empəθɪ/ n. power of identifying oneself mentally with person or object of contemplation. **empathize** v.

**emperor** /'empərə(r)/ n. ruler of empire.

**emphasis** /'emfəsəs/ n. (pl. -ses /-siːz/) significant stress on word(s); importance; vigour of expression etc.

**emphasize** /'emfəsaɪz/ v.t. lay stress on.

**emphatic** /əm'fætɪk/ a. forcible, strong; (of words) bearing emphasis.

**emphysema** /emfə'siːmə/ n. swelling due to air in body tissues.

**empire** /'empaɪə(r)/ n. extensive group of States or countries under single supreme authority; supreme dominion; large commercial etc. organization owned or directed by one person.

**empirical** /em'pɪrɪk(ə)l/ a. based or acting on observation and experiment, not on theory. **empiricism** n.; **empiricist** n.

**emplacement** /em'pleɪsmənt/ n. putting in position; platform for gun(s).

**employ** /em'plɔɪ/ 1 v.t. use services of esp. for wages; use (thing, time, ener-

# employee

**gies,** etc.); find occupation for. **2** *n.* **in the employ of** employed by.

**employee** /emplɔɪ'iː/ *n.* person employed for wages.

**employer** /em'plɔɪə(r)/ *n.* person who employs, esp. others for wages.

**employment** /em'plɔɪmənt/ *n.* employing or being employed; regular occupation or business.

**emporium** /em'pɔːrɪəm/ *n.* centre of commerce; large shop, store.

**empower** /em'paʊə(r)/ *v.t.* give power or authority to.

**empress** /'emprəs/ *n.* wife or widow of emperor; woman emperor.

**empty** /'emptɪ/ **1** *a.* containing nothing; devoid (*of*); vacant; *colloq.* hungry; vacuous, foolish. **2** *v.* remove contents of; transfer (contents of); become empty; (of river) discharge itself. **3** *n.* emptied box or bottle etc.

**emu** /'iːmjuː/ *n.* large flightless Aus. bird. **emu bush** Aus. shrub eaten by emu; **emu parade** *Aus.* group of soldiers or schoolchildren etc. picking up litter; **emu-wren** small Aus. bird with tail feathers like those of emu.

**emulate** /'emjʊleɪt/ *v.t.* try to equal or excel; imitate. **emulation** *n.*; **emulative** *a.*; **emulator** *n.*

**emulous** /'emjʊləs/ *a.* zealously imitative (*of*); actuated by rivalry.

**emulsify** /ɪ'mʌlsɪfaɪ/ *v.t.* make emulsion of.

**emulsion** /ɪ'mʌlʃ(ə)n/ *n.* fine dispersion of one liquid in another, esp. as paint or medicine etc.

**en** *n.* *Print.* unit of measurement equal to space occupied by n.

**enable** /ɪ'neɪb(ə)l/ *v.t.* supply with means (*to do*); make possible.

**enact** /ɪ'nækt/ *v.t.* ordain; play (part); make into legislative act. **enactment** *n.*

**enamel** /ɪ'næm(ə)l/ **1** *n.* glasslike coating on metal; any hard smooth coating; hard coating of teeth. **2** *v.t.* coat with enamel.

**enamour** /ɪ'næmə(r)/ *v.t.* inspire with love; make fond of.

**en bloc** /ɑ̃ 'blɒk/ in a block, all at the same time. [F]

**encamp** /en'kæmp/ *v.* settle in (esp. military) camp. **encampment** *n.*

**encase** /en'keɪs/ *v.t.* confine (as) in a case.

**encaustic** /en'kɒstɪk/ **1** *a.* (of painting) with wax colours fixed by heat; (of tile etc.) inlaid with coloured clays burnt in. **2** *n.* art or product of this.

**encephalitis** /ensefə'laɪtɪs/ *n.* inflammation of brain.

**enchain** /en'tʃeɪn/ *v.t.* chain up; hold fast.

**enchant** /en'tʃɑːnt/ or -'tʃænt/ *v.t.* bewitch; delight. **enchantment** *n.*; **enchantress** *n.*

**encircle** /en'sɜːk(ə)l/ *v.t.* surround. **encirclement** *n.*

**enclave** /'enkleɪv/ *n.* territory of one State surrounded by that of another.

**enclitic** /en'klɪtɪk/ **1** *a.* (of word) so unemphatic as to be pronounced as if part of preceding word. **2** *n.* enclitic word.

**enclose** /en'kləʊz/ *v.t.* shut in on all sides; surround, fence in; shut up in receptacle (esp. in envelope besides letter); in *p.p.* (of religious community) secluded from outside world.

**enclosure** /en'kləʊʒə(r)/ *n.* enclosing; enclosed space or area; thing enclosed.

**encode** /en'kəʊd/ *v.t.* put into code.

**encomium** /en'kəʊmɪəm/ *n.* (*pl.* **-iums** or **-ia**) formal or high-flown praise.

**encompass** /en'kʌmpəs/ *v.t.* surround, contain.

**encore** /'ɒŋkɔː(r)/ **1** *n.* call for further performance or repetition of item; such item. **2** *v.t.* call for repetition of or by. **3** *int.* again.

**encounter** /en'kaʊntə(r)/ **1** *v.t.* meet by chance; meet as adversary. **2** *n.* meeting by chance or in combat.

**encourage** /en'kʌrɪdʒ/ *v.t.* give courage to; urge; stimulate; promote. **encouragement** *n.*

**encroach** /en'krəʊtʃ/ *v.i.* intrude on others' territory etc. **encroachment** *n.*

**encrust** *v.* /en'krʌst/ cover with or form crust; overlay with crust of silver etc.

**encumber** /en'kʌmbə(r)/ *v.t.* be burden to; hamper, impede.

**encumbrance** /en'kʌmbrəns/ *n.* burden, impediment.

**encyclical** /en'sɪklɪk(ə)l/ **1** *a.* for wide circulation. **2** *n.* papal encyclical letter.

**encyclopaedia** /ensaɪklə'piːdɪə/ *n.* (also **encyclopedia**) book of information on many branches of know-

**end**          182          **engraving**

ledge or on many aspects of one subject. **encyclopaedic** *a*.

**end 1** *n*. limit; farthest point; extreme point or part; remnant; conclusion, latter part; destruction; death; result; object. **2** *v*. bring or come to end. **3 endpaper** blank leaf of paper at beginning or end of book; **end-product** final product of process of manufacture etc.; **end up** reach certain state or action eventually. **4 endways, endwise,** *advs*.

**endanger** /en'deɪndʒə(r)/ *v.t.* bring into danger.

**endear** /en'dɪə(r)/ *v.t.* make dear (*to*).

**endearment** *n*. act or words expressing affection.

**endeavour** /en'devə(r)/ **1** *v.i.* try, strive. **2** *n*. attempt, effort.

**endemic** /en'demɪk/ **1** *a*. regularly found among (specified) people or in (specified) area etc. **2** *n*. endemic disease or plant. **3 endemically** *adv*.

**ending** /'endɪŋ/ *n*. end of word or verse or story.

**endive** /'endaɪv/ *n*. curly-leaved plant used as salad.

**endless** /'endləs/ *a*. infinite; continual; incessant.

**endo-** *in comb.* internal.

**endocrine** /'endəʊkraɪn/ *a*. (of gland) secreting directly into blood.

**endogenous** /en'dɒdʒənəs/ *a*. growing or originating from within.

**endorse** /en'dɔːs/ *v.t.* confirm, approve; write on back of (document), esp. sign name on back of (cheque etc.); enter details of offence on (driving-licence etc.). **endorsement** *n*.

**endow** /en'daʊ/ *v.t.* give permanent income to; (esp. in *p.p.*) provide with talent or ability. **endowment** *n*.

**endue** /en'djuː/ *v.t.* provide (*with* quality etc.).

**endurance** /en'djʊərəns/ *n*. habit or power of enduring.

**endure** /en'djʊə(r)/ *v*. undergo; bear; last.

**enema** /'enəmə/ *n*. injection of liquid etc. into rectum esp. to expel its contents; liquid or syringe used for this.

**enemy** /'enəmɪ/ **1** *n*. person actively hostile to another; hostile army or nation; member of this; adversary, opponent. **2** *a*. of or belonging to enemy.

**energetic** /enə'dʒetɪk/ *a*. full of energy; powerfully active.

**energize** /'enədʒaɪz/ *v.t.* give energy to.

**energy** /'enədʒɪ/ *n*. force, vigour, activity; ability of matter or radiation to do work.

**enervate** /'enəveɪt/ *v.t.* deprive of vigour. **enervation** *n*.

**enfant terrible** /ɑ̃fɑ̃ te'riːbl/ person who causes embarrassment by indiscreet behaviour; unruly child. [F]

**enfeeble** /en'fiːb(ə)l/ *v.t.* make feeble. **enfeeblement** *n*.

**enfilade** /enfɪ'leɪd/ **1** *n*. gunfire directed along line from end to end. **2** *v.t.* direct enfilade at.

**enfold** /en'fəʊld/ *v.t.* wrap; embrace.

**enforce** /en'fɔːs/ *v.t.* compel observance of; persist in; impose. **enforcement** *n*.

**enfranchise** /en'fræntʃaɪz/ *v.t.* give (person) right to vote; free (slave etc.). **enfranchisement** /-tʃɪz- / *n*.

**engage** /en'geɪdʒ/ *v*. employ or hire; occupy; bind by contract or promise (esp. of marriage); cause parts (of gear) to interlock; fit, interlock (*with*); bring or come into conflict with enemy; take part *in*; pledge oneself. **engagement** *n*.

**engender** /en'dʒendə(r)/ *v.t.* give rise to.

**engine** /'endʒɪn/ *n*. mechanical contrivance of parts working together esp. as a source of mechanical power; railway locomotive; means, instrument.

**engineer** /endʒɪ'nɪə(r)/ **1** *n*. person who works in a branch of engineering; person who makes or is in charge of engines etc.; person who designs and constructs military works. **2** *v*. construct or manage as engineer; *colloq*. contrive, bring about.

**engineering** /endʒɪ'nɪərɪŋ/ *n*. application of science for control and use of power in machines; road-building etc.

**English** /'ɪŋglɪʃ/ **1** *a*. of England. **2** *n*. language of England, now used in UK, Australia, NZ, US, and most Commonwealth countries; *the* people of England. **3 Englishman, Englishwoman,** native of England.

**engraft** /en'grɑːft/ *v.t.* insert or incorporate *into*, (*up*)*on*.

**engrave** /en'greɪv/ *v.t.* inscribe or cut (design) on hard surface; inscribe (surface) thus; impress deeply (*on* memory etc.).

**engraving** *n*. print made from engraved plate.

**engross** /enˈgrəʊs/ v.t. fully occupy; write in large letters or in legal form. **engrossment** n.

**engulf** /enˈgʌlf/ v.t. flow over and swamp, overwhelm.

**enhance** /enˈhɑːns/ or -ˈhæns/ v.t. heighten, intensify. **enhancement** n.

**enigma** /əˈnɪgmə/ n. puzzling person or thing; riddle. **enigmatic** a.

**enjoin** /enˈdʒɔɪn/ v.t. command, order.

**enjoy** /enˈdʒɔɪ/ v.t. find pleasure in; have use or benefit of; experience. **enjoy oneself** find pleasure, be happy. **enjoyable** a.; **enjoyment** n.

**enkindle** /enˈkɪnd(ə)l/ v.t. cause to blaze up.

**enlarge** /enˈlɑːdʒ/ v. expand; grow larger; describe in greater detail; reproduce on larger scale. **enlargement** n.

**enlighten** /enˈlaɪt(ə)n/ v.t. instruct; inform; free from superstition. **enlightenment** n.

**enlist** /enˈlɪst/ v. enrol for military service; get co-operation or support of. **enlistment** n.

**enliven** /enˈlaɪv(ə)n/ v.t. make lively or cheerful; inspirit. **enlivenment** n.

**en masse** /ɑ̃ ˈmæs/ all together. [F]

**enmesh** /enˈmeʃ/ v.t. entangle (as) in net.

**enmity** /ˈenmətɪ/ n. hatred, state of being an enemy.

**ennoble** /ɪˈnəʊb(ə)l/ v.t. make noble. **ennoblement** n.

**ennui** /ˈɒnwiː/ n. boredom.

**enormity** /əˈnɔːmətɪ/ n. great wickedness; crime, monstrous offence.

**enormous** /əˈnɔːməs/ a. very large.

**enough** /əˈnʌf/ 1 a. as much or as many as required. 2 n. amount or quantity that is enough. 3 adv. to required degree; fairly; very, quite.

**enquire, enquiry** vars. of **inquire, inquiry**.

**enrage** /enˈreɪdʒ/ v.t. make furious.

**enrapture** /enˈræptʃə(r)/ v.t. delight intensely.

**enrich** /enˈrɪtʃ/ v.t. make rich(er). **enrichment** n.

**enrol** /enˈrəʊl/ v.t. insert name in list; enlist; incorporate as member; enrol oneself. **enrolment** n.

**en route** /ɑ̃ ruːt/ on the way. [F]

**ensconce** /enˈskɒns/ v.t. establish in snug place.

**ensemble** /ɑ̃ˈsɑ̃b(ə)l/ n. thing viewed as whole; set of matching items of dress; group of musicians or dancers etc.; *Mus.* concerted passage for ensemble.

**enshrine** /enˈʃraɪn/ v.t. enclose (as) in shrine; serve as shrine for.

**enshroud** /enˈʃraʊd/ v.t. cover completely (as) with shroud.

**ensign** /ˈensaɪn/ n. banner, flag, esp. military or naval flag of nation; *hist.* lowest commissioned officer in infantry; *US* lowest commissioned officer in navy.

**ensilage** /ˈensɪlɪdʒ/ n. silage.

**enslave** /enˈsleɪv/ v.t. make slave of. **enslavement** n.

**ensnare** /enˈsneə(r)/ v.t. entrap.

**ensue** /enˈsjuː/ v. happen later or as a result.

**ensure** /enˈʃʊə(r)/ v.t. make safe or certain; secure.

**ENT** abbr. *Med.* ear, nose, and throat.

**entail** /enˈteɪl/ 1 v.t. necessitate or involve unavoidably; settle (landed estate) on persons successively so that it cannot be bequeathed at pleasure. 2 n. entailing; entailed estate.

**entangle** /enˈtæŋg(ə)l/ v.t. cause to get caught in snare etc.; involve in difficulties; complicate. **entanglement** n.

**entente** /ɒnˈtɒnt/ n. friendly understanding esp. between States.

**enter** /ˈentə(r)/ v. go or come in or into; come on stage; penetrate; put (name, fact, etc.) into list or record etc.; become member of; name, or name oneself, as competitor *for*; admit, obtain admission for. **enter into** engage in, sympathize with, form part of, bind oneself by; **enter (up)on** assume possession of, begin, begin to deal with.

**enteric** /enˈterɪk/ a. of intestines.

**enteritis** /entəˈraɪtəs/ n. inflammation of intestines.

**enterprise** /ˈentəpraɪz/ n. bold undertaking; readiness to engage in enterprises.

**enterprising** a. showing courage or imaginativeness.

**entertain** /entəˈteɪn/ v.t. amuse; receive as guest; harbour; admit (idea) to consideration.

**entertainment** n. entertaining; thing that entertains, esp. before public audience.

**enthral** /enˈθrɔːl/ v.t. captivate; please greatly. **enthralment** n.

**enthrone** /enˈθrəʊn/ v.t. place on throne. **enthronement** n.

**enthuse** /enˈθjuːz/ v. colloq. show or fill with enthusiasm.

**enthusiasm** /enˈθjuːzɪæz(ə)m/ n. great eagerness, zeal. **enthusiast** n.; **enthusiastic** a.

**entice** /enˈtaɪs/ v.t. persuade by offer of pleasure or reward. **enticement** n.

**entire** /enˈtaɪə(r)/ a. complete; not broken; in one piece.

**entirely** adv. wholly.

**entirety** /enˈtaɪərəti/ n. completeness; sum total.

**entitle** /enˈtaɪt(ə)l/ v.t. give right or claim to; give title to. **entitlement** n.

**entity** /ˈentəti/ n. thing with real existence; thing's existence.

**entomb** /enˈtuːm/ v.t. place in tomb; serve as tomb for. **entombment** n.

**entomology** /entəˈmɒlədʒi/ n. study of insects. **entomological** a.; **entomologist** n.

**entourage** /ˈɒntuːrɑːʒ/ n. people attending important person.

**entr'acte** /ˈɒntrækt/ n. (performance in) interval in theatre etc.

**entrails** /ˈentreɪlz/ n.pl. inner parts; intestines.

**entrance**[1] /ˈentrəns/ n. coming or going in; right of admission; door or passage for entering.

**entrance**[2] /enˈtrɑːns or -ˈtræns/ v.t. enchant, delight; put into trance.

**entrant** /ˈentrənt/ n. person who enters examination or profession etc.

**entrap** /enˈtræp/ v.t. catch (as) in trap.

**entreat** /enˈtriːt/ v.t. ask earnestly; beg.

**entreaty** /enˈtriːti/ n. earnest request.

**entrecôte** /ˈɒntrəkəʊt/ n. boned steak cut off sirloin.

**entrée** /ˈɒntreɪ/ n. right of admission; dish served between fish and meat courses; US main dish of meal.

**entrench** /enˈtrentʃ/ v.t. establish firmly; surround or fortify with trench. **entrenchment** n.

**entrepreneur** /ɒntrəprəˈnɜː(r)/ n. person who undertakes an enterprise, with chance of profit or loss; contractor. **entrepreneurial** a.

**entropy** /ˈentrəpi/ n. measure of the unavailability of a system's thermal energy for conversion into mechanical work; measure of the disorganization of the universe.

**entrust** /enˈtrʌst/ v.t. charge with (duty, object of care); confide to.

**entry** /ˈentri:/ n. coming or going in; place of entrance; alley; entering, item entered.

**entwine** /enˈtwaɪn/ v.t. twine round, interweave.

**enumerate** /əˈnjuːməreɪt/ v.t. count; mention separately. **enumeration** n.; **enumerative** a.; **enumerator** n.

**enunciate** /əˈnʌnsɪeɪt/ v.t. pronounce (words); state definitely. **enunciation** n.; **enunciative** a.; **enunciator** n.

**envelop** /enˈveləp/ v.t. wrap up, cover; surround (enemy). **envelopment** n.

**envelope** /ˈenvələʊp/ n. folded paper cover for letter etc.; wrapper, covering.

**enviable** /ˈenvɪəb(ə)l/ a. such as to excite envy.

**envious** /ˈenvɪəs/ a. feeling or showing envy.

**environment** /enˈvaɪərənmənt/ n. surroundings; surrounding objects or conditions etc. **environmental** a.

**environmentalist** /envaɪərənˈmentəlɪst/ n. person who is concerned with protection of natural environment.

**environs** /enˈvaɪərənz/ n.pl. district round town etc.

**envisage** /enˈvɪzɪdʒ/ v.t. visualize, imagine, contemplate.

**envoy** /ˈenvɔɪ/ n. messenger; diplomatic minister ranking below ambassador.

**envy** /ˈenvi/ 1 n. feeling of discontented longing aroused by another's better fortune etc.; object of this. 2 v.t. feel envy of.

**enwrap** /enˈræp/ v.t. wrap, enfold.

**enzyme** /ˈenzaɪm/ n. Chem. substance produced by living cells catalysing reactions in organism.

**epaulette** /epəˈlet/ n. ornamental shoulder-piece worn on uniform.

**ephedrine** /ˈefədriːn/ n. alkaloid drug used to relieve asthma etc.

**ephemera** /əˈfemərə/ n.pl. things of only short-lived use.

**ephemeral** /əˈfemər(ə)l/ a. short-lived, transitory. **ephemerality** n.

**epic** /ˈepɪk/ 1 n. long poem narrating adventures of heroic figure etc.; book or film based on this. 2 a. like an epic, grand.

**epicene** /'epɪsiːn/ a. having characteristics of both sexes.

**epicentre** /'epɪsentə(r)/ n. point at which earthquake reaches earth's surface.

**epicure** /'epɪkjʊə(r)/ n. person with refined taste in food and drink. **epicurism** n.

**epicurean** /epɪkjuː'riːən/ 1 a. fond of pleasure and luxury. 2 n. person of epicurean tastes. 3 **epicureanism** n.

**epidemic** /epə'demɪk/ 1 a. (of disease) prevalent among community at particular time. 2 n. epidemic disease.

**epidemiology** /epədiːmiː'ɒlədʒi:/ n. branch of medicine concerned with epidemics.

**epidermis** /epɪ'dɜːməs/ n. outer layer of skin.

**epidiascope** /epɪ'daɪəskəʊp/ n. optical projector giving images of both opaque and transparent objects.

**epidural** /epɪ'djʊər(ə)l/ 1 a. (of anaesthetic) injected into matter round spinal cord. 2 n. epidural injection.

**epiglottis** /epɪ'glɒtəs/ n. cartilage at root of tongue, depressed in swallowing. **epiglottal** a.

**epigram** /'epɪgræm/ n. short poem with witty ending; pointed saying. **epigrammatic** a.; **epigrammatist** n.

**epigraph** /'epɪgrɑːf or -græf/ n. inscription. **epigraphic** a.; **epigraphy** n.

**epilepsy** /'epəlepsi:/ n. nervous disorder with recurrent attacks of unconsciousness and convulsions etc. **epileptic** a. & n.

**epilogue** /'epɪlɒg/ n. concluding part of book etc.; short speech at end of play etc.

**Epiphany** /ə'pɪfəni:/ n. festival (6 Jan.) commemorating manifestation of Christ to Magi.

**epiphyte** /'epɪfaɪt/ n. plant growing on another; vegetable parasite on animal.

**episcopacy** /ə'pɪskəpəsi:/ n. episcopal government; bishops collectively.

**episcopal** /ə'pɪskəp(ə)l/ a. (of church) governed by bishops.

**episcopalian** /əpɪskə'peɪliːən/ 1 a. of episcopacy. 2 n. adherent of episcopacy; member of Episcopal Church. 3 **episcopalianism** n.

**episcopate** /ə'pɪskəpət/ n. office or tenure of bishop; bishops collectively.

**episode** /'epəsəʊd/ n. incident in narrative; part of serial story; incidental narrative or digression. **episodic** /-'sɒd-/ a.

**epistemology** /əpɪstə'mɒlədʒi:/ n. theory of method or grounds of knowledge. **epistemological** a.

**epistle** /ə'pɪs(ə)l/ n. letter; poem etc. in form of letter.

**epistolary** /ə'pɪstələri:/ a. of or suitable for letters.

**epitaph** /'epɪtɑːf/ n. words inscribed on or suitable for tomb.

**epithelium** /epɪ'θiːliːəm/ n. Biol. tissue forming outer layer of body or lining open cavity. **epithelial** a.

**epithet** /'epəθet/ n. adjective expressing quality or attribute; descriptive word.

**epitome** /ə'pɪtəmi:/ n. person who embodies a quality etc. **epitomize** v.t.

**EPNS** abbr. electroplated nickel silver.

**epoch** /'iːpɒk/ n. period marked by special events; beginning of era. **epoch-making** notable, significant. **epochal** a.

**eponym** /'epənɪm/ n. person after whom place etc. is named. **eponymous** /ə'pɒnəməs/ a.

**epoxy resin** /ɪ'pɒksɪ/ synthetic thermosetting resin.

**Epsom salts** /'epsəm/ magnesium sulphate used as purgative.

**equable** /'ekwəb(ə)l/ a. even; moderate; not easily disturbed. **equability** n.

**equal** /'iːkw(ə)l/ 1 a. same in number or size or merit etc.; evenly matched; having same rights or status. 2 n. person etc. equal to another. 3 v.t. be equal to; do something that is equal to.

**equality** /ɪ'kwɒləti:/ n. being equal.

**equalize** /'iːkwəlaɪz/ v. make or become equal; (in games) equal opponent's score. **equalization** n.

**equanimity** /ekwə'nɪməti:/ n. composure, calm.

**equate** /iː'kweɪt/ v.t. regard as equal or equivalent.

**equation** /iː'kweɪʒ(ə)n/ n. making equal, balancing; Math. statement of equality between two expressions; Chem. formula representing chemical reaction by means of symbols.

**equator** /ə'kweɪtə(r)/ n. imaginary line round the earth or other body, equidistant from poles.

**equatorial** /ekwə'tɔːrɪəl/ *a.* of or near the equator.

**equerry** /'ekwəri/ *n.* officer of British royal household, attending sovereign etc.

**equestrian** /ɪ'kwestrɪən/ 1 *a.* of horse-riding; on horseback. 2 *n.* rider or performer on horseback. 3 **equestrianism** *n.*

**equiangular** /iːkwiː'æŋɡjələ(r)/ *a.* having equal angles.

**equidistant** /iːkwiː'dɪst(ə)nt/ *a.* at equal distances.

**equilateral** /iːkwiː'lætər(ə)l/ *a.* having all sides equal.

**equilibrium** /iːkwə'lɪbrɪəm/ *n.* (*pl.* -ia *or* -iums) state of balance; composure.

**equine** /'ekwaɪn/ *a.* of or like horse.

**equinoctial** /iːkwɪ'nɒkʃ(ə)l/ 1 *a.* of or happening at or near equinox. 2 *n.* celestial equator.

**equinox** /'ekwənɒks/ *n.* time or date at which sun crosses equator and day and night are of equal length.

**equip** /ɪ'kwɪp/ *v.t.* supply with what is needed.

**equipage** /'ekwəpɪdʒ/ *n.* requisites, outfit; carriage, horses, and attendants.

**equipment** /ɪ'kwɪpmənt/ *n.* equipping; necessary outfit, tools, apparatus, etc.

**equipoise** /'ekwəpɔɪz/ *n.* equilibrium; counterbalancing thing.

**equitable** /'ekwətəb(ə)l/ *a.* fair, just; valid in equity.

**equitation** /ekwə'teɪʃ(ə)n/ *n.* riding on horse.

**equity** /'ekwəti/ *n.* fairness; principles of justice supplementing law; value of shares issued by company; in *pl.* stocks and shares not bearing fixed interest.

**equivalent** /ɪ'kwɪvələnt/ 1 *a.* equal in value or meaning etc.; corresponding. 2 *n.* equivalent amount etc. 3 **equivalence** *n.*

**equivocal** /ɪ'kwɪvək(ə)l/ *a.* of double or doubtful meaning; dubious.

**equivocate** /ɪ'kwɪvəkeɪt/ *v.i.* use words ambiguously, esp. to conceal truth. **equivocation** *n.*

**ER** *abbr.* Queen Elizabeth (*Elizabeth Regina*); King Edward (*Edwardus Rex*).

**era** /'ɪərə/ *n.* system of chronology starting from particular point; historical or other period.

**eradicate** /ɪ'rædəkeɪt/ *v.t.* root out, get rid of. **eradication** *n.*

**erase** /ɪ'reɪz/ *v.t.* rub out, obliterate.

**eraser** *n.* piece of rubber etc. for rubbing out writing etc.

**erasure** /ɪ'reɪʒə(r)/ *n.* rubbing out; word etc. rubbed out.

**ere** /eə(r)/ *prep.* & *conj. arch.* before.

**erect** /ɪ'rekt/ 1 *a.* upright, vertical; (of part of body) enlarged and rigid esp. from sexual excitement. 2 *v.t.* raise, set upright; build. 3 **erection** *n.*; **erector** *n.*

**erectile** /ɪ'rektaɪl/ *a.* that can become erect.

**erg** *n. Phys.* unit of work or energy.

**ergo** /'ɜːɡəʊ/ *adv.* therefore.

**ergonomics** /ɜːɡə'nɒmɪks/ *n.* study of efficiency of persons in their working environment. **ergonomist** *n.*

**ergot** /'ɜːɡət/ *n.* disease of rye etc. caused by fungus.

**Erin** /'erɪn/ *n. poet.* Ireland.

**ermine** /'ɜːmɪn/ *n.* animal of weasel kind; its white winter fur.

**erne** /ɜːn/ *n.* sea eagle.

**erode** /ɪ'rəʊd/ *v.t.* eat away, wear out; destroy surface of.

**erogenous** /ɪ'rɒdʒənəs/ *a.* giving rise to sexual excitement.

**erosion** /ɪ'rəʊʒ(ə)n/ *n.* eroding or being eroded. **erosive** *a.*

**erotic** /ɪ'rɒtɪk/ *a.* of or arousing sexual desire or excitement. **eroticism** *n.*

**erotica** /ɪ'rɒtɪkə/ *n.pl.* erotic literature or art.

**err** /ɜː(r)/ *v.i.* make mistakes; be incorrect; sin.

**errand** /'erənd/ *n.* short journey on which person goes or is sent with message etc.; object of journey.

**errant** /'erənt/ *a.* erring; roaming in quest of adventure.

**erratic** /ɪ'rætɪk/ *a.* irregular or uncertain in movement or conduct etc.

**erratum** /ɪ'rɑːtəm/ *n.* (*pl.* -ta) error in printing etc.

**erroneous** /ɪ'rəʊnɪəs/ *a.* incorrect.

**error** /'erə(r)/ *n.* mistake; condition of being wrong in opinion or conduct; wrong opinion; amount of inaccuracy in calculation or measurement.

**ersatz** /'ɜːzæts/ *a* & *n.* substitute; imitation.

**erstwhile** /'ɜːstwaɪl/ *adv.* & *a. arch.* former(ly).

**eructation** /erʌk'teɪʃ(ə)n/ *n.* belch.

**erudite** /'eru:daɪt/ a. learned. **erudition** /-dɪʃ-/ n.

**erupt** /ə'rʌpt/ v.i. break out or through; (of volcano) shoot out lava etc.; (of rash) appear on skin. **eruption** n.; **eruptive** a.

**erysipelas** /erə'sɪpələs/ n. acute inflammation of skin, with deep red coloration.

**escalate** /'eskəleɪt/ v. increase or develop by successive stages. **escalation** n.

**escalator** /'eskəleɪtə(r)/ n. moving staircase.

**escalope** /'eskəlɒp/ n. thin slice of meat, esp. veal.

**escapade** /'eskəpeɪd/ n. piece of irresponsible or unorthodox conduct.

**escape** /ə'skeɪp/ 1 v. get free; find way out; leak; elude, avoid. 2 n. escaping; leakage; outlet; fire-escape. 3 **escape clause** clause releasing contracting party from obligation in specified circumstances.

**escapee** /eskeɪ'pi:/ n. person who has escaped.

**escapism** /ə'skeɪpɪz(ə)m/ n. tendency to seek distraction or relief from reality. **escapist** a. & n.

**escapology** /eskə'pɒlədʒi/ n. methods and technique of escaping from confinement. **escapologist** n.

**escarpment** /əs'kɑ:pmənt/ n. long steep slope at edge of plateau etc.

**eschatology** /eskə'tɒlədʒi/ n. doctrine of death and afterlife. **eschatological** a.

**escheat** /əs'tʃi:t/ 1 n. lapse of property to Crown etc.; property so lapsing. 2 v. revert by escheat; confiscate.

**eschew** /əs'tʃu:/ v.t. abstain from.

**escort** 1 /'eskɔ:t/ n. body of armed men as guard; person(s) etc. accompanying another for protection, or as courtesy, etc.; person accompanying another of opposite sex socially. 2 v.t. /ə'skɔ:t/ act as escort to.

**escritoire** /eskrɪ'twɑ:(r)/ n. writing-desk with drawers etc.

**esculent** /'eskjələnt/ 1 a. fit for food. 2 n. esculent substance.

**escutcheon** /ə'skʌtʃ(ə)n/ n. shield bearing coat of arms. **blot on one's escutcheon** stain on one's reputation.

**Eskimo** /'eskəməʊ/ 1 n. (pl. -mos) member of people inhabiting Arctic coasts of N. Amer. etc.; their language. 2 a. of the Eskimos or their language.

**Esky** /'eskɪ/ n. (P) Aus. portable insulated container for cold food and drink.

**esoteric** /i:səʊ'terɪk/ a. intelligible only to those with special knowledge.

**ESP** abbr. extra-sensory perception.

**espadrille** /espə'drɪl/ n. light canvas shoe with plaited fibre sole.

**espalier** /ə'spælɪə(r)/ n. framework for training tree etc.; tree trained on espalier.

**esparto** /ə'spɑ:təʊ/ n. kind of grass used in paper-making.

**especial** /ə'speʃ(ə)l/ a. special, exceptional.

**especially** adv. particularly, more than in other cases.

**Esperanto** /espə'ræntəʊ/ n. artificial universal language.

**espionage** /'espɪənɑ:ʒ/ n. spying or using spies.

**esplanade** /'espləneɪd/ n. level space, esp. in front of fortress or used as public promenade.

**espousal** /ə'spaʊz(ə)l/ n. espousing; (usu. in pl.) marriage, betrothal.

**espouse** /ə'spaʊz/ v.t. support (cause); marry.

**espresso** /e'spresəʊ/ n. (pl. -os) coffee made under steam pressure; machine for making this.

*esprit de corps* /espri: də 'kɔ:(r)/ regard for honour and interests of body one belongs to. [F]

**espy** /ə'spaɪ/ v.t. catch sight of.

**Esq.** abbr. Esquire.

**esquire** /ə'skwaɪə(r)/ n. title of courtesy appended in writing to man's name; arch. squire.

**essay** 1 /'eseɪ/ n. short prose composition on a subject; attempt. 2 /e'seɪ/ v.t. attempt.

**essayist** /'eseɪəst/ n. writer of essays.

**essence** /'es(ə)ns/ n. all that makes a thing what it is; indispensable quality or element; extract obtained by distillation etc.; perfume, scent.

**essential** /ə'senʃ(ə)l/ 1 a. necessary, indispensable; of or constituting a thing's essence. 2 n. indispensable element or thing. 3 **essential oil** volatile oil with characteristic odour etc.

**establish** /ə'stæblɪʃ/ v.t. set up; settle;

**establishment** *n.* establishing or being established; public institution; house of business; staff, household, etc.; church system established by law. **the Establishment** social group exercising authority or influence and resisting change.

**estate** /ə'steɪt/ *n.* landed property; residential or industrial district planned as a whole; person's collective assets and liabilities; order or class forming part of body politic. **estate agent** person whose business is sale and letting of houses and land; **estate duty** death duty.

**esteem** /ə'sti:m/ 1 *v.t.* think highly of; consider. 2 *n.* favourable opinion.

**ester** /estə(r)/ *n.* compound formed by interaction of an acid and an alcohol.

**estimable** /'estəməb(ə)l/ *a.* worthy of esteem.

**estimate** 1 /'estəmət/ *n.* approximate judgement of a number or value etc.; price quoted in advance for work. 2 /'estəmeɪt/ *v.t.* form estimate of; fix by estimate *at*.

**estimation** /estə'meɪʃ(ə)n/ *n.* judgement of worth.

**estrange** /ə'streɪndʒ/ *v.t.* turn away feelings or affections of. **estrangement** *n.*

**estuary** /'estjʊərɪ/ *n.* tidal mouth of river.

**etc.** *abbr.* etcetera.

**etcetera** /et'setərə/ and the rest; and so on. **etceteras** *n.pl.* extras, sundries.

**etch** *v.* reproduce (picture etc.) by engraving metal plate with acid esp. in order to print copies; engrave (plate) thus; practise this craft; *fig.* impress deeply *on*.

**etching** /'etʃɪŋ/ *n.* print made from etched plate.

**eternal** /ə'tɜ:n(ə)l/ *a.* existing always; without end or beginning; unchanging; constant, too frequent.

**eternity** /ə'tɜ:nətɪ/ *n.* infinite time; endless life after death; being eternal.

**ethane** /'i:θeɪn/ *n.* hydrocarbon gas of paraffin series.

**ether** /'i:θə(r)/ *n.* volatile liquid used as anaesthetic and solvent; clear sky, upper air; medium formerly assumed to permeate space.

**ethereal** /ə'θɪərɪəl/ *a.* light, airy; delicate, esp. in appearance; heavenly. **ethereality** *n.*; **etherealize** *v.t.*

**ethical** /'eθɪk(ə)l/ *a.* relating to or treating of morals or ethics; moral, honourable; (of drug etc.) sold only on prescription.

**ethics** /'eθɪks/ *n.pl.* (also treated as *sing.*) science of morals, moral principles or code.

**ethnic** /'eθnɪk/ *a.* of group of mankind having common national or cultural tradition; (of clothes etc.) resembling those of an ethnic group.

**ethnology** /eθ'nɒlədʒɪ/ *n.* comparative study of peoples. **ethnological** *a.*

**ethos** /'i:θɒs/ *n.* characteristic spirit of community or people or system.

**ethylene** /'eθɪli:n/ *n.* a hydrocarbon of the olefin series.

**etiolate** /'i:tɪəleɪt/ *v.t.* make pale by excluding light; give sickly hue to. **etiolation** *n.*

**etiquette** /'etɪkət/ *n.* conventional rules of social behaviour or professional conduct.

**étude** /eɪ'tju:d/ *n.* short musical composition or exercise.

**etymology** /etɪ'mɒlədʒɪ/ *n.* word's origin and sense-development; account of this. **etymological** *a.*

**eucalypt** /'ju:kəlɪpt/ *n.* eucalyptus tree.

**eucalyptus** /ju:kə'lɪptəs/ *n.* tall evergreen tree; oil obtained from it, used as antiseptic etc.

**Eucharist** /'ju:kərəst/ *n.* Christian sacrament in which bread and wine are consecrated and consumed; consecrated elements, esp. bread. **Eucharistic** *a.*

**euchre** /'ju:kə(r)/ *n.* Amer. card-game.

**euchred** /'ju:kəd/ *a.* Aus. done for, beaten; exhausted.

**eugenic** /ju:'dʒenɪk/ *a.* of or concerning eugenics. **eugenically** *adv.*

**eugenics** *n.pl.* (usu. treated as *sing.*) science of improving the population by control of inherited qualities.

**eulogize** /'ju:lədʒaɪz/ *v.t.* extol; praise.

**eulogy** /'ju:lədʒɪ/ *n.* speech or writing in praise or commendation. **eulogistic** *a.*

**eunuch** /'ju:nək/ *n.* castrated man.

**euphemism** /'ju:fəmɪz(ə)m/ *n.* substitution of mild for blunt expression; such substitute. **euphemistic** *a.*

**euphonium** /juːˈfəʊniːəm/ n. large brass wind instrument of tuba kind.

**euphony** /ˈjuːfəniː/ n. pleasantness or smoothness of sounds, esp. in words. **euphonious** a.

**euphoria** /juːˈfɔːriːə/ n. sense of well-being. **euphoric** a.

**euphuism** /ˈjuːfjuː(ə)m/ n. affectedly high-flown style of writing. **euphuistic** a.

**Eurasian** /jʊəˈreɪʒ(ə)n/ 1 a. of mixed European and Asian parentage; of Europe and Asia. 2 n. Eurasian person.

**eureka** /jʊəˈriːkə/ int. I have found it!

**euro** /ˈjʊərəʊ/ n. Aus. species of large kangaroo.

**Eurocrat** /ˈjʊərəʊkræt/ n. bureaucrat of EEC.

**Eurodollar** /ˈjʊərəʊdɒlə(r)/ n. dollar held in bank in Europe etc.

**European** /jʊərəˈpiːən/ 1 a. of or in or extending over Europe. 2 n. native or inhabitant of Europe; descendant of such.

**Eurovision** /ˈjʊərəʊvɪʒ(ə)n/ n. television of European range.

**Eustachian tube** /juːˈsteɪʃ(ə)n/ passage between middle ear and back of throat.

**euthanasia** /juːθəˈneɪziːə/ n. bringing about gentle and easy death, esp. in case of incurable and painful disease.

**evacuate** /ɪˈvækjuːeɪt/ v.t. send (people) away from place of danger; make empty, clear; withdraw from (place); empty (bowels). **evacuation** n.

**evacuee** /ɪvækjuːˈiː/ n. person sent away from place of danger.

**evade** /ɪˈveɪd/ v.t. escape from, avoid; avoid doing or answering directly.

**evaluate** /ɪˈvæljuːeɪt/ v.t. find or state amount or value of; appraise, assess. **evaluation** n.

**evanesce** /ɪvəˈnes/ v.t. fade from sight; disappear. **evanescence** n.; **evanescent** a.

**evangelical** /iːvænˈdʒelɪk(ə)l/ 1 a. of or according to gospel teaching; of Protestant school maintaining that doctrine of salvation by faith is essence of gospel. 2 n. member of evangelical school. 3 **evangelicalism** n.

**evangelist** /ɪˈvændʒəlɪst/ n. writer of one of four Gospels; preacher of gospel. **evangelism** n.; **evangelistic** a.

**evangelize** /ɪˈvændʒəlaɪz/ v.t. preach gospel to. **evangelization** n.

**evaporate** /ɪˈvæpəreɪt/ v: turn into vapour; (cause to) lose moisture as vapour; (cause to) be lost or disappear. **evaporation** n.

**evasion** /ɪˈveɪʒ(ə)n/ n. evading; evasive answer etc.

**evasive** /ɪˈveɪsɪv/ a. seeking to evade.

**eve** n. evening or day before festival etc.; time just before event; *arch.* evening.

**even**[1] /ˈiːv(ə)n/ 1 a. level, smooth; uniform; equal; equable, calm; divisible by two. 2 v.t. make even. 3 adv. inviting comparison with less strong assertion or negation etc. that might have been made.

**even**[2] /ˈiːv(ə)n/ n. evening. **evensong** evening service in Church of England; **eventide** *arch.* evening.

**evening** /ˈiːvnɪŋ/ n. end of day, esp. time from sunset to bedtime.

**event** /ɪˈvent/ n. thing that happens or takes place, esp. one of importance; fact of thing occurring; item in (esp. sports) programme. **in any event, at all events**, whatever happens.

**eventful** /ɪˈventfəl/ a. marked by noteworthy events.

**eventual** /ɪˈventjuːəl/ a. finally resulting.

**eventuality** /ɪventjuːˈælətiː/ n. possible event.

**eventuate** /ɪˈventjuːeɪt/ v.i. result, be the outcome.

**ever** /ˈevə(r)/ adv. at all times; always; at any time. **ever since** throughout period since (then); **ever so** *colloq.* very.

**evergreen** /ˈevəɡriːn/ 1 a. retaining green leaves throughout year; always green or fresh. 2 n. evergreen tree or shrub.

**everlasting** /evəˈlɑːstɪŋ/ 1 a. lasting for ever or a long time; (of plant) retaining colour when dried. 2 n. eternity; everlasting flower.

**evermore** /evəˈmɔː(r)/ adv. for ever; always.

**every** /ˈevriː/ a. each; all taken separately. **everybody** every person; **everyday** occurring every day, ordinary; **Everyman** ordinary or typical human being; **everyone** everybody; **every other** each alternate; **everything** all

**evict** /ɪ'vɪkt/ *v.t.* expel (tenant) by legal process. **eviction** *n*.

**evidence** /'evɪd(ə)ns/ **1** *n.* indication, sign; information given to establish fact etc.; statement etc. admissible in court of law. **2** *v.t.* be evidence of, indicate.

**evident** /'evɪd(ə)nt/ *a.* obvious, manifest.

**evidential** /evɪ'denʃ(ə)l/ *a.* of or providing evidence.

**evil** /'iːv(ə)l/ **1** *a.* harmful; wicked. **2** *n.* evil thing; sin; harm. **3 evildoer** sinner; **evil eye** supposed power of doing harm by look.

**evince** /ɪ'vɪns/ *v.t.* show, indicate.

**eviscerate** /ɪ'vɪsəreɪt/ *v.t.* disembowel. **evisceration** *n.*

**evocative** /ɪ'vɒkətɪv/ *a.* tending to evoke (feelings etc.).

**evoke** /ɪ'vəʊk/ *v.t.* call up (feeling etc.). **evocation** /evə'keɪʃ(ə)n/ *n.*

**evolution** /iːvə'luːʃ(ə)n/ *n.* evolving; origin of species by development from earlier forms; development; change of position of troops or ships. **evolutionary** *a.*

**evolutionism** /iːvə'luːʃənɪz(ə)m/ *n.* theory of evolution of species. **evolutionist** *n.*

**evolve** /ɪ'vɒlv/ *v.* develop gradually by natural process; work out or devise; unfold, open out; produce (heat etc.).

**ewe** /juː/ *n.* female sheep.

**ewer** /'juːə(r)/ *n.* pitcher; water-jug.

**ex¹** *prep.* (of goods) sold from (warehouse etc.); outside. **ex-directory** not listed in telephone directory at subscriber's wish; **ex dividend** (of stocks and shares) not including next dividend.

**ex²** *n. colloq.* former husband or wife etc.

**ex-** *in comb.* formerly.

**exacerbate** /ek'sæsəbeɪt/ *v.t.* make worse; irritate. **exacerbation** *n.*

**exact** /əg'zækt/ **1** *a.* precise, accurate, strictly correct. **2** *v.t.* enforce payment of (fees etc.); demand, insist upon.

**exaction** /əg'zækʃ(ə)n/ *n.* exacting; illegal or exorbitant demand.

**exactitude** /əg'zæktɪtjuːd/ *n.* exactness.

**exactly** /əg'zæktlɪ/ *adv.* precisely; I agree.

**exaggerate** /əg'zædʒəreɪt/ *v.t.* make seem larger or greater than it really is; carry beyond truth; overstate. **exaggeration** *n..*

**exalt** /əg'zɔːlt/ *v.t.* raise in rank or power etc.; praise, extol; make lofty or noble. **exaltation** *n.*

**exam** /əg'zæm/ *n. colloq.* examination.

**examination** /əgzæmə'neɪʃ(ə)n/ *n.* examining or being examined; testing of knowledge or ability by questions; formal questioning of witness etc. in court.

**examine** /əg'zæmən/ *v.* investigate or inquire into; look closely at; test knowledge or proficiency of (pupils etc.) by questions; question formally. **examinee** *n.*; **examiner** *n.*

**example** /əg'zɑːmp(ə)l or əg'zæmp(ə)l/ *n.* thing illustrating general rule; model, pattern; specimen; precedent; warning to others.

**exasperate** /əg'zæspəreɪt/ *v.t.* irritate (person). **exasperation** *n.*

**ex cathedra** /eks kə'θiːdrə/ with full authority, (esp. of papal pronouncement). [L]

**excavate** /'ekskəveɪt/ *v.t.* hollow out; make (hole etc.), reveal or extract by digging. **excavation** *n.*; **excavator** *n.*

**exceed** /ək'siːd/ *v.* be more or greater than; surpass; go beyond; be immoderate.

**exceedingly** /ək'siːdɪŋlɪ/ *adv.* very.

**excel** /ək'sel/ *v.* be superior to; be pre-eminent.

**excellence** /'eksələns/ *n.* great merit.

**Excellency** /'eksələnsɪ/ *n.* title of ambassador or governor etc.

**excellent** /'eksələnt/ *a.* extremely good.

**except** /ək'sept/ **1** *v.* exclude from general statement etc. **2** *prep.* not including, with exception of. **3 except for** if it were not for.

**excepting** /ək'septɪŋ/ *prep.* except.

**exception** /ək'sepʃ(ə)n/ *n.* excepting; thing or case excepted; objection.

**exceptionable** /ək'sepʃənəb(ə)l/ *a.* open to objection.

**exceptional** /ək'sepʃən(ə)l/ *a.* forming exception; unusual.

**excerpt 1** /'eksɜːpt/ *n.* short extract from book or film etc. **2** *v.t.* take excerpts from. **3 excerption** *n.*

**excess 1** /ək'ses/ *n.* fact of exceeding;

amount by which thing exceeds; intemperance in eating or drinking etc.; extreme degree. 2 /'ekses/ a. that exceeds a limit or given amount.

**excessive** /ək'sesɪv/ a. too much; too great.

**exchange** /əks'tʃeɪndʒ/ 1 n. giving one thing and receiving another in its place; exchanging of money for equivalent in other currency; central office where telephone connections are made. 2 v. give or receive in exchange; interchange. 3 **rate of exchange** price at which another country's money may be bought. 4 **exchangeable** a.

**exchequer** /əks'tʃekə(r)/ n. department charged with receipt and custody of public revenue; royal or national treasury.

**excise**[1] /'eksaɪz/ n. duty or tax levied on goods produced or sold within the country, and on various licences etc.

**excise**[2] /ək'saɪz/ v.t. cut out or away. **excision** /-'sɪʒ-/ n.

**excitable** /ək'saɪtəb(ə)l/ a. easily excited. **excitability** n.

**excitation** /eksə'teɪʃ(ə)n/ n. exciting, rousing; stimulation.

**excite** /ək'saɪt/ v.t. move to strong emotion; set in motion; stir up; stimulate to activity. **excitement** n.

**exclaim** /əks'kleɪm/ v. cry out, esp. in anger or delight etc.; utter or say thus.

**exclamation** /eksklə'meɪʃ(ə)n/ n. exclaiming; word(s) etc. exclaimed. **exclamation mark** punctuation mark (!) denoting exclamation. **exclamatory** /-'klæm-/ a.

**exclude** /əks'klu:d/ v.t. shut out (*from*), leave out; make impossible, preclude. **exclusion** n.

**exclusive** /əks'klu:sɪv/ 1 a. excluding; not inclusive; (of society etc.) tending to exclude outsiders; not to be had or not published etc. elsewhere. 2 n. *colloq*. exclusive item of news or film etc. 3 **exclusive of** not including, not counting.

**excommunicate** /ekskə'mju:nəkeɪt/ v.t. deprive (person) of membership and sacraments of Church. **excommunication** n.; **excommunicator** n.

**excoriate** /eks'kɔ:rɪeɪt/ v.t. remove part of skin of by abrasion etc.; remove (skin); *fig.* censure severely. **excoriation** n.

**excrement** /'ekskrəmənt/ n. faeces. **excremental** a.

**excrescence** /əks'kres(ə)ns/ n. abnormal or morbid outgrowth. **excrescent** a.

**excreta** /eks'kri:tə/ n.pl. faeces and urine.

**excrete** /əks'kri:t/ v.t. expel from the body as waste. **excretion** n.; **excretory** a.

**excruciating** /əks'kru:ʃɪ:eɪtɪŋ/ a. acutely painful; (of humour etc.) corny, very bad.

**exculpate** /'ekskʌlpeɪt/ v.t. free from blame. **exculpation** n.; **exculpatory** a.

**excursion** /əks'kɜ:ʃ(ə)n/ n. short journey or ramble; pleasure-trip, esp. one made by number of persons.

**excursive** /əks'kɜ:sɪv/ a. digressive.

**excuse** 1 /əks'kju:z/ v.t. try to lessen blame attaching to; forgive; grant exemption to; allow to leave. 2 /əks'kju:s/ n. reason put forward to mitigate or justify offence; apology. 3 **excuse me** polite formula of apology for interrupting or disagreeing with.

**ex-directory**, **ex dividend** see ex[1].

**execrable** /'eksəkrəb(ə)l/ a. abominable.

**execrate** /'eksəkreɪt/ v. express or feel abhorrence for; utter curses. **execration** n.

**executant** /əg'zekjətənt/ n. performer, esp. of music.

**execute** /'eksəkju:t/ v.t. carry out, perform; put to death.

**execution** /eksə'kju:ʃ(ə)n/ n. carrying out, performance; capital punishment; skill in performing music.

**executioner** n. person carrying out sentence of death.

**executive** /əg'zekjətɪv/ 1 a. concerned with execution of laws or policy etc. or with administration etc.; of an executive. 2 n. person or body having executive authority or in executive position in business etc.; executive branch of government etc.

**executor** /əg'zekjətə(r)/ n. (*fem.* **executrix**) person appointed by testator to carry out terms of will. **executorial** a.

**exegesis** /eksə'dʒi:sɪs/ n. explanation, esp. of Scripture. **exegetic** a.

**exemplar** /əg'zemplə(r)/ n. model; type.

# exemplary — expatriate

**exemplary** /ɪɡˈzempləri/ *a.* fit to be imitated; serving as example.

**exemplify** /ɪɡˈzemplɪfaɪ/ *v.t.* give or be example of. **exemplification** *n.*

**exempt** /ɪɡˈzempt/ 1 *a.* free from obligation or liability imposed on others; not liable to. 2 *v.t.* make exempt (*from*). 3 **exemption** *n.*

**exequies** /ˈeksəkwiːz/ *n.pl.* funeral rites.

**exercise** /ˈeksəsaɪz/ 1 *n.* use of muscles etc., esp. for health; task set for bodily or other training; employment (*of* faculties etc.); practice; (often in *pl.*) military drill or manœuvres. 2 *v.* use; give exercise to; take exercise; perplex, worry.

**exert** /ɪɡˈzɜːt/ *v.t.* use; bring to bear. **exert oneself** use efforts or endeavours. **exertion** *n.*

**exfoliate** /eksˈfəʊlieɪt/ *v.i.* come off in scales or layers. **exfoliation** *n.*

**ex gratia** /eks ˈɡreɪʃə/ done or given as concession and not under (esp. legal) compulsion. [L]

**exhale** /eksˈheɪl/ *v.* give off or be given off in vapour; breathe out. **exhalation** *n.*

**exhaust** /ɪɡˈzɔːst/ 1 *v.t.* consume, use up; drain of energy or resources etc., tire out; empty of contents; deal with exhaustively. 2 *n.* expulsion or exit of steam or products of combustion etc. from engine etc.; such gases etc.; pipe or system through which they are expelled. 3 **exhaustible** *a.*; **exhaustion** *n.*

**exhaustive** /ɪɡˈzɔːstɪv/ *a.* complete, comprehensive.

**exhibit** /ɪɡˈzɪbɪt/ 1 *v.t.* display; manifest; show publicly. 2 *n.* thing exhibited. 3 **exhibitor** *n.*

**exhibition** /eksəˈbɪʃ(ə)n/ *n.* display; public show; sum allowed to student from funds of college etc.

**exhibitioner** /eksəˈbɪʃənə(r)/ *n.* student receiving exhibition.

**exhibitionism** /eksəˈbɪʃənɪz(ə)m/ *n.* tendency towards display or extravagant behaviour; mental condition characterized by urge to expose genitals. **exhibitionist** *n.*

**exhilarate** /ɪɡˈzɪləreɪt/ *v.t.* enliven, gladden. **exhilaration** *n.*

**exhort** /ɪɡˈzɔːt/ *v.t.* admonish earnestly; urge (*to*). **exhortation** *n.*; **exhortative** *a.*; **exhortatory** *a.*

**exhume** /eksˈhjuːm/ *v.t.* dig out, unearth. **exhumation** *n.*

**exigency** /ˈeksɪdʒənsi/ *n.* (also **exigence**) urgent need; emergency. **exigent** *a.*

**exiguous** /ɪɡˈzɪɡjuːəs/ *a.* scanty, small. **exiguity** *n.*

**exile** /ˈeksaɪl/ 1 *n.* being expelled or long absence from one's country etc.; person in exile. 2 *v.t.* condemn to exile (*from*).

**exist** /ɪɡˈzɪst/ *v.i.* be, have being; occur, be found; live, sustain life.

**existence** /ɪɡˈzɪst(ə)ns/ *n.* fact or manner of existing or living; all that exists. **existent** *a.*

**existential** /eɡzɪˈstenʃ(ə)l/ *a.* of or relating to existence.

**existentialism** /eɡzɪˈstenʃəlɪz(ə)m/ *n.* philosophical theory emphasizing existence of individual as free and responsible agent determining his own development. **existentialist** *n.* & *a.*

**exit** /ˈeksɪt/ 1 *n.* going out; way out; departure. 2 *v.i.* make one's exit.

**exodus** /ˈeksədəs/ *n.* mass departure; **Exodus** that of Israelites from Egypt.

**ex officio** /eks əˈfɪʃɪəʊ/ by virtue of one's office.

**exonerate** /ɪɡˈzɒnəreɪt/ *v.t.* free or declare free from blame. **exoneration** *n.*

**exorbitant** /ɪɡˈzɔːbɪt(ə)nt/ *a.* grossly excessive. **exorbitance** *n.*

**exorcize** /ˈeksɔːsaɪz/ *v.t.* drive out (evil spirit) by invocation etc.; clear (person, place) thus. **exorcism** *n.*; **exorcist** *n.*

**exordium** /ɪɡˈzɔːdɪəm/ *n.* (pl. **-diums** or **-dia**) introductory part of discourse or treatise. **exordial** *a.*

**exotic** /ɪɡˈzɒtɪk/ 1 *a.* introduced from abroad; strange, bizarre. 2 *n.* exotic plant etc. 3 **exotically** *adv.*

**expand** /ɪkˈspænd/ *v.* increase in size or bulk etc.; spread out; express at length; become genial.

**expanse** /ɪkˈspæns/ *n.* wide area or extent of land or space etc.

**expansion** /ɪkˈspænʃ(ə)n/ *n.* expanding or being expanded.

**expansive** /ɪkˈspænsɪv/ *a.* able or tending to expand; extensive; genial.

**expatiate** /ɪkˈspeɪʃieɪt/ *v.i.* speak or write at length. **expatiation** *n.*

**expatriate** 1 /eksˈpætrɪeɪt/ *v.t.* expel, remove *oneself* from one's native

**expect** /əkˈspekt/ v.t. regard as likely; assume as future event; look for as due; suppose.

**expectant** /əkˈspekt(ə)nt/ a. expecting; expecting to become; pregnant. **expectancy** n.

**expectation** /ekspekˈteɪʃ(ə)n/ n. looking forward; what one expects; probability; in pl. prospects of inheritance.

**expectorant** /ekˈspektərənt/ 1 a. that causes one to expectorate. 2 n. expectorant medicine.

**expectorate** /ekˈspektəreɪt/ v. cough or spit out from chest or lungs; spit. **expectoration** n.

**expedient** /əkˈspiːdɪənt/ 1 a. suitable, advantageous; advisable on practical rather than moral grounds. 2 n. means of achieving one's end; resource. 3 **expedience** n.; **expediency** n.

**expedite** /ˈekspɪdaɪt/ v.t. assist progress of; accomplish quickly.

**expedition** /ekspəˈdɪʃ(ə)n/ n. journey or voyage for some definite purpose; people or ships etc. undertaking this; promptness, speed.

**expeditionary** /ekspəˈdɪʃənərɪ/ a. of or used in an expedition.

**expeditious** /ekspəˈdɪʃəs/ a. acting or done with speed and efficiency.

**expel** /əksˈpel/ v.t. throw out; eject.

**expend** /əkˈspend/ v.t. spend (money, time, care, etc.); use up, consume.

**expendable** /əkˈspendəb(ə)l/ a. that can be spared; that may be sacrificed to gain one's ends.

**expenditure** /ekˈspendətʃə(r)/ n. expending; amount expended.

**expense** /əkˈspens/ n. cost, charge; in pl. costs incurred in doing job etc., reimbursement of this.

**expensive** /əkˈspensɪv/ a. costing much; of high price.

**experience** /əkˈspɪərɪəns/ 1 n. personal observation or contact; knowledge or skill based on this; event that affects one. 2 v.t. feel, undergo; have experience of.

**experienced** a. wise or skilful through experience.

**experiment** /əkˈsperəmənt/ 1 n. procedure adopted or operation carried out to test hypothesis or demonstrate known fact etc. 2 (also /-ment/) v.i. make experiment(s).

**experimental** /əkspərəˈment(ə)l/ a. based on or done by way of experiment. **experimentalism** n.

**expert** /ˈekspɜːt/ 1 a. trained by practice, well-informed, skilful. 2 n. person having special skill or knowledge.

**expertise** /ekspɜːˈtiːz/ n. expert skill or knowledge.

**expiate** /ˈekspɪeɪt/ v.t. make amends for (wrong); pay penalty of. **expiable** a.; **expiation** n.; **expiatory** a.

**expire** /əkˈspaɪə(r)/ v. come to an end; become void; breathe out; die. **expiration** n.; **expiratory** a.

**expiry** /əkˈspaɪərɪ/ n. ceasing; end of period of validity.

**explain** /əksˈpleɪn/ v.t. make known; make intelligible; account for. **explanation** n.

**explanatory** /əkˈsplænətərɪ/ a. serving to explain.

**expletive** /əkˈspliːtɪv/ 1 n. oath or exclamation; word used to fill out sentence. 2 a. serving as expletive.

**explicable** /ˈeksplɪkəb(ə)l/ a. explainable.

**explicit** /əkˈsplɪsət/ a. expressly stated or shown; definite; outspoken.

**explode** /əkˈspləʊd/ v. expand violently with loud noise; cause (gas or bomb etc.) to do this; give vent suddenly to emotion or violence; (of population etc.) increase suddenly; discredit.

**exploit** 1 /ˈeksplɔɪt/ n. bold or daring feat. 2 /əkˈsplɔɪt/ v.t. use or develop for one's own ends; take advantage of. 3 **exploitation** n.

**explore** /əkˈsplɔː(r)/ v.t. examine (country etc.) by going through it; inquire into; examine by touch. **exploration** n.; **exploratory** a.

**explosion** /əkˈspləʊʒ(ə)n/ n. exploding; outbreak; sudden violent expansion.

**explosive** /əkˈspləʊsɪv/ 1 a. tending to explode; of or like explosion. 2 n. explosive substance. 3 **high explosive** one with violent local effect.

**exponent** /əkˈspəʊnənt/ n. person or thing that explains or interprets; type, representative; Math. symbol showing what power of a factor is to be taken.

**exponential** /ekspəˈnenʃ(ə)l/ a. (of increase) more and more rapid.

**export** /ˈekspɔːt/ 1 v.t. send (goods) for

**expose** /ək'spəʊz/ v.t. leave unprotected esp. from weather; disclose, reveal; subject (*to* risk etc.); *Photog.* subject (film, sensitized paper, etc.) to action of light.

**exposé** /ek'spəʊzeɪ/ n. disclosure (of discreditable thing).

**exposition** /ekspə'zɪʃ(ə)n/ n. expounding, explanation; exhibition.

***ex post facto*** /eks pəʊst 'fæktəʊ/ retrospective(ly). [L]

**expostulate** /ək'spɒstjəleɪt/ v.i. make protest, remonstrate. **expostulation** n.

**exposure** /ək'spəʊʒə(r)/ n. exposing, being exposed; length of time photographic film etc. is exposed; unmasking or revealing of error or crime etc.

**expound** /ək'spaʊnd/ v.t. set forth in detail; explain, interpret.

**express** /ək'spres/ 1 v.t. represent by symbols etc. or in language; put into words; squeeze out (juice etc.); send by express service. 2 a. definitely stated, explicit; operating at high speed; delivered by special messenger or service; (of train etc.) with few intermediate stops. 3 n. express train or messenger etc. 4 adv. with speed; by express train etc. 5 **expressible** a.

**expression** /ək'spreʃ(ə)n/ n. expressing; wording, word, phrase; expressive quality; aspect (of face), intonation (of voice); *Math.* symbols expressing quantity.

**expressionism** /ək'spreʃənɪz(ə)m/ n. style of painting etc. in which artist seeks to express emotional experience rather than depict external world. **expressionist** n. & a.

**expressive** /ək'spresɪv/ a. serving to express; significant.

**expressly** /ək'presli:/ adv. explicitly; on purpose.

**expropriate** /eks'prəʊprɪeɪt/ v.t. take away (property); dispossess. **expropriation** n.; **expropriator** n.

**expulsion** /ək'spʌlʃ(ə)n/ n. expelling, being expelled. **expulsive** a.

**expunge** /ək'spʌndʒ/ v.t. erase, strike out.

**expurgate** /'ekspəgeɪt/ v.t. remove matter considered objectionable from (book etc.); clear away (such matter). **expurgation** n.; **expurgator** n.

**exquisite** /'ekskwəzət/ 1 a. of extreme beauty or delicacy; acute, keen. 2 n. person of refined (esp. affected) tastes.

**ex-serviceman** /eks'sɜ:vəsmən/ n. (pl. -men) former member of armed services.

**extant** /ek'stænt/ a. still existing.

**extempore** /ek'stempəreɪ/ adv. & a. without preparation; off-hand. **extemporaneous** a.; **extemporary** a.

**extemporize** /ek'stempəraɪz/ v. produce or speak extempore. **extemporization** n.

**extend** /ək'stend/ v. lay out at full length; lengthen in space or time; reach or be continuous over certain area; have certain scope; offer or accord feeling or invitation etc.; tax powers of. **extendible** a.; **extensible** a.

**extension** /ək'stenʃ(ə)n/ n. extending; enlargement, additional part; subsidiary telephone on same line as main one; its number; extramural instruction by university etc.

**extensive** /ək'stensɪv/ a. large, far-reaching.

**extent** /ək'stent/ n. space covered; width of application, scope.

**extenuate** /ək'stenjʊ:eɪt/ v.t. lessen seeming seriousness of (guilt etc.) by partial excuse. **extenuation** n.

**exterior** /ək'stɪərɪə(r)/ 1 a. outer, outward. 2 n. exterior aspect or part.

**exterminate** /ək'stɜ:məneɪt/ v.t. destroy utterly. **extermination** n.; **exterminator** n.

**external** /ək'stɜ:n(ə)l/ 1 a. outside; of or consisting of or belonging or referring to etc. outward world or what is outside; (of evidence) derived from source independent of thing discussed. 2 n. in pl. external features or circumstances. 3 **externality** n.

**externalize** /ək'stɜ:nəlaɪz/ v.t. give or attribute external existence to.

**extinct** /ək'stɪŋkt/ a. no longer existing, obsolete; no longer burning; (of volcano) that has ceased eruption.

**extinction** /ək'stɪŋkʃ(ə)n/ n. making or becoming extinct; dying out.

**extinguish** /ək'stɪŋgwɪʃ/ v.t. put out, quench; terminate, destroy; wipe out (debt).

## extirpate

**extirpate** /'ekstəːpeɪt/ v.t. destroy; root out. **extirpation** n.

**extol** /ək'stəʊl/ v.t. praise enthusiastically.

**extort** /ək'stɔːt/ v.t. get by force or threats or intimidation etc.

**extortion** /ək'stɔːʃ(ə)n/ n. extorting, esp. of money; illegal exaction.

**extortionate** /ək'stɔːʃənət/ a. exorbitant.

**extra** /'ekstrə/ 1 a. additional; more than usual or necessary. 2 adv. more than usually; additionally. 3 n. extra thing; thing charged extra; person engaged to be one of crowd etc. in film etc.; special edition of newspaper; *Crick*. run not scored from hit with bat.

**extra-** /'ekstrə/ in comb. outside, not within scope of.

**extract** 1 /ək'strækt/ v.t. take out; draw forth; obtain (juices etc.) by pressure or distillation etc.; deduce, derive (from); copy out, quote; *Math.* find (root of number). 2 /'ekstrækt/ n. passage from book etc.; substance got by distillation etc.; concentrated preparation.

**extraction** /ək'strækʃ(ə)n/ n. extracting; lineage.

**extractive** /ək'stræktɪv/ a. (of industries) obtaining minerals etc. from the ground.

**extractor fan** /ək'stræktə(r)/ ventilating fan in window etc. to remove stale air.

**extraditable** /'ekstrədaɪtəb(ə)l/ a. liable to or (of crime) warranting extradition.

**extradite** /'ekstrədaɪt/ v.t. hand over (person accused of crime) to State where crime was committed. **extradition** n.

**extramarital** /ekstrə'mærɪt(ə)l/ a. (of sexual relationships) outside marriage.

**extramural** /ekstrə'mjʊːr(ə)l/ a. additional to ordinary university teaching etc.

**extraneous** /ək'streɪnɪəs/ a. of external origin; not belonging.

**extraordinary** /ək'strɔːdənərɪ/ a. unusual or remarkable; out of the usual course; specially employed.

**extrapolate** /ək'stræpəleɪt/ v. estimate from known values or data etc. (others which lie outside the range of those known). **extrapolation** n.

**extra-sensory** /ekstrə'sensərɪ/ a. derived by means other than known senses.

**extra-terrestrial** /ekstrətə'restrɪəl/ a. outside the earth or its atmosphere.

**extravagant** /ək'strævəgənt/ a. spending (esp. money) excessively; costing much; wild, absurd. **extravagance** n.

**extravaganza** /əkstrævə'gænzə/ n. fantastic composition; spectacular theatrical production.

**extreme** /ək'striːm/ 1 a. reaching a high or the highest degree; going to great lengths, not moderate; outermost; utmost. 2 n. one or other of two things as remote or different as possible; thing at either end; extreme degree etc. 3 **extreme unction** *RC Ch.* anointing by priest of dying person.

**extremely** adv. in extreme degree; very.

**extremism** /ək'striːmɪz(ə)m/ n. advocacy of extreme measures. **extremist** a. & n.

**extremity** /ək'streməti:/ n. extreme point, end; extreme adversity or danger etc.; in pl. hands and feet.

**extricate** /'ekstrɪkeɪt/ v.t. disentangle, release. **extrication** n.

**extrinsic** /ək'strɪnzɪk/ a. not inherent or intrinsic; extraneous. **extrinsically** adv.

**extrovert** /'ekstrəvɜːt/ 1 a. directing thoughts or interests to things outside oneself; sociable, unreserved. 2 n. extrovert person. 3 **extroversion** n.

**extrude** /ək'struːd/ v.t. thrust or squeeze out; shape by forcing through mould. **extrusion** n.; **extrusive** a.

**exuberant** /əg'zuːbərənt/ a. lively, effusive; high-spirited; luxuriant, prolific; copious, lavish. **exuberance** n.

**exude** /əg'zjuːd/ v. ooze out; give off. **exudation** n.

**exult** /əg'zʌlt/ v.i. rejoice, triumph (*at, in, over*); **exultant** a.; **exultation** n.

**eye** /aɪ/ 1 n. organ or faculty of sight; iris of eye; region round eye; gaze; perception; eyelike thing; leaf-bud of potato etc.; spot, hole, loop. 2 v.t.(*partic.* **eyeing**) observe, watch closely or suspiciously. 3 **eyeball** ball of eye within lids and socket; **eyebath** vessel for applying lotion to eye; **eyebrow** hair growing on ridge over eye; **eyeglass** lens for defective eye, in pl. pair of these joined by bar over bridge of nose; **eyehole** hole to look through; **eyelash** any of hairs on edge of eyelid; **eyelid** movable fold of skin that can cover eye; **eye-liner** cosmetic applied as line round eye; **eye-opener** surprising fact etc.; **eyepiece** lens(es) at eye-end of optical instrument; **eye-shade** device to protect eyes from strong light; **eye-shadow** cosmetic for eyelids; **eyesight** faculty or strength of sight; **eyesore** thing that offends sight; **eyes out** *Aus. sl.* using every effort; **eye-tooth** pointed tooth just under eye, canine; **eye-wash** *sl.* nonsense; **eyewitness** one who can testify from his own observation.

**eyeful** /'aɪfʊl/ *n.* thing thrown or blown into eye; *colloq.* remarkable or attractive person.

**eyelet** /'aɪlət/ *n.* small hole for passing cord etc. through.

**eyrie** /'aɪərɪ:/ *n.* nest of bird of prey or of bird that builds high up.

# F

**F** *abbr.* Fahrenheit.

**f** *abbr.* forte².

**FA** *abbr.* Football Association.

**FAA** *abbr.* Fellow of the Australian Academy of Science.

**fa** var. of **fah**.

**fable** /'feɪb(ə)l/ *n.* story not based on fact; short moral tale, esp. with animals for characters; myth, legend.

**fabled** *a.* celebrated in fable, legendary.

**fabric** /'fæbrɪk/ *n.* woven etc. material; walls, floor, and roof of building; structure; thing put together.

**fabricate** /'fæbrəkeɪt/ *v.t.* construct, manufacture; invent (fact), forge (document). **fabrication** *n.*

**fabulous** /'fæbjələs/ *a.* celebrated in fable; incredible; *colloq.* marvellous.

**façade** /fə'sɑːd/ *n.* face or front of building; outward (esp. deceptive) appearance.

**face 1** *n.* front of head; expression, grimace; surface; front, right side; dial-plate of clock etc.; striking surface of bat or racket or golf-club etc.; effrontery; aspect. **2** *v.* look or front towards; be opposite to; meet firmly; supply (garment, wall, etc.) with facing. **3 face-lift** operation for removing wrinkles by tightening skin of face, *fig.* improvement in appearance; **face value** that stated on coin or note etc., apparent value; **lose face** be humiliated; **on the face of it** to judge by appearance; **save face** spare oneself humiliation.

**faceless** /'feɪsləs/ *a.* without identity, not identifiable.

**facet** /'fæsət/ *n.* particular aspect of thing; one side of many-sided body, esp. cut gem.

**facetious** /fə'siːʃəs/ *a.* intending or meant to be amusing, esp. inopportunely.

**facia** /'feɪʃə/ *n.* instrument-panel of motor vehicle; plate over shop-front with name etc.

**facial** /'feɪʃ(ə)l/ **1** *a.* of face. **2** *n.* beauty-treatment for face.

**facile** /'fæsaɪl/ *a.* easily achieved but of little value; easy; working easily; fluent.

**facilitate** /fə'sɪlɪteɪt/ *v.t.* make easy, promote. **facilitation** *n.*

**facility** /fə'sɪlətɪ/ *n.* absence of difficulty; dexterity; (usu. in *pl.*) opportunity or equipment for doing something.

**facing** /'feɪsɪŋ/ *n.* material over part of garment etc. for contrast or strength; surface covering of different material.

**facsimile** /fæk'sɪmɪlɪ/ *n.* exact copy of writing or picture etc.

**fact** *n.* thing done; thing known to be true; what is true or existent, reality; **in fact** in reality, really, indeed.

**faction** /'fækʃ(ə)n/ *n.* small group with special aims within larger one, esp. political.

**factious** /'fækʃəs/ *a.* of a faction; characterized by factions.

**factitious** /fæk'tɪʃəs/ *a.* made for special purpose; artificial.

**factor** /'fæktə(r)/ *n.* thing contributing to result; any of numbers etc. whose product is given number etc.; business agent; *Sc.* land-steward.

**factorial** /fæk'tɔːrɪəl/ **1** *n.* the product of a number and all whole numbers below it. **2** *a.* of factor or factorial.

**factorize** /'fæktəraɪz/ *v.t.* resolve (number) into factors. **factorization** *n.*

**factory** /'fæktərɪ/ *n.* building(s) and equipment for manufacture of goods. **factory farm** one organized on industrial lines.

**factotum** /fæk'təʊtəm/ *n.* employee doing all kinds of work.

**factual** /'fæktjʊəl/ *a.* based on or concerned with fact.

**faculty** /'fækəltɪ/ *n.* aptitude for particular action; physical or mental power; teaching staff of department of learning at university etc.; (esp. *Eccl.*) authorization.

**fad** *n.* craze, pet notion. **faddish** *a.*

**faddy** /'fædɪ/ *a.* having arbitrary likes and dislikes, esp. about food.

**fade 1** *v.* (cause to) lose freshness or colour or strength; disappear gradually; bring sound or picture gradually *in* or *out* of perception. **2** *n.* action of fading.

**faeces** /'fiːsiːz/ *n.pl.* waste matter discharged from bowels. **faecal** /'fiːk(ə)l/ *a.*

**fag¹ 1** *v.* toil, grow or make weary **2** *n.* drudgery; *sl.* cigarette; **3 fag-end** inferior remnant, cigarette-end.

**fag** *n. US sl.* homosexual.

**faggot** /'fægət/ *n.* seasoned chopped liver etc. baked or fried as ball or roll; bundle of sticks for fuel; bundle of herbs or metal rods etc.; *sl.* unpleasant woman; *US sl.* homosexual.

**fah** *n. Mus.* fourth note of scale in tonic sol-fa.

**FAHA** *abbr.* Fellow of the Australian Academy of the Humanities.

**Fahrenheit** /'færənhaɪt/ *a.* of scale of temperature on which water freezes at 32° and boils at 212°.

**faience** /faɪ'ɑ̃s/ *n.* painted and glazed earthenware and porcelain.

**fail** 1 *v.* not succeed; be unsuccessful in (examination etc.); disappoint; neglect; not be able; be missing or deficient; break down; go bankrupt. 2 *n.* failure. 3 **fail-safe** reverting to safe condition in event of breakdown etc.; **without fail** for certain, whatever happens.

**failing** /'feɪlɪŋ/ 1 *n.* deficiency, fault; foible. 2 *prep.* in default of.

**failure** /'feɪljə(r)/ *n.* failing; non-performance; cessation or impairment of vital function; unsuccessful person, thing, or attempt.

**fain** *arch.* 1 *pred.a.* willing; glad. 2 *adv.* gladly.

**faint** 1 *a.* dim, pale; weak from hunger etc.; timid; feeble. 2 *v.i.* lose consciousness; become faint. 3 *n.* act or state of fainting. 4 **faint-hearted** cowardly.

**fair**[1] 1 *a.* just, equitable; blond, not dark; of moderate quality or amount; (of weather) favourable; beautiful. 2 *adv.* in fair manner. 3 **fair and square** equitably, exactly; **fair copy** transcript free from corrections; **fair dinkum** *Aus.* genuine, honestly; **fair go** *Aus.* a fair chance, fair treatment; **fair play** equitable conduct or conditions; **fairweather friend** one not good in a crisis.

**fair**[2] *n.* periodical gathering for sale of goods, often with entertainments; funfair; trade exhibition.

**Fair Isle** /'feər aɪl/ (of jersey etc.) knitted in characteristic coloured design.

**fairly** /'feəlɪ/ *adv.* in a fair manner; moderately; to a noticeable degree.

**fairway** /'feəweɪ/ *n.* navigable channel; mown grass between golf tee and green.

**fairy** /'feərɪ/ *n.* small imaginary being with magical powers; *sl.* male homosexual. **fairy godmother** *colloq.* benefactress; **fairyland** home of fairies; **fairy lights** small coloured lights esp. for outdoor decorations; **fairy ring** ring of darker grass caused by fungi; **fairy story, -tale**, tale about fairies, incredible story, falsehood.

*fait accompli* /feɪt ə'kɒmpli:/ thing done and past arguing about. [F]

**faith** *n.* trust; belief esp. in religious doctrine; religion; things believed; loyalty, trustworthiness. **faithcure, -healing**, cure etc. depending on faith rather than treatment.

**faithful** /'feɪθfəl/ *a.* loyal, constant; true, accurate. **faithfully** *adv.* **yours faithfully** formula at end of business etc. letter.

**faithless** /'feɪθləs/ *a.* disloyal, false.

**fake** 1 *n.* thing or person that is not genuine. 2 *a.* counterfeit, not genuine. 3 *v.t.* make (false thing) so that it appears genuine; feign.

**fakir** /'feɪkɪə(r)/ *n.* Muslim or Hindu religious mendicant or ascetic.

**falcon** /'fɔ:lkən/ *n.* small hawk trained to hunt game-birds for sport.

**falconer** /'fɔ:lkənə(r)/ *n.* person who keeps or trains or hunts with hawks.

**falconry** /'fɔ:lkənrɪ/ *n.* hunting with or breeding of hawks.

**fall** /fɔ:l/ 1 *v.* (*past* **fell**, *p.p.* **fallen**) go or come down freely; cease to stand, lose balance; become detached and descend; slope or hang down; become lower, subside; lose high position; yield to temptation; occur; become; *Aus.* fell (tree). 2 *n.* falling; amount that falls; descent; drop; downfall, ruin; (often in *pl.*) waterfall; *US* autumn. 3 **fall back on** have recourse to; **fall down (on)** *colloq.* fail (in); **fall for** be captivated or deceived by; **fall foul of** collide or quarrel with; **fall guy** *sl.* easy victim, scapegoat; **fall in** *Mil.* (cause to) take place in parade; **fall in with** meet (by chance), agree or coincide with; **fall off** decrease, deteriorate; **fall out** quarrel, result, occur, *Mil.* (cause to) leave place in parade; **fall-out** radioactive debris from nuclear explosion; **fall short of** fail to reach or amount to; **fall through** fail, come to nothing; **fall to** start working etc.

**fallacy** /'fæləsɪ/ *n.* mistaken belief;

**fallible** /ˈfæləb(ə)l/ *a.* capable of making mistakes. **fallibility** *n.*

**Fallopian tube** /fəˈləʊpiːən/ either of two tubes along which egg-cells travel from ovaries to womb.

**fallow**[1] /ˈfæləʊ/ **1** *a.* (of land) ploughed etc. but left unsown; uncultivated. **2** *n.* fallow land.

**fallow**[2] /ˈfæləʊ/ *a.* of pale brownish yellow. **fallow deer** kind smaller than red deer.

**false** /fɔːls/ *a.* wrong, incorrect; deceitful; treacherous; unfaithful *to*; deceptive; sham, artificial. **false alarm** alarm given without valid cause; **false pretences** misrepresentations meant to deceive. **falsity** *n.*

**falsehood** /ˈfɔːlshʊd/ *n.* untrue thing; lying, lie(s).

**falsetto** /fɔːlˈsetəʊ/ *n.* (*pl.* **-os**) high-pitched artificial voice esp. of male singer.

**falsify** /ˈfɔːlsəfaɪ/ *v.t.* fraudulently alter; misrepresent. **falsification** *n.*

**falter** /ˈfɔːltə(r)/ *v.* go unsteadily; say or speak hesitatingly; waver.

**fame** *n.* renown, glory; *arch.* reputation.

**famed** /feɪmd/ *a.* famous, much spoken of.

**familial** /fəˈmɪliəl/ *a.* of or relating to a family or its members.

**familiar** /fəˈmɪliə(r)/ **1** *a.* well acquainted (*with*); well known; often encountered; (excessively) informal. **2** *n.* intimate friend; demon attending witch etc. **familiarity** *n.*

**familiarize** /fəˈmɪliəraɪz/ *v.t.* make (person etc.) familiar (*with*). **familiarization** *n.*

**family** /ˈfæməli/ *n.* set of parents and children or of relatives; person's children; household; lineage; race; group of allied genera. **family allowance** allowance paid by State etc. to parent of family; **family man** man with family, domestic man; **family planning** birth-control; **family tree** genealogical chart.

**famine** /ˈfæmɪn/ *n.* extreme scarcity esp. of food.

**famish** /ˈfæmɪʃ/ *v.* reduce or be reduced to extreme hunger.

faulty reasoning; misleading argument. **fallacious** /-ˈleɪʃ/ *a.*

**famous** /ˈfeɪməs/ *a.* well-known; celebrated; *colloq.* excellent.

**fan**[1] *n.* rotating apparatus giving current of air; instrument, usu. folding and sector-shaped, for agitating air to cool face etc.; anything spreading out in fan shape. **2** *v.t.* move (air) with fan; drive air (as) with fan upon; increase (flames etc.) (as) by fanning; spread (*out*) in fan shape. **3 fan-belt** belt transmitting torque from motor-vehicle engine to fan that cools radiator; **fan heater** heater in which fan drives air over electric heater into room etc.; **fanlight** window (orig. semi-circular) over door; **fantail** pigeon with fan-shaped tail, *Aus.* member of genus of small flycatching birds with fan-shaped tail.

**fan**[2] *n.* enthusiast, devotee. **fanmail** letters from fans.

**fanatic** /fəˈnætɪk/ **1** *n.* person filled with excessive or mistaken enthusiasm, esp. in religion. **2** *a.* excessively enthusiastic. **3 fanatical** *a.*; **fanaticism** *n.*

**fancier** /ˈfænsɪə(r)/ *n.* connoisseur.

**fanciful** /ˈfænsəfəl/ *a.* imaginary; unreal; indulging in fancies.

**fancy** /ˈfænsɪ/ **1** *n.* faculty of imagination; supposition; caprice, whim; taste, liking. **2** *a.* ornamental, not plain; unusual. **3** *v.t.* imagine; *colloq.* feel inclination towards; *colloq.* find sexually attractive; *colloq.* have unduly high opinion of (*oneself*). **4 fancy dress** fanciful costume, often historical or exotic; **fancy-free** not in love.

**fandango** /fænˈdæŋgəʊ/ *n.* (*pl.* **-goes**) lively Spanish dance.

**fanfare** /ˈfænfeə(r)/ *n.* short showy or ceremonious sounding of trumpets etc.

**fang** *n.* canine tooth esp. of dog etc.; serpent's venom-tooth; root of tooth or its prong.

**fantasia** /fænˈteɪzɪə/ *n.* musical composition in which form is of minor importance.

**fantasize** /ˈfæntəsaɪz/ *v.* create fantasy (*about*).

**fantastic** /fænˈtæstɪk/ *a.* extravagantly fanciful; grotesque, quaint; *colloq.* excellent, extraordinary.

**fantasy** /ˈfæntəsɪ/ *n.* faculty of imagination; mental image, day-dream; fanciful invention or speculation etc.

**far 1** *adv.* at or to great distance; by

much. 2 *a.* distant, remote. 3 **far-away** remote, as if from distance, dreamy; **Far East** countries of eastern Asia; **far-fetched** strained, unconvincing; **far-flung** widely extended; **far gone** very ill or drunk, much in debt, etc.; **far-off** remote; **far out** *colloq.* avant-garde, excellent; **far-reaching** of wide application or influence; **far-seeing** showing foresight, prudent; **far-sighted** far-seeing, seeing distant things best.

**farad** /'færəd/ *n. Electr.* fundamental unit of capacitance.

**farce** *n.* comedy based on ludicrously improbable events; absurdly futile proceeding. **farcical** *a.*

**fare** /feə(r)/ 1 *n.* price charged to passenger on public transport; passenger; food. 2 *v.i.* progress; get on.

**farewell** /feə'wel/ *int. & n.* goodbye.

**farina** /fə'ramə/ *n.* flour or meal of corn or nuts or starchy roots. **farinaceous** /færɪ'neɪʃəs/ *a.*

**farm** 1 *n.* area of land and its buildings used for growing crops and raising animals etc.; place for breeding of animals; farmhouse. 2 *v.* use (land) for growing crops and raising animals etc.; breed (fish etc.) commercially; work as farmer; take proceeds of (tax) on payment of fixed sum. 3 **farmhouse** dwelling-place on farm; **farm out** delegate (work) to others; **farmstead** farm and its buildings; **farmyard** yard of farmhouse.

**farmer** /'fɑːmə(r)/ *n.* owner or manager of farm.

**faro** /'feərəʊ/ *n.* gambling card-game.

**farrago** /fə'rɑːgəʊ/ *n.* (*pl.* -gos) medley, hotchpotch.

**farrier** /'færɪə(r)/ *n.* smith who shoes horses. **farriery** *n.*

**farrow** /'færəʊ/ 1 *v.i.* give birth to pigs. 2 *n.* farrowing; litter of pigs.

**fart** *vulg.* 1 *v.i.* emit wind from anus. 2 *n.* emission of wind from anus.

**farther** var. of **further**.

**farthest** var. of **furthest**.

**farthing** /'fɑːðɪŋ/ *n. hist.* quarter of old penny.

**farthingale** /'fɑːðɪŋgeɪl/ *n. hist.* hooped petticoat.

**fascia** /'feɪʃə/ *n.* long flat surface of wood or stone (*Archit.*); facia.

**fascicle** /'fæsɪk(ə)l/ *n.* instalment of book.

**fascinate** /'fæsəneɪt/ *v.t.* capture interest of; charm irresistibly; paralyse (victim) with fear. **fascination** *n.*

**Fascism** /'fæʃɪz(ə)m/ *n.* extreme right-wing totalitarian political system or views, as orig. in Italy (1922–43). **Fascist** *n. & a.*

**fashion** /'fæʃ(ə)n/ 1 *n.* current popular custom or style, esp. in dress; manner of doing something. 2 *v.t.* form or make (*into*). 3 **in fashion** fashionable; **out of fashion** no longer fashionable.

**fashionable** /'fæʃənəb(ə)l/ *a.* of or conforming to (latest) fashion; characteristic of or patronized by those who are in fashion.

**FASSA** *abbr.* Fellow of the Academy of Social Sciences in Australia.

**fast**[1] /fɑːst/ 1 *a.* rapid; (of clock) showing later than correct time; firm, fixed; (of colour) not fading when washed etc.; (of person) dissipated. 2 *adv.* quickly, firmly, tightly. 3 **fast food** prepared food requiring minimum of further preparation before sale or serving etc.; **fast one** *sl.* unfair or deceitful action; **fast reactor** *Phys.* nuclear reactor using neutrons with high kinetic energy.

**fast**[2] /fɑːst/ 1 *v.i.* go without (some kinds of) food, esp. as religious observance. 2 *n.* fasting; going without food.

**fasten** /'fɑːs(ə)n/ *v.* attach, fix, secure; become tightly fixed.

**fastener** /'fɑːsənə(r)/ *n.* (also **fastening**) device that fastens something.

**fastidious** /fæ'stɪdɪəs/ *a.* easily disgusted, hard to please.

**fastness** /'fɑːstnəs/ *n.* stronghold.

**fat** 1 *a.* well-fed, plump; oily; fertile, rich, rewarding. 2 *n.* oily substance esp. that found in animal bodies; fat part of thing; in *pl. Aus.* fat cattle or sheep. 3 **a fat lot** *colloq.* very little.

**fatal** /'feɪt(ə)l/ *a.* causing or ending in death; destructive, ruinous.

**fatalism** /'feɪtəlɪz(ə)m/ *n.* belief that all is predetermined and therefore inevitable. **fatalist** *n.*; **fatalistic** *a.*

**fatality** /fə'tælɪtɪ/ *n.* death by accident, in war, etc.

**fate** 1 *n.* power predetermining events from eternity; what is destined; person's appointed lot; death, destruction. 2 *v.t.* in *p.p.* preordained.

**fateful** /ˈfeɪtfəl/ a. controlled by fate; decisive; important.

**father** /ˈfɑːðə(r)/ n. male parent; forefather; originator; early leader; in pl. elders; priest; venerable person; oldest member. 2 v.t. beget; originate; fix paternity of, or responsibility for, on. 3 **father-in-law** wife's or husband's father; **fatherland** native country. 4 **fatherhood** n.

**fatherly** /ˈfɑːðəlɪ/ a. of or like a father.

**fathom** /ˈfæðəm/ 1 n. measure of 6ft., esp. in soundings. 2 v.t. comprehend; measure depth of (water).

**fathomless** /ˈfæðəmləs/ a. too deep to fathom.

**fatigue** /fəˈtiːg/ 1 n. weariness from exertion; weakness in metals etc. from variations of stress; soldier's non-combatant duty. 2 v.t. tire.

**fatten** /ˈfæt(ə)n/ v. make or become fat.

**fatty** /ˈfætɪ/ a. like or containing fat.

**fatuous** /ˈfætjʊəs/ a. vacantly silly; purposeless. **fatuity** n.

**faucet** /ˈfɔːsɪt/ n. tap for barrel etc.; US any tap.

**fault** /fɔːlt/ 1 n. defect, blemish; offence, misdeed; responsibility for something wrong; Tennis etc. incorrect serve; Geol. break in continuity of strata etc. 2 v. find fault with; cause fault in (strata etc.), show fault. 3 **find fault** with criticize unfavourably; **to a fault** excessively. 4 **faulty** a.

**faun** /fɔːn/ n. Latin rural deity with goat's horns, legs, and tail.

**fauna** /ˈfɔːnə/ n. (pl. **-nas**) the animals of a region or period.

*faux pas* /fəʊ pɑː/ tactless mistake. [F]

**favour** /ˈfeɪvə(r)/ 1 n. liking, goodwill, approval; kind or helpful act; partiality; thing given or worn as mark of favour. 2 v.t. regard or treat with favour; support, facilitate, oblige; in p.p. having unusual advantages.

**favourable** /ˈfeɪvərəb(ə)l/ a. well disposed; approving; pleasing, satisfactory, helpful, suitable.

**favourite** /ˈfeɪvərɪt/ 1 a. preferred to all others. 2 n. favourite person or thing; person favoured by monarch or superior; competitor generally thought most likely to win.

**favouritism** /ˈfeɪvərɪtɪz(ə)m/ n. unfair favouring of one person or group.

**fawn**[1] n. fallow deer in first year; light yellowish brown. 2 a. fawn-coloured. 3 v.i. give birth to fawn.

**fawn**[2] v.i. (of dog etc.) show affection by frisking and grovelling etc.; lavish caresses *upon*; behave servilely.

**fay** n. poet. fairy.

**FBI** abbr. US Federal Bureau of Investigation.

**FC** abbr. Football Club.

**fealty** /ˈfɪəltɪ/ n. duty of feudal vassal to lord; faithful adherence.

**fear** /fɪə(r)/ 1 n. emotion caused by impending danger or pain etc.; alarm, dread. 2 v. be afraid (of); be anxious; hesitate; shrink from; revere (God).

**fearful** /ˈfɪəfəl/ a. afraid; causing fear; colloq. annoying, extreme.

**fearless** /ˈfɪələs/ a. feeling no fear; brave.

**fearsome** /ˈfɪəsəm/ a. formidable.

**feasible** /ˈfiːzəb(ə)l/ a. practicable, possible; plausible. **feasibility** n.

**feast** 1 n. sumptuous meal; religious festival; something giving great pleasure. 2 v. partake of feast; eat and drink heartily (on); give feast to; regale.

**feat** n. remarkable act or achievement.

**feather** /ˈfeðə(r)/ 1 n. appendage of bird's skin with central shaft fringed with thin narrow barbs; piece of this as decoration etc.; piece(s) of feathers attached to end of arrow or dart; plumage; game-birds. 2 v. cover or line with feathers; turn (oar) so as to pass through air edgeways. 3 **feather bed** mattress stuffed with feathers; **feather-bed** make things easy for, pamper; **feather-brained, -headed,** silly; **featherweight** light person or thing, boxing-weight (up to 57 kg.). 4 **feathery** a.

**feature** /ˈfiːtʃə(r)/ n. part of face, esp. with regard to appearance; characteristic or prominent part; prominent article in newspaper etc.; feature film. 2 v. give prominence to; make or be special feature of; take part (in). 3 **feature film** main item in cinema programme.

**featureless** /ˈfiːtʃələs/ a. lacking distinct features.

**Feb.** abbr. February.

**febrile** /ˈfiːbraɪl/ a. of fever.

**February** /ˈfebruːərɪ/ n. second month of year.

**feckless** /ˈfekləs/ a. feeble, incompetent, helpless.

**fecund** /'fi:kənd/ a. fertile. **fecundity** n.

**fecundate** /'fi:kəndeɪt/ v.t. make fruitful; impregnate. **fecundation** n.

**fed** past & p.p. of **feed**. **fed up** sl. discontented or bored (with).

**federal** /'fedər(ə)l/ a. of system of government in which several states unite, but remain independent in internal affairs; of such States or their central government; US hist. of Northern States in Civil War. **federalism** n.; **federalist** n.; **federalize** v.

**federate** 1 /'fedəreɪt/ v. unite on federal basis or for common object. 2 /'fedərət/ a. so united.

**federation** /fedə'reɪʃ(ə)n/ n. act of federating; federal group. **federative** a.

**fedora** /fə'dɔːrə/ n. kind of soft felt hat.

**fee** n. sum payable to official or professional person etc. for services; charge esp. for instruction at school or entrance for examination etc.; money paid for transfer of footballer etc.; inherited estate.

**feeble** /'fi:b(ə)l/ a. weak; lacking energy or strength or effectiveness.

**feed** 1 v. (past & p.p. **fed**) supply with food; put food in mouth of; eat; graze; keep supplied or supply with; put material (in)to; comfort (with); nourish. 2 n. feeding; pasturage; fodder; meal (esp. for babies or colloq.). 3 **feedback** return to input of part of output of system or process, information about result of experiment, response; **feed on** consume, be nourished by.

**feeder** /'fi:də(r)/ n. one that feeds in specified way; feeding apparatus in machine; child's bib; tributary; branch road or railway line.

**feel** 1 v. (past & p.p. **felt**) examine or perceive by touch; be conscious of, be consciously; experience; be affected by; have pity for; have vague or emotional impression; consider, think; seem. 2 n. sense of touch; sensation characterizing something. 3 **feel like** colloq. desire, be inclined towards doing.

**feeler** /'fi:lə(r)/ n. organ in certain animals for testing things by touch; tentative suggestion etc.

**feeling** /'fi:lɪŋ/ 1 n. sense of touch; physical sensation; emotion; in pl. susceptibilities; consideration for others; belief or opinion. 2 a. sensitive; sympathetic; heartfelt.

**feet** pl. of **foot**.

**feign** /feɪn/ v. pretend; simulate.

**feint** /feɪnt/ 1 n. sham attack or blow etc. to deceive opponent; pretence. 2 v.i. make feint. 3 a. (of paper etc.) having faintly ruled lines.

**feldspar** /'felspɑː(r)/ n. common white or flesh-red mineral containing silicates.

**felicitate** /fə'lɪsɪteɪt/ v.t. congratulate. **felicitation** n.

**felicitous** /fə'lɪsɪtəs/ a. well-chosen, apt.

**felicity** /fə'lɪsɪtɪ/ n. great happiness; pleasing manner or style.

**feline** /'fi:laɪn/ 1 a. of cats; catlike. 2 n. animal of cat family. 3 **felinity** /-'lɪn-/ n.

**fell**[1] v.t. cut down (tree); strike down; stitch down (seam).

**fell**[2] n. wild high stretch of country esp. in N. England.

**fell**[3] a. fierce; destructive.

**fell**[4] n. animal's hide or skin with hair.

**fell**[5] past of **fall**.

**fellow** /'feləʊ/ 1 n. comrade, associate; counterpart, equal; colloq. man or boy; incorporated senior member of college; member of learned society. 2 a. of same class; associated in joint action etc. 3 **fellow-feeling** sympathy; **fellow-traveller** sympathizer with but not member of political party.

**fellowship** /'feləʊʃɪp/ n. sharing; companionship; body of associates; position or income of college fellow.

**felon** /'felən/ n. person who has committed felony.

**felony** /'felənɪ/ n. crime regarded by law as grave. **felonious** a.

**felspar** var. of **feldspar**.

**felt**[1] 1 n. fabric of matted and pressed fibres of wool etc. 2 v. make into or form felt; cover with felt; become matted. 3 **felt pen** pen with felt point.

**felt**[2] past & p.p. of **feel**.

**female** /'fi:meɪl/ 1 a. of offspring-bearing sex; (of plants) fruit-bearing; of women or female animals or plants; (of screw, socket, etc.) made hollow to receive corresponding inserted part. 2 n. female person or animal.

**feminine** /'femənɪn/ a. of women;

**feminism** 203 **fetter**

womanly; *Gram.* of gender proper to women's names. **femininity** *n.*
**feminism** /ˈfemɪnɪz(ə)m/ *n.* advocacy of women's rights. **feminist** *n.* & *a.*
**femur** /ˈfiːmə(r)/ *n.* (*pl.* **femurs** or **femora**) thigh-bone.
**fen** *n.* low marshy tract of land. **fenny** *a.*
**fence** 1 *n.* barrier or railing enclosing field or garden etc.; guard in machine; receiver of stolen goods. 2 *v.* surround (as) with fence; practise sword play; be evasive.
**fencing** /ˈfensɪŋ/ *n.* fences, material for fences; sword-fighting, esp. as sport.
**fend** *v.* ward or keep *off*; provide *for* (*oneself* etc.).
**fender** /ˈfendə(r)/ *n.* frame round hearth to keep in falling coals; thing used to keep something off; *US* bumper of motor vehicle.
**fennel** /ˈfen(ə)l/ *n.* fragrant herb with yellow flowers, used for flavouring.
**fenugreek** /ˈfenjuːɡriːk/ *n.* leguminous plant with aromatic seeds.
**feoff** /fef/ *n.* fief.
**feral** /ˈfɪər(ə)l/ *a.* wild; in wild state after escape from captivity.
**ferial** /ˈfɪərɪəl/ *a.* (of day) not a festival or fast.
**ferment** 1 /ˈfɜːment/ *n.* fermenting agent; fermentation; excitement. 2 /fəˈment/ *v.* undergo or subject to fermentation; excite.
**fermentation** /fɜːmenˈteɪʃ(ə)n/ *n.* chemical change involving effervescence and production of heat, induced by organic substance such as yeast; excitement.
**fern** *n.* kind of flowerless plant usu. with feathery fronds.
**ferocious** /fəˈrəʊʃəs/ *a.* fierce, cruel. **ferocity** /-ˈrɒs-/ *n.*
**ferret** /ˈferɪt/ 1 *n.* small animal like weasel, used in catching rabbits or rats etc. 2 *v.* hunt with ferrets; rummage or search *about* (*for*), search *out*. 3 **ferrety** *a.*
**ferric, ferrous,** /ˈferɪk/ *adjs.* of or containing iron.
**Ferris wheel** /ˈferəs/ giant revolving vertical wheel with passenger cars, in amusement parks etc.
**ferro-** /ˈferəʊ/ *in comb.* of or containing iron.

**ferroconcrete** /ferəʊˈkɒŋkriːt/ *n.* reinforced concrete.
**ferrous:** see **ferric.**
**ferrule** /ˈferəl/ *n.* metal ring or cap at end of stick etc.
**ferry** /ˈferi/ 1 *v.* take or go in boat, or work boat, over river or lake etc.; transport (persons or things) from place to place, esp. as regular service. 2 *n.* boat etc. for ferrying; ferrying place or service.
**fertile** /ˈfɜːtaɪl/ *a.* (of soil) producing abundant vegetation; fruitful; (of seed, egg, etc.) capable of becoming new individual; able to conceive young or produce fruit; inventive. **fertility** /-ˈtɪl-/ *n.*
**fertilize** /ˈfɜːtəlaɪz/ *v.t.* make fertile; cause (egg etc. or female) to develop new individual. **fertilization** *n.*
**fertilizer** /ˈfɜːtəlaɪzə(r)/ *n.* chemical plant food; manure.
**fervent** /ˈfɜːv(ə)nt/ *a.* ardent, impassioned. **fervency** *n.*
**fervid** /ˈfɜːvɪd/ *a.* fervent.
**fervour** /ˈfɜːvə(r)/ *n.* passion, zeal.
**festal** /ˈfest(ə)l/ *a.* of feast; bright, cheerful.
**fester** /ˈfestə(r)/ *v.i.* make or become septic; cause continuing annoyance; rot; stagnate.
**festival** /ˈfestɪv(ə)l/ *n.* day or time of celebration; series of musical etc. performances held regularly in town etc.
**festive** /ˈfestɪv/ *a.* of feast; joyous.
**festivity** /feˈstɪvɪti/ *n.* gaiety, festive celebration; in *pl.* festive proceedings.
**festoon** /feˈstuːn/ 1 *n.* chain of flowers or ribbons etc. hung in curve. 2 *v.t.* adorn with or form into festoons.
**fetch** *v.t.* go for and bring back; be sold for; draw forth; deal (blow).
**fetching** /ˈfetʃɪŋ/ *a.* attractive.
**fête** /feɪt/ 1 *n.* outdoor function to raise money for charity. 2 *v.t.* entertain; make much of (person).
**fetid** /ˈfetɪd/ *a.* stinking.
**fetish** /ˈfetɪʃ/ *n.* object worshipped by primitive peoples; anything irrationally reverenced; abnormal object of sexual desire. **fetishism** *n.*; **fetishist** *n.*
**fetlock** /ˈfetlɒk/ *n.* part of back of horse's leg where tuft of hair grows above hoof.
**fetter** /ˈfetə(r)/ 1 *n.* shackle for feet; in

**fettle** / *pl.* captivity; restraint. **2** *v.t.* put into fetters, restrict.

**fettle** /ˈfet(ə)l/ *n.* condition, trim.

**fettler** /ˈfetlə(r)/ *n. Aus.* railway maintenance worker.

**feud**[1] /fjuːd/ **1** *n.* lasting mutual hostility esp. between two families or groups. **2** *v.i.* conduct feud.

**feud**[2] /fjuːd/ *n.* fief.

**feudal** /ˈfjuːd(ə)l/ *a.* of social system in medieval Europe whereby vassal held land from superior in exchange for allegiance and service. **feudalism** *n.*; **feudalistic** *a.*

**fever** /ˈfiːvə(r)/ **1** *n.* abnormally high body temperature; disease characterized by this; nervous agitation. **2** *v.t.* affect with fever or excitement.

**feverfew** /ˈfiːvəfjuː/ *n.* herb formerly used to reduce fever.

**feverish** /ˈfiːvərɪʃ/ *a.* having symptoms of fever; excited, restless.

**few 1** *a.* not many. **2** *n.* a small number. **3 a good few, quite a few,** *colloq.* a fair number.

**fey** /feɪ/ *a.* strange, other-worldly; *Sc.* fated to die soon.

**fez** *n.* flat-topped conical red cap with tassel, worn by men in some Muslim countries.

**ff.** *abbr.* following pages etc.

**ff** *abbr.* fortissimo.

**fiancé** /fiˈɒnseɪ/ *n.* (*fem.* **-cée** *pr.* same) person to whom a person is engaged to be married.

**fiasco** /fiˈæskəʊ/ *n.* (*pl.* **-cos**) failure; ignominious result.

**fiat** /ˈfaɪæt/ *n.* authorization; decree.

**fib 1** *n.* trivial lie. **2** *v.i.* tell fib.

**fibre** /ˈfaɪbə(r)/ *n.* one of the threadlike cells or filaments forming animal and vegetable tissue and textile substance; piece of glass in form of thread; roughage; substance formed of fibres; personal character. **fibre-board** board made of compressed wood etc. fibres; **fibreglass** glass in fibrous form woven as fabric or used as insulator etc.; **fibre optics** transmission of information by means of infra-red light signals along thin glass fibre.

**fibril** /ˈfaɪbrɪl/ *n.* small fibre.

**fibroid** /ˈfaɪbrɔɪd/ **1** *a.* like fibre or fibrous tissue. **2** *n.* fibroid tumour in uterus.

**fibrositis** /faɪbrəˈsaɪtɪs/ *n.* rheumatic inflammation of fibrous tissue.

**fibrous** /ˈfaɪbrəs/ *a.* of or like fibres.

**fibula** /ˈfɪbjələ/ *n.* (*pl.* **-lae** *or* **-las**) bone on outer side of lower leg.

**fiche** /fiːʃ/ *n.* (*pl.* same) microfiche.

**fickle** /ˈfɪk(ə)l/ *a.* inconstant, changeable.

**fiction** /ˈfɪkʃ(ə)n/ *n.* invention; invented statement or narrative; literature consisting of such narrative; conventionally accepted falsehood. **fictional** *a.*

**fictitious** /fɪkˈtɪʃəs/ *a.* imagined or made up, not real or genuine.

**fiddle** /ˈfɪd(ə)l/ **1** *n. colloq.* violin; *sl.* artful trick or piece of cheating. **2** *v.* fidget *with*; move aimlessly *about*; *sl.* falsify, swindle, get by cheating; play fiddle, play (tune) on fiddle. **3 fiddlesticks** nonsense. **4 fiddler** *n.*

**fiddling** /ˈfɪdlɪŋ/ *a. colloq.* petty, trivial.

**fiddly** /ˈfɪdlɪ/ *a.* awkward to do or use.

**fidelity** /fɪˈdelɪtɪ/ *n.* faithfulness, loyalty; accuracy, precision in sound reproduction.

**fidget** /ˈfɪdʒɪt/ **1** *v.* move restlessly; be or make uneasy, worry. **2** *n.* person who fidgets; restless state or mood. **3 fidgety** *a.*

**fiduciary** /fɪˈdjuːʃərɪ/ **1** *a.* held or given in trust; (of currency) depending for its value on public confidence. **2** *n.* trustee.

**fie** /faɪ/ *int.* expressing disgust or shame.

**fief** /fiːf/ *n.* land held under feudal system; one's sphere of operation or control.

**field** /fiːld/ **1** *n.* area of open land, esp. for pasture or tillage or playing game; area rich in some natural product; all competitors or all except specified one(s); *Crick.* etc. fielding side; expanse of sea or snow etc.; scene of battle; area or sphere of action or influence etc.; *Computers* part of a record, representing a unit of information. **2** *v.* act as fieldsman, stop and return (ball); select (team or individual) to play in game. **3 field-day** *Mil.* day of exercise in manoeuvres etc., review, day of brilliant or exciting events; **field-events** athletic events other than races; **fieldglasses** binoculars for outdoor use; **field hospital** temporary hospital near

**fielder** /ˈfiːldə(r)/ n. Crick. etc. fieldsman; **Field Marshal** Army officer of highest rank; **fieldsman** Crick. player (other than bowler) opposed to batsman; **field sports** outdoor sports, esp. hunting, shooting, and fishing.

**fieldfare** /ˈfiːldfeə(r)/ n. kind of thrush.

**fiend** /fiːnd/ n. devil; very wicked or cruel person; sl. addict, devotee. **fiendish** a.

**fierce** /fɪəs/ a. violent; ardent, eager; raging, vehemently aggressive; intense.

**fiery** /ˈfaɪərɪ/ a. consisting of fire, flaming; bright red; intensely hot; spirited, intense.

**fiesta** /fɪˈestə/ n. festival, holiday.

**fife** /faɪf/ n. small shrill flute.

**fifteen** /fɪfˈtiːn/ a. & n. one more than fourteen; Rugby Footb. side of fifteen players. **fifteenth** a. & n.

**fifth** /fɪfθ/ 1 a. next after fourth. 2 n. fifth person or thing; one of five equal parts of a thing. 3 **fifth column** group working for enemy within country at war etc.

**fifty** /ˈfɪftɪ/ a. & n. five times ten. **fifty-fifty** half-and-half, equally. **fiftieth** a. & n.

**fig**[1] n. soft pear-shaped fruit; tree bearing it; valueless thing. **fig-leaf** device for concealing something, esp. genitals.

**fig**[2] n. dress, equipment.

**fig.** abbr. figure.

**fight** /faɪt/ 1 v. (past & p.p. **fought** /fɔːt/) contend or struggle physically in battle or single combat; struggle (for); contend with; strive to overcome. 2 n. fighting; battle; power or inclination to fight; boxing-match. 3 **fight shy of** avoid.

**fighter** /ˈfaɪtə(r)/ n. person who fights; aircraft designed for attacking other aircraft.

**fighting** /ˈfaɪtɪŋ/ a. able and eager or bred or trained to fight; engaged in fighting. **fighting chance** chance of succeeding by great effort; **fighting fit** extremely fit.

**figment** /ˈfɪgmənt/ n. thing existing only in the imagination.

**figurative** /ˈfɪgjʊrətɪv/ a. metaphorical; of pictorial or sculptural representation.

**figure** /ˈfɪgə(r)/ 1 n. external form, bodily shape; person as seen or viewed mentally; representation of human form; image; expression using words differently from literal meaning; symbol of number, numeral, esp. 0-9; value, amount of money; in pl. arithmetical calculations; diagram, illustration; series of movements forming single unit in dancing or skating etc. 2 v. appear or be mentioned; represent in diagram or picture; imagine; embellish with pattern; calculate, estimate; US understand, consider; US colloq. be understandable. 3 **figure-head** carved image etc. over ship's prow, merely nominal leader etc.; **figure out** work out by arithmetic or logic.

**figurine** /fɪgəˈriːn/ n. statuette.

**filament** /ˈfɪləmənt/ n. threadlike strand or fibre; conducting wire or thread in electric bulb. **filamentary** a.

**filbert** /ˈfɪlbət/ n. nut of cultivated hazel; tree bearing it.

**filch** v.t. steal, pilfer.

**file**[1] 1 n. folder or box etc. for keeping papers for reference; papers so kept; collection of records for use by computer; row of persons or things one behind the other. 2 v.t. place in file or among records; submit (application for patent, petition for divorce, etc.); march in file.

**file**[2] 1 n. tool with rough surface for smoothing surfaces. 2 v.t. smooth or shape with file.

**filial** /ˈfɪlɪəl/ a. of or due from son or daughter.

**filibuster** /ˈfɪləbʌstə(r)/ 1 n. person who obstructs progress in legislative assembly; such obstruction. 2 v.i. act as filibuster.

**filigree** /ˈfɪlɪgriː/ n. fine ornamental tracery of gold or other wire; anything delicate and frail.

**filings** /ˈfaɪlɪŋz/ n.pl. particles rubbed off by file.

**fill** 1 v. make or become full; put filling into; spread over, pervade; block up (hole etc.); occupy. 2 n. as much as one wants; enough to fill thing. 3 **fill in** complete, fill completely, act as substitute, colloq. inform more fully; **fill out** enlarge, become enlarged, esp. to proper size; **fill up** fill completely, fill petrol tank of (motor vehicle).

**filler** /'filə(r)/ *n.* person or thing that fills; material used to fill cavity or increase bulk.

**fillet** /'filət/ 1 *n.* boneless piece of fish or meat; band worn round head; hair ribbon; *Archit.* narrow flat band between mouldings. 2 *v.t.* remove bones from (fish etc.); divide (fish etc.) into fillets; bind or provide with fillet(s).

**filling** /'filɪŋ/ *n.* material used to fill cavity in tooth; material between bread in sandwich. **filling-station** establishment selling petrol etc. to motorists.

**fillip** /'fɪləp/ 1 *n.* stimulus, incentive; flick with finger or thumb. 2 *v.* stimulate; flick.

**filly** /'fɪlɪ/ *n.* female foal; *sl.* young woman.

**film** 1 *n.* thin coating or layer; strip or sheet of plastic etc. coated with light-sensitive emulsion for exposure in camera; story etc. recorded on cinematographic film; slight veil of haze etc.; dimness over eyes. 2 *v.* make film or motion picture of; cover or become covered (as) with film. 3 **film star** well-known actor or actress in films. 4 **filmy** *a.*

**filter** /'fɪltə(r)/ 1 *n.* device for removing impurities from a liquid or gas; device for making coffee by letting hot water drip through ground beans; screen for absorbing or modifying light; electrical device for suppressing certain frequencies etc.; arrangement for filtering of traffic. 2 *v.* pass or flow through filter; make way (*through*, *into*, etc.), leak *out*; (of traffic) be allowed to pass in certain direction when other traffic is held up. 3 **filter-tip** (cigarette with) filter for purifying smoke.

**filth** /fɪlθ/ *n.* loathsome dirt; garbage; obscenity. **filthy** *a.*

**filtrate** /'fɪltreɪt/ 1 *v.* filter. 2 *n.* filtered liquid. **filtration** *n.*

**fin** *n.* organ for propelling and steering, projecting from body of fish etc.; fin-like projection on aircraft or rocket etc.

**finagle** /fə'neɪg(ə)l/ *v. colloq.* act or obtain dishonestly or by trickery.

**final** /'faɪn(ə)l/ 1 *a.* at the end, coming last; conclusive, decisive. 2 *n.* last or deciding heat or game or competition; last edition of day's newspaper; (usu. in *pl.*) final examination.

**finale** /fɪ'nɑːlɪ/ *n.* last movement or section of piece of music or drama etc.

**finalist** /'faɪnəlɪst/ *n.* competitor in final.

**finality** /faɪ'nælɪtɪ/ *n.* quality or fact of being final.

**finalize** /'faɪnəlaɪz/ *v.t.* put in final form; complete. **finalization** *n.*

**finance** /faɪ'næns/ 1 *n.* management of money; money support for enterprise; in *pl.* money resources. 2 *v.t.* find capital for. 3 **financial** *a.*

**financier** /faɪ'nænsɪə(r)/ *n.* person engaged in large-scale finance.

**finch** *n.* small passerine bird.

**find** /faɪnd/ 1 *v.t.* (*past & p.p.* **found** /faʊnd/) discover, or get possession of, by chance or search; become aware of, obtain; ascertain; supply; perceive, experience; *Law* judge and declare. 2 *n.* what is found; pleasing discovery. 3 **find out** discover, detect.

**finding** /'faɪndɪŋ/ *n.* conclusion reached by judicial etc. inquiry.

**fine**¹ 1 *a.* of high quality; excellent; pure, refined; handsome, imposing; bright, free from rain; small or thin, in small particles; smart, showy; fastidious. 2 *adv.* finely. 3 *v.i. Aus.* **fine up** (of weather) become fine. 4 **fine arts** arts appealing to sense of beauty, esp. painting, sculpture, and architecture; **fine-spun** delicate, too subtle.

**fine**² 1 *n.* sum of money (to be) paid as penalty for offence. 2 *v.t.* punish by fine.

**finery** /'faɪnərɪ/ *n.* showy dress or decoration.

**finesse** /fɪ'nes/ 1 *n.* subtle management; artfulness; *Cards* attempt to win trick by playing card that is not the highest held. 2 *v.* use finesse; manage by finesse; make finesse.

**finger** /'fɪŋgə(r)/ 1 *n.* any of terminal members of hand (usu. excluding thumb); corresponding part of glove; finger-like object; breadth of finger, esp. that depth of liquor in glass. 2 *v.t.* touch or turn about with fingers; play (music or instrument) with fingers. 3 **fingerbowl** bowl for rinsing fingers during meal; **fingerpost** signpost at road-junction; **fingerprint** impression made on surface by fingers, esp. used for identifying criminals, *fig.* distinctive charac-

**fingering** / ˈfɪŋgərɪŋ/ *n.* proper use of fingers in playing music; indication of this in score.

**fingering**² /ˈfɪŋgərɪŋ/ *n.* fine wool for knitting.

**finial** /ˈfɪnɪəl/ *n.* ornamental top to gable or canopy etc.

**finicky** /ˈfɪnɪkɪ/ *a.* (also **finical**, **finicking**) excessively detailed; overparticular; fastidious.

**finis** /ˈfɪnɪs/ *n.* end, esp. of book.

**finish** /ˈfɪnɪʃ/ 1 *v.* bring or come to an end, come to end of; put final touches to. 2 *n.* last stage, decisive result; completed state; mode of surface treatment.

**finite** /ˈfaɪnaɪt/ *a.* limited, not infinite; *Gram.* (of verb) having specific number and person.

**fiord** /fjɔːd/ *n.* narrow inlet of sea between cliffs.

**fir** *n.* kind of evergreen conifer with needles placed singly on shoots; its wood. **fir-cone** its fruit.

**fire** /faɪə(r)/ 1 *n.* state of combustion; flame, glow; destructive burning; burning fuel in grate etc.; electric or gas heater; firing of guns; fervour, spirit; burning heat. 2 *v.* shoot (gun etc. or missile from it); shoot gun or missile; detonate; dismiss (employee); set fire to; catch fire; supply with fuel; stimulate, fill with enthusiasm; bake or dry (pottery, bricks, etc.); become heated or excited. 3 **firearm** gun, pistol, etc.; **fire-ball** large meteor, ball of flame from nuclear explosion; **fire-bomb** incendiary bomb; **firebrand** piece of burning wood, trouble-maker; **firebreak** obstacle preventing spread of fire in forest or bush etc.; **fire-brick** fire-proof brick used for grates etc.; **fire brigade** organized body of firemen; **fire-clay** clay used for fire-bricks etc.; **firedog** andiron; **fire-drill** rehearsal of procedure to be used if fire breaks out; **fire-engine** vehicle carrying equipment for extinguishing fires; **fire-escape** apparatus or emergency staircase for escape from building on fire; **firefly** insect emitting phosphorescent light; **fire-irons** tongs, poker, and shovel for tending domestic fire; **fireman** man employed to extinguish fires, man who tends furnace etc.; **fireplace** grate or hearth for domestic fire, *Aus.* clearing in bush where fires may be lit; **fire-power** destructive capacity of guns etc.; **fire-practice** fire-drill; **fireside** area round fireplace, home, home-life; **fire-water** *colloq.* strong alcoholic liquor; **firework** device giving spectacular effect by use of combustible chemicals etc., *fig.* in *pl.* display of anger etc.; **under fire** being shot at, being criticized.

**firing** /ˈfaɪərɪŋ/ *n.* discharge of guns; fuel. **firing-line** front line of battle; **firing-squad** group which fires salute at military funeral or shoots condemned person.

**firm**¹ 1 *a.* of solid structure; fixed, steady; steadfast, resolute; (of offer etc.) not liable to cancellation after acceptance. 2 *v.* make or become firm or secure.

**firm**² 1 *n.* business concern or its members.

**firmament** /ˈfɜːməmənt/ *n.* sky regarded as vault.

**first** 1 *a.* foremost in time or order or importance. 2 *n.* first person or thing. 3 *adv.* before all or something else; for the first time. 4 **first aid** help given to injured until medical treatment is available; **first class** best category, best accommodation in train or ship etc., highest category of achievement in examination, class of mail most quickly delivered; **first-class** of or by first class; excellent; **firsthand** direct, original; **first night** first public performance of play etc.; **first-rate** excellent, very well. 5 **firstly** *adv.*

**firth** /fɜːθ/ *n.* inlet of sea, estuary.

**fiscal** /ˈfɪsk(ə)l/ 1 *a.* of public revenue.

**fish**¹ 1 *n.* (*pl.* usu. same) vertebrate cold-blooded animal living in water; flesh of fish as food. 2 *v.* try to catch fish (in); search *for*; draw *out*; seek by indirect means *for*. 3 **fish-eye lens** wide-angled lens; **fish finger** small oblong piece of fish in breadcrumbs; **fish-hook** barbed hook for catching fish; **fish-kettle** oval pan for boiling fish; **fishmeal** ground dried fish as fertilizer etc.; **fishmonger** dealer in fish; **fish-slice** cook's flat implement for turning fish etc.; **fishwife** woman selling fish.

**fish**² *n.* piece of wood or iron for

**fisherman** /ˈfɪʃəmən/ n. (pl. -men) man who lives by fishing, angler.

**fishery** /ˈfɪʃəri/ n. place where fish are caught; business of fishing.

**fishing** /ˈfɪʃɪŋ/ n. sport of trying to catch fish.

**fishy** /ˈfɪʃi/ a. of or like fish; sl. dubious, open to suspicion.

**fissile** /ˈfɪsaɪl/ a. capable of undergoing nuclear fission; tending to split.

**fission** /ˈfɪʃ(ə)n/ 1 n. Biol. division of cell etc. as mode of reproduction; (in full **nuclear fission**) splitting of atomic nucleus. 2 v. (cause to) undergo fission.

**fissure** /ˈfɪʃə(r)/ 1 n. narrow opening; split; cleavage. 2 v. split.

**fist** n. clenched hand.

**fistula** /ˈfɪstjələ/ n. pipe-like ulcer; surgically made body-passage. **fistular** a.; **fistulous** a.

**fit**[1] 1 a. qualified, competent, worthy; in good health or condition; becoming, proper. 2 v. be in harmony (with); be or make of or adjust to right size and shape; join (*on, together, up,* etc.) parts that fit; adapt; make competent *for* or *to*; supply *with*. 3 n. way thing fits. **fit in** make room or time for, adapt oneself, conform, be adapted; **fit out, up,** equip.

**fit**[2] n. sudden seizure of epilepsy or hysteria or fainting etc.; attack of strong feeling; sudden transitory state; mood.

**fitful** /ˈfɪtfəl/ a. active or occurring spasmodically or intermittently.

**fitment** /ˈfɪtmənt/ n. piece of fixed furniture.

**fitter** /ˈfɪtə(r)/ n. person who makes garments etc. fit; mechanic who fits together parts of engines etc.

**fitting** /ˈfɪtɪŋ/ 1 n. action of fitting on a garment; (usu. in *pl.*) fixture, fitment. 2 a. proper, befitting.

**five** a. & n. one more than four.

**fiver** /ˈfaɪvə(r)/ n. *UK colloq.* £5 note.

**fives** /faɪvz/ n. game in which ball is struck with hands or bat against walls of court.

**fix** 1 v. make firm or stable or permanent; fasten, secure; settle, specify; direct (eyes etc.) steadily on; attract and hold (attention etc.); identify, locate; mend, repair; arrange, make ready; *sl.* do for, get even with; *colloq.* tamper with or arrange result of etc., esp. by bribery; inject (*oneself*) with narcotic; (of plant) assimilate (gas) by forming non-gaseous compound. 2 n. dilemma, difficult position; position determined by bearings etc.; *sl.* dose of narcotic drug.

**fixate** /fɪkˈseɪt/ v.t. *Psych.* cause to acquire abnormal attachment to person or things.

**fixation** /fɪkˈseɪʃ(ə)n/ n. act or process of being fixated; obsession; fixing, coagulation; process of combining gas to form solid.

**fixative** /ˈfɪksətɪv/ 1 a. tending to fix. 2 n. substance used to fix colours etc.

**fixedly** /ˈfɪksɪdlɪ/ adv. intently.

**fixings** /ˈfɪksɪŋz/ n. pl. *US* equipment; trimmings of dress or dish.

**fixity** /ˈfɪksɪtɪ/ n. fixed state; stability, permanence.

**fixture** /ˈfɪkstʃə(r)/ n. thing fixed in position; in *pl.* articles belonging to land or house; (date fixed for) sporting event.

**fizz** 1 v.i. effervesce; hiss or splutter. 2 n. fizzing sound; effervescence; *colloq.* effervescent drink. 3 **fizzy** a.

**fizzle** /ˈfɪz(ə)l/ 1 v.i. hiss or splutter feebly. 2 n. fizzling sound. 3 **fizzle out** fail feebly.

**fjord** var. of **fiord**.

**fl.** abbr. fluid.

**flab** n. *colloq.* fat, flabbiness.

**flabbergast** /ˈflæbəɡɑːst/ v.t. *colloq.* overwhelm with astonishment.

**flabby** /ˈflæbɪ/ a. limp, not firm; feeble.

**flaccid** /ˈflæksɪd/ a. flabby. **flaccidity** n.

**flag**[1] 1 n. piece of cloth or other material, attached by one edge to pole or rope etc. and used as standard or ensign or signal. 2 v.t. inform or signal to (as) with flag; mark with flag or tag. 3 **flag-day** day on which money is raised for cause by sale of small paper flags; **flag-officer** admiral or vice- or rear-admiral; **flag-pole** flagstaff; **flagship** ship with admiral on board; **flagstaff** pole on which flag is hung.

**flag**[2] v.i. become limp, feeble, or uninteresting.

**flag**[3] 1 n. flat slab of stone for paving;

## flag

in *pl.* pavement of flags. **3 flagstone** flag.

**flag**⁴ *n.* plant with bladed leaf.

**flagellant** /ˈflædʒələnt/ **1** *n.* person who flagellates himself or others. **2** *a.* of flagellation.

**flagellate** /ˈflædʒəleɪt/ *v.t.* whip or flog, esp. as religious discipline or sexual stimulus. **flagellation** *n.*

**flageolet** /flædʒəˈlet/ *n.* small wind-instrument like recorder.

**flagon** /ˈflægən/ *n.* rounded vessel to hold liquor.

**flagrant** /ˈfleɪgrənt/ *a.* glaring, scandalous. **flagrancy** *n.*

**flail 1** *n.* hand threshing-implement. **2** *v.* wave or swing wildly; beat (as) with flail.

**flair** *n.* selective instinct for what is good or useful etc.

**flak** *n.* anti-aircraft fire; *fig.* barrage of criticism.

**flake 1** *n.* light fleecy piece esp. of snow; thin broad piece; layer. **2** *v.* take or come (*off* etc.) in flakes; fall in flakes, sprinkle with flakes. **3 flaky** *a.*

**flambé** /ˈflɑːbeɪ/ *a.* (of food) covered with spirit and served alight. [F]

**flamboyant** /flæmˈbɔɪənt/ *a.* florid, showy. **flamboyance** *n.*

**flame 1** *n.* (portion of) ignited gas; visible combustion; bright light; passion esp. of love; *colloq.* sweetheart. **2** *v.i.* emit flames; break *out*, blaze *up*, into anger; shine, gleam.

**flamenco** /fləˈmeŋkəʊ/ *n.* (*pl.* **-cos**) Spanish gipsy style of singing and dancing.

**flaming** /ˈfleɪmɪŋ/ *a.* burning with flames; very hot or bright; *colloq.* bloody, damned.

**flamingo** /fləˈmɪŋgəʊ/ *n.* (*pl.* **-goes**) tall long-necked wading-bird with pink, scarlet, and black plumage.

**flammable** /ˈflæməb(ə)l/ *a.* inflammable.

**flan** *n.* pastry or sponge case filled with spread with jam or fruit or savoury mixture etc.

**flange** /flændʒ/ *n.* projecting flat rim or collar or rib.

**flank 1** *n.* side of body between ribs and hip; side of mountain or body of troops etc. **2** *v.t.* be or be posted at or move along side(s) of.

**flannel** /ˈflæn(ə)l/ **1** *n.* woven woollen usu. napless cloth; in *pl.* flannel trousers; cloth used for washing oneself; *sl.* nonsense, flattery. **2** *v.* wash with flannel; *sl.* flatter.

**flannelette** /flænəˈlet/ *n.* napped cotton fabric resembling flannel.

**flap 1** *v.* (cause to) swing or sway about or move up and down; drive (flies etc.) *away* with flat object; *colloq.* be agitated or panicky. **2** *n.* broad piece hinged or held by one side and usu. hanging down; action or sound of flapping; light blow usu. with something flat; *colloq.* state of agitation or fuss. **3 flapjack** sweet oatcake, small pancake.

**flare** /fleə(r)/ **1** *v.* blaze with bright unsteady flame; (cause to) widen or spread gradually. **2** *n.* unshaded flame in open air, esp. used as signal or guide; outburst of flame; bright unsteady light; flared shape. **3 flare path** line of lights to guide aircraft landing or taking off; **flare up** burst into flame or anger etc.

**flash 1** *n.* sudden short blaze of flame or light; brief outburst or transient display; instant; brief news report; *Photog.* flashlight; *Mil.* cloth patch on uniform as emblem of unit etc. **2** *v.* produce a flash, gleam; *colloq.* show suddenly or ostentatiously; *sl.* briefly expose oneself indecently; send or reflect in flash(es); cause to shine briefly. **3** *a.* *colloq.* gaudy, showy. **4 flashback** return, esp. in a film, to past event; **flashbulb** bulb giving light for flashlight photograph; **flashlight** device producing brief bright light for indoor etc. photography, electric torch; **flash-point** temperature at which vapour from oil etc. ignites.

**flashing** /ˈflæʃɪŋ/ *n.* strip of metal to prevent flooding or leakage at joint of roofing etc.

**flashy** /ˈflæʃɪ/ *a.* gaudy, showy.

**flask** /flɑːsk/ *n.* vacuum flask; narrow-necked bulbous bottle; pocket-bottle of metal or glass.

**flat 1** *a.* horizontal, level; lying at full length; smooth, without bumps or indentation; absolute, downright; dull; dejected; without effervescence, insipid; (of battery) unable to generate electric current; (of tyre etc.) deflated or punctured; *Mus.* below correct or normal pitch. **2** *adv.* in a flat manner;

**flatten**            210            **flight**

*colloq.* downright, plainly; exactly. **3** *n.* group of rooms usu. on one floor, forming residence; flat surface or part; level ground; low-lying marshy land; *Mus.* note lowered by semitone, sign indicating this; section of stage scenery on frame; *colloq.* punctured tyre. **4 flat-fish** fish with flattened body, e.g. sole or plaice; **flat foot** foot with less than normal arch; **flat-footed** having flat feet, *colloq.* uninspired; **flat-iron** iron heated by external means, for smoothing linen; **flatlet** small flat; **flat out** at top speed, using all resources; **flat race** over level ground without jumps; **flat rate** unvarying rate or charge; **flat spin** aircraft's nearly horizontal spin, *colloq.* panic, consternation.

**flatten** /ˈflæt(ə)n/ *v.* make or become flat; *colloq.* defeat decisively.

**flatter** /ˈflætə(r)/ *v.t.* fawn upon; over-praise; cause to feel honoured; (of portrait) exaggerate good looks of. **flattery** *n.*

**flatulent** /ˈflætjələnt/ *a.* causing, caused by, or troubled with, formation of gas in alimentary canal; inflated, pretentious. **flatulence** *n.*

**flaunt** /flɔːnt/ *v.* display proudly; show off, parade.

**flautist** /ˈflɔːtɪst/ *n.* flute-player.

**flavour** /ˈfleɪvə(r)/ **1** *n.* mixed sensation of smell and taste; distinctive taste, characteristic quality. **2** *v.t.* give flavour to, season.

**flavouring** /ˈfleɪvərɪŋ/ *n.* thing used to flavour food or drink.

**flaw** **1** *n.* imperfection; blemish; crack, breach; defect in document etc. **2** *v.* make flaw in, spoil.

**flax** *n.* blue-flowered plant cultivated for its seeds and for textile fibre obtained from stem.

**flaxen** /ˈflæks(ə)n/ *a.* of flax; (of hair) pale yellow.

**flay** *v.t.* strip off skin or hide of; peel off; criticize severely.

**flea** *n.* small wingless jumping insect feeding on human or other blood. **flea market** *colloq.* street market selling second-hand goods etc.; **flea-pit** *sl.* dingy cinema.

**fleck** **1** *n.* spot of colour, freckle; small particle; speck. **2** *v.t.* mark with flecks.

**fled** *past* & *p.p.* of **flee**.

**fledge** *v.t.* provide with feathers or down; in *p.p.* able to fly, *fig.* mature.

**fledgeling** /ˈfledʒlɪŋ/ *n.* young bird; *fig.* inexperienced person.

**flee** *v.* (*past* & *p.p.* **fled**) run away (from); leave hurriedly.

**fleece** **1** *n.* woolly covering, esp. of sheep; wool shorn from sheep. **2** *v.t.* strip, plunder. **3 fleecy** *a.*

**fleet¹** *n.* naval force, navy; ships sailing together; number of vehicles owned by one proprietor. **2** *a.* swift, nimble.

**fleeting** /ˈfliːtɪŋ/ *a.* brief, passing rapidly.

**Flemish** /ˈflemɪʃ/ **1** *a.* of Flanders. **2** *n.* language of Flanders.

**flesh** *n.* soft substance between skin and bones; meat; body as opp. to mind or soul; pulpy substance of fruit etc.; plumpness, fat. **flesh and blood** human body, human nature, mankind, one's (*own*) near relations; **flesh-colour** yellowish-pink; **flesh-pots** luxurious living; **flesh-wound** one not reaching bone or vital organ.

**fleshly** /ˈfleʃlɪ/ *a.* worldly; carnal.

**fleshy** /ˈfleʃɪ/ *a.* of or like flesh; plump.

**fleur-de-lis** /flɜːdəˈliː/ *n.* (*pl.* **fleurs-** *pr. same*) heraldic device of three petals; former royal arms of France.

**flew** *past* of **fly¹**.

**flex¹** *n.* flexible insulated wire.

**flex²** *v.* bend (joint, limb); move (muscle) to bend joint.

**flexible** /ˈfleksəb(ə)l/ *a.* easily bent; pliable, adaptable. **flexibility** *n.*

**flexion** /ˈflekʃ(ə)n/ *n.* bending, bent state or part.

**flibbertigibbet** /ˈflɪbətɪdʒɪbət/ *n.* gossiping or frivolous or restless person.

**flick** **1** *n.* sudden release of bent finger or thumb; quick light blow or stroke; jerk; in *pl. sl.* cinema. **2** *v.t.* strike or knock *away* or *off* with flick. **3 flick-knife** weapon with blade that springs out when button etc. is pressed; **flick through** look cursorily through (book etc.).

**flicker** /ˈflɪkə(r)/ *v.i.* shine or burn unsteadily; show fitful vibration. **2** *n.* flickering light or motion; brief feeling of hope etc.

**flier** var. of **flyer**.

**flight¹** /flaɪt/ *n.* act or manner of flying; movement or path of thing through air; (regular) journey by airline; group of

**flight**

birds etc. flying together; volley (*of* arrows etc.); series (*of* stairs, hurdles etc. for racing, etc.); feather etc. on dart or arrow. **flight-deck** cockpit of large aircraft, deck of aircraft carrier; **flight lieutenant** air force officer next below squadron leader; **flight-recorder** device in aircraft to record technical details for use in case of accident.

**flight**² /flaɪt/ *n.* running away; hasty retreat.

**flighty** /'flaɪtɪ/ *a.* frivolous; changeable.

**flimsy** /'flɪmzɪ/ *a.* easily damaged or knocked apart.

**flinch** *v.i.* draw back, shrink; wince.

**Flinders grass** /'flɪndəz/ *Aus.* fodder grass resistant to dry weather.

**fling** 1 *v.* (*past & p.p.* **flung**) throw, hurl; rush, go violently. 2 *n.* throw, cast; vigorous dance; spell of self-indulgence.

**flint** *n.* hard stone found in pebbly lumps; piece of flint esp. as tool or weapon; piece of hard alloy used to produce spark. **flintlock** old type of gun discharged by spark from flint. **flinty** *a.*

**flip**¹ 1 *v.* turn over quickly, flick; toss (thing) so that it turns over. 2 *n.* action of flipping.

**flip**² *n.* drink of heated beer and spirit.

**flip**³ *a. colloq.* glib, flippant.

**flippant** /'flɪpənt/ *a.* treating serious things lightly; disrespectful. **flippancy** *n.*

**flipper** /'flɪpə(r)/ *n.* limb used by turtle or walrus etc. in swimming; rubber etc. attachment to foot for underwater swimming; *sl.* hand.

**flirt** 1 *v.* behave in amorous or enticing manner without serious intentions; superficially interest oneself *with.* 2 *n.* person who flirts. 3 **flirtation** *n.*; **flirtatious** *a.*

**flit** 1 *v.i.* pass lightly or rapidly (*about*); fly lightly and swiftly; abscond, disappear secretly, esp. to escape creditor. 2 *n.* act of flitting.

**flitch** *n.* side of bacon.

**flitter** /'flɪtə(r)/ *v.i.* flit about.

**float** 1 *v.* (cause to) rest or drift on surface of liquid; hover *before* eye or mind; (of currency) have fluctuating exchange rate; cause or allow to do this; launch (company, scheme). 2 *n.* thing

**florin**

that floats or rests on surface of liquid; raft; low-bodied cart etc. esp. used in procession; sum of money for minor expenditures or change-giving; tool for smoothing plaster etc.; in *sing.* or *pl.* footlights. 3 **floating dock** floating structure usable as dry dock; **floating rib** rib not attached to breastbone in front.

**floatation** var. of **flotation**.

**flocculent** /'flɒkjʊlənt/ *a.* like tufts of wool.

**flock**¹ 1 *n.* number of animals esp. birds, sheep, or goats, regarded as a unit; large crowd of people; congregation in relation to its pastor. 2 *v.i.* move or assemble *together* in large numbers.

**flock**² *n.* lock or tuft of wool etc.; wool or cotton waste used as stuffing.

**floe** *n.* sheet of floating ice.

**flog** *v.t.* beat with whip or stick etc.; *sl.* sell.

**flood** /flʌd/ 1 *n.* (coming of) great quantity of water, esp. over land; outburst, outpouring; inflow of tide. 2 *v.* overflow; cover or be covered with flood; come in great quantities. 3 **the Flood** that described in Genesis; **floodgate** gate for admitting or excluding water; **floodlight** (illuminate with) copious artificial lighting directed on building etc.; **floodlit** lit thus.

**floor** /flɔː(r)/ *n.* lower surface of room; bottom of sea or cave etc.; rooms on one level in house; storey; part of legislative chamber where members sit and speak; right of speaking; level area. 2 *v.t.* provide with floor; knock down; baffle, nonplus; overcome. 3 **floor show** cabaret.

**flop** 1 *v.* move or fall or sit etc. *down* awkwardly or negligently or with soft thud; sway about heavily and loosely; *sl.* collapse, fail. 2 *n.* flopping motion or sound; *sl.* failure. 3 *adv.* with a flop. 4 **floppy** *a.*

**flora** /'flɔːrə/ *n.* (*pl.* **-ras**) the plants of a region or period.

**floral** /'flɔːr(ə)l/ *a.* of or decorated with flowers.

**floret** /'flɔːrət/ *n.* any of the small flowers of composite flower.

**florid** /'flɒrɪd/ *a.* ornate, showy; ruddy, high-coloured. **floridity** *n.*

**florin** /'flɒrɪn/ *n. hist.* gold or silver coin, esp. English two-shilling coin.

**florist** /'florəst/ *n.* person who deals in or grows flowers.

**floruit** /'floru:ɪt/ *n.* period at which person was alive or worked.

**floss** *n.* rough silk enveloping silkworm's cocoon; dental floss. **floss silk** rough silk used in cheap goods. **flossy** *a.*

**flotation** /fləʊ'teɪʃ(ə)n/ *n.* launching of a commercial enterprise etc.

**flotilla** /flə'tɪlə/ *n.* small fleet, fleet of small ships.

**flotsam** /'flɒtsəm/ *n.* floating wreckage.

**flounce**[1] /flaʊns/ 1 *v.i.* go or move with agitated or violent motion. 2 *n.* flouncing movement.

**flounce**[2] /flaʊns/ 1 *n.* ornamental frill round woman's skirt etc. 2 *v.t.* trim with flounces.

**flounder**[1] /'flaʊndə(r)/ *v.t.* move or struggle clumsily; proceed in bungling or struggling fashion.

**flounder**[2] /'flaʊndə(r)/ *n.* small flatfish.

**flour** /flaʊə(r)/ 1 *n.* powdery substance got by milling and usu. sifting cereals, esp. wheat. 2 *v.t.* sprinkle with flour. 3 **floury** *a.*

**flourish** /'flʌrɪʃ/ 1 *v.* grow vigorously; thrive, prosper; wave or throw about. 2 *n.* ornamental curve in writing; sweeping gesture with weapon or hand etc.; *Mus.* florid passage; fanfare.

**flout** /flaʊt/ *v.t.* express contempt for by word or act.

**flow** /fləʊ/ 1 *v.i.* glide along as stream; move like liquid; gush out; circulate; move easily; (of dress etc.) hang easily; be in flood; result (*from*). 2 *n.* flowing; copious supply; rise of tide. 3 **flow chart, diagram,** diagram of movement or actions etc. of things or persons in complex activity; **flow-on** *Aus.* wage rise awarded to group of workers to match award made to another group.

**flower** /'flaʊə(r)/ 1 *n.* part of plant from which seed or fruit develops; flowering plant; state of blooming. 2 *v.* produce flowers; reach peak.

**flowery** /'flaʊərɪ/ *a.* abounding in flowers; full of fine words.

**flown** *p.p.* of **fly**[1].

**flu** *n. colloq.* influenza.

**fluctuate** /'flʌktjʊeɪt/ *v.i.* vary, rise and fall; be unstable. **fluctuation** *n.*

**flue** *n.* smoke-duct in chimney; channel for conveying heat.

**fluent** /'flu:ənt/ *a.* expressing oneself quickly and easily; copious and ready, flowing. **fluency** *n.*

**fluff** 1 *n.* light downy substance, e.g. that shed from fabric; *sl.* mistake made in speaking etc. 2 *v.* shake *up* or *out* into soft mass; *sl.* make mistake in speaking etc. 3 **fluffy** *a.*

**fluid** /'flu:ɪd/ 1 *n.* substance capable of flowing freely, gas or liquid; liquid secretion. 2 *a.* able to flow freely, not solid or rigid or stable. 3 **fluidify** *v.*; **fluidity** *n.*

**fluke**[1] 1 *n.* lucky accidental stroke or success. 2 *v.* get or hit etc. by fluke. 3 **fluky** *a.*

**fluke**[2] *n.* flat-fish, flounder; parasitic flatworm in liver of sheep etc.

**flummery** /'flʌmərɪ/ *n.* sweet milk dish; empty talk; nonsense.

**flummox** /'flʌməks/ *v.t. colloq.* bewilder.

**flung** *past* & *p.p.* of **fling**.

**flunk** *v. US sl.* fail, esp. in examination.

**flunkey** /'flʌŋkɪ/ *n.* usu. *derog.* footman.

**fluorescence** /flʊə'res(ə)ns/ *n.* light produced from some substances by action of radiation. **fluoresce** *v.i.*; **fluorescent** *a.*

**fluoridate** /'flʊərədeɪt/ *v.t.* add fluoride to (water supply). **fluoridation** *n.*

**fluoride** /'flʊəraɪd/ *n.* compound of fluorine with metal.

**fluorine** /'flʊəri:n/ *n.* pungent corrosive gaseous element.

**fluorspar** /'flʊəspɑ:(r)/ *n.* calcium fluoride as mineral.

**flurry** /'flʌrɪ/ 1 *n.* gust, squall; nervous hurry, agitation. 2 *v.t.* agitate, confuse.

**flush**[1] 1 *v.* (cause to) glow or blush; cleanse (drain, lavatory, etc.) by flow of water; dispose of thus; spurt, rush out. 2 *n.* glow, blush; feeling of feverish heat; rush of emotion or elation; rush of water; cleansing by flushing; freshness, vigour. 3 *a.* level (*with*); *colloq.* having plenty of money etc.

**flush**[2] *v.* (cause to) fly up suddenly; reveal, drive *out.*

**flush**[3] *n. Cards* hand of cards all of one suit.

**fluster** /'flʌstə(r)/ 1 *v.* confuse, agitate; bustle. 2 *n.* confused or agitated state.

**flute** 1 *n.* woodwind instrument, long pipe with holes stopped by keys and mouth-hole at side; vertical groove in pillar etc. 2 *v.* make grooves in; whistle or sing etc. in flute-like tones; play (on) flute.

**fluting** /'flu:tɪŋ/ *n.* series of ornamental grooves.

**flutter** /'flʌtə(r)/ 1 *v.* flap (wings) in flying or trying to fly; wave or flap quickly and irregularly; move restlessly; beat feebly and irregularly. 2 *n.* fluttering; tremulous excitement; rapid variation of pitch or loudness of sound; *colloq.* small bet or speculation.

**fluty** /'flu:tɪ/ *a.* soft and clear in tone.

**fluvial** /'flu:vɪəl/ *a.* of or found in rivers.

**flux** *n.* continuous succession of changes; flowing; inflow of tide; substance mixed with metal etc. to assist fusion.

**fly**[1] 1 *v.* (*past* flew; *p.p.* flown /fləʊn/) move through air with wings or in aircraft; control flight of (aircraft); flutter, wave, set or keep (flag, kite) flying; travel swiftly; hasten, rush; flee (from). 2 *n.* flying; flap on garment, esp. trousers, to contain or cover fastening; (*freq.* in *pl.*) this fastening; flap at entrance of tent; *Theatr.* in *pl.* space over proscenium; part of flag farthest from staff. 3 **fly-half** *Rugby footb.* halfback who stands off from scrum-half; **flyleaf** blank leaf at beginning or end of book; **flyover** bridge carrying road etc. over another; **fly-past** ceremonial flight of aircraft past person or place; **fly-post** display (handbills etc.) in unauthorized places; **flywheel** heavy wheel regulating machinery or accumulating power.

**fly**[2] *n.* two-winged insect; disease of plants or animals caused by flies; natural or artificial fly used as bait. **flyblown** tainted, *Aus. sl.* penniless; **flycatcher** bird that catches flies in air; **fly-spray** liquid sprayed from canister to kill flies; **flyweight** boxing-weight (up to 51 kg.).

**fly**[3] *a. sl.* knowing, clever.

**flyer** /'flaɪə(r)/ *n.* airman; fast animal or vehicle.

**flying** /'flaɪɪŋ/ 1 *n.* in flight. 2 *a.* that flies; hasty. 3 **flying boat** seaplane with boatlike fuselage; **flying buttress** buttress slanting from column etc. to wall, usu. on arch; **flying doctor** *Aus.* doctor visiting patients by aircraft; **flying fish** fish that can rise into air by winglike fins; **flying fox** fruit-eating bat, *Aus.* carrier operated by cables across gorge etc.; **flying officer** air force officer next below flight-lieutenant; **flying saucer** unidentified saucer-shaped object reported as seen in sky; **flying squad** detachment of police organized for rapid movement; **flying start** start in which starting-point is passed at full speed, vigorous start, initial advantage.

**FM** *abbr.* Field Marshal; frequency modulation.

**FO** *abbr.* Flying Officer.

**foal** 1 *n.* young of horse or ass etc. 2 *v.i.* give birth to foal.

**foam** 1 *n.* froth formed in liquid; froth of saliva or perspiration; rubber or plastic in cellular mass. 2 *v.i.* emit foam; froth, gather foam. 3 **foamy** *a.*

**fob**[1] *n.* ornamental attachment to watch-chain etc.; small pocket for watch etc. in waistband of trousers.

**fob**[2] *v.t.* (with *off*) deceive (person) into being satisfied (*with* inferior thing or excuse); palm or pass (off thing) *on* person.

**focal** /'fəʊk(ə)l/ *a.* of or at a focus. **focal length** distance between centre of lens etc. and its focus.

**fo'c's'le** var. of **forecastle**.

**focus** /'fəʊkəs/ 1 *n.* (*pl.* -cuses or -ci /-saɪ/) point at which rays etc. meet after reflection or refraction or from which rays etc. appear to proceed; point at which object must be situated to give clearly defined image; adjustment of eye or lens to produce clear image; state of clear definition; central or originating point. 2 *v.* bring into focus; adjust focus of (lens or eye); (cause to) converge to focus; concentrate or be concentrated *on*.

**fodder** /'fɒdə(r)/ 1 *n.* dried food, hay, etc. for cattle. 2 *v.t.* give fodder to.

**foe** *n.* enemy.

**foetid** var. of **fetid**.

**foetus** /'fi:təs/ *n.* developed embryo in womb or egg. **foetal** *a.*

**fog** 1 *n.* vapour suspended at or near earth's surface; thick mist; cloudiness on photographic negative. 2 *v.t.* (*past* & *p.p.* **fogged**) envelop (as) in fog; per-

**fogy** 3 **fog-horn** sounding instrument for warning ships in fog. 4 **foggy** *a*.
**fogy** /'fəʊgi:/ *n*. (also **fogey**) (**old**) **fogy** old-fashioned person.
**foible** /'fɔɪb(ə)l/ *n*. weak point, fault.
**foil**[1] *v*. baffle, frustrate, defeat.
**foil**[2] *n*. thin sheet or leaf of metal; thing that sets another off by contrast.
**foil**[3] *n*. blunt-edged fencing-sword.
**foist** *v.t*. fob (thing) (*off*) on person.
**fold**[1] /fəʊld/ 1 *v*. double (flexible thing) over upon itself; bend portion of; become or be able to be folded; clasp; envelop, wrap. 2 *n*. folding; hollow among hills; line made by folding. 3 **fold up** make more compact by folding, *colloq*. collapse, fail.
**fold**[2] /fəʊld/ 1 *n*. enclosure for sheep; body of believers. 2 *v.t*. enclose (sheep) in fold.
**folder** /'fəʊldə(r)/ *n*. folding cover or holder for loose papers etc.
**foliaceous** /fəʊli:'eɪʃəs/ *a*. of or like leaves; laminated.
**foliage** /'fəʊli:ədʒ/ *n*. leaves, leafage.
**foliate** 1 /'fəʊli:ət/ *a*. leaflike, having leaves. 2 /'fəʊli:eɪt/ *v*. split into thin layers. 3 **foliation** *n*.
**folio** /'fəʊli:əʊ/ 1 *n*. (*pl*. **-os**) leaf of paper etc. numbered only on front; sheet of paper folded once; volume made of such sheets. 2 *a*. (of book etc.) made of folios.
**folk** /fəʊk/ *n*. nation, race; in *pl*. people in general; people in general or of specified class; one's relatives; *attrib*. of popular origin. **folklore** traditional beliefs etc., study of these; **folk music** etc. music etc. traditional in a country, or in style of this; **folkweave** rough loosely-woven fabric.
**folksy** /'fəʊksi:/ *a*. having characteristics of ordinary people; resembling folk art.
**follicle** /'fɒlɪk(ə)l/ *n*. small sac or vesicle; small gland or cavity containing hair-root. **follicular** *a*.
**follow** /'fɒləʊ/ *v*. go or come after; go along; come next in order or time; take as guide; understand meaning of; be aware of present state or progress of; provide *with* sequel or successor; result *from*; be necessary inference. **follow on** continue, *Crick*. bat again immediately after first innings; **follow suit** play card of same suit as was led, *fig*. conform to another's actions; **follow through** continue (action etc.) to conclusion; **follow up** pursue, develop, supplement.
**follower** /'fɒləʊə(r)/ *n*. supporter, devotee.
**following** /'fɒləʊɪŋ/ 1 *n*. body of supporters. 2 *a*. now to be mentioned.
**folly** /'fɒli:/ *n*. foolishness; foolish act or conduct or idea etc.; costly ornamental building.
**foment** /fə'ment/ *v.t*. instigate, stir up (trouble etc.). **fomentation** *n*.
**fond** *a*. tender, loving; doting; foolishly credulous or optimistic. **fond of** having liking for.
**fondant** /'fɒnd(ə)nt/ *n*. soft sweet of flavoured sugar.
**fondle** /'fɒnd(ə)l/ *v*. caress.
**fondue** /'fɒndju:/ *n*. dish of flavoured melted cheese.
**font** *n*. receptacle for baptismal water.
**food** /fu:d/ *n*. substance taken into animal or plant to maintain life and growth; solid food. **food poisoning** illness due to bacteria etc. in food; **food processor** electric machine for chopping and mixing etc. food; **foodstuff** substance used as food.
**fool**[1] /fu:l/ 1 *n*. silly person, simpleton; unwise person; *hist*. jester, clown; dupe. 2 *v*. act in joking or teasing way; play or trifle; cheat, dupe. 3 **foolproof** so plain or simple as to be incapable of misuse or mistake; **fool's errand** fruitless one; **fool's paradise** illusory happiness; **make a fool of** make (person) look foolish; **play the fool** indulge in buffoonery.
**fool**[2] /fu:l/ *n*. dish of stewed crushed fruit mixed with cream, custard, etc.
**foolery** /'fu:ləri:/ *n*. foolish acts or behaviour.
**foolhardy** /'fu:lhɑ:di:/ *a*. foolishly bold; reckless.
**foolish** /'fu:lɪʃ/ *a*. lacking good sense; indiscreet; stupid.
**foolscap** /'fu:lskæp/ *n*. long folio writing or printing paper.
**foot** /fʊt/ 1 *n*. (*pl*. **feet**) end part of leg beyond ankle; lower part or end; linear measure of 12 in. (30.48 cm.); division of verse with one stressed syllable; step, pace, tread; *hist*. infantry. 2 *v.t*. pay (bill). 3 **foot-and-mouth** (**disease**) contagious virus disease of cattle etc.; **footfall** sound of footstep; **foothill** one

**footage** 215 **foredoom**

lying at base of mountain or range; **foothold** support for feet in climbing; **footlights** row of lights along front of stage; **footloose** free to act as one pleases; **footman** liveried servant; **footmark** footprint; **footnote** note at foot of page; **footpath** path for pedestrians only; **footplate** platform in locomotive for driver and fireman; **footprint** impression left by foot or shoe; **footsore** with sore feet, esp. from walking; **footstep** tread, footprint; **footstool** stool for resting feet on when sitting; **on foot** walking.

**footage** /'fʊtɪdʒ/ *n.* length in feet, esp. of cinema film.

**football** /'fʊtbɔːl/ *n.* large inflated usu. leather ball; game played with football. **football pool** form of gambling on results of football matches. **footballer** *n.*

**footing** /'fʊtɪŋ/ *n.* foothold; secure position; position or status of person etc. in relation to others.

**footling** /'fuːtlɪŋ/ *a.* trivial, silly.

**fop** *n.* dandy, vain man. **foppery** *n.*; **foppish** *a.*

**for 1** *prep.* in defence or favour of; representing; at price of; with the object of; during; as regards; in direction of; because of, on account of; notwithstanding. **2** *conj.* seeing that, since.

**forage** /'fɒrɪdʒ/ **1** *n.* food for horses and cattle; foraging. **2** *v.* rummage, search (*for*); collect forage (from).

**foray** /'fɒreɪ/ **1** *n.* sudden attack, raid. **2** *v.i.* make foray.

**forbad(e)** past of forbid.

**forbear**[1] /fɔː'beə(r)/ *v.* (*past* **forbore**; *p.p.* **forborne**) abstain or refrain (*from*); be patient. **forbearance** *n.*; **forbearing** *a.*

**forbear**[2] var. of forebear.

**forbid** /fə'bɪd/ *v.t.* (*past* **-bade** or **-bad** /-bæd/; *p.p.* **-bidden**) command not to do; not allow; prevent.

**forbidding** *a.* uninviting; repellent; stern.

**force 1** *n.* strength, violence, intense effort; body of men; in *pl.* troops; body of police; compulsion; influence, effectiveness. **2** *v.t.* constrain, compel; strain, urge; break open by force; drive, propel; impose or press (*up*)*on* (person); cause or produce by effort; artificially hasten maturity of; *Aus.* keep (stock) moving through race or yard, usu. with dog. **3 forced landing** unavoidable landing of aircraft in emergency; **forced march** lengthy and vigorous march, esp. by troops; **force-feed** feed (prisoner etc.) against his will; **force person's hand** compel him to act etc. prematurely or unwillingly; **forcing-dog** *Aus.* dog skilled in moving stock in a desired direction; **forcing-pen** *Aus.* pen into which sheep are driven.

**forceful** /'fɔːsfəl/ *a.* powerful; impressive.

**force majeure** /fɔːs mæˈʒɜː(r)/ *n.* irresistible compulsion; circumstances beyond one's control. [F]

**forcemeat** /'fɔːsmiːt/ *n.* meat or other food chopped and seasoned for use as stuffing.

**forceps** /'fɔːseps/ *n.* (*pl.* same) surgical pincers.

**forcible** /'fɔːsəb(ə)l/ *a.* done by or involving force; forceful.

**ford 1** *n.* shallow place where river etc. may be crossed. **2** *v.t.* cross (water) at ford.

**fore 1** *a.* situated in front. **2** *n.* front part; bow of ship. **3** *int.* Golf warning person in ball's line of flight. **4 fore-and-aft** (of sails or rigging) set lengthwise, not on yards; **to the fore** conspicuous.

**forearm**[1] /'fɔːrɑːm/ *n.* arm from elbow to wrist or fingertips.

**forearm**[2] /fɔːˈrɑːm/ *v.t.* arm beforehand, prepare.

**forebear** /'fɔːbeə(r)/ *n.* ancestor.

**forebode** /fɔːˈbəʊd/ *v.t.* be advance sign of; portend.

**foreboding** *n.* expectation of trouble.

**forecast** /'fɔːkɑːst/ **1** *v.t.* (*past* & *p.p.* **-cast** or **-casted**) predict or estimate beforehand. **2** *n.* prediction or estimate, esp. of coming weather.

**forecastle** /'fəʊks(ə)l/ *n.* forward part of ship where formerly crew were accommodated.

**foreclose** /fɔːˈkləʊz/ *v.* gain possession of mortgaged property of (person) on non-payment of money due; stop (mortgage) from being redeemable; exclude, prevent. **foreclosure** *n.*

**forecourt** /'fɔːkɔːt/ *n.* enclosed space in front of building.

**foredoom** /fɔːˈduːm/ *v.t.* doom beforehand; predestine.

**forefather** /ˈfɔːfɑːðə(r)/ n. (usu. in pl.) ancestor, member of past generation etc.

**forefinger** /ˈfɔːfɪŋgə(r)/ n. finger next to thumb.

**forefoot** /ˈfɔːfʊt/ n. (pl. -feet) front foot of animal.

**forefront** /ˈfɔːfrʌnt/ n. foremost part.

**foregoing** /fɔːˈgəʊɪŋ/ a. previously mentioned.

**foregone** /ˈfɔːgɒn/ a. previous, preceding. **foregone conclusion** easily foreseeable result.

**foreground** /ˈfɔːgraʊnd/ n. part of view nearest observer.

**forehand** /ˈfɔːhænd/ 1 n. Tennis etc. stroke made with palm turned forwards. 2 a. of or made with this stroke.

**forehead** /ˈfɒrɪd or ˈfɔːhed/ n. part of face above eyebrows.

**foreign** /ˈfɒrən/ a. of or in or with or characteristic of country or language other than one's own; of another district or society etc.; dissimilar or irrelevant to; introduced from outside.

**foreigner** /ˈfɒrənə(r)/ n. person born in or coming from another country.

**foreknow** /fɔːˈnəʊ/ v.t. (past -knew; p.p. -known) know beforehand. **foreknowledge** (/-ˈnɒlɪdʒ/) n.

**foreland** /ˈfɔːlənd/ n. promontory, cape.

**foreleg** /ˈfɔːleg/ n. animal's front leg.

**forelock** /ˈfɔːlɒk/ n. lock of hair just above forehead.

**foreman** /ˈfɔːmən/ n. (pl. -men) workman superintending others; principal juror.

**foremast** /ˈfɔːmɑːst/ n. mast nearest bow of ship.

**foremost** /ˈfɔːməʊst/ 1 a. first in place or order; chief, best. 2 adv. first.

**forename** /ˈfɔːneɪm/ n. first or Christian name.

**forenoon** /ˈfɔːnuːn/ n. arch. day till noon, morning.

**forensic** /fəˈrensɪk/ a. of courts of law. **forensic medicine** application of medical knowledge to legal problems.

**foreordain** /fɔːrɔːˈdeɪn/ v.t. predestine.

**foreplay** /ˈfɔːpleɪ/ n. stimulation preceding sexual intercourse.

**forerunner** /ˈfɔːrʌnə(r)/ n. predecessor; advance messenger.

**foresail** /ˈfɔːseɪl/ n. principal sail on foremast.

**foresee** /fɔːˈsiː/ v.t. (past -saw; p.p. -seen) see or be aware of beforehand.

**foreshadow** /fɔːˈʃædəʊ/ v.t. be warning or indication of (future event).

**foreshore** /ˈfɔːʃɔː(r)/ n. shore between high- and low-water marks.

**foreshorten** /fɔːˈʃɔːt(ə)n/ v.t. show or portray (object) with the apparent shortening due to visual perspective.

**foresight** /ˈfɔːsaɪt/ n. care for future; foreseeing.

**foreskin** /ˈfɔːskɪn/ n. loose skin covering end of penis.

**forest** /ˈfɒrɪst/ 1 n. large area of land covered chiefly with trees and undergrowth. 2 v.t. plant with trees; make into forest. 3 **forest oak** Aus. casuarina.

**forestall** /fɔːˈstɔːl/ v.t. act in advance of in order to prevent; deal with beforehand.

**forester** /ˈfɒrɪstə(r)/ n. officer in charge of forest; dweller in forest; Aus. large greyish kangaroo.

**forestry** /ˈfɒrɪstri/ n. management of forests.

**foretaste** /ˈfɔːteɪst/ n. taste or experience of something in advance.

**foretell** /fɔːˈtel/ v.t. (past & p.p. -told) predict, prophesy; be precursor of.

**forethought** /ˈfɔːθɔːt/ n. care for the future; deliberate intention.

**forever** /fəˈrevə(r)/ adv. always, constantly.

**forewarn** /fɔːˈwɔːn/ v.t. warn beforehand.

**forewoman** /ˈfɔːwʊmən/ n. (pl. -women /-ˈwɪmɪn/) woman worker supervising others; woman foreman of jury.

**foreword** /ˈfɔːwɜːd/ n. preface.

**forfeit** /ˈfɔːfɪt/ 1 n. thing surrendered as a penalty. 2 v.t. lose or surrender as penalty. 3 a. lost or surrendered as a penalty. 4 **forfeiture** n.

**forfend** /fɔːˈfend/ v.t. arch. avert.

**forgather** /fɔːˈgæðə(r)/ v.i. assemble; associate.

**forgave** past of **forgive**.

**forge**[1] 1 n. furnace etc. for melting or refining metal; workshop with this. 2 v. make or write in fraudulent imitation; shape by heating and hammering.

**forge**[2] v.i. advance gradually. **forge ahead** advance rapidly, take lead.

## forgery

**forgery** /ˈfɔːdʒəri/ *n.* (making of) forged document etc.

**forget** /fəˈget/ *v.* (*past* **-got**; *p.p.* **-gotten**) lose remembrance of; neglect, overlook; cease to think of. **forget-me-not** plant with small blue flowers; **forget oneself** act without due dignity, neglect one's interests.

**forgetful** /fəˈgetfəl/ *a.* liable to forget.

**forgive** /fəˈgɪv/ *v.t.* (*past* **-gave**; *p.p.* **-given** /-ˈgɪv(ə)n/) cease to resent; pardon; remit (debt). **forgiveness** *n.*

**forgo** /fɔːˈgəʊ/ *v.t.* (*past* **-went**; *p.p.* **-gone** /-gɒn/) go without, relinquish.

**fork** 1 *n.* pronged instrument used in eating and cooking etc.; pronged implement for digging etc.; (place of) divergence into branches or limbs etc.; forked part, esp. of bicycle frame. 2 *v.* form fork; branch; take one road at fork; dig with fork. 3 **fork-lift (truck)** vehicle with pronged device for lifting and carrying loads; **fork out** *sl.* pay, usu. unwillingly.

**forlorn** /fəˈlɔːn/ *a.* forsaken; in pitiful condition. **forlorn hope** the only faint hope that remains.

**form** 1 *n.* shape, arrangement of parts, visible aspect; mode in which thing exists or manifests itself; document with blanks to be filled up; class in school; behaviour according to rule or custom; set order of words; (of horse, athlete, etc.) condition of health and training; bench. 2 *v.* fashion, mould; take shape, become solid; make up, amount to; *Mil.* draw up in order, assume (formation).

**formal** /ˈfɔːm(ə)l/ *a.* according to recognized forms or rules; ceremonial, conventional; of or concerned with form; done as a matter of form, perfunctory; prim, stiff.

**formaldehyde** /fɔːˈmældəhaɪd/ *n.* colourless gas used in solution as preservative and disinfectant.

**formalin** /ˈfɔːməlɪn/ *n.* aqueous solution of formaldehyde.

**formalism** /ˈfɔːməlɪz(ə)m/ *n.* strict adherence to or concern with form. **formalist** *n.*

**formality** /fɔːˈmælətɪ/ *n.* formal act or conduct; rigid observance of rules or convention.

**formalize** /ˈfɔːməlaɪz/ *v.t.* make formal; give definite (esp. legal) form to.

## forth

**format** /ˈfɔːmæt/ 1 *n.* shape and size (of book etc.); style or manner of arrangement etc. 2 *v.* (*past* & *p.p.* **formatted**) arrange in format.

**formation** /fɔːˈmeɪʃ(ə)n/ *n.* forming; thing formed; particular arrangement (e.g. of troops); *Geol.* set of rocks or strata with common characteristic.

**formative** /ˈfɔːmətɪv/ *a.* serving to form; of formation.

**former** /ˈfɔːmə(r)/ 1 *a.* of the past, earlier. 2 *pron.* the first or first-named of two.

**formerly** *adv.* in former times.

**formic acid** /ˈfɔːmɪk/ colourless irritant volatile acid contained in fluid emitted by ants.

**formidable** /ˈfɔːmɪdəb(ə)l/ *a.* inspiring fear or dread; difficult to overcome or resist etc.

**formless** /ˈfɔːmləs/ *a.* without definite or regular form.

**formula** /ˈfɔːmjələ/ *n.* (*pl.* **-las** or **-lae** /-liː/) set of chemical symbols showing constituents of substance; rule or fact expressed in figures; fixed form of words; list of ingredients; classification of racing car esp. by engine capacity. **formulaic** /-ˈleɪɪk/ *a.*

**formulate** /ˈfɔːmjəleɪt/ *v.t.* express in a formula; express clearly and precisely. **formulation** *n.*

**fornication** /fɔːnəˈkeɪʃ(ə)n/ *n.* voluntary sexual intercourse between unmarried persons. **fornicate** *v.i.*; **fornicator** *n.*

**forsake** /fəˈseɪk/ *v.t.* (*past* **forsook**; *p.p.* **forsaken**) give up, renounce; desert, abandon.

**forsooth** /fəˈsuːθ/ *adv. arch.* indeed.

**forswear** /fɔːˈsweə(r)/ *v.t.* (*past* **-swore**; *p.p.* **-sworn**) abjure, renounce; perjure *oneself*; (in *p.p.*) perjured.

**forsythia** /fɔːˈsaɪθɪə/ *n.* ornamental shrub with bright yellow flowers.

**fort** *n.* fortified building or position. **hold the fort** act as temporary substitute.

**forte**[1] /ˈfɔːteɪ/ *n.* thing in which one excels.

**forte**[2] /ˈfɔːteɪ/ *Mus.* 1 *adv.* loudly. 2 *n.* passage to be performed thus.

**forth** /fɔːθ/ *adv.* forward; out of doors; onwards in time. **forthcoming** about to come forth, approaching, produced when wanted, informative or respons-

**fortiethe; forthright** straightforward, outspoken, decisive; **forthwith** immediately, without delay.

**fortieth** see **forty**.

**fortification** /ˌfɔːtəfəˈkeɪʃ(ə)n/ n. fortifying; (usu. in pl.) defensive work(s).

**fortify** /ˈfɔːtəfaɪ/ v.t. strengthen; provide with defensive works; strengthen (wine etc.) with spirits; add extra nutrients to (food).

**fortissimo** /fɔːˈtɪsɪməʊ/ *Mus.* 1 *adv.* very loudly. 2 n. (pl -mos) passage to be performed thus.

**fortitude** /ˈfɔːtɪtjuːd/ n. courage in pain or adversity.

**fortnight** /ˈfɔːtnaɪt/ n. two weeks.

**fortnightly** 1 a. done or produced or occurring once a fortnight. 2 adv. every fortnight. 3 n. fortnightly magazine etc.

**Fortran** /ˈfɔːtræn/ n. computer language used esp. for scientific calculations.

**fortress** /ˈfɔːtrəs/ n. fortified building or town.

**fortuitous** /fɔːˈtjuːɪtəs/ a. happening by chance. **fortuity** n.

**fortunate** /ˈfɔːtjənət/ a. lucky, auspicious.

**fortune** /ˈfɔːtjən/ n. chance as power in human affairs; luck; person's destiny; prosperity, wealth; large sum of money. **fortune-teller** foreteller of future events etc.

**forty** /ˈfɔːtɪ/ a. & n. four times ten. **forty winks** short sleep. **fortieth** a. & n.

**forum** /ˈfɔːrəm/ n. place of public discussion; court, tribunal.

**forward** /ˈfɔːwəd/ 1 a. lying in one's line of motion, onward or towards front; relating to the future; precocious, presumptuous, pert; well-advanced. 2 n. attacking player in football etc. 3 *adv.* towards future; to front; progressively. 4 *v.t.* send (letter etc.) on; dispatch; help to advance, promote.

**forwards** *adv.* forward.

**forwent** *past* of **forgo**.

**fosse** /fɒs/ n. canal, ditch, trench.

**fossick** /ˈfɒsɪk/ v. *Aus. & NZ* search for gold by digging out crevices or by digging in abandoned workings etc.; rummage or hunt *about*; dig *out*, hunt *up*.

**fossil** /ˈfɒs(ə)l/ 1 n. remains or impression of (usu. prehistoric) plant or animal hardened in rock; antiquated or unchanging person or thing. 2 a. of or like fossil; dug from the ground.

**fossilize** /ˈfɒsəlaɪz/ v. (cause to) become fossil. **fossilization** n.

**foster** /ˈfɒstə(r)/ 1 v.t. promote growth of; nurse or bring up as foster-child; encourage or harbour (feeling). 2 a. having family connection by fostering and not birth. 3 **foster home** home in which foster child is brought up.

**fought** *past & p.p.* of **fight**.

**foul** /faʊl/ 1 a. offensive, loathsome, stinking; dirty, soiled; obscene; (of weather) wet, rough; containing noxious matter; clogged, choked; unfair, against rules; in collision, entangled, etc. 2 n. foul blow or stroke etc.; collision, entanglement. 3 *adv.* unfairly. 4 v. make or become foul; commit foul on (player); entangle; become entangled; collide with. 5 **foul-mouthed** using obscene language; **foul play** unfair play, treacherous dealing, violence, murder; **foul up** block or jam (traffic etc.), make dirty or unpleasant. 6 **foully** /ˈfaʊlli/ *adv.*

**foulard** /fuːˈlɑːd/ n. thin soft smooth material of silk etc.

**found**[1] /faʊnd/ v.t. establish, originate; lay base of; base, build *up*.

**found**[2] /faʊnd/ v.t. melt and mould (metal), fuse (materials for glass); make thus.

**found**[3] *past & p.p.* of **find**.

**foundation** /faʊnˈdeɪʃ(ə)n/ n. (establishing of) endowed institution; solid ground or base; basis; underlying principle; base for application of cosmetics. **foundation garment** woman's supporting undergarment; **foundation-stone** one laid with ceremony to celebrate founding of building.

**founder** /ˈfaʊndə(r)/ v.i. (of horse) collapse, fall lame; (of rider) fall to ground; (of plan) fail; (of ship) fill with water and sink.

**foundling** /ˈfaʊndlɪŋ/ n. deserted infant of unknown parents.

**foundry** /ˈfaʊndrɪ/ n. factory or workshop for founding metal or glass etc.

**fount**[1] /faʊnt/ n. set of printing type of same size and face.

**fount**[2] /faʊnt/ n. source, spring, fountain.

**fountain** /ˈfaʊntɪn/ n. artificial jet(s) of water; spring; source. **fountain-head**

**four**

source; **fountain-pen** pen with reservoir holding ink.

**four** /fɔː(r)/ *a.* & *n.* one more than three; 4-oared boat or its crew. **four-in-hand** vehicle with 4 horses driven by one person; **four-poster** bed with 4 posts supporting canopy; **foursome** party of 4, game between two pairs; **four-square** firmly placed, steady; **four-wheel** acting on all 4 wheels of vehicle.

**fourfold** *a.* & *adv.*

**fourteen** /fɔːˈtiːn/ *a.* & *n.* one more than thirteen. **fourteenth** *a.* & *n.*

**fourth** /fɔːθ/ *a.* & *n.* next after third; one of four equal parts of thing.

**fowl** /faʊl/ 1 *n.* domestic cock or hen kept for eggs and flesh; bird. 2 *v.i.* hunt or shoot or snare wildfowl.

**fox** 1 *n.* wild four-legged animal with red fur and bushy tail; its fur; crafty person. 2 *v.t.* deceive; puzzle; *Aus.* pursue stealthily, shadow; *Aus.* chase and retrieve (cricket ball); discolour with brown spots. 3 **foxglove** tall plant with purple or white flowers; **foxhole** *Mil.* hole in ground as shelter against missiles or as firing-point; **foxhound** hound bred to hunt foxes; **fox-terrier** small short-haired terrier; **foxtrot** ballroom dance with slow and quick steps.

**foxie** /ˈfʊksɪ/ *n. Aus. colloq.* fox-terrier.

**foxy** /ˈfɒksɪ/ *a.* foxlike; sly or cunning; reddish-brown.

**foyer** /ˈfɔɪeɪ/ *n.* entrance hall or open space of hotel or theatre etc.

**Fr.** *abbr.* Father; French.

**fr.** *abbr.* franc(s).

**fracas** /ˈfrækɑː/ *n.* (*pl.* same *pr.* /-kɑːz/) noisy quarrel.

**fraction** /ˈfrækʃ(ə)n/ *n.* numerical quantity that is not a whole number; small part or amount etc.; portion of mixture obtainable by distillation etc. **fractional** *a.*

**fractious** /ˈfrækʃəs/ *a.* unruly, peevish.

**fracture** /ˈfræktʃə(r)/ 1 *n.* breakage, esp. of bone. 2 *v.* cause fracture in, suffer fracture.

**fragile** /ˈfrædʒaɪl/ *a.* easily broken; of delicate constitution. **fragility** /-ˈdʒɪl-/ *n.*

**fragment** /ˈfrægmənt/ 1 *n.* part broken off; remains of otherwise lost whole. 2 *v.* (also /fræɡˈment/) break into fragments. 3 **fragmentary** *a.*; **fragmentation** *n.*

**fragrance** /ˈfreɪɡrəns/ *n.* being fragrant; perfume.

**fragrant** /ˈfreɪɡrənt/ *a.* sweet-smelling.

**frail** *a.* fragile, delicate; morally weak.

**frailty** /ˈfreɪltɪ/ *n.* frail quality; weakness, foible.

**frame** 1 *v.t.* construct, put together or devise; adapt, fit; articulate (words); set in frame; serve as frame for; *sl.* concoct false accusation or contrive evidence against. 2 *n.* case or border enclosing picture etc.; construction, build, structure; framework; single picture on cinema film or transmitted by television; glazed structure to protect plants. 3 **frame-up** *sl.* conspiracy, esp. to make innocent person appear guilty; **framework** essential supporting structure, basic system.

**franc** /fræŋk/ *n.* French or Belgian or Swiss etc. monetary unit.

**franchise** /ˈfræntʃaɪz/ *n.* right to vote; citizenship; authorization to sell company's goods etc. in particular area.

**Franciscan** /frænˈsɪskən/ 1 *a.* of order of St Francis. 2 *n.* Franciscan monk or nun.

**frank** 1 *a.* candid, open; outspoken; undisguised. 2 *v.t.* mark (letter etc.) to record payment of postage. 3 *n.* franking signature or mark.

**frankfurter** /ˈfræŋkfɜːtə(r)/ *n.* seasoned smoked sausage.

**frankincense** /ˈfræŋkɪnsens/ *n.* aromatic gum resin burnt as incense.

**frantic** /ˈfræntɪk/ *a.* wildly excited; characterized by great hurry or anxiety; desperate, violent.

**fraternal** /frəˈtɜːn(ə)l/ *a.* of brothers, brotherly.

**fraternity** /frəˈtɜːnətɪ/ *n.* religious body, guild, etc.; brotherliness; *US* male students' society in university etc.

**fraternize** /ˈfrætənaɪz/ *v.i.* associate, make friends. **fraternization** *n.*

**fratricide** /ˈfrætrəsaɪd/ *n.* killing of one's brother or sister; person who does this.

**fraud** *n.* criminal deception; dishonest trick; impostor; disappointing person etc.

**fraudulent** /ˈfrɔːdjələnt/ *a.* of or involving or guilty of fraud. **fraudulence** n.

**fraught** /frɔːt/ a. filled or attended *with* (danger etc.); *colloq.* causing or suffering anxiety.

**fray**[1] v. rub; make or become ragged at edge.

**fray**[2] n. fight, conflict; brawl.

**frazzle** /ˈfræz(ə)l/ n. *colloq.* worn or exhausted state.

**FRG** abbr. Federal Republic of Germany (West Germany).

**freak** /friːk/ 1 n. capricious or unusual idea etc.; monstrosity; abnormal person or thing. 2 v. *sl.* (with *out*) (cause to) undergo drug etc. hallucinations or strong emotional experience; adopt unconventional life-style. 3 **freakish** a.

**freckle** /ˈfrek(ə)l/ 1 n. light brown spot on skin. 2 v. spot or be spotted with freckles.

**free** 1 a. (*compar.* **freer**; *superl.* **freest**) not a slave; at liberty; having personal rights and social and political liberty; unrestricted, unimpeded, not confined; spontaneous; not charged for; disengaged, available, permitted; lavish, unreserved; (of translation) not literal. 2 *adv.* freely; without cost or charge. 3 *v.t.* (*past* & *p.p.* **freed**) make free, set at liberty; disentangle. 4 **freeboard** part of ship's side between waterline and deck; **Free Church** a nonconformist Church; **free enterprise** freedom of private business from State control; **free fall** movement under force of gravity only; **free hand** liberty to act at one's own discretion; **free-hand** (of drawing) done without ruler or compasses etc.; **free lance** person working for no fixed employer; **free-loader** *sl.* person who eats etc. at other's expense; **freeman** holder of freedom of city etc.; **free port** one open to all traders alike; **free-range** (of hens etc.) given freedom of movement in seeking food; **free-selector** *Aus. hist.* person who could legally select a block of crown land and acquire freehold by annual payments; **free-select** v.; **free-standing** not supported by another structure; **freethinker** person who rejects authority in religious belief; **free trade** commerce left to its natural course without customs duties; **freeway** express highway; **free wheel** (in bicycle) drivingwheel able to revolve while pedals are at rest; **free-wheel** ride bicycle with pedals stationary, drive car with clutch disengaged; **free will** power of directing one's actions voluntarily.

**freebooter** /ˈfriːbuːtə(r)/ n. pirate.

**freedom** /ˈfriːdəm/ n. being free; personal or civil liberty; liberty of action; undue familiarity; exemption (*from*); unrestricted use (*of*); membership or honorary citizenship (*of* company, city, etc.).

**freehold** /ˈfriːhəʊld/ n. land etc. held by owner in absolute possession; this tenure. **freeholder** n.

**Freemason** /ˈfriːmeɪs(ə)n/ n. member of society for mutual help etc. having elaborate secret rituals. **Freemasonry** n.

**freesia** /ˈfriːzə/ n. fragrant flowering plant.

**freeze** 1 v. (*past* **froze**; *p.p.* **frozen**) turn into ice or other solid by cold; cover or be covered with ice; feel extreme cold; make or become cold and rigid, congeal or chill or be chilled by frost or cold or fear etc.; preserve (food) by refrigeration below freezing-point; fix at certain level; make (assets etc.) unrealizable, stabilize (prices etc.). 2 n. state of frost; coming or period of frost; fixing or stabilization of prices or wages etc. 3 **freeze-dry** freeze and dry by evaporation of ice in high vacuum; **freeze up** freeze completely, obstruct by formation of ice etc.; **freezing-point** temperature at which liquid freezes; **freezing-works** slaughterhouse where carcasses are frozen for export.

**freezer** n. refrigerated container or compartment in which food is preserved at very low temperature.

**freight** /freɪt/ 1 n. transport of goods by water or (*US*) land; goods transported, cargo; charge for transport of goods. 2 *v.t.* transport (goods) by freight; load (ship etc.).

**freighter** /ˈfreɪtə(r)/ n. ship or aircraft designed to carry freight.

**French** 1 a. of France. 2 n. French language; *the* French people. 3 **French bean** kind used as unripe pods or as ripe seeds; **French bread** bread in long crisp loaf; **French chalk** powdered talc used as marker or dry lubricant etc.;

**frenetic** /frəˈnetɪk/ *a.* frantic, frenzied. **frenetically** *adv.*

**frenzy** /ˈfrenzi/ 1 *n.* wild excitement; delirious fury. 2 *v.t.* (usu. in *p.p.*) drive to frenzy.

**frequency** /ˈfriːkwənsi/ *n.* frequent occurrence; *Phys.* rate of recurrence (of vibration etc.); *Electr.* number of cycles of carrier wave per second.

**frequent** 1 /ˈfriːkwənt/ *a.* often occurring, common; habitual. 2 /frɪˈkwent/ *v.t.* go often or habitually to.

**fresco** /ˈfreskəʊ/ *n.* (*pl.* **-cos** or **-coes**) painting done in water-colour on fresh plaster.

**fresh** 1 *a.* newly made or obtained; not previously known or used; lately arrived *from*; not stale or faded; (of food) not preserved by tinning or freezing etc.; (of water) not salt; pure, untainted; refreshing; cheeky, amorously impudent; inexperienced. 2 *adv.* newly, recently.

**freshen** /ˈfreʃ(ə)n/ *v.* make or become fresh.

**fresher** /ˈfreʃə(r)/ *n.* freshman.

**freshet** /ˈfreʃət/ *n.* river flood.

**freshman** /ˈfreʃmən/ *n.* (*pl.* **-men**) university student in first year.

**fret**[1] 1 *v.* worry; annoy; distress oneself with regret or discontent; consume by gnawing or rubbing. 2 *n.* irritation, vexation.

**fret**[2] 1 *n.* ornamental pattern of continuous combinations of straight lines joined usu. at right angles. 2 *v.t.* adorn with fret etc. 3 **fretsaw** narrow saw stretched on frame for cutting thin wood in patterns etc.; **fretwork** wood cut in patterns.

**fret**[3] *n.* bar or ridge on finger-board of guitar etc.

**fretful** /ˈfretfəl/ *a.* querulous.

**Freudian** /ˈfrɔɪdɪən/ 1 *a.* of Freud's system of psychoanalysis. 2 *n.* adherent of Freud. 3 **Freudian slip** unintentional error that seems to reveal subconscious feelings.

**Fri.** *abbr.* Friday.

**friable** /ˈfraɪəb(ə)l/ *a.* easily crumbled. **friability** *n.*

**friar** /ˈfraɪə(r)/ *n.* member of certain religious orders of men.

**friary** /ˈfraɪəri/ *n.* monastery of friars.

**fribby** /ˈfrɪbi/ *a. Aus.* 1 (of locks of wool) small short. 2 *n.* fribby lock.

**fricassee** /ˈfrɪkəsi/ 1 *n.* dish of fried or stewed pieces of meat with sauce. 2 *v.t.* make fricassee of.

**fricative** /ˈfrɪkətɪv/ 1 *a.* made by friction of breath in narrow opening. 2 *n.* fricative consonant.

**friction** /ˈfrɪkʃ(ə)n/ *n.* rubbing of one object against another; resistance object encounters in moving over another; *fig.* clash of wills or temperaments etc.

**Friday** /ˈfraɪdeɪ or -dɪ/ *n.* day of week following Thursday.

**fridge** *n. colloq.* refrigerator.

**friend** /frend/ *n.* person, usu. not relation or lover, who feels mutual affection and regard for another; sympathizer, helper; person who is not an enemy; **Friend** member of Society of Friends, Quaker.

**friendly** /ˈfrendli/ *a.* acting or disposed to act as friend; on amicable terms. **Friendly Society** society for insurance against sickness etc. **friendliness** *n.*

**friendship** /ˈfrendʃɪp/ *n.* friendly relationship or feeling.

**frieze** /friːz/ *n.* part of entablature between architrave and cornice; band of decoration, esp. along wall near ceiling.

**frigate** /ˈfrɪɡət/ *n.* naval escort vessel like large corvette.

**fright** /fraɪt/ *n.* sudden or violent fear; grotesque-looking person.

**frighten** /ˈfraɪt(ə)n/ *v.t.* fill with fright; drive *away* or *into* etc. by fright.

**frightful** /ˈfraɪtfʊl/ *a.* dreadful, shocking; ugly; *colloq.* very great.

**frigid** /ˈfrɪdʒɪd/ *a.* lacking enthusiasm; dull; (of woman) sexually unresponsive; cold. **frigidity** *n.*

**frill** 1 *n.* ornamental strip of material or paper etc. gathered at one edge; in *pl.* unnecessary elaboration. 2 *v.t.* decorate with frill. 3 **frill(ed) lizard** large N. Aus. lizard with neck encircled

**fringe** 222 **fruit**

by a broad erectile membrane. **4** frilly *a.*

**fringe** /frɪndʒ/ **1** *n.* bordering of loose threads or tassels or twists; front hair hanging over forehead; border, outskirts, margin; area or part of minor importance. **2** *v.t.* adorn with fringe; serve as fringe to. **3 fringe benefit** employee's benefit additional to wage or salary.

**frippery** /'frɪpəri/ *n.* finery, needless or tawdry ornament; trifles.

**frisk 1** *v.* leap or skip playfully; *sl.* search (person). **2** *n.* playful leap or skip.

**frisky** /'frɪski:/ *a.* lively, playful.

**fritter**[1] /'frɪtə(r)/ *v.t.* throw *away* in trifling and wasteful way.

**fritter**[2] /'frɪtə(r)/ *n.* fried batter containing slice of fruit or meat etc.

**fritz** *n. Aus.* = devon.

**frivolous** /'frɪvələs/ *a.* paltry, trifling; silly. **frivolity** /-'vɒl-/ *n.*

**frizz 1** *v.* form (hair) into mass of small curls. **2** *n.* frizzed hair or state. **3 frizzy** *a.*

**frizzle**[1] /'frɪz(ə)l/ *v.* fry or toast or grill with sputtering noise; burn or shrivel *up.*

**frizzle**[2] /'frɪz(ə)l/ **1** *v.* frizz (hair). **2** *n.* frizzed hair or state.

**fro** *adv.* **to and fro** backwards and forwards.

**frock** *n.* woman's or child's dress; monk's or priest's gown. **frock-coat** man's long-skirted coat not cut away in front.

**frog**[1] *n.* tailless amphibian with long web-footed hind legs. **frogman** underwater swimmer equipped with rubber suit and flippers; **frogmarch** hustle forward after seizing from behind and pinning arms.

**frog**[2] *n.* ornamental coat-fastening of spindle-shaped button and loop.

**frolic** /'frɒlɪk/ **1** *v.i.* play about cheerfully. **2** *n.* prank, merry-making.

**frolicsome** /'frɒlɪksəm/ *a.* playful.

**from** *prep.* expr. separation or origin.

**frond** *n.* leaf-like organ of ferns etc.

**front** /frʌnt/ **1** *n.* side or part normally nearer or towards spectator or direction of motion; scene of actual fighting; combination of forces etc. to achieve end; organized political group; appearance, demeanour; person etc. serving to cover subversive or illegal activities; part of seaside resort facing sea; *Meteor.* boundary between warm-air and cold-air masses; auditorium of theatre. **2** *a.* of or at front. **3** *v.* have front facing or directed (*on, to, towards,* etc.); *sl.* act as front for; furnish with front. **4 front bench** seats for leading members of Government and Opposition in Parliament; **front line** foremost portion of army in battle; **front runner** leading contestant.

**frontage** /'frʌntɪdʒ/ *n.* land abutting on street or water; extent of front; front of building.

**frontal** /'frʌnt(ə)l/ *a.* of or on front; of forehead.

**frontier** /'frʌntɪə(r)/ *n.* boundary between States; border of settled or inhabited part; limits of attainment in science etc.

**frontispiece** /'frʌntɪspi:s/ *n.* illustration facing title-page of book etc.

**frost 1** *n.* freezing; frozen dew or vapour. **2** *v.t.* cover (as) with frost; injure (plant etc.) with frost; roughen surface of (glass etc.), make opaque. **3 frostbite** injury to body tissue due to freezing.

**frosting** /'frɒstɪŋ/ *n.* icing for cakes.

**frosty** /'frɒsti:/ *a.* cold with frost; unfriendly.

**froth** /frɒθ/ **1** *n.* foam; idle talk. **2** *v.i.* emit or gather froth. **3 frothy** *a.*

**frown** /fraʊn/ **1** *v.* wrinkle brows; express displeasure or deep thought. **2** *n.* action of frowning, look of displeasure or deep thought.

**frowsty** /'fraʊsti:/ *a.* stuffy, fusty.

**frowzy** /'fraʊzi:/ *a.* fusty; slatternly, dingy.

**froze, frozen** *past* & *p.p.* of **freeze**.

**FRS** *abbr.* Fellow of the Royal Society.

**fructify** /'frʌktɪfaɪ/ *v.* bear fruit; make fruitful. **fructification** *n.*

**fructose** /'frʌktəʊz/ *n.* kind of sugar found in fruits and honey.

**frugal** /'fru:g(ə)l/ *a.* sparing, economical. **frugality** *n.*

**fruit** /fru:t/ **1** *n.* product of plant or tree that contains seed, this used as food; (usu. in *pl.*) vegetable products fit for food; product, result. **2** *v.i.* bear fruit. **3 fruit-cake** cake containing dried fruit; **fruit sugar** fructose.

**fruiterer** /ˈfruːtərə(r)/ n. dealer in fruit.

**fruitful** /ˈfruːtfəl/ a. fertile, prolific; productive.

**fruition** /fruːˈɪʃ(ə)n/ n. realization of aims or hopes etc.

**fruitless** /ˈfruːtləs/ a. not bearing fruit; useless, unsuccessful.

**fruity** /ˈfruːtɪ/ a. of or resembling fruit; of strong or rich quality. **fruitiness** n.

**frump** n. dowdy old-fashioned woman. **frumpish** a.; **frumpy** a.

**frustrate** /frʌsˈtreɪt/ v.t. prevent from achieving purpose; disappoint. **frustration** n.

**fry**[1] 1 v. cook in hot fat. 2 n. internal parts of animals, usu. eaten fried; fried food. 3 **frying-pan** shallow long-handled pan for frying.

**fry**[2] n. young or freshly hatched fishes. **small fry** unimportant people, children.

**ft.** abbr. foot, feet.

**fuchsia** /ˈfjuːʃə/ n. ornamental shrub with drooping flowers.

**fuddle** /ˈfʌd(ə)l/ 1 v.t. intoxicate; confuse. 2 n. intoxication; confusion.

**fuddy-duddy** /ˈfʌdɪdʌdɪ/ 1 a. sl. fussy or old-fashioned. 2 n. such person.

**fudge** 1 n. soft toffee-like sweet; nonsense. 2 v.t. fit together or make up in makeshift or dishonest way; deal with incompetently.

**fuel** /ˈfjuːəl/ 1 n. material for burning as fire or as source of heat or power; thing that sustains or inflames passion etc. 2 v.t. supply with fuel.

**fug** n. colloq. stuffy atmosphere.

**fugal** /ˈfjuːg(ə)l/ a. of or resembling fugue.

**fugitive** /ˈfjuːdʒɪtɪv/ 1 a. fleeing; fleeting, transient. 2 n. one who flees (*from*).

**fugue** /fjuːg/ n. piece of music in which short melodic theme is introduced by one part and successively taken up by others.

**fulcrum** /ˈfʊlkrəm/ n. (pl. -cra) point against or on which lever is supported.

**fulfil** /fʊlˈfɪl/ v.t. carry out; satisfy. **fulfilment** n.

**full**[1] /fʊl/ 1 a. holding all its limits will allow; replete; crowded; copious; abundant; complete, perfect; swelling; *Aus. sl.* drunk. 2 adv. quite, exactly. 3 **full back** football player behind half-backs; **full-blooded** vigorous, sensual, not hybrid; **full-bodied** rich in quality or tone etc.; **full brother, sister**, one having both parents the same; **full house** large or full attendance at theatre etc., *Poker* hand with three of a kind and a pair; **full-length** (of mirror, portrait, etc.) showing whole of human figure; **full moon** moon with whole disc illuminated; **full stop** punctuation mark (.) used at end of sentence, complete cessation.

**full**[2] /fʊl/ v.t. clean and thicken (cloth).

**fuller** /ˈfʊlə(r)/ n. person who fulls cloth. **fuller's earth** clay used in fulling.

**fully** /ˈfʊlɪ/ adv. completely, quite.

**fulminant** /ˈfʌlmənənt/ a. fulminating.

**fulminate** /ˈfʌlmɪneɪt/ v. express censure loudly and forcibly; explode, flash like lightning. **fulmination** n.

**fulsome** /ˈfʊlsəm/ a. cloying, disgustingly excessive.

**fumble** /ˈfʌmb(ə)l/ 1 v. grope about; handle or deal with awkwardly. 2 n. act of fumbling.

**fume** 1 n. exuded smoke or vapour or gas etc. 2 v. emit fumes; be angry or irritated; subject to fumes; darken (oak etc.) thus.

**fumigate** /ˈfjuːmɪgeɪt/ v.t. subject to fumes, disinfect or purify thus. **fumigation** n.; **fumigator** n.

**fun** n. sport, amusement; source of this. **fun-fair** fair consisting of amusements and side-shows; **make fun of, poke fun at**, ridicule.

**function** /ˈfʌŋkʃ(ə)n/ 1 n. work thing is designed to do; official duty; public ceremony or occasion; *Math.* quantity whose value depends on varying values (*of* others). 2 v.i. fulfil function; operate.

**functional** /ˈfʌŋkʃən(ə)l/ a. of or serving a function; shaped, designed, etc. with regard mainly to function; utilitarian.

**functionary** /ˈfʌŋkʃənərɪ/ n. official.

**fund** 1 n. permanently available stock; stock of money, esp. one set apart for purpose; in *pl.* pecuniary resources. 2 v.t. provide with money; make (debt) permanent at fixed interest.

**fundamental** /fʌndəˈment(ə)l/ 1 a. of or serving as base or foundation; essential, primary. 2 n. fundamental rule etc.

**fundamentalism** /fʌndəˈmentəlɪ-

**funeral**

**fundamentalism** /-z(ə)m/ *n.* strict maintenance of traditional scriptural beliefs. **fundamentalist** *n.*

**funeral** /'fju:nər(ə)l/ **1** *n.* burial or cremation of dead with ceremonies. **2** *a.* of or used at funeral.

**funerary** /'fju:nərəri/ *a.* of funeral(s).

**funereal** /fju:'nɪərɪəl/ *a.* of or appropriate to funeral; dismal, dark.

**fungicide** /'fʌndʒɪsaɪd/ *n.* substance that kills fungus.

**fungus** /'fʌŋgəs/ *n.* (*pl.* **-gi** /-gaɪ/) mushroom, toadstool, or allied plant; spongy morbid growth. **fungoid** *a.*; **fungous** *a.*

**funicular** /fə'nɪkjələ(r)/ *n.* (in full **funicular railway**) cable railway with ascending and descending cars counterbalanced.

**funk** **1** *n. sl.* fear, panic; coward. **2** *v.* be afraid of; evade, shirk.

**funky** /'fʌŋkɪ/ *a.* (of music etc.) uncomplicated, swinging, fashionable.

**funnel** /'fʌn(ə)l/ **1** *n.* narrowing tube for guiding liquid etc. into small opening; chimney of steam-engine or ship. **2** *v.* (cause to) move (as) through funnel. **3 funnel-web spider** *Aus.* large poisonous black spider.

**funny** /'fʌnɪ/ *a.* comical, amusing, strange. **funny-bone** part of elbow over which ulnar nerve passes.

**fur** **1** *n.* short fine hair of some animals; animal skin with fur on it; garment made of or trimmed or lined with this; *collect.* furred animals; crust or coating. **2** *v.* provide, clothe, coat, with fur; become coated with fur.

**furbelow** /'fɜ:bɪləʊ/ *n.* flounce; pleated border; in *pl.* showy ornaments.

**furbish** /'fɜ:bɪʃ/ *v.t.* polish *up*; renovate.

**furcate** /'fɜ:keɪt/ **1** *a.* forked, branched. **2** *v.* fork, divide. **3 furcation** *n.*

**furious** /'fjʊərɪəs/ *a.* very angry, violent; raging, frantic.

**furl** *v.* roll up (sail, umbrella); become furled.

**furlong** /'fɜ:lɒŋ/ *n.* eighth of mile.

**furlough** /'fɜ:ləʊ/ *n.* leave of absence.

**furnace** /'fɜ:nəs/ *n.* apparatus with chamber for applying intense heat; closed fireplace for heating building; very hot place.

**furnish** /'fɜ:nɪʃ/ *v.t.* fit up with furniture; provide (*with*).

**furniture** /'fɜ:nɪtʃə(r)/ *n.* movable contents of building or room; rigging and stores etc. of ship; accessories, e.g. handles and locks on doors.

**furore** /fjʊ'rɔ:rɪ/ *n.* uproar; outburst of popular enthusiasm.

**furphy** /'fɜ:fɪ/ *n. Aus.* false report, idle rumour.

**furrier** /'fʌrɪə(r)/ *n.* dealer in or dresser of furs.

**furrow** /'fʌrəʊ/ **1** *n.* narrow trench made by plough; rut; wrinkle. **2** *v.t.* plough; make furrows in.

**furry** /'fɜ:rɪ/ *a.* having or resembling fur.

**further** /'fɜ:ðə(r)/ **1** *adv.* more far in space or time; more, to greater extent; in addition. **2** *a.* more distant or advanced; more, additional. **3** *v.t.* promote, favour. **4 further education** education for persons above school age; **furthermore** in addition, besides; **furthermost** most distant.

**furtherance** /'fɜ:ðərəns/ *n.* furthering (*of* plan etc.).

**furthest** /'fɜ:ðəst/ **1** *a.* most distant. **2** *adv.* to or at the greatest distance.

**furtive** /'fɜ:tɪv/ *a.* sly, stealthy.

**fury** /'fjʊərɪ/ *n.* fierce passion, wild anger; violence; avenging spirit; angry woman.

**furze** *n.* spiny yellow-flowered shrub, gorse. **furzy** *a.*

**fuse**[1] /fju:z/ **1** *v.* melt with intense heat; blend (as) by melting; supply with fuse(s); be put out of action by blowing of fuse; cause fuse(s) of to blow. **2** *n.* easily melted wire in circuit, designed to melt when circuit is overloaded.

**fuse**[2] /fju:z/ **1** *n.* cord etc. made so as to burn in order to ignite explosive. **2** *v.t.* fit fuse to.

**fuselage** /'fju:zəlɑ:ʒ/ *n.* body of aircraft.

**fusible** /'fju:zəb(ə)l/ *a.* that may be melted. **fusibility** *n.*

**fusilier** /fju:zə'lɪə(r)/ *n.* soldier of some regiments formerly armed with light muskets.

**fusillade** /fju:zə'leɪd/ *n.* continuous discharge of firearms; sustained outburst of criticism etc.

**fusion** /'fju:ʒ(ə)n/ *n.* fusing; blending, coalition; (in full **nuclear fusion**) union of atomic nuclei to form heavier nuclei with release of energy.

**fuss** **1** *n.* bustle; excessive commotion; excessive concern about trivial thing;

**fussy** sustained protest. **2** *v.* make fuss; bustle; agitate, worry. **3 fuss-pot** *colloq.* person who is always making a fuss; **make a fuss** complain vigorously; **make a fuss of** treat with (excessive) attention.

**fussy** /'fʌsi:/ *a.* inclined to fuss; overelaborate; fastidious. **fussiness** *n.*

**fustian** /'fʌstjən/ **1** *n.* thick twilled cotton cloth; bombast. **2** *a.* made of fustian; bombastic, worthless.

**fusty** /'fʌsti:/ *a.* musty, stuffy; stale-smelling; antiquated. **fustiness** *n.*

**futon** /'fu:tɒn/ *n.* light orig. Japanese kind of mattress.

**futile** /'fju:taɪl/ *a.* useless, frivolous, worthless. **futility** /-'tɪl-/ *n.*

**future** /'fju:tʃə(r)/ **1** *a.* about to happen or be or become; of time to come; *Gram.* (of tense) describing event yet to happen. **2** *n.* time to come; future condition or events etc.; prospect of success etc.

**futurism** /'fju:tʃərɪz(ə)m/ *a.* artistic and literary movement departing violently from tradition. **futurist** *a.* & *n.*

**futuristic** /fju:tʃə'rɪstɪk/ *a.* ultra-modern; pertaining to future; of futurism.

**futurity** /fju:'tjuːrəti:/ *n.* future time, events, etc.

**fuzz** *n.* fluff; fluffy or frizzy hair; *sl.* police(man).

**fuzzy** /'fʌzi:/ *a.* fluffy, frizzy; blurred, indistinct. **fuzziness** *n.*

# G

**g.** *abbr.* gram(s).
**gab** *n. colloq.* talk, chatter.
**gabardine** /'gæbədi:n/ *n.* a strong twilled cloth.
**gabble** /'gæb(ə)l/ 1 *v.* talk or utter inarticulately or too fast. 2 *n.* rapid talk.
**gabby** /'gæbi:/ *a. colloq.* talkative.
**gaberdine** var. of **gabardine**.
**gable** /'geɪb(ə)l/ *n.* triangular part of wall at end of ridged roof.
**gad** *v.i.* go *about* idly or in search of pleasure. **gadabout** gadding person.
**gadfly** /'gædflaɪ/ *n.* cattle-biting fly.
**gadget** /'gædʒət/ *n.* small mechanical device or tool. **gadgetry** *n.*
**Gaelic** /'geɪlɪk or 'gælɪk/ *n.* Celtic language of Scots or Irish.
**gaff**[1] 1 *n.* stick with hook for landing fish; barbed fishing-spear. 2 *v.t.* seize with gaff.
**gaff**[2] *n. sl.* **blow the gaff** let out secret.
**gaffe** /gæf/ *n.* blunder, *faux pas.*
**gaffer** /'gæfə(r)/ *n. UK colloq.* old man; foreman, boss.
**gag** 1 *n.* thing thrust into mouth to prevent speech or hold it open etc.; joke, comic business, etc. 2 *v.* apply gag to, silence; make jokes; choke, retch.
**gaga** /'ga:ga:/ *a.* fatuous, senile.
**gage**[1] *n.* pledge, security; challenge.
**gage**[2] *n.* greengage.
**gaggle** /'gæg(ə)l/ *n.* flock (of geese); disorderly group.
**gaiety** /'geɪəti:/ *n.* being gay, mirth; amusement, merry-making.
**gaily** /'geɪli:/ *adv.* in gay manner.
**gain** 1 *v.* obtain, secure; acquire, earn; improve or advance; (of clock etc.) become fast (by); win; reach; persuade. 2 *n.* increase of wealth, profit; money-making.
**gainful** /'geɪnfəl/ *a.* lucrative; paid.
**gainsay** /geɪn'seɪ/ *v.t.* (*past* & *p.p.* **-said** /-'sed/) deny, contradict.
**gait** *n.* manner of or carriage in walking.
**gaiter** /'geɪtə(r)/ *n.* covering of leather etc. for leg or ankle.
**gal.** *abbr.* gallon(s).
**gala** /'gɑ:lə/ *n.* festive occasion; festive gathering for sports.
**galactic** /gə'læktɪk/ *a.* of galaxy.
**galah** /gə'lɑ:/ *n. Aus.* rose-breasted grey-backed cockatoo; *sl.* fool, simpleton.
**galantine** /'gæləntɪ:n/ *n.* cold dish of meat in jelly.
**galaxy** /'gæləksɪ/ *n.* independent system of stars etc. existing in space; brilliant company. **the Galaxy** Milky Way.
**gale** *n.* strong wind; outburst, esp. of laughter.
**gall**[1] /gɔ:l/ *n.* bile; *colloq.* impudence; asperity, rancour. **gall-bladder** sac in body containing bile; **gallstone** small hard mass that forms in gall-bladder.
**gall**[2] /gɔ:l/ 1 *n.* painful swelling, blister, etc.; sore; place rubbed bare. 2 *v.t.* rub sore; vex, humiliate.
**gall**[3] /gɔ:l/ *n.* growth produced on tree etc. by insect etc.
**gallant** /'gælənt/ 1 *a.* brave; fine, stately; (also /gə'lænt/) attentive to women. 2 *n.* (also /gə'lænt/) ladies' man.
**gallantry** /'gæləntrɪ/ *n.* bravery; polite act or speech.
**galleon** /'gælɪən/ *n. hist.* (usu. Spanish) ship of war.
**gallery** /'gælərɪ/ *n.* room for showing works of art; balcony over part of area of hall or church etc.; highest of such balconies in theatre; covered walk, colonnade; passage, corridor.
**galley** /'gælɪ/ *n. hist.* low flat one-decked vessel, usu. rowed by slaves or criminals; ship's or aircraft's kitchen; tray for set-up type; (in full **galley proof**) printer's proof in long narrow form.
**Gallic** /'gælɪk/ *a.* of Gaul or Gauls; French. **Gallicize** *v.*
**Gallicism** /'gælɪsɪz(ə)m/ *n.* French idiom.
**gallinaceous** /gælɪ'neɪʃəs/ *a.* of order of birds including domestic poultry.
**gallivant** /'gælɪvænt/ *v.i. colloq.* gad about.
**gallon** /'gælən/ *n.* measure of capacity (4546 cc).
**gallop** /'gæləp/ 1 *n.* horse's fastest pace; a ride at this pace. 2 *v.* go at gallop; make (horse) gallop; talk etc. very fast; progress rapidly.
**gallows** /'gæləʊz/ *n.pl.* (usu. treated as *sing.*) structure for hanging criminals.
**Gallup poll** /'gæləp/ assessment of

**galore** /gə'lɔː(r)/ *adv.* in plenty.

**galosh** /gə'lɒʃ/ *n.* waterproof overshoe.

**galumph** /gə'lʌmf/ *v.i. colloq.* go prancing exultantly; move noisily or clumsily.

**galvanic** /gæl'vænɪk/ *a.* producing an electric current by chemical action; (of electric current) produced thus; *fig.* stimulating, full of energy.

**galvanize** /'gælvənaɪz/ *v.t.* stimulate (as) by electricity; *fig.* rouse by shock etc.; coat (iron) with zinc to protect from rust.

**galvanometer** /gælvə'nɒmɪtə(r)/ *n.* instrument for measuring electric currents.

**galvo** /'gælvəʊ/ *n. Aus. colloq.* galvanized iron.

**gambit** /'gæmbɪt/ *n. Chess* opening with sacrifice of pawn etc.; trick, device.

**gamble** /'gæmb(ə)l/ 1 *v.i.* play games of chance for money stakes; take risks (*with*). 2 *n.* risk, risky undertaking.

**gambler** /'gæmblə(r)/ *n.* person who gambles habitually.

**gamboge** /gæm'buːdʒ/ *n.* gum-resin used as yellow pigment.

**gambol** /'gæmb(ə)l/ 1 *v.i.* jump about playfully. 2 *n.* caper.

**game**[1] 1 *n.* form of play or sport, esp. competitive one organized with rules etc.; portion of play forming scoring unit; winning score in game; in *pl.* athletic contests; scheme, undertaking; wild animals or birds etc. hunted for sport or food; their flesh as food. 2 *a.* spirited, ready. 3 *v.i.* gamble for money stakes. 4 **game-cock** kind bred for cock-fighting; **gamekeeper** person employed to breed game and prevent poaching etc.; **gamesmanship** art of winning games by psychological means.

**game**[2] *a.* (of leg etc.) crippled.

**gamete** /'gæmiːt/ *n.* mature germ-cell uniting with another in sexual reproduction.

**gamin** /'gæmən/ *n.* street urchin, impudent child.

**gamine** /gə'miːn/ *n.* girl with mischievous charm.

**gamma** /'gæmə/ *n.* third letter of Greek alphabet ($\Gamma$, $\gamma$). **gamma rays** very short X-rays emitted by radioactive substances.

**gammon** /'gæmən/ *n.* bottom piece of flitch of bacon with hind leg.

**gammy** /'gæmɪ/ *a. sl.* (of leg etc.) crippled.

**gamut** /'gæmət/ *n.* whole series of recognized notes in music; compass of voice; entire range or scope.

**gamy** /'geɪmɪ/ *a.* smelling or tasting like game kept until it is high.

**gander** /'gændə(r)/ *n.* male goose.

**gang** 1 *n.* set of associates, esp. for criminal purposes; set of workmen or slaves or prisoners. 2 *v.i. colloq.* join *up*; act in concert *with*.

**ganger** /'gæŋə(r)/ *n.* foreman of gang of workmen.

**gang-gang** /'gæŋgæŋ/ *n. Aus.* small grey cockatoo of which male has red crest.

**gangling** /'gæŋglɪŋ/ *a.* (of person) loosely built, lanky.

**ganglion** /'gæŋglɪən/ *n.* (*pl.* **-glia**) knot on nerve forming centre for reception and transmission of impulses.

**gangplank** /'gæŋplæŋk/ *n.* plank for walking into or out of boat etc.

**gangrene** /'gæŋgriːn/ *n.* death of body tissue. **gangrenous** *a.*

**gangster** /'gæŋstə(r)/ *n.* member of gang of violent criminals.

**gangue** /gæŋ/ *n.* valueless earth in which ore is found.

**gangway** /'gæŋweɪ/ *n.* passage, esp. between rows of seats; opening in ship's bulwarks; bridge.

**gannet** /'gænɪt/ *n.* large sea-bird.

**gantry** /'gæntrɪ/ *n.* structure supporting travelling crane or railway signals or equipment for rocket-launch etc.

**gaol** /dʒeɪl/ 1 *n.* prison. 2 *v.t.* put in prison. 3 **gaolbird** habitual criminal.

**gaoler** /'dʒeɪlə(r)/ *n.* person in charge of gaol or prisoners in it.

**gap** *n.* breach in hedge or wall; interval; deficiency; wide divergence.

**gape** 1 *v.i.* open mouth wide; stare *at*; yawn. 2 *n.* yawn; stare.

**garage** /'gærɑːdʒ/ 1 *n.* building for storing motor vehicle(s); establishment selling petrol etc. or repairing and selling motor vehicles. 2 *v.t.* put or keep in garage.

**garb** 1 *n.* clothing, esp. of distinctive kind. 2 *v.t.* dress.

# garbage

**garbage** /'gɑːbɪdʒ/ n. refuse; domestic waste; foul or rubbishy literature etc.

**garble** /'gɑːb(ə)l/ v.t. distort or confuse (facts, statements, etc.).

**garbo** /'gɑːbəʊ/ n. (pl. **-bos**) Aus. sl. garbage collector.

**garden** /'gɑːd(ə)n/ 1 n. piece of ground for growing flowers, fruit, and vegetables, esp. attached to a house; (esp. in pl.) pleasure-grounds. 2 v.i. cultivate or work in garden.

**gardenia** /gɑː'diːnɪə/ n. tree or shrub with fragrant white or yellow flower; this flower.

**garfish** /'gɑːfɪʃ/ n. Aus. edible fish with long spearlike snout.

**gargantuan** /gɑː'gæntjuːən/ a. gigantic.

**gargle** /'gɑːg(ə)l/ 1 v. rinse (throat) with liquid kept in motion by breath. 2 n. liquid so used.

**gargoyle** /'gɑːgɔɪl/ n. grotesque spout projecting from gutter of building.

**garish** /'geərɪʃ/ a. obtrusively bright, gaudy.

**garland** /'gɑːlənd/ 1 n. wreath of flowers etc. as decoration. 2 v.t. crown or deck with garland.

**garlic** /'gɑːlɪk/ n. plant with pungent bulb; this bulb used in cookery.

**garment** /'gɑːmənt/ n. article of clothing.

**garner** /'gɑːnə(r)/ 1 v.t. store up, collect. 2 n. storehouse for corn etc.

**garnet** /'gɑːnət/ n. vitreous mineral, esp. red kind used as gem.

**garnish** /'gɑːnɪʃ/ 1 v.t. decorate, esp. dish of food. 2 n. decorative addition.

**garret** /'gærət/ n. room, esp. small and poor, on top floor.

**garrison** /'gærəs(ə)n/ 1 n. troops stationed in town. 2 v.t. provide with or occupy as garrison.

**garrotte** /gə'rɒt/ 1 n. Spanish capital punishment by strangulation; apparatus for this. 2 v.t. execute by garotte.

**garrulous** /'gærələs/ a. talkative. **garrulity** n.

**garter** /'gɑːtə(r)/ n. band to keep sock or stocking up. **the Garter** (badge of) highest order of English knighthood; **garter stitch** pattern made by knitting all rows plain.

**gas** /gæs/ 1 n. (pl. **gases**) any airlike or completely elastic fluid, esp. one not liquid or solid at ordinary temperatures; such fluid, esp. coal gas or natural gas; gas used as anaesthetic; poisonous gas used in war; US colloq. petrol; colloq. empty talk, boasting. 2 v. expose to gas; colloq. talk emptily or boastfully. 3 **gasbag** derog. empty talker; **gas chamber** used to kill animals or prisoners by gas poisoning; **gasholder** gasometer; **gas mask** device worn over head for protection against harmful gases; **gas ring** ring pierced with small holes and fed with gas for cooking etc.; **gasworks** place where coal gas is manufactured.

**gaseous** /'gæsɪəs/ a. of or in form of gas.

**gash** 1 n. long deep cut or wound, cleft. 2 v.t. make gash in.

**gasify** /'gæsɪfaɪ/ v. convert into gas. **gasification** n.

**gasket** /'gæskɪt/ n. sheet or ring of rubber etc. to seal junction of metal surfaces; small cord securing furled sail to yard.

**gasoline** /'gæsəliːn/ n. US petrol.

**gasometer** /gæ'sɒmɪtə(r)/ n. large tank from which gas is distributed.

**gasp** /gɑːsp/ 1 v. catch breath with open mouth; utter with gasps. 2 n. convulsive catching of breath. 3 **at one's last gasp** at point of death, fig. exhausted.

**gassy** /'gæsɪ/ a. of or full of or like gas; verbose.

**gastric** /'gæstrɪk/ a. of stomach. **gastric flu** colloq. intestinal disorder of unknown cause; **gastric juice** digestive fluid secreted by stomach glands.

**gastronome** /'gæstrənəʊm/ n. connoisseur of cookery. **gastronomic** /-'nɒm/ a.; **gastronomy** /-'strɒn/ n.

**gastropod** /'gæstrəpɒd/ n. mollusc that moves by means of ventral organ.

**gate** n. barrier, usu. hinged, used to close opening in wall or fence etc.; such opening; means of entrance or exit; numbered place of access to aircraft at airport; device regulating passage of water in lock etc.; number entering by payment at gates to see football match etc., money thus taken. **gatecrash** attend social gathering uninvited; **gate-legged** (of table) with legs in gatelike frame swinging back to allow top to fold down; **gateway** opening closed by gate.

**gateau** /'gætəʊ/ n. (pl. **-teaus**) large rich elaborate cake.

**gather** /'gæðə(r)/ 1 v. bring or come together, collect; infer, deduce; pluck (flowers etc.); increase (speed); draw together in folds or wrinkles; develop purulent swelling. 2 n. small fold or pleat.

**gathering** n. assembly; purulent swelling.

**GATT** abbr. General Agreement on Tariffs and Trade.

**gauche** /gəʊʃ/ a. tactless, socially awkward. **gaucherie** n.

**gaucho** /'gaʊtʃəʊ/ n. (pl. **-os**) mounted herdsman in S. Amer. pampas.

**gaudy** /'gɔːdi/ a. tastelessly showy.

**gauge** /geɪdʒ/ 1 n. standard measure; instrument for measuring or testing; capacity, extent; criterion, test. 2 v.t. measure exactly; measure contents of; estimate.

**Gaul** /gɔːl/ n. inhabitant of ancient Gaul. **Gaulish** a. & n.

**gaunt** /gɔːnt/ a. lean, haggard, grim.

**gauntlet**[1] /'gɔːntlət/ n. glove with long loose wrist, esp. for driving etc.; hist. armoured glove.

**gauntlet**[2] /'gɔːntlət/ n. **run the gauntlet** pass between two rows of men etc. armed with sticks etc., as punishment, fig. undergo criticism.

**gauze** /gɔːz/ n. thin transparent fabric or wire mesh etc. **gauzy** a.

**gave** past of **give**.

**gavel** /'gæv(ə)l/ n. auctioneer's or chairman's or judge's hammer.

**gavotte** /gə'vɒt/ n. lively 18th-c. dance; music for this.

**gawk** 1 v.i. stare stupidly. 2 n. awkward or bashful person. 3 **gawky** a.

**gawp** v.i. colloq. stare stupidly.

**gay** a. light-hearted, mirthful; colloq. homosexual; showy; dissolute.

**gaze** 1 v.i. look fixedly. 2 n. intent look.

**gazebo** /gə'ziːbəʊ/ n. (pl. **-bos**) structure from which view may be had.

**gazelle** /gə'zel/ n. small graceful antelope.

**gazette** /gə'zet/ 1 n. newspaper, esp. official journal. 2 v.t. publish in official gazette.

**gazetteer** /gæzə'tɪə(r)/ n. geographical index.

**gazump** /gə'zʌmp/ v.t. raise price after accepting offer from (buyer); swindle.

**GB** abbr. Great Britain.

**GC** abbr. George Cross.

**GDR** abbr. German Democratic Republic (E. Germany).

**gear** /gɪə(r)/ 1 n. set of toothed wheels working together, esp. those connecting engine to road wheels; (often in pl.) particular setting of these; colloq. clothing, rigging. 2 v.t. put in gear; provide with gear; adjust or adapt to; harness (up). 3 **gearbox** case enclosing gears of machine or vehicle; **gearlever** lever moved to engage or change gear; **in gear** with gears engaged.

**gecko** /'gekəʊ/ n. (pl. **-os**) house lizard found in warm climates.

**gee** /dʒiː/ int. expr. surprise etc.

**geebung** /'dʒiːbʌŋ/ n. Aus. any of several trees or shrubs with an edible fruit; this fruit.

**geese** pl. of **goose**.

**geezer** /'giːzə(r)/ n. sl. man, esp. old one.

**Geiger counter** /'gaɪɡə(r)/ instrument for measuring radioactivity.

**geisha** /'geɪʃə/ n. Japanese professional hostess and entertainer.

**gel** /dʒel/ n. semi-solid colloidal solution or jelly.

**gelatine** /'dʒelətiːn/ n. (also **gelatin** /-tɪn/) transparent tasteless substance used in cookery for making jelly etc. and in photography etc. **gelatinous** /-'læt-/ a.

**geld** /geld/ v.t. castrate.

**gelding** /'geldɪŋ/ n. castrated horse etc.

**gelignite** /'dʒelɪɡnaɪt/ n. nitro-glycerine explosive.

**gem** /dʒem/ 1 n. precious stone; thing of great beauty or worth. 2 v.t. adorn (as) with gems.

**Gemini** /'dʒemənaɪ/ n. third sign of zodiac.

**gen** /dʒen/ colloq. 1 n. information. 2 v. (with up) gain or give information.

**Gen.** abbr. General.

**gendarme** /'ʒɒndɑːm/ n. soldier employed in police duties, esp. in France.

**gender** /'dʒendə(r)/ n. grammatical classification (or one of classes) roughly corresponding to two sexes and sexlessness.

**gene** /dʒiːn/ n. unit of heredity in chromosome, controlling particular inherited characteristic.

**genealogy** /dʒiːni'ælədʒi/ n. descent traced continuously from ancestor,

**genera** /'dʒenərə/ pl. of **genus**.

**general** /'dʒenər(ə)l/ 1 *a.* applicable to all, not partial or particular; prevalent, usual; vague, lacking detail; (in titles) chief, head. 2 *n.* Army officer next below Field Marshal; commander of army. 3 **general anaesthetic** one affecting whole body; **general election** election of representatives to parliament etc. from whole country; **general knowledge** knowledge of miscellaneous facts; **general practitioner** doctor treating cases of all kinds; **in general** usually, for the most part.

**generalissimo** /dʒenərə'lɪsəməʊ/ *n.* (*pl.* -mos) commander of combined forces.

**generality** /dʒenə'rælətɪ/ *n.* general statement; indefiniteness; majority *of.*

**generalize** /'dʒenərəlaɪz/ *v.* speak in general or indefinite terms, form general notion; reduce to general statement; infer (rule etc.) from particular cases; bring into general use. **generalization** *n.*

**generally** /'dʒenərəlɪ/ *adv.* in general sense; in most respects; usually.

**generate** /'dʒenəreɪt/ *v.t.* bring into existence, produce.

**generation** /dʒenə'reɪʃ(ə)n/ *n.* procreation; production, esp. of electricity; step in pedigree; all persons born about same time; period of about 30 years.

**generative** /'dʒenərətɪv/ *a.* of procreation, productive.

**generator** /'dʒenəreɪtə(r)/ *n.* dynamo; apparatus for producing gas or steam etc.

**generic** /dʒɪ'nerɪk/ *a.* characteristic of or applied to genus or class; not specific or special.

**generous** /'dʒenərəs/ *a.* giving or given freely; magnanimous; abundant. **generosity** *n.*

**genesis** /'dʒenəsɪs/ *n.* origin; mode of formation or generation.

**genetic** /dʒɪ'netɪk/ *a.* of genetics; of or in origin.

**genetics** *n.pl.* treated as *sing.* study of heredity and variation in animals and plants.

**genial** /'dʒiːnɪəl/ *a.* kindly, sociable; mild, warm; cheering. **geniality** /-'æl-/ *n.*

**genie** /'dʒiːnɪ/ *n.* (*pl.* **genii** /'dʒiːnɪaɪ/) sprite or goblin of Arabian tales.

**genital** /'dʒenɪt(ə)l/ 1 *a.* of animal reproduction or reproductive organs. 2 *n.* in pl. external genital organs.

**genitalia** /dʒenə'teɪlɪə/ *n.pl.* genitals.

**genitive** /'dʒenɪtɪv/ *Gram.* 1 *a.* (of case) corresponding to *of* or *from* etc., with noun representing possessor or source etc. 2 *n.* genitive case.

**genius** /'dʒiːnɪəs/ *n.* (*pl.* -iuses) very high natural ability; person having this; tutelary spirit.

**genocide** /'dʒenəsaɪd/ *n.* deliberate extermination of a people or nation.

**genre** /'ʒɑ̃nr/ *n.* kind or style etc. of art or literature; portrayal of scenes from ordinary life.

**gent** /dʒent/ *n. colloq.* gentleman.

**genteel** /dʒen'tiːl/ *a.* affectedly polite or refined.

**gentian** /'dʒenʃ(ə)n/ *n.* mountain plant with usu. blue flowers. **gentian violet** dye used as antiseptic.

**gentile** /'dʒentaɪl/ 1 *a.* not Jewish; heathen. 2 *n.* gentile person.

**gentility** /dʒen'tɪlətɪ/ *n.* social superiority; upper-class habits.

**gentle** /'dʒent(ə)l/ *a.* not rough or severe; kind, mild; well-born; quiet. **gently** *adv.*

**gentlefolk** /'dʒent(ə)lfəʊk/ *n.* people of good family.

**gentleman** /'dʒent(ə)lmən/ *n.* (*pl.* -men) man; chivalrous well-bred man; man of good social position.

**gentlemanly** *a.* behaving or looking like or befitting a gentleman.

**gentlewoman** /'dʒent(ə)lwʊmən/ *n. arch.* (*pl.* -women /-wɪmən/) woman of good birth or breeding.

**gentry** /'dʒentrɪ/ *n.* people next below nobility; *derog.* people.

**genuflect** /'dʒenjʊflekt/ *v.i.* bend knee, esp. in worship. **genuflexion** *n.*

**genuine** /'dʒenjʊən/ *a.* really coming from its reputed source; not sham; properly so called.

**genus** /'dʒiːnəs/ *n.* (*pl.* **genera** /'dʒenərə/) group of animals, plants, etc., with common structural characteristics, usu. containing several species; kind, class.

**geocentric** /dʒiːə'sentrɪk/ *a.* con-

**geode** /ˈdʒiːəʊd/ n. cavity lined with crystals; rock containing this.

**geodesic** /dʒiːəˈdiːsɪk/ a. (also **geodetic**) of geodesy. **geodesic line** shortest possible line on surface between two points.

**geodesy** /dʒiːˈɒdəsiː/ n. study of shape and area of the earth.

**geography** /dʒiːˈɒgrəfiː/ n. science of earth's form and physical features etc.; features of place. **geographer** n.; **geographic(al)** a.

**geology** /dʒiːˈɒlədʒiː/ n. science of earth's crust and strata. **geological** a.; **geologist** n.

**geometry** /dʒiːˈɒmɪtriː/ n. science of properties and relations of lines, surfaces, and solids. **geometric(al)** a.; **geometrician** n.

**georgette** /dʒɔːˈdʒet/ n. thin crêpe of silk or other fabric.

**Georgian** /ˈdʒɔːdʒ(ə)n/ a. of time of Kings George I-IV or George V and VI.

**geranium** /dʒəˈreɪnɪəm/ n. herb or shrub with fruit shaped like crane's bill; cultivated pelargonium.

**gerbil** /ˈdʒɜːbəl/ n. mouselike desert rodent with long hind legs.

**geriatrics** /dʒerɪˈætrɪks/ n.pl. treated as sing. branch of medical science dealing with old age and its diseases. **geriatric** a.; **geriatrician** n.

**germ** /dʒɜːm/ n. micro-organism or microbe; portion of organism capable of developing into new one; rudiment, elementary principle.

**German**[1] /ˈdʒɜːmən/ **1** a. of Germany. **2** n. native or language of Germany. **3 German measles** disease like mild measles; **German shepherd (dog)** dog of a wolfhound breed.

**german**[2] /ˈdʒɜːmən/ a. (placed after *brother* or *sister* etc.) having full relationship, not half-brother etc.

**germane** /dʒɜːˈmeɪn/ a. relevant or pertinent (*to*).

**Germanic** /dʒɜːˈmænɪk/ a. having German characteristics.

**germicide** /ˈdʒɜːmɪsaɪd/ n. substance that destroys germs. **germicidal** a.

**germinal** /ˈdʒɜːmən(ə)l/ a. of germs; in earliest stage of development.

**germinate** /ˈdʒɜːməneɪt/ v. sprout, bud; cause to shoot, produce. **germination** n.

**gerontology** /dʒerɒnˈtɒlədʒiː/ n. study of old age and ageing.

**gerrymander** /ˈdʒerɪˈmændə(r)/ v.t. manipulate boundaries of (constituency etc.) to gain unfair electoral advantage.

**gerund** /ˈdʒerənd/ n. verbal noun, in English ending in *-ing*.

**Gestapo** /geˈstɑːpəʊ/ n. Nazi secret police.

**gestation** /dʒeˈsteɪʃ(ə)n/ n. carrying in womb between conception and birth; period of this.

**gesticulate** /dʒeˈstɪkjʊleɪt/ v. use gestures with or instead of speech. **gesticulation** n.

**gesture** /ˈdʒestʃə(r)/ **1** n. significant movement of limb or body; action calculated to evoke response or convey intention. **2** v. gesticulate.

**get** /get/ v. (past **got**; p.p. **got** or US **gotten**) obtain, earn, gain, win, procure; fetch; go to reach or catch; prepare (meal); learn; experience or suffer; catch or contract, have inflicted; (cause to ) reach some state or become; succeed in coming or going *to* or *away* etc., succeed in bringing or placing etc.; in *perf.* possess, have, be bound *to do* or *be*; induce; *colloq.* understand; *colloq.* annoy, attract, or obsess; beget. **get at** reach, get hold of, *colloq.* imply, *colloq.* tamper with; **get away** escape; **getaway** n.; **get by** *colloq.* be acceptable, cope; **get down on** *Aus sl.* steal; **get in** win election, obtain place at college etc.; **get on** advance, fare, live harmoniously *with*, become elderly; **get out of** avoid or escape; **get over** surmount, recover from; **get-together** social assembly; **get up** rise esp. from bed, arrange appearance of; **get-up** style of equipment or costume etc.

**geum** /ˈdʒiːəm/ n. kind of rosaceous plant.

**gewgaw** /ˈgjuːgɔː/ n. gaudy plaything or ornament.

**geyser** /ˈgaɪzə(r)/ n. hot spring; /ˈgiːzə(r)/ apparatus for heating water.

**ghastly** /ˈgɑːstliː/ a. horrible, frightful, deathlike, pallid.

**ghat** /gɔːt/ n. (also **ghaut**) in India, steps leading to river; landing-place.

**ghee** /giː/ n. Indian clarified butter.

**gherkin** /ˈgɜːkən/ *n.* small cucumber for pickling.

**ghetto** /ˈgetəʊ/ *n.* (*pl.* **-os**) part of city occupied by minority group; Jews' quarter in city; segregated group or area.

**ghilgai** var. of **gilgai**.

**ghost** /gəʊst/ 1 *n.* apparition of dead person etc.; disembodied spirit; emaciated or pale person; semblance; secondary or duplicate image in defective telescope or television-picture. 2 *v.* act as ghost writer etc. 3 **ghost writer** writer doing work for which another takes credit. 4 **ghostly** *a.*

**ghoul** /guːl/ *n.* person morbidly interested in death etc.; spirit said to prey on corpses. **ghoulish** *a.*

**GHQ** *abbr.* General Headquarters.

**ghyll** var. of **gill**³.

**GI** /dʒiːˈaɪ/ 1 *n.* American private soldier. 2 *a.* of or for US armed forces.

**giant** /ˈdʒaɪənt/ 1 *n.* mythical being of human form but superhuman size; very tall or large person or animal etc.; person of extraordinary ability. 2 *a.* gigantic. 3 **giant-killer** person who defeats more powerful opponent. 4 **giantess** *n.*

**gibber**¹ /ˈdʒɪbə(r)/ *v.i.* chatter inarticulately.

**gibber**² /ˈgɪbə(r)/ *n. Aus.* boulder, large stone. **gibber-bird** small chat frequenting stony plains; **gibber-gunyah** Abor. cave-dwelling; **gibber-plain** flat land covered with gibbers.

**gibberish** /ˈdʒɪbərɪʃ/ *n.* unintelligible speech, meaningless sounds.

**gibbet** /ˈdʒɪbət/ *n. hist.* gallows; post on which body of executed criminal was exposed.

**gibbon** /ˈgɪbən/ *n.* long-armed ape.

**gibbous** /ˈgɪbəs/ *a.* convex; (of moon etc.) with bright part greater than semicircle. **gibbosity** *n.*

**gibe** /dʒaɪb/ 1 *v.* jeer or mock (at). 2 *n.* jeering remark, taunt.

**giblets** /ˈdʒɪblɪts/ *n.pl.* liver and gizzard etc. of bird removed before it is cooked.

**giddy** /ˈgɪdɪ/ *a.* dizzy; tending to fall or stagger; making dizzy; excitable, flighty.

**gidgee** /ˈgɪdʒiː/ *n. Aus.* a small acacia; its close-grained dark-red timber.

**gift** /gɪft/ 1 *n.* thing given, present; natural talent. 2 *v.t.* endow with gifts; present.

**gig**¹ /gɪg/ *n.* light two-wheeled one-horse carriage; light ship's-boat; rowing-boat esp. for race.

**gig**² /gɪg/ *Aus. sl.* 1 *n.* fool, victim. 2 *v.* hoax, fool; trick.

**gig**³ /gɪg/ *v. Aus. sl.* tease, taunt.

**gig**⁴ /gɪg/ *Aus. sl.* 1 *v.i.* stare at. 2 *n.* person who stares.

**gig**⁵ /gɪg/ *n. colloq.* engagement to play jazz etc. esp. for one night.

**gigantic** /dʒaɪˈgæntɪk/ *a.* giant-like, huge.

**giggle** /ˈgɪg(ə)l/ 1 *v.i.* give small bursts of half-suppressed laughter. 2 *n.* such laugh; *colloq.* amusing person or thing.

**gigolo** /ˈʒɪgələʊ/ *n.* (*pl.* **-los**) young man paid by older woman for his attentions.

**gild**¹ /gɪld/ *v.t.* (*p.p.* **gilded** or **gilt**) cover thinly with gold; tinge with golden colour.

**gild**² var. of **guild**.

**gilgai** /ˈgɪlgaɪ/ *n. Aus.* shallow depression forming natural reservoir for rain-water.

**gill**¹ /gɪl/ *n.* usu. in *pl.* respiratory organ of fish etc.; vertical radial plate on under side of mushroom etc.; flesh below person's jaws and ears.

**gill**² /dʒɪl/ *n.* quarter-pint measure.

**gill**³ /gɪl/ *n. UK* deep wooded ravine; narrow mountain torrent.

**gilt**¹ /gɪlt/ 1 *a.* overlaid with gold. 2 *n.* gilding. 3 **gilt-edged** (of securities) having high degree of reliability.

**gilt**² /gɪlt/ *n.* young sow.

**gimbals** /ˈdʒɪmb(ə)lz/ *n.pl.* contrivance of rings etc. for keeping things horizontal at sea.

**gimcrack** /ˈdʒɪmkræk/ 1 *a.* flimsy, worthless. 2 *n.* showy ornament etc.

**gimlet** /ˈgɪmlət/ *n.* small boring-tool.

**gimmick** /ˈgɪmɪk/ *n. colloq.* tricky device or idea etc., esp. to attract attention. **gimmickry** *n.*; **gimmicky** *a.*

**gimp** /gɪmp/ *n.* twist of silk etc. with cord or wire running through.

**gin**¹ /dʒɪn/ *n.* spirit distilled from grain or malt and flavoured with juniper etc.

**gin**² /dʒɪn/ 1 *n.* snare, trap; machine separating cotton from seeds; kind of crane or windlass. 2 *v.t.* treat (cotton) in gin; trap.

**gin**³ /dʒɪn/ *n. Aus.* Abor. woman.

**ginger** /ˈdʒɪndʒə(r)/ 1 *n.* hot spicy root

**gingerly** used in cooking and medicine; plant from which this comes; light reddish yellow; mettle, spirit. **2** *v.t.* flavour with ginger; liven *up*. **3 ginger-ale, -beer,** ginger-flavoured aerated drinks; **gingerbread** ginger-flavoured treacle cake; **ginger group** one urging party or movement to more decided action; **ginger-nut, -snap,** kinds of ginger-flavoured biscuit. **4 gingery** *a*.

**gingerly** /'dʒɪndʒəlɪ/ **1** *a*. showing extreme care or caution. **2** *adv.* in gingerly manner.

**gingham** /'gɪŋəm/ *n*. plain-woven cotton cloth, frequently striped or checked.

**gink** /gɪŋk/ *n*. Aus. colloq. a fellow; a look.

**gingivitis** /dʒɪndʒɪ'vaɪtɪs/ *n*. inflammation of the gums.

**ginkgo** /'gɪŋkəʊ/ *n*. (*pl.* **-gos**) yellow-flowered Chinese and Japanese tree.

**ginseng** /'dʒɪnseŋ/ *n*. medicinal plant found in E. Asia and N. America; root of this.

**gipsy** var. of **gypsy.**

**giraffe** /dʒə'rɑːf/ *n*. large African four-legged animal with long neck.

**gird** /ɡɜːd/ (*past* & *p.p.* **girded** or **girt**) encircle or fasten (on) with waistbelt etc. **gird up one's loins** prepare for action.

**girder** /'ɡɜːdə(r)/ *n*. iron or steel beam or compound structure forming span of bridge etc.; beam supporting joists.

**girdle**[1] /'ɡɜːd(ə)l/ **1** *n*. cord or belt used to gird waist; thing that surrounds; corset; bony support for limbs. **2** *v.t.* surround with girdle.

**girdle**[2] /'ɡɜːd(ə)l/ *n*. circular iron plate for baking scones etc. over heat.

**girl** /ɡɜːl/ *n*. female child; young woman; female servant; man's girlfriend. **girl guide** Guide. **girlhood** *n*.; **girlish** *a*.

**giro** /'dʒaɪrəʊ/ *n*. (*pl.* **-os**) UK system of credit transfer between banks or post offices etc.

**girt** *past* & *p.p.* of **gird.**

**girth** /ɡɜːθ/ *n*. distance round a thing; band round body of horse securing saddle.

**gist** /'dʒɪst/ *n*. substance or point or essence *of* a matter.

**give** /ɡɪv/ **1** *v*. (*past* **gave**; *p.p.* **given** /'ɡɪv(ə)n/) transfer possession of gratuitously; grant, accord; deliver, administer; consign, put; pledge; devote; present, offer (one's hand, arm, etc.); exert; impart, be source of; assume, grant, specify; allow to have; collapse, yield, shrink. **2** *n*. elasticity; yielding to pressure. **3 give and take** exchange of talk or ideas, willingness to make concessions etc. **give away** transfer as gift, hand over (bride) to bridegroom, betray or expose; **give-away** *colloq.* unintentional disclosure; **give in** yield; **give (it) away** *Aus.* abandon or give up something, desist; **give off** emit; **give out** distribute, announce, emit, be exhausted, run short; **give over** devote *to*, hand over, *colloq.* desist; **give up** cease from effort or *doing*, part with, resign, surrender, renounce hope (of); **give way** yield under pressure, give precedence.

**given** **1** *p.p.* of **give. 2** *a*. disposed, prone (*to*); granted as basis of reasoning etc.; fixed, specified. **3 given name** forename.

**gizzard** /'ɡɪzəd/ *n*. bird's second stomach, for grinding food.

**glacé** /'ɡlæseɪ/ *a*. iced, sugared; (of cloth etc.) smooth, polished.

**glacial** /'ɡleɪʃ(ə)l/ *a*. of ice, icy; *Geol.* characterized or produced by ice.

**glaciated** /'ɡleɪsɪeɪtɪd/ *a*. covered with glaciers; affected by friction of moving ice. **glaciation** *n*.

**glacier** /'ɡlæsɪə(r)/ *n*. slowly moving river or mass of ice.

**glad** *a*. pleased; joyful, cheerful. **glad rags** *colloq.* best clothes.

**gladden** /'ɡlæd(ə)n/ *v.t.* make glad.

**glade** *n*. clear space in forest.

**gladiator** /'ɡlædɪeɪtə(r)/ *n*. trained fighter in ancient Roman shows. **gladiatorial** *a*.

**gladiolus** /ɡlædɪ'əʊləs/ *n*. (*pl.* **-li** /-laɪ/) plant of iris kind with bright flower-spikes.

**gladsome** /'ɡlædsəm/ *a*. *poet.* joyful, cheerful.

**glair** *n*. white of egg; similar viscous substance.

**glamour** /'ɡlæmə(r)/ *n*. alluring or exciting beauty or charm. **glamorize** *v.t.*; **glamorous** *a*.

**glance** /ɡlɑːns/ or /ɡlæns/ **1** *v.i.* give brief or momentary look; glide *off.* **2** *n*. brief look; flash, gleam; swift oblique

# gland     glory

movement or impact. **3 glance at** make brief allusion to.

**gland** *n.* organ secreting substances required for particular function of body; similar organ in plant.

**glanders** /'glændəz/ *n.pl.* contagious horse-disease.

**glandular** /'glændjələ(r)/ *a.* of gland(s). **glandular fever** infectious disease with swelling of lymph-glands.

**glare** /gleə(r)/ **1** *v.i.* look fiercely; shine oppressively. **2** *n.* fierce look; oppressive light; tawdry brilliance.

**glass** /glɑːs/ **1** *n.* substance, usu. transparent, lustrous, hard, and brittle, made by fusing sand with soda and potash etc.; glass objects collectively; glass drinking-vessel; looking-glass; lens; in *pl.* pair of spectacles or binoculars; barometer; microscope. **2** *v.t.* fit or cover with glass. **3 glass-cloth** cloth for drying glasses; **glass fibre** fabric made from or plastic reinforced by glass filaments; **glasshouse** greenhouse, *sl.* military prison; **glass-paper** paper covered with powdered glass, for smoothing etc.; **glass wool** fine glass fibres for packing and insulation.

**glassy** /'glɑːsɪ/ *a.* like glass; (of eye) dull, fixed.

**glaucoma** /glɔː'kəʊmə/ *n.* eye-disease with pressure in eye-ball and gradual loss of sight.

**glaze 1** *v.* fit with glass or windows; cover (pottery etc.) with vitreous substance or (surface) with smooth lustrous coating; (of eye) become glassy. **2** *n.* substance used for or surface produced by glazing.

**glazier** /'gleɪzɪə(r)/ *n.* person who glazes windows etc. professionally.

**gleam 1** *n.* subdued or transient light; faint or momentary show. **2** *v.i.* emit gleams.

**glean** *v.* pick up (facts etc.); gather (corn left by reapers). **gleanings** *n.pl.*

**glebe** *n.* piece of land yielding revenue to benefice.

**glee** *n.* mirth, lively delight; musical composition for several voices. **gleeful** *a.*

**glen** *n.* narrow valley.

**glengarry** /glen'gærɪ/ *n.* kind of Highland cap.

**glib** *a.* speaking or spoken fluently but insincerely.

**glide 1** *v.* pass or proceed by smooth continuous movement; (of aircraft) fly without engines; go stealthily. **2** *n.* gliding motion or flight.

**glider** /'glaɪdə(r)/ *n.* light aircraft without engine.

**glimmer** /'glɪmə(r)/ **1** *n.* faint light or gleam. **2** *v.i.* shine faintly or intermittently.

**glimpse** /glɪmps/ **1** *n.* brief view; faint transient appearance. **2** *v.t.* have brief view of.

**glint** *v.i.* & *n.* flash; glitter.

**glissade** /glɪ'sɑːd/ **1** *v.i.* make controlled slide down slope of ice etc. **2** *n.* glissading movement.

**glisten** /'glɪs(ə)n/ **1** *v.* shine like wet or polished surface; sparkle. **2** *n.* glistening.

**glitter** /'glɪtə(r)/ **1** *v.i.* shine with brilliant tremulous light. **2** *n.* glittering; material that glitters.

**gloaming** /'gləʊmɪŋ/ *n.* evening twilight.

**gloat** *v.i.* look or ponder with greedy or malicious pleasure (*over*).

**global** /'gləʊb(ə)l/ *a.* world-wide; all-embracing.

**globe** *n.* spherical object; *the* earth; spherical map of earth or constellations; thing shaped like this. **globe-trotting** travelling through many foreign countries.

**globular** /'glɒbjələ(r)/ *a.* globe-shaped; composed of globules. **globularity** *n.*

**globule** /'glɒbjuːl/ *n.* small globe or round particle, esp. of liquid.

**glockenspiel** /'glɒkənspiːl/ *n.* musical instrument of bells or tuned metal bars played with hammers.

**gloom** /gluːm/ *n.* darkness; melancholy, depression. **2** *v.i.* look or be sullen or depressed; be dull.

**gloomy** /'gluːmɪ/ *a.* dark, depressed, depressing.

**glorify** /'glɔːrɪfaɪ/ *v.t.* make glorious; extol; make out to be more splendid than is the case; invest with radiance. **glorification** *n.*

**glorious** /'glɔːrɪəs/ *a.* possessing or conferring glory; splendid, excellent.

**glory** /'glɔːrɪ/ **1** *n.* renown, honourable fame; resplendent majesty or beauty etc.; halo of saint. **2** *v.i.* take pride (*in*). **3 glory box** *Aus.* box in which woman stores clothes etc. in preparation for marriage.

**gloss**[1] 1 *n.* lustre of surface; deceptively attractive appearance. 2 *v.t.* make glossy. 3 **gloss over** seek to conceal. 4 **glossy** *a.*

**gloss**[2] 1 *n.* explanatory comment added to text; comment, interpretation. 2 *v.t.* insert glosses in, make or write gloss on; explain.

**glossary** /'glɒsəri/ *n.* dictionary of technical or special words.

**glottal** /'glɒt(ə)l/ *a.* of the glottis. **glottal stop** sound produced by sudden opening or shutting of glottis.

**glottis** /'glɒtɪs/ *n.* opening at upper end of windpipe and between vocal cords.

**glove** /glʌv/ 1 *n.* hand-covering, usu. with separated fingers, for warmth or protection etc.; boxing-glove. 2 *v.t.* cover or provide with gloves. 3 **glove compartment** recess for small articles in motor-car dashboard.

**glow** /gləʊ/ 1 *v.* emit flameless light and heat; show warm colour; burn *with* bodily heat or emotion. 2 *n.* glowing state; ardour. 3 **glow-worm** beetle that emits green light from abdomen.

**glower** /'glaʊə(r)/ *v.i.* scowl (*at*).

**glucose** /'glu:kəʊs/ *n.* kind of sugar found in fruits and blood etc.

**glue** 1 *n.* sticky substance used as adhesive. 2 *v.t.* attach (as) with glue; hold closely. 3 **gluey** *a.*

**glum** *a.* dejected, sullen.

**glut** 1 *v.t.* feed or indulge to the full, satiate; overstock. 2 *n.* excessive supply; surfeit.

**gluten** /'glu:t(ə)n/ *n.* viscous part of flour.

**glutinous** /'glu:tɪnəs/ *a.* sticky, gluelike, viscous.

**glutton** /'glʌt(ə)n/ *n.* excessive eater; person insatiably eager *for*; voracious animal of weasel kind. **gluttonous** *a.*; **gluttony** *n.*

**glycerine** /'glɪsərɪn/ *n.* colourless sweet viscous liquid got from oils or fats.

**gm.** *abbr.* gram(s).

**G-man** /'dʒi:mæn/ *n. US sl.* Federal criminal-investigation officer.

**GMT** *abbr.* Greenwich Mean Time.

**gnamma** /'næmə/ *n. Aus.* natural hole in rock, containing water.

**gnarled** /nɑ:ld/ *a.* knobbly, rugged, twisted.

**gnash** /næʃ/ *v.* grind (one's teeth); (of teeth) strike together.

**gnat** /næt/ *n.* small biting fly.

**gnaw** /nɔ:/ *v.t.* bite persistently, wear *away* thus; corrode, torment.

**gneiss** /naɪs/ *n.* coarse-grained rock of quartz, feldspar, and mica.

**gnome** /nəʊm/ *n.* goblin, dwarf; *colloq.* person with sinister influence, esp. in finance.

**gnomic** /'nəʊmɪk/ *a.* of maxims, sententious.

**gnomon** /'nəʊmɒn/ *n.* rod etc. showing time by its shadow on marked surface of sundial.

**gnostic** /'nɒstɪk/ 1 *a.* of knowledge; having special mystic knowledge. 2 *n.* **Gnostic**, early Christian heretic claiming mystical knowledge 3 **Gnosticism** *n.*

**GNP** *abbr.* gross national product.

**gnu** /nu:/ *n.* oxlike antelope.

**go**[1] 1 *v.i.* (*past* **went**; *p.p.* **gone** /gɒn/) walk, travel, proceed; depart; move, pass; become; (of money) be spent *in* or *on*; be functioning, moving, etc.; collapse, give way, fail; extend, reach; be successful or acceptable; be sold; give forth sound. 2 *n.* (*pl.* **goes**) animation, dash; *colloq.* state of affairs; success; *Aus.* chance; turn, try (*at*). 3 **go-ahead** enterprising; **go-between** intermediary; **go by** be guided by, pass; **go-getter** enterprising pushful person; **go in for** compete or engage in; **go-kart** miniature racing-car with skeleton body; **go off** explode, deteriorate, (of event) succeed *well* etc., begin to dislike; **go out** leave room or house, be extinguished, cease to be fashionable, mix in society; **go round** pay informal visit, suffice for all; **go slow** work at deliberately slow pace as industrial protest; **go under** succumb, fail; **go without** not have, abstain from; **it's no go** *colloq.* nothing can be done; **on the go** *colloq.* in motion.

**go**[2] *n.* Japanese board-game.

**goad** 1 *n.* spiked stick for urging cattle; thing that incites or torments. 2 *v.t.* urge with goad; drive *by* annoyance.

**goal** *n.* structure into or through which ball is to be driven in certain games; point(s) so won; object of effort; des-

**goalie** /ˈgəʊlɪ/ n. colloq. goalkeeper.

**goanna** /gəʊˈænə/ n. Aus. large kind of lizard.

**goat** n. small horned ruminant; licentious man; fool. **get person's goat** sl. irritate him.

**goatee** /gəʊˈtiː/ n. beard like goat's.

**gob**[1] n. sl. mouth. **gob-stopper** large hard sweet for sucking.

**gob**[2] n. sl. clot of slimy substance.

**gobbet** /ˈgɒbət/ n. extract from text set for translation or comment.

**gobble**[1] /ˈgɒb(ə)l/ v. eat hurriedly and noisily.

**gobble**[2] /ˈgɒb(ə)l/ v.i. (of turkey-cock) make gurgling sound in throat; speak thus.

**gobbledegook** /ˈgɒbəldɪguːk/ n. colloq. pompous official etc. jargon.

**goblet** /ˈgɒblət/ n. drinking-vessel with foot and stem.

**goblin** /ˈgɒblɪn/ n. mischievous demon.

**goby** /ˈgəʊbɪ/ n. small fish with ventral fins joined into disc or sucker.

**god** n. superhuman being worshipped as possessing divine power; (**God**) creator and ruler of universe; idol; adored person. **the gods** Theatr. (occupants of) gallery; **godchild** child in relation to godparent; **god-daughter** female godchild; **godfather** male godparent; **God-fearing** religious; **God-forsaken** dismal, forlorn; **godmother** female godparent; **godparent** sponsor at baptism; **godsend** unexpected welcome event or acquisition; **godson** male godchild.

**goddess** /ˈgɒdes/ n. female deity; adored woman.

**godhead** /ˈgɒdhed/ n. divine nature, deity.

**godless** /ˈgɒdləs/ a. not believing in God; impious, wicked.

**godly** /ˈgɒdlɪ/ a. pious, devout.

**godwit** /ˈgɒdwɪt/ n. marsh bird like curlew.

**goer** /ˈgəʊə(r)/ n. person or thing that goes; lively or vivacious person; Aus. colloq. proposal or idea etc. that is acceptable or feasible.

**goggle** /ˈgɒg(ə)l/ 1 v.i. look with wide-open eyes; (of eyes) be rolled, project; roll (eyes). 2 a. (of eyes) protuberant, rolling. 3 n.pl. spectacles for protecting eyes from glare or dust etc. 4 **goggle-box** sl. television set.

**going** /ˈgəʊɪŋ/ 1 n. condition of ground for riding etc.; progress. 2 a. in action; existing, available; currently valid. 3 **goings-on** strange conduct.

**goitre** /ˈgɔɪtə(r)/ n. abnormal enlargement of thyroid gland. **goitrous** a.

**gold** /gəʊld/ 1 n. precious yellow metal; coins or articles of this; wealth; colour of gold. 2 a. of or coloured like gold. 3 **gold-digger** sl. woman who wheedles money out of men; **goldfinch** bright-coloured song-bird; **goldfish** small golden-red Chinese carp; **gold-leaf** gold beaten into thin sheet; **gold medal** medal given usu. as first prize; **gold rush** to newly-discovered goldfield; **goldsmith** worker in gold; **gold standard** financial system in which value of money is based on gold.

**golden** /ˈgəʊld(ə)n/ a. of gold; coloured or shining like gold; precious, excellent. **golden handshake** gratuity as compensation for dismissal or compulsory retirement; **golden mean** neither too much nor too little; **golden perch** edible Aus. freshwater fish, callop. **golden syrup** pale treacle; **golden wedding** 50th wedding anniversary.

**golf** n. game in which small hard ball is struck with clubs over ground into series of small holes. 2 v.i. play golf. 3 **golf ball** ball used in golf, colloq. spherical unit carrying type in some electric typewriters; **golf-course** area of land on which golf is played.

**golliwog** /ˈgɒlɪwɒg/ n. black-faced soft doll with bright clothes and fuzzy hair.

**golosh** var. of galosh.

**gonad** /ˈgəʊnæd/ n. animal organ producing gametes, e.g. testis or ovary.

**gondola** /ˈgɒndələ/ n. light Venetian canal-boat; car suspended from airship.

**gondolier** /gɒndəˈlɪə(r)/ n. rower of gondola.

**gone** p.p. of go[1].

**goner** /ˈgɒnə(r)/ n. sl. doomed or irrevocably lost person or thing.

**gong** n. metal disc giving resonant note when struck; saucer-shaped bell; sl. medal.

**gonorrhoea** /gɒnəˈriːə/ n. venereal disease with inflammatory discharge from urethra or vagina.

**goo** *n. colloq.* viscous or sticky substance. **gooey** *a.*

**good** /gʊd/ **1** *a.* (*compar.* **better**; *superl.* **best**) having right qualities, adequate; proper; virtuous, morally excellent; worthy; well-behaved; agreeable; suitable; considerable; valid. **2** *n.* good quality or circumstance; in *pl.* movable property, merchandise. **3 good-for-nothing** worthless (person); **good humour** genial mood; **good-looking** handsome; **good-nature** kindly disposition; **good on you** *Aus. colloq.* well done; **goodwill** kindly feeling, heartiness, established custom or business etc.

**goodbye** /gʊdˈbaɪ/ **1** *int.* expressing good wishes at parting. **2** *n.* leave-taking, saying goodbye.

**goodly** /ˈgʊdlɪ/ *a.* handsome, of imposing size etc.

**goodness** /ˈgʊdnəs/ *n.* virtue; excellence; kindness; nutriment.

**goodo** /gʊˈdəʊ/ *Aus. colloq.* **1** *int.* expr. approval or acquiescence. **2** *a.* good. **3** *adv.* well.

**goody** /ˈgʊdɪ/ **1** *n.* something good or attractive esp. to eat; good person. **2** *int.* expr. childish delight.

**goody-goody** /ˈgʊdɪgʊdɪ/ **1** *a.* obtrusively virtuous. **2** *n.* such person.

**goof** /guːf/ *sl.* **1** *n.* foolish or stupid person or mistake. **2** *v.* blunder, bungle. **3 goofy** *a.*

**googly** /ˈguːlɪ/ *n. Crick.* ball bowled so as to bounce in unexpected direction.

**goon** /guːn/ *n. sl.* stupid person; hired ruffian.

**goondie** /ˈguːndɪ/ *n. Aus.* a gunyah.

**goose** /guːs/ *n.* (*pl.* **geese** /giːs/) large web-footed bird; female of this; simpleton; (*pl.* **gooses**) tailor's smoothing-iron. **goose-flesh** bristling state of skin due to cold or fright; **goose-step** parading-step of marching soldiers with knees kept stiff.

**gooseberry** /ˈgʊzbərɪ/ *n.* small green usu. sour berry; thorny shrub bearing it.

**gopher** /ˈgəʊfə(r)/ *n.* Amer. burrowing rodent.

**gore**[1] *n.* clotted blood.

**gore**[2] *v.t.* pierce with horn or tusk etc.

**gore**[3] **1** *n.* wedge-shaped piece in garment; triangular or tapering piece in umbrella or balloon etc. **2** *v.t.* shape with gore.

**gorge 1** *n.* narrow opening between hills; surfeit; contents of stomach. **2** *v.* feed greedily; satiate.

**gorgeous** /ˈgɔːdʒəs/ *a.* richly coloured; splendid; *colloq.* very pleasant.

**gorgon** /ˈgɔːgən/ *n.* frightening or repulsive woman.

**Gorgonzola** /gɔːgənˈzəʊlə/ *n.* rich blue-veined Italian cheese.

**gorilla** /gəˈrɪlə/ *n.* large powerful anthropoid ape.

**gormandize** /ˈgɔːməndaɪz/ *v.i.* eat greedily.

**gormless** /ˈgɔːmləs/ *a. colloq.* foolish, lacking sense.

**gorse** /gɔːs/ *n.* prickly yellow-flowered shrub.

**gory** /ˈgɔːrɪ/ *a.* blood-stained; involving bloodshed.

**gosh** *int.* of surprise etc.

**goshawk** /ˈgɒshɔːk/ *n.* large short-winged hawk.

**gosling** /ˈgɒzlɪŋ/ *n.* young goose.

**gospel** /ˈgɒsp(ə)l/ *n.* teaching or revelation of Christ; **Gospel** each of four books of NT giving account of Christ's life; portion of this read at church service; thing regarded as absolutely true.

**gossamer** /ˈgɒsəmə(r)/ **1** *n.* filmy substance of small spiders' webs; delicate filmy material. **2** *a.* light and flimsy as gossamer.

**gossip** /ˈgɒsəp/ **1** *n.* idle talk; informal talk or writing esp. about persons; person indulging in gossip. **2** *v.i.* talk or write gossip. **3 gossip column** regular newspaper column of gossip. **4 gossipy** *a.*

**got** *past* & *p.p.* of **get**.

**Goth** /gɒθ/ *n.* member of Germanic people who invaded Roman Empire in 3rd-5th c.

**Gothic** /ˈgɒθɪk/ *a.* of Goths; *Archit.* in the pointed-arch style prevalent in W. Europe in 12th-16th c.; (of novel etc.) in a horrific style popular in 18th-19th c.

**gotten** *US p.p.* of **get**.

**gouache** /ɡuːˈɑːʃ/ *n.* painting with opaque water-colour; pigments used for this.

**Gouda** /ˈgaʊdə/ *n.* flat round usu. Dutch cheese.

**gouge** /gaʊdʒ/ **1** *n.* concave-bladed

## goulash

**goulash** /ˈguːlæʃ/ *n.* stew of meat and vegetables seasoned with paprika.

**gourd** /gʊəd/ *n.* fleshy fruit of trailing or climbing plant; this plant; dried rind of this fruit used as bottle.

**gourmand** /ˈgʊəmænd/ *n.* glutton; gourmet.

**gourmet** /ˈgʊəmeɪ/ *n.* connoisseur of good food.

**gout** /gaʊt/ *n.* disease with painful inflammation of small joints; drop or splash, esp. of blood. **gouty** *a.*

**govern** /ˈgʌv(ə)n/ *v.* rule with authority; conduct policy and affairs of (State etc.); influence or determine; curb, control.

**governance** /ˈgʌvənəns/ *n.* act or manner or function of governing.

**governess** /ˈgʌvənəs/ *n.* woman employed to teach children in private household.

**government** /ˈgʌvənmənt/ *n.* system of governing; persons governing State; particular ministry in office. **governmental** *a.*

**governor** /ˈgʌvənə(r)/ *n.* ruler; official governing province or town etc.; executive head of State of US; one of governing body of institution; *sl.* one's employer or father; automatic regulator controlling speed of engine etc.

**gown** /gaʊn/ *n.* woman's, esp. formal or elegant, dress; robe of alderman or judge or clergyman or member of university etc.; surgeon's overall.

**goy** *n.* (*pl.* **goyim** or **goys**) Jewish name for non-Jew.

**GP** *abbr.* general practitioner.

**GPO** *abbr.* General Post Office.

**gr.** *abbr.* gram(s); gross.

**grab** 1 *v.* seize suddenly, snatch; take greedily; capture. 2 *n.* sudden clutch or attempt to seize; *Mech.* device for clutching or gripping.

**grace** 1 *n.* attractiveness, charm, esp. of elegant proportions or ease and refinement of movement or manner etc.; attractive feature, accomplishment; courteous good will; divine inspiring influence; delay granted; thanksgiving at meals. 2 *v.t.* add grace to; bestow honour on. 3 **grace-note** *Mus.* note embellishing melody; **His, Her, Your, Grace** titles used of or in addressing duke, duchess, or archbishop.

**graceful** /ˈgreɪsfəl/ *a.* full of grace or charm.

**graceless** /ˈgreɪsləs/ *a.* lacking grace or charm.

**gracious** /ˈgreɪʃəs/ *a.* kindly, esp. to inferiors; merciful. **gracious living** elegant way of life.

**gradate** /grəˈdeɪt/ *v.* (cause to) pass by gradations from one shade to another; arrange in gradations.

**gradation** /grəˈdeɪʃ(ə)n/ *n.* stage of transition or advance; degree in rank or intensity etc.; arrangement in grades. **gradational** *a.*

**grade** 1 *n.* degree in rank or merit etc.; mark indicating quality of student's work; slope; *US* class or form in school. 2 *v.t.* arrange in grades; give grade to; reduce to easy gradients. 3 **make the grade** succeed.

**gradient** /ˈgreɪdiənt/ *n.* amount of slope in road etc.; sloping road etc.

**gradual** /ˈgrædjuəl/ *a.* happening by degrees; not steep or abrupt.

**graduate** 1 /ˈgrædjuət/ *n.* holder of academic degree. 2 /ˈgrædjueɪt/ *v.* take academic degree; mark in degrees or portions; arrange in gradations; apportion (tax) according to scale. **graduation** *n.*

**graffito** /grəˈfiːtəʊ/ *n.* (*pl.* **-ti** /-tiː/) drawing or writing on wall etc.

**graft**[1] /grɑːft/ 1 *n.* shoot or scion planted in slit made in another stock; piece of transplanted living tissue; *sl.* hard work. 2 *v.* insert (graft) *in* or *on*; transplant (living tissue); fix or join (thing) permanently to another; *sl.* work hard.

**graft**[2] /grɑːft/ 1 *n.* practices for securing illicit gains in politics or business; such gains. 2 *v.i.* seek or make graft.

**Grail** *n.* legendary cup or platter used by Christ at Last Supper.

**grain** 1 *n.* fruit or seed of cereal; *collect.* wheat or allied food-grass; corn; particle, least possible amount; unit of weight, 0.0648 gr.; texture in skin or wood or stone etc.; arrangement of lines of fibre in wood. 2 *v.* paint in imitation of grain of wood; form into grains.

**grallatorial** /grælæˈtɔːriəl/ *a.* of long-legged wading birds.

**gram** *n.* unit of weight in metric system.

**graminaceous** /græmə'neɪʃəs/ *a.* of or like grass.

**graminivorous** /græmə'nɪvərəs/ *a.* grass-eating.

**grammar** /'græmə(r)/ *n.* study or rules of a language's inflexions or other means of showing relation between words; book on grammar. **grammar school** *UK* secondary school with academic curriculum.

**grammarian** /grə'meərɪən/ *n.* expert in grammar.

**grammatical** /grə'mætɪk(ə)l/ *a.* of or according to grammar.

**gramme** var. of **gram**.

**gramophone** /'græməfəʊn/ *n.* instrument reproducing recorded sound by stylus resting on rotating grooved disc. **gramophone record** such disc.

**grampus** /'græmpəs/ *n.* sea-animal resembling dolphin.

**granary** /'grænərɪ/ *n.* storehouse for grain; region producing much corn.

**grand** 1 *a.* splendid, imposing; chief, of chief importance; of highest rank; *colloq.* excellent. 2 *n.* grand piano; *sl.* 1,000 pounds or dollars etc. 3 **grand jury** to examine validity of accusation before trial; **grand piano** one with horizontal strings; **grand total** sum of other totals.

**grandchild** /'græntʃaɪld/ *n.* one's child's child.

**granddaughter** /'grændɔːtə(r)/ *n.* one's child's daughter.

**grandee** /græn'diː/ *n.* Spanish or Portuguese noble of highest rank; great personage.

**grandeur** /'grændjə(r)/ *n.* majesty, splendour, dignity; high rank, eminence.

**grandfather** /'grænfɑːðə(r)/ *n.* one's parent's father. **grandfather clock** clock in tall wooden case.

**grandiloquent** /græn'dɪləkwənt/ *a.* pompous or inflated in language. **grandiloquence** *n.*

**grandiose** /'grændɪəʊs/ *a.* imposing; planned on large scale. **grandiosity** *n.*

**grandmother** /'grænmʌðə(r)/ *n.* one's parent's mother.

**grandparent** /'grænpeərənt/ *n.* one's parent's parent.

**Grand Prix** /grɒ̃ priː/ international motor-racing championship.

**grandson** /'grænsʌn/ *n.* one's child's son.

**grandstand** /'grænstænd/ *n.* main stand for spectators at racecourse etc.

**grange** /greɪndʒ/ *n. UK* country-house with farm buildings.

**granite** /'grænɪt/ *n.* granular crystalline rock of quartz and mica etc.

**granny** /'grænɪ/ *n. colloq.* grandmother; (in full **granny knot**) reef-knot crossed wrong way; **Granny Smith** bright green eating or cooking apple.

**grant** /grɑːnt/ 1 *v.t.* consent to fulfil; give formally, transfer legally; concede, admit. 2 *n.* thing, esp. money, granted; granting.

**grantor** /grɑːn'tɔː(r)/ *n.* person by whom property is legally transferred.

**granular** /'grænjələ(r)/ *a.* of or like grains or granules.

**granulate** /'grænjəleɪt/ *v.* form into grains; roughen surface of. **granulation** *n.*

**granule** /'grænjuːl/ *n.* small grain.

**grape** *n.* green or purple berry growing in clusters on vine. **grape-shot** small balls as scattering charge for cannon; **grapevine** vine, means of transmission of rumour.

**grapefruit** /'greɪpfruːt/ *n.* (*pl.* same) large round yellow citrus fruit.

**graph** /grɑːf or græf/ *n.* symbolic diagram representing relation between two or more variables.

**graphic** /'græfɪk/ *a.* of writing or drawing or painting or etching etc.; vividly descriptive.

**graphics** *n.pl.* (usu. treated as *sing.*) production or use of diagrams etc. in calculation and design.

**graphite** /'græfaɪt/ *n.* crystalline form of carbon used in pencils or as lubricant etc.

**graphology** /grə'fɒlədʒɪ/ *n.* study of handwriting. **graphologist** *n.*

**grapnel** /'græpn(ə)l/ *n.* iron-clawed instrument for dragging or grasping; small many-fluked anchor.

**grapple** /'græp(ə)l/ 1 *v.* seize with hands; come to close quarters with; contend in close fight *with*. 2 *n.* hold (as) of wrestler; close contest; clutching-instrument. 3 **grappling-iron** grapnel.

**grasp** /grɑːsp/ 1 *v.* clutch, seize greed-

**grasping** *a.* avaricious.

**grass** /grɑːs/ 1 *n.* herbage of which blade-like leaves are eaten by horses and cattle etc.; any species of this; pasture land; grass-covered ground; grazing; *sl.* marijuana; *sl.* informer. 2 *v.t.* cover with turf; *sl.* betray, inform police. 3 **grass roots** fundamental level or source, esp. (*Polit.*) the voters; **grass snake** small non-poisonous snake; **grass widow** woman whose husband is temporarily absent. 4 **grassy** *a.*

**grasshopper** /'grɑːshɒpə(r)/ *n.* jumping and chirping insect.

**grate**¹ *v.* rub to small particles on rough surface; grind, creak; have irritating effect.

**grate**² *n.* frame of metal bars holding fuel in fireplace etc.

**grateful** /'greɪtfəl/ *a.* thankful; feeling or showing gratitude.

**gratify** /'grætɪfaɪ/ *v.t.* please, delight; indulge. **gratification** *n.*

**grating** /'greɪtɪŋ/ *n.* framework of parallel or crossed metal bars.

**gratis** /'greɪtɪs/ or /'grɑː-/ *adv.* & *a.* (given, done) for nothing, free.

**gratitude** /'grætɪtjuːd/ *n.* being thankful.

**gratuitous** /grə'tjuːɪtəs/ *a.* given or done gratis; uncalled for, motiveless.

**gratuity** /grə'tjuːɪtɪ/ *n.* money given in recognition of services.

**gravamen** /grə'veɪmen/ *n.* essence or worst part of accusation.

**grave**¹ *n.* hole dug for burial of corpse; mound or monument over it; being dead, death. **gravestone** inscribed stone over grave; **grave-yard** burial-ground.

**grave**² *a.* serious, weighty; dignified, solemn; low-pitched.

**grave**³ *v.t.* (*p.p.* **graved** or **graven**) fix indelibly; *arch.* engrave, carve. **graven image** idol.

**grave**⁴ /grɑːv/ *n.* accent ( ` ) over vowel.

**grave**⁵ *v.t.* clean (ship's bottom) by burning and tarring. **graving dock** dry dock.

**gravel** /'græv(ə)l/ 1 *n.* coarse sand and small stones; formation of crystals in bladder. 2 *v.t.* lay with gravel; puzzle, nonplus.

**gravelly** /'grævəlɪ/ *a.* of or like gravel; (of voice) deep and rough-sounding.

**gravid** /'grævɪd/ *a.* pregnant.

**gravitate** /'grævɪteɪt/ *v.i.* be attracted (*towards*); move or tend by force of gravity; sink (as) by gravity.

**gravitation** /grævɪ'teɪʃ(ə)n/ *n.* falling of bodies to earth; attraction of each particle of matter on every other; movement or tendency towards centre of this attraction. **gravitational** *a.*

**gravity** /'grævɪtɪ/ *n.* force that attracts body to centre of earth etc.; intensity of this; weight; importance, seriousness; solemnity.

**gravy** /'greɪvɪ/ *n.* (sauce made from) juices exuding from meat in and after cooking.

**gray** var. of **grey**.

**grayling** /'greɪlɪŋ/ *n.* silver-grey N. hemis. freshwater fish; similar Aus. fish.

**graze**¹ 1 *v.* suffer slight abrasion of (part of body); touch lightly in passing, move (*along, against,* etc.) with such contact. 2 *n.* abrasion.

**graze**² *v.* feed on growing grass; pasture cattle.

**grazier** /'greɪzɪə(r)/ *n.* person who feeds cattle for market.

**grazing** /'greɪzɪŋ/ *n.* grassland suitable for pasturage.

**grease** /griːs/ 1 *n.* fatty or oily matter, esp. as lubricant; melted fat of dead animal. 2 *v.t.* lubricate or smear with grease. 3 **grease-paint** actor's make-up.

**greasy** /'griːsɪ/ *a.* of or like or smeared with or having too much grease; (of person, manner) too unctuous.

**great** /greɪt/ 1 *a.* large in bulk or number; considerable in extent or time; important, pre-eminent; of great ability; more than ordinary; *colloq.* very satisfactory. 2 *n.* great person or thing. 3 **greatcoat** large heavy overcoat.

**great-** /greɪt/ *in comb.* (of family relationships) one degree more remote (*great-grandfather, great-niece,* etc.).

**greatly** /'greɪtlɪ/ *adv.* much.

**grebe** *n.* a diving bird.

**Grecian** /'griːʃ(ə)n/ *a.* Greek.

**greed** *n.* excessive desire esp. for food or wealth.

# greedy

**greedy** /ˈgriːdi/ *a.* showing greed; gluttonous; eager *to do* thing.

**Greek 1** *a.* of Greece. **2** *n.* native or language of Greece.

**green 1** *a.* coloured like grass; unripe, young; inexperienced; not seasoned or dried or smoked etc. **2** *n.* green colour or paint or clothes etc.; piece of grassy public land; grass-plot for special purpose; in *pl.* green vegetables; **3 green ban** *Aus.* workers' ban on job for conservationist principle; **green belt** area of open land for preservation round city; **greenfinch** bird with greenish plumage; **green fingers** *colloq.* skill in gardening; **greenfly** green aphid; **greengage** roundish green plum; **greenhead** *Aus.* kind of ant with painful sting; **greenhorn** simpleton, novice; **greenhouse** structure with sides and roof mainly of glass, for rearing plants; **green-room** room in theatre etc. for actors when off stage; **greenstone** kind of jade; **greenstuff** green vegetables; **greensward** grassy turf; **greenwood** woodlands in summer.

**greenery** /ˈgriːnəri/ *n.* green foliage.

**greengrocer** /ˈgriːnɡrəʊsə(r)/ *n.* retailer of fruit and vegetables. **greengrocery** *n.*

**greenie** /ˈgriːni/ *n. Aus. colloq.* conservationist.

**greet** *v.t.* address on meeting or arrival; salute, receive (*with* words etc.); meet (eye, ear, etc.).

**greeting** /ˈgriːtɪŋ/ *n.* act or words used to greet. **greetings card** decorative card for conveying goodwill message etc.

**gregarious** /ɡrəˈɡeərɪəs/ *a.* fond of company; living in flocks etc.

**Gregorian** /ɡrəˈɡɔːrɪən/ *a.* of plainsong. **Gregorian calendar** calendar introduced in 1582 by Pope Gregory XIII.

**gremlin** /ˈɡremlɪn/ *n. sl.* mischievous sprite said to cause faults in machinery etc.

**grenade** /ɡrəˈneɪd/ *n.* small bomb thrown by hand or shot from rifle.

**grenadier** /ɡrenəˈdɪə(r)/ *n. hist.* soldier armed with grenades; **Grenadiers** first regiment of royal household infantry.

**grew** *past of* **grow**.

**grey** /ɡreɪ/ **1** *a.* coloured like ashes or lead; clouded, dull; (of hair) turning white, (of person) with grey hair; anonymous, unidentifiable. **2** *n.* grey colour or paint or clothes etc.; grey horse. **3** *v.* make or become grey. **4 Grey Friar** Franciscan monk; **grey matter** active part of brain; **grey nurse** *Aus.* large kind of shark.

**greyhound** /ˈɡreɪhaʊnd/ *n.* slender swift dog used in racing and coursing.

**grid** *n.* grating; system of numbered squares for map references; network of lines or electric-power connections etc.; *Aus. sl.* bicycle; gridiron.

**griddle** /ˈɡrɪd(ə)l/ *n.* = **girdle**².

**gridiron** /ˈɡrɪdaɪən/ *n.* barred metal frame for broiling or grilling.

**grief** /ɡriːf/ *n.* sorrow, deep trouble; **come to grief** meet with disaster.

**grievance** /ˈɡriːv(ə)ns/ *n.* real or imagined cause for complaint.

**grieve** /ɡriːv/ *v.* (cause to) feel grief.

**grievous** /ˈɡriːvəs/ *a.* severe; injurious, flagrant, heinous.

**griffin** /ˈɡrɪf(ə)n/ *n.* fabulous creature with eagle's head and wings and lion's body.

**griffon** /ˈɡrɪf(ə)n/ *n.* small coarse-haired terrier-like dog; large vulture; griffin.

**grill 1** *n.* device on cooker for radiating heat downwards; gridiron; grilled food; grill room. **2** *v.* cook on gridiron or under grill; subject to severe questioning. **3 grill room** small restaurant.

**grille** /ɡrɪl/ *n.* grating, latticed screen; metal grid protecting motor-vehicle radiator.

**grilse** /ɡrɪls/ *n.* young salmon that has been only once to the sea.

**grim** *a.* of harsh appearance; stern, merciless; ghastly, joyless; unpleasant.

**grimace** /ˈɡrɪməs/ **1** *n.* distortion of face made in disgust etc. or to amuse. **2** *v.i.* make grimace.

**grime 1** *n.* dirt deeply ingrained. **2** *v.t.* blacken, befoul. **3 grimy** *a.*

**grin 1** *v.i.* smile broadly, showing teeth. **2** *n.* act or action of grinning.

**grind** /ɡraɪnd/ **1** *v.* (*past* **ground** /ɡraʊnd/) crush to small particles; harass with exactions; sharpen; rub gratingly; study hard, toil. **2** *n.* grinding; hard dull work. **3 grindstone** thick revolving abrasive disc for grinding and sharpening etc.

**grip 1** *v.* grasp tightly; take firm hold;

**gripe** 1 v. cause colic; affect with colic; *sl.* complain; clutch, grip. 2 n. in *pl.* colic pains; *sl.* complaint. 3 **gripe-water** medicine to cure colic in babies.

**grisly** /'grɪzlɪ/ a. causing terror or horror.

**grist** n. corn for grinding.

**gristle** /'grɪs(ə)l/ n. tough flexible tissue; cartilage. **gristly** a.

**grit** 1 n. small particles of sand etc.; coarse sandstone; *colloq.* pluck, endurance. 2 v. grind or clench (teeth); make grating sound. **gritty** a.

**grits** n.pl. oats husked but unground; coarse oatmeal.

**grizzle** /'grɪz(ə)l/ v.i. *colloq.* cry fretfully.

**grizzled** a. grey-haired.

**grizzly** /'grɪzlɪ/ 1 a. grey-haired. 2 n. grizzly bear. 3 **grizzly bear** large fierce N. Amer. bear.

**groan** 1 v. make deep sound expressing pain or grief or disapproval; be oppressed or loaded. 2 n. sound made in groaning.

**groat** n. *hist.* silver fourpenny piece.

**groats** n.pl. hulled or crushed grain, esp. oats.

**grocer** /'grəʊsə(r)/ n. dealer in food and household provisions.

**grocery** /'grəʊsərɪ/ n. grocer's trade or shop or (in *pl.*) goods.

**grog** n. drink of spirit (esp. rum) and water.

**groggy** /'grɒgɪ/ a. unsteady, tottering.

**grogram** /'grɒgrəm/ n. coarse fabric of silk and mohair etc.

**groin** 1 n. depression between belly and thigh; edge formed by intersecting vaults. 2 v.t. build with groins.

**groom** /gru:m/ 1 n. servant who tends horses; bridegroom. 2 v.t. tend (horse); give neat or attractive appearance to; prepare (person) for office or occasion etc.

**groove** 1 n. channel or hollow; spiral cut in gramophone record for needle; routine. 2 v.t. make groove(s) in.

**groovy** /'gru:vɪ/ a. of or like a groove; *sl.* excellent.

**grope** v.i. feel about as in dark; search blindly. **grope one's way** move cautiously.

**groper** /'grəʊpə(r)/ n. *Aus.* any of several kinds of esp. tropical seafish.

**grosgrain** /'grəʊgreɪn/ n. corded fabric of silk etc.

**gross** /grəʊs/ 1 a. flagrant; total, not net; coarse; indecent; overfed, bloated; luxuriant, rank. 2 n. (*pl.* same) 12 dozen. 3 v.t. produce as gross profit.

**grotesque** /grəʊ'tesk/ 1 a. comically or repulsively distorted; incongruous, absurd. 2 n. decoration interweaving human and animal forms with foliage; comically distorted figure or design.

**grotto** /'grɒtəʊ/ n. (*pl.* -oes) picturesque cave; structure imitating cave.

**grotty** /'grɒtɪ/ a. *sl.* unpleasant, dirty, ugly.

**grouch** /graʊtʃ/ *colloq.* 1 v.i. grumble. 2 n. grumbler; complaint; sulky grumbling mood. 3 **grouchy** a.

**ground**[1] /graʊnd/ 1 n. surface of earth; land; foundation, motive; area of special kind; surface worked upon in painting; in *pl.* enclosed land attached to house; in *pl.* dregs; bottom of sea or water; floor or level. 2 v. run aground, strand; prevent from taking off or flying; instruct thoroughly; base upon cause or principle; alight on ground; fix or place on ground. 3 **ground bass** *Mus.* short bass phrase repeated with varied upper parts; **ground floor** storey on level of outside ground; **ground frost** frost on surface of ground; **ground-nut** peanut; **ground-rent** rent for land leased for building; **groundsman** person who maintains sports-ground etc.; **ground speed** aircraft's speed relative to ground; **ground swell** heavy sea due to distant or past storm etc.; **groundwork** preliminary or basic work.

**ground**[2] *past* & *p.p.* of **grind**.

**grounding** /'graʊndɪŋ/ n. basic instruction in subject.

**groundless** /'graʊndləs/ a. without motive or foundation.

**groundsel** /'graʊnds(ə)l/ n. yellow-flowered weed.

**group** /gru:p/ 1 n. number of persons or things near or belonging or classed together; pop group; division of air force. 2 v. form into group; place in

**grouse** 243 **guest**

group(s). **3 group captain** air force officer next below air commodore.

**grouse**[1] /graʊs/ n. game-bird with feathered feet.

**grouse**[2] /graʊs/ v.i. & n. sl. grumble.

**grout** /graʊt/ 1 n. thin fluid mortar. 2 v.t. apply grout to.

**grouter** /ˈgraʊtə(r)/ n. Aus. sl. unfair advantage. **come in on the grouter** exploit advantage.

**grove** n. small wood; group of trees.

**grovel** /ˈgrɒv(ə)l/ v.i. lie prone, humble oneself.

**grow** /grəʊ/ v. (past grew; p.p. grown) increase in size or height or amount etc.; develop or exist as living plant or natural product; become by degrees; produce by cultivation; let grow; in pass. be covered with growth. **grown-up** adult.

**growl** /graʊl/ 1 n. guttural sound of anger; rumble; murmur, complaint. 2 v. make growl.

**grown** p.p. of **grow**.

**growth** /grəʊθ/ n. increase; what has grown or is growing; tumour.

**groyne** /grɔɪn/ n. structure run out into sea etc. to stop shifting of beach.

**grub** 1 n. larva of insect; sl. food. 2 v. dig superficially; clear (ground) of roots etc.; dig up, out.

**grubby** /ˈgrʌbɪ/ a. dirty, grimy.

**grudge** 1 v.t. be unwilling to give or allow. 2 n. resentment, ill-will.

**gruel** /ˈgruəl/ n. liquid food of oatmeal etc. boiled in milk or water.

**gruelling** /ˈgruəlɪŋ/ a. exhausting, punishing.

**gruesome** /ˈgruːsəm/ a. grisly, disgusting.

**gruff** a. rough-voiced; surly.

**grumble** /ˈgrʌmb(ə)l/ 1 v. complain peevishly; be discontented; make rumbling sound. 2 n. act or sound of grumbling.

**grummet** /ˈgrʌmət/ n. insulating washer round electric conductor passing through hole in metal.

**grumpy** /ˈgrʌmpɪ/ a. ill-tempered.

**grunt** 1 n. low guttural sound characteristic of pig. 2 v. utter (with) grunt.

**Gruyère** /ˈgruːjeə(r)/ n. kind of orig. Swiss cheese with holes in.

**gryphon** var. of **griffin**.

**G-string** /ˈdʒiːstrɪŋ/ n. narrow strip of cloth etc. attached to string round waist, for covering genitals.

**guano** /ˈgwɑːnəʊ/ n. excrement of seafowl used as manure.

**guarantee** /gærənˈtiː/ 1 n. formal promise or assurance; giver of guaranty or security; thing serving as security. 2 v.t. give or serve as guarantee for; answer for; secure. 3 **guarantor** n.

**guaranty** /ˈgærəntɪ/ n. written or other undertaking to answer for performance of obligation; ground for security.

**guard** /gɑːd/ 1 n. vigilant state; watch; protector; sentry; official in charge of train; soldiers etc. protecting place or person; device to prevent injury or accident; defensive posture; in pl. household troops. 2 v. protect, defend; take precautions against; keep in check. 3 **guardhouse, guardroom**, room accommodating military guard or for keeping prisoners under guard; **guardsman** soldier of guards.

**guardian** /ˈgɑːdɪən/ n. keeper, protector; person having custody of person or property of minor etc. **guardianship** n.

**guava** /ˈgwɑːvə/ n. tropical Amer. tree; its edible orange acid fruit.

**gubernatorial** /guːbənəˈtɔːrɪəl/ a. US of governor.

**gudgeon**[1] /ˈgʌdʒ(ə)n/ n. small freshwater fish; credulous person.

**gudgeon**[2] /ˈgʌdʒ(ə)n/ n. kind of pivot or metal pin; socket for rudder.

**guelder rose** /ˈgeldə(r)/ shrub with round bunches of white flowers.

**guernsey** /ˈgɜːnzɪ/ n. thick knitted woollen jersey; Aus. coloured shirt worn by Aus. Rules player. **get a guernsey** Aus. be selected for team etc., get honourable mention.

**guerrilla** /gəˈrɪlə/ n. person engaged in irregular fighting by small independently acting groups.

**guess** /ges/ 1 v. estimate without calculation or measurement; conjecture, think likely; conjecture rightly. 2 n. rough estimate, conjecture. 3 **guess-work** guessing.

**guest** /gest/ n. person invited to visit one's house or have meal etc. at one's expense, or lodging at hotel etc. **guest-house** superior boarding-house.

**guffaw** /gʌˈfɔː/ 1 n. boisterous laugh. 2 v.i. utter guffaw.

**guidance** /ˈgaɪd(ə)ns/ n. guiding; advice.

**guide** /gaɪd/ 1 n. one who shows the way; professional conductor of travellers or climber etc.; **Guide** member of girls' organization similar to Scouts; adviser; directing principle; guidebook. 2 v.t. act as guide to; lead, direct. 3 **guidebook** book of information about place etc.; **guided missile** one under remote control or directed by equipment within itself; **guide-dog** dog trained to lead blind person; **guided tour** tour accompanied by guide.

**Guider** /ˈgaɪdə(r)/ n. adult leader of Guides.

**guild** /gɪld/ n. society for mutual aid or with common object; medieval association of craftsmen. **guildhall** meeting-place of medieval guild, town hall.

**guilder** /ˈgɪldə(r)/ n. monetary unit of Netherlands.

**guile** /gaɪl/ n. treachery, deceit. **guileful** a.; **guileless** a.

**guillotine** /ˈgɪlətiːn/ 1 n. beheading-machine; machine for cutting paper; *Parl.* method of shortening discussion of bill by fixing voting times. 2 v.t. use guillotine on.

**guilt** /gɪlt/ n. fact of having committed offence; (feeling of) culpability.

**guiltless** /ˈgɪltləs/ a. innocent; not having knowledge or possession *of*.

**guilty** /ˈgɪlti/ a. having or showing or due to guilt.

**guinea** /ˈgɪnɪ/ n. *hist.* gold coin worth twenty-one shillings; this sum. **guinea-pig** small S. Amer. rodent common as pet, person used as subject of experiment etc.

**guipure** /ˈgiːpʊə(r)/ n. heavy lace of linen pieces joined by embroidery.

**guise** /gaɪz/ n. external, esp. assumed, appearance; pretence.

**guitar** /gɪˈtɑː(r)/ n. six-stringed musical instrument played with fingers or plectrum. **guitarist** n.

**gulch** n. *US* ravine, gully.

**gulf** n. large area of sea partly surrounded by land; deep hollow, chasm; wide difference of opinion etc. **Gulf Stream** warm current from Gulf of Mexico to Europe.

**gull**[1] n. long-winged web-footed sea-bird.

**gull**[2] n. & v.t. dupe, fool.

**gullet** /ˈgʌlət/ n. food-passage from mouth to stomach.

**gullible** /ˈgʌləb(ə)l/ a. easily persuaded or deceived. **gullibility** n.

**gully** /ˈgʌli/ n. ravine cut by water; gutter, drain; *Crick.* fielding-position between point and slips.

**gulp** 1 v. swallow hastily or with effort; choke. 2 n. act of gulping; large mouthful.

**gum**[1] 1 n. sticky secretion of some trees and shrubs, used as glue etc.; chewing-gum; in pl. sweet made of gelatine etc. 2 v.t. apply gum to; fasten thus. 3 **gum arabic** gum exuded from some kinds of acacia; **gumboot** rubber boot; **gum-tree** tree exuding gum, esp. eucalyptus; **gum up** *colloq.* interfere with, spoil.

**gum**[2] n. firm flesh around roots of teeth. **gumboil** small abscess on gum.

**gummy**[1] /ˈgʌmi/ a. sticky, exuding gum.

**gummy**[2] /ˈgʌmi/ a. toothless.

**gumption** /ˈgʌmpʃ(ə)n/ n. *colloq.* common sense; resourcefulness, enterprise.

**gun** n. metal tube for throwing missiles with explosive propellant; starting-pistol; device for discharging grease or electrons etc. in desired direction; member of shooting-party; *Aus.* expert shearer. **gunboat** small warship with heavy guns; **gun-carriage** wheeled support for gun; **gun-cotton** cotton steeped in acids, used for blasting; **gun dog** dog trained to assist at shoot; **gunfire** firing of guns; **gunman** armed lawbreaker; **gun-metal** bluish-grey alloy of copper and tin or zinc; **gunpowder** explosive of saltpetre, sulphur, and charcoal; **gunroom** room in warship, for junior officers; **gun-running** bringing guns into country illegally; **gunshot** shot from gun, the range of a gun.

**gundy** *var.* of **goondie**.

**gunner** /ˈgʌnə(r)/ n. artillery soldier; *Naut.* warrant officer in charge of battery and magazine etc.; airman who operates gun.

**gunnery** /ˈgʌnəri/ n. construction and management of large guns.

**gunny** /'gʌni:/ *n.* coarse sacking usu. of jute fibre; sack made of this.

**gunwale** /'gʌn(ə)l/ *n.* upper edge of ship's or boat's side.

**gunyah** /'gʌnjə/ *n. Aus.* Abor. hut; bush hut.

**guppy** /'gʌpi:/ *n.* very small bright-coloured tropical fish.

**gurgle** /'gɜ:g(ə)l/ 1 *n.* bubbling sound. 2 *v.* make gurgles; utter with gurgles.

**gurnard** /'gɜ:nəd/ *n.* sea-fish with large spiny head.

**guru** /'guru:/ *n.* Hindu spiritual teacher; influential or revered teacher.

**gush** 1 *n.* sudden or copious stream; effusiveness. 2 *v.* flow with gush; emit gush of; speak or behave effusively.

**gusher** /'gʌʃə(r)/ *n.* oil-well emitting unpumped oil.

**gusset** /'gʌsət/ *n.* piece let into garment etc. to strengthen or enlarge it.

**gust** 1 *n.* sudden violent rush of wind; burst of rain or smoke or anger etc. 2 *v.i.* blow in gusts. 3 **gusty** *a.*

**gustatory** /'gʌstətəri/ *a.* connected with sense of taste.

**gusto** /'gʌstəʊ/ *n.* zest, enjoyment.

**gut** 1 *n.* intestine; in *pl.* bowels, entrails; in *pl. colloq.* force of character, staying power; material for violin etc. strings or surgical use or for fishing line. 2 *a.* instinctive, fundamental. 3 *v.t.* remove guts of; remove or destroy internal fittings of (building).

**gutser** /'gʌtsə(r)/ *n. Aus. sl.* a heavy fall. **come a gutser** fall heavily.

**gutsy** /'gʌtsi/ *a. colloq.* courageous; greedy.

**gutta-percha** /gʌtə'pɜ:tʃə/ *n.* tough plastic substance from latex of various Malayan trees.

**gutter** /'gʌtə(r)/ 1 *n.* shallow trough below eaves, or channel at side of street, for carrying off rain-water; channel, groove. 2 *v.* (of candle) burn unsteadily and melt away.

**guttering** /'gʌtərɪŋ/ *n.* material for gutters.

**guttersnipe** /'gʌtəsnaɪp/ *n.* street urchin.

**guttural** /'gʌtər(ə)l/ 1 *a.* throaty; (of sound) produced in throat. 2 *n.* guttural consonant.

**guy¹** /gaɪ/ 1 *n. UK* effigy of Guy Fawkes burnt on 5 Nov.; *colloq.* man; grotesquely dressed person. 2 *v.t.* ridicule.

**guy²** /gaɪ/ 1 *n.* rope or chain etc. to steady crane-load etc. or secure tent. 2 *v.t.* secure with guy(s).

**guzzle** /'gʌz(ə)l/ *v.* drink or eat greedily.

**gybe** /dʒaɪb/ *v.* (of fore-and-aft sail or boom) swing to other side; (of boat etc.) change course thus.

**gym** /dʒɪm/ *n. colloq.* gymnasium, gymnastics. **gym-slip** sleeveless usu. belted garment worn by schoolgirls.

**gymkhana** /dʒɪm'kɑ:nə/ *n.* meeting for competition between horse-riders etc.

**gymnasium** /dʒɪm'neɪzɪəm/ *n.* (*pl.* -siums) room etc. equipped for gymnastics.

**gymnast** /'dʒɪmnæst/ *n.* expert in gymnastics.

**gymnastic** /dʒɪm'næstɪk/ *a.* of gymnastics. **gymnastically** *adv.*

**gymnastics** *n.pl.* occas. treated as *sing.* exercises to develop muscles or demonstrate agility.

**gynaecology** /gaɪnə'kɒlədʒi:/ *n.* science of physiological functions and diseases of women. **gynaecological** *a.*; **gynaecologist** *n.*

**gypsum** /'dʒɪpsəm/ *n.* mineral used to make plaster of Paris.

**gypsy** /'dʒɪpsi:/ *n.* member of wandering dark-skinned people of Europe.

**gyrate** /dʒaɪ'reɪt/ *v.i.* move in circle or spiral. **gyration** *n.*; **gyratory** *a.*

**gyro** /'dʒaɪrəʊ/ *n.* (*pl.* -ros) *colloq.* gyroscope.

**gyroscope** /'dʒaɪrəskəʊp/ *n.* rotating wheel whose axis is free to turn but maintains fixed direction unless perturbed, esp. as used for stabilization. **gyroscopic** /-'skɒp/ *a.*

# H

**H** *abbr.* hard (pencil-lead).
**h.** *abbr.* hour(s); hot.
**ha** *int.* expr. surprise, triumph, etc.
**ha** *abbr.* hectare(s).
**habeas corpus** /ˈheɪbɪəs ˈkɔːpəs/ writ requiring person to be brought before judge etc., esp. to investigate lawfulness of his imprisonment.
**haberdasher** /ˈhæbədæʃə(r)/ *n.* dealer in small articles of dress and sewing-goods. **haberdashery** *n.*
**habiliments** /həˈbɪləmənts/ *n.pl.* clothing
**habit** /ˈhæbɪt/ *n.* settled tendency or practice; practice that is hard to give up; constitution (of body or mind); clothes esp. of religious order. **2** *v.t.* clothe.
**habitable** /ˈhæbətəb(ə)l/ *a.* suitable for living in. **habitability** *n.*
**habitat** /ˈhæbətæt/ *n.* natural home of plant or animal.
**habitation** /hæbəˈteɪʃ(ə)n/ *n.* house or home; inhabiting.
**habitual** /həˈbɪtjuːəl/ *a.* done as a habit; usual; given to a habit.
**habituate** /həˈbɪtjuːeɪt/ *v.t.* accustom (to). **habituation** *n.*
*habitué* /həˈbɪtjueɪ/ *n.* frequent visitor (*of*). [F]
**hacienda** /hæsiˈendə/ *n.* plantation etc. with dwelling-house, in Spanish-speaking country.
**hack**¹ **1** *v.* cut or chop roughly; kick shin of; deal cutting blows (*at*). **2** *n.* kick with toe of boot, wound from this. **3 hack-saw** saw for metal-cutting.
**hack**² **1** *n.* horse for ordinary riding; hired horse; person hired to do dull routine work, esp. as writer. **2** *v.i.* ride on horseback at ordinary pace. **3** *a.* used as hack; commonplace.
**hacking** *a.* (of cough) short, dry, and frequent.
**hacker** /ˈhækə(r)/ *n. colloq.* (excessively) enthusiastic computer user.
**hackle** /ˈhæk(ə)l/ *n.* long feathers on neck of domestic cock etc.; steel flax-comb. **with hackles up** angry, ready to fight.
**hackney** /ˈhæknɪ/ *v.t.* make common or trite by repetition. **hackney-cab, -carriage**, etc. taxi.

**had** *past* & *p.p.* of **have**.
**haddock** /ˈhædək/ *n.* common sea-fish used for food.
**Hades** /ˈheɪdiːz/ *n. Gk. myth.* abode of departed spirits; the underworld.
**hadji** /ˈhædʒiː/ *n.* Muslim who has been to Mecca on pilgrimage.
**haematite** /ˈhiːmətaɪt/ *n.* red or brown iron ore.
**haematology** /hiːməˈtɒlədʒɪ/ *n.* study of physiology of the blood.
**haemoglobin** /hiːməˈɡləʊbɪn/ *n.* oxygen-carrying substance in red blood-cells.
**haemophilia** /hiːməˈfɪlɪə/ *n.* (hereditary) tendency to severe bleeding from even a slight injury through failure of blood to clot. **haemophiliac** *a.* & *n.*
**haemorrhage** /ˈhemərɪdʒ/ **1** *n.* escape of blood from blood-vessels, bleeding. **2** *v.i.* undergo haemorrhage.
**haemorrhoid** /ˈhemərɔɪd/ *n.* (usu. in *pl.*) swollen vein in tissue near anus.
**haft** /hɑːft/ *n.* handle (of knife etc.).
**hag** *n.* ugly old woman. **hagridden** afflicted by nightmares or fears.
**haggard** /ˈhæɡəd/ *a.* wild-looking (esp. from fatigue or worry etc.).
**haggis** /ˈhæɡɪs/ *n.* minced offal of sheep boiled in bag with oatmeal etc.
**haggle** /ˈhæɡ(ə)l/ *v.i.* & *n.* dispute, esp. *about* price or terms.
**hagiography** /hæɡɪˈɒɡrəfɪ/ *n.* writing of lives of saints.
**ha ha** *int.* representing laughter.
**ha-ha** *n.* fence placed along bottom of ditch, bounding park or garden.
**haiku** /ˈhaɪkuː/ *n.* Japanese 3-line poem of usu. 17 syllables.
**hail**¹ **1** *n.* pellets of frozen rain falling in shower (**hailstorm**); shower *of* questions etc. **2** *v.* pour down as or like hail. **3 hailstone** pellet of hail.
**hail**² **1** *int.* of greeting. **2** *v.* salute; greet (*as*); call to; have come *from*. **3** *n.* hailing.
**hair** *n.* any or all of fine filaments growing from skin esp. of human head; hairlike thing. **haircloth** cloth made of hair; **haircut** (style of) cutting hair; **hair-do** *colloq.* style or process of woman's hairdressing; **hairdressing** cutting and styling of hair; **hair-grip** flat

# hajji     247     halt

hairpin with ends close together; **hair-line** edge of person's hair on forehead, very narrow crack or line; **hair-piece** false hair augmenting person's natural hair; **hairpin** U-shaped pin for fastening the hair; **hairpin bend** very sharp doubling-back of road; **hair-raising** terrifying; **hair's breadth** minute distance; **hair shirt** ascetic's or penitent's shirt of haircloth; **hair-slide** clip for keeping hair in position; **hairspring** fine spring regulating balance-wheel of watch; **hair-style** particular way of arranging hair; **hair-trigger** trigger acting on very slight pressure. **hairy** *a.*

**hajji** var. of **hadji**.

**hake** *n.* codlike sea-fish.

**hakea** /'hɑːkiːə/ *n. Aus.* genus of shrubs and small trees with hard woody fruit.

**halberd** /'hælbəd/ *n. hist.* combined spear and battle-axe.

**halcyon** /'hælsɪən/ *a.* peaceful, quiet; (of period) happy, prosperous.

**hale**[1] *a.* strong and healthy.

**hale**[2] *v.t. arch.* drag forcibly.

**half** /hɑːf/ **1** *n.* (*pl.* **halves** /hɑːvz/) either of two (esp. equal) parts into which a thing is divided; half-price ticket; school term; *colloq.* half-back, half-pint, etc. **2** *a.* forming a half. **3** *adv.* in part; equally. **4 half-and-half** being half one thing and half another; **half-back** player immediately behind forwards in football etc.; **half-baked** not thoroughly thought out; **half-breed** person of mixed race; **half-brother, -sister**, one having one parent in common; **half-caste** half-breed; **half-crown** former British coin worth 2s. 6d. (12½p); **half-hearted** lacking courage or zeal; **half-life** time after which radioactivity etc. is half its original value; **at half-mast** (of flag) lowered to half height of mast as symbol of mourning; **half moon** (shape of) moon with disc half illuminated; **half nelson** wrestling hold, with arm under opponent's arm and behind his head; **half-term** short holiday about halfway through school term; **half-timbered** having walls with spaces in timber frame filled with bricks or plaster; **half-time** time when half of game etc. is completed, interval occurring then; **half-tone** photograph representing tones by large or small dots; **half-truth** statement that conveys only part of truth; **half-volley** ball hit or returned as soon as it touches ground; **half-wit** stupid or foolish person; **half-witted** *a.*

**halfpenny** /'heɪpnɪ/ *n.* (*pl.* **halfpence** /'heɪpəns/ or **halfpennies** /'heɪpnɪːz/) former bronze coin worth half penny.

**halibut** /'hælɪbət/ *n.* large flat-fish.

**halitosis** /hælɪ'təʊsəs/ *n.* unpleasant-smelling breath.

**hall** /hɔːl/ *n.* entrance room or passage of house; large room or building for meetings or meals or concerts etc.; large country house, esp. with landed estate; building for residence or instruction of students etc.; college dining-room; large public room; corridor. **hallmark** mark used to show standard of gold, silver, and platinum, *fig.* token of excellence or quality.

**hallelujah** var. of **alleluia**.

**halliard** var. of **halyard**.

**hallo** /hə'ləʊ/ *int. & n.* calling attention or expr. surprise or greeting.

**halloo** /hə'luː/ **1** *int. & n.* cry inciting dogs to chase etc., or to attract attention. **2** *v.* cry halloo.

**hallow** /'hæləʊ/ *v.t.* make or honour as holy.

**Hallowe'en** /hæləʊ'iːn/ *n.* 31 Oct.

**hallucinate** /hə'luːsɪneɪt/ *v.i.* experience hallucination(s).

**hallucination** /həluːsɪ'neɪʃ(ə)n/ *n.* illusion of seeing objects or hearing sounds etc. not actually present. **hallucinatory** *a.*

**hallucinogen** /hə'luːsɪnədʒ(ə)n/ *n.* drug causing hallucinations. **hallucinogenic** /-'dʒen-/ *a.*

**halo** /'heɪləʊ/ **1** *n.* (*pl.* **-loes**) disc of light shown round head of saint etc. in paintings etc.; circle of light round sun or moon etc. **2** *v.t.* surround with halo.

**halogen** /'hælədʒ(ə)n/ *n.* any of group of non-metallic elements (fluorine, chlorine, etc.) which form a salt by simple union with a metal.

**halt**[1] /hɔːlt or hɒlt/ **1** *n.* stoppage on march or journey; interruption of progress; railway stopping-place without regular station-buildings etc. **2** *v.* (cause to) halt.

**halt**[2] /hɔːlt or hɒlt/ **1** *v.i.* walk hesitatingly; limp. **2** *a.* lame.

**halter** /ˈhɔːltə(r)/ n. rope or strap with headstall for horses or cattle; woman's dress etc. with top held up by strap passing round back of neck.

**halve** /hɑːv/ v.t. divide into halves; reduce to half.

**halyard** /ˈhæljəd/ n. Naut. rope or tackle for raising and lowering sail etc.

**ham** 1 n. upper part of pig's leg salted and dried for food; back of thigh; thigh and buttock; inexpert but flamboyant performer or actor; operator of amateur radio station. 2 v. overact. 3 **hamfisted** sl. heavy-handed, clumsy.

**hamburger** /ˈhæmbɜːgə(r)/ n. fried cake of chopped beef, often eaten in a soft bread roll.

**hamlet** /ˈhæmlət/ n. small village, esp. without church.

**hammer** /ˈhæmə(r)/ 1 n. tool with heavy metal head at right angles to handle, used for breaking, driving nails, etc.; similar device, as for exploding charge in gun or striking strings of piano etc.; auctioneer's mallet; metal ball attached to a wire for throwing as athletic contest. 2 v. strike or drive (as) with hammer; Aus. sl. back (of person's body). 3 **be on person's hammer** watch him closely, pester him; **hammer and tongs** with great energy; **hammer-toe** toe bent permanently downwards.

**hammock** /ˈhæmək/ n. bed of canvas or netting suspended by cords at ends.

**hamper**[1] /ˈhæmpə(r)/ n. basketwork packing-case; food etc. packed up esp. as a present.

**hamper**[2] /ˈhæmpə(r)/ v.t. obstruct movement of; impede, hinder.

**hamster** /ˈhæmstə(r)/ n. small rodent often kept as pet.

**hamstring** /ˈhæmstrɪŋ/ 1 n. any of five tendons at back of human knee; (in quadruped) tendon at back of hock. 2 v.t. (past & p.p. **hamstrung**) cripple by cutting hamstring(s).

**hand** 1 n. end part beyond wrist of human arm; similar member of monkey; control, disposal; share (in doing); agency; handlike thing, esp. pointer of clock etc.; (right or left) side; pledge of marriage; skill or style esp. of writing; person who does or makes something; person etc. as source; manual worker in factory etc.; playing-cards dealt to player, round or game of cards; colloq. round of applause; forefoot of quadruped; measure of horse's height, = 4 in. (10.16 cm). 2 v.t. deliver or transfer (as) with hand; serve (food round). 3 **at hand** near by; **give, lend, a hand** help; **handbag** small bag esp. used by woman to hold purse etc.; **handbill** printed notice circulated by hand; **handbook** short manual or guidebook; **handcuff** secure (prisoner) with **handcuffs**, pair of lockable metal rings joined by short chain; **hand-out** food etc. given to needy person, information etc. distributed to press etc.; **hand over fist** with rapid progress; **hand-picked** carefully chosen; **handrail** rail along edge of stairs etc.; **hands down** easily, without effort; **handwriting** (style of) writing by hand; **out of hand** without delay, out of control; **to hand** within reach.

**handful** /ˈhændfʊl/ n. enough to fill the hand; small number or quantity; colloq. troublesome person or task.

**handicap** /ˈhændɪkæp/ 1 n. disadvantage imposed on superior competitor to equalize chances; race etc. in which handicaps are imposed; disadvantage, disability. 2 v.t. impose handicap on; place at disadvantage; in p.p. suffering from physical or mental disability.

**handicraft** /ˈhændɪkrɑːft/ n. work that requires manual and artistic skill.

**handiwork** /ˈhændɪwɜːk/ n. thing done or made by hands or by particular person.

**handkerchief** /ˈhæŋkətʃɪf/ n. square of linen or cotton etc., used to wipe nose etc.

**handle** /ˈhænd(ə)l/ 1 n. part by which thing is held. 2 v.t. touch or feel with hands; manage, deal with; deal in (goods etc.). 3 **handlebar** steering-bar of bicycle etc.

**handler** /ˈhændlə(r)/ n. person in charge of trained dog etc.

**handmaid** /ˈhændmeɪd/ n. arch. (also **-maiden**) female servant.

**handsome** /ˈhænsəm/ a. good-looking; generous; considerable.

**handy** /ˈhændɪ/ a. convenient to handle; ready to hand; clever with hands. **handyman** person able to do odd jobs.

**hang** 1 v. (past & p.p. **hung** exc. as

below) (cause to) be supported from above; set up on hinges etc.; place (picture) on wall or in exhibition; attach (wallpaper); (*past* & *p.p.* **hanged**) suspend or be suspended by neck, esp. as capital punishment; let droop; remain or be hung. 2 *n.* way thing hangs. 3 **get the hang of** get knack of, understand. **hang about, around** loiter, not move away; **hangdog** shamefaced; **hang fire** delay acting; **hang-glider** airborne frame controlled by movements of person standing or lying in it; **hangman** executioner by hanging; **hangnail** agnail; **hangover** after-effects of excess of alcohol; **hang up** hang from hook etc., end telephone conversation; **hang-up** *sl.* emotional inhibition.

**hangar** /ˈhæŋə(r)/ *n.* shed for housing aircraft etc.

**hanger** /ˈhæŋə(r)/ *n.* person or thing that hangs; shaped piece of wood etc. from which clothes may be hung. **hanger-on** follower, dependant.

**hanging** /ˈhæŋɪŋ/ *n.* usu. in *pl.* drapery for walls etc.

**hank** *n.* coil of yarn etc.

**hanker** /ˈhæŋkə(r)/ *v.i.* crave or long *after* or *for*.

**hanky** /ˈhæŋkɪ/ *n. colloq.* handkerchief.

**hanky-panky** /hæŋkɪˈpæŋkɪ/ *n. sl.* trickery; misbehaviour.

**hansom** /ˈhænsəm/ *n.* (in full **hansom cab**) two-wheeled horse-drawn cab with driver seated behind.

**haphazard** /hæpˈhæzəd/ 1 *a.* casual, random. 2 *adv.* at random.

**hapless** /ˈhæplɪs/ *a.* unlucky.

**happen** /ˈhæpən/ *v.i.* occur; have the (good or bad) fortune (*to do* thing); be fate or experience of; come by chance *on*.

**happy** /ˈhæpɪ/ *a.* feeling or showing pleasure or contentment; fortunate; apt, pleasing. **happy-go-lucky** taking things cheerfully as they happen.

**hara-kiri** /hærəˈkɪrɪ/ *n.* Japanese suicide by ritual disembowelling.

**harangue** /həˈræŋ/ 1 *n.* lengthy and earnest speech. 2 *v.* make harangue (to).

**harass** /ˈhærəs/ *v.t.* worry, trouble; attack repeatedly. **harassment** *n.*

**harbinger** /ˈhɑːbɪndʒə(r)/ *n.* one who announces another's approach, forerunner.

**harbour** /ˈhɑːbə(r)/ 1 *n.* place of shelter for ships; shelter. 2 *v.t.* give shelter to; entertain (thoughts etc.).

**hard** 1 *a.* firm, solid; unyielding; difficult to bear or do or understand; unfeeling, harsh, severe; (of drinks) strongly alcoholic; (of drug) potent and addictive; strenuous. 2 *adv.* strenuously, severely. 3 **hard and fast** (of rule etc.) strict; **hardback** (book) bound in stiff covers; **hardbitten** tough; **hardboard** stiff board of compressed etc. woodpulp; **hard-boiled** (of eggs) boiled until white and yolk are solid, *fig.* tough, shrewd; **hard cash** coins and banknotes, not cheques etc.; **hard copy** printed material produced by computer; **hard core** heavy material as road-foundation; **hard court** lawn-tennis court of asphalt etc.; **hard currency** currency not likely to fluctuate much in value; **hard-headed** practical, not sentimental; **hard-hearted** unfeeling; **hard line** firm adherence to policy; **hard lines** worse fortune than one deserves; **hard of hearing** somewhat deaf; **hard-pressed** closely pursued, burdened with urgent business; **hard sell** aggressive salesmanship; **hard up** short of money; **hardware** ironmongery, weapons, machinery, etc.; **hard water** water containing mineral salts that prevent soap from lathering easily; **hardwood** wood of deciduous tree; **hard word** *Aus. sl.* request for favour.

**harden** /ˈhɑːd(ə)n/ *v.* make or become hard(er) or unyielding.

**hardihood** /ˈhɑːdɪhʊd/ *n.* boldness.

**hardly** /ˈhɑːdlɪ/ *adv.* with difficulty; scarcely; harshly, severely.

**hardship** /ˈhɑːdʃɪp/ *n.* severe suffering or privation.

**hardy** /ˈhɑːdɪ/ *a.* robust; capable of endurance; (of plant) able to grow in the open all year.

**hare** /heə(r)/ 1 *n.* mammal like large rabbit, with long ears, short tail, and divided upper lip. 2 *v.i.* run very fast. 3 **hare-brained** rash, wild; **harelip** congenital fissure of upper lip.

**harebell** /ˈheəbel/ *n.* plant with pale-blue bell-shaped flowers.

**harem** /ˈhɑːriːm/ *n.* women of a Muslim

## haricot

household, living in separate part of house; their quarters.

**haricot** /'hærəkəʊ/ *n*. (in full **haricot bean**) dried white seed of variety of bean.

**hark** *v.i.* listen. **hark back** revert (*to* subject).

**harlequin** /'hɑːləkwɪn/ 1 *a*. in various colours. 2 **Harlequin** *n*. pantomime character in mask and parti-coloured costume.

**harlot** /'hɑːlət/ *n. arch.* prostitute. **harlotry** *n*.

**harm** *n. & v.t.* damage, hurt.

**harmful** /'hɑːmfʊl/ *a*. that does harm.

**harmless** /'hɑːmləs/ *a*. that does no harm.

**harmonic** /hɑː'mɒnɪk/ 1 *a*. of or relating to harmony; harmonious. 2 *n*. harmonic tone; component frequency of wave motion. 3 **harmonic tone** one produced by vibration of aliquot parts of strings etc.

**harmonica** /hɑː'mɒnɪkə/ *n*. mouth-organ.

**harmonious** /hɑː'məʊnɪəs/ *a*. sweet-sounding; forming a pleasant or consistent whole; free from dissent.

**harmonium** /hɑː'məʊnɪəm/ *n*. keyboard musical instrument with bellows and metal reeds.

**harmonize** /'hɑːmənaɪz/ *v*. add notes to (melody) to form chords; bring into or be in harmony. **harmonization** *n*.

**harmony** /'hɑːmənɪ/ *n*. combination of notes to form chords; melodious sound; agreement, concord.

**harness** /'hɑːnəs/ 1 *n*. gear of draught-horse etc.; arrangement of straps etc. for fastening thing to person etc. 2 *v.t.* put harness on; utilize (natural forces) for motive power.

**harp** 1 *n*. musical instrument with strings of graduated lengths played with fingers. 2 *v.i.* play harp; dwell tediously *on*. 3 **harpist** *n*.

**harpoon** /hɑː'puːn/ 1 *n*. spear-like missile for catching whales etc. 2 *v.t.* spear with harpoon.

**harpsichord** /'hɑːpsɪkɔːd/ *n*. keyboard musical instrument with strings plucked mechanically.

**harpy** /'hɑːpɪ/ *n. Myth.* monster with woman's face and bird's wings and claws; rapacious woman.

## hatch

**harridan** /'hærəd(ə)n/ *n*. ill-tempered old woman.

**harrier** /'hærɪə(r)/ *n*. hound used in hunting hares; in *pl*. cross-country runners; kind of falcon.

**harrow** /'hærəʊ/ 1 *n*. frame with metal teeth or discs for breaking clods of earth. 2 *v.t.* draw harrow over; distress greatly.

**harry** /'hærɪ/ *v.t.* ravage, spoil (land, people); harass.

**harsh** *a*. rough to hear or taste etc.; severe, unfeeling.

**hart** *n*. male of (esp. red) deer.

**hartebeest** /'hɑːtəbiːst/ *n*. large Afr. antelope.

**harum-scarum** /heərəm'skeərəm/ *a*. reckless, wild.

**harvest** /'hɑːvəst/ 1 *n*. gathering in of crops etc.; season for this; season's yield; product of any action. 2 *v.t.* reap and gather in.

**harvester** *n*. reaper, reaping-machine.

**has** 3 pers. sing. pres. of **have**.

**hash** 1 *n*. dish of cooked meat cut into small pieces and recooked; mixture, jumble; re-used material. 2 *v.t.* make (meat) into hash. 3 **make a hash of** *colloq.* make a mess of, bungle; **settle person's hash** make end of or subdue him.

**hashish** /'hæʃɪʃ/ *n*. narcotic drug got from hemp.

**hasp** /hɑːsp/ *n*. hinged metal clasp passing over staple and secured by pin etc.

**hassle** /'hæs(ə)l/ 1 *n*. quarrel; struggle. 2 *v*. quarrel; harass.

**hassock** /'hæsək/ *n*. kneeling-cushion.

**haste** /heɪst/ 1 *n*. urgency of movement; hurry. 2 *v.i.* go in haste. 3 **make haste** be quick.

**hasten** /'heɪs(ə)n/ *v*. (cause to) proceed or go quickly.

**hasty** /'heɪstɪ/ *a*. hurried; acting or said or done too quickly.

**hat** *n*. head-covering esp. worn out of doors. **hat trick** *Crick.* taking 3 wickets with successive balls, *Footb.* etc. scoring of 3 goals by same player in same match.

**hatch**[1] *n*. opening in floor or wall etc.; opening or door in aircraft etc.; cover for hatchway. **hatchback** vehicle with rear door hinged at top; **hatchway** opening in ship's deck for lowering cargo.

# hatch — head

**hatch²** 1 v. bring or come forth from egg; incubate; devise (plot). 2 n. hatching; brood hatched.

**hatch³** v.t. mark with parallel lines.

**hatchet** /'hætʃət/ n. light short axe.

**hate** 1 n. hatred. 2 v.t. dislike strongly; bear malice to.

**hateful** /'heɪtfəl/ a. arousing hatred.

**hatred** /'heɪtrəd/ a. intense dislike; ill-will.

**hatter** /'hætə(r)/ n. maker or seller of hats; *Aus.* solitary bushman.

**haughty** /'hɔ:tɪ/ a. proud, arrogant.

**haul** /hɔ:l/ 1 v. pull or drag forcibly; transport by cart etc. 2 n. hauling; amount gained or acquired; distance to be traversed.

**haulage** /'hɔ:lɪdʒ/ n. (charge for) conveyance of goods.

**haulier** /'hɔ:lɪə(r)/ n. one who hauls, esp. firm or person engaged in road transport of goods.

**haulm** /hɔ:m/ n. stalks of beans or peas or potatoes etc.

**haunch** n. fleshy part of buttock and thigh; leg and loin of deer etc. as food.

**haunt** 1 v.t. (of ghost etc.) visit frequently usu. with signs of its presence; be persistently in or with; obsess. 2 n. place frequented by person.

**hautboy** /'əʊbɔɪ/ n. old name for oboe.

*haute couture* /əʊt ku:'tjʊə(r)/ (world of) high fashion. [F]

**hauteur** /əʊ'tɜ:(r)/ n. haughtiness.

**Havana** /həˈvænə/ n. cigar of Cuban tobacco.

**have** /hæv/ 1 v. (3 *sing. pres.* **has** /hæz/; *past* & *p.p.* **had**) hold in possession; possess, contain; enjoy, suffer; be burdened with; give birth to; engage in; permit (to); cause to be or do etc.; receive; *colloq.* deceive, get the better of. 2 v. *aux.* with *p.p.* of *vbs.* forming past tenses. 3 n. *sl.* one who has (esp. wealth etc.); **haves and have-nots** rich and poor); swindle. 4 **have on** wear (clothes), have (engagement), *colloq.* play trick on; **have to** be obliged to, must.

**haven** /'heɪv(ə)n/ n. refuge; harbour.

**haver** /'heɪvə(r)/ v.i. hesitate; talk foolishly.

**haversack** /'hævəsæk/ n. canvas etc. bag carried on back or over shoulder.

**havoc** /'hævək/ n. devastation, confusion.

**haw** n. hawthorn berry.

**hawk¹** 1 n. bird of prey with rounded wings; person who advocates aggressive policy. 2 v. hunt with hawk.

**hawk²** v. clear throat noisily; bring (phlegm etc.) *up* thus.

**hawk³** v.t. carry about for sale.

**hawker** /'hɔ:kə(r)/ n. person who hawks goods.

**hawser** /'hɔ:zə(r)/ n. *Naut.* thick rope or cable for mooring ship.

**hawthorn** /'hɔ:θɔ:n/ n. thorny shrub or tree bearing red berries.

**hay** n. grass mown and dried for fodder. **hay fever** allergic irritation of nose and throat etc. caused esp. by pollen; **haymaking** mowing grass and spreading it to dry; **haystack** packed pile of hay; **haywire** tangled, in disorder, out of control.

**hazard** /'hæzəd/ 1 n. danger, risk; obstacle on golf-course. 2 v.t. risk; venture on (guess etc.).

**hazardous** /'hæzədəs/ a. risky.

**haze** n. slight mist; mental obscurity, confusion.

**hazel** /'heɪz(ə)l/ n. nut-bearing bush or small tree; light brown colour.

**hazy** /'heɪzɪ/ a. misty; vague.

**HB** *abbr.* hard black (pencil-lead).

**H-bomb** /'eɪtʃbɒm/ n. hydrogen bomb.

**he** 1 *pron.* (*obj.* **him**, *poss.* **his**) the male person or animal in question. 2 n. & a. male. 3 **he-man** masterful or virile man.

**HE** *abbr.* high explosive; His or Her Excellency.

**head** /hed/ 1 n. uppermost part of human body; foremost part of body of animal; seat of intellect etc.; person, individual; top or front or upper end; thing like head in form or position; signal-converting device on tape-recorder etc.; foam on top of beer etc.; confined body of water or steam, pressure exerted by this; ruler, chief, leader, etc.; headmaster, headmistress; climax or crisis. 2 v. be or put oneself or be put or put thing at head of; form head of; *Footb.* strike (ball) with head; provide with head or heading. 3 **headache** continuous pain in head, *colloq.* troublesome problem; **head-dress** (esp. ornamental) covering for head; **headlamp, headlight**, lamp on front of car etc.; **headland** promontory; **headline**

**header** 252 **heaven**

line at top of page or newspaper article etc. containing title etc., in *pl.* summary of broadcast news; **headlong** with head foremost, precipitately; **headmaster, headmistress,** principal master, mistress, of school; **head-on** (of collision etc.) head to head or front to front; **head-phone** pair of earphones held by band fitting over head; **headroom** overhead space; **headstall** part of bridle or halter fitting round horse's head; **head start** advantage granted or gained at beginning of race; **headstone** stone set up at head of grave; **headstrong** self-willed, obstinate; **headway** progress; **head wind** one blowing from directly in front; **off one's head** *colloq.* crazy.

**header** /ˈhedə(r)/ *n. Footb.* act of heading a ball; *colloq.* dive or plunge head first.

**heading** /ˈhedɪŋ/ *n.* title etc. at head of page etc.

**headquarters** /hedˈkwɔːtəz/ *n.pl.* (occas. treated as *sing.*) centre of operations; chief place of business etc.

**heady** /ˈhedi/ *a.* (of liquor etc.) apt to intoxicate; impetuous.

**heal** *v.* restore to health; cure; become sound.

**health** /helθ/ *n.* state of being well in body or mind; condition of body; toast drunk in person's honour. **health food** food chosen for its unmodified natural qualities etc.

**healthful** /ˈhelθfəl/ *a.* health-giving.

**healthy** /ˈhelθɪ/ *a.* having or conducive to good health.

**heap 1** *n.* number of things lying one on another; in *sing.* or *pl. colloq.* large number or amount. **2** *v.t.* pile (*up*) in heap; load with large quantities.

**hear** *v.* (*past* & *p.p.* **heard** /hɜːd/) perceive with ear; listen to; listen judicially to; be informed; receive message etc. *from.* **hearsay** gossip.

**hearing** /ˈhɪərɪŋ/ *n.* faculty of perceiving sounds; range within which sounds may be heard; opportunity to be heard; giving of case in lawcourt. **hearing aid** small sound-amplifier worn by deaf peson.

**hearken** /ˈhɑːkən/ *v.i. arch.* listen (*to*).

**hearse** /hɜːs/ *n.* vehicle for conveying coffin.

**heart** /hɑːt/ *n.* organ in body keeping up circulation of blood by expanding and contracting; seat of emotions or affections; soul, mind; courage; central or innermost part, essence; compact head of cabbage etc.; (conventionally) heart-shaped thing; playing-card of suit marked with red hearts. **at heart** in inmost feelings; **by heart** in or from memory; **have the heart** be hardhearted enough (*to*); **heartache** mental anguish; **heart attack** sudden heart failure; **heart-breaking, heartbroken,** causing, crushed by, great distress; **heartburn** burning sensation in chest; **heartfelt** sincere; **heart-rending** distressing; **heartsick** despondent; **heart-strings** deepest affections or pity; **heart-throb** *sl.* object of romantic affections; **heart-to-heart** frank (talk); **heart-warming** emotionally moving and encouraging; **take to heart** be much affected by.

**hearten** /ˈhɑːt(ə)n/ *v.* encourage, cheer.

**hearth** /hɑːθ/ *n.* floor of fireplace; area in front of this.

**heartless** /ˈhɑːtləs/ *a.* unfeeling, pitiless.

**hearty** /ˈhɑːtɪ/ *a.* vigorous; genial; sincere; (of meal or appetite) copious.

**heat 1** *n.* being hot, sensation of this; hot weather; warmth of feeling; anger; preliminary contest, winner(s) of which compete in final; receptive period of sexual cycle esp. in female mammals. **2** *v.* make or become hot; inflame. **3 heat-stroke** illness caused by excessive heat; **heat wave** period of very hot weather.

**heated** /ˈhiːtɪd/ *a.* vehement, angry.

**heath** /hiːθ/ *n.* flat waste tract of land, esp. covered with low shrubs; undershrub of heather kind.

**heathen** /ˈhiːð(ə)n/ **1** *n.* person who is not a member of a widely-held religion. **2** *a.* of heathens, having no religion. **3 heathenish** *a.*

**heather** /ˈheðə(r)/ *n.* purple-flowered plant of moors and heaths.

**heave 1** *v.* lift, raise; utter (sigh, groan) with effort; *colloq.* throw; *Naut.* (*past* & *p.p.* **hove**) haul; pull (at rope etc.); swell, rise; retch. **2** *n.* heaving. **3 heave in sight** come into view; **heave to** bring vessel to standstill with head to wind.

**heaven** /ˈhev(ə)n/ *n.* place believed to

**heavenly** / **hellebore**

be abode of God and of the righteous after death; place of bliss; sky.

**heavenly** *a.* of heaven, divine; of the sky; *colloq.* very pleasing.

**heavy** /'hevi/ 1 *a.* of great weight; of great density; laden; abundant; severe, extensive; striking or falling with force; hard to digest; (of ground) difficult to travel over; dull, tedious, oppressive, sad; *sl.* serious, important. 2 *n. Theatr.* villain. 3 **heavy-duty** designed to withstand hard use; **heavy-handed** clumsy, oppressive; **heavy hydrogen** deuterium; **heavy industry** that concerned with production of metal and machines etc.; **heavy water** oxide of deuterium; **heavyweight** boxing-weight with no upper limit.

**Hebraic** /hi:'breɪk/ *a.* of Hebrew or the Hebrews. **Hebraist** *n.*

**Hebrew** /'hi:bru:/ 1 *n.* member of a Semitic people in ancient Palestine; their language; modern form of this used esp. in Israel. 2 *a.* of or in Hebrew; of the Jews.

**heckle** /'hek(ə)l/ *v.t.* interrupt or harass (speaker).

**hectare** /'hekteə(r)/ *n.* metric unit of square measure, about 2½ acres.

**hectic** /'hektɪk/ *a.* busy and confused; excited, feverish.

**hectogram** /'hektəgræm/ *n.* 100 grams.

**hectolitre** /'hektəli:tə(r)/ *n.* 100 litres.

**hectometre** /'hektəmi:tə(r)/ *n.* 100 metres.

**hector** /'hektə(r)/ *v.* bluster, bully.

**hedge** 1 *n.* fence of bushes or low trees; protection against loss. 2 *v.* surround with hedge; make or trim hedges; secure oneself against loss on (bet etc.); avoid committing oneself. 3 **hedge-hop** fly at low altitude; **hedgerow** row of bushes forming hedge; **hedge-sparrow** common brown-backed European bird.

**hedgehog** /'hedʒhɒg/ *n.* small spiny nocturnal insect-eating mammal.

**hedonism** /'hi:dənɪz(ə)m/ *n.* doctrine that pleasure is the only proper aim. **hedonist** *n.*; **hedonistic** *a.*

**heed** 1 *v.t.* attend to; take notice of. 2 *n.* care, attention.

**heedless** /'hi:dləs/ *a.* not giving care or attention.

**hee-haw** /'hi:hɔ:/ *n.* & *v.i.* bray.

**heel**[1] 1 *n.* back part of human foot; corresponding part of quadruped's hind limb; part of sock etc. that covers heel; part of boot etc. that supports heel; heel-like thing; *sl.* contemptible person. 2 *v.* fit or renew heel on (shoe); *Rugby footb.* pass ball *out* at back of scrum with heel. 3 **heelball** shoemaker's polishing mixture of wax etc., esp. used in brass-rubbing.

**heel**[2] 1 *v.* (of ship etc.) lean over; cause (ship) to do this. 2 *n.* heeling.

**hefty** /'heftɪ/ *a.* heavy; sturdy; stalwart.

**hegemony** /hɪ'geməni/ *n.* leadership.

**heifer** /'hefə(r)/ *n.* young cow that has not had a calf.

**heigh** /heɪ/ *int.* expr. encouragement or inquiry. **heigh-ho** expr. boredom etc.

**height** /haɪt/ *n.* measure from base to top; elevation above ground or other level; high point; top; utmost degree.

**heighten** /'haɪt(ə)n/ *v.t.* raise higher; intensify; exaggerate.

**heinous** /'heɪnəs/ *a.* atrocious.

**heir** /eə(r)/ *n.* person entitled to property or rank as legal successor of former holder. **heir apparent** one whose claim cannot be superseded by birth of nearer heir; **heirloom** piece of property that has been in family for generations; **heir presumptive** one whose claim may be superseded by birth of nearer heir. **heiress** *n.*

**held** *past* & *p.p.* of **hold**[1].

**helical** /'helɪk(ə)l/ *a.* spiral.

**helices** *pl.* of **helix**.

**helicopter** /'helɪkɒptə(r)/ *n.* aircraft lifted and propelled by engine-driven blades revolving horizontally.

**heliograph** /'hi:lɪəʊgrɑ:f/ 1 *n.* signalling apparatus reflecting flashes of sunlight. 2 *v.t.* send (message) thus.

**heliotrope** /'hi:lɪətrəʊp/ *n.* plant with small clustered purple flowers; light purple colour.

**heliport** /'helɪpɔ:t/ *n.* place where helicopters take off and land.

**helium** /'hi:lɪəm/ *n.* light non-inflammable gaseous element.

**helix** /'hi:lɪks/ *n.* (*pl.* **helices** /'hi:lɪsi:z/) spiral.

**hell** *n.* abode of dead or damned; place or state of misery. **hellish** *a.*

**hellebore** /'helɪbɔ:(r)/ *n.* plant of kind including Christmas rose.

**Hellene** /ˈheliːn/ n. Greek. **Hellenic** a.; **Hellenism** n.; **Hellenist** n.

**hello** var. of **hallo**.

**helm** n. tiller or wheel for managing rudder. **at the helm** in control; **helmsman** person who steers ship.

**helmet** /ˈhelmɪt/ n. protective headcover of soldier or fireman or motorcyclist etc.

**helot** /ˈhelət/ n. serf, esp. in ancient Sparta.

**help** 1 v.t. provide with means to what is needed or sought, be useful to; prevent, refrain from. 2 n. act of helping; person or thing that helps; domestic servant(s); employee(s); remedy etc. 3 **help oneself (to)** take without seeking help or permission.

**helpful** /ˈhelpfəl/ a. giving help, useful.

**helping** /ˈhelpɪŋ/ n. portion of food.

**helpless** /ˈhelpləs/ a. unable to manage without help; without help or power.

**helpmate** /ˈhelpmeɪt/ n. helpful companion, esp. husband or wife.

**helter-skelter** /heltəˈskeltə(r)/ 1 adv. in disordered haste. 2 n. spiral slide at fun-fair.

**helve** n. handle of weapon or tool.

**hem**¹ 1 n. border of cloth where edge is turned under and sewn down. 2 v.t. sew edge thus. 3 **hem in** enclose, confine; **hem-stitch** (make hem with) ornamental stitch.

**hem**² int. expr. hesitation or calling attention.

**hemisphere** /ˈhemɪsfɪə(r)/ n. half sphere; half earth, esp. as divided by equator or by line passing through poles; each half of brain. **hemispherical** /-ˈsfer-/ a.

**hemlock** /ˈhemlɒk/ n. poisonous plant with small white flowers; poison got from it.

**hemp** n. Asian herbaceous plant; its fibre used for rope etc.; any of several narcotic drugs got from it.

**hempen** /ˈhempən/ a. made of hemp.

**hen** n. female bird, esp. of domestic fowl; female crab or lobster or salmon. **hen-party** colloq. party of women only; **henpecked** (of husband) domineered over by his wife.

**henbane** /ˈhenbeɪn/ n. narcotic and poisonous plant.

**hence** adv. from now; for this reason.

**henceforth, henceforward**, from this time forward.

**henchman** /ˈhentʃmən/ n. (pl.-**men**) trusty supporter.

**henna** /ˈhenə/ n. tropical shrub; reddish dye made from it and used esp. for hair.

**hepatic** /həˈpætɪk/ a. of the liver.

**hepatitis** /hepəˈtaɪtɪs/ n. inflammation of the liver.

**hepta-** /ˈheptə/ in comb. seven.

**heptagon** /ˈheptəɡən/ n. plane figure with 7 sides and angles. **heptagonal** /-ˈtæɡ-/ a.

**her** pron., obj. and poss. case of **she**, with abs. form **hers**.

**herald** /ˈher(ə)ld/ 1 n. forerunner; messenger; hist. officer who made State proclamations etc. 2 v.t. proclaim approach of; usher in. 3 **heraldic** /-ˈræld-/ a.

**heraldry** /ˈherəldrɪ/ n. knowledge or art of a herald; armorial bearings.

**herb** n. plant used for flavouring or medicine etc.; soft-stemmed plant dying down to ground after flowering. **herby** a.

**herbaceous** /hɜːˈbeɪʃəs/ a. of or like herbs. **herbaceous border** border in garden etc. containing esp. perennial flowering plants.

**herbage** /ˈhɜːbɪdʒ/ n. herbs; pasturage.

**herbal** /ˈhɜːb(ə)l/ 1 a. of herbs. 2 n. book about herbs.

**herbalist** /ˈhɜːbəlɪst/ n. dealer in medicinal herbs; writer on herbs.

**herbarium** /hɜːˈbeərɪəm/ n. collection of dried plants.

**herbicide** /ˈhɜːbɪsaɪd/ n. preparation used to destroy unwanted vegetation.

**herbivorous** /hɜːˈbɪvərəs/ a. feeding on plants. **herbivore** n.

**herculean** /hɜːkjəˈliːən/ a. extremely strong; (of task) of great difficulty.

**herd** 1 n. number of cattle etc. feeding or travelling together; large number of people. 2 v. collect or drive or go in herd; tend. 3 **herd recording, testing**, testing of dairy herds to estimate quantity and quality of milk; **herdsman** keeper of herds.

**here** 1 adv. in or to this place; at this point. 2 n. this place or point. 3 **hereabout(s)** somewhere near here; **hereafter** (in) future, (in) next world; **hereby** by this means; **herein** in this

# heredditable — hiatus

place or book etc.; **hereinafter** below (in document); **hereof** of this; **hereto** to this; **heretofore** formerly; **hereupon** after or in consequence of this; **herewith** with this.

**hereditable** /həˈredɪtəb(ə)l/ a. that can be inherited. **hereditability** n.

**hereditary** /həˈredɪtəri/ a. descending by inheritance; transmitted from one generation to another; holding position by inheritance.

**heredity** /həˈredɪti/ n. transmission of physical or mental characteristics from parents to children; these characteristics; genetic constitution.

**heresy** /ˈherəsi/ n. opinion contrary to orthodox (Christian) belief or to accepted doctrine.

**heretic** /ˈherətɪk/ n. believer in heresy. **heretical** a.

**heritable** /ˈherɪtəb(ə)l/ a. that can be inherited.

**heritage** /ˈherɪtɪdʒ/ n. what is or may be inherited; one's portion or lot; inherited cultural influence or tradition etc.

**hermaphrodite** /hɜːˈmæfrədaɪt/ 1 n. person or animal with characteristics or organs of both sexes. 2 a. having such characteristics. 3 **hermaphroditic** /-ˈdɪt-/ a.

**hermetic** /hɜːˈmetɪk/ a. with an airtight seal.

**hermit** /ˈhɜːmɪt/ n. person living in solitude.

**hermitage** /ˈhɜːmɪtɪdʒ/ n. place of hermit's retreat; secluded residence.

**hernia** /ˈhɜːniə/ n. Med. protrusion of internal part of organ through aperture in enclosing membrane etc.

**hero** /ˈhɪərəʊ/ n. (pl. **-roes**) man admired for great or noble deeds; chief male character in poem or story etc.

**heroic** /həˈrəʊɪk/ 1 a. having qualities of or suited to a hero; very brave. 2 n. in pl. over-dramatic talk or behaviour; heroic verse. 3 **heroic verse** form used in epic poetry.

**heroin** /ˈherəʊɪn/ n. sedative addictive drug prepared from morphine.

**heroine** /ˈherəʊɪn/ n. female hero.

**heroism** /ˈherəʊɪz(ə)m/ n. heroic conduct.

**heron** /ˈherən/ n. long-necked long-legged wading bird.

**herpes** /ˈhɜːpiːz/ n. virus disease of various kinds, causing blisters.

**herring** /ˈherɪŋ/ n. N. Atlantic edible fish. **herring-bone** stitch or weave suggesting bones of herring, zigzag pattern.

**hers** see **her**.

**herself** /hɜːˈself/ pron., emphat. & refl. form of **she**.

**hertz** n. (pl. same) unit of frequency, one cycle per second.

**hesitant** /ˈhezɪt(ə)nt/ a. hesitating. **hesitancy** n.

**hesitate** /ˈhezɪteɪt/ v.i. feel or show indecision; pause, be reluctant. **hesitation** n.

**hessian** /ˈhesiən/ n. strong coarse cloth of mixed hemp and jute.

**het** a. **het up** sl. excited.

**heterodox** /ˈhetərədɒks/ a. not orthodox. **heterodoxy** n.

**heterodyne** /ˈhetərədaɪn/ a. Radio relating to production of lower (audible) frequency from combination of two high frequencies.

**heterogeneous** /hetərəˈdʒiːniəs/ a. diverse; composed of diverse elements. **heterogeneity** (/-ˈniːəti:/) n.

**heterosexual** /hetərəˈseksjuəl/ 1 a. characterized by being sexually attracted to opposite sex. 2 n. heterosexual person. 3 **heterosexuality** n.

**heuristic** /hjuːˈrɪstɪk/ a. serving to discover; using trial and error.

**hew** v. (p.p. **hewed** or **hewn**) chop or cut with axe or sword etc.; cut into shape.

**hexa-** /heksə/ in comb. six.

**hexagon** /ˈheksəgən/ n. plane figure with 6 sides and angles. **hexagonal** a.

**hexagram** /ˈheksəgræm/ n. 6-pointed star formed by 2 intersecting equilateral triangles.

**hexameter** /hekˈsæmətə(r)/ n. line of 6 metrical feet.

**hey** /heɪ/ int. calling attention or expr. surprise or question. **hey presto!** conjuror's formula of command.

**heyday** /ˈheɪdeɪ/ n. time of greatest success, prime.

**HF** abbr. high frequency.

**hi** /haɪ/ int. calling attention or used as greeting.

**hiatus** /haɪˈeɪtəs/ n. gap in series etc.; break between two vowels coming together but not in same syllable.

# hibernate — hillock

**hibernate** /ˈhaɪbəneɪt/ v.i. (of animal) spend winter in torpid state. **hibernation** n.

**Hibernian** /haɪˈbɜːnɪən/ 1 a. of Ireland. 2 n. native of Ireland.

**hibiscus** /həˈbɪskəs/ n. cultivated shrub with large bright-coloured flowers.

**hiccup** /ˈhɪkʌp/ (also **hiccough**) 1 n. involuntary audible spasm of respiratory organs. 2 v. make hiccup.

**hick** n. US yokel.

**hickory** /ˈhɪkərɪ/ n. N. Amer. tree related to walnut; its wood.

**hid** past of **hide**¹.

**hidalgo** /hɪˈdælgəʊ/ n. (pl. **-gos**) Spanish gentleman.

**hidden** p.p. of **hide**¹.

**hide**¹ 1 v. (past **hid**; p.p. **hidden**) put or keep out of sight; conceal (fact from person); conceal oneself. 2 n. place of concealment used in observing or hunting wild animals. 3 **hide-out** colloq. hiding-place.

**hide**² n. animal's skin, raw or dressed; joc. person's skin. **hidebound** rigidly conventional.

**hideous** /ˈhɪdɪəs/ a. repulsive, revolting.

**hiding** /ˈhaɪdɪŋ/ n. thrashing.

**hie** v.i. & refl., poet. go quickly.

**hielaman** /ˈhiːləmən/ n. Aus. narrow Abor. shield made of bark or wood.

**hierarchy** /ˈhaɪərɑːkɪ/ n. system in which grades of authority rank one above another. **hierarchical** a.

**hieroglyph** /ˈhaɪərəglɪf/ n. picture or symbol representing word or syllable, esp. in ancient Egyptian writing. **hieroglyphic** a.; **hieroglyphics** n.pl.

**hi-fi** /ˈhaɪfaɪ/ 1 a. colloq. high fidelity. 2 n. equipment for such sound-reproduction.

**higgledy-piggledy** /ˌhɪgəldɪˈpɪgəldɪ/ adv. & a. in utter disorder.

**high** /haɪ/ 1 a. of great or specified upward extent; coming above normal level; of exalted rank or position, of superior quality; extreme, intense; (of opinion) favourable; (of sound) shrill; (of meat etc.) beginning to go bad; colloq. intoxicated by or on alcohol or drugs. 2 n. high or highest level or number; area of high barometric pressure; sl. euphoric state caused by drug etc. 3 adv. far up, aloft; in or to high degree; at high price. 4 **highball** US drink of spirits and soda etc.; **highbrow** colloq. (person) of superior intellectual or cultural interests; **High Church** section of Church of England emphasizing ritual and priestly authority and sacraments; **High Commission** embassy from one Commonwealth country to another; **High Court** supreme court of justice for civil cases; **high explosive** explosive with violent local effect; **high fidelity** quality of sound-reproduction with little distortion; **high-flown** extravagant, bombastic; **high frequency** Radio 3-30 megahertz; **high-handed** overbearing; **high-level** conducted by persons of high rank, (of computer language) close to ordinary language; **highlight** moment or detail of vivid interest, bright part of picture, (v.t.) bring into prominence; **high-minded** of firm moral principles; **high priest** chief priest, head of cult; **high-rise** (of building) having many storeys; **high road** main road; **high school** school for secondary education; **high seas** seas outside territorial waters; **high-spirited** cheerful; **high tea** early evening meal of tea and cooked food; **high water** high tide; **high-water mark** recorded maximum in any fluctuation.

**highland** /ˈhaɪlənd/ 1 n. (usu. in pl.) mountainous country, esp. (**Highlands**) of N. Scotland. 2 a. of highland or Sc. Highlands. 3 **highlander** n.

**highly** /ˈhaɪlɪ/ adv. in high degree, favourably.

**Highness** /ˈhaɪnəs/ n. title of princes etc.

**highway** /ˈhaɪweɪ/ n. public road, main route; conductor transmitting signals in computer. **highwayman** hist. (usu. mounted) robber of stage-coaches.

**hijack** /ˈhaɪdʒæk/ 1 v.t. seize control of (lorry, aircraft in flight, etc.) illegally; steal (goods) in transit. 2 n. hijacking.

**hike** 1 n. long walk for pleasure or exercise. 2 v.i. go on hike.

**hilarious** /hɪˈleərɪəs/ a. cheerful, merry; extremely funny. **hilarity** n.

**hill** n. natural elevation of ground, small mountain; heap, mound. **hillbilly** US person from remote rural area. **hilly** a.

**hillock** /ˈhɪlək/ n. small hill, mound.

**hilt** *n.* handle of sword or knife etc.

**him** *pron., obj.* case of **he**.

**himself** /hɪmˈself/ *pron., emphat. & refl.* form of **he**.

**hind**[1] /haɪnd/ *a.* situated at back. **hindquarters** rump and hind legs of quadruped; **hindsight** wisdom after event. **hindmost** /hɪz/ *pron., poss.* case of **he**.

**hind**[2] /haɪnd/ *n.* female (esp. red) deer.

**hinder**[1] /ˈhɪndə(r)/ *v.t.* impede; prevent.

**hinder**[2] /ˈhaɪndə(r)/ *a.* rear, hind.

**Hindi** /ˈhɪndi/ *n.* one of official languages of India; literary form of Hindustani; group of spoken languages in N. India.

**hindrance** /ˈhɪndrəns/ *n.* obstruction.

**Hindu** /hɪnˈduː/ **1** *n.* adherent of Hinduism. **2** *a.* of Hindus or Hinduism.

**Hinduism** /ˈhɪnduːɪz(ə)m/ *n.* religious and social system esp. in India with worship of several gods etc.

**Hindustani** /hɪnduˈstɑːniː/ *n.* language based on Hindi, used in N. India and Pakistan.

**hinge 1** *n.* movable joint such as that by which door is hung on post; *fig.* principle on which all depends. **2** *v.* attach or be attached with hinge; depend (*on*).

**hinny** /ˈhɪni/ *n.* offspring of she-ass by stallion.

**hint 1** *n.* indirect suggestion; slight indication. **2** *v.* suggest indirectly. **3 hint at** refer indirectly to.

**hinterland** /ˈhɪntəlænd/ *n.* district behind that lying along coast etc.

**hip**[1] *n.* projection of pelvis and upper part of thigh-bone at side of body.

**hip**[2] *n.* fruit of rose.

**hip**[3] *int.* used to introduce cheer.

**hip**[4] *a. sl.* stylish; well-informed.

**hippie** /ˈhɪpiː/ *n. sl.* person (esp. in 1960s) rejecting materialism and formality in dress etc.

**hippo** /ˈhɪpəʊ/ *n.* (*pl.* **-os**) *colloq.* hippopotamus.

**Hippocratic oath** /hɪpəˈkrætɪk/ oath embodying code of medical ethics.

**hippodrome** /ˈhɪpədrəʊm/ *n.* course for chariot races etc.

**hippopotamus** /hɪpəˈpɒtəməs/ *n.* (*pl.* **-muses**) large Afr. mammal with short legs and thick skin, inhabiting rivers etc.

**hippy** var. of **hippie**.

**hipster** /ˈhɪpstə(r)/ *a.* (of garment) hanging from hips rather than waist.

**hire 1** *v.t.* obtain use of (thing) or services of (person) for payment; give use of thus. **2** *n.* hiring; payment for this. **3 hire-purchase** system by which hired thing becomes hirer's property after number of payments.

**hireling** /ˈhaɪəlɪŋ/ *n.* usu. *derog.* person who works for hire.

**hirsute** /ˈhɜːsuːt/ *a.* hairy.

**his** /hɪz/ *pron., poss.* case of **he**.

**Hispanic** /hɪˈspænɪk/ *a.* of Spain and other Spanish-speaking countries.

**hiss** /hɪs/ *n.* sharp sound of *s.* **2** *v.* make hiss; express disapproval of thus; utter with angry hiss.

**histamine** /ˈhɪstəmiːn/ *n.* substance occurring in animal tissues and causing some allergic reactions etc.

**histology** /hɪˈstɒlədʒi/ *n.* science of organic tissues.

**historian** /hɪˈstɔːrɪən/ *n.* writer of history books; person learned in history.

**historic** /hɪˈstɒrɪk/ *a.* famous in history or potentially so.

**historical** /hɪˈstɒrɪk(ə)l/ *a.* of history; belonging to or dealing with the past; not legendary; studying development over period of time.

**historicity** /hɪstəˈrɪsəti/ *n.* historical truth or authenticity.

**historiography** /hɪstɔːrɪˈɒɡrəfi/ *n.* writing of history; study of this. **historiographer** *n.*

**history** /ˈhɪstəri/ *n.* continuous record of important or public events; past events, study of these; (eventful) career; story.

**histrionic** /hɪstrɪˈɒnɪk/ **1** *a.* of acting; stagy. **2** *n.* in *pl.* theatricals; stagy behaviour (designed to impress others).

**hit 1** *v.* (*past & p.p.* **hit**) strike with blow or missile; aim blow; have effect on, cause to suffer; propel (ball etc.) with bat etc.; *colloq.* encounter; light upon, find. **2** *n.* blow; stroke of satire etc.; successful attempt; success. **3 hit it off** get on well (*with*); **hit-or-miss** *colloq.* casual, careless.

**hitch 1** *v.* move (thing) with jerk; fasten with loop etc.; hitch-hike. **2** *n.* jerk; kind of noose or knot; temporary difficulty; snag. **3 hitch-hike** travel by means of lifts in vehicles.

**hither** /ˈhɪðə(r)/ **1** *adv.* to this place. **2**

**hive** 258 **holding**

*a.* situated on this side; the nearer. **3 hitherto** *adv.* up to now.

**hive 1** *n.* artificial home for bees; scene of busy activity. **2** *v.* place or live or store etc. (as) in hive. **3 hive off** separate from larger group.

**hives** /haɪvz/ *n.pl.* skin eruption, esp. nettle-rash.

**HM** *abbr.* Her or His Majesty('s).

**HM(A)S** *abbr.* Her or His Majesty's (Australian) Ship.

**HMSO** *abbr.* Her or His Majesty's Stationery Office.

**ho** *int.* expr. triumph or derision etc., or calling attention etc.

**hoar** /hɔː(r)/ *a.* grey with age; white. **hoar-frost** frozen water vapour on lawns etc.

**hoard** /hɔːd/ **1** *n.* store (esp. of money or treasure) laid by. **2** *v.* amass and put away, store *up*.

**hoarding** /'hɔːdɪŋ/ *n.* temporary board fence round building etc.; structure erected to carry advertisements.

**hoarse** /hɔːs/ *a.* (of voice) rough, husky; having hoarse voice.

**hoary** /'hɔːrɪ/ *a.* white or grey with age; aged; old and trite.

**hoax 1** *v.t.* deceive esp. by way of joke. **2** *n.* such deception.

**hob** *n.* flat iron shelf at side of grate; array of hotplates etc. on top of cooker. **hob-nail** heavy-headed nail for boot-sole.

**hobble** /'hɒb(ə)l/ **1** *v.* walk lamely, limp; tie together legs of (horse etc.) to keep it from straying. **2** *n.* limping gait; rope etc. used to hobble horse.

**hobby** /'hɒbɪ/ *n.* favourite pursuit outside one's main work or business. **hobby-horse** stick with horse's head, used as toy, figure of horse used in morris-dancing, favourite theme, obsession.

**hobgoblin** /'hɒbgɒblɪn/ *n.* mischievous imp; bogy.

**hob-nob** *v.i.* associate or spend time (*with*).

**hobo** /'həʊbəʊ/ *n.* (*pl.* **-bos**) *US* wandering workman or tramp.

**hock**[1] *n.* joint of quadruped's hind leg between knee and fetlock.

**hock**[2] *n.* German white wine.

**hock**[3] *sl.* **1** *v.t.* pawn. **2** *n.* **in hock** in pawn, in prison, in debt.

**hockey** /'hɒkɪ/ *n.* team-game played with ball and curved sticks.

**hocus-pocus** /həʊkəs'pəʊkəs/ *n.* trickery; conjuring formula.

**hod** *n.* trough on pole for carrying bricks etc.; container for shovelling and holding coal.

**hodgepodge** var. of **hotchpotch**.

**hoe 1** *n.* tool for scraping up weeds etc. **2** *v.* use hoe; weed (crops), loosen (soil) or dig *out* or *up* etc. with hoe.

**hog 1** *n.* domesticated pig, esp. castrated male for slaughter; *colloq.* greedy person. **2** *v.* take greedily; hoard selfishly. **3 go the whole hog** *sl.* do thing thoroughly; **hog's back** sharp hill-ridge; **hogwash** *fig.* worthless stuff.

**hogmanay** /'hɒgmaneɪ/ *n. Sc.* New Year's Eve.

**hogshead** /'hɒgzhed/ *n.* large cask; measure of beer (usu. about 50 gals.).

**hoick** *v.t. sl.* lift or jerk (*out* etc.).

***hoi polloi*** /hɔɪ pə'lɔɪ/ ordinary people, the masses. [Gk]

**hoist 1** *v.t.* raise or haul (*up*); raise with ropes and pulleys etc. **2** *n.* apparatus for hoisting things.

**hoity-toity** /hɔɪtɪ'tɔɪtɪ/ *a. colloq.* haughty, petulant.

**hokum** /'həʊkəm/ *n. sl.* false sentiment, sentimental or melodramatic nonsense.

**hold**[1] /həʊld/ **1** *v.* (*past* & *p.p.* **held**) keep thing in some position or condition; grasp; possess; contain, have capacity for; conduct, celebrate; restrain; think, believe; not give way; keep going; be valid. **2** *n.* grasp; manner or means of holding; means of exerting influence *on* or *over*. **3 holdall** large soft travelling bag; **hold down** repress, *colloq.* be competent enough to keep (job); **hold forth** speak at length or tediously; **hold on** maintain grasp, wait, not ring off; **hold out** offer (inducement etc.), maintain resistance, continue to make demand *for*; **hold over** postpone; **hold up** obstruct, sustain, rob by (threat of) violence; **hold-up** robbery of this kind, stoppage, delay; **hold water** (of reasoning) be sound; **hold with** *colloq.* approve of.

**hold**[2] /həʊld/ *n.* cavity below ship's deck for cargo.

**holder** /'həʊldə(r)/ *n.* occupant of office etc.; device for holding something.

**holding** /'həʊldɪŋ/ *n.* tenure of land; land or stocks held. **holding company**

**hole** 1 *n.* cavity in solid body; opening through or sunken place on surface; burrow; *colloq.* small or gloomy place; *sl.* awkward situation; cavity into which ball must be got in some games, *Golf* section of course from tee to hole. 2 *v.* make hole(s) in; hit golf-ball into hole. **hole-and-corner** *a.* underhand; **hole up** *sl.* hide oneself. 3 **holey** *a.*

**holiday** /'hɒlədeɪ/ *n.* break from work esp. for recreation; (freq. in *pl.*) period of this, esp. spent away from home.

**holiness** /'həʊlɪnəs/ *n.* being holy or sacred. **His Holiness** title of Pope.

**holland** /'hɒlənd/ *n.* linen fabric, freq. unbleached.

**hollandaise** /hɒlən'deɪz/ *n.* creamy sauce of butter and egg-yolks and vinegar etc.

**holler** /'hɒlə(r)/ *v. & n. US* shout.

**hollow** /'hɒləʊ/ 1 *a.* having hole or cavity or depression; not solid; empty; echoing, not full-toned; false, insincere. 2 *n.* hollow place; hole; valley. 3 *adv.* completely. 4 *v.t.* make hollow in.

**holly** /'hɒlɪ/ *n.* evergreen prickly-leaved shrub with red berries.

**hollyhock** /'hɒlɪhɒk/ *n.* tall plant with large showy flowers.

**holm** /həʊm/ *n.* (in full **holm-oak**) evergreen oak.

**holocaust** /'hɒləkɔːst/ *n.* wholesale destruction.

**hologram** /'hɒləgræm/ *n.* photographic pattern that gives 3-dimensional image when specially illuminated.

**holograph** /'hɒləgrɑːf or 'hɒləgræf/ 1 *a.* wholly in handwriting of person in whose name it appears. 3 *n.* such document.

**holster** /'həʊlstə(r)/ *n.* leather case for carrying pistol or revolver on the person.

**holy** /'həʊlɪ/ *a.* of high moral or spiritual excellence; belonging or devoted to God. **Holy Ghost** Holy Spirit; **holy orders** those of bishop, priest, and deacon; **Holy Spirit** Third Person of Trinity; **Holy Week** that preceding Easter Sunday; **Holy Writ** Bible.

**homage** /'hɒmɪdʒ/ *n.* tribute paid *to* person etc.; formal acknowledgement of allegiance.

**Homburg** /'hɒmbɜːg/ *n.* man's soft felt hat with narrow curled brim.

**home** 1 *n.* place where one lives; residence; native land; *Aus. arch.* Great Britain; institution of refuge or rest; (in games) finishing line in race, home match or win etc. 2 *a.* of or connected with home; not foreign; played etc. on team's own ground; that affects one closely. 3 *adv.* to or at home; to point aimed at. 4 *v.i.* (of pigeon) make way home; (of missile etc.) be guided to destination. 5 **home and dried** or **hosed** *Aus.* having successfully completed journey or task etc.; **Home Counties** *UK* those lying round London; **homeland** native land; **homesick** depressed by absence from home; **homespun** of yarn spun at home, plain and homely; **homestead** house with outbuildings, farm, *Aus.* owner's residence on sheep- or cattle-station; **homework** lessons etc. to be done by schoolchild at home. 6 **homeward** *a. & adv.*; **homewards** *adv.*

**homely** /'həʊmlɪ/ *a.* plain; unpretentious; *US* unattractive.

**homer** /'həʊmə(r)/ *n.* homing pigeon.

**Homeric** /həʊ'merɪk/ *a.* of or in style of the ancient Gk poet Homer; of Bronze Age Greece.

**homicide** /'hɒməsaɪd/ *n.* killing of person by another; person who kills another. **homicidal** *a.*

**homily** /'hɒmɪlɪ/ *n.* sermon; moralizing lecture. **homilectic** *a.*

**homing** /'həʊmɪŋ/ *a.* (of pigeon) trained to fly home from a distance; (of device) for guiding to target etc.

**hominid** /'hɒmɪnɪd/ 1 *a.* of the mammal family of existing and fossil man. 2 *n.* member of this.

**hominoid** /'hɒmɪnɔɪd/ 1 *a.* manlike. 2 *n.* animal resembling man.

**homoeopathy** /həʊmɪ'ɒpəθɪ/ *n.* treatment of disease by drugs that in healthy person would produce similar symptoms. **homoeopath** n.; **homoeopathic** /-'pæθ-/ *a.*

**homogeneous** /hɒmə'dʒiːnɪəs/ *a.* of same kind or nature; uniform. **homogeneity** /-'niːətɪ/ *n.*

**homogenize** /hə'mɒdʒənaɪz/ *v.t.* treat (milk) so that cream does not separate.

**homologous** /hɒˈmɒləgəs/ *a.* having same relation or value; corresponding.

**homology** /hɒˈmɒlədʒi:/ *n.* homologous relation, correspondence.

**homonym** /ˈhɒmənɪm/ *n.* word of same form as another but different meaning. **homonymous** *a.*

**homophone** /ˈhɒməfəʊn/ *n.* word having same sound as another, but different meaning.

**homosexual** /həʊməʊˈseksjuːəl/ 1 *a.* characterized by being sexually attracted to persons of same sex. 2 *n.* homosexual person. 3 **homosexuality** *n.*

**Hon.** *abbr.* honorary; Honourable.

**hone** 1 *n.* whetstone, esp. for razors. 2 *v.t.* sharpen on hone.

**honest** /ˈɒnɪst/ *a.* sincere; not lying or cheating or stealing; fairly earned.

**honesty** /ˈɒnɪsti:/ *n.* being honest, truthfulness; plant with purple flowers and flat round pods.

**honey** /ˈhʌni:/ *n.* sweet sticky yellow fluid made by bees from nectar collected from flowers; sweetness; darling.

**honey-eater** *Aus.* any of several species of birds that eat nectar.

**honeycomb** /ˈhʌni:kəʊm/ 1 *n.* bees' wax structure of hexagonal cells for honey and eggs; pattern hexagonally arranged. 2 *v.t.* fill with cavities; mark with honeycomb pattern.

**honeydew** /ˈhʌni:dju:/ *n.* sweet substance excreted by aphids; sweet green-fleshed type of melon.

**honeyed** /ˈhʌni:d/ *a.* sweet, sweet-sounding.

**honeymoon** /ˈhʌni:mu:n/ 1 *n.* holiday of newly-married couple; *fig.* initial period of enthusiasm or goodwill. 2 *v.i.* spend honeymoon.

**honeysuckle** /ˈhʌni:sʌk(ə)l/ *n.* climbing shrub with fragrant flowers.

**honk** 1 *n.* cry of wild goose or sound of motor horn. 2 *v.i.* make honk.

**honorarium** /ɒnəˈreərɪəm/ *n.* (*pl.* -riums) voluntary payment for professional services.

**honorary** /ˈɒnərəri/ *a.* conferred as honour; unpaid.

**honorific** /ɒnəˈrɪfɪk/ *a.* implying respect.

**honour** /ˈɒnə(r)/ 1 *n.* high respect, reputation; allegiance to what is right; thing conferred as distinction (esp. official award for bravery or achievement); privilege; person or thing that does credit to another; chastity, reputation for this; mark of respect; in *pl.* specialized degree-course or special distinction in examination; *Golf* right of driving off first; in *pl. Cards* 4 or 5 top cards in trump suit. 2 *v.t.* respect highly; confer honour on; accept or pay (bill, cheque) when due. 3 **do the honours** perform duties of host etc.

**honourable** /ˈɒnərəb(ə)l/ *a.* deserving or bringing honour; **Honourable** courtesy title of MPs and certain officials and children of certain ranks of the nobility.

**hooch** /huːtʃ/ *n. US sl.* alcoholic spirits, esp. inferior or illicit.

**hood**¹ /hʊd/ 1 *n.* covering for head and neck; garment worn as part of academic dress; thing like hood in shape or use, collapsible top or cover of motor vehicle etc.; *US* bonnet of car. 2 *v.t.* cover with hood.

**hood**² /hʊd/ *n. US* gangster, gunman.

**hoodlum** /ˈhuːdləm/ *n.* hooligan; gangster.

**hoodoo** /ˈhuːduː/ *US* 1 *n.* bad luck; thing that brings or causes this. 2 *v.t.* bring bad luck to.

**hoodwink** /ˈhʊdwɪŋk/ *v.t.* deceive, delude.

**hooey** /ˈhuːɪ/ *n. sl.* nonsense.

**hoof** /huːf/ 1 *n.* (*pl.* **hoofs** or **hooves**) horny part of foot of horse etc. 2 *v.* **hoof it** *sl.* go on foot.

**hook** /hʊk/ 1 *n.* bent piece of wire etc. for catching hold or for hanging things on; curved cutting instrument; hooking stroke; short swinging blow in boxing. 2 *v.* grasp or secure or fasten or catch with hook; *Sport* send (ball) in curving or deviating path; *Rugby footb.* secure (ball) in scrum with foot. 3 **hook and eye** small hook and loop as dress fastener; **hook-up** connection, esp. interconnection in broadcast transmission; **hookworm** kind of worm infesting intestines of humans and animals.

**hookah** /ˈhʊkə/ *n.* tobacco-pipe with long tube, drawing smoke through vase of water.

**hooked** /hʊkt/ *a.* bent like hook, hook-shaped. **hooked on** *colloq.* addicted to or captivated by.

**hooker** /'hukə(r)/ n. *Rugby footb.* player in front row of scrum who tries to hook ball; *US sl.* prostitute.

**hooligan** /'hu:lɪgən/ n. young thug. **hooliganism** n.

**hoon** /hu:n/ n. *Aus. sl.* pimp; lout.

**hoop** /hu:p/ 1 n. circular band of metal or wood etc. esp. for binding cask etc.; wooden etc. circle trundled by child; iron arch through which balls are driven in croquet; *Aus. sl.* jockey. 2 *v.t.* bind with hoops. 3 **hoop-la** game in which rings are thrown to capture prizes; **hoop-pine** *Aus.* softwood tree.

**hoopoe** /'hu:pu:/ n. Eur. bird with variegated plumage and fan-like crest.

**hooray** var. of **hurrah**.

**hoot** /hu:t/ 1 n. owl's cry; sound of steam-whistle or car horn etc.; inarticulate shout of derision etc. 2 *v.* utter hoot(s); greet or drive away with hoots; sound (horn). 3 **not care a hoot** or **two hoots** not care at all.

**hooter** /'hu:tə(r)/ n. siren, steam whistle, esp. as signal for start or end of work; car horn; *sl.* nose.

**Hoover** /'hu:və(r)/ 1 (P) n. vacuum cleaner. 2 **hoover** *v.t. colloq.* clean with vacuum cleaner.

**hop**¹ 1 *v.* spring on one foot; (of bird etc.) jump; hop over; move or go quickly or with leaping motion. 2 n. hopping; spring; *colloq.* dance; short flight in aircraft. 3 **hop it** *sl.* go away; **hopscotch** child's game of hopping over lines marked on ground.

**hop**² 1 n. climbing plant with bitter cones used to flavour beer etc.; in *pl.* these cones. 2 *v.* flavour with hops. 3 **hoppy** *a.*

**hope** 1 n. expectation and desire; trust; ground of hope; person or thing that encourages hope; what is hoped for. 2 *v.* feel hope; expect and desire.

**hopeful** /'həupfəl/ *a.* feeling hope, promising.

**hopefully** *adv.* in a hopeful manner; *colloq.* (qualifying whole sentence) it is to be hoped that.

**hopeless** /'həupləs/ *a.* feeling or admitting no hope; inadequate, incompetent.

**hopper**¹ /'hɒpə(r)/ n. one who hops, hopping insect etc.; funnel-like device for feeding grain into mill etc.

**hopper**² /'hɒpə(r)/ n. hop-picker.

**horde** /hɔ:d/ n. large crowd or troop; troop of Tartar or other nomads.

**horehound** /'hɔ:haund/ n. herb with aromatic bitter juice.

**horizon** /hə'raɪz(ə)n/ n. line at which earth and sky appear to meet; limit of mental perception or interest etc.

**horizontal** /hɒrɪ'zɒnt(ə)l/ 1 *a.* parallel to plane of horizon; level, flat. 2 n. horizontal line or bar etc.

**hormone** /'hɔ:məun/ n. substance internally secreted that passes into the blood or sap and stimulates organs or growth etc.; similar synthetic substance. **hormonal** *a.*

**horn** n. hard outgrowth, often curved and pointed, on head of animal; hornlike projection; substance of horns, article made of this; brass wind instrument; instrument giving warning. **hornbeam** tough-wooded Eur. hedgerow tree; **hornbill** bird with hornlike excrescence on bill.

**hornblende** /'hɔ:nblend/ n. darkbrown etc. mineral constituent of granite etc.

**hornet** /'hɔ:nət/ n. large species of wasp.

**hornpipe** /'hɔ:npaɪp/ n. lively dance associated esp. with sailors; music for this.

**horny** /'hɔ:nɪ/ *a.* of or like horn; hard; *sl.* lecherous.

**horology** /hə'rɒlədʒɪ/ n. clock-making. **horological** /-'lɒdʒ-/ *a.*

**horoscope** /'hɒrəskəup/ n. prediction of person's future based on relative position of stars at his birth.

**horrible** /'hɒrəb(ə)l/ *a.* arousing horror; hideous, shocking; *colloq.* unpleasant.

**horrid** /'hɒrɪd/ *a.* horrible; *colloq.* disagreeable.

**horrific** /hə'rɪfɪk/ *a.* horrifying.

**horrify** /'hɒrəfaɪ/ *v.t.* arouse horror in; shock.

**horror** /'hɒrə(r)/ n. intense dislike or fear; horrifying thing.

**hors-d'oeuvre** /ɔ: 'dɜ:vr/ n. appetizer served at start of meal.

**horse** /hɔ:s/ 1 n. solid-hoofed quadruped used as beast of burden and draught and for riding on; *collect.* cavalry; vaulting-block in gymnasium; frame for supporting things. 2 *v.i. colloq.* fool *around*. 3 **horse-box** closed vehicle for transporting horse(s); **horse-chestnut** tree with conical clusters of white or pink flowers, its dark-brown fruit; **horsehair** hair from mane or tail of horse; **horse-laugh** loud coarse laugh; **horseman** (skilled) rider on horseback; **horsemanship** skill in riding; **horseplay** boisterous play; **horsepower** unit of rate of doing work; **horse-radish** plant with pungent root used to make sauce; **horse sense** *colloq*. plain common sense; **horseshoe** U-shaped iron shoe for horse, thing of this shape; **horsewhip** whip for horse, (*v.t.*) beat (person) with this; **horsewoman** (skilled) woman rider on horseback.

**horsy** /ˈhɔːsiː/ *a*. of or like horse; concerned with horses.

**hortative** /ˈhɔːtətɪv/ *a*. (also **hortatory**) serving to exhort.

**horticulture** /ˈhɔːtɪkʌltʃə(r)/ *n*. art of gardening. **horticultural** *a*.; **horticulturist** *n*.

**hosanna** /həʊˈzænə/ *n*. cry of adoration.

**hose** /həʊz/ 1 *n*. flexible tube for conveying liquids; stockings; *hist*. breeches. 2 *v*. water or wash *down* (as) with a hose.

**hosier** /ˈhəʊzɪə(r)/ *n*. dealer in stockings and socks. **hosiery** *n*.

**hospice** /ˈhɒspɪs/ *n*. travellers' house of rest kept by religious order etc.; home for destitute or (esp. terminally) ill.

**hospitable** /ˈhɒspɪtəb(ə)l/ *a*. disposed to give hospitality.

**hospital** /ˈhɒspɪt(ə)l/ *n*. institution providing medical and surgical treatment for ill and injured persons; *hist*. charitable institution.

**hospitality** /hɒspɪˈtælətɪ/ *n*. friendly and generous reception of guests or strangers.

**hospitalize** /ˈhɒspɪtəlaɪz/ *v.t.* send to or treat in hospital. **hospitalization** *n*.

**host**[1] /həʊst/ *n*. large number; *arch*. army.

**host**[2] /həʊst/ *n*. person who entertains another as guest; landlord of inn; animal having parasite.

**host**[3] /həʊst/ *n*. bread consecrated in celebration of Eucharist.

**hostage** /ˈhɒstɪdʒ/ *n*. person handed over or seized as pledge.

**hostel** /ˈhɒst(ə)l/ *n*. house of residence for students etc.

**hostelry** /ˈhɒstəlrɪ/ *n*. *arch*. inn.

**hostess** /ˈhəʊstes/ *n*. woman who entertains guests, or customers at night-club.

**hostie** /ˈhəʊstɪ/ *n*. *Aus*. *colloq*. air hostess.

**hostile** /ˈhɒstaɪl/ *a*. of enemy; unfriendly.

**hostility** /hɒˈstɪlətɪ/ *n*. being hostile; enmity; warfare; in *pl*. acts of war.

**hot** 1 *a*. of or at high temperature, very warm; giving or feeling heat; pungent; ardent; excited; (of news) fresh; skilful, formidable; (*sl*. of goods) stolen. 2 *v.t. colloq*. heat *up*. 3 **hot air** *sl*. excited or boastful talk; **hotbed** bed of earth heated by fermenting manure, *fig*. place that promotes growth; **hot dog** hot sausage sandwiched in bread roll; **hotfoot** in eager haste; **hothead** impetuous person; **hothouse** heated building with glass roof and sides, for growing plants; **hot line** direct communications link between distant places; **hotplate** heated metal plate for cooking food or keeping it hot; **hotpot** dish of stewed meat and vegetables; **hot seat** *sl*. awkward or responsible position, electric chair; **hot water** *colloq*. *fig*. disgrace, trouble; **hot-water bottle** container filled with hot water and used to warm bed etc.

**hotchpotch** /ˈhɒtʃpɒtʃ/ *n*. confused mixture, jumble, medley.

**hotel** /həʊˈtel/ *n*. place providing meals and accommodation for payment.

**hotelier** /həʊˈtelɪə(r)/ *n*. hotel-keeper.

**hound** /haʊnd/ 1 *n*. dog used in hunting; despicable man. 2 *v.t.* harass or pursue; urge *on*.

**hour** /aʊə(r)/ *n*. period of 60 minutes; period set aside for some purpose; in *pl*. fixed habitual time for work etc.; short time; time *for* action etc.; prayers said at any of 7 fixed times of day.

**hourglass** reversible device with two glass bulbs containing sand that takes an hour to pass from upper to lower bulb.

**houri** /ˈhʊərɪ/ *n*. beautiful young woman (in Muslim paradise).

**hourly** /ˈaʊəlɪ/ 1 *a*. occurring etc. every hour. 2 *adv*. every hour.

**house** 1 /haʊs/ *n*. (*pl. pr*. /ˈhaʊzəz/) building for habitation or specified pur-

**household**    263    **hull**

pose; building for keeping animals or goods; residential establishment, esp. of religious order; section of boarding-school etc.; family, dynasty; firm or institution; legislative etc. assembly, building where it meets; audience or performance in theatre etc. 2 /haʊz/ *v.t.* provide house for; receive or store (as) in house; fix in socket or mortise etc. 3 **house arrest** detention in one's own house; **houseboat** boat fitted up for living in; **house-bound** unable to leave one's house through illness etc.; **housebreaker** burglar; **housekeeper** woman managing affairs of house; **housemaid** female servant in house; **houseman** resident doctor of hospital or institution; **house-plant** one grown indoors; **house-proud** preoccupied with care etc. of home; **house-trained** (of domestic animal) trained to be clean in house; **house-warming** party etc. celebrating move to new house; **housewife** mistress of house, domestic manager, /ˈhʌzɪf/ case for sewing requisites; **housewifely** *a.*; **housework** cleaning and cooking etc. in home.

**household** /ˈhaʊshəʊld/ *n.* occupants of house; domestic establishment. **household troops** those nominally employed to guard sovereign; **household word** familiar saying or name.

**householder** *n.* person who occupies house as his own dwelling; head of household.

**housing** /ˈhaʊzɪŋ/ *n.* (provision of) houses; protective casing. **housing estate** residential estate planned as a unit.

**hove** *Naut. past & p.p.* of **heave**.

**hovel** /ˈhɒv(ə)l/ *n.* small miserable dwelling.

**hover** /ˈhɒvə(r)/ *v.i.* (of bird etc.) remain in one place in air; loiter about.

**hovercraft** /ˈhɒvəkrɑːft/ *n.* (*pl.* same) vehicle moving on air-cushion over surface of sea or land.

**how** /haʊ/ 1 *adv.* in what way; by what means; in what condition; to what extent. 2 *n.* way thing is done. 3 **howbeit** /-ˈbiːət/ *arch.* nevertheless. **however** nevertheless, in or to whatever way or degree; **howsoever** /-səʊˈevə(r)/ in or to whatever manner or degree.

**howdah** /ˈhaʊdə/ *n.* seat, usu. with canopy, on elephant's back.

**howitzer** /ˈhaʊɪtsə(r)/ *n.* short gun firing shell at high elevation.

**howl** /haʊl/ 1 *n.* long doleful cry (as) of dog etc.; similar sound; loud cry of rage or derision or laughter etc. 2 *v.* make howl; utter with howl.

**howler** *n. sl.* glaring blunder.

**hoy**[1] *int.* used to call attention.

**hoy**[2] *n. Aus.* game of chance resembling bingo, using playing-cards.

**hoyden** /ˈhɔɪd(ə)n/ *n.* boisterous girl.

**HP** *abbr.* hire-purchase; horsepower.

**HQ** *abbr.* headquarters.

**hr.** *abbr.* hour.

**HRH** *abbr.* His or Her Royal Highness.

**HT** *abbr.* high tension.

**hub** *n.* central part of wheel, from which spokes radiate; centre of interest etc.

**hubble-bubble** /ˈhʌb(ə)lbʌb(ə)l/ *n.* form of hookah.

**hubbub** /ˈhʌbʌb/ *n.* din; tumult.

**hubby** /ˈhʌbi/ *n. colloq.* husband.

**huckaback** /ˈhʌkəbæk/ *n.* rough-surfaced linen or cotton fabric for towels etc.

**huckleberry** /ˈhʌkəlberi/ *n.* low shrub common in N. Amer.; its fruit.

**huckster** /ˈhʌkstə(r)/ *n.* hawker; mercenary person. 2 *v.* haggle; be hawker.

**huddle** /ˈhʌd(ə)l/ 1 *v.* heap or crowd together; nestle closely. 2 *n.* confused heap etc., *sl.* (secret) conference.

**hue**[1] *n.* colour, tint.

**hue**[2] *n.* **hue and cry** loud outcry.

**huff** 1 *n.* fit of petulance. 2 *v.* blow; *Draughts* remove (opponent's man) as forfeit. 3 **huffy** *a.*

**hug** 1 *v.t.* squeeze tightly in one's arms; keep close to (shore etc.); cling to. 2 *n.* close or rough clasp.

**huge** /hjuːdʒ/ *a.* very large or great.

**hugely** /ˈhjuːdʒli/ *adv.* very much.

**hugger-mugger** /ˈhʌɡəmʌɡə(r)/ *a. & adv.* secret(ly); confused(ly), in a muddle.

**Hughie** /ˈhjuːi/ *n. Aus. joc.* **send her down Hughie!** make it rain!

**hula** /ˈhuːlə/ *n.* women's dance of Hawaiian origin. **hula hoop** large hoop for spinning round the body.

**hulk** *n.* body of dismantled ship; large clumsy-looking person or thing.

**hulking** /ˈhʌlkɪŋ/ *a. colloq.* bulky, clumsy.

**hull**[1] *n.* body of ship etc.

**hull**[2] 1 *n.* pod of beans etc.; calyx of

**hullabaloo** /hʌləbə'lu:/ n. uproar.

**hullo** var. of **hallo**.

**hum**¹ 1 v. make low continuous sound like bee; sing with closed lips; make slight inarticulate sound, esp. of hesitation. 2 n. humming sound; excl. of hesitation. 3 **humming-bird** bird of kind whose wings hum.

**hum**² Aus. sl. 1 v. borrow, scrounge. 2 n. scrounger.

**human** /'hju:mən/ 1 a. having or showing qualities distinctive of mankind; that is a person or consists of persons; not divine or animal or mechanical. 2 n. human being. 3 **human interest** (newspaper etc. story) involving personal emotions; **human rights** those held to belong to all persons.

**humane** /hju:'meɪn/ a. benevolent, compassionate; (of studies) tending to civilize.

**humanism** /'hju:mənɪz(ə)m/ n. doctrine emphasizing human needs and seeking solely rational ways of solving human problems; system of thought etc. concerned with human rather than religious values; literary culture, esp. in Renaissance. **humanist** n.; **humanistic** a.

**humanitarian** /hju:mænɪ'teərɪən/ 1 a. concerned with promoting human welfare. 2 n. humanitarian person. 3 **humanitarianism** n.

**humanity** /hju:'mænɪtɪ/ n. human nature; human race; humaneness; (usu. in pl.) learning or literature concerned with human culture.

**humanize** /'hju:mənaɪz/ v. make or become human or humane. **humanization** n.

**humanly** /'hju:mənlɪ/ adv. within human capabilities.

**humble** /'hʌmb(ə)l/ 1 a. having or showing low estimate of one's own importance; lowly, modest. 2 v.t. make humble; lower rank of. 3 **eat humble pie** submit to humiliation.

**humbug** /'hʌmbʌg/ 1 n. sham, deception; nonsense; impostor; kind of usu. peppermint-flavoured boiled sweet. 2 v.t. delude, cheat.

**humdinger** /'hʌmdɪŋə(r)/ n. sl. remarkable person or thing.

**humdrum** /'hʌmdrʌm/ a. dull, commonplace.

**humerus** /'hju:mərəs/ n. (pl. **-ri** /-raɪ/) bone of upper arm. **humeral** a.

**humid** /'hju:mɪd/ a. damp, moist.

**humidity** /hju:'mɪdɪtɪ/ n. humid state, degree of moisture esp. in atmosphere.

**humiliate** /hju:'mɪlɪeɪt/ v.t. harm dignity or self-respect of. **humiliation** n.

**humility** /hju:'mɪlɪtɪ/ n. humbleness; meekness.

**hummock** /'hʌmək/ n. low hill or hump.

**hummus** /'hʊməs/ n. paste of chickpeas and oil flavoured with lemon and garlic.

**humorist** /'hju:mərɪst/ n. humorous talker or writer etc.

**humorous** /'hju:mərəs/ a. full of humour, comic.

**humour** /'hju:mə(r)/ 1 n. quality of being amusing; ability to appreciate the comic; state of mind, mood; each of 4 fluids formerly held to determine physical and mental qualities. 2 v.t. keep (person) contented by indulging his wishes.

**hump** 1 n. protuberance esp. on back; rounded raised mass of earth etc.; sl. fit of depression. 2 v. make humpshaped; sl. hoist or carry (pack etc.). 3 **humpback** deformed back with hump, person having this; **humpback bridge** one with steep approach to top.

**humph** int. expr. dissatisfaction etc.

**humpy** /'hʌmpɪ/ n. Aus. Abor. hut; any small hut or shanty.

**humus** /'hju:məs/ n. organic constituent of soil formed by decomposition of plants etc.

**hunch** 1 v. bend or arch into a hump. 2 n. hump, hunk; intuitive feeling. 3 **hunchback** humpback.

**hundred** /'hʌndrəd/ n. & a. ten times ten; hist. subdivision of county. **hundredweight** 112lb., US 100 lb. **hundredth** a. & n.

**hundredfold** a. & adv. a hundred times as much or many; consisting of a hundred parts.

**hung** past & p.p. of **hang**.

**hunger** /'hʌŋgə(r)/ 1 n. discomfort or painful sensation caused by lack of food; strong desire. 2 v.i. feel hunger; crave for. 3 **hunger-strike** refusal to take food.

**hungry** /'hʌŋgri/ *a.* feeling or showing hunger; eager; *Aus.* mean, stingy.

**hunk** *n.* large piece cut off.

**hunt 1** *v.* pursue wild animals for food or sport; (of animal) pursue prey; *Aus.* drive away, dismiss; search *for*; drive *out*. **2** *n.* hunting; hunting district or society. **3 hunting-ground** place where one hunts (freq. *fig.*); **huntsman** hunter, person in charge of hounds; large flat-bodied Aus. spider.

**hunter** /'hʌntə(r)/ *n.* one who hunts; horse ridden for hunting; watch with cover protecting glass. **huntress** *n.*

**Huon pine** /'hjuːən/ large Tasmanian evergreen conifer, its wood.

**hurdle** /'hɜːd(ə)l/ **1** *n.* portable frame with bars etc. for temporary fence; frame to be jumped over in **hurdle-race**; in *pl.* hurdle-race; *fig.* obstacle. **2** *v.i.* run in hurdle-race.

**hurdler** /'hɜːdlə(r)/ *n.* hurdle-racer; hurdle-maker.

**hurdy-gurdy** /'hɜːdɪgɜːdɪ/ *n.* musical instrument having handle, with droning sound, played by turning handle; *colloq.* barrel-organ.

**hurl 1** *v.t.* throw violently. **2** *n.* violent throw.

**hurly-burly** /'hɜːlɪbɜːlɪ/ *n.* commotion, tumult.

**hurrah** /hə'rɑː/ *int.* & *n.* (also **hurray**) (shout) expr. joy or approval.

**hurricane** /'hʌrəkən/ *n.* violent storm-wind, esp. W. Ind. cyclone. **hurricane lamp** one with flame protected from wind.

**hurry** /'hʌrɪ/ **1** *n.* great haste; eagerness; need for haste. **2** *v.* (cause to) move or act with haste; in *p.p.* hasty, done rapidly. **3 hurry-scurry** (in) disorderly haste. **4 hurriedly** *adv.*

**hurt 1** *v.* (*past* & *p.p.* hurt) cause pain or injury or distress to; suffer pain. **2** *n.* injury; harm; offence. **3 hurtful** *a.*

**hurtle** /'hɜːt(ə)l/ *v.i.* move swiftly esp. with clattering sound, come with crash.

**husband** /'hʌzbənd/ **1** *n.* married man in relation to his wife. **2** *v.t.* manage thriftily.

**husbandry** /'hʌzbəndrɪ/ *n.* farming; management of resources.

**hush 1** *v.* silence; be silent. **2** *n.* silence. **3 hush-hush** *colloq.* highly secret; **hush-money** sum paid to avoid exposure; **hush up** suppress (fact).

**husk 1** *n.* dry outer covering of fruit or seed. **2** *v.t.* remove husk from.

**husky**[1] /'hʌskɪ/ *a.* full of or dry as husks; hoarse; *colloq.* big and strong.

**husky**[2] /'hʌskɪ/ *n.* Eskimo dog.

**hussar** /hə'zɑː(r)/ *n.* light-cavalry soldier.

**hussy** /'hʌsɪ/ *n.* pert girl; immoral woman.

**hustings** /'hʌstɪŋz/ *n.* (parliamentary) election proceedings.

**hustle** /'hʌs(ə)l/ **1** *v.* push roughly, jostle; hurry; push one's way, bustle. **2** *n.* hustling, bustle.

**hut** *n.* small simple or crude house or shelter; *Mil.* temporary housing for troops.

**hutch** *n.* boxlike pen for rabbits etc.

**hyacinth** /'haɪəsɪnθ/ *n.* bulbous plant with bell-shaped flowers.

**hyaena** /haɪ'iːnə/ *var.* of **hyena**.

**hybrid** /'haɪbrɪd/ **1** *n.* offspring of two animals or plants of different species etc.; thing of mixed origins. **2** *a.* bred as hybrid, cross-bred; heterogeneous. **3 hybridism** *n.*; **hybridization** *n.*; **hybridize** *v.*

**hydra** /'haɪdrə/ *n.* thing hard to get rid of; water-snake; freshwater polyp.

**hydrangea** /haɪ'dreɪndʒə/ *n.* shrub with globular clusters of white or blue or pink flowers.

**hydrant** /'haɪdrənt/ *n.* water-pipe with nozzle for hose.

**hydrate** /haɪ'dreɪt/ **1** *n.* chemical compound of water with another compound etc. **2** *v.* (cause to) combine with water. **3 hydration** *n.*

**hydraulic** /haɪ'drɔːlɪk/ *a.* of water etc. conveyed through pipes etc.; operated by movement of liquid.

**hydraulics** *n.pl.* usu. treated as *sing.* science of conveyance of liquids through pipes etc. esp. as motive power.

**hydro** /'haɪdrəʊ/ *n.* (*pl.* -os) *colloq.* hotel etc. providing hydropathic treatment; hydroelectric power plant.

**hydro-** /'haɪdrəʊ/ *in comb.* water; combined with hydrogen.

**hydrocarbon** /haɪdrəʊ'kɑːbən/ *n.* compound of hydrogen and carbon.

**hydrocephalus** /haɪdrəʊ'sefələs/ *n. Med.* condition, esp. in young children, with accumulation of fluid within cranium. **hydrocephalic** /-sə'fælɪk/ *a.*; **hydrocephalous** *a.*

**hydrodynamics** /haɪdrəʊdaɪ'næmɪks/ *n.pl.* usu. treated as *sing.* science of forces exerted by liquids.

**hydroelectric** /haɪdrəʊə'lektrɪk/ *a.* producing electricity by water-power; (of electricity) produced by water-power.

**hydrofoil** /'haɪdrəfɔɪl/ *n.* boat equipped with device for raising hull out of water at speed; this device.

**hydrogen** /'haɪdrədʒ(ə)n/ *n.* light colourless odourless gas combining with oxygen to form water. **hydrogen bomb** immensely powerful bomb utilizing explosive fusion of hydrogen nuclei.

**hydrogenate** /haɪ'drɒdʒəneɪt/ *v.t.* charge with or cause to combine with hydrogen. **hydrogenation** *n.*

**hydrography** /haɪ'drɒgrəfɪ:/ *n.* study of seas, lakes, rivers, etc.

**hydrolyse** /'haɪdrəlaɪz/ *v.t.* decompose by hydrolysis.

**hydrolysis** /haɪ'drɒləsəs/ *n.* decomposition by chemical reaction with water. **hydrolytic** /-lɪt-/ *a.*

**hydrometer** /haɪ'drɒmətə(r)/ *n.* instrument for measuring density of liquids.

**hydropathy** /haɪ'drɒpəθɪ:/ *n.* medical treatment by external and internal application of water. **hydropathic** /-'pæθ-/ *a.*

**hydrophobia** /haɪdrə'fəʊbɪ:ə/ *n.* aversion to water, esp. as symptom of rabies in man; rabies. **hydrophobic** *a.*

**hydroplane** /'haɪdrəpleɪn/ *n.* light fast motor boat; finlike device enabling submarine to rise or fall.

**hydroponics** /haɪdrə'pɒnɪks/ *n.pl.* (usu. treated as *sing.*) art of growing plants without soil, in water etc. impregnated with chemicals.

**hydrostatic** /haɪdrə'stætɪk/ *a.* of the equilibrium of liquids and the pressure exerted by liquids at rest.

**hydrostatics** *n.pl.* (usu. treated as *sing.*) study of properties of liquids.

**hydrous** /'haɪdrəs/ *a.* containing water.

**hyena** /haɪ'i:nə/ *n.* carnivorous mammal allied to dog.

**hygiene** /'haɪdʒi:n/ *n.* principles of maintaining health; sanitary science. **hygienic** *a.*; **hygienist** *n.*

**hygrometer** /haɪ'grɒmətə(r)/ *n.* instrument for measuring humidity of air etc.

**hygroscopic** /haɪgrə'skɒpɪk/ *a.* tending to absorb moisture from air.

**hymen** /'haɪmən/ *n.* membrane partially closing external orifice of virgin's vagina.

**hymenopterous** /haɪmə'nɒptərəs/ *a.* of order of insects including wasp and ant etc., with 4 membranous wings.

**hymn** /hɪm/ 1 *n.* song of praise esp. to God. 2 *v.t.* praise or celebrate in hymns.

**hymnal** /'hɪmn(ə)l/ *n.* book of hymns.

**hymnology** /hɪm'nɒlədʒɪ:/ *n.* composition or study of hymns. **hymnologist** *n.*

**hyoscine** /'haɪəsi:n/ *n.* alkaloid used as sedative etc.

**hyper-** /haɪpə(r)/ *in comb.* over-; excessive.

**hyperbola** /haɪ'pɜ:bələ/ *n.* curve produced when cone is cut by plane making larger angle with base than side of cone makes. **hyperbolic** /-'bɒl-/ *a.*

**hyperbole** /haɪ'pɜ:bəlɪ:/ *n.* statement exaggerated for effect. **hyperbolical** /-'bɒl-/ *a.*

**hypercritical** /haɪpə'krɪtɪk(ə)l/ *a.* too critical.

**hypermarket** /'haɪpəmɑ:kət/ *n. UK* & *US* very large self-service store.

**hypersensitive** /haɪpə'sensətɪv/ *a.* abnormally or excessively sensitive.

**hypersonic** /haɪpə'sɒnɪk/ *a.* of speeds more than 5 times that of sound.

**hypertension** /haɪpə'tenʃ(ə)n/ *n.* abnormally high blood-pressure; extreme tension.

**hypertrophy** /haɪ'pɜ:trəfɪ:/ *n.* enlargement (*of* organ) due to excessive nutrition. **hypertrophic** /-'trɒf-/ *a.*

**hyphen** /'haɪf(ə)n/ 1 *n.* sign (-) used to join or divide words. 2 *v.t.* hyphenate.

**hyphenate** /'haɪfəneɪt/ *v.t.* join or divide with hyphen.

**hypnosis** /hɪp'nəʊsəs/ *n. (pl.* **-noses** /-'nəʊsi:z/) state like sleep in which subject acts only on external suggestion; artificially induced sleep.

**hypnotic** /hɪp'nɒtɪk/ 1 *a.* of or causing hypnosis. 2 *n.* hypnotic drug or influence.

**hypnotism** /'hɪpnətɪz(ə)m/ *n.* production or process of hypnosis. **hypnotist** *n.*

**hypnotize** /ˈhɪpnətaɪz/ v.t. produce hypnosis in; fascinate.

**hypo** /ˈhaɪpəʊ/ n. Photog. sodium thiosulphate, used in fixing.

**hypocaust** /ˈhaɪpəkɔːst/ n. Rom. ant. hot-air channel under floor for heating house.

**hypochondria** /haɪpəˈkɒndrɪə/ n. abnormal anxiety about one's health.

**hypochondriac** /haɪpəˈkɒndrɪæk/ 1 n. person suffering from hypochondria. 2 a. of hypochondria.

**hypocrisy** /hɪˈpɒkrəsi/ n. simulation of virtue; insincerity.

**hypocrite** /ˈhɪpəkrɪt/ n. person guilty of hypocrisy. **hypocritical** a.

**hypodermic** /haɪpəˈdɜːmɪk/ 1 a. (of drug) introduced under the skin. 2 n. hypodermic injection or syringe. 3 **hypodermic syringe** syringe with hollow needle for injecting under the skin.

**hypostasis** /haɪˈpɒstəsəs/ n. (pl. **-ses** /-siːz/) Metaphys. underlying substance; Theol. any one of the three Persons of the Trinity. **hypostatic** a.

**hypotenuse** /haɪˈpɒtənjuːz/ n. side opposite right angle of right-angled triangle.

**hypothermia** /haɪpəˈθɜːmɪə/ n. Med. condition of having abnormally low body temperature.

**hypothesis** /haɪˈpɒθəsəs/ n. (pl. **-ses** /-siːz/) supposition made as basis for reasoning etc.

**hypothetical** /haɪpəˈθetɪk(ə)l/ a. of or resting on hypothesis.

**hyssop** /ˈhɪsəp/ n. small bushy aromatic herb.

**hysterectomy** /hɪstəˈrektəmi/ n. surgical removal of womb. **hysterectomize** v.t.

**hysteria** /hɪˈstɪərɪə/ n. uncontrollable emotion or excitement; functional disturbance of nervous system.

**hysteric** /hɪˈsterɪk/ n. hysterical person. in pl. fit of hysteria.

**hysterical** /hɪˈsterɪk(ə)l/ a. of or caused by hysteria; suffering from hysteria; colloq. extremely funny.

**Hz** abbr. hertz.

# I

**I¹, i**, Roman numeral 1.

**I²** /aɪ/ *pron.* (obj. **me**, poss. **my**) *pron.* of 1st person *sing*.

**I.** *abbr.* Island(s); Isle(s).

**IATA** *abbr.* International Air Transport Association.

**ibex** /'aɪbeks/ *n.* wild goat of Alps etc. with large backward-curving horns.

**ibid.** *abbr.* in same book or passage etc. (*ibidem*).

**ibis** /'aɪbɪs/ *n.* storklike bird with long curved bill.

**ICBM** *abbr.* intercontinental ballistic missile.

**ice 1** *n.* frozen water; portion of ice-cream etc. **2** *v.t.* become covered (as) with ice; freeze; cool with ice; cover with icing. **3 ice age** glacial period; **icebox** US refrigerator; **ice-breaker** boat with reinforced bow for breaking channel through ice; **ice-cap** mass of thick ice covering polar region etc.; **ice-cream** sweet creamy frozen food; **ice-field** extensive sheet of floating ice.

**iceberg** /'aɪsbɜːg/ *n.* mass of floating ice at sea; *Aus. sl.* person who swims regularly in winter.

**ichneumon** /ɪk'njuːmən/ *n.* mongoose of N. Africa etc. **ichneumon-fly** kind of insect parasitic on other insects.

**ichthyology** /ɪkθɪ'ɒlədʒɪ/ *n.* study of fishes. **ichthyological** *a.*; **ichthyologist** *n.*

**icicle** /'aɪsɪk(ə)l/ *n.* tapering hanging spike of ice.

**icing** /'aɪsɪŋ/ *n.* sugar etc. coating for cake etc.; formation of ice on aircraft. **icing sugar** finely powdered sugar.

**icon** /'aɪkɒn/ *n.* sacred painting or mosaic etc.

**iconoclast** /aɪ'kɒnəklæst/ *n.* person who assails cherished beliefs; breaker of images. **iconoclasm** *n.*; **iconoclastic** *a.*

**iconography** /aɪkə'nɒgrəfɪ/ *n.* illustration of subject by drawings etc.; study of portraits esp. of one person.

**ictus** /'ɪktəs/ *n.* rhythmical or metrical stress.

**icy** /'aɪsɪ/ *a.* very cold; covered with or abounding in ice; (of manner) unfriendly.

**id** *n.* *Psych.* part of mind comprising instinctive impulses of individual etc.

**idea** /aɪ'dɪə/ *n.* thing conceived by mind; vague belief, fancy; plan, intention, aim.

**ideal** /aɪ'dɪəl/ **1** *a.* perfect; existing only in idea; visionary. **2** *n.* perfect type; actual thing as standard for imitation.

**idealism** /aɪ'dɪəlɪz(ə)m/ *n.* forming or pursuing ideals; representation of things in ideal form; philosophy in which object of external perception is held to consist of ideas. **idealist** *n.*; **idealistic** *a.*

**idealize** /aɪ'dɪəlaɪz/ *v.t.* make or treat as ideal. **idealization** *n.*

**identical** /aɪ'dentɪk(ə)l/ *a.* same; agreeing in all details (with); (of twins) developed from single fertilized ovum and very similar in appearance.

**identify** /aɪ'dentɪfaɪ/ *v.* establish identity of; treat as identical; associate *with*; regard oneself as sharing characteristics *with*.

**identity** /aɪ'dentɪtɪ/ *n.* being specified person or thing; absolute sameness; individuality; *Aus.* old identity.

**ideograph** /'ɪdɪəgrɑːf/ *n.* character in pictorial writing indicating idea, not name, of thing.

**ideology** /aɪdɪ'ɒlədʒɪ/ *n.* scheme of ideas at basis of political etc. theory or system; characteristic way of thinking. **ideological** *a.*

**idiocy** /'ɪdɪəsɪ/ *n.* mental condition of idiot; utter foolishness.

**idiom** /'ɪdɪəm/ *n.* form of expression peculiar to language; language; characteristic mode of expression. **idiomatic** /-'mæt-/ *a.*

**idiosyncrasy** /ɪdɪəʊ'sɪŋkrəsɪ/ *n.* attitude or form of behaviour peculiar to person. **idiosyncratic** /-'kræt-/ *a.*

**idiot** /'ɪdɪət/ *n.* person too deficient in mind to be capable of rational conduct; *colloq.* stupid person. **idiotic** /-'ɒt-/*a.*

**idle** /'aɪd(ə)l/ **1** *a.* lazy, indolent, unoccupied; useless, purposeless. **2** *v.* be idle; pass (time) thus; (of engine) run slowly without doing any work. **3 idler** *n.*; **idly** *adv.*

**idol** /'aɪd(ə)l/ *n.* image as object of worship; object of devotion.

**idolater** /aɪ'dɒlətə(r)/ *n.* worshipper of idols; devout admirer. **idolatrous** *a.*; **idolatry** *n.*

**idolize** /'aɪdəlaɪz/ v.t. venerate or love to excess; treat as idol. **idolization** n.

**idyll** /'ɪdəl/ n. account of picturesque scene or incident etc.; such scene etc. **idyllic** a.

**i.e.** abbr. that is to say (id est).

**if** conj. on condition or supposition that; whenever; whether.

**igloo** /'ɪgluː/ n. Eskimo dome-shaped snow house.

**igneous** /'ɪgnɪəs/ a. produced by volcanic action; of fire.

**ignite** /ɪg'naɪt/ v. set fire to; catch fire.

**ignition** /ɪg'nɪʃ(ə)n/ n. igniting; mechanism for starting combustion in cylinder of motor engine.

**ignoble** /ɪg'nəʊb(ə)l/ a. mean, base; of low birth or position.

**ignominious** /ɪgnə'mɪnɪəs/ a. humiliating.

**ignominy** /'ɪgnəmɪnɪ/ n. dishonour, infamy.

**ignoramus** /ɪgnə'reɪməs/ a. ignorant person.

**ignorant** /'ɪgnərənt/ a. lacking knowledge; uninformed (of). **ignorance** n.

**ignore** /ɪg'nɔː(r)/ 1 v.t. refuse to take notice of. 2 n. Aus. sl. disregard.

**iguana** /ɪg'wɑːnə/ n. large S. Amer. tree lizard.

**iguanodon** /ɪg'wɑːnəd(ə)n/ n. large herbivorous dinosaur.

**ikebana** /ɪkɪ'bɑːnə/ n. Japanese art of flower-arrangement.

**ikon** var. of **icon**.

**ilex** /'aɪleks/ n. evergreen oak; Bot. plant of genus including holly.

**iliac** /'ɪlɪæk/ a. of flank or hip-bone.

**ilk** 1 a. Sc. same. 2 n. colloq. kind, sort. 3 **of that ilk** of ancestral estate of same name.

**ill** 1 a. in bad health, sick; harmful, unfavourable; faulty, deficient. 2 adv. badly, unfavourably; scarcely. 3 n. evil; harm; in pl. misfortunes. 4 **ill-advised** unwise; **ill-bred** rude; **ill-favoured** unattractive; **ill-gotten** gained by evil means; **ill-starred** unlucky; **ill-tempered** morose, irritable; **ill-timed** done or occurring at unsuitable time; **ill-treat, -use**, treat badly.

**illegal** /ɪ'liːg(ə)l/ a. contrary to law. **illegality** /-'gæl-/ n.

**illegible** /ɪ'ledʒəb(ə)l/ a. not legible, unreadable. **illegibility** /-'bɪl-/ n.

**illegitimate** /ɪlə'dʒɪtəmət/ a. (of child) born of parents not married to each other; not authorized by law; improper. **illegitimacy** n.

**illiberal** /ɪ'lɪbər(ə)l/ a. narrow-minded; sordid; stingy. **illiberality** n.

**illicit** /ɪ'lɪsət/ a. unlawful; forbidden.

**illiterate** /ɪ'lɪtərət/ a. unable to read; uneducated. 2 n. illiterate person. 3 **illiteracy** n.

**illness** /'ɪlnəs/ n. ill health; disease.

**illogical** /ɪ'lɒdʒɪk(ə)l/ a. devoid of or contrary to logic. **illogicality** n.

**illuminant** /ɪ'luːmɪnənt/ 1 n. means of illumination. 2 a. serving to illuminate.

**illuminate** /ɪ'luːmɪneɪt/ v.t. light up; enlighten; help to explain; decorate with lights as sign of festivity; decorate (manuscript etc.) with gold etc. **illumination** n.; **illuminative** a.; **illuminator** n.

**illumine** /ɪ'luːmɪn/ v.t. light up; enlighten.

**illusion** /ɪ'luːʒ(ə)n/ n. false belief; deceptive appearance. **illusive** a.; **illusory** a.

**illusionist** /ɪ'luːʒənɪst/ n. producer of illusions, conjuror.

**illustrate** /'ɪləstreɪt/ v.t. provide with pictures; make clear, esp. by examples or drawings; serve as example of. **illustrator** n.

**illustration** /ɪlə'streɪʃ(ə)n/ n. illustrating; drawing etc. in book; explanatory example.

**illustrative** /'ɪləstrətɪv/ a. explanatory (of).

**illustrious** /ɪ'lʌstrɪəs/ a. distinguished, renowned.

**illywhacker** /'ɪlɪwækə(r)/ n. Aus. sl. professional trickster.

**image** /'ɪmɪdʒ/ 1 n. imitation of object's external form, esp. figure of saint or divinity, idol; reputation, general impression of person or thing; simile, metaphor; mental representation; optical appearance produced by rays of light reflected from mirror or refracted through transparent medium; idea, conception. 2 v.t. make image of; mirror; picture.

**imagery** /'ɪmədʒərɪ/ n. figurative illustration; use of images in literature etc.; images, statuary.

**imaginary** /ɪ'mædʒənərɪ/ a. existing only in imagination.

**imagination** /ɪmædʒə'neɪʃ(ə)n/ n.

mental faculty forming images of objects not present to senses; creative faculty of mind.

**imaginative** /ɪˈmædʒənətɪv/ *a.* having or showing high degree of imagination.

**imagine** /ɪˈmædʒɪn/ *v.t.* form mental image of, conceive; *colloq.* suppose, think.

**imago** /ɪˈmeɪɡəʊ/ *n.* (*pl.* **-gines** /-dʒəniːz/) fully-developed stage of insect.

**imam** /ɪˈmɑːm/ *n.* prayer-leader of mosque; title of some Muslim leaders.

**imbalance** /ɪmˈbæləns/ *n.* lack of balance; disproportion.

**imbecile** /ˈɪmbəsiːl/ 1 *n.* person of abnormally weak intellect; *colloq.* stupid person. 2 *a.* mentally weak; *colloq.* stupid. 3 **imbecilic** *a.*; **imbecility** *n.*

**imbed** var. of **embed**.

**imbibe** /ɪmˈbaɪb/ *v.t.* drink in; drink; inhale; absorb.

**imbroglio** /ɪmˈbrəʊlɪəʊ/ *n.* (*pl.* **-os**) confused or complicated situation.

**imbue** /ɪmˈbjuː/ *v.t.* inspire; saturate; dye.

**imitable** /ˈɪmətəb(ə)l/ *a.* that can be imitated. **imitability** *n.*

**imitate** /ˈɪməteɪt/ *v.t.* follow example of; mimic; be like. **imitative** *a.*; **imitator** *n.*

**imitation** /ɪməˈteɪʃ(ə)n/ *n.* imitating; copy; counterfeit.

**immaculate** /ɪˈmækjələt/ *a.* pure, spotless; faultless.

**immanent** /ˈɪmənənt/ *a.* inherent; (of God) pervading universe. **immanence** *n.*

**immaterial** /ɪməˈtɪərɪəl/ *a.* not material; unimportant; irrelevant. **immateriality** *n.*

**immature** /ɪməˈtjʊə(r)/ *a.* not mature. **immaturity** *n.*

**immeasurable** /ɪˈmeʒərəb(ə)l/ *a.* not measurable, immense.

**immediate** /ɪˈmiːdɪət/ *a.* occurring at once; without intervening medium, direct; nearest. **immediacy** *n.*

**immemorial** /ɪməˈmɔːrɪəl/ *a.* ancient beyond memory.

**immense** /ɪˈmens/ *a.* vast, huge. **immensity** *n.*

**immensely** /ɪˈmenslɪ/ *adv.* vastly, very much.

**immerse** /ɪˈmɜːs/ *v.t.* dip, plunge; put under water; involve deeply, embed. **immersible** *a.*

**immersion** /ɪˈmɜːʃ(ə)n/ *n.* immersing or being immersed. **immersion heater** electric heater designed to be immersed in liquid to be heated.

**immigrant** /ˈɪməɡrənt/ 1 *n.* person who immigrates. 2 *a.* immigrating; of immigrants.

**immigrate** /ˈɪməɡreɪt/ *v.t.* come as permanent resident (*into* country). **immigration** *n.*

**imminent** /ˈɪmənənt/ *a.* soon to happen. **imminence** *n.*

**immobile** /ɪˈməʊbaɪl/ *a.* immovable; motionless. **immobility** *n.*

**immobilize** /ɪˈməʊbəlaɪz/ *v.t.* prevent from being moved.

**immoderate** /ɪˈmɒdərət/ *a.* excessive.

**immodest** /ɪˈmɒdəst/ *a.* indecent; impudent; conceited. **immodesty** *n.*

**immolate** /ˈɪməleɪt/ *v.t.* kill as sacrifice. **immolation** *n.*

**immoral** /ɪˈmɒr(ə)l/ *a.* not conforming to, or opposed to, (esp. sexual) morality; dissolute, **immorality** *n.*

**immortal** /ɪˈmɔːt(ə)l/ 1 *a.* living for ever; famous for all time. 2 *n.* immortal being, esp. (in *pl.*) gods of antiquity. 3 **immortality** *n.*; **immortalize** *v.t.*

**immovable** /ɪˈmuːvəb(ə)l/ *a.* not movable; unyielding. **immovability** *n.*

**immune** /ɪˈmjuːn/ *a.* having immunity, exempt.

**immunity** /ɪˈmjuːnətɪ/ *n.* living organism's power of resisting and overcoming infection; freedom or exemption (*from*).

**immunize** /ˈɪmjənaɪz/ *v.t.* make immune (*against*). **immunization** *n.*

**immure** /ɪˈmjʊə(r)/ *v.t.* imprison, shut in.

**immutable** /ɪˈmjuːtəb(ə)l/ *a.* unchangeable. **immutability** *n.*

**imp** *n.* little devil; mischievous child.

**impact** 1 /ˈɪmpækt/ *n.* collision, striking; (immediate) effect or influence. 2 /ɪmˈpækt/ *v.t.* drive or wedge together, in *p.p.* (of tooth) wedged between another tooth and jaw. 3 **impaction** *n.*

**impair** /ɪmˈpeə(r)/ *v.t.* damage, weaken. **impairment** *n.*

**impala** /ɪmˈpɑːlə/ *n.* small S. Afr. antelope.

**impale** /ɪmˈpeɪl/ *v.t.* transfix on stake. **impalement** *n.*

**impalpable** /ɪmˈpælpəb(ə)l/ *a.* imperceptible to touch; not easily grasped.

**impart** /ɪmˈpɑːt/ *v.t.* give share of; communicate (to).

**impartial** /ɪmˈpɑːʃ(ə)l/ *a.* fair, not partial. **impartiality** /-ʃɪˈæl-/ *n.*

**impassable** /ɪmˈpɑːsəb(ə)l/ *a.* that cannot be traversed. **impassability** *n.*

**impasse** /ˈæmpɑːs/ *n.* deadlock.

**impassible** /ɪmˈpæsəb(ə)l/ *a.* not subject to suffering; impassive. **impassibility** *n.*

**impassioned** /ɪmˈpæʃ(ə)nd/ *a.* deeply moved; ardent.

**impassive** /ɪmˈpæsɪv/ *a.* not feeling or showing emotion. **impassivity** *n.*

**impasto** /ɪmˈpæstəʊ/ *n.* laying on of paint thickly.

**impatient** /ɪmˈpeɪʃ(ə)nt/ *a.* not patient; intolerant; eager. **impatience** *n.*

**impeach** /ɪmˈpiːtʃ/ *v.t.* accuse, esp. of treason etc.; call in question; disparage. **impeachment** *n.*

**impeccable** /ɪmˈpekəb(ə)l/ *a.* faultless; not liable to sin. **impeccability** *n.*

**impecunious** /ɪmpɪˈkjuːnɪəs/ *a.* having little or no money. **impecuniosity** *n.*

**impedance** /ɪmˈpiːd(ə)ns/ *n.* total effective resistance of electric circuit etc. to alternating current.

**impede** /ɪmˈpiːd/ *v.t.* retard; hinder.

**impediment** /ɪmˈpedəmənt/ *n.* hindrance; defect in speech, esp. lisp or stammer.

**impedimenta** /ɪmpedəˈmentə/ *n.pl.* baggage esp. of army.

**impel** /ɪmˈpel/ *v.t.* drive, force; propel.

**impend** /ɪmˈpend/ *v.i.* be imminent; hang (over).

**impenetrable** /ɪmˈpenətrəb(ə)l/ *a.* not penetrable; inscrutable; impervious. **impenetrability** *n.*

**impenitent** /ɪmˈpenɪt(ə)nt/ *a.* not penitent. **impenitence** *n.*

**imperative** /ɪmˈperətɪv/ **1** *a.* urgent, obligatory; *Gram.* of mood expressing command; peremptory. **2** *n.* imperative mood.

**imperceptible** /ɪmpəˈseptəb(ə)l/ *a.* not perceptible; very slight or gradual.

**imperfect** /ɪmˈpɜːfəkt/ **1** *a.* not perfect; incomplete; faulty; *Gram.* of tense implying action going on but not completed. **2** *n.* imperfect tense.

**imperfection** /ɪmpəˈfekʃ(ə)n/ *n.* imperfectness; fault, blemish.

**imperial** /ɪmˈpɪərɪəl/ *a.* of empire or sovereign State ranking with this; of emperor; majestic; (of weights and measures) used by statute in UK.

**imperialism** /ɪmˈpɪərɪəlɪz(ə)m/ *n.* imperial system of government etc.; extension of country's power by acquisition of dependencies or (usu. *derog.*) through trade etc. **imperialist** *a.* & *n.*

**imperil** /ɪmˈperəl/ *v.t.* endanger.

**imperious** /ɪmˈpɪərɪəs/ *a.* domineering; urgent.

**imperishable** /ɪmˈperɪʃəb(ə)l/ *a.* that cannot perish.

**impermanent** /ɪmˈpɜːmənənt/ *a.* not permanent. **impermanence** *n.*

**impermeable** /ɪmˈpɜːmɪəb(ə)l/ *a.* not permeable. **impermeability** *n.*

**impersonal** /ɪmˈpɜːsən(ə)l/ *a.* having no personality or personal feeling or reference; *Gram.* (of verb) used only in 3rd person *sing.* **impersonality** *n.*

**impersonate** /ɪmˈpɜːsəneɪt/ *v.* pretend to be, play part of. **impersonation** *n.*; **impersonator** *n.*

**impertinent** /ɪmˈpɜːtənənt/ *a.* insolent, saucy; irrelevant. **impertinence** *n.*

**imperturbable** /ɪmpəˈtɜːbəb(ə)l/ *a.* not excitable; calm. **imperturbability** *n.*

**impervious** /ɪmˈpɜːvɪəs/ *a.* impenetrable, inaccessible (to).

**impetigo** /ɪmpəˈtaɪɡəʊ/ *n.* contagious skin disease.

**impetuous** /ɪmˈpetjʊəs/ *a.* acting rashly; moving violently or fast. **impetuosity** /-ˈɒs-/ *n.*

**impetus** /ˈɪmpətəs/ *n.* moving force; momentum; impulse.

**impiety** /ɪmˈpaɪətɪ/ *n.* lack of piety.

**impinge** /ɪmˈpɪndʒ/ *v.i.* make impact (*on*); encroach *upon*.

**impious** /ˈɪmpɪəs/ *a.* not pious; wicked.

**impish** /ˈɪmpɪʃ/ *a.* of or like imp, mischievous.

**implacable** /ɪmˈplækəb(ə)l/ *a.* not appeasable. **implacability** *n.*

**implant 1** /ɪmˈplɑːnt/ or ɪmˈplænt/ *v.t.* insert, fix; instil; plant. **2** /ˈɪmplɑːnt/ or ˈɪmplænt/ *n.* thing implanted. **3 implantation** *n.*

**implement 1** /ˈɪmpləmənt/ *n.* tool,

utensil. 2 /'ɪmpləment/ v.t. carry into effect. 3 **implementation** n.
**implicate** /'ɪmplɪkeɪt/ v.t. include; involve; imply. **implication** n.
**implicit** /ɪm'plɪsɪt/ a. implied though not expressed; unquestioning.
**implode** /ɪm'pləʊd/ v. (cause to) burst inwards. **implosion** n.
**implore** /ɪm'plɔː(r)/ v.t. beg earnestly.
**imply** /ɪm'plaɪ/ v.t. mean; involve truth of; insinuate, hint.
**impolite** /ɪmpə'laɪt/ a. uncivil, rude.
**impolitic** /ɪm'pɒlɪtɪk/ a. not politic, not advisable.
**imponderable** /ɪm'pɒndərəb(ə)l/ 1 a. that cannot be estimated; very light. 2 n. imponderable thing.
**import** 1 /ɪm'pɔːt/ v.t. bring in (esp. foreign goods) from abroad; imply, mean. 2 /'ɪmpɔːt/ n. article or (in pl.) amount imported; meaning, implication; importance. 3 **importation** n.
**important** /ɪm'pɔːt(ə)nt/ a. of great consequence; momentous; (of person) having position of authority or rank; pompous. **importance** n.
**importunate** /ɪm'pɔːtjʊnət/ a. making persistent or pressing requests. **importunity** /-'tjuːn-/ n.
**importune** /ɪm'pɔːtjuːn/ v.t. solicit pressingly; solicit for immoral purpose.
**impose** /ɪm'pəʊz/ v. lay (tax etc.) on; enforce compliance with; palm off (on). **impose (up)on** take advantage of, deceive, impress, overawe.
**imposing** /ɪm'pəʊzɪŋ/ a. impressive, esp. in appearance.
**imposition** /ɪmpə'zɪʃ(ə)n/ n. unfair demand or burden; tax, duty; work set as punishment at school; laying on (of hands in blessing etc.).
**impossible** /ɪm'pɒsəb(ə)l/ a. not possible; not easy or convenient; colloq. outrageous, intolerable. **impossibility** n.
**impost** /'ɪmpəʊst/ n. tax, duty.
**impostor** /ɪm'pɒstə(r)/ n. person who assumes false character; swindler.
**imposture** /ɪm'pɒstʃə(r)/ n. fraudulent deception.
**impotent** /'ɪmpət(ə)nt/ a. powerless; decrepit; (of male) unable to achieve sexual intercourse. **impotence** n.
**impound** /ɪm'paʊnd/ v.t. confiscate; shut up in pound.

**impoverish** /ɪm'pɒvərɪʃ/ v.t. make poor. **impoverishment** n.
**impracticable** /ɪm'præktɪkəb(ə)l/ a. impossible in practice. **impracticability** n.
**impractical** /ɪm'præktɪk(ə)l/ a. not practical; not practicable. **impracticality** n.
**imprecation** /ɪmprə'keɪʃ(ə)n/ n. cursing; curse. **imprecatory** a.
**impregnable** /ɪm'pregnəb(ə)l/ a. safe against attack. **impregnability** n.
**impregnate** /ɪm'pregneɪt/ v.t. fill, saturate; make pregnant. **impregnation** n.
**impresario** /ɪmprə'sɑːrɪəʊ/ n. (pl. -os) organizer of public entertainments.
**impress**[1] 1 /ɪm'pres/ v.t. affect or influence deeply; enforce, fix; imprint, stamp. 2 /'ɪmpres/ n. mark impressed; characteristic quality. 3 **impressible** a.
**impress**[2] /ɪm'pres/ v.t. hist. force to serve in army or navy. **impressment** n.
**impression** /ɪm'preʃ(ə)n/ n. effect produced on mind; belief; imitation of person or sound, done to entertain; impressing, mark impressed; unaltered reprint of book etc.; issue of book or newspaper etc.; print from type or engraving.
**impressionable** /ɪm'preʃənəb(ə)l/ a. easily influenced.
**impressionism** /ɪm'preʃənɪz(ə)m/ n. method of painting or writing so as to give general effect without detail. **impressionist** n.; **impressionistic** a.
**impressive** /ɪm'presɪv/ a. able to excite deep feeling esp. of approval or admiration.
**imprimatur** /ɪmprə'meɪtə(r)/ n. licence to print.
**imprint** 1 /ɪm'prɪnt/ v.t. impress mark on. 2 /'ɪmprɪnt/ n. impression; printer's or publisher's name in book etc.
**imprison** /ɪm'prɪz(ə)n/ v.t. put into prison; confine. **imprisonment** n.
**improbable** /ɪm'prɒbəb(ə)l/ a. not likely. **improbability** n.
**improbity** /ɪm'prəʊbətɪ/ n. wickedness.
**impromptu** /ɪm'prɒmptjuː/ 1 adv. & a. unrehearsed. 2 n. impromptu mu-

**improper** /ɪmˈprɒpə(r)/ *a.* unseemly, indecent; inaccurate, wrong.

**impropriety** /ɪmprəˈpraɪəti/ *n.* incorrectness, unfitness; indecency.

**improve** /ɪmˈpruːv/ *v.* make or become better; make good use of (occasion, opportunity). **improvement** *n.*

**improvident** /ɪmˈprɒvɪd(ə)nt/ *a.* heedless, thriftless. **improvidence** *n.*

**improvise** /ˈɪmprəvaɪz/ *v.t.* compose extempore; use or construct from materials etc. not intended for the purpose. **improvisation** *n.*

**imprudent** /ɪmˈpruːd(ə)nt/ *a.* rash, indiscreet. **imprudence** *n.*

**impudent** /ˈɪmpjəd(ə)nt/ *a.* impertinent; insolent. **impudence** *n.*

**impugn** /ɪmˈpjuːn/ *v.t.* challenge; call in question.

**impulse** /ˈɪmpʌls/ *n.* impelling; impetus; sudden tendency to act without reflection.

**impulsive** /ɪmˈpʌlsɪv/ *a.* apt to be moved or prompted by impulse.

**impunity** /ɪmˈpjuːnəti/ *n.* exemption from punishment or injurious consequences.

**impure** /ɪmˈpjʊə(r)/ *a.* adulterated, mixed; dirty; unchaste. **impurity** *n.*

**impute** /ɪmˈpjuːt/ *v.t.* ascribe (*to*); ascribe. **imputation** *n.*

**in** 1 *prep.* expr. inclusion or position within limits of space or time or circumstance etc. 2 *adv.* expr. position bounded by certain limits, or movement to point enclosed by them; into room etc.; at home etc.; in fashion or season or office; (of player etc.) having turn or right to play; (of fire etc.) burning. 3 *a.* internal, living etc. inside; fashionable. 4 **inasmuch as** because; **ins and outs** details; **in so far as** to the extent that; **insomuch** to such an extent; **in-tray** tray for incoming documents etc.

**in.** *abbr.* inch(es).

**inability** /ɪnəˈbɪləti/ *n.* being unable.

**inaccessible** /ɪnækˈsesəb(ə)l/ *a.* not accessible; unapproachable. **inaccessibility** *n.*

**inaccurate** /ɪnˈækjərət/ *a.* not accurate. **inaccuracy** *n.*

**inaction** /ɪnˈækʃ(ə)n/ *n.* absence of action; sluggishness. **inactive** *a.*; **inactivity** *n.*

**inadequate** /ɪnˈædəkwət/ *a.* insufficient; incompetent. **inadequacy** *n.*

**inadmissible** /ɪnədˈmɪsəb(ə)l/ *a.* not allowable. **inadmissibility** *n.*

**inadvertent** /ɪnədˈvɜːt(ə)nt/ *a.* unintentional; inattentive. **inadvertence** *n.*; **inadvertency** *n.*

**inalienable** /ɪnˈeɪliːənəb(ə)l/ *a.* not transferable to another owner.

**inane** /ɪˈneɪn/ *a.* silly, senseless; empty. **inanity** /-ˈnæn-/ *n.*

**inanimate** /ɪnˈænəmət/ *a.* not endowed with life; spiritless, dull.

**inanition** /ɪnəˈnɪʃ(ə)n/ *n.* exhaustion from lack of nourishment.

**inapplicable** /ɪnˈæplɪkəb(ə)l/ *a.* irrelevant; unsuitable. **inapplicability** *n.*

**inapposite** /ɪnˈæpəzət/ *a.* not apposite.

**inappropriate** /ɪnəˈprəʊpriːət/ *a.* not appropriate.

**inapt** /ɪnˈæpt/ *a.* not suitable; unskilful. **inaptitude** *n.*

**inarticulate** /ɪnɑːˈtɪkjələt/ *a.* unable to express oneself clearly; not articulate, indistinct; dumb; not jointed.

**inartistic** /ɪnɑːˈtɪstɪk/ *a.* not following principles of or unskilled in art.

**inattention** /ɪnəˈtenʃ(ə)n/ *n.* lack of attention; negligence. **inattentive** *a.*

**inaudible** /ɪnˈnɔːdəb(ə)l/ *a.* that cannot be heard. **inaudibility** *n.*

**inaugural** /ɪnˈnɔːgjər(ə)l/ 1 *a.* of inauguration. 2 *n.* inaugural speech or lecture.

**inaugurate** /ɪnˈnɔːgjəreɪt/ *v.t.* admit (person) to office; initiate or begin or introduce with ceremony. **inauguration** *n.*

**inauspicious** /ɪnɔːˈspɪʃəs/ *a.* not of good omen; unlucky.

**inborn** /ˈɪnbɔːn/ *a.* inherent by nature.

**inbred** /ɪnˈbred/ *a.* inborn; produced by inbreeding.

**inbreeding** /ɪnˈbriːdɪŋ/ *n.* breeding from closely related animals or persons.

**Inc.** *abbr.* Incorporated.

**incalculable** /ɪnˈkælkjələb(ə)l/ *a.* too great for calculation; uncertain. **incalculability** *n.*

**incandesce** /ɪnkænˈdes/ *v.* (cause to) glow with heat.

**incandescent** /ɪnkænˈdes(ə)nt/ *a.* glowing with heat, shining; (of artificial

**incantation** /mkæn'teɪʃ(ə)n/ n. spell, charm.

**incapable** /ɪn'keɪpəb(ə)l/ a. not capable; not capable of rational conduct. **incapability** n.

**incapacitate** /ɪnkə'pæsɪteɪt/ v.t. make incapable or unfit.

**incapacity** /ɪnkə'pæsɪti:/ n. inability; legal disqualification.

**incarcerate** /ɪn'kɑ:səreɪt/ v.t. imprison. **incarceration** n.

**incarnate** 1 /ɪn'kɑ:nət/ a. embodied in flesh, esp. human form. 2 /ɪn'kɑ:neɪt/ v.t. embody in flesh; be living embodiment of (quality etc.).

**incarnation** /ɪnkɑ:'neɪʃ(ə)n/ n. embodiment in flesh. **the Incarnation** incarnation of God in Christ.

**incautious** /ɪn'kɔ:ʃəs/ a. rash.

**incendiary** /ɪn'sendjəri:/ 1 a. (of bomb) filled with material for causing fires; inflammatory; guilty of arson. 2 n. incendiary person or bomb.

**incense**[1] /'ɪnsens/ n. gum or spice giving sweet smell when burned; smoke of this, esp. in religious ceremonial.

**incense**[2] /ɪn'sens/ v.t. make angry.

**incentive** /ɪn'sentɪv/ 1 n. thing inciting or encouraging to action; inducement, esp. to increase output etc. 2 a. inciting.

**inception** /ɪn'sepʃ(ə)n/ n. beginning.

**incertitude** /ɪn'sɜ:tətju:d/ n. uncertainty.

**incessant** /ɪn'ses(ə)nt/ a. continual; repeated.

**incest** /'ɪnsest/ n. sexual intercourse of near relations. **incestuous** a.

**inch** 1 n. twelfth of (linear) foot, 2.54 cm. 2 v. move gradually.

**inchoate** /'ɪnkəʊət/ a. undeveloped, just begun. **inchoation** n.

**incidence** /'ɪnsɪd(ə)ns/ n. falling on or contact with thing; range, scope, extent; manner or range of occurrence.

**incident** /'ɪnsɪd(ə)nt/ 1 n. event, occurrence; episode. 2 a. apt to occur, naturally attaching (*to*).

**incidental** /ɪnsɪ'dent(ə)l/ a. casual; not essential; (of music) played during or between scenes of play or film etc. **incidentally** *adv.* by the way.

**incinerate** /ɪn'sɪnəreɪt/ v.t. consume by fire. **incineration** n.

**incinerator** /ɪn'sɪnəreɪtə(r)/ n. furnace or device for incineration.

**incipient** /ɪn'sɪpi:ənt/ a. beginning, in early stage.

**incise** /ɪn'saɪz/ v.t. make cut in; engrave. **incision** /-'sɪʒ(ə)n/ n.

**incisive** /ɪn'saɪsɪv/ a. sharp; clear and effective.

**incisor** /ɪn'saɪzə(r)/ n. any of front teeth between canines.

**incite** /ɪn'saɪt/ v.t. urge on, stir up. **incitement** n.

**incivility** /ɪnsɪ'vɪləti:/ n. rudeness.

**inclement** /ɪn'klemənt/ a. (of weather) severe, cold or stormy. **inclemency** n.

**inclination** /ɪnklə'neɪʃ(ə)n/ n. propensity; liking, affection; slope, slant.

**incline** /ɪn'klaɪn/ 1 v. (cause to) lean; bend forward or downward; dispose, be disposed; tend. 2 n. (also /'ɪn-/) slope, inclined plane.

**include** /ɪn'klu:d/ v.t. comprise, regard or treat as part of whole. **inclusion** n.

**inclusive** /ɪn'klu:sɪv/ a. including; comprehensive; including all accessory payments.

**incognito** /ɪnkɒg'ni:təʊ/ 1 adv. under false name; with identity concealed. 2 a. acting incognito. 3 n. (pl. -tos) pretended identity; person who is incognito.

**incoherent** /ɪnkəʊ'hɪərənt/ a. not coherent. **incoherence** n.

**incombustible** /ɪnkəm'bʌstəb(ə)l/ a. that cannot be burnt up. **incombustibility** n.

**income** /'ɪnkʌm/ n. money received, esp. periodically, from work or investments etc. **income tax** tax levied on income.

**incoming** /'ɪnkʌmɪŋ/ a. coming in, succeeding.

**incommensurable** /ɪnkə'menʃərəb(ə)l/ a. not comparable in size or value etc.; having no common measure. **incommensurability** n.

**incommensurate** /ɪnkə'menʃərət/ a. out of proportion; inadequate.

**incommode** /ɪnkə'məʊd/ v.t. trouble, annoy; impede.

**incommodious** /ɪnkə'məʊdɪəs/ a. not affording comfort, inconvenient.

**incommunicable** /ɪnkə'mju:nɪkəb(ə)l/ a. that cannot be shared or told. **incommunicability** n.

**incommunicado** /ɪnkəmju:nə-

'ka:dəʊ/ *a.* without means of communication, in solitary confinement.

**incomparable** /ɪnˈkɒmpərəb(ə)l/ *a.* without an equal.

**incompatible** /ɪnkəmˈpætəb(ə)l/ *a.* opposed; discordant; inconsistent. **incompatibility** *n.*

**incompetent** /ɪnˈkɒmpət(ə)nt/ *a.* not competent; not legally qualified. **incompetence** *n.*

**incomplete** /ɪnkəmˈpli:t/ *a.* not complete.

**incomprehensible** /ɪnkɒmprəˈhensəb(ə)l/ *a.* that cannot be understood. **incomprehensibility** *n.*

**inconceivable** /ɪnkənˈsi:vəb(ə)l/ *a.* that cannot be imagined. **inconceivability** *n.*

**inconclusive** /ɪnkənˈklu:sɪv/ *a.* (of argument etc.) not convincing or decisive.

**incongruous** /ɪnˈkɒŋgru:əs/ *a.* out of keeping; absurd. **incongruity** *n.*

**inconsequent** /ɪnˈkɒnsəkwənt/ *a.* irrelevant, disconnected; not following logically. **inconsequence** *n.*

**inconsequential** /ɪnkɒnsəˈkwenʃ(ə)l/ *a.* unimportant; inconsequent.

**inconsiderable** /ɪnkənˈsɪdərəb(ə)l/ *a.* not worth considering; of small size or value etc.

**inconsiderate** /ɪnkənˈsɪdərət/ *a.* not considerate of others; thoughtless.

**inconsistent** /ɪnkənˈsɪst(ə)nt/ *a.* not consistent; incompatible. **inconsistency** *n.*

**inconsolable** /ɪnkənˈsəʊləb(ə)l/ *a.* that cannot be comforted.

**inconspicuous** /ɪnkənˈspɪkju:əs/ *a.* not readily seen or noticed.

**inconstant** /ɪnˈkɒnst(ə)nt/ *a.* fickle; variable; irregular. **inconstancy** *n.*

**incontestable** /ɪnkənˈtestəb(ə)l/ *a.* that cannot be disputed.

**incontinent** /ɪnˈkɒntɪnənt/ *a.* unable to control excretions voluntarily; lacking self-restraint. **incontinence** *n.*

**incontrovertible** /ɪnkɒntrəˈvɜ:təb(ə)l/ *a.* indisputable.

**inconvenience** /ɪnkənˈvi:ni:əns/ 1 *n.* lack of ease or comfort; instance of this. 2 *v.t.* cause inconvenience to. 3 **inconvenient** *a.*

**incorporate** 1 /ɪnˈkɔ:pəreɪt/ *v.t.* include as part or ingredient; constitute as legal corporation; combine into one substance or whole (*with, in, into*). 2 /ɪnˈkɔ:pərət/ *a.* incorporated. 3 **incorporation** *n.*

**incorporeal** /ɪnkɔ:ˈpɔ:ri:əl/ *a.* without substance or material existence.

**incorrect** /ɪnkəˈrekt/ *a.* untrue, inaccurate.

**incorrigible** /ɪnˈkɒrɪdʒəb(ə)l/ *a.* incurably bad.

**incorruptible** /ɪnkəˈrʌptəb(ə)l/ *a.* that cannot decay or be corrupted. **incorruptibility** *n.*

**increase** 1 /ɪnˈkri:s/ *v.* become or make greater or more numerous; intensify. 2 /ˈɪnkri:s/ *n.* growth, enlargement; increased amount. 3 **on the increase** increasing.

**incredible** /ɪnˈkredəb(ə)l/ *a.* that cannot be believed; *colloq.* surprising. **incredibility** *n.*

**incredulous** /ɪnˈkredjələs/ *a.* unbelieving, showing disbelief. **incredulity** /-ˈdju:l-/ *n.*

**increment** /ˈɪnkrəmənt/ *n.* amount of increase; added amount; profit.

**incriminate** /ɪnˈkrɪmɪneɪt/ *v.t.* indicate as guilty; charge with crime. **incrimination** *n.*; **incriminatory** *a.*

**incrustation** /ɪnkrʌsˈteɪʃ(ə)n/ *n.* encrusting, being encrusted; crust, hard coating.

**incubate** /ˈɪnkjəbeɪt/ *v.* hatch (eggs) by sitting on them or by artificial heat; sit on eggs; cause (bacteria etc.) to develop.

**incubation** /ɪnkjəˈbeɪʃ(ə)n/ *n.* incubating or being incubated; development of disease germs before first symptoms appear.

**incubator** /ˈɪnkjəbeɪtə(r)/ *n.* apparatus for hatching eggs or rearing babies born prematurely or for developing bacteria.

**incubus** /ˈɪnkjəbəs/ *n.* oppressive person or thing; evil spirit believed to visit sleeper; nightmare.

**inculcate** /ˈɪnkʌlkeɪt/ *v.t.* urge, impress persistently (*in* etc.). **inculcation** *n.*

**inculpate** /ˈɪnkʌlpeɪt/ *v.t.* incriminate; accuse, blame. **inculpation** *n.*

**incumbent** /ɪnˈkʌmbənt/ 1 *a.* resting as duty (*up*)*on.* 2 *n.* holder of office, esp. benefice. 3 **incumbency** *n.*

**incunabula** /ɪnkju:ˈnæbjələ/ *n.pl.* early printed books, esp. from before 1501.

**incur** /ɪnˈkɜ:(r)/ *v.t.* bring on oneself.

**incurable** /ɪnˈkjuːrəb(ə)l/ 1 *a.* that cannot be cured. 2 *n.* incurable person. 3 **incurability** *n.*

**incurious** /ɪnˈkjuːriːəs/ *a.* devoid of curiosity. **incuriosity** *n.*

**incursion** /ɪnˈkɜːʃ(ə)n/ *n.* invasion; sudden attack. **incursive** *a.*

**indebted** /ɪnˈdetəd/ *a.* owing money or gratitude (*to*).

**indecent** /ɪnˈdiːs(ə)nt/ *a.* unbecoming; offending against decency; unsuitable. **indecent assault** sexual attack not involving rape. **indecency** *n.*

**indecipherable** /ɪndəˈsaɪfərəb(ə)l/ *a.* that cannot be deciphered.

**indecision** /ɪndəˈsɪʒ(ə)n/ *n.* lack of decision, hesitation.

**indecisive** /ɪndəˈsaɪsɪv/ *a.* not decisive; irresolute.

**indecorous** /ɪnˈdekərəs/ *a.* improper, in bad taste.

**indeed** /ɪnˈdiːd/ *adv.* in truth; really.

**indefatigable** /ɪndəˈfætɪɡəb(ə)l/ *a.* unwearying. **indefatigability** *n.*

**indefeasible** /ɪndəˈfiːzəb(ə)l/ *a.* that cannot be forfeited or annulled. **indefeasibility** *n.*

**indefensible** /ɪndəˈfensəb(ə)l/ *a.* that cannot be defended. **indefensibility** *n.*

**indefinable** /ɪndəˈfaɪnəb(ə)l/ *a.* that cannot be defined or exactly described.

**indefinite** /ɪnˈdefənət/ *a.* vague, undefined.

**indelible** /ɪnˈdeləb(ə)l/ *a.* that cannot be blotted out; permanent. **indelibility** *n.*

**indelicate** /ɪnˈdelɪkət/ *a.* immodest, tactless. **indelicacy** *n.*

**indemnify** /ɪnˈdemnɪfaɪ/ *v.t.* secure against loss or legal responsibility; compensate (*for* loss etc.). **indemnification** *n.*

**indemnity** /ɪnˈdemnəti/ *n.* security against damage or loss; exemption from penalties etc.; compensation for damage.

**indent** 1 /ɪnˈdent/ *v.* make notches, dents, or recesses in; set back (beginning of line) inwards from margin; make requisition or written order *for*. 2 /ˈɪndent/ *n.* official requisition, order; indentation; indenture. 3 **indentation** *n.*

**indenture** /ɪnˈdentʃə(r)/ 1 *n.* (usu. in *pl.*) sealed agreement, esp. binding apprentice to master. 2 *v.t.* bind by indentures.

**independence** /ɪndəˈpend(ə)ns/ *n.* being independent. **Independence Day** US holiday (4 Jul.), anniversary of Declaration of Independence.

**independent** 1 *a.* not depending on authority (*of*); self-governing; not depending on something else for validity or efficiency etc. or on another person for one's livelihood or opinions; (of institution) not supported by public funds; (of income) making it unnecessary for one to earn one's livelihood; unwilling to be under obligation to others. 2 *n.* politician etc. independent of any political party.

**indescribable** /ɪndəˈskraɪbəb(ə)l/ *a.* beyond description; vague. **indescribability** *n.*

**indestructible** /ɪndəˈstrʌktəb(ə)l/ *a.* that cannot be destroyed. **indestructibility** *n.*

**indeterminable** /ɪndəˈtɜːmənəb(ə)l/ *a.* that cannot be ascertained or settled.

**indeterminate** /ɪndəˈtɜːmənət/ *a.* not fixed in extent or character etc.; vague.

**index** /ˈɪndeks/ 1 *n.* (*pl.* **-dexes** or **-dices** /-dɪsiːz/) alphabetical list of subjects etc. with references, usu. at end of book; number expressing prices etc. in terms of a standard value; *Math.* exponent. 2 *v.t.* furnish (book) with index, enter in index. 3 **index finger** forefinger.

**India paper** /ˈɪndiːə/ very thin tough opaque printing-paper.

**Indian** /ˈɪndiːən/ 1 *a.* of India; of the subcontinent comprising India and Pakistan and Bangladesh; of the original inhabitants of America and the W. Indies. 2 *n.* native of India; Red Indian. 3 **Indian club** bottle-shaped club for gymnastic exercises; **Indian corn** maize; **Indian file** single file; **Indian ink** black pigment; **Indian summer** period of calm dry warm weather in late autumn.

**indiarubber** /ɪndiːəˈrʌbə(r)/ *n.* rubber, esp. for rubbing out pencil marks etc.

**indicate** /ˈɪndɪkeɪt/ *v.t.* point out, make known, show; be sign of; require. **indication** *n.*

**indicative** /ɪnˈdɪkətɪv/ 1 *a.* suggestive, giving indications, *of*; *Gram.* of mood stating thing as fact, not conditional

# indicator — induction

or subjunctive. **2** *n. Gram.* indicative mood.

**indicator** /'ɪndəkeɪtə(r)/ *n.* person or thing that indicates; recording instrument on machine etc.; board giving current information; device to show intended turn by vehicle.

**indices** *pl.* of **index**.

**indict** /ɪn'daɪt/ *v.t.* accuse, esp. by legal process. **indictment** *n.*

**indictable** /ɪn'daɪtəb(ə)l/ *a.* rendering person liable to be indicted; so liable.

**indifference** /ɪn'dɪfərəns/ *n.* absence of interest or attention; unimportance.

**indifferent** *a.* showing indifference; neither good nor bad; rather bad.

**indigenous** /ɪn'dɪdʒənəs/ *a.* native or belonging naturally (*to* soil etc.).

**indigent** /'ɪndɪdʒ(ə)nt/ *a.* needy, poor. **indigence** *n.*

**indigestible** /ɪndə'dʒestəb(ə)l/ *a.* difficult or impossible to digest.

**indignant** /ɪn'dɪgnənt/ *a.* moved by anger and scorn or sense of injury. **indignation** *n.*

**indignity** /ɪn'dɪgnəti/ *n.* humiliating treatment, insult, slight.

**indigo** /'ɪndɪgəʊ/ *n.* (*pl.* **-gos**) deep violet-blue; dye of this colour.

**indirect** /ɪndə'rekt/ *a.* not direct. **indirect object** *Gram.* person or thing affected by action of verb but not acted on; **indirect speech** reported speech; **indirect tax** tax paid as price increase for taxed goods.

**indiscernible** /ɪndə'sɜːnəb(ə)l/ *a.* that cannot be discerned.

**indiscipline** /ɪn'dɪsəplən/ *n.* lack of discipline.

**indiscreet** /ɪndə'skriːt/ *a.* revealing secrets; injudicious, unwary.

**indiscretion** /ɪndə'skreʃ(ə)n/ *n.* indiscreet conduct or action.

**indiscriminate** /ɪndə'skrɪmɪnət/ *a.* confused; undiscriminating. **indiscrimination** *n.*

**indispensable** /ɪndə'spensəb(ə)l/ *a.* that cannot be dispensed with; necessary. **indispensability** *n.*

**indispose** /ɪndə'spəʊz/ *v.t.* make unfit or unable; make averse.

**indisposed** *a.* slightly unwell. **indisposition** *n.*

**indisputable** /ɪndə'spjuːtəb(ə)l/ *a.* beyond dispute.

**indissoluble** /ɪndə'sɒljəb(ə)l/ *a.* that cannot be dissolved; lasting, stable.

**indistinct** /ɪndə'stɪŋkt/ *a.* not distinct; confused, obscure.

**indistinguishable** /ɪndə'stɪŋgwɪʃəb(ə)l/ *a.* not distinguishable.

**indite** /ɪn'daɪt/ *v.t.* put into words; *joc.* write (letter etc.).

**individual** /ɪndə'vɪdjuəl/ **1** *a.* single; particular; characteristic of particular person etc.; of or for single person or thing. **2** *n.* single member of class or group etc.; single human being; *colloq.* person. **3 individuality** *n.*; **individualize** *v.t.*

**individualism** /ɪndə'vɪdjuəlɪz(ə)m/ *n.* self-reliant action by individual; social theory favouring free action by individuals; egoism. **individualist** *n.*; **individualistic** *a.*

**indivisible** /ɪndə'vɪzəb(ə)l/ *a.* not divisible.

**indoctrinate** /ɪn'dɒktrɪneɪt/ *v.t.* imbue with doctrine etc.; teach. **indoctrination** *n.*

**Indo-European** /ɪndəʊjʊərə'piːən/ **1** *n.* family of languages spoken over most of Europe and in Asia as far as N. India. **2** *a.* of these languages.

**indolent** /'ɪndələnt/ *a.* lazy, slothful. **indolence** *n.*

**indomitable** /ɪn'dɒmɪtəb(ə)l/ *a.* unyielding.

**indoor** /'ɪndɔː(r)/ *a.* done etc. in a building or under cover.

**indoors** /ɪn'dɔːz/ *adv.* in(to) a building; under roof.

**indorse** var. of **endorse**.

**indubitable** /ɪn'djuːbɪtəb(ə)l/ *a.* beyond doubt.

**induce** /ɪn'djuːs/ *v.t.* prevail on, persuade; bring about; bring on (labour) artificially; produce by induction; infer. **inducible** *a.*

**inducement** *n.* thing that induces, attraction, motive.

**induct** /ɪn'dʌkt/ *v.t.* install.

**inductance** /ɪn'dʌkt(ə)ns/ *n. Electr.* amount of induction of current.

**induction** /ɪn'dʌkʃ(ə)n/ *n.* inducting or inducing; *Med.* inducing (of labour); general inference from particular instances; *Electr.* production of electric or magnetic state by proximity of neighbouring circuit etc.

**inductive** /ɪn'dʌktɪv/ *a.* based on or using induction.

**indulge** /ɪn'dʌldʒ/ *v.* take one's pleasure freely *in*; yield freely to (desire etc.); gratify by compliance with wishes.

**indulgence** /ɪn'dʌldʒ(ə)ns/ *n.* indulging; privilege granted; *RC Ch.* remission of punishment still due for sin after sacramental absolution.

**indulgent** *a.* willing to overlook faults; too lenient.

**indurate** /'ɪndjuːreɪt/ *v.* make or become hard. **induration** *n.*

**industrial** /ɪn'dʌstrɪəl/ *a.* of industries; engaged in or connected with industry; having highly developed industries. **industrialize** *v.t.*

**industrialism** /ɪn'dʌstrɪəlɪz(ə)m/ *n.* system involving prevalence of industries.

**industrialist** /ɪn'dʌstrɪəlɪst/ *n.* person engaged in management of industry.

**industrious** /ɪn'dʌstrɪəs/ *a.* hard-working.

**industry** /'ɪndəstrɪ/ *n.* branch of trade or manufacture; trade or manufacture collectively; diligence.

**inebriate 1** /ɪ'niːbrɪət/ *a.* drunken. **2** /ɪ'niːbrɪət/ *n.* drunkard. **3** /ɪ'niːbrɪeɪt/ *v.t.* make drunk. **4 inebriation** *n.*; **inebriety** /ɪnə'braɪətɪ/ *n.*

**inedible** /ɪ'nedəb(ə)l/ *a.* not edible.

**ineducable** /ɪ'nedjəkəb(ə)l/ *a.* incapable of being educated.

**ineffable** /ɪ'nefəb(ə)l/ *a.* unutterable.

**ineffective** /ɪnə'fektɪv/ *a.* ineffectual.

**ineffectual** /ɪnə'fektjuːəl/ *a.* not producing desired effect; inefficient.

**inefficient** /ɪnə'fɪʃ(ə)nt/ *a.* not efficient or fully capable. **inefficiency** *n.*

**inelastic** /ɪnə'læstɪk/ *a.* not elastic or adaptable; rigid. **inelasticity** *n.*

**inelegant** /ɪ'nelɪgənt/ *a.* ungraceful, unrefined; unpolished. **inelegance** *n.*

**ineligible** /ɪ'nelɪdʒəb(ə)l/ *a.* not eligible, undesirable. **ineligibility** *n.*

**ineluctable** /ɪnə'lʌktəb(ə)l/ *a.* against which it is useless to struggle.

**inept** /ɪ'nept/ *a.* unskilful; absurd, silly; out of place. **ineptitude** *n.*

**inequality** /ɪnə'kwɒlətɪ/ *n.* lack of equality; variableness; unevenness.

**inequitable** /ɪ'nekwətəb(ə)l/ *a.* unfair, unjust.

**ineradicable** /ɪnə'rædəkəb(ə)l/ *a.* that cannot be rooted out.

**inert** /ɪ'nɜːt/ *a.* without inherent power of action; chemically inactive; sluggish, slow.

**inertia** /ɪ'nɜːʃə/ *n.* inertness; property by which matter continues in existing state of rest or motion unless acted on by external force. **inertia reel** reel allowing automatic adjustment of safety-belt rolled round it; **inertia selling** sending of unordered goods in hope they will not be refused.

**inescapable** /ɪnə'skeɪpəb(ə)l/ *a.* that cannot be escaped or avoided.

**inessential** /ɪnə'senʃ(ə)l/ *a.* & *n.* unnecessary (thing).

**inestimable** /ɪ'nestəməb(ə)l/ *a.* too great etc. to be estimated.

**inevitable** /ɪ'nevətəb(ə)l/ *a.* unavoidable; bound to happen or appear. **inevitability** *n.*

**inexact** /ɪnəg'zækt/ *a.* not exact. **inexactitude** *n.*

**inexcusable** /ɪnəks'kjuːzəb(ə)l/ *a.* that cannot be justified.

**inexhaustible** /ɪnəg'zɔːstəb(ə)l/ *a.* that cannot be exhausted.

**inexorable** /ɪ'neksərəb(ə)l/ *a.* relentless. **inexorability** *n.*

**inexpedient** /ɪnək'spiːdɪənt/ *a.* not expedient. **inexpediency** *n.*

**inexpensive** /ɪnək'spensɪv/ *a.* cheap, offering good value.

**inexperience** /ɪnək'spɪərɪəns/ *n.* lack of experience. **inexperienced** *a.*

**inexpert** /ɪ'nekspɜːt/ *a.* unskilful.

**inexpiable** /ɪ'nekspɪəb(ə)l/ *a.* that cannot be expiated.

**inexplicable** /ɪ'neksplɪkəb(ə)l/ *a.* that cannot be explained. **inexplicability** *n.*

**inexpressible** /ɪnək'spresəb(ə)l/ *a.* that cannot be expressed in words.

**in extremis** /ɪn ek'striːmɪs/ at point of death; in great difficulties. [L]

**inextricable** /ɪ'nekstrɪkəb(ə)l/ *a.* that cannot be loosened or resolved or escaped from.

**infallible** /ɪn'fæləb(ə)l/ *a.* incapable of erring; unfailing, sure. **infallibility** *n.*

**infamous** /'ɪnfəməs/ *a.* notoriously vile, evil; abominable.

**infamy** /'ɪnfəmɪ/ *n.* evil reputation; infamous conduct.

**infant** /'ɪnf(ə)nt/ *n.* child during earliest

# infanta / inflorescence

period of life; *Law* person under 18. **infancy** *n.*

**infanta** /ɪnˈfæntə/ *n. hist.* daughter of Spanish or Portuguese king.

**infanticide** /ɪnˈfæntɪsaɪd/ *n.* murder of infant soon after birth; person guilty of this.

**infantile** /ˈɪnfəntaɪl/ *a.* of or like infants. **infantile paralysis** poliomyelitis.

**infantry** /ˈɪnfəntri:/ *n.* foot-soldiers. **infantryman** soldier of infantry regiment.

**infatuate** /ɪnˈfætjʊeɪt/ *v.t.* inspire with intense fondness. **infatuation** *n.*

**infect** /ɪnˈfekt/ *v.t.* affect or contaminate with germ or virus or disease; imbue with opinion or feeling etc.

**infection** /ɪnˈfekʃ(ə)n/ *n.* infecting or being infected; disease; communication of disease.

**infectious** /ɪnˈfekʃəs/ *a.* transmissible by infection; apt to spread.

**infelicitous** /ɪnfəˈlɪsɪtəs/ *a.* not felicitous.

**infelicity** /ɪnfəˈlɪsɪti/ *n.* unhappiness; infelicitous expression.

**infer** /ɪnˈfɜ:(r)/ *v.t.* deduce, conclude. **inference** /ˈɪn-/ *n.*; **inferential** /-ˈren-/ *a.*

**inferior** /ɪnˈfɪəri:ə(r)/ 1 *a.* lower in rank etc.; of poor quality; situated below. 2 *n.* inferior person.

**inferiority** /ɪnfɪəri:ˈɒrəti:/ *n.* being inferior. **inferiority complex** unconscious feeling of inferiority to others, sometimes manifested in aggressive behaviour, *colloq.* sense of inferiority.

**infernal** /ɪnˈfɜ:n(ə)l/ *a.* of hell; hellish.

**inferno** /ɪnˈfɜ:nəʊ/ *n.* (*pl.* **-nos**) scene of horror or distress, esp. in fire; hell.

**infertile** /ɪnˈfɜ:taɪl/ *a.* not fertile. **infertility** /-ˈtɪl-/ *n.*

**infest** /ɪnˈfest/ *v.t.* overrun in large numbers. **infestation** *n.*

**infidel** /ˈɪnfəd(ə)l/ 1 *n.* disbeliever in (specified) religion. 2 *a.* unbelieving; of infidels.

**infidelity** /ɪnfəˈdelɪti/ *n.* being unfaithful.

**infighting** /ˈɪnfaɪtɪŋ/ *n.* hidden conflict in organization; boxing at closer quarters than arm's length.

**infiltrate** /ˈɪnfɪltreɪt/ *v.* enter (territory, political party, etc.) gradually and imperceptibly; pass (fluid) by filtration (*into*); permeate by filtration. **infiltration** *n.*; **infiltrator** *n.*

**infinite** /ˈɪnfənət/ *a.* boundless; endless; very great or many.

**infinitesimal** /ɪnfɪnəˈtesəm(ə)l/ *a.* infinitely or very small. **infinitesimal calculus** that dealing with such quantities.

**infinitive** /ɪnˈfɪnətɪv/ *a.* & *n. Gram.* (verb-form) expressing verbal notion without particular subject or tense etc.

**infinitude** /ɪnˈfɪnətju:d/ *n.* infinity; being infinite.

**infinity** /ɪnˈfɪnəti:/ *n.* infinite number or extent; immensity.

**infirm** /ɪnˈfɜ:m/ *a.* weak; irresolute. **infirmity** *n.*

**infirmary** /ɪnˈfɜ:məri:/ *n.* hospital; sick-quarters in school etc.

**in flagrante delicto** /ɪn flæˈgrænti:dəˈlɪktəʊ/ in act of committing offence. [L]

**inflame** /ɪnˈfleɪm/ *v.t.* provoke to strong feeling; cause inflammation in; (cause to) catch fire; make hot.

**inflammable** /ɪnˈflæməb(ə)l/ *a.* easily set on fire or excited. **inflammability** *n.*

**inflammation** /ɪnfləˈmeɪʃ(ə)n/ *n.* condition of living tissue marked by heat and swelling and redness and usu. pain.

**inflammatory** /ɪnˈflæmətəri:/ *a.* tending to inflame; of inflammation.

**inflate** /ɪnˈfleɪt/ *v.t.* distend with air or gas; puff up; raise (price) artificially; resort to inflation (of currency).

**inflated** /ɪnˈfleɪtəd/ *a.* (of language) bombastic.

**inflation** /ɪnˈfleɪʃ(ə)n/ *n.* inflating or being inflated; general rise in prices, increase in supply of money regarded as cause of such rise. **inflationary** *a.*

**inflect** /ɪnˈflekt/ *v.t.* change or vary pitch of; modify (word) to express grammatical relation.

**inflexible** /ɪnˈfleksəb(ə)l/ *a.* unbendable; unbending; unyielding. **inflexibility** *n.*

**inflexion** /ɪnˈflekʃ(ə)n/ *n.* modulation of voice etc.; inflected form; inflecting suffix etc.; inflecting. **inflexional** *a.*

**inflict** /ɪnˈflɪkt/ *v.t.* deal (blow etc.); impose (*up*)*on.* **infliction** *n.*

**inflorescence** /ɪnfləˈres(ə)ns/ *n.* arrangement of flowers or collective flower of plant; flowering.

**inflow** /'ɪnfləʊ/ n. flowing in; that which flows in.

**influence** /'ɪnfluːəns/ 1 n. action invisibly exercised; ascendancy, moral power; thing or person exercising this. 2 v.t. exert influence upon; affect.

**influential** /ˌɪnfluːˈenʃ(ə)l/ a. having great influence.

**influenza** /ˌɪnfluːˈenzə/ n. infectious virus disease with fever and severe aching and catarrh.

**influx** /'ɪnflʌks/ n. flowing in.

**inform** /ɪnˈfɔːm/ v. give information to; bring charge (*against*); in *p.p.* knowing the facts.

**informal** /ɪnˈfɔːm(ə)l/ a. not formal; without formality. **informal vote** *Aus.* & *NZ* spoilt voting-paper, invalid vote. **informality** n.

**informant** /ɪnˈfɔːmənt/ n. giver of information.

**information** /ˌɪnfəˈmeɪʃ(ə)n/ n. what is told; knowledge; news; charge or accusation. **information science** study of processes for storing and retrieving information.

**informative** /ɪnˈfɔːmətɪv/ a. giving information, instructive.

**infra dig.** /ˌɪnfrə 'dɪg/ beneath one's dignity.

**infraction** /ɪnˈfrækʃ(ə)n/ n. infringement.

**infra-red** /ˌɪnfrəˈred/ a. of or using invisible rays (just) beyond red end of spectrum.

**infrastructure** /'ɪnfrəstrʌktʃə(r)/ n. subordinate parts of an undertaking, esp. permanent installations forming basis of defence.

**infrequent** /ɪnˈfriːkwənt/ a. not frequent. **infrequency** n.

**infringe** /ɪnˈfrɪndʒ/ v.t. transgress, act contrary to. **infringement** n.

**infuriate** /ɪnˈfjʊərɪeɪt/ v.t. enrage.

**infuse** /ɪnˈfjuːz/ v. cause to be saturated or filled *with* quality; instil; steep or be steeped in liquid to extract properties.

**infusible** /ɪnˈfjuːzəb(ə)l/ a. that cannot be melted. **infusibility** n.

**infusion** /ɪnˈfjuːʒ(ə)n/ n. infusing; liquid extract so obtained; infused element.

**ingenious** /ɪnˈdʒiːnɪəs/ a. clever at contriving; cleverly contrived.

**ingénue** /ˈæʒemjuː/ n. artless young woman, esp. as stage type. [F]

**ingenuity** /ˌɪndʒəˈnjuːətɪ/ n. ingeniousness.

**ingenuous** /ɪnˈdʒenjʊəs/ a. artless; frank.

**ingest** /ɪnˈdʒest/ v.t. take in (food etc.). **ingestion** n.

**ingle-nook** /'ɪŋg(ə)lnʊk/ n. warm seat inside old-fashioned wide fireplace.

**inglorious** /ɪnˈglɔːrɪəs/ a. shameful; obscure.

**ingoing** /'ɪŋgəʊɪŋ/ a. going in.

**ingot** /'ɪŋgət/ n. mass of cast metal, esp. gold, silver, or steel.

**ingrained** /ɪnˈgreɪnd/ a. deeply embedded, inveterate.

**ingratiate** /ɪnˈgreɪʃɪeɪt/ v. bring *oneself* into favour *with*.

**ingratitude** /ɪnˈgrætɪtjuːd/ n. lack of gratitude.

**ingredient** /ɪnˈgriːdɪənt/ n. component part in mixture.

**ingress** /'ɪŋgres/ n. going in; right to go in.

**ingrowing** /'ɪŋgrəʊɪŋ/ a. (of nail) growing into the flesh.

**inhabit** /ɪnˈhæbɪt/ v.t. dwell in, occupy. **inhabitant** n.; **inhabitation** n.

**inhalant** /ɪnˈheɪlənt/ n. medicinal substance to be inhaled.

**inhale** /ɪnˈheɪl/ v. breathe in; take into lungs. **inhalation** n.

**inhaler** n. inhaling-apparatus.

**inharmonious** /ˌɪnhɑːˈməʊnɪəs/ a. not harmonious.

**inhere** /ɪnˈhɪə(r)/ v.i. be inherent.

**inherent** /ɪnˈhɪərənt/ a. existing or abiding in as essential quality.

**inherit** /ɪnˈherɪt/ v. receive as heir; derive from parents etc. **inheritor** n.

**inheritance** /ɪnˈherɪt(ə)ns/ n. what is inherited; inheriting.

**inhibit** /ɪnˈhɪbɪt/ v.t. hinder, restrain, or prevent; prohibit.

**inhibition** /ˌɪnhəˈbɪʃ(ə)n/ n. inhibiting or being inhibited; restraint of direct expression of instinct; *colloq.* emotional resistance to thought or action.

**inhospitable** /ɪnˈhɒspɪtəb(ə)l/ a. not hospitable; affording no shelter.

**inhuman** /ɪnˈhjuːmən/ a. brutal, unfeeling, barbarous. **inhumanity** /-ˈmæn-/ n.

**inimical** /ɪˈnɪmɪk(ə)l/ a. hostile; harmful.

**inimitable** /ɪˈnɪmɪtəb(ə)l/ a. that cannot be imitated.

**iniquity** /ɪ'nɪkwətɪ/ n. wickedness; gross injustice. **iniquitous** a.

**initial** /ɪ'nɪʃ(ə)l/ 1 a. of or existing or occurring at beginning. 2 n. first letter of (esp. person's) name. 3 v.t. mark or sign with initials. 4 **initially** adv.

**initiate** 1 /ɪ'nɪʃɪeɪt/ v.t. originate, set going; admit, introduce (*into*). 2 /ɪ'nɪʃɪət/ n. initiated person. 3 **initiation** n.; **initiatory** a.

**initiative** /ɪ'nɪʃətɪv/ n. ability to initiate, enterprise; first step; lead.

**inject** /ɪn'dʒekt/ v.t. force (fluid *into*) (as) by syringe; place (quality etc.) where needed in something. **injection** n.

**injudicious** /ɪndʒu:'dɪʃəs/ a. unwise, ill-judged.

**injunction** /ɪn'dʒʌŋkʃ(ə)n/ n. authoritative order; judicial process restraining from specified act or compelling restitution etc.

**injure** /'ɪndʒə(r)/ v.t. hurt, harm, impair; do wrong to.

**injurious** /ɪn'dʒʊərɪəs/ a. wrongful; harmful; defamatory.

**injury** /'ɪndʒərɪ/ n. wrong; damage, harm. **injury time** extra time added to football match etc. because of that lost in dealing with injuries.

**injustice** /ɪn'dʒʌstɪs/ n. unfairness; unjust act.

**ink** 1 n. coloured fluid for writing or printing; black liquid ejected by cuttlefish etc. 2 v.t. mark or cover or smear with ink. 3 **inky** a.

**inkling** /'ɪŋklɪŋ/ n. hint, slight knowledge or suspicion (*of*).

**inland** 1 /'ɪnlænd/ a. in interior of country; remote from sea or border within a country. 2 /ɪn'lænd/ adv. in or towards interior. 3 /'ɪnlænd/ n. interior of country.

**in-laws** /'ɪnlɔːz/ n.pl. colloq. relatives by marriage.

**inlay** 1 /ɪn'leɪ/ v.t. (*past* & *p.p.* -laid) embed (thing *in* another); decorate (thing) thus. 2 /'ɪnleɪ/ n. inlaid material or work.

**inlet** /'ɪnlət/ n. small arm of sea etc.; way of admission.

**inmate** /'ɪnmeɪt/ n. occupant (*of* house, hospital, prison, etc.).

***in memoriam*** /ɪn mə'mɔːrɪæm/ in memory of. [L]

**inmost** /'ɪnməʊst/ a. most inward.

**inn** n. house providing lodging etc. for payment, esp. for travellers; house providing alcoholic liquor. **innkeeper** keeper of inn; **Inns of Court** 4 legal societies admitting persons to practise at English bar.

**innards** /'ɪnədz/ n.pl. colloq. entrails.

**innate** /ɪ'neɪt/ a. inborn.

**inner** /'ɪnə(r)/ 1 a. interior, internal. 2 n. circle nearest bull's-eye of target. 3 **inner tube** separate inflatable tube in pneumatic tyre. 4 **innermost** a.

**innings** /'ɪnɪŋz/ n. (pl. same) *Crick*. etc. batsman's or side's turn at batting.

**innocent** /'ɪnəs(ə)nt/ 1 a. not guilty; sinless; guileless; harmless. 2 n. innocent person, esp. young child. 3 **innocence** n.

**innocuous** /ɪ'nɒkjʊəs/ a. harmless.

**innovate** /'ɪnəveɪt/ v.i. bring in new ideas etc.; make changes. **innovation** n.; **innovative** a.; **innovator** n.

**innuendo** /ɪnjuː'endəʊ/ n. (pl. **-oes**) allusive (usu. depreciatory) remark.

**innumerable** /ɪ'njuːmərəb(ə)l/ a. countless.

**innumerate** /ɪ'njuːmərət/ a. not knowing basic mathematics and science.

**inoculate** /ɪ'nɒkjəleɪt/ v.t. treat with vaccine or serum, esp. as protective measure. **inoculation** n.

**inoffensive** /ɪnə'fensɪv/ a. unoffending; not objectionable.

**inoperable** /ɪ'nɒpərəb(ə)l/ a. that cannot be cured by surgical operation.

**inoperative** /ɪ'nɒpərətɪv/ a. not working or taking effect.

**inopportune** /ɪ'nɒpətjuːn/ a. not appropriate, esp. as regards time.

**inordinate** /ɪ'nɔːdənət/ a. excessive.

**inorganic** /ɪnɔː'gænɪk/ a. *Chem.* mineral not organic; without organized physical structure.

**input** /'ɪnpʊt/ 1 n. what is put in; place of entry of energy or information etc. 2 v.t. (*past* & *p.p.* **-put** or **-putted**) put in; supply (data, programs, etc.) to computer.

**inquest** /'ɪnkwest/ n. inquiry held by coroner into cause of death.

**inquietude** /ɪn'kwaɪətjuːd/ n. uneasiness.

**inquire** /ɪn'kwaɪə(r)/ v. ask question; seek information; make inqiry (*into*).

**inquiry** /ɪn'kwaɪərɪ/ n. asking; question; investigation, esp. official.

**inquisition** /ɪnkwə'zɪʃ(ə)n/ n. investigation; official inquiry; **Inquisition** hist. RC Ch. ecclesiastical tribunal for suppression of heresy. **inquisitional** a.

**inquisitive** /ɪn'kwɪzətɪv/ a. curious, prying.

**inquisitor** /ɪn'kwɪzətə(r)/ n. investigator; officer of Inquisition.

**inquisitorial** /ɪnkwɪzə'tɔːrɪəl/ a. inquisitor-like; prying.

**inroad** /'ɪnrəʊd/ n. hostile incursion; encroachment.

**inrush** /'ɪnrʌʃ/ n. violent influx.

**insalubrious** /ɪnsə'luːbrɪəs/ a. unhealthy.

**insane** /ɪn'seɪn/ a. mad; extremely foolish.

**insanitary** /ɪn'sænətəri/ a. not sanitary.

**insanity** /ɪn'sænəti/ n. madness.

**insatiable** /ɪn'seɪʃəb(ə)l/ a. that cannot be satisfied; greedy. **insatiability** n.

**insatiate** /ɪn'seɪʃɪət/ a. never satisfied.

**inscribe** /ɪn'skraɪb/ v.t. write (in, on); mark with characters; *Geom.* trace (figure) within another so that some points of their boundaries coincide; enter on list.

**inscription** /ɪn'skrɪpʃ(ə)n/ n. words inscribed; inscribing.

**inscrutable** /ɪn'skruːtəb(ə)l/ a. mysterious, impenetrable. **inscrutability** n.

**insect** /'ɪnsekt/ n. small invertebrate animal with segmented body and 6 legs.

**insecticide** /ɪn'sektəsaɪd/ n. preparation used for killing insects.

**insectivorous** /ɪnsek'tɪvərəs/ a. insect-eating. **insectivore** /-'sekt-/ n.

**insecure** /ɪnsə'kjʊə(r)/ a. not secure or safe; not feeling safe.

**inseminate** /ɪn'semeneɪt/ v.t. introduce semen into; sow (seed etc.). **insemination** n.

**insensate** /ɪn'senseɪt/ a. without sensibility; stupid.

**insensible** /ɪn'sensəb(ə)l/ a. unconscious; unaware; callous, imperceptible. **insensibility** n.

**insensitive** /ɪn'sensətɪv/ a. not sensitive.

**insentient** /ɪn'senʃ(ə)nt/ a. inanimate.

**inseparable** /ɪn'sepərəb(ə)l/ a. that cannot be separated. **inseparability** n.

**insert 1** /ɪn'sɜːt/ v.t. place or put (thing into another). **2** /'ɪnsɜːt/ n. thing inserted.

**insertion** /ɪn'sɜːʃ(ə)n/ n. inserting, thing inserted.

**inset 1** /'ɪnset/ n. extra piece inserted in book or garment etc.; small map etc. within border of larger. **2** /ɪn'set/ v.t. (*past & p.p.* -**set**) put in as inset.

**inshore** /ɪn'ʃɔː(r)/ adv. & a. close to shore.

**inside** /ɪn'saɪd/ **1** n. inner side or part; position on inner side; *colloq.* stomach and bowels. **2** a. (*attrib.* /'ɪnsaɪd/) of or on or in the inside; nearer to centre of games field. **3** adv. on or in the inside; sl. in prison. **4** prep. within, on the inside of; in less than. **5 inside information** information not accessible to outsiders; **inside job** colloq. burglary etc. by person living or working on premises; **inside out** turned so that inner becomes outer side; **know inside out** know thoroughly.

**insidious** /ɪn'sɪdɪəs/ a. proceeding inconspicuously but harmfully.

**insight** /'ɪnsaɪt/ n. mental penetration.

**insignia** /ɪn'sɪgnɪə/ n.pl. badges or marks of office etc.

**insignificant** /ɪnsɪg'nɪfɪkənt/ a. unimportant; trivial. **insignificance** n.

**insincere** /ɪnsɪn'sɪə(r)/ a. not sincere or candid. **insincerity** /-'ser-/ n.

**insinuate** /ɪn'sɪnjʊeɪt/ v.t. hint obliquely; introduce gradually or subtly. **insinuation** n.

**insipid** /ɪn'sɪpɪd/ a. flavourless; dull, lifeless. **insipidity** n.

**insist** /ɪn'sɪst/ v. demand or maintain emphatically. **insistence** n.; **insistent** a.

**in situ** /ɪn 'sɪtjuː/ in its original place. [L]

**insobriety** /ɪnsə'braɪəti/ n. intemperance, esp. in drinking.

**insole** /'ɪnsəʊl/ n. removable inner sole for use in shoe.

**insolent** /'ɪnsələnt/ a. offensively contemptuous; insulting. **insolence** n.

**insoluble** /ɪn'sɒljəb(ə)l/ a. that cannot be dissolved or solved. **insolubility** n.

**insolvent** /ɪn'sɒlv(ə)nt/ **1** a. unable to pay debts. **2** n. insolvent debtor. **3 insolvency** n.

**insomnia** /ɪn'sɒmnɪə/ n. sleeplessness.

**insomniac** /ɪnˈsɒmniːæk/ *n.* person suffering from insomnia.

**insouciant** /ɪnˈsuːsiːənt/ *a.* carefree, unconcerned. **insouciance** *n.*

**inspect** /ɪnˈspekt/ *v.t.* look closely into; examine officially. **inspection** *n.*

**inspector** /ɪnˈspektə(r)/ *n.* official employed to inspect or supervise; police officer next below superintendent.

**inspectorate** /ɪnˈspektərət/ *n.* office of inspector; body of inspectors.

**inspiration** /ɪnspəˈreɪʃ(ə)n/ *n.* inspiring; sudden brilliant idea; source of inspiring influence; divine influence in poetry and Scripture.

**inspire** /ɪnˈspaɪə(r)/ *v.* stimulate (person) to creative activity; breathe in; animate; instil thought or feeling into.

**inspirit** /ɪnˈspɪrɪt/ *v.t.* put life into, animate; encourage.

**inst.** *abbr.* instant, of current month.

**instability** /ɪnstəˈbɪləti/ *n.* lack of stability.

**install** /ɪnˈstɔːl/ *v.t.* fix or establish (equipment, person, etc.); place *in* office with ceremony. **installation** *n.*

**instalment** *n.* any of successive parts of sum payable or of serial story etc.

**instance** /ˈɪnst(ə)ns/ 1 *n.* example; particular case. 2 *v.t.* cite as instance.

**instant** /ˈɪnst(ə)nt/ 1 *a.* immediate; (of food etc.) that can be prepared easily for immediate use; urgent, pressing; of current calendar month. 2 *n.* precise moment; short time, moment.

**instantaneous** /ɪnstənˈteɪnɪəs/ *a.* occurring or done in an instant.

**instantly** /ˈɪnstəntli/ *adv.* immediately.

**instead** /ɪnˈsted/ *adv.* as substitute or alternative; in place *of*.

**instep** /ˈɪnstep/ *n.* top of foot between toes and ankle; part of shoe etc. fitting this.

**instigate** /ˈɪnstɪɡeɪt/ *v.t.* incite (*to*); bring about by persuasion. **instigation** *n.*; **instigator** *n.*

**instil** /ɪnˈstɪl/ *v.t.* put (ideas etc. *into* mind etc.) gradually; put in by drops. **instillation** *n.*

**instinct** 1 /ˈɪnstɪŋkt/ *n.* inborn pattern of behaviour; innate impulse; intuition. 2 /ɪnˈstɪŋkt/ *a.* filled or charged (*with*). 3 **instinctive** *a.*; **instinctual** *a.*

**institute** /ˈɪnstɪtjuːt/ 1 *n.* organized body for promotion of scientific or other aim; its building. 2 *v.t.* establish; initiate.

**institution** /ɪnstɪˈtjuːʃ(ə)n/ *n.* instituting; (esp. charitable) institute; established law or custom; *colloq.* well-known person.

**institutional** /ɪnstɪˈtjuːʃən(ə)l/ *a.* of or like an institution; typical of charitable institutions. **institutionalize** *v.t.*

**instruct** /ɪnˈstrʌkt/ *v.t.* teach; inform; give information to; direct. **instructor** *n.*; **instructress** *n.*

**instruction** /ɪnˈstrʌkʃ(ə)n/ *n.* instructing; in *pl.* directions, orders. **instructional** *a.*

**instructive** /ɪnˈstrʌktɪv/ *a.* enlightening.

**instrument** /ˈɪnstrəmənt/ *n.* tool, implement; measuring-device, esp. in aircraft to find position in fog etc.; contrivance for producing musical sounds; formal (esp. legal) document.

**instrumental** /ɪnstrəˈment(ə)l/ *a.* serving as instrument or means (*to, in*); (of music) performed on instruments. **instrumentality** *n.*

**instrumentalist** /ɪnstrəˈmentəlɪst/ *n.* performer on musical instrument.

**instrumentation** /ɪnstrəmenˈteɪʃ(ə)n/ *n.* arrangement of music for instruments.

**insubordinate** /ɪnsəˈbɔːdənət/ *a.* disobedient; unruly. **insubordination** *n.*

**insubstantial** /ɪnsəbˈstænʃ(ə)l/ *a.* lacking solidity or substance; not real. **insubstantiality** *n.*

**insufferable** /ɪnˈsʌfərəb(ə)l/ *a.* unbearable.

**insufficient** /ɪnsəˈfɪʃ(ə)nt/ *a.* not enough, inadequate. **insufficiency** *n.*

**insular** /ˈɪnsjələ(r)/ *a.* narrow-minded; of or like islanders; of or forming an island. **insularity** *n.*

**insulate** /ˈɪnsjəleɪt/ *v.t.* isolate, esp. by non-conductor of electricity or heat or sound etc. **insulation** *n.*; **insulator** *n.*

**insulin** /ˈɪnsjəlɪn/ *n.* hormone produced in the pancreas, controlling sugar in body and used against diabetes.

**insult** 1 /ɪnˈsʌlt/ *v.t.* abuse scornfully; offend self-respect etc. of. 2 /ˈɪnsʌlt/ *n.* insulting remark or action.

**insuperable** /ɪnˈsuːpərəb(ə)l/ *a.* that cannot be got over. **insuperability** *n.*

# insupportable

**insupportable** /ɪnsə'pɔːtəb(ə)l/ *a.* unbearable.

**insurance** /ɪn'ʃʊərəns or -'ʃɔːr-/ *n.* procedure or contract securing compensation for loss or damage or injury on payment of premium; business of this; sum paid to effect insurance.

**insure** /ɪn'ʃʊə(r) or -'ʃɔː(r)/ *v.* effect insurance *against* or with respect to.

**insurgent** /ɪn'sɜːdʒ(ə)nt/ 1 *n.* rebel. 2 *a.* in revolt; rebellious. 3 **insurgency** *n.*

**insurmountable** /ɪnsə'maʊntəb(ə)l/ *a.* insuperable.

**insurrection** /ɪnsə'rekʃ(ə)n/ *n.* rising in resistance to authority; incipient rebellion. **insurrectionist** *n.*

**insusceptible** /ɪnsə'septəb(ə)l/ *a.* not susceptible. **insusceptibility** *n.*

**intact** /ɪn'tækt/ *a.* unimpaired; entire; untouched.

**intaglio** /ɪn'tɑːlɪəʊ/ *n.* (*pl.* -os) engraved design; gem with incised design.

**intake** /'ɪnteɪk/ *n.* action of taking in; place where water is taken into pipe, or fuel or air into engine; persons or things or quantity taken in.

**intangible** /ɪn'tændʒəb(ə)l/ *a.* that cannot be touched or mentally grasped. **intangibility** *n.*

**integer** /'ɪntədʒə(r)/ *n.* whole number.

**integral** /'ɪntəɡr(ə)l/ *a.* of or essential to a whole; complete; of or denoted by an integer.

**integrate** /'ɪntəɡreɪt/ *v.* combine (parts) into whole; bring or come into equal membership of society; end racial etc. segregation. **integrated circuit** small piece of material replacing electrical circuit of many components. **integration** *n.*

**integrity** /ɪn'teɡrəti/ *n.* honesty; wholeness; soundness.

**integument** /ɪn'teɡjəmənt/ *n.* skin, husk, or other (natural) covering.

**intellect** /'ɪntəlekt/ *n.* faculty of knowing and reasoning; understanding.

**intellectual** /ɪntə'lektjʊəl/ 1 *a.* of or requiring or using intellect; having highly-developed intellect. 2 *n.* intellectual person. 3 **intellectualism** *n.*; **intellectualize** *v.t.*

**intelligence** /ɪn'telɪdʒ(ə)ns/ *n.* intellect; quickness of understanding; news; (persons engaged in) obtaining of esp. secret information. **intelligence quo**tient ratio of person's intelligence to the normal or average.

**intelligent** *a.* having or showing good intelligence, clever.

**intelligentsia** /ɪntelɪ'dʒentsɪə/ *n.* intellectuals as a class, esp. regarded as cultured and politically enterprising.

**intelligible** /ɪn'telɪdʒəb(ə)l/ *a.* that can be understood. **intelligibility** *n.*

**intemperate** /ɪn'tempərət/ *a.* immoderate; excessive in indulgence of appetite; addicted to drinking. **intemperance** *n.*

**intend** /ɪn'tend/ *v.t.* have as one's purpose; design.

**intended** 1 *a.* done on purpose. 2 *n. colloq.* fiancé(e).

**intense** /ɪn'tens/ *a.* existing in high degree; vehement; strenuous; feeling or apt to feel strong emotion. **intensity** *n.*

**intensify** /ɪn'tensəfaɪ/ *v.* make or become (more) intense. **intensification** *n.*

**intensive** /ɪn'tensɪv/ *a.* thorough, vigorous; concentrated; increasing production of limited area etc.; emphasizing; of or in intensity. **intensive care** medical treatment with constant supervision of patient.

**intent** /ɪn'tent/ 1 *n.* intention; purpose. 2 *a.* resolved, bent (*on*); attentively occupied; eager. 3 **to all intents (and purposes)** practically.

**intention** /ɪn'tenʃ(ə)n/ *n.* intending; purpose, aim.

**intentional** /ɪn'tenʃən(ə)l/ *a.* done on purpose.

**inter** /ɪn'tɜː(r)/ *v.t.* place (corpse etc.) in earth or tomb; bury.

**inter-** /ɪntə(r)/ *in comb.* among, between; mutually, reciprocally.

**interact** /ɪntə'rækt/ *v.i.* act on each other. **interaction** *n.*; **interactive** *a.*

**interbreed** /ɪntə'briːd/ *v.* (*past & p.p.* -bred) (cause to) produce hybrid individual.

**intercalary** /ɪntə'kæləri/ *a.* inserted to harmonize calendar with solar year; having such additions; interpolated.

**intercalate** /ɪntəkə'leɪt/ *v.t.* interpose; insert. **intercalation** *n.*

**intercede** /ɪntə'siːd/ *v.i.* mediate; plead (*for* another).

**intercept** /ɪntə'sept/ *v.t.* seize or catch

# intercession

or stop etc. in transit; cut off. **interception** n.; **interceptor** n.

**intercession** /ɪntəˈseʃ(ə)n/ n. interceding. **intercessor** n.

**interchange** 1 /ɪntəˈtʃeɪndʒ/ v. put in each other's place; make exchange of; alternate. 2 /ˈɪntətʃeɪndʒ/ n. reciprocal exchange; alternation; road junction so arranged that paths of vehicles do not cross.

**intercom** /ˈɪntəkɒm/ n. colloq. system of intercommunication operating like telephone.

**intercommunicate** /ɪntəkəˈmjuːnəkeɪt/ v.i. have communication with each other. **intercommunication** n.

**intercommunion** /ɪntəkəˈmjuːnɪən/ n. mutual communion, esp. between religious bodies.

**interconnect** /ɪntəkəˈnekt/ v.i. connect with each other. **interconnection** n.

**intercontinental** /ɪntəkɒntəˈnent(ə)l/ a. connecting or travelling between continents.

**intercourse** /ˈɪntəkɔːs/ n. social communication, dealings; sexual intercourse.

**interdenominational** /ɪntədɪnɒməˈneɪʃən(ə)l/ a. of or involving more than one Christian denomination.

**interdependent** /ɪntədɪˈpend(ə)nt/ a. mutually dependent. **interdependence** n.

**interdict** 1 /ɪntəˈdɪkt/ v.t. forbid; prohibit; restrain. 2 /ˈɪntədɪkt/ n. authoritative prohibition. 3 **interdiction** n.

**interdisciplinary** /ɪntədɪsəˈplɪnərɪ/ a. of or involving different branches of learning.

**interest** /ˈɪntrest/ 1 n. concern or curiosity or attention; quality causing this; thing towards which one feels it; advantage; money paid for use of money borrowed etc.; legal concern or title or right. 2 v.t. arouse interest of; cause to take interest (in); in p.p. having private interest, not impartial.

**interesting** a. causing curiosity; holding the attention.

**interface** /ˈɪntəfeɪs/ n. surface forming common boundary of two regions; place where interaction occurs between two systems etc.

# interminable

**interfere** /ɪntəˈfɪə(r)/ v.i. meddle, intervene; be an obstacle; clash (with).

**interference** /ɪntəˈfɪərəns/ n. interfering; fading of received radio signals.

**interferon** /ɪntəˈfɪərɒn/ n. protein inhibiting development of virus in cell.

**interfuse** /ɪntəˈfjuːz/ v.t. mix, blend. **interfusion** n.

**interim** /ˈɪntərɪm/ 1 n. intervening time. 2 a. provisional, temporary.

**interior** /ɪnˈtɪərɪə(r)/ 1 n. inner part; inland region; inside of room etc.; home affairs of country. 2 a. situated within; inland; internal, domestic.

**interject** /ɪntəˈdʒekt/ v.t. make (remark etc.) abruptly or parenthetically.

**interjection** /ɪntəˈdʒekʃ(ə)n/ n. exclamation.

**interlace** /ɪntəˈleɪs/ v. bind intricately together; interweave.

**interlard** /ɪntəˈlɑːd/ v.t. mix (speech etc.) with.

**interleave** /ɪntəˈliːv/ v.t. insert (usu. blank) leaves between leaves of (book).

**interlink** /ɪntəˈlɪŋk/ v. link together.

**interlock** /ɪntəˈlɒk/ 1 v. engage with each other by overlapping etc.; lock together. 2 a. (of fabric) knitted with closely interlocking stitches. 3 n. such fabric.

**interlocutor** /ɪntəˈlɒkjətə(r)/ n. person who takes part in conversation. **interlocutory** a.

**interloper** /ˈɪntələʊpə(r)/ n. intruder; person who thrusts himself into others' affairs.

**interlude** /ˈɪntəluːd/ n. interval between parts of play etc., performance filling this; intervening time or event etc. of different kind.

**intermarriage** /ɪntəˈmærɪdʒ/ n. marriage between members of different families or races etc. **intermarry** v.i.

**intermediary** /ɪntəˈmiːdɪərɪ/ 1 n. mediator; acting between parties. 2 a. intermediate.

**intermediate** /ɪntəˈmiːdɪət/ 1 a. coming between in time or place or order. 2 n. intermediate thing.

**interment** /ɪnˈtɜːmənt/ n. burial.

**intermezzo** /ɪntəˈmetsəʊ/ n. (pl. -mezzi /-ˈmetsiː/) Mus. short connecting movement or composition.

**interminable** /ɪnˈtɜːmənəb(ə)l/ a. tediously long; endless.

**intermingle** /ɪntə'mɪŋg(ə)l/ v. mix together, mingle.

**intermission** /ɪntə'mɪʃ(ə)n/ n. pause, cessation; interval in cinema etc.

**intermittent** /ɪntə'mɪt(ə)nt/ a. occurring at intervals, not continuous or steady.

**intermix** /ɪntə'mɪks/ v. mix together.

**intern** 1 /ɪn'tɜːn/ v.t. confine within prescribed limits. 2 /'ɪntɜːn/ n. recent graduate etc. living in hospital and acting as assistant physician or surgeon. 3 **internee** n.; **internment** n.

**internal** /ɪn'tɜːn(ə)l/ a. of or in the inside of thing; relating to interior of the body; of domestic affairs of country; of students attending a university as well as taking its examinations; used or applying within an organization; intrinsic; of mind or soul. **internal-combustion engine** engine in which motive power comes from explosion of gas or vapour with air in cylinder.

**international** /ɪntə'næʃən(ə)l/ 1 a. existing or carried on between nations; agreed to by many nations. 2 n. contest (usu. in sports) between representatives of different nations; such representative; **International** one of four successive associations for socialist or communist action. 3 **internationality** n.

**internationalism** /ɪntə'næʃənəlɪz(ə)m/ n. advocacy of community of interests among nations; support of International. **internationalist** n.

**internationalize** /ɪntə'næʃənəlaɪz/ v.t. make international; bring under joint protection etc. of different nations.

**internecine** /ɪntə'niːsaɪn/ a. mutually destructive.

**interpenetrate** /ɪntə'penətreɪt/ v. pervade; penetrate each other. **interpenetration** n.

**interpersonal** /ɪntə'pɜːsən(ə)l/ a. between persons.

**interplanetary** /ɪntə'plænətəri/ a. between planets.

**interplay** /'ɪntəpleɪ/ n. reciprocal action.

**Interpol** /'ɪntəpɒl/ n. International Criminal Police Commission.

**interpolate** /ɪn'tɜːpəleɪt/ v.t. make (esp. misleading) insertions in; insert or introduce between other things. **interpolation** n.

**interpose** /ɪntə'pəʊz/ v. insert (thing *between* others); introduce or use or say etc. as interruption or interference; intervene; interrupt. **interposition** n.

**interpret** /ɪn'tɜːprɪt/ v. explain; render, represent; act as interpreter. **interpretation** n.

**interpreter** /ɪn'tɜːprətə(r)/ n. person who translates orally.

**interregnum** /ɪntə'regnəm/ n. (pl. **-na** or **-nums**) interval between successive reigns; interval, pause.

**interrelated** /ɪntərɪ'leɪtɪd/ a. related to each other. **interrelation(ship)** ns.

**interrogate** /ɪn'terəgeɪt/ v.t. question closely or formally. **interrogation** n.; **interrogator** n.

**interrogative** /ɪntə'rɒgətɪv/ 1 a. of or like or used in questions. 2 n. interrogative pronoun etc.

**interrogatory** /ɪntə'rɒgətəri/ 1 a. questioning. 2 n. formal set of questions.

**interrupt** /ɪntə'rʌpt/ v.t. break in upon; break continuity of; obstruct (view etc.). **interruption** n.

**intersect** /ɪntə'sekt/ v. divide by passing or lying across; cross or cut each other.

**intersection** /ɪntə'sekʃ(ə)n/ n. place where two roads intersect; point or line common to lines or planes that intersect.

**intersperse** /ɪntə'spɜːs/ v.t. diversify (*with* things scattered about); scatter, place here and there (*between*).

**interstate** /'ɪntəsteɪt/ a. existing etc. between states.

**interstellar** /ɪntə'stelə(r)/ a. between stars.

**interstice** /ɪn'tɜːstɪs/ n. chink, crevice, gap.

**interstitial** /ɪntə'stɪʃ(ə)l/ a. of or in interstices.

**intertwine** /ɪntə'twaɪn/ v. twine closely together.

**interval** /'ɪntəv(ə)l/ n. intervening time or space; pause; break; *Mus.* difference of pitch between two sounds. **at intervals** here and there, now and then.

**intervene** /ɪntə'viːn/ v.i. occur in meantime; come between persons or things; interfere, mediate.

**intervention** /ɪntə'venʃ(ə)n/ n. intervening; interference; mediation.

**interview** /'ɪntəvjuː/ 1 n. meeting between reporter and person whose views he wishes to publish; oral examination of applicant; meeting of persons, esp. for discussion. 2 *v.t.* have interview with.

**interweave** /ɪntə'wiːv/ *v.t.* (*past* -**wove**, *p.p.* -**woven**) weave together; blend intimately.

**intestate** /ɪn'testeɪt/ 1 *a.* not having made a will before death. 2 *n.* intestate person. 3 **intestacy** *n.*

**intestine** /ɪn'testən/ *n.* lower part of alimentary canal. **intestinal** *a.*

**intimate** 1 /'ɪntəmət/ *a.* closely acquainted; familiar; closely personal; close. 2 /'ɪntəmət/ *n.* intimate friend. 3 /'ɪntəmeɪt/ *v.t.* make known, state; imply. 4 **intimacy** *n.*; **intimation** *n.*

**intimidate** /ɪn'tɪmədeɪt/ *v.t.* frighten, esp. in order to influence conduct.

**into** /ɪntuː/ *prep.* expr. motion or direction to point within, or change or condition or result; *colloq.* interested in.

**intolerable** /ɪn'tɒlərəb(ə)l/ *a.* that cannot be endured.

**intolerant** /ɪn'tɒlərənt/ *a.* not tolerant (*of*). **intolerance** *n.*

**intonation** /ɪntə'neɪʃ(ə)n/ *n.* intoning; modulation of voice, accent.

**intone** /ɪn'təʊn/ *v.t.* recite with prolonged sounds, esp. in monotone.

***in toto*** /ɪn 'təʊtəʊ/ entirely. [L]

**intoxicant** /ɪn'tɒksəkənt/ 1 *n.* intoxicating substance. 2 *a.* intoxicating.

**intoxicate** /ɪn'tɒksəkeɪt/ *v.t.* make drunk; excite or elate beyond self-control. **intoxication** *n.*

**intractable** /ɪn'træktəb(ə)l/ *a.* not easily dealt with; stubborn. **intractability** *n.*

**intramural** /ɪntrə'mjʊə(r)əl/ *a.* situated or done within walls of city or house etc.

**intransigent** /ɪn'trænsədʒ(ə)nt/ 1 *a.* uncompromising. 2 *n.* such person. 3 **intransigence** *n.*

**intransitive** /ɪn'trænsətɪv/ *a. Gram.* (of verb) not taking direct object.

**intra-uterine** /ɪntrə'juːtəram/ *a.* within the womb.

**intravenous** /ɪntrə'viːnəs/ *a.* in(to) vein(s).

**intrepid** /ɪn'trepəd/ *a.* fearless; brave. **intrepidity** *n.*

**intricate** /'ɪntrəkət/ *a.* entangled; complicated. **intricacy** *n.*

**intrigue** /ɪn'triːg/ 1 *v.* carry on underhand plot; use secret influence; rouse interest or curiosity of. 2 *n.* (also /'ɪn-/) underhand plotting or plot; *arch.* secret love affair.

**intrinsic** /ɪn'trɪnzɪk/ *a.* inherent; essential.

**introduce** /ɪntrə'djuːs/ *v.t.* make (person) known to another; announce or present to audience; bring into use; bring before Parliament; draw attention to; insert; bring in; usher in, bring forward. **introducible** *a.*

**introduction** /ɪntrə'dʌkʃ(ə)n/ *n.* introducing; formal presentation; preliminary matter in book; introductory treatise. **introductory** *a.*

**introspection** /ɪntrə'spekʃ(ə)n/ *n.* examination of one's own thoughts. **introspective** *a.*

**introvert** /'ɪntrəvɜːt/ *n.* introverted person.

**introverted** *a.* principally interested in one's own thoughts; reserved, shy. **introversion** *n.*

**intrude** /ɪn'truːd/ *v.* thrust (*into*), force (*upon*); come uninvited, thrust oneself in. **intrusion** *n.*; **intrusive** *a.*

**intuition** /ɪntjuː'ɪʃ(ə)n/ *n.* immediate apprehension by mind without reasoning; immediate insight. **intuitional** *a.*

**intuitive** /ɪn'tjuːətɪv/ *a.* of or having or perceived by intuition.

**inundate** /'ɪnəndeɪt/ *v.t.* flood or overwhelm (*with*). **inundation** *n.*

**inure** /ɪ'njʊə(r)/ *v.t.* habituate, accustom. **inurement** *n.*

**invade** /ɪn'veɪd/ *v.t.* make hostile inroad into; encroach on.

**invalid**[1] /'ɪnvəlɪd/ 1 *n.* (also -/liːd/) person enfeebled or disabled by illness or injury. 2 *a.* of or for invalids; being an invalid. 3 *v.t.* (also -/liːd/) remove from active service, send *home* etc. as invalid. 4 **invalidism** *n.*

**invalid**[2] /ɪn'vælɪd/ *a.* not valid. **invalidity** *n.*

**invalidate** /ɪn'vælədeɪt/ *v.t.* make invalid. **invalidation** *n.*

**invaluable** /ɪn'væljʊəb(ə)l/ *a.* beyond price, inestimable.

**invariable** /ɪn'veərɪəb(ə)l/ *a.* always the same; *Math.* constant. **invariability** *n.*

**invasion** /ɪn'veɪʒ(ə)n/ *n.* invading or being invaded. **invasive** *a.*

# invective

**invective** /ɪnˈvektɪv/ n. violent attack in words.

**inveigh** /ɪnˈveɪ/ v.i. speak or write violently *against*.

**inveigle** /ɪnˈveɪg(ə)l/ v.t. entice, tempt (*into*). **inveiglement** n.

**invent** /ɪnˈvent/ v.t. create by thought; originate; fabricate. **inventor** n.

**invention** /ɪnˈvenʃ(ə)n/ n. inventing; thing invented; inventiveness.

**inventive** /ɪnˈventɪv/ a. able to invent.

**inventory** /ˈɪnvəntəri/ 1 n. list of goods etc. 2 v.t. make inventory of; enter in inventory.

**inverse** /ɪnˈvɜːs/ 1 a. inverted in position or order or relation; (of ratio etc.) between two quantities one of which increases as other decreases. 2 n. inverted state; direct opposition.

**inversion** /ɪnˈvɜːʃ(ə)n/ n. inverting, esp. reversal of normal order of words.

**invert** 1 /ɪnˈvɜːt/ v.t. turn upside down; reverse position or order or relation etc. of. 2 /ˈɪnvɜːt/ n. homosexual. **3 inverted commas** quotation-marks.

**invertebrate** /ɪnˈvɜːtɪbrət/ 1 a. without backbone or spinal column. 2 n. invertebrate animal.

**invest** /ɪnˈvest/ v.t. apply or use (money) for profit; endue (*with* qualities, insignia, etc.); clothe, dress; lay siege to. **invest in** put money into (stocks etc.), *colloq*. buy. **investor** n.

**investigable** /ɪnˈvestɪɡəb(ə)l/ a. that can be investigated.

**investigate** /ɪnˈvestɪɡeɪt/ v.t. examine, inquire into. **investigation** n.; **investigator** n.

**investiture** /ɪnˈvestɪtʃə(r)/ n. formal investing of person with honours etc.

**investment** /ɪnˈvestmənt/ n. investing; money invested; property in which money is invested.

**inveterate** /ɪnˈvetərət/ a. deep-rooted, confirmed. **inveteracy** n.

**invidious** /ɪnˈvɪdɪəs/ a. likely to excite ill-will against performer or possessor etc.

**invigilate** /ɪnˈvɪdʒɪleɪt/ v.i. supervise examinees. **invigilation** n.; **invigilator** n.

**invigorate** /ɪnˈvɪɡəreɪt/ v.t. give vigour to. **invigoration** n.; **invigorative** a.

**invincible** /ɪnˈvɪnsəb(ə)l/ a. unconquerable. **invincibility** n.

# iodine

**inviolable** /ɪnˈvaɪələb(ə)l/ a. not to be violated. **inviolability** n.

**inviolate** /ɪnˈvaɪələt/ a. not having been violated. **inviolacy** n.

**invisible** /ɪnˈvɪzəb(ə)l/ a. that cannot be seen. **invisible exports, imports**, items for which payment is made by or to another country but which are not goods. **invisibility** n.

**invite** 1 /ɪnˈvaɪt/ v.t. request courteously to come or to do etc.; solicit courteously; attract. 2 /ˈɪnvaɪt/ n. *colloq*. invitation. 3 **invitation** /ɪnvɪˈteɪʃ(ə)n/ n.

**inviting** a. attractive.

**invocation** /ɪnvəˈkeɪʃ(ə)n/ n. invoking; calling upon in prayer. **invocatory** /-ˈvɒk-/ a.

**invoice** /ˈɪnvɔɪs/ 1 n. list of goods sent, with prices etc. 2 v.t. make invoice of; send invoice to.

**invoke** /ɪnˈvəʊk/ v.t. call on in prayer or as witness; appeal to; summon (spirit) by charms; ask earnestly for.

**involuntary** /ɪnˈvɒləntərɪ/ a. done etc. without exercise of will, not controlled by will.

**involute** /ˈɪnvəluːt/ a. intricate; curled spirally.

**involution** /ɪnvəˈluːʃ(ə)n/ n. involving, intricacy; curling inwards, part so curled.

**involve** /ɪnˈvɒlv/ v.t. cause (person or thing) to share experience or effect; imply, make necessary; include or affect in its operation; in *p.p.* complicated. **involvement** n.

**involved** a. concerned (*in*); complicated.

**invulnerable** /ɪnˈvʌlnərəb(ə)l/ a. that cannot be wounded. **invulnerability** n.

**inward** /ˈɪnwəd/ 1 a. directed towards inside; situated within; mental, spiritual. 2 adv. inwards.

**inwardly** /ˈɪnwədlɪ/ adv. on the inside; not aloud; in mind or spirit.

**inwardness** /ˈɪnwədnəs/ n. inner nature, spirituality.

**inwards** /ˈɪnwədz/ adv. towards inside; within mind or soul.

**inwrought** /ɪnˈrɔːt/ a. decorated (*with*); wrought (*in*, *on*).

**iodine** /ˈaɪədiːn/ n. black solid halogen element; solution of this used as antiseptic.

**iodize** /ˈaɪədaɪz/ v.t. impregnate with iodine.

**ion** /ˈaɪən/ n. one of the electrically charged particles into which atoms and molecules of certain substances are dissociated by solution in water.

**ionic** /aɪˈɒnɪk/ a. of or using ions.

**ionize** /ˈaɪənaɪz/ v.t. convert or be converted into ion(s). **ionization** n.

**ionosphere** /aɪˈɒnəsfɪə(r)/ n. ionized region in upper atmosphere. **ionospheric** /-ˈsfer-/ a.

**iota** /aɪˈəʊtə/ n. ninth letter of Greek alphabet (*I*, ι); smallest amount.

**IOU** /aɪəʊˈjuː/ n. signed document acknowledging debt.

**IPA** abbr. International Phonetic Alphabet.

**ipecacuanha** /ɪpɪkækjuˈɑːnə/ n. root of S. Amer. plant used as emetic etc.

***ipso facto*** /ɪpsəʊ ˈfæktəʊ/ by that very fact. [L]

**IQ** abbr. intelligence quotient.

**IRA** abbr. Irish Republican Army.

**irascible** /ɪˈræsɪb(ə)l/ a. irritable; hot-tempered. **irascibility** n.

**irate** /aɪˈreɪt/ a. angry.

**ire** /aɪə(r)/ n. *poet.* anger. **ireful** a.

**iridaceous** /ɪrɪˈdeɪʃəs/ a. *Bot.* of iris family.

**iridescent** /ɪrɪˈdes(ə)nt/ a. showing rainbow-like colours. **iridescence** n.

**iris** /ˈaɪərɪs/ n. circular coloured membrane surrounding pupil of eye; bulbous or tuberous plant with sword-shaped leaves and showy flowers.

**Irish** /ˈaɪərɪʃ/ 1 a. of Ireland. 2 n. Celtic language of Ireland; *the* Irish people. 3 **Irish stew** dish of stewed mutton and onions and potatoes. 4 **Irishman** n.; **Irishwoman** n.

**irk** v.t. irritate or annoy.

**irksome** /ˈɜːksəm/ a. tiresome.

**iron** /ˈaɪən/ 1 n. common strong grey metallic element; tool etc. of iron; implement heated to smooth clothes etc.; golf-club with iron or steel head; in *pl.* fetters, leg-supports to rectify malformations. 2 a. of iron; robust; unyielding. 3 v.t. smooth (clothes etc.) with heated iron. 4 **Iron Age** era characterized by use of iron weapons etc.; **ironbark** any of several Aus. eucalypts with very hard bark; **Iron Curtain** *fig.* barrier to passage of persons and information at limit of Soviet sphere of influence; **ironing-board** narrow folding table etc. for ironing clothes on; **iron lung** rigid case over patient's body for prolonged artificial respiration; **ironmaster** manufacturer of iron; **ironmonger** dealer in tools and household implements etc.; **ironmongery** n.; **iron ration** (soldier's) small quantity of tinned etc. food for use in emergency; **ironstone** hard iron-ore, kind of hard white pottery.

**ironic** /aɪˈrɒnɪk/ a. (also **ironical**) using or displaying irony. **ironically** adv.

**irony** /ˈaɪərənɪ/ n. expression of meaning by use of words normally conveying opposite meaning; apparent perversity of fate or circumstances. **ironist** n.

**irradiate** /ɪˈreɪdɪeɪt/ v.t. subject to radiation; shine upon; throw light on; light up. **irradiation** n.

**irrational** /ɪˈræʃən(ə)l/ a. unreasonable, illogical; not endowed with reason; *Math.* not commensurable with the natural numbers. **irrationality** n.

**irreconcilable** /ɪrekənˈsaɪləb(ə)l/ a. implacably hostile; incompatible. **irreconcilability** n.

**irrecoverable** /ɪrəˈkʌvərəb(ə)l/ a. that cannot be recovered or remedied.

**irredeemable** /ɪrəˈdiːməb(ə)l/ a. that cannot be redeemed, hopeless.

**irreducible** /ɪrəˈdjuːsəb(ə)l/ a. not reducible.

**irrefutable** /ɪrəˈfjuːtəb(ə)l/ a. that cannot be refuted. **irrefutability** n.

**irregular** /ɪˈregjələ(r)/ 1 a. uneven, varying; contrary to rule; (of troops) not in regular army. 2 n. member of irregular military force. 3 **irregularity** n.

**irrelevant** /ɪˈreləv(ə)nt/ a. not relevant. **irrelevance** n.

**irreligion** /ɪrəˈlɪdʒ(ə)n/ n. hostility to or indifference to religion. **irreligious** a.

**irremediable** /ɪrəˈmiːdɪəb(ə)l/ a. that cannot be remedied.

**irremovable** /ɪrəˈmuːvəb(ə)l/ a. not removable. **irremovability** n.

**irreparable** /ɪˈrepərəb(ə)l/ a. that cannot be rectified or made good.

**irreplaceable** /ɪrəˈpleɪsəb(ə)l/ a. that cannot be replaced.

**irrepressible** /ɪrəˈpresəb(ə)l/ a. that cannot be repressed.

**irreproachable** /ɪrəˈprəʊtʃəb(ə)l/ a.

**irresistible** 290 **itinerant**

faultless, blameless. **irreproachability** n.
**irresistible** /ɪrə'zɪstəb(ə)l/ a. too strong or convincing or charming etc. to be resisted. **irresistibility** n.
**irresolute** /ɪ'rezəluːt/ a. hesitating; lacking in resolution. **irresolution** n.
**irrespective** /ɪrə'spektɪv/ a. irrespective of not taking into account, without reference to.
**irresponsible** /ɪrə'spɒnsəb(ə)l/ a. acting or done without due sense of responsibility; not responsible. **irresponsibility** n.
**irretrievable** /ɪrə'triːvəb(ə)l/ a. not retrievable.
**irreverent** /ɪ'revərənt/ a. lacking in reverence. **irreverence** n.
**irreversible** /ɪrə'vɜːsəb(ə)l/ a. that cannot be reversed. **irreversibility** n.
**irrevocable** /ɪ'revəkəb(ə)l/ a. unalterable; gone beyond recall. **irrevocability** n.
**irrigate** /'ɪrɪgeɪt/ v.t. supply (land) with water; water (land) by system of artificial channels; *Med.* moisten (wound etc.) with constant flow of liquid. **irrigation** n.
**irritable** /'ɪrətəb(ə)l/ a. easily annoyed; sensitive; inflamed, sore. **irritability** n.
**irritant** /'ɪrət(ə)nt/ 1 a. causing irritation. 2 n. irritant substance or agent.
**irritate** /'ɪrəteɪt/ v.t. excite to anger, annoy; inflame. **irritation** n.
**irruption** /ɪ'rʌpʃ(ə)n/ n. invasion; violent entry.
**is** /ɪz/ 3 pers. sing. pres. of **be**.
**isinglass** /'aɪzɪŋɡlɑːs/ n. kind of gelatin obtained from sturgeon etc.
**Islam** /'ɪzlɑːm/ n. religion of Muslims, revealed through Prophet Muhammad; the Muslim world. **Islamic** /-'læm-/ a.
**island** /'aɪlənd/ n. piece of land surrounded by water; traffic island; detached or isolated thing.
**islander** /'aɪləndə(r)/ n. inhabitant of island.
**isle** /aɪl/ n. (usu. small) island.
**islet** /'aɪlət/ n. small island.
**isobar** /'aɪsəbɑː(r)/ n. line on map etc. connecting places with same atmospheric pressure. **isobaric** /-'bær-/ a.
**isolate** /'aɪsəleɪt/ v.t. place apart or alone; separate (esp. infectious patient from others); insulate (electrical apparatus). **isolation** n.
**isolationism** /aɪsə'leɪʃənɪz(ə)m/ n. policy of holding aloof from affairs of other countries or groups. **isolationist** n.
**isomer** /'aɪsəmə(r)/ n. one of two or more substances whose molecules have same atoms in different arrangement. **isomeric** /-'mer-/ a.; **isomerism** /-'sɒm-/ n.
**isosceles** /aɪ'sɒsəliːz/ a. (of triangle) having two sides equal.
**isotherm** /'aɪsəθɜːm/ n. line on map etc. connecting places with same temperature. **isothermal** a.
**isotope** /'aɪsətəʊp/ n. any of two or more forms of chemical element with different atomic weight and different nuclear but not chemical properties. **isotopic** /-'tɒp-/ a.
**Israeli** /ɪz'reɪlɪ/ 1 a. of modern State of Israel. 2 n. Israeli person.
**issue** /'ɪʃuː/ 1 n. outgoing, outflow; giving out or circulation; copies of journal etc. issued at one time; one of regular series of magazine etc.; result, outcome; question, dispute; offspring. 2 v. go or come out; give or send out; publish, circulate; supply, supply *with* equipment etc.; emerge; be derived, result.
**isthmus** /'ɪsθməs/ n. neck of land; narrow connecting part.
**it** pron. (poss. **its**) thing named or in question; indefinite or undefined or impersonal action or condition or object etc.; sl. the very person or thing, perfection; sl. sexual intercourse, sex appeal.
**Italian** /ɪ'tæljən/ a. of Italy. 2 n. native or language of Italy.
**italic** /ɪ'tælɪk/ 1 a. (of type etc.) of sloping kind; **Italic** of ancient Italy. 2 n. in pl. italic type.
**italicize** /ɪ'tælɪsaɪz/ v.t. print in italics.
**itch** 1 n. irritation in skin; disease with itch; restless desire. 2 v.i. feel itch.
**item** /'aɪtəm/ n. any one of enumerated things; detail of news etc.
**itemize** /'aɪtəmaɪz/ v.t. state by items. **itemization** n.
**iterate** /'ɪtəreɪt/ v.t. repeat; state repeatedly. **iteration** n.; **iterative** a.
**itinerant** /aɪ'tɪnərənt/ 1 a. travelling from place to place. 2 n. itinerant person.

**itinerary** /aɪˈtɪnərəri/ n. route; record of travel; guide-book.

**its** pron., poss. case of **it**.

**itself** /ɪtˈself/ pron., emphat. & refl. form of **it**.

**IUD** abbr. intra-uterine (contraceptive) device.

**ivory** /ˈaɪvəri/ n. white substance of tusks of elephant etc.; colour of this; in pl. sl. dice, piano-keys, teeth, etc. **ivory tower** seclusion from harsh realities.

**ivy** /ˈaɪvi:/ n. climbing evergreen with shining leaves.

# J

**jab** 1 *v.t.* poke roughly; thrust abruptly. 2 *n.* abrupt blow with pointed thing or fist; *colloq.* hypodermic injection.

**jabber** /ˈdʒæbə(r)/ 1 *v.* chatter volubly; utter fast and indistinctly. 2 *n.* chatter, gabble.

**jabot** /ˈʒæbəʊ/ *n.* frill at neck or down front opening of shirt or blouse etc.

**jacaranda** /dʒækəˈrændə/ *n.* tropical Amer. tree with hard scented wood.

**jacinth** /ˈdʒæsɪnθ/ *n.* reddish-orange gem, kind of zircon.

**jack** 1 *n.* machine for lifting weights, esp. for lifting wheel of vehicle off ground; lowest-ranking court-card; ship's flag esp. one flown from bow and showing nationality; device using single plug to connect electrical circuit; device for turning spit; in *pl.* treated as *sing.* game played with jackstones; *Bowls* small white ball for players to aim at; (usu. young) pike. 2 *v.t.* hoist *up* (as) with jack. 3 *a. Aus. sl.* tired *of*; fed up with. 4 **jackboot** large boot with top reaching above knee, *fig.* oppressive behaviour; **jack in** *sl.* abandon; **jack-in-office** pompous official; **jack-in-the-box** toy figure that springs out when box is opened; **jackknife** large clasp-knife, accidental folding of articulated vehicle (also *v.*); **jack of all trades** person who can do many kinds of work; **jack up** *Aus. sl.* refuse, be obstinate.

**jackal** /ˈdʒæk(ə)l/ *n.* wild animal related to dog.

**jackanapes** /ˈdʒækəneɪps/ *n.* pert child or fellow.

**jackaroo** /dʒækəˈruː/ *n. Aus. & NZ* cadet or novice on sheep- or cattle-station.

**jackass** /ˈdʒækæs/ *n.* male ass; stupid person; *Aus.* kookaburra.

**jackdaw** /ˈdʒækdɔː/ *n.* bird of crow family.

**jackeroo** var. of **jackaroo**.

**jacket** /ˈdʒækɪt/ *n.* sleeved short outer garment; outer covering round boiler etc. to prevent heat loss; outside wrapper of book; skin of potato.

**jackpot** /ˈdʒækpɒt/ *n.* accumulating prize in lottery etc.

**Jacky Winter** /ˈdʒæki/ *Aus.* small brown flycatcher.

**Jacobean** /dʒækəˈbiːən/ *a.* of reign of James I of England.

**Jacobite** /ˈdʒækəbaɪt/ *n. hist.* supporter of exiled Stuarts.

**Jacuzzi** /dʒəˈkuːzi/ *n.* (P) large bath with underwater jets of water.

**jade**[1] *n.* hard translucent green or blue or white stone; green colour of this.

**jade**[2] *n.* poor or worn-out horse; *joc.* hussy.

**jaded** /ˈdʒeɪdɪd/ *a.* tired out, sated.

**jadeite** /ˈdʒeɪdaɪt/ *n.* jadelike stone.

**jag** 1 *n.* sharp projection of rock etc. 2 *v.t.* cut or tear unevenly; make indentations in.

**jagged** /ˈdʒægɪd/ *a.* with unevenly cut or torn edge.

**jaguar** /ˈdʒægjʊə(r)/ *n.* large Amer. carnivorous spotted animal of cat family.

**jail** var. of **gaol**.

**jake** *a. Aus. sl.* all right; fine, excellent.

**jalap** /ˈdʒæləp/ *n.* purgative drug.

**jalopy** /dʒəˈlɒpi/ *n. colloq.* dilapidated old motor vehicle.

**jalousie** /ˈʒæluːziː/ *n.* blind or shutter with slats sloped upwards from outside.

**jam**[1] *v.* squeeze; (cause to) become wedged; cause (machinery) to become wedged etc. so that it cannot work, become thus wedged; force or cram together; block by crowding; make (radio transmission) unintelligible by causing interference. 2 *n.* squeeze; stoppage; crowded mass esp. of traffic on road.

**jam**[2] *n.* conserve of fruit and sugar boiled until thick; *colloq.* something easy or pleasant to deal with. **jammy** *a.*

**jamb** /dʒæm/ *n.* side post or side of doorway or window arch.

**jamboree** /dʒæmbəˈriː/ *n.* celebration, merry-making; large rally of Scouts.

**Jan.** *abbr.* January.

**jangle** /ˈdʒæŋg(ə)l/ 1 *v.* (cause to) make harsh metallic sound. 2 *n.* such sound.

**janitor** /ˈdʒænɪtə(r)/ *n.* doorkeeper; caretaker of building.

**January** /ˈdʒænjʊəri/ *n.* first month of the year.

**japan** /dʒəˈpæn/ 1 *n.* hard usu. black varnish. 2 *v.t.* make black and glossy (as) with japan.

**Japanese** /dʒæpəˈniːz/ 1 n. native or language of Japan. 2 a. of Japan.
**jape** n. practical joke.
**japonica** /dʒəˈpɒnɪkə/ n. ornamental variety of quince with red flowers.
**jar**[1] 1 v. strike discordantly, grate; be at variance (with). 2 n. jarring sound or shock or vibration.
**jar**[2] n. glass or pottery or plastic etc. vessel, usu. cylindrical.
**jardinière** /ˌʒɑːdəˈnjeə(r)/ n. ornamental pot or stand for display of growing flowers.
**jargon** /ˈdʒɑːgən/ n. language peculiar to class or profession etc.; barbarous or debased language.
**jarrah** /ˈdʒærə/ n. W. Aus. eucalypt; its durable brown-red wood.
**jasmine** /ˈdʒæzmɪn/ n. shrub with white or yellow flowers.
**jasper** /ˈdʒæspə(r)/ n. red or yellow or brown opaque quartz.
**jaundice** /ˈdʒɔːndɪs/ 1 n. condition due to obstruction of bile and marked by yellowness of skin etc. 2 v.t. affect with jaundice; fig. affect (person etc.) with envy or resentment etc.
**jaunt** 1 n. pleasure excursion. 2 v.i. take a jaunt.
**jaunty** /ˈdʒɔːntɪ/ a. cheerful and self-confident; sprightly.
**javelin** /ˈdʒævəlɪn/ n. light spear thrown as weapon or in sports.
**jaw** 1 n. bone(s) containing teeth; in pl. mouth, gripping part of machine etc.; colloq. long or sermonizing talk. 2 v. sl. speak at length; admonish, lecture. 3 **jaw-bone** lower jaw of mammals.
**jay** n. noisy European bird with vivid plumage. **jay-walker** pedestrian who walks in, or crosses, road carelessly.
**jazz** 1 n. music of US Negro origin usu. characterized by improvisation, syncopation, and marked rhythm. 2 v. brighten or liven up; play or dance to jazz.
**jazzy** /ˈdʒæzɪ/ a. of or like jazz; vivid.
**jealous** /ˈdʒeləs/ a. watchfully tenacious; suspicious or resentful of rivalry in love or affection; envious. **jealousy** n.
**jean** n. twilled cotton cloth; in pl. trousers of jean or denim.
**Jeep** n. (P) small sturdy motor vehicle with four-wheel drive.

**jeer** 1 v. scoff (at); deride. 2 n. gibe, taunt.
**Jehovah** /dʒɪˈhəʊvə/ n. OT name of God. **Jehovah's Witness** member of a fundamentalist Christian sect.
**jejune** /dʒɪˈdʒuːn/ a. meagre; poor, barren.
**jell** v.i. colloq. set as jelly; take definite form.
**jellied** /ˈdʒelɪd/ a. (of food etc.) set in jelly.
**jelly** /ˈdʒelɪ/ n. soft stiffish usu. semi-transparent food made of or with gelatine or of fruit-juice and sugar; substance of similar consistency; sl. gelignite. **jelly baby** gelatinous sweet in shape of baby; **jellyfish** marine animal with gelatinous body and stinging tentacles.
**jemmy** /ˈdʒemɪ/ n. burglar's crowbar.
**jeopardize** /ˈdʒepədaɪz/ v.t. endanger.
**jeopardy** /ˈdʒepədɪ/ n. danger esp. of severe harm.
**jerboa** /dʒɜːˈbəʊə/ n. small Afr. jumping rodent with long hind legs.
**jeremiad** /dʒerəˈmaɪəd/ n. doleful complaint.
**jerk**[1] 1 n. sharp sudden pull or twist etc.; spasmodic twitch of muscle; sl. fool, stupid person. 2 v. move with a jerk; throw with suddenly arrested motion. 3 **jerky** a.
**jerk**[2] v.t. cure (esp. beef) by cutting in long slices and drying in the sun.
**jerkin** /ˈdʒɜːkɪn/ n. sleeveless jacket.
**jeroboam** /dʒerəˈbəʊəm/ n. wine-bottle of 6-12 times ordinary size.
**jerrican** var. of **jerrycan**.
**jerry**[1] /ˈdʒerɪ/ n. sl. chamber-pot.
**jerry**[2] /ˈdʒerɪ/ v. Aus. sl. **jerry to** become aware of.
**jerry-building** building of unsubstantial houses with bad materials. **jerry-builder** n.; **jerry-built** a.
**jerrycan** /ˈdʒerɪkæn/ n. kind of petrol- or water-can.
**jersey** /ˈdʒɜːzɪ/ n. knitted usu. woollen pullover; knitted fabric.
**Jerusalem artichoke** /dʒəˈruːsələm/ kind of sunflower with edible tuber; this tuber.
**jest** 1 n. joke; fun; object of derision. 2 v. joke, make jests.
**jester** /ˈdʒestə(r)/ n. hist. professional joker at court etc.

**Jesuit** /ˈdʒezjuːət/ n. member of RC Society of Jesus. **Jesuitical** a.

**jet**[1] n. stream of water or steam or flame etc. shot esp. from small opening; spout or nozzle for emitting water etc. thus; jet engine or plane. 2 v. spurt out in jet(s); *colloq.* travel or send by jet plane. 3 **jet engine** one using jet propulsion for forward thrust esp. of aircraft; **jet lag** delayed bodily effects felt after long flight; **jet plane** one with jet engine; **jet-propelled** having jet propulsion, *fig.* very fast; **jet propulsion** propulsion by backward ejection of high-speed jet of gas etc.; **jet set** wealthy élite.

**jet**[2] n. hard black lignite taking brilliant polish. **jet-black** deep glossy black.

**jetsam** /ˈdʒetsəm/ n. goods thrown out of ship to lighten it and washed ashore.

**jettison** /ˈdʒetɪs(ə)n/ v.t. throw out (goods) from ship or aircraft esp. to lighten load; *fig.* abandon.

**jetty** /ˈdʒetɪ/ n. pier or breakwater constructed to defend harbour etc.; landing-pier.

**Jew** n. person of Hebrew descent or whose religion is Judaism. **jewfish** *Aus.* mulloway, catfish, perch-like W. Aus. fish. **Jewess** n.; **Jewish** a.

**jewel** /ˈdʒuːəl/ 1 n. precious stone; personal ornament containing jewel(s); precious thing etc. 2 v.t. adorn with jewels; fit (watch) with jewels for the pivot-holes.

**jeweller** /ˈdʒuːələ(r)/ n. dealer in jewels or jewellery.

**jewellery** /ˈdʒuːəlrɪ/ n. jewels or jewelled ornaments.

**Jewry** /ˈdʒuːrɪ/ n. Jews collectively.

**Jezebel** /ˈdʒezəbel/ n. shameless woman.

**jib** 1 n. triangular staysail from outer end of jib-boom to top of foremast or from bowsprit to mast-head. 2 v.i. (of horse or *fig.* of person) stop and refuse to go on. 3 **jib at** object strongly to; **jib-boom** spar from end of bowsprit.

**jibe**[1] var. of **gibe**.

**jibe**[2] var. of **gybe**.

**jiff** n. *colloq.* (also **jiffy**) short time, moment.

**jig** 1 n. lively dance; music for this. 2 v. dance jig; move quickly up and down.

**jigger**[1] /ˈdʒɪgə(r)/ n. small glass or measure esp. for spirits.

**jigger**[2] /ˈdʒɪgə(r)/ var. of **chigoe**.

**jiggery-pokery** /dʒɪgərɪˈpəʊkərɪ/ *colloq.* deceitful or dishonest dealing; trickery.

**jiggle** /ˈdʒɪg(ə)l/ v.t. rock or jerk lightly.

**jigsaw** /ˈdʒɪgsɔː/ n. machine fretsaw; (in full **jigsaw puzzle**) picture pasted on board etc. and cut into irregular pieces to be reassembled as pastime.

**jilt** v.t. capriciously discard encouraged lover.

**Jindyworobak** /dʒɪndɪˈwʊrəbæk/ n. *Aus.* member of group founded in 1938 to promote Aus. values in literature and art etc.

**jingle** /ˈdʒɪŋg(ə)l/ 1 n. mixed noise as of small bells or links of chain etc.; repetition of same sounds in words; short verse of this kind used in advertising etc. 2 v. (cause to) make jingle.

**jingo** /ˈdʒɪŋgəʊ/ n. (pl. **-goes**) blustering patriot. **jingoism** n.; **jingoist** n.; **jingoistic** a.

**jink** 1 v. move elusively; elude by dodging. 2 n. act of jinking. 3 **high jinks** boisterous fun.

**jinker** /ˈdʒɪŋkə(r)/ n. *Aus.* wheeled conveyance for logs.

**jinnee** /dʒɪˈniː/ n. (pl. **jinn**, also used as *sing.*) (in Muslim mythology) spirit of supernatural power.

**jinx** n. person or thing that brings bad luck.

**jitter** /ˈdʒɪtə(r)/ *colloq.* 1 v.i. be nervous, act nervously. 2 n. in pl. extreme nervousness. 3 **jittery** a.

**jive** *sl.* 1 n. fast lively jazz music; dance done to this. 2 v. play or dance jive.

**job**[1] 1 n. piece of work (to be) done; paid employment; *sl.* a crime, esp. a robbery; *colloq.* difficult task. 2 v. do jobs; hire, let out for time or job; buy and sell (stock etc.) as middleman; deal with corruptly. 3 **job lot** miscellaneous group of articles, esp. bought as speculation.

**job**[2] v. *Aus. sl.* punch; deal heavy blow.

**jobber** /ˈdʒɒbə(r)/ n. stockjobber.

**jobbery** /ˈdʒɒbərɪ/ n. corrupt dealing.

**jockey** /ˈdʒɒkɪ/ 1 n. rider in horse-races. 2 v. cheat, trick; manoeuvre *for* advantageous position. 3 **jockey spider** *Aus.* red-backed spider.

**jock-strap** /ˈdʒɒkstræp/ n. support or protection for male genitals worn esp. by sportsmen.

**jocose** /dʒəˈkəʊs/ a. jocular. **jocosity** /-ˈkɒs-/ n.

**jocular** /ˈdʒɒkjələ(r)/ a. given to joking; humorous. **jocularity** n.

**jocund** /ˈdʒɒkənd/ a. merry, cheerful. **jocundity** n.

**jodhpurs** /ˈdʒɒdpəz/ n.pl. long riding-breeches, tight from knee to ankle.

**joey** /ˈdʒəʊɪ/ n. Aus. young kangaroo; sl. odd-job man.

**jog 1** v. stimulate (memory); nudge, push, jerk; run slowly for exercise; walk or run or ride with jolting pace. **2** n. spell of jogging; slow walk or trot; push, jerk, nudge. **3 jog-trot** slow regular trot.

**joggle** /ˈdʒɒg(ə)l/ **1** v. move to and fro in jerks. **2** n. slight shake.

*joie de vivre* /ʒwɑː də ˈviːvr/ feeling of exuberant enjoyment of life. [F]

**join 1** v. put together, fasten, unite; connect (points) by line etc.; become member of; take one's place with or in; take part with others (*in*); unite or be united in marriage or alliance etc.; (of river or road) become continuous or connected with (another). **2** n. point or line or surface of junction.

**joiner** /ˈdʒɔɪnə(r)/ n. maker of furniture and light woodwork. **joinery** n.

**joint 1** n. place at which or means by which two things join; structure by which two bones fit together; section of animal's carcase used for food; sl. place of meeting for drinking etc.; sl. marijuana cigarette. **2** a. held or done by, or belonging to, two or more persons etc. in common; sharing *with* others in possession etc. **3** v.t. connect by joint(s); divide (carcase) into joints or at a joint. **4 joint stock** capital held jointly.

**jointure** /ˈdʒɔɪntʃə(r)/ n. estate settled on wife for period during which she survives husband.

**joist** n. one of parallel timbers stretched from wall to wall to carry ceiling or floor boards.

**jojoba** /həʊˈhəʊbə/ n. desert shrub with bean yielding oil.

**joke 1** n. thing said or done to excite laughter. **2** v.i. make jokes. **3 jokey** a.

**joker** /ˈdʒəʊkə(r)/ n. person who jokes; extra playing-card used in some games.

**jollification** /dʒɒləfɪˈkeɪʃ(ə)n/ n. merry-making.

**jolly** /ˈdʒɒlɪ/ **1** a. joyful; festive, jovial; colloq. pleasant, delightful. **2** adv. colloq. very. **3** v.t. colloq. coax or humour (person) *along*. **4 jollity** n.

**jolt** /dʒəʊlt/ **1** v. jerk from seat etc.; move along with jerks; give mental shock to. **2** n. such jerk or shock.

**jonquil** /ˈdʒɒŋkwɪl/ n. kind of narcissus with white or yellow fragrant flowers.

**josh** US sl. **1** v. make fun of, hoax. **2** n. good-natured joke.

**joss** n. Chinese idol. **joss-stick** stick of fragrant tinder and clay for incense.

**jostle** /ˈdʒɒs(ə)l/ **1** v. knock or shove (*against*); struggle. **2** n. jostling.

**jot 1** n. small amount, whit. **2** v.t. write (*down*) briefly or hastily.

**jotter** /ˈdʒɒtə(r)/ n. small notebook etc.

**joule** /dʒuːl/ n. unit of work or energy.

**jounce** /dʒaʊns/ v. bump, bounce, jolt.

**journal** /ˈdʒɜːn(ə)l/ n. daily record of events etc.; log-book; newspaper or other periodical; part of shaft or axle resting on bearings.

**journalese** /dʒɜːnəˈliːz/ n. hackneyed style of language characteristic of some newspaper writing.

**journalism** /ˈdʒɜːnəlɪz(ə)m/ n. work of journalist.

**journalist** /ˈdʒɜːnəlɪst/ n. person employed to write for journal or newspaper.

**journey** /ˈdʒɜːnɪ/ **1** n. act of going from one place to another; distance travelled. **2** v.i. make journey. **3 journeyman** qualified mechanic or artisan working for another.

**joust** /dʒaʊst/ hist. **1** n. combat with lances between two mounted knights. **2** v.i. engage in joust.

**jovial** /ˈdʒəʊvɪəl/ a. merry, convivial, hearty. **joviality** n.

**jowl** /dʒaʊl/ n. jaw, jawbone; cheek; loose skin on throat.

**joy** n. gladness, pleasure; cause of this. **joy-ride** colloq. (unauthorized) pleasure-ride in motor car etc.; **joystick** control lever of aircraft, Computers device for moving cursor on screen. **joyful** a; **joyous** a.

**JP** abbr. Justice of the Peace.

**Jr.** abbr. Junior.

**jubilant** /ˈdʒuːbələnt/ a. exultant.

**jubilation** /dʒuːbəˈleɪʃ(ə)n/ n. exulting; rejoicing.

**jubilee** /ˈdʒuːbəliː/ n. (esp. 50th) anniversary; time of rejoicing.

**Judaic** /dʒuːˈdeɪɪk/ a. Jewish.

**Judaism** /ˈdʒuːdeɪɪz(ə)m/ n. religion of the Jews.

**Judas** /ˈdʒuːdəs/ n. infamous traitor.

**judder** /ˈdʒʌdə(r)/ 1 v.i. shake, shudder noisily. 2 n. instance of juddering.

**judge** 1 n. officer appointed to try causes in court of justice etc.; person appointed to decide dispute or contest; person fit to decide on merits of thing or question. 2 v. try (cause); pronounce sentence on (person); decide (contest, question); form opinion about, estimate; conclude, consider; act as judge.

**judgement** /ˈdʒʌdʒmənt/ n. critical faculty, discernment, good sense; opinion; decision of court of justice etc.; misfortune as sign of divine displeasure. **Last Judgement** judgement by God at end of world.

**judicature** /ˈdʒuːdəkətʃə(r)/ n. administration of justice; body of judges.

**judicial** /dʒuːˈdɪʃ(ə)l/ a. of or by court of law; of or proper to a judge; impartial.

**judiciary** /dʒuːˈdɪʃəri/ n. judges collectively.

**judicious** /dʒuːˈdɪʃəs/ a. sensible, prudent.

**judo** /ˈdʒuːdəʊ/ n. modern development of ju-jitsu.

**jug** 1 n. deep vessel for liquids, with handle and usu. spout; sl. prison. 2 v.t. stew (hare) in covered vessel.

**juggernaut** /ˈdʒʌɡənɔːt/ n. large heavy motor vehicle; overpowering force or object.

**juggins** /ˈdʒʌɡɪnz/ n. sl. simpleton.

**juggle** /ˈdʒʌɡ(ə)l/ v. perform feats of dexterity (*with* objects tossed up and caught); manipulate or arrange to suit purpose.

**Jugoslav** var. of **Yugoslav**.

**jugular** /ˈdʒʌɡjʊlə(r)/ 1 a. of neck or throat. 2 n. jugular vein. 3 **jugular vein** either of veins of neck conveying blood from head.

**juice** /dʒuːs/ n. liquid content of vegetable or fruit or meat; bodily secretion; sl. petrol, electricity.

**juicy** /ˈdʒuːsi/ a. full of juice; colloq. interesting, (esp.) scandalous.

**ju-jitsu** /dʒuːˈdʒɪtsuː/ n. Japanese system of wrestling.

**ju-ju** /ˈdʒuːdʒuː/ n. W.Afr. charm, fetish; magic attributed to them.

**jujube** /ˈdʒuːdʒuːb/ n. sweet fruit-flavoured lozenge of gelatin etc.

**juke-box** /ˈdʒuːkbɒks/ n. slot-machine that plays selected gramophone record.

**Jul.** abbr. July.

**julep** /ˈdʒuːlep/ n. drink of spirit and water iced and flavoured esp. with mint.

**julienne** /dʒuːliˈen/ 1 n. vegetables etc. cut into thin strips; clear soup to which such vegetables are added. 2 a. cut into thin strips.

**July** /dʒuːˈlaɪ/ n. seventh month of the year.

**jumble** /ˈdʒʌmb(ə)l/ 1 v.t. mix (*up*) in confusion. 2 n. confused heap etc.; muddle; articles for jumble sale. 3 **jumble sale** sale of miscellaneous usu. second-hand articles to raise funds for charity etc.

**jumbo** /ˈdʒʌmbəʊ/ 1 n. (pl. **-bos**) big animal (esp. elephant) or person or thing; jumbo jet. 2 a. very large of its kind. 3 **jumbo jet** large jet plane able to carry several hundred passengers.

**jumbuck** /ˈdʒʌmbʌk/ n. Aus. sheep.

**jump** 1 v. leap or spring from ground etc.; rise or move with sudden start; clear (obstacle) by jumping; come *to* or arrive *at* (conclusion etc.) hastily; (of train etc.) leave (rails); abscond from; pass over. 2 n. act of jumping; abrupt rise in price etc.; obstacle to be jumped, esp. by horse; sudden movement caused by shock etc. 3 **jump at** accept eagerly; **jumped-up** a. upstart; **jump the gun** make premature start; **jump-jet** jet plane that can take off and land vertically; **jump-lead** cable for conveying current from one battery to another; **jump the queue** take unfair precedence; **jump suit** one-piece garment for whole body; **jump to it** act promptly and energetically.

**jumper** /ˈdʒʌmpə(r)/ n. knitted pullover; loose outer jacket worn by sailors; US pinafore dress.

**jumpy** /ˈdʒʌmpi/ a. nervous, easily startled.

**Jun.** abbr. June; Junior.

**junction** /ˈdʒʌŋkʃ(ə)n/ n. joining-point; place where railway lines or roads meet. **junction box** box containing junction of electric cables etc.

**juncture** /'dʒʌŋktʃə(r)/ n. state of affairs, crisis.

**June** n. sixth month of the year.

**jungle** /'dʒʌŋg(ə)l/ n. land overgrown with tangled vegetation esp. in tropics; tangled mass; place of bewildering complexity or ruthless struggle.

**junior** /'dʒu:niə(r)/ 1 a. the younger; inferior in age or standing or position. 2 n. junior person. 3 **junior school** one for younger pupils.

**juniper** /'dʒu:nəpə(r)/ n. evergreen shrub, esp. with purple berry-like aromatic cones.

**junk**[1] n. discarded articles, rubbish; sl. narcotic drug, esp. heroin. **junk food** food which is not nutritious.

**junk**[2] n. flat-bottomed sailing vessel in China seas.

**junket** /'dʒʌŋkət/ 1 n. dish of milk curdled by rennet and sweetened and flavoured; feast; official's tour at public expense. 2 v.i. feast, picnic.

**junkie** /'dʒʌŋki/ n. sl. drug-addict.

**junta** /'dʒʌntə/ n. political clique or faction holding power after revolution etc.

**juridical** /dʒu:'rɪdɪk(ə)l/ a. of judicial proceedings, relating to the law.

**jurisdiction** /dʒu:rəs'dɪkʃ(ə)n/ n. administration of justice; (extent or area of) authority.

**jurisprudence** /dʒu:rəs'pru:d(ə)ns/ n. science or philosophy of law.

**jurist** /'dʒu:rəst/ n. person versed in law. **juristic** a.

**juror** /'dʒu:rə(r)/ n. member of jury.

**jury** /'dʒu:ri:/ n. body of persons sworn to render verdict in court of justice or coroner's court; judges of competition. **jury-box** enclosure in court for jury; **juryman**, **jurywoman**, juror.

**just** 1 a. upright, fair; deserved, due; well-grounded, right. 2 adv. exactly; barely; exactly or nearly at this or that moment; colloq. simply, merely, positively, quite; sl. really. 3 **just now** at this moment, a little time ago.

**justice** /'dʒʌstəs/ n. justness, fairness; judicial proceedings; judge, magistrate. **Justice of the Peace** lay magistrate.

**justiciary** /dʒʌs'tɪʃəri:/ n. administrator of justice.

**justify** /'dʒʌstəfaɪ/ v.t. show justice or truth of; be adequate ground for, warrant; Print. adjust (line of type) to fill space evenly. **justifiable** a.; **justification** n.; **justificatory** a.

**jut** 1 v.i. protrude. 2 n. projection.

**jute** n. fibre from bark of E. Ind. plants, used for sacking and mats etc.

**juvenile** /'dʒu:vənaɪl/ 1 a. youthful; of or for young persons. 2 n. young person; actor playing such part. 3 **juvenile delinquency** offences committed by persons below age of legal responsibility; **juvenile delinquent** such offender. 4 **juvenility** /-'nɪl-/ n.

**juvenilia** /dʒu:və'nɪli:ə/ n.pl. works produced by author or artist in youth.

**juxtapose** /dʒʌkstə'pəʊz/ v.t. put side by side. **juxtaposition** n.

# K

**K.** *abbr.* Köchel (list of Mozart's works).
**k** *abbr.* kilo-.
**kaftan** var. of **caftan**.
**kaiser** /'kaɪzə(r)/ *n. hist.* emperor esp. of Germany.
**kale** *n.* variety of cabbage, esp. **curly kale** with wrinkled leaves. **kaleyard** *Sc.* kitchen garden.
**kaleidoscope** /kə'laɪdəskəʊp/ *n.* tube containing angled mirrors and pieces of coloured glass, producing symmetrical patterns which can be altered by rotating the end of the tube; *fig.* constantly changing scene etc. **kaleidoscopic** /-'skɒp-/ *a.*
**kamikaze** /kæmɪ'kɑ:zi/ *n. hist.* Japanese aircraft laden with explosives deliberately crashed by pilot on target.
**kangaroo** /kæŋgə'ru:/ *n.* Aus. marsupial with hind quarters strongly developed for jumping. **kangaroo apple** *Aus.* flowering shrub; **kangaroo bar** *Aus.* bull bar; **kangaroo court** illegal court held by strikers etc.; **kangaroo dog** *Aus.* large dog trained to hunt kangaroos; **kangaroo grass** a tall Aus. fodder grass; **kangaroo-paw** sedge-like Aus. plant with woolly-coated flowers; **kangaroo-rat** *Aus.* rat-kangaroo.
**kaolin** /'keɪəlɪn/ *n.* fine white clay used for porcelain.
**kapok** /'keɪpɒk/ *n.* fine cotton-like material from tropical tree used to stuff cushions etc.
**kaput** /kə'pʊt/ *a. sl.* done for, ruined, out of order.
**karate** /kə'rɑ:tɪ/ *n.* Japanese system of unarmed combat using hands and feet as weapons.
**karma** /'kɑ:mə/ *n.* Buddhist's or Hindu's destiny as determined by his actions.
**katydid** /'keɪtɪdɪd/ *n.* large green grasshopper common in US.
**kauri** /'kaʊrɪ/ *n.* coniferous NZ timber-tree.
**kayak** /'kaɪæk/ *n.* Eskimo one-man canoe.
**KBE** *abbr.* Knight Commander of the Order of the British Empire.
**KC** *abbr.* King's Counsel.
**kea** /'keɪə/ *n.* green NZ parrot.

**kebab** /kə'bæb/ *n.* (usu. in *pl.*) small piece(s) of meat and vegetables etc. cooked on skewer.
**kedge** 1 *v.* move (ship) by hawser attached to small anchor. 2 *n.* small anchor for this purpose.
**kedgeree** /'kedʒərɪ/ *n.* dish of fish and rice and hard-boiled eggs etc.
**keel** 1 *n.* lengthwise timber on which ship's framework is built up. 2 *v.* turn (ship) keel upwards. 3 **keelhaul** haul (person) under keel as punishment; **keel over** capsize, (of person) fall over.
**keen**[1] *a.* eager, ardent; sharp; strong; acute, penetrating; competitive.
**keen**[2] 1 *n.* Irish funeral song accompanied with wailing. 2 *v.* utter the keen; utter in wailing tone.
**keep** 1 *v.* (*past & p.p.* **kept**) have charge of; retain possession of; maintain; provide for; maintain or remain in good or specified condition; restrain; pay due regard to, observe; protect; conduct or maintain, esp. for profit. 2 *n.* maintenance, food; *hist.* tower, stronghold. 3 **for keeps** *colloq.* permanently.
**keeper** /'ki:pə(r)/ *n.* person who keeps or looks after something; gamekeeper; custodian of museum etc. or forest; wicket-keeper.
**keeping** /'ki:pɪŋ/ *n.* custody, charge; agreement, harmony.
**keepsake** /'ki:pseɪk/ *n.* thing treasured for sake of giver.
**keg** *n.* small barrel.
**kelp** *n.* large seaweed; calcined ashes of this yielding iodine etc.
**kelpie**[1] /'kelpɪ/ *n. Sc.* malevolent water-spirit.
**kelpie**[2] /'kelpɪ/ *n.* Aus. breed of sheep-dog.
**Kelt** var. of **Celt**.
**ken** 1 *v. Sc.* know. 2 *n.* range of knowledge or sight.
**kendo** /'kendəʊ/ *n.* Japanese sport of fencing with bamboo swords.
**kennel** /'ken(ə)l/ 1 *n.* small structure for shelter of house-dog or hounds; in *pl.* establishment where dogs are bred, or cared for during owners' absence. 2 *v.t.* put or keep in kennel.
**kept** *past & p.p.* of **keep**.
**kerb** *n.* stone edging to pavement etc.

**kerchief** /'kɜːtʃəf/ n. cloth used to cover head.

**kerfuffle** /kəˈfʌf(ə)l/ n. colloq. fuss, commotion.

**kermes** /'kɜːmɪz/ n. female of an insect that lives on an evergreen oak; red dye made from these.

**kernel** /'kɜːn(ə)l/ n. part within hard shell of nut or stone fruit; seed within husk etc.; central or essential part.

**kerosene** /'kerəsiːn/ n. US fuel-oil distilled from petroleum or from coal or bituminous shale.

**kestrel** /'kestr(ə)l/ n. kind of small falcon.

**ketch** n. small two-masted coasting-vessel.

**ketchup** /'ketʃəp/ n. sauce made from tomatoes or mushrooms etc.

**kettle** /'ket(ə)l/ n. metal vessel with spout and handle, for boiling water. **kettledrum** tuned drum of hollow metal hemisphere with parchment etc. stretched across.

**key** /kiː/ 1 n. instrument for turning bolt of lock; instrument for winding clock etc. or for grasping screw or nut etc.; mechanical device for making or breaking electric circuit; one of set of levers pressed by finger on musical instrument or typewriter etc.; Mus. system of notes definitely related and based on particular note; solution; explanation, word or system for solving cipher or code; roughness of surface helping adhesion of plaster etc. 2 v. fasten with pin or wedge or bolt etc.; strike key(s) on keyboard of computer etc. 3 a. essential, of vital importance. 4 **keyboard** set of keys on piano or typewriter or computer etc.; **keyhole** hole by which key is put into lock; **keynote** Mus. note on which key is based, fig. dominant idea etc.; **key-pad** computer etc. keyboard, esp. small one held in hand; **key-ring** ring for keeping keys on; **keystone** central stone of arch, central principle; **key up** stimulate, increase nervous tension in.

**KG** abbr. Knight of the Order of the Garter.

**kg.** abbr. kilogram(s).

**KGB** n. secret police of USSR.

**khaki** /'kɑːkiː/ 1 a. dull brownish yellow. 2 n. khaki colour or cloth or uniform.

**khan** /kɑːn/ n. title of rulers and officials in Central Asia. **khanate** n.

**kHz** abbr. kilohertz.

**kibbutz** /kɪˈbʊts/ n. (pl. **kibbutzim** /-tsiːm/) communal esp. farming settlement in Israel.

**kibosh** /'kaɪbɒʃ/ n. sl. **put the kibosh on** put an end to.

**kick** 1 v. strike out with foot; strike or move with foot; score (goal) by a kick; protest; sl. abandon (habit). 2 n. kicking action or blow; recoil of gun; colloq. temporary enthusiasm, sharp stimulant effect, thrill. 3 **kickback** recoil, payment esp. for illegal help; **kick off** Footb. begin or restart game, colloq. start; **kick-off** n.; **kick out** colloq. expel forcibly, dismiss; **kick-start(er)** device to start engine of motor cycle etc. by downward thrust of pedal; **kick up a fuss** make vigorous protest etc.

**kid** 1 n. young goat; kid-skin leather; colloq. child. 2 v. give birth to kid; sl. hoax, deceive.

**kidnap** /'kɪdnæp/ v.t. carry off (person) illegally esp. to obtain ransom.

**kidney** /'kɪdnɪ/ n. either of pair of glandular organs serving to excrete urine; kidney of sheep or pig etc. as food; nature, kind. **kidney-bean** scarlet runner or dwarf French bean; **kidney machine** apparatus able to take over function of damaged kidney.

**kidstakes** /'kɪdsteɪks/ n. Aus. sl. joking, pretence.

**kill** 1 v. deprive of life, put to death; put an end to; switch off; colloq. cause severe pain to; overwhelm (person) with amusement etc. 2 n. act of killing; animal(s) killed by sportsman. 3 **killjoy** depressing person.

**killer** /'kɪlə(r)/ n. person or thing that kills, esp. murderous person; Aus. animal to be killed for meat.

**killing** /'kɪlɪŋ/ 1 n. causing death; great financial success. 2 a. colloq. very attractive or amusing.

**kiln** n. furnace or oven for burning, baking, or drying.

**kilo** /'kiːləʊ/ n. (pl. **-os**) kilogram.

**kilo-** /'kɪləʊ/ in comb. 1,000.

**kilocycle** /'kɪləsaɪk(ə)l/ n. kilohertz.

**kilogram** /'kɪləgræm/ n. 1,000 grams.

**kilohertz** /'kɪləhɜːts/ n. unit of frequency, = 1,000 cycles per second.

**kilolitre** /'kɪləliːtə(r)/ n. 1,000 litres.

**kilometre** /ˈkɪləmiːtə(r)/ n. 1,000 metres, approx. 0.62 mile.

**kiloton** /ˈkɪlətʌn/ n. unit of explosive force equal to 1,000 tons of TNT.

**kilotonne** /ˈkɪlətɒn/ n. metric unit equivalent to kiloton.

**kilowatt** /ˈkɪləwɒt/ n. 1,000 watts. **kilowatt-hour** energy equal to 1 kilowatt working for 1 hour.

**kilt** 1 n. pleated skirt usu. of tartan, esp. worn by Highland man. 2 v.t. tuck up (skirts) round body; gather in vertical pleats.

**kimono** /kɪˈməʊnəʊ/ n. (pl. **-os**) long Japanese robe with wide sleeves; dressing-gown like this.

**kin** n. one's relatives or family. 2 pred. a. related.

**kind** /kaɪnd/ 1 n. class of similar or related things or animals etc.; natural way, fashion; character. 2 a. gentle, benevolent; friendly, considerate. 3 **in kind** (of payment) in goods etc. instead of money, in same form.

**kindergarten** /ˈkɪndəɡɑːt(ə)n/ n. school for young children.

**kindle** /ˈkɪnd(ə)l/ v. set on fire, light; fig. inspire; become kindled, glow.

**kindling** /ˈkɪndlɪŋ/ n. small pieces of wood etc. for lighting fires.

**kindly** /ˈkaɪndlɪ/ 1 a. kind, good-natured. 2 adv. in a kind manner; please.

**kindred** /ˈkɪndrəd/ 1 n. blood relationship; one's relations. 2 a. related, allied, similar.

**kine** n.pl. arch. cows.

**kinetic** /kəˈnetɪk/ a. of or due to motion. **kinetic energy** body's ability to do work by virtue of its motion.

**king** n. male sovereign ruler of independent state; man pre-eminent in specified field; largest kind of thing; chess piece to be protected from checkmate; crowned piece in draughts; courtcard with picture of king. **kingfish** any of several large Aus. fish; **king-hit** Aus. sl. sudden knock-out blow; **kingpin** main or large bolt, fig. essential person or thing; **king-size(d)** large. **kingly** a.

**kingdom** /ˈkɪŋdəm/ n. state or territory ruled by a king or queen; domain; division of nature. **kingdom-come** sl. the next world.

**kingfisher** /ˈkɪŋfɪʃə(r)/ n. small bird with brilliant blue plumage, which dives for fish.

**kink** 1 n. short backward twist in something straight or smooth; fig. mental twist. 2 v. (cause to) form kink.

**kinky** /ˈkɪŋkɪ/ a. having (many) kinks; bizarre; perverted.

**kinsfolk** /ˈkɪnzfəʊk/ n.pl. relations by blood. **kinsman** n.; **kinswoman** n.

**kinship** /ˈkɪnʃɪp/ n. blood relationship; similarity.

**kiosk** /ˈkiːɒsk/ n. light open structure for sale of newspapers or food etc.; structure in street etc. for public telephone.

**kip**[1] sl. n. sleep, bed. 2 v.i. sleep.

**kip**[2] n. Aus. sl. small flat board from which coins are spun in two-up.

**kipper**[1] /ˈkɪpə(r)/ 1 n. kippered fish, esp. herring. 2 v. cure (herring etc.) by splitting open, salting, drying, and smoking.

**kipper**[2] /ˈkɪpə(r)/ n. Aus. young Abor. who has been initiated and admitted to the rites of manhood.

**kipsie** /ˈkɪpsiː/ n. Aus. sl. (also **kipsy**) house, home; lean-to, shelter.

**kirk** n. Sc. church.

**kirsch** /kɪəʃ/ n. spirit distilled from wild cherries.

**kismet** /ˈkɪsmet/ n. destiny.

**kiss** 1 n. touch given with lips. 2 v.t. touch with lips, esp. as sign of love or affection or reverence etc.; touch gently. 3 **kiss-curl** small curl of hair on forehead or nape of neck; **kiss hands** kiss those of sovereign on appointment to high office.

**kit** 1 n. equipment or clothing etc. for particular activity; soldier's or traveller's pack or equipment; set of parts sold together from which whole thing can be made. 2 v.t. supply, fit out with kit. 3 **kitbag** usu. cylindrical canvas etc. bag for carrying soldier's or traveller's kit.

**kitchen** /ˈkɪtʃən/ n. place where food is cooked. **kitchen evening** or **tea** Aus. & NZ party to which guests bring gifts of kitchen articles for bride-to-be; **kitchen garden** garden for growing fruit and vegetables.

**kitchenette** /kɪtʃəˈnet/ n. small room or alcove fitted out as kitchen.

**kite** n. light framework covered with paper etc. and flown in wind at end of

# kith

long string as toy; bird of prey of hawk family.
**kith** /kɪθ/ *n.* **kith and kin** friends and relations.
**kitsch** /kɪtʃ/ *n.* worthless pretentiousness in art; art of this type.
**kitten** /ˈkɪt(ə)n/ **1** *n.* young of cat. **2** *v.* give birth to (kittens).
**kittiwake** /ˈkɪtiːweɪk/ *n.* kind of small sea-gull.
**kitty** /ˈkɪtɪ/ *n.* joint fund; pool in some card games.
**kiwi** /ˈkiːwiː/ *n.* flightless NZ bird; **Kiwi** *colloq.* New Zealander.
**kleptomania** /klɛptəˈmeɪmɪə/ *n.* irresistible tendency to steal. **kleptomaniac** *a.* & *n.*
**km.** *abbr.* kilometre(s).
**knack** /næk/ *n.* acquired dexterity; trick, habit.
**knacker** /ˈnækə(r)/ **1** *n.* buyer of useless horses for slaughter. **2** *v.t. sl.* kill; exhaust, wear out.
**knapsack** /ˈnæpsæk/ *n.* soldier's or traveller's bag strapped to back.
**knapweed** /ˈnæpwiːd/ *n.* weed with purple flowers on globular head.
**knave** /neɪv/ *n.* unprincipled man, rogue; jack in cards. **knavery** *n.*; **knavish** *a.*
**knead** /niːd/ *v.t.* work up into dough or paste; make (bread, pottery) thus; massage.
**knee** /niː/ *n.* joint between thigh and lower leg; upper surface of thigh of sitting person; part of garment covering knee. **kneecap** convex bone in front of knee.
**kneel** /niːl/ *v.i.* (*past* & *p.p.* **knelt**) rest or lower oneself on knees.
**kneeler** /ˈniːlə(r)/ *n.* mat etc. for kneeling on.
**knell** /nɛl/ *n.* sound of bell esp. after death or at funeral; omen of death or extinction.
**knelt** *past* & *p.p.* of **kneel**.
**knew** *past* of **know**.
**knickerbockers** /ˈnɪkəbɒkəz/ *n.pl.* loose-fitting breeches gathered in at knee.
**knickers** /ˈnɪkəz/ *n.pl.* woman's or girl's undergarment covering body below waist and having separate legs or leg-holes.
**knick-knack** /ˈnɪknæk/ *n.* trinket or small ornament.

# knock

**knife** /naɪf/ **1** *n.* (*pl.* **knives**) blade with long sharpened edge fixed in handle and used as cutting instrument or weapon; cutting-blade in machine. **2** *v.t.* cut or stab with knife. **3 the knife** *colloq.* surgery; **knife-edge** edge of knife, *fig.* position of extreme uncertainty; **knife-pleat** one of series of overlapping narrow flat pleats.
**knight** /naɪt/ **1** *n.* man raised to rank below baronetcy as reward for personal merit or services; *hist.* man raised to honourable military rank by king etc.; chess piece usu. with shape of horse's head. **2** *v.t.* confer knighthood on. **3 knight errant** medieval knight wandering in search of chivalrous adventures; **knight errantry** practice or conduct of knight errant. **4 knighthood** *n.*; **knightly** *a.*
**knit** /nɪt/ *v.* (*past* & *p.p.* **knitted** or **knit**) form (texture, garment) by interlocking loops of yarn or thread; treat (yarn etc.) thus; make (plain stitch) in knitting; wrinkle (brow); make or become close or compact; join, unite. **knitwear** knitted garments.
**knitting** /ˈnɪtɪŋ/ *n.* work being knitted. **knitting-needle** slender pointed rod used usu. in pairs in knitting.
**knob** /nɒb/ *n.* rounded protuberance e.g. handle of door or drawer etc., or for adjusting radio etc.; small lump (of butter, coal, etc.). **knobby** *a.*
**knobbly** /ˈnɒblɪ/ *a.* hard and lumpy.
**knock** /nɒk/ **1** *v.* strike with audible sharp blow; strike door or *at* door etc. for admittance; drive by striking; make by knocking; make knocking sound; *sl.* criticize. **2** *n.* sharp or audible blow; rap esp. at door. **3 knock about** treat roughly, wander about aimlessly; **knockabout** boisterous; **knock back** eat or drink quickly, *Aus. sl.* refuse, rebuff; **knock-back** *n.*; **knock down** strike to ground, demolish, dispose of *to* bidder at auction, *Aus. sl.* spend (money); **knock-down** (of price) very low, overwhelming; **knock knees** abnormal condition with legs curved inward at the knee; **knock-kneed** *a.*; **knock off** strike off with blow, leave off (work), *colloq.* do or make rapidly esp. without effort, *sl.* steal or kill; **knock out** render unconscious by blow to head, disable (boxer) so that he

# knocker

cannot recover in required time, defeat in knock-out competition, *Aus. sl.* earn; **knock-out** (blow) that knocks boxer out, (competition) in which loser of each match is eliminated, *sl.* outstanding person or thing; **knock together** construct hurriedly; **knock up** drive upwards with bat, make or arrange hastily, score (runs) at cricket, arouse (person) by knocking at door; **knock-up** practice game etc.

**knocker** /'nɒkə(r)/ *n.* hinged metal device on door for knocking to call attention. **on the knocker** *Aus.* promptly.

**knoll** /nəʊl/ *n.* small hill, mound.

**knop** /nɒp/ *n.* ornamental knob; loop or tuft in yarn.

**knot** /nɒt/ **1** *n.* intertwining of parts of one or more ropes or strings etc., as fastening; tangled mass etc., cluster; hard mass formed in tree-trunk where branch grew out; round cross-grained piece in board caused by this; difficulty, problem; unit of ship's or aircraft's speed equal to one nautical mile per hour. **2** *v.* tie in knot; form knots; entangle. **3 knot-grass** weed with intricate stems and pink flowers; **knot-hole** hole in wooden board, where knot has fallen out.

**knotty** /'nɒtɪ/ *a.* full of knots; puzzling.

**know** /nəʊ/ *v.* (*past* **knew**; *p.p.* **known**) be aware (of); have learnt; have understanding of; recognize, identify; be acquainted with. **in the know** knowing secret or inside information; **know-how** practical knowledge or skill.

**knowing** /'nəʊɪŋ/ *a.* cunning, shrewd.

**knowingly** *adv.* in a knowing manner; consciously, intentionally.

**knowledge** /'nɒlɪdʒ/ *n.* knowing; person's range of information; sum of what is known.

**knowledgeable** /'nɒlɪdʒəb(ə)l/ *a.* having much knowledge; well-informed.

**known** *p.p.* of **know**.

**knuckle** /'nʌk(ə)l/ **1** *n.* bone at finger-joint; projection of knee- or ankle-joint of quadruped; this as joint of meat. **2**

# kung fu

*v.* strike or rub etc. with knuckles. **3 knuckle down** apply oneself earnestly (*to* work etc.); **knuckle-duster** metal guard worn over knuckles in fist-fighting esp. to increase violence of blow; **knuckle under** give in, submit.

**knurl** /nɜːl/ *n.* small projecting ridge.

**KO** *abbr.* knock-out.

**koala** /kəʊˈɑːlə/ *n. Aus.* tailless arboreal marsupial with thick grey fur.

**kohl** /kəʊl/ *n.* powder used in eastern countries to darken eyelids etc.

**kohlrabi** /kəʊlˈrɑːbɪ/ *n.* cabbage with turnip-like edible stem.

**kookaburra** /ˈkʊkəbʌrə/ *n.* large Aus. kingfisher with loud discordant cry.

**kooky** /ˈkʊkɪ/ *a. US sl.* crazy or eccentric.

**Koran** /kɔːˈrɑːn/ *n.* sacred book of Muslims.

**kosher** /ˈkəʊʃə(r)/ **1** *a.* (of food or foodshop) fulfilling requirements of Jewish law; *colloq.* correct, genuine. **2** *n.* kosher food or shop.

**kowtow** /kaʊˈtaʊ/ **1** *v.i.* act obsequiously; perform kowtow. **2** *n.* Chinese custom of touching ground with forehead as sign of worship or submission.

**kraal** /krɑːl/ *n. S.Afr.* village of huts enclosed by fence; enclosure for cattle.

**kremlin** /ˈkremlɪn/ *n.* citadel within Russian town, esp. that of Moscow. **the Kremlin** USSR government.

**krill** *n.* tiny plankton crustaceans eaten by whales etc.

**kris** /kriːs/ *n.* Malay dagger with wavy blade.

**krugerrand** /ˈkruːɡərænd/ *n.* S. Afr. gold coin bearing portrait of President Kruger.

**Kt.** *abbr.* knight.

**kudos** /ˈkjuːdɒs/ *n. colloq.* glory, renown.

**kümmel** /ˈkʊm(ə)l/ *n.* liqueur flavoured with caraway seeds.

**kumquat** /ˈkʌmkwɒt/ *n.* tiny variety of orange.

**kung fu** /kʌŋ ˈfuː/ Chinese form of karate.

# L

**L, l,** *n.* Roman numeral 50.
**L** *abbr.* learner(-driver).
**L.** *abbr.* Lake; Liberal.
**l.** *abbr.* left; line; litre(s).
**la** var. of **lah**.
**lab** *n. colloq.* laboratory.
**Lab.** *abbr.* Labo(u)r.
**label** /'leɪb(ə)l/ 1 *n.* slip attached to object to give some information about it; classifying phrase etc. 2 *v.t.* attach label to; assign to category.
**labial** /'leɪbɪəl/ 1 *a.* of lips; *Phonet.* pronounced with (closed) lips. 2 *n. Phonet.* labial sound.
**labor** var. of **labour**.
**laboratory** /lə'bɒrətəri/ *n.* place used for scientific experiments and research.
**laborious** /lə'bɔːrɪəs/ *a.* needing much work; hard-working; showing signs of effort.
**labour** /'leɪbə(r)/ 1 *n.* bodily or mental work, exertion; task; the body of workers esp. as political force; **Labo(u)r** the Labo(u)r Party; process of giving birth, pains of this. 2 *v.* exert oneself, work hard; work as labourer; have difficulty; elaborate, work out in excessive detail. 3 **labour force** body of workers employed; **Labour** (*Aus.* **Labor**) **Party** *Polit.* party representing esp. workers' interests; **labour-saving** designed to reduce or eliminate work.
**labourer** /'leɪbərə(r)/ *n.* person who labours, esp. one employed to do unskilled manual work.
**Labrador** /'læbrədɔː(r)/ *n.* (dog of) retriever breed with usu. black or golden coat.
**laburnum** /lə'bɜːnəm/ *n.* poisonous tree with yellow hanging flowers.
**labyrinth** /'læbərɪnθ/ *n.* network of passages, maze; tangled affairs. **labyrinthine** /-θaɪm/ *a.*
**lace** 1 *n.* cord etc. passed through eyelets or hooks for fastening or tightening shoes etc.; trimming-braid; fine open fabric usu. with pattern. 2 *v.* fasten or tighten (*up*) with lace(s); trim with lace; add dash of spirits to.
**lacerate** /'læsəreɪt/ *v.t.* tear roughly; wound (feelings etc.). **laceration** *n.*
**lachrymal** /'lækrəm(ə)l/ *a.* of tears.
**lachrymose** /'lækrəməʊz/ *a.* tearful, often weeping.
**lack** 1 *n.* deficiency or want *of*. 2 *v.* not have when needed, be without. 3 **lacklustre** dull, lacking enthusiasm.
**lackadaisical** /lækə'deɪzɪk(ə)l/ *a.* languid; unenthusiastic.
**lackey** /'lækɪ/ *n.* footman; obsequious person.
**lacking** /'lækɪŋ/ *a.* undesirably absent; deficient (*in*).
**laconic** /lə'kɒnɪk/ *a.* using or expressed in few words. **laconicism** *n.*
**lacquer** /'lækə(r)/ 1 *n.* hard shiny shellac or synthetic varnish; substance sprayed on hair to keep it in place. 2 *v.t.* coat with lacquer.
**lacrosse** /lə'krɒs/ *n.* team game played with ball carried in net at end of stick.
**lactation** /læk'teɪʃ(ə)n/ *n.* suckling; secretion of milk.
**lacteal** /'læktɪəl/ *a.* of milk; conveying chyle.
**lactic** /'læktɪk/ *a.* of milk.
**lactose** /'læktəʊs/ *n.* sugar present in milk.
**lacuna** /lə'kjuːnə/ *n.* (*pl.* **-nas** or **-nae** /-niː/) gap, esp. in manuscript; missing part.
**lacy** /'leɪsɪ/ *a.* like lace fabric.
**lad** *n.* boy, young fellow.
**ladder** /'lædə(r)/ 1 *n.* pair of long pieces of wood or metal etc. joined at intervals by cross-pieces, used as means of ascent; vertical flaw in stocking etc.; *fig.* means of progress in career etc. 2 *v.* cause ladder in (stocking etc.); develop ladder.
**lade** *v.t.* (*p.p.* **laden**) load (ship); ship (goods); in *p.p.* loaded or burdened (*with*). **bill of lading** detailed list of ship's cargo.
**la-di-da** /lɑːdiː'dɑː/ *a.* pretentious or affected, esp. in pronunciation.
**ladle** /'leɪd(ə)l/ 1 *n.* long-handled large bowled spoon for transferring liquids. 2 *v.t.* transfer with ladle.
**lady** /'leɪdɪ/ *n.* woman of good social standing; (polite or formal for) woman; **Lady** title used as prefix to name of peeress below duchess or to surname of knight's or baronet's wife or widow. **ladybird** small kind of beetle usu.

## ladyship

reddish-brown with black spots; **Lady chapel** chapel dedicated to Virgin Mary; **Lady Day** 25 Mar.; **ladylike** like or appropriate to a lady; **lady's maid** personal maidservant of lady.

**ladyship** /ˈleɪdiʃɪp/ *n.* (with *her, your,* etc.) title used in adressing or referring to woman with rank of Lady.

**lag**[1] 1 *v.i.* go too slow; not keep pace; fall behind. 2 *n.* lagging, delay; *sl.* convict.

**lag**[2] *v.t.* enclose (boiler etc.) with insulating material.

**lager** /ˈlɑːgə(r)/ *n.* kind of light beer.

**laggard** /ˈlægəd/ *n.* person lagging behind.

**lagging** /ˈlægɪŋ/ *n.* material used to lag boiler etc.

**lagoon** /ləˈguːn/ *n.* salt-water lake separated from sea by sandbank or enclosed by atoll.

**lah** *n. Mus.* sixth note of scale in tonic sol-fa.

**laicize** /ˈleɪəsaɪz/ *v.t.* make secular.

**laid** *past* & *p.p.* of **lay**[1].

**lain** *p.p.* of **lie**[1].

**lair**[1] *n.* place where animal habitually rests or eats; *fig.* hiding-place.

**lair**[2] *n. Aus. sl.* flashily-dressed youth or man.

**laird** *n.* landed proprietor in Scotland.

**lairy** /ˈleəri/ *a. Aus. sl.* of a **lair**[2]; flashily-dressed.

**laissez-faire** /leɪseɪˈfeə(r)/ *n.* policy of non-interference. [F]

**laity** /ˈleɪəti/ *n.* laymen.

**lake**[1] *n.* large body of water surrounded by land.

**lake**[2] *n.* usu. reddish pigment made from dye and mordant.

**lam** *v. sl.* hit hard, thrash.

**lama** /ˈlɑːmə/ *n.* Tibetan or Mongolian Buddhist priest.

**lamasery** /ləˈmɑːsəri/ *n.* lama monastery.

**lamb** /læm/ 1 *n.* young sheep; its flesh as food; innocent or weak or dear person. 2 *v.i.* give birth to lamb.

**lambaste** /læmˈbeɪst/ *v.t. colloq.* thrash, beat.

**lambent** /ˈlæmbənt/ *a.* (of flame etc.) playing about a surface; gently brilliant. **lambency** *n.*

**lame** 1 *a.* disabled by injury or defect esp. in foot or leg; limping or unable to walk; (of excuse etc.) unsatisfactory; (of metre) halting. 2 *v.t.* make lame, disable. 3 **lame duck** person or firm unable to cope without help.

**lamé** /ˈlɑːmeɪ/ *n.* fabric with gold or silver thread woven in.

**lament** /ləˈment/ 1 *n.* passionate expression of grief, elegy. 2 *v.* express or feel grief for or about; utter lament; in *p.p.* mourned for.

**lamentable** /ˈlæməntəb(ə)l/ *a.* deplorable, regrettable.

**lamentation** /læmənˈteɪʃ(ə)n/ *n.* lament, lamenting.

**lamina** /ˈlæmɪnə/ *n.* (*pl.* **-nae** /-niː/) thin plate or scale or flake or layer. **laminar** *a.*

**laminate** 1 /ˈlæmɪneɪt/ *v.t.* beat or roll into laminae, split into layers; overlay with plastic layer etc. 2 /ˈlæmɪnət/ *n.* laminated structure, esp. of layers fixed together. 3 **lamination** *n.*

**lamington** /ˈlæmɪŋtən/ *n. Aus.* square of sponge-cake covered in chocolate and coconut.

**lamp** *n.* apparatus for giving light from electricity or gas or oil etc. **lampblack** pigment made from soot; **lamppost** post supporting street lamp; **lampshade** shade placed over lamp.

**lampoon** /læmˈpuːn/ 1 *n.* virulent or scurrilous satire. 2 *v.t.* write lampoon against.

**lamprey** /ˈlæmpri/ *n.* eel-like fish with sucker mouth.

**lance** /lɑːns or læns/ 1 *n.* long spear, esp. one used by horseman. 2 *v.t.* prick or open with lancet. 3 **lance-corporal** NCO below corporal.

**lanceolate** /ˈlænsɪələt/ *a.* shaped like spearhead, tapering to each end.

**lancer** /ˈlɑːnsə(r) or ˈlænsə(r)/ *n.* soldier of cavalry regiment orig. armed with lances; in *pl.* kind of square dance.

**lancet** /ˈlɑːnsɪt or ˈlænsɪt/ *n.* surgical instrument with point and two edges for small incisions; narrow pointed arch or window.

**land** 1 *n.* solid part of earth's surface; ground, soil, expanse of country; landed property; in *pl.* estates; country, State. 2 *v.* set or go ashore; bring (aircraft) down or come down to ground; bring to or reach certain place; deal (person blow etc.); bring (fish) to land; *fig.* win (prize, appointment, etc.). 3 **landfall** approach to land after sea or air journey; **landlady** woman keeping

**landau**     305     **largess**

inn or lodgings, or having tenants; **land-locked** (almost) enclosed by land; **landlord** keeper of inn or lodgings, person who has tenants; **landlubber** person unfamiliar with sea and ships; **landmark** conspicuous object, notable event; **land mass** large area of land; **land-mine** explosive mine laid in or on ground; **land rights** *Aus.* right of original inhabitants to possess land, esp. sacred tribal grounds; **landslide** landslip, *fig.* overwhelming majority for one side in election etc.; **landslip** sliding down of mass of land on cliff or mountain. **4 landward** *a.*, *adv.*, & *n.*; **landwards** *adv.*

**landau** /'lændɔː/ *n.* kind of 4-wheeled horse-drawn carriage.

**landed** /'lændəd/ *a.* possessing or consisting of land.

**landing** /'lændɪŋ/ *n.* process of coming or bringing to land; place for disembarking; platform or passage at top of flight of stairs. **landing-craft** naval craft for putting ashore troops and equipment; **landing-gear** undercarriage of aircraft; **landing-stage** platform for disembarking passengers and goods.

**landscape** /'lændskeɪp/ **1** *n.* piece of inland scenery; picture of it. **2** *v.t.* improve by or engage in landscape gardening. **3 landscape gardening** laying-out of grounds to imitate natural scenery.

**lane** *n.* narrow road or street; passage between rows of persons etc.; strip of road for one line of traffic; strip of track or water for competitor in race; regular course followed by ship or aircraft.

**language** /'læŋgwɪdʒ/ *n.* words and their use; speech; form of this prevalent in one or more countries; method or style of expression; system of symbols and rules for computer programs.

**languid** /'læŋgwɪd/ *a.* inert, lacking vigour etc.; apathetic; slow-moving.

**languish** /'læŋgwɪʃ/ *v.i.* lose or lack vitality; live *under* depressing conditions; pine (*for*).

**languor** /'læŋgə(r)/ *n.* languid state, soft or tender mood or effect. **languorous** *a.*

**lank** *a.* lean and tall; (of grass, hair, etc.) long and limp.

**lanky** /'læŋkɪ/ *a.* ungracefully lean and tall or long.

**lanolin** /'lænəlɪn/ *n.* fat from sheep-wool used in ointments.

**lantern** /'læntən/ *n.* transparent case protecting flame of candle etc.; light-chamber of lighthouse; erection on top of dome or room, with glazed sides. **lantern jaws** long thin jaws.

**lanyard** /'lænjəd/ *n.* short cord for fastening or holding something.

**lap**[1] **1** *n.* front of sitting person's body from waist to knees; part of dress covering this; one circuit of race-track etc.; amount of overlap; single turn of thread etc. round reel etc. **2** *v.* lead (competitor in race) by one or more laps; fold or wrap (garment etc. *about*, *round*); enfold; (cause to) overlap. **3 lap-dog** small pet dog.

**lap**[2] **1** *v.* drink by scooping with tongue; drink (*up*) greedily; make lapping sound. **2** *n.* act or sound of lapping.

**lapel** /lə'pel/ *n.* part of coat-front folded back.

**lapidary** /'læpədərɪ/ **1** *a.* concerned with stones; engraved on stone. **2** *n.* cutter or polisher or engraver of gems.

**lapis lazuli** /ˌlæpɪs 'læzjəlɪ/ *n.* bright blue gem mineral, colour, and pigment.

**lappet** /'læpət/ *n.* flap or fold of garment etc. or flesh.

**lapse** /læps/ **1** *n.* slight mistake; slip of memory etc.; passage *of* time. **2** *v.i.* fail to maintain position or state; fall back (*into* former state); become void, elapse.

**lapwing** /'læpwɪŋ/ *n.* peewit.

**larboard** /'lɑːbəd/ *n.* & *a. Naut.* = **port**[3].

**larceny** /'lɑːsənɪ/ *n. Law* theft of personal property. **larcenous** *a.*

**larch** *n.* bright-foliaged deciduous N. Hemis. coniferous tree; its wood.

**lard 1** *n.* pig fat prepared for use in cooking etc. **2** *v.t.* insert strips of bacon in (meat etc.) before cooking; garnish (talk etc.) *with* strange terms etc.

**larder** /'lɑːdə(r)/ *n.* room or cupboard for storing provisions.

**large** *a.* of considerable or relatively great size or extent; of wide range, comprehensive. **at large** at liberty, as a body or whole, without specific aim.

**largely** /'lɑːdʒlɪ/ *adv.* to a great or preponderating extent.

**largess** /lɑː'ʒes/ *n.* (also **largesse**)

**largo** 306 **latter**

money or gifts freely given esp. on occasion of rejoicing.

**largo** /'lɑːgəʊ/ *Mus.* **1** *adv.* in slow time with broad dignified treatment. **2** *n.* (*pl.* **-gos**) passage to be played thus.

**lariat** /'læriət/ *n.* tethering-rope; lasso.

**lark**[1] *n.* kind of small bird, esp. skylark.

**lark**[2] **1** *n.* frolic, spree; amusing incident; type of activity etc. **2** *v.i.* play *about*.

**larkspur** /'lɑːkspə(r)/ *n.* plant with spur-shaped calyx.

**larrikin** /'lærəkən/ *n. Aus.* hooligan.

**larva** /'lɑːvə/ *n.* (*pl.* **-vae** /-viː/) insect in the stage between egg and pupa. **larval** *a.*

**laryngeal** /lə'rɪndʒ(ə)l/ *a.* of the larynx.

**laryngitis** /lærən'dʒaɪtɪs/ *n.* inflammation of larynx.

**larynx** /'lærɪŋks/ *n.* cavity in throat holding vocal cords.

**Lascar** /'læskə(r)/ *n.* E. Indian seaman.

**lascivious** /lə'sɪvɪəs/ *a.* lustful.

**laser** /'leɪzə(r)/ *n.* device giving strong beam of radiation in one direction.

**lash 1** *v.* make sudden whiplike movement; pour, rush; hit or kick *out*; castigate in words; urge as with lash; fasten (*down*, *together*) with cord or twine. **2** *n.* stroke with whip etc.; flexible part of whip; eyelash. **3 have a lash at** *Aus. sl.* have a try at, attempt.

**lashings** /'læʃɪŋz/ *n.pl. sl.* plenty.

**lass** *n.* (also **lassie**) girl.

**lassitude** /'læsɪtjuːd/ *n.* languor; disinclination to exert or interest oneself.

**lasso** /læ'suː/ **1** *n.* (*pl.***-os**) rope etc. with running noose used esp. for catching cattle. **2** *v.t.* catch with lasso.

**last**[1] /lɑːst/ **1** *a.* after all others; coming at end; most recent, utmost. **2** *adv.* after all others; on the last occasion before the present. **3** *n.* last-mentioned person or thing; end; last performance of certain acts. **4 at (long) last** in the end, after much delay.

**last**[2] /lɑːst/ *v.i.* remain unexhausted or adequate or alive for specified or long time.

**last**[3] /lɑːst/ *n.* shoemaker's model on which shoe etc. is shaped.

**lasting** /'lɑːstɪŋ/ *a.* permanent, durable.

**lastly** /'lɑːstlɪ/ *adv.* finally, in the last place.

**lat.** *abbr.* latitude.

**latch 1** *n.* bar with catch as fastening of gate etc.; spring-lock as fastening of outer door. **2** *v.t.* fasten with latch. **3 latchkey** key of outer door; **latch on to** *colloq.* attach oneself to, understand.

**late 1** *a.* (doing or done) after due or usual time; far on in day or night or period etc.; flowering or ripening etc. towards end of season; no longer alive or having specified status; of recent date. **2** *adv.* after due or usual time; far on in time; at or till late hour; formerly but not now. **3 of late** recently.

**lateen sail** /lə'tiːn/ triangular sail on long yard at angle of 45° to mast.

**lately** /'leɪtlɪ/ *adv.* not long ago; in recent times.

**latent** /'leɪt(ə)nt/ *a.* concealed, dormant; existing but not developed or manifest. **latency** *n.*

**lateral** /'lætər(ə)l/ **1** *a.* of or at or towards or from side(s). **2** *n.* lateral shoot or branch. **3 lateral thinking** seeking to solve problems by indirect methods.

**latex** /'leɪteks/ *n.* milky fluid of (esp. rubber) plant; synthetic substance like this.

**lath** /lɑːθ/ *n.* thin narrow strip of wood.

**lathe** /leɪð/ *n.* machine for shaping wood or metal etc. by rotating article against cutting tools.

**lather** /'lɑːðə(r)/ **1** *n.* froth of soap etc. and water; frothy state of horse; state of agitation. **2** *v.* (of soap) form lather; cover with lather; thrash.

**Latin** /'lætɪn/ **1** *n.* language of ancient Rome; member of modern Latin people. **2** *a.* of or in Latin; (of peoples) speaking a language developed from Latin; of Roman Catholic Church. **3 Latin America** parts of Central and S. Amer. where Spanish or Portuguese is main language; **Latin Church** Western Church.

**Latinate** /'lætɪneɪt/ *a.* having character of Latin.

**latitude** /'lætɪtjuːd/ *n.* place's angular distance N. or S. of equator; (usu. in *pl.*) regions with reference to temperature; freedom from restriction in action or opinion.

**latrine** /lə'triːn/ *n.* communal lavatory, esp. in camp etc.

**latter** /'lætə(r)/ **1** *a.* mentioned later of two or last of three or more; recent;

## latterly

belonging to end of period etc. **2** *n*. the latter thing or person. **3 latter-day** modern, newfangled.

**latterly** /ˈlætəli/ *adv*. in later part of life or a period; of late.

**lattice** /ˈlætəs/ *n*. structure of laths or bars crossing each other with spaces between; arrangement resembling this. **lattice window** one with small panes set in lead.

**laud** *v.t.* praise, extol.

**laudable** /ˈlɔːdəb(ə)l/ *a*. commendable. **laudability** *n*.

**laudanum** /ˈlɔːdənəm/ *n*. tincture of opium.

**laudatory** /ˈlɔːdətəri/ *a*. praising.

**laugh** /lɑːf/ **1** *v*. make sounds etc. usual in expressing amusement or exultation or scorn etc.; utter with laugh. **2** *n*. sound or act of laughing; *colloq*. comical person or thing. **3 laugh at** ridicule.

**laughable** /ˈlɑːfəb(ə)l/ *a*. amusing; ridiculous.

**laughing** /ˈlɑːfɪŋ/ *n*. laughter. **laughing-gas** nitrous oxide as anaesthetic; **laughing jackass** kookaburra; **laughing-stock** object of general derision.

**laughter** /ˈlɑːftə(r)/ *n*. act or sound of laughing.

**launch**[1] /lɔːntʃ/ **1** *v*. set (vessel) afloat; hurl, send forth; start or send off (*on* career etc.; *into* expense, abuse, etc.). **2** *n*. launching of ship.

**launch**[2] /lɔːntʃ/ *n*. large motor-boat; man-of-war's largest boat.

**launcher** *n*. structure to hold rocket during launching.

**launder** /ˈlɔːndə(r)/ *v*. wash and iron etc. (linen or other clothes).

**launderette** /lɔːndəˈret/ *n*. establishment with coin-operated automatic washing-machines for public use.

**laundress** /ˈlɔːndrəs/ *n*. woman who launders.

**laundry** /ˈlɔːndri/ *n*. place for laundering clothes etc.; batch of clothes to be laundered.

**laureate** /ˈlɒrɪət/ *a*. wreathed with laurel. **poet laureate** poet appointed to write poems for State occasions.

**laurel** /ˈlɒr(ə)l/ *n*. kind of shrub with dark green glossy leaves; in *sing*. or *pl*. wreath of bay-leaves as emblem of victory or poetic merit.

**lava** /ˈlɑːvə/ *n*. matter flowing from volcano and solidifying as it cools.

## lay

**lavatory** /ˈlævətəri/ *n*. receptacle for urine and faeces, usu. with means of disposal; room etc. containing this.

**lave** *v.t. literary* wash, bathe; wash against, flow along.

**lavender** /ˈlævəndə(r)/ *n*. fragrant-flowered shrub; pale purplish colour of its flower. **lavender-water** a light perfume.

**laver** /ˈleɪvə(r)/ or /ˈlɑː-/ *n*. kind of edible seaweed.

**lavish** /ˈlævɪʃ/ **1** *v.t.* bestow or spend lavishly. **2** *a*. profuse, prodigal; (too) abundant.

**law** *n*. rule or body of rules established in a community and enjoining or prohibiting certain actions; such rules as social system or branch of study; *the* legal profession; *colloq. the* police; law-courts, judicial remedy; statement of invariable sequence between specified conditions and phenomena. **law-abiding** obedient to the laws; **lawcourt** court of law; **lawsuit** prosecution of claim in lawcourt.

**lawful** /ˈlɔːfəl/ *a*. permitted or appointed or recognized by law; not illegal.

**lawless** /ˈlɔːləs/ *a*. having no laws; disobedient to laws; unbridled.

**lawn**[1] *n*. close-mown turf in gardens etc. **lawn-mower** machine for cutting grass of lawns; **lawn tennis** form of tennis played on outdoor grass or hard court.

**lawn**[2] *n*. kind of fine linen or cotton.

**lawyer** /ˈlɔːjə(r)/ *n*. person pursuing law as a profession, esp. solicitor; expert in law.

**lax** *a*. negligent, not strict, vague. **laxity** *n*.

**laxative** /ˈlæksətɪv/ **1** *a*. tending to cause evacuation of bowels. **2** *n*. laxative medicine.

**lay**[1] **1** *v.t.* (*past & p.p.* **laid**) place on surface; put or bring into required position or state; make by laying; (of hen) produce (egg); cause to subside or lie flat; put down as wager; impose (*up*)*on*; make ready (trap, plan); prepare (table) for meal; put fuel ready to light (fire). **2** *n*. way or position or direction in which something lies. **3 layabout** habitual loafer; **lay bare** expose, reveal; **lay-by** *Aus*. reservation of an article by payment of a deposit and regular

**lay** instalments, *UK* extra strip beside road for vehicles to park; **lay down** relinquish, pay or wager, formulate (rule), store (wine) in cellar, sacrifice (one's life); **lay in** provide oneself with stock of; **lay into** *sl.* punish or scold; **lay off** discharge temporarily owing to shortage of work, *colloq.* desist; **lay on** provide supply of; **lay out** spread, expose to view, prepare (body) for burial, expend (money), dispose (grounds etc.) according to a plan; **layout** disposing or arrangement of ground or printed matter etc.; **lay up** store, save (money), in *p.p.* confined to bed.

**lay²** *a.* not ordained into the clergy; not professionally qualified, esp. in law or medicine etc.; of or done by such persons. **layman** person not in holy orders or without professional or special knowledge; **lay reader** layman licensed to conduct some religious services.

**lay³** *n.* minstrel's song, ballad.

**lay⁴** *past of* **lie¹**.

**layer** /'leɪə(r)/ 1 *n.* thickness of matter, esp. one of several, spread over surface; shoot fastened down to take root. 2 *v.t.* arrange in layers; propagate by layers.

**layette** /leɪ'et/ *n.* clothes etc. prepared for new-born child.

**lay figure** artist's jointed wooden model of human figure; unreal character in novel etc.; person lacking individuality.

**laze** *colloq.* 1 *v.i.* indulge in laziness. 2 *n.* spell of lazing.

**lazy** /'leɪzɪ/ *a.* averse to work, doing little work; of or inducing idleness. **lazy-bones** lazy person.

**lb.** *abbr.* pound(s) weight.

**l.b.w.** *abbr.* leg before wicket.

**l.c.** *abbr.* lower case.

**L/Cpl.** *abbr.* lance-corporal.

**lea** *n.* piece of meadow or arable or pasture land.

**leach** *v.t.* make (liquid) percolate through some material; subject (material) to this; purge *away* or *out* thus.

**lead¹** /liːd/ 1 *v.* (*past & p.p.* led) conduct or guide, esp. by going in front; direct movements or actions or opinions of; guide by persuasion (*to*); (of road etc.) go *to*; pass or spend (life); have first place in; go or be first; play (card) as first player in trick. 2 *n.* guidance, example; leader's place; amount by which competitor is ahead of others; strap etc. for leading dog etc.; *Electr.* conductor conveying current to place of use; chief part in play etc.; player of this; *Cards* act or right of playing first. 3 **lead on** entice into going farther than was intended; **lead story** news item made most prominent; **lead to** have as result; **lead up to** form preparation for, serve to introduce, direct conversation towards.

**lead²** /led/ 1 *n.* heavy soft grey metal; graphite used in pencils; lump of lead used in sounding; in *pl.* strips of lead covering roof, piece of lead-covered roof; *Print.* metal strip to give space between lines. 2 *v.t.* cover or weight or frame or space with lead(s).

**leaden** /'led(ə)n/ *a.* of or like lead; heavy, inert, lead-coloured.

**leader** /'liːdə(r)/ *n.* person or thing that leads; person followed by others; leading performer in orchestra or quartet etc.; leading article; shoot at apex of stem or main branch.

**leading** /'liːdɪŋ/ *a.* chief, most important. **leading aircraftman** one ranking just below NCO; **leading article** editorial expression of opinion in newspaper; **leading lady, man**, person taking chief part in play etc.; **leading light** prominent influential person; **leading note** seventh note of ascending scale; **leading question** one framed to prompt desired answer.

**leaf** 1 *n.* (*pl.* **leaves**) broad flat usu. green part of plant often on a stem; *collect.* leaves; single thickness of folded paper esp. in book; very thin sheet of metal etc.; hinged flap of table etc.; extra section that can be added to table. 2 *v.i.* **leaf through** turn over pages of (book etc.). 3 **leaf mould** soil composed chiefly of decaying leaves. 4 **leafy** *a.*

**leafage** /'liːfɪdʒ/ *n.* leaves of plants.

**leaflet** /'liːflət/ *n.* division of compound leaf; printed paper, single or folded, esp. for free distribution.

**league¹** /liːg/ 1 *n.* agreement for mutual help, parties to it; group of sports clubs who contend for championship; class of contestants. 2 *v.* join in league. 3 **in league** allied.

**league²** /liːg/ *n. arch.* measure of travelling-distance, usu. about 3 miles.

**leak** 1 *n.* hole through which liquid etc. passes wrongly in or out; liquid etc. thus passing through; similar escape of electric charge; disclosure of secret information. 2 *v.* (let) pass out or in through leak; disclose (secret); 3 **leak out** become known. 4 **leaky** *a.*

**leakage** /'liːkɪdʒ/ *n.* action or result of leaking.

**lean**[1] 1 *v.* (*past & p.p.* **leaned** or **leant** /lent/) take or be in or put in sloping position; rely *against* for support; rely or depend *on*; be inclined or partial *to*. 2 *n.* inclination, slope. 3 **lean-to** building with roof resting against larger building or wall.

**lean**[2] 1 *a.* having no superfluous fat; (of meat) consisting chiefly of muscular tissue, not fat; meagre. 2 *n.* lean part of meat. 3 **lean years** time of scarcity.

**leaning** /'liːnɪŋ/ *n.* tendency or inclination.

**leap** *v.* (*past & p.p.* **leaped** or **leapt** /lept/) & *n.* jump. **leap-frog** game in which player vaults with parted legs over another bending down; **leap year** year with 29 Feb. as extra day.

**learn** /lɜːn/ *v.* (*past* **learned** or **learnt**) get knowledge of or skill in by study, experience, or being taught; commit to memory; find out.

**learned** /'lɜːnəd/ *a.* deeply read, showing or requiring learning.

**learner** *n.* person learning, beginner; (in full **learner-driver**) person who is learning to drive motor vehicle but has not yet passed driving test.

**learning** *n.* knowledge got by study.

**lease** /liːs/ 1 *n.* contract by which owner of land or building allows another to use it for specified time usu. for rent. 2 *v.t.* grant or take on lease. 3 **leasehold** tenure of or property held by lease; **leaseholder** *n.*; **a new lease of life** improved prospect of living or of use after repair.

**leash** 1 *n.* thong for holding dog(s). 2 *v.* put leash on, hold in leash.

**least** 1 *a.* smallest, slightest. 2 *n.* least amount. 3 *adv.* in the least degree.

**leather** /'leðə(r)/ 1 *n.* skin of animal prepared for use by tanning etc.; article or piece of leather; polishing-cloth etc. 2 *v.t.* cover or polish with leather; beat, thrash. 3 **leather-head** *Aus.* kind of honey-eater; **leather-jacket** larva of crane-fly, *Aus.* kind of pancake, *Aus.* any of various thick-skinned fishes or tree with tough bark.

**leatherette** /leðə'ret/ *n.* imitation leather.

**leathery** /'leðəri/ *a.* like leather; tough.

**leave**[1] *v.* (*past & p.p.* **left**) go away (from); cause to or let remain; depart without taking; cease to reside at or belong to or work for etc.; abandon; bequeath; trust or commit *to* another; not consume or deal with.

**leave**[2] *n.* permission; permission to be absent from duty; period for which this lasts. **on leave** absent thus; **take one's leave of** bid farewell to.

**leaven** /'lev(ə)n/ 1 *n.* substance used to make dough ferment and rise; admixture *of* some quality. 2 *v.t.* ferment with leaven; permeate, transform; modify *with* tempering element.

**leavings** /'liːvɪŋz/ *n.pl.* what is left.

**lecher** /'letʃə(r)/ *n.* fornicator; debauchee.

**lecherous** /'letʃərəs/ *a.* lustful. **lechery** *n.*

**lectern** /'lektɜːn/ *n.* desk for holding bible etc. in church; similar desk for lecturer etc.

**lecture** /'lektʃə(r)/ 1 *n.* discourse delivered to class or other audience; admonition. 2 *v.* deliver lecture(s); admonish.

**lecturer** *n.* person who gives lectures, esp. in university.

**lectureship** /'lektʃəʃɪp/ *n.* university post as lecturer.

**led** *past & p.p.* of **lead**[1].

**ledge** *n.* narrow shelf or projection from vertical surface.

**ledger** /'ledʒə(r)/ *n.* book in which a firm's accounts are kept.

**lee** *n.* shelter given by neighbouring object; side of thing away from the wind. **lee shore** shore to leeward of ship; **leeway** drift of ship to leeward, *fig.* allowable deviation.

**leech** *n.* blood-sucking worm formerly used medicinally for bleeding; *fig.* person who extorts profit from others.

**leek** *n.* vegetable of onion family with cylindrical white bulb.

**leer** *n.* & *v.i.* glance with lascivious or malign or sly expression.

**leery** /'lɪərɪ/ *a. sl.* knowing, sly; wary *of*.

**lees** /liːz/ *n.pl.* sediment of wine etc.; dregs.

**leeward** /'liːwəd *or Naut.* 'luːəd/ **1** *a. & adv.* on or towards sheltered side. **2** *n.* this direction.

**left**[1] **1** *a.* on or towards side opposite **right**; of left in politics. **2** *adv.* on or to left side. **3** *n.* left part or region or direction; *Polit.* radicals collectively, more innovative etc. section of any group. **4 left-handed** using left hand in preference to right, made by or for left hand, turning to left, awkward, clumsy, (of compliment etc.) ambiguous; **left-hander** left-handed person or blow; **left wing** group on left of army, football etc. team, or political party; **left-winger** member of this. **5 leftward** *a. & adv.;* **leftwards** *adv.*

**left**[2] past & p.p. of **leave**[1].

**leg 1** *n.* each of limbs on which person or animal walks and stands; leg of animal as food; artificial leg; part of garment covering leg; support of chair or other piece of furniture; *Crick.* part of field on side where batsman places his feet; each of progression of stages in journey or competition etc. **2** *v.t.* **leg it** walk or run hard. **3 leg before wicket** (of batsman) out because of illegal obstruction of ball that would otherwise have hit his wicket; **leg-rope** *Aus.* rope used for securing animal by hind leg; **pull person's leg** deceive him jokingly; **stretch one's legs** go for a walk.

**legacy** /'legəsɪ/ *n.* gift left by will; anything handed down by predecessor.

**legal** /'liːg(ə)l/ *a.* of or based on or concerned with law; appointed or required or permitted by law.

**legalism** /'liːgəlɪz(ə)m/ *n.* unduly high regard for law or formula. **legalist** *n.;* **legalistic** *a.*

**legality** /lɪ'gælətɪ/ *n.* lawfulness.

**legalize** /'liːgəlaɪz/ *v.t.* make lawful; bring into harmony with law. **legalization** *n.*

**legate** /'legət/ *n.* papal ambassador.

**legatee** /legə'tiː/ *n.* recipient of legacy.

**legation** /lə'geɪʃ(ə)n/ *n.* diplomatic minister and his suite; his residence.

**legato** /lə'gɑːtəʊ/ *Mus.* **1** *adv.* in smooth connected manner. **2** *n. (pl.* **-tos)** passage to be performed thus.

**legend** /'ledʒ(ə)nd/ *n.* traditional story, myth; inscription on coin or medal etc.; caption; explanation on map of symbols used.

**legendary** /'ledʒəndərɪ/ *a.* famous or existing only in legend.

**legerdemain** /ledʒədəmeɪn/ *n.* sleight of hand; trickery, sophistry.

**leger line** /'ledʒə(r)/ short line added above or below staff for note(s) outside range of staff.

**legging** /'legɪŋ/ *n.* (usu. in *pl.*) outer covering of leather etc. for leg from knee to ankle.

**leggy** /'legɪ/ *a.* long-legged.

**leghorn** /'legho:n/ *n.* fine plaited straw; hat of this; **Leghorn** breed of domestic fowl.

**legible** /'ledʒəb(ə)l/ *a.* easily read. **legibility** *n.*

**legion** /'liːdʒ(ə)n/ *n.* division of 3,000–6,000 men in ancient Roman army; other large organized body.

**legionary** /'liːdʒənərɪ/ **1** *a.* of legions. **2** *n.* member of legion.

**legionnaire** /liːdʒə'neə(r)/ *n.* member of legion. **legionnaire's disease** form of bacterial pneumonia.

**legislate** /'ledʒəsleɪt/ *v.i.* make laws. **legislator** *n.*

**legislation** /ledʒə'sleɪʃ(ə)n/ *n.* making laws; laws made.

**legislative** /'ledʒəslətɪv/ *a.* of or empowered to make legislation.

**legislature** /'ledʒəslətʃə(r)/ *n.* legislative body of a State.

**legitimate** /lə'dʒɪtəmət/ *a.* (of child) born of parents married to one another; lawful, proper, regular; logically admissible. **legitimate theatre** plays of established merit or containing spoken lines only. **legitimacy** *n.;* **legitimation** *n.*

**legitimatize** /lə'dʒɪtəmətaɪz/ *v.t.* legitimize.

**legitimize** /lə'dʒɪtəmaɪz/ *v.t.* make legitimate; serve as justification for. **legitimization** *n.*

**legume** /'legjuːm/ *n.* leguminous plant; fruit or pod etc. of this.

**leguminous** /lə'gjuːmɪnəs/ *a.* of the family of plants with seeds in pods, e.g. peas and beans.

**lei** /'leɪiː/ *n.* Polynesian garland of flowers.

**leisure** /'leʒə(r)/ *n.* free time, time at one's own disposal. **at leisure** not occupied, in unhurried manner; **at one's leisure** when one has time.

**leisured** *a.* having ample leisure.

**leisurely** 1 *a.* deliberate, unhurried. 2 *adv.* without hurry.

**leitmotiv** /'laɪtməʊtiːf/ *n. Mus.* etc. theme associated throughout piece or work with some person or idea.

**lemming** /'lemɪŋ/ *n.* small arctic rodent reputed to rush in large numbers headlong into sea and drown, during migration.

**lemon** /'lemən/ *n.* yellow acid citrus fruit; its colour; tree bearing it. **lemon cheese, curd,** thick creamy lemon spread. **lemony** *a.*

**lemon sole** /'lemən/ *n.* kind of plaice.

**lemonade** /lemə'neɪd/ *n.* drink made from or flavoured like lemons, freq. aerated.

**lemur** /'liːmə(r)/ *n.* nocturnal mammal allied to monkeys.

**lend** *v.t.* (*past & p.p.* **lent**) grant temporary use of (thing); allow use of (money) at interest; bestow, contribute; accommodate *oneself to*.

**length** /leŋθ/ *n.* measurement from end to end; greatest of body's three dimensions; extent in or of or with regard to time; long stretch or extent; piece of certain length; full extent. **at length** in detail, at last, after a long time. **lengthways** *adv.*; **lengthwise** *adv. & a.*

**lengthen** /'leŋθ(ə)n/ *v.* make or become longer.

**lengthy** /'leŋθiː/ *a.* of unusual length, prolix, tedious.

**lenient** /'liːnɪənt/ *a.* merciful, not severe, mild. **lenience** *n.*; **leniency** *n.*

**lenity** /'lenɪtiː/ *n.* gentleness, mercifulness.

**lens** /lenz/ *n.* piece of transparent substance with one or both sides curved, used in spectacles and telescopes and cameras etc.; transparent substance behind iris of eye.

**Lent**[1] *n.* period of fasting and penitence from Ash Wednesday to Easter Eve. **Lenten** *a.*

**lent**[2] *past & p.p.* of **lend**.

**lentil** /'lentəl/ *n.* edible seed of leguminous plant; this plant.

**lento** /'lentəʊ/ *a. & adv.* slow(ly).

**Leo** /'liːəʊ/ *n.* fifth sign of zodiac.

**leonine** /'liːənaɪn/ *a.* lionlike; of lions.

**leopard** /'lepəd/ *n.* large feline carnivore with dark-spotted fawn coat; panther.

**leotard** /'liːətɑːd/ *n.* close-fitting one-piece garment worn by dancers etc.

**leper** /'lepə(r)/ *n.* person with leprosy.

**lepidopterous** /lepɪ'dɒptərəs/ *a.* of the order of insects including moths and butterflies, with four scale-covered wings. **lepidopterist** *n.*

**leprechaun** /'leprəkɔːn/ *n.* small mischievous sprite in Irish folklore.

**leprosy** /'leprəsiː/ *n.* chronic infectious disease of skin and nerves, causing mutilations and deformities. **leprous** *a.*

**lerp** *n. Aus.* sweet waxy secretion of certain insects, eaten by Aborigines.

**lesbian** /'lezbɪən/ 1 *n.* homosexual woman. 2 *a.* of homosexuality in women. 3 **lesbianism** *n.*

**lèse-majesté** /liːz'mædʒəstiː/ *n.* treason; affront to sovereign etc.; presumptuous conduct.

**lesion** /'liːʒ(ə)n/ *n.* damage, injury; *Path.* morbid change in action or texture of organ.

**less** 1 *a.* smaller; of smaller quantity; not so much. 2 *adv.* to smaller extent, in lower degree. 3 *n.* smaller amount, quantity, or number. 4 *prep.* minus, deducting.

**lessee** /le'siː/ *n.* person holding property by lease.

**lessen** /'les(ə)n/ *v.* diminish.

**lesser** /'lesə(r)/ *a.* not so great as the other or the rest; minor.

**lesson** /'les(ə)n/ *n.* spell of teaching; thing learnt by pupil; experience that serves to warn or encourage; passage from Bible read aloud during church service.

**lessor** /'lesɔː(r)/ *n.* person who lets property by lease.

**lest** *conj.* in order that not, for fear that.

**let**[1] 1 *v.* (*past & p.p.* **let**) allow or enable or cause to; grant use of (rooms, land) for rent or hire. 2 *n.* act of letting. 3 **let alone** not interfere with, attend to, or do, not to mention; **let down** lower, fail to support at need, disappoint; **let fly**

release, discharge; **let go** release, lose hold of, cease to restrain; **let in(to)** allow to enter, insert into surface of, make acquainted with (secret etc.); **let in for** involve in; **let loose** release; **let off** discharge, allow to go or escape, let (part of house etc.); **let on** *sl.* reveal secret; **let out** open door for exit of, allow to escape, slacken; **let-out** opportunity to escape; **let up** *colloq.* become less severe, diminish; **let-up** cessation, diminution.

**let**² 1 *n. Tennis* etc. obstruction of ball or player after which ball must be served again. 2 *v.t.* (*past* **letted** or **let**) *arch.* hinder, obstruct. 3 **without let or hindrance** unimpeded.

**lethal** /ˈliːθ(ə)l/ *a.* causing or sufficient to cause death.

**lethargy** /ˈleθədʒɪ/ *n.* torpid or apathetic state. **lethargic** /ləˈθɑːdʒɪk/ *a.*

**letter** /ˈletə(r)/ 1 *n.* any of the symbols of which written words are composed; written or printed communication usu. sent by post or messenger; precise terms of statement; in *pl.* literature. 2 *v.t.* inscribe letters on; classify with letters. 3 **letter-bomb** terrorist explosive device sent by post; **letter-box** box for delivery or posting of letters, slit in door for delivery of letters; **letterhead** printed heading on stationery; **letterpress** printing from raised type.

**lettuce** /ˈletəs/ *n.* garden plant with crisp leaves used as salad.

**leucocyte** /ˈljuːkəsaɪt/ *n.* white or colourless blood-corpuscle.

**leukaemia** /luːˈkiːmɪə/ *n.* progressive disease with abnormal accumulation of white corpuscles in tissues.

**Levant** /ləˈvænt/ *n.* the East-Mediterranean region.

**Levantine** /ləˈvæntaɪn/ 1 *a.* of or trading to the Levant. 2 *n.* inhabitant of the Levant.

**levee**¹ /ˈlevi:/ *n.* assembly of visitors esp. at formal reception; *hist.* sovereign's assembly for men only.

**levee**² /ˈlevi:/ *n. US* embankment against river floods.

**level** /ˈlev(ə)l/ 1 *n.* horizontal line or plane; social or moral or intellectual standard; plane of rank or authority; instrument for giving or testing a horizontal line or plane; height etc. reached; level surface, flat country. 2 *a.* horizontal; on a level or equality (*with*); even, uniform, well-balanced. 3 *v.* make or become level or even or uniform; place on same level; raze, abolish; take aim *at.* 4 **level-crossing** crossing of road and railway etc. at same level; **level-headed** mentally well-balanced, cool; **on the level** *colloq.* truthfully, honestly.

**lever** /ˈliːvə(r)/ 1 *n.* tool used in prizing; bar or other rigid structure used as lifting device; *fig.* means of moral pressure. 2 *v.* use lever; lift or move etc. (as) with lever.

**leverage** /ˈliːvərɪdʒ/ *n.* action or power of lever; *fig.* means of accomplishing a purpose.

**leveret** /ˈlevərɪt/ *n.* young hare.

**leviathan** /ləˈvaɪəθ(ə)n/ *n. Bibl.* sea monster; anything very large of its kind.

**levitate** /ˈlevɪteɪt/ *v.* (cause to) rise and float in air. **levitation** *n.*

**levity** /ˈlevɪtɪ/ *n.* disposition to make light of weighty matters; frivolity.

**levy** /ˈlevɪ/ 1 *v.t.* impose or collect (payment etc.) compulsorily; enrol (troops etc.). 2 *n.* levying; payment etc. or (in *pl.*) troops levied.

**lewd** *a.* lascivious, indecent.

**lexical** /ˈleksɪk(ə)l/ *a.* of the words of a language; (as) of a lexicon.

**lexicography** /leksɪˈkɒɡrəfɪ:/ *n.* making of dictionaries. **lexicographer** *n.*; **lexicographical** *a.*

**lexicon** /ˈleksɪkən/ *n.* dictionary.

**LF** *abbr.* low frequency.

**l.h.** *abbr.* left hand.

**liability** /laɪəˈbɪlətɪ/ *n.* being liable; troublesome person or thing; in *pl.* debts for which one is liable.

**liable** /ˈlaɪəb(ə)l/ *pred.a.* legally bound; subject *to*; exposed or apt *to*; answerable *for.*

**liaise** /liːˈeɪz/ *v.i. colloq.* establish co-operation or act as a link *with* or *between.*

**liaison** /liːˈeɪzɒn/ *n.* comunication, co-operation; illicit sexual relationship.

**liana** /liːˈɑːnə/ *n.* climbing and twining plant in tropical forests.

**liar** /ˈlaɪə(r)/ *n.* person who tells lies.

**Lib.** *abbr.* Liberal; liberation.

**libation** /laɪˈbeɪʃ(ə)n/ *n.* drink-offering to god.

**libel** /ˈlaɪb(ə)l/ 1 *n.* false statement dam-

**liberal** aging to person's reputation; publishing of this; false defamatory statement. 2 v.t. (past & p.p. **libelled**) utter or publish libel against. 3 **libellous** a.

**liberal** /'lɪbər(ə)l/ 1 a. given or giving freely; generous; abundant; unprejudiced; not rigorous; (of studies) directed to general broadening of mind; *Polit.* favouring moderate reforms. 2 n. person of liberal views, etc. **Liberal** member of Liberal Party. 3 **liberalism** n.; **liberalize** v.t.; **liberalization** n.

**liberality** /lɪbə'rælətɪ/ n. generosity; breadth of mind.

**liberate** /'lɪbəreɪt/ v.t. set at liberty, release *from*; free from oppressive social conventions. **liberation** n.; **liberator** n.

**libertarian** /lɪbə'teərɪən/ 1 a. believing in free will; advocating liberty. 2 n. libertarian person.

**libertine** /'lɪbətiːn/ n. dissolute or licentious man.

**liberty** /'lɪbətɪ/ n. being free, freedom; right or power to do as one pleases; piece of presumption; in *pl.* privileges enjoyed by prescription or grant. **at liberty** free, disengaged, having right *to do.*

**libidinous** /lɪ'bɪdɪnəs/ a. lustful.

**libido** /lɪbɪːdəʊ/ n. (pl. **-dos**) psychic impulse or drive esp. that associated with sex instinct. **libidinal** a.

**Libra** /'liːbrə/ n. seventh sign of zodiac.

**librarian** /laɪ'breərɪən/ n. chief executive or assistant in library.

**library** /'laɪbrərɪ/ n. a collection of books or of films or records etc.; room or building etc. where these are kept; series of books issued in similar bindings.

**libretto** /lɪ'bretəʊ/ n. (pl. **-ti** /-tiː/ or **-tos**) text of opera etc. **librettist** n.

**lice** pl. of **louse**.

**licence** /'laɪs(ə)ns/ n. permit from government to carry out some action etc. which without this would be illegal; permission, leave; excessive liberty of action, licentiousness.

**license** /'laɪs(ə)ns/ v.t. grant licence to; authorize use of (premises) for purpose esp. sale etc. of alcoholic liquor.

**licensee** /laɪsən'siː/ n. holder of licence esp. to sell alcoholic liquor.

**licentiate** /laɪ'senʃɪət/ n. holder of certificate of competence to practise certain profession.

**licentious** /laɪ'senʃəs/ a. immoral in sexual relations.

**lichee** var. of **litchi**.

**lichen** /'laɪkən/ n. plant organism composed of fungus and alga in association, growing on rocks and trees etc.

**lich-gate** /'lɪtʃgeɪt/ n. roofed gateway of churchyard.

**licit** /'lɪsɪt/ a. not forbidden.

**lick** 1 v. pass tongue over; take *off* or *up* by licking; play lightly over; *sl.* thrash, defeat. 2 n. act of licking with tongue; smart blow; *sl.* pace, speed.

**lid** n. hinged or removable cover esp. at top of container; eyelid.

**lie**[1] /laɪ/ 1 v.i. (past **lay**; p.p. **lain**; *partic.* **lying**) be in or assume horizontal position on supporting surface; be at rest on something; be situated or spread out to view etc.; remain, be; exist or be in certain position or manner; *Law* be admissible or sustainable. 2 n. way, position, or direction in which something lies. 3 **lie in** *colloq.* remain in bed late in morning; **lie-in** n.; **lie low** keep quiet or unseen; **lie of the land** state of affairs.

**lie**[2] /laɪ/ 1 n. intentional false statement; imposture, false belief. 2 v.i. (*partic.* **lying**) tell lie(s); be deceptive.

**lief** /liːf/ adv. *arch.* willingly.

**liege** /liːdʒ/ *hist.* 1 a. entitled to receive or bound to give feudal service or allegiance. 2 n. liege lord; (usu. in *pl.*) vassal, subject. 3 **liege lord** feudal superior.

**lien** /'liːən/ n. right to hold another's property till debt on it is paid.

**lieu** /ljuː/ n. **in lieu** instead (*of*).

**Lieut.** *abbr.* Lieutenant.

**lieutenant** /lef'ten(ə)nt/ n. deputy or substitute who acts for a superior; army officer next below captain; naval officer next below lieutenant-commander. **lieutenant-colonel, -commander, -general,** officers ranking next below colonel etc. **lieutenancy** n.

**life** n. (pl. **lives**) capacity for growth and functional activity and continual change peculiar to animals and plants; state of existence as living individual; living things and their activity; period during which life lasts; period from birth to present time or from present

# lifeless · like

**time to death; manner of existence or particular aspect of this; energy, liveliness; business and pleasures of the world; written account of person's life; time for which manufactured or perishable product continues to function or be satisfactory etc.; sentence of imprisonment for life. lifebelt** ring of buoyant material to support body in water; **lifeblood** vitalizing influence; **lifeboat** boat for rescue in storms, ship's boat for emergency use; **lifebuoy** lifebelt; **life cycle** *Biol.* cyclic series of changes undergone by an organism; **life insurance** insurance for payment on death of insured person; **life jacket** upper garment of buoyant material to support body in water; **lifeline** rope used for life-saving, *fig.* sole means of communication; **life peer** peer whose title lapses at death; **life-size(d)** of same size as person or thing represented; **life-style** individual's way of life; **lifetime** duration of person's life.

**lifeless** /ˈlaɪflɪs/ *a.* dead; lacking in animation.

**lifelike** /ˈlaɪflaɪk/ *a.* (of representation) realistic or vivid.

**lifer** /ˈlaɪfə(r)/ *n. sl.* person sentenced to imprisonment for life; such sentence.

**lift 1** *v.* raise to higher level, take up, hoist; give upward direction to; elevate; (of cloud etc.) rise, disperse; go up, be raised; remove (restriction etc.); steal, plagiarize. **2** *n.* lifting; carrying of person without charge as passenger in vehicle; apparatus for raising and lowering persons or things from floor to floor in building, or for carrying persons up or down mountain etc.; supporting or elevating influence. **liftoff** vertical take-off of spacecraft or rocket.

**ligament** /ˈlɪgəmənt/ *n.* band of tough fibrous tissue binding bones together.

**ligature** /ˈlɪgətʃə(r)/ **1** *n.* tie or bandage; *Mus.* slur, tie; *Print.* two or more letters joined (*æ, fl,* etc.). **2** *v.t.* bind or connect with ligature.

**light¹** /laɪt/ **1** *n.* natural agent that makes things visible; medium or condition of space in which this is present; brightness of eyes or aspect; source of light; means of procuring fire; traffic light; aspect in which thing is viewed; mental illumination; in *pl.* one's mental powers; word to be deduced from crossword clue. **2** *a.* well-provided with light, not dark; (of colours) pale. **3** *v.* (*past* **lit**; *p.p.* **lit** or **lighted**) set burning, begin to burn; give light to; show way etc. with light; (cause to) brighten (*up*) with animation. **4 lighthouse** structure with beacon light to warn or guide ships at sea; **lightship** anchored ship with beacon light; **light-year** distance which light travels in one year.

**light²** /laɪt/ **1** *a.* of little weight, not heavy, easy to lift; relatively low in weight or amount or density or strength; deficient in weight; easy to digest; easily borne or done; intended only as entertainment, not profound; free from sorrow, cheerful; nimble; elegant. **2** *adv.* lightly; with light load. **3** *v.i.* (*past & p.p.* **lit** or **lighted**) come by chance (*upon*). **4 light-fingered** apt to steal; **light-headed** giddy, delirious; **light-hearted** cheerful, untroubled; **light industry** that producing small or light articles; **light on** *Aus. colloq.* in short supply scarce; **lightweight** below average weight, of little ability or importance, (*n.*) lightweight person or thing, boxing weight (up to 60 kg.).

**lighten¹** /ˈlaɪt(ə)n/ *v.* make or become less heavy; reduce weight or load of; bring relief to; mitigate.

**lighten²** /ˈlaɪt(ə)n/ *v.* shed light upon, make or become bright; emit lightning.

**lighter¹** /ˈlaɪtə(r)/ *n.* device for lighting cigarettes etc.

**lighter²** /ˈlaɪtə(r)/ *n.* boat for transporting goods between ship and wharf etc.

**lightning** /ˈlaɪtnɪŋ/ *n.* visible electric discharge between clouds or cloud and ground. **lightning-conductor** metal rod or wire fixed to building etc. to divert lightning to earth.

**lights** /laɪts/ *n.pl.* lungs of sheep or pigs etc. as food, esp. for pets.

**lightsome** /ˈlaɪtsəm/ *a.* gracefully light; merry; agile.

**ligneous** /ˈlɪgnɪəs/ *a.* of the nature of wood.

**lignite** /ˈlɪgnaɪt/ *n.* brown coal of woody texture.

**lignum** /ˈlɪgnəm/ *n.* tall almost leafless shrub of Aus. interior.

**lignum vitae** /ˈlɪgnəm ˈvaɪtiː/ a hardwooded tree.

**like¹ 1** *a.* similar, resembling; such as;

**like**     315     **line**

characteristic of; in suitable state or mood for. **2** *prep.* in the manner of, to the same degree as. **3** *conj.* *incorrect* as; *US colloq.* as if. **4** *n.* counterpart, equal; like thing or person.

**like²** **1** *v.* find agreeable or satisfactory; feel attracted by, wish, prefer. **2** *n.* (usu. in *pl.*) thing one likes or prefers.

**likeable** /ˈlaɪkəb(ə)l/ *a.* pleasant, easy to like.

**likelihood** /ˈlaɪklihʊd/ *n.* probability.

**likely** /ˈlaɪkli/ **1** *a.* probable; such as might well happen or be or prove true; to be expected *to*; promising, apparently suitable. **2** *adv.* probably.

**liken** /ˈlaɪkən/ *v.t.* find or point out resemblance in (*to*).

**likeness** /ˈlaɪknəs/ *n.* resemblance, semblance; representation, portrait.

**likewise** /ˈlaɪkwaɪz/ *adv.* also, moreover; similarly.

**liking** /ˈlaɪkɪŋ/ *n.* one's taste; fondness or taste or fancy *for*.

**lilac** /ˈlaɪlək/ **1** *n.* shrub with fragrant pale violet or white flowers; pale violet colour. **2** *a.* of lilac colour.

**liliaceous** /lɪliˈeɪʃəs/ *a.* of the lily family.

**lilliputian** /lɪləˈpjuːʃ(ə)n/ *a.* diminutive.

**lilly-pilly** /ˈlɪliːpɪli/ *n.* E. Aus. tree with edible purplish to white berries; its fruit.

**lilt** **1** *n.* light pleasant rhythm; song or tune with this. **2** *v.* move or utter with lilt.

**lily** /ˈlɪli/ *n.* bulbous plant with large showy flowers; its flower; heraldic fleur-de-lis. **lily of the valley** spring plant with fragrant white bell-shaped flowers.

**limb¹** /lɪm/ *n.* leg, arm, or wing; large branch of tree; branch of cross. **out on a limb** *fig.* isolated, stranded.

**limb²** /lɪm/ *n. Astron.* specified edge of sun etc.

**limber¹** /ˈlɪmbə(r)/ **1** *a.* flexible; lithe, agile. **2** *v.* make oneself limber in preparation for athletic etc. activity.

**limber²** /ˈlɪmbə(r)/ **1** *n.* detachable front of gun-carriage. **2** *v.t.* attach limber to (gun).

**limbo¹** /ˈlɪmbəʊ/ *n.* (*pl.* **-bos**) supposed abode of pre-Christian righteous persons and of unbaptized infants; intermediate state or condition; condition of neglect or oblivion.

**limbo²** /ˈlɪmbəʊ/ *n.* (*pl.* **-bos**) W. Ind. dance in which dancer bends backwards to pass under horizontal bar.

**lime¹** **1** *n.* white caustic substance got by heating limestone etc. **2** *v.t.* treat with lime. **3 lime-kiln** kiln for heating limestone.

**lime²** *n.* round green acid fruit of lemon kind. **lime-green** yellowish-green colour.

**lime³** *n.* ornamental tree with heart-shaped leaves.

**limelight** /ˈlaɪmlaɪt/ *n.* intense white light used formerly in theatres; glare of publicity.

**limerick** /ˈlɪmərɪk/ *n.* humorous 5-line stanza.

**limestone** /ˈlaɪmstəʊn/ *n.* rock composed mainly of calcium carbonate.

**Limey** /ˈlaɪmi/ *n. US sl.* British person.

**limit** /ˈlɪmɪt/ **1** *n.* line etc. that may not or cannot be passed; greatest or smallest amount permitted. **2** *v.t.* set limits to, serve as limit to; restrict *to*.

**limitation** /lɪmɪˈteɪʃ(ə)n/ *n.* limiting or being limited; lack of ability; limiting rule or circumstance.

**limn** /lɪm/ *v.t. literary* paint (picture), portray.

**limousine** /ˈlɪməziːn/ *n.* motor car with closed body and partition behind driver.

**limp¹** **1** *v.i.* walk lamely; proceed slowly or with difficulty; (of verse) be defective. **2** *n.* lame walk.

**limp²** *a.* easily bent and not springing back to shape; *fig.* without will or energy.

**limpet** /ˈlɪmpət/ *n.* mollusc with low conical shell adhering tightly to rocks.

**limpid** /ˈlɪmpɪd/ *a.* transparently clear. **limpidity** *n.*

**linage** /ˈlaɪnɪdʒ/ *n.* number of lines in page etc.; payment by the line.

**linchpin** /ˈlɪntʃpɪn/ *n.* pin passed through axle-end to keep wheel on; *fig.* person or thing vital to organization etc.

**linctus** /ˈlɪŋktəs/ *n.* medicine, esp. soothing syrupy cough-mixture.

**linden** /ˈlɪnd(ə)n/ *n.* lime³.

**line¹** **1** *n.* long narrow mark traced on surface; band of colour, furrow, wrinkle; extent of length without breadth;

**line** 316 **lip**

limit, boundary; row of persons or things; piece of cord or rope etc. serving usu. specified purpose; wire or cable for telephone or telegraph; connection by this; contour, outline, lineament; course of procedure or conduct; in *pl.* plan, draft, manner of procedure; row of printed or written words; a verse or in *pl.* a piece of poetry; in *pl.* words of actor's part; track or branch of railway; regular succession of ships or buses or aircraft etc. plying between certain places, company conducting this; lineage, stock; direction, track; department of activity, branch of business; class of commercial goods; *Mil.* connected series of field-works, arrangement of soldiers side by side; one of the very narrow horizontal sections forming television picture. **2** *v.* mark with lines; position or stand at intervals along. **3 do a line with** *Aus. colloq.* (try to) enter amorous relationship with; **line printer** machine that prints output from computer a line at a time; **linesman** umpire's or referee's assistant who decides whether ball falls within playing area or not; **line up** arrange or be arranged in lines; **line-up** *n.*

**line²** *v.t.* apply layer of usu. different material to inside of; serve as lining for; fill (purse etc.).

**lineage** /ˈlɪnɪɪdʒ/ *n.* lineal descent, ancestry.

**lineal** /ˈlɪnɪəl/ *a.* in the direct line of descent or ancestry.

**lineament** /ˈlɪnɪəmənt/ *n.* usu. in *pl.* distinctive feature or characteristic esp. of face.

**linear** /ˈlɪnɪə(r)/ *a.* of or in lines; long and narrow and of uniform breadth.

**linen** /ˈlɪnən/ **1** *n.* cloth woven from flax; articles made or orig. made of this, such as sheets, shirts, undergarments, etc. **2** *a.* made of linen.

**liner¹** /ˈlaɪnə(r)/ *n.* ship or aircraft belonging to regular line and used for passenger transport.

**liner²** /ˈlaɪnə(r)/ *n.* removable lining.

**ling¹** /lɪŋ/ *n.* long slender sea-fish.

**ling²** *n.* kind of heather.

**linger** /ˈlɪŋɡə(r)/ *v.i.* be slow to depart; stay about, dally; be protracted.

**lingerie** /ˈlæʒəriː/ *n.* women's underwear and night-clothes.

**lingo** /ˈlɪŋɡəʊ/ *n.* (*pl.* **-gos**) *derog.* foreign language.

**lingual** /ˈlɪŋɡw(ə)l/ *a.* of tongue; of speech or languages.

**linguist** /ˈlɪŋɡwɪst/ *n.* person skilled in languages or linguistics.

**linguistic** /lɪŋˈɡwɪstɪk/ *a.* of the study of languages; of language. **linguistically** *adv.*

**linguistics** *n.pl.* (usu. treated as *sing.*) study of languages.

**liniment** /ˈlɪnɪmənt/ *n.* embrocation, usu. made with oil.

**lining** /ˈlaɪnɪŋ/ *n.* layer of material used to line surface.

**link 1** *n.* one loop or ring of chain etc.; thing or person that unites or provides continuity; member of series. **2** *v.* connect or join (*to, together, with*); clasp or intertwine.

**linkage** /ˈlɪŋkɪdʒ/ *n.* system of links; state of being linked.

**links** *n.pl.* (occas. treated as *sing.*) golf-course.

**Linnaean** /lɪˈniːən/ *a.* of Linnaeus or his classification of plants.

**linnet** /ˈlɪnɪt/ *n.* kind of song-bird.

**lino** /ˈlaɪnəʊ/ *n.* (*pl.* **-nos**) linoleum.

**linocut** design cut in relief on block of linoleum, print made from this.

**linoleum** /ləˈnəʊlɪəm/ *n.* floor-covering of canvas thickly coated with a preparation of linseed oil etc.

**Linotype** /ˈlaɪnətaɪp/ *n.* (**P**) composing-machine producing lines of words as single slugs of metal.

**linseed** /ˈlɪnsiːd/ *n.* seed of flax.

**linsey-woolsey** /lɪnzɪˈwʊlzɪ/ *n.* fabric of coarse wool woven on cotton warp.

**lint** *n.* linen with one side made fluffy, used for dressing wounds; fluff.

**lintel** /ˈlɪnt(ə)l/ *n.* horizontal timber or stone over door or window.

**lion** /ˈlaɪən/ *n.* large powerful tawny carnivorous animal of cat family; celebrated person; brave person. **lioness** *n.*

**lionize** /ˈlaɪənaɪz/ *v.t.* treat as celebrity.

**lip** *n.* either edge of opening of mouth; edge of vessel or cavity etc.; *sl.* impudence. **lip-reading** method used esp. by deaf persons to understand speech from lip movements; **lip-read** *v.*; **lip-service** insincere expression of support; **lipstick** stick of cosmetic for colouring lips.

**liquefy** /ˈlɪkwəfaɪ/ v. make or become liquid. **liquefaction** n.

**liqueur** /lɪˈkjuːə(r)/ n. drink made from a spirit sweetened and flavoured.

**liquid** /ˈlɪkwəd/ 1 a. having consistency like that of water or oil; neither solid nor gaseous; having clearness of water; (of sounds) clear, pure; (of assets) easily convertible into cash. 2 n. liquid substance; sound of l or r. 3 **liquid crystal** liquid in state approaching that of crystalline solid.

**liquidate** /ˈlɪkwədeɪt/ v.t. wind up affairs of (company etc.); pay off (debt); put an end to, get rid of (often by violent means). **liquidator** n.

**liquidation** /lɪkwəˈdeɪʃ(ə)n/ n. liquidating of company etc. **go into liquidation** be wound up and have assets apportioned.

**liquidity** /lɪˈkwɪdəti/ n. state of being liquid or having liquid assets.

**liquidize** /ˈlɪkwədaɪz/ v.t. reduce to liquid state.

**liquidizer** n. machine used for making purées etc.

**liquor** /ˈlɪkə(r)/ n. alcoholic (esp. distilled) drink; liquid used in or resulting from some process.

**liquorice** /ˈlɪkərəs/ n. black substance used as sweet and in medicine; plant from whose root it is obtained.

**lira** /ˈlɪərə/ n. (pl. **lire** /ˈlɪəreɪ/ or **liras**) currency unit in Italy and Turkey.

**lisle** /laɪl/ n. fine smooth cotton thread used for stockings etc.

**lisp** 1 v. pronounce sibilants with sound like /θ/ or /ð/; say lispingly. 2 n. such pronunciation.

**lissom** /ˈlɪsəm/ a. lithe, agile.

**list**[1] 1 n. number of connected items or names etc. written or printed together; in pl. palisades enclosing tilting-ground. 2 v.t. arrange as or include in list. 3 **enter the lists** issue or accept challenge.

**list**[2] 1 v.i. (of ship etc.) lean over to one side. 2 n. listing position, tilt.

**listen** /ˈlɪs(ə)n/ v.i. make effort to hear something, hear with attention; give attention with ear *to*; take notice. **listen in** tap communication made by telephone, listen to radio broadcast.

**listless** /ˈlɪstləs/ a. without energy or enthusiasm.

**lit** past & p.p. of **light**[1,2].

**litany** /ˈlɪtəni/ n. series of supplications to God used in church services.

**litchi** /ˈlɪtʃi/ n. sweetish pulpy shelled fruit; tree bearing this.

**literacy** /ˈlɪtərəsi/ n. ability to read and write.

**literal** /ˈlɪtər(ə)l/ a. taking words in their usual sense without metaphor etc.; exactly corresponding to original. **literalism** n.

**literary** /ˈlɪtərəri/ a. of or concerned with or interested in literature.

**literate** /ˈlɪtərət/ 1 a. able to read and write. 2 n. literate person.

**literati** /lɪtəˈrɑːtiː/ n.pl. literary or learned persons.

**literature** /ˈlɪtərətʃə(r)/ n. books and written works esp. of kind valued for form and style; the writings of a country or period etc.; colloq. printed matter.

**lithe** /laɪð/ a. flexible, supple.

**litho** /ˈlaɪθəʊ/ 1 n. (pl. **-thos**) lithographic process. 2 a. lithographic. 3 v.t. lithograph.

**lithograph** /ˈlɪθəɡrɑːf or -ɡræf/ 1 n. print produced by lithography. 2 v.t. produce such print of.

**lithography** /lɪˈθɒɡrəfi/ n. process of printing from stone or metal surface so treated that ink adheres only to the design to be printed. **lithographer** n.; **lithographic** a.

**litigant** /ˈlɪtɪɡənt/ 1 n. party to lawsuit. 2 a. engaged in lawsuit.

**litigate** /ˈlɪtɪɡeɪt/ v. go to law; contest (point) at law. **litigation** n.

**litigious** /ləˈtɪdʒəs/ a. fond of litigation; contentious.

**litmus** /ˈlɪtməs/ n. blue colouring-matter turned red by acid and restored to blue by alkali.

**litre** /ˈliːtə(r)/ n. unit of capacity in metric system, about 1.75 pints.

**litter** /ˈlɪtə(r)/ 1 n. refuse, esp. paper, discarded on streets etc., odds and ends lying about; vehicle containing couch and carried on men's shoulders or by beasts of burden; kind of stretcher for sick and wounded; young animals brought forth at a birth; bedding for animals; material for filling receptacle for domestic cat etc. to urinate etc. in. 2 v.t. make (place) untidy; give birth to (young); provide (horse etc.) with bedding.

**little** /ˈlɪt(ə)l/ 1 *a.* small, not great or big; short in stature; of short distance or duration; working etc. on only small scale; trivial, mean; not much. 2 *n.* not much, only a small amount; *a* certain but no great amount; short time or distance. 3 *adv.* to a small extent only; not at all. 4 **little by little** by degrees; **the little people** fairies.

**littoral** /ˈlɪtər(ə)l/ 1 *a.* of or on the shore. 2 *n.* region lying along the shore.

**liturgy** /ˈlɪtədʒi/ *n.* fixed form of public worship used in church. **liturgical** /-ˈtɜːdʒɪ-/ *a.*

**live¹** /lɪv/ *v.* be alive, have life; continue alive; subsist or feed *on*; have one's home; conduct oneself; pass or spend; enjoy life to the full.

**live²** /laɪv/ *a.* that is alive, living; burning or glowing; capable of being exploded or kindled; charged with electricity; (of broadcast) heard or seen during occurrence of event, or undertaken with audience present; not obsolete or exhausted. **livestock** animals kept or dealt in for use or profit; **live wire** highly energetic forceful person.

**liveable** /ˈlɪvəb(ə)l/ *a.* worth living; fit to live in or *with*.

**livelihood** /ˈlaɪvlɪhʊd/ *n.* means of living; sustenance.

**livelong** /ˈlɪvlɒŋ/ *a.* in its entire length.

**lively** /ˈlaɪvli:/ *a.* full of life or energy or interest or vividness; cheerful, keen.

**liven** /ˈlaɪv(ə)n/ *v.* brighten or cheer (*up*).

**liver¹** /ˈlɪvə(r)/ *n.* large glandular organ secreting bile; flesh of animal's liver as food; dark reddish-brown colour.

**liver²** /ˈlɪvə(r)/ *n.* person who lives in specified way.

**liverish** /ˈlɪvərɪʃ/ *a.* suffering from disorder of liver; peevish.

**liverwort** /ˈlɪvəwɜːt/ *n.* lichen-like plant with lobed leaves.

**livery** /ˈlɪvəri:/ *n.* distinctive clothes worn by male servant or member of London City Company; distinctive guise or marking; allowance of provender for horses. **livery company** one of the London City Companies that formerly had distinctive costume; **livery stable** stable where horses are kept for owner or let out for hire.

**livid** /ˈlɪvɪd/ *a.* of bluish leaden colour; *colloq.* very angry.

**living** /ˈlɪvɪŋ/ 1 *n.* livelihood; position held by clergyman, providing income. 2 *a.* now alive; (of likeness) exact; (of language) still in vernacular use. 3 **living-room** room for general day use; **living wage** wage on which one can live without privation; **withing living memory** that can still be remembered by living persons.

**lizard** /ˈlɪzəd/ *n.* reptile having usu. 4 legs and tail.

**llama** /ˈlɑːmə/ *n.* S. Amer. woolly-haired ruminant used as beast of burden.

**Lloyd's** /lɔɪdz/ *n.* incorporated society of underwriters in London. **Lloyd's Register** annual classified list of shipping.

**lo** *int. arch.* drawing attention.

**loach** *n.* small freshwater fish.

**load** 1 *n.* what is (to be) carried; amount usu. or actually carried; *fig.* weight of care or responsibility; *Electr.* amount of power supplied by generating station or carried by electric circuit; material object or force acting as a burden; in *pl. colloq.* plenty *of*. 2 *v.* put load on or aboard; place (load) aboard ship or on vehicle etc.; burden, strain; supply or assail overwhelmingly *with*; put ammunition in (firearm etc.); insert film in (camera); put (program, data, etc.) in computer memory. 3 **load line** Plimsoll line.

**loaded** /ˈləʊdəd/ *a.* (of question) carrying hidden implication; *sl.* rich, drunk, *US* drugged.

**loadstone** /ˈləʊdstəʊn/ *n.* magnetic oxide of iron; piece of it used as magnet; *fig.* thing that attracts.

**loaf¹** *n.* (*pl.* **loaves**) quantity of bread baked alone or as part of batch; loaflike block of cooked minced meat etc.

**loaf²** *v.i.* spend time idly, hang about.

**loam** *n.* rich soil of clay and sand and decayed vegetable matter. **loamy** *a.*

**loan** 1 *n.* thing lent; sum to be returned with or without interest. 2 *v.t.* grant loan of. 3 **loan-word** word adopted by one language from another.

**loath** /ləʊθ/ *pred.a.* disinclined, reluctant.

**loathe** /ləʊð/ *v.t.* regard with disgust. **loathing** *n.*

**loathsome** /ˈləʊðsəm/ *a.* repulsive, odious.

**loaves** pl. of **loaf¹**.

**lob** 1 v. send (ball) or send ball with slow or high-pitched motion. 2 n. such ball. 3 **lob in** Aus. sl. arrive.

**lobar** /ˈləʊbə(r)/ a. of a lobe.

**lobate** /ˈləʊbeɪt/ a. having lobe(s).

**lobby** /ˈlɒbɪ/ 1 n. porch, entrance-hall; ante-room, corridor; (in legislative building) large hall open to public used esp. for interviews between MPs and others, one of two corridors to which members retire to vote; body of those who lobby. 2 v. seek to influence (MP etc.) by interviews etc. in lobby; solicit members' votes or influence of (person).

**lobbyist** /ˈlɒbɪəst/ n. person who lobbies MP etc.

**lobe** /ləʊb/ n. lower soft pendulous part of outer ear; similar part of other organ.

**lobelia** /ləˈbiːlɪə/ n. herbaceous plant with brightly-coloured flowers.

**lobotomy** /ləˈbɒtəmɪ/ n. incision into frontal lobe of brain to relieve mental disorder.

**lobster** /ˈlɒbstə(r)/ n. large edible sea crustacean with heavy pincer-like claws; its flesh as food. **lobster-pot** basket in which lobsters are trapped.

**local** /ˈləʊk(ə)l/ 1 a. of place; belonging to or peculiar to certain place(s); of one's own neighbourhood; of or affecting a part and not the whole. 2 n. inhabitant of particular district; *colloq.* the local public house. 3 **local colour** touches of detail in story etc. designed to provide convincing background; **local government** system of administration of county or district etc. by elected representatives of those who live there.

**locale** /ləʊˈkɑːl/ n. scene or locality of operations or events.

**locality** /ləʊˈkælətɪ/ n. thing's position; site or scene of something.

**localize** /ˈləʊkəlaɪz/ v.t. assign to particular place; invest with characteristics of place; decentralize. **localization** n.

**locate** /ləʊˈkeɪt/ v.t. discover exact place of; establish in a place; state locality of; in *pass.* be situated.

**location** /ləʊˈkeɪʃ(ə)n/ n. locating or being located; particular place; place other than studio where (part of) film is made.

**loch** /lɒx or lɒk/ n. Scottish lake or land-locked arm of the sea.

**lock**[1] 1 n. mechanism for fastening door or lid etc.; section of canal or river confined within sluiced gates for shifting boats from one level to another; mechanism for exploding charge of gun; turning of front wheels of vehicle; interlocked or jammed state. 2 v. fasten with lock; shut *up* (house etc.); shut (person or thing) *up*, *in(to)*, or *out* by locking; be lockable; bring or come into rigidly fixed position; (cause to) jam or catch; store inaccessibly *up* or *away*. 3 **lockjaw** variety of tetanus in which jaws are rigidly closed; **lock-keeper** keeper of canal etc. lock; **lock-out** refusal by employer to allow employees access to place of work until they accept his conditions; **locksmith** maker and mender of locks; **lock-up** time or process of locking up, house or room for temporary detention of prisoners that is able to be locked.

**lock**[2] n. one of the portions into which the hair groups itself; in *pl.* the hair.

**locker** /ˈlɒkə(r)/ n. small lockable cupboard.

**locket** /ˈlɒkɪt/ n. small case containing portrait etc. usu. hung from neck.

**locomotion** /ləʊkəˈməʊʃ(ə)n/ n. (power of) motion from place to place, travel.

**locomotive** /ləʊkəˈməʊtɪv/ 1 n. locomotive engine. 2 a. of or effecting locomotion, not stationary. 3 **locomotive engine** engine for drawing trains.

**locum** /ˈləʊkəm/ n. deputy acting esp. for clergyman or doctor.

**locus** /ˈləʊkəs/ n. (pl. **loci** /ˈləʊsaɪ/) *Math.* curve etc. made by all points satisfying certain conditions or by defined motion of point or line or surface.

**locust** /ˈləʊkəst/ n. grasshopper migrating in swarms and consuming all vegetation; any of various kinds of tree and their fruit.

**locution** /ləˈkjuːʃ(ə)n/ n. phrase or idiom; style of speech.

**lode** n. vein of metal ore. **lodestar** star used as guide in navigation, esp. polestar; **lodestone** var. of **loadstone**.

**lodge** 1 n. small house, esp. one at entrance to park or grounds of large house; *Aus.* Prime Minister's house in

Canberra; porter's room etc.; members or meeting-place of branch of society such as Freemasons; beaver's or otter's lair. 2 v. provide with sleeping-quarters; reside as lodger; deposit for security or attention; fix in; settle, place.

**lodger** n. person paying for accommodation in another's house.

**lodging** n. accommodation in hired rooms, dwelling-place; in pl. room(s) rented for lodging in.

**loft** 1 n. attic; room over stable; gallery in church or hall; pigeon-house. 2 v.t. hit or throw or kick etc. (ball) high up.

**lofty** /'lɒftɪ/ a. of imposing height; haughty, keeping aloof; exalted, sublime.

**log**¹ 1 n. unhewn piece of felled tree; any large rough piece of wood; apparatus for ascertaining ship's speed; detailed record of ship's or aircraft's voyage or of progress or performance. 2 v.t. enter in ship's log-book; enter (data etc.) in regular record; cut into logs. 3 **log-book** log of ship etc.; **log in, out**, begin, finish, operations at terminal of esp. multi-access computer.

**log**² n. logarithm.

**loganberry** /'ləʊɡənberɪ/ n. hybrid between raspberry and Amer. blackberry.

**logan** /'ləʊɡən/ n. (in full **logan-stone**) poised heavy stone rocking at a touch.

**logarithm** /'lɒɡərɪð(ə)m/ n. one of a series of reckoning-numbers tabulated to simplify computation. **logarithmic** a.

**loggerhead** /'lɒɡəhed/ n. **at loggerheads** disagreeing or disputing (with).

**loggia** /'ləʊdʒə/ n. open-sided gallery or arcade; open-sided extension to house.

**logging** /'lɒɡɪŋ/ n. felling, cutting, and transporting timber.

**logic** /'lɒdʒɪk/ n. science of reasoning, chain of reasoning, use of or ability in argument. **logician** n.

**logical** /'lɒdʒɪk(ə)l/ a. of logic; in conformity with laws of logic; rightly deducible; capable of correct reasoning. **logicality** n.

**Logie** /'ləʊɡɪ/ n. Aus. award for excellence in television acting or directing etc.

**logistics** /lə'dʒɪstɪks/ n.pl. art of supplying and organizing (orig. military) services and equipment. **logistic** a.; **logistically** adv.

**logo** /'ləʊɡəʊ/ n. (pl. **-gos**) logotype.

**logotype** /'lɒɡəʊtaɪp/ n. non-heraldic device as badge of an organization; piece of type with this.

**loin** n. in pl. part of body on both sides of spine between ribs and hip-bones; in sing. joint of meat cut from loins. **loincloth** cloth worn round loins esp. as sole garment.

**loiter** /'lɔɪtə(r)/ v.i. linger on way; hang about.

**loll** v. recline or sit or stand in lazy attitude; (of tongue) hang out.

**lollipop** /'lɒlɪpɒp/ n. large boiled sweet on stick.

**lollop** /'lɒləp/ v.i. colloq. move or proceed in lounging or ungainly way; flop about.

**lolly** /'lɒlɪ/ n. colloq. Aus. sweet; UK lollipop; sl. money.

**lone** a. poet. solitary, uninhabited, lonely. **lone hand** hand played or player playing against the rest at cards, fig. person or action without allies; **lone wolf** loner.

**lonely** /'ləʊnlɪ/ a. lacking friends or companions; sad because of this; solitary, isolated. **loneliness** n.

**loner** /'ləʊnə(r)/ n. person or animal preferring not to associate with others.

**lonesome** /'ləʊnsəm/ a. lonely; causing loneliness.

**long**¹ 1 a. measuring much from end to end in space or time; of specified length; seemingly more than stated amount; lasting or reaching far back or forward in time; of elongated shape; remarkable for or concerned with length or duration. 2 n. long interval or period; long vowel or syllable. 3 adv. for or by a long time; throughout specified time; in compar. after implied point of time. 4 **in the long run** ultimately; **longboat** sailing ship's largest boat; **longbow** one drawn by hand and shooting long arrow; **long-distance** travelling or operating between distant places; **long face** dismal expression; **long-fin** Aus. pinkish-red fish of groper family; **longhand** ordinary handwriting; **long johns** colloq. underpants with full-length legs; **long jump** jump measured along ground; **long odds** very uneven chances; **long-playing** (of gramophone record) playing about 15-30 minutes on each side; **long-range** having a long range, relating to long period of future time; **long-shore** found or employed on or frequenting the shore; **long shot** wild guess or venture; **long sight** ability to see clearly only what is comparatively distant; **long-sighted** having long sight or foresight; **long-sleever** *Aus. colloq.* tall glass, long drink; **long-suffering** bearing provocation patiently; **long-term** occurring in or relating to long period of time; **long-winded** inclined to talk or write at tedious length.

**long**[2] *v.i.* wish earnestly or vehemently (*for*, *to*).

**long.** *abbr.* longitude.

**longevity** /lɒnˈdʒevəti/ *n.* long life.

**longitude** /ˈlɒŋɡətjuːd/ *n.* angular distance E. or W. of the meridian of Greenwich.

**longitudinal** /lɒŋɡəˈtjuːdən(ə)l/ *a.* of longitude; of or in length; lying longways.

**longways** /ˈlɒŋweɪz/ *adv.* (also **longwise**) in direction parallel with thing's length.

**loo** *n. colloq.* lavatory.

**loofah** /ˈluːfə/ *n.* dried pod of a kind of gourd used as rough sponge.

**look** /lʊk/ **1** *v.* use or direct one's eyes; make search; have specified appearance, seem; contemplate, examine; face or be turned in specified direction; indicate by looks; expect *to do* thing. **2** *n.* act of looking; gaze or glance; expression of face; appearance; in *pl.* personal appearance. **3 look after** attend to; **look down (up)on** consider oneself superior to; **look forward** to await eagerly or with specified feelings; **look in** make short visit; **look-in** chance of success; **looking-glass** glass mirror; **look into** investigate; **look on** be mere spectator; **look out** be vigilant or prepared (*for*); **look-out** watch, observation-post, person etc. stationed to look out, prospect of luck, person's own concern; **look up** search for in book of reference, improve; **look up to** respect.

**loom**[1] /luːm/ *n.* apparatus for weaving.

**loom**[2] /luːm/ *v.i.* appear dimly; be seen in vague and often magnified shape.

**loony** /ˈluːni/ *n. sl.* lunatic.

**loop** /luːp/ **1** *n.* figure produced by curve or doubled string etc. crossing itself; similarly shaped attachment or ornament used as fastening etc.; endless strip of tape or film allowing continuous repetition. **2** *v.* form (string etc.) into loop; enclose (as) with loop; fasten with loops; form loop. **3 loopline** railway or telegraph line that diverges from main line and joins it again.

**loophole** /ˈluːphəʊl/ *n.* means of evading rule etc. without infringing letter of it; narrow vertical slit in wall.

**loopy** /ˈluːpi/ *a. sl.* crazy.

**loose** /luːs/ **1** *a.* released from bonds or restraint; detached or detachable from its place; not held together or dense; slack; not compact or dense; inexact, vague; morally lax. **2** *v.* release, free, untie, undo; detach from moorings; relax. **3 at a loose end** without definite occupation; **loose box** stall in which horse can move about; **loose change** money as coins in pocket etc.; **loose cover** removable cover for chair etc.; **loose-leaf** (of book) with each leaf separately removable; **on the loose** having a spree.

**loosen** /ˈluːs(ə)n/ *v.* make or become less tight or compact or firm.

**loot** /luːt/ **1** *n.* booty, spoil; *sl.* money. **2** *v.* take loot (from); carry off (as) loot.

**lop**[1] *v.t.* cut away branches or twigs of; cut away.

**lop**[2] *v.i.* hang limply. **lop-eared** having drooping ears; **lop-sided** with one side lower, unevenly balanced.

**lope 1** *v.i.* run with long bounding stride. **2** *n.* such stride.

**loquacious** /lɒˈkweɪʃəs/ *a.* talkative. **loquacity** *n.*

**lord 1** *n.* master, ruler; *hist.* feudal superior; peer of realm; **Lord** prefixed as designation of certain ranks of peerage, or to Christian name of younger son of duke or marquis. **2** *int.* expr. surprise or consternation. **3** *v.* **lord it** domineer. **4 the Lord** God or Christ; **the Lords** the House of Lords; **Lord's day** Sunday; **Lord's Prayer** that beginning 'Our Father'; **Lord's Supper** Eucharist.

**lordly** /ˈlɔːdli/ *a.* haughty, imperious; suitable for a lord.

**lordship** /ˈlɔːdʃɪp/ *n.* title used in ad-

**lore** *n.* body of tradition and facts on a subject.

**lorgnette** /lɔːˈnjet/ *n.* pair of eyeglasses held to eyes by long handle.

**lorikeet** /ˈlɒrikiːt/ *n.* any of various small brightly-coloured parrots of Australia etc.

**lorilet** /ˈlɒrəlɛt/ *n.* small short-tailed parrot of N. Australia and New Guinea.

**lorn** *a. arch.* desolate, forlorn.

**lorry** /ˈlɒriː/ *n.* motor truck for transporting goods etc.

**lory** /ˈlɔːriː/ *n.* any of various brightly-coloured parrots of Australia etc.

**lose** /luːz/ *v.* (*past & p.p.* **lost**) be deprived of; cease to have; be unable to find; fail to keep in sight etc.; let pass from one's control; get rid of; be defeated in; forfeit; suffer loss or detriment; cause person the loss of; (of clock) become slow; in *pass.* disappear, perish.

**loser** /ˈluːzə(r)/ *n.* person who loses contest or game etc.; *colloq.* person who regularly fails.

**loss** *n.* losing; what is lost; detriment resulting from losing. **at a loss** sold etc. for less than was paid to buy it; **be at a loss** be puzzled or uncertain; **loss-leader** article sold at a loss to attract customers.

**lost** 1 *past & p.p.* of **lose**. 2 *a.* vanished; dead; deprived of help or salvation; astray.

**lot** *n. colloq.* considerable or (in *pl.*) great quantity or amount or number; each of set of objects used in securing chance selection; this method of deciding, share or office etc. given by it; destiny, fortune; piece or allotment of land; article or set of articles for sale at auction etc.; number or quantity of associated persons or things. **bad lot** disreputable etc. person; **the lot** total number or quantity.

**loth** var. of **loath**.

**lotion** /ˈləʊʃ(ə)n/ *n.* liquid preparation for skin as healing or cosmetic agent.

**lottery** /ˈlɒtəriː/ *n.* arrangement for distributing prizes by chance among purchasers of numbered tickets, as a means of raising money.

**lotto** /ˈlɒtəʊ/ *n.* game of chance with numbers drawn at random.

**lotus** /ˈləʊtəs/ *n.* legendary plant inducing luxurious languour in the eater; kind of water-lily. **lotus position** cross-legged position of meditation.

**loud** /laʊd/ 1 *a.* strongly audible; noisy; obtrusive. 2 *adv.* loudly. 3 **loudspeaker** apparatus that converts electrical signals into sounds.

**lough** /lɒk or lɒx/ *n. Ir.* loch.

**lounge** /laʊndʒ/ 1 *v.i.* loll, recline; stand or move lazily, idle. 2 *n.* spell of or place for lounging; place in airport etc. with seats for waiting passengers; sitting-room in house. 3 **lounge-suit** man's suit for ordinary day wear.

**lour** /ˈlaʊə(r)/ *v.i.* frown, look sullen; (of sky etc.) look dark and threatening.

**louse** /laʊs/ *n.* (*pl.* **lice**) kind of parasitic insect; *sl.* (*pl.* **louses**) contemptible person.

**lousy** /ˈlaʊziː/ *a.* infested with lice; *sl.* disgusting or bad; *sl.* abundantly supplied, swarming, *with*.

**lout** /laʊt/ *n.* hulking or rough-mannered fellow. **loutish** *a.*

**louvre** /ˈluːvə(r)/ *n.* one of set of overlapping boards etc. to admit air and exclude light or rain; domed erection on roof with side-openings for ventilation etc.

**lovable** /ˈlʌvəb(ə)l/ *a.* inspiring affection.

**love** /lʌv/ 1 *n.* fondness, warm affection; sexual passion; sweetheart, beloved one; *colloq.* delightful person or thing; (in games) no score, nil. 2 *v.* be in love (with); feel affection for; delight in, admire; *colloq.* like, be delighted. 3 **in love (with)** inspired with sexual love (for); **love-affair** relationship between two people in love; **love-bird** kind of parakeet; **love-in-a-mist** blue-flowered garden plant; **lovelorn** pining with unrequited love; **lovesick** languishing with love; **make love** pay amorous attentions *to*, have sexual intercourse.

**loveless** /ˈlʌvləs/ *a.* unloving, unloved.

**lovely** /ˈlʌvliː/ *a.* exquisitely beautiful; *colloq.* delightful. **loveliness** *n.*

**lover** /ˈlʌvə(r)/ *n.* person (esp. man) in love; admirer or devotee (*of*); in *pl.* pair in love.

**loving** /ˈlʌvɪŋ/ *a.* affectionate. **loving-cup** two-handled drinking-cup passed round at banquets.

**low**[1] /ləʊ/ 1 *a.* not high or tall or

**low** reaching far up; not elevated in position; of humble rank; of small or less than normal amount; lacking vigour, dejected; not shrill or loud; (of opinion) unfavourable; mean, vulgar. **2** *n.* low or lowest level or number; area of low barometric pressure. **3** *adv.* in or to low position; in low tone, at low pitch. **4 keep a low profile** remain inconspicuous; **lowbrow** *colloq.* (person) not highly intellectual or cultured; **Low Church** section of Church of England giving low place to ritual and priestly authority and sacraments; **low-down** abject, dishonourable, (*n.*) *sl.* relevant information *on*; **Low Sunday** next Sunday after Easter; **low water** low tide.

**low²** /ləʊ/ **1** *n.* sound made by cows. **2** *v.i.* make this sound.

**lowan** /ˈləʊən/ *n.* Aus. mallee-fowl.

**lower¹** /ˈləʊə(r)/ *v.* let or haul down; make or become lower; diminish height or elevation of; degrade.

**lower²** var. of **lour**.

**lowland** /ˈləʊlənd/ **1** *n.* (usu. in *pl.*) low-lying country esp. (**Lowlands**) less mountainous part of Scotland. **2** *a.* of lowland or Sc. Lowlands. **3 lowlander** *n.*

**lowly** /ˈləʊlɪ/ *a.* humble, unpretending. **lowliness** *n.*

**lowry** var. of **lory**.

**loyal** /ˈlɔɪəl/ *a.* faithful; true to allegiance; devoted to legitimate sovereign etc. **loyalty** *n.*

**loyalist** /ˈlɔɪəlɪst/ **1** *a.* remaining loyal to ruler or government etc. **2** *n.* loyalist person.

**lozenge** /ˈlɒzɪndʒ/ *n.* small sweet or medicinal etc. tablet to be dissolved in mouth; rhombus, diamond figure; lozenge-shaped thing.

**LP** *abbr.* long-playing (record).

**L-plate** /ˈelpleɪt/ *n.* sign bearing letter L, affixed to front and rear of motor vehicle to indicate that it is being driven by learner driver.

**LSD** *abbr.* lysergic acid diethylamide, a powerful hallucinogenic drug.

**LT** *abbr.* low tension.

**Lt.** *abbr.* Lieutenant.

**Ltd.** *abbr.* Limited.

**lubber** /ˈlʌbə(r)/ *n.* clumsy fellow, lout.

**lubberly** *a.* awkward, unskilful.

**lumber**

**lubra** /ˈluːbrə/ *n.* Aus. (occas. *derog.*) Abor. woman.

**lubricant** /ˈluːbrɪkənt/ *n.* substance used to reduce friction in machinery etc.

**lubricate** /ˈluːbrɪkeɪt/ *v.t.* apply lubricant to (machinery); make slippery. **lubrication** *n.*

**lubricious** /luːˈbrɪʃəs/ *a.* slippery, lewd. **lubricity** *n.*

**lucerne** /luːˈsɜːn/ *n.* alfalfa.

**lucid** /ˈluːsɪd/ *a.* expressing or expressed clearly. **lucidity** *n.*

**luck** *n.* good or ill fortune, chance; success due to chance.

**luckless** /ˈlʌkləs/ *a.* invariably having ill luck; ending in failure.

**lucky** /ˈlʌkɪ/ *a.* having or resulting from good luck; bringing good luck. **the Lucky Country** Australia (often *iron.*); **lucky dip** tub containing articles from which one chooses at random.

**lucrative** /ˈluːkrətɪv/ *a.* yielding considerable profit.

**lucre** /ˈluːkə(r)/ *n.* pecuniary gain as motive; *joc.* money.

**luderick** /ˈluːdərɪk/ *n.* Aus. a kind of blackfish.

**ludicrous** /ˈluːdɪkrəs/ *a.* absurd, ridiculous, laughable.

**lug** **1** *v.* drag with effort or violence; pull hard *at*. **2** *n.* hard or rough pull; projection on object by which it may be carried or fixed in place etc.; *colloq.* ear.

**luggage** /ˈlʌgɪdʒ/ *n.* bags etc. for containing traveller's belongings.

**lugger** /ˈlʌgə(r)/ *n.* small ship with 4-cornered sails (**lugsails**) set fore and aft.

**lugubrious** /luːˈguːbrɪəs/ *a.* doleful.

**lukewarm** /luːkˈwɔːm/ *a.* moderately warm, tepid; indifferent.

**lull** **1** *v.* send to sleep; soothe; (of suspicion) usu. by deception; (of storm or noise) lessen, fall quiet. **2** *n.* intermission in storm etc., interval of quiet.

**lullaby** /ˈlʌləbaɪ/ *n.* soothing song to send child to sleep.

**lumbago** /lʌmˈbeɪgəʊ/ *n.* rheumatic pain in muscles of loins.

**lumbar** /ˈlʌmbə(r)/ *a.* of loins.

**lumber** /ˈlʌmbə(r)/ **1** *n.* disused and cumbersome articles; useless stuff; partly prepared timber. **2** *v.* obstruct,

**luminary** encumber, *with*; move in blundering noisy way; cut and prepare forest timber. **3 lumberjack, lumberman**, feller or dresser or conveyor of lumber; **lumber-room** room where disused articles are kept.

**luminary** /'lu:mənəri:/ *n.* natural light-giving body, esp. sun or moon; person noted for learning etc.

**luminescent** /lu:mə'nes(ə)nt/ *a.* emitting light without heat. **luminescence** *n.*

**luminous** /'lu:mənəs/ *a.* emitting light; phosphorescent and so visible in darkness. **luminosity** *n.*

**lump¹** 1 *n.* compact shapeless mass; protuberance or swelling; heavy ungainly person etc. 2 *v.* class or mass *together*. **3 lump sugar** sugar in small lumps or cubes; **lump sum** sum including number of items or paid down all at once.

**lump²** *v.t. colloq.* (in contrast with *like*) put up with ungraciously.

**lumpish** /'lʌmpɪʃ/ *a.* heavy, clumsy, dull.

**lumpy** /'lʌmpi:/ *a.* full of or covered with lumps.

**lunacy** /'lu:nəsi:/ *n.* insanity; great folly.

**lunar** /'lu:nə(r)/ *a.* of or like or concerned with or determined by the moon. **lunar month** lunation, *pop.* period of four weeks.

**lunate** /'lu:neɪt/ *a.* crescent-shaped.

**lunatic** /'lu:nətɪk/ 1 *a.* insane; eccentric, outrageously foolish. 2 *n.* lunatic person.

**lunation** /lu:'neɪʃ(ə)n/ *n.* interval between new moons, about 29½ days.

**lunch** 1 *n.* midday meal; light refreshment at mid-morning. 2 *v.* take lunch; provide lunch for.

**luncheon** /'lʌntʃ(ə)n/ *n. formal* midday meal.

**lung** *n.* either of pair of air-breathing organs in man and most vertebrates.

**lunge** 1 *n.* sudden throwing forward of body in thrusting or hitting; thrust. 2 *v.* deliver or make lunge; drive (weapon etc.) violently.

**lupin** /'lu:pən/ *n.* garden or fodder plant with long tapering spikes of flowers.

**lupine** /'lu:paɪn/ *a.* of or like wolves.

**lupus** /'lu:pəs/ *n.* ulcerous disease of skin.

**lurch¹** 1 *n.* sudden shift of weight to one side. 2 *v.i.* make lurch, stagger.

**lurch²** *n.* **leave in the lurch** desert in difficulties.

**lurcher** /'lɜ:tʃə(r)/ *n.* cross-bred dog between collie and greyhound.

**lure** 1 *v.t.* entice; recall with lure. 2 *n.* thing used to entice, enticing quality; falconer's apparatus for recalling hawk.

**lurid** /'lʊərɪd/ *a.* strong and glaring in colour etc.; sensational; horrifying; ghastly.

**lurk** 1 *v.i.* keep out of sight, be hidden; be latent or elusive. 2 *n. Aus. colloq.* scheme, stratagem; occupation.

**luscious** /'lʌʃəs/ *a.* richly sweet in taste or smell; voluptuously attractive.

**lush** *a.* luxuriant and succulent.

**lust** 1 *n.* strong sexual desire; passionate desire *for* or enjoyment *of*; sensuous appetite. 2 *v.i.* have strong or excessive (esp. sexual) desire (*after, for*). **3 lustful** *a.*

**lustre** /'lʌstə(r)/ *n.* gloss; shining surface; brilliance, splendour; (pottery or porcelain with) iridescent glaze. **lustrous** *a.*

**lusty** /'lʌsti:/ *a.* healthy and strong; vigorous, lively.

**lute¹** *n.* guitar-like musical instrument with pear-shaped body. **lutanist, lutenist**, *n.*

**lute²** *n.* composition for making joints airtight.

**Lutheran** /'lu:θərən/ 1 *a.* of Martin Luther or the Protestant doctrines associated with him. 2 *n.* follower of Luther; member of Lutheran Church. **3 Lutheranism** *n.*

**luxuriant** /lʌg'ʒʊəri:ənt/ *a.* growing profusely; exuberant, florid. **luxuriance** *n.*

**luxuriate** /lʌg'ʒʊəri:eɪt/ *v.i.* revel or feel keen delight *in*.

**luxurious** /lʌg'ʒʊəri:əs/ *a.* supplied with luxuries; very comfortable; fond of luxury.

**luxury** /'lʌkʃəri:/ *n.* choice or costly food, furniture, etc.; habitual use of these; thing desirable for comfort or enjoyment but not essential.

**lychgate** var. of **lichgate**.

**lye** /laɪ/ *n.* water made alkaline with wood ashes etc.; other alkaline solution for washing.

**lying** *partic.* of **lie**¹,².
**lymph** /lɪmf/ *n.* colourless fluid from tissues or organs of body.
**lymphatic** /lɪmˈfætɪk/ *a.* of or secreting or conveying lymph; (of person) flabby, pale.
**lynch** /lɪntʃ/ *v.t.* execute by mob action without legal trial.
**lynx** /lɪŋks/ *n.* animal of cat family with short tail, spotted fur, and proverbially keen sight.
**lyre** /laɪə(r)/ *n.* ancient U-shaped stringed instrument used esp. for accompanying song. **lyrebird** Aus. bird of which male has lyre-shaped tail.
**lyric** /ˈlɪrɪk/ 1 *a.* (of poem) expressing writer's emotions; (of poet) writing lyric poetry; meant to be sung; of the nature of song. 2 *n.* lyric poem; (often in *pl.*) words of song. 3 **lyricism** /-sɪz(ə)m/ *n.*
**lyrical** /ˈlɪrɪk(ə)l/ *a.* resembling or using language appropriate to lyric poetry; *colloq.* highly enthusiastic.
**lyricist** /ˈlɪrəsɪst/ *n.* writer of lyrics.

# M

**M, m,** *n.* Roman numeral 1,000.
**M** *abbr.* mega-.
**M.** *abbr.* Master; *Monsieur*.
**m.** *abbr.* metre(s); mile(s); million(s); milli-; minute(s); masculine; married; male.
**ma** /mɑː/ *n. colloq.* mother.
**MA** *abbr.* Master of Arts.
**ma'am** /mɑːm/ *n.* madam (esp. used in addressing royal lady or female officer etc.).
**mac** *n. colloq.* mackintosh.
**macabre** /məˈkɑːbr/ *a.* gruesome, grim.
**macadam** /məˈkædəm/ *n.* material for road-making with successive layers of broken stone compacted; tar macadam. **macadamize** *v.t.*
**macadamia** /mækəˈdeɪmiːə/ *n.* Aus. tree bearing edible nuts; this nut.
**macaroni** /mækəˈrəʊni/ *n.* pasta formed into tubes.
**macaroon** /mækəˈruːn/ *n.* biscuit made of ground almonds etc.
**macaw** /məˈkɔː/ *n.* kind of parrot.
**mace**[1] *n.* staff of office, esp. symbol of Speaker's authority in House of Commons; *hist.* heavy usu. spiked club.
**mace**[2] *n.* dried outer covering of nutmeg used as spice.
**macédoine** /mæsəˈdwɑːn/ *n.* mixture of fruits or vegetables, esp. cut up small.
**macerate** /ˈmæsəreɪt/ *v.* make or become soft by soaking. **maceration** *n.*
**machete** /məˈtʃeti:/ *n.* broad heavy knife used in Central America and W. Indies.
**machiavellian** /mækiːəˈveliːən/ *a.* unscrupulous, cunning.
**machination** /mæʃəˈneɪʃ(ə)n/ *n.* (usu. in *pl.*) intrigue, scheme, plot.
**machine** /məˈʃiːn/ **1** *n.* apparatus for applying mechanical power, having several parts each with definite function; bicycle, motor cycle, etc.; aircraft; computer; controlling system of an organization. **2** *v.t.* make or operate on with machine (esp. of sewing or printing). **3 machine-gun** mounted automatic gun giving continuous fire; **machine readable** in form that computer can process; **machine tool** mechanically operated tool for working on metal, wood, or plastics.

**machinery** /məˈʃiːnəri/ *n.* machines; mechanism; organized system, means arranged.
**machinist** /məˈʃiːnəst/ *n.* person who works machine.
**machismo** /məˈtʃɪzməʊ/ *n.* virility, masculine pride.
**Mach number** /mɑːk/ ratio of speed of body to speed of sound in surrounding medium.
**macho** /ˈmætʃəʊ/ *a.* ostentatiously manly or virile.
**mack** var. of **mac**.
**mackerel** /ˈmækər(ə)l/ *n.* edible seafish. **mackerel sky** sky dappled with rows of small fleecy white clouds.
**mackintosh** /ˈmækɪntɒʃ/ *n.* waterproof coat or cloak; cloth waterproofed with rubber.
**macramé** /məˈkrɑːmiː/ *n.* art of knotting cord or string in patterns; work so made.
**macrobiotic** /mækrəʊbaɪˈɒtɪk/ *a.* relating to or following diet intended to prolong life.
**macrocosm** /ˈmækrəʊkɒz(ə)m/ *n.* universe; any great whole.
**mad** *a.* with disordered mind, insane; frenzied; wildly foolish; infatuated; *colloq.* annoyed. **madcap** reckless person; **madhouse** *hist.* mental home or hospital, confused uproar; **madman, -woman**, mad person. **madness** *n.*
**madam** /ˈmædəm/ *n.* polite formal address to woman; woman brothel-keeper; *colloq.* conceited etc. young woman.
***Madame*** /məˈdɑːm/ *n.* (*pl.* ***Mesdames*** /meɪˈdɑːm/) title uesd of or to French-speaking woman. [F]
**madden** /ˈmæd(ə)n/ *v.t.* make mad; irritate.
**madder** /ˈmædə(r)/ *n.* herbaceous climbing plant; red dye obtained from its root; synthetic substitute for this dye.
**made** *past* & *p.p.* of **make**.
**Madeira** /məˈdɪərə/ *n.* fortified wine from Madeira. **Madeira cake** kind of rich sweet sponge-cake.
***Mademoiselle*** /mædəmwəˈzel/ *n.* (*pl.* ***Mesdemoiselles*** /meɪdmwəˈzel/) title used of or to unmarried French-speaking woman. [F]

**madonna** /məˈdɒnə/ n. (pl. -as) (picture or statue of) Virgin Mary.

**madras** /məˈdræs/ n. cotton fabric woven with coloured stripes etc.

**madrigal** /ˈmædrɪg(ə)l/ n. Mus. part-song for several voices, usu. unaccompanied.

**maelstrom** /ˈmeɪlstrɒm/ n. great whirlpool.

**maenad** /ˈmiːnæd/ n. bacchante.

**maestro** /ˈmaɪstrəʊ/ n. (pl. -os) eminent musical teacher or conductor.

**Mafia** /ˈmæfiːə/ n. organized international body of criminals.

**Mafioso** /mæfiˈəʊsəʊ/ n. (pl. -si /-sɪ/) member of the Mafia.

**magazine** /mægəˈziːn/ n. periodical publication containing contributions by various writers; store for explosives, arms, or military provisions; chamber containing supply of cartridges fed automatically to breech of gun; similar device in camera, slide-projector, etc.

**magenta** /məˈdʒentə/ n. shade of crimson; aniline dye of this colour.

**maggot** /ˈmægət/ n. larva, esp. of bluebottle.

**maggoty** /ˈmægəti/ a. infested with or resembling maggots; Aus. sl. angry, bad-tempered.

**Magi** /ˈmeɪdʒaɪ/ n. pl. priests of ancient Persia; the 'wise men from the East' in the Gospel.

**magic** /ˈmædʒɪk/ 1 n. art of influencing events by occult control of nature or spirits; conjuring tricks; inexplicable or remarkable influence. 2 a. of or involving magic. 3 **magic carpet** mythical carpet able to transport person on it to any place; **magic lantern** simple form of image-projector using slides.

**magical** /ˈmædʒɪk(ə)l/ a. of magic; resembling or involving or produced as if by magic.

**magician** /məˈdʒɪʃ(ə)n/ n. person skilled in magic; conjurer.

**magisterial** /mædʒəˈstɪərɪəl/ a. authoritative; dictatorial; of a magistrate.

**magistracy** /ˈmædʒəstrəsɪ/ n. magisterial office; magistrates.

**magistrate** /ˈmædʒəstreɪt/ n. civil officer administering law, esp. one trying minor offences etc.

**magnanimous** /mægˈnænəməs/ a. noble, generous, not petty, in feelings or conduct. **magnanimity** /-ˈnɪm-/ n.

**magnate** /ˈmægneɪt/ n. person of wealth, authority, etc.

**magnesia** /mægˈniːʃə or -ˈniːʒə/ n. magnesium oxide; hydrated magnesium carbonate used as antacid and laxative.

**magnesium** /mægˈniːzɪəm/ n. silver-white metallic element.

**magnet** /ˈmægnət/ n. piece of iron, steel, etc., having properties of attracting iron and of pointing approx. north when suspended; fig. person or thing that attracts.

**magnetic** /mægˈnetɪk/ a. having properties of magnet; produced or acting by magnetism; fig. very attractive. **magnetic field** area of influence of magnet; **magnetic north** point indicated by north end of compass-needle; **magnetic storm** disturbance of earth's magnetic field; **magnetic tape** impregnated or coated plastic strip for recording and reproduction of signals.

**magnetism** /ˈmægnətɪz(ə)m/ n. magnetic phenomena; science of these; fig. personal charm.

**magnetize** /ˈmægnətaɪz/ v.t. make into magnet; attract like magnet. **magnetization** n.

**magneto** /mægˈniːtəʊ/ n. (pl. -tos) electric generator using permanent magnets (esp. for ignition in internal combustion engine).

**magnificent** /mægˈnɪfɪs(ə)nt/ a. splendid; imposing; excellent. **magnificence** n.

**magnify** /ˈmægnəfaɪ/ v.t. make (thing) appear larger than it is, as with lens (**magnifying glass**) etc.; exaggerate; arch. extol. **magnification** n.

**magnitude** /ˈmægnətjuːd/ n. largeness, size; importance.

**magnolia** /mægˈnəʊlɪə/ n. kind of flowering tree; very pale pinkish colour of its flowers.

**magnum** /ˈmægnəm/ n. two-quart bottle.

**magpie** /ˈmægpaɪ/ n. kind of crow with long tail and black-and-white plumage; random collector; similar unrelated Aus. bird. **magpie-lark** small black-and-white Aus. bird.

**Magyar** /ˈmægjɑː(r)/ 1 n. member of the people now predominant in Hungary; their language. 2 a. of this people.

**maharaja** /mɑːhəˈrɑːjə/ n. hist. (also **maharajah**) title of some Indian princes.

**maharanee** /mɑːhəˈrɑːniː/ n. hist. (also **maharani**) maharaja's wife or widow.

**maharishi** /mɑːhəˈrɪʃiː/ n. great Hindu sage.

**mahatma** /məˈhætmə/ n. (in India etc.) person regarded with reverence.

**mah-jong** /mɑːˈdʒɒŋ/ n. (also **-jongg**) orig. Chinese game played with 136 or 144 pieces.

**mahogany** /məˈhɒɡəni/ n. reddish-brown wood used for furniture etc.; colour of this; any of various Aus. eucalypts with reddish-brown wood.

**mahout** /məˈhaʊt/ n. elephant-driver.

**maid** n. female domestic servant; arch. girl, young woman. **maidservant** female domestic servant.

**maiden** /ˈmeɪd(ə)n/ 1 n. arch. girl, virgin, young unmarried woman; Crick. maiden over. 2 a. unmarried; (of voyage, speech by MP, etc.) first. 3 **maidenhair** delicate kind of fern; **maiden name** woman's surname before marriage; **maiden over** Crick. over in which no runs are scored. 4 **maidenly** a.

**mail**[1] n. letters etc. conveyed by post; the post; vehicle carrying mail. 2 v.t. send by mail. 3 **mail order** purchase of goods by post.

**mail**[2] n. armour of metal rings or plates.

**maim** v.t. cripple, mutilate.

**main** 1 a. chief, principal, most important. 2 n. principal channel for water or gas etc. or (usu. in pl.) electricity; arch. high seas. 3 **in the main** for the most part; **mainland** continuous extent of land excluding neighbouring islands etc.; **mainmast** principal mast; **mainsail** lowest sail or sail set on after part of mainmast; **mainspring** principal spring of watch or clock, fig. chief motive power etc.; **mainstay** chief support; **mainstream** prevailing trend of opinion, fashion, etc.

**mainly** /ˈmeɪnli/ adv. for the most part, chiefly.

**maintain** /meɪnˈteɪn/ v.t. keep up; keep going; keep in repair; support; assert as true.

**maintenance** /ˈmeɪntənəns/ n. maintaining or being maintained; (provision of) enough to support life; alimony.

**maisonette** /meɪzəˈnet/ n. part of house let or sold separately; small house.

**maize** /meɪz/ n. N. Amer. cereal plant; grain of this.

**Maj.** abbr. Major.

**majestic** /məˈdʒestɪk/ a. stately and dignified; imposing. **majestically** adv.

**majesty** /ˈmædʒəsti/ n. stateliness of aspect, language, etc.; sovereign power; title used in speaking to or of sovereign or sovereign's wife or widow.

**majolica** /məˈjɒlɪkə/ n. kind of ornamented Italian earthenware.

**major** /ˈmeɪdʒə(r)/ 1 a. greater or relatively great in size etc.; of full legal age; unusually serious or significant; Mus. of or based on scale having semitone next above third and seventh notes. 2 n. army officer next below lieutenant-colonel; person of full legal age; student's special subject or course. 3 v.i. undertake course, qualify in as a major. 4 **major-domo** (pl. **-mos**) house-steward; **major-general** army officer next below lieutenant-general.

**majority** /məˈdʒɒrəti/ n. greater number or part (of); number by which winning vote exceeds next; full legal age; rank of major.

**make** 1 v. (past & p.p. **made**) construct, frame, create, from parts or other substance; bring about, give rise to; prepare for consumption or use; write, compose; frame in the mind; establish, enact; gain, acquire, obtain as result; secure advancement or success of; cause to be or become; compel (to); execute, perform; represent as, consider (to be); constitute, amount to; accomplish; achieve place in. 2 n. way thing is made; origin of manufacture, brand. 3 **make believe** pretend; **make-believe** pretended, pretence; **make do** manage (with substitute etc.); **make for** be conducive to, proceed towards; **make good** compensate for, repair, fulfil (promise), succeed in an undertaking; **make off** depart hastily; **make out** draw up, write out, understand, distinguish by sight or hearing, pretend, make progress; **makeshift** (serving as) temporary substitute or device; **make up** serve or act to over-

**maker** /'meɪkə(r)/ n. one who makes, esp. (**Maker**) God.

**making** /'meɪkɪŋ/ n. in pl. essential qualities for becoming. **be the making of** ensure success etc. of; **in the making** in the course of being made.

**mako** /'mɑːkəʊ/ n. (pl. **-kos**) Aus. blue pointer shark.

**malachite** /'mæləkaɪt/ n. green mineral used for ornament.

**maladjusted** /mælə'dʒʌstəd/ a. (of person) not satisfactorily adjusted to his environment etc. **maladjustment** n.

**maladminister** /mæləd'mɪnɪstə(r)/ v.t. manage badly or improperly. **maladministration** n.

**maladroit** /mælə'drɔɪt/ a. bungling, clumsy.

**malady** /'mælədi/ n. ailment, disease.

**malaise** /mə'leɪz/ n. feeling of illness or uneasiness.

**malapropism** /'mæləprɒpɪz(ə)m/ n. ludicrous confusion between words.

**malaria** /mə'leərɪə/ n. fever transmitted by mosquitoes. **malarial** a.

**malcontent** /'mækəntent/ 1 n. discontented person. 2 a. discontented.

**male** 1 a. of sex that can beget offspring by performing fertilizing function; (of parts of machinery) designed to enter or fill corresponding female part. 2 n. male person or animal.

**malediction** /mælə'dɪkʃ(ə)n/ n. curse. **maledictory** a.

**malefactor** /'mæləfæktə(r)/ n. criminal; evil-doer. **malefaction** n.

**malevolent** /mə'levələnt/ a. wishing ill to others. **malevolence** n.

**malformation** /mælfɔː'meɪʃ(ə)n/ n. faulty formation. **malformed** a.

**malfunction** /mæl'fʌŋkʃ(ə)n/ 1 n. failure to function in normal manner. 2 v.i. function faultily.

**malice** /'mælɪs/ n. ill-will; desire to do harm.

**malicious** /mə'lɪʃəs/ a. given to or arising from malice.

**malign** /mə'laɪn/ 1 a. malevolent, injurious. 2 v.t. speak ill of; slander. 3 **malignity** n.

**malignant** /mə'lɪgnənt/ a. (of tumour) cancerous; (of disease) very virulent; feeling or showing intense ill-will. **malignancy** n.

**malinger** /mə'lɪŋgə(r)/ v.i. pretend illness to escape duty.

**mallard** /'mælɑːd/ n. kind of wild duck.

**malleable** /'mælɪəb(ə)l/ a. that can be shaped by hammering; pliable. **malleability** n.

**mallee** /'mælɪ/ n. Aus. any of several eucalypts flourishing in dry areas; scrub formed by this. **mallee-fowl** a large mound-building bird.

**mallet** /'mælət/ n. hammer, usu. of wood; implement for striking croquet or polo ball.

**mallow** /'mæləʊ/ n. kind of flowering plant with hairy stems and leaves.

**malmsey** /'mɑːmzɪ/ n. strong sweet wine.

**malnutrition** /mælnju:'trɪʃ(ə)n/ n. insufficient nutrition.

**malodorous** /mæl'əʊdərəs/ a. evil-smelling.

**malpractice** /mæl'præktəs/ n. wrongdoing; illegal action for one's own benefit while in position of trust; physician's improper or negligent treatment of patient.

**malt** /mɔːlt or mɒlt/ 1 n. barley or other grain prepared for brewing etc.; malt whisky. 2 v.t. convert (grain) into malt. 3 **malted milk** drink made from dried milk and extract of malt; **malt whisky** whisky made from malted barley.

**Maltese** /mɔːl'tiːz or mɒl'tiːz/ 1 a. of Malta. 2 n. native or language of Malta. 3 **Maltese cross** one with four equal limbs broadened at ends.

**maltreat** /mæl'triːt/ v.t. ill-treat. **maltreatment** n.

**malversation** /mælvə'seɪʃ(ə)n/ n. corrupt handling of public or trust money.

**mamba** /'mæmbə/ n. kind of venomous Afr. snake.

**mamma** /mə'mɑː/ n. arch. mother.

**mammal** /'mæm(ə)l/ n. animal of class characterized by secretion of milk to feed young. **mammalian** (/-'meɪlɪən/) a.

**mammary** /'mæmərɪ/ a. of breasts.

**Mammon** /ˈmæmən/ n. wealth regarded as idol or evil influence.

**mammoth** /ˈmæməθ/ 1 n. large extinct species of elephant. 2 a. huge.

**man** 1 n. (pl. **men**) adult human male; human being; collect. the human race; person; husband; employee, workman; (usu. in pl.) soldiers, sailors, etc.; one of set of objects used in playing chess, draughts, etc. 2 v.t. furnish with man or men or person(s) for service or defence. 3 **manhole** opening giving person access to sewer, conduit, etc.; **man-hour** work done by one person in one hour; **man-of-war** armed ship of country's navy; **manpower** number of persons available for work or military service; **manservant** (pl. **menservants**) male domestic servant; **mantrap** trap set to catch esp. trespassers.

**mana** /ˈmɑːnə/ n. Aus. authority; prestige; supernatural power.

**manacle** /ˈmænək(ə)l/ 1 n. (usu. in pl.) fetter. 2 v.t. put manacles on.

**manage** /ˈmænɪdʒ/ v. organize or regulate; succeed in achieving, contrive; succeed with limited resources, cope; gain one's ends with; have effective control of. **manageable** a.

**management** /ˈmænɪdʒmənt/ n. managing or being managed; administration; persons managing a business.

**manager** /ˈmænədʒə(r)/ n. person conducting business etc.; person controlling activities of person or team etc.; person who manages money etc. in specified way. **manageress** n.; **managerial** /-ˈdʒɪəriəl/ a.

**mañana** /mænˈjɑːnə/ adv. & n. tomorrow, indefinite future. [Sp.]

**manatee** /ˌmænəˈtiː/ n. large tropical aquatic mammal feeding on plants.

**mandarin** /ˈmændərɪn/ n. influential person, esp. bureaucrat; hist. Chinese official; (**Mandarin**) former standard spoken language in China; small flat loose-skinned orange.

**mandatary** /ˈmændətəri/ n. receiver or holder of a mandate.

**mandate** /ˈmændeɪt/ 1 n. authoritative command; commission to act for another; political instructions from electorate. 2 v.t. give authority to (delegate); commit (territory) to mandatary.

**mandatory** /ˈmændətəri/ a. compulsory; of or conveying a command.

**mandible** /ˈmændɪb(ə)l/ n. jaw-bone, esp. lower one; either part of bird's beak; either half of crushing organ in mouth-parts of insect etc.

**mandolin** /ˈmændəlɪn/ n. musical instrument with paired metal strings, played with a plectrum.

**mandrake** /ˈmændreɪk/ n. narcotic plant with forked root.

**mandrill** /ˈmændrəl/ n. kind of large baboon.

**mane** n. long hair on horse's or lion's neck; person's long hair.

**manège** /mæˈneɪʒ/ n. training of horses; movements of trained horse.

**manful** /ˈmænfəl/ a. brave, resolute.

**manganese** /ˈmæŋɡəniːz/ n. grey brittle metallic element; black oxide of this.

**mange** /meɪndʒ/ n. skin disease of dogs etc.

**mangel-wurzel** /ˈmæŋɡ(ə)l ˈwɜːz(ə)l/ n. large kind of beet used as cattle-food.

**manger** /ˈmeɪndʒə(r)/ n. eating-trough in stable.

**mangle**¹ /ˈmæŋɡ(ə)l/ v.t. hack, cut about; mutilate, spoil.

**mangle**² /ˈmæŋɡ(ə)l/ 1 n. machine with rollers for pressing water out of washed clothes. 2 v.t. put through mangle.

**mango** /ˈmæŋɡəʊ/ n. (pl. **-goes**) tropical fruit with yellow flesh; tree bearing it.

**mangrove** /ˈmæŋɡrəʊv/ n. tropical sea-shore tree with interlacing roots above ground.

**mangy** /ˈmeɪndʒi/ a. having mange; squalid, shabby.

**manhandle** /ˈmænhænd(ə)l/ v.t. move by human effort alone, handle roughly.

**manhood** /ˈmænhʊd/ n. state of being a man; manliness; men of a country.

**mania** /ˈmeɪnɪə/ n. mental derangement marked by great excitement and (freq.) violence; craze, passion (for).

**maniac** /ˈmeɪnɪæk/ 1 n. person affected with mania. 2 a. of or affected with mania. 3 **maniacal** /məˈnaɪək(ə)l/ a.

**manic** /ˈmænɪk/ a. of or affected with mania. **manic-depressive** relating to mental disorder with alternating periods of elation and depression, person having such disorder.

**manicure** /ˈmænɪkjuːə(r)/ 1 *n.* cosmetic care and treatment of the hands. 2 *v.t.* apply manicure to. 3 **manicurist** *n.*

**manifest** /ˈmænɪfest/ 1 *a.* clear to sight or mind; indubitable. 2 *v.t.* make manifest; reveal *itself*; appear. 3 *n.* cargo or passenger list. 4 **manifestation** *n.*

**manifesto** /mænɪˈfestəʊ/ *n.* (*pl.* -tos) public declaration of policy or principles.

**manifold** /ˈmænɪfəʊld/ 1 *a.* many and various; having various forms or applications or component parts etc. 2 *n.* pipe etc. with several outlets.

**manikin** /ˈmænɪkɪn/ *n.* little man, dwarf.

**manila** /məˈnɪlə/ *n.* strong fibre of Philippine tree; brown wrapping-paper or cardboard made of this.

**manipulate** /məˈnɪpjʊleɪt/ *v.t.* handle; deal skilfully with; manage craftily. **manipulation** *n.*; **manipulator** *n.*

**mankind** /mænˈkaɪnd/ *n.* human species.

**manly** /ˈmænlɪ/ *a.* having qualities associated with or befitting a man.

**manna** /ˈmænə/ *n.* food miraculously supplied to Israelites in wilderness.

**mannequin** /ˈmænəkɪn/ *n.* person, usu. woman, employed to model clothes; dummy for display of clothes in shop.

**manner** /ˈmænə(r)/ *n.* way thing is done or happens; in *pl.* social behaviour; sort or kind; style.

**mannered** /ˈmænəd/ *a.* behaving in specified way; showing mannerism.

**mannerism** /ˈmænərɪz(ə)m/ *n.* distinctive gesture or feature of style; excessive use of these in art etc.

**mannerly** /ˈmænəlɪ/ *a.* well-behaved, polite.

**mannish** /ˈmænɪʃ/ *a.* characteristic of man as opp. to woman; (of woman, usu. *derog.*) like a man.

**manoeuvre** /məˈnuːvə(r)/ 1 *n.* planned movement of vehicle or body of troops; in *pl.* large-scale exercise of troops etc.; deceptive or elusive movement; skilful plan. 2 *v.* perform or cause to perform manoeuvres; force or drive or manipulate by scheming or adroitness; employ artifice. 3 **manoeuvrable** *a.*

**manor** /ˈmænə(r)/ *n.* large landed estate or its house; *hist.* territorial unit of feudal period. **manorial** *a.*

**mansard roof** /ˈmænsɑːd/ roof with each face having two slopes, the steeper below.

**manse** /mæns/ *n.* (esp. Sc. Presbyterian) minister's house.

**mansion** /ˈmænʃ(ə)n/ *n.* large grand house; in *pl.* block of flats.

**manslaughter** /ˈmænslɔːtə(r)/ *n.* criminal homicide without malice aforethought.

**mantel** /ˈmænt(ə)l/ *n.* structure above and around fireplace; mantelpiece. **mantelpiece** shelf above fireplace.

**mantilla** /mænˈtɪlə/ *n.* Spanish woman's lace scarf worn over head and shoulders.

**mantis** /ˈmæntɪs/ *n.* kind of predacious insect.

**mantle** /ˈmænt(ə)l/ 1 *n.* loose sleeveless cloak; covering; fragile hood round gas-jet to give incandescent light. 2 *v.t.* cover (as) with mantle; conceal, envelop.

**manual** /ˈmænjʊəl/ 1 *a.* of or done with hands. 2 *n.* book of instructions, reference book; organ keyboard played with hands not feet.

**manufacture** /mænjʊˈfæktʃə(r)/ 1 *v.t.* produce by labour, esp. on large scale; invent, fabricate. 2 *n.* manufacturing of articles; branch of such industry.

**manure** /məˈnjʊə(r)/ 1 *n.* fertilizer, esp. dung. 2 *v.t.* treat with manure.

**manuscript** /ˈmænjʊskrɪpt/ 1 *n.* book or document written by hand or typed, not printed. 2 *a.* written by hand.

**many** /ˈmenɪ/ 1 *a.* numerous, great in number. 2 *n.* many people or things; *the* multitude.

**Maori** /ˈmaʊrɪ/ 1 *n.* member of aboriginal NZ race; their language. 2 *a.* of this people.

**map** 1 *n.* flat representation of (part of) earth's surface, or of sky; diagram. 2 *v.t.* represent on map. 3 **map out** arrange in detail.

**maple** /ˈmeɪp(ə)l/ *n.* kind of tree. **maple leaf** emblem of Canada; **maple sugar** sugar got by evaporating sap of some kinds of maple; **maple syrup** syrup got from maple sap or maple sugar.

**maquette** /məˈket/ *n.* preliminary model or sketch.

**mar** *v.t.* impair, spoil.

**Mar.** *abbr.* March.

**marabou** /ˈmærəbuː/ *n.* large W. Afr. stork; its down as trimming etc.

**maraca** /məˈrækə/ *n.* hand-held club-like gourd containing beans or beads etc., shaken as percussion instrument.

**maraschino** /mærəˈskiːnəʊ/ *n.* liqueur made from cherries. **maraschino cherry** one preserved in this.

**marathon** /ˈmærəθ(ə)n/ *n.* long-distance foot-race; feat of endurance; undertaking of long duration.

**maraud** /məˈrɔːd/ *v.i.* make raid, pillage.

**marble** /ˈmɑːb(ə)l/ 1 *n.* kind of limestone used in sculpture and architecture; in *pl.* collection of sculpture; small ball of glass etc. as toy; in *pl.* game played with these. 2 *v.t.* give veined or mottled appearance to (esp. paper).

**marcasite** /ˈmɑːkəsaɪt/ *n.* crystalline iron sulphide; piece of this as ornament.

**March**[2] *n.* third month of year. **March hare** hare in (N. hemisphere) breeding season.

**march**[2] 1 *v.* walk in military manner or with regular paces; proceed steadily; cause to march or walk. 2 *n.* marching of troops; procession as protest etc.; progress; piece of music suitable for marching to; distance covered in marching. 3 **marching girl** *Aus. & NZ* girl trained to march in formation; **march past** ceremonial march of troops past saluting-point.

**march**[3] *hist.* 1 *n.* boundary (often in *pl.*); tract of (often disputed) land between countries etc. 2 *v.i.* have common boundary (*with*).

**marchioness** /ˈmɑːʃənes/ *n. fem.* marquess's wife or widow; woman with own rank of marquess.

**mare** /meə(r)/ *n.* female of horse or other equine animal. **mare's nest** illusory discovery.

**margarine** /mɑːdʒəˈriːn/ *n.* butter-substitute made from edible oils etc.

**marge** /mɑːdʒ/ *n. colloq.* margarine.

**margin** /ˈmɑːdʒɪn/ *n.* border, strip near edge of something; plain space round printed page etc.; extra amount over what is necessary. **margin of error** difference allowed for miscalculation or mischance.

**marginal** /ˈmɑːdʒɪn(ə)l/ *a.* written in margin; of or at edge; (of constituency) having elected MP with small majority; close to limit esp. of profitability; barely adequate or provided for.

**marguerite** /mɑːgəˈriːt/ *n.* ox-eye daisy or similar flower.

**marigold** /ˈmærɪgəʊld/ *n.* plant with golden or bright yellow flowers.

**marijuana** /mærɪˈhwɑːnə/ *n.* dried leaves etc. of common hemp smoked as intoxicant.

**marimba** /məˈrɪmbə/ *n.* Afr. and Central Amer. xylophone; orchestral instrument developed from this.

**marina** /məˈriːnə/ *n.* place with moorings for pleasure-boats.

**marinade** /mærɪˈneɪd/ 1 *n.* mixture esp. of wine or vinegar with oil and herbs etc., for steeping fish or meat. 2 *v.* steep or be steeped in marinade.

**marinate** /ˈmærɪneɪt/ *v.* marinade.

**marine** /məˈriːn/ 1 *a.* of, found in, or produced by, the sea; for use at sea; of shipping. 2 *n.* member of corps trained to fight on land or sea; country's shipping fleet or navy.

**mariner** /ˈmærɪnə(r)/ *n.* sailor, seaman.

**marionette** /mærɪəˈnet/ *n.* puppet worked with strings.

**marital** /ˈmærɪt(ə)l/ *a.* of or between husband and wife; of marriage.

**maritime** /ˈmærɪtaɪm/ *a.* situated or living or found near the sea; connected with seafaring.

**marjoram** /ˈmɑːdʒərəm/ *n.* aromatic herb used in cookery.

**mark**[1] 1 *n.* visible sign left by person or thing; stain, scar etc.; written or printed symbol; this as assessment of conduct or proficiency; sign or indication (*of*); lasting effect or influence; unit of numerical award in examination; target, thing aimed at; *Aus. Rules Footb.* catching on full a ball kicked at least 10 m; line etc. serving to indicate position; (followed by numeral) particular design of piece of equipment. 2 *v.* make mark on; distinguish with mark; give distinctive character to, be a feature of; allot marks to (student's work etc.); in *pass.* have natural marks; see, notice, observe mentally; keep close to (opposing player) in games. 3 **mark down** reduce price of; **mark off** separate by boundary; **mark out** trace

**mark** out boundary of, plan (course), destine; **mark time** lift feet as though marching while halted, *fig.* await opportunity to advance; **mark up** increase price of; **mark-up** amount added by seller to cost-price of goods to cover profit margin etc.

**mark**² *n.* currency unit in Germany, Finland, etc.

**marked** /mɑːkt/ *a.* noticeable, conspicuous. **markedly** /-kədli/ *adv.*

**marker** /'mɑːkə(r)/ *n.* thing that marks a position; scorer esp. at billiards.

**market** /'mɑːkɪt/ **1** *n.* gathering for sale of commodities or livestock etc.; space or building used for this; demand (*for* goods etc.); place where there is such demand; conditions as regards or opportunity for buying and selling. **2** *v.* sell, offer for sale; buy or sell goods in market. **3 market garden** place where vegetables are grown for market; **market-place** open space where market is held, *fig.* scene of actual dealings; **market research** study of possible buyers for one's goods; **market town** town where market is held; **market value** value as saleable thing; **on the market** offered for sale.

**marking** /'mɑːkɪŋ/ *n.* identification mark; colouring of feathers, skin, etc.

**marksman** /'mɑːksmən/ *n.* (*pl.* **-men**) skilled shot, esp. with rifle. **marksmanship** *n.*

**marl** *n.* soil composed of clay and lime, used as fertilizer.

**marlinspike** /'mɑːlənspaɪk/ *n.* pointed tool used to separate strands of rope or wire.

**marmalade** /'mɑːməleɪd/ *n.* conserve of oranges or other citrus fruit, made like jam.

**marmoreal** /mɑː'mɔːrɪəl/ *a.* of or like marble.

**marmoset** /'mɑːməzet/ *n.* small bushy-tailed monkey.

**marmot** /'mɑːmət/ *n.* burrowing rodent related to squirrel.

**marocain** /'mærəkeɪn/ *n.* thin fine dress-fabric of crêpe type.

**maroon**¹ /məˈruːn/ or /məˈrəʊn/ *a.* & *n.* brownish-crimson.

**maroon**² /məˈruːn/ *v.t.* put and leave ashore on desolate island or coast; leave stranded.

**marquee** /mɑːˈkiː/ *n.* large tent.

**marquess** /'mɑːkwəs/ *n.* peer ranking between duke and earl.

**marquetry** /'mɑːkətri/ *n.* inlaid work in wood etc.

**marquis** /'mɑːkwɪs/ *n.* rank in some European nobilities.

**marquise** /mɑːˈkiːz/ *n.* marquis's wife or widow; woman with own rank of marquis.

**marriage** /'mærɪdʒ/ *n.* condition of man and woman legally united for the purpose of living together; act or ceremony etc. establishing this; particular matrimonial union. **marriage certificate, lines**, certificate stating that marriage has taken place.

**marriageable** /'mærɪdʒəb(ə)l/ *a.* old enough or fit for marriage.

**marron** /'mærən/ *n.* *Aus.* large WA freshwater crayfish.

**marrow** /'mærəʊ/ *n.* gourd with whitish flesh, cooked as vegetable; fatty substance in cavity of bones. **marrowbone** bone containing edible marrow.

**marry** /'mæri/ *v.* take or join or give in marriage; *fig.* unite intimately.

**Marsala** /mɑːˈsɑːlə/ *n.* dark sweet fortified wine.

**Marseillaise** /mɑːseɪˈjeɪz/ *n.* national anthem of France.

**marsh** *n.* low-lying watery ground. **marsh gas** methane; **marsh mallow** shrubby herb, confection made from root of this; **marshmallow** soft sweet made from sugar and albumen and gelatine etc. **marshy** *a.*

**marshal** /'mɑːʃ(ə)l/ **1** *n.* high-ranking officer of state or in armed forces; officer arranging ceremonies, controlling procedure at races, etc. **2** *v.t.* arrange in due order; conduct (person) ceremoniously. **3 marshalling yard** railway yard in which goods trains etc. are assembled.

**marsupial** /mɑːˈsuːpɪəl/ **1** *n.* mammal of kind in which females usu. have pouch in which to carry their young. **2** *a.* of this class.

**mart** *n.* market.

**Martello tower** /mɑːˈteləʊ/ small circular tower for coastal defence.

**marten** /'mɑːtən/ *n.* kind of weasel with valuable fur.

**martial** /'mɑːʃ(ə)l/ *a.* warlike; suited to or loving war. **martial arts** fighting sports such as judo or karate; **martial**

**martin** /'mɑ:tən/ n. bird of swallow family.

**martinet** /mɑ:tə'net/ n. strict disciplinarian.

**Martini** /mɑ:'ti:ni:/ n. (P) vermouth; cocktail of gin and vermouth.

**martyr** /'mɑ:tə(r)/ 1 n. person who undergoes death or suffering for great cause, esp. adherence to Christian faith. 2 v.t. put to death as martyr; torment. 3 **martyr to** constant sufferer from.

**martyrdom** /'mɑ:tədəm/ n. sufferings and death of martyr; torment.

**marvel** /'mɑ:v(ə)l/ 1 n. wonderful thing; wonderful example *of*. 2 v.i. feel surprise or wonder.

**marvellous** /'mɑ:vələs/ a. astonishing; excellent.

**Marxism** /'mɑ:ksɪz(ə)m/ n. doctrines of Marx, predicting abolition of private ownership of means of production. Marxist n. & a.

**marzipan** /'mɑ:zəpæn/ n. paste of ground almonds, sugar, etc.

**mascara** /mæs'kɑ:rə/ n. cosmetic for darkening eyelashes.

**mascot** /'mæskɒt/ n. person or animal or thing supposed to bring luck.

**masculine** /'mæskjələn/ a. of men, manly; mannish; *Gram*. of gender proper to men's names. **masculinity** /-'lɪn-/ n.

**maser** /'meɪzə(r)/ n. device for amplifying microwaves.

**mash** 1 n. mashed potatoes (*colloq*.); mixture of boiled bran etc. given to horses. 2 v.t. reduce (potatoes etc.) to uniform mass by crushing; crush to pulp.

**mask** /mɑ:sk/ 1 n. covering for all or part of face, worn as disguise or for protection, or by surgeon etc. to prevent infection of patient; respirator used to filter inhaled air or to supply gas for inhalation; likeness of person's face, esp. one made by taking mould from face; disguise. 2 v.t. cover or disguise with mask; conceal or protect.

**masochism** /'mæsəkɪz(ə)m/ n. pleasure in suffering physical or mental pain, e.g. as form of sexual perversion. masochist n.; masochistic a.

**mason** /'meɪs(ə)n/ n. person who builds with stone; **Mason** Freemason.

**Masonic** /mə'sɒnɪk/ a. of Freemasons.

**masonry** /'meɪsənrɪ/ n. mason's work; stonework; **Masonry** Freemasonry.

**masque** /mɑ:sk/ n. amateur dramatic and musical entertainment, esp. in 16th-17th c.

**masquerade** /mɑ:skə'reɪd/ 1 n. false show, pretence; masked ball. 2 v.i. appear in disguise; assume false appearance.

**mass**[1] n. 1 n. coherent body of matter; dense aggregation, large number or amount (*of*); *Phys*. quantity of matter body contains; *the* majority or main part (*of*); in pl. the ordinary people. 2 v. gather into mass; assemble into one body. 3 a. of or relating to large numbers of people or things. 4 **mass media** means of communication to large numbers of people; **mass production** production of large quantities of standardized article by mechanical processes.

**mass**[2] n. celebration of Eucharist, esp. in RC Church; (musical setting of) liturgy used in this.

**massacre** /'mæsəkə/ 1 n. general slaughter. 2 v.t. make massacre of.

**massage** /'mæsɑ:ʒ/ 1 n. kneading and rubbing of muscles etc., usu. with hands. 2 v.t. treat thus.

**masseur** /mæ'sɜ:(r)/ n. (*fem*. **masseuse** /mæ'sɜ:z/) person who provides massage professionally.

**massif** /'mæsi:f/ n. mountain heights forming compact group.

**massive** /'mæsɪv/ a. large and heavy or solid; substantial; unusually large.

**mast**[1] /mɑ:st/ n. upright to which ship's yards and sails are attached; post etc. to support radio or television aerial; flag-pole.

**mast**[2] /mɑ:st/ n. fruit of beech or oak etc. esp. as food for pigs.

**mastectomy** /mæ'stektəmɪ/ n. surgical removal of a breast.

**master** /'mɑ:stə(r)/ 1 n. person having control; male head of household; head of college etc.; owner of animal or slave; ship's captain; male teacher; skilled workman; holder of university degree above bachelor's; great artist; thing from which series of copies is made; **Master** title prefixed to name of boy. 2

**masterful** /ˈmɑːstəfəl/ *a.* self-willed, imperious.

**masterly** /ˈmɑːstəli/ *a.* worthy of a master; very skilful.

**mastery** /ˈmɑːstəri/ *n.* sway, dominion; masterly skill or knowledge.

**mastic** /ˈmæstɪk/ *n.* gum or resin exuded from certain trees; type of cement.

**masticate** /ˈmæstəkeɪt/ *v.t.* chew. **mastication** *n.*

**mastiff** /ˈmæstɪf/ *n.* large strong kind of dog.

**mastodon** /ˈmæstədɒn/ *n.* extinct animal resembling elephant.

**mastoid** /ˈmæstɔɪd/ 1 *a.* shaped like woman's breast. 2 *n.* conical prominence on temporal bone; *colloq.* inflammation of mastoid.

**masturbate** /ˈmæstəbeɪt/ *v.* produce sexual arousal (of) by manual stimulation of genitals. **masturbation** *n.*; **masturbatory** *a.*

**mat**¹ 1 *n.* piece of coarse fabric as floor-covering or for wiping shoes on; small rug; piece of material laid on table etc. to protect surface. 2 *v.* bring or come into thickly tangled state. 3 **on the mat** *colloq.* being reprimanded.

**mat**² var. of **matt**.

**matador** /ˈmætədɔː(r)/ *n.* bullfighter whose task is to kill bull.

**match**¹ 1 *n.* contest, game; person or thing equal to or nearly resembling or corresponding to another; marriage; person in respect of eligibility for marriage. 2 *v.* be equal, correspond; find or be match for; place in competition *with* or contest *against*. 3 **matchboard** board fitting into others by tongue along one edge and groove along other; **matchmaker** person fond of scheming to bring about marriages; **match point**
state of game when one side needs only one point to win match.

**match**² *n.* short thin piece of wood etc., tipped with composition that ignites when rubbed on rough or specially prepared surface. **matchbox** box for holding matches; **matchstick** stem of match; **matchwood** wood suitable for matches, minute splinters.

**matchless** /ˈmætʃləs/ *a.* incomparable.

**mate**¹ 1 *n.* companion, fellow worker; *colloq.* general form of address to equal; one of a pair esp. of birds; *colloq.* partner in marriage; subordinate officer on merchant ship; assistant to worker. 2 *v.* come or bring together for marriage or for breeding. 3 **mateship** *n.*

**mate**² *n.* & *v.t.* checkmate.

**material** /məˈtɪərɪəl/ 1 *n.* that from which thing is made; cloth, fabric; in *pl.* things needed for activity etc.; elements. 2 *a.* composed of or connected with matter; not spiritual; important, essential.

**materialism** /məˈtɪərɪəlɪz(ə)m/ *n.* belief that only matter is real or important; rejection of spiritual values etc. **materialist** *n.* & *a.*; **materialistic** *a.*

**materialize** /məˈtɪərɪəlaɪz/ *v.* become fact, happen; represent in or assume bodily form. **materialization** *n.*

**maternal** /məˈtɜːn(ə)l/ *a.* of or like a mother; motherly; related on mother's side.

**maternity** /məˈtɜːnəti/ *n.* motherhood; *attrib.* for women in pregnancy or childbirth.

**matey** /ˈmeɪti/ *a.* familiar and friendly (*with*). **matily** *adv.*

**mathematics** /mæθəˈmætɪks/ *n. pl.* (also treated as *sing.*) science of space, number, and quantity. **mathematical** *a.*; **mathematician** /-əˈtɪʃ(ə)n/ *n.*

**maths** /mæθs/ *n. colloq.* mathematics.

**matilda** /məˈtɪldə/ *n.* Aus. *sl.* bushman's bundle, swag.

**matinée** /ˈmætɪneɪ/ *n.* theatrical etc. performance in afternoon. **matinee coat** baby's short coat.

**matins** /ˈmætɪnz/ *n.* morning prayer.

**matriarch** /ˈmeɪtrɪɑːk/ *n.* woman who is head of family or tribe. **matriarchal** *a.*

**matriarchy** /ˈmeɪtrɪɑːki/ *n.* social organization in which mother is head of family.

**matricide** /'meɪtrəsaɪd/ n. killing of one's mother; person who kills his mother. **matricidal** a.

**matriculate** /mə'trɪkjəleɪt/ v. admit (student) to university; be thus admitted. **matriculation** n.

**matrimony** /'mætrəməni/ n. marriage. **matrimonial** /-'məʊniəl/ a.

**matrix** /'meɪtrɪks/ n. (pl. **-trices** /-trɪsiːz/) mould in which thing is cast or shaped; mass of rock etc. enclosing gems etc.; Math. rectangular array of quantities treated as single quantity.

**matron** /'meɪtrən/ n. married woman; woman managing domestic arrangements of school etc.; woman in charge of nursing in hospital.

**matronly** /'meɪtrənli/ a. of or like a matron, esp. stately or portly.

**matt** a. dull, without lustre.

**matter** /'mætə(r)/ 1 n. physical substance; thing(s), material; content as opp. form, substance; affair, concern; *the* thing that is amiss (*with*); purulent discharge. 2 v.i. be of importance; make difference (*to*). 3 **matter-of-fact** prosaic, unimaginative.

**matting** /'mætɪŋ/ n. fabric for mats.

**mattock** /'mætək/ n. tool like pickaxe with adze and chisel edge as ends of head.

**mattress** /'mætrəs/ n. fabric case filled with soft or firm material or springs, used on or as bed.

**mature** /mə'tjʊə(r)/ 1 a. fully developed, ripe; adult; (of bill etc.) due for payment. 2 v. bring to or reach mature state. 3 **maturity** n.

**matutinal** /mætju:'taɪn(ə)l/ a. of or in morning.

**maty** var. of matey.

**maudlin** /'mɔːdlɪn/ a. weakly sentimental.

**maul** /mɔːl/ 1 v.t. beat and bruise; injure by clawing etc.; handle roughly, damage. 2 n. heavy hammer, usu. of wood.

**maulstick** /'mɔːlstɪk/ n. stick used to support hand in painting.

**maunder** /'mɔːndə(r)/ v.i. talk ramblingly.

**Maundy** /'mɔːndi/ n. distribution of **Maundy money**, silver coins minted for English sovereign to give to the poor on **Maundy Thursday**, next before Easter.

**mausoleum** /mɔːsə'liːəm/ n. building erected as tomb and monument.

**mauve** /məʊv/ n. & a. pale purple.

**maverick** /'mævərɪk/ n. unorthodox or undisciplined person; *US* unbranded calf etc.

**maw** n. stomach of animal.

**mawkish** /'mɔːkɪʃ/ a. feebly sentimental.

**maxillary** /mæk'sɪləri/ a. of the jaw.

**maxim** /'mæksɪm/ n. general truth or rule of conduct expressed in a sentence.

**maximal** /'mæksəm(ə)l/ a. greatest possible in size, duration, etc.

**maximum** /'mæksəməm/ 1 n. (pl. **-ima**) highest or greatest degree or magnitude or quantity. 2 a. greatest.

**may**¹ v. aux. (3 sing. may; past **might** /maɪt/) expr. possibility, permission, request, wish, etc.

**May**² fifth month of year; (**may**) hawthorn blossom. **May Day** 1 May, esp. as international holiday in honour of workers; **mayfly** insect which lives briefly in spring; **maypole** flower-decked pole danced round at spring festival; **may queen** girl chosen as queen of maypole games.

**maybe** /'meɪbi/ adv. perhaps.

**mayday** /'meɪdeɪ/ n. international radio distress-signal used by ships and aircraft.

**mayhem** /'meɪhem/ n. violent or damaging action; *hist.* crime of maiming.

**mayonnaise** /meɪə'neɪz/ n. creamy dressing of oil, egg-yolk, vinegar, etc.; dish dressed with this.

**mayor** /meə(r)/ n. elected head of city or town or borough. **mayoral** a.

**mayoralty** /'meərəlti/ n. office of mayor; period of this.

**mayoress** /'meərəs/ n. mayor's wife or woman fulfilling ceremonial duties of mayor's wife; woman mayor.

**mazarine** /mæzə'riːn/ n. & a. deep blue.

**maze** n. complex and baffling network of paths, lines, etc.; tangle, confusion.

**mazurka** /mə'zɜːkə/ n. lively Polish dance in triple time; music for this.

**MB** abbr. Bachelor of Medicine.

**MBE** abbr. Member of the Order of the British Empire.

**MC** abbr. Master of Ceremonies; Military Cross.

**MCC** abbr. Marylebone Cricket Club.

**MD** *abbr.* Doctor of Medicine; Managing Director.

**me**[1] /miː/ *pron., obj.* case of **I**.

**me**[2] /miː/ *n. Mus.* third note of scale in tonic sol-fa.

**mead** *n.* alcoholic drink of fermented honey and water.

**meadow** /'medəʊ/ *n.* piece of grassland, esp. used for hay; low-lying ground, esp. near river. **meadowsweet** a fragrant flowering plant.

**meagre** /'miːgə(r)/ *a.* of poor quality and scanty in amount.

**meal**[1] *n.* occasion when food is eaten; food eaten on one occasion. **mealticket** source of income.

**meal**[2] *n.* grain or pulse ground to powder.

**mealy** /'miːlɪ/ *a.* of, like, or containing meal; dry and powdery. **mealy-mouthed** afraid to speak plainly.

**mean**[1] *v.* (*past & p.p.* **meant** /ment/) have as one's purpose, design; be resolved; intend to convey or indicate; involve, portend; be of (specified) significance *to* person.

**mean**[2] *a.* niggardly; not generous; ignoble; of low degree or poor quality; *US* vicious, nastily behaved.

**mean**[3] 1 *n.* condition or quality or course of action equally far from two extremes; quotient of the sum of several quantities and their number. 2 *a.* (of quantity) equally far from two extremes. 3 **in the mean time** meanwhile.

**meander** /mɪ'ændə(r)/ 1 *v.i.* wind about; wander at random. 2 *n.* in *pl.* sinuous winding; winding path or course etc.

**meaning** /'miːnɪŋ/ 1 *n.* what is meant; significance. 2 *a.* expressive; significant. 3 **meaningful** *a.*; **meaningless** *a.*

**means** *n.pl.* (usu. treated as *sing.*) that by which result is brought about; money resources. **means test** official inquiry into financial resources of applicant for assistance etc.

**meantime, meanwhile,** *advs.* in the intervening time; at the same time.

**measles** /'miːz(ə)lz/ *n.* as *pl.* or *sing.* infectious virus disease with red rash.

**measly** /'miːzlɪ/ *a.* of or affected with measles; *sl.* inferior or contemptible.

**measure** /'meʒə(r)/ 1 *n.* size or quantity found by measuring; vessel, rod, tape, etc., for measuring; degree, extent; suitable action; legislative enactment; that by which thing is measured; prescribed extent or amount; rhythm, metre, musical time. 2 *v.* find size, quantity, proportions, etc. of with measure; be of specified length etc.; deal *out*; bring into competition *with*. 3 **measurement** *n.*

**measureless** /'meʒələs/ *a.* not measurable; infinite.

**meat** *n.* animal flesh as food; chief part *of*. **meat-ant** large black Aus. ant.

**meaty** *a.* of or like meat; fleshy; full of meat or *fig.* substance.

**mechanic** /mɪ'kænɪk/ *n.* skilled worker, esp. one who makes or repairs or uses machinery.

**mechanical** /mɪ'kænɪk(ə)l/ *a.* of, working, or produced by, machines or mechanism; automatic; lacking originality; of mechanics as a science.

**mechanics** /mɪ'kænɪks/ *n.pl.* (usu. treated as *sing.*) branch of applied mathematics dealing with motion; science of machinery; method of construction or operation.

**mechanism** /'mekənɪz(ə)m/ *n.* structure or parts of machine; way machine works.

**mechanize** /'mekənaɪz/ *v.t.* introduce or use machines in; equip with machines; give mechanical character to. **mechanization** *n.*

**medal** /'med(ə)l/ *n.* piece of metal, usu. coin-shaped, commemorating event etc. or awarded as distinction.

**medallion** /mə'dælɪən/ *n.* large medal; thing so shaped, e.g. portrait.

**medallist** /'medəlɪst/ *n.* winner of (specified) medal.

**meddle** *v.i.* busy oneself unduly (*with*); interfere (*in*).

**meddlesome** /'med(ə)lsəm/ *a.* fond of meddling.

**media** *pl.* of **medium.**

**mediaeval** var. of **medieval.**

**medial** /'miːdɪəl/ *a.* situated in the middle.

**median** /'miːdɪən/ 1 *a.* medial. 2 *n.* line from angle of triangle to middle of opposite side.

**mediate** 1 /'miːdɪeɪt/ *v.i.* act as go-between or peace-maker. 2 /'miːdɪət/ *a.* connected through some other person or thing. 3 **mediation** *n.*

# medical

**medical** /ˈmedɪk(ə)l/ 1 a. of medicine in general or as distinct from surgery. 2 n. colloq. medical examination. 3 **medical certificate** certificate of fitness or unfitness to work etc.; **medical examination** examination to determine person's physical fitness.

**medicament** /məˈdɪkəmənt/ n. substance used in curative treatment.

**Medicare** /ˈmedɪkeə(r)/ n. Aus. Federal system of basic health insurance.

**medicate** /ˈmedɪkeɪt/ v.t. treat medically; impregnate with medicinal substance. **medication** n.

**medicinal** /məˈdɪsɪn(ə)l/ a. of medicine; having healing properties.

**medicine** /ˈmedəsən/ n. art of preserving and restoring health, esp. by other means than surgery; substance, esp. one taken internally, used in this. **medicine-man** witch-doctor.

**medieval** /medɪˈiːv(ə)l/ a. of or imitating Middle Ages.

**mediocre** /miːdiːˈəʊkə(r)/ a. of middling quality, second-rate.

**mediocrity** /miːdiːˈɒkrəti/ n. mediocre quality or person.

**meditate** /ˈmedɪteɪt/ v. exercise the mind in (esp. religious) contemplation; plan mentally. **meditation** n.; **meditative** /med-/ a.

**Mediterranean** /medɪtəˈreɪnɪən/ a. of or characteristic of the sea between Europe and N. Africa, or the countries bordering on it.

**medium** /ˈmiːdɪəm/ 1 n. (pl. -dia or -diums) middle quality or degree; environment; agency, means; in pl.=mass media; (pl. -diums) person claiming to communicate with spirits of the dead. 2 a. intermediate; average; moderate.

**mediumistic** /miːdɪəˈmɪstɪk/ a. of a spiritualist medium.

**medlar** /ˈmedlə(r)/ n. fruit like small apple, eaten when decayed; tree bearing it.

**medley** /ˈmedlɪ/ n. varied mixture.

**medulla** /məˈdʌlə/ n. bone or spinal marrow; hindmost segment of the brain. **medullary** a.

**meek** a. humbly submissive.

**meerschaum** /ˈmɪəʃəm/ n. creamy clay mineral used esp. for pipe-bowls; tobacco-pipe with meerschaum bowl.

**meet**[1] v. (past & p.p. **met**) come into contact or company (with); make acquaintance of; be present at arrival of; assemble; confront; become perceptible to; satisfy (need etc.); experience. 2 n. assembly for hunting etc.

**meet**[2] a. arch. fitting, proper.

**meeting** n. assembly of people for discussion or (Quaker) worship etc.

**mega-** in comb. great, large; one million.

**megabyte** /ˈmegəbaɪt/ n. one million bytes, esp. as unit of computer storage etc.

**megalith** /ˈmegəlɪθ/ n. large stone, esp. as monument. **megalithic** a.

**megalomania** /megələˈmeɪnɪə/ n. mental disorder involving exaggerated idea of one's own importance; passion for grandiose things. **megalomaniac** a. & n.

**megaphone** /ˈmegəfəʊn/ n. large funnel-shaped device for sending sound of voice to a distance.

**megaton** /ˈmegətʌn/ n. unit of explosive force equal to one million tons of TNT.

**meiosis** /maɪˈəʊsɪs/ n. (pl. **-ses** /-siːz/) ironical understatement.

**melamine** /ˈmeləmiːn/ n. resilient kind of plastic.

**melancholia** /melənˈkəʊlɪə/ n. mental illness marked by depression.

**melancholic** /melənˈkɒlɪk/ a. melancholy; liable to melancholy.

**melancholy** /ˈmelənkɒlɪ/ 1 n. pensive sadness; depression; tendency to this. 2 a. sad; depressing.

**melée** /ˈmeleɪ/ n. confused fight or struggle.

**mellifluous** /meˈlɪflʊəs/ a. sweet-sounding.

**mellow** /ˈmeləʊ/ 1 a. soft and rich in flavour, colour, or sound; softened by age etc.; genial. 2 v. make or become mellow.

**melodic** /məˈlɒdɪk/ a. of melody.

**melodious** /məˈləʊdɪəs/ a. of or producing melody, sweet-sounding.

**melodrama** /ˈmelədrɑːmə/ n. drama marked by crude appeals to emotion. **melodramatic** /-ˈmæt-/ a.

**melody** /ˈmelədɪ/ n. sweet music; arrangement of notes in musically expressive succession; principal part in harmonized music.

**melon¹** /'melən/ n. sweet fruit of various gourds.

**melon²** /'melən/ n. Aus. colloq. pademelon. **melon hole** gilgai.

**melt** v. change from solid to liquid by heat; dissolve; soften, be softened; vanish (away). **melt down** reduce (metal) to molten state; **melting-point** temperature at which solid melts; **melting-pot** fig. place of reconstruction or vigorous mixing.

**member** n. person belonging to society, order, etc.; part of complex structure; limb or other bodily organ. **Member of Parliament** person elected to House of Representatives etc.

**membership** n. being a member; number or body of members.

**membrane** /'membreɪn/ n. layer of connective tissue round organ, lining cavity, etc. in living organism. **membranous** a.

**memento** /mə'mentəʊ/ n. (pl. **-toes**) object serving as reminder or kept as memorial.

**memo** /'meməʊ/ n. (pl. **-mos**) colloq. memorandum.

**memoir** /'memwɑː(r)/ n. record of events written from personal knowledge etc.; (esp. in pl.) (auto)biography.

**memorable** /'memərəb(ə)l/ a. likely or worthy to be remembered.

**memorandum** /memə'rændəm/ n. (pl. **-dums** or **-da**) note or record for future use; informal written message esp. in business pl.

**memorial** /mə'mɔːrɪəl/ 1 n. object or custom established in memory of person or event. 2 a. commemorative.

**memorize** /'meməraɪz/ v.t. learn by heart.

**memory** /'memərɪ/ n. faculty by which things are recalled to or kept in mind; what is remembered; posthumous repute; store for data etc. in computer.

**men** pl. of **man**.

**menace** /'menəs/ 1 n. threat; dangerous thing or person. 2 v.t. threaten.

**ménage** /meɪ'nɑːʒ/ n. domestic establishment.

**menagerie** /mə'nædʒərɪ/ n. collection of wild animals in captivity.

**mend** 1 v. restore to sound condition; repair; improve. 2 n. place where thing has been mended. 3 **on the mend** improving.

**mendacious** /men'deɪʃəs/ a. lying, untruthful. **mendacity** /-'dæs-/ n.

**mendicant** /'mendɪkənt/ 1 a. begging. 2 n. beggar. 3 **mendicancy** n.

**menfolk** /'menfəʊk/ n. men in general; men in family.

**menhir** /'menhɪə(r)/ n. prehistoric monumental monolith.

**menial** /'miːnɪəl/ 1 a. (of work) degrading, servile. 2 n. lowly domestic servant.

**meningitis** /menən'dʒɑːtɪs/ n. inflammation of membrane enclosing brain and spinal cord.

**meniscus** /mə'nɪskəs/ n. lens convex on one side and concave on the other.

**menopause** /'menəpɔːz/ n. period of life when menstruation ceases.

**menses** /'mensiːz/ n.pl. monthly flow of blood etc. from lining of womb.

**menstrual** /'menstrʊəl/ a. of menses.

**menstruate** /'menstrʊeɪt/ v.i. discharge menses. **menstruation** n.

**mensurable** /'mensjərəb(ə)l/ a. measurable.

**mensuration** /mensjə'reɪʃ(ə)n/ n. measuring; mathematical rules for computing length, area, etc.

**mental** /'ment(ə)l/ a. of or in mind; sl. affected with mental disorder. **mental age** stage of mental development reached by average child at specified age; **mental arithmetic** arithmetic performed without use of written figures; **mental hospital** establishment for care of mental patients; **mental patient** sufferer from mental illness.

**mentality** /men'tælətɪ/ n. mental character or outlook.

**menthol** /'menθɒl/ n. camphor-like substance got from oil of peppermint etc., used as flavouring or to relieve local pain etc.

**mention** /'menʃ(ə)n/ 1 v.t. speak of, refer to. 2 n. mentioning.

**mentor** /'mentɔː(r)/ n. adviser, councillor.

**menu** /'menjuː/ n. list of dishes to be served or available in restaurant etc.; list of options displayed on computer screen.

**mercantile** /'mɜːkəntaɪl/ a. of trade, commercial; trading. **mercantile marine** merchant navy.

**mercenary** /'mɜːsənərɪ/ 1 a. working

**mercer** /'mɜːsə(r)/ n. dealer in textile fabrics.

merely for money or reward; hired. 2 n. hired soldier in foreign service.

**mercerized** /'mɜːsəraɪzd/ a. (of cotton) having silky lustre given by treatment with caustic alkali.

**merchandize** /'mɜːtʃəndaɪz/ 1 n. commodities of commerce; goods for sale. 2 v. promote sales of; trade.

**merchant** /'mɜːtʃənt/ n. wholesale trader, esp. with foreign countries; US retail trader. **merchant bank** one dealing in commercial loans and financing; **merchant navy** shipping engaged in commerce; **merchantman**, **merchant ship**, ship carrying merchandise; **merchant prince** wealthy merchant.

**merchantable** /'mɜːtʃəntəb(ə)l/ a. saleable.

**merciful** /'mɜːsəfəl/ a. having or feeling or showing mercy.

**merciless** /'mɜːsələs/ a. cruel, pitiless.

**mercurial** /mɜː'kjʊərɪəl/ a. of lively temperament; of or containing mercury.

**mercury** /'mɜːkjərɪ/ n. silver-white heavy normally liquid metal used in barometers, thermometers, etc. **mercuric** a.; **mercurous** a.

**mercy** /'mɜːsɪ/ n. refraining from infliction of suffering or punishment; disposition to forgive; act of mercy; thing to be thankful for. **at the mercy of** wholly in the power of or subject to; **mercy killing** killing out of pity for suffering person or animal.

**mere**[1] a. barely or only what it is said to be, nothing more than.

**mere**[2] n. poet. lake.

**merely** /'mɪəlɪ/ adv. just, only.

**meretricious** /merə'trɪʃəs/ a. showily but falsely attractive.

**merganser** /mɜː'gænsə(r)/ n. a diving duck.

**merge** v. join or blend gradually (into, with); lose or cause to lose character or identity in something else.

**merger** /'mɜːdʒə(r)/ n. combining of two commercial companies into one.

**meridian** /mə'rɪdɪən/ n. circle passing through given place and N. & S. poles; corresponding line on map etc.

**meridional** /mə'rɪdɪən(ə)l/ a. of the south, esp. of Europe, or its inhabitants.

**meringue** /mə'ræŋ/ n. mixture of sugar and beaten egg-white baked crisp.

**merino** /mə'riːnəʊ/ n. (pl. **-nos**) kind of sheep; fine yarn or soft fabric of its wool; fine woollen yarn.

**merit** /'merɪt/ 1 n. quality of deserving well; excellence, worth; (usu. in pl.) thing that entitles to reward or gratitude. 2 v.t. deserve.

**meritocracy** /merɪ'tɒkrəsɪ/ n. government by persons selected for merit.

**meritorious** /merɪ'tɔːrɪəs/ a. praiseworthy.

**mermaid** /'mɜːmeɪd/ n. legendary sea-creature with woman's head and trunk and fish's tail.

**merriment** /'merɪmənt/ n. hilarious enjoyment; mirth.

**merry** /'merɪ/ a. joyous, full of laughter or gaiety; colloq. slightly drunk. **merry-go-round** revolving machine carrying wooden horses, cars, etc., for riding on at fair etc.; **merry-making** festivity.

**mesa** /'meɪsə/ n. US high steep-sided tableland.

**mésalliance** /meɪ'zælɪɑ̃ns/ n. marriage with social inferior. [F]

**mescal** /'meskæl/ n. peyote cactus. **mescal buttons** its disc-shaped dried tops.

**mescaline** /'meskəliːn/ n. hallucinogenic alkaloid present in mescal buttons.

**Mesdames, Mesdemoiselles**, pl. of **Madame, Mademoiselle**.

**mesh** 1 n. open space in net, sieve, etc.; network fabric; in pl. network. 2 v. (of toothed wheel etc.) engage, interlock; catch in net.

**mesmerize** /'mezməraɪz/ v.t. hypnotize; fascinate. **mesmerism** n.

**meso-** /mesəʊ/ in comb. middle.

**mesolithic** /mesəʊ'lɪθɪk/ a. of Stone Age between palaeolithic and neolithic.

**meson** /'miːzɒn/ n. Phys. elementary particle intermediate in mass between proton and electron.

**Mesozoic** /mesə'zəʊɪk/ 1 a. of second geological era. 2 n. this era.

**mess** 1 n. dirty or untidy state; state of confusion or trouble; spilt liquid etc.; domestic animal's excreta; disagreeable concoction; group of people who

**message**

take meals together, esp. in armed services; room where such meals are taken; meal so taken; portion of liquid or pulpy food. 2 v. make dirty or untidy, muddle, bungle, (often with *up*); potter *about*; take meals *with*. 3 **make a mess of** bungle.

**message** /'mesɪdʒ/ n. communication sent from one person to another; inspired communication of prophet, writer, etc. **message stick** *Aus.* stick carved with marks, used as identification by Abor. messengers.

**messenger** /'mesəndʒə(r)/ n. person who carries message(s).

**Messiah** /mə'saɪə/ n. promised deliverer of Jews; Christ regarded as this. **Messianic** /mesɪ'ænɪk/ a.

**Messieurs** pl. of **Monsieur**.

**messmate** /'mesmeɪt/ n. member of same mess; *Aus.* any of various eucalypts, esp. stringybark.

**Messrs** /'mesəz/ abbr. pl. of **Mr**, as prefix to name of firm etc. or list of men's names.

**messuage** /'meswɪdʒ/ n. *Law* dwelling-house with outbuildings and land.

**messy** /'mesɪ/ a. untidy; causing or accompanied by a mess; difficult to deal with.

**met** past & p.p. of **meet**.

**metabolism** /mə'tæbəlɪz(ə)m/ n. process by which food is built up into living material or used to supply energy in living organism. **metabolic** /-'bɒl-/ a.

**metacarpus** /metə'kɑːpəs/ n. (pl. -**pi** /-paɪ/) part of hand between wrist and fingers. **metacarpal** a.

**metal** /'met(ə)l/ 1 n. any of class of elements such as gold, silver, iron, etc.; alloy of these; in pl. rails of railway; broken stone for roads. 2 a. made of metal. 3 v.t. furnish or supply with metal; make or mend (road) with metal.

**metallic** /mə'tælɪk/ a. (characteristic) of metal(s); sounding like struck metal.

**metallurgy** /mə'tælədʒɪ/ n. science of properties of metals; art of working metals, esp. of extracting them from ores. **metallurgical** a.; **metallurgist** n.

**metamorphic** /metə'mɔːfɪk/ a. *Geol.* (of rock) that has undergone transformation by natural agencies. **metamorphism** n.

**metamorphose** /metə'mɔːfəʊz/ v. subject to or undergo metamorphosis or metamorphism.

**metamorphosis** /metə'mɔːfəsɪs/ n. (pl. -**ses** /-siːz/) change of form, esp. by magic or natural development; change of character or circumstances etc.

**metaphor** /'metəfɔː(r)/ n. application of name or descriptive term to object to which it is not literally applicable

**metaphysics** /metə'fɪzɪks/ n.pl. (often treated as *sing.*) theoretical philosophy of being, knowing, etc. **metaphysical** a.

**metatarsus** /metə'tɑːsəs/ n. (pl. -**si** /-saɪ/) part of foot between ankle and toes. **metatarsal** n.

**mete** v.t. portion *out*.

**meteor** /'miːtɪə(r)/ n. small mass of matter from outer space made luminous by entering earth's atmosphere.

**meteoric** /miːtɪ'ɒrɪk/ a. of meteors; *fig.* dazzling, rapid.

**meteorite** /'miːtɪəraɪt/ n. fallen meteor; fragment of rock etc. reaching earth's surface from outer space.

**meteorology** /miːtɪə'rɒlədʒɪ/ n. study of atmospheric phenomena, esp. for weather forecasting. **meteorological** a.; **meteorologist** n.

**meter** /'miːtə(r)/ 1 n. instrument for recording quantity of substance supplied or time elapsed etc. 2 v.t. measure by meter.

**methane** /'miːθeɪn/ n. inflammable hydrocarbon gas of paraffin series.

**methinks** /mɪ'θɪŋks/ v.i. impers. (past **methought** /mɪ'θɔːt/) arch. it seems to me.

**metho** /'meθəʊ/ n. (pl. -**thos**) *Aus. sl.* methylated spirits; person who drinks methylated spirits.

**method** /'meθəd/ n. way of doing something; orderliness.

**methodical** /mə'θɒdɪk(ə)l/ a. characterized by method or order.

**Methodism** /'meθədɪz(ə)m/ n. evangelistic religious movement founded in 18th. c. **Methodist** a. & n.

**methought** past of **methinks**.

**meths** /meθs/ n. *colloq.* methylated spirit.

**methyl alcohol** /'meθəl/ n. a colourless volatile inflammable liquid.

**methylate** /'meθəleɪt/ v.t. mix with methyl alcohol, esp. alcohol to make it unfit for drinking.

**meticulous** /məˈtɪkjələs/ a. (over-) scrupulous about minute details; very careful or accurate.

**métier** /ˈmetjeɪ/ n. one's trade or profession; one's forte. [F]

**metonymy** /məˈtɒnəmɪ/ n. substitution of name of attribute for that of thing.

**metre** /ˈmiːtə(r)/ n. metric unit of length (about 39.4 in.); any form of poetic rhythm.

**metric** /ˈmetrɪk/ a. of or based on the metre. **metric system** decimal measuring system with metre, litre, and gram as units of length, capacity, and weight; **metric ton** 1,000 kg.

**metrical** /ˈmetrɪk(ə)l/ a. of or in metre; involving measurement.

**metrication** /metrɪˈkeɪʃ(ə)n/ n. conversion from imperial to metric system.

**metronome** /ˈmetrənəʊm/ n. instrument marking musical time.

**metropolis** /məˈtrɒpəlɪs/ n. chief city.

**metropolitan** /metrəˈpɒlɪt(ə)n/ 1 a. of metropolis. 2 n. bishop with authority over bishops of province.

**mettle** /ˈmet(ə)l/ n. quality of person's disposition or temperament; spirit, courage.

**mettlesome** /ˈmetəlsəm/ a. spirited.

**mew**¹ 1 n. cat's cry. 2 v.i. utter mew.

**mew**² n. sea-gull.

**mews** n. series of private stables round open yard or lane, now often converted into dwellings.

**mezzanine** /ˈmetsəniːn/ n. extra storey between two others, esp. ground and first floors.

**mezzo** /ˈmetsəʊ/ adv. Mus. moderately, half. **mezzo forte, piano**, moderately loud, soft. [It.]

**mezzo-soprano** /metsəʊsəˈprɑːnəʊ/ n. woman's singing voice between soprano and contralto in pitch; singer with mezzo-soprano voice; music for mezzo-soprano voice.

**mezzotint** /ˈmetsəʊtɪnt/ n. kind of copper or steel engraving.

**mf** abbr. mezzo-forte.

**mg** abbr. milligram(s).

**Mgr.** abbr. Monseigneur; Monsignor.

**MHR** abbr. Member of the House of Representatives.

**mi** var. of me³.

**MI** abbr. Military Intelligence.

**mia-mia** /ˈmaɪəmaɪə/ n. Aus. Aboriginal hut.

**miaow** /mɪˈaʊ/ n. & v.i. = mew¹.

**miasma** /mɪˈæzmə/ n. infectious or noxious emanation. **miasmic** a.

**mica** /ˈmaɪkə/ n. kind of mineral found as small glittering scales or crystals separable into thin plates.

**mice** pl. of mouse.

**Michaelmas** /ˈmɪkəlməs/ n. feast of St. Michael, 29 Sept. **Michaelmas daisy** aster flowering in autumn.

**mickery** /ˈmɪkərɪ/ n. Aus. water-holding depression in sandy inland riverbed.

**mickey** /ˈmɪkɪ/ n. **take the mickey (out of)** tease or mock.

**micky** /ˈmɪkɪ/ n. Aus. young wild bull.

**micro** /ˈmaɪkrəʊ/ n. colloq. microcomputer.

**micro-** in comb. small; one millionth of.

**microbe** /ˈmaɪkrəʊb/ n. micro-organism, esp. one causing disease or fermentation. **microbial** a.

**microbiology** /maɪkrəʊbaɪˈɒlədʒɪ/ n. study of micro-organisms.

**microchip** /ˈmaɪkrəʊtʃɪp/ n. tiny piece of semiconductor carrying many electrical circuits.

**microcomputer** /maɪkrəʊkəmˈpjuːtə(r)/ n. computer in which central processor is contained on microchip(s).

**microcosm** /ˈmaɪkrəkɒz(ə)m/ n. complex thing regarded as epitome of greater system; miniature representation (of).

**microdot** /ˈmaɪkrəʊdɒt/ n. photograph of document etc. reduced to very small size.

**microfiche** /ˈmaɪkrəʊfiːʃ/ 1 n. (pl. same) piece of film bearing photograph of document etc. reduced to very small size.

**microfilm** /ˈmaɪkrəʊfɪlm/ 1 n. length of film bearing series of document etc. reduced to very small size. 2 v.t. record on microfilm.

**micrometer** /maɪˈkrɒmətə(r)/ n. instrument for measuring small lengths or angles.

**micron** /ˈmaɪkrɒn/ n. millionth of a metre.

**micro-organism** /ˈmaɪkrəʊɔːgənɪz(ə)m/ n. organism too small to be visible to the naked eye.

**microphone** /'maɪkrəfəʊn/ n. instrument for converting sound-waves into electrical energy.

**microprocessor** /'maɪkrəʊprəʊsesə(r)/ n. data processor contained on microchip(s).

**microscope** /'maɪkrəskəʊp/ n. instrument for magnifying objects by means of lens(es) so as to reveal details invisible to naked eye.

**microscopic** /maɪkrə'skɒpɪk/ a. too small to be visible (in detail) without microscope; of the microscope.

**microscopy** /maɪ'krɒskəpɪ/ n. use of the microscope.

**microsurgery** /'maɪkrəʊsɜːdʒərɪ/ n. surgery using microscope to see tissues and instruments.

**microwave** /'maɪkrəʊweɪv/ n. electromagnetic wave of length between about 50 cm and 1 mm. **microwave oven** one using such waves to heat food quickly.

**micturition** /mɪktjə'rɪʃ(ə)n/ n. urination.

**mid** a. that is in the middle (of); intermediate. **midday** (time near) noon; **mid-off, -on,** *Crick.* fielder near bowler on off, on, side.

**midden** /'mɪd(ə)n/ n. dunghill; refuse-heap.

**middle** /'mɪd(ə)l/ 1 a. at equal distance from extremities; intermediate in rank, quality, etc.; average. 2 n. middle point or position; waist. 3 **in the middle of** while or during; **middle age** middle part of normal lifetime; **Middle Ages** about 1000–1400; **middle class** social class including professional and business workers; **middleman** any of traders who handle commodity between its producer and its consumer; **middleweight** boxing-weight (up to 75 kg).

**middling** /'mɪdlɪŋ/ 1 a. moderately good; *colloq.* fairly well in health. 2 *adv.* fairly or moderately.

**midge** n. gnatlike insect.

**midget** /'mɪdʒɪt/ n. extremely small person or thing.

**midland** /'mɪdlənd/ a. of the middle part of country. **the Midlands** the inland counties of central England.

**midnight** /'mɪdnaɪt/ n. 12 o'clock at night; middle of night. **midnight sun** sun visible at midnight during summer in polar regions.

**midriff** /'mɪdrɪf/ n. region of front of body just above waist.

**midshipman** /'mɪdʃɪpmən/ n. (*pl.* -men) naval officer ranking next below sub-lieutenant.

**midst** n. middle.

**midsummer** /'mɪdsʌmə(r)/ n. period of or near summer solstice, about 21 June. **Midsummer's Day** 24 June.

**midwife** /'mɪdwaɪf/ n. (*pl.* -**wives**) person trained to assist at childbirth. **midwifery** /-'wɪfərɪ/ n.

**mien** /miːn/ n. person's bearing or look.

**might**[1] *past of* **may**[1].

**might**[2] /maɪt/ n. great power or strength or resources.

**mighty** /'maɪtɪ/ 1 a. powerful, great. 2 *adv. colloq.* very.

**mignonette** /mɪnjə'net/ n. plant with fragrant grey-green flowers.

**migraine** /'miːgreɪn/ or /'maɪ-/ n. severe recurrent form of headache, often with disturbance of vision.

**migrant** /'maɪgrənt/ 1 a. that migrates. 2 n. immigrant; migrant bird etc.

**migrate** /maɪ'greɪt/ v.i. move from one place, esp. one country, to another; (of bird etc.) come and go with seasons. **migration** n.; **migratory** a.

**mikado** /mɪ'kɑːdəʊ/ n. (*pl.* -**dos**) Emperor of Japan.

**mike** n. *colloq.* microphone.

**milch** /mɪltʃ/ a. (of domestic animal) giving or kept for milk.

**mild** /maɪld/ a. gentle; not severe or harsh or drastic; not strong or bitter. **mild steel** steel that is tough but not easily tempered.

**mildew** /'mɪldjuː/ 1 n. growth of minute fungi forming on surfaces exposed to damp. 2 v. taint or be tainted with mildew.

**mile** n. unit of linear measure (approx. 1.6 km); race over one mile. **milestone** stone etc. set up on roadside to mark distance in miles, stage (in career etc.).

**mileage** /'maɪlɪdʒ/ n. number of miles travelled; advantage to be gained from something.

**miler** /'maɪlə(r)/ n. person or horse trained specially to run a mile.

**milfoil** /'mɪlfɔɪl/ n. common yarrow.

**milieu** /miː'ljɜː/ n. environment, social surroundings.

**militant** /'mɪlɪt(ə)nt/ 1 a. aggressively

## militarism

active; combative; engaged in warfare. 2 *n*. militant person. 3 **militancy** *n*.

**militarism** /'mɪlətərɪz(ə)m/ *n*. military spirit; reliance on military force and methods. **militarist** *n*.; **militaristic** *a*.

**military** /'mɪlətəri/ 1 *a*. of or for or done by soldiers or the armed forces. 2 *n*. **the** army. 3 **military band** combination of woodwind, brass, and percussion.

**militate** /'mɪlɪteɪt/ *v.i.* serve as argument or influence *against*.

**militia** /mə'lɪʃə/ *n*. military force, esp. one raised from civilian population and supplementing regular army in emergency.

**milk** 1 *n*. opaque white fluid secreted by female mammals for feeding young; cow's milk as food; milk-like liquid. 2 *v.t.* draw milk from; get money out of, exploit. **milkmaid** *arch*. woman who milks or works in dairy; **milkman** man who sells or delivers milk; **milk run** routine expedition or mission; **milk shake** drink of milk, flavouring, etc., mixed by shaking or whisking; **milksop** spiritless man or youth; **milk tooth** temporary tooth in young mammals.

**milko** /'mɪlkəʊ/ *n*. (*pl*. **-kos**) *Aus. sl.* milkman.

**milky** /'mɪlkɪ/ *a*. of, like, or mixed with milk; (of liquid) cloudy. **Milky Way** the Earth's galaxy.

**mill** 1 *n*. building fitted with mechanical apparatus for grinding corn; such apparatus; grinding-machine; building fitted with machinery for manufacturing process etc.; such machinery. 2 *v*. grind or treat in mill; produce grooves etc. in (metal, edge of coin, etc.); (of people or animals) move around in aimless manner. 3 **mill-pond** pond formed by damming stream to use water in mill; **mill-race** current of water driving mill-wheel; **millstone** circular stone for grinding corn, *fig*. heavy burden; **mill-wheel** wheel used to drive water-mill.

**millenium** /mə'leniəm/ *n*. thousand-year period; supposed coming time of happiness on earth. **millenial** *a*.

**millepede** /'mɪlɪpiːd/ *n*. small many-legged crawling animal.

## mince

**miller** /'mɪlə(r)/ *n*. person who works or owns a mill.

**millesimal** /mɪ'lesɪm(ə)l/ 1 *a*. thousandth; consisting of thousandths. 2 *n*. thousandth part.

**millet** /'mɪlɪt/ *n*. cereal plant with small nutritious seeds.

**milli-** *in comb*. one-thousandth.

**milliard** /'mɪljəd/ *n*. one thousand millions.

**millibar** /'mɪləbɑː(r)/ *n*. one-thousandth of a **bar**².

**milligram** /'mɪlɪɡræm/ *n*. one-thousandth of a gram.

**millilitre** /'mɪlɪliːtə(r)/ *n*. one-thousandth of a litre.

**millimetre** /'mɪlɪmiːtə(r)/ *n*. one-thousandth of a metre.

**milliner** /'mɪlɪnə(r)/ *n*. maker or seller of women's hats. **millinery** *n*.

**million** /'mɪljən/ *n*. one thousand thousand; million pounds, dollars, etc. **gone a million** *Aus. sl.* hopelessly defeated. **millionth** *a*. & *n*.

**millionaire** /mɪljə'neə(r)/ *n*. person possessing a million pounds etc.; very rich person.

**millipede** var. of **millepede**.

**milt** *n*. roe of male fish.

**mime** 1 *n*. acting with gestures and usu. without words; performance involving this. 2 *v*. act or represent in mime.

**mimeograph** /'mɪmɪəɡrɑːf or -ɡræf/ 1 *n*. apparatus for making copies from stencils. 2 *v.t.* reproduce thus.

**mimetic** /mɪ'metɪk/ *a*. of or given to imitation or mimicry.

**mimic** /'mɪmɪk/ 1 *v.t.* ridicule by imitating; imitate or resemble closely. 2 *n*. person who mimics. 3 **mimicry** *n*.

**mimosa** /mɪ'məʊzə/ *n*. kind of shrub esp. with small globular flower-heads.

**min.** *abbr*. minute(s); minimum.

**Min.** *abbr*. Minister; Ministry.

**mina** /'maɪnə/ *n*. talking bird of starling family.

**minaret** /mɪnə'ret/ *n*. tall slender tower of mosque.

**minatory** /'mɪnətəri/ *a*. threatening.

**mince** /mɪns/ 1 *v*. cut (meat etc.) very small, esp. in a machine; walk in affected way. 2 *n*. minced meat. 3 **mincemeat** mixture of currants, spices, suet, etc., chopped small; **mince pie** (usu. small round) pie of mincemeat.

# mind

**mind** /maɪnd/ 1 *n.* seat of consciousness, thought, volition, and feeling; intellectual powers; memory; opinion. 2 *v.* object to; take care or heed (of); have charge of; bear in mind.

**minded** /'maɪndəd/ *a.* disposed, inclined *to* do etc.

**minder** /'maɪndə(r)/ *n.* person whose business it is to look after person or thing.

**mindful** /'maɪndfəl/ *a.* taking thought or care (*of*).

**mindless** /'maɪndləs/ *a.* stupidly ill-behaved; not involving mental effort.

**mine**[1] *pron.* & *a.* the one(s) belonging to me.

**mine**[2] 1 *n.* excavation for extracting metal or coal or salt etc.; *fig.* abundant source (*of*); receptacle filled with explosive placed in or on ground or in water. 2 *v.* obtain (minerals) from mine; dig in (earth etc.) for ore etc.; *Mil.* lay mines under or in. 3 **minefield** area where mines have been laid; **minesweeper** ship for clearing away explosive mines.

**miner**[1] /'maɪnə(r)/ *n.* worker in mine. **miner's right** *Aus.* licence to dig for gold.

**miner**[2] /'maɪnə(r)/ *n.* any of various Aus. honey-eating birds.

**mineral** /'mɪnər(ə)l/ 1 *n.* substance obtained by mining; natural inorganic substance in earth; artificial mineral water. 2 *a.* obtained by mining; not animal or vegetable. 3 **mineral water** water naturally or artificially impregnated with mineral substance, other non-alcoholic effervescent drink.

**mineralogy** /mɪnə'rælədʒi/ *n.* science of minerals. **mineralogical** *a.*; **mineralogist** *n.*

**minestrone** /mɪnə'strəʊni/ *n.* soup containing vegetables and pasta or rice.

**mingle** /'mɪŋɡ(ə)l/ *v.* mix, blend.

**mingy** /'mɪndʒi/ *a. colloq.* stingy.

**mini** /'mɪni/ *n. colloq.* miniskirt; small car.

**mini-** /'mɪni/ *in comb.* miniature, very small of its kind.

**miniature** /'mɪnɪtʃə(r)/ 1 *a.* much smaller than normal; represented on small scale. 2 *n.* small painted portrait etc.; miniature thing.

**miniaturist** /'mɪnɪtʃərəst/ *n.* painter of miniatures.

# minstrel

**miniaturize** /'mɪnɪtʃəraɪz/ *v.t.* make miniature; produce in smaller version.

**minim** /'mɪnɪm/ *n. Mus.* note half as long as semibreve.

**minimal** /'mɪnɪm(ə)l/ *a.* being or related to a minimum; very minute or slight.

**minimize** /'mɪnɪmaɪz/ *v.t.* reduce to or estimate at minimum; represent at less than true value etc.

**minimum** /'mɪnɪməm/ 1 *n.* (*pl.* **-ima**) least amount attainable, usual, etc. 2 *a.* that is a minimum.

**minion** /'mɪnjən/ *n. derog.* subordinate, assistant.

**minister** /'mɪnɪstə(r)/ 1 *n.* person at head of government department; clergyman, esp. in Presbyterian and Nonconformist Churches; diplomatic agent usu. ranking below ambassador; person employed in execution *of.* 2 *v.i.* render aid or service (*to*).

**ministerial** /mɪnɪ'stɪərɪəl/ *a.* of minister or his office; of government.

**ministration** /mɪnɪ'streɪʃ(ə)n/ *n.* (act of) ministering.

**ministry** /'mɪnɪstri/ *n.* office or building or department of minister of State; ministers forming government; office as religious minister etc.

**mink** *n.* small stoatlike animal; its fur.

**minnow** /'mɪnəʊ/ *n.* small freshwater fish.

**Minoan** /mɪ'nəʊən/ 1 *a.* of Cretan Bronze-Age civilization. 2 *n.* person of this civilization.

**minor** /'maɪnə(r)/ 1 *a.* lesser of two things, classes, etc.; under full legal age; comparatively unimportant; *Mus.* of or based on scale that has semitone next above second note. 2 *n.* person under full legal age; *US* student's subsidiary subject. 3 *v.i. US* (of student) undertake study *in* as minor.

**minority** /maɪ'nɒrɪti/ *n.* smaller number or part, esp. in voting; group of persons differing from others in race, religion, language, etc.; state of being under full legal age, period of this.

**minster** /'mɪnstə(r)/ *n. UK* large church.

**minstrel** /'mɪnstr(ə)l/ *n.* medieval singer or musician; (usu. in *pl.*) one of band of entertainers with blackened faces etc.

**minstrelsy** /ˈmɪnstrəlsiː/ *n*. minstrel's art or poetry.

**mint**[1] *n*. aromatic culinary herb; peppermint.

**mint**[2] **1** *n*. place where money is coined. **2** *v.t.* coin (money); invent.

**minuet** /mɪnjuːˈet/ *n*. slow stately dance in triple time; music for this or in same style.

**minus** /ˈmaɪnəs/ **1** *prep*. with subtraction of; *colloq*. deprived of. **2** *n*. minus sign (−); negative quantity.

**minuscule** /ˈmɪnəskjuːl/ **1** *a*. extremely small; lower-case. **2** *n*. lower-case letter.

**minute**[1] /ˈmɪnɪt/ **1** *n*. sixtieth part of hour or degree; short time; memorandum, summary; in *pl*. official record of proceedings. **2** *v.t.* record in minutes; send minute to.

**minute**[2] /maɪˈnjuːt/ *a*. very small; precise, going into details.

**minutiae** /maɪˈnjuːʃiː/ *n. pl*. trivial points, small details.

**minx** *n*. pert or sly girl.

**miracle** /ˈmɪrək(ə)l/ *n*. event due to supernatural agency; remarkable event or object. **miracle play** medieval dramatic representation based on Bible or lives of saints.

**miraculous** /məˈrækjələs/ *a*. supernatural; surprising.

**mirage** /məˈrɑːʒ/ *n*. optical illusion produced by atmospheric conditions; illusory thing.

**mire** /maɪə(r)/ **1** *n*. swampy ground, mud. **2** *v*. sink in or besmatter with mud.

**mirror** /ˈmɪrə(r)/ **1** *n*. smooth surface, esp. of amalgam-coated glass, reflecting image; *fig*. what gives faithful reflection. **2** *v.t.* reflect as in mirror. **3 mirror image** reflection or copy in which left and right sides are reversed.

**mirth** /mɜːθ/ *n*. merriment, laughter. **mirthful** *a*.

**miry** /ˈmaɪəriː/ *a*. muddy.

**misadventure** /mɪsədˈventʃə(r)/ *n*. piece of bad luck. **by misadventure** by accident.

**misalliance** /mɪsəˈlaɪəns/ *n*. unsuitable marriage.

**misanthrope** /ˈmɪsənθrəʊp/ *n*. hater of mankind. **misanthropic** /-ˈθrɒpɪk/ *a*.; **misanthropy** /-ˈænθrəpiː/ *n*.

**misapply** /mɪsəˈplaɪ/ *v.t.* apply or use wrongly. **misapplication** *n*.

**misapprehend** /mɪsæprəˈhend/ *v.t.* misunderstand. **misapprehension** *n*.

**misappropriate** /mɪsəˈprəʊprɪeɪt/ *v.t.* apply (another's money etc.) dishonestly to one's own use. **misappropriation** *n*.

**misbegotten** /mɪsbəˈɡɒt(ə)n/ *a*. contemptible; bastard.

**misbehave** /mɪsbəˈheɪv/ *v.i.* behave improperly. **misbehaviour** *n*.

**miscalculate** /mɪsˈkælkjəleɪt/ *v*. calculate wrongly. **miscalculation** *n*.

**miscall** /mɪsˈkɔːl/ *v.t.* call by wrong name; call wrongly.

**miscarriage** /mɪsˈkærɪdʒ/ *n*. spontaneous abortion; miscarrying of plan etc.

**miscarry** /mɪsˈkæriː/ *v.i.* be unsuccessful, go astray; have miscarriage.

**miscast** /mɪsˈkɑːst/ *v.t.* (*past* & *p.p.* **-cast**) cast (actor) in unsuitable part.

**miscegenation** /mɪsədʒəˈneɪʃ(ə)n/ *n*. interbreeding between races.

**miscellaneous** /mɪsəˈlemiːəs/ *a*. of various kinds; of mixed composition or character.

**miscellany** /məˈseləniː/ *n*. mixture, medley.

**mischance** /mɪsˈtʃɑːns or -ˈtʃæns/ *n*. bad luck; misfortune.

**mischief** /ˈmɪstʃəf/ *n*. troublesome but not malicious conduct, esp. of children; harm or injury caused esp. by person. **mischievous** /ˈmɪstʃəvəs/ *a*.

**misconceive** /mɪskənˈsiːv/ *v*. have wrong idea of; misunderstand. **misconception** *n*.

**misconduct** /mɪsˈkɒndʌkt/ *n*. improper conduct.

**misconstrue** /mɪskənˈstruː/ *v.t.* misinterpret. **misconstruction** *n*.

**miscount** /mɪsˈkaʊnt/ **1** *v*. make wrong count, count (things) wrongly. **2** *n*. wrong count, esp. of votes.

**miscreant** /ˈmɪskriːənt/ *n*. villain.

**misdeal** /mɪsˈdiːl/ **1** *v*. (*past* & *p.p.* **-dealt** /-ˈdelt/) make mistake in dealing. **2** *n*. wrong deal.

**misdeed** /mɪsˈdiːd/ *n*. wrong action.

**misdemeanour** /mɪsdəˈmiːnə(r)/ *n*. misdeed; *Law* indictable offence.

**misdirect** /mɪsdəˈrekt/ *v.t.* direct wrongly. **misdirection** *n*.

**mise en scène** /miːz ɑ̃ ˈsen/ *n*. scenery etc.

**miser** /'maɪzə(r)/ n. person who hoards wealth and lives miserably. **miserly** a.

**miserable** /'mɪzərəb(ə)l/ a. wretchedly unhappy or uncomfortable; pitiable; mean, stingy.

**misericord** /mɪ'zerəkɔːd/ n. projection under hinged seat in choir stall to support person standing.

**misery** /'mɪzərɪ/ n. wretched state of mind or outward circumstances; *colloq.* constantly grumbling person.

**misfire** /mɪs'faɪə(r)/ 1 v.i. fail to go off or start action or function regularly or have intended effect. 2 n. such failure.

**misfit** /'mɪsfɪt/ n. person ill-adapted to surroundings etc.; garment etc. that does not fit.

**misfortune** /mɪs'fɔːtjuːn/ n. (instance of) bad luck.

**misgive** /mɪs'gɪv/ v.t. (past **-gave**; p.p. **given**) (of person's mind etc.) fill him with suspicion or foreboding.

**misgiving** /mɪs'gɪvɪŋ/ n. feeling of mistrust or apprehension.

**misgovern** /mɪs'gʌvən/ v.t. govern badly. **misgovernment** n.

**misguided** /mɪs'gaɪdɪd/ a. mistaken in thought or action.

**mishandle** /mɪs'hænd(ə)l/ v.t. deal with ineffectually; handle roughly.

**mishap** /'mɪshæp/ n. unlucky accident.

**mishear** /mɪs'hɪə(r)/ v. (past & p.p. **-heard** /-'hɜːd/) hear incorrectly or imperfectly.

**misinform** /mɪsɪn'fɔːm/ v.t. give wrong information to. **misinformation** n.

**misinterpret** /mɪsɪn'tɜːprət/ v.t. interpret wrongly. **misinterpretation** n.

**misjudge** /mɪs'dʒʌdʒ/ v.t. judge wrongly. **misjudgement** n.

**mislay** /mɪs'leɪ/ v.t. (past & p.p. **-laid**) put (thing) by accident where it cannot readily be found.

**mislead** /mɪs'liːd/ v.t. (past & p.p. **-led**) lead astray; give wrong impression to.

**mismanage** /mɪs'mænɪdʒ/ v.t. manage badly or wrongly. **mismanagement** n.

**misnomer** /mɪs'nəʊmə(r)/ wrongly applied name.

**misogynist** /mɪ'sɒdʒənɪst/ n. person who hates all women. **misogyny** n.

**misplace** /mɪs'pleɪs/ v.t. put in wrong place; bestow on ill-chosen object. **misplacement** n.

**misprint** 1 n. /'mɪsprɪnt/ error in printing. 2 v.t. /mɪs'prɪnt/ print wrongly.

**mispronounce** /mɪsprə'naʊns/ v.t. pronounce wrongly. **mispronunciation** n.

**misquote** /mɪs'kwəʊt/ v.t. quote wrongly. **misquotation** n.

**misread** /mɪs'riːd/ v.t. (past & p.p. **-read** /-'red/) read or interpret wrongly.

**misrepresent** /mɪsreprɪ'zent/ v.t. give false account of; represent wrongly. **misrepresentation** n.

**misrule** /mɪs'ruːl/ 1 v.t. govern badly. 2 n. bad government.

**miss**¹ 1 v. fail to hit, reach, meet, find, catch, or perceive; pass over; regret absence of; fail. 2 n. failure. 3 **give thing a miss** avoid it, leave it alone; **miss out** omit.

**Miss**² n. title prefixed to name of or used to address unmarried woman or girl.

**missal** /'mɪs(ə)l/ n. RC mass-book.

**missel-thrush** /'mɪs(ə)l/ large kind of thrush.

**misshapen** /mɪs'ʃeɪpən/ a. deformed, distorted.

**missile** /'mɪsaɪl/ n. object or weapon capable of being thrown or projected; weapon directed by remote control or automatically.

**missing** /'mɪsɪŋ/ a. not present; not found; (of person) not traced but not known to be dead.

**mission** /'mɪʃ(ə)n/ n. persons sent out as envoys or evangelists; missionary post; task; operational sortie; vocation.

**missionary** /'mɪʃənərɪ/ 1 a. of religious etc. missions. 2 n. person doing missionary work.

**missis** var. of **missus**.

**missive** /'mɪsɪv/ n. letter.

**misspell** /mɪs'spel/ v.t. (past & p.p. **-spelt** or **-spelled**) spell wrongly.

**misspend** /mɪs'spend/ v.t. (past & p.p. **-spent**) spend wrongly or wastefully.

**misstate** /mɪs'steɪt/ v.t. state wrongly. **misstatement** n.

**missus** /'mɪsəz/ n. **the missus** *colloq.* my or your wife.

**mist** 1 n. water-vapour in drops smaller than rain; dimness, blurring, caused by tears etc. 2 v. cover or be covered (as) with mist.

**mistake** /mɪˈsteɪk/ 1 *n.* incorrect idea or opinion; thing incorrectly done or thought. 2 *v.* (*past* -took; *p.p.* -taken) come to wrong conclusion about, misinterpret; wrongly take (person or thing) *for* another; in *p.p.* due to error, misjudged.

**mistime** /mɪsˈtaɪm/ *v.t.* say or do at wrong time.

**mistletoe** /ˈmɪsəltəʊ/ *n.* parasitic white-berried plant.

**mistral** /ˈmɪstr(ə)l/ *n.* cold N. or NW wind in S. France.

**mistress** /ˈmɪstrəs/ *n.* woman in authority or with power; female head of household; female teacher; woman having illicit sexual relationship with man.

**mistrial** /mɪsˈtraɪəl/ *n.* trial vitiated by error.

**mistrust** /mɪsˈtrʌst/ 1 *v.t.* feel no confidence in. 2 *n.* lack of confidence; suspicion. 3 **mistrustful** *a.*

**misty** /ˈmɪsti/ *a.* of, in, or like mist; of dim outline; obscure.

**misunderstand** /mɪsʌndəˈstænd/ *v.* (-stood) not understand rightly.

**misuse** 1 /mɪsˈjuːz/ *v.t.* use wrongly; illtreat. 2 /mɪsˈjuːs/ *n.* wrong use.

**mite** *n.* small arachnid esp. of kind found in cheese etc.; modest contribution; small object or child.

**mitigate** /ˈmɪtɪɡeɪt/ *v.t.* make milder or less intense or severe. **mitigation** *n.*

**mitre** /ˈmaɪtə(r)/ 1 *n.* bishop's tall pointed head-dress; joint of two pieces of wood such that line of junction bisects angle between them. 2 *v.t.* bestow mitre on; join with mitre.

**mitt** *n.* mitten; *sl.* hand.

**mitten** /ˈmɪt(ə)n/ *n.* glove with only one compartment for the 4 fingers; knitted etc. glove leaving fingertips and thumbtip bare.

**mix** 1 *v.* put together, combine, (substances, groups, qualities, etc.) so that particles or members etc. of each are diffused among those of the other(s); prepare (compound, cocktail, etc.) by mixing ingredients; be sociable (*with*); join, be mixed; be compatible. 2 *n.* mixing, mixture; ingredients prepared commercially for making cake etc. or for process such as concrete-making.

**mixed** /mɪkst/ *a.* of diverse qualities or elements; of or for various classes, both sexes, etc. **mixed marriage** one between persons of different race or religion; **mixed-up** *colloq.* muddled, ill-adjusted.

**mixer** /ˈmɪksə(r)/ *n.* apparatus for mixing foods etc.; person who manages socially in specified way.

**mixture** /ˈmɪkstʃə(r)/ *n.* mixing; what is mixed; combination of ingredients, qualities, etc.

**mizen-mast** /ˈmɪz(ə)n/ *Naut.* mast next aft of mainmast.

**ml.** *abbr.* mile(s); millilitre(s).

**Mlle(s)** *abbr. Mademoiselle, Mesdemoiselles.*

**MM** *abbr. Messieurs;* Military Medal.

**mm.** *abbr.* millimetre(s).

**Mme(s)** *abbr. Madame, Mesdames.*

**mnemonic** /nəˈmɒnɪk/ 1 *a.* of or designed to aid memory. 2 *n.* mnemonic device; in *pl.* art of or system for improving memory.

**mo** *n.* (*pl.* mos) *sl.* moment.

**MO** *abbr.* Medical Officer; money order.

**moan** 1 *n.* low inarticulate sound expressing pain or grief; complaint. 2 *v.* utter moan; lament, complain.

**moat** *n.* defensive ditch round castle, town, etc., usu. filled with water.

**mob** 1 *n.* riotous crowd; rabble; *sl.* gang, associated group of persons; *Aus.* collection of things, flock or drove of animals, Abor. community. 2 *v.t.* attack in mob; crowd round and molest.

**mob-cap** *n. hist.* woman's indoor cap covering all the hair.

**mobile** /ˈməʊbaɪl/ 1 *a.* movable (readily or freely); (of face) of changing expression; (of shop etc.) accommodated in vehicle; (of person) able to change social status. 2 *n.* ornamental structure that may be hung so as to turn freely. 3 **mobility** /-ˈbɪl-/ *n.*

**mobilize** /ˈməʊbəlaɪz/ *v.* call up, assemble, prepare, for warfare etc. **mobilization** *n.*

**mobster** /ˈmɒbstə(r)/ *n. sl.* gangster.

**moccasin** /ˈmɒkəsən/ *n.* soft heelless shoe as orig. worn by N. Amer. Indians.

**mock**[1] 1 *v.* ridicule, scoff *at*; mimic; jeer, scoff. 2 *a.* sham; imitation. 3 **mock-olive** *Aus.* olive with succulent fruit and hard wood; **mock-orange** *Aus.* native laurel with citrus-like leaves; **mock turtle soup** soup made from calf's head etc.; **mock-up** experimental model.

**mock**[2] *n. Aus. sl.* (also **mocker**) put the **mock(s)** or **mocker(s)** on inconvenience, hinder.

**mockery** /'mɒkəri/ *n.* derision, subject or occasion of this; travesty.

**modal** /'məʊd(ə)l/ *a.* of mode or form as opp. to substance; *Gram.* of or expressing mood or manner.

**mode** *n.* way in which thing is done; current fashion; *Mus.* scale system.

**model** /'mɒd(ə)l/ 1 *n.* representation in three dimensions of existing person or thing or of proposed structure, esp. on smaller scale; simplified description of system etc.; design or style of structure, esp. of motor vehicle; person or thing proposed for imitation; person employed to pose for artist, or to display clothes etc. by wearing them; (copy of) garment etc. by well-known designer. 2 *a.* exemplary, ideally perfect. 3 *v.* fashion or shape (figure) in clay, wax, etc.; form (thing) *after* or (*up*)*on* model; (of person acting as model) display (garment).

**modem** /'məʊdem/ *n.* device for sending and receiving computer data by means of telephone line.

**moderate** 1 /'mɒdərət/ *a.* avoiding extremes, temperate; not excessive; middling in quantity or quality. 2 /'mɒdərət/ *n.* person of moderate views. 3 /'mɒdəreɪt/ *v.t.* make or become less violent or excessive; act as moderator. 4 **moderation** *n.*

**moderator** /'mɒdəreɪtə(r)/ *n.* arbitrator, mediator; Presbyterian minister presiding over any ecclesiastical body.

**modern** /'mɒd(ə)n/ 1 *a.* of present and recent times; in current fashion, not antiquated. 2 *n.* person living in modern times. 3 **modernity** /-'dɜːn-/ *n.*

**modernism** /'mɒdənɪz(ə)m/ *n.* modern ideas or methods. **modernist** *a.* & *n.*

**modernize** /'mɒdənaɪz/ *v.* make modern; adapt to modern ideas, taste, etc. **modernization** *n.*

**modest** /'mɒdɪst/ *a.* having humble or moderate estimate of one's own merit; bashful; decorous; not excessive; unpretentious. **modesty** *n.*

**modicum** /'mɒdɪkəm/ *n.* small quantity.

**modify** /'mɒdɪfaɪ/ *v.t.* make less severe; tone down; make partial changes in. **modification** *n.*

**modish** /'məʊdɪʃ/ *a.* fashionable.

**modular** /'mɒdjʊlə(r)/ *a.* based on module(s).

**modulate** /'mɒdjʊleɪt/ *v.* regulate, adjust; adjust or vary tone or pitch of; alter amplitude or frequency of (wave) by wave of lower frequency to convey signal; *Mus.* pass from one key to another. **modulation** *n.*

**module** /'mɒdjuːl/ *n.* standardized part or independent unit in construction esp. of furniture, building, spacecraft, or electronic system.

**modus operandi** /ˌməʊdəs ɒpəˈrændiː/ method of working. [L]

**modus vivendi** /ˌməʊdəs vɪˈvendiː/ compromise pending settlement of dispute. [L]

**mogo** /'məʊgəʊ/ *n.* (*pl.* **-gos**) *Aus.* Abor. stone hatchet.

**mogul** /'məʊg(ə)l/ *n.* great or important person.

**mohair** /'məʊheə(r)/ *n.* hair of Angora goat; yarn or fabric from this.

**Mohammedan** var. of **Muhammaddan**.

**moiety** /'mɔɪəti/ *n.* half.

**moil** *v.i.* drudge.

**moiré** /'mwɑːreɪ/ *a.* (of silk) watered; like watered silk in appearance.

**moist** *a.* slightly wet, damp; rainy.

**moisten** /'mɔɪs(ə)n/ *v.* make or become moist.

**moisture** /'mɔɪstʃə(r)/ *n.* liquid diffused as vapour or condensed on surface.

**moisturize** /'mɔɪstʃəraɪz/ *v.t.* make less dry (esp. skin by use of cosmetic).

**moke** *n. sl.* donkey.

**molar** /'məʊlə(r)/ 1 *a.* serving to grind. 2 *n.* molar tooth.

**molasses** /məˈlæsəz/ *n.* syrup drained from raw sugar.

**mole**[1] *n.* small burrowing animal with short soft fur; *colloq.* spy established deep within organization. **molehill** mound thrown up by mole in burrowing.

**mole**[2] *n.* small permanent dark spot on human skin.

**mole**[3] *n.* massive stone etc. structure as pier or breakwater.

**molecule** /'mɒlɪkjuːl/ *n.* smallest particle (usu. group of atoms) to which

**molest** /mə'lest/ v.t. subject to intentional annoyance. **molestation** n.

**moll** n. colloq. prostitute; gangster's female companion.

**mollify** /'mɒlɪfaɪ/ v.t. soften, appease. **mollification** n.

**mollusc** /'mɒləsk/ n. one of a group of soft-bodied usu. hard-shelled animals including snails, oysters, etc.

**mollycoddle** /'mɒlɪkɒd(ə)l/ 1 v.t. coddle. 2 n. milksop.

**mollydooker** /'mɒlɪdu:kə(r)/ n. Aus. colloq. left-handed person.

**moloch** /'məʊlɒk/ n. slow-moving spiny Aus. lizard.

**molten** /'məʊlt(ə)n/ a. liquefied by heat.

**molto** /'mɒltəʊ/ adv. Mus. very.

**molybdenum** /mə'lɪbdənəm/ n. silverwhite metallic element used in steel for making high-speed tools etc.

**moment** /'məʊmənt/ n. point or brief space of time; importance, weight; Phys. product of force and distance of its line of action from centre of rotation.

**momentary** /'məʊməntərɪ/ a. lasting only a moment.

**momentous** /mə'mentəs/ a. having great importance.

**momentum** /mə'mentəm/ n. (pl. -ta) quantity of motion of moving body; impetus gained by movement.

**Mon.** abbr. Monday.

**monarch** /'mɒnək/ n. sovereign with title of king, queen, emperor, etc.; supreme ruler. **monarchic(al)** etc.

**monarchism** /'mɒnəkɪz(ə)m/ n. advocacy or principals of monarchy. **monarchist** n.

**monarchy** /'mɒnəkɪ/ n. monarchical government; State with this.

**monastery** /'mɒnəstərɪ/ n. residence of community, usu. of monks.

**monastic** /mə'næstɪk/ a. of or like monks, nuns, etc.; of monasteries. **monasticism** /-'næs-/ n.

**Monday** /'mʌndeɪ or -dɪ/ n. day of week following Sunday.

**monetarism** /'mʌnətərɪz(ə)m/ n. control of money as chief method of stabilizing economy. **monetarist** a. & n.

**monetary** /'mʌnətərɪ/ a. of the currency in use, (consisting of) money.

**money** /'mʌnɪ/ n. current medium of exchange in form of coins and banknotes etc.; in pl. (**moneys** or **monies**) sums of money; wealth. **moneychanger** person whose business it is to change money at stated rate; **moneylender** person lending money at interest; **money-market** sphere of operation of dealers in stocks and bills; **money order** post-office order for payment of specified sum; **money-spinner** thing that brings in much profit, kind of small spider.

**moneyed** /'mʌnɪd/ a. rich.

**mong** /mʌŋ/ n. Aus. sl. mongrel.

**Mongol** /'mɒŋg(ə)l/ 1 a. of Asian people now inhabiting Mongolia; (**mongol**) having Down's syndrome. 2 n. Mongol person; (**mongol**) person with Down's syndrome.

**Mongolian** /mɒŋ'gəʊlɪən/ 1 a. of Mongolia; Mongol; Mongoloid. 2 n. native or language of Mongolia.

**mongolism** /'mɒŋgəlɪz(ə)m/ n. Down's syndrome.

**Mongoloid** /'mɒŋgəlɔɪd/ 1 a. resembling Mongolians in racial origin or in having broad flat (yellowish) face; mongol. 2 n. Mongoloid person.

**mongoose** /'mɒŋgu:s/ n. small carnivorous tropical mammal.

**mongrel** /'mʌŋgr(ə)l/ 1 n. dog of no definable breed or type; any animal or plant resulting from crossings of different breeds or types. 2 a. of mixed origin or character.

**monitor** /'mɒnɪtə(r)/ 1 n. pupil in school with disciplinary etc. duties; television receiver used in selecting or verifying the broadcast picture; person who listens to and reports on foreign broadcasts etc.; detector of radioactive contamination. 2 v. act as monitor (of); maintain regular surveillance (over).

**monk** /mʌŋk/ n. member of community of men living apart under religious vows. **monkish** a.

**monkey** /'mʌŋkɪ/ 1 n. mammal of a group closely allied to man. 2 v.i. play tricks (*with*). 3 **monkey-nut** peanut; **monkey-puzzle** kind of prickly tree; **monkey-wrench** wrench with adjustable jaw.

**mono** /'mɒnəʊ/ 1 a. monophonic. 2 n. such sound, reproduction, etc.

**mono-** in comb. one, alone, single.

**monochromatic** /mɒnəkrə'mætɪk/ a. (of light) containing only one colour or wavelength; executed in monochrome.

**monochrome** /'mɒnəkrəʊm/ a. having or using only one colour.

**monocle** /'mɒnək(ə)l/ n. single eyeglass.

**monocular** /mə'nɒkjələ(r)/ a. with or for one eye.

**monody** /'mɒnədɪ/ n. dirge or elegy.

**monogamy** /mə'nɒɡəmɪ/ n. state or practice of being married to only one person at a time. **monogamous** a.

**monogram** /'mɒnəɡræm/ n. two or more letters, esp. initials, interwoven.

**monograph** /'mɒnəɡrɑːf or -ɡræf/ n. treatise on single subject or aspect of it.

**monolith** /'mɒnəlɪθ/ n. single block of stone, esp. shaped into pillar etc.; person or thing like monolith in being massive, immovable, or solidly uniform. **monolithic** a.

**monologue** /'mɒnəlɒɡ/ n. scene in drama where person speaks alone; dramatic composition for one speaker; long speech by one person.

**monomania** /mɒnə'meɪnɪə/ n. obsession of mind by one idea or interest. **monomaniac** n.

**monophonic** /mɒnə'fɒnɪk/ a. (of reproduction of sound) using only one channel of transmission.

**monoplane** /'mɒnəpleɪn/ n. aeroplane with one set of wings.

**monopolist** /mə'nɒpəlɪst/ n. holder or supporter of monopoly.

**monopolize** /mə'nɒpəlaɪz/ v.t. obtain exclusive possession or control of. **monopolization** n.

**monopoly** /mə'nɒpəlɪ/ n. exclusive trading privilege; sole possession or control.

**monorail** /'mɒnəʊreɪl/ n. railway in which track consists of single rail.

**monosodium glutamate** /mɒnə'səʊdɪəm 'ɡluːtəmeɪt/ substance added to food to enhance its flavour.

**monosyllable** /'mɒnəsɪləb(ə)l/ n. word of one syllable. **monosyllabic** a.

**monotheism** /'mɒnəθiːɪz(ə)m/ n. doctrine that there is only one God. **monotheist** n; **monotheistic** a.

**monotone** /'mɒnətəʊn/ n. sound continuing or repeated on one note or without change of pitch.

**monotonous** /mə'nɒtənəs/ a. lacking in variety, wearisome through sameness. **monotony** n.

**monoxide** /mə'nɒksaɪd/ n. oxide containing one oxygen atom.

*Monseigneur* /mɔ̃sen'jɜː(r)/ n. French title of princes, cardinals, etc. [F]

*Monsieur* /mə'sjɜː(r)/ n. (pl. *Messieurs* /mes'jɜː/) title used of or to French-speaking man. [F]

*Monsignor* /mɒnsiː'njɔː(r)/ n. title of some RC prelates etc. [It.]

**monsoon** /mɒn'suːn/ n. seasonal wind prevailing in S. Asia; rainy season accompanying SW monsoon.

**monster** /'mɒnstə(r)/ 1 n. imaginary large and frightening creature; misshapen animal or plant; inhumanly cruel or wicked person; huge animal or thing. 2 a. huge.

**monstrance** /'mɒnstrəns/ n. RC Ch. vessel in which consecrated Host is exposed.

**monstrosity** /mɒn'strɒsətɪ/ n. misshapen or outrageous thing; monstrousness.

**monstrous** /'mɒnstrəs/ a. like a monster; huge; outrageous.

**montage** /mɒn'tɑːʒ/ n. selection, cutting, and arrangement of shots in cinema film etc.; (picture etc. produced by) juxtaposition of (parts of) photographs etc.

**month** /mʌnθ/ n. any of 12 divisions of calendar year; any period between same dates in successive such portions; period of 28 days.

**monthly** /'mʌnθlɪ/ 1 a. produced or occurring once every month. 2 adv. every month. 3 n. monthly periodical.

**monument** /'mɒnjəmənt/ n. anything designed or serving to commemorate someone or something.

**monumental** /mɒnjə'ment(ə)l/ a. of or serving as monument; massive and permanent; great, stupendous.

**moo** 1 n. characteristic sound of cow. 2 v.i. make this sound.

**mooch** /muːtʃ/ v.i. colloq. loiter *about*; slouch *along*.

**mood**[1] /muːd/ n. state of mind or feeling.

**mood**[2] /muːd/ n. Gram. form(s) of verb serving to indicate whether it is to express fact or command or wish etc.; group of such forms.

**moody** /ˈmuːdi/ a. gloomy, sullen.
**Moomba** /ˈmʊmbə/ n. Aus. festival held in Melbourne in March.
**moon** /muːn/ 1 n. natural satellite of the earth, revolving round it monthly, reflecting light from the sun; *poet.* month; natural satellite of any planet. 2 v.i. move or look listlessly. 3 **moonbeam** ray of moonlight; **moonlight** light of moon, *colloq.* have other paid occupation besides official one; **moonlit** lighted by the moon; **moonshine** visionary talk, illicit liquor; **moonshot** launching of spacecraft to moon; **moonstone** feldspar with pearly appearance; **moonstruck** deranged in mind.
**moony** /ˈmuːni/ a. stupidly dreamy.
**moor**[1] /mʊə(r)/ n. UK tract of open waste land esp. if covered with heather. **moorhen** small water-hen; **moorland** country abounding in heather.
**moor**[2] /mʊə(r)/ v.t. attach (boat etc.) to fixed object.
**Moor**[3] /mʊə(r)/ n. one of a Muslim people of NW Africa. **Moorish** a.
**mooring** /ˈmʊərɪŋ/ n. (usu.in pl.) permanent anchors and chains for ships to be moored to; place where vessel is moored.
**moose** /muːs/ n. (pl. same) N. Amer. elk.
**moot** /muːt/ 1 v.t. raise (question etc.) for discussion. 2 a. debatable. 3 n. *hist.* assembly.
**mop** 1 n. sponge or bundle of yarn etc. fixed to stick for use in cleaning; thick untidy head of hair. 2 v. clean or wipe (as) with mop; wipe up (as) with mop. 3 **mop up** *sl.* absorb, dispose of, *Mil.* complete occupation of (area etc.) by capturing or killing remaining enemy troops etc.
**mope** v.i. be dull, dejected, and spiritless.
**moped** /ˈməʊped/ n. motorized bicycle.
**mopoke** /ˈməʊpəʊk/ n. Aus. boobook.
**moquette** /məˈket/ n. fabric with pile, used for upholstery etc.
**moraine** /mɒˈreɪn/ n. pile of debris carried down and deposited by glacier.
**moral** /ˈmɒr(ə)l/ 1 a. concerned with character etc. or with right and wrong; good, virtuous. 2 n. moral lesson; *Aus.* certainty; in pl. moral habits. 3 **moral certainty** probability so great as to allow no reasonable doubt; **moral support** psychological rather than physical help.
**morale** /mɒˈrɑːl/ n. mental attitude or bearing of person or group.
**moralist** /ˈmɒrəlɪst/ n. person who teaches morality. **moralistic** a.
**morality** /məˈrælɪti/ n. degree of conformity to moral principles; moral conduct; moralizing.
**moralize** /ˈmɒrəlaɪz/ v.i. indulge in moral reflection or talk. **moralization** n.
**morass** /məˈræs/ n. marsh, bog; entanglement.
**moratorium** /mɒrəˈtɔːriəm/ n. (pl. -iums) legal authorization to debtor to postpone payment; temporary prohibition or suspension.
**morbid** /ˈmɔːbɪd/ a. not natural and healthy; indicative etc. of disease. **morbidity** n.
**mordant** /ˈmɔːd(ə)nt/ 1 a. caustic, biting; (of acids etc.) corrosive. 2 n. mordant acid or substance.
**more** /mɔː/ 1 a. greater in quantity or degree. 2 n. greater quantity or number. 3 adv. to greater degree or extent or amount.
**morello** /məˈreləʊ/ n. (pl. -os) dark-coloured bitter cherry.
**moreover** /mɔːˈrəʊvə(r)/ adv. besides, in addition.
**morepork** /ˈmɔːpɔːk/ n. Aus. boobook.
**mores** /ˈmɔːriːz/ n.pl. social customs and moral principles etc. of class or group etc.
**Moreton bay** /ˈmɔːtən/ Aus. **Moreton bay bug** an edible crustacean; **Moreton bay chestnut** black bean; **Moreton bay fig** large fig-tree with smooth bark and glossy leaves.
**morganatic** /mɔːɡəˈnætɪk/ a. (of marriage) between man of high rank and woman of lower rank who remains in her former station.
**morgue** /mɔːɡ/ n. mortuary; materials kept for reference by newspaper etc.
**moribund** /ˈmɒrɪbʌnd/ a. at point of death.
**Mormon** /ˈmɔːmən/ n. member of Church of Latter-day Saints. **Mormonism** n.
**morn** n. *poet.* morning.
**morning** /ˈmɔːnɪŋ/ n. early part of day till noon or midday meal. **morning coat** tail-coat with front sloped away;

**morocco** /məˈrɒkəʊ/ n. (pl. -os) fine flexible leather of goatskin tanned with sumac.

**moron** /ˈmɔːrɒn/ n. adult with mental development of child of about 8 or 12; *colloq.* stupid person. **moronic** /-ˈrɒn-/ a.

**morose** /məˈrəʊs/ a. sullen, gloomy, and unsocial.

**morphia** /ˈmɔːfiə/ n. morphine.

**morphine** /ˈmɔːfiːn/ n. narcotic constituent of opium.

**morphology** /mɔːˈfɒlədʒi/ n. study of forms of animals and plants or of words and their structure. **morphological** a.

**morris dance** /ˈmɒrɪs/ traditional dance in fancy costume.

**morrow** /ˈmɒrəʊ/ n. following day.

**Morse** /mɔːs/ 1 n. the alphabet or code in which letters are represented by combinations of long and short signals. 2 a. of this alphabet or code.

**morsel** /ˈmɔːs(ə)l/ n. small quantity; mouthful, bit.

**mortal** /ˈmɔːt(ə)l/ 1 a. subject to or causing death; (of enemy) implacable. 2 n. human being. 3 **mortal sin** one fatal to salvation.

**mortality** /mɔːˈtælətɪ/ n. being subject to death; loss of life on large scale; death-rate.

**mortar** /ˈmɔːtə(r)/ n. mixture of lime and sand and water, for joining stones or bricks; short gun for throwing shells etc. at high angles; vessel in which drugs, food, etc. are pounded with pestle. **mortar-board** board for holding mortar, stiff square-topped academic cap.

**mortgage** /ˈmɔːgɪdʒ/ 1 n. conveyance of property as security for debt until money is repaid; sum of money lent by this. 2 v.t. make over by mortgage; pledge in advance.

**mortgagee** /mɔːgəˈdʒiː/ n. creditor in mortgage.

**mortgager** /ˈmɔːgədʒə(r)/ n. (in *Law* **mortgagor**) debtor in mortgage.

**mortician** /mɔːˈtɪʃ(ə)n/ n. *US* undertaker.

**mortify** /ˈmɔːtɪfaɪ/ v. humiliate, wound; bring (body etc.) into subjection by self-denial etc.; be affected with gangrene. **mortification** n.

**mortise** /ˈmɔːtɪs/ 1 n. hole in framework to receive another part, esp. tenon. 2 v.t. join by mortise and tenon; cut mortise in. 3 **mortise lock** one recessed in frame of door etc.

**mortuary** /ˈmɔːtjʊərɪ/ 1 n. building in which dead bodies may be kept for a time. 2 a. of death or burial.

**morwong** /ˈmɔːwɒŋ/ n. Aus. edible seafish.

**mosaic**[1] /məʊˈzeɪɪk/ 1 n. picture or pattern made with small coloured pieces of stone, glass, etc. 2 a. of or like such work.

**Mosaic**[2] /məʊˈzeɪɪk/ of Moses.

**moselle** /məʊˈzel/ n. dry German white wine.

**Moslem** /ˈmɒzləm/ var. of **Muslim**.

**mosque** /mɒsk/ n. Muslim place of worship.

**mosquito** /mɒsˈkiːtəʊ/ n. (pl. **-toes**) gnat, esp. with long blood-sucking proboscis. **mosquito-net** net to keep off mosquitoes.

**moss** n. small flowerless plant growing on moist surfaces; swamp, peat-bog. **moss-rose** rose with mosslike growth on calyx and stalk. **mossy** a.

**mossie** /ˈmɒzɪ/ n. Aus. *colloq.* mosquito.

**most** /məʊst/ 1 a. greatest in quantity or degree; the majority of. 2 n. the greatest quantity or degree; the majority. 3 adv. in great or greatest degree.

**mostly** /ˈməʊstlɪ/ adv. for the most part.

**mot** /məʊ/ n. (pl. **mots** /məʊz/) witty saying. **mot juste** /ʒuːst/ exactly appropriate expression. [F]

**mote** n. particle of dust.

**motel** /məʊˈtel/ n. roadside hotel or group of cabins for motorists.

**moth** /mɒθ/ n. mainly nocturnal lepidopterous insect like butterfly; kind of moth breeding in cloth etc. on which its larvae feed. **mothball** ball of naphthalene etc. kept with clothes etc. to repel moths; **moth-eaten** damaged by moths, *fig.* antiquated.

**mother** /ˈmʌðə(r)/ 1 n. female parent; head of female religious community etc.; old woman. 2 v.t. act like mother

**mothy** /ˈmɒθi/ *a.* infested with moths.

**motif** /məʊˈtiːf/ *n.* distinctive feature or dominant idea of design, music, etc.; ornament sewn or fastened on garment, vehicle, etc.

**motion** /ˈməʊʃ(ə)n/ **1** *n.* moving; gesture; formal proposal in deliberative assembly; application to judge or court for order etc.; evacuation of bowels. **2** *v.* make motion esp. to direct or guide person. **3 motion picture** cinema film.

**motionless** *a.* not moving.

**motivate** /ˈməʊtɪveɪt/ *v.t.* supply motive or inducement to; be motive of; stimulate interest of. **motivation** *n.*

**motive** /ˈməʊtɪv/ **1** *n.* what induces person to act. **2** *a.* productive of motion or action.

**motley** /ˈmɒtli/ **1** *a.* diversified in colour; of varied character. **2** *n. hist.* particoloured dress of jester.

**motor** /ˈməʊtə(r)/ **1** *n.* motive agent or force; apparatus, esp. internal combustion engine, supplying motive power for vehicle or machinery; motor car. **2** *a.* giving, imparting, or producing motion; driven by motor; of or for motor vehicles. **3** *v.* go or convey by car. **4 motor bike** *colloq.*, **cycle**, 2-wheeled motor-driven road vehicle; **motor car** motor-driven usu. 4-wheeled passenger road vehicle; **motorway** fast highway for motor vehicles.

**motorcade** /ˈməʊtəkeɪd/ *n.* procession or parade of motor cars.

**motorist** /ˈməʊtərɪst/ *n.* driver of motor car.

**motorize** /ˈməʊtəraɪz/ *v.t.* equip with motor transport; furnish with motor.

**mottle** /ˈmɒt(ə)l/ *v.t.* mark with spots or smears of colour.

**motto** /ˈmɒtəʊ/ *n.* (*pl.* **-oes**) maxim adopted as rule of conduct; inscription expressing appropriate sentiment or aspiration.

**mould**[1] /məʊld/ **1** *n.* hollow vessel in which fluid or plastic material is shaped or cast; pudding etc. shaped in mould; form or character. **2** *v.t.* shape (as) in mould; model.

**mould**[2] /məʊld/ *n.* furry growth of fungus on damp surface of organic material.

**mould**[3] /məʊld/ *n.* loose earth; soil rich in organic matter.

**moulder** /ˈməʊldə(r)/ *v.i.* decay to dust; crumble *away*.

**moulding** /ˈməʊldɪŋ/ *n.* ornamental strip applied to building etc.; material, esp. of wood, for this.

**mouldy** /ˈməʊldi/ *a.* covered with mould; out-of-date; *sl.* dull or miserable.

**moult** /məʊlt/ **1** *v.* shed (feathers) or shed feathers in changing plumage; (of animal) shed (hair) or shed hair etc. **2** *n.* moulting.

**mound** /maʊnd/ **1** *n.* heap or bank esp. of earth. **2** *v.t.* heap up in mounds.

**mount** /maʊnt/ **1** *v.* climb on to; put upon or provide with animal for riding; ascend; provide with or fix on or in support(s) or setting; organize, arrange. **2** *n.* mountain, hill; horse for person to ride; margin round picture etc.; card etc. on which drawing etc. is mounted; setting for gem etc. **3 mount guard** perform duty of guarding *over* thing etc.; **mount up** increase in amount.

**mountain** /ˈmaʊntən/ *n.* hill of impressive height; large heap or pile; large surplus stock. **mountain ash** scarlet-berried tree, any of several Aus. eucalypts; **mountain devil** *Aus.* moloch.

**mountaineer** /maʊntəˈnɪə(r)/ **1** *n.* person skilled in mountain-climbing. **2** *v.i.* climb mountains as recreation.

**mountainous** /ˈmaʊntənəs/ *a.* having many mountains, huge.

**mountebank** /ˈmaʊntəbæŋk/ *n.* swindler, charlatan.

**Mountie** /ˈmaʊnti/ *n. colloq.* member of Royal Canadian Mounted Police.

**mourn** /mɔːn/ *v.* feel sorrow or regret (for); grieve for loss of.

**mourner** *n.* person who mourns; person who attends funeral.

**mournful** /ˈmɔːnfəl/ *a.* doleful, sad.

**mourning** /ˈmɔːnɪŋ/ *n.* (wearing of) black clothes as sign of sorrow.

**mouse** /maʊs/ **1** *n.* (*pl.* **mice**) small rodent; small vole or shrew; shy or timid person; *Computers* device for

# mousse — mug

**moving** cursor on screen. **2** *v.i.* hunt mice. **3 mousy** *a.*

**mousse** /muːs/ *n.* dish of cold flavoured whipped cream, eggs, etc.

**moustache** /məˈstɑːʃ/ *n.* hair on upper lip.

**mouth 1** /maʊθ/ *n.* (*pl.* /maʊðz/) external opening in head, with cavity behind it containing organs for eating and speaking; opening of bag, cave, trumpet, volcano, etc.; place where river enters sea. **2** /maʊð/ *v.* utter or speak pompously; declaim; grimace; move lips silently. **3 mouth-organ** thin rectangular musical instrument played by blowing and sucking air through it; **mouthpiece** part of pipe, musical instrument, telephone, etc., placed between or near lips; **mouthwash** liquid antiseptic etc. for use in mouth.

**mouthful** /ˈmaʊθfʊl/ *n.* quantity of food or drink that fills the mouth; something difficult to say.

**move** /muːv/ **1** *v.* (cause to) change position, posture, place, or abode; move house; stir or rouse; affect with emotion; propose as resolution. **2** *n.* act or process of moving; change of residence, business premises, etc.; moving of piece at chess etc.; step or proceeding. **3** *mov* in take possession of new residence etc., so **move out**. **4 movable** *a.*

**movement** *n.* moving or being moved; moving part of mechanism; principal division of musical work; (group organized for) combined action or endeavour for particular end.

**movie** /ˈmuːvi/ *n. colloq.* cinema film.

**mow** /məʊ/ *v.* (*p.p.* **mowed** or **mown** /məʊn/) cut (grass etc.) with scythe or machine. **mower** *n.*

**moz** var. of **mock**².

**mozzle** /ˈmɒz(ə)l/ *n. Aus. colloq.* luck.

**MP** *abbr.* Member of Parliament.

**mp** *abbr.* mezzo piano.

**Mr** /ˈmɪstə(r)/ *n.* title prefixed to name of man.

**Mrs** /ˈmɪsəz/ *n.* title prefixed to name of married woman.

**Ms** /məz/ *n.* title prefixed to name of woman.

**MS** *abbr.* manuscript; multiple sclerosis.

**M.Sc.** *abbr.* Master of Science.

**MSS** /eˈmesəz/ *abbr.* manuscripts.

**Mt.** *abbr.* Mount.

**much** /mʌtʃ/ **1** *a.* existing in great quantity. **2** *n.* great quantity; noteworthy thing. **3** *adv.* in great degree; often; by great deal. **4 much of a muchness** very nearly the same.

**mucilage** /ˈmjuːsəlɪdʒ/ *n.* viscous substance got from plants; adhesive gum.

**muck 1** *n.* manure; dirt, filth; rubbish. **2** *v.* manure; make dirty; clean *out*; *sl.* fool or mess *about*. **3 muck in** *sl.* share tasks etc. (*with*); **muck-raking** seeking out and publishing of scandals etc.; **muck up** *sl.* bungle, make mess of. **4 mucky** *a.*

**mucous** /ˈmjuːkəs/ *a.* secreting or covered by mucus. **mucous membrane** skin lining nostrils and other cavities of body.

**mucus** /ˈmjuːkəs/ *n.* slimy substance secreted by mucous membrane.

**mud** *n.* wet soft earthy matter. **mud crab** large edible Aus. crab; **mudguard** hood on wheel as protection against mud; **mud map** *Aus. colloq.* sketch drawn in dirt with stick to give directions; **mud-slinging** abuse, slander.

**muddie** /ˈmʌdi/ *n. Aus. colloq.* mud crab.

**muddle** /ˈmʌd(ə)l/ **1** *v.* bewilder, confuse; bungle, mix *up*; act in confused ineffective manner. **2** *n.* muddled condition.

**muddy** /ˈmʌdi/ **1** *a.* like, covered in, or full of mud; confused; obscure. **2** *v.t.* make muddy.

**mudlark** /ˈmʌdlɑːk/ *n.* street urchin; *Aus.* magpie-lark.

**muesli** /ˈmuːzli/ *n.* food of crushed cereals, dried fruit, nuts, etc.

**muezzin** /muːˈezɪn/ *n.* Muslim crier who proclaims hours of prayer from minaret.

**muff**¹ *n.* cover of fur etc. for hands.

**muff**² *v.t.* fail in, bungle; miss (catch etc.).

**muffin** /ˈmʌfɪn/ *n.* light flat yeast cake eaten toasted and buttered.

**muffle** /ˈmʌf(ə)l/ *v.t.* wrap *up* for warmth; wrap up to deaden sound.

**muffler** *n.* wrap or scarf worn for warmth.

**mufti** /ˈmʌfti/ *n.* plain clothes as opp. uniform.

**mug**¹ **1** *n.* drinking-vessel, usu. cylindrical and with handle; *sl.* mouth, face;

**mug** *sl.* fool, gullible person. **2** *v.* rob with violence, esp. in public place; *sl.* make faces.

**mug**[2] *v. sl.* learn (subject) by hard study (with *up*).

**muggins** /'mʌgɪnz/ *n. colloq.* person who allows himself to be outwitted.

**muggy** /'mʌgi:/ *a.* warm, damp, and oppressive.

**Muhammadan** /məˈhæməd(ə)n/ **1** *a.* of Muhammad; Muslim. **2** *n.* a Muslim.

**mulatto** /mjuːˈlætəʊ/ *n.* (*pl.* -os) person of mixed White and Black parentage.

**mulberry** /'mʌlbəri/ *n.* tree bearing purple or white edible berries; fruit of this.

**mulch** /mʌltʃ/ **1** *n.* wet straw, leaves, etc. put round plant's roots. **2** *v.t.* treat with mulch.

**mulct** /mʌlkt/ *v.t.* extract money from by fine or taxation or fraudulent means.

**mule**[1] /mjuːl/ *n.* offspring of mare and he-ass; obstinate person; kind of spinning-machine.

**mule**[2] /mjuːl/ *n.* backless slipper or shoe.

**muleteer** /mjuːləˈtɪə(r)/ *n.* muledriver.

**mulga** /'mʌlgə/ *n. Aus.* scrubby variety of acacia; scrub, bush; club or shield made of mulga wood. **mulga snake** large brown snake; **mulga wire** *colloq.* bush telegraph.

**mulish** /'mjuːlɪʃ/ *a.* obstinate.

**mull**[1] *v.* ponder (*over*).

**mull**[2] *v.t.* heat and spice (wine, beer).

**mullah** /'mʌlə/ *n.* Muslim learned in Islamic law.

**mullet** /'mʌlɪt/ *n.* edible sea-fish.

**mulligatawny** /mʌlɪgəˈtɔːniː/ *n.* highly seasoned soup orig. from India.

**mullion** /'mʌljən/ *n.* vertical bar dividing panes of window.

**mullock** /'mʌlək/ *n. Aus.* mining refuse; rubbish. **poke mullock at** *sl.* ridicule.

**mulloway** /'mʌləweɪ/ *n.* large Aus. sea-fish.

**multi-** /'mʌltɪ/ *in comb.* many.

**multicoloured** /-kʌləd/ *a.* of many colours.

**multicultural** /-ˈkʌltʃər(ə)l/ *a.* promoting a number of cultures.

**multifarious** /-ˈfeərɪəs/ *a.* having great variety.

**multiform** *a.* having many forms, of many kinds.

**multilateral** /-ˈlætər(ə)l/ *a.* (of treaty etc.) in which 3 or more parties participate; having many sides.

**multilingual** /-ˈlɪŋgw(ə)l/ *a.* in or using many languages.

**multinational** /-ˈnæʃən(ə)l/ **1** *a.* of manufacturing company etc.) operating in several countries. **2** *n.* such company.

**multiple** /'mʌltəp(ə)l/ **1** *a.* having several or many parts, components, branches, kinds, etc. **2** *n. Math.* quantity exactly divisible by another. **3 multiple sclerosis** kind spreading to all or many parts of body.

**multiplicand** /mʌltɪpləˈkænd/ *n.* quantity to be multiplied.

**multiplication** /mʌltɪpləˈkeɪʃ(ə)n/ *n.* multiplying.

**multiplicity** /mʌltɪˈplɪsətɪ/ *n.* manifold variety, great number (*of*).

**multiplier** /'mʌltɪplaɪə(r)/ *n.* quantity by which multiplicand is multiplied.

**multiply** /'mʌltɪplaɪ/ *v.* find quantity produced by taking given quantity given number of times; make or become many.

**multi-purpose** *a.* serving more than one purpose.

**multiracial** /-ˈreɪʃ(ə)l/ *a.* composed of or concerning people of several races.

**multitude** /'mʌltɪtjuːd/ *n.* great number; throng; *the* common people. **multitudinous** *a.*

**mum**[1] *a.* silent. **mum's the word** say nothing.

**mum**[2] *n. colloq.* mother.

**mumble** /'mʌmb(ə)l/ **1** *v.* speak or utter indistinctly. **2** *n.* indistinct utterance.

**mumbo-jumbo** /mʌmbəʊˈdʒʌmbəʊ/ *n.* meaningless ritual; mystification, obscurity of language etc.

**mummer** /'mʌmə(r)/ *n.* actor in traditional mime.

**mummery** /'mʌmərɪ/ *n.* performance by mummers; ridiculous (esp. religious) ceremonial.

**mummify** /'mʌməfaɪ/ *v.* preserve (body) as mummy. **mummification** *n.*

**mummy**[1] /'mʌmɪ/ *n.* dead body preserved by embalming, esp. by ancient Egyptians.

**mummy**[2] /'mʌmɪ/ *n. colloq.* & *childish* mother.

**mumps** *n.pl.* infectious disease with swelling of neck and face.

**munch** /mʌntʃ/ *v.* chew steadily.

**mundane** /mʌn'deɪn/ *a.* dull, routine; of this world.

**municipal** /mju:'nɪsɪp(ə)l/ *a.* of municipality.

**municipality** /mju:nɪsɪ'pælɪtɪ/ *n.* town or district with local self-government; its governing body.

**munificent** /mju:'nɪfɪs(ə)nt/ *a.* splendidly generous. **munificence** *n.*

**muniment** /'mju:nɪmənt/ *n.* (usu. in *pl.*) document kept as evidence of rights or privileges.

**munitions** /mju:'nɪʃ(ə)nz/ *n.pl.* military weapons and ammunition and equipment and stores.

**mural** /'mjʊər(ə)l/ 1 *a.* of or in or on wall. 2 *n.* mural painting etc.

**murder** /'mɜ:də/ 1 *n.* unlawful and intentional killing of human being by another. 2 *v.t.* kill (human being) unlawfully; *colloq.* spoil by bad performance, mispronunciation, etc. 3 **murderer** *n.*; **murderess** *n.*; **murderous** *a.*

**murky** /'mɜ:kɪ/ *a.* dark, gloomy.

**murmur** /'mɜ:mə(r)/ 1 *n.* subdued continuous sound; hushed speech; subdued expression of discontent. 2 *v.* produce, say or speak in, murmur. 3 **murmurous** *a.*

**murrain** /'mʌrən/ *n.* infectious disease in cattle.

**Murray cod** /'mʌrɪ/ large edible mottled-green Aus. freshwater fish.

**muscadine** /'mʌskədɪn/ *n.* musk-flavoured kind of grape.

**muscat** /'mʌskət/ *n.* muscadine; wine made from this.

**muscatel** /mʌskə'tel/ *n.* muscadine; wine or raisin made from this.

**muscle** /'mʌs(ə)l/ 1 *n.* contractile fibrous band or bundle producing movement in animal body; lean flesh or meat; strength, power. 2 *v.i. sl.* force one's way *in.* 3 **muscle-bound** with muscles stiff through excessive exercise.

**muscular** /'mʌskjʊlə(r)/ *a.* of or affecting muscles; with well-developed muscles. **muscularity.** *n.*

**muse**[1] /mju:z/ *v.i.* ponder, meditate.

**Muse**[2] /mju:z/ *n.* Gk. *myth.* any of nine sister goddesses presiding over arts and sciences; **muse** poet's inspiration or genius.

**museum** /mju:'zi:əm/ *n.* place where objects illustrating antiquity, art, science, etc. are exhibited, studied, etc. **museum piece** object fit for museum, old-fashioned person etc.

**mush** /mʌʃ/ *n.* soft pulp; *fig.* feeble sentimentality; *US* maize porridge. **mushy** *a.*

**mushroom** /'mʌʃru:m/ 1 *n.* edible fungus with stem and domed cap. 2 *v.i.* expand rapidly; take mushroom shape; gather mushrooms. 3 **mushroom cloud** characteristic cloud produced by nuclear explosion.

**music** /'mju:zɪk/ *n.* art of combining sounds for reproduction by voice or instrument(s) in rhythmic, melodic, and harmonic form; sounds so produced; record or score of these for reproduction; any pleasant sound. **music centre** piece of equipment combining radio, record player, and tape recorder; **music-hall** variety theatre.

**musical** /'mju:zɪk(ə)l/ 1 *a.* of, fond of, skilled in, music; set to or accompanied by music; melodious. 2 *n.* play or film of which (esp. light) music is essential part.

**musician** /mju:'zɪʃ(ə)n/ *n.* person skilled in science or practice of music. **musicianship** *n.*

**musicology** /mju:zi:'kɒlədʒɪ/ *n.* study of history and forms of music. **musicological** *a.*; **musicologist** *n.*

**musk** *n.* substance secreted by male musk-deer used as basis of perfumes; plant with musky smell. **musk-deer** small hornless ruminant of Central Asia; **musk-melon** common melon; **musk-rat** (fur of) large N. Amer. aquatic rodent; **musk-rose** climbing rose with fragrant white flowers. **musky** *a.*

**musket** /'mʌskɪt/ *n. hist.* infantryman's (esp. smooth-bored) gun.

**musketeer** /mʌskɪ'tɪə(r)/ *n. hist.* soldier armed with musket.

**musketry** /'mʌskɪtrɪ/ *n.* muskets; art of using rifles or muskets.

**Muslim** /'mʊzlɪm/ 1 *n.* person believing in Allah as God according to revelations of Muhammad. 2 *a.* of Muslims or their religion.

**muslin** /'mʌzlɪn/ *n.* fine cotton fabric.

**musquash** /'mʌskwɒʃ/ *n.* musk-rat; its fur.

**mussel** /'mʌs(ə)l/ *n.* edible bivalve mollusc.

**must**[1] *v.aux.* (3 *sing.* **must**) be obliged to; be certain to. 2 *n. colloq.* something that cannot or should not be missed.

**must**[2] *n.* grape-juice before end of fermentation; new wine.

**mustang** /'mʌstæŋ/ *n.* wild horse of Mexico etc.

**mustard** /'mʌstəd/ *n.* plant with yellow flowers, seeds of which are ground and made into paste for use as condiment. **mustard gas** colourless oily liquid whose vapour is powerful irritant.

**muster** /'mʌstə(r)/ 1 *v.* bring or come together, collect; *Aus.* round up stock; summon *up* (courage etc.). 2 *n.* assembling of persons for inspection etc.; the process of rounding up stock. 3 **pass muster** be accepted as adequate.

**musty** /'mʌsti/ *a.* mouldy; antiquated, stale.

**mutable** /'mju:təb(ə)l/ *a.* liable to change; fickle. **mutability** *n.*

**mutant** /'mju:t(ə)nt/ 1 *a.* resulting from mutation. 2 *n.* mutant form.

**mutation** /mju:'teɪʃ(ə)n/ *n.* change; genetic change which when transmitted to offspring gives rise to heritable variation.

**mute** /mju:t/ 1 *a.* silent; refraining from speech; dumb; soundless. 2 *n.* dumb person; device to deaden sound of musical instrument. 3 *v.t.* muffle or deaden sound of.

**mutilate** /'mju:təleɪt/ *v.t.* injure, make imperfect, by depriving of part. **mutilation** *n.*

**mutineer** /mju:tə'nɪə(r)/ *n.* person who mutinies.

**mutinous** /'mju:tənəs/ *a.* rebellious.

**mutiny** /'mju:təni/ 1 *n.* open revolt against authority, esp. by members of armed forces. 2 *v.i.* engage in mutiny.

**mutt** *n. sl.* stupid person.

**mutter** /'mʌtə(r)/ 1 *v.* speak, utter, in low tone; grumble. 2 *n.* muttering.

**mutton** /'mʌt(ə)n/ *n.* flesh of sheep as food. **mutton-bird** *Aus.* short-tailed shearwater.

**mutual** /'mju:tjʊəl/ *a.* felt or done by each to other; bearing same relation to each other; *colloq.* common to two or more. **mutuality** *n.*

**muzzle** /'mʌz(ə)l/ 1 *n.* projecting part of animal's head including nose and mouth; open end of gun-barrel; cage etc. put on animal's muzzle. 2 *v.t.* put muzzle on; silence.

**muzzy** /'mʌzi/ *a.* confused, dazed; indistinct.

**MW** *abbr.* megawatt(s).

**my** /maɪ/ *pron., poss.* case of **I**, with *abs.* form **mine**.

**myall**[1] /'maɪəl/ *Aus.* 1 *n.* Aboriginal living in traditional way. 2 *a.* wild, uncivilized.

**myall**[2] /'maɪəl/ *n. Aus.* any of several acacias with hard sweet-scented wood.

**mycology** /maɪ'kɒlədʒi:/ *n.* study of fungi.

**myna(h)** var. of **mina**.

**myopia** /maɪ'əʊpiə/ *n.* short-sightedness. **myopic** /-'ɒp-/ *a.*

**myriad** /'mɪriəd/ 1 *n.* vast number. 2 *a.* innumerable.

**myrmidon** /'mɜ:mɪd(ə)n/ *n.* hired ruffian, menial servant.

**myrrh** /mɜː/ *n.* gum resin used in perfumes and medicine and incense.

**myrtle** /'mɜːt(ə)l/ *n.* evergreen shrub with fragrant white flowers.

**myself** /maɪ'self/ *pron. emphat.* and *refl.* form of **I**.

**mysterious** /mɪs'tɪəriəs/ *a.* full of or wrapped in or enjoying mystery.

**mystery** /'mɪstəri/ *n.* inexplicable matter; secrecy, obscurity; fictional work dealing with puzzling crime; revealed religious truth, esp. one beyond human understanding; in *pl.* secret religious rites; miracle-play. **mystery tour** pleasure excursion to unspecified destination.

**mystic** /'mɪstɪk/ 1 *n.* person who seeks union with deity through contemplation etc. or believes in spiritual apprehension of truths beyond understanding. 2 *a.* spiritually symbolic; esoteric; enigmatic. 3 **mystical** *a.*; **mysticism** *n.*

**mystify** /'mɪstɪfaɪ/ *v.t.* bewilder; confuse utterly. **mystification** *n.*

**mystique** /mɪs'tiːk/ *n.* atmosphere of mystery attending some activity or person.

**myth** /mɪθ/ *n.* traditional narrative usu. embodying esp. ancient popular belief or idea; fictitious person or thing; widely held but false idea. **mythical** *a.*

**mythology** /məˈθɒlədʒɪ/ *n.* body or study of myths. **mythological** *a.*; **mythologist** *n.*

**myxomatosis** /mɪksəməˈtəʊsəs/ *n.* virus disease in rabbits.

# N

**N.** *abbr.* North(ern).

**n** *n. Math.* indefinite number.

**n.** *abbr.* name; neuter; note.

**nab** *v.t. sl.* catch, arrest.

**nacre** /'neɪkə/ *n.* mother-of-pearl; shellfish yielding this. **nacreous** /'neɪkrɪəs/ *a.*

**nadir** /'neɪdɪə/ *n.* point of heavens opposite zenith; *fig.* lowest point.

**nag**¹ *v.* find fault (with) or scold persistently (*at*); (of pain etc.) be persistent.

**nag**² *n. colloq.* horse, esp. for riding.

**naiad** /'naɪæd/ *n.* water-nymph.

**nail** 1 *n.* horny covering of upper surface of tip of finger or toe; small usu. pointed and broad-headed metal spike. 2 *v.t.* fasten with nail(s); fix or hold tight; secure, catch. 3 **nail-tailed wallaby** kind of wallaby with nail-like tip to tail.

**nainsook** /'neɪnsʊk/ *n.* fine cotton fabric.

**naïve** /naː'iːv/ *a.* artless, unaffected; amusingly simple. **naïvety** /naː'iːvətɪ/ *n.*

**naked** /'neɪkəd/ *a.* unclothed, nude; without usual coverings or furnishings; unprotected; (of eye) unassisted.

**namby-pamby** /næmbɪ'pæmbɪ/ *a.* insipidly pretty; weakly sentimental.

**name** 1 *n.* word by which individual person, animal, place, or thing is spoken of or to; reputation, fame; family, clan. 2 *v.t.* give name to; speak of or to by name; nominate, appoint; identify; mention. 3 **name-day** day of saint after whom one is named; **namesake** person or thing of same name.

**nameless** /'neɪmləs/ *a.* obscure, left unnamed.

**namely** /'neɪmlɪ/ *adv.* that is to say, in other words.

**namma** var. of **gnamma**.

**nancy** /'nænsɪ/ *n. sl.* effeminate or homosexual young man.

**nankeen** /næŋ'kiːn/ *n.* yellow cotton cloth.

**nanny** /'nænɪ/ *n. UK* child's nurse or minder. **nanny goat** female goat.

**nannygai** /'nænɪɡaɪ/ *n.* small red edible Aus. salt-water fish.

**nano-** /'nænəʊ/ *in comb.* one thousand millionth.

**nap**¹ 1 *n.* short sleep, esp. by day. 2 *v.i.* have nap.

**nap**² *n.* surface of cloth consisting of fibre-ends raised, cut even, and smoothed.

**nap**³ 1 *n.* card-game; racing tip claimed to be almost a certainty. 2 *v.t.* name (horse) as almost certain winner. 3 **go nap** risk everything one has.

**napalm** /'neɪpɑːm/ *n.* jellied petrol for use as incendiary.

**nape** *n.* back of neck.

**naphtha** /'næfθə/ *n.* inflammable oil distilled from coal etc.

**naphthalene** /'næfθəliːn/ *n.* white crystalline substance used in manufacture of dyes etc. and in moth-balls.

**napkin** /'næpkən/ *n.* piece of linen etc. for wiping lips etc. at table; nappy.

**nappy** /'næpɪ/ *n.* piece of absorbent material wrapped round waist and between legs of baby.

**narcissism** /naː'sɪsɪz(ə)m/ *n.* abnormal self-love or self-admiration. **narcissistic** *a.*

**narcissus** /naː'sɪsəs/ *n.* kind of flowering bulb including daffodil.

**narcosis** /naː'kəʊsəs/ *n.* unconsciousness induced by narcotics.

**narcotic** /naː'kɒtɪk/ 1 *a.* inducing drowsiness, sleep, or insensibility. 2 *n.* narcotic drug or influence.

**nark** *sl.* 1 *v.t.* annoy, infuriate. 2 *n.* police spy, informer; *Aus.* unpleasant or obstructive thing or person etc.

**narrate** /nə'reɪt/ *v.t.* recount, relate, give continuous account of. **narration** *n.*; **narrator** *n.*

**narrative** /'nærətɪv/ 1 *n.* spoken or written recital of connected events in order. 2 *a.* of or by narration.

**narrow** /'nærəʊ/ 1 *a.* of small width in proportion to length; restricted; with little margin; narrow-minded. 2 *n.* (usu. in *pl.*) narrow part of sound, strait, river, or pass. 3 *v.* make or become narrower; lessen, contract. 4 **narrow boat** canal boat; **narrow-minded** intolerant, restricted in one's views.

**narwhal** /'naː(w)əl/ *n.* Arctic mammal of which male has long tusk.

**nasal** /'neɪz(ə)l/ 1 *a.* of nose; (of sounds) produced with nose passage open; (of

# nascent

voice etc.) having many nasal sounds. 2 *n.* nasal letter or sound.

**nascent** /'næs(ə)nt/ *a.* in process of birth; just beginning to be. **nascence** *n.*

**nasho** /'næʃəʊ/ *n. Aus. sl.* national service; man doing this.

**nasturtium** /nə'stɜːʃəm/ *n.* trailing garden plant with bright orange, red, or yellow flowers.

**nasty** /'nɑːstiː/ *a.* unpleasant, disagreeable; ill-natured, spiteful.

**Nat.** *abbr.* National(ist).

**natal** /'neɪt(ə)l/ *a.* of or from birth.

**nation** /'neɪʃ(ə)n/ *n.* community of people having common descent, language, history, or political institutions.

**national** /'næʃən(ə)l/ 1 *a.* of nation; common to or characteristic of whole nation. 2 *n.* citizen of specified State. **national service** service by conscription in armed forces.

**nationalism** /'næʃənəlɪz(ə)m/ *n.* patriotic feeling or principles; policy of national independence. **nationalist** *n.*

**nationality** /næʃə'nælətiː/ *n.* membership of nation; being national.

**nationalize** /'næʃənəlaɪz/ *v.t.* make national; convert (industry, etc.) into public ownership. **nationalization** *n.*

**native** /'neɪtɪv/ 1 *a.* inborn; by reason of (place of) one's birth; born in place, indigenous; of natives; occurring naturally; applied in Australia to many plants and animals similar but not necessarily related to European species. 2 *n.* person born in place; indigenous animal or plant. 3 **native cat** any of several predatory Aus. marsupials; **native companion** *Aus.* brolga.

**nativity** /nə'tɪvətiː/ *n.* birth, esp. of Christ.

**NATO** /'neɪtəʊ/ *abbr.* (also **Nato**) North Atlantic Treaty Organization.

**natter** /'nætə/ *colloq.* 1 *v.i.* chatter idly, grumble. 2 *n.* aimless chatter.

**natty** /'nætiː/ *a.* neat and trim.

**natural** /'nætʃər(ə)l/ 1 *a.* of or according to or provided by nature; physically existing; normal, not artificial; innate; to be expected; *Mus.* not flat or sharp. 2 *n.* person etc. naturally endowed, easy or obvious choice (*for*); *Mus.* natural note, sign indicating this. 3 **natural gas** fuel gas found in earth's crust; **natural history** study of animal and vegetable life; **natural selection** process favouring survival of organisms best adapted to environment.

**naturalism** /'nætʃərəlɪz(ə)m/ *n.* adherence to nature in art and literature, realism; philosophy based on nature alone. **naturalistic** *a.*

**naturalist** /'nætʃərəlɪst/ *n.* student of animals and plants.

**naturalize** /'nætʃərəlaɪz/ *v.t.* admit (alien) to citizenship; adopt (foreign word etc.), introduce (plant etc.) into new environment. **naturalization** *n.*

**naturally** /'nætʃərəliː/ *adv.* in natural manner; as might be expected, of course.

**nature** /'neɪtʃə/ *n.* phenomena of material world, physical power causing these; thing's essential qualities; innate character; kind, sort, class. **nature strip** *Aus.* piece of lawn in front of house or between fence or footpath and roadway or between carriageways of major road.

**naturist** /'neɪtʃərəst/ *n.* nudist. **naturism** *n.*

**naught** /nɔːt/ *arch.* 1 *n.* nothing. 2 *pred.a.* worthless.

**naughty** /'nɔːtiː/ *a.* badly behaved; disobedient; wicked; indecent.

**nausea** /'nɔːzɪə/ *n.* feeling of sickness, loathing.

**nauseate** /'nɔːzɪeɪt/ *v.t.* affect with nausea.

**nauseous** /'nɔːzɪəs/ *a.* loathsome.

**nautical** /'nɔːtɪk(ə)l/ *a.* of sailors or navigation. **nautical mile** approx. 1.85 km.

**nautilus** /'nɔːtələs/ *n.* kind of mollusc with spiral shell.

**naval** /'neɪv(ə)l/ *a.* of navy; of ships.

**nave**[1] *n.* body of church not including chancel and aisles.

**nave**[2] *n.* hub of wheel.

**navel** /'neɪv(ə)l/ *n.* depression on belly left by detachment of umbilical cord; central point of anything. **navel orange** one with navel-like formation at top.

**navigable** /'nævɪgəb(ə)l/ *a.* affording passage for ships; that can be steered. **navigability** *n.*

**navigate** /'nævɪgeɪt/ *v.* voyage, sail ship; sail or steam on or through (sea, river, air); manage, direct course of; indicate correct route. **navigator** *n.*

# navigation

**navigation** /nævə'geɪʃ(ə)n/ *n.* navigating; methods of determining ship's or aircraft's position and course.

**navvy** /'nævi:/ *n.* labourer excavating for canals, roads, etc.

**navy** /'neɪvi:/ *n.* State's warships with their crews and organization; officers and men of navy; fleet. **navy (blue)** very dark blue.

**nay** 1 *adv.* no; or rather, and even. 2 *n.* refusal.

**Nazi** /'nɑːtsiː/ 1 *n.* member of German National Socialist party. 2 *a.* of this party.

**NB** *abbr.* note well (*nota bene*).

**NCO** *abbr.* non-commissioned officer.

**NE** *abbr.* North-East(ern).

**Neanderthal** /niː'ændəθ(ə)l/ *a.* of type of man found in palaeolithic Europe.

**neap** *n.* (in full **neap tide**) tide of minimum height.

**Neapolitan** /niːə'pɒlɪtən/ 1 *a.* of Naples. 2 *n.* native of Naples.

**near** /nɪə(r)/ 1 *adv.* in or at a short distance in space or time; nearly; closely. 2 *prep.* near to in space, time, condition, or semblance. 3 *a.* close (*to*); closely related; (of way) direct, short; with little difference; left-hand; parsimonious. 4 *v.* draw near (to). 5 **nearsighted** short-sighted.

**nearby** /nɪə'baɪ/ *a.* close in position.

**nearly** /'nɪəliː/ *adv.* closely, almost. **not nearly** nothing like.

**neat** *a.* nicely made or proportioned; tidy, methodical; undiluted; cleverly done, phrased, etc.; deft, dextrous.

**neaten** /'niːt(ə)n/ *v.t.* make neat.

**neath** /niːθ/ *prep. poet.* beneath.

**nebula** /'nebjələ/ *n.* (*pl.* **-lae** /-liː/) luminous or dark patch in sky made by distant star-cluster or gas or dust. **nebular** *a.*

**nebulous** /'nebjələs/ *a.* cloudlike; hazy, vague. **nebulosity** *n.*

**necessary** /'nesəseri:/ 1 *a.* indispensable; that must be done; inevitable. 2 *n.* thing without which life cannot be maintained or is unduly harsh.

**necessitate** /nə'sesɪteɪt/ *v.t.* make necessary; involve as condition, result, etc.

**necessitous** /nə'sesɪtəs/ *a.* poor, needy.

**necessity** /nə'sesɪtiː/ *n.* constraint or compulsion regarded as law governing all human action; imperative need; indispensable thing; in *sing.* or *pl.* pressing need.

**neck** 1 *n.* part of body connecting head with shoulders; narrow part of anything, esp. connecting wider parts; part of garment round neck. 2 *v.i. sl.* kiss and caress amorously. 3 **necktie** band of material tied round shirt-collar.

**necklace** /'nekləs/ *n.* ornament of jewels, beads, etc. round neck.

**necklet** /'neklət/ *n.* ornament or fur garment for neck.

**necromancy** /'nekrəmænsɪ/ *n.* dealings with dead as means of divination; magic. **necromancer** *n.*

**necrophilia** /nekrə'fɪlɪə/ *n.* abnormal attraction to corpses.

**necropolis** /ne'krɒpələs/ *n.* cemetery.

**necrosis** /ne'krəʊsəs/ *n.* (*pl.* **-ses** /-siːz/) death of piece of bone or tissue. **necrotic** /-'krɒt-/ *a.*

**nectar** /'nektə/ *n.* sweet fluid produced by plants and made into honey by bees; *Myth.* drink of gods.

**nectarine** /'nektərɪːn/ *n.* downless kind of peach.

**née** /neɪ/ *a.* (before married woman's maiden name) born.

**need** 1 *n.* circumstances requiring some course of action; want, requirement; time of difficulty; destitution, poverty. 2 *v.* be in need of, require; be under necessity to do.

**needful** /'niːdfʊl/ *a.* requisite.

**needle** /'niːd(ə)l/ 1 *n.* pointed slender instrument pierced with eye for thread etc.; knitting-pin; instrument transmitting vibrations from revolving gramophone record; pointer of compass etc.; pointed instrument used in etching, surgery, etc.; pointed end of hypodermic syringe; leaf of fir or pine; sharp rock, peak; obelisk. 2 *v.t. colloq.* annoy, provoke. 3 **needlecord** finely ribbed fabric; **needle game, match**, etc., one closely contested or arousing exceptional personal feeling; **needlework** sewing or embroidery.

**needless** /'niːdləs/ *a.* unnecessary.

**needy** /'niːdiː/ *a.* poor, destitute.

**ne'er** /neə/ *adv. poet.* never. **ne'er-do-well** good-for-nothing person.

**nefarious** /nə'feərɪəs/ *a.* wicked.

**negate** /nə'geɪt/ *v.t.* nullify, deny existence of.

**negation** /nəˈgeɪʃ(ə)n/ n. denying; negative statement etc.; negative or unreal thing.

**negative** /ˈnegətɪv/ a. expressing or implying denial, prohibition, or refusal; lacking positive attributes; *Alg.* (of quantity) less than zero, to be subtracted; *Electr.* of, containing, producing, kind of charge carried by electrons, opposite to positive. 2 n. negative statement or word; *Photog.* developed film etc. bearing image having lights and shades of actual object reversed. 3 v.t. veto; serve to disprove; contradict; neutralize.

**neglect** /nəˈglekt/ 1 v.t. pay too little or no attention to; leave uncared for; leave undone. 2 n. neglecting or being neglected; negligence. 3 **neglectful** a.

**négligé** /ˈneglɪʒeɪ/ n. woman's light flimsy dressing-gown.

**negligence** /ˈneglɪdʒəns/ n. lack of proper care or attention; carelessness. **negligent** a.

**negligible** /ˈneglɪdʒəb(ə)l/ a. that need not be considered.

**negotiate** /nəˈgəʊʃiːeɪt/ v. confer with view to compromise or agreement; get or give money value for (bill, cheque); deal successfully with. **negotiable** a.; **negotiation** n.; **negotiator** n.

**Negress** /ˈniːgres/ n. female Negro.

**Negro** /ˈniːgrəʊ/ 1 n. (pl. -groes) member of black-skinned (orig.) African race. 2 a. of this race.

**Negroid** /ˈniːgrɔɪd/ 1 a. of group having characteristics typical of Negroes. 2 n. Negroid person.

**negus** /ˈniːgəs/ n. hot sweetened wine and water.

**neigh** /neɪ/ 1 n. cry of horse. 2 v.i. utter neigh.

**neighbour** /ˈneɪbə(r)/ n. person who lives next door or near by; fellow human being. 2 v. adjoin, border on or (*up*)on.

**neighbourhood** n. district; people of a district, vicinity.

**neighbourly** a. like good neighbour, friendly, helpful.

**neither** /ˈnaɪðə(r) or ˈniːðə(r)/ 1 adv. not either. 2 a. & pron. not the one or the other. 3 conj. arch. nor; nor yet.

**nelson** /ˈnels(ə)n/ n. wrestling hold in which arm is passed under opponent's arm from behind and hand applied to his neck.

**nem. con.** abbr. with no one dissenting (*nemine contradicente*).

**nemesis** /ˈneməsɪs/ n. justice bringing deserved punishment.

**neo-** in comb. new.

**neolithic** /niːəˈlɪθɪk/ a. of later Stone Age.

**neologism** /niːˈɒlədʒɪz(ə)m/ n. new word; word-coining.

**neon** /ˈniːɒn/ n. inert gas giving orange-red glow when electricity is passed through it.

**neophyte** /ˈniːəfaɪt/ n. new convert; religious novice; beginner.

**Neozoic** /niːəˈzəʊɪk/ a. of later period of geological history.

**nephew** /ˈnefjuː/ n. brother's or sister's son.

**nephritic** /nəˈfrɪtɪk/ a. of or in kidneys.

**nephritis** /neˈfraɪtɪs/ n. inflammation of kidneys.

**nepotism** /ˈnepətɪz(ə)m/ n. favouritism to relatives esp. in conferring offices etc.

**nereid** /ˈnɪərɪəd/ n. *Gk myth.* sea-nymph; *Zool.* kind of marine worm.

**nerve** /nɜːv/ 1 n. fibrous connection conveying impulses of sensation or motion between brain and other parts; presence of mind; coolness in danger; *colloq.* impudent boldness; in *pl.* nervousness, condition of mental and physical stress; *Bot.* rib of leaf. 2 v.t. give strength, vigour, or courage to.

**nerveless** /ˈnɜːvləs/ a. lacking vigour or spirit.

**nervous** /ˈnɜːvəs/ a. having disordered or delicate nerves; highly strung; timid; of the nerves; full of nerves. **nervous breakdown** severe disorder of the nerves; **nervous system** nerves as a whole.

**nervy** /ˈnɜːvi/ a. nervous, tense.

**ness** n. headland.

**nest** 1 n. structure or place in which bird lays eggs and shelters young; breeding-place or lair; snug retreat, shelter; brood, swarm; cluster or accumulation of similar objects. 2 v.i. make or have nest; (of objects) fit one inside another. 3 **nest-egg** money saved up as reserve.

**nestle** /ˈnes(ə)l/ v. settle oneself or be

**nestling** /ˈneslɪŋ/ n. bird too young to leave nest.

**net**¹ n. meshed fabric of cord, thread, hair, etc.; piece of this used for catching fish, keeping hair in place, enclosing area of ground e.g. in sport, etc. 2 v. cover, confine, catch, with net; send (ball) into net; make (cord etc.) into net. 3 **netball** game similar to basketball.

**net**² 1 a. remaining after necessary deductions; (of price) off which discount is not allowed; (of weight) not including wrappings etc. 2 v.t. yield (sum) as net profit.

**nether** /ˈneðə/ a. lower. **nethermost** a.

**nett** var. of **net**².

**netting** /ˈnetɪŋ/ n. netted fabric.

**nettle** /ˈnet(ə)l/ 1 n. plant covered with stinging hairs; plant resembling this. 2 v.t. irritate, provoke. 3 **nettle-rash** skin eruption like nettle-stings.

**network** /ˈnetwɜːk/ 1 n. arrangement of intersecting lines, complex system of; group of broadcasting stations connected for simultaneous broadcast of same programme. 2 v.t. broadcast thus.

**neural** /ˈnjʊər(ə)l/ a. of nerves.

**neuralgia** /njʊˈrældʒə/ n. intermittent pain in nerves esp. of face and head. **neuralgic** a.

**neurasthenia** /njʊərəsˈθiːnɪə/ n. debility of nerves causing fatigue etc. **neurasthenic** a.

**neuritis** /njʊˈraɪtɪs/ n. inflammation of nerve(s).

**neurology** /njʊˈrɒlədʒɪ/ n. scientific study of nerve systems. **neurological** a.; **neurologist** n.

**neurone** /ˈnjʊərəʊn/ n. (also **neuron**) nerve-cell and its appendages.

**neurosis** /njʊˈrəʊsɪs/ n. (pl. **-ses** /-siːz/) disorder of nervous system producing depression or irrational behaviour.

**neurotic** /njʊˈrɒtɪk/ 1 a. caused by or suffering from neurosis; colloq. obsessively anxious. 2 n. neurotic person.

**neuter** /ˈnjuːtə/ 1 a. Gram. neither masculine nor feminine. 2 n. neuter word etc.; neutered animal. 3 v.t. castrate.

**neutral** /ˈnjuːtr(ə)l/ a. taking neither side; impartial; vague, indeterminate; (of colours) not strong or positive; Chem. neither acid nor alkaline; Electr. neither positive nor negative. 2 n. neutral State or person; position of gear mechanism in which engine is disconnected from driven parts. 3 **neutrality** n.

**neutralize** /ˈnjuːtrəlaɪz/ v.t. make neutral; counterbalance; render ineffective. **neutralization** n.

**neutrino** /nuːˈtriːnəʊ/ n. Phys. (pl. **-nos**) elementary particle with zero electric charge and prob. zero mass.

**neutron** /ˈnjuːtrɒn/ n. Phys. elementary particle of about same mass as proton but without electric charge.

**never** /ˈnevə/ adv. at no time, not ever; not at all; colloq. surely not. **never mind** it does not matter; **the never-never** colloq. hire-purchase, Aus. colloq. remote areas esp. in Qld and NT.

**nevermore** /nevəˈmɔː/ adv. at no future time.

**nevertheless** /nevəðəˈles/ adv. for all that, notwithstanding.

**new** a. now first made, introduced, or discovered; fresh; additional; different, changed; recent; not worn. **New Australian** Aus. immigrant (esp. non-English-speaking one) to Australia; **new chum** Aus. sl. newcomer, esp. recent British immigrant, novice, inexperienced person; **newcomer** person recently arrived; **newfangled** different from what one is used to; **new moon** moon when first visible as crescent; **New Testament** part of Bible dealing with Christ and his followers; **New World** N. and S. America; **New Year's Day, Eve**, 1 Jan., 31 Dec.

**newel** /ˈnjuːəl/ n. centre pillar of winding stair; top or bottom post of stair-rail.

**newly** /ˈnjuːlɪ/ adv. recently, afresh.

**news** /njuːz/ n. new or interesting information; fresh events reported; broadcast report of news. **newsagent** dealer in newspapers etc.; **newsletter** printed informal bulletin of club etc.; **newspaper** /ˈnjuːs-/ printed publication usu. daily or weekly with news etc.; **newsprint** paper for newspapers; **newsreader** radio or television broadcaster of news reports; **newsreel** cinema film of recent news; **newsroom** room where news is prepared for publication or broadcasting; **newsworthy** worth reporting as news. **newsy** *a.*

**newt** /njuːt/ *n.* small tailed amphibian.

**next** 1 *a.* nearest; immediately following or preceding. 2 *adv.* in next place or degree, on next occasion. 3 *n.* next person or thing. 4 *prep. arch.* next to. 5 **next of kin** nearest living relative.

**nexus** /'nɛksəs/ *n.* connected group or series.

**niacin** /'naɪəsən/ *n.* nicotinic acid.

**nib** *n.* pen-point; in *pl.* crushed coffee- or cocoa-beans.

**nibble** /'nɪb(ə)l/ 1 *v.* take small bites at; bite gently or cautiously. 2 *n.* act of nibbling, esp. at bait.

**nice** /naɪs/ *a.* agreeable; kind, friendly, considerate; subtle, fine; fastidious.

**nicety** /'naɪsəti/ *n.* precision; subtle distinction or detail. **to a nicety** exactly.

**niche** /nɪtʃ, niːʃ/ *n.* shallow recess, esp. in wall; suitable place or position.

**nick** 1 *n.* small cut or notch; *sl.* prison, police station; *sl.* state, condition. 2 *v.t.* make nick(s) in; *sl.* catch, arrest, steal. 3 **in the nick of time** only just in time; **nick off** *Aus. sl.* depart rapidly.

**nickel** /'nɪk(ə)l/ *n.* silver-white metallic element used esp. in alloys and as plating; *US* 5-cent piece.

**nickname** /'nɪkneɪm/ 1 *n.* name jokingly added to or substituted for regular name. 2 *v.t.* give nickname to.

**nicotine** /'nɪkətiːn/ *n.* poisonous oily liquid got from tobacco.

**nicotinic acid** /nɪkə'tɪnɪk/ vitamin of B group.

**nictitate** /'nɪktɪteɪt/ *v.i.* blink, wink. **nictitation** *n.*

**niece** /niːs/ *n.* brother's or sister's daughter.

**nifty** /'nɪfti/ *a. colloq.* neat, smart, clever.

**niggard** /'nɪɡəd/ *n.* stingy person.

**niggardly** /'nɪɡədli/ *a.* stingy; given or giving grudgingly.

**niggle** /'nɪɡ(ə)l/ *v.* fuss over details, find fault in petty way; nag. **niggling** *a.*

**nigh** /naɪ/ *adv.* & *prep. arch.* near.

**night** /naɪt/ *n.* time from sunset to sunrise; (period of) darkness; nightfall; evening. **nightcap** drink before going to bed; **night-club** club open late at night; **night-dress**, **nightgown**, woman's or girl's loose garment for sleeping in; **nightfall** end of daylight; **nightjar** nocturnal bird with harsh cry; **night-life** entertainment available at night; **nightmare** terrifying dream or *colloq.* experience; **nightshade** any of various kinds of poisonous plant; **nightshirt** long shirt for sleeping in.

**nightingale** /'naɪtɪŋɡeɪl/ *n.* small bird of thrush family, the male of which sings much at night.

**nightly** /'naɪtli/ 1 *a.* happening or done or existing in the night; recurring every night. 2 *adv.* every night.

**nihilism** /'naɪɪlɪz(ə)m/ *n.* rejection of all religious and moral principles. **nihilist** *n.*; **nihilistic** *a.*

**nil** *n.* nothing.

**nimble** /'nɪmb(ə)l/ *a.* quick and light in movement; (of mind etc.) quick, clever.

**nimbus** /'nɪmbəs/ *n.* (*pl.* **-bi** /-baɪ/ or **-buses**) halo, aureole; *Meteor.* storm-cloud.

**nincompoop** /'nɪŋkəmpuːp/ *n.* foolish person.

**nine** *a.* & *n.* one more than eight. **ninepins** kind of skittles. **ninefold** *a.* & *adv.* **ninth** *a.* & *n.*

**nineteen** /naɪn'tiːn/ *a.* & *n.* one more than eighteen. **nineteenth** *a.* & *n.*

**ninety** /'naɪnti/ *a.* & *n.* nine times ten. **ninetieth** *a.* & *n.*

**ninny** /'nɪni/ *n.* foolish person.

**nip**¹ 1 *v.* pinch, squeeze sharply, bite; check growth of; *sl.* go nimbly. 2 *n.* pinch, sharp squeeze, bite; biting cold. 3 **nip in the bud** *fig.* stop at very beginning; **put the nips in** *Aus. sl.* ask for loan.

**nip**² *n.* small quantity of spirits.

**nipper** /'nɪpə/ *n.* claw of crab etc.; in *pl.* implement with jaws for gripping or cutting; *sl.* young boy or girl.

**nipple** /'nɪp(ə)l/ *n.* point of mammal's breast; teat of baby's bottle; nipple-like protuberance.

**nippy** /'nɪpi/ *a. colloq.* cold; nimble.

**nirvana** /nɜː'vɑːnə/ *n.* (in Buddhism and Hinduism) perfect bliss attained by extinction of individuality.

**nit**¹ *n.* egg of louse or other parasite; *sl.* stupid person. **nit-picking** *colloq.* petty fault-finding.

**nit**² *n. Aus. sl.* **keep nit** keep watch.

**nitrate** /'naɪtreɪt/ *n.* salt of nitric acid.

**nitre** /'naɪtə/ *n.* saltpetre.

**nitric acid** /'naɪtrɪk/ pungent corrosive caustic liquid.

**nitrogen** /'naɪtrədʒ(ə)n/ n. gas forming four-fifths of atmosphere.

**nitrogenous** /naɪ'trɒdʒənəs/ a. containing nitrogen.

**nitro-glycerine** /naɪtrəʊ'glɪsəriːn/ n. yellowish oily violently explosive liquid.

**nitrous** /'naɪtrəs/ a. of, like, or impregnated with nitre.

**nitty-gritty** /nɪti'grɪti/ n. sl. realities or basic facts of a matter.

**nitwit** /'nɪtwɪt/ n. colloq. stupid person.

**nix** n. sl. nothing.

**NNE** abbr. north north-east.

**NNW** abbr. north north-west.

**no** /nəʊ/ **1** particle used to express negative reply to question, request, etc. **2** a. not any, not one; not a. **3** adv. not; by no amount; not at all. **4** n. (pl. **noes**) word no, denial or refusal; in pl. voters against motion. **5 no-ball** unlawfully delivered ball in cricket etc.; **no-hoper** Aus. colloq. useless person etc; **no one** nobody; **no way** colloq. it is impossible.

**No.** abbr. number.

**nob**[1] n. sl. person of wealth or high social standing. **nobby** a.

**nob**[2] n. sl. head.

**nobble** /'nɒb(ə)l/ v.t. sl. tamper with (racehorse etc.); get hold of dishonestly; catch.

**nobbler** /'nɒblə(r)/ n. Aus. sl. glass or drink of alcoholic liquor.

**nobility** /nəʊ'bɪləti/ n. nobleness of character or rank; class of nobles.

**noble** /'nəʊb(ə)l/ **1** a. belonging to the aristocracy; of excellent character; magnanimous; of imposing appearance. **2** n. nobleman; noblewoman. **3 nobleman, -woman**, peer(ess).

**noblesse oblige** /nə'bles ə'bliːʒ/ privilege entails responsibility. [F]

**nobody** /'nəʊbədi/ **1** pron. no person. **2** n. person of no importance.

**nock** n. notch on bow or arrow for bowstring.

**nocturnal** /nɒk'tɜːn(ə)l/ a. of or done or active in the night.

**nocturne** /'nɒktɜːn/ n. dreamy musical piece; picture of night scene.

**nod 1** v. incline head slightly and quickly; let head droop, be drowsy; bend and sway; make slip or mistake. **2** n. nodding of head esp. in assent.

**noddle** /'nɒd(ə)l/ n. colloq. head.

**node** n. knob on root or branch; point at which leaves spring; hard swelling; point or line of rest in vibrating body; point at which curve crosses itself; intersecting-point esp. of planet's orbit and ecliptic. **nodal** a.

**nodule** /'nɒdjuːl/ n. small rounded lump of anything; small knotty tumour, ganglion. **nodular** a.

**noggin** /'nɒgɪn/ n. small mug; small measure of liquor.

**Noh** /nəʊ/ n. traditional Japanese drama.

**noise** /nɔɪz/ **1** n. sound, esp. loud or unpleasant one. **2** v.t. make public, spread abroad.

**noisome** /'nɔɪsəm/ a. noxious, disgusting.

**noisy** /'nɔɪzi/ a. loud; full of or making much noise; rowdy. **noisy miner** Aus. a honey-eating bird.

**nomad** /'nəʊmæd/ n. member of tribe roaming from place to place for pasture; wanderer. **nomadic** a.

**nom de plume** /nɒm də 'pluːm/ writer's assumed name. [F]

**nomenclature** /nə'menklətʃə/ n. system of names or naming; terminology.

**nominal** /'nɒmən(ə)l/ a. of or like noun; in name or word only; not real or substantial.

**nominate** /'nɒməneɪt/ v.t. appoint to or propose for election to office. **nomination** n.; **nominator** n.

**nominative** /'nɒmənətɪv/ Gram. **1** n. case expressing subject of verb. **2** a. of or in nominative. **3 nominatival** /-'taɪv-/ a.

**nominee** /nɒmə'niː/ n. person who is nominated.

**non-** in comb. not. For the meanings of combinations not given below the main word should be consulted.

**nonage** /'nəʊnɪdʒ/ n. being under age.

**nonagenarian** /nəʊnədʒə'neəriːən/ n. person between 90 and 99 years old.

**non-belligerent 1** a. taking no active or open part in war. **2** n. such State.

**nonce** /nɒns/ n. time being, present. **nonce-word** one coined for one occasion.

**nonchalant** /'nɒnʃəl(ə)nt/ a. unmoved, indifferent, cool. **nonchalance** n.

**non-combatant 1** a. not fighting, esp.

**non-commissioned** *a.* not holding commission (esp. of Army officers below second lieutenant).

**non-committal** *a.* not committing oneself to definite view, course of action, etc.

**non-conductor** *n.* substance that does not conduct heat or electricity.

**nonconformist** *n.* person who does not conform, esp. (**Nonconformist**) member of Protestant sect dissenting from Anglican Church. **nonconformity** *n.*

**non-contributory** *a.* not involving contributions.

**nondescript** /'nɒndəskrɪpt/ **1** *a.* hard to classify, indeterminate. **2** *n.* such person or thing.

**none** /nʌn/ **1** *pron.* not any of; no person(s). **2** *a.* no, not any. **3** *adv.* by no amount, not at all.

**nonentity** /nɒ'nentətɪ/ *n.* person of no importance; non-existence.

**nonesuch** var. of **nonsuch**.

**non-event** *n.* occurrence of no significance.

**non-existent** *a.* not existing. **non-existence** *n.*

**non-fiction** *n.* literary matter based on fact (opp. novels etc.).

**nong** *n.* Aus. sl. foolish person.

**non-interference** *n.* policy of non-intervention.

**non-intervention** *n.* policy of not interfering in affairs of other State(s).

**nonpareil** /'nɒnpər(ə)l/ **1** *a.* unrivalled, unique. **2** *n.* such person or thing.

**non-party** *a.* independent of political parties.

**nonplus** /nɒn'plʌs/ *v.t.* (**nonplussed**) completely perplex.

**nonsense** /'nɒnsəns/ **1** *n.* absurd or meaningless words or ideas; foolish conduct. **2** *int.* you are talking nonsense. **3 nonsensical** /-'sen-/ *a.*

**non sequitur** /nɒn 'sekwətə/ conclusion that does not follow from the premises. [L]

**non-skid** *a.* that does not or is designed not to skid.

**non-smoker** *n.* person who does not smoke; compartment in train etc. where smoking is forbidden.

**non-starter** *n. fig.* idea, person, etc., not worth considering.

**non-stick** *a.* to which food will not adhere in cooking.

**non-stop 1** *a.* (of train etc.) not stopping at intermediate stations; done without stopping. **2** *adv.* without stopping.

**nonsuch** /'nʌnsʌtʃ/ *n.* unrivalled person or thing; paragon.

**noodle**¹ /'nu:d(ə)l/ *n.* strip of pasta used in soup etc.

**noodle**² /'nu:d(ə)l/ *n.* simpleton.

**noodle**³ /'nu:d(ə)l/ *v.i.* Aus. look for opals in mullock.

**nook** /nʊk/ *n.* secluded corner or recess.

**noon** /nu:n/ *n.* 12 o'clock in day, midday. **noonday** midday.

**noose** /nu:s/ **1** *n.* loop with running knot; snare. **2** *v.t.* catch with or enclose in noose.

**nor** *conj.* and not, neither, and no more.

**Nordic** /'nɔːdɪk/ *a.* of tall blond Germanic people of N. Europe, esp. Scandinavia.

**Norfolk pine** /'nɔːfək/ (also **Norfolk Island pine**) Aus. a coniferous evergreen tree.

**nork** *n.* Aus. sl. (usu. in *pl.*) woman's breast.

**norm** *n.* standard, type; standard amount; customary behaviour.

**normal** /'nɔːm(ə)l/ **1** *a.* conforming to standard, usual, regular, typical. **2** *n.* usual state, level, etc. **3 normalcy** *n.*; **normality** *n.*; **normalize** *v.t.*

**Norman** /'nɔːm(ə)n/ **1** *n.* native of Normandy. **2** *a.* of Normans or their style of medieval architecture; of Normandy.

**Norse** /nɔːs/ **1** *n.* the Scandinavian language-group. **2** *a.* of ancient Scandinavia, esp. Norway.

**north** /nɔːθ/ **1** *n.* point of horizon to left of person facing east; northern part of country etc. **2** *a.* situated etc. in or towards north; facing north; (of wind) blowing from north. **3** *adv.* towards or in north. **4 north-east, -west,** (compass-point) half-way between north and east, west; **North Star** pole-star. **5 northward** *a., adv., & n.;* **northwards** *adv.*

**northerly** /'nɔːðəlɪ/ *a. & adv.* in northern position or direction; (of wind) blowing from north.

**northern** /'nɔːð(ə)n/ *a.* of or in the

**north. northern lights** aurora borealis.

**northerner** /ˈnɔːðənə(r)/ *n.* native or inhabitant of the north.

**Norwegian** /nɔːˈwiːdʒən/ **1** *a.* of Norway. **2** *n.* native or language of Norway.

**nose** /nəʊz/ *n.* organ on face or head above mouth, used for smelling and breathing; sense of smell; odour or perfume; open end of nozzle of pipe etc.; projecting part, front end. **2** *v.* perceive smell of, discover by smell; smell *out*; thrust nose against or into; pry or search; make one's way cautiously forward. **3 nosebag** fodder-bag hung on horse's head; **nosebleed** bleeding from nose; **nose-cone** cone-shaped nose of rocket, etc.; **nosedive** (make) steep downward plunge; **on the nose** *Aus. sl.* no good, objectionable.

**nosegay** /ˈnəʊzgeɪ/ *n.* small bunch of flowers.

**nosh** *sl.* **1** *v.* eat or drink. **2** *n.* food or drink. **3 nosh-up** large meal.

**nostalgia** /nɒsˈtældʒə/ *n.* homesickness; sentimental yearning for the past. **nostalgic** *a.*

**nostril** /ˈnɒstrəl/ *n.* either of two openings in nose.

**nostrum** /ˈnɒstrəm/ *n.* quack remedy, patent medicine; pet scheme.

**nosy** /ˈnəʊzɪ/ *a.* inquisitive, prying.

**not** *adv.* expressing negation, refusal, or denial. **not half** *sl.* very much, very.

**notable** /ˈnəʊtəb(ə)l/ **1** *a.* worthy of note, striking, eminent. **2** *n.* eminent person. **3 notability** *n.*

**notary** /ˈnəʊtərɪ/ *n.* person with authority to draw up deeds and perform other legal formalities. **notarial** /-ˈteərɪ-/ *a.*

**notation** /nəʊˈteɪʃ(ə)n/ *n.* representing of numbers, quantities, etc. by symbols; set of such symbols.

**notch 1** *n.* V-shaped indentation on edge or surface. **2** *v.t.* make notches in; score (*up*) by notches.

**note 1** *n.* brief record of facts etc.; short letter; annotation in book; banknote; formal diplomatic communication; notice, attention; eminence; written sign representing pitch and duration of musical sound; single tone of definite pitch made by instrument, voice, etc.; sign, characteristic. **2** *v.t.* observe, notice; set *down* as thing to be remembered; in *p.p.* celebrated, well known *for.* **3 notebook** book for memoranda etc.; **notecase** wallet for banknotes; **notepaper** paper for private correspondence.

**notelet** /ˈnəʊtlət/ *n.* small folded card etc. for informal letter.

**noteworthy** /ˈnəʊtwɜːðɪ/ *a.* worthy of attention; remarkable.

**nothing** /ˈnʌθɪŋ/ **1** *n.* no thing, not anything, nought; thing of no importance; no amount. **2** *adv.* not at all; in no way.

**nothingness** *n.* non-existence; worthlessness.

**notice** /ˈnəʊtɪs/ **1** *n.* heed, attention, intimation, warning, announcement; formal declaration of intention to end agreement or employment; review or comment in newspaper etc. **2** *v.t.* perceive, take notice of; remark upon. **3 noticeable** *a.*

**notifiable** /ˈnəʊtɪfaɪəb(ə)l/ *a.* (of disease etc.) that must be notified to the authorities.

**notify** /ˈnəʊtɪfaɪ/ *v.t.* report, give notice of; inform. **notification** *n.*

**notion** /ˈnəʊʃ(ə)n/ *n.* concept, idea; view, opinion; intention.

**notional** /ˈnəʊʃənəl/ *a.* speculative, imaginary.

**notorious** /nəʊˈtɔːrɪəs/ *a.* well-known, esp. for unfavourable reason. **notoriety** /nəʊtəˈraɪətɪ/ *n.*

**notwithstanding** /nɒtwɪðˈstændɪŋ/ **1** *prep.* in spite of. **2** *adv.* nevertheless.

**nougat** /ˈnuːgɑː/ *n.* sweet made of sugar and honey and nuts etc.

**nought** /nɔːt/ *n.* figure 0; nothing.

**noun** /naʊn/ *n.* word used as name of person or thing etc.

**nourish** /ˈnʌrɪʃ/ *v.t.* sustain with food; foster, cherish, nurse.

**nourishment** *n.* sustenance, food.

**nous** /naʊs/ *n. colloq.* common sense.

**Nov.** *abbr.* November.

**nova** /ˈnəʊvə/ *n.* (*pl.* **-vae** /-viː/ *or* **-vas**) star showing sudden large increase of brightness and then subsiding.

**novel** /ˈnɒv(ə)l/ **1** *a.* of new kind, strange, hitherto unknown. **2** *n.* fictitious prose story published as complete book.

**novelette** /nɒvəˈlet/ *n.* short (esp. romantic) novel.

**novelist** /ˈnɒvəlɪst/ *n.* writer of novels.

**novella** /nə'velə/ *n.* short novel or narrative tale.

**novelty** /'nɒvəlti:/ *n.* newness; new thing or occurrence; small toy etc.

**November** /nəʊ'vembə/ *n.* eleventh month of year.

**novena** /nə'vi:nə/ *n. RC Ch.* special prayers or services on 9 successive days.

**novice** /'nɒvəs/ *n.* probationary member of religious order; beginner.

**noviciate** /nə'vɪʃi:ət/ *n.* (also **novitiate**) period of being a novice; religious novice.

**now** /naʊ/ 1 *adv.* at present or mentioned time; in immediate past. 2 *conj.* (also with *that*) as, since. 3 *n.* this time; present. 4 **now and then** occasionally.

**nowadays** /'naʊədeɪz/ 1 *adv.* at the present day. 2 *n.* the present day.

**nowhere** /'nəʊweə/ 1 *adv.* in or to no place. 2 *pron.* no place.

**noxious** /'nɒkʃəs/ *a.* harmful, unwholesome.

**nozzle** /'nɒz(ə)l/ *n.* spout of hose-pipe etc.

**nr.** *abbr.* near.

**NSW** *abbr.* New South Wales.

**NT** *abbr.* New Testament; Northern Territory.

**nuance** /'nju:ɑ̃s/ *n.* subtle difference in or shade of meaning, colour, etc.

**nub** *n.* point or gist (*of* matter etc.).

**nubile** /'nju:baɪl/ *a. n.* (of woman) marriageable, sexually attractive. **nubility** /-'bɪl-/ *n.*

**nuclear** /'nju:kli:ə/ *a.* of or relating to or constituting a nucleus; using nuclear energy. **nuclear energy** energy released or absorbed during reactions in atomic nuclei; **nuclear family** father, mother, and child(ren); **nuclear fuel** source of nuclear energy; **nuclear physics** dealing with atomic nuclei; **nuclear power** power derived from nuclear energy.

**nucleic acid** /nju:'kli:ɪk/ either of two acids (DNA and RNA) present in all living cells.

**nucleus** /'nju:kli:əs/ *n.* (*pl.* **-clei** /-kli:aɪ/) central part or thing round which others collect; central part of atom, of seed, or of plant or animal cell; kernel.

**nude** /nju:d/ 1 *a.* naked, unclothed. 2 *n.* nude figure in painting etc.; nude person. 3 **the nude** unclothed state. 4 **nudity** *n.*

**nudge** /nʌdʒ/ 1 *v.t.* push with elbow to draw attention privately; push in gradual manner. 2 *n.* such push.

**nudist** /'nju:dəst/ *n.* person who advocates or practises going unclothed. **nudism** *n.*

**nugatory** /'nju:gətəri:/ *a.* futile, trifling; inoperative, not valid.

**nugget** /'nʌgət/ *n.* rough lump of gold etc.

**nuggety** /'nʌgəti:/ *a. Aus.* thickset; short and sturdy.

**nuisance** /'nju:səns/ *n.* source of annoyance; obnoxious act or circumstance or thing or person.

**null** *a.* void, not valid; expressionless. **nullity** *n.*

**nulla** /'nʌlə/ *n.* (also **nulla nulla**) hardwood club used by Aborigines.

**nullify** /'nʌləfaɪ/ *v.t.* neutralize; make invalid. **nullification** *n.*

**numb** /nʌm/ 1 *a.* deprived of feeling or power of motion. 2 *v.t.* make numb.

**numbat** /'nʌmbæt/ *n.* small slender reddish-brown insectivorous Aus. marsupial.

**number** /'nʌmbə/ 1 *n.* aggregate of units, sum, company; word or symbol stating how many; numbered person or thing, esp. single issue of periodical etc.; item, song, etc., in programme. 2 *v.t.* count; mark or distinguish with number; include *in, with,* etc.; have or amount to specified number; in *p.p.* be restricted in number. 3 **number one** *colloq.* oneself; **number-plate** plate bearing number esp. of motor vehicle.

**numberless** /'nʌmbələs/ *a.* innumerable.

**numeral** /'nju:mər(ə)l/ 1 *n.* word or symbol denoting a number. 2 *a.* of or denoting a number.

**numerate** /'nju:mərət/ *a.* familiar with basic elements of mathematics or science. **numeracy** *n.*

**numeration** /nju:mə'reɪʃ(ə)n/ *n.* numbering.

**numerator** /'nju:məreɪtə/ *n. Math.* number above line in vulgar fraction.

**numerical** /nju:'merɪk(ə)l/ *a.* of, in, denoting, etc. number(s).

**numerology** /nju:mə'rɒlədʒi:/ *n.* study of occult significance of numbers.

**numerous** /'nju:mərəs/ *a.* many; consisting of many.

**numinous** /'nju:mənəs/ *a.* indicating presence or influence of a god.

**numismatic** /nju:məz'mætɪk/ *a.* of coins or medals.

**numismatics** *n.pl.* (usu. treated as *sing.*) study of coins and medals. **numismatist** /-'mɪz-/ *n.*

**nun** *n.* member of community of women living apart under religious vows.

**nuncio** /'nʌnʃi:əʊ/ *n.* (*pl.* **-cios**) Pope's diplomatic representative.

**nunnery** /'nʌnəri/ *n.* convent of nuns.

**nuptial** /'nʌpʃ(ə)l/ **1** *a.* of marriage or wedding. **2** *n.* in *pl.* wedding.

**nurse** /nɜ:s/ **1** *n.* person trained for care of sick; woman employed to take charge of young children. **2** *v.* work as nurse; be nurse (of), tend; suckle; cherish; hold or treat carefully. **3 nursing home** private hospital.

**nursemaid** /'nɜ:smeɪd/ *n.* young woman in charge of child(ren).

**nursery** /'nɜ:səri/ *n.* room or place for children; place where plants are reared esp. for sale. **nurseryman** grower of plants etc. for sale; **nursery rhyme** traditional verse story for young children; **nursery school** school for young children under school age.

**nurture** /'nɜ:tʃə(r)/ **1** *n.* bringing up, fostering, care; nourishment. **2** *v.t.* bring up, rear.

**nut** *n.* fruit consisting of hard shell enclosing edible kernel; this kernel; small usu. hexagonal piece of metal with hole through it, screwed on end of bolt for securing it; *sl.* head; *sl.* crazy person; small lump of coal, butter, etc. **2** *v.* seek or gather nuts; *sl.* strike with the head. **3 nutcase** *sl.* crazy person; **nutcrackers** instrument for cracking nuts.

**nutation** /nju:'teɪʃ(ə)n/ *n.* nodding; oscillation of earth's axis.

**nuthatch** /'nʌthætʃ/ *n.* small climbing bird.

**nutmeg** /'nʌtmeg/ *n.* hard aromatic seed of E. Ind. tree used ground or grated as spice etc.

**nutria** /'nju:trɪə/ *a.* fur of coypu.

**nutrient** /'nju:trɪ(ə)nt/ **1** *a.* serving as or providing nourishment. **2** *n.* nutrient substance.

**nutriment** /'nju:trɪmənt/ *n.* nourishing food.

**nutrition** /nju:'trɪʃ(ə)n/ *n.* food, nourishment. **nutritional** *a.*

**nutritious** /nju:'trɪʃəs/ *a.* efficient as food.

**nutritive** /'nju:trətɪv/ *a.* of nutrition; nutritive.

**nuts** *pred.a. sl.* crazy.

**nutshell** /'nʌtʃel/ *n.* hard covering of nut. **in a nutshell** in a few words.

**nutter** /'nʌtə/ *n. sl.* crazy person.

**nutty** /'nʌti/ *a.* full of nuts; tasting of nuts; *sl.* crazy.

**nux vomica** /nʌks 'vɒmɪkə/ seed of E. Indian tree, yielding strychnine.

**nuzzle** /'nʌz(ə)l/ *v.* prod or rub gently with nose; nestle, lie snug.

**NW** *abbr.* North-West(ern).

**NY** *abbr.* New York.

**nylon** /'naɪlɒn/ *n.* strong light synthetic polymer; fabric of this; in *pl.* stockings of nylon.

**nymph** /nɪmf/ *n.* mythological semi-divine female spirit of sea or woods etc.; *Zool.* immature form of some insects.

**nymphomania** /nɪmfə'meɪnɪə/ *n.* excessive sexual desire in women. **nymphomaniac** *n.* & *a.*

**NZ** *abbr.* New Zealand.

# O

**O¹** /əʊ/ *n.* nought, zero.

**O²** /əʊ/ *int.* prefixed to name in vocative or expr. wish, entreaty, etc.

**oaf** *n.* awkward lout. **oafish** *a.*

**oak** *n.* forest tree with hard wood, acorns, and lobed leaves; its wood. **oak-apple, -gall,** kinds of excrescence produced on oak by gall-flies.

**oakum** /ˈəʊkəm/ *n.* loose fibre got by picking old rope to pieces.

**OAM** *abbr.* Medal of the Order of Australia.

**oar** /ɔː(r)/ *n.* pole with blade used to propel boat by leverage against water; rower.

**oarsman** /ˈɔːzmən/ *n.* (*pl.* **-men**) rower. **oarswoman** (*pl.* **-women**) *n.*

**oasis** /əʊˈeɪsɪs/ *n.* (*pl.* **oases** /-siːz/) fertile spot in desert.

**oast** *n.* hop-drying kiln. **oast-house** building containing this.

**oat** *n.* in *pl.* cereal grown as food; grain of this; tall grass resembling oats. **oatcake** thin unleavened cake of oatmeal; **oatmeal** meal ground from oats, greyish-fawn colour. **oaten** *a.*

**oath** /əʊθ/ *n.* (*pl.* /əʊðz/) solemn declaration or undertaking naming God etc. as witness; profanity, obscenity.

**ob.** *abbr.* died (*obiit*).

**obbligato** /ɒblɪˈɡɑːtəʊ/ *n.* (*pl.* **-tos**) *Mus.* part or accompaniment forming integral part of a composition.

**obdurate** /ˈɒbdjʊərət/ *a.* hardened; stubborn. **obduracy** *n.*

**OBE** *abbr.* Officer of the Order of the British Empire.

**obedient** /əʊˈbiːdɪənt/ *a.* obeying or ready to obey; submissive to another's will. **obedience** *n.*

**obeisance** /əʊˈbeɪs(ə)ns/ *n.* gesture expressing submission, respect, etc.; homage. **obeisant** *a.*

**obelisk** /ˈɒbəlɪsk/ *n.* tapering stone pillar of rectangular section; obelus.

**obelus** /ˈɒbələs/ *n.* (*pl.* **-li** /-laɪ/) dagger-shaped mark of reference (†).

**obese** /əʊˈbiːs/ *a.* very fat. **obesity** *n.*

**obey** /əʊˈbeɪ/ *v.* carry out command of; be obedient (to).

**obfuscate** /ˈɒbfəskeɪt/ *v.t.* darken; obscure, confuse; bewilder. **obfuscation** *n.*

**obituary** /əˈbɪtjəri/ **1** *n.* notice of death(s); brief biography of deceased person. **2** *a.* of or serving as obituary.

**object 1** /ˈɒbdʒɪkt/ *n.* material thing; person or thing to which action or feeling is directed; thing sought or aimed at; *Gram.* word governed by transitive verb or preposition. **2** /əbˈdʒekt/ *v.* express opposition or feel dislike or reluctance (*to*); state as reason (*against*). **3 no object** not an important factor; **object-glass** lens in telescope etc. nearest to object. **4 objector** *n.*

**objectify** /ɒbˈdʒektəfaɪ/ *v.t.* make objective, embody.

**objection** /əbˈdʒekʃ(ə)n/ *n.* expression of disapproval or dislike; objecting; adverse reason or statement.

**objectionable** *a.* open to objection; unpleasant, offensive.

**objective** /əbˈdʒektɪv/ **1** *a.* external to the mind; actually existing; dealing with outward things not thoughts or feelings; *Gram.* constructed as or appropriate to object. **2** *n.* object or purpose aimed at; *Gram.* objective case. **3 objectivity** *n.*

**objet d'art** /ɒbʒeɪ ˈdɑː/ (*pl.* **-jets** pr. same) small decorative object.

**objurgate** /ˈɒbdʒəɡeɪt/ *v.t.* chide, scold.

**oblate** /ˈɒbleɪt/ *a.* (of spheroid) flattened at poles.

**oblation** /əˈbleɪʃ(ə)n/ *n.* thing offered to God; pious donation.

**obligate** /ˈɒblɪɡeɪt/ *v.t.* bind *to* do; oblige.

**obligation** /ɒblɪˈɡeɪʃ(ə)n/ *n.* duty; binding agreement; indebtedness for service or benefit.

**obligatory** /əˈblɪɡətəri/ *a.* binding, compulsory.

**oblige** /əˈblaɪdʒ/ *v.* constrain, compel, require; be binding on; perform service (for); in *pass.* be bound (*to*) by gratitude.

**obliging** *a.* helpful, accommodating.

**oblique** /əˈbliːk/ **1** *a.* slanting; diverging from straight line or course; not going straight to the point, indirect; *Gram.* (of case) other than nominative or vocative. **2** *n.* oblique stroke. **3 obliquity** *n.*

**obliterate** /əˈblɪtəreɪt/ *v.t.* blot out, leave no clear trace of. **obliteration** *n.*

**oblivion** /əˈblɪvɪən/ *n.* state of being forgotten or of being oblivious.

# oblivious     372     occupational

**oblivious** /ə'blɪvɪəs/ *a.* unaware or unconscious (with *of* or *to*).

**oblong** /'ɒblɒŋ/ **1** *a.* rectangular with adjacent sides unequal. **2** *n.* oblong figure or object.

**obloquy** /'ɒblǝkwi:/ *n.* abuse, being ill spoken of.

**obnoxious** /əb'nɒkʃəs/ *a.* offensive, objectionable; disliked.

**oboe** /'əʊbəʊ/ *n.* double-reeded wood-wind musical instrument.

**obscene** /əb'si:n/ *a.* offensive, indecent; *Law* (of publication) tending to deprave and corrupt; *colloq.* highly offensive. **obscenity** /-'sen/- *n.*

**obscure** /əb'skjʊə(r)/ **1** *a.* not clearly expressed or easily understood; dark, indistinct; hidden, undistinguished. **2** *v.t.* make obscure or invisible. **3 obscurity** *n.*

**obsequies** /'ɒbsəkwiːz/ *n.pl.* funeral.

**obsequious** /əb'siːkwɪəs/ *a.* fawning, servile.

**observance** /əb'zɜːv(ə)ns/ *n.* keeping or performance (*of* law, occasion, etc.); rite, ceremonial act.

**observant** *a.* good at observing.

**observation** /ɒbzə'veɪʃ(ə)n/ *n.* observing or being observed; comment, remark.

**observatory** /əb'zɜːvətəri:/ *n.* building for astronomical or other observation.

**observe** /əb'zɜːv/ *v.* perceive, become aware of; watch; keep (rules etc.); celebrate (rite etc.); note and record; say esp. by way of comment.

**obsess** /əb'ses/ *v.t.* preoccupy, fill mind of. **obsession** *n.*; **obsessional** *a.* **obsessive** *a.*

**obsidian** /əb'sɪdɪən/ *n.* dark vitreous lava.

**obsolescent** /ɒbsə'les(ə)nt/ *a.* becoming obsolete. **obsolescence** *n.*

**obsolete** /'ɒbsəliːt/ *a.* no longer used, antiquated.

**obstacle** /'ɒbstək(ə)l/ *n.* thing obstructing progress.

**obstetrics** /əb'stetrɪks/ *n.pl.* usu. treated as *sing*. branch of medicine or surgery dealing with childbirth. **obstetrical** *a.*; **obstetrician** /-'trɪʃ/- *n.*

**obstinate** /'ɒbstənət/ *a.* stubborn, intractable. **obstinacy** *n.*

**obstreperous** /əb'strepərəs/ *a.* noisy, unruly.

**obstruct** /əb'strʌkt/ *v.t.* block up; make hard or impossible to pass along or through; retard or prevent progress of.

**obstruction** /əb'strʌkʃ(ə)n/ *n.* obstructing, being obstructive; thing that obstructs; hindering. **obstructionist** *n.*

**obstructive** /əb'strʌktɪv/ *a.* causing or meant to cause obstruction.

**obtain** /əb'teɪn/ *v.* acquire; get; have granted; be prevalent or established.

**obtrude** /əb'truːd/ *v.t.* thrust importunately forward. **obtrusion** *n.*; **obtrusive** *a.*

**obtuse** /əb'tjuːs/ *a.* dull-witted, slow to understand; blunt, not sharp or pointed; (of angle) greater than one right angle and less than two.

**obverse** /'ɒbvɜːs/ *n.* side of coin or medal that bears head or principal design; front or top side; counterpart.

**obviate** /'ɒbvɪeɪt/ *v.t.* clear away, get rid of; get round.

**obvious** /'ɒbvɪəs/ *a.* easily seen or recognized or understood.

**OC** *abbr.* Officer Commanding.

**ocarina** /ɒkə'riːnə/ *n.* egg-shaped musical wind instrument.

**occasion** /ə'keɪʒ(ə)n/ **1** *n.* special event or happening; time marked by this; suitable juncture, opportunity; reason. **2** *v.t.* be occasion or cause of.

**occasional** /ə'keɪʒən(ə)l/ *a.* happening irregularly and infrequently; made or meant for, acting on, etc. special occasion(s). **occasional table** small table for use as required.

**occasionally** *adv.* sometimes; intermittently.

**Occident** /'ɒksəd(ə)nt/ *n. the* West, esp. opp. Orient. **occidental** *a.*

**occiput** /'ɒksɪpʌt/ *n.* back of head. **occipital** /-'sɪp/- *a.*

**occlude** /ə'kluːd/ *v.t.* stop up; obstruct; *Chem.* absorb (gases). **occlusion** *n.*

**occult** /'ɒkʌlt or ə'kʌlt/ *a.* involving the supernatural, mystical, magical; esoteric; recondite.

**occupant** /'ɒkjəp(ə)nt/ *n.* person occupying a dwelling or office or position. **occupancy** *n.*

**occupation** /ɒkjə'peɪʃ(ə)n/ *n.* profession or employment; occupying or being occupied, esp. by armed forces of another country.

**occupational** *a.* pertaining to one's or an occupation. **occupational disease**,

**occupier** /'ɒkjəpaɪə(r)/ *n.* person residing in house etc. as owner or tenant.

**occupy** /'ɒkjəpaɪ/ *v.t.* reside in; take up, fill, be in; take military possession of; place oneself in (building etc.) esp. as political demonstration; hold (office); keep busy or engaged.

**occur** /ə'kɜː(r)/ *v.i.* take place, happen; come into one's mind; be met with or found in some place or conditions.

**occurrence** /ə'kʌr(ə)ns/ *n.* happening; incident.

**ocean** /'əʊʃ(ə)n/ *n.* sea surrounding continents of the earth, esp. one of the five named divisions of this; *the* sea; immense expanse or quantity. **oceanic** /əʊʃɪ'ænɪk/ *a.*

**oceanography** /əʊʃə'nɒgrəfiː/ *n.* study of the oceans. **oceanographer** *n.*

**ocelot** /'ɒsəlɒt/ *n.* S. Amer. feline animal resembling leopard.

**ochre** /'əʊkə(r)/ *n.* earth used as pigment; pale brownish-yellow colour. **ochrous** *a.*

**ocker** /'ɒkə(r)/ *Aus. sl.* **1** *n.* boorish (esp. aggressively Australian) person. **2** *a.* of ockers.

**o'clock** *adv.* of the clock, used to specify hour.

**oct-, octa-,** *in comb.* eight.

**Oct.** *abbr.* October.

**octagon** /'ɒktəgən/ *n.* plane figure with 8 sides and angles. **octagonal** /-'tæg-/ *a.*

**octahedron** /ɒktə'hiːdrən/ *n.* solid figure contained by 8 plane faces (usu. triangles). **octahedral** *a.*

**octane** /'ɒkteɪn/ *n.* hydrocarbon of paraffin series. **high-octane** (of fuel used in internal combustion engines) not detonating rapidly during power stroke.

**octave** /'ɒktɪv/ *n. Mus.* note 7 diatonic degrees above or below another; interval between note and its octave; series of notes filling this.

**octavo** /ɒk'teɪvəʊ/ *n.* (*pl.* **-vos**) size of book or page with sheets folded into 8 leaves.

**octet** /ɒk'tet/ *n. Mus.* composition for 8 performers; the performers; group of 8.

**octo-** *in comb.* eight.

**October** /ɒk'təʊbə(r)/ *n.* tenth month of year.

**octogenarian** /ɒktədʒə'neərɪən/ *n.* person between 80 and 89 years old.

**octopus** /'ɒktəpəs/ *n.* mollusc with 8 suckered tentacles.

**ocular** /'ɒkjələ(r)/ *a.* of or connected with the eyes or sight, visual.

**oculist** /'ɒkjəlɪst/ *n.* specialist in treatment of eye disorders or defects.

**odd** *a.* extraordinary, strange; left over, detached from a set; casual; (of number) not even, not divisible by two. **oddball** eccentric person; **odd job** casual isolated piece of work.

**oddity** /'ɒdɪtɪ/ *n.* strangeness; peculiar trait; strange person or thing.

**oddment** /'ɒdm(ə)nt/ *n.* odd article; something left over.

**odds** *n.pl.* occas. treated as *sing.* ratio between amounts staked by parties to a bet; chances in favour of or against result; balance of advantage; advantageous difference. **at odds** in conflict (*with*); **odds and ends** remnants, stray articles; **odds-on** a state when success is more likely than failure; **over the odds** above general price etc.

**ode** *n.* lyric poem of exalted style and tone.

**odious** /'əʊdɪəs/ *a.* hateful, repulsive.

**odium** /'əʊdɪəm/ *n.* general dislike or disapproval.

**odoriferous** /əʊdə'rɪfərəs/ *a.* diffusing (usu. pleasant) odours.

**odour** /'əʊdə(r)/ *n.* smell or fragrance; favour or repute. **odorous** *a.*

**odyssey** /'ɒdəsɪ/ *n.* long adventurous journey.

**OED** *abbr.* Oxford English Dictionary.

**Oedipus complex** /'iːdɪpəs/ attraction of child to parent of opposite sex (esp. son to mother). **Oedipal** *a.*

**oesophagus** /iː'sɒfəgəs/ *n.* canal from mouth to stomach, gullet.

**of** /ɒv/ *prep.* belonging to, from; concerning; out of; among; relating to.

**off 1** *adv.* away, at or to distance; out of position; loose, separate, gone; discontinued, stopped. **2** *prep.* from; no longer upon. **3** *a.* further; far; right-hand; (of food) decaying; *Crick.* towards or from or in side of field which batsman faces

**offal** /ˈɒf(ə)l/ *n*. edible organs of animal; refuse, waste stuff.

**offence** /əˈfens/ *n*. illegal act; transgression; wounding of person's feelings, wounded feelings; aggressive action.

**offend** /əˈfend/ *v*. cause offence to, upset; displease or anger; do wrong.

**offensive** /əˈfensɪv/ 1 *a*. causing offence; insulting; disgusting, nauseous; aggressive; intended for or used in attack. 2 *n*. aggressive attitude or action or campaign.

**offer** /ˈɒfə(r)/ 1 *v*. present for acceptance or refusal; express readiness or show intention (*to* do); attempt; present by way of sacrifice. 2 *n*. expression of readiness to do or give or sell; proposal, esp. of marriage; bid.

**offering** *n*. thing offered.

**offertory** /ˈɒfətəri/ *n*. collection of money at religious service.

**office** /ˈɒfɪs/ *n*. room or building where administrative or clerical work is done; place for transacting business; department or local branch etc. for specified purpose; position with duties attached to it; tenure of official position; duty, task, function; authorized form of worship; in *pl*. parts of house devoted to household work etc.

**officer** /ˈɒfɪsə(r)/ *n*. person holding position of authority or trust, esp. one with commission in armed forces; policeman; president, treasurer, etc. of society etc.

**official** /əˈfɪʃ(ə)l/ 1 *a*. of office or its tenure; characteristic of persons in office; properly authorized. 2 *n*. person holding office or engaged in official duties. 3 **officialdom** *n*.

**officialese** /əfɪʃəˈliːz/ *n*. officials' jargon.

**officiate** /əˈfɪʃɪeɪt/ *v.i*. act in official capacity; perform divine service.

**officious** /əˈfɪʃəs/ *a*. aserting one's authority; intrusively kind.

**offing** *n*. **in the offing** *fig*. at hand, ready or likely to happen etc.

**offset** /ˈɒfset/ 1 *n*. side-shoot of plant serving for propagation; compensation; sloping ledge; (in full **offset process**) method of printing by transferring ink from plate etc. to rubber roller and thence to paper. 2 *v.t*. (**-set**) counterbalance, compensate; print by offset process.

**offsider** /ˈɒfˈsaɪdə(r)/ *n. Aus. colloq*. assistant, partner, second-in-command.

**offspring** /ˈɒfsprɪŋ/ *n*. person's child(ren) or descendants; animal's young or descendants.

**oft** *adv. arch*. often.

**often** /ˈɒf(ə)n/ *adv*. frequently; many times; at short intervals; in many instances.

**ogee** /ˈəʊdʒiː/ *n*. S-shaped curve; moulding with such section.

**ogive** /ˈəʊdʒaɪv/ *n*. diagonal rib of vault; pointed arch.

**ogle** /ˈəʊg(ə)l/ 1 *v*. look flirtatiously (at). 2 *n*. flirtatious glance.

**ogre** /ˈəʊgə(r)/ *n*. man-eating giant. **ogress** *n*.; **ogrish** *a*.

**oh** /əʊ/ *int*. expr. surprise, pain, etc.

**ohm** /əʊm/ *n*. unit of electrical resistance.

**OHMS** *abbr*. On Her (or His) Majesty's Service.

**oho** /əʊˈhəʊ/ *int*. expressing surprise or exultation.

**oil** 1 *n*. viscous liquid with smooth and sticky feel; (often in *pl*.) oil-colour. 2 *v.t*. apply oil to, lubricate; treat with oil. 3 **oilcake** compressed linseed etc. as cattle-food or manure; **oilcloth** fabric, esp. canvas, waterproofed with oil; **oil-colour** paint made by mixing powdered pigment in oil; **oilfield** district yielding mineral oil; **oil-painting** use of or picture in oil-colours; **oil rig** equipment for drilling an oil well; **oilskin** cloth waterproofed with oil, garment or (in *pl*.) suit of it; **oil-well** well from which mineral oil is drawn.

**oily** /ˈɔɪli:/ *a*. of, like, covered or soaked with, oil; (of manner) fawning.

**ointment** /'ɔɪntm(ə)nt/ n. smooth greasy healing or beautifying preparation for skin.

**OK** /əʊ'keɪ/ colloq. 1 a. & adv. all right. 2 n. approval, sanction. 3 v.t. sanction.

**okapi** /əʊ'kɑːpiː/ n. rare Afr. ruminant mammal.

**okay** var. of **OK**.

**okra** /'ɒkrə/ n. tall orig. Afr. plant with seed-pods used as food.

**old** /əʊld/ 1 a. advanced in age; not young or near its beginning; of specified age; dating from far back; long established; former. 2 n. old time. 3 **old age** later part of normal lifetime; **old-age pension** pension paid by state to persons of specified age; **old boy** former member of school; **Old Dart** Aus colloq. England; **old-fashioned** in or according to fashion no longer current, antiquated; **old girl** former member of school; **Old Glory** US Stars and Stripes; **old guard** original or past or conservative members of group; **old hand** experienced or practised person; **old hat** colloq. thing tediously familiar; **old identity** Aus. & NZ well-known old resident in community; **old maid** elderly spinster; **old man** colloq. one's father or husband or employer etc., (a., Aus.) big, remarkable; **old man kangaroo** Aus. full-grown male kangaroo; **old man saltbush** fodder plant of inland Australia; **old master** great painter of former times, painting by such painter; **Old Testament** part of Bible dealing with pre-Christian times; **old-time** of former times, long-established; **old woman** colloq. one's wife or mother, fig. fussy or timid man.

**olden** /'əʊld(ə)n/ a. arch. of an earlier period.

**oldie** /'əʊldiː/ n. colloq. old person or thing.

**oleaginous** /əʊliː'ædʒənəs/ a. having properties of or producing oil; oily.

**oleander** /əʊliː'ændə(r)/ n. evergreen flowering Mediterranean shrub.

**oleaster** /əʊliː'æstə(r)/ n. wild olive.

**olefin** /'əʊləfɪn/ n. hydrocarbon of type containing less than maximum amount of hydrogen.

**olfactory** /ɒl'fæktəriː/ a. concerned with smelling.

**oligarch** /'ɒləɡɑːk/ n. member of oligarchy.

**oligarchy** /'ɒləɡɑːkiː/ n. government or State governed by small group of persons; members of such government. **oligarchic(al)** a.

**olive** /'ɒlɪv/ 1 n. oval hard-stoned fruit yielding oil; tree bearing it; colour of unripe olive, dull yellowish green. 2 a. coloured like unripe olive; (of complexion) yellowish-brown. 3 **olive-branch** fig. something done or offered for peace or reconciliation.

**Olympiad** /ə'lɪmpiːæd/ n. period of 4 years between Olympic games.

**Olympian** /ə'lɪmpiːən/ a. of Olympus; magnificent, condescending; aloof.

**Olympic** /ə'lɪmpɪk/ a. of the Olympic Games. 2 n. in pl. Olympic games. 3 **Olympic Games** ancient-Greek festival held every 4 years, or modern international revival of this.

**OM** abbr. (member of the) Order of Merit.

**ombudsman** /'ɒmbʊdzmən/ n. (pl. -men) official appointed to investigate individuals' complaints against public authorities.

**omega** /'əʊmɪɡə/ n. last letter of Greek alphabet (Ω, ω); last of series.

**omelette** /'ɒmlət/ n. dish of beaten eggs cooked in a frying-pan.

**omen** /'əʊmən/ n. sign portending good or evil, prophetic significance.

**ominous** /'ɒmɪnəs/ a. of evil omen, inauspicious.

**omit** /ə'mɪt/ v.t. leave out, not include; leave undone, neglect. **omission** n.

**omni-** in comb. all.

**omnibus** /'ɒmnɪbəs/ 1 n. bus; volume containing several novels etc. previously published separately. 2 a. serving several objects at once; comprising several items.

**omnipotent** /ɒm'nɪpət(ə)nt/ a. all-powerful. **omnipotence** n.

**omnipresent** /ɒmnə'prez(ə)nt/ a. present everywhere. **omnipresence** n.

**omniscient** /ɒm'nɪsɪənt/ a. knowing everything. **omniscience** n.

**omnivorous** /ɒm'nɪvərəs/ a. feeding on many kinds of food; joc. reading everything that comes one's way.

**on** 1 prep. (so as to be) supported by or covering or attached to, etc.; (so as to be) close to, in direction of; at, near, concerning, about; added to. 2 adv. (so as to be) on something; in some

**onager** /'ɒnədʒə(r)/ n. wild ass.

**onanism** /'əʊnənɪz(ə)m/ n. masturbation.

**once** /wʌns/ 1 adv. on one occasion only; at some time in past. 2 conj. as soon as. 3 n. one time, performance, etc. 4 **at once** immediately, simultaneously; **once-over** colloq. rapid preliminary inspection.

**oncoming** /'ɒnkʌmɪŋ/ a. approaching from the front.

**one** /wʌn/ 1 a. single and integral in number; only, without others, identical, same. 2 n. lowest cardinal numeral; thing numbered with it; unit, unity; single thing, person, or example. 3 pron. any person; the speaker. 4 **one-horse** sl. small, poorly equipped; **one-man** involving or operated by one person only; **one-off** colloq. made as the only one, not repeated; **one-sided** unfair, partial; **one-track mind** preoccupied with one subject; **one-way** allowing movement etc. in one direction only.

**oneness** /'wʌnnəs/ n. singleness; uniqueness; agreement, sameness.

**onerous** /'əʊnərəs/ a. burdensome.

**oneself** /wʌn'self/ pron., emphat. & refl. form of **one**.

**ongoing** /'ɒŋɡəʊɪŋ/ a. continuing, in progress.

**onion** /'ʌnjən/ n. vegetable with edible bulb of pungent smell and flavour.

**onlooker** /'ɒnlʊkə(r)/ n. spectator.

**only** /'əʊnlɪ/ 1 a. existing alone of its or their kind. 2 adv. solely, merely, exclusively. 3 conj. except that; but then. 4 **if only** I wish that.

**o.n.o.** abbr. or near offer.

**onomatopoeia** /ɒnəmætə'pi:ə/ n. formation of word from sound associated with thing named. **onomatopoeic** a.

**onset** /'ɒnset/ n. attack, impetuous beginning.

**onslaught** /'ɒnslɔ:t/ n. fierce attack.

**ontology** /ɒn'tɒlədʒɪ/ n. department of metaphysics concerned with nature of being. **ontological** a.; **ontologist** n.

**onus** /'əʊnəs/ n. burden, duty, responsibility.

**onward** /'ɒnwəd/ 1 adv. onwards. 2 a. directed onwards.

**onwards** adv. further on; towards front; with advancing motion.

**onyx** /'ɒnɪks/ n. kind of chalcedony with coloured layers.

**oodles** /'u:d(ə)lz/ n.pl. colloq. very great amount.

**ooh** /u:/ int. expr. surprised pleasure, pain, excitement, etc.

**oolite** /'əʊəlaɪt/ n. granular limestone. **oolitic** /-'lɪt/ a.

**oomph** /ʊmf/ n. sl. energy, enthusiasm.

**ooze** 1 v. pass slowly through pores etc.; exude; leak out or away. 2 n. wet mud; sluggish flow. 3 **oozy** a.

**op** n. colloq. operation.

**op.** abbr. opus.

**opacity** /ə'pæsɪtɪ/ n. opaqueness.

**opal** /'əʊp(ə)l/ n. milk-white or bluish stone with iridescent reflections.

**opalescent** /əʊpə'les(ə)nt/ a. iridescent. **opalescence** n.

**opaline** /'əʊpəlaɪm/ a. opal-like; opalescent.

**opaque** /əʊ'peɪk/ a. not transmitting light, not transparent; obscure.

**op. cit.** abbr. in the work already quoted (opere citato).

**OPEC** /'əʊpek/ abbr. Organization of Petroleum Exporting Countries.

**open** /'əʊpən/ 1 a. not closed or locked or blocked up; not covered or confined; exposed; expanded, unfolded, spread out; manifest, public; accessible to visitors or customers; not restricted; communicative, frank. 2 n. the open air; open competition etc. 3 v. make or become open or more open; begin, make start; declare open. 4 **open air** outdoors; **opencast** (of mining) on surface; **open-ended** with no limit or restriction; **open-handed** generous; **open-heart surgery** surgery with heart exposed and blood made to by-pass it; **open letter** one printed in newspaper etc. but addressed to person by name; **open mind** accessibility to new ideas, unprejudiced or undecided state; **open-plan** (of house, office, etc.) with few interior walls; **open question** matter on which differences of opinion

**opener** *n.* device for opening tins or bottles etc.

**opening 1** *n.* gap, aperture; beginning, initial part; opportunity. **2** *a.* initial, first.

**openly** *adv.* publicly, frankly.

**opera**[1] /ˈɒpərə/ *n.* musical drama with sung or spoken dialogue. **opera-glasses** small binoculars for use in theatres etc.; **opera-hat** man's collapsible top hat; **opera-house** theatre for operas.

**opera**[2] /ˈɒpərə/ *pl.* of **opus**.

**operable** /ˈɒpərəb(ə)l/ *a.* that can be operated; suitable for treatment by surgical operation.

**operate** /ˈɒpəreɪt/ *v.* be in action, produce effect; perform or carry on operation(s); work (machine etc.); direct working of. **operating theatre** place in hospital where surgical operations are performed.

**operatic** /ɒpəˈrætɪk/ *a.* of or like opera.

**operation** /ɒpəˈreɪʃ(ə)n/ *n.* action, working; performance of surgery on a patient; military manœuvre; financial transaction. **operational** *a.*

**operative** /ˈɒpərətɪv/ **1** *a.* in operation; practical; having principal relevance; of or by surgery. **2** *n.* worker, artisan.

**operator** /ˈɒpəreɪtə(r)/ *n.* person who operates machine, esp. person making connections of lines in telephone exchange; person engaging in business.

**operetta** /ɒpəˈretə/ *n.* light opera.

**ophidian** /əˈfɪdɪən/ **1** *n.* member of sub-order of reptiles including snakes. **2** *a.* of this order.

**ophthalmia** /ɒfˈθælmɪə/ *n.* inflammation of eye.

**ophthalmic** /ɒfˈθælmɪk/ *a.* of or for the eye; of or for or affected by ophthalmia. **ophthalmic optician** one qualified to prescribe as well as dispense spectacles.

**ophthalmology** /ɒfθælˈmɒlədʒɪ/ *n.* scientific study of the eye.

**ophthalmoscope** /ɒfˈθælməskəʊp/ *n.* instrument for examining the eye.

**opiate** /ˈəʊpɪət/ **1** *a.* containing opium; soporific. **2** *n.* drug containing opium and easing pain or inducing sleep.

**opine** /əʊˈpaɪn/ *v.t.* express or hold opinion (*that*).

**opinion** /əˈpɪnjən/ *n.* belief based on grounds short of proof; professional advice; estimate.

**opinionated** /əˈpɪnjəneɪtɪd/ *a.* unduly confident in one's opinions.

**opium** /ˈəʊpɪəm/ *n.* drug made from juice of kind of poppy and used as narcotic or sedative.

**opossum** /əˈpɒsəm/ *n.* kind of small Amer. marsupial; *Aus.* possum.

**opponent** /əˈpəʊnənt/ *n.* person who opposes or belongs to opposing side.

**opportune** /ˈɒpətjuːn/ *a.* (of time) suitable, favourable, well-selected; done etc. at opportune time.

**opportunism** /ˈɒpətjuːnɪz(ə)m/ *n.* adaptation of policy to circumstances, esp. regardless of principle. **opportunist** *n.*

**opportunity** /ɒpəˈtjuːnətɪ/ *n.* favourable occasion; good chance, opening. **opportunity shop** *Aus.* shop selling second-hand goods for charity.

**oppose** /əˈpəʊz/ *v.t.* place in opposition or contrast (to); set oneself against; resist; argue against. **as opposed to** in contrast with.

**opposite** /ˈɒpəzɪt/ **1** *a.* having position on other side; facing; of contrary kind; diametrically different. **2** *n.* opposite thing or person or term. **3** *adv.* in opposite position. **4** *prep.* opposite to. **5 opposite number** person in corresponding position in another set etc.

**opposition** /ɒpəˈzɪʃ(ə)n/ *n.* antagonism, resistance; contrast; diametrically opposite position. **the Opposition** chief parliamentary party, or group of parties, opposed to that in office.

**oppress** /əˈpres/ *v.t.* govern tyrannically; treat with gross harshness or injustice; weigh down. **oppression** *n.;* **oppressor** *n.*

**oppressive** /əˈpresɪv/ *a.* that oppresses; (of weather) sultry, close.

**opprobrious** /əˈprəʊbrɪəs/ *a.* severely scornful; abusive.

**opprobrium** /əˈprəʊbrɪəm/ *n.* disgrace, bad reputation; cause of this.

**oppugn** /əˈpjuːn/ *v.t.* controvert, call in question.

**opt** *v.i.* make choice; decide. **opt out (of)** choose not to take part etc. (in).

**optic** /ˈɒptɪk/ *a.* of eye or sight.

**optical** /ˈɒptɪk(ə)l/ *a.* visual; aiding

**optician** /ɒpˈtɪʃ(ə)n/ n. maker or prescriber of optical instruments, esp. spectacles.

**optics** /ˈɒptɪks/ n.pl. usu. treated as sing. science of light and vision.

**optimal** /ˈɒptəm(ə)l/ a. best or most favourable.

**optimism** /ˈɒptəmɪz(ə)m/ n. hopeful view or disposition; tendency or inclination to expect favourable outcome. **optimist** n.; **optimistic** a.

**optimum** /ˈɒptəməm/ 1 n. (pl. **-ma**) most favourable conditions; best compromise. 2 a. optimal.

**option** /ˈɒpʃ(ə)n/ n. choice, choosing; right to choose; purchased right to buy, sell, etc., on specified conditions at specified time.

**optional** /ˈɒpʃ(ə)n(ə)l/ a. not obligatory.

**opulent** /ˈɒpjʊl(ə)nt/ a. wealthy; abundant; luxurious. **opulence** n.

**opus** /ˈəʊpəs/ n. (pl. **opera**) musical composition numbered as one of composer's works.

**or** conj. introducing alternatives.

**oracle** /ˈɒrək(ə)l/ n. place at which ancient Greeks etc. consulted gods for advice or prophecy; response received there; person or thing regarded as source of wisdom etc. **oracular** /ɒˈrækjʊlə(r)/ a.

**oral** /ˈɔːr(ə)l/ or /ˈɒr(ə)l/ 1 a. spoken, verbal; by word of mouth; done or taken by mouth. 2 n. colloq. spoken examination.

**orange** /ˈɒrɪndʒ/ 1 n. roundish reddish-yellow citrus fruit; its colour; tree bearing it. 2 a. orange-coloured.

**orangeade** /ɒrɪnˈdʒeɪd/ n. drink made from or flavoured like oranges, freq. aerated.

**orang-utan** /ɔːræŋuːˈtæn/ n. large anthropoid ape.

**oration** /əˈreɪʃ(ə)n/ n. formal or ceremonial speech.

**orator** /ˈɒrətə(r)/ n. maker of a speech; eloquent public speaker.

**oratorio** /ɒrəˈtɔːrɪəʊ/ n. (pl. **-ios**) semi-dramatic musical composition usu. on sacred theme.

**oratory** /ˈɒrətərɪ/ n. art of or skill in public speaking; small private chapel. **oratorical** /-ˈtɒr-/ a.

**orb** n. sphere, globe; globe surmounted by cross as part of regalia; poet. eye.

**orbicular** /ɔːˈbɪkjʊlə(r)/ a. spherical or circular.

**orbit** /ˈɔːbɪt/ 1 n. curved course of planet, comet, satellite, etc. round another body; range or sphere of action. 2 v. go round in orbit; put into orbit. **orbital** a.

**orchard** /ˈɔːtʃəd/ n. enclosed piece of land with fruit-trees.

**orchestra** /ˈɔːkəstrə/ n. body of instrumental performers; area in theatre etc. assigned to them.

**orchestral** /ɔːˈkestr(ə)l/ a. of or for or performed by orchestra.

**orchestrate** /ˈɔːkəstreɪt/ v.t. compose or arrange or score, for orchestral performance.

**orchid** /ˈɔːkɪd/ n. any of various plants, freq. with brilliantly coloured or grotesquely shaped flowers.

**ordain** /ɔːˈdeɪn/ v.t. confer holy orders on; destine; appoint, enact.

**ordeal** /ɔːˈdiːl/ n. severe or testing trial or experience.

**order** /ˈɔːdə(r)/ 1 n. state of regular arrangement and normal functioning; natural or moral system with observed tendencies; arrangement of things relative to each other, sequence; prevalence of obedience to law; system of rules or procedure; authoritative direction or instruction; direction to supply something, thing (to be) supplied; Banking etc. instruction to pay money or deliver property; social class or rank; kind or sort; religious fraternity; grade of Christian ministry; company of persons distinguished by particular honour or reward, insignia worn by its members; stated form of divine service; mode of treatment in architecture; Biol. grouping of animals or plants below class and above family. 2 v.t. put in order; ordain; command, prescribe, direct; direct manufacturer, tradesman, etc., to supply waiter to serve.

**orderly** /ˈɔːdəlɪ/ 1 a. methodically arranged; tidy; not unruly. 2 n. soldier in attendance on officer; hospital attendant. 3 **orderly room** room in barracks for company's business.

**ordinal** /ˈɔːdɪn(ə)l/ 1 a. (of number)

**ordinance** /'ɔːdənəns/ n. decree; religious rite.

**ordinand** /'ɔːdənænd/ n. candidate for ordination.

**ordinary** /'ɔːdənəri/ a. normal; not exceptional; commonplace. **ordinary seaman** one of lower rating than able seaman.

**ordination** /ɔːdə'neɪʃ(ə)n/ n. ordaining; conferring of holy orders.

**ordnance** /'ɔːdnəns/ n. artillery and military supplies; department for military stores etc.

**ordure** /'ɔːdjʊə(r)/ n. dung.

**ore** n. naturally-occurring mineral yielding metal.

**oregano** /ɒrə'ɡɑːnəʊ/ n. dried wild marjoram as seasoning.

**organ** /'ɔːɡən/ n. musical instrument consisting of pipes that sound when air is forced through them, operated by keys and pedals; part of body serving some special function; medium of opinion, esp. newspaper. **organ-grinder** player of barrel-organ; **organ-stop** set of organ-pipes of similar tone-quality, handle bringing this into action.

**organdie** /'ɔːɡəndi/ n. fine usu. stiffened muslin.

**organic** /ɔː'ɡænɪk/ a. of or affecting bodily organ(s); (of animals and plants) having organs or organized physical structure; (of food) produced without artificial fertilizers or pesticides; organized; inherent, structural; *Chem.* (of compound) containing carbon in its molecules. **organic chemistry** that of carbon compounds. **organically** adv.

**organism** /'ɔːɡənɪz(ə)m/ n. individual animal or plant; organized body.

**organist** /'ɔːɡənɪst/ n. player of organ.

**organization** /ɔːɡənaɪ'zeɪʃ(ə)n/ n. organized body or system or society; organizing or being organized.

**organize** /'ɔːɡənaɪz/ v. give orderly structure to; make arrangements for; make organic or into living tissue.

**orgasm** /'ɔːɡæz(ə)m/ n. climax of sexual excitement. **orgasmic** /-'ɡæz-/ a.

**orgy** /'ɔːdʒi/ n. drunken or licentious party; excessive indulgence in an activity. **orgiastic** a.

**oriel** /'ɔːrɪəl/ n. window projecting from wall of house at upper level.

**orient 1** /'ɔːrɪənt/ n. **Orient**, *the* East, the countries east of Mediterranean, esp. E. Asia. **2** /'ɔːriːent/ v.t. establish *oneself* in relation to surroundings; place (building etc.) to face east; turn in specified direction; determine position of with regard to compass.

**oriental** /ɔːri'ent(ə)l/ **1** a. of Eastern or Asian world or its civilization. **2** n. native of East. **3 orientalize** v.

**orientate** /'ɔːrɪənteɪt/ v.t. orient. **orientation** n.

**orienteering** /ɔːriːən'tɪərɪŋ/ n. competitive sport of traversing rough country on foot with map and compass.

**orifice** /'ɒrɪfɪs/ n. aperture; mouth of cavity.

**origami** /ɒrə'ɡɑːmi/ n. Japanese art of folding paper into decorative shapes.

**origanum** /ɒrə'ɡɑːnəm/ n. wild marjoram.

**origin** /'ɒrɪdʒɪn/ n. source; starting-point; parentage.

**original** /ə'rɪdʒən(ə)l/ **1** a. existing from the first; primitive; earliest; not imitative or derived; creative. **2** n. pattern, archetype; thing from which another is copied or translated. **3 original sin** innate sinfulness held to be common to all human beings. **4 originality** n.

**originate** /ə'rɪdʒəneɪt/ v. have origin; initiate or give origin to, be origin of. **origination** n.; **originator** n.

**oriole** /'ɒriːəʊl/ n. kind of bird.

**ormolu** /'ɔːməluː/ n. gilded bronze; gold-coloured alloy; articles made of or decorated with these.

**ornament 1** /'ɔːnəmənt/ n. thing used to adorn or decorate; decoration; quality or person bringing honour or distinction. **2** /'ɔːnəment/ v.t. adorn, beautify. **3 ornamental** a.; **ornamentation** n.

**ornate** /ɔː'neɪt/ a. elaborately adorned.

**ornithology** /ɔːnə'θɒlədʒi/ n. study of birds. **ornithological** a.; **ornithologist** n.

**orotund** /'ɒrətʌnd/ a. (of utterance) dignified, imposing, pompous.

**orphan** /'ɔːf(ə)n/ **1** n. child whose parents are dead. **2** a. being an orphan. **3** v.t. bereave of parent(s).

**orphanage** /'ɔ:fənɪdʒ/ n. institution for orphans.

**orrery** /'ɒrəri/ n. clockwork model of planetary system.

**orris-root** /'ɒrəs/ n. violet-scented iris root.

**ortho-** in comb. straight, correct.

**orthodontics** /ɔ:θə'dɒntɪks/ n.pl. usu. treated as sing. correction of irregularities in teeth and jaws.

**orthodox** /'ɔ:θədɒks/ a. holding usual or accepted views; not heretical; conventional. **Orthodox Church** Eastern or Greek branch of Christian Church and Russian etc. Churches in communion with it. **orthodoxy** n.

**orthography** /ɔ:'θɒgrəfɪ/ n. spelling, esp. with reference to its correctness. **orthographic(al)** a.

**orthopaedic** /ɔ:'θə'pi:dɪk/ a. curing or treating deformity in bone or muscle.

**orthopaedics** n.pl. usu. treated as sing. orthopaedic surgery.

**OS** abbr. Ordinary Seaman; outsize.

**Oscar** /'ɒskə(r)/ n. statuette awarded annually for excellence in film acting, directing, etc.; **oscar** Aus. sl. money.

**oscillate** /'ɒsəleɪt/ v. (cause to) swing to and fro; vacillate; Electr. (of current) undergo high-frequency alternations. **oscillation** n.; **oscillator** n.

**oscilloscope** /ə'sɪləskəʊp/ n. device for recording oscillations esp. on screen of cathode ray tube.

**osier** /'əʊzɪə(r)/ n. willow used in basketwork; shoot of this.

**Oslo lunch** /'ɒzləʊ/ Aus. school lunch of uncooked health foods.

**osmosis** /ɒz'məʊsəs/ n. diffusion of fluid through semi-permeable partition into another fluid. **osmotic** /-'mɒt-/ a.

**osprey** /'ɒspreɪ/ n. large bird preying on inshore fish.

**osseous** /'ɒsɪəs/ a. bony; having bones.

**ossify** /'ɒsəfaɪ/ v. turn into bone; harden; make or become rigid. **ossification** n.

**ostensible** /ɒs'tensəb(ə)l/ a. professed; used to conceal real purpose or nature.

**ostentation** /ɒsten'teɪʃ(ə)n/ n. pretentious display; showing off. **ostentatious** a.

**osteopath** /'ɒstɪəpæθ/ n. person who treats disease by manipulation of bones. **osteopathy** /-'ɒp-/ n.

**ostler** /'ɒslə(r)/ n. stableman at inn.

**ostracize** /'ɒstrəsaɪz/ v.t. exclude from society, refuse to associate with. **ostracism** n.

**ostrich** /'ɒstrɪtʃ/ n. large flightless swift-running bird.

**OT** abbr. Old Testament.

**other** /'ʌðə(r)/ 1 a. not same; separate in identity; distinct in kind; alternative, further, or additional; *the* only remaining. 2 n. or pron. other person or thing. 3 adv. otherwise. 4 **the other day, week,** etc., a few days etc. ago; **other world** life after death.

**otherwise** /'ʌðəwaɪz/ adv. in a different way; if circumstances are or were or had been different; in other respects; or else.

**otiose** /'əʊtɪəʊz/ a. not required, serving no practical purpose.

**otter** /'ɒtə(r)/ n. furred aquatic fish-eating mammal.

**Ottoman** /'ɒtəmən/ 1 a. hist. of Turkish Empire. 2 n. (pl. **-mans**) Turk of Ottoman period; **ottoman** cushioned seat without back or arms, storage-box with padded top.

**oubliette** /u:bli:'et/ n. secret dungeon with trapdoor entrance.

**ouch** /aʊtʃ/ int. expr. sharp or sudden pain.

**ought** /ɔ:t/ v.aux. (3rd sing. ought) expr. duty, rightness, probability, etc.

**Ouija** /'wi:dʒə/ n. (P) (in full **Ouija-board**) board marked with alphabet used with movable pointer to obtain messages in spiritualist seances.

**ounce** /aʊns/ n. unit of weight, 1/16 lb. or 28 g.

**our** /aʊə(r)/ pron. & a., poss. case of **we**, with abs. form **ours**.

**ourself** /aʊə'self/ pron. corresponding to **myself** when used by sovereign, newspaper-writer, etc. who uses *we* instead of *I*.

**ourselves** /aʊə'selvz/ pron., emphat. and refl. form of **we**.

**ousel** var. of **ouzel**.

**oust** /aʊst/ v.t. eject; drive out of office or power; seize place of.

**out** /aʊt/ 1 adv. away from or not in place, not in right or normal state; not at home; so as to be excluded; in(to) open, sight, notice, etc.; to or at an end; not in fashion, office, etc.; not burning. 2 prep. out of. 3 **out of date** obsolete, antiquated; **out of doors** in(to) open

**out-** 381 **outpost**

air; **out of the way** unusual, remote, disposed cf.

**out-** *in comb.* out of, external, to excess, so as to defeat or excel, etc.

**outback** /'aʊtbæk/ *Aus.* **1** *n.* remote inland districts. **2** *a.* of the outback. **3** *abv.* in or to the outback.

**outbacker** *n. Aus.* dweller in outback.

**outbackery** *n. Aus.* excessive cultivation of outback values etc.

**outbid** /aʊt'bɪd/ *v.t.* (*past & p.p.* **-bid**) bid higher than.

**outboard** /'aʊtbɔːd/ *a.* towards outside of ship, aircraft, or vehicle, (of motor) attached externally to stern of boat; (of boat) using such motor.

**outbreak** /'aʊtbreɪk/ *n.* breaking out of emotion, war, disease, fire, etc.

**outbuilding** /'aʊtbɪldɪŋ/ *n.* outhouse.

**outburst** /'aʊtbɜːst/ *n.* bursting out, esp. of emotion in vehement words.

**outcast** /'aʊtkɑːst/ **1** *n.* person cast out from home and friends. **2** *a.* homeless, rejected.

**outclass** /aʊt'klɑːs/ *v.t.* surpass in quality.

**outcome** /'aʊtkʌm/ *n.* result, issue.

**outcrop** /'aʊtkrɒp/ *n.* rock etc. emerging at surface; *fig.* notable manifestation.

**outcry** /'aʊtkraɪ/ *n.* loud protest; clamour.

**outdated** /aʊt'deɪtəd/ *a.* out of date, obsolete.

**outdistance** /aʊt'dɪst(ə)ns/ *v.t.* get far ahead of.

**outdo** /aʊt'duː/ *v.t.* (*past* **-did**; *p.p.* **-done** /-'dʌn/) surpass, excel.

**outdoor** /'aʊtdɔː(r)/ *a.* of or done for use etc. out of doors.

**outdoors 1** *n. the* open air. **2** *adv.* in(to) the open air.

**outer** /'aʊtə(r)/ **1** *a.* farther from centre or inside; on outside. **2** *n. Aus.* part of sports ground without shelter; open-air betting-place near race-course. **3 on the outer** *Aus. sl.* unpopular, penniless; **outer space** universe beyond earth's atmosphere. **4 outermost** *a.*

**outface** /aʊt'feɪs/ *v.t.* disconcert by staring or by confident manner.

**outfall** /'aʊtfɔːl/ *n.* mouth of river, drain, etc.

**outfield** /'aʊtfiːld/ *n.* outer part of cricket or baseball pitch.

**outfit** /'aʊtfɪt/ *n.* set of equipment or clothes; *colloq.* (organized) group or company.

**outfitter** /'aʊtfɪtə(r)/ *n.* supplier of equipment, esp. men's clothes.

**outflank** /aʊt'flæŋk/ *v.t.* get round the flank of; outmanœuvre.

**outflow** /'aʊtfləʊ/ *n.* outward flow; what flows out.

**outgoing** /'aʊtgəʊɪŋ/ **1** *a.* going out; retiring from office; friendly. **2** *n.* in *pl.* expenditure.

**outgrow** /aʊt'grəʊ/ *v.t.* (*past* **-grew**; *p.p.* **-grown** /-'grəʊn/) grow faster or get taller than; get too big for (clothes, etc.); leave behind as one develops.

**outgrowth** /'aʊtgrəʊθ/ *n.* offshoot.

**outhouse** /'aʊthaʊs/ *n.* shed etc., esp. adjoining main house.

**outing** /'aʊtɪŋ/ *n.* pleasure-trip.

**outlandish** /aʊt'lændɪʃ/ *a.* looking or sounding strange or foreign; bizarre.

**outlast** /aʊt'lɑːst/ *v.t.* last longer than.

**outlaw** /'aʊtlɔː/ **1** *n.* person deprived of protection of law; lawless person. **2** *v.t.* declare outlaw; make illegal; proscribe.

**outlawry** *n.*

**outlay** /'aʊtleɪ/ *n.* expenditure.

**outlet** /'aʊtlət/ *n.* means of exit; means of expressing feelings; market for goods.

**outline** /'aʊtlaɪn/ **1** *n.* external boundary; line(s) enclosing visible object; contour; rough draft, summary; in *pl.* main features. **2** *v.t.* draw or describe in outline; mark outline of.

**outlive** /aʊt'lɪv/ *v.t.* live longer than or beyond or through.

**outlook** /'aʊtlʊk/ *n.* view, prospect; what seems likely to happen; *fig.* mental attitude.

**outlying** /'aʊtlaɪɪŋ/ *a.* far from centre; remote.

**outmanœuvre** /aʊtmə'nuːvə(r)/ *v.t.* outdo in manœuvring.

**outmatch** /aʊt'mætʃ/ *v.t.* be more than a match for.

**outmoded** /aʊt'məʊdəd/ *a.* out of fashion; obsolete.

**outnumber** /aʊt'nʌmbə(r)/ *v.t.* exceed in number.

**outpace** /aʊt'peɪs/ *v.t.* go faster than; outdo in contest.

**out-patient** /'aʊtpeɪʃ(ə)nt/ *n.* one not residing in hospital during treatment.

**outpost** /'aʊtpəʊst/ *n.* detachment on

guard at some distance from army; outlying settlement etc.

**output** /'aʊtpʊt/ **1** *n.* amount produced; place where energy, information, etc., leaves a system; results etc. supplied by computer. **2** *v.t.* (*past & p.p.* **-put** or **-putted**) (of computer) supply (results etc.).

**outrage** /'aʊtreɪdʒ/ **1** *n.* forcible violation of others' rights, sentiments, etc.; gross offence or indignity; fierce resentment. **2** *v.t.* subject to outrage; insult; infringe violently; shock and anger.

**outrageous** /aʊt'reɪdʒəs/ *a.* immoderate, shocking; grossly cruel or offensive etc.

**outrank** /aʊt'ræŋk/ *v.t.* be superior in rank to.

**outré** /'uːtreɪ/ *a.* eccentric, violating decorum. [F]

**outrider** /'aʊtraɪdə(r)/ *n.* motor cyclist riding ahead of car(s) etc.

**outrigger** /'aʊtrɪgə(r)/ *n.* spar or framework projecting from or over ship's side; bracket bearing rowlocks outside boat; boat with these.

**outright** **1** /aʊt'raɪt/ *adv.* altogether, entirely; not gradually; without reservation; not by degrees or instalments. **2** /'aʊtraɪt/ *a.* complete; thorough.

**outrun** /aʊt'rʌn/ *v.t.* (*past* **-ran**; *p.p.* **-run**) run faster or farther than; escape; go beyond.

**outsell** /aʊt'sel/ *v.t.* (*past & p.p.* **-sold** /-'səʊld/) sell more than; be sold in greater quantities than.

**outset** /'aʊtset/ *n.* beginning.

**outshine** /aʊt'ʃaɪn/ *v.t.* (*past & p.p.* **-shone** /-'ʃɒn/) be more brilliant than.

**outside** /'aʊtsaɪd/ **1** *n.* external surface, outer part(s); external appearance; position on outer side; highest computation. **2** *a.* of, on, or nearer outside; not belonging to some circle or institution; greatest existent or possible. **3** /aʊt'saɪd/ *adv.* on or to outside; not within. **4** /aʊt'saɪd/ *prep.* not in; to, or at the outside of; external to; beyond outside of. **5 outside broadcast** one not made from a studio.

**outsider** /aʊt'saɪdə(r)/ *n.* non-member of circle, party, profession, etc.; competitor thought to have no chance.

**outsize** /'aʊtsaɪz/ **1** *a.* unusually large. **2** *n.* outsize garment etc.

**outskirts** /'aʊtskɜːts/ *n.pl.* outer area of town etc.

**outsmart** /aʊt'smɑːt/ *v.t. colloq.* outwit; be too clever for.

**outspoken** /aʊt'spəʊkən/ *a.* frank, unreserved.

**outspread** /aʊt'spred/ *a.* spread out.

**outstation** /'aʊtsteɪʃ(ə)n/ *n. Aus.* sheep- or cattle-station distant from head station.

**outstanding** /aʊt'stændɪŋ/ *a.* conspicuous, esp. from excellence; still to be dealt with.

**outstay** /aʊt'steɪ/ *v.t.* stay longer than.

**outstretched** /'aʊtstretʃt/ *a.* stretched out.

**outstrip** /aʊt'strɪp/ *v.t.* go faster than; surpass in progress, competition, etc.

**outvote** /aʊt'vəʊt/ *v.t.* defeat by majority of votes.

**outward** /'aʊtwəd/ **1** *a.* directed towards outside; going out; physical; external, superficial. **2** *adv.* outwards.

**outwardly** *adv.* in outward appearance; on the surface.

**outwards** *adv.* in outward direction; towards outside.

**outweigh** /aʊt'weɪ/ *v.t.* exceed in weight, value, influence, etc.

**outwit** /aʊt'wɪt/ *v.t.* be too clever for; overcome by greater ingenuity.

**outwork** /'aʊtwɜːk/ *n.* advanced or detached part of fortress etc.; work done outside shop, factory, etc.

**outworn** /aʊt'wɔːn/ *a.* worn out, obsolete.

**ouzel** /'uːz(ə)l/ *n.* small bird of thrush family.

**ouzo** /'uːzəʊ/ *n.* Greek drink of aniseed-flavoured spirits.

**ova** *pl.* of **ovum**.

**oval** /'əʊv(ə)l/ **1** *a.* shaped like egg, elliptical. **2** *n.* elliptical closed curve; thing with oval outline.

**ovary** /'əʊvərɪ/ *n.* ovum-producing organ in female animal; seed-vessel in plant. **ovarian** /-'veər-/ *a.*

**ovation** /əʊ'veɪʃ(ə)n/ *n.* enthusiastic applause or reception.

**oven** /'ʌv(ə)n/ *n.* enclosed chamber for baking or cooking in. **ovenware** dishes in which food can be cooked in oven.

**over** /'əʊvə(r)/ **1** *adv.* outward and downward from brink or from erect position; above in place or position; more than; covering whole surface;

from one side, end, etc. to other; from beginning to end; at end; done with. 2 n. Crick. number of balls bowled from one end before change is made to other; play during this time. 3 prep. above; concerning; across; on or to other side, end, etc. of.

**over-** in comb. over; upper, outer; superior; excessive(ly).

**overact** /əʊvə'rækt/ v. act with exaggeration.

**over-active** /əʊvə'ræktɪv/ a. too active.

**overall** /'əʊvərɔːl/ 1 a. taking everything into account, inclusive, total. 2 adv. in all parts; taken as a whole. 3 n. protective outer garment; in pl. protective trousers or suit.

**overarm** /'əʊvəraːm/ a. & adv. with arm raised above shoulder.

**overawe** /əʊvə'rɔː/ v.t. awe into submission.

**overbalance** /əʊvə'bæl(ə)ns/ v. (cause to) lose balance and fall.

**overbear** /əʊvə'beə(r)/ v.t. (past -**bore**, p.p. -**borne**) bear down by weight or force; repress.

**overbearing** /əʊvə'beərɪŋ/ a. domineering, bullying.

**overblown** /əʊvə'bləʊn/ a. inflated or pretentious; past its prime.

**overboard** /'əʊvəbɔːd/ adv. from within ship into water. **go overboard** colloq. show extreme enthusiasm.

**overbook** /əʊvə'bʊk/ v. make too many bookings (for).

**overcast** /əʊvə'kaːst/ a. (of sky) covered with cloud; (in sewing) edged with stitching.

**overcharge** /əʊvə'tʃaːdʒ/ v. charge too high a price for or to; put too much (explosive, electric, etc.) charge into.

**overcoat** /'əʊvəkəʊt/ n. large coat worn over ordinary clothing.

**overcome** /əʊvə'kʌm/ v.t. (past -**came**, p.p. -**come**) prevail over, master; be victorious; in p.p. greatly affected or made helpless.

**overcrowd** /əʊvə'kraʊd/ v.t. cause too many people or things to be in (a place).

**overdevelop** /əʊvədə'veləp/ v. develop too much.

**overdo** /əʊvə'duː/ v.t. (past -**did**, p.p. -**done** /-'dʌn/) carry to excess; cook too long; exhaust.

**overdose** /'əʊvədəʊs/ n. excessive dose esp. of drug etc.

**overdraft** /'əʊvədraːft/ n. overdrawing of bank account; amount by which account is overdrawn.

**overdraw** /əʊvə'drɔː/ v. (past -**drew**; p.p. -**drawn**) draw more from bank account) than amount in credit; in p.p. having overdrawn one's account.

**overdress** /əʊvə'dres/ v. dress ostentatiously or with too much formality.

**overdrive** /'əʊvədraɪv/ n. mechanism in vehicle providing gear ratio higher than that of ordinary top gear.

**overdue** /əʊvə'djuː/ a. past the time when due or ready; late, in arrears.

**overestimate** 1 /əʊvə'restəmeɪt/ v.t. form too high an estimate of. 2 /əʊvə'restɪmət/ n. too high an estimate.

**over-expose** /əʊvərɪks'pəʊz/ v.t. expose too much or for too long.

**overfish** /əʊvə'fɪʃ/ v.t. fish (stream, sea, etc.) to depletion.

**overflow** 1 /əʊvə'fləʊ/ v. flow over, flood; extend beyond limits or capacity of; be so full that contents overflow; be very abundant. 2 /'əʊvəfləʊ/ n. what overflows or is superfluous; outlet for excess liquid.

**overgrown** /əʊvə'grəʊn/ a. covered with plants, weeds, etc.; grown too big.

**overhang** 1 /əʊvə'hæŋ/ v. (past & p.p. -**hung**) project or hang (over). 2 /'əʊvəhæŋ/ n. fact or amount of overhanging.

**overhaul** /əʊvə'hɔːl/ v.t. check over thoroughly and make necessary repairs to; overtake.

**overhead** 1 /əʊvə'hed/ adv. above one's head; in sky. 2 /'əʊvəhed/ a. placed overhead. 3 /'əʊvəhed/ n. in pl. routine administrative and maintenance expenses of a business.

**overhear** /əʊvə'hɪə(r)/ v.t. (past & p.p. -**heard** /-'hɜːd/) hear as unperceived or unintentional listener.

**overjoyed** /əʊvə'dʒɔɪd/ a. filled with extreme joy.

**overkill** /'əʊvəkɪl/ n. excess of capacity to kill or destroy.

**overland** 1 /əʊvə'lænd/ adv. by land and not sea. 2 /'əʊvəlænd/ a. entirely or partly by land. 3 v. Aus. go, esp. driving stock, a long distance overland. 4 **overlander** n.

**overlap** 1 /əʊvə'læp/ v. partly cover;

cover and extend beyond; partly coincide. 2 /ˈəʊvəlæp/ n. overlapping; overlapping part or amount.

**overlay** 1 /əʊvəˈleɪ/ v.t. (past & p.p. -laid) cover surface of *with* coating etc. 2 /ˈəʊvəleɪ/ n. thing laid over another.

**overleaf** /ˈəʊvəˈliːf/ adv. on other side of leaf of book.

**overlie** /əʊvəˈlaɪ/ v.t. (past -lay; p.p. -lain) lie on top of.

**overload** 1 /əʊvəˈləʊd/ v.t. load too heavily. 2 /ˈəʊvələʊd/ n. amount by which thing is overloaded.

**overlook** /əʊvəˈlʊk/ v.t. fail to observe, take no notice of, condone; have view of from above.

**overlord** /ˈəʊvəlɔːd/ n. supreme lord.

**overly** /ˈəʊvəli/ adv. excessively, too.

**overman** /əʊvəˈmæn/ v.t. provide with too many men as crew, staff, etc.

**overmuch** /əʊvəˈmʌtʃ/ a., n., & adv. too much.

**overnight** 1 /əʊvəˈnaɪt/ adv. during course of a night; on preceding evening; *colloq.* suddenly. 2 /ˈəʊvənaɪt/ a. done or for use etc. overnight.

**overpass** /ˈəʊvəpɑːs/ n. road that crosses another by a bridge.

**overpower** /əʊvəˈpaʊə(r)/ v.t. subdue, reduce to submission; be too intense or violent for.

**over-produce** /əʊvəprəˈdjuːs/ v.t. produce in excess of demand or of defined amount. **overproduction** n.

**overrate** /əʊvəˈreɪt/ v.t. have too high an opinion of.

**overreach** /əʊvəˈriːtʃ/ v. outwit, circumvent; **overreach oneself** defeat one's object by going too far.

**over-react** /əʊvəriˈækt/ v.i. respond more violently etc. than is justified.

**override** /əʊvəˈraɪd/ v.t. (past -rode; p.p. -ridden) have precedence or superiority over, intervene and make ineffective.

**overrider** /əʊvəˈraɪdə(r)/ n. vertical attachment on motor vehicle bumper to prevent its becoming interlocked with another vehicle.

**overrule** /əʊvəˈruːl/ v.t. set aside by superior authority; annul decision of thus.

**overrun** /əʊvəˈrʌn/ v. (past -ran; p.p. -run) swarm or spread over; exceed time etc. allowed.

**overseas** /əʊvəˈsiːz/ a. & adv. across or beyond sea.

**oversee** /əʊvəˈsiː/ v.t. (past -saw; p.p. -seen) superintend. **overseer** n.

**oversew** /ˈəʊvəsəʊ/ v.t. (p.p. -sewn) sew (two edges) with stitches lying over them.

**overshadow** /əʊvəˈʃædəʊ/ v.t. appear much more prominent or important than; cast into shade.

**overshoe** /ˈəʊvəʃuː/ n. shoe worn over another for protection in wet weather etc.

**overshoot** /əʊvəˈʃuːt/ v. (past & p.p. -shot) pass or send beyond (target or limit).

**oversight** /ˈəʊvəsaɪt/ n. failure to notice; inadvertent omission or mistake; supervision.

**oversimplify** /əʊvəˈsɪmplɪfaɪ/ v.t. distort by putting in too simple terms.

**oversleep** /əʊvəˈsliːp/ v.i. (past & p.p. -slept) sleep beyond intended time of waking.

**overspend** /əʊvəˈspend/ v.i. (past & p.p. -spent) spend beyond one's means.

**overspill** /ˈəʊvəspɪl/ n. what is spilt over or overflows; *fig.* surplus population leaving one area for another.

**overspread** /əʊvəˈspred/ v.t. (past & p.p. -spread) cover surface of; in *pass.* be covered *with.*

**overstate** /əʊvəˈsteɪt/ v.t. state too strongly; exaggerate. **overstatement** n.

**overstep** /əʊvəˈstep/ v.t. pass beyond.

**overstrain** /əʊvəˈstreɪn/ v.t. damage by exertion; stretch too far.

**overstrung** /əʊvəˈstrʌŋ/ a. too highly strung or intensely strained.

**oversubscribed** /əʊvəsəbˈskraɪbd/ a. (of shares offered for sale) not enough to meet amount subscribed.

**overt** /əʊˈvɜːt/ a. openly done, unconcealed.

**overtake** /əʊvəˈteɪk/ v.t. (past -took; p.p. -taken) catch up and pass; come suddenly upon.

**overtax** /əʊvəˈtæks/ v.t. make excessive demands on; tax too highly.

**overthrow** 1 /əʊvəˈθrəʊ/ v.t. (past -threw; p.p. -thrown) remove forcibly from power; put an end to; conquer; knock down. 2 /ˈəʊvəθrəʊ/ n. defeat; downfall.

**overtime** /ˈəʊvətaɪm/ 1 n. time worked

**overtone** /ˈəʊvətəʊn/ n. subtle extra quality or implication; *Mus.* any of tones above lowest in harmonic series.

**overtop** /əʊvəˈtɒp/ v.t. be or become higher than, surpass.

**overtrump** /əʊvəˈtrʌmp/ v. play higher trump (than).

**overture** /ˈəʊvətjʊə(r)/ n. *Mus.* orchestral prelude; opening of negotiations; formal proposal or offer.

**overturn** /əʊvəˈtɜːn/ v. (cause to) fall down or over; upset, overthrow.

**overview** /ˈəʊvəvjuː/ n. general survey.

**overweening** /əʊvəˈwiːnɪŋ/ a. arrogant.

**overweight** 1 /əʊvəˈweɪt/ a. beyond the weight allowed or desirable. 2 /ˈəʊvəweɪt/ n. excess weight.

**overwhelm** /əʊvəˈwelm/ v.t. overpower with emotion or with excess of business etc.; bury, submerge utterly.

**overwhelming** /əʊvəˈwelmɪŋ/ a. irresistible through force of numbers, influence, amount, etc.

**overwork** /əʊvəˈwɜːk/ 1 v. (cause to) work too hard; weary or exhaust with work. 2 n. excessive work.

**overwrought** /əʊvəˈrɔːt/ a. suffering reaction from excitement.

**oviduct** /ˈəʊvɪdʌkt/ n. tube through which ova pass from ovary.

**oviform** /ˈəʊvɪfɔːm/ a. egg-shaped.

**ovine** /ˈəʊvaɪn/ a. of or like sheep.

**oviparous** /əʊˈvɪpərəs/ a. egg-laying.

**ovoid** /ˈəʊvɔɪd/ a. (of solid) egg-shaped.

**ovulate** /ˈɒvjəleɪt/ v.i. discharge ovum or ova from ovary; produce ova. **ovulation** n.

**ovule** /ˈɒvjuːl/ n. structure containing germ-cell in female plant.

**ovum** /ˈəʊvəm/ n. (pl. **ova**) female germ-cell in animals, from which by fertilization with male sperm the young is developed; egg.

**ow** /aʊ/ int. expr. sudden pain.

**owe** /əʊ/ v. be under obligation to (re)pay or render; be in debt (*for*); be indebted for (*to*).

**owing** /ˈəʊɪŋ/ pred.a. owed, yet to be paid. **owing to** caused by, because of.

**owl** /aʊl/ n. night bird of prey.

**owlet** /ˈaʊlət/ n. small or young owl.

**owlish** /ˈaʊlɪʃ/ a. like an owl; solemn and dull.

**own** /əʊn/ 1 a. (after possessive) not another's; (*absol.*) own property, kindred, etc. 2 v. have as property, possess; acknowledge authorship or paternity of; admit as valid, true, etc. 3 **hold one's own** maintain one's position, not be defeated; **of one's own** belonging to one; **on one's own** alone, independently, unaided; **own up** *colloq.* confess.

**owner** /ˈəʊnə(r)/ n. possessor. **owner-occupier** person who owns house he lives in. **ownership** n.

**ox** n. (pl. **oxen**) individual of kinds of large usu. horned ruminant; castrated male of domestic species of this. **ox-eye daisy** kind of plant with large white or yellow flowers.

**oxalic acid** /ɒkˈsælɪk/ intensely sour poisonous acid found in wood sorrel and other plants.

**oxidation** /ɒksəˈdeɪʃ(ə)n/ n. oxidization.

**oxide** /ˈɒksaɪd/ n. compound of oxygen with another element or with radical.

**oxidize** /ˈɒksədaɪz/ v. (cause to) combine with oxygen; rust; cover with coating of oxide. **oxidization** n.

**oxy-acetylene** /ɒksɪəˈsetɪliːn/ a. of or using mixture of oxygen and acetylene, esp. in cutting or welding metals.

**oxygen** /ˈɒksədʒ(ə)n/ n. colourless odourless tasteless gas essential to life and to combustion. **oxygen tent** enclosure to allow patient to breathe air with increased oxygen content.

**oxygenate** /ˈɒksədʒəneɪt/ v.t. supply or treat or mix with oxygen; oxidize.

**oxymoron** /ɒksɪˈmɔːrɒn/ n. figure of speech with pointed conjunction of apparent contradictions.

**oyez** /əʊˈjez/ int. uttered by public crier or court officer to call for attention.

**oyster** /ˈɔɪstə(r)/ n. bivalve mollusc used as food; white colour with grey tinge.

**oz.** *abbr.* ounce(s).

**ozone** /ˈəʊzəʊn/ n. form of oxygen with pungent odour; *pop.* invigorating seaside air.

# P

**p** *abbr.* penny, pence.
**p.** *abbr.* page.
**p** *abbr. Mus.* piano².
**pa** /pɑː/ *n. colloq.* father.
**PA** *abbr.* personal assistant; public address.
**p.a.** *abbr.* per annum.
**pace**¹ /peɪs/ **1** *n.* single step in walking or running; space traversed in this; speed, rate of progression; gait. **2** *v.* walk (over, about), esp. with slow or regular step; measure (distance) by pacing; set pace for. **3 pacemaker** person who sets pace, natural or electrical device for stimulating heart muscle.
**pace**² /ˈpeɪsi/ *prep.* with all due deference to.
**pachyderm** /ˈpækɪdɜːm/ *n.* large thick-skinned mammal, esp. elephant or rhinoceros. **pachydermatous** *a.*
**pacific** /pəˈsɪfɪk/ *a.* tending to peace, of peaceful disposition.
**pacifist** /ˈpæsɪfəst/ *n.* person opposed to war. **pacifism** *n.*
**pacify** /ˈpæsɪfaɪ/ *v.t.* appease; bring to state of peace. **pacification** *n.*
**pack**¹ *n.* **1** collection of things wrapped or tied together for carrying; *Aus.* rucksack; lot or set; set of playing-cards; group of wild animals or hounds; forwards of Rugby football team; medicinal or cosmetic substance applied to face; area of large crowded pieces of floating ice in sea; method of packing. **2** *v.* put (things) together into bundle, box, etc., fill (bag etc.) with clothes etc., for transport or storing; put closely together, cram, crowd together, form into pack; wrap tightly. **3 go to the pack** *Aus. sl.* collapse, go to pieces; **pack-drill** military punishment of walking up and down in full marching equipment; **pack-horse** horse for carrying packs; **pack up** *sl.* stop working, break down, retire from contest, activity, etc.; **packing-case** (usu. wooden) case for packing goods in; **send packing** *colloq.* dismiss summarily.
**pack**² *v.t.* select (jury etc.) so as to secure biased decision in one's favour.
**package** /ˈpækɪdʒ/ **1** *n.* parcel; box etc. in which goods are packed. **2** *v.t.* make up into or enclose in package. **3 package deal** *colloq.* transaction agreed to as a whole; **package holiday, tour**, etc., one with fixed inclusive price.
**packer** /ˈpækə(r)/ *n.* person who packs; *Aus.* pack-animal.
**packet** /ˈpækɪt/ *n.* small package; *colloq.* large sum of money; mail-boat.
**pact** *n.* agreement, treaty.
**pad**¹ **1** *n.* piece of soft stuff used to diminish jarring, raise surface, absorb fluid, etc.; number of sheets of blank paper fastened together at one edge; fleshy cushion forming sole of foot of some animals; leg-guard in games; flat surface for helicopter take-off; *sl.* lodging. **2** *v.t.* provide with pad, stuff; fill out or *out* with superfluous matter.
**pad**² **1** *n. Aus.* track, path. **2** *v.* walk softly; tramp (along) on foot; travel on foot.
**padding** /ˈpædɪŋ/ *n.* material used to pad.
**paddle**¹ /ˈpæd(ə)l/ **1** *n.* short oar with broad blade at one or each end; strikingboard in paddle-wheel; fin or flipper; action or spell of paddling. **2** *v.* propel with paddle(s); row gently. **3 paddlewheel** wheel for propelling ship, with boards round circumference so as to press backward against water.
**paddle**² /ˈpæd(ə)l/ **1** *v.i.* wade about in shallow water. **2** *n.* action or spell of paddling.
**paddock** /ˈpædək/ *n. Aus.* fenced piece of land; *UK* small field for keeping horses in; enclosure where horses or cars are assembled before race.
**paddy**¹ /ˈpædi/ *n.* field where rice is grown (in full **paddy-field**); rice before threshing or in the husk.
**paddy**² /ˈpædi/ *n. colloq.* rage, temper.
**paddymelon** /ˈpædiːmelən/ *n.* (also **pademelon**) *Aus.* small wallaby of coastal scrub.
**padlock** /ˈpædlɒk/ **1** *n.* detachable lock hanging by hinged or pivoted hook. **2** *v.t.* secure with padlock.
**padre** /ˈpɑːdreɪ/ *n. colloq.* chaplain in army etc.
**paean** /ˈpiːən/ *n.* song of praise or triumph.
**paederast** var. of **pederast**.

**paediatrics** /piːdiˈætrɪks/ n. branch of medicine dealing with children's diseases. **paediatric** a.; **paediatrician** /-ˈtrɪʃ-/ n.

**paella** /pɑːˈelə/ n. Spanish dish of rice, chicken, seafood, etc.

**pagan** /ˈpeɪɡən/ n. & a. heathen. **paganism** n.

**page**[1] n. leaf of book etc.; one side of this. 2 v.t. number pages of.

**page**[2] 1 n. boy employed as liveried servant or personal attendant. 2 v.t. call name of (person sought) in public rooms of hotel etc.

**pageant** /ˈpædʒ(ə)nt/ n. spectacular performance, usu. illustrative of historical events; any brilliant show.

**pageantry** /ˈpædʒəntri/ n. spectacular show or display; what serves to make a pageant.

**paginate** /ˈpædʒəneɪt/ v.t. number pages of (book etc.). **pagination** n.

**pagoda** /pəˈɡəʊdə/ n. temple or sacred tower in China etc.; ornamental imitation of this.

**pah** int. expr. disgust.

**paid** past & p.p. of **pay**. **put paid to** colloq. finish off.

**pail** n. bucket.

**pain** 1 n. bodily suffering caused by injury or disease; mental distress; in pl. trouble taken; in pl. throes of childbirth. 2 v.t. inflict pain on. 3 **painstaking** /ˈpeɪnz-/ careful, industrious.

**painful** /ˈpeɪnfəl/ a. causing or suffering pain; causing trouble or difficulty.

**painless** /ˈpeɪnlɪs/ a. not causing pain.

**paint** 1 n. colouring matter prepared for application to surface. 2 v. cover surface of with paint; portray or make pictures in colours; depict in words; apply liquid or cosmetic to.

**painter**[1] /ˈpeɪntə(r)/ n. person who paints, esp. as artist or decorator.

**painter**[2] /ˈpeɪntə(r)/ n. rope at bow of boat for tying it up.

**painting** /ˈpeɪntɪŋ/ n. art of representing by colours on a surface; product of this.

**pair** /peə(r)/ 1 n. set of 2; thing with 2 corresponding parts not used separately; engaged or married or mated couple; (either of) 2 MPs etc. on opposite sides arranging both to be absent from division etc. 2 v. arrange or unite as pair or in pairs; mate. 3 **pair off** form into pairs.

**Paisley** /ˈpeɪzli/ a. having characteristic pattern of curved abstract figures.

**pajamas** var. of **pyjamas**.

**pal** colloq. 1 n. friend. 2 v.i. (with up) make friends.

**palace** /ˈpæləs/ n. official residence of sovereign, archbishop, or bishop; stately mansion or building.

**paladin** /ˈpælədɪn/ n. peer of Charlemagne's court; knight errant.

**palaeo-** /ˈpælɪəʊ/ in comb. ancient.

**palaeography** /pælɪˈɒɡrəfi/ n. study of ancient writing and inscriptions.

**palaeolithic** /pælɪəʊˈlɪθɪk/ a. of earlier Stone Age.

**palaeontology** /pælɪɒnˈtɒlədʒɪ/ n. study of life in geological past.

**Palaeozoic** /pælɪəʊˈzəʊɪk/ 1 a. of geological era containing oldest forms of highly organized life. 2 n. this era.

**palais** /ˈpæleɪ/ n. dance hall.

**palanquin** /pælənˈkiːn/ n. (also **palankeen**) Eastern covered litter.

**palatable** /ˈpælətəb(ə)l/ a. pleasant to taste; agreeable to the mind.

**palatal** /ˈpælət(ə)l/ 1 a. of the palate; (of sound) made with tongue against palate. 2 n. palatal sound.

**palate** /ˈpælət/ n. roof of mouth; sense of taste; liking.

**palatial** /pəˈleɪʃ(ə)l/ a. like palace, splendid.

**palaver** /pəˈlɑːvə(r)/ 1 n. fuss and bother; idle talk. 2 v. talk profusely; flatter, wheedle.

**pale**[1] a. (of complexion etc.) whitish, not ruddy; faintly coloured; (of colour) faint, (of light) dim. 2 v. grow or make pale.

**pale**[2] n. stake etc. as part of fence; boundary. **beyond the pale** outside bounds of acceptable behaviour.

**palette** /ˈpælɪt/ n. artist's flat tablet for mixing colours on. **palette-knife** knife with long round-ended flexible blade.

**palimpsest** /ˈpælɪmpsest/ n. writing-material used for second time after original writing has been erased.

**palindrome** /ˈpælɪndrəʊm/ n. word or phrase etc. that reads same backwards as forwards. **palindromic** /-ˈdrɒm-/ a.

**paling** /ˈpeɪlɪŋ/ n. in sing. or pl. fence of pales; pale.

**palisade** /ˈpæləˈseɪd/ 1 n. fence of pointed stakes. 2 v.t. enclose with palisade.

**pall**¹ /pɔːl/ n. cloth spread over coffin etc.; ecclesiastical vestment; *fig.* dark covering. **pallbearer** person helping to carry coffin at funeral.

**pall**² /pɔːl/ v.i. become tiresome.

**pallet**¹ /ˈpælət/ n. straw bed, mattress.

**pallet**² /ˈpælət/ n. portable platform for transporting and storing loads.

**palliasse** /ˈpælɪæs/ n. straw mattress.

**palliate** /ˈpælɪeɪt/ v.t. alleviate without curing; excuse, extenuate. **palliation** n.; **palliative** a. & n.

**pallid** /ˈpælɪd/ a. pale, sickly-looking.

**pallor** /ˈpælə(r)/ n. paleness.

**pally** /ˈpælɪ/ a. *colloq.* friendly.

**palm** /pɑːm/ 1 n. inner surface of hand between wrist and fingers; kind of tree with unbranched stem and crown of large esp. fan-shaped leaves; leaf of this as symbol of victory; (prize for) supreme excellence. 2 v.t. conceal in hand. 3 **palm off** impose or thrust fraudulently (*on*); **Palm Sunday** Sunday before Easter.

**palmar** /ˈpælmə(r)/ a. of or in palm of hand.

**palmate** /ˈpælmeɪt/ a. shaped like palm of hand.

**palmetto** /pælˈmetəʊ/ n. (*pl.* -os) palm-tree, esp. of small size.

**palmist** /ˈpɑːmɪst/ n. teller of character or fortune from lines etc. in palm of hand. **palmistry** n.

**palmy** /ˈpɑːmɪ/ a. of or like or abounding in palms; flourishing.

**palomino** /pæləˈmiːnəʊ/ n. (*pl.* -nos) golden or cream-coloured horse with light-coloured mane and tail.

**palpable** /ˈpælpəb(ə)l/ a. that can be touched or felt; readily perceived. **palpability** n.

**palpate** /pælˈpeɪt/ v.t. *Med.* examine by touch. **palpation** n.

**palpitate** /ˈpælpɪteɪt/ v.i. pulsate, throb; tremble. **palpitation** n.

**palsy** /ˈpɔːlzɪ/ 1 n. paralysis, esp. with involuntary tremors. 2 v.t. affect with palsy.

**paltry** /ˈpɔːltrɪ/ a. worthless; contemptible; trifling.

**pampas** /ˈpæmpəs/ n.pl. large treeless S. Amer. plains. **pampas-grass** large ornamental grass.

**pamper** /ˈpæmpə(r)/ v.t. over-indulge.

**pamphlet** /ˈpæmflət/ n. small unbound esp. controversial treatise.

**pamphleteer** /pæmfləˈtɪə(r)/ n. writer of (esp. political) pamphlets.

**pan**¹ 1 n. flat-bottomed usu. metal vessel used in cooking etc.; shallow receptacle or tray; bowl of scales or of lavatory; hollow in ground. 2 v. *colloq.* criticize harshly. 3 **pan out** (of gravel) yield gold, *fig.* succeed (*well* etc.).

**pan**² 1 v. cause film-camera to turn horizontally to follow movement etc.; (of camera) be moved thus. 2 n. panning movement.

**pan-** in *comb.* of or for all.

**panacea** /pænəˈsiːə/ n. universal remedy.

**panache** /pəˈnæʃ/ n. assertively confident style.

**panama** /ˈpænəmɑː/ n. hat of strawlike material made from leaves of a pine-tree.

**panatella** /pænəˈtelə/ n. long thin cigar.

**pancake** /ˈpænkeɪk/ n. thin flat usu. fried batter-cake.

**panchromatic** /pænkrəˈmætɪk/ a. (of film etc.) sensitive to all visible colours of spectrum.

**pancreas** /ˈpæŋkrɪəs/ n. gland near stomach supplying digestive fluid and insulin. **pancreatic** /-ˈæt-/ a.

**panda** /ˈpændə/ n. large rare bear-like black-and-white animal of China (also **giant panda**); raccoon-like Himalayan animal. **panda car** police patrol car.

**pandemic** /pænˈdemɪk/ a. (of disease) of world-wide distribution.

**pandemonium** /pændəˈməʊnɪəm/ n. uproar; utter confusion; scene of this.

**pander** /ˈpændə(r)/ 1 v.i. (with *to*) indulge perverse or weakness. 2 n. go-between in illicit love affairs; procurer.

**p. & p.** *abbr.* postage and packing.

**pane** n. single sheet of glass in window or door.

**panegyric** /pænəˈdʒɪrɪk/ n. laudatory discourse; eulogy. **panegyrist** n.; **panegyrize** v.t.

**panel** /ˈpæn(ə)l/ n. distinct or separate part of surface, esp. of wall or door etc.; surface holding or displaying controls and switches and recording dials etc.; group of people assembled for discussion, consultation, etc.; list of jury.

**panellist**

2 *v.t.* fit with panels. 3 **panel game** quiz etc. played by panel of entertainers.
**panellist** /'pænəlɪst/ *n.* member of panel.
**pang** *n.* sudden sharp pain.
**pangolin** /pæŋ'gəʊlɪn/ *n.* scaly anteater.
**panic** /'pænɪk/ 1 *n.* sudden alarm; infectious fright. 2 *a.* of or connected with panic. 3 *v.* affect or be affected with panic. 4 **panic-stricken, -struck**, affected with panic. 5 **panicky** *a.*
**panicle** /'pænɪk(ə)l/ *n. Bot.* loose branching cluster of flowers.
**panjandrum** /pæn'dʒændrəm/ *n.* mock title of great personage.
**pannier** /'pænɪə(r)/ *n.* one of pair of baskets or bags etc. carried by beast of burden or on bicycle or motor cycle etc.
**panoply** /'pænəplɪ/ *n.* full armour; *fig.* complete or splendid array.
**panorama** /pænə'rɑːmə/ *n.* picture or photograph containing wide view; continuous passing scene; unbroken view of surrounding region. **panoramic** /-'ræm-/ *a.*
**pansy** /'pænzɪ/ *n.* garden plant of violet family; *colloq.* effeminate man, male homosexual.
**pant** 1 *v.* gasp for breath; throb; yearn. 2 *n.* gasp; throb.
**pantaloons** /pæntə'luːnz/ *n.pl. hist.* trousers.
**pantechnicon** /pæn'teknɪkən/ *n.* furniture van.
**pantheism** /'pænθiːɪz(ə)m/ *n.* doctrine that God is everything and everything God. **pantheist** *n.*; **pantheistic** *a.*
**pantheon** /'pænθɪən/ *n.* temple of all gods; building with memorials of illustrious dead.
**panther** /'pænθə(r)/ *n.* leopard.
**panties** /'pæntɪz/ *n.pl. colloq.* shortlegged or legless knickers.
**pantile** /'pæntaɪl/ *n.* curved roof-tile.
**pantograph** /'pæntəgrɑːf or græf/ *n.* instrument for copying plan etc. on any scale.
**pantomime** /'pæntəmaɪm/ *n.* dramatic usu. Christmas entertainment based on fairy-tale; dumb show.
**pantry** /'pæntrɪ/ *n.* room in which provisions, crockery, cutlery, etc. are kept.
**pants** *n.pl. colloq.* underpants; knickers; trousers.

**pap**[1] *n.* soft or semi-liquid food; mash, pulp.
**pap**[2] *n. arch.* nipple of breast.
**papa** /pə'pɑː/ *n. arch.* child's name for father.
**papacy** /'peɪpəsɪ/ *n.* Pope's office or tenure; papal system.
**papal** /'peɪp(ə)l/ *a.* of the Pope or his office.
**papaw** /pə'pɔː/ *n.* pulpy orange edible fruit; tropical Amer. tree bearing it.
**paper** /'peɪpə(r)/ 1 *n.* substance made in thin flexible sheets from pulp of wood or other fibrous material, used for writing, printing, wrapping, etc.; documents; newspaper; set of examination questions or answers; essay, memorandum. 2 *a.* made of paper; written on paper. 3 *v.t* decorate (wall etc.) with paper. 4 **paperbark** *Aus.* any of several trees with papery bark; **paper-boy, -girl**, one who delivers or sells newspapers; **paper-clip** clip of bent wire or plastic for holding sheets of paper together; **paper-hanger** person who decorates walls etc. with wallpaper; **paper-knife** blunt knife for opening envelopes etc.; **paper money** banknotes etc.; **paperweight** small heavy object to hold papers down; **paperwork** office administration and recordkeeping.
**paperback** /'peɪpəbæk/ 1 *a.* bound in stiff paper, not boards. 2 *n.* paperback book.
**papier mâché** /pæpjeɪ 'mæʃeɪ/ moulded paper pulp used for making models etc.
**papilla** /pə'pɪlə/ *n.* (*pl.* **-lae** /-liː/) small nipple-like protuberance. **papillary** *a.*
**papist** /'peɪpɪst/ *n. derog.* Roman Catholic. **papistical** *a.*; **papistry** *n.*
**papoose** /pə'puːs/ *n.* young N. Amer. Indian child.
**paprika** /'pæprɪkə/ *n.* ripe red pepper; red condiment made from this.
**papyrus** /pə'paɪərəs/ *n.* (*pl.* **-ri** /riː/) aquatic plant of sedge family; ancient writing-material made from stem of this; manuscript written on this.
**par** *n.* average or normal value or degree; equality, equal footing; *Golf* number of strokes needed by first-class player for hole or course; face value.
**para-** *in comb.* beside, beyond.

**parable** /'pærəb(ə)l/ n. narrative used to illustrate moral or spiritual truth.

**parabola** /pə'ræbələ/ n. plane curve formed by intersection of cone with plane parallel to its side.

**parabolic** /pærə'bɒlɪk/ a. of or expressed in parable; of or like parabola. **parabolically** adv.

**paracetamol** /pærə'si:təmɒl/ n. compound used to relieve pain and reduce fever; tablet of this.

**parachute** /'pærəʃu:t/ 1 n. umbrella-shaped apparatus allowing person or heavy object to descend safely from a height, esp. from aircraft. 2 v. convey or descend by parachute. 3 **parachutist** n.

**parade** /pə'reɪd/ 1 n. muster of troops etc. for inspection, public procession; display, ostentation; public square, parade-ground. 2 v. assemble for parade; march with display (through); display ostentatiously. 3 **parade-ground** place for muster of troops.

**paradigm** /'pærədaɪm/ n. example, pattern, esp. of inflexion of word.

**paradise** /'pærədaɪs/ n. heaven; region or state of supreme bliss; garden of Eden. **paradisiacal** /-dɪ'saɪək(ə)l/ a.

**paradox** /'pærədɒks/ n. seemingly absurd or self-contradictory though perhaps well-founded statement etc. **paradoxical** a.

**paraffin** /'pærəfɪn/ n. inflammable waxy or oily substance got by distillation from petroleum etc. **paraffin wax** solid paraffin.

**paragon** /'pærəgən/ n. model of excellence; excellent person or thing.

**paragraph** /'pærəgrɑ:f or -græf/ n. distinct passage in book etc. usually marked by indentation of first line; mark of reference (¶); short separate item in newspaper etc.

**parakeet** /'pærəki:t/ n. small long-tailed parrot.

**parallax** /'pærəlæks/ n. apparent difference in position or direction of object caused by change of observation point; angular amount of this. **parallactic** a.

**parallel** /'pærəlel/ 1 a. (of lines) continuously equidistant; precisely similar, analogous, or corresponding. 2 n. person or thing analogous to another; comparison; imaginary line on earth's surface or line on map marking degree of latitude. 3 v.t. be parallel or correspond to; represent as similar; compare. 4 **parallelism** n.

**parallelepiped** /pærəlelə'paɪped/ n. solid bounded by parallelograms.

**parallelogram** /pærə'leləgræm/ n. 4-sided rectilinear figure whose opposite sides are parallel.

**paralyse** /'pærəlaɪz/ v.t. affect with paralysis; render powerless, cripple.

**paralysis** /pə'rælǝsǝs/ n. (pl. **-ses** /-si:z/) incapacity to move or feel; powerless or immobile state.

**paralytic** /pærə'lɪtɪk/ 1 a. affected with paralysis; sl. very drunk. 2 n. person affected with paralysis.

**paramedical** /pærə'medɪk(ə)l/ a. supplementing and supporting medical work.

**parameter** /pə'ræmətə(r)/ n. Math. quantity constant in case considered, but varying in different cases; (esp. measurable or quantifiable) characteristic or feature.

**paramilitary** /pærə'mɪlɪtəri/ a. ancillary to and similarly organized to military forces.

**paramount** /'pærəmaʊnt/ a. supreme. **paramountcy** n.

**paramour** /'pærəmʊə(r)/ n. arch. illicit lover.

**paranoia** /pærə'nɔɪə/ n. mental derangement with delusions of grandeur, persecution, etc.; abnormal tendency to suspect and mistrust others. **paranoiac** a. & n.; **paranoid** a. & n.

**paranormal** /pærə'nɔ:m(ə)l/ a. lying outside the range of normal scientific investigations etc.

**parapet** /'pærəpət/ n. low wall at edge of roof, balcony, bridge, etc.; mound along front of trench.

**paraphernalia** /pærəfə'neɪlɪə/ n.pl. personal belongings, miscellaneous accessories, etc.

**paraphrase** /'pærəfreɪz/ 1 n. restatement of sense of passage etc. in other words. 2 v.t. express meaning of in other words.

**paraplegia** /pærə'pli:dʒə/ n. paralysis of lower part of body. **paraplegic** a. & n.

**parapsychology** /pærəpsaɪ'kɒlədʒɪ:/ n. study of mental phenomena outside sphere of ordinary psychology.

**parasite** /'pærəsaɪt/ n. animal or plant living in or on another; self-seeking hanger-on. **parasitic** /-'sɪt-/ a.; **parasitism** n.

**parasol** /'pærəsɒl/ n. sunshade.

**paratroops** /'pærətruːps/ n.pl. airborne troops landing by parachute. **paratrooper** n.

**paratyphoid** /pærə'taɪfɔɪd/ n. fever resembling typhoid but caused by different bacterium.

**parboil** /'pɑːbɔɪl/ v.t. partly cook by boiling.

**parcel** /'pɑːs(ə)l/ 1 n. goods etc. packed up in single wrapping; piece of land. 2 v.t. wrap (*up*) into parcel; divide (*out*) into portions.

**parch** v. make or become hot and dry; slightly roast.

**parchment** /'pɑːtʃm(ə)nt/ n. skin, esp. of sheep or goat, prepared for writing etc.; manuscript written on this.

**pardalote** /'pɑːdələʊt/ n. a small Aus. insectivorous bird.

**pardon** /'pɑːd(ə)n/ 1 n. forgiveness; remission of punishment; courteous forbearance. 2 v.t. forgive; excuse.

**pardonable** /'pɑːdənəb(ə)l/ a. easily excused.

**pare** /peə(r)/ v.t. trim or reduce by cutting away edge or surface of; peel (fruit etc.); whittle away.

**paregoric** /pærə'gɒrɪk/ n. camphorated tincture of opium.

**parent** /'peər(ə)nt/ n. one who has begotten or borne offspring, father or mother; forefather; source, origin. **parentage** n.; **parental** /-'rent-/ a.

**parenthesis** /pə'renθəsɪs/ n. (pl. -ses /-siːz/) word or clause or sentence inserted as explanation etc. into passage independently of grammatical sequence; in pl. pair of round brackets used for this; *fig.* interlude. **parenthesize** v.t.; **parenthetic** /-'θet-/ a.

**par excellence** /pɑːr 'eksəlɑːs/ above all others that may be so called. [F]

**parfait** /'pɑːfeɪ/ n. rich iced pudding of whipped cream, eggs, etc.; layers of ice cream, fruit, etc., served in tall glass.

**parget** /'pɑːdʒət/ 1 v.t. plaster (wall etc.) with ornamental pattern; roughcast. 2 n. plaster, roughcast.

**pariah** /'pɑːrɑɪə/ n. member of low or no caste; social outcast.

**parietal** /pə'raɪət(ə)l/ a. of wall of body or any of its cavities. **parietal bone** one of pair forming part of skull.

**paring** /'peərɪŋ/ n. strip pared off.

**parish** /'pærɪʃ/ n. division of diocese having its own church and clergyman; local-government district; inhabitants of parish.

**parishioner** /pə'rɪʃənə(r)/ n. inhabitant of parish.

**parity** /'pærətɪ/ n. equality; equal status etc.; equivalence; being at par.

**park** 1 n. large public garden in town; large enclosed piece of ground attached to country house or laid out or preserved for public use; place where vehicles may be parked. 2 v.t. place and leave (vehicle) temporarily. 3 **parking-meter** mechanical device for collecting parking-fee esp. in street; **parking-ticket** notice of fine etc. imposed for parking vehicle illegally.

**parka** /'pɑːkə/ n. jacket with hood, as worn by Eskimos and mountaineers etc.

**parker** /'pɑːkə(r)/ n. Aus. parking-light on vehicle.

**parlance** /'pɑːl(ə)ns/ n. way of speaking.

**parley** /'pɑːlɪ/ 1 n. meeting between representatives of opposed forces to discuss terms. 2 v.i. hold discussion on terms.

**parliament** /'pɑːləm(ə)nt/ n. legislative assembly.

**parliamentarian** /pɑːləmən'teərɪən/ n. skilled debater in parliament.

**parliamentary** /pɑːlə'mentərɪ/ a. of or in or concerned with or enacted by parliament.

**parlour** /'pɑːlə(r)/ n. sitting-room in private house; room in hotel or convent etc. for private conversation. **parlour game** indoor game, esp. word-game.

**parlous** /'pɑːləs/ a. *arch.* perilous; hard to deal with.

**Parmesan** /'pɑːmɪzæn/ n. hard cheese of kind made at Parma.

**parochial** /pə'rəʊkɪəl/ a. of a parish; of narrow range, merely local. **parochialism** n.

**parody** /'pærədɪ/ 1 n. humorous exaggerated imitation of author or style etc.; travesty. 2 v.t. write or be parody of. 3 **parodist** n.

**parole** /pə'rəʊl/ 1 n. release of prisoner for special purpose or before end of

## parotid

sentence, on promise of good behaviour; such promise; word of honour. 2 *v.t.* put (prisoner) on parole.
**parotid** /pəˈrɒtɪd/ 1 *a.* situated near ear. 2 *n.* parotid gland. 3 **parotid gland** salivary gland in front of ear.
**paroxysm** /ˈpærəksəz(ə)m/ *n.* fit (*of* pain, rage, etc.).
**parquet** /ˈpɑːkeɪ/ 1 *n.* flooring of wooden blocks arranged in a pattern. 2 *v.t.* floor (room) thus.
**parramatta** /pærəˈmætə/ *n. Aus.* a light dress-fabric of wool and silk or cotton.
**parricide** /ˈpærəsaɪd/ *n.* person who kills his or her father, killing of one's father. **parricidal** *a.*
**parrot** /ˈpærət/ 1 *n.* kind of mainly tropical bird with short hooked bill, of which some species can be taught to repeat words; unintelligent imitator or chatterer. 2 *v.t.* (*past* & *p.p.* **parroted**) repeat mechanically.
**parry** /ˈpæri/ 1 *v.t.* ward off, avert. 2 *n.* act of parrying.
**parse** /pɑːz/ *v.t.* describe (word) or analyse (sentence) in terms of grammar.
**parsec** /ˈpɑːsek/ *n.* unit of stellar distance, about 3.25 light-years.
**parsimony** /ˈpɑːsɪməni/ *n.* carefulness in use of money etc.; meanness. **parsimonious** /-ˈməʊn-/ *a.*
**parsley** /ˈpɑːsli/ *n.* herb used for seasoning and garnishing.
**parsnip** /ˈpɑːsnɪp/ *n.* plant with pale yellow tapering root used as vegetable; this root.
**parson** /ˈpɑːs(ə)n/ *n.* parish clergyman; *colloq.* any clergyman. **parson's nose** rump of cooked fowl. **parsonical** /-ˈsɒn-/ *a.*
**parsonage** /ˈpɑːsənɪdʒ/ *n.* parson's house.
**part** 1 *n.* some but not all; component, division, portion; share, allotted portion; assigned character or role; *Mus.* one of melodies making up harmony of concerted music; side in agreement or dispute; region, direction, way; in *pl.* abilities. 2 *v.* divide into parts; separate; make parting (in hair). 3 *adv.* partly, in part. 4 **part and parcel** essential part *of*; **part exchange** transaction in which article is given as part of payment for more expensive one; **part-song** song for 3 or more voice-parts; **part-time** employed for or taking up only part of working day etc.; **part-timer** part-time worker; **part with** give up, relinquish.
**partake** /pɑːˈteɪk/ *v.i.* (*past* -**took**; *p.p.* -**taken**) take share (*in, of, with*); eat or drink some *of*; have some (*of* quality etc.).
**parterre** /pɑːˈteə(r)/ *n.* level garden space filled with flower-beds etc.; pit of theatre.
**partial** /ˈpɑːʃ(ə)l/ *a.* not total or complete; biased, unfair. **be partial to** like. **partiality** /-ˈæl-/ *n.*
**participate** /pɑːˈtɪsɪpeɪt/ *v.i.* have share or take part (*in*). **participant** *n.*; **participation** *n.*
**participle** /ˈpɑːtɪsɪp(ə)l/ *n.* adjective formed by inflexion from verb. **participial** /-ˈsɪp-/ *a.*
**particle** /ˈpɑːtɪk(ə)l/ *n.* minute portion of matter; smallest possible amount; minor esp. indeclinable part of speech; prefix or suffix with distinct meaning.
**particoloured** /ˈpɑːtiˌkʌləd/ *a.* partly of one colour and partly of another.
**particular** /pəˈtɪkjələ(r)/ 1 *a.* relating to one as distinguished from others; special; scrupulously exact; fastidious. 2 *n.* detail, item; in *pl.* detailed account. 3 **particularity** /-ˈlær-/ *n.*
**particularize** /pəˈtɪkjələraɪz/ *v.t.* name specially one by one; specify (items). **particularization** *n.*
**particularly** *adv.* very; to a special extent.
**parting** /ˈpɑːtɪŋ/ *n.* leave-taking; dividing line of combed hair.
**partisan** /pɑːtəˈzæn/ *n.* adherent of party or side or cause; guerrilla. **partisanship** *n.*
**partition** /pɑːˈtɪʃ(ə)n/ *n.* division into parts; such part; structure separating two such parts; thin wall. 2 *v.t.* divide into parts; divide *off* by partition.
**partitive** /ˈpɑːtɪtɪv/ *Gram.* 1 *a.* (of word) denoting part of collective whole. 2 *n.* partitive word.
**partly** /ˈpɑːtli/ *adv.* with respect to a part; in some degree; not wholly.
**partner** /ˈpɑːtnə(r)/ *n.* sharer; person associated with others in business; either of pair in marriage etc. or dancing or game. 2 *v.t.* associate as partners; be partner of. 3 **partnership** *n.*

**partridge** /'pɑ:trɪdʒ/ n. kind of gamebird.

**parturition** /pɑ:tjə'rɪʃ(ə)n/ n. act of bringing forth young; childbirth.

**party** /'pɑ:tɪ/ n. social gathering; body of persons travelling or working together; body of persons united in cause or in opposition to another body; person consenting or contributing to affair; either side in lawsuit, contract, or other transaction. **party line** set policy of political party; shared telephone line; **party-wall** wall common to two adjoining rooms or buildings etc.

**parvenu** /'pɑ:vənju:/ n. (fem. **-nue**) person who has risen from obscurity; upstart.

**Pascal** /'pæskæl/ n. computer language designed for training.

**paschal** /'pæsk(ə)l/ a. of Passover; of Easter.

**pasha** /'pɑ:ʃə/ n. hist. Turkish officer of high rank.

**pasque-flower** /'pæskflaʊə(r)/ n. kind of anemone.

**pass¹** /pɑ:s/ 1 v. (p.p. **passed**, or as adj. **past**) move onward, proceed; go past; leave on one side or behind; surpass; (cause to) go; spend (time etc.); Footb. etc. kick, hand, or hit (ball etc.) to or to player of one's own side; discharge from body as or with excreta; be successful in (examination); (of candidate) satisfy examiner; change (into, from); die, come to an end; happen; be accepted as adequate; utter (judgement etc.); be sanctioned; allow (bill in Parliament, candidate for examination, etc.) to proceed after scrutiny; hand round. 2 n. passing, esp. of examination; status of degree without honours; written permission or ticket or order; Footb. etc. passing of ball; thrust in fencing; critical position. 3 **make a pass at** colloq. make advances to; **pass away** die; **passbook** book recording customer's transactions with bank etc.; **passer-by** person who goes past, esp. casually; **pass for** be accepted as; **pass-key** master-key; **pass off** fade away, be carried through, misrepresent as something false, lightly dismiss; **pass out** become unconscious, complete military training; **pass over** omit, make no remark upon; **pass up** colloq. refuse or neglect (opportunity etc.);

**password** agreed secret word uttered to sentry etc. to allow one to proceed.

**pass²** /pɑ:s/ n. narrow passage through mountains.

**passable** /'pɑ:səb(ə)l/ a. adequate, fairly good.

**passage** /'pæsɪdʒ/ n. passing, transit; passageway; right of conveyance as passenger by sea or air; journey by sea or air; transition from one state to another; short part of book or piece of music etc.; in pl. interchange of words.

**passageway** /'pæsɪdʒweɪ/ n. narrow way for passing along; corridor.

**passé** /'pæseɪ/ a. behind the times; past the prime. [F]

**passenger** /'pæsəndʒə(r)/ n. traveller in public conveyance; traveller in car etc. who is not driving; ineffective member of team etc.

**passerine** /'pæsəraɪn/ 1 a. of sparrow kind. 2 n. passerine bird.

**passim** /'pæsɪm/ adv. throughout. [L]

**passion** /'pæʃ(ə)n/ n. strong emotion; anger; sexual love; strong enthusiasm; **Passion** the sufferings of Christ on cross, Gospel narrative of this or musical setting of it. **passion-flower** plant with flower supposed to suggest instruments of Crucifixion; **passion-fruit** edible fruit of some species of passion-flower.

**passionate** /'pæʃənət/ a. dominated by or easily moved to strong feeling; showing or caused by passion.

**passive** /'pæsɪv/ 1 a. acted upon, not acting; inert; submissive; Gram. of or in passive voice. 2 n. Gram. passive voice or form. 3 **passive voice** Gram. voice of verb indicating that subject undergoes action of the verb. 4 **passivity** /-'sɪv-/ n.

**Passover** /'pɑ:səʊvə(r)/ n. Jewish spring festival commemorating deliverance of Israelites from bondage in Egypt.

**passport** /'pɑ:spɔ:t/ n. official document showing identity and nationality etc. of traveller abroad.

**past** /pɑ:st/ 1 a. (p.p. of **pass¹**) gone by; just over. 2 n. past time; person's past life or career. 3 prep. beyond. 4 adv. by. 5 **past master** thorough master, expert.

**pasta** /'pæstə/ n. flour paste produced in various shapes; dish of this.

**paste** /peɪst/ 1 n. any moist fairly stiff mixture; dough of flour with fat and water etc.; flour and water or similar mixture as adhesive; easily spread preparation of pounded fish, meat, etc.; material used to make imitation gems. 2 v.t. fasten or coat with paste; sl. beat, thrash. 3 **pasteboard** stiff substance made by pasting together sheets of paper.

**pastel** /ˈpæst(ə)l/ n. crayon made of dry pigment-paste; drawing in pastel; light subdued colour.

**pastern** /ˈpæstɜːn/ n. part of horse's foot between fetlock and hoof.

**pasteurize** /ˈpɑːstʃəraɪz/ v.t. partially sterilize (milk etc.) by keeping for some time at high temperature. **pasteurization** n.

**pastiche** /pæsˈtiːʃ/ n. musical or other medley made up from various sources; literary or other work imitating style of author or period etc.

**pastille** /ˈpæstəl/ n. small sweet or lozenge.

**pastime** /ˈpɑːstaɪm/ n. recreation; sport or game.

**pastor** /ˈpɑːstə(r)/ n. minister of congregation; spiritual adviser.

**pastoral** /ˈpɑːstər(ə)l/ 1 a. of shepherds; of rural life; of pastor. 2 n. pastoral poem or picture; letter from bishop or other pastor to clergy or people.

**pastoralist** /ˈpɑːstərəlɪst/ n. Aus. sheep- or cattle-farmer; squatter.

**pastrami** /pæsˈtrɑːmiː/ n. seasoned smoked beef.

**pastry** /ˈpeɪstriː/ n. dough of flour, fat, and water; (item of) food made wholly or partly of this.

**pasturage** /ˈpɑːstʃərɪdʒ/ n. pasture land; pasturing.

**pasture** /ˈpɑːstʃə(r)/ 1 n. land covered with grass etc. for grazing animals; herbage for cattle. 2 v. put (cattle) to pasture; graze.

**pasty**[1] /ˈpæstiː/ n. pie of meat etc. enclosed in pastry crust and baked without dish.

**pasty**[2] /ˈpeɪstiː/ a. of or like paste; pallid.

**pat**[1] 1 v.t. strike gently with open hand or other flat surface. 2 n. patting touch or sound; small mass, esp. of butter, made (as) by patting. 3 a. apposite, opportune; ready for any occasion. 4 adv. in a pat manner.

**pat**[2] n. Aus. colloq. **on one's pat** alone.

**patch** 1 n. piece put on in mending; piece of plaster over wound; cover protecting injured eye; large or irregular spot on surface, distinct area or period; small plot of ground. 2 v.t. mend with patch(es); piece together; appear as patches on (surface). 3 **not a patch on** very much inferior to; **patch-pocket** pocket sewn on like patch; **patch up** repair, set to rights, esp. hastily; **patchwork** needlework using small pieces of different colours etc. sewn together.

**patchy** /ˈpætʃiː/ a. uneven in quality; having patches.

**pate** n. colloq. head.

**pâté** /ˈpæteɪ/ n. smooth paste of meat etc. **pâté de foie gras** /də fwɑː ɡrɑː/ pâté made from livers of fatted geese.

**patella** /pəˈtelə/ n. (pl. **-lae** /-liː/) kneecap.

**paten** /ˈpæt(ə)n/ n. plate for bread at Eucharist.

**patent** /ˈpeɪt(ə)nt, ˈpæt-/ 1 n. official document conferring right, title, etc., esp. sole right to make, use, or sell some invention; right granted by this; invention or process so protected. 2 a. conferred or protected by patent; (of food, medicine, etc.) proprietary; plain, obvious. 3 v.t. obtain patent for (invention). 4 **patent leather** leather with glossy varnished surface.

**patentee** /peɪtənˈtiː/ n. holder of patent.

**paternal** /pəˈtɜːn(ə)l/ a. of father, fatherly; related through father, on father's side.

**paternalism** /pəˈtɜːnəlɪz(ə)m/ n. government etc. restricting freedom and responsibility by well-meant regulations. **paternalistic** a.

**paternity** /pəˈtɜːnɪtiː/ n. fatherhood; one's paternal origin.

**paternoster** /pætəˈnɒstə(r)/ n. Lord's Prayer, esp. in Latin.

**path** /pɑːθ/ n. footway; track; line along which person or thing moves.

**pathetic** /pəˈθetɪk/ a. exciting pity or sadness or contempt.

**pathogen** /ˈpæθədʒ(ə)n/ n. agent causing disease. **pathogenic** /-ˈdʒen-/ a.

**pathological** /pæθəˈlɒdʒɪk(ə)l/ a. of pathology; of or caused by mental or physical disorder.

**pathology** /pəˈθɒlədʒiː/ n. study of disease. **pathologist** n.

**pathos** /'peɪθɒs/ n. quality that excites pity or sadness.

**patience** /'peɪʃ(ə)ns/ n. endurance of hardship, provocation, pain, delay, etc.; perseverance; card-game, usu. for one person.

**patient** /'peɪʃ(ə)nt/ 1 a. having or showing patience. 2 n. person under medical etc. treatment.

**patina** /'pætɪnə/ n. incrustation, usu. green, on surface of old bronze; gloss produced by age on woodwork etc.

**patio** /'pætɪəʊ/ n. (pl. **-os**) paved usu. roofless area adjoining house; roofless inner courtyard.

**patois** /'pætwɑː/ n. (pl. same /-wɑːz/) dialect of the common people of a district.

**patriarch** /'peɪtrɪɑːk/ n. male head of family or tribe; bishop of certain sees in Orthodox and R.C. Churches; venerable old man. **patriarchal** a.

**patriarchate** /'peɪtrɪɑːkət/ n. office or see or residence of patriarch.

**patriarchy** /'peɪtrɪɑːkɪ/ n. patriarchal system of society etc.

**patrician** /pə'trɪʃ(ə)n/ 1 n. person of noble birth. 2 a. of nobility; aristocratic.

**patricide** /'pætrɪsaɪd/ n. parricide.

**patrimony** /'pætrɪmənɪ/ n. property inherited from father or ancestors.

**patriot** /'pætrɪət, 'peɪ-/ n. person devoted to and ready to defend his country. **patriotic** /-'ɒt-/ a.; **patriotism** n.

**patrol** /pə'trəʊl/ 1 v. walk or travel round (area etc.) to protect or supervise it; act as patrol. 2 n. patrolling; person(s) or vehicle(s) assigned or sent out to patrol. 3 **patrol car** car used by police etc. for patrol; **patrolman** US police constable.

**patron** /'peɪtrən/ n. person who gives financial or other support to; customer of shop etc. **patron saint** saint regarded as protecting person or place etc.

**patronage** /'pætrənɪdʒ/ n. patron's or customer's support; right of bestowing or recommending for appointments; patronizing airs.

**patronize** /'pætrənaɪz/ v.t. act as patron to; support, encourage; treat condescendingly.

**patronymic** /pætrə'nɪmɪk/ n. name derived from that of father or ancestor.

**patter**¹ 1 v.i. (of rain etc.) make tapping sound; run with quick short steps. 2 n. sound of pattering.

**patter**² /'pætə(r)/ 1 n. language of profession or class; rapid often glib or deceptive talk. 2 v. say or talk with rapid utterance.

**pattern** /'pæt(ə)n/ 1 n. decorative design on surface; model or design or working instructions from which thing is to be made; excellent example; sample, esp. of cloth. 2 v.t. decorate with pattern.

**patty** /'pætɪ/ n. small pie or pasty.

**paucity** /'pɔːsɪtɪ/ n. smallness of number or quantity.

**paunch** /pɔːntʃ/ n. belly, stomach.

**pauper** /'pɔːpə(r)/ n. very poor person; *hist.* recipient of poor-law relief. **pauperism** n.; **pauperize** v.t.

**pause** /pɔːz/ 1 n. interval of inaction or silence; break made in speech or reading; *Mus.* mark denoting lengthening of note or rest. 2 v.i. make a pause; wait.

**pavan** /pə'væn/ n. (also **pavane**) stately dance in slow duple time; music for this.

**pave** v.t. cover with durable surface. **pave the way** make preparations *for*.

**pavement** /'peɪvm(ə)nt/ n. paved footway at side of road.

**pavilion** /pə'vɪlɪən/ n. light ornamental building; building on sports ground for spectators or players; large tent.

**pavlova** /pæv'ləʊvə/ n. meringue cake with cream and fruit.

**paw** 1 n. foot of animal with claws; *colloq.* person's hand. 2 v. touch with paw; *colloq.* handle awkwardly, rudely, etc.; (of horse) strike (ground) with hoof.

**pawky** /'pɔːkɪ/ a. Sc. & dial. drily humorous; shrewd.

**pawl** n. lever with catch for teeth of wheel or bar; bar to prevent capstan etc. from recoiling.

**pawn**¹ n. chess-man of smallest size and value; *fig.* unimportant person subservient to others' plans.

**pawn**² 1 v.t. deposit (thing) as security for money borrowed; pledge. 2 n. state of being pawned. 3 **pawnbroker** person who lends money at interest on security of personal property deposited with him; **pawnshop** his place of business.

**pawpaw** var. of **papaw**.

**pay** v. (past & p.p. **paid**) give as due; discharge debt to; bear cost; suffer penalty for; render, bestow (attention etc.); yield adequate return; let out (rope) by slackening it. 2 n. wages, salary. **3 in the pay of** employed by; **pay-as-you-earn** collection of income-tax by deduction at source from wages etc.; **pay-claim** demand for increase in pay; **payload** part of (esp. aircraft's) load from which revenue is derived; **pay off** pay in full and discharge, colloq. yield good results; **pay-off** sl. climax, denouement; **payphone** coinbox telephone; **payroll** list of employees receiving regular pay.

**payable** /'peɪəb(ə)l/ a. that must or may be paid.

**PAYE** abbr. pay-as-you-earn.

**payee** /peɪ'i:/ n. person to whom money is (to be) paid.

**payment** /'peɪm(ə)nt/ n. paying, amount paid; recompense.

**payola** /peɪ'əʊlə/ n. bribe offered in return for illicit or unfair help in promoting commercial product.

**PC** abbr. Police Constable; Privy Councillor; personal computer.

**p.c.** abbr. per cent; postcard.

**pd.** abbr. paid.

**PE** abbr. physical education.

**pea** n. climbing plant bearing round seeds in pods and cultivated for food; one of the seeds; similar plant.

**peace** /pi:s/ n. quiet, calm; harmonious relations; freedom from or cessation of war; civil order. **peacemaker** person who brings about peace; **peacetime** time when country is not at war.

**peaceable** /'pi:səb(ə)l/ a. disposed or tending to peace, peaceful.

**peaceful** /'pi:sfəl/ a. characterized by or concerned with peace.

**peach**[1] /pi:tʃ/ n. large roundish stone-fruit with downy delicately coloured skin; tree bearing it; sl. thing of superlative merit. **peach Melba** dish of ice cream and peaches. **peachy** a.

**peach**[2] v.i. sl. turn informer; inform.

**peacock** /'pi:kɒk/ n. male peafowl, bird with splendid plumage and fanlike tail. **peacock blue** bright lustrous blue of peacock's neck.

**peafowl** /'pi:faʊl/ n. kind of pheasant, peacock or peahen.

**peahen** /'pi:hen/ n. female peafowl.

**pea-jacket** /'pi:dʒækət/ n. sailor's short thick double-breasted overcoat.

**peak**[1] n. pointed top, esp. of mountain; projecting part of brim of cap; highest point of achievement, intensity, etc. 2 v.i. reach highest value, quality, etc.

**peak**[2] v.i. waste away; in p.p. pinched-looking.

**peaky** /'pi:kɪ/ a. sickly, puny.

**peal** 1 n. loud ringing of bell(s); set of bells; outburst of sound. 2 v. sound forth or ring (bells) in peal.

**peanut** /'pi:nʌt/ n. plant bearing underground pods containing seeds used as food and yielding oil; its seed; in pl. sl. trivial amount esp. of money. **peanut butter** paste of ground roasted peanuts.

**pear** /peə(r)/ n. fleshy fruit tapering towards stalk; tree bearing it.

**pearl** /pɜ:l/ 1 n. lustrous usu. white concretion found in shell of certain oyster and prized as gem; imitation of this; precious thing, finest example. 2 v. fish for pearls; (of moisture) form drops, form drops on. **3 Pearl barley** barley rubbed into small rounded grains; **pearl button** button of (real or imitation) mother-of-pearl; **pearl onion** very small onion used in pickles.

**pearly** /'pɜ:lɪ/ 1 a. resembling a pearl; adorned with pearls. 2 n. in pl. costermongers' clothes decorated with pearl buttons. **3 Pearly Gates** gates of Heaven; **pearly king**, **queen**, wearers of pearlies.

**peasant** /'pez(ə)nt/ n. (in some countries) worker on land, farm labourer; small farmer.

**peasantry** /'pezəntrɪ/ n. peasants of a district etc.

**pease pudding** /pi:z/ pudding of dried peas boiled in a cloth.

**peat** n. vegetable matter decomposed by water and partly carbonized; piece of this as fuel. **peat-bog** bog composed of peat. **peaty** a.

**pebble** /'peb(ə)l/ n. small stone rounded by action of water. **pebble-dash** mortar with pebbles in it as wall-coating. **pebbly** a.

**pecan** /'pi:kən/ n. pinkish-brown

**peccadillo** /pekə'dɪləʊ/ n. trivial offence.

**peccary** /'pekərɪ/ n. small wild pig of S. and Central Amer.

**peck**¹ 1 v. strike or pick up or pluck out or make (hole) with beak; eat fastidiously. 2 n. stroke with beak; hasty or perfunctory kiss.

**peck**² n. measure of capacity for dry goods, =2 gallons.

**pecker** n. **keep your pecker up** sl. stay cheerful.

**peckish** /'pekɪʃ/ a. colloq. hungry.

**pectin** /'pektɪn/ n. gelatinous substance in ripe fruits, causing jam etc. to set.

**pectoral** /'pektər(ə)l/ 1 a. of or for breast or chest. 2 n. pectoral fin or muscle.

**peculate** /'pekjʊleɪt/ v. embezzle. **peculation** n.; **peculator** n.

**peculiar** /pɪ'kju:lɪə(r)/ a. odd; exclusive *to*; belonging to the individual; particular, special.

**peculiarity** /pəkju:lɪ'ærətɪ/ n. being peculiar; characteristic; oddity.

**pecuniary** /pə'kju:nɪərɪ/ a. of or in money.

**pedagogue** /'pedəgɒg/ n. schoolmaster; pedant.

**pedagogy** /'pedəgɒdʒɪ/ n. science of teaching. **pedagogic(al)** a.

**pedal** /'ped(ə)l/ 1 n. lever or key operated by foot, esp. in bicycle or motor vehicle or some musical instruments. 2 v. work pedals (of); ride bicycle. 3 a. of foot or feet.

**pedant** /'ped(ə)nt/ n. person who overrates or parades learning or knowledge, or insists on strict adherence to formal rules. **pedantic** /-'dænt-/ a.; **pedantry** n.

**peddle** /'ped(ə)l/ v. be pedlar; trade or deal in as pedlar.

**pederast** /'pedəræst/ n. man who commits pederasty.

**pederasty** /'pedəræstɪ/ n. sodomy with a boy.

**pedestal** /'pedɪst(ə)l/ n. base of column; block on which something stands.

**pedestrian** /pɪ'destrɪən/ 1 n. walker, traveller on foot. 2 a. prosaic, dull; going or performed on foot; of walking; for those on foot.

**pedicure** /'pedɪkjʊə(r)/ n. care or treatment of feet, esp. of toe-nails.

**pedigree** /'pedɪgri:/ 1 n. genealogical table; ancestral line; ancient descent. 2 a. having known line of descent.

**pediment** /'pedɪm(ə)nt/ n. triangular part crowning front of building.

**pedlar** /'pedlə(r)/ n. travelling seller of small wares.

**pedometer** /pɪ'dɒmɪtə(r)/ n. instrument for estimating distance travelled on foot.

**peduncle** /pɪ'dʌŋk(ə)l/ n. Bot. stalk of flower or fruit or cluster, esp. main stalk bearing solitary flower.

**pee** colloq. 1 v.i. urinate. 2 n. urination; urine.

**peek** n. & v.i. peep, glance.

**peel** 1 n. rind or outer coating of fruit or potato etc. 2 v. strip peel or rind etc. from; take *off* (skin, peel, etc.); become bare of bark, skin, etc.; come off or *off* like peel.

**peeling** /'pi:lɪŋ/ n. piece peeled off.

**peep**¹ 1 v.i. look furtively or through narrow aperture; come cautiously or partly into view; begin to appear. 2 n. furtive or peering glance; first light (*of dawn, day*). 3 **peep-hole** small hole to peep through; **Peeping Tom** furtive voyeur; **peep-show** exhibition of pictures etc. viewed through lens in peephole.

**peep**² n. & v.i. cheep, squeak.

**peer**¹ v.i. look searchingly; peep out.

**peer**² n. equal (esp. in civil standing or rank); duke, marquis, earl, viscount, or baron. **peer group** person's associates of same status.

**peerage** /'pɪərɪdʒ/ n. the peers; book listing these; rank of peer or peeress.

**peeress** /'pɪərɪs/ n. female holder of peerage; peer's wife.

**peerless** /'pɪələs/ a. unequalled.

**peeve** /pi:v/ sl. 1 v.t. irritate. 2 n. cause of annoyance.

**peevish** /'pi:vɪʃ/ a. querulous, irritable.

**peewit** /'pi:wɪt/ n. magpie-lark.

**peg** 1 n. wooden or metal etc. bolt or pin for holding things together or hanging things on, or as stopper or position indicator; forked wooden peg or similar device for hanging washing on line; drink, esp. of spirits. 2 v. fix or mark or hang out (as) with peg(s); keep (prices etc.) stable. 3 **off the peg** (of clothes)

# pejorative / pennant

ready-made; **peg away** work persistently (*at*); **peg-board** board with holes and pegs; **peg out** mark out boundaries of, *sl.* die.

**pejorative** /pəˈdʒɒrətɪv/ **1** *a.* derogatory. **2** *n.* derogatory word.

**peke** *n. colloq.* Pekinese dog.

**Pekinese** /piːkəˈniːz/ *n.* (also **Pekingese**) dog of small short-legged snub-nosed breed with long silky hair.

**pelargonium** /peləˈɡəʊniːəm/ *n.* plant with showy flowers.

**pelf** *n.* money, wealth.

**pelican** /ˈpelɪkən/ *n.* large water-bird with pouch in bill for storing fish.

**pellagra** /pəˈlæɡrə/ *n.* deficiency disease with cracking of skin.

**pellet** /ˈpelət/ *n.* small ball of a substance; pill; small shot.

**pellicle** /ˈpelɪk(ə)l/ *n.* thin skin; membrane; film.

**pell-mell** /ˈpelˈmel/ *adv.* in disorder; headlong.

**pellucid** /pəˈljuːsɪd/ *a.* transparent, clear; free from obscurity.

**pelmet** /ˈpelmət/ *n.* pendent border concealing curtain-rods etc.

**pelt**[1] **1** *v.* assail with missiles, abuse, etc.; (of rain) come down hard; run at full speed. **2** *n.* pelting.

**pelt**[2] *n.* skin of animal, esp. with hair or fur still on it.

**pelvis** /ˈpelvəs/ *n.* lower abdominal cavity formed by haunch bones etc. **pelvic** *a.*

**pen**[1] **1** *n.* implement for writing with ink; writing or literary style. **2** *v.t.* compose and write (letter etc.). **3 penfriend** person with whom one corresponds without meeting; **penknife** small pocket-knife; **penmanship** skill in or style of handwriting; **pen-name** literary pseudonym.

**pen**[2] **1** *n.* small enclosure for cows, sheep, poultry, etc. **2** *v.t.* enclose; put or keep in confined space.

**pen**[3] *n.* female swan.

**penal** /ˈpiːn(ə)l/ *a.* of or involving punishment; punishable.

**penalize** /ˈpiːnəlaɪz/ *v.t.* subject to penalty or comparative disadvantage; make punishable.

**penalty** /ˈpenəltɪ/ *n.* fine or other punishment; disadvantage imposed by circumstances or for breaking rule or failing to fulfil condition etc.; (goal scored by) penalty kick. **penalty area** *Footb.* area in front of goal within which breach of rules involves penalty kick; **penalty kick** free kick at goal from close range.

**penance** /ˈpen(ə)ns/ *n.* act, esp. one imposed by priest, performed as expression of penitence.

**pence** *pl.* of **penny**.

**penchant** /pɑ̃ʃɑ̃/ *n.* inclination or liking (*for*). [F]

**pencil** /ˈpens(ə)l/ **1** *n.* instrument for drawing or writing, esp. of graphite enclosed in wooden cylinder or metal case with tapering end; something used or shaped like this. **2** *v.t.* draw or mark or write with pencil.

**pendant** /ˈpend(ə)nt/ *n.* ornament hung from necklace etc.

**pendent** /ˈpend(ə)nt/ *a.* hanging; overhanging; pending.

**pending** /ˈpendɪŋ/ **1** *a.* awaiting decision or settlement. **2** *prep.* until; during.

**pendulous** /ˈpendjʊləs/ *a.* hanging down; swinging.

**pendulum** /ˈpendjʊləm/ *n.* body suspended so as to be free to swing, esp. regulating movement of clock's works.

**penetrate** /ˈpenətreɪt/ *v.* make way into or through; pierce; permeate; see into or through; make a way. **penetrable** *a.*

**penetrating** *a.* having or showing insight; easily heard through or above other sounds.

**penetration** /penəˈtreɪʃ(ə)n/ *n.* act or extent of penetrating; acute insight.

**penguin** /ˈpeŋɡwɪn/ *n.* flightless seabird of southern hemisphere.

**penicillin** /penəˈsɪlɪn/ *n.* antibiotic obtained from mould.

**peninsula** /pəˈnɪnsjʊlə/ *n.* piece of land almost surrounded by water or projecting far into sea etc. **peninsular** *a.*

**penis** /ˈpiːnɪs/ *n.* sexual and (in mammals) urinary organ of male animal.

**penitent** /ˈpenɪt(ə)nt/ **1** *a.* repentant, contrite. **2** *n.* penitent person; person doing penance. **3 penitence** *n.*

**penitential** /penɪˈtenʃ(ə)l/ *a.* of penitence or penance.

**penitentiary** /penɪˈtenʃərɪ/ **1** *n. US* reformatory prison. **2** *a.* of penance or reformatory treatment.

**pennant** /ˈpenənt/ *n.* tapering flag, esp.

## penniless

**penniless** /'penələs/ *a.* destitute.
**pennon** /'penən/ *n.* long narrow triangular or swallow-tailed flag; long pointed streamer of ship.
**penny** /'peni/ *n.* (*pl.* **pence** *or* **pennies**) British bronze coin worth 1/100 of pound, or formerly 1/12 of shilling. **penny farthing** early kind of bicycle with large front wheel and small rear one; **penny-pinching** niggardly; **a pretty penny** a large sum of money.
**pennyroyal** /peni'rɔɪəl/ *n.* kind of mint formerly used in medicine.
**penology** /pi:'nɒlədʒi:/ *n.* study of punishment and prison management. **penological** *a.*
**pension** /'penʃ(ə)n/ **1** *n.* periodic payment made to person above specified age or to retired or widowed or disabled etc. person. **2** *v.t.* grant pension to. **3 pension off** dismiss with pension.
**pensionable** *a.* entitled or entitling person to pension.
**pensionary** /'penʃənəri/ **1** *a.* of pension. **2** *n.* recipient of pension.
**pensioner** /'penʃənə(r)/ *n.* recipient of (esp. retirement) pension.
**pensive** /'pensɪv/ *a.* deep in thought.
**pent** *a.* closely confined, shut in or up.
**penta-** *in comb.* five.
**pentacle** /'pentək(ə)l/ *n.* figure used as symbol, esp. in magic, e.g. pentagram.
**pentagon** /'pentəgən/ *n.* plane figure with 5 sides and angles. **the Pentagon** headquarters of leaders of US defence forces. **pentagonal** /-'tæg-/ *a.*
**pentagram** /'pentəgræm/ *n.* 5-pointed star.
**pentameter** /pen'tæmətə(r)/ *n.* line of 5 metrical feet.
**Pentateuch** /'pentətju:k/ *n.* first 5 books of OT.
**pentathlon** /pen'tæθlən/ *n.* athletic contest comprising 5 different events for competitor.
**Pentecost** /'pentɪkɒst/ *n.* Jewish harvest festival 50 days after Passover; Whit Sunday. **pentecostal** *a.*
**penthouse** /'penthaʊs/ *n.* flat, house, etc. on roof of tall building; sloping roof supported against wall of building.
**penultimate** /pɪ'nʌltɪmət/ **1** *a.* & *n.* last but one.
**penumbra** /pɪ'nʌmbrə/ *n.* (*pl.* **-rae** /-ri:/) partly shaded region round shadow of opaque body; partial shadow. **penumbral** *a.*
**penurious** /pənjʊ'ri:əs/ *a.* poor; stingy.
**penury** /'penjəri/ *n.* destitution, poverty.
**peon** /pjuːn/ *n.* Sp. Amer. day-labourer.
**peony** /'pi:əni/ *n.* garden plant with large globular flowers.
**people** /'pi:p(ə)l/ **1** *n.* race or nation; persons in general; subjects; *the* body of enfranchised citizens; parents or other relatives. **2** *v.t.* fill with people; populate; inhabit.
**pep 1** *n.* vigour, spirit. **2** *v.t.* fill *up*, inspire, with energy and vigour. **3 pep pill** one containing stimulant drug; **pep talk** exhortation to greater effort or courage.
**pepper** /'pepə(r)/ **1** *n.* pungent aromatic condiment from dried berries of some plants; capsicum plant, its fruit. **2** *v.t.* sprinkle or flavour with pepper; pelt with missiles. **3 pepper-and-salt** of closely mingled dark and light; **peppercorn** dried pepper berry, nominal rent; **pepper-mill** mill for grinding peppercorns.
**peppermint** /'pepəmɪnt/ *n.* species of mint grown for its strong fragrant oil; sweet flavoured with this oil; the oil.
**peppery** /'pepəri/ *a.* of or like or abounding in pepper; *fig.* hot-tempered.
**pepsin** /'pepsɪn/ *n.* enzyme contained in gastric juice.
**peptic** /'peptɪk/ *a.* digestive. **peptic ulcer** one in stomach or duodenum.
**per** *prep.* for each; by, by means or instrumentality of.
**peradventure** /pərəd'ventʃə(r)/ *adv. arch.* perhaps, perchance; by chance.
**perambulate** /pə'ræmbjəleɪt/ *v.* walk through or over or about. **perambulation** *n.*; **perambulatory** *a.*
**perambulator** /pə'ræmbjəleɪtə(r)/ *n.* pram.
**per annum** /pɜ:r 'ænəm/ for each year.
**per capita** /pɜ: 'kæpɪtə/ for each person.
**perceive** /pə'siːv/ *v.t.* become aware of by one of senses; apprehend; understand.
**per cent** /pə 'sent/ in every hundred; percentage; one part in every hundred.

**percentage** /pə'sentɪdʒ/ n. rate or proportion per cent; proportion.

**perceptible** /pə'septəb(ə)l/ a. that can be perceived. **perceptibility** n.

**perception** /pə'sepʃ(ə)n/ n. act or faculty of perceiving.

**perceptive** /pə'septɪv/ a. of perception; quick to perceive or understand. **perceptivity** n.

**perch**[1] 1 n. bird's resting place; *fig.* elevated position; measure of length (5½ yds.). 2 v. rest or place on or as if on perch.

**perch**[2] n. kind of freshwater fish.

**perchance** /pə'tʃɑːns/ adv. *arch.* maybe.

**percipient** /pə'sɪpɪənt/ 1 a. perceiving; conscious.

**percolate** /'pɜːkəleɪt/ v. filter, esp. through pores or perforations. **percolation** n.

**percolator** n. apparatus for making coffee by percolation.

**percussion** /pə'kʌʃ(ə)n/ n. forcible striking of body against another; *Mus.* instruments struck with stick or hand or struck together in pairs. **percussion cap** small metal or paper device containing explosive powder and exploded by fall of hammer. **percussive** a.

**perdition** /pə'dɪʃ(ə)n/ n. damnation.

**peregrine** /'perəgrɪn/ n. kind of falcon.

**peremptory** /pə'remptəri/ a. imperious; urgent.

**perennial** /pə'renɪəl/ 1 a. lasting through the year; lasting long or for ever; (of plant) living several years. 2 n. perennial plant.

**perentie** /pə'renti/ n. large burrowing monitor lizard of N. and Central Australia.

**perfect** /'pɜːfɪkt/ 1 a. complete, faultless; not deficient; exact, precise; entire, unqualified; *Gram.* (of tense) expressing completed action. 2 n. perfect tense. 3 v.t. (also /pə'fekt/) make perfect. 4 **perfect pitch** *Mus.* ability to recognize pitch of note. 5 **perfectible** /-'fekt-/ a.; **perfectibility** n.

**perfection** /pə'fekʃ(ə)n/ n. being or making perfect; perfect state; perfect person, specimen, etc.

**perfectionist** /pə'fekʃənɪst/ n. person who aspires constantly to perfection.

**perfectly** adv. quite, completely.

**perfidy** /'pɜːfɪdɪ/ n. breach of faith, treachery. **perfidious** /-'fɪd-/ a.

**perforate** /'pɜːfəreɪt/ v. pierce, make hole(s); make row of small holes in (paper). **perforation** n.

**perforce** /pə'fɔːs/ adv. unavoidably, necessarily.

**perform** /pə'fɔːm/ v. carry into effect; accomplish; go through, execute; act, sing, recite. esp. in public; (of animals) do tricks etc.

**performance** /pə'fɔːməns/ n. carrying out, doing; execution; notable feat; performing of or in play etc.

**perfume** /'pɜːfjuːm/ 1 n. sweet smell; fragrant liquid, esp. for application to the body, scent. 2 v.t. impart perfume to.

**perfumer** /pə'fjuːmə(r)/ n. maker or seller of perfumes. **perfumery** n.

**perfunctory** /pə'fʌŋktərɪ/ a. done merely for sake of getting through a duty; superficial.

**pergola** /'pɜːgələ/ n. arbour or covered walk arched with climbing plants.

**perhaps** /pə'hæps/ adv. it may be, possibly.

**perianth** /'perɪænθ/ n. outer part of flower.

**perigee** /'perɪdʒiː/ n. point nearest to earth in orbit of moon etc.

**perihelion** /perɪ'hiːlɪən/ n. (pl. **-lia**) point nearest to sun in orbit of planet or comet etc. round it.

**peril** /'perəl/ n. danger, risk. **perilous** a.

**perimeter** /pə'rɪmɪtə(r)/ n. circumference or outline of closed figure; length of this; outer boundary.

**period** /'pɪərɪəd/ 1 n. amount of time during which something runs its course; distinct portion of history, life, etc.; occurrence of menstruation, time of this; complete sentence; full stop. 2 a. of or characteristic of past period.

**periodic** /pɪərɪ'ɒdɪk/ a. appearing or recurring at regular intervals. **periodic table** arrangement of chemical elements by atomic number.

**periodical** /pɪərɪ'ɒdɪk(ə)l/ 1 a. periodic. 2 n. magazine etc. published at regular intervals.

**periodicity** /pɪərɪə'dɪsətɪ/ n. recurrence at intervals.

**peripatetic** /perəpə'tetɪk/ a. going from place to place; itinerant.

# peripheral

**peripheral** /pəˈrɪfər(ə)l/ 1 *a.* of periphery; of minor importance. 2 *n.* input or output device connected to computer.

**periphery** /pəˈrɪfəri:/ *n.* bounding line, esp. of round surface; outer or surrounding surface or area etc.

**periphrasis** /pəˈrɪfrəsəs/ *n.* (*pl.* **-ses** /-si:z/) roundabout speech or phrase, circumlocution. **periphrastic** /-ˈfræst-/ *a.*

**periscope** /ˈperəskəʊp/ *n.* apparatus with tube and mirrors for viewing objects otherwise out of sight.

**perish** /ˈperɪʃ/ *v.* suffer destruction, lose life; come to untimely end; (cause to) lose natural qualities; (of cold etc.) reduce to distress. **do a perish** *Aus. colloq.* come near to death esp. by starvation and lack of water.

**perishable** 1 *a.* subject to speedy decay. 2 *n.* in *pl.* perishable goods (esp. foods).

**perisher** *n. sl.* annoying person.

**perishing** *a. colloq.* intensely cold; confounded.

**peritoneum** /perɪtəˈni:əm/ *n.* (*pl.* **-neums**) membrane lining abdominal cavity. **peritoneal** *a.*

**peritonitis** /perətəˈnaɪtəs/ *n.* inflammation of peritoneum.

**periwig** /ˈperɪwɪg/ *n.* wig.

**periwinkle**[1] /ˈperɪwɪŋk(ə)l/ *n.* evergreen trailing plant with light-blue flower.

**periwinkle**[2] /ˈperɪwɪŋk(ə)l/ *n.* winkle.

**perjure** /ˈpɜ:dʒə(r)/ *v.refl.* **perjure oneself** commit perjury; in *p.p.* guilty of perjury.

**perjury** /ˈpɜ:dʒəri:/ *n.* wilful utterance of false evidence while on oath.

**perk**[1] *v. colloq.* (cause to) recover courage or confidence (usu. with *up*); raise (head etc.) briskly.

**perk**[2] *n. sl.* (usu. in *pl.*) perquisite.

**perky** /ˈpɜ:ki:/ *a.* lively and cheerful.

**perm**[1] 1 *n. colloq.* permanent wave. 2 *v.t.* give permanent wave to.

**perm**[2] 1 *n.* permutation. 2 *v.t.* make permutation of.

**permafrost** /ˈpɜ:məfrɒst/ *n.* permanently frozen subsoil in polar regions.

**permanence** /ˈpɜ:mənəns/ *n.* being permanent.

**permanency** /ˈpɜ:mənənsi:/ *n.* permanent thing or arrangement.

**permanent** /ˈpɜ:mənənt/ *a.* lasting or intended to last indefinitely. **permanent wave** long-lasting artificial wave in hair; **permanent way** finished roadbed of railway.

# perplex

**permeable** /ˈpɜ:mi:əb(ə)l/ *a.* admitting passage of fluid etc. **permeability** *n.*

**permeate** /ˈpɜ:mi:eɪt/ *v.* penetrate, saturate, pervade; be diffused. **permeation** *n.*

**permissible** /pəˈmɪsəb(ə)l/ *a.* allowable, that may be permitted. **permissibility** *n.*

**permission** /pəˈmɪʃ(ə)n/ *n.* consent or liberty (*to* do).

**permissive** /pəˈmɪsɪv/ *a.* tolerant, liberal; giving permission.

**permit** 1 /pəˈmɪt/ *v.* give consent to or opportunity for; admit *of*. 2 /ˈpɜ:mɪt/ *n.* written order giving permission.

**permutation** /pɜ:mjəˈteɪʃ(ə)n/ *n. Math.* variation of order of set of things; any one such arrangement; combination or selection of specified number of items from larger group.

**pernicious** /pəˈnɪʃəs/ *a.* destructive, injurious.

**pernickety** /pəˈnɪkəti:/ *a. colloq.* fastidious, over-precise.

**peroration** /perəˈreɪʃ(ə)n/ *n.* lengthy concluding part of speech.

**peroxide** /pəˈrɒksaɪd/ 1 *n.* oxide containing maximum proportion of oxygen; (in full **hydrogen peroxide**) colourless liquid used in water solution, esp. to bleach hair. 2 *v.t.* bleach (hair) with hydrogen peroxide.

**perpendicular** /pɜ:pənˈdɪkjələ(r)/ 1 *a.* at right angles (*to* given line, plane, or surface); upright; very steep; **Perpendicular** of or in style of English Gothic architecture of 15th-16th c. 2 *n.* perpendicular line etc. 3 **perpendicularity** *n.*

**perpetrate** /ˈpɜ:pətreɪt/ *v.t.* be guilty of; commit. **perpetration** *n.*; **perpetrator** *n.*

**perpetual** /pəˈpetjuːəl/ *a.* lasting for ever or indefinitely; continuous; *colloq.* frequent, repeated.

**perpetuate** /pəˈpetjuːeɪt/ *v.t.* make perpetual; cause to be always remembered. **perpetuation** *n.*

**perpetuity** /pɜ:pəˈtjuːəti:/ *n.* perpetual continuance or possession. **in perpetuity** for ever.

**perplex** /pəˈpleks/ *v.t.* bewilder, puzzle; complicate, tangle. **perplexity** *n.*

**per pro.** *abbr.* by proxy, through an agent (*per procurationem*).

**perquisite** /'pɜːkwəzət/ *n.* extra profit additional to main income etc.; customary extra right or privilege.

**perry** /'peri/ *n.* drink made from fermented pear-juice.

*per se* /pɜː 'seɪ/ by or in itself, intrinsically. [L]

**persecute** /'pɜːsəkjuːt/ *v.t.* subject to constant hostility and ill-treatment; harass, worry. **persecution** *n.*; **persecutor** *n.*

**persevere** /pɜːsə'vɪə(r)/ *v.i.* continue steadfastly, persist. **perseverance** *n.*

**Persian** /'pɜː(ə)n/ **1** *n.* native or language of Persia (now Iran). **2** *a.* of Persia (Iran). **3 Persian cat** kind with long silky hair.

**persiflage** /'pɜːsəflɑːʒ/ *n.* banter; light raillery.

**persimmon** /pɜː'sɪmən/ *n.* Amer. or E. Asian tree; its edible orange plumlike fruit.

**persist** /pə'sɪst/ *v.i.* continue to exist or do something in spite of obstacles. **persistence** *n.*; **persistent** *a.*

**person** /'pɜːs(ə)n/ *n.* individual human being; living body of human being; *Gram.* one of three classes of pronouns, verb-forms, etc., denoting respectively person etc. speaking, spoken to, or spoken of.

**persona** /pɜː'səʊnə/ *n.* (*pl.* **-nae** /-niː/) *Psychol.* aspect of personality as perceived by others. ***persona grata*** /-'ɡrɑːtə/ person, esp. diplomat, acceptable to certain others; ***persona non grata*** /-nɒn-/ person not acceptable.

**personable** /'pɜːsənəb(ə)l/ *a.* pleasing in appearance or demeanour.

**personage** /'pɜːsənɪdʒ/ *n.* person, esp important one.

**personal** /'pɜːsən(ə)l/ *a.* one's own; individual, private; done etc. in person; directed to or concerning individual; *Gram.* of or denoting one of the three persons. **personal column** part of newspaper devoted to short personal advertisements; **personal property** all property except land.

**personality** /pɜːsə'næləti/ *n.* distinctive personal character; personal existence or identity; (esp. well-known) person; in *pl.* personal remarks.

**personalize** /'pɜːsənəlaɪz/ *v.t.* identify as belonging to particular person.

**personally** /'pɜːsənəli/ *adv.* in person; for one's own part.

**personate** /'pɜːsəneɪt/ *v.t.* play part of; pretend to be. **personation** *n.*

**personify** /pə'sɒnɪfaɪ/ *v.t.* attribute personal nature to; symbolize by human figure; (esp. in *p.p.*) embody, exemplify typically. **personification** *n.*

**personnel** /pɜːsə'nel/ *n.* body of employees; persons engaged in particular service, profession, etc. **personnel department** department of firm etc. dealing with appointment and welfare of employees.

**perspective** /pə'spektɪv/ **1** *n.* art of drawing so as to give effect of solidity and relative position and size; relation or proportion between visible objects, parts of subject, etc.; view, prospect. **2** *a.* of or in perspective. **3 in perspective** according to rules of perspective, in proportion.

**Perspex** /'pɜːspeks/ *n.* (P) tough light transparent plastic.

**perspicacious** /pɜːspə'keɪʃəs/ *a.* having mental penetration or discernment. **perspicacity** /-'kæs-/ *n.*

**perspicuous** /pə'spɪkjuːəs/ *a.* expressed with clearness; lucid. **perspicuity** /-'kjuː-/ *n.*

**perspire** /pə'spaɪə(r)/ *v.* sweat. **perspiration** /pɜːspə'reɪʃ(ə)n/ *n.*

**persuade** /pə'sweɪd/ *v.t.* cause (person) by argument etc. to believe or do something; convince.

**persuasion** /pə'sweɪʒ(ə)n/ *n.* persuading; conviction; religious belief or sect.

**persuasive** /pə'sweɪsɪv/ *a.* able or tending to persuade.

**pert** *a.* forward, saucy.

**pertain** /pə'teɪn/ *v.i.* belong, relate.

**pertinacious** /pɜːtə'neɪʃəs/ *n.* persistent, obstinate. **pertinacity** /-'næs-/ *n.*

**pertinent** /'pɜːtən(ə)nt/ *a.* relevant; to the point. **pertinence** *n.*

**perturb** /pə'tɜːb/ *v.t.* throw into agitation; disquiet. **perturbation** *n.*

**peruke** /pə'ruːk/ *n.* wig.

**peruse** /pə'ruːz/ *v.t.* read; scan. **perusal** *n.*

**pervade** /pə'veɪd/ *v.t.* spread through, permeate, saturate. **pervasion** *n.*; **pervasive** *a.*

**perve** *Aus. sl.* **1** *n.* pervert; voyeur; erotic gaze. **2** *v.i.* act as voyeur.

**perverse** /pə'vɜːs/ *a.* obstinately or wilfully in the wrong; wayward; peevish; wicked. **perversity** *n.*

**perversion** /pə'vɜːʃ(ə)n/ *n.* perverting or being perverted; preference for abnormal form of sexual activity.

**pervert 1** /pə'vɜːt/ *v.t.* turn (thing) aside from proper or normal use; lead astray from right behaviour or belief etc.; in *p.p.* showing perversion. **2** /'pɜːvɜːt/ *n.* person who is perverted, esp. sexually.

**pervious** /'pɜːvɪəs/ *a.* permeable; allowing passage or access.

**peseta** /pə'seɪtə/ *n.* Spanish monetary unit.

**peso** /'peɪsəʊ/ *n.* (*pl.* **-sos**) monetary unit in several S. Amer. countries.

**pessary** /'pesərɪ/ *n.* instrument worn in vagina; vaginal suppository.

**pessimism** /'pesɪmɪz(ə)m/ *n.* tendency to take worst view or expect worst outcome. **pessimist** *n.*; **pessimistic** *a.*

**pest** *n.* troublesome or destructive person, animal, or thing. **pest plant** *Aus.* noxious weed.

**pester** /'pestə(r)/ *v.t.* trouble or annoy, esp. with persistent requests.

**pesticide** /'pestɪsaɪd/ *n.* substance for destroying harmful insects etc.

**pestiferous** /pes'tɪfərəs/ *a.* noxious; spreading infection; *fig.* pernicious.

**pestilence** /'pestɪl(ə)ns/ *n.* fatal epidemic disease, esp. bubonic plague.

**pestilent** /'pestɪlənt/ *a.* deadly or pestiferous; troublesome; obnoxious.

**pestilential** /pestɪ'lenʃ(ə)l/ *a.* of pestilence; pestilent.

**pestle** /'pes(ə)l/ *n.* instrument for pounding substances in a mortar.

**pet**[1] **1** *n.* domestic animal kept for pleasure or companionship; favourite. **2** *a.* of or for a pet; favourite; expressing fondness. **3** *v.t.* make pet of; fondle (esp. erotically).

**pet**[2] *n.* ill-humour, fit of peevishness.

**petal** /'pet(ə)l/ *n.* each division of flower corolla.

**petard** /pə'tɑːd/ *n. hist.* small bomb for breaking down door etc.

**peter**[1] /'piːtə(r)/ *v.i.* peter out give out, come to an end.

**peter**[2] /'piːtə(r)/ *n. Aus. sl.* till; cash-register. **tickle the peter** embezzle.

**petersham** /'piːtəʃ(ə)m/ *n.* thick ribbed silk ribbon.

**petiole** /'petɪəʊl/ *n.* leaf-stalk.

**petit** /'petɪ/ *a.* **petit four** /fʊə(r)/ very small fancy cake etc.; **petit point** /pwæ/ embroidery on canvas using small stitches. [F]

**petite** /pə'tiːt/ *a.* (of woman) of small dainty build.

**petition** /pə'tɪʃ(ə)n/ **1** *n.* request, supplication; formal written request, esp. one signed by many people, to authorities etc. **2** *v.* make petition (to); ask humbly.

**petrel** /'petr(ə)l/ *n.* small sea-bird with black-and-white plumage.

**petrify** /'petrɪfaɪ/ *v.* paralyse with terror or astonishment etc.; turn or be turned into stone. **petrifaction** *n.*

**petrochemical** /petrəʊ'kemɪk(ə)l/ *n.* substance obtained from petroleum or natural gas.

**petrodollar** /'petrəʊdɒlə(r)/ *n.* dollar available in petroleum-exporting country.

**petrol** /'petr(ə)l/ *n.* refined petroleum used as fuel in motor vehicles, aircraft, etc. **petrol-pump** machine for transferring petrol esp. from underground reservoir to tank in motor vehicle; **petrol station** place where petrol can be bought.

**petroleum** /pə'trəʊlɪəm/ *n.* hydrocarbon oil found in upper strata of earth, refined for use as fuel etc. **petroleum jelly** translucent solid mixture of hydrocarbons got from petroleum and used as lubricant etc.

**petticoat** /'petɪkəʊt/ *n.* woman's or child's undergarment hanging from waist or shoulders.

**pettifogging** /'petɪfɒgɪŋ/ *a.* quibbling; petty; dishonest.

**pettish** /'petɪʃ/ *a.* fretful, peevish.

**petty** /'petɪ/ *a.* unimportant, trivial; small-minded; minor, inferior. **petty cash** money kept for small items of expenditure; **petty officer** naval NCO.

**petulant** /'petjʊlənt/ *a.* peevishly impatient or irritable. **petulance** *n.*

**petunia** /pə'tjuːnɪə/ *n.* plant with vivid funnel-shaped flowers.

**pew** *n.* (in church) enclosed compartment or fixed bench with back; *colloq.* seat.

**pewit** var. of peewit.

**pewter** /ˈpjuːtə(r)/ n. grey alloy of tin and lead etc.; articles made of this.

**peyote** /peɪˈəʊtiː/ n. a Mexican cactus; hallucinogenic drug prepared from it.

**pfennig** /ˈpfenɪɡ/ n. small German coin worth 1/100 of a mark.

**PGR** abbr. Aus. Parental Guidance Recommended.

**phagocyte** /ˈfæɡəsaɪt/ n. blood corpuscle etc. capable of absorbing foreign matter, esp. bacteria, in the body.

**phalanger** /fəˈlændʒə(r)/ n. any of several Aus. arboreal thick furred marsupials, e.g. possums.

**phalanx** /ˈfælæŋks/ n. (pl. **-lanxes**) body of infantry in close formation; united or organized party or company.

**phallus** /ˈfæləs/ n. image of penis. **phallic** a.

**phantasm** /ˈfæntæz(ə)m/ n. illusion; phantom. **phantasmal** a.

**phantasmagoria** /ˌfæntæzməˈɡɔːriːə/ n. shifting scene of real or imaginary figures. **phantasmagoric** a.

**phantom** /ˈfæntəm/ 1 n. spectre, apparition; mental illusion. 2 a. merely apparent, illusory.

**Pharaoh** /ˈfeərəʊ/ n. title of ruler of ancient Egypt.

**Pharisee** /ˈfærəsiː/ n. member of ancient Jewish sect distinguished by strict observance of traditional and written law; self-righteous person; hypocrite. **Pharisaic** /-ˈseɪɪk/ a.

**pharmaceutical** /ˌfɑːməˈsjuːtɪk(ə)l/ a. of pharmacy; of use or sale of medicinal drugs. **pharmaceutics** n.

**pharmacist** /ˈfɑːməsəst/ n. person qualified to practise pharmacy.

**pharmacology** /ˌfɑːməˈkɒlədʒi/ n. science of action of drugs on the body. **pharmacological** a.; **pharmacologist** n.

**pharmacopoeia** /ˌfɑːməkəˈpiːə/ n. book with list of drugs and directions for use; stock of drugs.

**pharmacy** /ˈfɑːməsi/ n. preparation and dispensing of drugs; pharmacist's shop; dispensary.

**pharynx** /ˈfærɪŋks/ n. cavity behind mouth and nose. **pharyngeal** /fæˈrɪndʒɪəl/ a.

**phase** /feɪz/ 1 n. stage of development or process or recurring sequence; aspect of moon or planet. 2 v.t. carry out by phases. 3 **phase in, out**, bring gradually into, out of, use.

**Ph.D.** abbr. Doctor of Philosophy.

**pheasant** /ˈfez(ə)nt/ n. long-tailed bright-plumaged game-bird.

**phenomenal** /fəˈnɒmən(ə)l/ a. of or concerned with phenomena; extraordinary, remarkable.

**phenomenon** /fəˈnɒmənən/ n. (pl. **-na**) observed or apparent object or fact or occurrence; remarkable person or thing.

**phew** /fjuː/ int. expr. disgust, relief, etc.

**phial** /ˈfaɪəl/ n. small bottle.

**philander** /fəˈlændə(r)/ v.i. (of man) flirt (with woman); flirt habitually.

**philanthropy** /fəˈlænθrəpi/ n. love of all mankind; practical benevolence. **philanthropic** /-ˈθrɒp-/ a.; **philanthropist** n.

**philately** /fəˈlætəli/ n. stamp-collecting. **philatelic** /-ˈtel-/ a.; **philatelist** n.

**philharmonic** /ˌfɪlhɑːˈmɒnək/ a. devoted to music.

**philippic** /fəˈlɪpɪk/ n. bitter invective.

**philistine** /ˈfɪləstaɪn/ 1 n. person who is hostile or indifferent to culture. 2 a. hostile or indifferent to culture. 3 **philistinism** n.

**philology** /fəˈlɒlədʒi/ n. science of language. **philological** a.; **philologist** n.

**philosopher** /fəˈlɒsəfə(r)/ n. person engaged in or learned in philosophy; person who acts philosophically.

**philosophic(al)** /ˌfɪləˈsɒfək(ə)l/ a. of or according to philosophy; calm under adverse circumstances.

**philosophize** /fəˈlɒsəfaɪz/ v.i. theorize; moralize.

**philosophy** /fəˈlɒsəfi/ n. pursuit of wisdom or knowledge, esp. of ultimate reality or of general causes and principles; philosophical system; system for conduct of life; serenity, calmness.

**philtre** /ˈfɪltə(r)/ n. love-potion.

**phlebitis** /flɪˈbaɪtəs/ n. inflammation of walls of vein. **phlebitic** /-ˈbɪt-/ a.

**phlegm** /flem/ n. bronchial mucus ejected by coughing; calmness; sluggishness.

**phlegmatic** /fleɡˈmætɪk/ a. not easily agitated, sluggish.

**phlox** /flɒks/ n. plant with clusters of white or coloured flowers.

**phobia** /ˈfəʊbiːə/ n. abnormal fear or aversion. **phobic** a. & n.

**phoenix** /ˈfiːnɪks/ n. bird fabled to burn itself and rise from its ashes; unique person or thing.

**phone** /fəʊn/ n. & v. colloq. telephone. **phone-in** broadcast programme in which listeners participate by telephone.

**phonetic** /fəˈnetɪk/ a. of or representing vocal sound; (of spelling) corresponding to pronunciation.

**phonetics** n.pl. usu. treated as sing. study or representation of vocal sounds. **phonetician** /fəʊ-/ n.

**phoney** /ˈfəʊniː/ sl. 1 a. false, sham, counterfeit. 2 n. phoney person or thing.

**phonic** /ˈfɒnɪk/ a. of (vocal) sound.

**phonograph** /ˈfəʊnəɡrɑːf or -ɡræf/ n. early form of gramophone.

**phonology** /fəˈnɒlədʒiː/ n. study of sounds in a language. **phonological** a.

**phosphate** /ˈfɒsfeɪt/ n. salt of phosphoric acid, esp. used as fertilizer.

**phosphoresce** /fɒsfəˈres/ v.i. show phosphorescence.

**phosphorescence** /fɒsfəˈres(ə)ns/ n. emission of light without combustion or perceptible heat. **phosphorescent** a.

**phosphoric, phosphorous**, /fɒsˈfɒrɪk, ˈfɒsfərəs/ adjs. of or containing phosphorus.

**phosphorus** /ˈfɒsfərəs/ n. non-metallic waxlike substance appearing luminous in dark.

**photo** /ˈfəʊtəʊ/ n. (pl. -tos) colloq. photograph. **photo finish** close finish of race in which winner is identified by photography.

**photo-** in comb. light; photography.

**photocopier** /ˈfəʊtəʊkɒpiːə(r)/ n. machine for photocopying documents.

**photocopy** /ˈfəʊtəʊkɒpiː/ 1 n. photographic copy of document. 2 v.t. make photocopy of.

**photoelectric** /fəʊtəʊəˈlektrɪk/ a. with or using emission of electrons from substances exposed to light. **photoelectric cell** device using this effect to generate current.

**photogenic** /fəʊtəʊˈdʒenɪk/ a. apt to be a good subject for photographs; producing light.

**photograph** /ˈfəʊtəɡrɑːf or -ɡræf/ 1 n. picture formed by chemical action of light on sensitive film. 2 v. take photograph (of). 3 **photographer** /-ˈtɒɡ-/ n.; **photographic** /-ˈɡræf-/ a.; **photography** /-ˈtɒɡ-/ n.

**photogravure** /fəʊtəʊɡrəˈvjʊə(r)/ n. picture produced from photographic negative transferred to metal plate and etched in.

**photolithography** /fəʊtəʊləˈθɒɡrəfiː/ n. lithographic process in which plates are made photographically.

**photometer** /fəʊˈtɒmətə(r)/ n. instrument for measuring light. **photometric** /-ˈmet-/ a.; **photometry** n.

**photon** /ˈfəʊtɒn/ n. quantum of electromagnetic radiation energy.

**Photostat** /ˈfəʊtəʊstæt/ 1 (P) n. photocopy. 2 v.t. make Photostat of.

**photosynthesis** /fəʊtəʊˈsɪnθəsəs/ n. process in which energy of sunlight is used by green plants to form complex substances from carbon dioxide and water. **photosynthesize** v.

**phrasal** /ˈfreɪz(ə)l/ a. consisting of a phrase.

**phrase** /freɪz/ 1 n. group of words forming conceptual unit but not sentence; short pithy expression; Mus. short sequence of notes. 2 v.t. express in words; group in phrases. 3 **phrasebook** book listing phrases and their foreign equivalents, for use by tourists etc.

**phraseology** /freɪziːˈɒlədʒiː/ n. choice or arrangement of words. **phraseological** a.

**phrenetic** var. of frenetic.

**phrenology** /frəˈnɒlədʒiː/ n. study of external form of cranium as supposed indication of mental faculties etc. **phrenologist** n.

**phthisis** /ˈθaɪsəs/ n. pulmonary tuberculosis. **phthisical** /ˈθɪzɪk(ə)l/ a.

**phut** adv. colloq. **go phut** collapse, lit. or fig.

**phylactery** /fəˈlæktəriː/ n. small box containing Hebrew texts, worn by Jews at prayer.

**phylum** /ˈfaɪləm/ n. (pl. -la) major division of plant or animal kingdom.

**physic** /ˈfɪzɪk/ n. medical art or profession; arch. medicine.

**physical** /ˈfɪzək(ə)l/ a. of matter; of the

**physician** /fəˈzɪʃ(ə)n/ n. doctor, esp. specialist in medical diagnosis and treatment.

**physics** /ˈfɪzɪks/ n.pl. usu. treated as sing. science of properties and interaction of matter and energy. **physicist** n.

**physiognomy** /fɪzɪˈɒnəmɪ/ n. features or type of face; art of judging character from face and form; characteristic aspect. **physiognomist** n.

**physiography** /fɪzɪˈɒɡrəfɪ/ n. description of natural phenomena; physical geography. **physiographical** a.

**physiology** /fɪzɪˈɒlədʒɪ/ n. science of functioning of living organisms. **physiological** a.; **physiologist** n.

**physiotherapy** /fɪzɪəʊˈθerəpɪ/ n. treatment of injury or disease by exercise, heat, or other physical agencies. **physiotherapist** n.

**physique** /fɪˈziːk/ n. bodily structure and development.

**pi** /paɪ/ n. sixteenth letter of Greek alphabet (Π, π); Math. symbol of ratio of circumference of circle to diameter (approx. 3.14).

**pia mater** /piːə ˈmeɪtə(r)/ inner membrane enveloping brain and spinal cord.

**pianissimo** /piːəˈnɪsɪməʊ/ Mus. 1 adv. very softly. 2 n. (pl. **-os**) passage to be performed thus.

**pianist** /ˈpiːənɪst/ n. player of piano.

**piano**[1] /pɪˈænəʊ/ n. (pl. **-nos**) musical instrument played by keys which cause hammers to strike metal strings. **piano-accordion** accordion with melody played from small piano-like keyboard.

**piano**[2] /pɪˈɑːnəʊ/ Mus. 1 adv. softly. 2 n. (pl. **-nos**) passage to be performed thus.

**pianoforte** /piːænəʊˈfɔːtɪ/ n. piano[1].

**pibroch** /ˈpiːbrɒk/ n. martial or funeral bagpipe music.

**picador** /ˈpɪkədɔː(r)/ n. mounted man with lance in bull-fight.

**picaresque** /pɪkəˈresk/ a. (of fiction) dealing with adventures of rogues.

**piccalilli** /pɪkəˈlɪlɪ/ n. pickle of chopped vegetables, mustard, and spices.

**piccaninny** /pɪkəˈnɪnɪ/ n. small Black or Aus. Aboriginal child.

**piccolo** /ˈpɪkələʊ/ n. (pl. **-los**) small high-pitched flute.

**pick** 1 v. select, esp. carefully; pluck, gather (flower, fruit, etc.); make hole in or break surface of with fingers or sharp instrument; make (hole) thus; open (lock) with skeleton key etc.; probe with pointed instrument; clear (bone etc.) of adherent flesh. 2 n. picking, selection; *the* best part *of*; pickaxe; instrument for picking. 3 **pick on** nag at, find fault with, select; **pickpocket** person who steals from pockets; **pick up** take hold of and lift, learn routinely, stop for and take with one, (of police) take into custody, acquire casually, make acquaintance of casually, detect, manage to receive (broadcast signal etc.), recover health, improve; **pick-up** picking up, person met casually, part of record-player carrying stylus, small open motor truck.

**pick-a-back** var. of *piggy-back*.

**pickaxe** /ˈpɪkæks/ n. tool with sharp-pointed iron cross-bar for breaking up ground etc.

**picket** /ˈpɪkɪt/ 1 n. one or more person(s) stationed to dissuade workers from working during strike etc.; small body of men on military police duty; pointed stake driven into ground. 2 v.t. place or act as picket outside; post as military picket; secure with stakes.

**pickings** /ˈpɪkɪŋz/ n.pl. perquisites, gleanings.

**pickle** /ˈpɪk(ə)l/ 1 n. vegetables etc. preserved in vinegar etc.; liquor used for preserving food etc.; *colloq.* plight. 2 v.t. preserve in or treat with pickle; in *p.p. sl.* drunk.

**picnic** /ˈpɪknɪk/ 1 n. pleasure party including outdoor meal; Aus. sl. awkward task or situation. 2 v.i. (past & p.p. **picnicked**) take part in picnic. 3 **picnic races** Aus. a horse-race meeting in country area, often on improvised track.

**picot** /ˈpiːkəʊ/ n. one of series of small loops forming edging to lace etc.

**pictograph** /ˈpɪktəɡrɑːf/ or **-græf/** (also **pictogram**) n. pictorial symbol used as form of writing.

**pictorial** /pɪkˈtɔːrɪəl/ a. of or expressed in a picture.

**picture** /ˈpɪktʃə(r)/ 1 n. likeness or representation of subject produced by

**picturesque** /ˌpɪktʃəˈresk/ a. striking and pleasant to look at; (of language etc.) strikingly graphic.

**piddle** /ˈpɪd(ə)l/ v.i. work or act in trifling way; colloq. urinate.

**pidgin** /ˈpɪdʒɪn/ n. simplified language esp. used between persons of different nationality etc.; colloq. (a person's) business or particular concern.

**pie**[1] n. dish of meat or fruit etc., encased in or covered with pastry etc. and baked. **pie chart** diagram representing various quantities as sectors of circle.

**pie**[2] n. magpie.

**piebald** /ˈpaɪbɔːld/ 1 a. having light and dark colour in irregular patches. 2 n. piebald animal.

**piece** /piːs/ 1 n. one of the distinct portions of which thing is composed or into which it is divided or broken; detached portion; example, specimen; item; picture, literary or musical composition; chess-man, draughts, etc. 2 v.t. form into a whole; join pieces of *together*. 3 **in pieces** broken; **of a piece** uniform or consistent (*with*); **piece-goods** textile fabrics woven in standard lengths; **-work**, work paid for according to amount done.

**pièce de résistance** /pjɛs də reɪˈzɪstɑ̃s/ most important or remarkable item. [F]

**piecemeal** /ˈpiːsmiːl/ 1 adv. piece by piece, part at a time. 2 a. done etc. piecemeal.

**pied** /paɪd/ a. of black and white or of mixed colours.

**pied-à-terre** /ˌpjeɪd ɑː ˈteə(r)/ n. (pl. **pieds-** pr. same) place kept available as temporary quarters when needed. [F]

**pier** /pɪə(r)/ n. structure running out into sea used as promenade and landing-stage or breakwater; support of spans of bridge; pillar; solid part of wall between windows etc. **pier-glass** large tall mirror.

**pierce** /pɪəs/ v. go through or into like spear or needle; make hole in.

**pierrot** /ˈpɪərəʊ/ n. French pantomime character; itinerant musical entertainer.

**pietà** /pjeɪˈtɑː/ n. picture or sculpture of Virgin Mary holding dead body of Christ. [It.]

**pietism** /ˈpaɪətɪz(ə)m/ n. extreme or affected piety.

**piety** /ˈpaɪətɪ/ n. piousness.

**piffle** /ˈpɪf(ə)l/ sl. 1 n. nonsense. 2 v.i. talk or act feebly.

**pig** 1 n. wild or domesticated animal with broad snout and stout bristly body; pork; colloq. greedy, dirty, obstinate, or annoying person; oblong mass of smelted iron or other metal. 2 v.i. live or behave like pig (esp. **pig it**). 3 **pigheaded** obstinate; **pig-iron** crude iron from smelting-furnace; **pigsty** sty for pigs; **pig-tail** plait of hair hanging from back of head.

**pigeon** /ˈpɪdʒən/ n. bird of dove family; person who is easily swindled. **pigeonhole** one of set of compartments in cabinet etc. for papers etc., (v.t.) put in pigeon-hole, put aside for future consideration, classify mentally; **pigeon-toed** having toes turned inwards.

**piggery** /ˈpɪɡərɪ/ n. place where pigs are bred; pigsty.

**piggish** /ˈpɪɡɪʃ/ a. greedy, dirty.

**piggy** /ˈpɪɡɪ/ n. little pig. **piggy-back** a ride on shoulders and back of another person; **piggy bank** pig-shaped hollow pot for saving money in.

**piglet** /ˈpɪɡlət/ n. young pig.

**pigment** /ˈpɪɡmənt/ 1 n. colouring-matter. 2 v.t. colour (as) with natural pigment. 3 **pigmentation** n.

**pigmy** var. of **pygmy**.

**pike** 1 n. large voracious freshwater fish; peaked top of hill; spear formerly used by infantry. **pikestaff** wooden shaft of pike (**plain as a pikestaff** quite obvious).

**pilaff** /ˈpɪlæf/ n. Oriental dish of rice with meat, spices, etc.

**pilaster** /pəˈlæstə(r)/ n. rectangular column, esp. one fastened into wall.

**pilchard** /ˈpɪltʃəd/ n. small sea-fish related to herring.

**pile**[1] 1 n. heap of things laid on one another; colloq. large amount esp. of money; building of imposing height;

**pile** pyre; series of plates of dissimilar metals laid alternately for producing electric current; (in full **atomic pile**) nuclear reactor. 2 v. heap *up* or *on*; load; crowd *in(to)*, *on*, *out of*, etc. 3 **pile up** accumulate, cause (vehicle or aircraft) to crash; **pile-up** collision of several motor vehicles.

**pile**² n. heavy beam driven vertically into ground as support for building etc.

**pile**³ n. nap of velvet or carpet etc.

**pile**⁴ n. (usu. in pl.) haemorrhoid.

**pilfer** /'pɪlfə(r)/ v. steal or thieve in petty way. **pilferage** n.

**pilgrim** /'pɪlgrɪm/ n. person who journeys to sacred place; traveller. **Pilgrim Fathers** English Puritans who founded colony in Massachusetts 1620.

**pilgrimage** /'pɪlgrəmɪdʒ/ n. pilgrim's journey.

**pill** n. small ball or flat piece of medicinal substance to be swallowed whole. **the pill** *colloq.* contraceptive pill; **pillbox** small round shallow box for pills, hat shaped like this, *Mil.* small round concrete shelter, mainly underground.

**pillage** /'pɪlɪdʒ/ n. & v.t. plunder.

**pillar** /'pɪlə(r)/ n. slender upright structure used as support of ornament; column. **pillar-box** *UK* hollow pillar for posting letters in.

**pillion** /'pɪljən/ n. seat for passenger behind motor-cyclist etc.

**pillory** /'pɪlərɪ/ 1 n. *hist.* frame with holes for head and hands of offender exposed to public ridicule. 2 v.t. set in pillory; *fig.* expose to ridicule.

**pillow** /'pɪləʊ/ 1 n. cushion as support for head, esp. in bed; pillow-shaped thing. 2 v.t. rest, prop up, (as) on pillow. 3 **pillowcase**, **-slip**, washable cover for pillow.

**pilot** /'paɪlət/ 1 n. person operating flying controls of aircraft; person in charge of ships entering or leaving harbour etc.; guide. 2 v.t. act as pilot to; guide course of. 3 a. experimental, small-scale. 4 **pilot-light** small gas-burner kept alight to light another; **pilot officer** lowest commissioned rank in air force, next below flying officer.

**pimento** /pə'mentəʊ/ n. (pl. **-tos**) allspice; sweet pepper.

**pimp** 1 n. person who solicits clients for prostitute or brothel; *Aus.* tell-tale, informer. 2 v.i. act as pimp.

**pimpernel** /'pɪmpənel/ n. plant with small scarlet or blue flower.

**pimple** /'pɪmp(ə)l/ n. small hard inflamed spot on skin. **pimply** a.

**pin** 1 n. piece of thin stiff wire with point and head used as fastening; wooden or metal peg, rivet, etc.; skittle; in pl. sl. legs. 2 v.t. fasten with pin(s); fix responsibility for *on*; seize and hold fast; transfix with pin, lance, etc. 3 **pin-ball** game in which small metal balls are shot across sloping board and strike against obstacles; **pincushion** small pad for sticking pins in ready for use; **pin down** make (person) declare position or intentions; **pin-money** small sum of money, esp. earned by woman; **pin-point** locate or define (target etc.) with minute precision; **pinprick** petty irritation; **pins and needles** tingling sensation in limb recovering from numbness; **pin-stripe** very narrow stripe in cloth; **pin-table** table used in pin-ball; **pintail** duck or grouse with pointed tail; **pin-tuck** narrow ornamental tuck; **pin-up** picture of attractive or famous person, pinned up on wall etc.; **pin-wheel** small Catherine wheel.

**pinafore** /'pɪnəfɔː(r)/ n. apron covering front of body above and below waist. **pinafore dress** dress without collar or sleeves, worn over blouse or jumper.

**pince-nez** /'pæsneɪ/ n. pair of eye-glasses with spring that clips on nose.

**pincers** /'pɪnsəz/ n.pl. gripping-tool forming pair of jaws; pincer-shaped claw in crustaceans etc. **pincer movement** *Mil.* converging movement against enemy position.

**pinch** 1 v. grip tightly between two surfaces, esp. tips of finger and thumb; affect painfully; (of cold etc.) nip, shrivel; stint, be niggardly; *sl.* steal, arrest. 2 n. pinching, squeezing; stress of poverty etc.; small amount; *Aus.* steep hill. 3 **at a pinch** in an emergency.

**pinchbeck** /'pɪntʃbek/ 1 n. goldlike copper and zinc alloy used in cheap jewellery etc. 2 a. spurious, sham.

**pine**¹ n. evergreen needle-leaved coniferous tree; its wood. **pine-cone** fruit

**pine** of pine; **pine kernel** edible seed of some pine-trees.

**pine**² *v.i.* waste *away* with grief, disease, etc.; long (*for*).

**pineal** /'pɪnɪəl/ *a.* shaped like pine-cone. **pineal gland** conical gland in brain.

**pineapple** /'paɪnæp(ə)l/ *n.* large juicy tropical fruit with yellow flesh and tough skin.

**ping** 1 *n.* abrupt single ringing sound. 2 *v.i.* emit ping.

**ping-pong** /'pɪŋpɒŋ/ *n.* table tennis.

**pinion**¹ /'pɪnjən/ *n.* small cog-wheel engaging with larger.

**pinion**² /'pɪnjən/ 1 *n.* outer joint of bird's wing; *poet.* wing; flight-feather. 2 *v.t.* cut off pinions to prevent flight; restrain by binding arms to sides.

**pink**¹ 1 *n.* pale-red colour; garden plant with clove-scented flowers; *the point of perfection or excellence.* 2 *a.* pink-coloured; *sl.* mildly socialist. 3 **pinkwood** a Tasmanian and E. Aus. tree, its pale reddish wood.

**pink**² *v.t.* pierce slightly; cut scalloped or zigzag edge on. **pinking shears** dressmaker's serrated shears for cutting zigzag edge.

**pink**³ *v.i.* (of vehicle engine) emit high-pitched explosive sounds when running faultily.

**pinkie** /'pɪŋkɪ/ *n. Aus. sl.* cheep red wine.

**pinnace** /'pɪnəs/ *n.* ship's small boat.

**pinnacle** /'pɪnək(ə)l/ *n.* small ornamental turret crowning buttress, roof, etc.; culmination or climax.

**pinnate** /'pɪnət/ *a. Bot.* (of compound leaf) with leaflets on each side of leaf-stalk.

**pinny** /'pɪnɪ/ *n. colloq.* pinafore.

**pint** /paɪnt/ *n.* measure of capacity, 0.56 l.

**pintle** /'pɪnt(ə)l/ *n.* bolt or pin, esp. one on which some other part turns.

**pioneer** /paɪə'nɪə(r)/ 1 *n.* original explorer or settler etc.; beginner of enterprise etc. 2 *v.* act as pioneer (in).

**pious** /'paɪəs/ *a.* devout, religious; dutiful. **pious fraud** deception meant to benefit victim.

**pip**¹ *n.* seed of apple, pear, orange, etc.

**pip**² *n.* each spot on dominoes, dice, or playing-cards; star on army officer's shoulder.

**pip**³ *v.t. colloq.* forestall; defeat.

**pip**⁴ *n.* short high-pitched sound.

**pip**⁵ *n.* disease of poultry etc. **the pip** *sl.* (fit of) depression or boredom or bad temper.

**pipe** 1 *n.* tube of earthenware, metal, etc., esp. for conveying gas, water, etc.; narrow tube with bowl at one end containing tobacco for smoking; quantity of tobacco held by this; musical wind-instrument; each tube by which sound is produced in organ; in *pl.* bagpipes; tubular organ etc. in body; boatswain's whistle; measure of capacity for wine (105 gals.). 2 *v.* convey (as) through pipes; transmit (recorded music etc.) by wire or cable; play on pipe; utter shrilly; summon or lead etc. by sound of pipe or whistle; trim with piping; furnish with pipe(s). 3 **pipeclay** fine white clay for tobacco-pipes or for whitening leather etc.; **pipe-cleaner** piece of flexible tuft-covered wire to clean inside tobacco pipe; **pipe down** *colloq.* be quiet; **pipe-dream** extravagant fancy, impossible wish, etc.; **pipeline** pipe conveying oil etc. across country, *fig.* channel of supply or communication etc.; **pipe up** begin to play or sing etc.

**piper** /'paɪpə(r)/ *n.* person who plays on pipe, esp. bagpipes.

**pipette** /pɪ'pet/ *n.* slender tube used for transferring or measuring small quantities of liquid.

**pipi** /'pɪpɪ/ *n. Aus.* bivalve mollusc often used as bait.

**piping** /'paɪpɪŋ/ 1 *n.* length or system of pipes; ornamentation of dress or upholstery etc. by means of cord enclosed in pipelike fold; ornamental cordlike lines of sugar on cake. 2 *a.* **piping hot** (of food or water) extremely hot.

**pipit** /'pɪpɪt/ *n.* small bird resembling lark.

**pippin** /'pɪpɪn/ *n.* apple grown from seed; dessert apple.

**piquant** /'piːkənt/ *a.* agreeably pungent, sharp, appetizing, stimulating. **piquancy** *n.*

**pique** /piːk/ 1 *v.t.* wound pride or stir curiosity of. 2 *n.* enmity, resentment.

**piquet** /pɪ'ket/ *n.* card-game for 2 players.

**piracy** /'paɪrəsɪ/ *n.* activity of pirate.

**piranha** /pəˈrɑːnə/ n. voracious S. Amer. freshwater fish.

**pirate** /ˈpaɪərət/ 1 n. sea-faring robber attacking other ships; ship used by pirate; person who infringes copyright or regulations or encroaches on rights of others etc. 2 v.t. reproduce (book etc.) without permission for one's own benefit. 3 piratical /-ˈræt-/ a.

**pirouette** /pɪruˈet/ 1 n. ballet-dancer's spin on one foot or point of toe. 2 v.i. perform pirouette.

**piscatorial** /pɪskəˈtɔːrɪəl/ a. of fishing.

**Pisces** /ˈpaɪsiːz/ n. twelfth sign of zodiac.

**pisciculture** /ˈpɪsɪkʌltʃə(r)/ n. artificial rearing of fish.

**piscina** /pəˈsiːnə/ n. (pl. **-nae** /-niː/ or **-nas**) stone basin in niche on south side of altar in church.

**piss** vulg. 1 v. urinate; discharge with urine; in p.p. sl. drunk. 2 n. urinating; urine. 3 **piss off** sl. go away, annoy, depress.

**pistachio** /pɪsˈtæʃɪəʊ/ n. (pl. **-chios**) kind of nut with green kernel.

*piste* /piːst/ n. ski-track of compacted snow. [F]

**pistil** /ˈpɪstɪl/ n. female organ in flowers.

**pistillate** /ˈpɪstɪleɪt/ a. having pistils.

**pistol** /ˈpɪst(ə)l/ 1 n. small fire-arm. 2 v.t. shoot with pistol.

**piston** /ˈpɪst(ə)n/ n. sliding cylinder fitting closely in tube and moving up and down in it, used in steam or petrol engine to impart motion; sliding valve in trumpet etc. **piston-rod** rod connecting piston to other parts of machine.

**pit**[1] 1 n. large hole in ground, esp. one made in digging for minerals etc.; coalmine; covered hole as trap; depression in skin or any surface; floor of theatre auditorium, sunken area accommodating orchestra; sunken area in floor of workshop etc. for inspection or repair of underside of vehicle etc.; area to side of track where racing cars are refuelled etc. during race. 2 v.t. match *against*; make pit(s) in; store in pit. 3 **pitfall** unsuspected snare or danger, covered pit as trap; **pit-head** top of shaft of coal-mine, area surrounding this; **pit of the stomach** hollow below bottom of breastbone.

**pita** /ˈpiːtə/ n. kind of flat bread orig. from Greece and Middle East.

**pit-a-pat** /ˈpɪtəpæt/ 1 n. sound as of light quick steps. 2 adv. with this sound.

**pitch**[1] 1 v. set up in chosen position; encamp; give chosen altitude or gradient or intensity or musical pitch or style or level etc. to; throw, fling, fall; (of ship etc.) plunge in longitudinal direction; sl. tell (yarn etc.). 2 n. act or process of pitching; area marked out for play in esp. outdoor game; Crick. part of ground between or near wickets; Mus. degree of highness or lowness of tone; place, esp. in street or market, where one is stationed; height, degree, intensity, gradient; distance between successive ridges of screw, teeth of cogwheel, etc. 3 **pitched battle** one planned beforehand, not casual; **pitchfork** long-handled two-pronged fork for tossing hay etc., (v.t.) thrust forcibly or hastily *into* (office, position, etc.); **pitch in** colloq. set to work vigorously; **pitch into** colloq. attack vigorously.

**pitch**[2] 1 n. dark resinous tarry substance. 2 v.t. coat, smear, etc. with pitch. 3 **pitch black, pitch dark**, intensely dark; **pitch-pine** resinous kinds of pine.

**pitchblende** /ˈpɪtʃblend/ n. uranium oxide yielding radium.

**pitcher**[1] /ˈpɪtʃə(r)/ n. large jug, ewer. **pitcher-plant** plant with pitcher-shaped leaves.

**pitcher**[2] /ˈpɪtʃə(r)/ n. player who delivers ball in baseball.

**pitchi** /ˈpɪtʃiː/ n. Aus. receptacle hollowed out of solid log.

**pitchy** /ˈpɪtʃɪ/ a. of, like, dark etc. as, pitch.

**piteous** /ˈpɪtɪəs/ a. deserving or arousing pity.

**pith** /pɪθ/ n. spongy tissue in stems of plants or lining rind of orange etc.; chief part; vigour, energy. **pith helmet** one made from dried pith of sola etc.

**pithy** /ˈpɪθɪ/ a. condensed and forcible, terse.

**pitiable** /ˈpɪtɪəb(ə)l/ a. deserving or arousing pity or contempt.

**pitiful** /ˈpɪtɪfəl/ a. arousing pity; contemptible.

**pitiless** /ˈpɪtɪləs/ a. showing no pity.

**piton** /ˈpiːtɒn/ n. peg driven in to support climber or rope.

**pittance** /ˈpɪt(ə)ns/ n. scanty allowance, small amount.

**pittosporum** /pə'tɒspərəm/ n. evergreen shrub or small tree with fragrant flowers and seeds embedded in a viscous substance.

**pituitary** /pɪ'tju:ətəri/ n. (in full **pituitary gland**) small ductless gland at base of brain.

**pity** /'pɪti/ 1 n. sorrow for another's suffering; cause for regret. 2 v.t. feel pity for.

**pivot** /'pɪvət/ 1 n. shaft or pin on which something turns; cardinal or crucial person or point. 2 v. turn (as) on pivot; hinge (*on*); provide with pivot. 3 **pivotal** a.

**pixie** /'pɪksi/ (also **pixy**) n. supernatural being akin to fairy. **pixie hood** hood with pointed crown.

**pizza** /'pi:tsə/ n. flat piece of dough baked with savoury topping.

**pizzicato** /pɪtsə'kɑ:təʊ/ 1 adv. with the string of violin etc. plucked, not played with bow. 2 n. (*pl.* **-tos**) note or passage to be performed thus.

**pl.** *abbr.* place; plate; plural.

**placable** /'plækəb(ə)l/ a. easily appeased; mild-tempered. **placability** n.

**placard** /'plækɑ:d/ 1 n. large notice for public display. 2 v.t. post placards on; advertise by placards.

**placate** /plə'keɪt/ v.t. conciliate, pacify. **placatory** /-'keɪt-/ a.

**place** 1 n. particular part of space; space or room of or for person etc.; city, town, village, residence, building; building or spot devoted to specified purpose; office or employment; duties of this; rank, station, position. 2 v.t. put or dispose in place; assign rank or order of class to; give (order for goods etc.) to firm etc.; in *pass.* be among first 3 in race. 3 **all over the place** in disorder; **in place** suitable, appropriate; **in place of** instead of; **out of place** unsuitable, inappropriate; **place-kick** *Footb.* kick made with ball placed on ground; **place-mat** small mat on table at person's place; **place-setting** set of dishes and implements for one person to eat with; **take place** happen; **take the place of** be substituted for. 4 **placement** n.

**placebo** /plə'si:bəʊ/ n. (*pl.* **-bos**) medicine given to humour rather than cure patient; dummy pill etc.

**placenta** /plə'sentə/ n. organ in uterus of pregnant mammal that nourishes foetus. **placental** a.

**placer** /'pleɪsə(r)/ n. deposit of gravel, sand, etc., on bed of stream containing minerals, esp. gold.

**placid** /'plæsɪd/ a. calm, unruffled; not easily disturbed. **placidity** /-'sɪd-/ n.

**placket** /'plækɪt/ n. opening or slit at top of skirt, for fastenings or access to pocket.

**plagiarize** /'pleɪdʒɪəraɪz/ v. take and use (another's writings etc.) as one's own. **plagiarism** n.; **plagiarist** n.

**plague** /pleɪg/ 1 n. deadly contagious disease; infestation *of* pest; great trouble or affliction. 2 v.t. afflict with plague; *colloq.* annoy, bother.

**plaice** /pleɪs/ n. kind of flat-fish.

**plaid** /plæd/ 1 n. long piece of woollen cloth as part of Highland costume; tartan cloth. 2 a. made of plaid, having plaidlike pattern.

**plain** /pleɪn/ 1 a. clear, evident; straightforward; ordinary, homely; not decorated or embellished or luxurious; not good-looking. 2 n. level tract of country; ordinary stitch in knitting. 3 adv. simply; clearly. 3 **plain chocolate** chocolate made without milk; **plain clothes** civilian clothes as distinct from uniform; **plain sailing** simple situation or course of action; **plainsong** traditional church music sung in unison in medieval modes and free rhythm; **plain-spoken** frank.

**plaint** n. *Law* accusation, charge; *poet.* lamentation.

**plaintiff** /'pleɪntɪf/ n. party who brings suit into lawcourt.

**plaintive** /'pleɪntɪv/ a. mournful-sounding.

**plait** /plæt/ 1 n. interlacing of 3 or more strands of hair or ribbon etc.; material thus interlaced. 2 v.t. form into plait.

**plan** 1 n. method or procedure by which thing is to be done; drawing exhibiting relative position and size of parts of building etc., diagram, map. 2 v. arrange beforehand, scheme; make plan of; design.

**planchette** /plɑːn'ʃet/ n. small board on castors, with pencil, said to trace letters etc. without conscious direction.

**plane**[1] n. level surface; level of attainment etc.; aeroplane; main aerofoil. 2 a. level as or lying in a plane.

## plane

**plane²** 1 *n.* tool for smoothing surface of wood by paring shavings from it. 2 *v.t.* smooth, pare (*away* etc.), with plane.

**plane³** *n.* tall spreading broad-leaved tree.

**planet** /'plænɪt/ *n.* any of heavenly bodies revolving round sun. **planetary** *a.*

**planetarium** /plænə'teərɪəm/ *n.* (*pl.* -iums) device for projecting image of night sky as seen at various times and places; building containing this.

**plangent** /'plændʒ(ə)nt/ *a.* loudly lamenting. **plangency** *n.*

**plank** 1 *n.* long flat piece of timber; item of political or other programme. 2 *v.t.* lay etc. with planks; *colloq.* put *down* (esp. money).

**plankton** /'plæŋkt(ə)n/ *n.* (chiefly microscopic) drifting or floating organisms found in sea or fresh water.

**planner** /'plænə(r)/ *n.* person who plans or makes plans, esp. with reference to controlled design of buildings and development of land. **planning** *n.*

**plant** /plɑːnt or plænt/ 1 *n.* organism capable of living wholly on inorganic matter and lacking power of locomotion; small plant (other than trees and shrubs); equipment for industrial process; *Aus.* the portable equipment and stock of a drover or other bush worker; *sl.* thing deliberately placed for discovery by others, hoax, trap. 2 *v.t.* place (seed etc.) in ground to grow; furnish (land etc.) with plants; fix firmly, establish; deliver (blow etc.); *sl.* conceal (stolen goods, evidence of complicity, etc.), esp. with view to misleading later discoverer.

**plantain¹** /'plæntɪn/ *n.* herb yielding seed used as food for cage-birds.

**plantain²** /'plæntɪn/ *n.* tropical fruit like banana; treelike plant bearing it.

**plantation** /plæn'teɪʃ(ə)n/ *n.* number of growing plants, esp. trees, planted together; estate for cultivation of cotton, tobacco, etc.; *hist.* colony.

**planter** /'plɑːntə(r) or 'plænt-/ *n.* owner or manager of plantation; container for house plants.

**plaque** /plɑːk/ *n.* ornamental tablet of metal, porcelain, etc.; film on teeth, where bacteria proliferate.

**plasma** /'plæzmə/ *n.* colourless coagulable part of blood in which corpuscles etc. float; protoplasm; *Phys.* gas of positive ions and free electrons in about equal numbers.

**plaster** /'plɑːstə(r)/ 1 *n.* mixture esp. of lime and sand and water spread on walls etc.; medicinal or protective substance etc. spread on fabric and applied to body; sticking-plaster; plaster of Paris. 2 *v.t.* cover with or like plaster; apply, stick, etc., like plaster to; coat, bedaub; *sl.* bomb heavily; in *p.p. sl.* drunk. 3 **plasterboard** board with core of plaster used for walls etc.; **plaster of Paris** fine white powder of gypsum used for making moulds or casts.

**plastic** /'plæstɪk/ 1 *n.* synthetic resinous etc. substance that can be moulded by heat or pressure. 2 *a.* made of plastic; capable of being moulded; giving form to clay, wax, etc. 3 **plastic arts** those concerned with modelling; **plastic surgery** repair or restoration of lost or damaged etc. tissue. 4 **plasticity** *n.*; **plasticize** *v.t.*

**Plasticine** /'plæstɪsiːn/ (**P**) *n.* plastic substance used for modelling.

**plate** 1 *n.* shallow usu. circular vessel from which food is eaten or served; table utensils of gold, silver, or other metal; engraved piece of metal; illustration printed from engraved plate etc.; thin sheet of metal, glass, etc. coated with sensitive film for photography; flat thin sheet of metal etc.; part of denture fitting to mouth and holding teeth. 2 *v.* cover (other metal) with thin coating of silver, gold, etc.; cover with plates of metal. 3 **plate glass** thick finequality glass for mirrors, windows, etc.; **platelayer** workman laying and repairing railway lines.

**plateau** /'plætəʊ/ *n.* (*pl.* -teaux /-təʊz/) area of level high ground; state of little variation following an increase.

**platelet** /'pleɪtlət/ *n.* small disc in blood, involved in clotting.

**platen** /'plæt(ə)n/ *n.* plate in printing-press by which paper is pressed against type; corresponding part in typewriter etc.

**platform** /'plætfɔːm/ *n.* raised level surface, esp. one from which speaker addresses audience, or one along side of line at railway station; thick sole of shoe; declared policy of political party.

**platinum** /'plætənəm/ n. white heavy metallic element that does not tarnish. **platinum blonde** woman with silvery blonde hair, this colour.

**platitude** /'plætɪtjuːd/ n. commonplace remark. **platitudinous** a.

**Platonic** /plə'tɒnɪk/ a. of Plato or his philosophy; **platonic** confined to words or theory; (of love or friendship) purely spiritual, not sexual. **Platonism** n.; **Platonist** n.

**platoon** /plə'tuːn/ n. Mil. subdivision of infantry company.

**platter** /'plætə(r)/ n. flat plate or dish, esp. for food.

**platypus** /'plætəpəs/ n. Aus. egg-laying mammal with ducklike beak.

**plaudit** /'plɔːdɪt/ n. (usu. in pl.) round of applause; commendation.

**plausible** /'plɔːzəb(ə)l/ a. seeming reasonable or probable, (of person) persuasive but deceptive. **plausibility** n.

**play 1** v. occupy or amuse oneself with some recreation or game or exercise etc.; do this *with* another; perform on (musical instrument), perform (piece of music etc.); perform (drama, role); act in drama etc., perform, execute; take part in (game); have as opponent in game; move piece in game, put card on table, strike ball, etc.; move about in lively or unrestrained manner; touch gently (*on*); allow (fish) to exhaust itself pulling against line. **2** n. recreation; amusement; playing of game, ball, etc.; dramatic piece; freedom of movement; fitful or light movement; gambling. **3 play along** pretend to co-operate; **play back** make audible (what has been recorded); **play-back** n.; **playbill** poster announcing theatre programme; **playboy** pleasure-seeking usu. wealthy man; **play down** minimize; **playfellow** companion in childhood; **playgoer** person who goes often to the theatre; **playground** outdoor area for children to play on; **playgroup** group of pre-school children who play together under supervision; **playhouse** theatre; **playing-card** small oblong card used in games, one of set of usu. 52 divided into 4 suits; **playmate** playfellow; **play-off** extra match played to decide draw or tie; **plaything** toy; **play up to** flatter to win favour etc.; **playwright** dramatist.

**plea** n. appeal, entreaty; *Law* formal statement by or on behalf of defendant; excuse.

**pleach** v.t. entwine, interlace, (esp. branches to form a hedge).

**plead** v. address court as advocate or party; allege as plea; make appeal or entreaty. **plead guilty, not guilty**, admit, deny, liability or guilt; **plead with** make earnest appeal to.

**pleading** /'pliːdɪŋ/ n. (usu. in pl.) formal statement of cause of action or defence.

**pleasant** /'plez(ə)nt/ a. agreeable; giving pleasure.

**pleasantry** /'plezntrɪ/ n. joking remark.

**please** /pliːz/ **1** v. be agreeable to; give joy or gratification to; choose, be willing, like. **2** int. or adv. as courteous qualification to request etc.

**pleasurable** /'pleʒərəb(ə)l/ a. causing pleasure.

**pleasure** /'pleʒə(r)/ n. satisfaction, delight; sensuous enjoyment; will, discretion, choice.

**pleat 1** n. flattened fold in cloth etc. **2** v.t. make pleat(s) in.

**pleb** n. & a. colloq. plebeian.

**plebeian** /plə'biːən/ a. of common people. **2** n. plebeian person.

**plebiscite** /'plebɪsaɪt/ n. direct vote of all electors of State on important public question.

**plectrum** /'plektrəm/ n. small implement for plucking strings of musical instrument.

**pledge 1** n. thing given to person as security for fulfilment of contract, payment of debt, etc.; thing put in pawn; token; solemn promise; drinking of health. **2** v.t. deposit as security, pawn; promise solemnly by pledge; bind by solemn promise; drink to the health of.

**Pleiades** /'plaɪədiːz/ n.pl. cluster of stars in constellation Taurus.

**plenary** /'pliːnərɪ/ a. not subject to limitation or exceptions; (of assembly) to be attended by all members.

**plenipotentiary** /plenɪpə'tenʃərɪ/ **1** n. person (esp. diplomat) having full power of independent action. **2** a. having such power.

**plenitude** /'plenɪtjuːd/ n. abundance; fullness; completeness.

**plenteous** /'plentɪəs/ a. plentiful.

# plentiful

**plentiful** /'plentəfəl/ a. existing in ample quantity.

**plenty** /'plenti/ 1 n. abundance; quite enough. 2 adv. colloq. fully.

**pleonasm** /'pli:ənæz(ə)m/ n. use of more words than are needed to express meaning. **pleonastic** a.

**plethora** /'pleθərə/ n. over-supply, glut.

**pleurisy** /'pluərɪsi/ n. inflammation of membrane enclosing lungs. **pleuritic** /-'rɪt-/ a.

**plexus** /'pleksəs/ n. Anat. network of nerves or vessels in animal body.

**pliable** /'paɪəb(ə)l/ a. easily bent or influenced; supple; accommodating. **pliability** n.

**pliant** /'plaɪənt/ a. pliable. **pliancy** n.

**pliers** /'plaɪəz/ n.pl. pincers with flat grip for bending wire etc.

**plight**[1] /plaɪt/ n. condition, state, esp. unfortunate one.

**plight**[2] /plaɪt/ v.t. arch. pledge; engage *oneself*.

**plimsoll** /'plɪmsəʊl/ n. UK rubber-soled canvas shoe. **Plimsoll line**, **mark**, marking on ship's side showing limit of legal submersion under various conditions.

**plinth** /plɪnθ/ n. base supporting vase or statue etc.

**plod** v.i. 1 walk or work laboriously. 2 n. Aus. piece of ground on which a miner is working; yarn or excuse.

**plonk** n. sl. cheap or inferior wine.

**plop** 1 n. sound of smooth object dropping into water. 2 v. (cause to) fall with plop. 3 adv. with a plop.

**plot** 1 n. small piece of land; plan or essential facts of tale, play, etc.; secret plan, conspiracy. 2 v. make chart, diagram, graph, etc. of; hatch secret plans; devise secretly.

**plough** /plaʊ/ 1 n. implement for furrowing and turning up soil; similar instrument for clearing away snow etc. 2 v. turn up with plough; furrow, make (furrow); advance laboriously *through*; cut or force way. 3 **plough back** plough (crop) into soil to enrich it, reinvest (profits etc.) in business etc.; **ploughman** guider of plough; **ploughshare** blade of plough.

**plover** /'plʌvə(r)/ n. medium-sized wading bird.

# plunder

**ploy** n. colloq. manœuvre to gain advantage.

**pluck** 1 v. pick or pull out or away; strip (bird) of feathers; pull at, twitch; tug or snatch *at*; plunder or swindle. 2 n. courage; animal's heart, liver, and lungs. 3 **pluck up courage** summon up one's courage.

**plucky** /'plʌki/ a. brave, spirited.

**plug** 1 n. something fitting into and stopping or filling hole or cavity; device of metal pins etc. for making electrical connection; (piece of) tobacco pressed into cake or stick. 2 v. stop with plug; put plug into; sl. seek to make popular by frequent repetition, commendation, etc.; sl. shoot; colloq. work *away at*. 3 **plug in** connect electrically by inserting plug into socket.

**plum** n. roundish fleshy stone-fruit; tree bearing it; currant or raisin; good thing, best thing, prize. **plum pudding** Christmas pudding.

**plumage** /'plu:mɪdʒ/ n. bird's feathers.

**plumb** /plʌm/ 1 n. ball of lead attached to line for testing whether wall etc. is vertical; perpendicularity; sounding-lead. 2 a. vertical. 3 adv. exactly; vertically; US sl. quite, utterly. 4 v. sound (water); measure (depth); ascertain depth of or get to bottom of; make vertical; work as plumber; fit as part of plumbing system. 5 **plumb-line** string with plumb attached.

**plumber** /'plʌmə(r)/ n. workman who fits and repairs water-pipes, cisterns, etc.

**plumbing** /'plʌmɪŋ/ n. system or apparatus of water-supply; plumber's work.

**plume** /plu:m/ 1 n. feather, esp. large and showy one; feathery ornament in hat, hair, etc.; feather-like formation, esp. of smoke. 2 v.t. furnish with plume; pride *oneself* (*on*); preen (feathers).

**plummet** /'plʌmət/ 1 n. plumb or plumb-line; sounding-lead. 2 v.i. fall rapidly.

**plummy** /'plʌmi/ a. colloq. good, desirable, (of voice) rich in tone.

**plump** 1 a. having full rounded fleshy shape. 2 v. make or become plump; vote *for* (candidate, or one of alternative choices). 3 adv. colloq. with sudden or heavy fall.

**plunder** /'plʌndə(r)/ 1 v. rob forcibly,

**plunge** esp. as in war; rob, steal, embezzle. **2** *n.* plundering; property plundered; *sl.* profit.

**plunge** **1** *v.* immerse completely; put suddenly, throw oneself, dive, (*into*); move with a rush; *sl.* run up gambling debts. **2** *n.* plunging; dive; *fig.* decisive step.

**plunger** /'plʌndʒə(r)/ *n.* part of mechanism that works with plunging or thrusting motion; rubber cup on handle for removing blockages by plunging action; *sl.* reckless gambler.

**pluperfect** /plu:'pɜːfɪkt/ *Gram.* **1** *a.* expressing action completed prior to some past point of time. **2** *n.* pluperfect tense.

**plural** /'plʊər(ə)l/ **1** *a.* more than one in number. **2** *n.* plural number or form.

**pluralism** /'plʊərəlɪz(ə)m/ *n.* holding of more than one office at a time; form of society in which minority groups retain independent traditions. **pluralist** *n.*; **pluralistic** *a.*

**plurality** /plʊə'rælətɪ/ *n.* state of being plural; majority (*of* votes etc.).

**pluralize** /'plʊərəlaɪz/ *v.t.* make plural; express as plural.

**plus** /plʌs/ **1** *prep.* with addition of; *colloq.* having gained. **2** *n.* symbol (+); additional or positive quantity; advantage. **3** *a.* additional, extra; (after number etc.) at least, rather better than; *Math.* positive.

**plush** /plʌʃ/ **1** *n.* cloth of silk, cotton, etc. with long soft pile. **2** *a.* made of plush, plushy.

**plushy** /'plʌʃɪ/ *a.* stylish, luxurious.

**plutocracy** /plu:'tɒkrəsɪ/ *n.* State in which power belongs to rich; wealthy class. **plutocrat** *n.*; **plutocratic** *a.*

**plutonium** /plu:'təʊnɪəm/ *n.* radioactive metallic element.

**pluvial** /'plu:vɪəl/ *a.* of or caused by rain.

**ply**[1] /plaɪ/ *n.* fold, thickness, strand.

**ply**[2] /plaɪ/ *v.* wield vigorously; work *at*; continuously or assail vigorously (*with*); (of ship, vehicle, etc.) go to and fro (*between*).

**plywood** /'plaɪwʊd/ *n.* strong thin board made by gluing layers with the direction of the grain alternating.

**PM** *abbr.* Prime Minister.

**p.m.** *abbr.* after noon (*post meridiem*).

**pneumatic** /nju:'mætɪk/ *a.* filled with wind or air; working by means of compressed air.

**pneumonia** /nju:'məʊnɪə/ *n.* inflammation of lungs.

**po** *n.* (*pl.* **pos**) *colloq.* chamber-pot. **po-faced** solemn-faced, humourless.

**PO** *abbr.* Post Office; postal order; Petty Officer; Pilot Officer.

**poach** /pəʊtʃ/ *v.* cook (egg) without shell in boiling water; cook (fish etc.) by simmering in small amount of liquid; catch (game or fish) illicitly; encroach, trespass.

**pock** *n.* eruptive spot esp. in smallpox. **pock-marked** bearing marks like those left by smallpox.

**pocket** /'pɒkɪt/ **1** *n.* small bag inserted in or attached to garment for carrying small articles; pouchlike compartment in suitcase, car door, etc.; pecuniary resources; pouch at corner or on side of billiard-table into which balls are driven; cavity in earth, rock, etc., esp. filled with ore etc.; isolated area. **2** *a.* of suitable size for carrying in pocket; small, diminutive. **3** *v.t.* put into pocket; appropriate; submit to (affront etc.), conceal (feelings). **4 in, out of, pocket** having gained, lost, in transaction; **pocket-book** notebook, small booklike case for papers, paper money, etc.; **pocket-knife** small folding knife; **pocket-money** money for occasional expenses, esp. allowance given to child.

**pod 1** *n.* long seed-vessel esp. of pea or bean etc. **2** *v.* form pods; remove (peas etc.) from pods.

**podgy** /'pɒdʒɪ/ *a.* short and fat.

**podium** /'pəʊdɪəm/ *n.* (*pl.* **-dia**) continuous projecting base or pedestal round house etc.; conductor's or speaker's rostrum.

**poem** /'pəʊɪm/ *n.* metrical composition; elevated composition in prose or verse; something with poetic qualities.

**poesy** /'pəʊzɪ/ *n. arch.* poems or poetry.

**poet** /'pəʊɪt/ *n.* writer of poems. **poet Laureate** poet appointed to write poems for State occasions. **poetess** *n.*

**poetaster** /pəʊɪ'tæstə(r)/ *n.* inferior poet.

**poetic** /pəʊ'etɪk/ *a.* of or like poets or poetry. **poetic justice** well-deserved punishment or reward; **poetic licence** departure from truth etc. for effect.

**poetical** /pəʊˈetɪk(ə)l/ a. poetic; written in verse.

**poetry** /ˈpəʊətri/ n. poet's art or work; poems; quality calling for poetical expression.

**pogo** /ˈpəʊgəʊ/ n. (pl. -gos) stiltlike toy with spring, used to jump about on.

**pogrom** /ˈpɒgrəm/ n. organized massacre (orig. of Jews in Russia).

**poignant** /ˈpɔɪnjənt/ a. painfully sharp, deeply moving; pleasantly piquant; arousing sympathy. **poignancy** n.

**poinsettia** /pɔɪnˈsetɪə/ n. plant with large scarlet bracts surrounding small yellowish flowers.

**point** 1 n. sharp end, tip, projection; very small mark on surface; particular place; stage or degree in progress or increase; precise moment; single item or particular; unit of scoring in games etc., or in evaluation etc.; significant thing, thing actually intended or under discussion; distinctive or salient feature; effectiveness, value; one of 32 directions marked on compass; (usu. in pl.) tapering movable rail to direct railway train from one line to another; power point; Crick. (position of) fielder near batsman on off side; promontory. 2 v. direct (finger, weapon, etc.) at; direct attention (as) by extending finger; aim or be directed; provide with point(s); give force to (words, action); fill joints of (brickwork etc.) with smoothed mortar or cement; (of dog) indicate presence of game by standing rigid looking towards it. 3 **on the point of** on the verge of; **point-blank** with aim or weapon level, at close range, directly, flatly; **point-duty** (of policeman etc.) position at particular point to control traffic; **point of view** position from which thing is viewed, way of thinking about a matter; **point out** indicate, draw attention to; **point-to-point** horse-race over course defined only by landmarks; **point up** emphasize.

**pointed** /ˈpɔɪntɪd/ a. having point; (of remark etc.) cutting, emphasized.

**pointer** /ˈpɔɪntə(r)/ n. indicator on gauge etc.; rod used to point to words etc. on screen, blackboard, etc.; breed of dog trained to point at game; colloq. hint.

**pointless** /ˈpɔɪntləs/ a. having no point; meaningless, purposeless.

**poise** /pɔɪz/ 1 v. balance or be balanced; hold suspended or supported. 2 n. equilibrium; composure; carriage (of head etc.).

**poison** /ˈpɔɪz(ə)n/ 1 n. substance that when absorbed by living organism kills or injures it; harmful influence. 2 v.t. administer poison to; kill or injure with poison; fill with prejudice; corrupt, pervert; spoil. 3 **poison ivy** N. Amer. climbing plant secreting irritant oil from leaves; **poison pen** anonymous writer of scurrilous or libellous letters.

**poke** 1 v. push with (end of) finger, stick, etc.; stir (fire), make thrusts (at etc.) with stick etc.; thrust forward. 2 n. poking; thrust, nudge. 3 **poke fun at** ridicule.

**poker**¹ /ˈpəʊkə(r)/ n. metal rod for poking fire.

**poker**² /ˈpəʊkə(r)/ n. card-game in which players bet on value of their hands. **poker-face** impassive countenance appropriate to poker-player, person with this; **poker machine** Aus. gambling-device operated by pulling down armlike handle.

**pokie** /ˈpəʊki/ n. Aus. colloq. poker-machine.

**poky** /ˈpəʊki/ a. (of room etc.) small and cramped.

**polar** /ˈpəʊlə(r)/ a. of or near either pole of earth; having electric or magnetic polarity; directly opposite in character. **polar bear** large white bear living in Arctic.

**polarity** /pəˈlærəti/ n. tendency of magnet etc. to point to earth's magnetic poles or of body to lie with axis in particular direction; possession of two poles having contrary qualities; electrical condition of body as positive or negative.

**polarize** /ˈpəʊləraɪz/ v. restrict vibrations of (light-waves etc.) so that they have different amplitudes in different planes; give polarity to; fig. divide into two opposing groups. **polarization** n.

**pole**¹ n. long slender rounded piece of wood or metal esp. as support for scaffolding, tent, etc.; measure of length (=**perch**¹). **pole-jump, -vault**, vault over high bar with aid of pole held in

**pole** hands; **pole on** *Aus.* sponge on; **up the pole** *colloq.* completely wrong.

**pole²** *n.* either end of earth's axis; either of two points in celestial sphere about which stars appear to revolve; each of two opposite points on surface of magnet at which magnetic forces are concentrated; positive or negative terminal point of electric cell or battery etc.; each of two opposed principles etc. **pole-star** star near N. pole of heavens, thing serving as guide.

**Pole³** *n.* native of Poland.

**pole-axe** 1 *n.* battle-axe; butcher's slaughtering axe. 2 *v.t.* kill or strike with pole-axe.

**polecat** /'pəʊlkæt/ *n.* small dark brown mammal of weasel family.

**polemic** /pə'lemɪk/ 1 *n.* verbal attack; controversy. 2 *a.* controversial, involving dispute. 3 **polemical** *a.*

**police** /pə'liːs/ 1 *n.* civil force responsible for maintaining public order; (as *pl.*) its members; similar force employed to enforce regulations etc. 2 *v.t.* control or provide with police; keep order in, control. 3 **police dog** dog trained and used by police to track criminals etc.; **policeman, police-officer, policewoman,** member of police force; **police state** totalitarian State regulated by esp. secret police; **police station** office of local police force.

**policy¹** /'pɒlɪsɪ/ *n.* course of action adopted by government, party, etc.; prudent conduct.

**policy²** /'pɒlɪsɪ/ *n.* document containing contract of insurance.

**polio** /'pəʊlɪəʊ/ *n. colloq.* poliomyelitis.

**poliomyelitis** /ˌpəʊlɪəʊmaɪə'laɪtɪs/ *n.* infectious viral inflammation of nerve cells in spinal cord, with temporary or permanent paralysis.

**polish¹** /'pɒlɪʃ/ 1 *v.* make or become smooth or glossy by rubbing; make elegant or cultured; smarten *up*; finish *off* quickly. 2 *n.* substance used to produce polished surface; smoothness, glossiness; refinement.

**Polish²** /'pəʊlɪʃ/ 1 *a.* of Poland. 2 *n.* language of Poland.

**polite** /pə'laɪt/ *a.* having refined manners, courteous; cultivated, cultured; refined, elegant.

**politic** /'pɒlɪtɪk/ *a.* judicious, expedient; sagacious, prudent.

**political** /pə'lɪtɪk(ə)l/ *a.* of or taking part in politics; of State or its government; of public affairs; relating to person's or organization's status etc. **political economy** study of economic problems of government; **political geography** that dealing with boundaries etc. of States; **political prisoner** person imprisoned for political offence.

**politician** /pɒlə'tɪʃ(ə)n/ *n.* person engaged or interested in politics.

**politicize** /pə'lɪtɪsaɪz/ *v.t.* give political character to.

**politics** /'pɒlɪtɪks/ *n.pl.* also treated as *sing.* science and art of government; political affairs or life or principles etc.

**polity** /'pɒlɪtɪ/ *n.* form of civil administration; organized society, State.

**polka** /'pɒlkə/ *n.* lively dance in duple time; music for this. **polka-dot** round dot as one of many forming regular pattern on textile fabric etc.

**poll** /pəʊl/ 1 *n.* voting; counting of voters; result of voting, number of votes recorded; questioning of sample of population to estimate trend of public opinion; head. 2 *v.* take votes of, vote, receive votes of; cut off top of (tree etc.) or horns of (cattle). 3 **polling-booth** place where vote is recorded at election; **poll-tax** tax levied on every person.

**pollack** /'pɒlək/ *n.* marine food-fish related to cod.

**pollard** /'pɒləd/ 1 *n.* tree polled to produce close head of young branches; hornless animal. 2 *v.t.* make pollard of (tree).

**pollen** /'pɒlən/ *n.* fertilizing powder discharged from flower's anther. **pollen count** index of amount of pollen in air.

**pollie** /'pɒlɪ/ *n. Aus. sl.* politician.

**pollinate** /'pɒlɪneɪt/ *v.t.* sprinkle stigma of (flower) with pollen. **pollination** *n.*

**pollock** var. of **pollack.**

**pollster** /'pəʊlstə(r)/ *n.* person who organizes public opinion poll.

**pollute** /pə'ljuːt/ *v.t.* destroy purity of; contaminate or defile. **pollution** *n.*

**polo** /'pəʊləʊ/ *n.* game like hockey played on horseback. **polo-neck** high round turned-over collar.

**polonaise** /pɒlə'neɪz/ *n.* slow processional dance; music for this.

## polony

**polony** /pə'ləʊni/ n. kind of sausage.

**poltergeist** /'pɒltəgaist/ n. ghost manifesting itself by noise, mischievous behaviour, etc.

**poltroon** /pɒl'truːn/ n. coward. **poltroonery** n.

**poly-** in comb. many.

**polyandry** /pɒli'ændri/ n. polygamy in which one woman has more than one husband.

**polyanthus** /pɒli'ænθəs/ n. cultivated primula.

**polychromatic** /pɒlikrəʊ'mætɪk/ a. many-coloured.

**polychrome** /'pɒlikrəʊm/ 1 a. in many colours. 2 n. polychrome work of art.

**polyester** /pɒli'estə(r)/ n. a synthetic resin or fibre.

**polyethylene** /pɒli'eθəliːn/ n. polythene.

**polygamy** /pə'lɪgəmi/ n. practice of having more than one wife or husband at once. **polygamist** n.; **polygamous** a.

**polyglot** /'pɒli:glɒt/ 1 a. knowing or using or written in several languages. 2 n. polyglot person.

**polygon** /'pɒli:gən/ n. figure with many sides and angles. **polygonal** a.

**polyhedron** /pɒli'hiːdrən/ n. (pl. **-dra**) solid figure with many faces. **polyhedral** a.

**polymath** /'pɒli:mæθ/ n. person of varied learning, great scholar.

**polymer** /'pɒləmə(r)/ n. compound whose molecule is formed from many repeated units of one or more compounds. **polymeric** /-'mer-/ a.

**polymerize** /'pɒləməraɪz/ v. combine or be combined into polymer. **polymerization** n.

**polyp** /'pɒlɪp/ n. simple organism with tube-shaped body; small growth on mucous membrane.

**polyphony** /pə'lɪfəni/ n. Mus. simultaneous combination of several individual melodies. **polyphonic** /-'fɒn-/ a.

**polystyrene** /pɒli'staɪriːn/ n. kind of hard plastic.

**polysyllabic** /pɒli:sə'læbɪk/ a. (of word) having many syllables; marked by polysyllables.

**polysyllable** /pɒli'sɪləb(ə)l/ n. polysyllabic word.

**polytechnic** /pɒli'teknɪk/ n. UK institution for higher education maintained by local authority and providing courses in esp. vocational subjects.

**polytheism** /'pɒli:θiːɪz(ə)m/ n. belief in or worship of more than one god. **polytheist** n.; **polytheistic** a.

**polythene** /'pɒləθiːn/ n. a tough light plastic.

**polyunsaturated** /pɒli:ʌn'sætʃəreɪtəd/ a. of those kinds of fat or oil not associated with formation of cholesterol.

**polyurethane** /pɒli:'jʊərəθeɪn/ n. a synthetic resin or plastic used esp. as foam.

**polyvinyl chloride** /pɒli:'vaɪnəl/ n. a vinyl plastic used for insulation or as fabric.

**pom** n. Aus. sl. pommy.

**pomade** /pə'mɑːd/ n. scented ointment for hair.

**pomander** /pə'mændə(r)/ n. ball of mixed aromatic substances; container for this.

**pomegranate** /'pɒməgrænət/ n. large tough-rinded many-seeded fruit.

**Pomeranian** /pɒmə'reɪnɪən/ n. breed of small silky-haired dogs.

**pommel** /'pʌm(ə)l/ n. knob of sword-hilt; projecting front part of saddle.

**pommy** /'pɒmi:/ n. Aus. & NZ sl. British person, esp. recent immigrant.

**pomp** n. splendour, splendid display; grandeur.

**pom-pom**[1] /'pɒmpɒm/ n. automatic quick-firing gun.

**pom-pom**[2] var. of **pompon**.

**pompon** /'pɒmpɒn/ n. decorative tuft or ball on hat or shoe etc.; small-flowered kind of chrysanthemum or dahlia.

**pompous** /'pɒmpəs/ a. showing self-importance; (of language) pretentious, unduly grand. **pomposity** /-'pɒs-/ n.

**ponce** 1 n. man who lives off prostitute's earnings; sl. effeminate man. 2 v.i. act as ponce; sl. move about effeminately.

**poncho** /'pɒntʃəʊ/ n. (pl. **-chos**) (orig. S. Amer.) cloak of rectangular piece of material with slit in middle for head.

**pond** n. small area of still water.

**ponder** /'pɒndə(r)/ v. think (over), muse.

**ponderable** /'pɒndərəb(ə)l/ a. having appreciable weight. **ponderability** n.

# ponderous

**ponderous** /'pɒndərəs/ *a.* heavy; unwieldy; dull, tedious. **ponderosity** *n.*
**pong** *n.* & *v.i. colloq.* stink.
**poniard** /'pɒnjəd/ *n.* dagger.
**pontiff** /'pɒntɪf/ *n.* bishop; chief priest; Pope.
**pontifical** /pɒn'tɪfɪk(ə)l/ *a.* of or befitting pontiff; solemnly dogmatic.
**pontificate** 1 /pɒn'tɪfəkeɪt/ *v.i.* speak or act pompously or dogmatically; officiate as bishop. 2 /pɒn'tɪfəkət/ *n.* office of bishop or Pope; period of this.
**pontoon**[1] /pɒn'tu:n/ *n.* card-game in which players try to acquire cards with face-value totalling 21.
**pontoon**[2] /pɒn'tu:n/ *n.* flat-bottomed boat etc. as one of supports of temporary bridge.
**pony** /'pəʊnɪ/ *n.* horse of any small breed. **pony-tail** hair drawn back, tied, and hanging down behind head.
**poodle** /'pu:d(ə)l/ *n.* breed of dog with thick curling hair.
**pooh** /pu:/ *int.* of contempt. **pooh-pooh** express contempt for, ridicule.
**pool**[1] /pu:l/ *n.* small area of still water; puddle; deep place in river; swimming-pool.
**pool**[2] /pu:l/ 1 *n.* common fund, e.g. of profits or of players' stakes in gambling, football pool; common supply of persons, vehicles, etc., for sharing by group; group of persons sharing duties etc.; arrangement between competing parties to fix prices and share business; game like billiards with usu. 16 balls. 2 *v.t.* put into common fund; share in common; *Aus. sl.* implicate, involve (person) against his will; *Aus. sl.* inform on.
**poon** /pu:n/ *n. Aus. sl.* a foolish person.
**poop** /pu:p/ *n.* stern of ship; aftermost and highest deck.
**poor** /pʊə(r)/ *a.* having little money or means; deficient (*in*); inadequate; deserving pity; inferior; despicable, insignificant. **poor man's** inferior substitute for.
**poorly** /'pʊəlɪ/ 1 *adv.* in a poor manner; badly. 2 *pred. a.* unwell.
**pop**[1] 1 *n.* abrupt explosive sound; effervescing drink. 2 *v.* (cause to) make pop; go or come unexpectedly or suddenly; put quickly (*in, down,* etc.); *sl.* pawn. 3 *adv.* with sound of pop; suddenly. 4 **popcorn** maize which when heated bursts open to form fluffy balls; **pop-eyed** *colloq.* with eyes bulging or wide open; **popgun** toy gun shooting pellet etc. by compressed air or spring. **popping-crease** *Crick.* line in front of and parallel to wicket.
**pop**[2] 1 *a.* in popular modern style; performing or concerned with pop music. 2 *n.* pop music. 3 **pop music** music in popular modern style.
**pop**[3] *n. colloq.* father.
**pope** *n.* bishop of Rome as head of RC Ch.
**popery** *n. derog.* papal system, RC religion.
**popinjay** /'pɒpɪndʒeɪ/ *n.* fop, conceited person.
**popish** /'pəʊpɪʃ/ *a. derog.* of popery.
**poplar** /'pɒplə(r)/ *n.* tree with straight trunk and often tremulous leaves.
**poplin** /'pɒplɪn/ *n.* closely-woven corded fabric.
**poppadam** /'pɒpədəm/ *n.* large thin crisp savoury Indian biscuit.
**poppet** /'pɒpɪt/ *n. colloq.* (esp. as term of endearment) small or dainty person.
**poppy** /'pɒpɪ/ *n.* plant with bright flowers and milky narcotic juice; artificial poppy worn on **Poppy Day** Remembrance Sunday.
**poppycock** /'pɒpɪkɒk/ *n. sl.* nonsense.
**populace** /'pɒpjələs/ *n.* the common people.
**popular** /'pɒpjələ(r)/ *a.* generally liked or admired; of or for the general public. **popularity** *n.*; **popularize** *v.t.*
**populate** /'pɒpjəleɪt/ *v.t.* form population of; supply with inhabitants.
**population** /pɒpjə'leɪʃ(ə)n/ *n.* inhabitants of town, country, etc.; total number of these; degree to which place is populated.
**populous** /'pɒpjələs/ *a.* thickly inhabited.
**porcelain** /'pɔ:səlɪn/ *n.* fine earthenware, china; things made of this.
**porch** *n.* covered approach to entrance of building.
**porcine** /'pɔ:saɪn/ *a.* of or like pigs.
**porcupine** /'pɔ:kjəpaɪn/ *n.* rodent with body and tail covered with erectile spines; **porcupine ant-eater** *Aus.* echidna; **porcupine grass** *Aus.* a grass with stiff sharp-pointed leaves.
**pore**[1] *n.* minute opening in surface through which fluids may pass.

**pore**² *v.i.* **pore over** be absorbed in studying (book etc.).

**pork** *n.* flesh of pig used as food.

**porker** /'pɔːkə(r)/ *n.* pig raised for pork.

**pornography** /pɔːˈnɒɡrəfi/ *n.* explicit presentation of sexual activity in literature or films etc., to stimulate erotic rather than aesthetic feelings. **pornographer** *n.*; **pornographic** *a.*

**porous** /'pɔːrəs/ *a.* having pores; permeable. **porosity** *n.*

**porphyry** /'pɔːfəri/ *n.* hard rock with large crystals in fine-grained ground mass.

**porpoise** /'pɔːpəs/ *n.* sea mammal related to whale.

**porridge** /'pɒrɪdʒ/ *n.* oatmeal or other meal boiled in water or milk.

**porringer** /'pɒrɪndʒə(r)/ *n.* small soup-basin.

**port**¹ *n.* harbour; town or place possessing harbour.

**port**² *n.* strong sweet red fortified wine.

**port**³ 1 *n.* left-hand side of boat or aircraft etc. looking forward. 2 *v.* turn (helm) to port.

**port**⁴ *n.* opening in ship's side for entrance, loading, etc., porthole. **porthole** (esp. glazed) aperture in ship's side to admit light and air.

**port**⁵ *v.t. Mil.* hold (rifle) diagonally in front of body.

**port**⁶ *n. Aus.* portmanteau, suitcase; *Qland* satchel, shopping-bag.

**portable** /'pɔːtəb(ə)l/ *a.* that can be carried about, movable. **portability** *n.*

**portage** /'pɔːtɪdʒ/ *n.* carrying of boats or goods between two navigable waters.

**portal** /'pɔːt(ə)l/ *n.* gate; doorway.

**portcullis** /pɔːtˈkʌlɪs/ *n.* strong heavy grating raised and lowered in grooves as defence of gateway.

**portend** /pɔːˈtend/ *v.t.* foreshadow, as an omen; give warning of.

**portent** /'pɔːtent/ *n.* omen, significant sign; prodigy.

**portentous** /pɔːˈtentəs/ *a.* of or like portent; solemn; pompous.

**porter**¹ /'pɔːtə(r)/ *n.* person employed to carry luggage etc.; dark beer brewed from charred or browned malt. **porterhouse steak** a choice cut of beef.

**porter**² /'pɔːtə(r)/ *n.* gate-keeper or door-keeper, esp. of large building.

**porterage** /'pɔːtərɪdʒ/ *n.* hire of porters.

**portfolio** /pɔːtˈfəʊlɪəʊ/ *n.* (*pl.* -lios) case for loose drawings, sheets of paper, etc.; list of investments held by investor etc.; office of minister of State.

**portico** /'pɔːtɪkəʊ/ *n.* (*pl.* -coes) colonnade serving as porch to building.

**portion** /'pɔːʃ(ə)n/ 1 *n.* part allotted, share; helping; dowry; destiny or lot. 2 *v.t.* divide into portions, share *out*; give dowry to.

**Port Jackson** /'dʒæks(ə)n/ *Aus.* **Port Jackson fig** an evergreen tree with inedible figs; **Port Jackson shark** a small harmless Aus. shark.

**Portland** *n.* **Portland cement** cement manufactured from chalk and clay; **Portland stone** valuable building limestone.

**portly** /'pɔːtli/ *a.* corpulent and dignified.

**portmanteau** /pɔːtˈmæntəʊ/ *n.* (*pl.* -teaus) case for clothes etc. opening into two equal parts. **portmanteau word** invented word combining sounds and meanings of two others.

**portrait** /'pɔːtrət/ *n.* likeness of person or animal made by drawing or painting or photography; graphic description.

**portraiture** /'pɔːtrətʃə(r)/ *n.* portraying; portrait; graphic description.

**portray** /pɔːˈtreɪ/ *v.t.* make likeness of; describe. **portrayal** *n.*

**Portuguese** /pɔːtjəˈɡiːz/ 1 *a.* of Portugal. 2 *n.* native or language of Portugal.

**pose** /pəʊz/ 1 *v.* assume attitude, esp. for artistic purpose; set up, give oneself out, *as*; propound (question, problem); arrange in required attitude. 2 *n.* attitude of body or mind; affectation or pretence.

**poser** /'pəʊzə(r)/ *n.* puzzling question or problem.

**poseur** /pəʊˈzɜː(r)/ *n.* (*fem.* -seuse /-ˈzɜːz/) person who poses for effect.

**posh** *a. colloq.* smart, stylish; high-class.

**posit** /'pɒzɪt/ *v.t.* assume as fact, postulate.

**position** /pəˈzɪʃ(ə)n/ 1 *n.* place occupied by person or thing; proper place; way thing is placed; mental attitude; state of affairs; situation; rank or status; paid (official or domestic) employment; strategic point. 2 *v.t.* place in position. 3 **positional** *a.*

**positive** /'pɒzətɪv/ 1 *a.* formally or ex-

## positivism

plicitly stated, definite, unquestionable; confident in opinion, cocksure; absolute, not relative; constructive; not negative; dealing only with matters of fact, practical; *Alg.* (of quantity) greater than zero; *Electr.* of, containing, producing, kind of charge produced by rubbing glass with silk; *Gram.* (of adj. etc.) expressing simple quality without comparison; *Photog.* showing lights and shades as seen in original image cast on film etc. 2 *n.* positive adjective, quantity, photograph, etc.

**positivism** /'pɒzɪtɪvɪz(ə)m/ *n.* philosophical system recognizing only positive facts and observable phenomena. **positivist** *n. & a.*; **positivistic** *a.*

**positron** /'pɒzɪtrɒn/ *n.* elementary particle with mass of electron and charge same as electron's but positive.

**posse** /'pɒsɪ/ *n.* body (*of* constables); strong force or company.

**possess** /pə'zes/ *v.t.* hold as property; own, have; (of demon etc.) occupy, dominate mind of. **possessor** *n.*

**possession** /pə'zeʃ(ə)n/ *n.* possessing or being possessed; thing possessed; occupancy; in *pl.* property.

**possessive** /pə'zesɪv/ 1 *a.* showing desire to possess or retain what one possesses; *Gram.* of or indicating possession. 2 *n. Gram.* possessive case or word.

**possibility** /pɒsə'bɪlətɪ/ *n.* state or fact of being possible; thing that may exist or happen.

**possible** /'pɒsəb(ə)l/ 1 *a.* that can exist, be done, or happen; that may be or become. 2 *n.* possible candidate, member of team, etc.; highest possible score.

**possibly** /'pɒsəblɪ/ *adv.* in accordance with possibility; perhaps, maybe.

**possie** /'pɒzɪ/ *n. Aus. colloq.* place or position.

**possum** /'pɒsəm/ *n. colloq.* opossum. **play possum** pretend to be unconscious; **stir the possum** *colloq.* create a disturbance, cause trouble.

**post**[1] /pəʊst/ 1 *n.* upright of timber or metal as support in building; stake or stout pole to mark boundary, carry notices, etc.; pole etc. marking start or finish in race. 2 *v.t.* (also with *up*) display (notice etc.) in prominent place; advertise by placard or in published list.

## postilion

**post**[2] /pəʊst/ 1 *n.* official conveying of letters and parcels; single collection or delivery of these; place where letters etc. are dealt with. 2 *v.* put (letter etc.) into post; supply with latest information; enter in ledger. 3 **post-box** box for posting letters; **postcard** card conveying message by post without envelope; **postcode** group of letters and figures in postal address to assist sorting; **post-haste** with great speed; **postman** person who collects or delivers post; **postmark** official mark stamped on letters; **postmaster, postmistress,** official in charge of post office; **post office** room or building for postal business; **Post Office** public department or corporation providing postal etc. services.

**post**[3] 1 *n.* situation of paid employment; appointed place of soldier etc. on duty; fort, trading-station. 2 *v.t.* place (soldier etc.) at his post, appoint to post or command.

**post-** *in comb.* after, behind.

**postage** /'pəʊstɪdʒ/ *n.* amount charged for sending letter etc. by post. **postage stamp** small adhesive label indicating amount of postage paid.

**postal** /'pəʊst(ə)l/ *a.* of or by post. **postal note, order,** kind of money order issued by Post Office.

**postdate** /pəʊst'deɪt/ *v.t.* follow in time; give later than true date to.

**poster** /'pəʊstə(r)/ *n.* placard in public place; large printed picture.

**poste restante** /pəʊst re'stɑ̃t/ department in post office where letters are kept till called for.

**posterior** /pɒs'tɪərɪə(r)/ 1 *a.* hinder; later in time or order. 2 *n.* buttocks.

**posterity** /pɒs'terɪtɪ/ *n.* later generations; descendants.

**postern** /'pɒst(ə)n/ *n.* back or side entrance.

**postgraduate** /pəʊst'grædjuːət/ 1 *a.* (of course of study) carried on after taking first degree. 2 *n.* student taking such course.

**posthumous** /'pɒstjʊməs/ *a.* occurring after death; published after author's death; born after father's death.

**postie** /'pəʊstɪ/ *n. Aus. colloq.* postman.

**postilion** /pə'tɪljən/ *n.* rider on near horse drawing coach etc. without coachman.

**Post-Impressionism** /pəʊst-/ n. artistic aims and methods directed to expressing individual artist's conception of objects represented. **Post-Impressionist** n. & a.

**post-mortem** /pəʊst'mɔːtəm/ 1 n. examination of body made after death; *colloq.* discussion after conclusion (of game etc.). 2 a. & adv. after death.

**postnatal** /pəʊst'neɪt(ə)l/ a. existing or occurring etc. after birth.

**postpone** /pəʊst'pəʊn/ v.t. cause to take place at later time. **postponement** n.

**postscript** /'pəʊstskrɪpt/ n. addition at end of letter etc. after signature.

**postulant** /'pɒstjʊlənt/ n. candidate esp. for admission to religious order.

**postulate** 1 /'pɒstjʊleɪt/ v.t. assume or require to be true; claim; take for granted. 2 /'pɒstjʊlət/ n. thing postulated.

**posture** /'pɒstʃə(r)/ 1 n. attitude of body or mind; relative position of parts esp. of body; condition or state (of affairs etc.). 2 v.i. assume posture esp. for effect.

**post-war** /pəʊst-/ a. occurring or existing after a war.

**posy** /'pəʊzi/ n. small bunch of flowers.

**pot**[1] 1 n. vessel of earthenware or metal or glass etc.; chamber-pot; teapot; contents of pot; *colloq.* large sum, cup, etc. won as prize; pot-belly. 2 v.t. plant in pot; pocket (ball) in billiards etc.; shoot; bag (game etc.); abridge, epitomize; preserve (food) in sealed pot. 3 **go to pot** *colloq.* be ruined; **pot-belly** protuberant belly; **pot-boiler** work of literature etc. done merely to earn money; **pot-herb** herb used in cooking; **pot-hole** deep cylindrical hole in rock, rough hole in road-surface; **pot luck** whatever is available; **pot-roast** braise, (n.) braised meat; **potsherd** piece of broken earthenware; **pot-shot** random shot; **put someone's pot on** *Aus. colloq.* inform on him.

**pot**[2] n. sl. marijuana.

**potable** /'pəʊtəb(ə)l/ a. drinkable.

**potash** /'pɒtæʃ/ n. potassium carbonate.

**potassium** /pə'tæsɪəm/ n. soft silver-white metallic element.

**potation** /pə'teɪʃ(ə)n/ n. drinking; a drink.

**potato** /pə'teɪtəʊ/ n. (pl. **-toes**) plant with tubers used as food; its tuber.

**potch** n. *Aus.* inferior kind of opal.

**poteen** /pɒ'tiːn/ n. *Ir.* whisky from illicit still.

**potent** /'pəʊt(ə)nt/ a. powerful; strong; cogent; influential; (of a man) able to procreate. **potency** n.

**potentate** /'pəʊtənteɪt/ n. monarch, ruler.

**potential** /pə'tenʃ(ə)l/ 1 a. capable of coming into being. 2 n. capability for use or development; usable resources; quantity determining energy of mass in gravitational field or of charge in electric field etc. 3 **potentiality** n.

**potheen** var. of **poteen**.

**pother** /'pɒðə(r)/ n. fuss; din.

**potion** /'pəʊʃ(ə)n/ n. draught of medicine or poison.

**potoroo** /pɒtə'ruː/ n. *Aus.* long-nosed rat kangaroo.

**pot-pourri** /pəʊpʊri/ n. scented mixture of dried petals and spices; musical or literary medley.

**pottage** /'pɒtɪdʒ/ n. *arch.* soup or stew.

**potter**[1] /'pɒtə(r)/ v.i. move (*about* etc.), work, etc. in aimless or desultory manner.

**potter**[2] /'pɒtə(r)/ n. maker of earthenware vessels.

**pottery** /'pɒtəri/ n. vessels etc. made of baked clay; potter's work or workshop.

**potty**[1] /'pɒti/ a. sl. crazy; insignificant.

**potty**[2] /'pɒti/ n. *colloq.* chamber-pot, esp. for child.

**pouch** /paʊtʃ/ 1 n. small bag; detachable pocket; baglike receptacle in which marsupials carry undeveloped young, other baglike natural receptacle. 2 v. put into pouch; take shape of or hang like pouch.

**pouffe** /puːf/ n. low stuffed seat or cushion.

**poulterer** /'pəʊltərə(r)/ n. dealer in poultry and usu. game.

**poultice** /'pəʊltɪs/ 1 n. soft usu. hot dressing applied to sore or inflamed part of body; *Aus. colloq.* mortgage, large sum of money. 2 v.t. apply poultice to.

**poultry** /'pəʊltri/ n. domestic fowls.

**pounce** /paʊns/ 1 v.i. make sudden attack (*up*)*on*; seize eagerly (*up*)*on*. 2 n. pouncing; sudden swoop.

**pound**[1] /paʊnd/ n. unit of weight equal to 16 oz. (454 g.); monetary unit of UK

**pound** (**pound sterling**) and some other countries.

**pound²** /paʊnd/ v. crush or beat with repeated strokes; thump, pummel; walk or run etc. heavily.

**pound³** /paʊnd/ n. enclosure where stray animals or officially removed vehicles etc. are kept until claimed.

**poundage** /ˈpaʊndɪdʒ/ n. commission or fee of so much per pound sterling or weight.

**pounder** /ˈpaʊndə(r)/ n. thing that, or gun carrying shell that, weighs a pound or (**-pounder**) so many pounds (e.g. *six-pounder*).

**pour** /pɔː(r)/ v. (cause to) flow in stream or shower; rain heavily; discharge copiously.

**pout** /paʊt/ 1 v. protrude lips, (of lips etc.) protrude, esp. as sign of displeasure. 2 n. pouting expression.

**pouter** /ˈpaʊtə(r)/ n. kind of pigeon with great power of inflating crop.

**poverty** /ˈpɒvətɪ/ n. being poor; want, scarcity or lack; inferiority, poorness. **poverty-stricken** poor.

**POW** *abbr.* prisoner of war.

**powder** /ˈpaʊdə(r)/ 1 n. mass of fine dry particles; cosmetic or medicine in this form; gunpowder. 2 v. apply powder to; reduce to powder. 3 **powder blue** soft pale blue; **powder-puff** soft pad for applying cosmetic powder to skin; **powder-room** ladies' lavatory. 4 **powdery** a.

**power** /ˈpaʊə(r)/ 1 n. ability to do or act; vigour, energy; control, influence, ascendancy; authority; influential person etc.; State with international influence; capacity for exerting mechanical force; electricity supply; *Math.* product obtained by multiplying a number by itself a specified number of times; magnifying capacity of lens. 2 v.t. supply with mechanical or electrical energy. 3 **power cut** temporary withdrawal or failure of electric power supply; **powerhouse** power-station, *fig.* source of drive or energy; **power-point** socket for connection of electrical appliance etc. to mains; **power-station** building etc. where electric power is generated for distribution.

**powerful** /ˈpaʊəfəl/ a. having great power or influence.

**powerless** /ˈpaʊələs/ a. without power; wholly unable (*to*).

**pow-wow** /ˈpaʊwaʊ/ n. conference or meeting for discussion (orig. among N. Amer. Indians).

**pox** n. virus disease with pocks; *colloq.* syphilis.

**pp.** *abbr.* pages.

**p.p.** *abbr.* per pro.

**pp** *abbr.* pianissimo.

**PPS** *abbr.* further postscript (*post postscriptum*).

**PR** *abbr.* proportional representation; public relations.

**practicable** /ˈpræktɪkəb(ə)l/ a. that can be done or used etc. **practicability** n.

**practical** /ˈpræktɪk(ə)l/ a. of or concerned with or shown in practice; inclined to action; able to do functional things well; that is such in effect though not in name, virtual. **practical joke** trick played on person. **practicality** n.

**practically** adv. virtually, almost; in a practical way.

**practice** /ˈpræktɪs/ n. habitual action, established method; exercise to improve skill; action as opposed to theory; lawyer's or doctor's professional business. **in practice** in the realm of action, skilled by having recently had practice; **out of practice** no longer having former skill.

**practise** /ˈpræktɪs/ v. carry out in action; do repeatedly to improve skill; exercise oneself in or on; pursue profession; (in *p.p.*) expert.

**practitioner** /prækˈtɪʃənə(r)/ n. professional worker, esp. in medicine.

**praetorian guard** /prɪˈtɔːrɪən/ bodyguard of Roman emperor etc.

**pragmatic** /prægˈmætɪk/ a. dealing with matters from a practical point of view; treating facts of history with reference to their practical lessons.

**pragmatism** /ˈprægmətɪz(ə)m/ n. matter-of-fact treatment of things; *Philos.* doctrine that evaluates assertions solely by practical consequences. **pragmatist** n.

**prairie** /ˈpreərɪ/ n. large treeless tract of grassland esp. in N. Amer.

**praise** /preɪz/ 1 v.t. express warm approval of; commend; glorify. 2 n. praising; commendation. 3 **praiseworthy** worthy of praise.

**praline** /ˈprɑːliːn/ *n.* sweet made of almonds etc. browned in boiling sugar.

**pram** *n.* carriage for baby, pushed by person on foot.

**prance** /prɑːns/ 1 *v.i.* walk or move in elated or arrogant manner; (of horse) spring from hind legs. 2 *n.* prancing; prancing movement.

**prank** *n.* practical joke.

**prat** *n. sl.* fool; buttocks.

**prate** *v.i.* chatter foolishly; talk too much.

**prattle** 1 *v.i.* talk in childish or artless way. 2 *n.* prattling talk.

**prawn** *n.* edible shellfish like large shrimp. **come the raw prawn** *Aus. sl.* try to impose on someone.

**pray** *v.* say prayers; make devout supplication (to); ask earnestly (for).

**prayer** /preə(r)/ *n.* solemn request or thanksgiving to God or object of worship; formula used in praying; entreaty.

**prayer-book** book of forms of prayer, esp. liturgy of Church of England.

**prayer-mat** small carpet used by Muslims when praying.

**pre-** *pref.* before (in time, place, order, or importance), freely used with Eng. words, only the more important of which are given below.

**preach** /priːtʃ/ *v.* deliver sermon; proclaim (the Gospel etc.); give obtrusive moral advice; advocate, inculcate.

**preamble** /priːˈæmb(ə)l/ *n.* introductory part of statute, deed, etc.

**pre-arrange** /priːəˈreɪndʒ/ *v.t.* arrange beforehand. **pre-arrangement** *n.*

**prebend** /ˈprebənd/ *n.* stipend of canon or member of chapter; portion of land etc. from which this is drawn. **prebendal** *a.*

**prebendary** /ˈprebəndəri/ *n.* holder of prebend; honorary canon.

**precarious** /prɪˈkeərɪəs/ *a.* uncertain; dependent on chance; perilous.

**pre-cast** /priːˈkɑːst/ *a.* (of concrete) cast in blocks before use.

**precaution** /prɪˈkɔːʃ(ə)n/ *n.* action taken beforehand to avoid risk or ensure good result. **precautionary** *a.*

**precede** /prɪˈsiːd/ *v.t.* come or go before in importance or place or time; cause to be preceded by.

**precedence** /ˈpresɪd(ə)ns/ *n.* priority; right of preceding others.

**precedent** /ˈpresɪd(ə)nt/ *n.* previous case taken as example or justification etc.

**precentor** /prɪˈsentə(r)/ *n.* member of cathedral clergy in general charge of music there.

**precept** /ˈpriːsept/ *n.* rule for action or conduct; writ, warrant.

**preceptor** /prɪˈseptə(r)/ *n.* teacher, instructor. **preceptorial** *a.*

**precession** /prɪˈseʃ(ə)n/ *n.* change by which equinoxes occur earlier in each successive sidereal year.

**precinct** /ˈpriːsɪŋkt/ *n.* space within boundaries of place or building; district in town where traffic is excluded; in *pl.* environs.

**preciosity** /preʃɪˈɒsəti/ *n.* over-refinement in art.

**precious** /ˈpreʃəs/ 1 *a.* of great price; valuable, highly valued; affectedly refined. 2 *adv. colloq.* extremely, very.

**precipice** /ˈpresəpəs/ *n.* vertical steep face of rock, cliff, mountain, etc.

**precipitance** /prɪˈsɪpɪt(ə)ns/ *n.* (also **precipitancy**) rash haste.

**precipitate** 1 /prɪˈsɪpɪteɪt/ *v.t.* hasten occurrence of; cause to go hurriedly or violently; throw down headlong; *Chem.* cause (substance) to be deposited in solid form from solution; *Phys.* condense (vapour) into drops. 2 /prɪˈsɪpɪtət/ *a.* headlong; rash; done too soon. 3 /prɪˈsɪpɪtət/ *n.* solid matter precipitated; moisture condensed from vapour.

**precipitation** /prɪsɪpɪˈteɪʃ(ə)n/ *n.* precipitating or being precipitated; rash haste; rain, snow, etc., falling to ground.

**precipitous** /prɪˈsɪpɪtəs/ *a.* of or like precipice; steep.

**précis** /ˈpreɪsiː/ 1 *n.* (*pl.* same) summary, abstract. 2 *v.t.* make précis of.

**precise** /prɪˈsaɪs/ *a.* accurately worded; definite, exact; punctilious.

**precisely** *adv.* in precise manner; in exact terms; quite so.

**precision** /prɪˈsɪʒ(ə)n/ *n.* accuracy; *attrib.* designed for exact work.

**preclude** /prɪˈkluːd/ *v.t.* prevent; make impossible.

**precocious** /prɪˈkəʊʃəs/ *a.* prematurely developed in some faculty or characteristic. **precocity** /-ˈkɒs-/ *n.*

**precognition** /priːkɒgˈnɪʃ(ə)n/ *n.* (esp. supernatural) foreknowledge.

**preconceive** /priːkənˈsiːv/ v.t. form (opinion etc.) beforehand.

**preconception** /ˌpriːkənˈsepʃ(ə)n/ n. preconceiving; prejudice.

**pre-condition** /priːkənˈdɪʃ(ə)n/ n. condition that must be fulfilled beforehand.

**precursor** /priːˈkɜːsə(r)/ n. forerunner, harbinger; person who precedes in office etc.

**predacious** /prəˈdeɪʃəs/ a. (of animal) predatory.

**pre-date** /priːˈdeɪt/ v.t. antedate.

**predator** /ˈpredətə(r)/ n. predatory animal.

**predatory** /ˈpredətəri/ a. (of animal) preying naturally on others; plundering or exploiting others.

**predecease** /priːdəˈsiːs/ v.t. die before (another).

**predecessor** /ˈpriːdəsesə/ n. former holder of office or position; thing to which another has succeeded.

**predestine** /priːˈdestɪn/ v.t. determine or appoint beforehand; ordain by divine will or as if by fate. **predestination** n.

**predetermine** /priːdəˈtɜːmən/ v.t. decree beforehand, predestine. **predetermination** n.

**predicable** /ˈpredəkəb(ə)l/ a. that can be predicated or affirmed.

**predicament** /prəˈdɪkəmənt/ n. difficult or unpleasant situation.

**predicate** 1 /ˈpredɪkeɪt/ v.t. assert, affirm, as true or existent. 2 /ˈpredɪkət/ n. what is predicated; *Gram.* what is said about subject of sentence. 3 **predication** n.

**predicative** /prəˈdɪkətɪv/ a. *Gram.* (of adjective or noun) forming part or all of predicate.

**predict** /prəˈdɪkt/ v.t. forecast; prophesy. **prediction** n.; **predictive** a.

**predilection** /priːdəˈlekʃ(ə)n/ n. preference or special liking (*for*).

**predispose** /priːdɪsˈpəʊz/ v.t. render liable or inclined (*to*) beforehand. **predisposition** n.

**predominate** /prəˈdɒmɪneɪt/ v.i. have chief power or influence; prevail; preponderate. **predominance** n.; **predominant** a.

**pre-eminent** /priːˈemɪnənt/ a. excelling others. **pre-eminence** n.

**pre-empt** /priːˈempt/ v.t. obtain by pre-emption; forestall.

**pre-emption** /priːˈempʃ(ə)n/ n. purchase of thing before it is offered to others; right to first refusal.

**pre-emptive** /priːˈemptɪv/ a. pre-empting; *Mil.* intended to prevent attack by disabling threatening enemy.

**preen** v.t. (of bird) trim (feathers) with beak; (of person) smarten (*oneself*). **preen oneself** show self-satisfaction.

**pre-exist** /priːəɡˈzɪst/ v.i. exist previously. **pre-existence** n.; **pre-existent** a.

**prefab** /ˈpriːfæb/ n. *colloq.* prefabricated building.

**prefabricate** /priːˈfæbrəkeɪt/ v.t. manufacture sections of (building etc.) prior to assembly on a site. **prefabrication** n.

**preface** /ˈprefəs/ 1 n. introduction to book stating subject, scope, etc.; preliminary part of speech etc. 2 v.t. introduce or begin (as) with preface. 3 **prefatory** /ˈpref-/ a.

**prefect** /ˈpriːfekt/ n. chief administrative officer of certain departments in France etc.; senior pupil in school, authorized to maintain discipline. **prefectorial** a.

**prefecture** /ˈpriːfektjə(r)/ n. district under government of prefect; prefect's office or tenure.

**prefer** /prəˈfɜː(r)/ v.t. choose rather, like better; submit (accusation etc. *against* offender); promote *to* office.

**preferable** /ˈprefərəb(ə)l/ a. to be preferred, more desirable.

**preference** /ˈprefərəns/ n. preferring, thing preferred; favouring of one person etc. before others; prior right.

**preferential** /prefəˈrenʃ(ə)l/ a. of or giving or receiving preference.

**preferment** /prəˈfɜːmənt/ n. promotion to office.

**prefigure** /priːˈfɪɡə(r)/ v.t. represent or imagine beforehand.

**prefix** /ˈpriːfɪks/ 1 n. verbal element placed at beginning of word to qualify meaning; title placed before name. 2 v.t. add as introduction; join as prefix (*to* word).

**pregnant** /ˈpreɡnənt/ a. (of woman or female animal) having developing child or young in womb; significant, suggestive; plentifully furnished *with* (con-

## prehensile

**pregnancy** *n.*
**prehensile** /pri:'hensaɪl/ *a.* (of tail or limb etc.) capable of grasping.
**prehistoric** /pri:hɪs'tɒrɪk/ *a.* of period before written records. **prehistory** *n.*
**prejudge** /pri:'dʒʌdʒ/ *v.t.* pass judgement on before trial or proper inquiry. **prejudgement** *n.*
**prejudice** /'predʒədəs/ 1 *n.* preconceived opinion, bias; injury or detriment resulting from action or judgement. 2 *v.t.* impair validity of; cause (person) to have prejudice. 3 **prejudicial** /-'dɪʃ-/ *a.*
**prelacy** /'prelasi:/ *n.* church government by prelates; prelates collectively; office or rank of prelate.
**prelate** /'prelət/ *n.* high ecclesiastical dignitary, e.g. bishop.
**preliminary** /prə'lɪmənəri:/ 1 *a.* preparatory, introductory. 2 *n.* (usu. in *pl.*) preliminary step or arrangement. 3 *adv.* preparatory.
**prelude** /'prelju:d/ 1 *n.* action or event etc. serving as introduction (*to*); *Mus.* introductory movement or first piece of suite, short piece of music of similar type. 2 *v.t.* serve as prelude to, introduce (with prelude).
**pre-marital** /pri:'mærət(ə)l/ *a.* occurring before marriage.
**premature** /'premətjə(r)/ *a.* occurring or done before right or usual time; too hasty; (of baby) born 3-12 weeks before expected time. **prematurity** *n.*
**premedication** /pri:medə'keɪʃ(ə)n/ *n.* medication in preparation for operation.
**premeditate** /pri:'medəteɪt/ *v.t.* (esp. in *p.p.*) think out or plan beforehand. **premeditation** *n.*
**pre-menstrual** /pri:'menstru:əl/ *a.* of the time immediately before menstruation.
**premier** /'premɪə(r)/ 1 *a.* first in importance or order or time. 2 *n. Aus.* leader of a State government; *UK* etc. prime minister.
**première** /'premɪeə(r)/ 1 *n.* first performance or showing of play, film, etc. 2 *v.t.* give premiere of.
**premise** /'preməs/ *n.* premiss; in *pl.* house or building with grounds etc.; in *pl. Law* the aforesaid houses, lands, or tenements. **on the premises** in the house etc. concerned.
**premiss** /'preməs/ *n.* previous statement from which another is inferred.
**premium** /'pri:mɪəm/ *n.* amount to be paid for contract of insurance; sum added to interest, wages, etc.; reward, prize. **at a premium** above nominal or usual price, *fig.* highly valued; **Premium (Savings) Bond** government security not bearing interest but with periodical chance of prize.
**premonition** /pri:mə'nɪʃ(ə)n/ *n.* forewarning; presentiment. **premonitory** /-'mɒn-/ *a.*
**pre-natal** /pri:'neɪt(ə)l/ *a.* existing or occurring before birth.
**preoccupation** /pri:ɒkjə'peɪʃ(ə)n/ *n.* state of being preoccupied; thing that engages one's mind.
**preoccupy** /pri:'ɒkjəpaɪ/ *v.t.* dominate or engross mind of.
**pre-ordain** /pri:ɔ:'deɪn/ *v.t.* ordain or determine beforehand.
**prep** *n. colloq.* preparation of school work; time when this is done.
**preparation** /prepə'reɪʃ(ə)n/ *n.* preparing or being prepared; substance specially prepared; work done by school pupils to prepare for lesson; (usu. in *pl.*) thing done to make ready.
**preparatory** /prə'pærətəri:/ 1 *a.* serving to prepare; introductory. 2 *adv.* as a preparation (with *to*). 3 **preparatory school** where pupils are prepared for higher school or (*US*) for college.
**prepare** /prə'peə(r)/ *v.* make or get ready; get oneself ready.
**prepay** /pri:'peɪ/ *v.* (*past* & *p.p.* **-paid**) pay (charge) beforehand; pay postage on beforehand. **prepayment** *n.*
**preponderate** /prə'pɒndəreɪt/ *v.i.* be superior in influence, quantity, or number; be heavier. **preponderance** *n.*; **preponderant** *a.*
**preposition** /prepə'zɪʃ(ə)n/ *n.* word governing (and normally preceding) noun or pronoun, expressing latter's relation to another word. **prepositional** *a.*
**prepossess** /pri:pə'zes/ *v.t.* take possession of; prejudice, usu. favourably. **prepossessing** *a.*; **prepossession** *n.*
**preposterous** /prə'pɒstərəs/ *a.* utterly absurd; perverse; contrary to reason.
**prepuce** /'pri:pju:s/ *n.* foreskin.

## Pre-Raphaelite / press

**Pre-Raphaelite** /priːˈræfəlaɪt/ *n.* member of group of 19th-c. Eng. artists.

**prerequisite** /priːˈrekwəzɪt/ 1 *a.* required as previous condition. 2 *n.* prerequisite thing.

**prerogative** /prɪˈrɒgətɪv/ *n.* right or privilege exclusive to individual or class.

**Pres.** *abbr.* President.

**presage** /ˈpresɪdʒ/ 1 *n.* omen; presentiment. 2 (also /prɪˈseɪdʒ/) *v.t.* portend; foretell, foresee.

**presbyter** /ˈprezbətə(r)/ *n.* priest of Episcopal Church; elder of Presbyterian Church.

**Presbyterian** /prezbəˈtɪərɪən/ 1 *a.* (of church) governed by elders all of equal rank, esp. national Church of Scotland. 2 *n.* member of Presbyterian church. 3 **Presbyterianism** *n.*

**presbytery** /ˈprezbətəri/ *n.* body of presbyters, esp. court next above kirk-session; eastern part of chancel; RC priest's house.

**prescient** /ˈpresɪənt/ *a.* having foreknowledge or foresight. **prescience** *n.*

**prescribe** /prɪˈskraɪb/ *v.t.* lay down authoritatively; advise use of (medicine etc.).

**prescript** /ˈpriːskrɪpt/ *n.* ordinance, command.

**prescription** /prɪˈskrɪpʃ(ə)n/ *n.* prescribing; physician's (usu. written) direction for composition and use of medicine, medicine thus prescribed.

**prescriptive** /prɪˈskrɪptɪv/ *a.* prescribing; laying down rules; based on prescription; prescribed by custom.

**presence** /ˈprez(ə)ns/ *n.* being present; place where person is; personal appearance; person or thing that is present.

**present**[1] /ˈprez(ə)nt/ 1 *a.* being in place in question; now existing or occurring or being dealt with etc.; *Gram.* denoting present action etc. 2 *n.* the present time; present tense. 3 **at present** now; **for the present** for this time, just now.

**present**[2] /ˈprez(ə)nt/ *n.* gift.

**present**[3] /prɪˈzent/ *v.t.* introduce; exhibit; hold out; offer, deliver, give. **present arms** hold rifle etc. in saluting position; **present person with** present to him, cause him to have.

**presentable** /prɪˈzentəb(ə)l/ *a.* of decent appearance; fit to be shown. **presentability** *n.*

**presentation** /prezənˈteɪʃ(ə)n/ *n.* presenting or being presented; thing presented.

**presentiment** /prɪˈzentəmənt/ *n.* vague expectation, foreboding.

**presently** /ˈprezntli/ *adv.* before long; *US & Sc.* at present.

**preservative** /prɪˈzɜːvətɪv/ 1 *n.* substance for preserving food etc. 2 *a.* tending to preserve.

**preserve** /prɪˈzɜːv/ 1 *v.t.* keep safe; keep alive; maintain, retain; keep from decay; treat (food etc.) to prevent decomposition or fermentation; keep (game etc.) undisturbed for private use. 2 *n.* preserved fruit, jam; place where game etc. is preserved; *fig.* sphere regarded by person as being for him alone. 3 **preservation** /prezəˈveɪʃ(ə)n/ *n.*

**pre-shrink** /ˈpriːʃrɪŋk/ *v.t.* treat (fabric, garment) so as to shrink during manufacture, not after.

**preside** /prɪˈzaɪd/ *v.i.* be chairman or president; exercise control or authority.

**presidency** /ˈprezədənsi/ *n.* office of president; period of this.

**president** /ˈprezəd(ə)nt/ *n.* elected head of republic; head of college or council or company etc.; person presiding over meetings and proceedings of society etc. **presidential** /-den-/ *a.*

**presidium** /prɪˈzɪdɪəm/ *n.* standing committee esp. in Communist organization.

**press**[1] 1 *v.* apply steady force to; squeeze; flatten, shape, take *out* (crease etc.), smooth (esp. clothes), etc. thus; exert pressure (on); be urgent, urge; crowd; hasten, urge one's way, *on* etc.; force (offer etc.) *on.* 2 *n.* pressing; device for compressing, flattening, extracting juice, etc.; machine for printing; *the* newspapers; printing-house; publishing company; crowding, crowd; pressure of affairs etc.; large usu. shelved cupboard for clothes, books, etc. 3 **press agent** person employed to attend to advertising and press publicity; **press conference** meeting with journalists; **press cutting** article, review, etc. cut from newspaper etc.; **press-gallery** gallery for reporters, esp. in legislative assembly; **press-stud** small device fastened by pressing to engage two parts; **press-up** (usu. in *pl.*) exercise in which prone body is raised by pressing down on hands to straighten arms.

**press**² /presː/ *v.t. hist.* force to serve in army or navy; bring into use as makeshift. **press-gang** body of men employed to press men for navy; (*v.t.*) force into service.

**pressing** /ˈpresɪŋ/ 1 *a.* urgent; insistent. 2 *n.* thing made by pressing, esp. gramophone record; series of records made at one time.

**pressure** /ˈpreʃə(r)/ 1 *n.* exertion of continuous force, force so exerted, amount of this; urgency; constraining or compelling influence. 2 *v.t.* apply pressure to, coerce, persuade. 3 **pressure-cooker** apparatus for cooking under high pressure in short time; **pressure group** group seeking to influence policy by concerted action.

**pressurize** /ˈpreʃəraɪz/ *v.t.* raise to high pressure; (esp. in *p.p.*) maintain normal atmospheric pressure in (aircraft cabin etc.) at high altitude.

**prestidigitator** /prestɪˈdɪdʒɪteɪtə(r)/ *n.* conjuror. **prestidigitation** *n.*

**prestige** /preˈstiːʒ/ 1 *n.* influence or reputation. 2 *a.* having or conferring prestige.

**prestigious** /preˈstɪdʒəs/ *a.* having or showing prestige.

**presto** /ˈprestəʊ/ *Mus.* 1 *adv.* in quick tempo. 2 *n.* (*pl.* **-tos**) movement etc. to be played thus.

**pre-stressed** /priːˈstrest/ *a.* (of concrete) strengthened by means of stretched wires etc. in it.

**presumably** /prɪˈzjuːməblɪ/ *adv.* it is or may reasonably be presumed.

**presume** /prɪˈzjuːm/ *v.* suppose to be true; take for granted; venture (*to*); be presumptuous. **presume upon** make unscrupulous use of.

**presumption** /prɪˈzʌmpʃ(ə)n/ *n.* arrogance, presumptuous behaviour; taking for granted; thing presumed to be true; ground for presuming.

**presumptive** /prɪˈzʌmptɪv/ *a.* giving ground for presumption.

**presumptuous** /prɪˈzʌmptjuːəs/ *a.* unduly confident, arrogant.

**presuppose** /priːsəˈpəʊz/ *v.t.* assume beforehand; imply. **presupposition** /-ˈzɪʃ-/ *n.*

**pre-tax** /priːˈtæks/ *a.* (of income) before deduction of taxes.

**pretence** /prɪˈtens/ *n.* pretending, make-believe; pretext; claim; ostentation.

**pretend** /prɪˈtend/ *v.* claim or assert falsely; imagine in play; in *p.p.* falsely claimed to be. **pretend to** profess to have.

**pretender** *n.* person who claims throne or title etc.

**pretension** /prɪˈtenʃ(ə)n/ *n.* assertion of claim; pretentiousness.

**pretentious** /prɪˈtenʃəs/ *a.* making claim to great merit or importance, ostentatious.

**preterite** /ˈpretərət/ *Gram.* 1 *a.* expressing past action or state. 2 *n.* past tense.

**preternatural** /priːtəˈnætʃər(ə)l/ *a.* outside ordinary course of nature, supernatural.

**pretext** /ˈpriːtekst/ *n.* ostensible reason; excuse.

**pretty** /ˈprɪtɪ/ 1 *a.* attractive in delicate way; fine, good. 2 *adv.* fairly, moderately. 3 **pretty-pretty** too pretty; **sitting pretty** *colloq.* comfortably placed. 4 **prettiness** *n.*

**pretzel** /ˈprets(ə)l/ *n.* crisp knot-shaped salted biscuit.

**prevail** /prɪˈveɪl/ *v.i.* be victorious (*against* etc.); be the more usual or prominent; exist or occur in general use. **prevail (up)on** persuade.

**prevalent** /ˈprevələnt/ *a.* generally existing or occurring. **prevalence** *n.*

**prevaricate** /prɪˈværɪkeɪt/ *v.i.* make evasive or misleading statements. **prevarication** *n.*; **prevaricator** *n.*

**prevent** /prɪˈvent/ *v.t.* hinder, stop. **prevention** *n.*

**preventative** /prɪˈventətɪv/ *a.* preventive.

**preventive** /prɪˈventɪv/ 1 *a.* serving to prevent, esp. *Med.* to keep off disease. 2 *n.* preventive agent, measure, drug, etc.

**preview** /ˈpriːvjuː/ 1 *n.* showing of film or play etc. before it is seen by general public. 2 *v.t.* view or show in advance of public presentation.

**previous** /ˈpriːvɪəs/ *a.* coming before in time or order; prior *to*; done or acting hastily. **previous to** before.

**pre-war** /priːˈwɔː(r)/ a. occurring or existing before a war.

**prey** /preɪ/ 1 n. animal hunted or killed by other animal for food; victim. 2 v.i. **prey (up)on** seek or take as prey, exert harmful influence on.

**price** 1 n. money for which thing is bought or sold; what must be given, done, etc. to obtain thing; odds. 2 v.t. fix or find price of; estimate value of. 3 **at a price** at high cost.

**priceless** /ˈpraɪsləs/ a. invaluable; sl. very amusing or absurd.

**pricey** /ˈpraɪsi/ a. colloq. expensive.

**prick** 1 v. pierce slightly, make small hole in; mark with pricks or dots; trouble mentally; feel pricking sensation. 2 n. pricking, mark of it; vulg. penis. 3 **prick out** plant (seedlings etc.) in small holes pricked in earth; **prick up one's ears** (of dog) erect the ears when on the alert, (of person) become suddenly attentive.

**prickle** /ˈprɪk(ə)l/ 1 n. small thorn; hard-pointed spine; prickling sensation. 2 v.i. feel sensation as of prick(s).

**prickly** /ˈprɪkli/ a. having prickles; irritable; tingling. **prickly heat** inflammation of skin near sweat glands with prickly sensations; **prickly pear** cactus with pear-shaped edible fruit, its fruit.

**pride** 1 n. feeling of elation and pleasure at one's achievements or possessions etc.; unduly high opinion of oneself; proper sense of one's own worth or position etc.; group (of lions etc.) 2 v.refl. **pride oneself (up)on** be proud of. 3 **take a pride in** be proud of.

**prie-dieu** /priːˈdjɜː/ n. kneeling-desk for prayer.

**priest** /priːst/ n. minister of religious worship; clergyman, esp. above deacon and below bishop.

**priestess** /ˈpriːstes/ n. female priest of non-Christian religion.

**priesthood** /ˈpriːsthʊd/ n. office or position of priest; *the* priests in general.

**priestly** /ˈpriːstli/ a. of or like or befitting priest.

**prig** n. self-righteously correct or moralistic person. **priggish** a.

**prim** a. consciously precise, formal; prudish.

**prima** /ˈpriːmə/ a. **prima ballerina** chief female performer in ballet; **prima donna** chief female singer in opera, temperamental person.

**primacy** /ˈpraɪməsi/ n. pre-eminence; office of primate.

**prima facie** /praɪmə ˈfeɪʃɪ/ at first sight, (of evidence) based on first impression.

**primal** /ˈpraɪm(ə)l/ a. primitive, primeval; fundamental.

**primary** /ˈpraɪməri/ 1 a. original; holding or sharing first place in time or importance or development. 2 n. thing that is primary; primary feather; US primary election. 3 **primary battery** one producing electricity by irreversible chemical action; **primary colour** one not obtained by mixing others; **primary education** first stage of education; **primary election** US election to select candidate(s) for principal election; **primary feather** large flight-feather of bird's wing; **primary school** school where primary education is given. 4 **primarily** adv.

**primate** /ˈpraɪmət/ n. archbishop; member of highest order of mammals including man and apes etc.

**prime**[1] a. chief, most important; of highest quality; primary, fundamental. 2 n. state of highest perfection; best part; prime number. 3 **prime minister** chief minister of government; **prime number** number divisible only by itself and unity; **prime time** time at which television etc. audience is largest.

**prime**[2] v.t. prepare (explosive) for detonation; pour liquid into (pump) to start it working; cover (wood etc.) with first coat of paint or with oil etc. to prevent paint from being absorbed; equip (person *with* information).

**primer**[1] /ˈpraɪmə(r)/ n. substance used to prime wood etc.

**primer**[2] /ˈpraɪmə(r)/ n. elementary school-book; small introductory book.

**primeval** /praɪˈmiːv(ə)l/ a. of first age of world; primitive, ancient.

**primitive** /ˈprɪmətɪv/ 1 a. ancient; at early stage of civilization; crude, simple. 2 n. untutored painter with naïve style; picture by such painter.

**primogeniture** /praɪməʊˈdʒenətʃə(r)/

**primordial**     430     **private**

*n.* principle by which property descends to eldest son.

**primordial** /praɪˈmɔːdɪəl/ *a.* existing at or from beginning, primeval.

**primrose** /ˈprɪmrəʊz/ *n.* plant bearing pale-yellow spring flower; this flower; pale yellow. **the primrose path** unjustified pursuit of pleasure.

**primula** /ˈprɪmjələ/ *n.* herbaceous perennial with flowers of various colours.

**Primus** /ˈpraɪməs/ *n.* (**P**) brand of portable stove burning vaporized oil.

**prince** /prɪns/ *n.* male member of royal family other than king; ruler esp. of small State; nobleman of some countries; *fig.* the greatest (*of*). **prince consort** husband of reigning queen who is himself a prince.

**princely** /ˈprɪnsli/ *a.* of or worthy of a prince, sumptuous, splendid.

**princess** /ˈprɪnses/ *n.* prince's wife; female member of royal family other than queen.

**principal** /ˈprɪnsəp(ə)l/ 1 *a.* first in importance; chief, leading. 2 *n.* head of some institutions; principal actor or singer etc.; capital sum lent or invested; person for whom another acts as agent etc. 3 **principal boy** actress playing leading male part in pantomime.

**principality** /prɪnsəˈpælətɪ/ *n.* government of or State ruled by a prince. **the Principality** Wales.

**principally** /ˈprɪnsəpəlɪ/ *adv.* for the most part, chiefly.

**principle** /ˈprɪnsəp(ə)l/ *n.* fundamental truth or law as basis of reasoning or action; personal code of conduct; fundamental source or element. **in principle** as regards fundamentals but not necessarily in detail; **on principle** from settled moral motive.

**principled** *a.* based on or having (esp. praiseworthy) principles of behaviour.

**prink** *v.* smarten, dress *up*.

**print** 1 *n.* mark left on surface by pressure; impression left on paper by inked type or photography; reading-matter produced from type etc.; engraving, newspaper, photograph; printed fabric. 2 *v.t.* produce by means of printing-types etc.; express or publish in print; stamp or impress; write (letters etc.) without joining in imitation of printing; produce (photograph) from negative. 3 **in print** in printed form, (of book etc.) available from publisher; **out of print** (of book etc.) no longer available from publisher; **printed circuit** *Electr.* one with thin conducting strips printed on flat sheet; **printing-press** machine for printing from types etc.; **printout** computer output in printed form.

**printer** *n.* person who prints books; owner of printing-business; device that prints esp. computer output.

**prior** /ˈpraɪə(r)/ 1 *a.* earlier; coming before in time, order, or importance, (*to*). 2 *n.* superior of religious house; (in abbey) deputy of abbot. 3 *adv.* **prior to** before. 4 **prioress** *n.*

**priority** /praɪˈɒrətɪ/ *n.* being earlier; precedence in rank etc.; interest having prior claim to attention.

**priory** /ˈpraɪərɪ/ *n.* religious house governed by prior or prioress.

**prise** /praɪz/ *v.t.* force open or out by leverage.

**prism** /ˈprɪz(ə)m/ *n.* solid figure whose two ends are equal parallel rectilineal figures, and whose sides are parallelograms; transparent body of this form with refracting surfaces.

**prismatic** /prɪzˈmætɪk/ *a.* of or like prism; (of colours) formed, distributed, etc. (as if) by transparent prism.

**prison** /ˈprɪz(ə)n/ *n.* place of captivity or confinement, esp. building to which persons are consigned while awaiting trial or for punishment.

**prisoner** /ˈprɪzənə(r)/ *n.* person kept in prison; *fig.* person or thing confined by illness, another's grasp, etc. **prisoner of war** one who has been captured in war.

**prissy** /ˈprɪsɪ/ *a.* prim, prudish.

**pristine** /ˈprɪstiːn/ *a.* in original condition; unspoilt.

**privacy** /ˈprɪvəsɪ/ *n.* being private, freedom from publicity or observation.

**private** /ˈpraɪvət/ 1 *a.* belonging to an individual, personal; secret, confidential; not public or official; secluded; not provided or supported or managed by State. 2 *n.* private soldier. 3 **in private** privately; **private detective** person who undertakes special enquiries for pay; **private enterprise** business(es) not under State control; **private eye** *colloq.* private detective; **private member** MP not holding Government appointment; **private parts** genitals;

**private soldier** ordinary soldier, not officer.

**privateer** /praɪvə'tɪə(r)/ *n.* privately owned and commissioned warship.

**privation** /praɪ'veɪʃ(ə)n/ *n.* lack of necessaries or comforts; hardship.

**privatize** /'praɪvətaɪz/ *v.t.* transfer from State to private ownership.

**privet** /'prɪvɪt/ *n.* bushy evergreen shrub used for hedges.

**privilege** /'prɪvəlɪdʒ/ **1** *n.* right or advantage or immunity belonging to person or class or office; special advantage or benefit. **2** *v.t.* invest with privilege.

**privy** /'prɪvɪ/ **1** *a.* hidden, secluded, secret. **2** *n. arch.* lavatory. **3 Privy Council** body of advisers chosen by sovereign; **Privy Counsellor** member of this; **privy purse** allowance from public revenue for monarch's private expenses; **privy seal** State seal formerly affixed to documents of minor importance (**Lord Privy Seal** senior UK cabinet minister without official duties); **privy to** in the secret of.

**prize**[1] **1** *n.* reward in lottery, competition, etc.; reward given as symbol of victory or superiority; thing (to be) striven for. **2** *a.* to which prize is awarded; excellent of its kind. **3** *v.t.* value highly. **4 prize-fight** boxing-match for money.

**prize**[2] *n.* ship or property captured in naval warfare.

**prize**[3] var. of **prise**.

**pro**[1] *n.* (*pl.* **pros**) *colloq.* professional.

**pro**[2] **1** *a.* & *prep.* in favour (of). **2** *n.* reason in favour (esp. in **pros and cons**).

**PRO** *abbr.* public relations officer.

**probability** /prɒbə'bɪlətɪ/ *n.* being probable; likelihood; (most) probable event; extent to which thing is likely to occur, measured by ratio of favourable cases to all cases possible. **in all probability** most probably.

**probable** /'prɒbəb(ə)l/ **1** *a.* that may be expected to happen or prove true or correct; likely. **2** *n.* probable candidate or member of team etc.

**probate** /'prəʊbeɪt/ *n.* official proving of will.

**probation** /prə'beɪʃ(ə)n/ *n.* testing of person's conduct or character; system of suspending sentence on selected offenders subject to good behaviour under supervision of **probation officer**. **probationary** *a.*

**probationer** /prə'beɪʃənə(r)/ *n.* person on probation.

**probe 1** *n.* blunt-ended surgical instrument for exploring wound etc.; unmanned exploratory spacecraft; probing, investigation. **2** *v.t.* explore with probe; *fig.* examine closely.

**probity** /'prəʊbətɪ/ *n.* uprightness, honesty.

**problem** /'prɒbləm/ *n.* doubtful or difficult question; thing hard to understand or deal with.

**problematic** /prɒblə'mætɪk/ *a.* (also **problematical**) attended by difficulty; doubtful, questionable.

**proboscis** /prə'bɒsɪs/ *n.* elephant's trunk; long flexible snout; elongated part of mouth of some insects.

**procedure** /prə'siːdjə(r)/ *n.* mode of conducting business; series of actions. **procedural** *a.*

**proceed** /prə'siːd/ *v.i.* go forward or on further; make one's way; continue or resume; adopt course of action; take legal proceedings; issue, originate.

**proceeding** /prə'siːdɪŋ/ *n.* action, piece of conduct; in *pl.* legal action, published report of discussions or conference.

**proceeds** /'prəʊsiːdz/ *n.pl.* money produced by sale or performance, etc.

**process**[1] /'prəʊses/ *n.* course of action or proceeding, esp. series of stages in manufacture etc.; progress or course; natural or involuntary operation or series of changes; action at law; summons or writ; *Biol.* natural appendage or outgrowth of organism. **2** *v.t.* subject to manufacturing or legal process.

**process**[2] /prə'ses/ *v.i. colloq.* go in procession.

**procession** /prə'seʃ(ə)n/ *n.* array of persons etc. going along in orderly succession esp. as ceremony or on festive occasion.

**processional** /prə'seʃən(ə)l/ **1** *a.* of processions; used or carried or sung etc. in processions. **2** *n.* processional hymn.

**processor** /'prəʊsesə(r)/ *n.* machine that processes things; part of computer that controls activities of other units and performs actions specified in program.

**proclaim** /prə'kleɪm/ *v.t.* announce

**proclivity** /prəˈklɪvəti:/ n. natural tendency.

**procrastinate** /prəˈkræstəneɪt/ v.i. defer action, be dilatory. **procrastination** n.

**procreate** /ˈprəʊkri:eɪt/ v. bring (offspring) into existence by natural process of reproduction; beget offspring. **procreation** n.; **procreative** a.

**procuration** /ˌprɒkjəˈreɪʃ(ə)n/ n. procuring, action as another's agent.

**procurator** /ˈprɒkjərəeɪtə(r)/ n. agent or proxy esp. with power of attorney.

**procure** /prəˈkjʊə(r)/ v. succeed in getting; bring about or cause by others' agency; act as procurer. **procurement** n.

**procurer** n. person who obtains women for prostitution. **procuress** n.

**prod** 1 v.t. poke with finger or end of stick etc.; stimulate to action. 2 n. poke, thrust; stimulus to action.

**prodigal** /ˈprɒdəɡ(ə)l/ 1 a. wasteful; lavish (of). 2 n. spendthrift. 3 **prodigality** /-ˈɡæl/ n.

**prodigious** /prəˈdɪdʒəs/ a. marvellous; enormous; abnormal.

**prodigy** /ˈprɒdədʒi:/ n. person with exceptional qualities, esp. precocious child; marvellous thing.

**produce** 1 /prəˈdju:s/ v.t. bring forward for inspection etc.; make or manufacture; bear or yield; bring into existence; cause or bring about; bring (play etc.) before public. 2 /ˈprɒdju:s/ n. what is produced, esp. agricultural or natural products; amount produced.

**producer** n. person who produces articles or produce; person who directs performance of play or programme etc.; person in charge of financing and scheduling of film production.

**product** /ˈprɒdʌkt/ n. thing produced by natural process or manufacture; *Math.* quantity obtained by multiplying.

**production** /prəˈdʌkʃ(ə)n/ n. producing or being produced; thing(s) produced; literary or artistic work.

**productive** /prəˈdʌktɪv/ a. producing esp. abundantly.

**productivity** /ˌprɒdʌkˈtɪvəti:/ n. capacity to produce; effectiveness of productive effort esp. in industry.

**proem** /ˈprəʊəm/ n. introductory discourse.

**Prof.** *abbr.* Professor.

**profane** /prəˈfeɪn/ 1 a. not sacred; irreverent, blasphemous. 2 v.t. treat with irreverence; pollute, violate. 3 **profanation** /ˌprɒf-/ n.

**profanity** /prəˈfænəti:/ n. blasphemy.

**profess** /prəˈfes/ v. claim openly to have; pretend; declare; affirm one's faith in or allegiance to.

**professed** a. self-acknowledged; alleged, ostensible. **professedly** /-ˈsɪdlɪ/ adv.

**profession** /prəˈfeʃ(ə)n/ n. occupation, esp. in branch of advanced learning or science; persons engaged in such branch; declaration, avowal.

**professional** /prəˈfeʃənl/ 1 a. of or belonging to or connected with or appropriate to a profession; engaged in specified activity as paid occupation. 2 n. professional person.

**professionalism** /prəˈfeʃənəlɪz(ə)m/ n. qualities or typical features of professionals.

**professor** /prəˈfesə(r)/ n. holder of university chair, *US* university teacher; person who makes profession (of religion etc.). **professorial** /ˌprɒfəˈsɔ:rɪəl/ a.; **professorship** n.

**professoriate** /ˌprɒfəˈsɔ:rɪət/ n. the professors of a university etc.

**proffer** /ˈprɒfə(r)/ v.t. offer.

**proficient** /prəˈfɪʃ(ə)nt/ a. expert, adept. **proficiency** n.

**profile** /ˈprəʊfaɪl/ n. side view or outline, esp. of human face; short biographical sketch.

**profit** /ˈprɒfɪt/ 1 n. advantage, benefit; pecuniary gain, excess of returns over outlay. 2 v. be of advantage (to); obtain advantage.

**profitable** /ˈprɒfɪtəb(ə)l/ a. beneficial, yielding profit, lucrative.

**profiteer** /ˌprɒfɪˈtɪə(r)/ 1 v.i. make or seek excessive profits out of others' needs esp. in times of scarcity. 2 n. person who profiteers.

**profiterole** /prəˈfɪtərəʊl/ n. small hollow cake of choux pastry with filling.

**profligate** /ˈprɒflɪɡət/ 1 a. licentious, dissolute; recklessly extravagant. 2 n. profligate person. 3 **profligacy** n.

## pro forma

**pro forma** /prəʊ 'fɔːmə/ for form's sake; (in full **pro forma invoice**) invoice sent to purchaser in advance of goods for completion of business formalities.

**profound** /prə'faʊnd/ a. having or showing great knowledge or insight; requiring much study or thought; deep; intense. **profundity** n.

**profuse** /prə'fjuːs/ a. lavish, extravagant, copious, excessive. **profusion** n.

**progenitor** /prə'dʒenətə(r)/ n. ancestor; predecessor, original.

**progeny** /'prɒdʒəni/ n. offspring; fig. issue, outcome.

**progesterone** /prə'dʒestərəʊn/ n. a sex hormone that maintains pregnancy.

**prognosis** /prɒg'nəʊsəs/ n. (pl. **-ses** /-siːz/) forecast of course of disease.

**prognostic** /prɒg'nɒstɪk/ 1 n. advance indication or omen; prediction. 2 a. foretelling, predictive (of).

**prognosticate** /prɒg'nɒstɪkeɪt/ v.t. foretell; betoken. **prognostication** n.

**programme** /'prəʊgræm/ (US & Computers **program**) 1 n. plan of intended proceedings; descriptive notice, list, of series of events etc.; such series of events; broadcast performance or entertainment; series of instructions to control operation of computer etc. 2 v.t. make programme of; express (problem) or instruct (computer) by means of program. 3 **programmatic** a.

**progress** 1 /'prəʊgres/ n. forward movement; advance; development; arch. state journey, esp. by royal person. 2 /prə'gres/ v.i. move forward or onward; advance, develop. 3 **in progress** in course of occurrence, going on.

**progression** /prə'greʃ(ə)n/ n. progressing; succession, series.

**progressive** /prə'gresɪv/ 1 a. moving forward; proceeding step by step; successive; favouring progress or reform; advanced in social conditions etc.; (of disease etc.) continuously increasing; (of taxation) at rates increasing with the sum taxed. 2 n. advocate of progressive policy.

**prohibit** /prə'hɪbət/ v.t. forbid, prevent.

**prohibition** /prəʊə'bɪʃ(ə)n/ n. forbidding or being forbidden; edict or order that forbids; forbidding by law of manufacture and sale of intoxicants.

**prohibitive** /prə'hɪbətɪv/ a. prohibiting; (of price) so high as to preclude purchase.

**project** 1 /'prɒdʒekt/ n. plan, scheme; planned undertaking, esp. piece of individual research by student(s). 2 /prə'dʒekt or prəʊ-/ v. make plans for; cause (light, image) to fall on surface; send or throw outward or forward; protrude, jut out.

**projectile** /prə'dʒektaɪl/ 1 n. object to be hurled. 2 a. of or serving as a projectile.

**projection** /prə'dʒekʃ(ə)n/ n. projecting or being projected; part that protrudes; representation of earth etc. on plane surface; mental image viewed as objective reality.

**projectionist** /prə'dʒekʃənəst/ n. person who operates projector.

**projector** /prə'dʒektə(r)/ n. apparatus for projecting image or film etc. on screen.

**prolapse** 1 /'prəʊlæps/ n. slipping downward or forward of part or organ, esp. of womb or rectum. 2 /prə'læps/ v.i. undergo prolapse.

**prolate** /'prəʊleɪt/ a. (of spheroid) lengthened along polar diameter.

**prolegomena** /prəʊlə'gɒmənə/ n.pl. preliminary matter prefixed to book etc.

**proletarian** /prəʊlə'teərɪən/ 1 a. of proletariat. 2 n. member of proletariat.

**proletariat** /prəʊlə'teərɪət/ n. class of industrial workers.

**proliferate** /prə'lɪfəreɪt/ v. reproduce itself or grow by multiplication of elementary parts; increase rapidly, multiply. **proliferation** n.

**prolific** /prə'lɪfɪk/ a. producing much offspring or output; abundantly productive.

**prolix** /'prəʊlɪks/ a. lengthy; long-winded; tedious. **prolixity** n.

**prologue** /'prəʊlɒg/ n. introduction to poem or play etc.; act or event serving as introduction (to).

**prolong** /prə'lɒŋ/ v.t. make longer; cause to continue. **prolongation** /prəʊlɒŋ'geɪʃ(ə)n/ n.

**prom** n. colloq. promenade; promenade concert.

**promenade** /prɒmə'nɑːd/ 1 n. place for

## prominent

walking, esp. paved area at seaside; leisure walk. **2** *v.* make promenade (on, through, etc.); lead about, esp. for display. **3 promenade concert** one at which (part of) audience is not provided with seats; **promenade deck** upper deck on liner.

**prominent** /ˈprɒmən(ə)nt/ *a.* jutting out, conspicuous; distinguished; well-known. **prominence** *n.*

**promiscuous** /prəˈmɪskjuːəs/ *a.* having casual sexual relations with many people; indiscriminate; of mixed and disorderly composition. **promiscuity** /ˌprɒmɪsˈkjuːətɪ/

**promise** /ˈprɒmɪs/ **1** *n.* explicit undertaking to do or not to do something; thing promised; favourable indications. **2** *v.* make promise (to) *to* give, do, etc.; seem likely (*to*), hold out good etc. prospect.

**promising** /ˈprɒmɪsɪŋ/ *a.* likely to turn out well; hopeful; full of promise.

**promissory** /ˈprɒmɪsərɪ/ *a.* conveying or implying promise. **promissory note** signed document containing promise to pay stated sum.

**promontory** /ˈprɒməntərɪ/ *n.* point of high land jutting out into sea etc.; headland.

**promote** /prəˈməʊt/ *v.t.* advance (person) to higher office or position; help forward or initiate process or formation of; publicize and sell. **promotion** *n.*; **promotional** *a.*

**promoter** *n.* person who promotes an enterprise financially, esp. formation of joint-stock company or holding of sporting event or theatrical production etc.

**prompt 1** *a.* acting or done at once or without delay; punctual. **2** *adv.* punctually. **3** *v.t.* incite, move, inspire; help out (actor, speaker) by supplying words that come next. **4** *n.* thing said to help memory jog of actor. **5 prompt side** side of stage to actor's left.

**prompter** /ˈprɒmptə(r)/ *n. Theatr.* person unseen by audience who prompts actors.

**promptitude** /ˈprɒmptɪtjuːd/ *n.* promptness.

**promulgate** /ˈprɒməlgeɪt/ *v.t.* make known to the public; proclaim. **promulgation** *n.*

## propeller

**prone** *a.* lying face downwards; lying flat, prostrate; inclined, disposed (*to*).

**prong** *n.* spike of fork.

**pronominal** /prəˈnɒmɪn(ə)l/ *a.* of or of the nature of a pronoun.

**pronoun** /ˈprəʊnaʊn/ *n.* word serving as grammatical substitute for noun.

**pronounce** /prəˈnaʊns/ *v.* utter or speak, esp. with reference to correct manner; utter formally; give (as) one's opinion; pass judgement. **pronounceable** *a.*

**pronounced** *a.* strongly marked.

**pronouncement** *n.* formal statement, declaration.

**pronto** /ˈprɒntəʊ/ *adv. sl.* promptly, quickly.

**pronunciation** /prənʌnsɪˈeɪʃ(ə)n/ *n.* way in which word is pronounced; person's way of pronouncing words.

**proof** /pruːf/ **1** *n.* fact or evidence or reasoning that proves truth or existence of something; test or trial; trial impression of printed matter for correction; standard of strength of distilled alcoholic liquors. **2** *a.* impervious to penetration or damage or undesired action. **3** *v.t.* make proof, esp. against water or bullets. **4 proof-read** read and correct (printed proof); **proof-reader** person who does this; **proof spirit** mixture of alcohol and water used in computing alcoholic strength.

**prop¹ 1** *n.* thing used to support something or keep it upright; supporter of cause etc; *Aus.* sudden stop by horse going at speed. **2** *v.* support (as) by prop, hold *up* thus; *Aus.* (of horse) make prop.

**prop²** *n. colloq.* aircraft propeller.

**prop³** *n. Theatr.* stage property.

**propaganda** /ˌprɒpəˈgændə/ *n.* organized scheme for propagation of a doctrine etc.; ideas etc. so propagated; *colloq.* biased information.

**propagate** /ˈprɒpəgeɪt/ *v.* breed or reproduce from parent stock; (of plant etc.) reproduce (*itself*); disseminate. **propagation** *n.*

**propane** /ˈprəʊpeɪn/ *n.* a hydrocarbon of the paraffin series.

**propel** /prəˈpel/ *v.t.* drive or push forward; give onward motion to.

**propellant** /prəˈpelənt/ *n.* propelling agent.

**propeller** /prəˈpelə(r)/ *n.* revolving de-

**propensity** /prəˈpensəti/ n. inclination, tendency.

**proper** /ˈprɒpə(r)/ a. suitable, appropriate; accurate, correct; respectable, decent; strictly so called, genuine; belonging or relating exclusively or distinctively (to); colloq. thorough. **proper name** name of person or place etc.

**property** /ˈprɒpəti/ n. thing owned; landed estate; owning; being owned; attribute or quality; Theatr. movable article used on stage during performance of play.

**prophecy** /ˈprɒfəsi/ n. prophesying; prophetic utterance; prediction.

**prophesy** /ˈprɒfəsaɪ/ v. speak as prophet; predict.

**prophet** /ˈprɒfɪt/ n. inspired teacher; revealer or interpreter of divine will; person who predicts. **prophetess** n.

**prophetic** /prəˈfetɪk/ a. of prophet; predicting or containing a prediction of.

**prophylactic** /prɒfɪˈlæktɪk/ 1 a. tending to prevent disease or other misfortune. 2 n. prophylactic medicine or course of action.

**prophylaxis** /prɒfɪˈlæksəs/ n. (pl. -xes /-ksiːz/) preventive treatment against disease etc.

**propinquity** /prəˈpɪŋkwəti/ n. nearness; close kinship.

**propitiate** /prəˈpɪʃieɪt/ v.t. appease. **propitiation** n.; **propitiatory** a.

**propitious** /prəˈpɪʃəs/ a. well-disposed, favourable (to); suitable for.

**proponent** /prəˈpəʊnənt/ n. person who puts forward proposal.

**proportion** /prəˈpɔːʃ(ə)n/ 1 n. comparative part; share; comparative relation, ratio; correct relation between things or parts of thing; in pl. dimensions. 2 v.t. make proportionate.

**proportional** /prəˈpɔːʃən(ə)l/ a. in correct proportion; corresponding in degree or amount. **proportional representation** representation of parties etc. in parliament in proportion to votes they receive.

**proportionate** /prəˈpɔːʃənət/ a. in due proportion (to).

**proposal** /prəˈpəʊz(ə)l/ n. proposing; scheme etc. proposed; offer of marriage.

**propose** /prəˈpəʊz/ v. put forward for consideration; intend; set up as an aim; offer marriage (to); offer as subject for drinking of toast; nominate as member of society etc.

**proposition** /prɒpəˈzɪʃ(ə)n/ 1 n. proposal; scheme proposed; statement, assertion; Math. formal statement of theorem or problem; colloq. task, problem, opponent. 2 v.t. colloq. put (esp. indecent) proposition to.

**propound** /prəˈpaʊnd/ v.t. offer for consideration or solution.

**proprietary** /prəˈpraɪətəri/ a. of proprietor; holding property; held in private ownership; manufactured and sold by one particular firm. **proprietary company** Aus. company whose membership and transfer of shares are limited by law.

**proprietor** /prəˈpraɪətə(r)/ n. owner. **proprietorial** /-ˈtɔːr-/ a.; **proprietress** n.

**propriety** /prəˈpraɪəti/ n. fitness, rightness; correctness of behaviour or morals; in pl. the conventions of polite behaviour.

**propulsion** /prəˈpʌlʃ(ə)n/ n. driving or pushing forward. **propulsive** a.

**pro rata** /prəʊ ˈrɑːtə/ proportional; in proportion.

**prorogue** /prəˈrəʊg/ v. discontinue meetings of (parliament) without dissolving it; be prorogued. **prorogation** n.

**prosaic** /prəʊˈzeɪɪk/ a. like prose; unpoetic; commonplace. **prosaically** adv.

**proscenium** /prəˈsiːnɪəm/ n. (pl. -niums or -nia) part of theatre stage in front of curtain, esp. with enclosing arch.

**proscribe** /prəˈskraɪb/ v.t. denounce or forbid; outlaw; banish, exile. **proscription** n.; **proscriptive** a.

**prose** /prəʊz/ 1 n. ordinary non-metrical form of language; plain speech. 2 v.i. talk tediously.

**prosecute** /ˈprɒsɪkjuːt/ v.t. institute legal proceedings against; pursue or carry on.

**prosecution** /prɒsɪˈkjuːʃ(ə)n/ n. prosecuting; prosecuting party.

**prosecutor** /ˈprɒsɪkjuːtə(r)/ n. person who prosecutes esp. in criminal court.

**proselyte** /ˈprɒsɪlaɪt/ n. Gentile convert to Jewish faith; any convert.

# proselytism

**proselytism** /'prɒsəlɪtɪz(ə)m/ *n.* being a proselyte; practice of proselytizing.

**proselytize** /'prɒsəlɪtaɪz/ *v.t.* seek to make proselyte of.

**prosody** /'prɒsədi:/ *n.* science of versification. **prosodist** *n.*

**prospect** 1 /'prɒspekt/ *n.* what one is to expect; extensive view; mental scene; *colloq.* possible or likely customer etc. 2 /prə'spekt/ *v.* explore (*for* gold etc.). 3 **prospector** *n.*

**prospective** /prəs'pektɪv/ *a.* concerned with or applying to the future; expected, some day to be.

**prospectus** /prəs'pektəs/ *n.* pamphlet etc. containing description of chief features of school or business etc.

**prosper** /'prɒspə(r)/ *v.i.* succeed, thrive.

**prosperity** /prɒ'sperəti/ *n.* state of prospering.

**prosperous** /'prɒspərəs/ *a.* successful, thriving; auspicious.

**prostate gland** /'prɒsteɪt/ large gland round neck of bladder, accessory to male genital organs. **prostatic** /-'tæt-/ *a.*

**prostitute** /'prɒstɪtju:t/ 1 *n.* person who offers sexual intercourse for payment. 2 *v.t.* make prostitute of; sell or make use of unworthily. 3 **prostitution** *n.*

**prostrate** 1 /'prɒstreɪt/ *a.* lying with face to ground, esp. in submission or humility; lying horizontally; overthrown; exhausted. 2 /prɒs'treɪt/ *v.t.* throw or lay flat on ground; overcome; reduce to extreme physical weakness. 3 **prostration** *n.*

**prosy** /'prəʊzi:/ *a.* tedious, commonplace, dull.

**protagonist** /prə'tægənɪst/ *n.* chief person in drama or story etc.

**protean** /'prəʊti:ən/ *a.* variable, versatile.

**protect** /prə'tekt/ *v.t.* keep safe; shield; secure.

**protection** /prə'tekʃ(ə)n/ *n.* protecting, defence; person or thing that protects; system or policy of protecting home industries by tariffs etc. **protectionism** *n.*; **protectionist** *n.* & *a.*

**protective** /prə'tektɪv/ *a.* protecting; giving or intended for protection. **protective custody** detention of person for his own protection.

# protractor

**protector** /prə'tektə(r)/ *n.* person or thing that protects; regent in charge of kingdom during minority or absence of sovereign. **protectorship** *n.*; **protectress** *n.*

**protectorate** /prə'tektərət/ *n.* office of protector of kingdom or State; period of this; protectorship of weak or underdeveloped State by stronger one; such territory.

**protégé** /'prɒteʒeɪ/ *n.* (*fem.* **-gée** *pr.* same) person under protection or patronage of another.

**protein** /'prəʊti:n/ *n.* one of a class of nitrogenous compounds important in all living organisms.

**pro tem** /prəʊ 'tem/ *abbr.* for the time being (*pro tempore*).

**protest** 1 /prə'test/ *v.* express disapproval or dissent; *US* object to; declare solemnly. 2 /'prəʊtest/ *n.* expression of dissent or disapproval; remonstrance. 3 **protestor** *n.*

**Protestant** /'prɒtɪst(ə)nt/ 1 *n.* member or adherent of any of the Christian bodies that separated from the Roman communion in the Reformation, or their offshoots. 2 *a.* of Protestants. 3 **Protestantism** *n.*

**protestation** /prɒtəs'teɪʃ(ə)n/ *n.* solemn affirmation.

**protocol** /'prəʊtəkɒl/ *n.* official formality and etiquette; observance of this; draft of diplomatic document, esp. of agreed terms of treaty.

**proton** /'prəʊtɒn/ *n. Phys.* elementary particle with unit positive electric charge, forming part or (in hydrogen) whole of atomic nucleus.

**protoplasm** /'prəʊtəʊplæz(ə)m/ *n.* viscous translucent substance forming main constituent of cells in organisms. **protoplasmic** *a.*

**prototype** /'prəʊtəʊtaɪp/ *n.* original thing or person in relation to a copy, improved form, etc.; trial model, esp. of aeroplane etc.

**protozoon** /prəʊtə'zəʊən/ *n.* (*pl.* **-zoa**) one-celled microscopic animal. **protozoan** *a.* & *n.*

**protract** /prə'trækt/ *v.t.* prolong, lengthen; make last long(er). **protraction** *n.*

**protractor** /prə'træktə(r)/ *n.* instrument for measuring angles, usu. in form of graduated semicircle.

**protrude** /prə'truːd/ v. stick out; thrust out. **protrusion** n.; **protrusive** a.

**protuberant** /prə'tjuːbərənt/ a. bulging out; prominent. **protuberance** n.

**proud** /praʊd/ a. feeling or showing (proper) pride; haughty, arrogant; feeling greatly honoured; imposing, splendid; slightly projecting; (of flesh) overgrown round healing wound. **do proud** treat with great generosity or honour.

**prove** /pruːv/ v. (p.p. **proved** or esp. US, Sc., or literary **proven**) demonstrate to be true by evidence or argument; be found (to be); establish validity of (will); rise or cause (dough) to rise; arch. test.

**provenance** /'prɒvənəns/ n. origin; place of origin.

**provender** /'prɒvəndə(r)/ n. fodder; joc. food for humans.

**proverb** /'prɒvɜːb/ n. short pithy saying in general use; person or thing that is widely known.

**proverbial** /prə'vɜːbɪəl/ a. of or expressed in proverbs; notorious.

**provide** /prə'vaɪd/ v. cause to have possession or use of; supply, make available; make due preparation; stipulate. **provide for** supply necessities of life for; **provided** (or **providing**) **(that)** on condition or understanding that.

**providence** /'prɒvəd(ə)ns/ n. foresight, timely care; beneficent care of God or nature; **Providence** God.

**provident** /'prɒvəd(ə)nt/ a. having or showing foresight, thrifty.

**providential** /prɒvə'denʃ(ə)l/ a. of or by divine foresight or intervention; opportune, lucky.

**province** /'prɒvəns/ n. principal administrative division of country; in pl. the whole of country outside capital; sphere of action; concern.

**provincial** /prə'vɪnʃ(ə)l/ 1 a. of province(s); having restricted views or the interests or manners etc. attributed to inhabitants of the provinces. 2 n. inhabitant of province(s). 3 **provincialism** n.

**provision** /prə'vɪʒ(ə)n/ n. providing; preparation for future contingency; provided amount of; in pl. supply of food and drink; formally stated condition.

**provisional** /prə'vɪʒən(ə)l/ a. providing for immediate needs only, temporary.

**proviso** /prə'vaɪzəʊ/ n. (pl. -sos) stipulation; limiting clause. **provisory** a.

**provocation** /prɒvə'keɪʃ(ə)n/ n. incitement esp. to anger etc.; irritation; cause of annoyance.

**provocative** /prə'vɒkətɪv/ a. tending or intended to cause provocation (of anger, lust, etc.).

**provoke** /prə'vəʊk/ v.t. rouse, incite, (to); irritate; call forth, cause.

**prow** /praʊ/ n. part adjoining stem of boat or ship; pointed projecting front part.

**prowess** /'praʊəs/ n. skill, expertise; valour; gallantry.

**prowl** /praʊl/ 1 v. go about stealthily in search of prey or plunder; traverse (place) thus. 2 n. prowling.

**prox.** abbr. proximo.

**proximate** /'prɒksəmət/ a. nearest, next before or after.

**proximity** /prɒk'sɪmətɪ/ n. nearness; neighbourhood.

**proximo** /'prɒksɪməʊ/ a. of next month.

**proxy** /'prɒksɪ/ n. person authorized to act for another; agency of such a person; document authorizing person to vote on another's behalf; vote so given.

**prude** n. person of extreme propriety in conduct or speech, esp. as regards sexual matters. **prudery** n.; **prudish** a.

**prudent** /'pruːd(ə)nt/ a. showing care and foresight; discreet. **prudence** n.

**prudential** /prʊ'denʃ(ə)l/ a. of or involving or marked by prudence.

**prune**¹ v.t. trim (tree etc.) by cutting away dead or overgrown parts; remove (superfluities); reduce (costs etc.); clear (of) what is superfluous.

**prune**² n. dried plum.

**prurient** /'prʊərɪənt/ a. given to or arising from indulgence of lewd ideas. **prurience** n.

**Prussian** /'prʌʃ(ə)n/ 1 a. of Prussia. 2 n. native of Prussia. 3 **Prussian blue** deep blue pigment.

**prussic acid** /'prʌsɪk/ a highly poisonous liquid.

**pry** /praɪ/ v.i. look or inquire etc. (into) inquisitively.

**PS** abbr. postscript.

**psalm** /sɑːm/ n. sacred song, hymn; **(Book of) Psalms** book of these in OT.
**psalmist** /'sɑːməst/ n. author of psalms.
**psalmody** /'sɑːmədiː/ n. practice or art of singing psalms.
**psalter** /'sɔːltə(r)/ n. version or copy of Book of Psalms.
**psaltery** /'sɔːltəriː/ n. ancient and medieval plucked stringed instrument.
**psephology** /se'fɒlədʒiː/ n. study of trends in elections and voting. **psephologist** n.
**pseudo-** /'sjuːdəʊ/ in comb. false, apparent, supposed but not real.
**pseudonym** /'sjuːdənɪm/ n. fictitious name, esp. one assumed by author.
**pseudonymous** /sjuː'dɒnəməs/ a. written under fictitious name.
**psoriasis** /sɔː'raɪəsəs/ n. skin disease with red scaly patches.
**PSV** abbr. public service vehicle.
**psyche** /'saɪkiː/ n. soul, spirit, mind.
**psychedelic** /saɪkə'delɪk/ a. hallucinatory, expanding the mind's awareness; having vivid colours or sounds etc.
**psychiatry** /saɪ'kaɪətriː/ n. study and treatment of mental disease. **psychiatric(al)** /saɪkɪ'ætrək(ə)l/ a.; **psychiatrist** n.
**psychic** /'saɪkɪk/ 1 a. psychical; able to exercise psychical or occult powers. 2 n. person susceptible to psychical influence, medium.
**psychical** /'saɪkək(ə)l/ a. of the soul or mind; of phenomena and conditions apparently outside domain of physical law.
**psycho-** /'saɪkəʊ/ in comb. mind, soul.
**psycho-analysis** /saɪkəʊə'næləsəs/ n. therapeutic method for treating mental disorders by investigating interaction of conscious and unconscious elements in the mind. **psycho-analyse** v.t.; **psycho-analyst** n.; **psycho-analytical** /-'lɪt-/ a.
**psychological** /saɪkə'lɒdʒɪk(ə)l/ a. of the mind; of psychology. **psychological moment** the psychologically appropriate moment, colloq. the most appropriate time; **psychological warfare** achieving aims by acting on enemy's minds.
**psychology** /saɪ'kɒlədʒiː/ n. science of human mind; treatise on or system of this; colloq. mental characteristics. **psychologist** n.
**psychoneurosis** /saɪkəʊnjuː'rəʊsəs/ n. (pl. **-ses** /-siːz/) neurosis esp. with indirect expression of emotional feelings. **psychoneurotic** /-'rɒt-/ a.
**psychopath** /'saɪkəʊpæθ/ n. person suffering chronic mental disorder esp. with abnormal social behaviour; mentally or emotionally unstable person. **psychopathic** a.
**psychosis** /saɪ'kəʊsəs/ n. (pl. **-ses** /-siːz/) severe mental derangement involving whole personality.
**psychosomatic** /saɪkəʊsə'mætɪk/ a. of mind and body; (of disease) caused or aggravated by mental stress.
**psychosurgery** /saɪkəʊ'sɜːdʒəriː/ n. brain surgery as means of treating mental disorder.
**psychotherapy** /saɪkəʊ'θerəpiː/ n. treatment of mental disorder by psychological means. **psychotherapist** n.
**psychotic** /saɪ'kɒtɪk/ 1 a. of or suffering from psychosis. 2 n. psychotic person.
**PT** abbr. physical training.
**pt.** abbr. part; pint; point; port.
**PTA** abbr. parent–teacher association.
**ptarmigan** /'tɑːməgən/ n. bird of grouse family.
**Pte.** abbr. Private (soldier).
**pterodactyl** /terə'dæktəl/ n. extinct winged reptile.
**PTO** abbr. please turn over.
**ptomaine** /'təʊmeɪn/ n. one of a group of compounds (some toxic) in putrefying animal and vegetable matter.
**Pty** abbr. Aus. Proprietary.
**pub** n. colloq. public house.
**puberty** /'pjuːbətiː/ n. stage at which person becomes capable of procreating.
**pubes** /'pjuːbiːz/ n. lower part of abdomen.
**pubescence** /pjuː'bes(ə)ns/ n. arrival at puberty; soft down on plant or animal. **pubescent** a.
**pubic** /'pjuːbɪk/ a. of pubes or pubis.
**pubis** /'pjuːbəs/ n. (pl. **-bes** /-biːz/) bone forming front of each half of pelvis.
**public** /'pʌblɪk/ 1 a. of or concerning community as a whole; open to or shared by people in general; open to general observation, done etc. in public. 2 n. (members of) community as

a whole; section of community. **3 in public** publicly, openly; **public-address system** equipment of loud-speakers etc.; **public house** place licensed for and chiefly concerned with selling of alcoholic drink; **public lending right** right of authors to payment when their books are lent by public libraries; **public relations** relations between organization etc. and the public; **public school** endowed independent fee-paying school, *Sc. & US etc.* school managed by public authorities; **public-spirited** ready to do things for the benefit of people in general; **public transport** buses, trains, etc., available to public and having fixed routes; **public utility** organization supplying water or gas or electricity etc. **4 publicly** *adv.*

**publican** /'pʌblɪkən/ *n.* keeper of public house.

**publication** /ˌpʌblɪˈkeɪʃ(ə)n/ *n.* publishing; published book, periodical, etc.

**publicist** /'pʌblɪsɪst/ *n.* publicity agent; writer on public concerns.

**publicity** /pʌbˈlɪsəti/ *n.* public attention or the means of attracting it; business of advertising; being open to general observation.

**publicize** /'pʌblɪsaɪz/ *v.t.* bring to public notice, esp. by advertisement etc.

**publish** /'pʌblɪʃ/ *v.t.* prepare and issue copies of (book, magazine, etc.) for sale to public; make generally known; formally announce.

**publisher** *n.* person or firm that issues copies of book, magazine, etc.

**puce** /pjuːs/ *a. & n.* brownish-purple.

**puck**[1] *n.* rubber disc used in ice-hockey.

**puck**[2] *n.* mischievous sprite. **puckish** *a.*

**pucker** /'pʌkə(r)/ **1** *v.* contract or gather (*up*) into wrinkles or folds or bulges. **2** *n.* such bulge etc.

**pudding** /'pʊdɪŋ/ *n.* sweet food eaten as course of meal; food containing or enclosed in mixture of flour etc. and cooked by baking or boiling; kind of sausage.

**puddle** /'pʌd(ə)l/ *n.* small dirty pool; clay made into watertight coating.

**pudenda** /pjuːˈdendə/ *n.pl.* genitals, esp. of woman.

**puerile** /'pjʊəraɪl/ *a.* childish; trivial. **puerility** /-'rɪl-/ *n.*

**puerperal** /pjuːˈɜːpər(ə)l/ *a.* of or due to childbirth.

**puff 1** *n.* short quick blast of breath or wind; sound (as) of this; smoke or vapour sent out by it; pad for applying powder to skin; (piece of) light pastry; unduly laudatory review or advertisement etc. **2** *v.* emit puff or puffs; smoke in puffs; pant; blow *out* or *up*, inflate; advertise in exaggerated terms. **3 puff-adder** large venomous Afr. viper; **puff-ball** ball-shaped fungus; **puff pastry** light flaky pastry; **puff sleeve** short full sleeve gathered into band.

**puffin** /'pʌfɪn/ *n.* N. Atlantic auk with short striped bill.

**puffy** /'pʌfi/ *a.* puffed out, swollen; short-winded.

**pug** *n.* small snub-nosed breed of dog. **pug-nosed** having short snub or flat nose.

**pugilist** /'pjuːdʒɪlɪst/ *n.* boxer. **pugilism** *n.* **pugilistic** *a.*

**pugnacious** /pʌgˈneɪʃəs/ *a.* disposed to fight. **pugnacity** /-'næs-/ *n.*

**puisne** /'pjuːni/ *n.* judge of superior court who is inferior in rank to chief justice.

**puissant** /'pwiːs(ə)nt/ *a. literary* wielding great power; mighty. **puissance** *n.*

**puke** /pjuːk/ *v. & n.* vomit.

**pukka** /'pʌkə/ *a. colloq.* real, genuine.

**pulchritude** /'pʌlkrɪtjuːd/ *n.* beauty. **pulchritudinous** *a.*

**pull** /pʊl/ **1** *v.* exert force on (thing etc.) to move it to oneself; cause to move towards oneself or in direction so regarded; exert pulling force; damage (muscle etc.) by abnormal strain; proceed with effort; attract; make (grimace) by distorting muscles. **2** *n.* act of pulling; force thus exerted; means of exerting influence; advantage; deep draught of liquor; handle etc. for applying pull; printer's rough proof. **3 pull back** retreat; **pull down** demolish, lower in health etc.; **pull in** move towards near side, into parking-place, etc., **pull-in** place for doing this; **pull off** win, manage successfully; **pull oneself together** recover control of oneself; **pull out** move away, move towards off side; **pull one's punches** fail to give full force in boxing or argument etc.; **pull round, through,** recover from (illness); **pull strings** exert

**pullet** /ˈpʊlət/ n. young domestic fowl before first moult.

**pulley** /ˈpʊli/ n. grooved wheel for cord etc. to run over, mounted in block and used to lift weight etc.; wheel or drum mounted on shaft and turned by belt, used to increase speed or power.

**Pullman** /ˈpʊlmən/ n. railway carriage or motor coach with specially comfortable seats etc.; sleeping-car.

**pullover** /ˈpʊləʊvə(r)/ n. knitted garment put on over the head.

**pullulate** /ˈpʌljəleɪt/ v. grow or develop; abound *with*. **pullulation** n.

**pulmonary** /ˈpʊlmənəri/ a. of or in or connected with lungs; affected with or subject to lung-disease.

**pulp 1** n. fleshy part of fruit, animal body, etc.; soft shapeless mass, esp. of materials for paper-making. **2** v. reduce to pulp; become pulp. **3 pulpy** a.

**pulpit** /ˈpʊlpɪt/ n. raised enclosed platform for preaching from; *the* profession of preaching.

**pulsar** /ˈpʌlsɑː(r)/ n. cosmic source of regularly and rapidly pulsating radio signals.

**pulsate** /pʌlˈseɪt/ v.i. expand and contract rhythmically; throb, vibrate, quiver. **pulsation** n.

**pulse**[1] /pʌls/ **1** n. rhythmical throbbing of arteries; point where this can be felt externally; single vibration of sound or light or electric signal etc.; throb, thrill, of life or emotion. **2** v.i. pulsate.

**pulse**[2] /pʌls/ n. as *sing.* or *pl.* edible seeds of peas, beans, lentils, etc.

**pulverize** /ˈpʌlvəraɪz/ v. reduce or crumble to powder or dust; demolish, crush, smash. **pulverization** n.

**puma** /ˈpjuːmə/ n. large tawny Amer. feline.

**pumice** /ˈpʌməs/ n. (also **pumice-stone**) light porous lava used as abrasive; piece of this.

**pummel** /ˈpʌm(ə)l/ v.t. strike repeatedly, esp. with fists.

**pump**[1] **1** n. machine or device of various kinds for raising or moving liquids or gases. **2** v. work pump; remove or raise or compress or inflate etc. (as) by pumping; elicit information from (person) by persistent or artful questions. **3 pump-room** room at spa where medicinal water is dispensed; **pump up** inflate (pneumatic tyre etc.)

**pump**[2] n. plimsoll; light shoe for dancing etc.

**pumpernickel** /ˈpʌmpənɪkəl/ n. wholemeal rye bread.

**pumpkin** /ˈpʌmpkən/ n. large orange-coloured fruit used as vegetable; plant bearing it.

**pun 1** n. humorous use of word to suggest different meanings, or of different words of same sound, etc. **2** v.i. make pun(s).

**punch**[1] **1** v. strike with fist; make hole in (as) with punch; pierce (hole) thus. **2** n. blow with fist; *sl.* vigour, effective force; instrument or machine for cutting holes or impressing design in leather or metal or paper etc. **3 punch-ball** inflated or stuffed ball used for practice in punching; **punch-drunk** stupefied with repeated punches; **punch-line** words giving point of joke etc.; **punch-up** *sl.* fight with fists, brawl.

**punch**[2] n. mixture of spirit or wine with (hot) water and spices etc. **punch-bowl** bowl in which punch is mixed; round deep hollow in hill(s).

**punch**[3] n. short-legged thickset draught horse.

**Punch**[4] n. grotesque humpbacked figure in puppet-show called *Punch and Judy*.

**punchy** /ˈpʌntʃi/ a. having vigour, forceful.

**punctilio** /pʌŋkˈtɪliəʊ/ n. (pl. **-lios**) delicate point of ceremony or honour; petty formality.

**punctilious** /pʌŋkˈtɪliəs/ a. attentive to formality or etiquette; precise in behaviour.

**punctual** /ˈpʌŋktjʊəl/ a. observant of appointed time; not late. **punctuality** n.

**punctuate** /ˈpʌŋktjʊeɪt/ v.t. insert punctuation marks in; interrupt at intervals.

**punctuation** /pʌŋktjʊˈeɪʃ(ə)n/ n. punctuating. **punctuation mark** any of the marks used in writing to separate sentences and phrases etc.

**puncture** /ˈpʌŋktʃə(r)/ **1** n. prick or

**pundit** /'pʌndɪt/ n. learned Hindu; learned person, expert.

**pungent** /'pʌndʒ(ə)nt/ a. having strong sharp taste or smell; stinging, caustic, biting. **pungency** n.

**punish** /'pʌnɪʃ/ v.t. cause (offender) to suffer for offence; inflict penalty for (offence); tax severely the powers of; subject to severe treatment. **punishment** n.

**punitive** /'pju:nətɪv/ a. inflicting or intended to inflict punishment.

**punk** n. colloq. worthless person or thing; colloq. punk rock, fan of this. **punk rock** type of pop music using aggressive and outrageous effects.

**punkah** /'pʌŋkə/ n. large swinging fan on frame worked by cord or electrically.

**punnet** /'pʌnət/ n. small basket for fruit etc.

**punster** /'pʌnstə(r)/ n. maker of puns.

**punt**[1] 1 n. flat-bottomed boat propelled by long pole thrust against bottom of river etc. 2 v. propel with or use punt-pole; travel or convey in punt.

**punt**[2] 1 v. kick (football) dropped from hands before it reaches ground. 2 n. such kick.

**punt**[3] v.i. (in some card games) lay stake against bank; colloq. bet, speculate in shares, etc.

**puny** /'pju:nɪ/ a. undersized, feeble.

**pup** 1 n. puppy; young wolf, rat, seal, etc. 2 v.i. (of bitch) give birth to pups.

**pupa** /'pju:pə/ n. (pl. **-pae** /-pi:/) insect in passive development between larva and imago.

**pupil** /'pju:pəl/ n. person being taught; opening in centre of iris of eye.

**puppet** /'pʌpɪt/ n. kind of doll representing human being etc. and moved by various means as entertainment; person whose acts are controlled by another. **puppet state** country apparently independent but actually under control of some greater power. **puppetry** n.

**puppy** /'pʌpɪ/ n. young dog; conceited young man. **puppy-fat** temporary fatness of child or adolescent.

**purblind** /'pɜ:blaɪnd/ a. partly blind, dim-sighted; obtuse, dull.

**purchase** /'pɜ:tʃəs/ 1 v.t. buy. 2 n. buying; thing bought; firm hold on thing, leverage.

**purdah** /'pɜ:də/ n. system of screening Muslim or Hindu women from strangers, by means of curtain.

**pure** /pjʊə(r)/ a. unmixed, unadulterated; morally or sexually undefiled; guiltless; mere, simple; not discordant; (of science) dealing with abstract concepts and not practical applications.

**purée** /'pjʊreɪ/ 1 n. pulp of vegetables or fruit etc. reduced to uniform mass. 2 v.t. (past & p.p. **puréed**) make purée of.

**purely** /'pjʊəlɪ/ adv. merely; exclusively; solely; entirely.

**purgative** /'pɜ:ɡətɪv/ 1 a. serving to purify; strongly laxative. 2 n. purgative thing.

**purgatory** /'pɜ:ɡətərɪ/ n. condition or place of spiritual cleansing; place of temporary suffering or expiation. **purgatorial** a.

**purge** /pɜ:dʒ/ 1 v.t. make physically or spiritually clean; remove by cleansing process; rid of persons regarded as undesirable; clear (bowels) by evacuation; Law atone for or wipe out (offence etc.). 2 n. purging; purgative. **purgation** n.

**purification** /pjʊərɪfɪ'keɪʃ(ə)n/ n. purifying; ritual cleansing.

**purify** /'pjʊərɪfaɪ/ v.t. make pure, cleanse; clear of extraneous elements.

**purist** /'pjʊərɪst/ n. stickler for correctness esp. in language. **purism** n.

**Puritan** /'pjʊərɪtən/ 1 n. hist. member of English Protestant party regarding Reformation as incomplete; **puritan** person of extreme strictness in religion or morals. 2 a. **puritan** of Puritans; scrupulous in religion or morals. 3 **puritanical** a.; **puritanism** n.

**purity** /'pjʊərɪtɪ/ n. freedom from physical or moral pollution.

**purl** 1 n. stitch in knitting with needle moved in opposition to normal direction; chain of minute loops. 2 v.t. make (stitch) purl.

**purler** /'pɜ:lə(r)/ n. colloq. heavy fall.

**purlieu** /'pɜ:lju:/ n. (usu. in pl.) outskirts, outlying region.

**purlin** /'pɜ:lɪn/ n. horizontal beam running along length of roof.

**purloin** /pɜ:'lɔɪn/ v.t. steal, pilfer.

**purple** /'pɜ:p(ə)l/ 1 n. colour between

red and blue; purple robe, esp. as dress of emperor etc.; cardinal's scarlet official dress. 2 *a.* of purple. 3 *v.* make or become purple.

**purport** 1 /'pɜːpət/ *n.* ostensible meaning; tenor of document or speech. 2 /pə'pɔːt/ *v.t.* profess, be intended to seem (*to* do); have as its meaning.

**purpose** /'pɜːpəs/ 1 *n.* object to be attained, thing intended; intention to act; resolution, determination. 2 *v.t.* have as one's purpose, intend. 3 **on purpose** intentionally; **to good, little, no,** etc. **purpose** with good, little, etc. effect or result; **to the purpose** relevant.

**purposeful** /'pɜːpəsfəl/ *a.* having or indicating purpose; intentional.

**purposely** /'pɜːpəslɪ/ *adv.* on purpose.

**purposive** /'pɜːpəsɪv/ *a.* having or serving or done with a purpose; purposeful.

**purr** /pɜː(r)/ 1 *v.* make low vibratory sound of cat expressing pleasure; (of machinery etc.) make similar sound. 2 *n.* such sound.

**purse** /pɜːs/ 1 *n.* small pouch for carrying money in; funds; sum given as present or prize. 2 *v.* contract (esp. lips) in wrinkles; become wrinkled. 3 **hold the purse strings** have control of expenditure.

**purser** /'pɜːsə(r)/ *n.* ship's officer who keeps accounts, esp. head steward in passenger vessel.

**pursuance** /pə'sjuːəns/ *n.* carrying out or observance (*of* plan, rules, etc.)

**pursuant** /pə'sjuːənt/ *adv.* conformably *to*.

**pursue** /pə'sjuː/ *v.* follow with intent to overtake or capture or do harm to; seek after; persistently assail; proceed along; continue; continue to investigate etc.; follow (profession etc.).

**pursuit** /pə'sjuːt/ *n.* pursuing; occupation or activity pursued.

**purulent** /'pjʊərələnt/ *a.* of or containing or discharging pus. **purulence** *n.*

**purvey** /pə'veɪ/ *v.* provide or supply (provisions) as one's business. **purveyor** *n.*

**purview** /'pɜːvjuː/ *n.* range of physical or mental vision.

**pus** /pʌs/ *n.* yellowish viscous matter produced from inflamed or infected tissue.

**push** /pʊʃ/ 1 *v.* exert force on (thing etc.)

to move it away from oneself; cause to move thus; exert such force; thrust forward or upward or *out* or *forth*; make one's way forcibly or persistently; make persistent demands *for*; urge, impel; sell (drug) illegally; tax abilities or tolerance of. 2 *n.* act of pushing; force thus exerted; vigorous effort; determination; use of influence to advance person; *Aus.* gang, *hist.* crowd of larrikins; **the push** *sl.* dismissal; **push-bike** *colloq.* pedal cycle; **push-chair** child's folding chair on wheels; **push off** *sl.* go away; **pushover** opponent or difficulty easily overcome.

**pusher** *n.* illegal seller of drugs; *Aus.* push-chair.

**pushing** *a. colloq.* pushy; having nearly reached (specified age).

**pushy** *a. colloq.* self-assertive; showing determination to get on.

**pusillanimous** /pjuːsɪ'lænɪməs/ *a.* lacking courage, timid. **pusillanimity** /-'nɪm-/ *n.*

**puss** /pʊs/ *n.* cat; playful or coquettish girl.

**pussy** /'pʊsɪ/ *n. colloq.* cat. **pussyfoot** tread softly or lightly, move or act warily; **pussy-willow** kind of willow with silky catkins.

**pustulate** /'pʌstjʊleɪt/ *v.* form into pustules.

**pustule** /'pʌstjuːl/ *n.* pimple. **pustular** *a.*

**put** /pʊt/ 1 *v.* (*past & p.p.* **put**) move to or cause to be in specified place or position or state; impose; substitute (thing *for* another); express in words; hurl (*the shot*) from hand as athletic exercise. 2 *n.* throw of shot. 3 **put about** spread (rumour); **put across** make acceptable or effective or understood; **put away** *colloq.* imprison, *colloq.* consume (food or drink); **put down** suppress, snub, record in writing, consider *as*, attribute *to*, kill (old etc. animal); **put in** install, formally present, perform (spell of work), *colloq.* spend (time); **put off** postpone, evade (person *with* excuse), dissuade, repel, disconcert; **put on** clothe (oneself) with, cause (electric light, apparatus) to operate, feign, develop additional (weight of body); **put out** disconcert, annoy, extinguish, dislocate; **put over** = **put**

**putative** /ˈpjuːtətɪv/ *a.* reputed, supposed.

**putrefy** /ˈpjuːtrəfaɪ/ *v.* become putrid, go bad, rot; fester. **putrefaction** *n.*; **putrefactive** *a.*

**putrescent** /pjuːˈtres(ə)nt/ *a.* of or in process of rotting. **putrescence** *n.*

**putrid** /ˈpjuːtrɪd/ *a.* decomposed, rotten; stinking. **putridity** *n.*

**putsch** /pʊtʃ/ *n.* attempt at revolution.

**putt** /pʌt/ 1 *v.* strike (golf-ball) gently to roll it into hole. 2 *n.* putting stroke. 3 **putting-green** smooth turf round hole.

**puttee** /ˈpʌtiː/ *n.* long strip of cloth wound spirally round leg for protection and support.

**putter** /ˈpʌtə(r)/ *n.* golf-club used in putting.

**putty** /ˈpʌtiː/ 1 *n.* paste of chalk and linseed oil etc. for fixing panes of glass etc. 2 *v.t.* fix or fill with putty. 3 **up to putty** *Aus. sl.* of poor quality, worthless.

**puzzle** /ˈpʌz(ə)l/ 1 *n.* difficult or confusing problem; problem or toy designed to test ingenuity etc. 2 *v.* perplex, be perplexed; make *out* by exercising ingenuity etc. 3 **puzzlement** *n.*

**PVC** *abbr.* polyvinyl chloride.

**pyaemia** /paɪˈiːmɪə/ *n.* severe bacterial infection of blood.

**pygmy** /ˈpɪgmɪ/ 1 *n.* one of group of very short people in equatorial Africa; very small person or thing. 2 *a.* of pygmies; dwarf.

**pyjamas** /pəˈdʒɑːməz/ *n.pl.* suit of trousers and top for sleeping in etc.

**pylon** /ˈpaɪlɒn/ *n.* tall structure erected as support, esp. for overhead electric cables.

**pyorrhoea** /paɪəˈriːə/ *n.* discharge of pus, esp. in disease of tooth-sockets.

**pyramid** /ˈpɪrəmɪd/ *n.* monumental (esp. ancient Egyptian) stone structure with square base and sloping sides meeting at apex; solid of this shape with base of three or more sides; pyramid-shaped thing. **pyramidal** /-ˈræm-/ *a.*

**pyre** /paɪə(r)/ *n.* pile of combustible material esp. for burning corpse.

**pyrethrum** /paɪˈriːθrəm/ *n.* chrysanthemum with finely divided leaves; insecticide made from its dried flowers.

**Pyrex** /ˈpaɪreks/ *n.* (**P**) a hard heat-resistant glass.

**pyrites** /paɪˈraɪtiːz/ *n.* native sulphide of iron or copper and iron.

**pyromania** /paɪrəʊˈmeɪnɪə/ *n.* uncontrollable impulse to start fires. **pyromaniac** *n.* & *a.*

**pyrotechnics** /paɪrəˈtekniks/ *n.pl.* art of making fireworks; display of fireworks. **pyrotechnic** *a.*

**pyrrhic** /ˈpɪrɪk/ *a.* (of victory) achieved at too great cost.

**python** /ˈpaɪθ(ə)n/ *n.* large snake that crushes its prey.

**pyx** /pɪks/ *n.* vessel in which concrated bread for Eucharist is kept.

# Q

**Q** *abbr.* Queen.
**QANTAS** /'kwɒntəs/ *abbr.* Australia's international airline (originally Queensland and Northern Territory Aerial Service).
**QC** *abbr.* Queen's Counsel.
**QED** *abbr.* which was to be proved (*quod erat demonstrandum*).
**QM** *abbr.* Quartermaster.
**qr.** *abbr.* quarter(s).
**qt.** *abbr.* quart(s).
**qua** /kwɑ:/ *conj.* in the capacity of.
**quack**[1] 1 *n.* harsh cry of ducks. 2 *v.i.* utter quack; talk loudly and foolishly.
**quack**[2] *n.* pretender to skill esp. in medicine etc.; charlatan; *Aus. colloq.* any medical doctor. **quackery** *n.*
**quad** /kwɒd/ *colloq.* 1 *n.* quadrangle; quadruplet; quadraphony. 2 *a.* quadraphonic.
**quadrangle** /'kwɒdræŋg(ə)l/ *n.* 4-sided figure, esp. square or rectangle; 4-sided court esp. in college etc. **quadrangular** *a.*
**quadrant** /'kwɒdrənt/ *n.* quarter of circle or sphere; instrument for taking angular measurements etc.
**quadraphonic** /kwɒdrə'fɒnɪk/ *a.* (of sound-reproduction) using 4 transmission channels. **quadraphony** *n.*
**quadratic** /kwɒd'rætɪk/ 1 *a.* involving the square and no higher power of unknown quantity or variable. 2 *n.* quadratic equation.
**quadrennial** /kwɒd'renɪəl/ *a.* lasting 4 years; recurring every 4 years.
**quadrilateral** /kwɒdrɪ'lætər(ə)l/ 1 *a.* 4-sided. 2 *n.* quadrilateral figure.
**quadrille** /kwə'drɪl/ *n.* square dance, music for it.
**quadroon** /kwɒ'dru:n/ *n.* person of quarter-Negro blood.
**quadruped** /'kwɒdrəped/ *n.* 4-footed animal.
**quadruple** /'kwɒdrəp(ə)l/ 1 *a.* fourfold; of 4 parts or parties; being 4 times as many or much as. 2 *n.* quadruple number or amount. 3 *v.* multiply by 4.
**quadruplet** /'kwɒdrəplet/ *n.* one of 4 children born at one birth.
**quadruplicate** 1 /kwɒ'dru:plɪkət/ *a.* fourfold; of which 4 copies are made. 2 /kwɒ'dru:plɪkeɪt/ *v.t.* multiply by 4; make 4 copies of.

**quaff** /kwɒf/ *v.* drink in copious draughts.
**quagmire** /'kwægmaɪə(r)/ *n.* quaking bog, marsh, slough.
**quail**[1] *n.* bird related to partridge.
**quail**[2] *v.i.* flinch, show fear.
**quaint** *a.* unfamiliar or old-fashioned; daintily odd.
**quake** 1 *v.i.* tremble; rock to and fro. 2 *n. colloq.* earthquake.
**Quaker** /'kweɪkə(r)/ *n.* member of Society of Friends. **Quakerism** *n.*
**qualification** /kwɒlɪfɪ'keɪʃ(ə)n/ *n.* qualifying; accomplishment; thing that modifies or limits. **qualificatory** *a.*
**qualify** /'kwɒlɪfaɪ/ *v.* make or become competent or fit or entitled or eligible etc. (*for*, *to*); modify, limit, moderate, mitigate; attribute quality to, describe *as*.
**qualitative** /'kwɒlətətɪv/ *a.* concerned with or depending on quality.
**quality** /'kwɒlətɪ/ *n.* degree of excellence, attribute; relative nature or kind or character; timbre.
**qualm** /kwɑ:m/ *n.* misgiving; scruple of conscience; momentary faint or sick feeling.
**quandary** /'kwɒndərɪ/ *n.* perplexed state; dilemma.
**quandong** /'kwɒndɒŋ/ *n.* any of several Aus. fruit-bearing trees; (also **quandong nut**) its edible seed.
**quanta** *pl.* of **quantum**.
**quantify** /'kwɒntɪfaɪ/ *v.t.* express as quantity.
**quantitative** /'kwɒntɪtətɪv/ *a.* of or measured or measurable by quantity.
**quantity** /'kwɒntɪtɪ/ *n.* size or extent or weight or amount or number; in *pl.* large amounts or numbers; length or shortness of sound or syllable; thing having quantity. **quantity surveyor** person who measures and prices the work of builders.
**quantum** /'kwɒntəm/ *n.* (*pl.* **-ta**) unit quantity of energy proportional to frequency of radiation; required or desired or allowed amount.
**quarantine** /'kwɒrənti:n/ 1 *n.* isolation imposed on ship or person or animal etc. to prevent infection or contagion; period of this. 2 *v.t.* put in quarantine.

**quark** /kwɑːk/ *n. Phys.* component of elementary particles.

**quarrel** /ˈkwɒr(ə)l/ 1 *n.* severe or angry dispute; break in friendly relations; cause of complaint. 2 *v.i.* have quarrel, dispute fiercely; find fault *with*. 3 **quarrelsome** *a.*

**quarry**[1] /ˈkwɒri/ 1 *n.* place from which stone is extracted for building etc. 2 *v.* extract from quarry. 3 **quarry tile** unglazed floor-tile.

**quarry**[2] /ˈkwɒri/ *n.* intended prey; object of pursuit.

**quart** /kwɔːt/ *n.* liquid measure equal to a quarter of gallon.

**quarter** /ˈkwɔːtə(r)/ 1 *n.* one of 4 equal parts; period of 3 months, esp. ending on quarter-day; point of time 15 minutes before or after any hour o'clock; 25 US or Canadian cents, coin worth this; division of town; point of compass, region at this; direction, district; source of supply; in *pl.* lodgings, abode, station of troops; mercy towards enemy etc. on condition of surrender; grain-measure of 8 bushels, weight of 28 or *US* 25 lb. 2 *v.t.* divide into quarters; put (troops, etc.) into quarters; provide with lodgings. 3 **quarter-day** day on which quarterly payments are due; **quarterdeck** part of upper deck extending from stern and after-mast; **quarter-final** match or round preceding semifinal; **quarter-finalist** *n.*; **quartermaster** *Mil.* regimental officer in charge of quartering, rations, etc., *Naut.* officer in charge of steering, hold-stowing, etc.

**quartering** *n.* division into quarters; in *pl. Her.* coats of arms arranged on one shield to denote alliances of families.

**quarterly** /ˈkwɔːtəli/ 1 *adv.* once in every quarter of year. 2 *a.* done or published or due quarterly. 3 *n.* quarterly magazine.

**quartet** /kwɔːˈtet/ *n. Mus.* composition for group of 4 performers; the performers; group of 4.

**quarto** /ˈkwɔːtəʊ/ *n.* (*pl.* **-os**) size of book or page given by folding sheet of standard size to form 4 leaves; book or page of this size.

**quartz** /kwɔːts/ *n.* silica in various mineral forms. **quartz clock** one operated by electric vibrations of quartz crystal.

**quasar** /ˈkweɪzɑː(r)/ *n.* starlike object with large red-shift.

**quash** /kwɒʃ/ *v.t.* annul; reject as not valid; suppress, crush.

**quasi-** /ˈkweɪzaɪ/ *in comb.* seeming(ly), not real(ly), almost.

**quassia** /ˈkwɒʃə/ *n.* S. Amer. tree; its wood or bark or root; bitter tonic made from this.

**quaternary** /kwəˈtɜːnəri/ *a.* having 4 parts.

**quatrain** /ˈkwɒtreɪn/ *n.* 4-line stanza.

**quatrefoil** /ˈkætrəfɔɪl/ *n.* 4-cusped figure; 4-lobed leaf or flower.

**quaver** /ˈkweɪvə(r)/ 1 *v.* (of voice or sound) vibrate, shake, tremble; say in trembling tones. 2 *n.* tremulousness in speech; trill; *Mus.* note equal to half crotchet. 3 **quavery** *a.*

**quay** /kiː/ *n.* artificial landing-place for loading or unloading ships.

**queasy** /ˈkwiːzɪ/ *a.* inclined to sickness or nausea; liable to qualms or scruples.

**queen** 1 *n.* female sovereign of kingdom; king's wife; woman or country etc. pre-eminent in specified field; perfect fertile female of bee or ant etc.; most powerful piece in chess; court-card bearing representation of queen; *sl.* male homosexual. 2 *v.* convert (pawn in chess) to queen when it reaches opponent's end of board; (of pawn) be thus converted. 3 **queen it** act like queen; **queen mother** king's widow who is mother of sovereign; **Queen's** or **King's Counsel** counsel to the Crown, taking precedence over other barristers. 4 **queenly** *a.*

**Queensland** /ˈkwiːnzlænd or -lənd/ *n.* **Queensland bean** tall leguminous Aus. climbing plant; **Queensland hemp** Aus. shrub with strong soft fibre; **Queensland lungfish** Aus. freshwater fish with lungs as well as gills; **Queensland nut** macadamia.

**queer** /kwɪə(r)/ 1 *a.* strange, odd, eccentric; of questionable character; out of sorts; *sl.* (esp. of man) homosexual. 2 *n. sl.* (esp. male) homosexual. 3 *v.t. sl.* spoil, put out of order.

**quell** *v.t.* suppress, crush.

**quench** *v.t.* satisfy (thirst); extinguish (fire); cool; stifle or suppress.

**quern** *n.* hand-mill for grinding corn etc.

## querulous

**querulous** /ˈkweru:ləs/ a. complaining; peevish.

**query** /ˈkwɪəri:/ 1 n. question, question mark, esp. indicating doubt of correctness of statement etc. 2 v.t. call in question, question accuracy of.

**quest** 1 n. search, seeking; thing sought; inquiry. 2 v.i. search *about*.

**question** /ˈkwestʃ(ə)n/ 1 n. sentence phrased, punctuated, or spoken so as to elicit information; doubt or dispute; subject of discussion; problem for solution; matter depending on conditions *of*. 2 v.t. ask questions of; subject to examination; throw doubt on. 3 **in question** being mentioned or discussed; **out of the question** too impracticable to be worth discussing; **question mark** punctuation mark (?) indicating question; **question-master** chairman of broadcast quiz etc.; **question time** period in parliament when MPs may question ministers.

**questionable** /ˈkwestʃənəb(ə)l/ a. of doubtful truth or honesty or wisdom.

**questionnaire** /ˌkwestʃəˈneə(r)/ n. series of questions for obtaining information on special points.

**queue** /kju:/ 1 n. line of persons or vehicles etc. awaiting their turn; pigtail. 2 v.i. (often with *up*) stand in or join queue.

**quibble** /ˈkwɪb(ə)l/ 1 n. petty objection; merely verbal or trivial point of criticism; play on words; equivocation, evasion. 2 v.i. use quibbles.

**quiche** /ki:ʃ/ n. open pie with usu. savoury filling.

**quick** 1 a. taking only a short time (to do thing or things); arriving after only a short time, prompt; lively, alert, intelligent. 2 adv. quickly. 3 n. sensitive flesh below nails or skin; seat of feeling or emotion. 4 **quicklime** unslaked lime; **quicksand** loose wet sand readily swallowing up heavy objects; **quickset** (of hedge) formed of living plants set to grow in ground; **quicksilver** mercury; **quickstep** fast foxtrot.

**quicken** v. make or become quicker; accelerate; give life to; (of foetus) make perceptible movements.

**quid**[1] n. sl. (pl. same) one pound sterling.

**quid**[2] n. lump of tobacco for chewing.

## quintuple

**quiddity** /ˈkwɪdəti:/ n. essence, real nature.

**quid pro quo** /kwɪd prəʊ ˈkwəʊ/ thing given as compensation.

**quiescent** /kwaɪˈes(ə)nt/ a. inert, dormant. **quiescence** n.

**quiet** /ˈkwaɪət/ 1 a. with little or no sound or motion; of gentle disposition; unobtrusive; tranquil. 2 n. undisturbed state; tranquillity, repose; calm, silence. 3 v. quieten.

**quieten** /ˈkwaɪətən/ v. make or become quiet, calm.

**quietism** /ˈkwaɪətɪz(ə)m/ n. passive attitude towards life, esp. as form of religious mysticism. **quietist** n. & a.

**quietude** /ˈkwaɪətju:d/ n. quietness.

**quietus** /kwaɪˈeɪtəs/ n. death; finishing stroke.

**quiff** n. lock of hair brushed upwards in front.

**quill** n. large feather of wing or tail; hollow stem of this; pen etc. made of quill; (usu. in *pl.*) porcupine's spine(s).

**quilt**[1] n. bed-cover, esp. of quilted material. 2 v.t. make from padding kept in place between two layers of material by lines of stitching.

**quilt**[2] v.t. *Aus. sl.* thrash, hit with fist.

**quin** n. *colloq.* quintuplet.

**quince** n. (tree bearing) hard pear-shaped fruit used in jams etc. **get on person's quince** *Aus. sl.* irritate him.

**quincentenary** /ˌkwɪnsenˈti:nəri:/ 1 n. 500th anniversary; celebration of this. 2 a. of a quincentenary.

**quinella** /kwɪˈnelə/ n. betting on first two place-getters in a race.

**quinine** /ˈkwɪni:n/ n. bitter drug used in treatment of malaria and as tonic.

**Quinquagesima** /ˌkwɪŋkwəˈdʒesəmə/ n. Sunday before Lent.

**quinquennial** /kwɪŋˈkweni:əl/ a. lasting 5 years; recurring every 5 years.

**quinsy** /ˈkwɪnsi:/ n. abscess that forms around tonsils.

**quintessence** /kwɪnˈtes(ə)ns/ n. purest form or manifestation *of* some quality etc.; highly refined extract. **quintessential** /-ˈsen-/ a.

**quintet** /kwɪnˈtet/ n. *Mus.* composition for group of 5 performers; the performers; group of 5.

**quintuple** /ˈkwɪntəp(ə)l/ 1 a. fivefold; having 5 parts; being 5 times as many

**quintuplet** or much as. **2** *n.* quintuple number or amount. **3** *v.* multiply by 5.

**quintuplet** /'kwɪntjəplət/ *n.* one of 5 children born at one birth.

**quip 1** *n.* clever saying, epigram. **2** *v.i.* make quips.

**quire** /kwaɪə(r)/ *n.* 25 sheets of writing-paper; one of the folded sheets that are sewn together in book-binding.

**quirk** *n.* trick of action or behaviour. **quirky** *a.*

**quisling** /'kwɪzlɪŋ/ *n.* collaborator with invading enemy.

**quit 1** *v.* give up, abandon; leave; stop. **2** *pred.a.* rid *of.*

**quitch** *n.* couch-grass.

**quite** *adv.* completely, altogether, absolutely; rather, to some extent.

**quits** *pred.a.* on even terms by retaliation or repayment.

**quittance** /'kwɪt(ə)ns/ *n.* release *from* obligation; acknowledgement of payment.

**quiver**[1] /'kwɪvə(r)/ **1** *v.i.* tremble or vibrate with slight rapid motion. **2** *n.* quivering motion or sound.

**quiver**[2] /'kwɪvə(r)/ *n.* case for arrows.

**qui vive** /ki:'vi:v/ **on the qui vive** on the alert. [F]

**quixotic** /kwɪk'sɒtɪk/ *a.* extravagantly and romantically chivalrous. **quixotically** *adv.*

**quiz 1** *n.* questioning or series of questions, esp. as entertainment or competition. **2** *v.t.* examine by questioning.

**quizzical** /'kwɪzɪk(ə)l/ *a.* mocking, gently amused.

**quod** *n. sl.* prison.

**quoin** /kɔɪn/ *n.* external angle of building, corner-stone; wedge used in printing or gunnery.

**quoit** /kɔɪt/ *n.* rubber ring thrown at mark or to encircle peg etc.; in *pl.* game played with quoits.

**quokka** /'kwɒkə/ *n.* small W. Aus. scrub-wallaby.

**quondam** /'kwɒndæm/ *a.* that was; former.

**quorate** /'kwɔːreɪt/ *a.* (of meeting etc.) having quorum present.

**quorum** /'kwɔːrəm/ *n.* number that must be present to constitute valid meeting.

**quota** /'kwəʊtə/ *n.* share to be contributed to or received from total by one of parties concerned; total number or amount required or permitted.

**quotable** /'kwəʊtəb(ə)l/ *a.* worth quoting. **quotability** *n.*

**quotation** /kwəʊ'teɪʃ(ə)n/ *n.* quoting; passage or price quoted. **quotation-marks** punctuation marks (' ' or " ") used at beginning and end of quoted words.

**quote 1** *v.* cite as example, authority, etc.; repeat or copy out passage from; make quotations (*from*); state price (of). **2** *n. colloq.* passage or price quoted; (usu. in *pl.*) quotation-mark.

**quoth** /kwəʊθ/ *v.t. arch.* (only with *I* or *he* or *she* placed after) said.

**quotidian** /kwɒ'tɪdɪən/ *a.* daily, of every day; commonplace.

**quotient** /'kwəʊʃ(ə)nt/ *n.* result given by dividing one quantity by another.

**q.v.** *abbr.* which see (*quod vide*).

**qy.** *abbr.* query.

# R

**R** *abbr.* registered as trademark.

**R.** *abbr. Regina; Rex;* River.

**r.** *abbr.* right.

**RA** *abbr.* Royal Academician; Royal Academy; Royal Artillery.

**RAAF** *abbr.* Royal Australian Air Force.

**rabbet** /ˈræbət/ 1 *n.* step-shaped channel cut along edge or face of wood etc. to receive edge or tongue of another piece. 2 *v.t.* join with rabbet; cut rabbet in.

**rabbi** /ˈræbaɪ/ *n.* Jewish religious leader; Jewish scholar or teacher esp. of the law. **rabbinical** /-ˈbɪn-/ *a.*

**rabbit** /ˈræbɪt/ 1 *n.* gregarious burrowing mammal of hare family; *colloq.* poor performer at game. 2 *v.i.* hunt rabbits; *sl.* talk at length. **3 rabbit punch** punch on back of neck. **4 rabbity** *a.*

**rabble** /ˈræb(ə)l/ *n.* disorderly crowd, mob; contemptible or inferior set of people; *the* lowest classes. **rabble-rouser** person who stirs up rabble for social or political change.

**Rabelaisian** /ræbəˈleɪz(ə)n/ *a.* exuberantly and coarsely humorous.

**rabid** /ˈræbɪd/ *a.* furious, unreasoning, affected with rabies, mad. **rabidity** *n.*

**rabies** /ˈreɪbiːz/ *n.* contagious virus disease of dogs etc., hydrophobia.

**raccoon** var. of racoon.

**race**¹ 1 *n.* contest of speed; in *pl.* series of these for horses etc.; onward movement; strong current in sea or river; channel; *Aus.* fenced passageway for drafting livestock. 2 *v.* compete in race (with); cause to race; go at full speed; attend races. **3 not in the race** *Aus.* with no chance; **racecourse** ground for horse-racing; **racehorse** one bred or kept for racing; **race-meeting** horse-racing fixture; **race off** *Aus. sl.* seduce or abduct; **race-track** course for racing horses or vehicles etc.

**race**² *n.* each of the major divisions of mankind; group of persons or animals etc. (regarded as) of common stock; posterity *of.*

**raceme** /rəˈsiːm/ *n.* flower-cluster with flowers attached by short stalks along central stem.

**racial** /ˈreɪʃ(ə)l/ *a.* of or characteristic of race²; concerning or caused by race².

**racialism** /ˈreɪʃəlɪz(ə)m/ *n.* belief in superiority of particular race; antagonism between races. **racialist** *n.* & *a.*

**racism** /ˈreɪsɪz(ə)m/ *n.* racialism; theory that human abilities etc. are determined by race. **racist** *n.* & *a.*

**rack**¹ 1 *n.* framework, usu. with rails or bars etc. for holding things; cogged or indented rail or bar gearing with wheel, pinion, etc.; *hist.* instrument of torture for stretching victim's joints. 2 *v.t.* torture on rack; inflict suffering on. **3 rack one's brains** make great mental effort; **rack-rent** extortionate rent.

**rack**² *n.* destruction (usu. **rack and ruin**).

**rack**³ *v.* **rack off** *Aus. sl.* go away, get lost.

**racket**¹ *n.* network of cord, catgut, etc. stretched across round or oval frame with handle, used as bat in tennis etc.; in *pl.* ball-game with rackets in court of 4 plain walls.

**racket**² 1 *n.* uproar, din; way of making money etc. by dubious or illegal means; *sl.* game, line of business. 2 *v.i.* move *about* noisily.

**racketeer** /rækəˈtɪə(r)/ *n.* person who operates dishonest scheme. **racketeering** *n.*

**rackety** /ˈrækɪtɪ/ *a.* noisy, rowdy.

**raconteur** /rækɒnˈtɜː(r)/ *n.* teller of anecdotes.

**racoon** /rəˈkuːn/ *n.* bushy-tailed N. Amer. nocturnal mammal.

**racy** /ˈreɪsɪ/ *a.* lively, spirited; of distinctive quality or vigour.

**radar** /ˈreɪdɑː(r)/ *n.* system for determination of direction and range of objects by radio devices; apparatus used for this. **radar trap** arrangement using radar to detect vehicles travelling faster than speed limit.

**raddle** /ˈræd(ə)l/ 1 *n.* red ochre. 2 *v.t.* colour with raddle, or with much rouge crudely used.

**radial** /ˈreɪdɪəl/ 1 *a.* of or arranged like rays or radii; having spokes or lines radiating from a centre; acting or moving along such lines; (of tyre) having fabric layers parallel and tread strengthened. 2 *n.* radial-ply tyre. **3 radial-ply** (of tyre) radial.

**radian** /ˈreɪdiːən/ *a.* angle at centre of circle formed by radii of arc with length equal to radius.

**radiant** /ˈreɪdiːənt/ **1** *a.* emitting rays; beaming with joy etc.; bright or dazzling; issuing in rays. **2** *n.* point or object from which heat or light radiates. **3 radiance** *n.*; **radiancy** *n.*

**radiate** /ˈreɪdiːeɪt/ *v.* diverge or emit from centre; emit rays of light, heat, etc.; be arranged like spokes; disseminate; show clearly.

**radiation** /reɪdiːˈeɪʃ(ə)n/ *n.* radiating; emission of energy as electromagnetic waves; energy thus transmitted, esp. invisibly. **radiation sickness** that caused by exposure to excessive radiation.

**radiator** /ˈreɪdiːeɪtə(r)/ *n.* apparatus for heating room etc. by radiation of heat; engine-cooling apparatus in motor vehicle or aeroplane.

**radical** /ˈrædɪk(ə)l/ **1** *a.* fundamental, far-reaching, thorough; advocating fundamental reforms; forming the basis, primary; of the root of a number. **2** *n.* person holding radical political opinions; atom or group of atoms forming base of compound and remaining unchanged during reactions; quantity forming or expressed as root of another. **radicalism** *n.*

**radicle** /ˈrædɪk(ə)l/ *n.* part of seed that develops into root.

**radio** /ˈreɪdiːəʊ/ **1** *n.* (*pl.* **-os**) transmission and reception of messages etc. by electromagnetic waves without connecting wires; apparatus for receiving signals by radio; broadcasting station; sound broadcasting. **2** *a.* of or relating to or sent by or used in or using radio. **3** *v.* send (message), send message to (person), by radio; communicate or broadcast by radio. **4 radio car** etc. vehicle equipped with radio for communication.

**radio-** *in comb.* connected with rays, radiation, radioactivity, or radio.

**radioactive** /reɪdiːəʊˈæktɪv/ *a.* of or exhibiting radioactivity.

**radioactivity** /reɪdiːəʊækˈtɪvəti/ *n.* property of spontaneous disintegration of atomic nuclei usu. with emission of penetrating radiation or particles.

**radio-carbon** /reɪdiːəʊˈkɑːbən/ *n.* radioactive isotope of carbon used in dating ancient organic materials.

**radiogram** /ˈreɪdiːəʊɡræm/ *n.* combined radio and gramophone; telegram sent by radio; picture obtained by X-rays etc.

**radiograph** /ˈreɪdiːəʊɡrɑːf/ or -ɡræf/ **1** *n.* picture obtained by X-rays etc. **2** *v.t.* obtain such picture of. **3 radiographer** /-ˈɒɡ-/ *n.*; **radiography** /-ˈɒɡ-/ *n.*

**radiology** /reɪdiːˈɒlədʒiː/ *n.* scientific study of X-rays and other high-energy radiation. **radiologist** *n.*

**radioscopy** /reɪdiːˈɒskəpiː/ *n.* examination by X-rays etc. of objects opaque to light. **radioscopic** /-ˈskɒp-/ *a.*

**radio-telegraphy** /reɪdiːəʊtɪˈlegrəfiː/ *n.* telegraphy using radio.

**radio-telephony** /reɪdiːəʊtɪˈlefəniː/ *n.* telephony using radio.

**radio-therapy** /reɪdiːəʊˈθerəpiː/ *n.* treatment of disease by X-rays or other forms of radiation.

**radish** /ˈrædɪʃ/ *n.* plant with crisp pungent root eaten raw; this root.

**radium** /ˈreɪdiːəm/ *n.* radioactive metallic element.

**radius** /ˈreɪdiːəs/ *n.* (*pl.* **-dii** /-dɪaɪ/) straight line from centre to circumference of circle or sphere; any of set of lines diverging from point like radii of circle; bone of forearm on same side as thumb.

**radix** /ˈreɪdɪks/ *n.* (*pl.* **-dices** /-dɪsiːz/) number or symbol used as basis of numeration scale.

**RAF** *abbr. UK* Royal Air Force.

**Rafferty rules** /ˈræfətiː/ *Aus. colloq.* no rules at all.

**raffia** /ˈræfiːə/ *n.* soft fibre from leaves of kind of palm.

**raffish** /ˈræfɪʃ/ *a.* of dissipated appearance; disreputable.

**raffle** /ˈræf(ə)l/ **1** *n.* sale of articles by lottery. **2** *v.t.* sell by raffle.

**raft** /rɑːft/ *n.* flat floating structure of wood or fastened logs etc., used in water for transport or as emergency boat.

**rafter** /ˈrɑːftə(r)/ *n.* any of sloping beams forming framework of roof.

**rag**[1] *n.* torn or frayed piece of woven material; remnant; in *pl.* tattered clothes; *derog.* newspaper. **rag doll** stuffed cloth doll; **ragtime** form of jazz with much syncopation; **rag trade**

*colloq.* the clothing business; **ragwort** yellow-flowered wild plant.

**rag**² 1 *n.* annual programme of stunts etc. staged by students esp. to collect money for charity; *colloq.* prank; disorderly scene, rowdy celebration. 2 *v. sl.* tease; play rough jokes on; engage in rag.

**ragamuffin** /ˈrægəmʌfɪn/ *n.* person in ragged dirty clothes.

**rage** 1 *n.* violent anger; fit of this; object of widespread temporary popularity. 2 *v.i.* rave, storm; be violent, be at the height; be full of anger.

**ragged** /ˈrægɪd/ *a.* torn, frayed; in ragged clothes; having broken jagged outline or surface; lacking finish or smoothness or uniformity.

**raglan** /ˈræglən/ *n.* garment in which top of sleeve is carried up to neck. **raglan sleeve** one of this kind.

**ragout** /ræˈguː/ *n.* stew of meat with vegetables.

**raid** 1 *n.* rapid surprise attack, in warfare or to steal or do harm; surprise visit by police etc. to arrest suspected persons or seize illicit goods. 2 *v.* make raid (on).

**rail**¹ 1 *n.* level or sloping bar or series of bars used to hang things on or as protection against falling etc. or as part of fence etc.; steel bar making part of track of railway; railway. 2 *v.t.* provide or enclose with rail(s). 3 **railhead** furthest point reached by railway, point where rail transport ends; **railroad** *US* railway.

**rail**² *v.i.* complain fiercely or abusively.

**rail**³ *n.* small wading bird.

**railing** *n.* fence or barrier with rails.

**raillery** /ˈreɪləri:/ *n.* good-humoured ridicule.

**railway** /ˈreɪlweɪ/ *n.* track or set of tracks for passage of trains; organization and persons required for their working. **railwayman** railway employee.

**raiment** /ˈreɪmənt/ *n. arch.* clothing.

**rain** 1 *n.* condensed moisture of atmosphere falling in drops; fall of these; in *pl.* season of these; falling liquid or particles or objects etc., rainlike descent of these. 2 *v.* fall or send down like rain; send down rain. 3 **it rains** rain falls; **raincoat** waterproof coat; **rainfall** total amount of rain falling within given area in given time; **rain forest** tropical forest with heavy rainfall; **rainmaker** *Aus.* (very) high kick (in football).

**rainbow** /ˈreɪnbəʊ/ 1 *n.* arch showing sequence of colours formed in sky by refraction and dispersion of sun's rays in falling raindrops etc. 2 *a.* many-coloured. 3 **rainbow trout** large trout orig. of N. Amer.

**rainy** /ˈreɪni:/ *a.* (of weather, day, region, etc.) in or on which rain is falling or much rain usually falls. **rainy day** *fig.* time of need.

**raise** /reɪz/ 1 *v.t.* put or take into higher position, cause to stand up or *up*, bring to vertical position; rouse; build up or *up*; levy, collect; cause to be heard or considered; educate; breed; increase amount of; remove (barrier). 2 *n.* increase in amount; *US* rise in salary. 3 **raise Cain, hell,** etc. *colloq.* raise a disturbance; **raise a laugh** cause others to laugh; **raise one's eyebrows** look supercilious or shocked; **raising agent** substance causing bread and cakes etc. to rise.

**raisin** /ˈreɪz(ə)n/ *n.* dried grape.

**raison d'être** /reɪzɔ̃ ˈdetr/ *n.* purpose that accounts for or justifies or originally caused thing's existence. [F]

**raj** /rɑːdʒ/ *n.* British rule in India.

**raja** /ˈrɑːdʒə/ (also **rajah**) *n. hist.* Indian king or prince.

**rake**¹ 1 *n.* implement of pole with comblike crossbar for drawing hay etc. together, smoothing loose soil, etc.; implement resembling rake used for other purposes. 2 *v.* collect, draw *together*, (as) with rake; use rake; ransack, search (*through* etc.); sweep with eyes, shot, etc. 3 **rake-off** *colloq.* (share of) profit, commission.

**rake**² *n.* dissipated or immoral man of fashion.

**rake**³ 1 *v.* set or be set at sloping angle; (of mast, funnel, etc.) incline towards stern or rear. 2 *n.* raking position or build; amount by which thing rakes.

**rakish** /ˈreɪkɪʃ/ *a.* like a rake²; dashing, jaunty.

**rallentando** /rælənˈtændəʊ/ *Mus.* 1 *adv.* with gradual decrease of speed. 2 *n.* (*pl.* **-dos**) passage to be played thus.

**rally**¹ /ˈræli:/ 1 *v.* bring or come together for united effort; revive by effort

**rally** ... of will; throw off illness; (of prices etc.) increase after fall. **2** *n.* act of rallying; recovery of energy or spirit; mass meeting; competition for motor vehicles over public roads; *Tennis* etc. series of strokes before point is decided.

**rally**² /'ræli:/ *v.t.* subject to good-humoured ridicule.

**ram** **1** *n.* uncastrated male sheep; battering-ram; pile-driving or hydraulic or pumping-machine or parts of them. **2** *v.t.* beat firm; force home; pack closely; collide violently with, charge or crash *into*; impress by repetition.

**RAM** *abbr.* random-access memory.

**Ramadan** /'ræmədɑ:n/ *n.* ninth month of Muslim year, with strict fast during daylight hours.

**ramble** /'ræmb(ə)l/ **1** *v.i.* walk for pleasure; talk in desultory or irrelevant way. **2** *n.* walk taken for pleasure.

**rambler** /'ræmblə(r)/ *n.* person who rambles; straggling or climbing rose.

**rambling** /'ræmblɪŋ/ *a.* irregularly arranged; (of plant) straggling, climbing.

**ramekin** /'ræməkɪn/ *n.* small dish for baking and serving individual portion of food; food served in this.

**ramify** /'ræmɪfaɪ/ *v.* form branches or sub-divisions; develop into complicated system. **ramification** *n.*

**ramp** **1** *n.* slope joining two levels of ground or floor etc.; *Aus.* cattle-grid; stairs for entering or leaving aircraft. **2** *v.* furnish or construct with ramp; take threatening posture.

**ramp**² *n. sl.* swindle; charging of extortionate prices.

**rampage** **1** /ræm'peɪdʒ/ *v.i.* rush *about*; rage, storm. **2** /'ræmpeɪdʒ/ *n.* violent behaviour. **3 on the rampage** rampaging. **4 rampageous** *a.*

**rampant** /'ræmpənt/ *a. Her.* (esp. of lion etc.) standing on one hind leg with forefeet in air; extravagant, unrestrained, rank, luxuriant. **rampancy** *n.*

**rampart** /'ræmpɑ:t/ *n.* defensive broad-topped wall; defence, protection.

**ramrod** /'ræmrɒd/ *n. hist.* rod for ramming home charge of muzzle-loading firearm; *fig.* thing that is very straight or rigid.

**ramshackle** /'ræmʃæk(ə)l/ *a.* rickety, tumbledown.

**ran** *past* of **run**.

**ranch** /rɑ:ntʃ/ or /ræntʃ/ **1** *n.* cattle-breeding establishment esp. in US & Canada; farm where other animals are bred. **2** *v.i.* conduct ranch.

**rancid** /'rænsɪd/ *a.* smelling or tasting like rank stale fat. **rancidity** *n.*

**rancour** /'ræŋkə(r)/ *n.* malignant hate; bitterness. **rancorous** *a.*

**rand** *n.* monetary unit of S. Afr. countries.

**R & D** *abbr.* research and development.

**random** /'rændəm/ *a.* made or done etc. without method or conscious choice. **at random** without aim or purpose or principle; **random-access** (of computer memory) having all parts directly accessible.

**randy** /'rændi/ *a. colloq.* lustful.

**ranee** /'rɑ:ni:/ *n.* raja's wife or widow.

**rang** *past* of **ring**².

**range** /reɪndʒ/ **1** *n.* area over which thing is found or has effect or relevance; scope; region between limits of variables, such limits; distance attainable or to be covered by gun or projectile; distance that can be covered by vehicle etc. without refuelling; row or series, esp. of mountains; open or enclosed area with targets for shooting; cooking fireplace; stretch of grazing or hunting ground. **2** *v.* place in row(s) or in specified arrangement; rove, wander; extend, reach; vary between limits; go all about. **3 range-finder** instrument for estimating distance of object for shooting or photography.

**ranger** /'reɪndʒə(r)/ *n.* keeper of park or forest; **Ranger Guide**.

**rangy** /'reɪndʒi:/ *a.* tall and slim.

**rani** var. of **ranee**.

**rank**¹ *n.* position in hierarchy; grade of advancement; distinct social class, grade of dignity, high social position; place in scale; row, queue; soldiers in single line abreast; place where taxis await customers. **2** *v.* have rank or place; assign rank to; arrange in rank. **3 rank and file** ordinary undistinguished people; **the ranks** common soldiers.

**rank**² *a.* too luxuriant; coarse; offensive, loathsome; flagrant; gross.

**rankle** /'ræŋk(ə)l/ *v.i.* cause persistent annoyance or pain or resentment.

**ransack** /'rænsæk/ *v.t.* pillage, plunder; thoroughly search.

**ransom** /'rænsəm/ 1 *n*. sum of money or value paid for release of prisoner; liberation of prisoner in return for this. 2 *v*. buy freedom or restoration of; hold to ransom; release for a ransom. 3 **hold to ransom** keep prisoner and demand ransom.

**rant** 1 *v*. use bombastic language; preach noisily. 2 *n*. piece of ranting.

**ranunculus** /rə'nʌŋkjələs/ *n*. (*pl*. -luses) plant of genus including buttercup.

**rap**¹ 1 *n*. smart slight blow; sound (as) of this; *sl*. blame, punishment. 2 *v*. strike smartly; make sound of rap; criticize adversely. 3 **rap out** utter abruptly.

**rap**² *n*. the least bit.

**rapacious** /rə'peɪʃəs/ *a*. grasping, extortionate, predatory. **rapacity** /-'pæs-/ *n*.

**rape**¹ 1 *n*. forcible or fraudulent sexual intercourse esp. imposed on woman; violent assault or interference. 2 *v.t*. commit rape on.

**rape**² *n*. plant grown as fodder and for its oil-yielding seed.

**rapid** /'ræpɪd/ 1 *a*. speedy, swift. 2 *n*. (usu. in *pl*.) steep descent in river-bed with swift current. 3 **rapidity** /-'pɪd-/ *n*.

**rapier** /'reɪpɪə(r)/ *n*. light slender sword used for thrusting.

**rapine** /'ræpaɪn/ *n*. plundering.

**rapist** /'reɪpɪst/ *n*. man who commits rape.

**rapport** /ræ'pɔː(r)/ *n*. communication, sympathetic relationship.

*rapprochement* /ræ'prɒʃmɑ̃/ *n*.. restoration of harmonious relations esp. between States. [F]

**rapscallion** /ræp'skælɪən/ *n*. *arch*. rascal.

**rapt** *a*. absorbed; intent; carried away in spirit.

**raptorial** /ræp'tɔːrɪəl/ 1 *a*. predatory. 2 *n*. predatory animal or bird.

**rapture** /'ræptʃə(r)/ *n*. ecstatic delight; in *pl*. great enthusiasm or expression of it. **rapturous** *a*.

**rare**¹ *a*. seldom done or found or occurring; uncommon; exceptionally good; of less than usual density.

**rare**² *a*. (of meat) underdone.

**rarebit**: see **Welsh rabbit**.

**rarefy** /'reərəfaɪ/ *v*. lessen density or solidity of; refine, become less dense. **rarefaction** *n*.

**rarely** /'reəlɪ/ *adv*. seldom, not often.

**raring** /'reərɪŋ/ *a*. *colloq*. eager (*to go* etc.).

**rarity** /'reərətɪ/ *n*. rareness; rare thing.

**rascal** /'rɑːsk(ə)l/ *n*. dishonest or mischievous person. **rascally** *a*.

**rase** var. of **raze**.

**rash**¹ *a*. hasty, impetuous; reckless.

**rash**² *n*. skin eruption in spots or patches; *fig*. sudden widespread onset of.

**rasher** /'ræʃə(r)/ *n*. thin slice of bacon or ham.

**rasp** /rɑːsp/ 1 *n*. coarse file; grating sound or effect. 2 *v*. scrape with rasp; scrape roughly; grate upon; make grating sound.

**raspberry** /'rɑːzbərɪ/ *n*. small usu. red fruit like blackberry; bramble bearing this; *sl*. sound expressing derision or dislike. **raspberry-jam tree** W. Aus. acacia with wood scented like jam.

**Rastafarian** /ræstə'feərɪən/ 1 *n*. member of orig. Jamaican sect. 2 *a*. of this sect.

**rat** 1 *n*. rodent like large mouse; *sl*. unpleasant or treacherous person. 2 *v.i*. hunt or kill rats; act as informer. 3 **rat kangaroo** small rat-like Aus. marsupial; **rat on** desert or betray (person); **rat race** fiercely competitive struggle; **smell a rat** begin to suspect treachery etc.

**ratafia** /rætə'fiːə/ *n*. liqueur flavoured with almonds or fruit-kernels; biscuit similarly flavoured.

**ratbag** /'rætbæg/ *n*. Aus. *colloq*. an eccentric.

**ratchet** /'rætʃət/ *n*. set of teeth on edge of bar or wheel with catch allowing motion in one direction only; ratchetwheel. **ratchet-wheel** wheel with rim so toothed.

**rate**¹ 1 *n*. stated numerical proportion between two sets of things; standard or way of reckoning; value or cost, measure of this; (relative) speed; assessment on buildings and land owned, levied by local authorities; in *pl*. amount thus paid by householder. 2 *v*. estimate worth or value of; consider, regard as; rank or be rated *as*; subject to payment of local rate. 3 **ratepayer** person liable to pay rates.

**rate²** v.t. scold angrily.

**rateable** /ˈreɪtəb(ə)l/ a. liable to local rates. **rateable value** value at which house etc. is assessed for rates.

**rather** /ˈrɑːðə(r)/ adv. by preference; more truly; to a greater extent; somewhat; *colloq.* most emphatically, assuredly.

**ratify** /ˈrætɪfaɪ/ v.t. confirm or accept by signature or other formality. **ratification** n.

**rating** /ˈreɪtɪŋ/ n. placing in rank or class; non-commissioned sailor; estimated standing of person as regards credit etc.; estimated size of audience to show popularity of a broadcast.

**ratio** /ˈreɪʃɪəʊ/ n. (pl. **-ios**) quantitative relation between similar magnitudes; proportion.

**ratiocinate** /rætɪˈɒsɪneɪt/ v.i. reason, esp. formally. **ratiocination** n.

**ration** /ˈræʃ(ə)n/ 1 n. fixed allowance or individual share of provisions, fuel, clothing, etc. 2 v.t. limit (food etc.) to fixed ration; share (*out*) in fixed quantities.

**rational** /ˈræʃən(ə)l/ a. able to reason; sensible; moderate; of or based on reasoning; *Math.* expressible as ratio of integers. **rationality** n.

**rationale** /ræʃəˈnɑːl/ n. fundamental reason or logical basis.

**rationalism** /ˈræʃənəlɪz(ə)m/ n. practice of treating reason as basis of belief and knowledge. **rationalist** n. & a.; **rationalistic** a.

**rationalize** /ˈræʃənəlaɪz/ v. offer rational but specious explanation of (behaviour or attitude); make logical and consistent; make (an industry etc.) more efficient by reducing waste. **rationalization** n.

**ratline** /ˈrætlɪn/ n. (also **ratlin**) n. any of the small lines fastened across ship's shrouds like ladder-rungs.

**rattan** /rəˈtæn/ n. palm with long thin many-jointed stems; cane of this.

**rattle** /ˈræt(ə)l/ 1 v. give out rapid succession of short sharp sounds; cause such sounds by shaking something; move or travel with rattling noise; say or recite rapidly; *sl.* disconcert, alarm. 2 n. rattling sound; instrument or plaything made to rattle. 3 **rattlesnake** venomous Amer. snake making rattling noise with tail; **rattletrap** rickety vehicle etc.

**rattling** 1 a. brisk, vigorous. 2 adv. remarkably (*good* etc.).

**raucous** /ˈrɔːkəs/ a. harsh-sounding; hoarse.

**ravage** /ˈrævɪdʒ/ 1 v. lay waste, plunder; make havoc. 2 n. (esp. in *pl.*) destructive effects *of*.

**rave** 1 v. talk wildly or deliriously; speak with rapturous admiration (*about*, *over*). 2 n. *colloq.* highly enthusiastic review. 3 **rave-up** *sl.* lively party.

**ravel** /ˈræv(ə)l/ v. entangle, become entangled; confuse, complicate; fray out.

**raven¹** /ˈreɪv(ə)n/ 1 n. large black hoarse-voiced crow. 2 a. of glossy black.

**raven²** /ˈræv(ə)n/ v. seek *after* prey or plunder; devour voraciously.

**ravenous** /ˈrævənəs/ a. very hungry; voracious; rapacious.

**ravine** /rəˈviːn/ n. deep narrow gorge.

**ravioli** /rævɪˈəʊlɪ/ n. small pasta cases containing meat etc.

**ravish** /ˈrævɪʃ/ v.t. enrapture, fill with delight; commit rape on.

**raw** a. uncooked; in natural state, not processed or manufactured; inexperienced, unskilled; stripped of skin; sore, sensitive to touch; (of weather) damp and chilly; crude. **in the raw** in its natural state, naked; **raw-boned** gaunt; **raw deal** unfair treatment; **rawhide** untanned leather; **raw material** that from which process of manufacture makes articles.

**ray¹** n. single line or narrow beam of light or other radiant energy; remnant or beginning of enlightening influence; any of set of radiating lines, parts, or things; marginal part of daisy etc.

**ray²** n. large marine food-fish related to skate.

**ray³** n. *Mus.* second note of scale in tonic sol-fa.

**rayon** /ˈreɪɒn/ n. textile fibre or fabric made from cellulose.

**raze** v.t. completely destroy, tear down.

**razor** /ˈreɪzə(r)/ n. instrument for shaving. **razor-back** sharp ridge, *Aus. sl.* lean bullock or cow; **razor-bill** auk with sharp-edged bill; **razor-blade** flat piece of metal with usu. two sharp edges, used in safety razor; **razor-edge** keen edge, sharp mountain ridge, critical situation, sharp line of division;

**razor-grinder** kind of Aus. flycatcher with rasping call.

**razzle** /ˈræz(ə)l/ *n. sl.* spree.

**razzle-dazzle** *n.* excitement, bustle.

**RC** *abbr.* Roman Catholic.

**Rd.** *abbr.* Road.

**re**[1] /riː/ *prep.* in the matter of; *colloq.* about, concerning.

**re**[2] var. of **ray**[3].

**re-** *pref.* attachable to almost any verb or verbal derivative, denoting once more, again, anew, afresh, repeated, back. For words with this prefix, if not found below, the root-words should be consulted.

**reach** /riːtʃ/ **1** *v.* stretch *out*, extend; stretch out hand etc.; get as far as, attain to, arrive at; amount to; pass or take with outstretched hand etc.; *Naut.* sail with wind abeam. **2** *n.* act of reaching; range of hand etc.; scope; continuous extent, tack. **3 reach-me-down** *colloq.* ready-made.

**react** /riːˈækt/ *v.i.* respond *to* stimulus; undergo change or show behaviour under some influence; be activated by repulsion *against*; tend in reverse or backward direction.

**reaction** /riːˈækʃ(ə)n/ *n.* reacting; responsive feeling; occurrence of condition after its opposite; *Polit.* tendency to oppose change or to return to former system.

**reactionary** /riːˈækʃənərɪ/ **1** *a. Polit.* showing reaction. **2** *n.* reactionary person.

**reactivate** /riːˈæktəveɪt/ *v.t.* restore to state of activity.

**reactive** /riːˈæktɪv/ *a.* showing reaction.

**reactor** /riːˈæktə(r)/ *n.* (in full **nuclear reactor**) assembly of materials in which controlled nuclear chain reaction takes place.

**read** /riːd/ *v.* (*past & p.p.* **read** /red/) reproduce mentally or vocally (written or printed words etc.) while following their symbols with the eyes; (be able to) convert into intended words or meaning (written or printed words, figures, markings, etc.); interpret in certain sense; find written or printed; show, convey when read, record, indicate; study by reading; (of computer) copy or transfer (data).

**readable** /ˈriːdəb(ə)l/ *a.* able to be read esp. with interest. **readability** *n.*

**reader** /ˈriːdə(r)/ *n.* person who reads, esp. aloud; book containing passages for instruction or exercise etc.; device to produce image that can be read from microfilm etc.; senior university lecturer; publisher's employee who reports on submitted MSS; printer's proof-corrector.

**readership** /ˈriːdəʃɪp/ *n.* readers of a newspaper etc.

**readily** /ˈredɪlɪ/ *adv.* without reluctance; willingly; easily.

**readiness** /ˈredɪnəs/ *n.* prepared state; willingness, facility; quickness in argument or action.

**reading** /ˈriːdɪŋ/ *n.* entertainment at which something is read; literary knowledge; figure etc. shown by instrument or dial etc.; interpretation or view taken, rendering; word(s) read or given by editor as text; presentation of bill to legislative assembly. **reading-lamp** lamp giving light for reading.

**ready** /ˈredɪ/ **1** *a.* with preparations complete; in fit state; willing; within reach; fit for immediate use or action; prompt, enthusiastic. **2** *adv.* beforehand; in readiness. **3** *n. sl.* ready money. **4** *v.t.* prepare. **5 at the ready** ready for action; **ready-made** (esp. of clothes) made in standard shapes and sizes, not to measure; **ready money** cash, actual coin; **ready reckoner** book or table of results of arithmetical calculations.

**reagent** /riːˈeɪdʒ(ə)nt/ *n.* substance used to produce chemical reaction.

**real 1** *a.* actually existing or occurring; objective; genuine; consisting of immovable property; appraised by purchasing power. **2** *adv. Sc. & US colloq.* really, very. **3 real tennis** original form of tennis played on indoor court.

**realism** /ˈrɪəlɪz(ə)m/ *n.* practice of regarding things in their true nature and dealing with them as they are; fidelity to nature in representation. **realist** *n.*

**realistic** /rɪəˈlɪstɪk/ *a.* regarding things as they are; based on facts rather than ideals.

**reality** /riːˈælətɪ/ *n.* what is real or existent or underlies appearances; real existence; being real; likeness to original. **in reality** in fact.

**realize** /ˈriːəlaɪz/ *v.t.* be fully aware of;

present or conceive as real; understand clearly; convert into fact; convert into money; be sold for. **realization** *n.*

**really** /'rɪəli/ *adv.* in fact; I assure you; as expression of mild protest or surprise.

**realm** /relm/ *n.* kingdom; sphere, domain.

**realty** /'ri:əlti/ *n.* real estate.

**ream** *n.* twenty quires of paper; (usu. in *pl.*) large quantity of writing.

**reap** *v.* cut (grain etc.) with sickle or machine; harvest; *fig.* receive as consequences of actions.

**rear**[1] 1 *n.* back part of anything; space or position at back. 2 *a.* at the back. 3 **bring up the rear** come last; **rear-admiral** flag officer below vice-admiral; **rearguard** troops etc. detached to protect rear, esp. in retreat; **rearguard action** engagement between rearguard and enemy. 4 **rearmost** *a.*

**rear**[2] *v.* bring up, foster, educate; cultivate; (of horse etc.) rise on hind feet; raise, build.

**rearm** /ri:'ɑ:m/ *v.* arm again, esp. with improved weapons. **rearmament** *n.*

**rearward** /'rɪəwəd/ 1 *n.* rear. 2 *a.* at the rear. 3 *adv.* rearwards.

**rearwards** *adv.* towards the rear.

**reason** /'ri:z(ə)n/ 1 *n.* motive or cause or justification; fact adduced or serving as this; intellectual faculty by which conclusions are drawn from premisses; sense, sanity; sensible conduct; moderation. 2 *v.* form or try to reach conclusions by connected thought; think *out*; use argument *with* by way of persuasion.

**reasonable** /'ri:zənəb(ə)l/ *a.* having sound judgement; sensible, moderate; inexpensive, not extortionate; tolerable.

**reassure** /ri:ə'ʃʊə(r) or -'ʃɔ:(r)/ *v.t.* restore confidence to; confirm again in opinion etc.

**rebarbative** /rə'bɑ:bətɪv/ *a.* forbidding, repellent.

**rebate**[1] /'ri:beɪt/ *n.* deduction from sum to be paid, discount.

**rebate**[2] /'ræbət, rə'beɪt/ var. of **rabbet**.

**rebel** 1 /'reb(ə)l/ *n.* person who fights against or resists or refuses allegiance to established government; person who resists authority or control. 2 /rɪ'bel/ *v.i.* act as rebel (*against*); feel or show opposition, repugnance, etc. (*against*).

**rebellion** /rə'beljən/ *n.* open resistance to any authority, esp. organized armed resistance to established government.

**rebellious** /rə'beljəs/ *a.* in rebellion; disposed to rebel; unmanageable, refractory.

**rebound** 1 /rɪ'baʊnd/ *v.i.* spring back after impact; recoil. 2 /'ri:baʊnd/ *n.* rebounding, recoil; reaction after emotion.

**rebuff** /rə'bʌf/ 1 *n.* rejection of person who makes advances or offers help etc.; repulse. 2 *v.t.* give rebuff to.

**rebuke** /rə'bju:k/ 1 *v.t.* express condemnation or censure authoritatively. 2 *n.* rebuking or being rebuked.

**rebus** /'ri:bəs/ *n.* riddling representation of name or word etc. by pictures etc. suggesting its parts.

**rebut** /rə'bʌt/ *v.t.* refute, disprove; force back. **rebuttal** *n.*

**recalcitrant** /rə'kælsətrənt/ *a.* obstinately disobedient or refractory. **recalcitrance** *n.*

**recall** /rə'kɔ:l/ 1 *v.t.* summon back; bring back *to* memory; (cause to) remember; revive, resuscitate; revoke, annul. 2 *n.* recalling or being recalled.

**recant** /rə'kænt/ *v.* withdraw and renounce as erroneous or heretical; disavow former opinion etc. **recantation** *n.*

**recap** /'ri:kæp/ 1 *v. colloq.* recapitulate. 2 *n.* recapitulation.

**recapitulate** /ri:kə'pɪtjʊleɪt/ *v.* summarize, restate briefly. **recapitulation** *n.*

**recast** /ri:'kɑ:st/ *v.t.* (*past* & *p.p.* **-cast**) put into new form; improve arrangement of.

**recce** /'reki:/ *sl.* 1 *n.* reconnaissance. 2 *v.* reconnoitre.

**recede** /rə'si:d/ *v.i.* go or shrink back; be left at an increasing distance; slope backwards; decline in force or value etc.

**receipt** /rə'si:t/ 1 *n.* receiving or being received; written acknowledgement of receipt of payment etc.; (usu. in *pl.*) amount of money received. 2 *v.t.* write or give receipt on or for.

**receive** /rə'si:v/ *v.* take into one's hands or possession, have sent to one; acquire,

**receiver** /rə'siːvə(r)/ n. person appointed to administer property of bankrupt etc. or property under litigation; person who receives stolen goods; apparatus for receiving transmitted signals.

**recent** /'riːs(ə)nt/ a. not long past, that happened or existed lately; not long established, modern.

**receptacle** /rə'septək(ə)l/ n. vessel, space, or place for receiving or holding.

**reception** /rə'sepʃ(ə)n/ n. receiving or being received; way in which person or thing is received; social occasion for receiving guests, esp. after wedding; place where visitors register on arriving at hotel, business premises, etc.; receiving of broadcast signals; quality of this. **reception room** one available or suitable for receiving guests.

**receptionist** /rə'sepʃənəst/ n. person employed to receive guests, patients, clients, etc.

**receptive** /rə'septɪv/ a. able or quick to receive ideas etc. **receptivity** /-'tɪv-/ n.

**recess** /rə'ses/ 1 n. space set back from line of wall etc.; remote or secret place; temporary cessation from work etc., esp. of Parliament. 2 v. set back; provide with recess(es); US take recess.

**recession** /rə'seʃ(ə)n/ n. temporary decline in activity or prosperity; receding, withdrawal.

**recessive** /rə'sesɪv/ a. tending to recede; (of inherited characteristic) remaining latent when dominant contrary characteristic is present.

**recherché** /rə'ʃeəʃeɪ/ a. (excessively) far-fetched or carefully thought out.

**recidivism** /rə'sɪdəvɪz(ə)m/ n. habitual relapse into crime. **recidivist** n.

**recipe** /'resəpi/ n. statement of ingredients and procedure for preparing dish etc.

**recipient** /rə'sɪpɪənt/ n. person who receives thing.

**reciprocal** /rə'sɪprək(ə)l/ 1 a. in return; mutual; *Gram.* expressing mutual relation. 2 n. *Math.* function or expression so related to another that their product is unity.

**reciprocate** /rə'sɪprəkeɪt/ v. interchange; require, make return (*with*); go with alternate backward and forward motion. **reciprocation** n.

**reciprocity** /resə'prosəti/ n. reciprocal condition, mutual action; give-and-take.

**recital** /rə'saɪt(ə)l/ n. act of reciting; detailed account or narration *of* facts etc.; programme of music performed by one musician with or without accompanist, or by small group of musicians.

**recitation** /resə'teɪʃ(ə)n/ n. reciting esp. as entertainment; piece recited.

**recitative** /resətə'tiːv/ n. musical declamation of kind usual in narrative and dialogue parts of opera and oratorio.

**recite** /rə'saɪt/ v. repeat aloud or declaim from memory; mention in order, enumerate.

**reckless** /'rekləs/ a. regardless of consequences or danger etc.

**reckon** /'rekən/ v. ascertain number or amount (of) by counting or calculation; count; settle accounts *with*; rely or base plans (*up*)*on*; *colloq.* conclude, suppose.

**reckoning** n. calculating; opinion; settlement of account. **day of reckoning** time when something must be atoned for or avenged.

**reclaim** /rə'kleɪm/ v.t. ask for return of (one's property); bring (land) under cultivation from sea or from waste state; win back from vice or error. **reclamation** /rek-/ n.

**recline** /rə'klaɪn/ v. (cause to) assume or be in horizontal or leaning position.

**recluse** /rə'kluːs/ n. person living in retirement or isolation.

**recognition** /rekəg'nɪʃ(ə)n/ n. recognizing or being recognized.

**recognizable** /'rekəgnaɪzəb(ə)l/ a. that can be recognized, identified, or detected. **recognizability** n.

**recognizance** /rə'kɒgnɪz(ə)ns/ n. bond by which person engages before court or magistrate to observe some condition; sum pledged as surety for such observance.

**recognize** /'rekəgnaɪz/ v.t. know again, identify as known before; accord notice or consideration to; acknowledge or

**recoil** /rɪˈkɔɪl/ 1 v.i. start back, shrink, in horror or disgust or fear; rebound; (of gun) be driven backwards by discharge. 2 (also /ˈriːkɔɪl/) n. act or fact or sensation of recoiling.

**recollect** /rekəˈlekt/ v.t. succeed in remembering, call to mind.

**recollection** /rekəˈlekʃ(ə)n/ n. act or power of recollecting; thing recollected; person's memory, time over which it extends.

**recommend** /rekəˈmend/ v.t. suggest as fit for favour or trial; advise (course of action etc., person *to* do etc.); make acceptable or desirable; commit *to* care of. **recommendation** n.

**recompense** /ˈrekəmpens/ 1 v.t. make amends for; requite; compensate. 2 n. reward; requital; compensation.

**reconcile** /ˈrekənsaɪl/ v.t. make friendly after estrangement; make resigned; harmonize; make compatible; show compatibility of. **reconciliation** n.

**recondite** /ˈrekəndaɪt/ a. abstruse; obscure.

**recondition** /riːkənˈdɪʃ(ə)n/ v.t. overhaul, renovate, make usable again.

**reconnaissance** /rɪˈkɒnəs(ə)ns/ n. military etc. examination of region to locate enemy or ascertain strategic features; preliminary survey.

**reconnoitre** /rekəˈnɔɪtə(r)/ v. make reconnaissance (of).

**reconsider** /riːkənˈsɪdə(r)/ v.t. consider again, esp. for possible change of decision.

**reconstitute** /riːˈkɒnstɪtjuːt/ v.t. reconstruct or reorganize; restore previous constitution of. **reconstitution** n.

**reconstruct** /riːkənˈstrʌkt/ v.t. build again; restore mentally; reorganize. **reconstruction** n.

**record** 1 /rɪˈkɔːd/ v. put in writing or other permanent form; set down for remembrance or reference; put into permanent form for later reproduction. 2 /ˈrekɔːd/ n. being recorded, recorded state; recorded evidence or information etc.; document or monument preserving it; facts known about person's past; disc from which recorded sound can be reproduced; best performance or most remarkable event of its kind. 3 **have a record** have been convicted on previous occasion; **off the record** unofficially, confidentially; **on record** legally or otherwise recorded; **record-player** gramophone.

**recorder** /rɪˈkɔːdə(r)/ n. judge in certain courts; recording apparatus; woodwind musical instrument.

**recording** /rɪˈkɔːdɪŋ/ n. process of recording sound etc. for later reproduction; sound etc. thus recorded; television programme recorded on film.

**recount** /rɪˈkaʊnt/ v.t. narrate; tell in detail.

**re-count** 1 /riːˈkaʊnt/ v.t. count again. 2 /ˈriːkaʊnt/ n. re-counting, esp. of votes.

**recoup** /rɪˈkuːp/ v. recover or regain (loss); compensate or reimburse for loss. **recoup oneself** recover loss. **recoupment** n.

**recourse** /rɪˈkɔːs/ n. resorting to possible source of help; person or thing resorted to.

**recover** /rɪˈkʌvə(r)/ v. regain possession or use or control of; come back to life or health or normal state or position; secure by legal process; make up for; retrieve. **recovery** n.

**recreant** /ˈrekrɪənt/ 1 a. craven, cowardly. 2 n. coward.

**re-create** /riːkrɪˈeɪt/ v.t. create anew.

**recreation** /rekrɪˈeɪʃ(ə)n/ n. (means of) entertaining oneself; pleasurable exercise or employment.

**recriminate** /rɪˈkrɪməneɪt/ v.i. make mutual or counter accusations. **recrimination** n.; **recriminatory** a.

**recrudesce** /riːkruːˈdes/ v.i. (of disease or sore etc.) break out again. **recrudescence** n.; **recrudescent** a.

**recruit** /rɪˈkruːt/ 1 n. newly enlisted soldier; person who joins society etc. 2 v. enlist recruits (for), enlist (person); replenish, reinvigorate. 3 **recruitment** n.

**rectal** /ˈrekt(ə)l/ a. of or by means of rectum.

**rectangle** /ˈrektæŋɡ(ə)l/ n. 4-sided plane rectilinear figure with 4 right angles. **rectangular** /-ˈtæŋ-/ a.

**rectify** /ˈrektɪfaɪ/ v.t. adjust or make right; *Chem.* purify, esp. by redistilling;

**rectilinear** /rektɪ'lɪnɪə(r)/ *a.* bounded or characterized by straight lines; in or forming straight line.

**rectitude** /'rektɪtjuːd/ *n.* moral uprightness.

**recto** /'rektəʊ/ *n.* (*pl.* **-tos**) right-hand page of open book; front of leaf.

**rector** /'rektə(r)/ *n.* incumbent of parish where all tithes formerly passed to incumbent; head priest of church etc.; head of university or college or religious institution. **rectorship** *n.*

**rectory** /'rektərɪ/ *n.* rector's house.

**rectum** /'rektəm/ *n.* (*pl.* **-tums**) final section of large intestine.

**recumbent** /rɪ'kʌmbənt/ *a.* lying down, reclining.

**recuperate** /rɪ'kuːpəreɪt/ *v.* recover from exhaustion or illness or loss etc.; regain (health or losses etc.). **recuperation** *n.*; **recuperative** *a.*

**recur** /rɪ'kɜː(r)/ *v.i.* occur again; go back in thought or speech; *Math.* (of decimal figure etc.) be repeated indefinitely.

**recurrent** /rɪ'kʌrənt/ *a.* recurring. **recurrence** *n.*

**recusant** /'rekjʊz(ə)nt/ *n.* person refusing submission or compliance; *hist.* person who refused to attend Anglican services. **recusancy** *n.*

**recycle** /riː'saɪk(ə)l/ *v.t.* return (material) to previous stage of cyclic process, esp. convert (waste) to reusable material.

**red** 1 *a.* of colour from crimson to orange; (of hair) reddish-brown; having to do with bloodshed, burning, violence, or revolution; communist. 2 *n.* red colour, paint, clothes, etc.; debit side of account; socialist or communist. 3 **in the red** in debt; **red-back spider** venomous Aus. spider with red stripe on its back; **red-blooded** virile, vigorous; **redbreast** robin; **redcoat** *hist.* British soldier; **Red Cross** international relief organization; **redfish** *Aus.* nannygai; **red flag** symbol of revolution, danger signal; **red-handed** in act of crime; **redhead** person with red hair; **red herring** irrelevant diversion; **red-hot** heated to redness, furious, excited; **Red Indian** N. Amer. Indian; **red kangaroo** large kangaroo of Central Australia; **red lead** red oxide of lead as pigment etc.; **red-letter day** joyfully memorable day; **red light** stop signal, warning; **red Ned** *Aus. sl.* rough red wine; **red pepper** cayenne pepper, red capsicum; **red rag** thing that excites rage; **red-shift** *Astron.* movement of spectrum to longer wavelengths in light from distant galaxies; **redskin** Red Indian; **red tape** excessive bureaucracy or formalities esp. in public business; **redwing** kind of thrush; **redwood** tree yielding red wood. **reddish** *a.*

**redcurrant** /'redkʌrənt/ *n.* small round red berry; shrub bearing it.

**redden** /'red(ə)n/ *v.* make or become red.

**redeem** /rɪ'diːm/ *v.t.* recover by expenditure of effort; make single payment to cancel (regular charge etc.); convert (tokens or bonds) into goods or cash; deliver from sin and damnation; make amends or compensate for; save, rescue, reclaim; fulfil (promise).

**redeemer** *n.* one who redeems, esp. Christ.

**redemption** /rɪ'dempʃ(ə)n/ *n.* redeeming or being redeemed. **redemptive** *a.*

**redeploy** /riːdɪ'plɔɪ/ *v.t.* send (troops, workers) to new place or task. **redeployment** *n.*

**rediffusion** /riːdɪ'fjuːʒ(ə)n/ *n.* relaying of broadcast programmes esp. by wire from central receiver.

**redolent** /'redələnt/ *a.* strongly smelling or suggestive *of*. **redolence** *n.*

**redouble** /riː'dʌb(ə)l/ *v.* make or grow greater or more intense or numerous; double again.

**redoubt** /rɪ'daʊt/ *n.* detached outwork without flanking defences.

**redoubtable** /rɪ'daʊtəb(ə)l/ *a.* formidable.

**redound** /rɪ'daʊnd/ *v.i.* make great contribution *to* one's advantage etc.; recoil *on* or *upon*.

**redress** /rɪ'dres/ 1 *v.t.* remedy, make up for; put right again. 2 *n.* compensation, reparation; redressing.

**reduce** /rɪ'djuːs/ *v.* make or become smaller or less; bring by force or necessity *to* some new state or action; convert to or *to* other (esp. simpler) form; subdue; bring lower; lessen one's weight or size; weaken; impoverish. **reducible** *a.*

**reduction** /rəˈdʌkʃ(ə)n/ *n.* reducing or being reduced; amount by which prices etc. are reduced; reduced copy of picture etc.

**redundant** /rəˈdʌnd(ə)nt/ *a.* superfluous; that can be omitted without loss of significance; (of worker) no longer needed for any available job and therefore liable to dismissal. **redundancy** *n.*

**reduplicate** /rəˈdjuːplɪkeɪt/ *v.t.* make double; repeat. **reduplication** *n.*

**re-echo** /riːˈekəʊ/ *v.* echo repeatedly; resound.

**reed** *n.* firm-stemmed water or marsh plant; tall straight stalk of this; vibrating part of some musical wind instruments; in *pl.* such instruments. **reedmace** tall waterside plant with brown flower-spikes.

**reedy** /ˈriːdɪ/ *a.* full of reeds; like reed; like reed instrument in tone.

**reef**¹ *n.* ridge of rock or sand etc. at or near surface of water; lode of ore, bedrock surrounding this.

**reef**² 1 *n.* one of several strips along top or bottom of sail that can be taken in and rolled up. 2 *v.t.* take in reef(s) of (sail). 3 **reef-knot** symmetrical double knot.

**reefer** /ˈriːfə(r)/ *n.* marijuana cigarette.

**reek** 1 *v.i.* smell unpleasantly (*of*); have suspicious associations. 2 *n.* foul or stale smell; smoke, vapour, exhalation.

**reel** 1 *n.* cylindrical device on which thread, paper, film, wire, etc., are wound; device for winding and unwinding line as required esp. in fishing; lively Sc. dance; music for this. 2 *v.* wind on reel; draw *in* or *up* by means of reel; rattle *off* without pause or apparent effort; stand or walk unsteadily; be shaken physically or mentally; dance reel.

**re-entrant** /riːˈentrənt/ *a.* (of angle) pointing inwards.

**re-entry** /riːˈentrɪ/ *n.* act of entering again, esp. (of spacecraft etc.) of re-entering earth's atmosphere.

**reeve**¹ *n. hist.* chief magistrate of town or district.

**reeve**² *v.t.* (*past* **rove**) *Naut.* thread (rope, rod, etc.) *through* ring etc.; fasten (rope, block) thus.

**ref** *n. colloq.* referee.

**refectory** /rəˈfektərɪ/ *n.* room for meals in monastery, college, etc. **refectory table** long narrow table.

**refer** /rəˈfɜː(r)/ *v.* (*past & p.p.* **referred**) trace or ascribe *to*; assign *to*; send on or direct *to* some authority or source of information; make allusion or have relation *to*. **referable** *a.*

**referee** /refəˈriː/ 1 *n.* arbitrator, person chosen to decide between opposing parties; umpire, esp. in football or boxing; person willing to testify to character of applicant for employment etc. 2 *v.* act as referee (for).

**reference** *n.* referring to some authority; scope given to such authority; relation or respect or allusion etc. *to*; direction *to* page, book, etc. where information may be found; written testimonial, person giving it. **reference book** book for occasional consultation at particular points for information; **reference library** library of books that may be consulted but not taken away. **referential** *a.*

**referendum** /refəˈrendəm/ *n.* (*pl.* **-dums**) referring of question to electorate for direct decision.

**referral** /rəˈfɜːr(ə)l/ *n.* referring esp. of person to medical specialist etc.

**refill** 1 /riːˈfɪl/ *v.t.* fill again. 2 /ˈriːfɪl/ *n.* what serves to refill anything.

**refine** /rəˈfaɪn/ *v.* free from impurities or defects; make or become more elegant or cultured.

**refinement** *n.* refining or being refined; fineness of feeling or taste; elegance; instance of added development; piece of subtle reasoning, fine distinction.

**refinery** /rəˈfaɪnərɪ/ *n.* place where oil etc. is refined.

**refit** 1 /riːˈfɪt/ *v.* make or become fit again (esp. of ship undergoing repairs etc.) 2 /ˈriːfɪt/ *n.* refitting. 3 **refitment** *n.*

**reflate** /riːˈfleɪt/ *v.t.* cause reflation of (currency, economy, etc.).

**reflation** /riːˈfleɪʃ(ə)n/ *n.* inflation of financial system to restore previous condition after deflation.

**reflect** /rəˈflekt/ *v.* throw back (light, heat, sound); (of mirror etc.) show image of, reproduce to eye or mind; bring credit, discredit, etc., on; meditate, consider.

**reflection** /rəˈflekʃ(ə)n/ *n.* reflecting or

**reflective** /rəˈflektɪv/ *a.* (of surface) giving back reflection or image; concerned in reflection or thought; thoughtful, given to meditation.

**reflector** /rəˈflektə(r)/ *n.* piece of glass or metal for reflecting light etc. in required direction; telescope etc. using mirror to produce images.

**reflex** /ˈriːfleks/ 1 *a.* (of angle) larger than 180°; (of action) independent of the will. 2 *n.* reflex action; reflected light or image. 3 **reflex camera** camera in which image is reflected by mirror to allow focusing up to moment of exposure.

**reflexion** var. of **reflection**.

**reflexive** /rəˈfleksɪv/ 1 *a. Gram.* (of word or form) implying subject's action on himself or itself. 2 *n.* reflexive word or form.

**reform** /rəˈfɔːm/ 1 *v.* make or become better; abolish or cure (abuse etc.). 2 *n.* removal of abuses esp. in politics; improvement. 3 **reformative** *a.*

**reformation** /ˌrefəˈmeɪʃ(ə)n/ *n.* reforming or being reformed, esp. radical change for the better in political or religious or social affairs; **the Reformation** 16th-c. movement for reform of abuses in Roman Church ending in establishment of Reformed or Protestant Churches.

**reformatory** /rəˈfɔːmətəri/ 1 *a.* tending or intended to produce reform. 2 *n. US* institution to which young offenders are sent to be reformed.

**reformer** /rəˈfɔːmə(r)/ *n.* advocate of reform; leader in Reformation.

**refract** /rəˈfrækt/ *v.t.* deflect (light) at certain angle when it enters obliquely a medium of different density. **refraction** *n.*; **refractive** *a.*

**refractor** /rəˈfræktə(r)/ *n.* refracting medium or lens; telescope using lens to produce image.

**refractory** /rəˈfræktəri/ *a.* stubborn, unmanageable; rebellious; resistant to heat, treatment, etc.

**refrain**[1] /rɪˈfreɪn/ *v.* hold back, keep oneself (*from* thing or action).

**refrain**[2] /rɪˈfreɪn/ *n.* recurring phrase or lines esp. at end of stanzas.

**refresh** /rɪˈfreʃ/ *v.t.* give fresh spirit or vigour to; freshen up (memory).

**refresher** *n.* extra fee to counsel in prolonged lawsuit.

**refreshment** *n.* refreshing or being refreshed in mind or body; thing esp. (usu. in *pl.*) food or drink that refreshes.

**refrigerant** /rəˈfrɪdʒərənt/ 1 *n.* substance used for refrigeration. 2 *a.* refrigerating.

**refrigerate** /rəˈfrɪdʒəreɪt/ *v.* make or become cool or cold; subject (food etc.) to low temperature, esp. to preserve it. **refrigeration** *n.*

**refrigerator** /rəˈfrɪdʒəreɪtə(r)/ *n.* cabinet or room in which food etc. is refrigerated.

**reft** *pred. a.* taken or torn (*away, from*).

**refuge** /ˈrefjuːdʒ/ *n.* shelter from pursuit or danger or trouble; person or place offering this.

**refugee** /ˌrefjuːˈdʒiː/ *n.* person taking refuge, esp. in foreign country from war or persecution or natural disaster.

**refulgent** /rəˈfʌldʒ(ə)nt/ *a.* shining, gloriously bright. **refulgence** *n.*

**refund** 1 /rəˈfʌnd/ *v.* pay back; reimburse. 2 /ˈriːfʌnd/ *n.* repayment, money etc. repaid.

**refurbish** /riːˈfɜːbɪʃ/ *v.t.* brighten up, redecorate.

**refusal** /rəˈfjuːz(ə)l/ *n.* refusing or being refused; chance of taking thing before it is offered to others.

**refuse**[1] /rəˈfjuːz/ *v.* withhold acceptance of or consent to; indicate unwillingness; not grant request made by (person); (of horse) be unwilling to jump (fence etc.).

**refuse**[2] /ˈrefjuːs/ *n.* what is rejected as worthless; waste.

**refute** /rəˈfjuːt/ *v.t.* prove falsity or error of; rebut by argument. **refutation** /ˌrefjuːˈteɪʃ(ə)n/ *n.*

**regain** /riːˈɡeɪn/ *v.t.* gain back possession of; reach (place) again.

**regal** /ˈriːɡ(ə)l/ *a.* of or by king(s); magnificent. **regality** *n.*

**regale** /rəˈɡeɪl/ *v.t.* entertain lavishly (*with*); give delight to.

**regalia** /rəˈɡeɪliə/ *n.pl.* insignia of royalty used at coronation etc.; insignia of an order or of civic dignity.

**regard** /rəˈɡɑːd/ 1 *v.* gaze upon; give heed to, take into account; look upon or contemplate mentally in specified

# regardful

way. **2** *n.* look; attention, heed, care, concern; esteem; in *pl.* expression of friendly feelings. **3 as regards** about, in respect of; **with regard to** in respect of.

**regardful** /rə'gɑːdfəl/ *a.* not neglectful *of*.

**regarding** /rə'gɑːdɪŋ/ *prep.* concerning, related to.

**regardless** /rə'gɑːdləs/ **1** *a.* without regard or consideration (*of*); without paying attention.

**regatta** /rə'gætə/ *n.* meeting for boat or yacht races.

**regency** /'riːdʒənsɪ/ **1** *n.* office of regent; commission acting as regent; regent's or regency commission's period of office. **the Regency** 1810-20. **2** *a.* of or in style of Regency.

**regenerate 1** /rɪ'dʒenəreɪt/ *v.* generate again, bring or come into renewed existence; improve moral condition of; breathe more vigorous life into; invest with new and higher spiritual nature. **2** /rɪ'dʒenərət/ *a.* spiritually born again; reformed. **3 regeneration** *n.*; **regenerative** *a.*

**regent** /'riːdʒ(ə)nt/ **1** *n.* person appointed to administer kingdom during minority, absence, or incapacity of monarch. **2** *a.* (placed after *n.*) acting as regent.

**reggae** /'regeɪ/ *n.* W. Ind. style of music with strongly accented subsidiary beat.

**regicide** /'redʒəsaɪd/ *n.* person who kills or takes part in killing a king; killing of a king. **regicidal** *a.*

**regime** /reɪ'ʒiːm/ *n.* method of government; prevailing system of things.

**regimen** /'redʒəmen/ *n.* prescribed course of treatment, way of life, or esp. diet.

**regiment** /'redʒəmənt/ **1** *n.* permanent unit of army consisting of several battalions or troops or companies; large array or number. **2** *v.t.* organize in groups or according to system; form into regiment(s). **3 regimentation** *n.*

**regimental** /redʒə'ment(ə)l/ **1** *a.* of a regiment. **2** *n.* in *pl.* military uniform, esp. of particular regiment.

**region** /'riːdʒ(ə)n/ *n.* area of land or division of the earth's surface, having definable characteristics; administrative district, esp. in Scotland; part of body; sphere or realm *of.* **regional** *a.*

# regular

**register** /'redʒəstə(r)/ **1** *n.* official list; book in which items are recorded for reference; device recording speed etc.; adjustable plate for regulating draught etc.; compass of voice or instrument. **2** *v.* record in writing; enter or cause to be entered in register; send (letter) by registered post; enter one's name in register; record automatically, indicate; make mental note of; show (emotion etc.) in face etc.; make impression. **3 registered post** postal procedure with special precautions and compensation in case of loss.

**registrar** /ˌredʒɪ'strɑː(r)/ *n.* person charged with keeping register; doctor undergoing hospital training as specialist.

**registration** /ˌredʒəs'treɪʃ(ə)n/ *n.* registering or being registered. **registration mark, number,** combination of letters and numbers identifying motor vehicle.

**registry** /'redʒəstrɪ/ *n.* place where registers or records are kept. **registry office** place where civil marriages are conducted.

**Regius professor** /'riːdʒəs/ holder of British university chair founded by sovereign or filled by Crown appointment.

**regress 1** /rɪ'gres/ *v.t.* move backwards. **2** /'riːgres/ *n.* going back; backward tendency.

**regression** /rə'greʃ(ə)n/ *n.* backward movement; relapse; return to earlier stage of development. **regressive** *a.*

**regret** /rə'gret/ **1** *v.t.* feel or express sorrow or repentance or distress over (action or loss); say with sorrow or remorse. **2** *n.* sorrow or repentance etc. over action or loss etc. **3 regretful** *a.*

**regrettable** *a.* undesirable, unwelcome; deserving censure.

**regular** /'regjələ(r)/ **1** *a.* conforming to a rule or principle; consistent; systematic; habitual; (of soldier) being member of regular army; not capricious or casual; acting or done uniformly in time or manner; correct; *Eccl.* bound by religious rule, belonging to monastic order. **2** *n.* regular soldier; regular customer or visitor etc.; one of regular clergy. **3 regular army** of professional soldiers. **4 regularity** *n.*; **regularize** *v.t.*; **regularization** *n.*

**regulate** /ˈregjəleɪt/ v.t. control by rule, subject to restrictions; adapt to requirements; adjust (clock, watch, etc.) to work accurately. **regulator** n.

**regulation** /regjəˈleɪʃ(ə)n/ 1 n. regulating or being regulated; prescribed rule. 2 a. in accordance with regulations, of correct pattern etc.

**regurgitate** /riːˈgɜːdʒɪteɪt/ v.t. bring (swallowed food) up again to mouth; pour or cast out again. **regurgitation** n.

**rehabilitate** /riːhəˈbɪlɪteɪt/ v.t. restore to rights or reputation etc. or to previous condition or normal health or capacity, etc. **rehabilitation** n.

**rehash** 1 /riːˈhæʃ/ v.t. put into new form, without significant change or improvement. 2 /ˈriːhæʃ/ n. rehashing, material rehashed.

**rehearsal** /rɪˈhɜːs(ə)l/ n. rehearsing; trial performance or practice.

**rehearse** /rɪˈhɜːs/ v. practise before performing in public; recite or say over; give list of, enumerate.

**Reich** /raɪx/ n. the former German State, esp. (**Third Reich**) Nazi regime.

**reign** /reɪn/ 1 n. sovereignty, rule; sovereign's period of rule. 2 v.i. be king or queen; prevail.

**reimburse** /riːɪmˈbɜːs/ v.t. repay (person); refund. **reimbursement** n.

**rein** /reɪn/ 1 n. long narrow strap used to guide horse; fig. means of control. 2 v.t. check, pull back or up or hold in with reins; fig. govern, control.

**reincarnation** /riːɪnkɑːˈneɪʃ(ə)n/ n. rebirth of soul in new body. **reincarnate** /-ˈkɑːnət/ a.

**reindeer** /ˈreɪndɪə(r)/ n. subarctic deer with large antlers.

**reinforce** /riːɪmˈfɔːs/ v.t. support or strengthen by additional men or material. **reinforced concrete** concrete with metal bars etc. embedded in it.

**reinforcement** n. reinforcing or being reinforced; in pl. additional men, ships, aircraft, etc., for military or naval force.

**reinstate** /riːɪmˈsteɪt/ v.t. re-establish in or restore to lost position or privileges etc. **reinstatement** n.

**reinsure** /riːɪmˈʃʊə(r)/ or /-ˈʃɔː(r)/ v. insure again (esp. of insurer securing himself by transferring risk to another insurer). **reinsurance** n.

**reiterate** /riːˈɪtəreɪt/ v.t. repeat over again or several times. **reiteration** n.; **reiterative** a.

**reject** 1 /rəˈdʒekt/ v.t. refuse to accept or believe in; put aside or send back as not to be used or done or complied with. 2 /ˈriːdʒekt/ n. rejected thing or person. 3 **rejection** n.

**rejoice** /rəˈdʒɔɪs/ v. feel joy, be glad; take delight in or at; cause joy to.

**rejoin**[1] /riːˈdʒɔɪn/ v. join again; reunite.

**rejoin**[2] /rəˈdʒɔɪn/ v. say in answer; retort.

**rejoinder** /rəˈdʒɔɪndə(r)/ n. what is rejoined or said in reply.

**rejuvenate** /rəˈdʒuːvəneɪt/ v.t. make young again. **rejuvenation** n.; **rejuvenator** n.

**relapse** /rəˈlæps/ 1 v.i. fall back into worse state after improvement. 2 n. relapsing, esp. deterioration in patient's condition after partial recovery.

**relate** /rəˈleɪt/ v. narrate, recount; bring into relation; have reference to; bring oneself into relation to; in p.p. connected, akin by blood or marriage.

**relation** /rəˈleɪʃ(ə)n/ n. connection between persons or things; kinsman, kinswoman, relative; narration, narrative. **relational** a.

**relationship** /rəˈleɪʃənʃɪp/ n. state of being related; condition or character due to being related; connection between persons or things; kinship.

**relative** /ˈrelətɪv/ 1 a. in relation or proportion to something else; implying comparison or relation; having application or reference to; Gram. (of word, clause, etc.) referring to expressed or implied antecedent, attached to antecedent by such word. 2 n. person connected by blood or marriage; species related to another by common origin; relative word, esp. pronoun.

**relativity** /reləˈtɪvətiː/ n. relativeness; theory based on principle that all motion is relative and that light has constant velocity in a vacuum.

**relax** /rəˈlæks/ v. make or become less stiff or rigid or tense or formal or strict; reduce or abate.

**relaxation** /riːlækˈseɪʃ(ə)n/ n. relaxing; recreation, amusements.

**relay** /ˈriːleɪ/ 1 n. fresh set of people or horses to replace tired ones; gang of men, supply of materials, etc. similarly

**release** /rə'li:s/ 1 *v.t.* set free, liberate, unfasten; allow to move from fixed position; make (information) public; exhibit etc. (film etc.) generally or for first time. 2 *n.* liberation from confinement or fixed position or trouble etc.; handle or catch etc. that releases part of machine etc.; document etc. made available for publication; film or record etc. that is released; releasing of document or film etc.

**relegate** /'reləgeɪt/ *v.t.* consign or dismiss to inferior position; transfer (team) to lower division of league. **relegation** *n.*

**relent** /rə'lent/ *v.i.* relax severity; yield to compassion.

**relentless** /rə'lentləs/ *a.* unrelenting.

**relevant** /'reləv(ə)nt/ *a.* bearing upon or pertinent *to* matter in hand. **relevance** *n.*

**reliable** /rə'laɪəb(ə)l/ *a.* that may be relied upon. **reliability** *n.*

**reliance** /rə'laɪəns/ *n.* trust, confidence. **reliant** *a.*

**relic** /'relɪk/ *n.* part of holy person's body or belongings kept as object of reverence; in *pl.* dead body, remains, of person, what has survived destruction or wasting; surviving trace or memorial *of.*

**relict** /'relɪkt/ *n.* object which has survived in primitive form.

**relief** /rə'li:f/ *n.* alleviation of or deliverance from pain or distress etc.; feature etc. that diversifies monotony or relaxes tension; assistance given to persons in special danger or need; replacing of person(s) on duty by another or others; persons thus bringing relief; thing supplementing another in some service; method of carving, moulding, etc., in which design projects from surface; piece of sculpture etc. in relief; effect of being done in relief given by colour or shading etc.; delivery of place from siege. **relief map** one showing hills and valleys by shading or colouring etc.

**relieve** /rə'li:v/ *v.t.* bring or give or be relief to; release (person) from duty by taking his place or providing a substitute. **relieve oneself** urinate or defecate.

**religion** /rə'lɪdʒ(ə)n/ *n.* belief in superhuman controlling power, esp. in a personal God or gods entitled to obedience; system of faith and worship; life under monastic conditions.

**religious** /rə'lɪdʒəs/ 1 *a.* imbued with religion, devout; of or concerned with religion. 2 *n.* (*pl.* same) person bound by monastic vows.

**relinquish** /rə'lɪŋkwɪʃ/ *v.t.* give up, let go, resign, surrender. **relinquishment** *n.*

**reliquary** /'reləkwəri/ *n.* receptacle for relics.

**relish** /'relɪʃ/ 1 *n.* liking or enjoyment *for*; appetizing flavour, attractive quality; thing eaten with plainer food to add flavour; distinctive flavour or taste *of.* 2 *v.* get pleasure out of, enjoy greatly.

**reluctant** /rə'lʌkt(ə)nt/ *a.* unwilling, disinclined. **reluctance** *n.*

**rely** /rə'laɪ/ *v.i.* depend with confidence (*up*)*on* (person or thing).

**relocate** /ri:ləʊ'keɪt/ *v.* locate in or move to new place. **relocation** *n.*

**remain** /rə'meɪn/ *v.i.* be left over; stay in same place or condition; be left behind; continue to be.

**remainder** /rə'meɪndə(r)/ 1 *n.* residue; remaining persons or things; *Arith.* number left after subtraction or division; copies of book left unsold. 2 *v.t.* dispose of remaining stocks of (book) at reduced price.

**remains** /rə'meɪnz/ *n.pl.* what remains over; surviving parts or amount; relics of antiquity etc.; dead body.

**remand** /rə'mɑ:nd or -mænd/ 1 *v.t.* send back (prisoner) into custody to allow of further inquiry. 2 *n.* recommittal to custody. 3 **remand centre, home,** place of detention for juvenile offenders.

**remark** /rə'mɑ:k/ *v.* say by way of comment; make comment (*up*)*on*; take notice of. 2 *n.* comment; noticing; thing said.

**remarkable** /rə'mɑ:kəb(ə)l/ *a.* worth notice; exceptional, striking.

**remedial** /rə'mi:dɪəl/ *a.* affording or intended as a remedy; (of teaching) for slow or backward children.

**remedy** /'remədi/ 1 n. healing medicine or treatment; means of removing anything undesirable; redress. 2 v.t. rectify, make good. 3 **remediable** /-'mi:d-/ a.

**remember** /rə'membə(r)/ v.t. retain in or recall to memory; not forget; convey greetings from; make present to, tip.

**remembrance** /rə'membrəns/ n. remembering or being remembered; keepsake, souvenir; in pl. greetings conveyed through third person.

**remind** /rə'maɪnd/ v.t. cause (person) to remember or think of.

**reminder** /rə'maɪndə(r)/ n. thing that reminds or is memento (of).

**reminisce** /remə'nɪs/ v.i. indulge in reminiscence(s).

**reminiscence** /remə'nɪs(ə)ns/ n. remembering of things past; in pl. account of things remembered, esp. in literary form.

**reminiscent** /remə'nɪs(ə)nt/ a. reminding or suggestive of; concerned with reminiscence.

**remiss** /rə'mɪs/ a. careless of duty; negligent.

**remission** /rə'mɪʃ(ə)n/ n. shortening of prison sentence on account of good behaviour; remittance of debt etc.; diminution of force etc.; forgiveness of sins etc.

**remit** 1 /rə'mɪt/ v. (past & p.p. **remitted**) refrain from exacting or inflicting (debt, punishment, etc.); abate, slacken; send (esp. money); refer to some authority, send back to lower court; postpone, defer; pardon (sins, etc.). 2 /'ri:mæt/ n. terms of reference of committee etc.

**remittance** /rə'mɪt(ə)ns/ n. money sent to person; sending of money. **remittance man** Aus. hist. English immigrant supported by remittances from home.

**remittent** /rə'mɪt(ə)nt/ a. that abates at intervals.

**remnant** /'remn(ə)nt/ n. small remaining quantity; piece of cloth etc. left when greater part has been used or sold.

**remonstrate** /'remənstreɪt/ v. make protest with (person). **remonstrance** /-'mɒn-/ n.; **remonstration** n.

**remorse** /rə'mɔ:s/ n. bitter repentance; compunction. **remorseful** a.

**remorseless** /rə'mɔ:sləs/ a. without compassion.

**remote** /rə'məʊt/ a. far apart or away in place or time; out-of-the-way, secluded; not closely related; aloof, not friendly. **remote control** control of apparatus etc. from a distance.

**remould** 1 /ri:'məʊld/ v.t. mould again, refashion; reconstruct tread of (tyre). 2 /'ri:məʊld/ n. remoulded tyre.

**removal** /rə'mu:v(ə)l/ n. removing or being removed; transfer of furniture etc. to different house.

**removalist** /rə'mu:vəlɪst/ n. Aus. furniture etc. remover.

**remove** /rə'mu:v/ 1 v. take off or away from place occupied; convey to another place; dismiss; change one's residence, go away from; in p.p. distant or remote from. 2 n. distance, degree of remoteness; stage in gradation; form or division in some schools.

**removed** /rə'mu:vd/ a. (of cousins) **once, twice,** etc. **removed** with difference of one, two, etc., generations.

**remunerate** /rə'mju:nəreɪt/ v.t. pay for service rendered.

**remuneration** /rəmju:nə'reɪʃ(ə)n/ n. remunerating or being remunerated; what is received as pay.

**remunerative** /rə'mju:nərətɪv/ a. profitable.

**Renaissance** /rə'neɪs(ə)ns/ n. revival of arts and literature in 14th-16th cc.; style of art and architecture developed by it; **renaissance** any similar revival.

**renal** /'ri:n(ə)l/ a. of kidneys.

**renascent** /rə'næs(ə)nt/ a. springing up anew; being reborn. **renascence** n.

**rend** v. (past & p.p. **rent**) arch. tear or wrench; split or divide.

**render** /'rendə(r)/ v.t. cause to be or become; give in return; pay as due; present, submit; reproduce, portray; perform, translate; melt (fat) down; give (first) coat of plaster etc. to.

**rendezvous** /'rɒndeɪvu:/ 1 n. (pl. same /-vu:z/) agreed or regular meeting-place; meeting by appointment. 2 v.i. (3 sing. **-vouses** /-vu:z/; past & p.p. **-voused** /-vu:d/; partic. **-vousing** /-vu:ɪŋ/) meet at rendezvous.

**rendition** /ren'dɪʃ(ə)n/ n. rendering, performance, interpretation.

**renegade** /'renəgeɪd/ n. deserter of party or principles.

**renege** /rɪˈniːg/ v.i. go back *on* promise; back out.

**renew** /rɪˈnjuː/ v. make new again; restore to original state; replace; repeat; continue or resume; grant or be granted continuation of (licence etc.). **renewal** n.

**rennet** /ˈrenɪt/ n. curdled milk from calf's stomach, or artificial preparation, used in curdling milk for cheese or junket etc.

**renounce** /rɪˈnaʊns/ v.t. consent formally to abandon; repudiate; decline further association with.

**renovate** /ˈrenəveɪt/ v.t. restore to good condition; repair. **renovation** n.

**renown** /rɪˈnaʊn/ n. fame, high distinction.

**renowned** /rɪˈnaʊnd/ a. famous; celebrated.

**rent**[1] n. periodical payment for use of land or premises; payment for hire of machinery etc. 2 v. take or occupy or use for rent; let or hire for rent; be let (*at*).

**rent**[2] n. tear in garment etc.; gap, cleft, fissure.

**rent**[3] past & p.p. of **rend**.

**rental** /ˈrent(ə)l/ n. amount paid or received as rent; act of renting; income from rents.

**rentier** /ˈrãtieɪ/ n. person living on income from property or investments. [F]

**renunciation** /rɪnʌnsɪˈeɪʃ(ə)n/ n. renouncing, self-denial, giving up of things.

**rep**[1] n. corded upholstery fabric.

**rep**[2] n. *colloq.* representative, esp. commercial traveller.

**rep**[3] n. *colloq.* repertory theatre or company.

**repair**[1] v.t. restore to good condition after damage or wear; set right or make amends for. 2 n. restoring to sound condition; good or relative condition for working or using.

**repair**[2] v.i. resort; go (*to*).

**reparable** /ˈrepərəb(ə)l/ a. that can be repaired or made good.

**reparation** /repəˈreɪʃ(ə)n/ n. making of amends; compensation.

**repartee** /repɑːˈtiː/ n. witty retort; making of witty retorts.

**repast** /rɪˈpɑːst/ n. meal.

**repatriate** 1 /riːˈpætrɪeɪt/ v.t. return to native land. 2 /riːˈpætrɪət/ n. repatriated person. 3 **repatriation** n.

**repay** /riːˈpeɪ/ v. (*past & p.p.* **-paid**) pay back; return, retaliate; requite, recompense. **repayment** n.

**repeal** /rɪˈpiːl/ 1 v.t. annul, revoke. 2 n. repealing.

**repeat** /rɪˈpiːt/ 1 v.t. say or do over again; recite, report; reproduce; recur. 2 n. repeating; repeated broadcast programme; *Mus.* passage intended to be repeated.

**repeatedly** /rɪˈpiːtədlɪ/ adv. several times.

**repeater** /rɪˈpiːtə(r)/ n. person or thing that repeats; firearm that fires several shots without reloading; watch that strikes last quarter etc. again when required.

**repel** /rɪˈpel/ v.t. (*past & p.p.* **repelled**) drive back; ward off; be repulsive or distasteful to.

**repellent** /rɪˈpelənt/ 1 a. that repels. 2 n. substance that repels, esp. insects etc.

**repent** /rɪˈpent/ v. feel sorrow or regret for what one has done or left undone; think with regret or contrition *of*. **repentance** n.; **repentant** a.

**repercussion** /riːpəˈkʌʃ(ə)n/ n. indirect effect or reaction (*of*); recoil after impact.

**repertoire** /ˈrepətwɑː(r)/ n. stock of pieces etc. that performer or company knows or is prepared to perform.

**repertory** /ˈrepətərɪ/ n. repertoire; theatrical performance of various plays for short periods by one company.

**repetition** /repəˈtɪʃ(ə)n/ n. repeating or being repeated; thing repeated, copy. **repetitious** a.; **repetitive** /-ˈpet-/ a.

**repine** /rɪˈpaɪn/ v.i. fret, be discontented.

**replace** /rɪˈpleɪs/ v.t. put back in place; take or fill up place of, be or provide substitute for; in *pass.* be succeeded or superseded (*by*).

**replacement** n. replacing or being replaced; person or thing that takes the place of another.

**replay** 1 /riːˈpleɪ/ v.t. play (match, recording, etc.) again. 2 /ˈriːpleɪ/ n. replaying (of match, recording of incident in game, etc.).

**replenish** /rɪˈplenɪʃ/ v.t. fill up again (*with*). **replenishment** n.

**replete** /rɪˈpliːt/ a. filled or well supplied *with*; sated. **repletion** n.

**replica** /ˈreplɪkə/ n. exact copy, model; duplicate made by original artist.

**replicate** /ˈreplɪkeɪt/ v.t. make replica of. **replication** n.

**reply** /rɪˈplaɪ/ 1 v. make an answer, respond. 2 n. replying; what is replied.

**report** /rɪˈpɔːt/ 1 v. bring back or give account of; tell as news; make official or formal statement; inform against; take down, write description of, etc., for publication; present oneself *to* (person); be responsible *to*. 2 n. account given or opinion formally expressed after investigation; description, reproduction, or epitome of speech, law case, scene, etc., esp. for newspaper publication; common talk, rumour; repute; account by teacher of pupil's conduct and progress; sound of explosion.

**reporter** n. person employed to report news etc. for newspaper or broadcast.

**repose**[1] /rɪˈpəʊz/ 1 n. rest; sleep; peaceful state, tranquillity; restful effect. 2 v. rest, lay to rest, give rest to; be lying; be supported or based *on*. 3 **reposeful** a.

**repose**[2] /rɪˈpəʊz/ v.t. place (trust etc.) *in*.

**repository** /rɪˈpɒzɪtəri/ n. place where things are stored or may be found; receptacle; recipient *of* secrets etc.

**repp** var. of **rep**[1].

**reprehend** /reprɪˈhend/ v.t. rebuke, blame.

**reprehensible** /reprɪˈhensəb(ə)l/ a. blameworthy.

**represent** /reprɪˈzent/ v.t. stand for, correspond to; symbolize; present likeness of to mind or senses; describe or depict *as*; declare *to* be; allege *that*; show or play part of in action or show; be substitute or deputy for, esp. be accredited deputy for in legislative assembly etc. **representation** n.

**representational** /reprɪzenˈteɪʃən(ə)l/ a. (of art) seeking to portray objects etc. realistically.

**representative** /reprɪˈzentətɪv/ 1 a. typical of class; containing typical specimens of all or many classes; of or based on representation of body of persons, esp. whole people, in government or legislation. 2 n. sample, specimen; typical embodiment *of*; agent; person representing another or a section of community etc.

**repress** /rɪˈpres/ v.t. keep under; put down; suppress. **repression** n.; **repressive** a.

**reprieve** /rɪˈpriːv/ 1 v.t. postpone or remit execution of. 2 n. remission or commutation of capital sentence; respite.

**reprimand** /ˈreprəmɑːnd/ or -mænd/ 1 n. official rebuke. 2 v.t. rebuke officially.

**reprint** 1 /riːˈprɪnt/ v.t. print again. 2 /ˈriːprɪnt/ n. new printing of book etc., esp. without alterations; book etc. reprinted.

**reprisal** /rɪˈpraɪz(ə)l/ n. act of retaliation.

**reprise** /rɪˈpriːz/ n. *Mus.* repeated passage or song etc.

**reproach** /rɪˈprəʊtʃ/ 1 v.t. express disapproval to (person) for fault etc.; rebuke. 2 n. rebuke, censure; thing that brings discredit.

**reproachful** /rɪˈprəʊtʃfəl/ a. inclined to or expressing reproach.

**reprobate** /ˈreprəbeɪt/ n. unprincipled or immoral person.

**reprobation** /reprəˈbeɪʃ(ə)n/ n. strong condemnation.

**reproduce** /riːprəˈdjuːs/ v. produce copy or representation of; produce further members of same species by natural means; produce offspring of (one*self*, it*self*). **reproducible** a.

**reproduction** /riːprəˈdʌkʃ(ə)n/ n. reproducing; copy of painting etc.; *attrib.* (of furniture etc.) made in imitation of earlier style. **reproductive** a.

**reproof** /rɪˈpruːf/ n. blame; words expressing blame.

**reprove** /rɪˈpruːv/ v.t. rebuke, scold.

**reptile** /ˈreptaɪl/ n. member of class of cold-blooded vertebrates including snakes; mean grovelling person. **reptilian** /-ˈtɪl-/ a.

**republic** /rɪˈpʌblɪk/ n. State in which supreme power is held by the people or its elected representatives.

**republican** /rɪˈpʌblɪkən/ 1 a. of or characterizing etc. republic(s); advocating or supporting republican government. 2 n. supporter or advocate

**repudiate** /rɪˈpjuːdɪeɪt/ v. disown, disavow, deny; refuse to recognize or obey (authority) or discharge (obligation or debt). **repudiation** n.

**repugnance** /rɪˈpʌgn(ə)ns/ n. aversion, antipathy; inconsistency or incompatibility of ideas, tempers, etc.

**repugnant** /rɪˈpʌgn(ə)nt/ a. distasteful, contradictory, (to).

**repulse** /rɪˈpʌls/ 1 v.t. drive back; rebuff, reject. 2 n. defeat, rebuff.

**repulsion** /rɪˈpʌlʃ(ə)n/ n. aversion, disgust; *Phys.* tendency of bodies to repel each other.

**repulsive** /rɪˈpʌlsɪv/ a. causing aversion or loathing.

**reputable** /ˈrepjətəb(ə)l/ a. of good repute, respectable.

**reputation** /repjəˈteɪʃ(ə)n/ n. what is generally said or believed about character of person or thing; credit, respectability; credit or discredit.

**repute** /rɪˈpjuːt/ 1 n. reputation. 2 v.t. in *pass.* be generally considered.

**request** /rɪˈkwest/ 1 n. asking for something, thing asked for; being sought after, demand. 2 v.t. make request for or of; seek permission *to* do.

**requiem** /ˈrekwɪəm/ n. Mass for the dead; musical setting for this.

**require** /rɪˈkwaɪə(r)/ v.t. need; depend on for success etc.; lay down as imperative; demand or insist on.

**requirement** n. thing required; need.

**requisite** /ˈrekwəzɪt/ 1 a. required, necessary. 2 n. thing needed (*for* some purpose).

**requisition** /rekwəˈzɪʃ(ə)n/ 1 n. official order laying claim to use of property or materials; formal demand, usu. in writing. 2 v.t. demand use or supply of.

**requite** /rɪˈkwaɪt/ v.t. make return for; reward or avenge; give in return. **requital** n.

**reredos** /ˈrɪədɒs/ n. ornamental screen covering wall above back of altar.

**resale** /riːˈseɪl/ n. sale of thing bought.

**rescind** /rɪˈsɪnd/ v.t. abrogate, revoke, cancel. **rescission** /-ˈsɪʒ(ə)n/ n.

**rescript** /ˈriːskrɪpt/ n. edict or official pronouncement.

**rescue** /ˈreskjuː/ 1 v.t. save or set free from danger or harm. 2 n. rescuing or being rescued.

**research** /rɪˈsɜːtʃ/ 1 n. careful search or inquiry into subject to discover facts by study or investigation. 2 v. make researches (into or for).

**resemble** /rɪˈzemb(ə)l/ v.t. be like; have similarity to. **resemblance** n.

**resent** /rɪˈzent/ v.t. show or feel indignation at; feel injured or insulted by. **resentment** n.

**resentful** /rɪˈzentfəl/ a. feeling resentment.

**reservation** /rezəˈveɪʃ(ə)n/ n. reserving or being reserved; thing reserved (e.g. room in hotel); express or tacit limitation or exception; strip of land between carriageways of road; tract of land reserved esp. for exclusive occupation of group, tribe, etc.

**reserve** /rɪˈzɜːv/ 1 v.t. put aside or keep back for later occasion or special use; order to be retained or allocated for person at particular time; retain or secure; in *p.p.* reticent, uncommunicative. 2 n. thing reserved for future use; limitation or exception attached to something; self-restraint, coolness of manner; company's profit added to capital; in *sing.* or *pl.* assets kept readily available; troops withheld from action to reinforce or protect others; forces outside regular ones but available in emergency; extra player chosen as possible substitute in team; tract of land reserved for special use, esp. for occupation by animals; *Aus.* public park; *Aus.* area set aside for Aboriginals. 3 **reserve bank** *Aus.* central bank holding currency reserves; **reserve-grade** *Aus.* of second rank among teams in a sports club.

**reservist** /rɪˈzɜːvɪst/ n. member of reserve forces.

**reservoir** /ˈrezəvwɑː(r)/ n. large natural or artificial lake as source of area's water supply; receptacle for fluid; supply *of* facts etc.

**reshuffle** /riːˈʃʌf(ə)l/ 1 v.t. shuffle again; interchange posts of (Government ministers etc.). 2 n. reshuffling.

**reside** /rɪˈzaɪd/ v.i. have one's home; (of right etc.) be vested *in*; (of quality) be present *in*.

**residence** /ˈrezɪd(ə)ns/ n. residing;

place where one resides; abode. **in residence** dwelling at specified place.

**resident** /ˈrezəd(ə)nt/ **1** *n.* permanent inhabitant; guest staying at hotel. **2** *a.* having quarters on the spot; located *in*; residing; in residence.

**residential** /rezəˈdenʃ(ə)l/ *a.* suitable for or occupied by private houses; used as residence; connected with residence.

**residual** /rəˈzɪdjuːəl/ *a.* left as residue or residuum.

**residuary** /rəˈzɪdjuːəri/ *a.* of the residue of an estate; residual.

**residue** /ˈrezɪdjuː/ *n.* remainder, what is left over; what remains of estate when liabilities have been discharged.

**residuum** /rəˈzɪdjuːəm/ *n.* (*pl.* **-dua**) what remains esp. after combustion or evaporation.

**resign** /rəˈzaɪn/ *v.* give up office; relinquish, surrender; reconcile *oneself to*.

**resignation** /rezɪgˈneɪʃ(ə)n/ *n.* resigning esp. of an office; uncomplaining endurance.

**resigned** /rəˈzaɪnd/ *a.* having resigned oneself; content to endure; full or indicative of resignation.

**resilient** /rəˈzɪliːənt/ *a.* resuming original form after compression etc.; (of person) readily recovering from depression etc. **resilience** *n.*

**resin** /ˈrezɪn/ **1** *n.* sticky secretion of trees and plants; similar synthetic substance, esp. organic compound made by polymerization etc. and used in plastics. **2** *v.t.* rub or treat with resin. **3 resinous** *a.*

**resist** /rəˈzɪst/ *v.* withstand action or effect of; abstain from (pleasure etc.); strive against, oppose; offer resistance. **resistible** *a.*

**resistance** /rəˈzɪst(ə)ns/ *n.* act of resisting; power to resist; impeding effect exerted by material thing on another; *Phys.* property of resisting passage of electric current or heat etc.; *Electr.* resistor; secret organization resisting authority, esp. in conquered country. **resistant** *a.*

**resistor** /rəˈzɪstə(r)/ *n. Electr.* device having resistance to passage of current.

**resoluble** /rəˈzɒljəb(ə)l/ *a.* resolvable, analysable *into*.

**resolute** /ˈrezəluːt/ *a.* determined; bold; not vacillating or shrinking.

**resolution** /rezəˈluːʃ(ə)n/ *n.* resolute

temper or character or conduct; thing resolved on; formal expression of opinion of meeting; solving *of* question etc.; resolving or being resolved.

**resolve** /rəˈzɒlv/ **1** *v.* make up one's mind; cause to do this; pass resolution by vote; (cause to) separate into constituent parts, analyse; solve, settle; *Mus.* convert (discord), or be converted, into concord. **2** *n.* mental decision; determination.

**resonant** /ˈrezən(ə)nt/ *a.* echoing, resounding; continuing to sound; causing reinforcement or prolongation of sound, esp. by vibration. **resonance** *n.*

**resonate** /ˈrezəneɪt/ *v.i.* produce or show resonance. **resonator** *n.*

**resort** /rəˈzɔːt/ **1** *n.* place frequented esp. for holidays etc.; thing to which recourse is had, recourse; frequenting or being frequented. **2** *v.i.* turn for aid etc. *to*; go often or in numbers *to*. **3 in the last resort** when all else has failed.

**resound** /rəˈzaʊnd/ *v.i.* ring or echo; produce echoes, go on sounding, fill place with sound; be much mentioned or repeated.

**resounding** *a.* unmistakable, emphatic.

**resource** /rəˈzɔːs/ *n.* expedient, device; in *pl.* means of supplying what is needed; stock that can be drawn on; skill in devising expedients.

**resourceful** /rəˈzɔːsfəl/ *a.* good at devising expedients.

**respect** /rəˈspekt/ **1** *n.* deferential esteem; heed or regard *of*; detail, aspect; reference or relation (*to*); in *pl.* polite greetings. **2** *v.* treat or regard with deference or esteem; treat with consideration, spare.

**respectable** /rəˈspektəb(ə)l/ *a.* deserving respect; of fair social standing, honest and decent; of acceptably great amount or size or merit; befitting respectable persons. **respectability** *n.*

**respectful** /rəˈspektfəl/ *a.* showing deference.

**respecting** *prep.* with regard to.

**respective** /rəˈspektɪv/ *a.* concerning or appropriate to each of several individually; comparative.

**respectively** *adv.* for each separately or in turn, and in the order mentioned.

**respiration** /respəˈreɪʃ(ə)n/ *n.* breathing; plant's absorption of oxygen and

**respirator**

emission of carbon dioxide; single inspiration and expiration. **respiratory** /-'spɪr-/ *a.*

**respirator** /'respəreɪtə(r)/ *n.* apparatus worn over mouth and nose to filter etc. inhaled air; apparatus for maintaining artificial respiration.

**respire** /rə'spaɪə(r)/ *v.* breathe; take breath; (of plant) carry out respiration.

**respite** /'respaɪt/ **1** *n.* interval of rest or relief; delay permitted in discharge of obligation or suffering of penalty. **2** *v.t.* grant or bring respite to.

**resplendent** /rə'splend(ə)nt/ *a.* brilliant, glittering. **resplendence** *n.*

**respond** /rə'spɒnd/ *v.i.* make answer; act etc. in response (*to*).

**respondent** /rə'spɒnd(ə)nt/ **1** *n.* defendant esp. in appeal or divorce case. **2** *a.* in position of defendant.

**response** /rə'spɒns/ *n.* answer; action, feeling, etc. caused by stimulus etc.; part of liturgy said or sung in answer to priest.

**responsibility** /rəspɒnsə'bɪlətɪ/ *n.* being responsible; charge, trust.

**responsible** /rə'spɒnsəb(ə)l/ *a.* liable to be called to account; morally accountable for actions; of good credit and repute; trustworthy; involving responsibility.

**responsive** /rə'spɒnsɪv/ *a.* responding readily *to* some influence; sympathetic; answering; by way of answer.

**respray 1** /riː'spreɪ/ *v.t.* spray again (esp. to change colour of paint on vehicle). **2** /'riːspreɪ/ *n.* respraying.

**rest**[1] **1** *v.* cease from exertion or action; be still; lie in sleep or death; give relief or repose to; place or lie or lean or rely or base or depend etc. (*up*)*on*. **2** *n.* repose or sleep; resting; prop or support for steadying something; *Mus.* interval of silence, sign denoting this. **3 at rest** not moving, not agitated or troubled; **lay to rest** bury; **set at rest** settle, reassure.

**rest**[2] **1** *n.* the remainder or remaining parts or individuals (*of*). **2** *v.i.* remain in specified state. **3 for the rest** as regards anything else; **rest with** be in hands or charge or choice of.

**restaurant** /'restərɒnt/ *n.* public premises where meals may be had.

**restaurateur** /restərə'tɜː(r)/ *n.* restaurant-keeper.

**restful** /'restfəl/ *a.* quiet, soothing.

**restitution** /restɪ'tjuːʃ(ə)n/ *n.* restoring of property etc. to its owner; reparation.

**restive** /'restɪv/ *a.* fidgety; intractable, resisting control.

**restless** /'restləs/ *a.* finding or affording no rest; uneasy, agitated, fidgeting.

**restoration** /restə'reɪʃ(ə)n/ *n.* restoring or being restored; model or drawing representing supposed original form of extinct animal, ruined building, etc. **the Restoration** return of Charles II to throne of England in 1660.

**restorative** /rə'stɔːrətɪv/ **1** *a.* tending to restore health or strength. **2** *n.* restorative food or medicine etc.

**restore** /rə'stɔː(r)/ *v.t.* bring back to original state by rebuilding, repairing, etc.; give back; reinstate; bring back to former place or condition or use; make restoration of (extinct animal, ruined building, etc.).

**restrain** /rə'streɪn/ *v.t.* check or hold in (*from*); keep under control; repress; confine.

**restraint** /rə'streɪnt/ *n.* restraining or being restrained; agency or influence that restrains; self-control; avoidance of exaggeration; reserve.

**restrict** /rə'strɪkt/ *v.t.* confine, limit. **restriction** *n.*

**restrictive** /rə'strɪktɪv/ *a.* restricting. **restrictive practice** agreement or practice that limits efficiency or output in industry etc.

**result** /rə'zʌlt/ **1** *n.* consequence; issue; answer etc. got by calculation; (often in *pl.*) announcement of score or winner etc. in sporting event or examination. **2** *v.i.* arise as consequence, effect, or conclusion (*from*); end *in*.

**resultant** /rə'zʌlt(ə)nt/ **1** *a.* resulting. **2** *n.* force etc. equivalent to two or more forces acting in different directions at same point.

**resume** /rə'zjuːm/ *v.* begin again; recommence; take again or back. **resumption** *n.*; **resumptive** *a.*

**résumé** /'rezjuːmeɪ/ *n.* summary.

**resurface** /riː'sɜːfɪs/ *v.* put new surface on; return to surface.

**resurgent** /rə'sɜːdʒ(ə)nt/ *a.* rising or arising again. **resurgence** *n.*

**resurrect** /rezə'rekt/ *v.t.* revive practice or memory of; take from grave.

**resurrection** /rezə'rekʃ(ə)n/ n. rising from the dead; revival from disuse or decay etc.

**resuscitate** /rə'sʌsəteɪt/ v. revive from unconsciousness or apparent death; revive (old custom etc.). **resuscitation** n.

**retail** /'riːteɪl/ 1 n. sale of goods to the public in small quantities. 2 a. of retail. 3 adv. by retail. 4 v. sell by retail; be retailed; (also /rə'teɪl/) recount.

**retain** /rə'teɪn/ v.t. keep possession of, continue to have or use or recognize etc.; keep in mind; keep in place, hold fixed; secure services of (esp. barrister) by preliminary fee.

**retainer** /rə'teɪnə(r)/ n. person or thing that retains; fee for retaining barrister etc.; hist. dependant or follower of person of rank.

**retaliate** /rə'tælɪeɪt/ v. repay in kind; attack in return. **retaliation** n.; **retaliatory** a.

**retard** /rə'tɑːd/ v.t. make slow or late; delay progress or accomplishment of; in p.p. backward in mental or physical development. **retardation** n.

**retch** v.i. make motion of vomiting.

**retention** /rə'tenʃ(ə)n/ n. retaining or being retained.

**retentive** /rə'tentɪv/ a. tending to retain; (of memory) not forgetful.

**rethink** 1 /riː'θɪŋk/ v.t. (past & p.p. **-thought** /-'θɔːt/) consider afresh, esp. with view to making changes. 2 /'riːθɪŋk/ n. rethinking.

**reticence** /'retəs(ə)ns/ n. avoidance of expressing all one knows or feels; uncommunicativeness. **reticent** a.

**reticulate** 1 /rə'tɪkjəleɪt/ v. divide or be divided in fact or appearance into network. 2 /rə'tɪkjələt/ a. reticulated. 3 **reticulation** n.

**reticule** /'retəkjuːl/ n. arch. woman's handbag.

**retina** /'retənə/ n. (pl. **-nas**) layer at back of eyeball sensitive to light. **retinal** a.

**retinue** /'retənjuː/ n. suite or train of persons attending important person.

**retire** /rə'taɪə(r)/ v. leave office or employment, esp. because of age; cause (employee) to retire; withdraw, retreat, seek seclusion or shelter; go to bed.

**retired** a. who has retired; withdrawn from society, secluded.

**retirement** n. condition of having retired; seclusion, secluded place.

**retiring** /rə'taɪərɪŋ/ a. shy, fond of seclusion.

**retort**[1] /rə'tɔːt/ 1 n. incisive or witty or angry reply. 2 v. say by way of retort; repay in kind.

**retort**[2] /rɪ'tɔːt/ n. vessel with long downward-bent neck for distilling liquids; vessel for heating coal to generate gas.

**retouch** /riː'tʌtʃ/ v.i. amend or improve (esp. photograph) by new touches.

**retrace** /riː'treɪs/ v.t. go back over; trace back to source or beginning.

**retract** /rə'trækt/ v. draw or be drawn back or in; withdraw (statement or opinion). **retraction** n.

**retractile** /rə'træktaɪl/ a. retractable. **retractility** n.

**retread** 1 /riː'tred/ v.t. put new tread on (tyre). 2 /'riːtred/ n. retreaded tyre.

**retreat** /rə'triːt/ 1 v.i. go back, retire; recede. 2 n. act of retreating; withdrawing into seclusion; place of seclusion or shelter; temporary retirement for religious exercises; military signal for retreating.

**retrench** /rə'trentʃ/ v. reduce amount of, cut down; economize. **retrenchment** n.

**retrial** /riː'traɪəl/ n. retrying of case.

**retribution** /retrə'bjuːʃ(ə)n/ n. recompense, usu. for evil, vengeance. **retributive** /-'trɪb-/ a.

**retrieve** /rə'triːv/ v. regain possession of; find again; (of dog) find and bring in game; rescue *from* bad state etc., restore to good state; repair. **retrieval** n.

**retriever** /rə'triːvə(r)/ n. dog of breed used for retrieving game.

**retro-** /retrəʊ/ in comb. backwards, back.

**retroactive** /retrəʊ'æktɪv/ a. having retrospective effect.

**retrograde** /'retrəʊɡreɪd/ 1 a. directed backwards; reverting, esp. to inferior state. 2 v.i. move backwards; decline, revert.

**retrogress** /retrəʊ'ɡres/ v.i. move backwards; deteriorate. **retrogression** n.; **retrogressive** a.

**retro-rocket** /'retrəʊrɒkət/ n. auxiliary rocket for slowing down spacecraft etc.

**retrospect** /'retrəspekt/ n. survey of or

**retrospection** /retrə'spekʃ(ə)n/ n. action of looking back, esp. into the past.

**retrospective** /retrə'spektɪv/ a. looking back on or dealing with the past; (of statute etc.) applying to the past as well as to the future.

*retroussé* /rə'truːseɪ/ a. (of nose) turned up at tip. [F]

**retry** /riː'traɪ/ v.t. (past & p.p. -tried) try (defendant, law case) again.

**return** /rə'tɜːn/ 1 v. come or go back; bring or put or send back; give in response; say in reply; send (ball) back in tennis etc.; state in answer to formal demand; elect as MP. 2 n. returning or being returned; coming round again; return ticket; what is returned; proceeds or profit; coming in of these; formal report. 3 **returned serviceman** Aus. & NZ serviceman who has served overseas; **returning officer** official conducting election in constituency etc. and announcing result; **return match** second match between same opponents; **return ticket** ticket for journey to place and back again.

**reunion** /riː'juːnɪən/ n. reuniting or being reunited; social gathering.

**reunite** /riːjuː'naɪt/ v. bring or come together again; join again.

**rev** colloq. 1 n. revolution (of engine). 2 v. (past & p.p. **revved**) (of engine) revolve; rev up. 3 **rev up** cause (engine) to run quickly.

**Rev.** abbr. Reverend.

**revamp** /riː'væmp/ v.t. renovate, revise; patch up.

**Revd** abbr. Reverend.

**reveal** /rə'viːl/ v.t. display, show, allow to appear; disclose, divulge.

**reveille** /rə'vælɪ/ n. military waking-signal.

**revel** /'rev(ə)l/ 1 v.i. (past & p.p. **revelled**) make merry, be riotously festive; take keen delight **in**. 2 n. revelling; in sing. or pl. merry-making.

**revelation** /revə'leɪʃ(ə)n/ n. revealing; knowledge disclosed by divine or supernatural agency; striking disclosure; **(the) Revelation** last book of NT.

**revelry** /'revəlrɪ/ n. revelling.

**revenge** /rə'vendʒ/ 1 n. (act of) retaliation; desire for this. 2 v.t. inflict punishment or exact retribution for; avenge.

**revengeful** /rə'vendʒfəl/ a. eager for revenge.

**revenue** /'revənjuː/ n. annual income, esp. of State; department collecting State revenue.

**reverberate** /rə'vɜːbəreɪt/ v. (of sound, light, heat) be returned or reflected; return (sound etc.) thus. **reverberant** a.; **reverberation** n.; **reverberative** a.

**revere** /rə'vɪə(r)/ v.t. regard with deep and affectionate or religious respect.

**reverence** /'revərəns/ 1 n. revering or being revered; deep respect. 2 v.t. revere.

**reverend** /'revərənd/ a. deserving reverence; **Reverend** title of clergyman.

**reverent** /'revərənt/ a. feeling or showing reverence.

**reverential** /revə'renʃ(ə)l/ a. of the nature of or due to or characterized by reverence.

**reverie** /'revərɪ/ n. fit of musing; daydream.

**revers** /rə'vɪə(r)/ n. turned-back front edge of garment.

**reversal** /rə'vɜːs(ə)l/ n. reversing or being reversed.

**reverse** /rə'vɜːs/ 1 v. turn the other way round or up or inside out; convert to opposite character or effect; make (vehicle) travel backwards; (of vehicle) travel backwards; make work in contrary direction; revoke, annul. 2 a. opposite or contrary (to); inverted, back(ward); upside down. 3 n. the contrary (of); piece of misfortune, disaster; reverse gear or motion; reverse side; side of coin etc. bearing secondary design; verso of leaf. 4 **reverse the charges** make recipient of telephone call responsible for payment; **reverse gear** gear used to make vehicle etc. travel backwards; **reversing light** light at rear of vehicle operated when vehicle is in reverse gear. 5 **reversible** a.

**reversion** /rə'vɜːʃ(ə)n/ n. legal right (esp. of original owner) to possess or succeed to property on death of present possessor; return to previous state or earlier type.

**revert** /rə'vɜːt/ v.i. return **to** former condition or practice etc.; recur **to** in

**review**

thought or talk; return by reversion. **revertible** a.

**review** /rə'vju:/ 1 n. general survey, inspection; retrospect; revision, reconsideration; published account or criticism of book etc.; periodical in which events, books, etc. are reviewed. 2 v. survey, look back on; hold review of (troops, etc.); write review of (book etc.).

**revile** /rə'vaɪl/ v.t. criticize abusively.

**revise** /rə'vaɪz/ 1 v.t. examine and improve or amend; read again. 2 n. proof-sheet embodying corrections made in earlier proof.

**revision** /rə'vɪʒ(ə)n/ n. revising; revised edition or form.

**revisionism** /rə'vɪʒənɪz(ə)m/ n. policy of revision or modification, esp. of Marxist-Leninist doctrine.

**revisory** /rə'vaɪzərɪ/ a. of revision.

**revival** /rə'vaɪv(ə)l/ n. reviving or being revived; new production of old play; reawakening of religious fervour; campaign to promote this.

**revivalism** /rə'vaɪvəlɪz(ə)m/ n. organization of religious revival. **revivalist** n.

**revive** /rə'vaɪv/ v. come or bring back to consciousness, life, vigour, use, or notice.

**revivify** /ri:'vɪvɪfaɪ/ v.t. restore to life or strength or activity. **revivification** n.

**revocable** /'revəkəb(ə)l/ a. that can be revoked.

**revoke** /rə'vəʊk/ 1 v. rescind, withdraw, cancel; *Cards* fail to follow suit though able to. 2 n. revoking at cards. 3 **revocation** n.

**revolt** /rə'vəʊlt/ 1 v. rise in rebellion against authority; affect with disgust; feel revulsion. 2 n. insurrection; sense of loathing; rebellious mood.

**revolting** a. disgusting, horrible.

**revolution** /revə'lu:ʃ(ə)n/ n. forcible substitution of new government or ruler for old; fundamental change; revolving; single completion of orbit or rotation.

**revolutionary** /revə'lu:ʃənərɪ/ 1 a. involving great change; of political revolution. 2 n. instigator or supporter of political revolution.

**revolutionize** /revə'lu:ʃənaɪz/ v.t. completely change or reconstruct.

**rhino**

**revolve** /rə'vɒlv/ v. turn round; rotate; move in orbit; ponder in the mind.

**revolver** n. pistol with revolving chambers enabling user to fire several shots without reloading.

**revue** /rə'vju:/ n. theatrical entertainment consisting of a series of items.

**revulsion** /rə'vʌlʃ(ə)n/ n. abhorrence; sudden violent change of feeling.

**reward** /rə'wɔ:d/ 1 n. return or recompense for service or merit; requital for good or evil; sum offered for detection of criminal or recovery of lost property etc. 2 v.t. give or serve as reward to.

**rewind** /ri:'waɪnd/ v.t. (past & p.p. -wound /-'waʊnd/) wind (film, tape, etc.) back towards beginning.

**rewire** /ri:'waɪə(r)/ v.t. renew electrical wiring of (building).

**rhapsodize** /'ræpsədaɪz/ v.i. utter or write rhapsodies. **rhapsodist** n.

**rhapsody** /'ræpsədɪ/ n. enthusiastic high-flown utterance or composition. **rhapsodical** a.

**rhesus** /'ri:səs/ n. small Indian monkey. **Rhesus factor** antigen occurring in red blood cells of most persons and some animals. **Rhesus-positive** (or **-negative**) having (or not having) Rhesus factor.

**rhetoric** /'retərɪk/ n. art of persuasive speaking or writing; inflated or exaggerated language. **rhetorician** /-'rɪʃ-/ n.

**rhetorical** /rə'tɒrɪk(ə)l/ a. expressed with a view to persuasive or impressive effect; of the nature of rhetoric. **rhetorical question** question asked not for information but to produce effect.

**rheumatic** /ru:'mætɪk/ 1 a. of or caused by or suffering from rheumatism. 2 n. in pl. colloq. rheumatism. 3 **rheumatic fever** fever with pain in the joints. 4 **rheumatically** a.

**rheumatism** /'ru:mətɪz(ə)m/ n. disease marked by inflammation and pain in the joints etc.

**rheumatoid** /'ru:mətɔɪd/ a. having the character of rheumatism. **rheumatoid arthritis** chronic progressive disease causing inflammation and stiffening of joints.

**rhinestone** /'raɪnstəʊn/ n. imitation diamond.

**rhino** /'raɪnəʊ/ n. (pl. **-nos**) colloq. rhinoceros.

**rhinoceros** /raɪˈnɒsərəs/ n. large thick-skinned animal with horn or two horns on nose.

**rhizome** /ˈraɪzəʊm/ n. rootlike stem growing along or under ground and producing both roots and shoots.

**rhododendron** /rəʊdəˈdendrən/ n. evergreen shrub with large flowers.

**rhomboid** /ˈrɒmbɔɪd/ 1 a. like a rhombus. 2 n. quadrilateral of which only opposite sides and angles are equal. 3 **rhomboidal** a.

**rhombus** /ˈrɒmbəs/ n. (pl. -buses) oblique equilateral parallelogram, e.g. diamond on playing-card.

**rhubarb** /ˈruːbɑːb/ n. plant with fleshy leaf-stalks cooked and eaten as fruit; these stalks.

**rhyme** /raɪm/ 1 n. identity of sound at ends of words or verse-lines; rhymed verse; word providing rhyme; poem, poetry. 2 v. (of words or lines) end in rhymes; be or use as rhyme (to, with); versify, write rhymes.

**rhythm** /ˈrɪð(ə)m/ n. measured flow of words in verse or prose; Mus. periodical accent and duration of notes; movement or pattern with regulated succession of strong and weak elements; regularly occurring sequence of events. **rhythm method** contraception by avoiding sexual intercourse near times of ovulation. **rhythmic(al)** a.

**rib** 1 n. each of the curved bones protecting thoracic cavity and its organs; ridge or long raised piece often of stronger or thicker material across surface or through structure, serving to support or strengthen; combination of plain and purl stitches producing ribbed somewhat elastic fabric. 2 v.t. provide or mark (as) with ribs; colloq. tease.

**ribald** /ˈrɪbəld/ a. irreverent, coarsely humorous. **ribaldry** n.

**riband** /ˈrɪbənd/ n. ribbon.

**ribbing** a. ribs or riblike structure.

**ribbon** /ˈrɪbən/ n. narrow strip or band of fabric; material in this form; ribbon of special colour worn to indicate some honour or membership of sports team etc.; long narrow strip; in pl. ragged strips. **ribbon development** building of houses along main road outwards from town.

**ribonucleic acid** /raɪbəʊnjuːˈkliːɪk/ substance controlling protein synthesis in cells.

**rice** n. grain from a kind of grass grown esp. in Asia; this grass. **rice-paper** edible paper made from pith of an oriental tree and used for painting and in cookery.

**rich** /rɪtʃ/ a. having much wealth; splendid, costly; abundant, ample; abounding in; fertile; (of food) containing much fat or spice etc.; mellow, strong and full; highly amusing.

**riches** /ˈrɪtʃəz/ n.pl. abundant means; valuable possessions.

**richly** /ˈrɪtʃli/ adv. fully, thoroughly.

**rick¹** n. stack of hay etc.

**rick²** v.t. slightly strain or sprain. 2 n. slight sprain or strain.

**rickets** /ˈrɪkəts/ n. as sing. or pl. children's disease with softening of the bones.

**rickety** /ˈrɪkɪti/ a. shaky, insecure; suffering from rickets.

**rickshaw** /ˈrɪkʃɔː/ n. light two-wheeled hooded vehicle drawn by one or more persons.

**ricochet** /ˈrɪkəʃeɪ/ 1 n. rebounding of projectile etc. from object it strikes; hit made after this. 2 v.i. skip or rebound once or more on surface.

**rid** v.t. (past & p.p. rid) make (person, place) free of.

**riddance** /ˈrɪd(ə)ns/ n. **good riddance** welcome freedom from unwanted thing or person.

**ridden** p.p. of **ride**.

**riddle¹** /ˈrɪd(ə)l/ 1 n. question designed to test ingenuity in divining answer or meaning; puzzling fact or thing or person. 2 v.i. speak in or propound riddles.

**riddle²** /ˈrɪd(ə)l/ 1 v.t. sift; make many holes in esp. with gunshot; in p.p. filled with (faults etc.). 2 n. coarse sieve.

**ride** 1 v. (past **rode**; p.p. **ridden**) sit on and be carried by horse etc.; go on horseback or bicycle or in train or other conveyance; manage horse; lie at anchor; float buoyantly; in p.p. dominated or infested (with). 2 n. journey in vehicle; spell of riding; path (esp. through woods) for riding on. 3 **ride up** (of garment) work upwards when worn; **take for a ride** sl. make fool of.

**rider** /ˈraɪdə(r)/ n. person riding; additional clause amending or

**ridge** *n.* line of junction in which two sloping surfaces meet; long narrow hilltop; mountain range; any narrow elevation along surface. **ridge-pole** horizontal pole of long tent; **ridgeway** road along ridge.

**ridicule** /'rɪdɪkju:l/ **1** *n.* derision, mockery. **2** *v.t.* make fun of; subject to ridicule; laugh at.

**ridiculous** /rə'dɪkjələs/ *a.* deserving to be laughed at; unreasonable.

**riding** /'raɪdɪŋ/ *n.* former division of Yorkshire.

**rife** *pred. a.* of common occurrence; prevailing, current, numerous.

**riff** *n.* short repeated phrase in jazz and similar music.

**riff-raff** /'rɪfræf/ *n. the* rabble, disreputable people.

**rifle** /'raɪf(ə)l/ **1** *n.* gun with rifled barrel; in *pl.* troops armed with rifles. **2** *v.t.* search and rob; make spiral grooves in (gun, etc.) to make bullets spin.

**rift** *n.* crack, split; cleft; disagreement, dispute. **rift valley** one formed by subsidence of section of earth's crust.

**rig**[1] *v.t.* provide (ship) with spars and ropes etc.; fit (*out*, *up*) with clothes or equipment; set *up* hastily or as makeshift. **2** *n.* arrangement of ship's masts and sails etc.; equipment for special purpose; oil-rig. **3 rig-out** *colloq.* outfit, costume.

**rig**[2] *v.t.* manage or conduct fraudulently.

**rigging** /'rɪgɪŋ/ *n.* ropes etc. used to support masts and work or set sails etc.

**right** /raɪt/ **1** *a.* morally good; just; correct, true; in good or normal condition; not mistaken; on or towards side of human body which in majority of persons has the more-used hand, on or towards that part of an object which is analogous to person's right side. **2** *n.* what is just; fair treatment; fair claim; being entitled to privilege or immunity, thing one is entitled to; in *pl.* right condition, true state; right part, region, or direction; *Polit.* conservatives collectively. **3** *v.t.* restore to proper or straight or vertical position; make reparation for, avenge; vindicate, rehabilitate; correct, set in order. **4** *adv.* straight; all the way (*round*, *to*, etc.), completely; quite, very; justly, properly, correctly, truly; on or to right side. **5 by rights** if right were done; **in the right** having justice or truth on one's side; **right angle** angle of 90° (**at right angles** placed with right angle); **right-hand** placed on right side; **right-handed** using right hand in preference to left, made by or for right hand, turning to right; **right-hander** right-handed person or blow; **right-hand man** indispensable or chief assistant; **right-minded** having sound views and principles; **right of way** right to pass over another's ground, path subject to such right, precedence in passing granted to one vehicle over another; **right side** of fabric etc. meant to show; **right wing** group on right of army or football etc. team or political party; **right-winger** member of this; **set to rights** arrange properly. **6 rightward** *a.* & *adv.*; **rightwards** *adv.*

**righteous** /'raɪtʃəs/ *a.* virtuous, upright, just, honest.

**rightful** /'raɪtf(ə)l/ *a.* legitimately entitled to position etc.; that one is entitled to.

**rightly** /'raɪtlɪ/ *adv.* justly, correctly, properly, justifiably.

**rigid** /'rɪdʒɪd/ *a.* not flexible; that cannot be bent; inflexible, harsh. **rigidity** *n.*

**rigmarole** /'rɪgmərəʊl/ *n.* rambling or meaningless talk.

**rigor mortis** /ˌrɪgə 'mɔ:tɪs/ stiffening of body after death.

**rigour** /'rɪgə(r)/ *n.* severity, strictness, harshness; strict application or observance etc. (*of.* **rigorous** *a.*

**rile** *v.t. colloq.* anger, irritate.

**rill** *n.* tiny stream.

**rim** *n.* raised edge or border; outer ring of wheel on which tyre is fitted.

**rime**[1] **1** *n.* hoar-frost. **2** *v.t.* cover with rime.

**rime**[2] var. of **rhyme**.

**rimmed** /rɪmd/ *a.* edged, bordered.

**rind** /raɪnd/ *n.* tough outer layer or covering of fruit and vegetables or cheese or bacon etc.

**ring**[1] **1** *n.* circlet usu. of precious metal and often set with gem(s) worn esp. on finger; circular band of any material; line or band round cylindrical or circular object; mark or part etc. having form of circular band; *Aus. vulg.* anus; enclosure for circus, boxing, betting at races, etc.; persons or things arranged in circle, such arrangement; combination of traders, politicians, spies, etc., acting together for control of operations. 2 *v.t.* encompass; encircle; put ring on (bird etc.). 3 **ringbark** cut away bark in a ring round (tree) to kill it; **ring-dove** large species of pigeon; **ring-finger** third finger esp. of left hand; **ring-in** *Aus.* substitute; **ringleader** instigator in crime or mischief etc.; **ring main** electrical supply through cable in continuous ring; **ringmaster** director of circus performance; **ring-tail (possum)** any of several Aus. possums with prehensile tails; **ringworm** skin-disease forming circular patches.

**ring²** 1 *v.* (*past* **rang**; *p.p.* **rung**) give clear resonant sound; make (bell) ring; make telephone call (to); (of place) resound, re-echo; (of ears) be filled with sensation of ringing; ring bell; announce or signal or summon by sound of bell. 2 *n.* ringing sound or tone; act of ringing bell, sound caused by this; *colloq.* telephone call; set of (church) bells. 3 **ring off** end telephone call; **ring up** make telephone call (to), record (amount) on cash register.

**ring³** *v. Aus.* beat (shedful of men) at sheep-shearing.

**ringer** /'rɪŋə(r)/ *n. Aus.* fastest shearer in a shed; the best of anything; stationhand, stockman.

**ringlet** /'rɪŋlɪt/ *n.* curly lock of hair.

**rink** *n.* stretch or sheet of ice (used for skating or game of curling); floor for roller-skating; strip of bowling-green used for match.

**rinse** /rɪns/ 1 *v.t.* pour water into and out of to remove dirt etc.; wash lightly, pour liquid over; put through clean water to remove soap; remove by rinsing. 2 *n.* rinsing; solution for temporary tinting of hair.

**riot** /'raɪət/ 1 *n.* tumult, disorder; disturbance of peace by crowd; loud revelry; lavish display *of*; very amusing thing or person. 2 *v.i.* make or engage in riot. 3 **run riot** throw off all restraint. 4 **riotous** *a.*

**rip¹** 1 *v.* cut or tear quickly or forcibly away or apart; make (hole etc.) thus; make long cut or tear in; come violently apart, split. 2 *n.* long tear or cut; act of ripping. 3 **let rip** not check speed of or interfere; **rip-cord** cord for releasing parachute from its pack; **rip off** *sl.* defraud, steal; **rip-off** *n.*

**rip²** *n.* dissolute person, rake.

**RIP** *abbr.* may he or she or they rest in peace.

**riparian** /raɪˈpeərɪən/ *a.* of or on riverbank.

**ripe** *a.* ready to be reaped or picked or eaten; mature, in fit state *for*.

**ripen** /'raɪpən/ *v.* make or become ripe.

**riposte** /rɪˈpɒst/ 1 *n.* retort; quick return thrust in fencing. 2 *v.i.* deliver riposte.

**ripple** /'rɪp(ə)l/ 1 *n.* ruffling of water's surface; small wave(s); gentle lively sound that rises and falls. 2 *v.* form or flow in ripples; sound like ripples; make ripples in.

**rise** /raɪz/ 1 *v.i.* (*past* **rose** /rəʊz/; *p.p.* **risen** /'rɪz(ə)n/) come up or go up; project or swell upwards; come to surface; get up from lying or sitting or kneeling; get out of bed; cease to sit for business; make revolt; ascend, soar; have origin, begin to flow. 2 *n.* rising; upward slope; social advancement; increase in rank or price or amount or wages etc.; origin. 3 **give rise to** cause, induce; **take a rise out of** cause to display temper etc.

**riser** /'raɪzə(r)/ *n.* vertical piece between treads of staircase.

**risible** /'rɪzɪb(ə)l/ *a.* laughable; inclined to laugh. **risibility** *n.*

**rising** /'raɪzɪŋ/ *n.* insurrection.

**risk** 1 *n.* chance of injury or loss or bad consequence; person or thing causing risk. 2 *v.t.* expose to risk; venture on, take chances of.

**risky** /'rɪskɪ/ *a.* full of risk; *risqué*.

**risotto** /rɪˈzɒtəʊ/ *n.* (*pl.* **-tos**) Italian dish of rice with stock, meat, onions, etc.

**risqué** /'rɪskeɪ/ *a.* (of story etc.) slightly indecent. [F]

**rissole** /'rɪsəʊl/ *n.* fried ball or cake of minced meat with breadcrumbs etc.

**rite** *n.* religious or solemn ceremony or observance.

**ritual** /'rɪtjʊəl/ 1 *n.* prescribed order for performing religious service; performance of actions in rite; procedure regularly followed. **2** *a.* of or done with rites.

**ritualism** /ˈrɪtjuːəlɪz(ə)m/ *n.* regular or excessive practice of ritual. **ritualist** *n.*; **ritualistic** *a.*

**rival** /ˈraɪv(ə)l/ **1** *n.* person or thing that competes with another. **2** *v.t.* be rival of or comparable to.

**rivalry** /ˈraɪvəlrɪ/ *n.* being rivals; emulation.

**riven** /ˈrɪv(ə)n/ *a.* split, torn violently.

**river** /ˈrɪvə(r)/ *n.* large natural stream of water flowing in channel; copious flow *of*.

**rivet** /ˈrɪvɪt/ **1** *n.* nail or bolt for holding together metal plates etc. **2** *v.t.* (*past & p.p.* **riveted**) join or fasten with rivets; concentrate, direct intently (*upon*); engross attention of.

**rivulet** /ˈrɪvjʊlət/ *n.* small stream.

**RM** *abbr.* Royal Marines.

**RN** *abbr.* Royal Navy.

**RNA** *abbr.* ribonucleic acid.

**roach** /rəʊtʃ/ *n.* small freshwater fish.

**road** *n.* way, esp. with prepared surface, for pedestrians, riders, and vehicles; way of getting *to*; route; (usu. in *pl.*) piece of water near shore in which ships can ride at anchor. **on the road** travelling; **road-block** obstruction on road to detain traffic; **road-hog** reckless or inconsiderate motorist etc.; **road-house** inn or restaurant on main road in country district; **roadstead** sea road for ships; **road test** test of vehicle by use on road; **road-train** *Aus.* truck pulling one or more large trailers; **roadway** part of road, bridge, etc. used by vehicles; **road-works** construction or repair of roads; **roadworthy** (of vehicle) fit to be used on road.

**roadie** /ˈrəʊdiː/ *n. colloq.* assistant of touring pop group etc., responsible for equipment.

**roadster** /ˈrəʊdstə(r)/ *n.* open car without rear seats; horse or bicycle for use on roads.

**roam** *v.* ramble, wander or travel unsystematically (about).

**roan 1** *a.* (of animal) with coat of which prevailing colour is thickly interspersed with another. **2** *n.* roan horse or cow.

**roar** /rɔː(r)/ **1** *n.* loud deep hoarse sound as of lion. **2** *v.* utter roar; say or shout in roar; travel in vehicle at high speed.

**roaring** /ˈrɔːrɪŋ/ *a.* riotous, noisy, brisk.

**roast 1** *v.* cook or heat by exposure to an open fire or in oven; undergo roasting. **2** *attrib.a.* roasted. **3** *n.* dish of roast meat; meat for roasting.

**rob** *v.* take unlawfully from or deprive *of* esp. by violence; deprive (*of*); commit robbery. **robbery** *n.*

**robe 1** *n.* long loose garment, esp. as indication of rank, office, etc.; dressing-gown. **2** *v.* dress; put on robes; clothe in robe.

**robin** /ˈrɒbɪn/ *n.* small brown red-breasted bird.

**robot** /ˈrəʊbɒt/ *n.* automaton with human appearance; automatic mechanical device; machine-like person. **robotic** /-ˈbɒt-/ *a.*

**robust** /rəʊˈbʌst/ *a.* of strong health and physique; not slender or weakly; vigorous.

**roc** *n.* gigantic bird of Eastern legend.

**rock**[1] *n.* solid part of earth's crust; material or mass of this; large detached stone or boulder; hard sweet usu. in form of stick and flavoured with peppermint. **on the rocks** *colloq.* short of money, having broken down, (of drink) served with ice cubes; **rock-bottom** *colloq.* very lowest; **rock-cake** bun with rugged surface; **rock crystal** crystallized quartz; **rock-garden** rockery; **rock kangaroo** *Aus.* wallaroo; **rock lily** *Aus.* orchid with fragrant white flowers; **rock lobster** *Aus.* marine crayfish; **rock parakeet, parrot**, *Aus.* parakeet that frequents rocks or crags; **rock-plant** plant that grows on or among rocks; **rock salmon** dogfish as sold for food; **rock-salt** common salt as solid mineral; **rock wallaby** *Aus.* any of several small wallabies living in rocky country.

**rock**[2] **1** *v.* move gently to and fro; set or keep or be in such motion; sway from side to side; oscillate; shake, reel. **2** *n.* rocking motion; popular modern music with strong beat. **3 rock and roll** popular music with heavy beat and simple melody; **rock group** group playing rock music; **rocking-chair** chair mounted on rockers; **rocking-horse** wooden horse on rockers for child.

**rocker** n. each of the curved bars on which cradle etc. rocks; rocking-chair.

**rockery** /'rɒkəri/ n. pile of rough stones with soil between them for growing rock-plants on.

**rocket** /'rɒkɪt/ 1 n. firework or signal in form of cylindrical case that can be projected to distance or height by ignition of contents; shell or bomb or spacecraft projected by rocket propulsion. 2 v.t. (past & p.p. **rocketed**) move rapidly upwards or away; bombard with rockets. 3 **rocket propulsion** propulsion by reaction of jet of gases released in combustion of propellant.

**rocketry** /'rɒkɪtri/ n. science or practice of rocket propulsion.

**rocky**[1] /'rɒkɪ/ a. of or like rock; full of rocks.

**rocky**[2] /'rɒkɪ/ a. colloq. unsteady, tottering.

**rococo** /rə'kəʊkəʊ/ 1 a. of ornate style of art, music, and literature in 18th-c. Europe. 2 n. this style.

**rod** n. slender straight round stick or metal bar; cane or birch for flogging; fishing-rod; measure of length (= perch[1]).

**rode** past of ride.

**rodent** /'rəʊd(ə)nt/ n. animal with strong incisors and no canine teeth (e.g. rat, squirrel, beaver).

**rodeo** /'rəʊdɪəʊ/ n. (pl. -deos) exhibition of cowboys' skills; round-up of cattle for branding etc.

**roe**[1] n. **hard roe** mass of eggs in female fish; **soft roe** male fish's milt.

**roe**[2] n. small kind of deer. **roebuck** male roe.

**roentgen** /'rʌntjən/ n. unit of ionizing radiation.

**rogation** /rə'geɪʃ(ə)n/ n. (usu. in pl.) litany of the saints chanted on the 3 days (**Rogation days**) before Ascension Day.

**roger** /'rɒdʒə(r)/ int. used to indicate that message has been received and understood; sl. I agree.

**rogue** /rəʊg/ n. dishonest or unprincipled person; mischievous person; wild animal driven or living apart from herd and of savage temper; inferior or defective specimen among many acceptable ones. **roguery** n.; **roguish** a.

**roister** /'rɔɪstə(r)/ v.i. revel noisily, be uproarious.

**role** n. actor's part; person's or thing's function.

**roll** /rəʊl/ 1 n. cylinder formed by turning paper, cloth, etc. over and over on itself without folding; thing of similar form; small loaf of bread for one person; official list or register; rolling motion or gait; continuous sound of thunder or drum or shouting. 2 v. move or send or go in some direction by turning over and over on axis; make into or form roll; make by rolling; flatten with roller; walk with swaying gait; sway or rock; undulate, show undulating motion or surface; sound with vibration. 3 **roll-call** calling of list of names to establish presence; **rolled gold** thin coating of gold applied by roller to base metal; **rolling-mill** machine or factory for rolling metal into shape; **rolling-pin** roller for pastry; **rolling-stock** company's railway or (US) road vehicles; **rollmop** rolled pickled herring fillet; **roll-top desk** desk with flexible cover sliding in curved grooves; **strike off the rolls** debar from practising as solicitor.

**roller** /'rəʊlə(r)/ n. hard cylinder used for smoothing or flattening or crushing or spreading ink or paint etc.; small cylinder on which hair is rolled for setting; long swelling wave. **roller-coaster** switchback at fair etc.; **roller-skate** skate mounted on set of small rollers; **roller-towel** towel with ends joined, hung on roller.

**rollicking** /'rɒlɪkɪŋ/ a. jovial and boisterous.

**roly-poly** /rəʊlɪ'pəʊlɪ/ 1 n. pudding of suet pastry covered with jam and rolled up and boiled; Aus. bushy plant or tufted grass that breaks free and is rolled about by the wind. 2 a. podgy, plump.

**Roman** /'rəʊmən/ 1 a. of ancient Rome or its territory or people; of medieval or modern Rome; Roman Catholic. 2 n. inhabitant of Rome, member of ancient-Roman State; Roman Catholic; **roman** roman type. 3 **Roman alphabet** letters A–Z as in W. Eur. languages; **Roman candle** tubular firework discharging coloured sparks; **Roman Catholic** of part of Christian Church acknowledging Pope as its head, member of this; **Roman nose** one with high

**romance** /rə'mæns/ 1 *n.* episode or story centred on imaginative scenes of love or heroism etc.; romantic character or quality; love affair; medieval tale of chivalry; exaggeration, picturesque falsehood. 2 *a.* **Romance** of any of the languages developed from Latin. 3 *v.i.* exaggerate, invent or tell fantastic stories.

**Romanesque** /rəumə'nesk/ *n.* style in architecture etc. prevalent between classical and Gothic periods.

**romanize** /'rəumənaɪz/ *v.t.* make Roman or Roman Catholic in character; put into Roman alphabet or roman type. **romanization** *n.*

**romantic** /rə'mæntɪk/ 1 *a.* marked by or suggestive of or given to romance; imaginative, visionary; (of literature or music etc.) concerned more with emotion than with form. 2 *n.* romantic person, esp. writer, painter, or musician.

**romanticism** /rə'mæntɪsɪz(ə)m/ *n.* adherence to romantic style in literature or art etc. **romanticist** *n.*

**romanticize** /rə'mæntɪsaɪz/ *v.* make romantic; indulge in romance.

**Romany** /'rɒmənɪ/ *n.* gypsy; language of gypsies.

**romp** 1 *v.i.* play in lively and boisterous manner; *colloq.* succeed easily. 2 *n.* spell of romping.

**rompers** *n.pl.* young child's play-garment.

**rondeau** /'rɒndəʊ/ *n.* short poem with two rhymes only, and opening words used as refrains.

**rondel** /'rɒnd(ə)l/ *n.* rondeau.

**rondo** /'rɒndəʊ/ *n.* (*pl.* -**os**) *Mus.* movement or composition in which principal theme recurs several times.

**Röntgen rays** /'rʌntjən/ X-rays.

**roo** *n. Aus. colloq.* kangaroo. **roo-bar** bull bar.

**rood** /ruːd/ *n.* crucifix, esp. on roodscreen; quarter-acre. **rood-screen** carved screen separating nave and chancel.

**roof** /ruːf/ 1 *n.* upper covering of building; top of covered vehicle etc. 2 *v.t.* cover with roof; be roof of. 3 **roof of the mouth** palate; **roof-rack** framework to carry luggage etc. on motorcar roof.

**rook**[1] /rʊk/ 1 *n.* black bird of crow kind that nests in colonies. 2 *v.t.* swindle or cheat, esp. at cards etc.; charge extortionately.

**rook**[2] /rʊk/ *n.* chess piece with battlement-shaped top.

**rookery** /'rʊkərɪ/ *n.* colony of rooks or penguins or seals.

**rookie** /'rʊkɪ/ *n. sl.* recruit.

**room** /ruːm/ 1 *n.* space that is or might be occupied by something; part of house etc. enclosed by walls or partitions; in *pl.* apartments or lodgings; opportunity, scope. 2 *v.i. US* have room(s), lodge.

**roomy** /'ruːmɪ/ *a.* having much room, spacious.

**roost** /ruːst/ 1 *n.* bird's resting-place. 2 *v.i. n.* (of bird) settle for sleep; be perched or lodged for the night.

**rooster** /'ruːstə(r)/ *n. US* domestic cock.

**root**[1] /ruːt/ 1 *n.* part of plant that fixes it to earth etc. and conveys nourishment from soil; in *pl.* fibres or branches of this; plant with edible root, such root; embedded part of hair or tooth etc.; in *pl.* emotional attachment to a place; source, means of growth, basis; *Math.* number which multiplied by itself a given number of times yields a given number, esp. *square root*; ultimate element of language. 2 *v.* (cause to) take root; fix or establish firmly; pull up by root. 3 **root out** find and get rid of; **root-stock** rhizome, source from which offshoots have arisen; **take root** begin to draw nourishment from the soil, become established.

**root**[2] /ruːt/ *v.* turn up ground, turn *up* (ground etc.) in search of food; search *out*, hunt *up.* **root for** *US sl.* encourage by applause or support.

**ropable** /'rəʊpəb(ə)l/ *a. Aus.* angry.

**rope** 1 *n.* stout cord made by twisting together strands of hemp or wire etc.; string of pearls; in *pl.* the ropes enclosing boxing-ring etc. 2 *v.t.* fasten or secure or connect with rope, put rope on; enclose or mark *off* with rope. 3 **know the ropes** be familiar with conditions in some sphere of action; **rope in** persuade to take part.

**ropy** /'rəʊpɪ/ *a. colloq.* poor in quality.

**Roquefort** /ˈrɒkfɔː(r)/ n. (P) blue cheese orig. made from ewe's milk.

**rorqual** /ˈrɔːkw(ə)l/ n. kind of whale with dorsal fin.

**rort** n. Aus. rowdy party; trick, dishonest practice.

**rosaceous** /rəʊˈzeɪʃəs/ a. of the family of plants including the rose.

**rosary** /ˈrəʊzəri/ n. RC Ch. form of devotion made up of repeated prayers; string of beads for keeping count in this.

**rose**[1] /rəʊz/ 1 n. prickly shrub bearing fragrant flower usu. of red, yellow, or white colour; similar flowering plant; light crimson colour, pink; representation of the flower; rose-shaped design or object; nozzle of watering-can etc. 2 a. coloured like pale red rose, of warm pink. 3 **rosebud** bud of rose, pretty girl; **rose-coloured** rosy, fig. sanguine, cheerful, optimistic; **rose-water** fragrant liquid distilled from roses; **rose-window** circular window, usu. with roselike tracery; **rosewood** close-grained fragrant kind used in making furniture, any of several similar Aus. woods.

**rose**[2] past of **rise**.

*rosé* /ˈrəʊzeɪ/ n. light pink wine. [F]

**roseate** /ˈrəʊzɪət/ a. rose-coloured.

**rosella** /rəˈzelə/ n. any of several brightly-coloured Aus. parakeets.

**rosemary** /ˈrəʊzməri/ n. evergreen fragrant shrub used as culinary herb.

**rosette** /rəʊˈzet/ n. rose-shaped ornament made of ribbons etc. or carved in stone etc.

**rosin** /ˈrɒzɪn/ 1 n. resin, esp. in solid form. 2 v.t. rub with rosin.

**roster** /ˈrɒstə(r)/ n. list or plan showing turns of duty etc.

**rostrum** /ˈrɒstrəm/ n. (pl. -tra) platform for public speaking etc.

**rosy** /ˈrəʊzɪ/ a. coloured like pink or red rose; cheerful, hopeful.

**rot** 1 v. undergo decay by putrefaction or from lack of use; cause to rot, make rotten. 2 n. decay, rottenness; sl. nonsense; sl. series of failures. 3 **rot-gut** inferior or harmful liquor.

**rota** /ˈrəʊtə/ n. list of persons acting, or duties to be done, in rotation.

**rotary** /ˈrəʊtəri/ a. rotating, acting by rotation.

**rotate** /rəʊˈteɪt/ v. move round axis or centre, revolve; arrange or take in rotation. **rotatory** a.

**rotation** /rəʊˈteɪʃ(ə)n/ n. rotating or being rotated; recurrent series or period; regular succession of members of a group. **rotational** a.

**rote** n. mechanical process of memory.

**rotisserie** /rəˈtɪsəri/ n. cooking-device for roasting food on revolving spit.

**rotor** /ˈrəʊtə(r)/ n. rotary part of machine; rotating system of helicopter.

**rotten** /ˈrɒt(ə)n/ a. perishing from decay; morally or politically corrupt; worthless; sl. disagreeable, ill-advised.

**rotter** /ˈrɒtə(r)/ n. sl. objectionable person.

**rotund** /rəʊˈtʌnd/ a. rounded, plump; sonorous, grandiloquent. **rotundity** n.

**rotunda** /rəʊˈtʌndə/ n. circular building, esp. one with dome.

**rouble** /ˈruːb(ə)l/ n. monetary unit of USSR.

**roué** /ˈruːeɪ/ n. debauchee, rake.

**rouge** /ruːʒ/ 1 n. red cosmetic used to colour cheeks and lips. 2 v. colour with rouge; adorn oneself thus.

**rough** /rʌf/ 1 a. having uneven surface, not smooth or level; not mild or quiet or gentle; violent, harsh, unfeeling, unpleasant; deficient in finish etc.; approximate, preliminary. 2 adv. in rough manner. 3 n. hardship; hooligan; rough ground; the unfinished or natural state. 4 v.t. make rough; sketch in or plan out roughly. 5 **rough-and-ready** rough or crude but effective, not elaborate or over-particular; **rough-and-tumble** irregular, disorderly, (n.) haphazard fight; **roughcast** plaster of lime and gravel, (v.t.) coat with this; **rough house** disturbance, rough fight; **rough it** do without ordinary comforts; **rough justice** treatment that is approximately fair; **roughneck** colloq. driller on oil rig, US sl. rough person; **roughshod** (of horse) having shoes with nail-heads projecting (**ride roughshod over** treat inconsiderately or arrogantly).

**roughage** /ˈrʌfɪdʒ/ n. indigestible material in food that stimulates intestinal action.

**roughen** /ˈrʌf(ə)n/ v. make or become rough.

**roulette** /ruːˈlet/ n. gambling game played on table with revolving

**round** /raʊnd/ 1 *a.* shaped like circle or sphere or cylinder; done with circular motion; (of number etc.) without odd units; entire, continuous, complete, candid. 2 *n.* round object; revolving motion, circular or recurring course, series; route on which goods are regularly delivered; single provision (*of* drinks etc.); one spell of play etc., one stage in competition; playing of all holes in golf-course once; ammunition to fire one shot; slice of bread, sandwich made from whole slices of bread; rung of ladder; circumference, extent, *of*; *Mus.* canon for voices at same pitch or in octaves. 3 *adv.* with circular motion, with return to starting-point or change to opposite position; to or at or affecting all or many points of circumference or area or members of company etc.; in every direction from a centre; measuring (specified distance) in girth. 4 *prep.* so as to encircle or enclose; at or to points on circumference of; in various directions from; so as to pass in curved course, having thus passed. 5 *v.* give or take round shape; make (number etc.) round by omitting units etc.; pass round (corner etc.). 6 **in the round** with all features shown or considered, with audience all round theatre stage; **Roundhead** member of Parliamentary party in English Civil War; **round off** bring to complete or symmetrical state; **round on** attack unexpectedly; **round robin** petition with signatures in circle to conceal order of writing; **roundsman** tradesman's employee who delivers goods; **round-table conference** one with discussion by members round table; **round trip** circular tour, outward and return journey; **round-up** rounding up, summary.

**roundabout** /'raʊndəbaʊt/ 1 *n.* road junction with traffic passing in one direction round central island; merry-go-round. 2 *a.* circuitous.

**roundel** /'raʊnd(ə)l/ *n.* small disc; rondeau.

**roundelay** /'raʊndəleɪ/ *n.* short simple song with refrain.

**rounders** /'raʊndəz/ *n.* team-game with bat and ball where players run round a series of bases.

**roundly** /'raʊndlɪ/ *adv.* bluntly, severely.

**rouse**[1] /raʊz/ *v.* stir up from sleep or quiescence; cease to sleep; become active.

**rouse**[2] /raʊs/ *v.* Aus. colloq. (usu. with *on*) scold, revile.

**rouseabout** /'raʊsəbaʊt/ *n.* Aus. & NZ odd-job man on sheep-station or farm or in shearing-shed.

**rout**[1] /raʊt/ 1 *n.* disorderly retreat of defeated troops. 2 *v.t.* defeat utterly.

**rout**[2] var. of **root**[2].

**route** /ruːt/ 1 *n.* way taken in getting from starting-point to destination. 2 *v.t.* (*partic.* **routeing**) send etc. along particular route. 3 **route march** training-march of soldiers etc.

**routine** /ruːˈtiːn/ 1 *n.* regular course of procedure, unvarying performance of certain acts; set sequence in performance, esp. dance; sequence of instructions to computer. 2 *a.* performed as routine.

**rove**[1] *v.* wander without settled destination; (of eyes) look in changing directions.

**rove**[2] var. of **reeve**[2].

**rover**[1] /'rəʊvə(r)/ *n.* wanderer.

**rover**[2] /'rəʊvə(r)/ *n.* pirate.

**row**[1] /rəʊ/ *n.* line of persons or things; line of seats in theatre etc. **in a row** *colloq.* in succession.

**row**[2] /rəʊ/ 1 *v.* propel boat with oars; convey in boat. 2 *n.* spell of rowing. 3 **rowing-boat** boat propelled with oars.

**row**[3] /raʊ/ 1 *n. colloq.* disturbance, noise, dispute; being reprimanded. 2 *v.t.* make or engage in a row; reprimand.

**rowan** /'raʊən, 'rəʊən/ *n.* mountain ash; its scarlet berry.

**rowdy** /'raʊdɪ/ 1 *a.* noisy and disorderly. 2 *n.* rowdy person. 3 **rowdyism** *n.*

**rowel** /'raʊəl/ *n.* spiked revolving disc at end of spur.

**rowlock** /'rɒlək/ *n.* appliance serving as point of support for oar.

**royal** /'rɔɪəl/ 1 *a.* of or suited to or worthy of king or queen; in service or under patronage of king or queen; belonging to or of family of king or queen; splendid, on great scale. 2 *n.*

**royalist** /'rɔɪəlɪst/ n. supporter of monarchy or of the royal side in civil war etc.

**royalty** /'rɔɪəltɪ/ n. being royal; royal persons; member of royal family; sum paid to patentee for use of patent or to author etc. for each copy of his book etc. sold or for each public performance of his work; royal right (now esp. over minerals) granted by sovereign to individual or corporation.

**r.p.m.** abbr. revolutions per minute.

**RSL** abbr. Aus. Returned Services League.

**RSM** abbr. Regimental Sergeant-Major.

**RSPCA** abbr. Royal Society for the Prevention of Cruelty to Animals.

**RSVP** abbr. please answer (*répondez s'il vous plaît*).

**Rt. Hon.** abbr. Right Honourable.

**Rt. Revd.** abbr. Right Reverend.

**rub** 1 v. slide hand or object along or over surface of; polish or clean or abrade or chafe or make dry or sore by rubbing; take (stain etc.) *out*; freshen or brush *up*; come into or be in sliding contact, exercise friction *against* etc.; get frayed or worn by friction; get *along* etc. with more or less restraint or difficulty. 2 n. action or spell of rubbing; impediment or difficulty. 3 **rub off** be transferred by contact; **rub (up) the wrong way** irritate.

**rubato** /ruː'bɑːtəʊ/ n. Mus. (pl. -tos) temporary disregarding of strict tempo.

**rubber**[1] /'rʌbə(r)/ n. elastic substance made from latex of tropical plants or synthetically; piece of this or other substance for erasing pencil-marks; *US* in pl. galoshes. **rubber band** loop of rubber to hold papers etc.; **rubber-neck** *US* (be) gaping sightseer; **rubber plant** plant yielding rubber, esp. kind grown as house plant; **rubber stamp** device for inking and imprinting on surface; **rubber-stamp** approve automatically without proper consideration. **rubbery** a.

**rubber**[2] /'rʌbə(r)/ n. three successive games between same sides or persons at bridge etc. or cricket.

**rubbish** /'rʌbɪʃ/ n. waste or worthless matter; litter; trash, nonsense. 2 v.t. colloq. disparage, criticize. 3 **rubbishy** a.

**rubbity** /'rʌbətɪ/ n. Aus. sl. pub.

**rubble** /'rʌb(ə)l/ n. waste fragments of stone, brick, etc.

**rubella** /ruː'belə/ n. German measles.

**rubicund** /'ruːbɪkənd/ a. ruddy, red-faced.

**rubric** /'ruːbrɪk/ n. direction for conduct of divine service inserted in liturgical book; explanatory words; general instruction; heading or passage in red or special lettering.

**ruby** /'ruːbɪ/ 1 n. crimson or rose-coloured precious stone; glowing red colour. 2 a. ruby-coloured.

**ruche** /ruːʃ/ 1 n. frill or gathering of lace etc. 2 v.t. gather into or trim with ruche(s).

**ruck**[1] n. main body of competitors not likely to overtake leaders; undistinguished crowd of persons or things.

**ruck**[2] v. crease, wrinkle.

**rucksack** /'rʌksæk/ n. bag slung by straps from both shoulders and resting on back.

**ruction** /'rʌkʃ(ə)n/ n. colloq. dispute, row.

**rudder** /'rʌdə(r)/ n. flat piece hinged to vessel's stern or rear of aeroplane for steering with.

**ruddy** /'rʌdɪ/ a. freshly or healthily red; reddish; sl. bloody, damnable.

**rude** a. impolite, offensive; roughly made; primitive; uneducated; abrupt, sudden; vigorous, hearty.

**rudiment** /'ruːdəmənt/ n. in pl. elements or first principles (*of*), imperfect beginning of something undeveloped; in *sing.* part or organ imperfectly developed as having no function.

**rudimentary** /ruːdə'mentərɪ/ a. not advanced or developed; of the nature of a rudiment.

**rue**[1] v.t. (*partic.* ruing) repent of; wish undone or non-existent.

**rue**[2] n. evergreen shrub with bitter strong-scented leaves.

**rueful** /'ruːfəl/ a. expressing (mock) sorrow.

**ruff**[1] n. projecting starched frill worn round neck; projecting or conspicuous band of feathers or hair round bird's or animal's neck; kind of pigeon.

**ruff**[2] 1 v. trump at cards. 2 n. trumping.

# ruffian

**ruffian** /'rʌfiːən/ n. violent lawless person. **ruffianly** a.

**ruffle** /'rʌf(ə)l/ **1** v.t. disturb smoothness or tranquillity of. **2** n. frill of lace etc.; ripple.

**rufous** /'ruːfəs/ a. reddish-brown.

**rug** n. floor-mat; thick woollen wrap or coverlet.

**Rugby** /'rʌgbiː/ n. (in full **Rugby football**) game played with oval ball that may be kicked or carried.

**rugged** /'rʌgəd/ a. of rough uneven surface; harsh; austere.

**rugger** /'rʌgə(r)/ n. colloq. Rugby football.

**ruin** /'ruːən/ **1** n. fallen or wrecked state; downfall; loss of property or position; (often in pl.) remains of building etc. that has suffered ruin; cause of ruin. **2** v.t. reduce to ruins; bring to ruin; damage irrecoverably, destroy, bankrupt. **3 ruination** n.

**ruinous** /'ruːənəs/ a. bringing ruin; disastrous; in ruins.

**rule** /ruːl/ **1** n. principle to which action conforms or should conform; prevailing custom, standard, normal state of things; government, dominion; graduated straight measure; Print. thin line or dash; code of discipline of religious order. **2** v. exercise sway or decisive influence over; keep under control; have sovereign control of or over; pronounce authoritatively (that); make parallel lines across (paper), make (straight line) with ruler etc. **3 as a rule** usually; **rule of thumb** method or procedure based on experience or practice, not theory; **rule out** exclude; **Rules** Aus. Australian Rules.

**ruler** /'ruːlə(r)/ n. person exercising government or dominion; straight strip of wood etc. used for drawing or measuring lines.

**ruling** /'ruːlɪŋ/ n. authoritative pronouncement.

**rum**[1] n. spirit distilled from sugar-cane or molasses.

**rum**[2] a. colloq. queer, strange. **rum 'un** Tas. colloq. remarkable person, a character.

**rumba** /'rʌmbə/ n. ballroom dance of Cuban origin; music for this.

**rumble**[1] /'rʌmb(ə)l/ **1** v. make continuous deep sound as of thunder; (of person or vehicle) go *along* making such sound. **2** n. rumbling sound.

**rumble**[2] /'rʌmb(ə)l/ v.t. sl. see through, detect.

**rumbustious** /rʌm'bʌstʃəs/ a. colloq. boisterous, uproarious.

**ruminant** /'ruːmən(ə)nt/ **1** n. animal that chews the cud. **2** a. of ruminants; ruminating.

**ruminate** /'ruːmənent/ v.i. chew the cud; meditate, ponder. **rumination** n.; **ruminative** a.

**rummage** /'rʌmɪdʒ/ **1** v. search thoroughly or untidily (in); find among other things. **2** n. search. **3 rummage sale** jumble sale.

**rummy** /'rʌmiː/ n. card-game played usu. with two packs.

**rumour** /'ruːmə(r)/ **1** n. general talk or report or hearsay, often of doubtful accuracy. **2** v.t. report by way of rumour.

**rump** n. tail-end or buttocks of animal or bird or person. **rump steak** cut of beef from rump.

**rumple** /'rʌmp(ə)l/ v.t. crease, crumple.

**rumpus** /'rʌmpəs/ n. colloq. row, uproar.

**run 1** v. (past **ran**; p.p. **run**) go at pace faster than walk; flee; go or travel hurriedly or briefly etc.; advance (as) by rolling or on wheels or smoothly; be in action or operation; be current or operative or valid; (of bus or train etc.) travel or be travelling on its route; extend; compete in race etc.; enter for race or contest; seek election; flow or emit contents; spread rapidly; set or keep going, control operations of; own and use (vehicle); smuggle. **2** n. act or spell of running; short excursion; distance travelled; general tendency; regular route; continuous stretch or spell or course; high general demand; general or average type or class; point scored in cricket or baseball; permission for free use *of*; animal's regular track; Aus. sheep- or cattle-station; enclosure for fowls etc.; range of pasture; ladder in stocking. **3 on the run** fleeing; **run across** happen to meet; **run after** pursue; **run away** leave quickly or secretly; **runaway** fugitive; **run down** knock down or collide with, reduce numbers of (staff), (of clockwork) stop for lack of winding, (of person or

**rune** 483 **rusticate**

health etc.) become enfeebled, discover after search, disparage; **run-down** reduction in numbers, detailed analysis, (*a.*) decayed from prosperity; **run dry** cease to flow; **run in** bring (new engine etc.) into good working order, *colloq.* arrest; **run into** incur (debt), collide with, happen to meet, reach as many as; **run low** become depleted, have few left; **run off** flee, produce (copies) on machine, decide (race) after tie or heats, write or recite fluently; **run-of-the-mill** ordinary, not special; **run out** come to an end, exhaust one's stock *of*, put down wicket of (running batsman); **run out on** desert; **run over** overflow, (of vehicle) pass over (animal, prostrate person, etc.), review; **run short** = *run low*; **run through** examine or rehearse briefly, deal successively with; **run to** have money or ability for, reach (amount etc.), show tendency to; **run up** accumulate quickly, build or make hurriedly, raise (flag); **run up against** meet with (difficulty etc.); **runway** specially prepared airfield surface for taking off and landing.

**rune** *n.* letter of earliest Germanic alphabet; similar character of mysterious or magic significance. **runic** *a.*

**rung**[1] *n.* short stick fixed as crossbar, esp. in ladder.

**rung**[2] *p.p.* of **ring**[2].

**runnel** /'rʌn(ə)l/ *n.* brook; gutter.

**runner** /'rʌnə(r)/ *n.* racer; messenger; creeping plant-stem that can take root; groove or rod for thing to slide along; sliding ring on rod etc.; long narrow ornamental cloth or rug. **runner bean** kind of climbing bean; **runner-up** competitor taking second place.

**running** 1 *n.* act or manner of running; management. 2 *a.* continuous; consecutive. 3 **in the running** with chance of winning or success; **make the running** set the pace; **running commentary** oral description of events in progress; **running jump** one in which jumper runs to take-off; **running knot** one that slips along rope etc. and changes size of loop; **running repairs** minor repairs and replacements; **running water** water available from stream or taps.

**runny** /'rʌnɪ/ *a.* tending to run or flow; excessively fluid.

**runt** *n.* undersized person or animal; smallest of litter.

**rupee** /ruː'piː/ *n.* monetary unit of India, Pakistan, etc.

**rupture** /'rʌptʃə(r)/ 1 *n.* breaking, breach; breach of harmonious relations; abdominal hernia. 2 *v.* burst (cell, membrane, etc.); sever (connection); affect with or suffer hernia.

**rural** /'rʊər(ə)l/ *a.* in or of suggesting country. **rurality** /-'ræl-/ *n.*; **ruralize** *v.t.*

**ruse** /ruːz/ *n.* stratagem, trick.

**rush**[1] 1 *v.* go or move or pass precipitately or with great speed; impel or carry along rapidly; force (person) to act hastily; attack or capture by sudden assault. 2 *n.* act of rushing; violent advance or attack; period of great activity; sudden migration of large numbers, esp. to a gold discovery; strong run *on* or *for* a commodity; in *pl. Cinema* preliminary showings of film before cutting. 3 **rush-hour** time each day when traffic etc. is heaviest.

**rush**[2] *n.* marsh plant with slender pith-filled stem; its stem; rushes as material. **rushlight** candle made by dipping pith of rush in tallow.

**rusk** *n.* slice of bread rebaked as kind of light biscuit esp. for infants.

**russet** /'rʌsət/ 1 *a.* reddish-brown. 2 *n.* russet colour; rough-skinned russet apple.

**Russian** /'rʌʃ(ə)n/ 1 *a.* of Russia. 2 *n.* native or language of Russia. 3 **Russian roulette** firing of revolver held to one's head after spinning cylinder with one chamber loaded; **Russian salad** mixed diced cooked vegetables with mayonnaise.

**rust** 1 *n.* reddish- or yellowish-brown corrosive coating formed on iron by oxidation; plant-disease with rust-coloured spots. 2 *v.* become rusty; affect with rust; lose quality or efficiency by disuse or inactivity. 3 **rust bucket** Aus. *colloq.* rusty old car.

**rustic** /'rʌstɪk/ 1 *a.* of or like country people or peasants; uncouth; of simple workmanship; made of untrimmed branches or rough timber, with rough surface. 2 *n.* countryman. 3 **rusticity** *n.*

**rusticate** /'rʌstəkeɪt/ *v.* expel temporarily from university as punishment;

**rustle** retire to or live in the country. **rustication** n.

**rustle** /'rʌs(ə)l/ 1 v. (cause to) make sound as of dry leaves blown in breeze; go with rustle; steal (cattle or horses). 2 n. rustling sound. 3 **rustle up** colloq. produce when needed.

**rusty** /'rʌsti/ a. rusted, affected with rust; impaired by age or disuse; discoloured by age.

**rut**[1] n. track sunk by passage of wheels; fixed pattern of behaviour difficult to change.

**rut**[2] 1 n. periodic sexual excitement of male deer etc. 2 v.i. be affected with rut. 3 **ruttish** a.

**ruthless** /'ru:θləs/ a. having no pity or compassion.

**RV** abbr. Revised Version (of Bible).

**rye** /raɪ/ n. cereal plant used for bread and as fodder etc.; grain of this; (in full **rye whisky**) whisky distilled from rye.

# S

**S.** *abbr.* south; southern.

**s.** *abbr.* second(s); shilling(s); singular; son.

**SA** *abbr.* Salvation Army; sex appeal; South Africa; South Australia.

**sabbatarian** /sæbə'teərɪən/ *n.* person observing sabbath strictly. **sabbatarianism** *n.*

**sabbath** /'sæbəθ/ *n.* religious rest-day appointed for Jews on last, and for Christians on first, day of the week.

**sabbatical** /sə'bætɪk(ə)l/ 1 *a.* of sabbath; (of leave) granted at intervals to university teacher etc. for study or travel. 2 *n.* period of sabbatical leave.

**sable** /'seɪb(ə)l/ 1 *n.* small dark-furred arctic mammal; its skin or fur; the colour black. 2 *a.* black, gloomy.

**sabot** /'sæbəʊ/ *n.* wooden or wooden-soled shoe.

**sabotage** /'sæbətɑːʒ/ 1 *n.* deliberate destruction or damage, esp. for industrial or political purpose. 2 *v.t.* commit sabotage on; damage or destroy.

**saboteur** /sæbə'tɜː(r)/ *n.* person who commits sabotage.

**sabre** /'seɪbə(r)/ *n.* cavalry sword with curved blade; light fencing-sword. **sabre-rattling** display or threats of military force.

**sac** *n.* membranous bag in animal or vegetable organism.

**saccharin** /'sækərɪn/ *n.* very sweet substance used as substitute for sugar.

**saccharine** /'sækəriːn/ *a.* intensely sweet, cloying.

**sacerdotal** /sækə'dəʊt(ə)l/ *a.* of priests or priestly office.

**sachet** /'sæʃeɪ/ *n.* small bag or packet esp. of perfumed substance or shampoo etc.

**sack**[1] 1 *n.* large bag made of coarse flax or hemp etc.; amount held by sack. 2 *v.t.* put in sack(s); *colloq.* dismiss from employment. 3 **the sack** *colloq.* dismissal; **sackcloth** coarse fabric of flax or hemp etc.

**sack**[2] 1 *v.t.* plunder and destroy. 2 *n.* sacking of town etc.

**sack**[3] *n. hist.* white wine from Spain etc.

**sackbut** /'sækbʌt/ *n.* early form of trombone.

**sacking** /'sækɪŋ/ *n.* sackcloth.

**sacral** /'seɪkr(ə)l/ *a.* of sacrum.

**sacrament** /'sækrəmənt/ *n.* symbolic religious ceremony, esp. Eucharist; sacred thing, influence, etc. **sacramental** *a.*

**sacred** /'seɪkrɪd/ *a.* connected with religion; dedicated or appropriated to a god or *to* some person or purpose; safeguarded or required by religion or tradition etc.; inviolable. **sacred cow** idea or institution unreasonably held to be above criticism.

**sacrifice** /'sækrɪfaɪs/ 1 *n.* giving up something for sake of something else, thing given up thus; loss entailed; slaughter of animal or person or surrender of a possession as offering to a deity; what is thus slaughtered or surrendered. 2 *v.* give up, devote *to*; offer or kill (as) sacrifice. 3 **sacrificial** /-'fɪʃ-/ *a.*

**sacrilege** /'sækrɪlɪdʒ/ *n.* violation of what is sacred. **sacrilegious** *a.*

**sacristan** /'sækrɪst(ə)n/ *n.* person in charge of sacristy and church contents.

**sacristy** /'sækrɪstɪ/ *n.* repository for church's vestments and vessels etc.

**sacrosanct** /'sækrəsæŋkt/ *a.* most sacred; inviolable. **sacrosanctity** *n.*

**sacrum** /'seɪkrəm/ *n.* composite bone forming back of pelvis.

**sad** *a.* sorrowful; showing or causing sorrow; incorrigible; deplorably bad.

**sadden** /'sæd(ə)n/ *v.* make or become sad.

**saddle** /'sæd(ə)l/ 1 *n.* seat of leather etc. fastened on horse etc.; seat for rider of bicycle etc.; joint of meat consisting of the two loins; ridge rising to a summit at each end. 2 *v.t.* put saddle on (horse etc.); burden *with* task etc. 3 **saddlebag** one of pair of bags laid across back of horse etc.; bag attached behind saddle of bicycle etc.

**saddler** /'sædlə(r)/ *n.* maker of or dealer in saddles and harness. **saddlery** *n.*

**sadism** /'seɪdɪz(ə)m/ *n.* enjoyment of cruelty to others; sexual perversion characterized by this. **sadist** *n.*; **sadistic** /-'dɪs-/ *a.*

**s.a.e.** *abbr.* stamped addressed envelope.

# safari

**safari** /sə'fɑːriː/ *n.* hunting or scientific expedition esp. in Africa. **safari park** area where wild animals are kept in open for viewing.

**safe 1** *a.* free of danger or injury; affording security or not involving danger; reliable; sure; prevented from escaping or doing harm; cautious. **2** *n.* strong lockable cupboard for valuables; ventilated cupboard for provisions. **3 safe conduct** immunity from arrest or harm; **safe deposit** building containing safes or strong-rooms kept separately.

**safeguard** /'seɪfgɑːd/ **1** *n.* proviso or circumstance etc. that tends to prevent something undesirable. **2** *v.t.* guard or protect (rights etc.).

**safety** /'seɪftɪ/ *n.* being safe; freedom from danger. **safety belt** strap securing person safely, esp. seat-belt; **safety-catch** contrivance for locking gun-trigger or preventing accidental operation of machinery; **safety curtain** fireproof curtain in theatre to divide auditorium from stage in case of fire etc.; **safety match** match that ignites only on specially prepared surface; **safety net** net placed to catch acrobat etc. in case he falls; **safety-pin** pin with point that is bent back to head and held in guard when closed; **safety razor** razor with guard protecting skin from cuts; **safety-valve** valve relieving excessive pressure of steam, *fig.* means of harmlessly releasing excitement or anger etc.

**saffron** /'sæfrən/ **1** *n.* orange-coloured stigmas of crocus used for colouring and flavouring; colour of this. **2** *a.* saffron-coloured.

**sag 1** *v.i.* sink or subside; have downward bulge or curve in middle. **2** *n.* state or amount of sagging.

**saga** /'sɑːgə/ *n.* medieval Icelandic or Norwegian prose tale; story of heroic achievement or adventure; long family chronicle.

**sagacious** /sə'geɪʃəs/ *a.* having or showing insight or good judgement. **sagacity** /-'gæs-/ *n.*

**sage¹** *n.* aromatic herb with dull greyish-green leaves.

**sage² 1** *a.* wise, judicious, experienced. **2** *n.* person credited with profound wisdom.

# sal ammoniac

**Sagittarius** /sædʒə'teərɪəs/ *n.* ninth sign of zodiac.

**sago** /'seɪgəʊ/ *n.* starch prepared from palm-pith and used for puddings etc.

**sahib** /sɑːɪb/ *n.* former title of address to European men in India.

**said** *past & p.p.* of SAY.

**sail 1** *n.* piece of canvas etc. extended on rigging to catch wind and propel vessel; *collect.* ship's sails; voyage or excursion in sailing-vessel; wind-catching apparatus attached to arm of windmill. **2** *v.* travel on water by use of sails or engine-power; traverse sea; navigate ship; start on voyage; glide or move smoothly or easily. **3 sailcloth** canvas for sails, kind of coarse linen; **sailing-boat, -ship**, etc. one moved by sails; **sailplane** kind of glider.

**sailor** /'seɪlə(r)/ *n.* seaman or mariner, esp. below officer's rank. **bad, good, sailor** person very liable, not liable, to seasickness.

**sainfoin** /'sænfɔɪn/ *n.* pink-flowered fodder-plant.

**saint 1** *n.* holy or canonized person, regarded as having place in heaven; very virtuous person. **2** *attrib.* as prefix to name. **3** *v.t.* canonize; in *p.p.* sacred, worthy of sainthood. **4 sainthood** *n.*; **saintly** *a.*

**sake¹** /seɪk/ *n.* **for the sake of, for my etc. sake** out of consideration for, in the interest of, in order to please or get etc.

**sake²** /'sɑːkɪ/ *n.* Japanese fermented liquor made from rice.

**salaam** /sə'lɑːm/ **1** *n.* oriental salutation; low bow. **2** *v.i.* make salaam.

**salacious** /sə'leɪʃəs/ *a.* erotic; lecherous. **salacity** /-'læs-/ *n.*

**salad** /'sæləd/ *n.* mixture of raw or cold vegetables etc. often eaten with or including cold meat or cheese etc.; vegetable or herb suitable for eating raw. **salad days** one's period of youthful inexperience; **salad-dressing** mixture of oil and vinegar etc., used with salad.

**salamander** /'sæləmændə(r)/ *n.* lizard-like animal formerly supposed to live in fire; kind of tailed amphibian.

**salami** /sə'lɑːmɪ/ *n.* highly-seasoned sausage, orig. Italian.

**sal ammoniac** /sælə'məʊnɪæk/ ammonium chloride.

**salary** /'sæləri:/ 1 *n.* fixed regular payment made by employer to employee. 2 *v.t.* (esp. in *p.p.*) pay salary to.

**sale** *n.* exchange of commodity for money etc.; act or instance of selling; amount sold; occasion when goods are sold; offering of goods at reduced prices for a period. **for, on, sale** offered for purchase; **sale-room** room where auctions are held; **salesman, salesperson, saleswoman,** person employed to sell goods etc.

**salesmanship** /'seɪlzmənʃɪp/ *n.* skill in selling.

**saleable** /'seɪləb(ə)l/ *a.* fit to be sold; finding purchasers. **saleability** *n.*

**salient** /'seɪlɪənt/ 1 *a.* prominent, conspicuous; standing or pointing outwards. 2 *n.* salient angle; *Mil.* bulge in line of attack or defence.

**saline** /'seɪlaɪn/ 1 *a.* of salt(s); containing or tasting of salt(s). 2 *n.* saline substance; salt lake or spring etc. **salinity** /-'lɪn-/ *n.*

**saliva** /sə'laɪvə/ *n.* colourless liquid produced by glands in mouth. **salivary** *a.*

**salivate** /'sælɪveɪt/ *v.i.* secrete or discharge saliva esp. in excess.

**sallee** /'sæli:/ *n. Aus.* any of several species of acacia or eucalyptus.

**sallow**[1] /'sæləʊ/ *a.* (of complexion) of sickly yellow or yellowish brown.

**sallow**[2] /'sæləʊ/ *n.* low-growing willow; shoot or wood of this.

**sally** /'sæli:/ 1 *n.* rush from besieged place upon enemy; witticism, piece of banter. 2 *v.i.* make sally; go *forth* or *out* for walk etc.

**salmon** /'sæmən/ 1 *n.* large silver-scaled fish with orange-pink flesh. 2 *a.* orange-pink. 3 **salmon-trout** sea trout.

**salmonella** /sælmə'nelə/ *n.* kind of bacterium causing food poisoning.

**salon** /'sælɒn/ *n.* reception-room of large house; meeting here of eminent people; room or establishment where hairdresser or couturier etc. receives clients.

**saloon** /sə'lu:n/ *n.* large room or hall for assemblies etc. or for specified purpose; public room on ship; *US* drinking-bar; saloon car. **saloon bar** first-class bar in public house; **saloon car** motor car with closed body and no partition behind driver.

**salsify** /'sælsəfi:/ *n.* plant with long fleshy root cooked as vegetable.

**salt** /sɔ:lt or sɒlt/ 1 *n.* substance that gives sea-water its characteristic taste, got by mining or by evaporation of sea-water etc., and used esp. for seasoning or preserving food; *Chem.* substance formed when part of the hydrogen in an acid is replaced by a metal or metal-like radical; (often in *pl.*) substance resembling salt in taste or form etc.; in *pl.* such substance used as laxative; piquancy, pungency, wit. 2 *a.* containing or tasting of or treated with salt. 3 *v.t.* preserve or season or treat with salt; *sl.* make fraudulent entries in (accounts etc.). 4 **salt away, down,** *colloq.* save or put away for the future; **saltbush** any of a large group of wild herbs and shrubs of the Aus. interior; **salt-cellar** vessel holding salt for table use; **salt damp** *S. Aus.* saline rising damp; **salt-marsh** marsh overflowed by sea; **salt-mine** mine yielding rock-salt, *fig.* place of unremitting toil; **salt of the earth** finest people, those who keep society wholesome; **saltpan** hollow near sea where salt is got by evaporation; **take with a grain** or **pinch of salt** be sceptical about; **worth one's salt** having merit.

**SALT** *abbr.* Strategic Arms Limitation Talks.

**salting** /'sɔ:ltɪŋ/ *n.* salt marsh.

**saltire** /'sɔ:ltaɪə(r)/ *n.* X-shaped cross.

**saltpetre** /'sɔ:ltpi:tə(r)/ *n.* white crystalline salty substance used in gunpowder, in preserving meat, and medicinally.

**salty** /'sɔ:lti: or 'sɒl-/ *a.* containing or tasting of salt; pungent, witty.

**salubrious** /sə'lu:brɪəs/ *a.* health-giving. **salubrity** *n.*

**saluki** /sə'lu:ki:/ *n.* large slender silky-coated dog.

**salutary** /'sæljətəri:/ *a.* producing good effects.

**salutation** /sælju:'teɪʃ(ə)n/ *n.* sign or expression of greeting or respect; use of these.

**salute** /sə'lu:t/ 1 *n.* gesture expressing respect or courteous recognition etc.; *Mil.* etc. prescribed movement or use of flags or discharge of gun(s) in sign

**salvage**

of respect. 2 v. make salute to; greet with polite gesture; express respect for.

**salvage** /'sælvɪdʒ/ 1 n. rescue of property from loss at sea or by fire, payment made or due for this; saving and utilization of waste material; property or materials salvaged. 2 v.t. save from wreck or fire etc.; make salvage of.

**salvation** /sæl'veɪʃ(ə)n/ n. act of saving or being saved, esp. from sin and its consequences; person or thing that preserves from loss or calamity etc. **Salvation Army** religious missionary body organized on quasi-military lines.

**Salvationist** /sæl'veɪʃənɪst/ n. member of Salvation Army. **Salvationism** n.

**salve¹** /sælv/ 1 n. healing ointment; something that soothes. 2 v.t. soothe.

**salve²** /sælv/ v.t. save from wreck or fire etc.

**salver** /'sælvə(r)/ n. tray for handing refreshments or letters etc.

**salvo** /'sælvəʊ/ n. (pl. **-voes**) simultaneous firing of artillery or other guns; round of applause.

**sal volatile** /sæl və'lætəlɪ/ solution of ammonium carbonate, used as restorative in faintness etc.

**Samaritan** /sə'mærɪt(ə)n/ n. charitable or helpful person (also **good Samaritan**).

**samba** /'sæmbə/ 1 n. ballroom dance of Brazilian origin; music for this. 2 v.i. dance samba.

**same** 1 a. identical; unchanged; unvarying; previously referred to. 2 pron. **the same** the same thing. 3 adv. **the same** in the same manner. 4 **just the same** nevertheless.

**samovar** /'sæməvɑː(r)/ n. Russian urn for making tea.

**Samoyed** /'sæməjed/ n. white Arctic breed of dog.

**sampan** /'sæmpæn/ n. small boat used in Far East.

**samphire** /'sæmfaɪə(r)/ n. cliff plant used in pickles.

**sample** /'sɑːmp(ə)l/ 1 n. small part taken from quantity to show what whole is like; specimen; typical example. 2 v.t. take samples of, try qualities of; get representative experience of. 3 **sample-bag** Aus. show-bag.

**sampler** /'sɑːmplə(r)/ n. piece of embroidery worked to show proficiency.

**samurai** /'sæmʊraɪ/ n. (pl. same) Japanese army officer; hist. member of military caste in Japan.

**sanatorium** /sænə'tɔːrɪəm/ n. (pl. **-iums**) establishment for treatment of invalids, esp. convalescents and the chronically sick; accommodation for sick persons in school etc.

**sanctify** /'sæŋktɪfaɪ/ v.t. consecrate, make or observe as holy; purify from sin. **sanctification** n.

**sanctimonious** /sæŋktɪ'məʊnɪəs/ a. making a show of being holy.

**sanction** /'sæŋkʃ(ə)n/ 1 n. approval given to action etc. by custom or tradition; express permission; penalty or reward attached to law; consideration causing any rule to be obeyed; in pl. economic or military action to coerce a State to conform to agreement etc. 2 v.t. authorize, countenance, permit.

**sanctity** /'sæŋktɪtɪ/ n. sacredness, holiness.

**sanctuary** /'sæŋktjʊərɪ/ n. holy place; place where wild animals and birds etc. are protected; esp. hist. place of refuge.

**sanctum** /'sæŋktəm/ n. holy place; person's private room.

**sand** 1 n. substance resulting from wearing down of esp. siliceous rocks; in pl. grains of sand, expanse of sand, sandbank. 2 v.t. smooth or polish with sandpaper; sprinkle or treat with sand. 3 **sandbag** bag filled with sand esp. for making temporary defences, (v.t.) defend or hit with sandbag(s); **sandbank** deposit of sand forming shallow place in sea or river; **sand-blast** jet of sand driven by compressed air or steam, (v.t.) clean or treat with this; **sand-castle** structure of sand made esp. by child on beach; **sand-hill** dune; **sand-martin** bird nesting in sandy banks; **sandpaper** paper with abrasive coating for smoothing or polishing, (v.t.) treat with this; **sandpiper** bird inhabiting wet sandy places; **sandstone** sedimentary rock of compressed sand; **sandstorm** storm with clouds of sand raised by wind.

**sandal** /'sænd(ə)l/ n. shoe with openwork upper or no upper, fastened with straps.

**sandalwood** /'sændəlwʊd/ n. kind of scented wood; tree with this.

**sandwich** /ˈsænwɪdʒ/ 1 n. two or more slices of bread or toast etc. with filling between; cake of two or more layers with jam or cream etc. between. 2 v.t. put (thing, statement, etc.) between two others of different kind. 3 **sandwich-board** board carried by sandwich-man; **sandwich course** course of study in which periods of theoretical and practical work alternate; **sandwich-man** man walking in street with advertisement boards hanging in front and behind.

**sandy** /ˈsændɪ/ a. covered with sand; sand-coloured, (of hair) yellowish-red.

**sandy-blight** Aus. kind of ophthalmia.

**sane** a. of sound mind, not mad; (of opinion etc.) sensible, rational.

**sang** past of sing.

**sanger** /ˈsæŋə(r)/ n. Aus. colloq. sandwich.

**sang-froid** /sɑ̃ˈfrwɑː/ n. calmness in danger or difficulty.

**sanguinary** /ˈsæŋɡwɪnərɪ/ a. accompanied by or delighting in bloodshed; bloodthirsty; bloody.

**sanguine** /ˈsæŋɡwɪn/ a. optimistic; (of complexion) bright and florid.

**Sanhedrin** /ˈsænɪdrən/ n. court of justice and supreme council in ancient Jerusalem.

**sanitarium** /sænɪˈteərɪəm/ n. US sanatorium.

**sanitary** /ˈsænɪtərɪ/ a. of or aimed at or assisting the protection of health; hygienic. **sanitary towel** absorbent pad used during menstruation.

**sanitation** /sænɪˈteɪʃ(ə)n/ n. sanitary conditions, maintenance or improvement of these; disposal of sewage and refuse etc.

**sanitize** /ˈsænɪtaɪz/ v.t. make sanitary.

**sanity** /ˈsænɪtɪ/ n. being sane.

**sank** past of sink.

**Sanskrit** /ˈsænskrɪt/ 1 n. ancient and sacred language of Hindus in India. 2 a. of or in Sanskrit. 3 **Sanskritic** a.

**Santa Claus** /ˈsæntə klɔːz/ person said to fill children's stockings with presents at Christmas.

**sap**[1] 1 n. vital juice of plants; vitality; sl. foolish person. 2 v.t. drain of sap; exhaust vigour of. 3 **sappy** a.

**sap**[2] 1 n. tunnel or trench to conceal assailants' approach to fortified place. 2 v. make saps; undermine (wall etc.); destroy insidiously, weaken.

**sapid** /ˈsæpɪd/ a. savoury; not tasteless; not insipid. **sapidity** n.

**sapient** /ˈseɪpɪənt/ a. wise; pretending to be wise. **sapience** n.

**sapling** /ˈsæplɪŋ/ n. young tree.

**sapper** /ˈsæpə(r)/ n. private of Royal Engineers.

**sapphire** /ˈsæfaɪə(r)/ 1 n. transparent blue precious stone; its colour. 2 a. of sapphire blue.

**saprophyte** /ˈsæprəfaɪt/ n. vegetable organism living on dead organic matter.

**saraband** /ˈsærəbænd/ n. slow Spanish dance; music for this.

**Saracen** /ˈsærəs(ə)n/ n. Arab or Muslim of time of crusades. **Saracenic** a.

**sarcasm** /ˈsɑːkæz(ə)m/ n. bitter or wounding remark(s), esp. ironically worded. **sarcastic** a.

**sarcophagus** /sɑːˈkɒfəɡəs/ n. (pl. **-gi** /-ɡaɪ/) stone coffin.

**sardine** /sɑːˈdiːn/ n. small fish related to herring, often tinned tightly packed in oil.

**sardonic** /sɑːˈdɒnɪk/ a. grimly jocular; full of bitter mockery; cynical.

**sardonyx** /ˈsɑːdənɪks/ n. onyx in which white layers alternate with yellow or orange ones.

**sargasso** /sɑːˈɡæsəʊ/ n. (pl. **-os**) seaweed with berry-like air-vessels.

**sarge** /sɑːdʒ/ n. sl. sergeant.

**sari** /ˈsɑːrɪ/ n. length of material wrapped round body, worn as main garment by Hindu women.

**sarong** /səˈrɒŋ/ n. garment of long strip of cloth tucked round waist or under armpits.

**sarsaparilla** /sɑːsəpəˈrɪlə/ n. tropical Amer. smilax; its dried roots; tonic made from these.

**sarsen** /ˈsɑːs(ə)n/ n. sandstone etc. boulder, relict carried by ice in glacial period.

**sarsenet** /ˈsɑːsənət/ n. soft silk fabric used for linings etc.

**sartorial** /sɑːˈtɔːrɪəl/ a. of clothes or tailoring.

**sash**[1] n. long strip or loop of cloth worn over one shoulder or round waist esp. as part of uniform or insignia.

**sash**[2] n. frame holding window-glass,

**sassafras** /'sæsəfræs/ n. a medicinal bark; N. Amer. tree with this.

**Sassenach** /'sæsənæx/ n. Sc. & Ir. usu. derog. English person.

**sat** past & p.p. of **sit**.

**Sat.** abbr. Saturday.

**Satan** /'seɪt(ə)n/ n. the Devil.

**satanic** /sə'tænɪk/ a. of or like Satan; devilish, evil.

**satchel** /'sætʃ(ə)l/ n. small bag, esp. for carrying school-books.

**sate** v.t. satiate.

**sateen** /sæ'tiːn/ n. glossy cotton fabric woven like satin.

**satellite** /'sætəlaɪt/ n. heavenly or artificial body revolving round earth or other planet; hanger-on, follower; country etc. controlled by or dependent on another.

**satiate** /'seɪʃɪeɪt/ v.t. gratify fully, surfeit. **satiation** n.

**satiety** /sə'taɪətɪ/ n. state of being glutted; feeling of having had too much.

**satin** /'sætɪn/ n. silk etc. fabric with glossy surface on one side. **satin (bower-)bird** Aus. bower-bird with glossy plumage; **satin sparrow** a Tasmanian flycatcher; **satinwood** kind of choice glossy timber, any of several Aus. timber trees or their wood. **satiny** a.

**satire** /'sætaɪə(r)/ n. use of ridicule or irony etc. to expose folly or vice etc.; work or composition using satire. **satirical** /-'tɪr-/ a.

**satirist** /'sætərɪst/ n. writer or performer of satires.

**satirize** /'sætəraɪz/ v.t. attack with satire; describe satirically.

**satisfaction** /sætɪs'fækʃ(ə)n/ n. satisfying or being satisfied; thing that satisfies desire or gratifies feeling; payment of debt; atonement; amends for injury.

**satisfactory** /sætɪs'fæktərɪ/ a. causing satisfaction; adequate.

**satisfy** /'sætɪsfaɪ/ v.t. meet expectations or wishes of; be accepted by (person etc.) as adequate; please; pay, fulfil, comply with; put an end to (an appetite or want), rid (person) of an appetite or want; convince.

**satsuma** /sæt'suːmə/ n. kind of mandarin orange.

**saturate** /'sætʃəreɪt/ v.t. fill with moisture, soak; imbue with or steep in; cause (substance) to absorb, hold, or combine with greatest possible amount of another substance.

**saturation** /sætʃə'reɪʃ(ə)n/ n. act or result of being saturated. **saturation point** stage beyond which no more can be absorbed or accepted.

**Saturday** /'sætədeɪ or -dɪ/ n. day of week following Friday.

**Saturnalia** /sætə'neɪlɪə/ n. ancient-Roman festival of Saturn; **saturnalia** scene or time of wild revelry.

**saturnine** /'sætənaɪn/ a. of gloomy temperament or appearance.

**satyr** /'sætə(r)/ n. Gk. & Rom. myth. half-human half-animal woodland deity; lustful or sensual man.

**sauce** /sɔːs/ 1 n. liquid or soft preparation used as relish with food; something that adds piquancy; colloq. sauciness. 2 v.t. colloq. be impudent to. 3 **sauce-boat** shallow jug in which sauce is served; **saucepan** metal cooking-vessel with long handle, for use on top of stove.

**saucer** /'sɔːsə(r)/ n. small shallow dish, esp. for standing cup on.

**saucy** /'sɔːsɪ/ a. impudent, cheeky; colloq. smart-looking.

**sauerkraut** /'saʊəkraʊt/ n. German dish of pickled cabbage.

**sauna** /'sɔːnə/ n. Finnish-style steam-bath.

**saunter** /'sɔːntə(r)/ 1 v.i. walk in leisurely way. 2 n. leisurely ramble or gait.

**saurian** /'sɔːrɪən/ 1 n. animal of lizard family. 2 a. of or like a lizard.

**sausage** /'sɒsɪdʒ/ n. minced meat seasoned and stuffed into cylindrical case of thin membrane; sausage-shaped object. **sausage-dog** colloq. dachshund; **sausage roll** sausage-meat baked in cylindrical pastry-case.

**sauté** /'səʊteɪ/ 1 a. quickly and lightly fried in a little fat. 2 n. food cooked thus. 3 v.t. (past & p.p. **sautéd**) cook thus.

**savage** /'sævɪdʒ/ 1 a. uncivilized, in primitive state; fierce, cruel; colloq. angry. 2 n. member of savage tribe; brutal or barbarous person. 3 v.t. attack and bite or trample; attack fiercely.

**savagery** /'sævɪdʒərɪ/ n. savage behaviour or state.

**savannah** /sə'vænə/ n. grassy plain in tropical or subtropical region.

**savant** /'sæv(ə)nt/ n. learned person.

**save 1** v. rescue or preserve *from* danger or harm; keep for future use (also with *up*); obviate need for, avoid wasting; relieve from need or obligation or experience; prevent loss of; effect spiritual salvation of; *Footb.* etc. prevent opponent from scoring. **2** n. act of saving in football etc. **3** prep. except, but.

**saveloy** /'sævəlɔɪ/ n. highly seasoned sausage.

**saving** /'seɪvɪŋ/ **1** n. act of rescuing or preserving; in *pl.* amount of money saved. **2** a. redeeming; that makes economical use of; making reservation or exception. **3** prep. except. **4 savings-bank** bank receiving small deposits at interest.

**saviour** /'seɪvɪə(r)/ n. deliverer, redeemer; person who saves others from harm or danger.

**savoir-faire** /sævwɑː'feə(r)/ n. quickness to see and do right thing; tact.

**savory** /'seɪvərɪ/ n. aromatic herb used in cookery.

**savour** /'seɪvə(r)/ **1** n. characteristic taste or flavour; tinge or hint *of.* **2** v. appreciate flavour of, enjoy; suggest presence *of.*

**savoury** /'seɪvərɪ/ **1** a. with appetizing taste or smell; of stimulating or piquant flavour, not sweet. **2** n. savoury dish, esp. at end of meal or as appetizer.

**savoy** /sə'vɔɪ/ n. rough-leaved winter cabbage.

**savvy** /'sævɪ/ *sl.* **1** v. know. **2** n. knowingness, understanding.

**saw**[1] **1** n. implement with toothed blade for cutting wood etc. **2** v. (*p.p.* **sawn** or **sawed**) cut or make with saw; make to-and-fro motion as of saw or sawing. **3 sawdust** fine wood-fragments produced in sawing; **sawfish** large sea-fish with toothed end of snout; **sawmill** mill for mechanical sawing of wood into planks etc.; **saw-toothed** serrated.

**saw**[2] n. old saying, maxim.

**saw**[3] *past* of **see**[1].

**sawyer** /'sɔːjə(r)/ n. workman who saws timber.

**sax** n. *colloq.* saxophone.

**saxe** /sæks/ n. (also **saxe blue**) light blue with greyish tinge.

**saxifrage** /'sæksəfrɪdʒ/ n. kind of rock plant.

**Saxon** /'sæks(ə)n/ **1** a. of Germanic people by whom parts of England were occupied in 5th–6th cc.; Anglo-Saxon. **2** n. member or language of the Saxon people.

**saxophone** /'sæksəfəʊn/ n. keyed brass reed instrument with gradually widening tube. **saxophonist** /sæk'sɒfə-/ n.

**say 1** v. (3rd. *sing. pres.* **says** /sez/; *past* & *p.p.* **said** /sed/) utter; state; speak words of; express; convey information, indicate; adduce or plead; decide. **2** n. what one wishes to say, opportunity of saying this; share in decision. **3 say-so** power of decision, mere assertion.

**saying** /'seɪɪŋ/ n. common remark, maxim.

**sc.** *abbr.* scilicet.

**scab** n. crust formed over sore in healing; kind of skin-disease or plant-disease; blackleg in strike.

**scabbard** /'skæbəd/ n. sheath of sword etc.

**scabby** /'skæbɪ/ a. like a scab; covered with scabs. **scabby mouth** *Aus.* contagious disease of sheep and goats.

**scabies** /'skeɪbiːz/ n. contagious skin-disease causing itching.

**scabious** /'skeɪbɪəs/ n. a wild or garden flower.

**scabrous** /'skeɪbrəs/ a. rough-surfaced; indecent.

**scaffold** /'skæf(ə)ld/ n. platform on which criminal is executed; scaffolding.

**scaffolding** n. temporary structure of poles and planks providing builders etc. with platform(s); materials for this.

**scald** /skɔːld/ **1** v. burn with hot liquid or vapour; heat (liquid, esp. milk) to near boiling-point; cleanse with boiling water. **2** n. injury to skin by scalding.

**scale**[1] **1** n. set of marks at measured distances on line for use in measuring; basis of numerical notation; relative dimensions, ratio of reduction or enlargement in map or picture etc.; series of degrees; ladder-like arrangement, graded system; *Mus.* set of sounds belonging to a key, arranged in order of pitch. **2** *v.t.* climb up with ladder or by clambering; represent in dimensions different from but proportional to actual ones. **3 scale down** or **up** make

**scale** smaller or larger in proportion, reduce or increase in size; **to scale** with uniform reduction or enlargement.

**scale²** 1 *n.* one of thin horny overlapping plates protecting skin of many fishes and reptiles; thin plate or flake resembling this; incrustation inside boiler etc.; tartar on teeth. 2 *v.t.* remove scale(s) from; form or come off in scales. 3 **scaly** *a.*

**scale³** 1 *n.* pan of weighing-balance; in *pl.* weighing-instrument. 2 *v.t.* be found to weigh (specified amount).

**scalene** /'skeɪliːn/ *a.* (of triangle) having unequal sides.

**scallion** /'skæliːən/ *n.* spring onion.

**scallop** /'skɒləp/ 1 *n.* bivalve shellfish with fan-shaped ridged shells; one shell of this esp. used for cooking or serving food on; in *pl.* ornamental edging in fabric etc. 2 *v.t.* cook in scallop; ornament with scallops.

**scallywag** /'skæliːwæg/ *n. sl.* scamp, rascal.

**scalp** 1 *n.* skin and hair of top of head; this cut off as trophy by Amer. Indian. 2 *v.t.* take scalp of.

**scalpel** /'skælp(ə)l/ *n.* small surgical knife.

**scamp** 1 *n.* rascal, rogue. 2 *v.t.* do (work etc.) perfunctorily or inadequately.

**scamper** /'skæmpə(r)/ 1 *v.i.* move or run hastily or impulsively. 2 *n.* act of scampering.

**scampi** /'skæmpiː/ *n.pl.* large prawns.

**scan** 1 *v.* look at all parts of successively; look round quickly; traverse systematically with radar beam etc.; resolve (picture) into elements of light and shade for television transmission; analyse metre of (line etc.) by examining feet and syllables; be metrically correct. 2 *n.* act or process of scanning.

**scandal** /'skænd(ə)l/ *n.* general feeling of outrage or indignation, thing causing this; malicious gossip. **scandalmonger** /-mʌŋgə(r)/ person who spreads scandal.

**scandalize** /'skændəlaɪz/ *v.t.* offend moral feelings or sense of propriety of.

**scandalous** /'skændələs/ *a.* containing or arousing scandal; outrageous, shocking.

**Scandinavian** /skændɪ'neɪviːən/ 1 *a.* of Scandinavia. 2 *n.* native or inhabitant, or family of languages, of Scandinavia.

**scansion** /'skænʃ(ə)n/ *n.* metrical scanning.

**scant** *a.* barely sufficient; deficient.

**scanty** /'skæntiː/ *a.* of small amount or extent; barely sufficient.

**scapegoat** /'skeɪpgəʊt/ *n.* person blamed or punished for faults of others.

**scapula** /'skæpjʊlə/ *n.* (*pl.* **-lae** /-liː/) shoulder-blade.

**scapular** /'skæpjʊlə(r)/ 1 *a.* of scapula. 2 *n.* monastic short cloak.

**scar¹** 1 *n.* mark left on skin etc. by wound etc. 2 *v.* mark with or form scar(s).

**scar²** *n.* precipitous craggy part of mountain-side.

**scarab** /'skærəb/ *n.* gem cut in form of beetle.

**scarce** /skeəs/ 1 *a.* not plentiful; insufficient, rare. 2 *adv. arch.* scarcely. 3 **make oneself scarce** go away, keep out of the way.

**scarcely** /'skeəsliː/ *adv.* hardly, only just; surely not.

**scarcity** /'skeəsətiː/ *n.* being scarce; insufficiency.

**scare** /skeə(r)/ 1 *v.t.* strike with sudden terror, frighten (*away, off,* etc.); in *p.p.* frightened (*of, to do*). 2 *n.* sudden fright or alarm, esp. general alarm caused by baseless or exaggerated rumours. 3 **scarecrow** device for frightening birds away from crops, badly dressed or grotesque person; **scaremonger** /-mʌŋgə(r)/ person who starts or spreads scare(s).

**scarf¹** *n.* (*pl.* **scarves**) long strip of material worn round neck for ornament or warmth; square piece of material worn round neck or over woman's hair.

**scarf²** 1 *n.* joint made by thinning ends of two pieces of timber etc. so that they overlap without increase of thickness. 2 *v.t.* join with scarf.

**scarify** /'skeərɪfaɪ/ *v.t.* loosen surface of (soil etc.); *Surg.* make slight incisions in; scratch; criticize etc. mercilessly. **scarification** *n.*

**scarlatina** /skɑːlə'tiːnə/ *n.* scarlet fever.

**scarlet** /'skɑːlət/ 1 *a.* of brilliant red colour inclining to orange. 2 *n.* scarlet colour or pigment or clothes etc. 3

# scarp

**scarlet fever** infectious fever with scarlet rash; **scarlet runner** scarlet-flowered climbing bean.

**scarp** 1 *n.* steep slope, esp. inner side of ditch in fortification. 2 *v.t.* make steep or perpendicular.

**scarper** /ˈskɑːpə(r)/ *v.i. sl.* escape, run away.

**scat** *n.* wordless jazz song using voice as instrument.

**scathing** /ˈskeɪðɪŋ/ *a.* (of criticism etc.) harsh, severe.

**scatology** /skæˈtɒlədʒiː/ *n.* preoccupation with the obscene or with excrement. **scatological** *a.*

**scatter** /ˈskætə(r)/ 1 *v.* throw or send or go in many different directions; cover by scattering; rout or be routed; dissipate; *Phys.* deflect or diffuse (light, particles, etc.); in *p.p.* not situated together, wide apart. 2 *n.* act of scattering; small amount scattered; extent of distribution. 3 **scatter-brain** thoughtless or flighty person; **scatter cushions** ones to be placed here and there in a room.

**scatty** /ˈskætiː/ *a. sl.* lacking concentration, disorganized.

**scavenge** /ˈskævɪndʒ/ *v.* be or act as scavenger; remove dirt or waste etc. from.

**scavenger** /ˈskævəndʒə(r)/ *n.* person who searches among or collects things unwanted by others; animal or bird that feeds on carrion.

**scenario** /səˈnɑːrɪəʊ/ *n.* (*pl.* **-rios**) script or synopsis of film or play etc.; imagined sequence of future events.

**scene** /siːn/ *n.* place of actual or fictitious occurrence; piece of continuous action that forms part of play; action, episode, situation; stormy action or encounter or outburst, esp. with display of temper; landscape or view; painted canvas and properties etc. representing scene of action, stage set with these; *sl.* area or subject of activity or interest. **behind the scenes** out of view of audience, out of sight or hearing or knowledge of general public; **scene-shifter** person who changes scenes in theatre.

**scenery** /ˈsiːnərɪ/ *n.* furnishings used in theatre to represent scene; features (esp. picturesque) of landscape.

# schmaltz

**scenic** /ˈsiːnɪk/ *a.* picturesque; of or on stage; of scenery.

**scent** /sent/ 1 *n.* characteristic odour of something; fragrance; liquid perfume; smell or trail left by animal; line of investigation etc.; power of scenting. 2 *v.t.* discern by smell; begin to suspect presence or existence of; make fragrant, perfume.

**sceptic** /ˈskeptɪk/ *n.* person who questions truth of (esp. religious) doctrine cr theory etc.; sceptical person. **scepticism** *n.*

**sceptical** /ˈskeptɪk(ə)l/ *a.* of scepticism; critical, doubtful, incredulous, hard to convince.

**sceptre** /ˈseptə(r)/ *n.* staff borne as symbol of sovereignty.

**schedule** /ˈʃedjuːl/ 1 *n.* timetable or programme of planned events; table of details etc., esp. as appendix to document. 2 *v.t.* make schedule of; include in schedule; appoint time for; include (building etc.) in list of those to be preserved. 3 **on schedule** at time appointed; **scheduled flight** one operated on regular timetable.

**schematic** /skəˈmætɪk/ *a.* of or like scheme or diagram; systematic, formalized.

**schematize** /ˈskiːmətaɪz/ *v.t.* put in schematic form.

**scheme** /skiːm/ 1 *n.* systematic arrangement; outline, syllabus; plan of action; artful or underhand design. 2 *v.i.* make plans, plan esp. in secret or underhand way.

**scherzo** /ˈskeətsəʊ/ *n.* (*pl.* **-zos**) *Mus.* vigorous and lively movement or composition.

**schism** /ˈsɪz(ə)m/ *n.* separation or division in religious group. **schismatic** *a.*

**schist** /ʃɪst/ *n.* fine-grained rock with components arranged in layers.

**schizo** /ˈskɪtsəʊ/ *n.* (*pl.* **-zos**) *colloq.* schizophrenic.

**schizoid** /ˈskɪtsɔɪd/ 1 *a.* of or resembling schizophrenia or a schizophrenic. 2 *n.* schizoid person.

**schizophrenia** /skɪtsəˈfriːnɪə/ *n.* mental disorder marked by disconnection between thought, feelings, etc., and actions. **schizophrenic** /-ˈfren/-*a.* & *n.*

**schmaltz** /ʃmɔːlts/ *n.* sickly sentimentality.

**schnapps** /ʃnæps/ n. strong kind of gin.

**schnitzel** /'ʃnɪts(ə)l/ n. veal cutlet.

**schnorkel** var. of **snorkel**.

**scholar** /'skɒlə(r)/ n. learned person; person who learns; holder of scholarship. **scholarly** a.

**scholarship** /'skɒləʃɪp/ n. award of money towards education; learning, erudition.

**scholastic** /skə'læstɪk/ a. of schools or education; academic.

**school**[1] /sku:l/ 1 n. institution for educating children or giving instruction; its buildings; its pupils; time given to teaching; being educated in school; circumstances etc. serving to discipline or instruct; branch of study at university; group of artists or disciples etc. following or holding similar principles or opinions etc; group of gamblers. 2 v.t. send to school; discipline, bring under control, train or accustom to. 3 **schoolboy, schoolchild, schoolgirl,** one who attends school; **school-leaver** person who has just left school; **schoolmaster, schoolmistress, schoolteacher,** teacher in school; **schoolroom** room used for lessons, esp. in private house.

**school**[2] /sku:l/ n. shoal of fish or whales etc.

**schoolie** /'sku:li/ n. Aus. sl. schoolteacher.

**schooner** /'sku:nə(r)/ n. two-masted fore-and-aft rigged ship; large glass of sherry.

**schottische** /ʃɒ'ti:ʃ/ n. kind of slow polka.

**sciatic** /saɪ'ætɪk/ a. of hip or sciatic nerve; of or having sciatica. **sciatic nerve** large nerve from pelvis to thigh.

**sciatica** /saɪ'ætɪkə/ n. neuralgia of hip and thigh.

**science** /'saɪəns/ n. branch of knowledge, esp. one dealing with material phenomena and based on observation, experiment, and induction; systematic and formulated knowledge; pursuit of this; skilful technique. **science fiction** imaginative fiction based on postulated scientific discoveries etc.

**scientific** /saɪən'tɪfɪk/ a. of or concerned with science; according to principles of science; having or requiring trained skill.

**scientist** /'saɪəntɪst/ n. student or expert in science.

**scilicet** /'saɪlɪset/ adv. that is to say, namely.

**scimitar** /'sɪmɪtə(r)/ n. curved oriental sword.

**scintillate** /'sɪntɪleɪt/ v.i. sparkle, twinkle; talk or act cleverly or wittily. **scintillation** n.

**scion** /'saɪən/ n. shoot cut for grafting; young member of family.

**scissors** /'sɪzəz/ n.pl. (also **pair of scissors**) cutting-instrument of pair of blades pivoted together.

**sclerosis** /sklə'rəʊsɪs/ n. abnormal hardening of tissue. **sclerotic** /-'rɒt-/ a.

**scoff**[1] 1 v.i. speak derisively; mock or jeer at. 2 n. mocking words; taunt.

**scoff**[2] v.t. sl. eat greedily.

**scold** /skəʊld/ 1 v. rebuke severely or noisily; find fault noisily. 2 n. nagging or complaining woman.

**sconce** /skɒns/ n. wall-bracket holding candlestick or light-fitting.

**scone** /skɒn/ n. soft flat cake of flour etc. baked quickly.

**scoop** /sku:p/ 1 n. short-handled deep shovel; long-handled ladle; excavating part of digging-machine etc.; device for serving portions of ice cream etc.; act or motion of scooping; large profit made quickly; exclusive item in newspaper etc. 2 v. lift (up) or hollow (out) (as) with scoop; secure by sudden action or stroke of luck; forestall (rival newspaper etc.) with news scoop.

**scoot** /sku:t/ v.i. colloq. dart, shoot along; make off.

**scooter** /'sku:tə(r)/ n. child's toy of narrow foot-board on wheels propelled by pushes of one foot on ground; low-powered kind of motor cycle.

**scope** n. reach or sphere of observation or action, range; opportunity, outlet.

**scorch** /skɔ:tʃ/ 1 v. burn or discolour surface of with dry heat; become so discoloured etc.; sl. go at very high speed. 2 n. mark of scorching. 3 **scorched earth policy** policy of destroying everything that might be of use to invading enemy.

**scorcher** /'skɔ:tʃə(r)/ n. colloq. extremely hot day.

**score** n. number of points or goals etc. made by player or side in game etc.; detailed table of these; (set of) 20; Mus.

copy of composition with parts on series of staves; point or reason; *colloq.* remark or act by which person scores off another; scratch or notch or line made on surface; record of money owing. 2 *v.* make (points etc.) in game; win or gain; record or keep score; enter in score, record, esp. mentally (often with *up*); secure an advantage, have good luck; mark with incisions or lines; make (line etc.) with something that marks; *Mus.* orchestrate or arrange (*for* instruments). **3 score off** *colloq.* defeat in argument etc., humiliate.

**scoria** /'skɔ:riːə/ *n.* (*pl.* **-riae** /-riːiː/) slag; clinker-like mass of lava.

**scorn 1** *n.* disdain, contempt, derision; object of contempt. **2** *v.t.* hold in contempt; abstain from or refuse to do as unworthy.

**scornful** /'skɔ:nfəl/ *a.* contemptuous (*of*).

**Scorpio** /'skɔ:piːəʊ/ *n.* eighth sign of zodiac.

**scorpion** /'skɔ:piːən/ *n.* lobster-like arachnid with jointed stinging tail.

**Scot** *n.* native of Scotland.

**Scotch**[1] **1** *a.* Scots, Scottish. **2** *n.* Scotch whisky. **3 Scotch broth** soup made from beef or mutton with pearl barley and vegetables; **Scotch egg** hard-boiled egg enclosed in sausage-meat; **Scotch fir** common N. Eur. pine; **Scotch mist** thick mist and drizzle; **Scotch terrier** small rough-coated short-legged terrier; **Scotch whisky** whisky distilled in Scotland.

**scotch**[2] *v.t.* decisively put an end to; *arch.* wound without killing.

**scot-free** *a.* unharmed, unpunished.

**Scots 1** *a.* of Scotland. **2** *n.* form of English spoken in (esp. Lowlands of) Scotland. **3 Scotsman, Scotswoman**, native of Scotland; **Scots pine** = **Scotch fir**.

**Scottish** /'skɒtɪʃ/ *a.* of Scotland or its inhabitants.

**scoundrel** /'skaʊndr(ə)l/ *n.* unscrupulous person; villain. **scoundrelly** *a.*

**scour**[1] /'skaʊə(r)/ **1** *v.t.* rub bright or clean; clean out; clear *off*, *out*, etc. **2** *n.* act or process of scouring.

**scour**[2] /'skaʊə(r)/ *v.* search rapidly or thoroughly; hasten esp. in search or pursuit.

**scourer** /'skaʊərə(r)/ *n.* abrasive pad or powder for scouring.

**scourge** /skɜːdʒ/ *n.* person or thing regarded as instrument of divine or other vengeance etc.; whip. **2** *v.t.* chastise; afflict; whip.

**scouse** /skaʊs/ *sl.* **1** *a.* of Liverpool. **2** *n.* native of Liverpool; Liverpool dialect.

**scout**[1] /skaʊt/ **1** *n.* person sent out to get information or reconnoitre; **Scout** member of boys' organization intended to develop character. **2** *v.i.* act as scout. **3 scout about, around**, search (*for*).

**scout**[2] /skaʊt/ *v.t.* reject with scorn or ridicule.

**Scouter** /'skaʊtə(r)/ *n.* adult leader in Scout Association.

**scowl** /skaʊl/ **1** *n.* sullen or bad-tempered look. **2** *v.i.* wear scowl.

**scrabble** /'skræb(ə)l/ **1** *v.i.* scratch or grope busily (*about*). **2** *n.* **Scrabble (P)** game in which players build up words from letter-blocks on board.

**scrag 1** *n.* inferior end of neck of mutton (also **scrag end**); skinny person or animal. **2** *v.t.* strangle; hang; seize roughly by the neck; beat up.

**scraggy** /'skrægɪ/ *a.* thin and bony.

**scram** *v.i. sl.* go away.

**scramble** /'skræmb(ə)l/ **1** *v.* make way by clambering etc.; struggle with competitors (*for* thing or share of it); cook (eggs) by stirring in heated pan with butter etc.; alter frequency of sound etc. in telephoning etc. so as to make message unintelligible without special receiver; go rapidly or hastily. **2** *n.* climb or rough walk; motor-cycle race over rough ground; eager struggle or competition (*for*).

**scrap**[1] **1** *n.* small detached piece; shred or fragment; waste material, discarded metal for reprocessing; in *pl.* odds and ends, bits of uneaten food. **2** *v.t.* discard as useless. **3 scrap-book** book in which cuttings etc. are kept; **scrap-heap** collection of waste material; **scrap yard** place where scrap is collected.

**scrap**[2] *colloq.* **1** *n.* fight or rough quarrel. **2** *v.i.* have scrap.

**scrape 1** *v.* clean or abrade etc. by causing hard edge to move across surface; take *away* or *off* or *out* etc. by scraping; draw or move with sound (as) of scraping; produce such sound (*from*); move while (almost) touching; get

**scraper** 496 **scripture**

*along* or *by* or *through* etc. with difficulty; gain with effort or by parsimony; be economical; make clumsy bow. **2** *n.* act or sound of scraping; awkward predicament esp. resulting from escapade.

**scraper** /'skreɪpə(r)/ *n.* device used for scraping.

**scrappy** /'skræpɪ/ *a.* consisting of scraps, incomplete.

**scratch 1** *v.* score or wound superficially with sharp or pointed thing; rub with the nails to relieve itching; make hole or strike out or mark through etc. by scratching; erase name of or withdraw from list of competitors etc. **2** *n.* wound or mark or sound made by scratching; act of scratching oneself; *colloq.* trifling wound; starting-line for race etc.; position of those receiving no handicap. **3** *a.* collected by chance, collected or made from whatever is available; with no handicap given. **4 from scratch** from the beginning without any help or advantage; **up to scratch** up to required standard.

**scratchy** /'skrætʃɪ/ *a.* tending to make scratches or scratching noise; tending to cause itchiness; done in scratches or carelessly.

**scrawl 1** *v.* write in hurried untidy way. **2** *n.* hurried writing; scrawled note.

**scrawny** /'skrɔːnɪ/ *a.* lean, scraggy.

**scream 1** *v.* utter piercing cry (as) of terror or pain; utter in or with scream; laugh uncontrollably. **2** *n.* screaming cry or sound; *colloq.* irresistibly funny occurrence or person etc.

**scree** *n.* in *sing.* or *pl.* small loose stones; mountain slope covered with these.

**screech** /skriːtʃ/ **1** *n.* loud shrill harsh cry or sound. **2** *v.* make or utter with screech. **3 screech-owl** barn-owl.

**screed** *n.* long and tiresome letter or harangue.

**screen 1** *n.* fixed or movable upright partition designed to shelter from observation or draughts or excess of heat etc.; thing used as shelter, esp. from observation; measure adopted for concealment; windscreen; blank surface on which images are projected; *the* cinema industry; large sieve; system for showing presence or absence of disease or quality etc. **2** *v.t.* shelter, hide partly or completely; protect from detection or censure etc.; show (film etc.) on screen; prevent from causing electrical interference; sieve; test (person) for presence or absence of disease or quality etc., esp. for reliability or loyalty. **3 screen off** shut off or hide with screen; **screenplay** script of film; **screen-printing** process like stencilling with ink forced through prepared sheet of fine material.

**screw 1** *n.* cylinder or cone with spiral ridge running round it outside (**male screw**) or inside (**female screw**); metal male screw with slotted head for holding pieces of wood etc. together; wooden or other screw used to exert pressure; revolving shaft with spiral blades for propelling ship or aircraft etc.; one turn of screw; small twisted-up paper (*of*); oblique curling motion; *sl.* prison warder; *sl.* salary. **2** *v.* fasten or tighten (as) with screw; press hard on, oppress; extort *out of*; contort, distort. **3 screwball** *US sl.* crazy or eccentric person; **screwdriver** tool for turning screws by slot; **screw up** contract or contort, summon up (courage etc.), *sl.* bungle or mismanage.

**screwy** /'skruːɪ/ *a. sl.* mad, eccentric, absurd.

**scribble** /'skrɪb(ə)l/ **1** *v.* write hurriedly or carelessly; be author or writer. **2** *n.* scrawl; hasty note etc.

**scribbly gum** /'skrɪblɪ/ Aus. eucalypt with smooth white bark on which insects make marks like scribbling.

**scribe** *n.* ancient or medieval copyist of manuscripts. **scribal** *a.*

**scrim** *n.* open-weave fabric for lining or upholstery etc.

**scrimmage** /'skrɪmɪdʒ/ **1** *n.* tussle, confused struggle, brawl. **2** *v.i.* engage in scrimmage.

**scrimp** *v.* skimp.

**scrip** *n.* provisional certificate of money subscribed to company etc.; *collect.* such certificates.

**script 1** *n.* handwriting; type-face imitating handwriting; alphabet or system of writing; text of play or film or broadcast etc.; examinee's written answer. **2** *v.t.* write script for (film etc.).

**scripture** /'skrɪptʃə(r)/ *n.* sacred book; the Bible. **scriptural** *a.*

**scrivener** /'skrɪvənə(r)/ *n. hist.* drafter of documents; notary.

**scrofula** /'skrɒfjələ/ *n.* disease with glandular swellings. **scrofulous** *a.*

**scroll** /skrəʊl/ **1** *n.* roll of parchment or paper; book of ancient roll form; ornamental design imitating roll of parchment. **2** *v.t.* move (display on VDU screen) up or down etc. as new material appears.

**scrotum** /'skrəʊtəm/ *n.* (*pl.* **-ta**) pouch of skin enclosing testicles. **scrotal** *a.*

**scrounge** /skraʊndʒ/ *v. colloq.* obtain (things) illicitly or by cadging.

**scrub**[1] **1** *v.* rub hard so as to clean, esp. with hard brush; pass (gas etc.) through scrubber; *sl.* cancel (plan, order, etc.). **2** *n.* scrubbing or being scrubbed.

**scrub**[2] *n.* brushwood or stunted trees etc.; land covered with this; stunted or insignificant person etc. **scrub wallaby** *Aus.* paddymelon. **scrubby** *a.*

**scrubber**[1] /'skrʌbə(r)/ *n.* scrubbing-brush; apparatus for removing impurities from gases.

**scrubber**[2] /'skrʌbə(r)/ *n. Aus.* animal that lives in the scrub; domestic animal that has run wild; *sl.* inferior person or animal.

**scruff** *n.* back of neck.

**scruffy** /'skrʌfɪ/ *a.* shabby, slovenly, untidy.

**scrum** *n.* scrummage. **scrum-half** half-back who puts ball into scrum.

**scrummage** /'skrʌmɪdʒ/ *n. Rugby footb.* grouping of all forwards on each side to push against those of the other and seek possession of ball thrown on ground between them.

**scrumptious** /'skrʌmpʃəs/ *a. colloq.* delicious.

**scrunch** *n.* & *v.* crunch.

**scruple** /'skru:p(ə)l/ **1** *n.* doubt or hesitation in regard to morality or propriety of an action; unit of apothecaries' weight (20 grains). **2** *v.t.* hesitate owing to scruples *to do.*

**scrupulous** /'skru:pjələs/ *a.* careful to avoid doing wrong; conscientious even in small matters; (over-)attentive to details. **scrupulosity** *n.*

**scrutineer** /skru:tɪ'nɪə(r)/ *n.* person who scrutinizes ballot-papers.

**scrutinize** /'skru:tɪnaɪz/ *v.t.* subject to scrutiny.

**scrutiny** /'skru:tənɪ/ *n.* critical gaze; close or detailed examination; official examination of ballot-papers to check their validity or accuracy of their counting.

**scuba** /'sku:bə/ *n.* self-contained underwater breathing apparatus.

**scud** *v.i.* run or fly straight and fast; skim along; *Naut.* run before wind.

**scuff** **1** *v.* walk with dragging feet; graze or brush against; mark or wear out (shoes etc.) thus. **2** *n.* mark of scuffing.

**scuffle** /'skʌf(ə)l/ **1** *n.* confused struggle or disorderly fight. **2** *v.i.* engage in scuffle.

**scull** **1** *n.* each of pair of small oars; oar used to propel boat from stern. **2** *v.* row or propel with scull(s).

**scullery** /'skʌlərɪ/ *n.* back kitchen where dishes are washed etc.

**sculpt** *v. colloq.* sculpture.

**sculptor** /'skʌlptə(r)/ *n.* person who does sculpture. **sculptress** *n.*

**sculpture** /'skʌlptʃə(r)/ **1** *n.* art of forming representations by chiselling, carving, casting, or modelling; a work of sculpture. **2** *v.* represent in or adorn with sculpture; practise sculpture. **3 sculptural** *a.*

**scum** **1** *n.* impurities that rise to surface of liquid; *the* worst part, refuse (*of*). **2** *v.* remove scum from; form scum (on). **3 scummy** *a.*

**scupper** /'skʌpə(r)/ **1** *n.* hole in ship's side draining water from deck. **2** *v.t. sl.* sink (ship, crew); defeat or ruin (plan etc.).

**scurf** *n.* flakes of dead skin, esp. in hair. **scurfy** *a.*

**scurrilous** /'skʌrɪləs/ *a.* grossly or obscenely abusive. **scurrility** /-'rɪl-/ *n.*

**scurry** /'skʌrɪ/ **1** *v.i.* run hurriedly, scamper. **2** *n.* scurrying, bustle, rush; flurry (*of* snow etc.).

**scurvy** /'skɜ:vɪ/ **1** *n.* deficiency disease resulting from lack of vitamin C. **2** *a. arch.* paltry, contemptible.

**scut** *n.* short tail, esp. of rabbit, hare, or deer.

**scutter** /'skʌtə(r)/ *v.i. colloq.* scurry.

**scuttle**[1] /'skʌt(ə)l/ *n.* receptacle for carrying and holding small supply of coal; part of motor-car body between windscreen and bonnet.

**scuttle**[2] /'skʌt(ə)l/ **1** *n.* hole with lid in ship's deck or side. **2** *v.t.* let water in (ship) esp. to sink it.

**scuttle**³ /'skʌt(ə)l/ 1 *v.i.* scurry; make off, retreat in undignified way. 2 *n.* hurried gait; precipitate flight or departure.

**scythe** /saɪð/ 1 *n.* mowing and reaping implement with long thin slightly curved blade. 2 *v.t.* cut with scythe.

**SE** *abbr.* South-East(ern).

**sea** *n.* expanse of salt water; ocean; swell of sea, large wave; vast quantity or expanse *of*. **at sea** in ship on the sea, confused; **sea anchor** bag to retard drifting of ship; **sea-dog** old sailor; **seafaring** travelling by sea, esp. regularly; **seafood** edible marine fish or shellfish; **sea front** part of seaside town facing sea; **seagoing** designed for open sea; **sea-gull** = **gull**¹; **sea-horse** small fish with head suggestive of horse's; **seakale** herb with young shoots used as vegetable; **sea-legs** ability to walk on deck of rolling ship; **sea-level** mean level of sea's surface, used in reckoning heights of hills etc. and as barometric standard; **sea-lion** large kind of seal; **seaman** sailor, navigator, sailor below rank of officer; **seaplane** aircraft designed to take off from and land on water; **seaport** town with harbour; **sea-salt** salt got by evaporating seawater; **seascape** picture or view of the sea; **sea shell** shell of salt-water mollusc; **seasick** suffering sickness caused by motion of ship etc.; **seaside** sea coast, esp. as holiday resort; **sea trout** trout resembling salmon; **sea-urchin** marine animal covered with spines; **seaweed** plant growing in sea; **seaworthy** fit to put to sea.

**seal**¹ 1 *n.* piece of wax etc. impressed with design and attached to document as evidence of authenticity etc., or to envelope or receptacle or door to prevent its being opened without owner's knowledge; metal stamp etc. used in making seal; act or thing etc. regarded as confirmation or guarantee; decorative adhesive stamp. 2 *v.t.* stamp or fasten or certify as correct with seal; fix seal to; close securely or hermetically; *Aus.* surface (road) with tar macadam; settle or decide. 3 **sealing-wax** mixture of shellac and rosin softened by heating and used for seals; **seal off** prevent entry to and exit from (area).

**seal**² 1 *n.* kind of amphibious marine animal with flippers. 2 *v.i.* hunt seals.

**sealer** /'siːlə(r)/ *n.* ship or man engaged in seal-hunting.

**Sealyham** /'siːlɪəm/ *n.* wiry-haired short-legged terrier.

**seam** 1 *n.* line of junction between two edges, esp. those of two pieces of cloth etc. sewn together; fissure between parallel edges; wrinkle; stratum of coal etc. 2 *v.t.* join with seam; (esp. in *p.p.*) mark or score with seam or fissure or scar.

**seamstress** /'semstrəs/ *n.* woman who sews, esp. professionally.

**seamy** /'siːmɪ/ *a.* showing seams. **seamy side** disreputable or unattractive side.

**seance** /'seɪɑ̃s/ *n.* meeting for exhibition or investigation of spiritualistic phenomena.

**sear** /sɪə(r)/ *v.t.* scorch, cauterize; make callous.

**search** /sɜːtʃ/ 1 *v.* examine thoroughly, esp. to find something; make search or investigation. 2 *n.* act of searching, investigation. 3 **searchlight** lamp designed to throw strong beam of light in any desired direction, light or beam from this; **search-party** group of persons going out to look for lost person or thing; **search-warrant** official authority to enter and search building.

**season** /'siːz(ə)n/ 1 *n.* each of four divisions of year; proper or suitable time, time when something is plentiful or active or in vogue etc.; indefinite period; season-ticket 2 *v.* flavour or make palatable with condiments etc.; temper, moderate; make or become suitable or in desired condition, esp. by exposure to air or weather. 3 **in season** (of food) available plentifully, (of animal) on heat; **season-ticket** one entitling holder to any number of journeys or admittances etc. in a given period.

**seasonable** /'siːzənəb(ə)l/ *a.* suitable to season; opportune.

**seasonal** /'siːzən(ə)l/ *a.* of or depending on or varying with seasons.

**seasoning** /'siːzənɪŋ/ *n.* flavouring for food.

**seat** 1 *n.* thing made or used for sitting on; buttocks, part of garment covering them; part of chair etc. on which sitter's

**seating** /'si:tɪŋ/ *n.* seats collectively; sitting accommodation.

**sebaceous** /sə'beɪʃəs/ *a.* fatty; secreting or conveying oily matter.

**sec** *a.* (of wine) dry. [F]

**Sec.** *abbr.* Secretary.

**sec.** *abbr.* second(s).

**secateurs** /'sekətɜ:z/ *n.pl.* pruning-clippers.

**secede** /sə'si:d/ *v.i.* withdraw formally from political or religious body.

**secession** /sə'seʃ(ə)n/ *n.* seceding. **secessionist** *n.*

**seclude** /sə'klu:d/ *v.t.* keep retired or away from company, screen from view.

**seclusion** /sə'klu:ʒ(ə)n/ *n.* secluded state or place.

**second**[1] /'sekənd/ **1** *a.* next after first; other, another, additional; of subordinate importance or value; inferior. **2** *n.* second person or class etc.; supporter or helper esp. of boxer or duellist; in *pl.* goods of second quality, second helping of food. **3** *v.t.* back up, give one's support to; /sɪ'kɒnd/ transfer (person) temporarily to another department etc. **4 second-best** next after the best; **second class** second-best group or category or accommodation; **second cousin** child of parent's first cousin; **second fiddle** subordinate position; **second-hand** (of goods) bought after use etc. by previous owner, (of information etc.) obtained from others and not by original observation etc.; **second nature** acquired tendency that has become instinctive; **second-rate** inferior; **second sight** supposed power of perceiving future events; **second string** person or thing kept in reserve; **second thoughts** new opinion reached after consideration; **second wind** renewed capacity for effort after tiredness.

**second**[2] /'sekənd/ *n.* sixtieth part of minute of time or angle.

**secondary** /'sekəndəri/ *a.* coming after or next below what is primary; derived from or depending on or supplementing what is primary. **secondary colour** one made by mixing two primary colours; **secondary education** education for those who have had primary education; **secondary school** school where secondary education is given.

**secondly** /'sekəndli/ *adv.* in the second place, furthermore.

**secrecy** /'si:krəsi/ *n.* keeping of secrets; being secret.

**secret** /'si:krət/ **1** *a.* kept from general knowledge or view; not (to be) made known; working etc. in secret. **2** *n.* thing (to be) kept secret; thing for which explanation is unknown or not widely known. **3 in secret** secretly; **secret agent** spy; **secret police** police operating in secret for political ends; **secret service** government department concerned with espionage.

**secretariat** /sekrə'teəriət/ *n.* administrative office or department; its members or premises.

**secretary** /'sekrətəri/ *n.* person employed to deal with correspondence and keep records and make appointments etc.; principal assistant of minister or ambassador etc. **secretary-bird** long-legged crested Afr. bird; **Secretary-General** principal administrative officer of organization etc.; **Secretary of State** head of major government department, *US* Foreign Secretary. **secretarial** *a.*

**secrete** /sə'kri:t/ *v.t.* conceal; *Physiol.* separate (substance) in gland etc. from blood or sap for function in the organism or for excretion.

**secretion** /sə'kri:ʃ(ə)n/ *n.* act of secreting; secreted substance.

**secretive** /'si:krətɪv/ *a.* inclined to make or keep secrets, uncommunicative.

**secretory** /sə'kri:təri/ *a.* of physiological secretion.

**sect** *n.* body of persons sharing (usu. unorthodox) religious doctrines; religious denomination.

**sectarian** /sek'teəriən/ **1** *a.* of or concerning sect(s); bigoted in following one's sect. **2** *n.* member of a sect. **sectarianism** *n.*

**section** /'sekʃ(ə)n/ **1** *n.* part cut off;

**sectional**     500     **seed**

one of parts into which something is divided; subdivision of book or statute or group of people etc.; *US* area of land, district of town; *Aus. hist.* area of one square mile of undeveloped land; *Aus. & NZ* fare stage on bus or train route; subdivision of platoon; separation by cutting; cutting of solid by plane, resulting figure or area of this; thin slice cut off for microscopic examination. **2** *v.t.* arrange in or divide into sections. **3 section mark** sign (§) used to indicate start of section of book etc.

**sectional** /'sekʃən(ə)l/ *a.* of a section; made up of sections; local rather than general.

**sector** /'sektə(r)/ *n.* branch of an activity; *Geom.* plane figure enclosed between two radii of circle etc.; *Mil.* portion of battle area.

**secular** /'sekjələ(r)/ *a.* concerned with the affairs of this world; not sacred; not monastic or ecclesiastical; occurring once in an age or century. **secularity** *n.*; **secularize** *v.t.*

**secularism** /'sekjələrɪz(ə)m/ *n.* doctrine that morality or education should not be based on religion. **secularist** *n.*

**secure** /sɪ'kjʊə(r)/ **1** *a.* untroubled by danger or fear; impregnable; safe, reliable, firmly fixed or fastened or established etc. **2** *v.t.* make secure or safe; fasten or close securely; obtain.

**security** /sɪ'kjʊərɪtɪ/ *n.* secure condition or feeling; thing that guards or guarantees; safety of State or company etc. against espionage or theft etc.; organization for ensuring this; thing deposited or pledged as guarantee of fulfilment of undertaking or repayment of loan; document as evidence of loan, certificate of stock or bond etc. **security risk** person of doubtful loyalty.

**sedan** /sɪ'dæn/ *n.* sedan-chair; *US* saloon car. **sedan-chair** *hist.* vehicle for one person, usu. carried on poles by two men.

**sedate** /sɪ'deɪt/ **1** *a.* tranquil, equable, serious. **2** *v.t.* treat with sedation.

**sedation** /sɪ'deɪʃ(ə)n/ *n.* treatment by sedatives.

**sedative** /'sedətɪv/ **1** *a.* tending to calm or soothe. **2** *n.* sedative medicine etc.

**sedentary** /'sedəntərɪ/ *a.* sitting (of work etc.) characterized by much sitting and little physical exercise; (of person) having or inclined to work etc. of this kind.

**sedge** *n.* grasslike plant growing in marshes or by water. **sedgy** *a.*

**sediment** /'sedəmənt/ *n.* matter that settles to bottom of liquid, dregs; *Geol.* material carried by water or wind which settles and consolidates to make rock. **sedimentary** /-'men-/ *a.*; **sedimentation** *n.*

**sedition** /sɪ'dɪʃ(ə)n/ *n.* conduct or language inciting to rebellion. **seditious** *a.*

**seduce** /sɪ'dju:s/ *v.t.* tempt or entice into sexual activity or into wrongdoing; coax or lead astray.

**seduction** /sɪ'dʌkʃ(ə)n/ *n.* seducing or being seduced; tempting or attractive thing or quality.

**seductive** /sɪ'dʌktɪv/ *a.* tending to seduce; alluring, enticing.

**sedulous** /'sedjələs/ *a.* persevering, diligent, painstaking. **sedulity** *n.*

**see**[1] *v.* (*past* **saw**; *p.p.* **seen**) have or use power of perceiving with eye; discern mentally; understand; consider, foresee; watch, look at; meet, grant interview to; take view of; visit to consult; imagine; escort or conduct. **see about** attend to; **see off** accompany to place of departure; **see over** tour and examine; **see red** become enraged; **see through** not be deceived by, support (person) during difficult time, not abandon (project) before its completion; **see-through** transparent; **see to** attend to, repair.

**see**[2] *n.* office or position or jurisdiction of bishop.

**seed 1** *n.* flowering plant's unit of reproduction capable of developing into another such plant; *collect.* seeds in any quantity esp. as collected for sowing; semen; prime cause, beginning; offspring; seeded player. **2** *v.* place seed(s) in; sow seeds; sprinkle (as) with seed; produce or drop seed; remove seeds from (fruit etc.); place crystal etc. in (cloud) to produce rain; *Tennis* etc. designate (competitor in knock-out tournament) so that strong competitors do not meet each other until later rounds. **3 go, run, to seed** cease flowering as seed develops, *fig.* become degenerate or unkempt etc.; **seed-bed** bed of fine soil in which to sow seeds; **seed**

**seedling** /ˈsiːdlɪŋ/ n. young plant raised from seed.

**seedy** /ˈsiːdi/ a. full of seed; shabby; unwell.

**seeing** /ˈsiːɪŋ/ 1 n. use of eyes. 2 conj. (also **seeing that**) considering that; since, because.

**seek** v. (past & p.p. **sought** /sɔːt/) go in search of, look for; make a search; try to obtain or bring about, try to do; ask for, request.

**seem** v.i. have air or appearance of; appear to be or exist or be true etc. or to be or do.

**seeming** /ˈsiːmɪŋ/ a. apparent but not real.

**seemly** /ˈsiːmli/ a. decorous, becoming.

**seen** p.p. of **see**¹.

**seep** v.i. ooze, percolate.

**seepage** /ˈsiːpɪdʒ/ n. act of seeping; quantity that seeps.

**seer** /sɪə(r)/ n. person who sees; person who sees visions; prophet.

**seersucker** /ˈsɪəsʌkə(r)/ n. thin cotton etc. fabric with puckered surface.

**see-saw** /ˈsiːsɔː/ 1 a. & adv. with backward-and-forward or up-and-down motion. 2 n. long board supported in middle so that ends on which children etc. sit move alternately up and down; game played on this. 3 v.i. play at or move up and down as on see-saw; vacillate.

**seethe** /siːð/ v. boil, bubble; be agitated.

**segment** /ˈsɛɡmənt/ n. part cut off or separable from other parts; Geom. part of circle or sphere cut off by line or plane intersecting it. 2 v. divide into segments. 3 **segmental** a.; **segmentation** n.

**segregate** /ˈsɛɡrɪɡeɪt/ v. put or come apart, isolate; separate (esp. racial group) from the rest of the community. **segregation** n.

**seigneur** /seɪnˈjɜː(r)/ n. feudal lord. **seigneurial** a.

**seine** /seɪn/ n. large vertical fishing-net with ends drawn together to enclose fish.

**seismic(al)** /ˈsaɪzmɪk/ a. (also **seismical**) of earthquake(s).

**seismograph** /ˈsaɪzməɡrɑːf/ n. instrument for recording earthquake tremors.

**seismography** /saɪzˈmɒɡrəfi/ n. study or recording of seismic phenomena. **seismographer** n.

**seismology** /saɪzˈmɒlədʒi/ n. seismography. **seismologist** n.

**seize** /siːz/ v. take or hold possession of esp. forcibly or suddenly or by legal power; comprehend quickly or clearly; Law put in possession of. **seize up** (of mechanism) become stuck or jammed from undue heat or friction etc.

**seizure** /ˈsiːʒə(r)/ n. seizing or being seized; sudden attack of apoplexy etc., stroke.

**seldom** /ˈsɛldəm/ adv. rarely; not often.

**select** /sɪˈlɛkt/ 1 v.t. choose, esp. as best or most suitable. 2 a. chosen for excellence; picked, choice; exclusive. 3 **selector** n.

**selection** /sɪˈlɛkʃ(ə)n/ n. selecting; what is selected; Aus. free-selection, piece of land taken up by free-selection; things from which choice may be made; Biol. process by which some animals or plants thrive more than others, as factor in evolution.

**selective** /sɪˈlɛktɪv/ a. using or characterized by selection; able to select. **selectivity** n.

**selenium** /sɪˈliːnɪəm/ n. non-metallic element of sulphur group.

**self** 1 n. (pl. **selves**) person's or thing's own individuality or essence; person or thing as object of reflexive action; one's own interests or pleasure, concentration on these; Commerc. or colloq. myself, yourself, himself, etc. 2 a. of same colour throughout.

**self-** in comb. expr. reflexive action, automatic or independent action, or sameness. **self-abuse** masturbation; **self-addressed** addressed to oneself; **self-assertive** determined to assert oneself or one's claims etc.; **self-assertion** n.; **self-assurance** self-confidence; **self-catering** providing one's own meals; **self-centred** preoccupied with oneself or one's own affairs; **self-confident** having confidence in one's own abilities etc.; **self-confidence** n.; **self-conscious** embarrassed or ill at ease from awareness of oneself; **self-contained** complete in itself, uncommunicative; **self-control** control of

**selfish** oneself or one's behaviour etc.; **self-defence** defence of oneself or one's reputation etc.; **self-denial** going without things one would like; **self-determination** free will, choice of form of government or allegiance exercised by nation; **self-employed** working as owner of business etc.; **self-esteem** good opinion of oneself; **self-evident** needing no demonstration; **self-governing** governing itself or oneself; **self-government** n.; **self-help** use of one's own abilities etc. to achieve success; **self-important** having exaggerated idea of one's own importance; **self-importance** n.; **self-indulgent** indulging one's own desires for ease or pleasure etc.; **self-indulgence** n.; **self-interest** one's personal interests or advantage; **self-interested** activated by self-interest; **self-made** having risen from obscurity or poverty by one's own efforts; **self-opinionated** obstinate in one's own opinion; **self-pity** pity for oneself; **self-portrait** artist's portrait of himself; **self-possessed** unperturbed, cool; **self-possession** n.; **self-preservation** keeping oneself from death and harm, instinct for this; **self-raising** (of flour) containing its own raising agent; **self-reliant** relying on one's own abilities; **self-reliance** n.; **self-respect** proper regard for one's dignity or standard of conduct etc.; **self-righteous** convinced of one's own righteousness; **self-sacrifice** sacrifice of one's interests and desires to those of others; **selfsame** *the* very same; **self-satisfied** conceited; **self-satisfaction** n.; **self-seeking** seeking one's own welfare before that of others; **self-service** in or at which customers help themselves and pay cashier afterwards; **self-starter** electric device for starting internal-combustion engine; **self-styled** having taken name or description without justification; **self-sufficient** capable of supplying one's own needs; **self-sufficiency** n.; **self-willed** determined to follow one's own wishes or intentions etc.

**selfish** /'selfɪʃ/ a. deficient in consideration for others; actuated by or appealing to self-interest.

**selfless** /'selfləs/ a. disregarding oneself, unselfish.

**sell** 1 v. (*past* & *p.p.* **sold** /səʊld/) make over or dispose of in exchange for money; deal in, keep stock of for sale; betray for money or other reward; promote sales (of); advertise or publish merits of; persuade or convince of value or importance of something; cause to be sold. 2 n. *colloq*. manner of selling; deception, disappointment. 3 **seller's market** situation when goods are scarce and expensive; **sell off** sell remainder of at reduced prices; **sell out** sell (all) one's stock or shares etc., betray, be treacherous; **sell-out** selling of all tickets for show etc., commercial success, betrayal; **sell short** disparage, underestimate; **sell up** sell one's business or house etc.

**Sellotape** /'seləteɪp/ n. (**P**) adhesive usu. transparent cellulose tape.

**selvage** /'selvɪdʒ/ n. edge of cloth so woven that it cannot unravel.

**semantic** /sə'mæntɪk/ a. of meaning in language.

**semantics** n.pl. (usu. treated as *sing*.) branch of linguistics concerned with meanings.

**semaphore** /'seməfɔː(r)/ 1 n. signalling by person holding flag in each hand. 2 v. signal or send by semaphore.

**semblance** /'sembləns/ n. outward or superficial appearance of something.

**semen** /'siːmən/ n. reproductive fluid of males, containing spermatozoa.

**semester** /sə'mestə(r)/ n. half-year term in (esp. German and US) universities.

**semi** /'semi/ n. *colloq*. semi-detached house.

**semi-** *in comb*. half-, partly, occurring etc. twice in specified period.

**semibreve** /'semibriːv/ n. *Mus*. longest note in common use.

**semicircle** /'semisɜːk(ə)l/ n. half of circle or its circumference. **semicircular** a.

**semicolon** /semi'kəʊlən/ n. punctuation mark (;) of intermediate value between comma and full stop.

**semiconductor** /semikən'dʌktə(r)/ n. substance that in certain conditions has electrical conductivity intermediate between insulators and metals.

**semi-detached** /ˌsemiːdəˈtætʃt/ a. (of house) joined to another on one side only.

**semifinal** /ˌsemiːˈfaɪm(ə)l/ n. match or round preceding final. **semifinalist** n.

**seminal** /ˈsemən(ə)l/ a. of seed or semen; germinal, reproductive; (of idea etc.) providing basis for future development.

**seminar** /ˈsemənɑː(r)/ n. small class for discussion etc.; short intensive course of study.

**seminarist** /ˈsemənərɪst/ n. student in seminary.

**seminary** /ˈsemənərɪ/ n. training-college for priests etc.

**semi-permeable** /ˌsemiːˈpɜːmɪəb(ə)l/ a. (of membrane etc.) allowing small molecules to pass through but not large ones.

**semiprecious** /ˌsemiːˈpreʃəs/ a. (of gem) of less value than a precious stone.

**semiquaver** /ˈsemiːkweɪvə(r)/ n. *Mus.* note equal to half a quaver.

**Semite** /ˈsiːmaɪt/ n. member of any of races supposedly descended from Shem, including Jews and Arabs.

**Semitic** /sɪˈmɪtɪk/ a. of languages of family including Hebrew and Arabic; of Semites, esp. of Jews.

**semitone** /ˈsemiːtəʊn/ n. half a tone in musical scale.

**semi-trailer** /ˌsemiːˈtreɪlə(r)/ n. trailer having wheels at back and supported at front by towing vehicle.

**semivowel** /ˈsemiːvaʊəl/ n. sound intermediate between vowel and consonant; letter representing this.

**semolina** /ˌseməˈliːnə/ n. hard round grains of wheat used for puddings etc.

**sempstress** var. of **seamstress**.

**Sen.** *abbr.* Senator; Senior.

**senate** /ˈsenət/ n. upper house of legislature in some countries; governing body of some universities; *Rom. hist.* State council.

**senator** /ˈsenətə(r)/ n. member of senate. **senatorial** a.

**send** v. (past & p.p. **sent**) order or cause to go or be conveyed (*to*); send message or letter; grant, bestow, inflict, cause to be. **send down** rusticate or expel from university; **send for** summon, order by post; **send off** get despatched, witness departure of; **send away** (*for*), attend departure of; **send-off** demonstration of goodwill etc. at departure of person; **send on** transmit to further destination; **send up** *colloq.* satirize; **send-up** n.

**senescent** /sɪˈnes(ə)nt/ a. growing old. **senescence** n.

**seneschal** /ˈsenɪʃ(ə)l/ n. steward of medieval great house.

**senile** /ˈsiːnaɪl/ a. of or characteristic of old age; having symptoms and weakness of old age. **senility** /-ˈnɪl-/ n.

**senior** /ˈsiːnɪə(r)/ 1 a. older in age or standing; of higher degree. 2 n. person of advanced age or long service; one's elder or superior. 3 **senior citizen** old person, esp. old-age pensioner. 4 **seniority** /-ˈɒr-/ n.

**senna** /ˈsenə/ n. cassia; laxative prepared from this.

**señor** /senˈjɔː(r)/ n. (*pl.* **señores** /senˈjɔːrez/) title used of or to Spanish-speaking man. [Sp.]

**señora** /senˈjɔːrə/ n. title used of or to Spanish-speaking married woman. [Sp.]

**señorita** /ˌsenjəˈriːtə/ n. title used of or to Spanish-speaking unmarried woman. [Sp.]

**sensation** /senˈseɪʃ(ə)n/ n. consciousness of perceiving or seeming to perceive some condition of body or senses or mind etc.; excited or violent feeling esp. in community; cause or manifestation of this.

**sensational** /senˈseɪʃən(ə)l/ a. causing or intended to cause a sensation. **sensationalism** n.; **sensationalist** a. & n.

**sense** /sens/ 1 n. any of special bodily faculties through which sensation is caused; ability to perceive; consciousness *of*; appreciation or instinct; practical wisdom; conformity to this; meaning of word etc.; intelligibility or coherence; prevailing opinion; in *pl.* person's sanity or normal state of mind. 2 *v.t.* perceive by sense(s); be vaguely aware of; (of machine) detect.

**senseless** /ˈsenslas/ a. unconscious; wildly foolish; meaningless, purposeless.

**sensibility** /ˌsensəˈbɪlɪtɪ/ n. capacity to feel; sensitiveness or susceptibility; in *pl.* tendency to feel offended etc.

**sensible** /ˈsensəb(ə)l/ a. having or showing good sense; judicious; perceptible by senses; aware *of*.

**sensitive** /ˈsensɪtɪv/ a. acutely affected

by external impressions; having sensibility *to*; touchy or quick to take offence; responsive *to* or recording slight changes of condition, readily affected by or susceptible to (light, agency, etc.); (of topic) subject to restriction of discussion to prevent embarrassment etc. **sensitive plant** kind of mimosa that droops or closes when touched. **sensitivity** *n*.

**sensitize** /'sensətaɪz/ *v.t.* make sensitive. **sensitization** *n*.

**sensor** /'sensə(r)/ *n*. device to detect or record or measure a physical property.

**sensory** /'sensəri/ *a*. of sensation or senses.

**sensual** /'sensjʊəl/ *a*. of or connected with the body and the senses; self-indulgent, esp. sexually. **sensualism** *n*.; **sensuality** /-'æl-/ *n*.

**sensuous** /'sensjʊəs/ *a*. of or derived from or affecting senses, esp. aesthetically.

**sent** past & p.p. of **send**.

**sentence** /'sent(ə)ns/ **1** *n*. series of words grammatically complete in itself; punishment allotted to person convicted in criminal trial; declaration of this. **2** *v.t.* declare sentence of, condemn *to*.

**sententious** /sen'tenʃəs/ *a*. affectedly or pompously moralizing; aphoristic, moralistic.

**sentient** /'senʃ(ə)nt/ *a*. that feels or is capable of feeling. **sentience** *n*.

**sentiment** /'sentəmənt/ *n*. mental feeling, view; emotional thought expressed in words etc.; tendency to be swayed by feeling; mawkish tenderness.

**sentimental** /sentə'ment(ə)l/ *a*. of or characterized by sentiment; showing or affected by emotion rather than reason. **sentimentalism** *n*.; **sentimentalist** *n*.; **sentimentality** *n*.; **sentimentalize** *v*.

**sentinel** /'sentɪn(ə)l/ *n*. sentry.

**sentry** /'sentri/ *n*. soldier etc. stationed to keep guard. **sentry-box** wooden cabin large enough to shelter standing sentry; **sentry-go** duty of pacing up and down as sentry.

**sepal** /'sep(ə)l/ *n*. leaf or division of calyx.

**separable** /'sepərəb(ə)l/ *a*. that can be separated. **separability** *n*.

**separate 1** /'sepərət/ *a*. divided or withdrawn from others; independent, distinct, individual, of individuals. **2** /'sepərət/ *n*. in *pl*. separate articles of dress suitable for wearing together in various combinations. **3** /'sepəreɪt/ *v*. make separate, sever; prevent union or contact of; cease to live together as married couple; go different ways; secede *from*; divide or sort into parts or sizes. **4 separator** *n*.

**separation** /sepə'reɪʃ(ə)n/ *n*. separating or being separated; separation of husband and wife without dissolution of marriage.

**separatist** /'sepərətɪst/ *n*. person who favours separation, esp. for political or ecclesiastical independence. **separatism** *n*.

**sepia** /'siːpɪə/ *n*. dark reddish-brown colour or paint.

**sepoy** /'siːpɔɪ/ *n*. *hist*. Indian soldier under European, esp. British, discipline.

**sepsis** /'sepsɪs/ *n*. (*pl*. **-ses** /-siːz/) septic condition.

**sept** *n*. clan, esp. in Ireland.

**Sept.** *abbr*. September.

**September** /sep'tembə(r)/ *n*. ninth month of year.

**septet** /sep'tet/ *n*. musical composition for 7 performers; the performers; group of 7.

**septic** /'septɪk/ *a*. putrefying; contaminated by bacteria. **septic tank** tank in which sewage is disintegrated through bacterial activity.

**septicaemia** /septɪ'siːmɪə/ *n*. blood-poisoning.

**septuagenarian** /septjuːədʒə'neərɪən/ *n*. person between 70 and 79 years old.

**Septuagesima** /septjuːə'dʒesəmə/ *n*. third Sunday before Lent.

**Septuagint** /'septjuːədʒɪnt/ *n*. ancient-Greek version of OT.

**septum** /'septəm/ *n*. (*pl*. **-ta**) partition such as that between nostrils.

**sepulchral** /sə'pʌlkr(ə)l/ *a*. of tomb or burial; gloomy, dismal.

**sepulchre** /'sepəlkə(r)/ **1** *n*. tomb, burial vault or cave. **2** *v.t.* lay in sepulchre.

**sequel** /'siːkw(ə)l/ *n*. what follows after; novel or film etc. that continues story of earlier one.

**sequence** /'siːkwəns/ *n*. succession;

# sequential                                                                 505                                                                 service

order of succession; set of things belonging next to one another; unbroken series; episode or incident in film etc.

**sequential** /sɪˈkwenʃ(ə)l/ *a.* forming sequence or consequence.

**sequester** /sɪˈkwestə(r)/ *v.t.* seclude, isolate; sequestrate.

**sequestrate** /sɪˈkwestreɪt/ *v.t. Law* confiscate, take temporary possession of (debtor's estate etc.). **sequestration** /sɪkwɪˈstreɪʃ(ə)n/ *n.*

**sequin** /ˈsiːkwɪn/ *n.* circular spangle on dress etc.

**sequoia** /sɪˈkwɔɪə/ *n.* Californian coniferous tree of immense height.

**sera** *pl.* of **serum**.

**seraglio** /seˈrɑːlɪəʊ/ *n.* (*pl.* **-ios**) harem; *hist.* Turkish palace.

**seraph** /ˈserəf/ *n.* (*pl.* **-phim** or **-phs**) member of highest of 9 orders of angels. **seraphic** /-ˈræf-/ *a.*

**serenade** /serəˈneɪd/ 1 *n.* piece of music (suitable to be) sung or played at night, esp. by lover under lady's window; orchestral suite for small ensemble. 2 *v.t.* sing or play serenade to.

**serendipity** /serənˈdɪpɪtɪ/ *n.* faculty of making happy discoveries by accident. **serendipitous** *a.*

**serene** /sɪˈriːn/ *a.* clear and calm; placid, unperturbed. **serenity** /-ˈren-/ *n.*

**serf** *n. hist.* labourer not allowed to leave the land on which he worked; oppressed person, drudge. **serfdom** *n.*

**serge** *n.* durable twilled worsted etc. fabric.

**sergeant** /ˈsɑːdʒ(ə)nt/ *n.* non-commissioned army or air force officer next below warrant officer; police officer next below inspector. **sergeant-major** warrant officer assisting adjutant of regiment or battalion.

**serial** /ˈsɪərɪəl/ 1 *n.* story published or broadcast etc. in instalments. 2 *a.* of or in or forming series; (of story etc.) in form of serial.

**serialize** /ˈsɪərɪəlaɪz/ *v.t.* publish or produce in instalments. **serialization** *n.*

**series** /ˈsɪəriːz/ *n.* (*pl.* same) number of things or events etc. of which each is similar to or connected with the preceding one; number of radio or television programmes or films etc. with same actors and theme etc. but each complete in itself. **in series** (of set of electrical circuits) arranged so that same current passes through each circuit.

**serif** /ˈserɪf/ *n.* fine cross-line finishing off stroke of letter.

**serious** /ˈsɪərɪəs/ *a.* thoughtful, earnest; important; requiring thought; not slight or negligible; sincere, in earnest.

**serjeant** /ˈsɑːdʒ(ə)nt/ *n. hist.* barrister of highest rank. **serjeant-at-arms** official of court or city or parliament with ceremonial duties.

**sermon** /ˈsɜːmən/ *n.* discourse on religious or moral subject, esp. delivered from pulpit; admonition, reproof.

**sermonize** /ˈsɜːmənaɪz/ *v.* deliver moral lecture (to).

**serous** /ˈsɪərəs/ *a.* of or like serum, watery.

**serpent** /ˈsɜːp(ə)nt/ *n.* snake, esp. of large kind; treacherous or cunning person.

**serpentine** /ˈsɜːpəntaɪn/ 1 *a.* of or like serpent; writhing, coiling, sinuous. 2 *n.* soft usu. dark green rock, sometimes mottled.

**serrated** /səˈreɪtɪd/ *a.* with toothed edge like a saw. **serration** *n.*

**serried** /ˈserɪd/ *a.* (of ranks esp. of soldiers) close together.

**serum** /ˈsɪərəm/ *n.* (*pl.* **-ra** or **-rums**) liquid separating from clot when blood coagulates, esp. used for inoculation; watery fluid in animal bodies.

**servant** /ˈsɜːv(ə)nt/ *n.* person who carries out orders of employer, esp. one engaged in household work; person willing to serve another.

**serve** 1 *v.* be servant to; do service for; carry out duty; be employed (*in* organization, esp. armed forces); meet needs (of), perform function, be suitable, suffice; go through due period of (office or apprenticeship or prison sentence etc.); set (food) on table, distribute, dish *out* or *up*; act as waiter; act towards or treat in specified way; make legal delivery of (writ etc.); set (ball) in play at tennis etc.; (of male animal) copulate with (female). 2 *n. Tennis* etc. act or manner of serving ball; person's turn to serve. 3 **serve person right** be his deserved misfortune.

**server** /ˈsɜːvə(r)/ *n.* person who serves, esp. *Eccl.* celebrant's lay assistant.

**service** /ˈsɜːvɪs/ 1 *n.* work done or doing

of work for employer or for community etc.; assistance or benefit given to someone; provision of some public need, e.g. transport or (in *pl.*) water, gas, etc.; being servant; employment or position as servant; department of royal or public employ, persons or employment in it; in *pl. the* armed forces; meeting of congregation for worship; liturgical form for use on some occasion; maintenance and repair work, esp. by vendor or manufacturer after sale; serving of food etc.; set of dishes etc. for serving meal; serve in tennis etc., game in which one serves. 2 *v.t.* provide service for, do routine maintenance work on. 3 **at person's service** ready to serve him; **of service** useful; **service-car** rural bus etc. carrying passengers and mail etc.; **service charge** additional charge for service rendered; **service flat** one in which domestic service etc. is provided by the management; **service industry** one providing services not goods; **serviceman, servicewoman**, person in armed services; **service road** one giving access to houses lying back from main road; **service station** place beside road selling petrol etc. to motorists.

**serviceable** /'sɜːvəsəb(ə)l/ *a.* useful or usable; durable, hard-wearing.

**serviette** /sɜːvɪˈet/ *n.* table-napkin.

**servile** /'sɜːvaɪl/ *a.* of or like slave(s); slavish, fawning, completely dependent. **servility** /-'vɪl-/ *n.*

**servitor** /'sɜːvətə(r)/ *n. arch.* attendant, servant.

**servitude** /'sɜːvɪtjuːd/ *n.* slavery, subjection.

**servo-** *in comb.* power-assisted.

**sesame** /'sesəmɪ/ *n.* E. Ind. herbaceous plant with oil-yielding seeds; its seeds.

**sesqui-** *in comb.* one and a half.

**sessile** /'sesaɪl/ *a. Biol.* attached directly by base without stalk or peduncle etc.

**session** *n.* assembly for deliberative or judicial business; single meeting for such purpose; period during which such meetings are regularly held; academic year; period devoted to an activity. **in session** assembled for business, not on vacation. **sessional** *a.*

**set**[1] 1 *v. (past & p.p.* **set**) put or lay or stand in certain position; fix or place ready; dispose suitably for use or action or display; (of sun, moon, etc.) move towards or below earth's horizon; adjust hands or mechanism of (clock, trap, etc.); lay (table) for meal; solidify or harden; fix (hair) while damp so that it dries in desired style; (of face) assume hard expression; insert (jewel) in ring or framework etc.; ornament or provide (surface) *with*; bring into specified state, cause to be; present or impose as work to be done or material to be dealt with or problem to be solved etc.; initiate (fashion etc.); establish (a record etc.); determine, decide; join, attach, fasten; appoint, establish; (of tide, current, etc.) have certain motion or direction; put parts of (broken or dislocated bone, limb, etc.) into correct position for healing; provide (song, words) with music; arrange (type) or type for (book etc.); (of blossom) form into fruit; (of hunting dog) take rigid attitude indicating presence of game. 2 *n.* direction or position in which something sets or is set; setting or stage furniture etc. for play or film etc.; setting of sun or hair etc.; (also **sett**) badger's burrow, paving-block, young plant or bulb ready to be planted. 3 *a.* prescribed or determined in advance; unchanging, fixed; prepared for action. 4 **have a set on person** *Aus. colloq.* have a grudge against him; **set about** begin, take steps towards, attack; **set back** impede or reverse progress of, *sl.* cost (person) specified amount; **set-back** reversal or arrest of progress; **set down** record in writing; **set eyes on** catch sight of; **set forth** begin journey or expedition; **set in** begin, become established, insert; **set off** begin journey, initiate, stimulate, cause (person) to start laughing etc., serve as adornment or foil to, use as compensating item *against*; **set on** set upon, instigate, (*a.*) determined to get or achieve etc.; **set out** begin journey, exhibit, arrange; **set piece** formal or elaborate arrangement esp. in art or literature, fireworks arranged on scaffolding etc.; **set square** right-angled triangular plate for drawing lines at certain angles; **set to** begin doing something vigorously; **set-to** fight or argument; **set up** place in position or view, start or establish, prepare,

**set**              507              **sexton**

equip; **set-up** arrangement or organization, manner or structure of this; **set upon** attack, cause or urge to attack.

**set²** n. see **set¹**.

**sett** n. see **set¹**.

**settee** /se'ti:/ n. long seat with back and usu. arms, for more than one person.

**setter** /'setə(r)/ n. kind of sporting dog trained to stand rigid on scenting game.

**setting** /'setɪŋ/ n. position or manner in which thing is set; surroundings, environment, scene; scenery etc. of play or film etc.; frame in which jewel etc. is set; music to which words are set; cutlery for one person at table.

**settle¹** /'set(ə)l/ v. establish or become established in abode or place or way of life; (cause to) sit or come down to stay; cease from wandering or change or disturbance etc.; determine, agree upon, decide, appoint; deal effectually with; get rid of; pay (bill); subside, sink; become colonists or dwellers in. **settle down** begin to live routine life; **settle on** give (property etc.) to (person) esp. for rest of his life; **settle up** pay money owed etc.

**settle²** /'set(ə)l/ n. bench with high back and arms.

**settlement** /'setəlmənt/ n. settling or being settled; place occupied by settlers; arrangement ending dispute; terms on which property is given to person; deed stating these.

**settler** /'setlə(r)/ n. person who settles in newly developed (tract of) country.

**settler's clock** Aus. kookaburra.

**seven** /'sev(ə)n/ a. & n. one more than six. **seventh** a. & n.

**seventeen** /sevən'ti:n/ a. & n. one more than sixteen. **seventeenth** a. & n.

**seventy** /'sevəntɪ/ a. & n. seven times ten. **seventieth** a. & n.

**sever** /'sevə(r)/ v. divide, break, make separate, esp. by cutting; end employment contract of (person).

**several** /'sevər(ə)l/ a. & pron. a few, more than two; separate or respective.

**severally** adv. separately, respectively.

**severance** /'sevərəns/ n. severing; severed state. **severance pay** amount paid to employee on termination of contract.

**severe** /sə'vɪə(r)/ a. harsh and rigorous; serious; extreme or forceful; arduous, exacting; unadorned. **severity** /-'ver-/ n.

**sew** /səʊ/ v. (p.p. **sewn** or **sewed**) fasten or join or make etc. by passing thread again and again through material by means of a needle; use needle and thread or sewing-machine. **sewing-machine** machine for sewing or stitching.

**sewage** /'su:ɪdʒ/ n. waste matter conveyed in sewers. **sewage farm, works**, place where sewage is treated.

**sewer** /'su:ə(r)/ n. (usu. underground) pipe or conduit for carrying off drainage water and waste matter.

**sewerage** /'su:ərɪdʒ/ n. system of or drainage by sewers.

**sewn** p.p. of **sew**.

**sex** 1 n. being male or female; males or females collectively; sexual instincts or desire or activity etc.; sexual intercourse. 2 v.t. determine sex of; in p.p. having specified sexual appetite. 3 **sex appeal** sexual attractiveness; **sex change** apparent change of sex by surgical means.

**sexagenarian** /seksədʒə'neərɪən/ n. person between 60 and 69 years old.

**Sexagesima** /seksə'dʒesəmə/ n. second Sunday before Lent.

**sexism** /'seksɪz(ə)m/ n. prejudice or discrimination against people (esp. women) because of their sex. **sexist** a. & n.

**sexless** /'sekslas/ a. neither male nor female; lacking sexual desire or attractiveness.

**sextant** /'sekst(ə)nt/ n. instrument with graduated arc of 60° used in navigation and surveying for measuring angular distance of objects by means of mirrors.

**sextet** /seks'tet/ n. musical composition for 6 performers; the performers; group of 6.

**sexton** /'sekst(ə)n/ n. person who looks after church and churchyard, often acting as bell-ringer and grave-digger.

**sextuple** /'sekstjəp(ə)l/ a. sixfold.

**sextuplet** /'sekstjəplət/ n. each of 6 children born at one birth.

**sexual** /'seksjuːəl/ a. of or connected with sex or sexes. **sexual intercourse** insertion of man's penis into woman's vagina.

**sexuality** /seksjuːˈælətɪ/ n. sexual characteristics or activity.

**sexy** /'seksɪ/ a. colloq. sexually attractive or provocative.

**SF** abbr. science fiction.

**Sgt.** abbr. Sergeant.

**sh** int. hush.

**shabby** /'ʃæbɪ/ a. dingy and faded from wear or exposure; worn, dilapidated; poorly dressed; contemptible, dishonourable.

**shack** 1 n. roughly built hut or cabin. 2 v.i. sl. **shack up** cohabit with or together.

**shackle** /'ʃæk(ə)l/ 1 n. metal loop or link closed by bolt, coupling link; fetter, fig. restraint. 2 v.t. fetter, impede.

**shad** n. large edible fish.

**shade** 1 n. comparative darkness caused by shelter from direct light and heat; place or area sheltered from the sun; darker part of picture etc.; a colour, esp. with regard to its depth or as distinguished from one nearly like it; slight amount or difference; translucent cover for lamp etc.; screen excluding or moderating light; ghost. 2 v. screen from light; darken, esp. with parallel pencil lines to represent shadow etc.; change or pass by degrees. 3 **in the shade** in comparative obscurity.

**shadow** /'ʃædəʊ/ 1 n. shade; patch of shade; dark figure projected by body intercepting rays of light; person's inseparable attendant or companion; person secretly following another; insubstantial remnant; shaded part of picture; gloom or sadness. 2 v.t. cast shadow over; follow closely, persistently, and usu. secretly. 3 **shadow-boxing** boxing against imaginary opponent; **Shadow Cabinet** members of opposition party serving as spokesmen for affairs for which Cabinet ministers have responsibility. 4 **shadowy** a.

**shady** /'ʃeɪdɪ/ a. giving or situated in shade; of doubtful honesty, disreputable.

**shaft** /ʃɑːft/ n. arrow or spear; its long slender stem; fig. remark aimed to hurt or stimulate; ray (of light); stroke (of lightning); handle of tool etc.; long narrow space, usu. vertical, for access to a mine or for a lift in a building or for ventilation etc.; long and narrow part supporting or connecting or driving part(s) of greater thickness etc.; part of column between base and capital; one of pair of poles between which horse of vehicle is harnessed.

**shag** n. rough mass of hair; coarse tobacco; (crested) cormorant.

**shaggy** /'ʃægɪ/ a. hairy, rough-haired; tangled. **shaggy-dog story** long inconsequential narrative or joke.

**shagreen** /ʃæˈgriːn/ n. kind of untanned leather with granulated surface; shark-skin.

**shah** /ʃɑː/ n. former ruler of Iran.

**shake** 1 v. (past **shook** /ʃʊk/; p.p. **shaken** /'ʃeɪkən/) move violently or quickly up and down or to and fro; (cause to) tremble or rock or vibrate; agitate, shock, disturb; Aus. sl. steal; weaken or impair. 2 n. shaking or being shaken; jerk, shock; colloq. moment. 3 **shake down** settle or cause to fall by shaking, become comfortably settled or established; **shake-down** makeshift bed esp. on floor; **shake hands** clasp hands (with person), esp. at meeting or parting or as sign of bargain; **shake off** get rid of, evade; **shake up** mix (ingredients) by shaking, disturb or make uncomfortable, rouse from lethargy etc.; **shake-up** upheaval, reorganization.

**shaker** n. container for shaking together ingredients of cocktails etc.

**Shakespearian** /ʃeɪkˈspɪərɪən/ a. of Shakespeare.

**shako** /'ʃækəʊ/ n. (pl. -**kos**) military cap with peak and upright plume or tuft.

**shaky** /'ʃeɪkɪ/ a. unsteady, trembling, infirm, tottering, wavering.

**shale** /ʃeɪl/ n. soft rock that splits easily, resembling slate. **shaly** a.

**shall** v. aux. (pres. **shall**, past **should** /ʃʊd/) expr. future event or situation etc. or (strong) intention or condition or command or duty or obligation or likelihood or tentative suggestion.

# shallot     shave

**shallot** /ʃəˈlɒt/ *n.* onion-like plant with cluster of small bulbs.

**shallow** /ˈʃæləʊ/ 1 *a.* of little depth; superficial, trivial. 2 *n.* shallow place. 3 *v.* make or become shallow(er).

**sham** 1 *n.* imposture, pretence; person or thing pretending or pretended to be what he or it is not. 2 *a.* pretended, counterfeit. 3 *v.* feign; pretend (to be).

**shamble** /ˈʃæmb(ə)l/ 1 *v.i.* walk or run in shuffling or ungainly way. 2 *n.* shambling gait.

**shambles** *n.pl.* (usu. treated as *sing.*) *colloq.* mess, muddle; butchers' slaughter-house; scene of carnage.

**shambolic** /ʃæmˈbɒlɪk/ *a. colloq.* disorganized, chaotic.

**shame** 1 *n.* feeling of humiliation excited by consciousness of guilt or folly; capacity for experiencing this; state of disgrace or ignominy or discredit; person or thing that brings disgrace; *colloq.* regrettable or unlucky thing. 2 *v.t.* make ashamed, bring disgrace on; force by shame *into* or *out of* etc. 3 **shamefaced** bashful, ashamed, abashed.

**shameful** /ˈʃeɪmfəl/ *a.* disgraceful, scandalous.

**shameless** /ˈʃeɪmləs/ *a.* having or showing no shame; impudent.

**shammy** /ˈʃæmɪ/ *n.* chamois-leather.

**shampoo** /ʃæmˈpuː/ 1 *n.* liquid or cream used to wash hair; similar substance for washing carpet or car etc. 2 *v.t.* wash with shampoo.

**shamrock** /ˈʃæmrɒk/ *n.* kind of trefoil, used as national emblem of Ireland.

**shandy** /ˈʃændɪ/ *n.* mixture of beer with ginger-beer or lemonade.

**shanghai** /ʃæŋˈhaɪ/ 1 *v.t.* force (person) to be sailor on ship, usu. by trickery; *Aus.* shoot with catapult. 2 *n. Aus.* catapult.

**shank** *n.* leg, lower part of leg; stem or shaft of nail or key or anchor etc.

**shan't** /ʃɑːnt/ *colloq.* = *shall not*.

**shantung** /ʃænˈtʌŋ/ *n.* soft undressed Chinese silk, usu. undyed.

**shanty**[1] /ˈʃæntɪ/ *n.* hut, cabin. **shanty town** suburb etc. of shanties.

**shanty**[2] /ˈʃæntɪ/ *n.* song sung by sailors while hauling ropes etc.

**shape** 1 *n.* configuration, form; external appearance, guise; orderly arrangement, proper condition; pattern or mould. 2 *v.* fashion into desired or definite shape; form, devise, plan; direct (one's course etc.); develop (*into*).

**shapeless** /ˈʃeɪpləs/ *a.* lacking proper shape or shapeliness.

**shapely** /ˈʃeɪplɪ/ *a.* well-formed; of pleasing shape.

**shard** /ʃɑːd/ *n.* broken piece of pottery or glass etc.

**share** /ʃeə(r)/ 1 *n.* portion that person gives to or receives from common amount or commitment; each of equal parts into which company's capital is divided entitling owner to proportion of profits. 2 *v.* get or give or have share (of); participate in; divide and distribute (often with *out*); give away part of. 3 **share-farmer** tenant farmer who shares profits with owner; **shareholder** owner of shares in a company; **share index** number indicating how prices of shares have fluctuated; **share-out** division and distribution.

**shark** *n.* large voracious sea-fish; extortioner, swindler. **sharkbait** *Aus. sl.* swimmer who swims too far out to sea; **shark-skin** skin of shark, smooth fabric with dull surface.

**sharp** 1 *a.* having edge or point able to cut or pierce; tapering to a point or edge; abrupt or angular or steep; severe; intense; shrill, piercing; harsh; acute, sensitive; clever; unscrupulous; acid, pungent; vigorous or brisk; *Mus.* above true pitch, a semitone higher than note named. 2 *n. Mus.* sharp note; sign indicating this; *colloq.* swindler, cheat. 3 *adv.* punctually, suddenly; at a sharp angle; *Mus.* above true pitch. 4 **sharp practice** barely honest dealings; **sharp-shooter** skilled marksman.

**sharpen** /ˈʃɑːpən/ *v.* make or become sharp.

**sharper** /ˈʃɑːpə(r)/ *n.* swindler esp. at cards.

**sharpie** /ˈʃɑːpɪ/ *n. Aus.* member of teenage gang distinguished by very short hair.

**shatter** /ˈʃætə(r)/ *v.* break suddenly in pieces; wreck, utterly destroy; *colloq.* severely discompose.

**shave** 1 *v.* (*p.p.* **shaved** or esp. as *a.* **shaven**) cut (growing hair) from face etc. with razor; remove hair from face etc. (of); cut thin slices from surface of (wood etc.) to shape it; pass close to without touching, miss narrowly. **2** *n.* shaving or being shaved; narrow miss or escape; tool for shaving wood etc. **3 shaving-brush** brush for lathering chin etc. before shaving; **shaving-cream, -soap,** etc. substance applied to chin etc. to assist shaving.

**shaver** /ˈʃeɪvə(r)/ *n.* electrical appliance for shaving face etc.; *colloq.* youngster.

**Shavian** /ˈʃeɪvɪən/ *a.* of the writer G. B. Shaw.

**shaving** /ˈʃeɪvɪŋ/ *n.* (esp. in *pl.*) thin paring of wood.

**shawl** *n.* rectangular piece of fabric freq. folded into triangle, worn over shoulders etc. or wrapped round baby.

**she 1** *pron.* (*obj.* **her**, *poss.* **her**) the female person or animal in question; in Australia often used of any material or immaterial thing. **2** *n.* & *a.* female. **3 she-oak** *Aus.* casuarina; **she's apples** *Aus. colloq.* everything's fine; **she'll be right** *Aus. colloq.* there's no need to worry.

**sheaf 1** *n.* (*pl.* **sheaves**) group of things laid lengthwise together and usu. tied, esp. bundle of corn-stalks tied after reaping. **2** *v.t.* make into sheaves.

**shear** *v.* (*p.p.* **shorn** *or* **sheared**) cut (off) with scissors or shears etc.; clip wool off (sheep etc.); *fig.* strip bare *of*, deprive *of*; distort or be distorted or break *off*. **2** *n.* strain produced by pressure in structure of substance; in *pl.* (also **pair of shears**) clipping or cutting instrument shaped like scissors. **3 off the shears** *Aus.* (of sheep) having just been shorn.

**sheath** /ʃiːθ/ *n.* close-fitting cover, esp. for blade or tool; condom. **sheath-knife** dagger-like knife carried in sheath.

**sheathe** /ʃiːð/ *v.t.* put into sheath; encase or protect with sheath.

**shed¹** /ʃed/ *n.* one-storeyed building for storage or shelter or as workshop etc.

**shed²** *v.t.* (*past* & *p.p.* **shed**) let fall off, lose; cause to fall or flow; disperse, diffuse, radiate.

**sheen** *n.* brightness, lustre. **sheeny** *a.*

**sheep** *n.* (*pl.* same) animal with thick woolly coat, esp. kept in flocks for its wool or meat; bashful or timid or silly person; (usu. in *pl.*) member of minis-ter's congregation. **sheep-dip** preparation for cleansing sheep of vermin etc., place where sheep are dipped in this; **sheep-dog** dog trained to guard and herd sheep, type of dog suitable for this; **sheep-fold** enclosure for sheep; **sheepshank** knot used to shorten rope temporarily; **sheepskin** garment or rug of sheep's skin with wool on.

**sheepish** /ˈʃiːpɪʃ/ *a.* bashful or embarrassed in manner.

**sheer¹** *1 a.* mere, unqualified, absolute; (of cliff, ascent, etc.) perpendicular; (of textile) thin, diaphanous. **2** *adv.* perpendicularly; directly.

**sheer²** *v.i.* swerve or change course. **sheer off** go away, esp. from person that one dislikes or fears.

**sheet¹ 1** *n.* rectangular piece of cotton or linen etc. as part of bedclothes; broad thin flat piece of glass or paper etc.; wide expanse *of* water or flame etc. **2** *v.* cover with sheet; form into sheets. **3 sheet metal** metal formed into thin sheets by rolling or hammering etc.; **sheet music** music published in separate sheets.

**sheet²** *n.* rope or chain at lower corner of sail to extend it or alter its direction. **sheet-anchor** large anchor used only in emergencies, thing depended on as one's last hope.

**sheikh** /ʃeɪk/ *n.* chief or head of Arab tribe or family etc.; Muslim leader.

**sheila** /ˈʃiːlə/ *n. Aus. & NZ sl.* young woman, girl.

**shekel** /ˈʃek(ə)l/ *n.* currency unit of Israel; ancient Jewish etc. weight and coin; in *pl. colloq.* money.

**sheldrake** /ˈʃeldreɪk/ *n.* (*fem.* & *pl.* **shelduck**) bright-plumaged wild duck.

**shelf 1** *n.* (*pl.* **shelves**) horizontal slab or board projecting from wall or forming one tier of bookcase or cupboard; ledge on cliff-face etc.; reef or sand-bank; *Aus. sl.* an informer. **2** *v.t. Aus. sl.* inform on. **3 on the shelf** put aside, (of unmarried woman) considered past marriageable age; **shelf-life** time for which stored thing remains usable; **shelf-mark** mark on book to show its place in library.

**shell 1** *n.* hard outer case enclosing nut-kernel or egg or seed or fruit or animal or part of it; framework or case for something; walls of unfinished or gut-

**shellac**

ted building or ship etc.; explosive artillery projectile; light rowing-boat for racing; outward show, mere semblance. 2 *v.t.* take out of shell, remove shell or pod from; fire shells at. **3 come out of one's shell** become communicative; **shellfish** water animal with shell (mollusc or crustacean); **shell out** *sl.* pay (money); **shell-shock** nervous breakdown resulting from prolonged exposure to battle conditions.

**shellac** /ʃəˈlæk/ 1 *n.* resinous substance used for making varnish etc. 2 *v.t.* (*past* & *p.p.* **shellacked**) varnish with shellac.

**shelter** /ˈʃeltə(r)/ 1 *n.* protection from danger or the elements etc.; place providing this. 2 *v.* act or serve as shelter to; shield; take shelter.

**shelve** *v.* put on shelf; defer consideration of; remove from active work etc.; provide with shelves; (of ground) slope gently.

**shelving** /ˈʃelvɪŋ/ *n.* shelves; material for shelves.

**shepherd** /ˈʃepəd/ 1 *n.* man who tends sheep; *fig.* pastor. 2 *v.t.* tend or drive sheep; marshal or guide like sheep. **3 shepherd's pie** minced meat baked with covering of (esp. mashed) potato. **4 shepherdess** *n.*

**sherbet** /ˈʃɜːbət/ *n.* fizzy flavoured drink; the powder for making this.

**sherd** *n.* potsherd.

**sheriff** /ˈʃerɪf/ *n.* chief executive officer of Crown in county, with legal and ceremonial duties; *Sc.* chief judge of county or district; *US* chief law-enforcing officer of county.

**sherry** /ˈʃerɪ/ *n.* white usu. fortified wine orig. from Spain, drunk esp. as aperitif.

**Shetland** /ˈʃetlənd/ *a.* **Shetland pony** pony of small hardy breed; **Shetland wool** fine wool from Shetland sheep.

**shew** /ʃəʊ/ *arch.* var. of **show**.

**shibboleth** /ˈʃɪbəleθ/ *n.* old-fashioned doctrine or formula of party etc., catchword; word or custom etc. regarded as revealing person's orthodoxy.

**shicer** /ˈʃaɪsə(r)/ *n.* *Aus.* unproductive claim or mine; *sl.* swindler, cheat.

**shickered** /ˈʃɪkəd/ *a.* *Aus.* *sl.* drunk.

**shield** /ʃiːld/ 1 *n.* piece of defensive armour carried in hand or on arm to

**shingle**

protect the body when fighting; person or thing serving as protection or defence; representation of shield for displaying person's coat of arms; shield-shaped thing, esp. sports trophy; protective plate etc. in machinery etc. 2 *v.t.* protect or defend.

**shift** 1 *v.* change or move from one position to another; change form or character; use expedients; manage, get along; *sl.* move quickly. 2 *n.* change of place or character etc.; group of workers working at same time; period for which they work; expedient, device, trick; woman's loose straight dress; change of position of typewriter type-bars to type capitals etc.; displacement of lines of spectrum; *US* gear-change in motor vehicle.

**shiftless** /ˈʃɪftləs/ *a.* lazy, inefficient; lacking in resource.

**shifty** /ˈʃɪftɪ/ *a.* not straightforward, evasive, deceitful.

**Shiite** /ˈʃiːaɪt/ 1 *n.* member of esp. Iranian Muslim sect opposed to Sunnites. 2 *a.* of this sect.

**shillelagh** /ʃəˈleɪlɪ/ *n.* Irish cudgel.

**shilling** /ˈʃɪlɪŋ/ *n.* former British monetary unit and coin, worth 1/20 of pound; monetary unit in some other countries.

**shilly-shally** /ˈʃɪlɪˌʃælɪ/ *v.i.* vacillate, hesitate or be undecided.

**shimmer** /ˈʃɪmə(r)/ 1 *n.* tremulous or faint diffused light. 2 *v.i.* shine with shimmer. 3 **shimmery** *a.*

**shin** 1 *n.* front of leg below knee. 2 *v.i.* climb (*up*) by using arms and legs. 3 **shin-bone** inner and usu. larger of two bones from knee to ankle.

**shindig** /ˈʃɪndɪɡ/ (also **shindy**) *n.* *colloq.* festive gathering, esp. boisterous one; brawl, disturbance.

**shine** 1 *v.* (*past* & *p.p.* **shone** /ʃɒn/) emit or reflect light, be bright, glow; be brilliant, excel; cause to shine; *colloq.* (*past* and *p.p.* **shined**) polish (boots etc.). 2 *n.* light, brightness, sunshine; lustre, sheen; polishing. **3 take a shine to** *colloq.* take a liking to.

**shiner** /ˈʃaɪnə(r)/ *n.sl.* black eye.

**shingle**¹ /ˈʃɪŋɡ(ə)l/ *n.* small rounded pebbles on sea-shore. **shingly** *a.*

**shingle**² /ˈʃɪŋɡ(ə)l/ 1 *n.* rectangular piece of wood used as roof-tile etc.; shingled hair. 2 *v.t.* roof with shingles;

# shingles     512     shoot

cut (woman's hair) short and tapering from back of head to nape of neck. **3 be or have a shingle short** *Aus. colloq.* be mentally deficient.

**shingles** /ˈʃɪŋg(ə)lz/ *n.pl.* painful virus infection of nerves with outbreaks of small blisters, esp. round waist.

**shinty** /ˈʃɪnti/ *n.* game resembling hockey.

**shiny** /ˈʃaɪni/ *a.* shining, polished, rubbed bright.

**ship 1** *n.* large seagoing vessel; *colloq.* spacecraft, *US* aircraft. **2** *v.* send or take or put in ship; deliver (goods) to agent for forwarding; fix (mast, rudder) in its place on ship; embark; (of sailor) engage for service on ship; take (oars) from rowlocks and lay them inside boat. **3 ship-canal** canal allowing ships to go inland; **shipmate** person sailing on same ship as another; **shipshape** in good order, neat and tidy; **shipwreck** destruction of ship by storm or collision etc., ruin *of* one's hopes etc., (*v.*) suffer this, cause to suffer this; **shipwright** shipbuilder, ship's carpenter; **shipyard** place where ships are built.

**shipment** /ˈʃɪpmənt/ *n.* putting of goods etc. on board; goods shipped.

**shipper** /ˈʃɪpə(r)/ *n.* importer or exporter.

**shipping** /ˈʃɪpɪŋ/ *n.* ships collectively.

**shiralee** /ʃɪrəˈliː/ *n. Aus. sl.* a swag.

**shire** /ˈʃaɪə(r)/ *n.* rural local government area in some parts of Australia; *UK* county. **shire-horse** heavy powerful draught-horse.

**shirk** *v.t.* avoid or get out of (duty, work, etc.) from laziness or cowardice.

**shirr** *v.t.* gather with several parallel threads. **shirring** *n.*

**shirt** *n.* loose sleeved garment of cotton etc. for upper part of body; **in shirt-sleeves** not wearing jacket; **shirt dress** dress with bodice like shirt; **shirtwaister** shirt dress.

**shirting** /ˈʃɜːtɪŋ/ *n.* material for shirts.

**shirty** /ˈʃɜːti/ *a. sl.* annoyed.

**shiver¹** /ˈʃɪvə(r)/ **1** *v.i.* tremble esp. with cold or fear. **2** *n.* momentary shivering movement. **3 shivery** *a.*

**shiver²** /ˈʃɪvə(r)/ **1** *n.* small fragment, splinter. **2** *v.* break into shivers.

**shivoo** /ʃɪˈvuː/ *n. Aus. colloq.* party or celebration, esp. boisterous one.

**shoal¹ 1** *n.* crowd, great number, esp. of fish swimming together. **2** *v.i.* form shoal(s).

**shoal² 1** *n.* shallow place in sea; submerged sandbank. **2** *v.i.* become shallow.

**shock¹ 1** *n.* violent concussion or impact; sudden and disturbing physical or mental impression; acute state of prostration following sudden violent emotion or severe injury etc.; electric shock; violent shake or tremor of earth's surface in earthquake; great disturbance of or injury to organization, stability, etc. **2** *v.t.* affect with electrical or mental shock; appear scandalous or outrageous to. **3 shock absorber** device on vehicle etc. for absorbing vibration and shock; **shock therapy** electroconvulsive therapy.

**shocker** /ˈʃɒkə(r)/ *n.* person or thing that shocks; very bad specimen of anything; sensational novel or film etc.

**shocking** /ˈʃɒkɪŋ/ *a.* scandalous; improper; *colloq.* very bad.

**shod** *past & p.p.* of **shoe**.

**shoddy** /ˈʃɒdi/ *a.* of poor quality, counterfeit, shabby.

**shoe** /ʃuː/ **1** *n.* outer covering of leather etc. for foot, esp. one not reaching above ankle; thing like shoe in shape or use; metal rim nailed to underside of horse's hoof. **2** *v.* (*past & p.p.* **shod**; *partic.* **shoeing**) fit with shoe(s); (in *p.p.*) having shoes of specified kind. **3 shoehorn** curved piece of metal etc. for easing heel into back of shoe; **shoe-lace** cord for lacing shoe; **shoe-string** shoe-lace, *colloq.* small or inadequate amount of money; **shoe-tree** shaped block for keeping shoe in shape.

**shone** *past & p.p.* of **shine**.

**shonky** /ˈʃɒŋki/ *a. Aus. sl.* unreliable, dishonest.

**shoo 1** *int.* used to frighten birds etc. away. **2** *v.* utter such sound; drive *away* thus.

**shook** *past* of **shake**. **shook on** *Aus. colloq.* keen on, enthusiastic about.

**shoot** /ʃuːt/ **1** *v.* (*past & p.p.* **shot**) cause (weapon) to discharge missile; kill or wound (person, animal) with missile from weapon; send out or discharge rapidly; hunt game etc. with gun; come or go swiftly or suddenly; *Assoc. Footb.* etc. take shot at goal; take film or photo-

**shop** 513 **shot**

graph of; (of plant) put forth buds, (of bud) appear. **2** *n.* young branch or sucker; expedition or party for shooting game; land on which game is shot. **3 shooting-brake** station-wagon; **shooting-gallery** place for shooting at targets with rifles etc.; **shooting star** small meteor appearing like star, moving quickly and disappearing; **shooting-stick** spiked walking-stick with handle that can be used as seat; **shoot through** *Aus. colloq.* depart suddenly.

**shop 1** *n.* place for retail sale of goods or services etc.; workshop or place of manufacture; one's work or profession as subject of conversation. **2** *v.* go to shops to make purchases; *sl.* inform against. **3 shop around** look for best bargain; **shop-assistant** employee in retail shop; **shop-floor** production area in factory etc., workers as distinct from management; **shopkeeper** owner or manager of shop; **shoplifting** stealing of goods from display in shop; **shop-soiled** soiled or faded by being shown in shop; **shop-steward** person elected by fellow workmen as their spokesman; **shopwalker** supervisor in large shop.

**shopping** /ˈʃɒpɪŋ/ *n.* going to shops; goods bought in shop(s). **shopping centre** area containing many shops.

**shore**[1] *n.* land that adjoins sea or large body of water; **on shore** ashore.

**shore**[2] **1** *n.* prop, beam set obliquely against wall etc. as support. **2** *v.t.* support or prop *up* with shore(s).

**shorn** *p.p.* of **shear**.

**short 1** *a.* measuring little from end to end in space or time, or from head to foot; concise, brief; curt, uncivil; deficient, inadequate in quantity, scarce; (of pastry) easily crumbled; (of vowel or syllable) having the less of two recognized durations. **2** *adv.* abruptly, suddenly; before the natural or expected time or place; in short manner. **3** *n.* short thing, esp. short syllable or vowel or film; *colloq.* short circuit, short drink; in *pl.* trousers reaching only to or above knees, *US* underpants. **4** *v.* short-circuit. **5 shortbread, shortcake**, rich crumbly cake made of flour and butter and sugar; **short-change** rob or cheat esp. by giving insufficient change; **short circuit** electric circuit through small resistance, esp. instead of through normal circuit; **short-circuit** cause short circuit in, have short circuit, *fig.* shorten or avoid by taking short cut; **shortcoming** failure to reach required standard, deficiency; **short cut** path or course shorter than usual or normal; **short drink** small drink of spirits etc.; **shortfall** deficit; **shorthand** method of rapid writing for keeping pace with speaker, *fig.* abbreviated or symbolic means of expression; **short-handed** undermanned, understaffed; **shorthorn** breed of cattle; **short list** list of candidates from whom final selection will be made; **short-list** put on short list; **short-lived** having short life, ephemeral; **short of** not having enough of, less than, without reaching; **short-range** having short range, relating to short period of future time; **short shrift** curt attention or treatment; **short sight** ability to see clearly only what is comparatively near; **short-sighted** having short sight, *fig.* lacking imagination or foresight; **short-tempered** easily angered; **short-term** occurring in or relating to a short period of time; **short-winded** easily becoming breathless.

**shortage** /ˈʃɔːtɪdʒ/ *n.* deficiency; amount of this.

**shorten** /ˈʃɔːt(ə)n/ *v.* become or make short(er).

**shortening** /ˈʃɔːtənɪŋ/ *n.* fat used for making esp. short pastry.

**shortly** /ˈʃɔːtlɪ/ *adv.* soon, in a short time; in a short manner.

**shot**[1] *n.* discharge of gun etc.; sound of this; *Aus. sl.* approved thing to do; attempt to hit something by shooting or throwing etc.; stroke or kick in ball-game; attempt to do something; *Aus. sl.* attempt to injure or annoy person; person of specified skill in shooting; single missile for gun or cannon etc.; small lead pellet of which several are used for single charge; (as *pl.*) these collectively; heavy metal ball thrown in shot-put; scene etc. photographed, photograph, photographing, injection of drug etc.; *colloq.* dram of spirits. **shotgun** gun for firing small shot at short range; **shotgun wedding** wedding enforced esp. because of bride's

**shot** pregnancy; **shot-put** athletic contest of throwing heavy metal ball.

**shot²** 1 *past* & *p.p.* of **shoot**. 2 *a.* woven or dyed so as to show different colours at different angles.

**should** *v.aux.* expr. duty or obligation, possible or expected future event, or conditional or indefinite mood.

**shoulder** /ˈʃəʊldə(r)/ 1 *n.* part of body to which arm or foreleg or wing is attached; part of garment covering shoulder; animal's upper foreleg as joint of meat; in *pl.* upper part of back; part or projection resembling human shoulder; strip of land adjoining metalled road-surface. 2 *v.* push with shoulder, jostle; take (burden) on one's shoulder, assume (responsibility etc.). 3 **shoulder-blade** either flat bone of upper back; **shoulder-strap** strap passing over shoulder to support something, strap from shoulder to collar of garment, esp. with indication of military rank.

**shout** /ʃaʊt/ 1 *n.* loud cry calling attention or expr. joy or defiance or approval etc; *Aus. colloq.* turn to buy drinks etc. 2 *v.* utter shout; speak or say loudly, call out; *Aus. colloq.* buy round of drinks. 3 **shout down** reduce to silence by shouting.

**shove** /ʃʌv/ 1 *n.* (strong) push. 2 *v.* push, esp. vigorously or roughly; *colloq.* put. 3 **shove-halfpenny** game in which coins etc. are driven along polished board by blow with hand; **shove off** *colloq.* depart.

**shovel** /ˈʃʌv(ə)l/ 1 *n.* spadelike scoop used to shift earth or coal etc. 2 *v.t.* move (as) with shovel or spade. **shovelboard** game played on ship's deck by pushing discs over marked surface.

**shoveller** /ˈʃʌvələ(r)/ *n.* duck with shovel-like beak.

**show** /ʃəʊ/ 1 *v.* (*p.p.* **shown** or **showed**) allow or cause to be seen; disclose, manifest; offer for inspection; exhibit; demonstrate, make understand; be or become visible or noticeable. 2 *n.* showing; spectacle, exhibition, display; agricultural show with competitions and sideshows; public entertainment or performance; *Aus. colloq.* chance, opportunity; *sl.* concern, undertaking, business; outward appearance, impression produced; ostentation, mere display. 3 **show-bag** *Aus.* bag of advertisers' samples distributed at show; **show business** the entertainment profession; **show-case** glazed case for displaying goods or exhibits; **show-down** final test or battle etc., disclosure of achievements or possibilities; **show-jumping** competitive jumping on horseback; **showman** proprietor or organizer of public entertainment, person skilled in showmanship; **showmanship** capacity for exhibiting one's wares or capabilities to best advantage; **show off** display to advantage, try to impress people by displaying one's skill or wealth etc.; **show-piece** excellent specimen suitable for display; **show-place** place that tourists etc. go to see; **showroom** room where goods are exhibited or kept for inspection; **show round** take (person) to all points of interest; **show trial** judicial trial regarded as intended to impress public opinion; **show up** make or be visible or conspicuous, expose, humiliate, *colloq.* appear or arrive.

**shower** /ˈʃaʊə(r)/ 1 *n.* brief fall of rain or hail or sleet; great number of missiles or gifts or questions or kisses etc.; shower-bath; *Aus. colloq.* party for bride-to-be. 2 *v.* descend or send or give in shower; bestow lavishly *upon*; take showerbath. 3 **shower-bath** bath in which water is sprayed from above.

**showery** /ˈʃaʊəri/ *a.* of or characterized by rain-showers.

**showing** /ˈʃəʊɪŋ/ *n.* quality or appearance of performance or achievement etc.; evidence, putting of case etc.

**shown** *p.p.* of **show**.

**showy** /ˈʃəʊi/ *a.* striking, making good display; gaudy.

**shrank** *past* of **shrink**.

**shrapnel** /ˈʃræpn(ə)l/ *n.* fragments of metal scattered from exploding projectile.

**shred** 1 *n.* small torn or broken or cut piece; scrap, fragment; least amount. 2 *v.* tear or cut etc. to shreds.

**shrew** *n.* small long-snouted mouselike animal; scolding woman.

**shrewd** *a.* showing astute powers of judgement; clever.

**shrewd-head** *Aus.* cunning or shrewd person.

**shrewdie** /ˈʃruːdi/ n. Aus. colloq. shrewd person or tick.

**shrewish** /ˈʃruːɪʃ/ a. ill-tempered and scolding.

**shriek** /ʃriːk/ 1 n. loud shrill piercing cry or sound. 2 v. make a shriek; say in shrill tones.

**shrike** n. bird with strong hooked beak.

**shrill** 1 a. piercing and high-pitched. 2 v. sound or utter shrilly.

**shrimp** n. small edible crustacean; *derog.* very small person.

**shrine** n. casket or tomb holding relics; sacred or revered place.

**shrink** v. (past **shrank**; p.p. **shrunk** or as a. **shrunken**) become or make smaller, esp. by action from moisture or heat or cold; recoil or flinch (from). **shrink-wrap** enclose (article) in material that shrinks tightly round it.

**shrinkage** /ˈʃrɪŋkɪdʒ/ n. process or degree of shrinking; allowance for loss by theft or wastage.

**shrivel** /ˈʃrɪv(ə)l/ v. contract into wrinkled or curled-up state.

**shroud** /ʃraʊd/ 1 n. wrapping for a corpse; something which conceals; in *pl.* ropes supporting ship's mast. 2 v.t. clothe (corpse) for burial; cover or disguise

**Shrove Tuesday** day before Ash Wednesday.

**shrub** n. woody plant smaller than tree and usu. branching from near ground. **shrubby** a.

**shrubbery** /ˈʃrʌbəri/ n. area planted with shrubs.

**shrug** 1 v. draw up shoulders momentarily as gesture of indifference etc. 2 n. shrugging movement.

**shrunk(en)** p.p. of shrink.

**shudder** /ˈʃʌdə(r)/ 1 n. sudden or convulsive shivering due to horror or cold etc. 2 v.i. experience shudder; have vibrating movement.

**shuffle** /ˈʃʌf(ə)l/ 1 v. move with dragging or sliding or difficult motion; intermingle or rearrange (esp. cards); keep shifting one's position; prevaricate, be evasive. 2 n. shuffling action or movement; general change of relative positions; shuffling dance. 3 **shuffle off** remove or get rid of.

**shun** v.t. avoid, keep clear of.

**shunt** 1 v. move (train etc.) to another track; (of train) be shunted; redirect. 2 n. shunting or being shunted; *Electr.* conductor joining two points in electric circuit for diversion of current; *sl.* collision.

**shush** /ʃʊʃ/ v. & int. colloq. hush.

**shut** v. (past & p.p. **shut**) move (door, window, lid, etc.) into position to block opening; become or admit of being shut; shut door etc. of; bring (book, hand, telescope) into folded or contracted state; bar access to (place). **shut down** close, cease working; **shut-eye** *sl.* sleep; **shut off** stop flow of (water, gas, etc.), separate, cut off; **shut out** exclude, prevent; **shut up** close securely or decisively or permanently, imprison, put away in box etc., colloq. stop talking.

**shutter** /ˈʃʌtə(r)/ 1 n. movable hinged cover for window; device for opening and closing aperture of camera. 2 v.t. provide or close (window) with shutter(s). 3 **put up the shutters** close business for the day or permanently.

**shuttle** /ˈʃʌt(ə)l/ 1 n. weaving-implement by which weft-thread is carried between threads of warp; thread-carrier for lower thread in sewing-machine; train or bus or aircraft etc. used in shuttle service; space shuttle. 2 v. (cause to) move to and fro like shuttle. 3 **shuttlecock** object struck to and fro in badminton, consisting of rounded piece of cork with feathers in or of imitation of this; **shuttle service** transport system operating to and fro over relatively short distance.

**shy¹** 1 a. self-conscious or uneasy in company, bashful; easily startled, wary; (as suffix) showing fear or distaste for. 2 v.i. (esp. of horse) start aside in alarm (at). 3 n. shying.

**shy²** v. & n. colloq. throw, fling.

**shyster** /ˈʃaɪstə(r)/ n. colloq. person, esp. lawyer, who acts unscrupulously or unprofessionally.

**si** /siː/ n. Mus. te.

**SI** abbr. international system of units of measurement (*Système International*).

**Siamese** /saɪəˈmiːz/ 1 a. of Siam (now Thailand). 2 n. native or language of Siam. 3 **Siamese cat** cream-coloured brown-faced short-haired breed of cat;

**Siamese twins** twins joined together at birth.

**sibilant** /'sɪbələnt/ 1 *a.* hissing, sounding like hiss. 2 *n.* sibilant speech sound. 3 **sibilance** *n.*

**sibling** /'sɪblɪŋ/ *n.* one of two or more children having one or both parents in common.

**sibyl** /'sɪbəl/ *n.* pagan prophetess.

**sibylline** /'sɪbəlʌm/ *a.* uttered by or characteristic of a sibyl, mysteriously prophetic.

**sic** *adv.* thus used or spelt etc. (confirming form of quoted words). [L]

**sick** 1 *a.* ill, unwell; vomiting or disposed to vomit; of or for those who are sick; surfeited and tired *of*; (of humour) making fun of misfortune or macabre things. 2 *v.t.* colloq. vomit (esp. with *up*). 3 *n.* vomit. 4 **sick-bay** place for sick persons.

**sicken** /'sɪkən/ *v.* make or become sick or disgusted etc. **sicken for** be in first stages of (illness).

**sickie** /'sɪki/ *n. Aus. sl.* day's sick leave, esp. fraudulent one.

**sickle** /'sɪk(ə)l/ *n.* short-handled implement with semicircular blade for reaping or lopping etc.

**sickly** /'sɪklɪ/ *a.* liable to be ill, of weak health; causing or suggesting sickness; faint, pale; mawkish, weakly sentimental.

**sickness** /'sɪknəs/ *n.* being ill; disease; vomiting, nausea.

**side** 1 *n.* one of inner or outer surfaces of object, esp. as distinct from top and bottom or front and back or ends; one of lines bounding triangle or rectangle etc.; either surface of thing regarded as having only two; right or left part of person's or animal's body; part of object or place etc. that faces specified direction or that is on observer's right or left; region nearer or farther than, or to right or left of, a real or imaginary dividing line; marginal part of area or thing; each of sets of opponents in war or game etc.; cause represented by this; team; line of descent through father or mother; spinning motion given to ball by striking it on side; *sl.* swagger, assumption of superiority. 2 *a.* of or on or from or to side; oblique, indirect; subordinate, subsidiary, not main. 2 *v.i.* take part or be on same side *with*. 3 **side-bet** one additional to ordinary stakes; **sideboard** table or flat-topped chest with drawers and cupboards for crockery etc.; **sideburns** short sidewhiskers; **side by side** standing close together esp. for mutual encouragement; **side-car** passenger car attachable to side of motor cycle; **side-drum** small double-headed drum; **sidekick** colloq. close associate; **sidelight** light from side, small light at front of vehicle etc., piece of incidental information etc.; **sideline** work etc. carried on in addition to one's main activity, in *pl.* lines bounding sides of football-pitch or tennis-court etc., space just outside these, place for spectators as opp. participants; **side-saddle** saddle esp. for woman made so that rider may have both feet on same side of horse, (*adv.*) sitting thus on horse; **side-show** minor show attached to principal one (freq. *fig.*); **sideslip** skid, movement sideways, (*v.i.*) move sideways (esp. of aircraft); **sidesman** assistant churchwarden; **side-step** step taken sideways, (*v.t.*) avoid, evade; **sidetrack** divert from course or purpose etc.; **sidewalk** *US* pavement at side of road; **side-whiskers** hair left unshaven on cheeks.

**sidelong** /'saɪdlɒŋ/ 1 *a.* directed to the side. 2 *adv.* to the side.

**sidereal** /saɪ'dɪərɪəl/ *a.* of or measured or determined by stars.

**sideways** /'saɪdweɪz/ *a. & adv.* with side foremost; to or from a side.

**siding** /'saɪdɪŋ/ *n.* short track by side of railway line for shunting etc.

**sidle** /'saɪd(ə)l/ *v.i.* walk obliquely, esp. in furtive or unobtrusive manner.

**siege** /siːdʒ/ 1 *n.* surrounding and blockading of fortified place. **lay siege to** conduct siege of; **raise siege** end it.

**sienna** /sɪ'enə/ *n.* kind of clay used as pigment; its colour of reddish- or yellowish-brown.

**sierra** /sɪ'erə/ *n.* long jagged mountain-chain in Spain or Spanish America.

**siesta** /sɪ'estə/ *n.* afternoon nap or rest in hot countries.

**sieve** /sɪv/ 1 *n.* utensil with network or perforated bottom through which liquids or fine particles can pass. 2 *v.t.* sift.

**sift** *v.* separate with or cause to pass

through sieve; sprinkle; closely examine details of, analyse; fall (as) from or through sieve.

**sigh** /saɪ/ 1 *n.* long deep audible breath expressing dejection or weariness or longing or relief etc. 2 *v.* give sigh or sound resembling it; express with sighs; yearn *for*.

**sight** /saɪt/ 1 *n.* faculty of seeing; seeing or being seen; range of or region open to vision; thing seen or visible or worth seeing; *colloq.* person or thing of ridiculous or repulsive appearance; in *pl.* noteworthy or attractive features of a place; precise aim with gun or observation with optical instrument; device for assisting this; *colloq.* a great quantity. 2 *v.t.* get sight of; observe presence of; aim (gun etc.) with sights. 3 **at first sight** on first glimpse or impression; **on sight** as soon as person or thing is seen; **out of sight** not visible; **sight-read** play (music) at sight; **sight-screen** *Crick.* large white screen placed near boundary in line with wicket to help batsman see ball; **sightseer** person visiting sights of place; **sight-seeing** *n.*

**sightless** /ˈsaɪtləs/ *a.* blind.

**sightly** /ˈsaɪtlɪ/ *a.* attractive to sight.

**sign** /saɪn/ 1 *n.* indication or suggestion or symptom *of* or *that*; symbol or word etc. representing phrase or idea or instruction etc.; mark traced on surface etc.; motion or gesture used instead of words to convey information or demand etc.; one of the 12 divisions of the zodiac; signboard. 2 *v.* write one's name on (document etc.) to show that one is the author etc. or that one accepts or agrees with contents; write (one's name) thus; communicate by gesture. 3 **signboard** board bearing name or symbol etc. displayed outside shop or inn etc.; **sign-language** series of signs used esp. by deaf or dumb people for communication; **sign off** end contract or work etc.; **sign on** register to obtain unemployment benefit; **signpost** post etc. showing directions of roads, (*v.t.*) provide with signpost(s).

**signal** /ˈsɪgn(ə)l/ 1 *n.* sign, esp. prearranged one, conveying information or direction esp. to person(s) at a distance; message made up of such signs; device on railway giving instructions or warnings to train-drivers etc.; event which causes immediate activity; *Electr.* transmitted impulses or radio waves; sequence of these. 2 *v.* make signal(s) (to); transmit or announce or direct (*to* do) by signal(s). 3 *a.* remarkably good or bad, noteworthy. 4 **signalbox** building from which railway signals are controlled; **signalman** person responsible for displaying or operating signals.

**signalize** /ˈsɪgnəlaɪz/ *v.t.* make conspicuous or remarkable.

**signatory** /ˈsɪgnətərɪ/ 1 *a.* that has signed an agreement, esp. a treaty. 2 *n.* signatory party.

**signature** /ˈsɪgnətʃ(ə)r/ *n.* person's name or initials used in signing; act of signing; *Mus.* indication of key or tempo following clef; section of book made from one sheet folded and cut; letter or figure indicating sequence of these. **signature tune** tune used esp. in broadcasting to announce a particular programme or performer etc.

**signet** /ˈsɪgnət/ *n.* small seal, esp. one set in finger-ring (**signet ring**).

**significance** /sɪgˈnɪfɪkəns/ *n.* being significant; meaning, import; importance.

**significant** /sɪgˈnɪfɪkənt/ *a.* having or conveying meaning; highly expressive; important. **significant figure** *Math.* digit conveying information about a number containing it, not a zero filling vacant place at beginning or end.

**signification** /sɪgnəfɪˈkeɪʃ(ə)n/ *n.* exact meaning or sense.

**signify** /ˈsɪgnəfaɪ/ *v.* be sign or symbol of; represent, mean, denote; make known, be of importance, matter.

**signor** /ˈsiːnjɔː(r)/ *n.* (*pl.* **-ri** /-riː/) title used of or to Italian man. [It.]

**signora** /siːˈnjɔːrə/ *n.* title used of or to Italian married woman. [It.]

**signorina** /siːnjəˈriːnə/ *n.* title used of or to Italian unmarried woman. [It.]

**silage** /ˈsaɪlɪdʒ/ *n.* storage in silo; green fodder so stored.

**silence** /ˈsaɪləns/ 1 *n.* absence of sound; abstinence from speech or noise; reticence; neglect or omission to mention or write etc. 2 *v.t.* make silent, reduce to silence; put down, repress.

**silencer** /ˈsaɪlənsə(r)/ *n.* device for re-

**silent** /'saɪlənt/ a. making or accompanied by little or no sound or speech. **silent cop** Aus. sl. small raised dome in street to control turning traffic.

**silhouette** /sɪluː'et/ 1 n. dark outline or shadow in profile against lighter background; contour, outline, profile; portrait in profile cut from paper or done in solid black on white. 2 v.t. represent or show in silhouette.

**silica** /'sɪləkə/ n. hard mineral occurring as quartz and as main constituent of sand etc. **siliceous** /sɪ'lɪʃəs/ a.

**silicate** /'sɪləkət/ n. compound of metal(s), silicon, and oxygen.

**silicon** /'sɪlɪkən/ n. non-metallic element occurring in silica and silicates. **silicon chip** tiny piece of silicon containing integrated circuit.

**silicone** /'sɪlɪkəʊn/ n. any of group of silicon compounds, used in polishes and paints and lubricants etc.

**silicosis** /sɪlɪ'kəʊsɪs/ n. lung disease caused by inhaling dust containing silica.

**silk** n. fine strong soft lustrous fibre produced by silkworms; thread or cloth made from this; in pl. kinds or garments of silk; colloq. KC or QC; attrib. made of silk. **silk hat** tall cylindrical hat covered with silk plush; **silk-screen printing** = screen-printing; **silkworm** caterpillar which spins cocoon of silk; **take silk** become KC or QC.

**silken** /'sɪlkən/ a. of or resembling silk; soft or smooth or lustrous.

**silky** /'sɪlkɪ/ a. like silk in smoothness or softness etc.; suave. **silky oak** Aus. tall tree with fern-like foliage and mottled wood.

**sill** n. shelf or slab of wood or stone etc. at base of window or doorway.

**sillabub** var. of **syllabub**.

**silly** /'sɪlɪ/ a. foolish, imprudent, thoughtless; weak-minded; Crick. (of fielder or his position) very close to batsman. 2 n. colloq. silly person.

**silo** /'saɪləʊ/ n. (pl. -los) pit or airtight structure in which green crops are stored for fodder; tower or pit for storage of grain or cement etc.; underground place where guided missile is kept ready for firing.

**silt** 1 n. sediment deposited by water in channel or harbour etc. 2 v. block or be blocked (up) with silt.

**silvan** /'sɪlv(ə)n/ a. of the woods; wooded; rural.

**silver** /'sɪlvə(r)/ 1 n. white lustrous precious metal; coins or articles made of or looking like this; colour of silver. 2 a. of or coloured like silver. 3 v. coat or plate with silver; give silvery appearance to; provide (mirror-glass) with backing of tin amalgam etc.; (of hair) turn grey or white. 4 **silver beet** Aus. & NZ variety of chard; **silver birch** Old World birch with silver-coloured bark; **silver-eye** small Aus. honey-eater with pale feathers round eye; **silver-fish** silver-coloured fish, silvery wingless insect; **silver jubilee** 25th anniversary; **silver medal** medal awarded as second prize; **silver paper** tin foil; **silver plate** articles plated with silver; **silver-plated** plated with silver; **silver sand** fine pure kind used in gardening; **silverside** upper side of round of beef; **silversmith** worker in silver; **silvertail** Aus. sl. rich and influential person; **silver wedding** 25th anniversary of wedding.

**silvery** /'sɪlvərɪ/ a. like silver in colour or appearance; having clear soft ringing sound.

**simian** /'sɪmɪən/ 1 a. resembling ape or monkey. 2 n. ape or monkey.

**similar** /'sɪmələ(r)/ a. like, alike, having resemblance (to), of same kind or nature or shape or amount. **similarity** /-'lær-/ n.

**simile** /'sɪmɪlɪ/ n. comparison of two things for purpose of illustration or ornament.

**similitude** /sə'mɪlɪtjuːd/ n. guise or outward appearance; simile.

**simmer** /'sɪmə(r)/ 1 v. be or keep just below boiling-point; be in state of suppressed anger or laughter. 2 n. simmering state. 3 **simmer down** become less agitated.

**simnel** /'sɪmn(ə)l/ n. rich decorated fruit-cake, usu. with almond paste.

**simony** /'saɪmənɪ/ n. buying or selling of ecclesiastical offices.

**simoom** /sɪ'muːm/ n. hot dry dust-laden desert wind.

**simper** /'sɪmpə(r)/ 1 v. smile in silly affected way; utter with simper. 2 n. such smile.

# simple — sink

**simple** /'sɪmp(ə)l/ *a.* easily understood or done, presenting no difficulty; not complicated or elaborate; unsophisticated, natural; consisting of or involving only one element or operation etc.; foolish, feeble-minded. **simple-minded** unsophisticated, ingenuous, feeble-minded.

**simpleton** /'sɪmplt(ə)n/ *n.* stupid or gullible person.

**simplicity** /sɪm'plɪsəti/ *n.* quality of being simple.

**simplify** /'sɪmpləfaɪ/ *v.t.* make simple, make easy to do or understand. **simplification** *n.*

**simplistic** /sɪm'plɪstɪk/ *a.* excessively simple or simplified. **simplistically** *adv.*

**simply** /'sɪmpli/ *adv.* in simple manner; absolutely; merely.

**simulate** /'sɪmjəleɪt/ *v.t.* pretend to be or have or feel; counterfeit; imitate conditions of (situation etc.) e.g. for training. **simulation** *n.*; **simulator** *n.*

**simultaneous** /sɪml'teɪnɪəs/ *a.* occurring or operating at same time (*with*). **simultaneity** *n.*

**sin** 1 *n.* transgression against divine law or principles of morality; offence against good taste etc. 2 *v.i.* commit sin; offend *against*.

**since** 1 *prep.* from (specified time) till now, within period between (specified past time) and now. 2 *conj.* from time that; seeing that, because. 3 *adv.* since that time or event.

**sincere** /sɪn'sɪə(r)/ *a.* free from pretence or deceit, genuine, frank, not assumed or put on. **sincerity** /-'ser-/ *n.*

**sincerely** *adv.* in sincere manner; **yours sincerely** formula for closing letter.

**sine** *n. Math.* ratio of side opposite angle (in right-angled triangle) to hypotenuse.

**sinecure** /'saɪnəkjʊə(r)/ *n.* position that requires little or no work but usu. yields profit or honour.

**sine die** /'saɪni 'daɪiː/ *adv.* adjourned indefinitely with no appointed date. [L]

**sine qua non** /'saɪneɪ kwaː nəʊn/ indispensable condition or qualification. [L]

**sinew** /'sɪnjuː/ *n.* tough fibrous tissue joining muscle to bone; piece of this; in *pl.* muscles; strength; *fig.* that which strengthens or sustains. **sinewy** *a.*

**sinful** /'sɪnfəl/ *a.* committing or involving sin; wicked.

**sing** *v.* (*past* **sang**; *p.p.* **sung**) utter words or sounds in tuneful succession, esp. in set tune; produce vocal melody, utter (song, tune); make melodious humming or whistling etc. sounds; celebrate in verse. **sing out** *colloq.* call out loudly; **singsong** uttered with monotonous rhythm or cadence, singsong manner, session of informal singing.

**singe** /sɪndʒ/ 1 *v.* (*partic.* **singeing**) burn superficially or slightly, burn ends or edges (of); suffer singeing. 2 *n.* superficial burn; singeing.

**Singhalese** var. of Sinhalese.

**single** /'sɪŋg(ə)l/ 1 *a.* one only, not double or multiple; individual; of or for one person or thing; solitary, unaided; unmarried; taken separately; (of ticket) valid for one journey only, not return. 2 *n.* single ticket; pop record with one piece of music on each side; hit for one run in cricket; (usu. in *pl.*) game with one player on each side. 3 *v.t.* choose *out* for special attention. **single-breasted** (of coat etc.) with only one set of buttons, not overlapping; **single file** line of persons etc. going one behind another; **single-handed** without assistance from others; **single-minded** keeping one purpose in view.

**singlet** /'sɪŋglət/ *n.* knitted or woven undergarment worn on upper part of body; athlete's garment like singlet.

**singleton** /'sɪŋgəlt(ə)n/ *n.* player's only card of suit.

**singular** /'sɪŋgjələ(r)/ 1 *a.* extraordinary, uncommon, surprising; strange, peculiar; *Gram.* denoting one person or thing. 2 *n. Gram.* singular word or form. 3 **singularity** /-'lær-/ *n.*

**Sinhalese** /sɪnhə'liːz/ 1 *a.* of a people from N. India now forming majority of population of Sri Lanka. 2 *n.* member or language of this people.

**sinister** /'sɪnɪstə(r)/ *a.* suggestive of evil; harmful; wicked, corrupt, evil; villainous; *Her.* on left side of shield etc.

**sink** 1 *v.* (*past* **sank**; *p.p.* **sunk** or as *a.* **sunken**) fall or come slowly downwards, decline, disappear below horizon or surface of liquid; go to bottom of sea etc.; settle down, droop, gradually expire or perish or cease; cause or allow to sink; dig (well), bore (shaft); invest

**sinker**    520    **situate**

(money) so that it is not readily realizable or is lost; cause (ball) to enter pocket at billiards or hole at golf etc.; cause failure of; penetrate or make way in or *into*; be absorbed *in* or *into* mind etc. **2** *n.* fixed basin with water supply and outflow pipe; place where foul liquid collects, *fig.* place of rampant vice etc. **3 sinking-fund** money set aside for gradual repayment of debt.

**sinker** /'sɪŋkə(r)/ *n.* weight used to sink fishing- or sounding-line.

**Sino-** /'saɪnəʊ/ *in comb.* Chinese.

**sinology** /saɪ'nɒlədʒi:/ *n.* study of China and its language and history etc. **sinologist** *n.*; **sinologue** /'sɪnəlɒg/ *n.*

**sinter** /'sɪntə(r)/ **1** *n.* solid coalesced by heating. **2** *v.* form into sinter.

**sinuous** /'sɪnjuːəs/ *a.* with many curves, undulating. **sinuosity** *n.*

**sinus** /'saɪnəs/ *n.* cavity, esp. either of cavities in skull communicating with nostrils.

**sinusitis** /saɪnə'saɪtɪs/ *n.* inflammation of sinus.

**sip 1** *v.* drink in repeated small mouthfuls or spoonfuls. **2** *n.* small mouthful of liquid; action of taking this.

**siphon** /'saɪf(ə)n/ **1** *n.* pipe or tube bent so that one leg is longer than other, used for drawing off liquids by atmospheric pressure; bottle from which aerated water is forced out by pressure of gas. **2** *v.* conduct or flow (as) through siphon.

**sir** /sɜː(r)/ *n.* polite or respectful form of address or reference to a man; **Sir** title of honour placed before Christian name of knight or baronet.

**sire** /saɪə(r)/ **1** *n.* male parent of animal, esp. stallion kept for breeding; *arch.* as form of address to king; *arch.* father or other male ancestor. **2** *v.t.* beget.

**siren** /'saɪərən/ *n.* device for making loud prolonged signal or warning sound; *Gk. Myth.* any of several women or winged creatures whose singing lured unwary sailors on to rocks; dangerously fascinating woman.

**sirloin** /'sɜːlɔɪn/ *n.* best part of loin of beef.

**sirocco** /sə'rɒkəʊ/ *n.* (*pl.* -**os**) hot moist wind in S. Europe.

**sisal** /'saɪz(ə)l/ *n.* fibre from leaves of agave.

**siskin** /'sɪskən/ *n.* small song-bird.

**sissy** /'sɪsi:/ **1** *n.* effeminate or cowardly man. **2** *a.* characteristic of sissy.

**sister** /'sɪstə(r)/ *n.* daughter of same parents; female fellow-member of class or sect or human race; member of religious sisterhood; head nurse of ward in hospital etc. **sister-in-law** husband's or wife's sister, brother's wife. **sisterly** *a.*

**sisterhood** /'sɪstəhʊd/ *n.* relationship (as) of sisters; society of women bound by monastic vows or devoting themselves to religious or charitable work.

**sit** *v.* (*past* & *p.p.* **sat**) take or be in position in which body is supported more or less upright by buttocks; cause to sit, place in sitting position; (of bird) perch; (of animal) rest with hind legs bent and body close to ground; pose *for* portrait; be MP *for* constituency; (of bird) remain on nest to hatch eggs; be candidate *for* examination; undergo (examination etc.); (of parliament, court, etc.) be in session; keep or have one's seat on (horse etc.). **sit back** relax one's efforts; **sit down** sit after standing, cause to sit, suffer tamely (*under* humiliation etc.); **sit in** occupy place as protest; **sit-in** *n.*; **sit in on** be present as guest etc. at (meeting); **sit on** be member of (committee etc.), *colloq.* delay action about, *sl.* repress or snub; **sit out** take no part in, stay till end of, sit outdoors; **sit tight** *colloq.* remain firmly in one's place, not yield; **sit up** rise from lying to sitting position, sit erect without lolling, not go to bed.

**sitar** /sɪ'tɑː(r)/ *n.* long-necked Indian guitar-like instrument.

**sitcom** /'sɪtkɒm/ *n. colloq.* situation comedy.

**site 1** *n.* ground on which town or building etc. stands or stood or is to stand; ground set apart for some purpose. **2** *v.t.* locate, place.

**sitter** /'sɪtə(r)/ *n.* person who sits for portrait etc.; baby-sitter; *sl.* easy catch or shot.

**sitting** /'sɪtɪŋ/ **1** *n.* time during which person or assembly etc. sits. **2** *a.* having sat down; (of animal or bird) not running or flying. **3 sitting-room** room containing easy chairs.

**situate 1** /'sɪtjʊeɪt/ *v.t.* place or put in position or situation etc. **2** /'sɪtjʊət/ *a. arch.* situated.

**situation** /sɪtjuːˈeɪʃ(ə)n/ n. place and its surroundings; set of circumstances, position of affairs, condition; employee's position or job. **situation comedy** broadcast comedy involving same characters in series of episodes. **situational** a.

**six** a. & n. one more than five. **hit, knock, for six**, colloq. utterly surprise or defeat; **six-gun, -shooter**, 6-chambered revolver.

**sixpence** /ˈsɪkspəns/ n. formerly sum of 6d, silver coin worth this. **sixpenny** a.

**sixteen** /sɪksˈtiːn/ a. & n. one more than fifteen. **sixteenth** a. & n.

**sixth** 1 a. next after fifth. 2 n. one of 6 equal parts. 3 **sixth form** form in secondary school for pupils of 16-18 years old; **sixth sense** supposed faculty giving intuitive or extra-sensory knowledge.

**sixty** /ˈsɪkstɪ/ a. & n. six times ten. **sixtieth** a. & n.

**size**[1] 1 n. relative bigness or extent of a thing; dimensions, magnitude; each of classes into which things are divided by size. 2 v.t. sort in sizes or by size. 3 **size up** estimate size of, colloq. form judgement of.

**size**[2] 1 n. gelatinous solution used for glazing paper and stiffening textiles etc. 2 v.t. treat with size.

**sizeable** /ˈsaɪzəb(ə)l/ a. fairly large.

**sizzle** /ˈsɪz(ə)l/ 1 v.i. make sputtering or hissing noise, as of frying. 2 n. sizzling sound.

**SJ** abbr. Society of Jesus.

**skate**[1] 1 n. each of pair of steel blades (or boots with blades attached) for gliding over ice; roller-skate. 2 v. move or glide or perform (as) on skates; pass lightly over. 3 **skateboard** short narrow board on roller-skate wheels for riding on standing up; **skating-rink** place with specially-prepared surface for skating.

**skedaddle** /skəˈdæd(ə)l/ v.i. colloq. run away, retreat hastily.

**skein** /skeɪn/ n. quantity of yarn etc. coiled and usu. loosely twisted; flock of wild geese etc. in flight.

**skeleton** /ˈskelɪt(ə)n/ n. hard framework of bones or shell or woody fibre etc. supporting or containing animal or vegetable body; dried bones of body fastened together in same relative position as in life; very thin person or animal; remaining part of something after usefulness etc. has gone; outline sketch; attrib. having only the essential or minimum number of persons or parts etc. **skeleton key** key fitting many locks. **skeletal** /ˈskelɪt(ə)l/ a.

**skep** n. wooden or wicker basket or hamper; straw or wicker beehive.

**skerrick** /ˈskerɪk/ n. Aus. colloq. small fragment or amount.

**skerry** /ˈskerɪ/ n. rocky reef or islet.

**sketch** 1 n. rough or unfinished drawing or painting; rough draft, general outline; short usu. humorous play. 2 v. make or give sketch of; make sketches.

**sketchy** /ˈsketʃɪ/ a. insubstantial or imperfect, esp. through haste.

**skew** 1 a. oblique, slanting, not symmetrical. 2 n. slant. 3 v. make skew; move obliquely.

**skewbald** /ˈskjuːbɔːld/ 1 a. (of animal) with irregular patches of white and another colour. 2 n. skewbald animal, esp. horse.

**skewer** /ˈskjuːə(r)/ 1 n. wooden or metal pin for holding meat compactly together while cooking. 2 v.t. fasten together or pierce (as) with skewer.

**ski** /skiː/ 1 n. each of pair of long narrow pieces of wood etc. fastened under feet for travelling over snow; similar device under vehicle. 2 v.i. (past & p.p. **ski'd** or **skied** /skiːd/; partic. **skiing**) travel on skis. 3 **skier** n.

**skid** 1 v. (of vehicle etc.) slide esp. sideways or obliquely on slippery road etc.; cause (vehicle) to skid. 2 n. act of skidding; braking device, esp. wooden or metal shoe, on wheel of vehicle; runner used as part of landing-gear of aircraft. 3 **skid-pan** slippery surface prepared for vehicle-drivers to practise control of skidding; **skid row** US sl. district frequented by vagrants.

**skied**[1] past & p.p. of **ski**.

**skied**[2] past & p.p. of **sky**.

**skiff** n. small light boat, esp. for rowing or sculling.

**skilful** /ˈskɪlfəl/ a. having or showing skill.

**skill** n. practised ability, expertness, facility; craft or art etc. requiring skill.

**skilled** /skɪld/ a. skilful; properly trained or experienced; requiring skill and experience.

# skillet

**skillet** /ˈskɪlət/ n. metal cooking utensil, usu. with feet and long handle; US frying-pan.

**skillion** /ˈskɪljən/ n. Aus. a lean-to, esp. for sheep waiting to be shorn.

**skim** v. take scum or cream etc. from surface of (liquid); pass over surface or along etc. rapidly and lightly with close approach or very slight contact; read superficially. **skim milk** milk with cream removed.

**skimp** v. supply meagrely, use too little of; be parsimonious.

**skimpy** /ˈskɪmpi/ a. meagre, insufficient.

**skin** 1 n. flexible continuous covering of human or animal body; skin removed from animal, material made from this; complexion; outer layer or covering; container for liquid, made of animal's skin; ship's planking or plating. 2 v. strip skin from; cover or become covered (as) with skin; sl. swindle, fleece. 3 **skin-deep** merely superficial; **skin-diver** person who swims under water without diving-suit; **skin-diving** n.; **skinflint** miserly person; **skin-graft** surgical transplanting of skin, skin thus transferred; **skin-tight** very close-fitting.

**skinful** /ˈskɪnfʊl/ n. colloq. enough alcoholic liquor to make one drunk.

**skinny** /ˈskɪni/ a. thin, emaciated.

**skint** a. sl. having no money.

**skip**[1] v. move along lightly, esp. by taking two steps with each foot in turn; jump lightly from ground; spring or leap over rope revolved over head and under feet; shift quickly from one subject etc. to another; omit or make omissions in reading; colloq. not participate in; colloq. leave hurriedly. 2 n. skipping movement or action.

**skip**[2] n. large container for refuse etc.; cage or bucket etc. in which men or materials are lowered or raised in mines or quarries.

**skip**[3] n. Aus. sl. derog. Australian of British descent.

**skipjack** /ˈskɪpdʒæk/ n. Aus. trevally.

**skipper** /ˈskɪpə(r)/ 1 n. captain of ship or aircraft or team etc. 2 v.t. act as captain of.

**skirl** 1 n. shrill sound of bagpipes. 2 v.i. make skirl.

**skirmish** /ˈskɜːmɪʃ/ 1 n. minor fight esp. between detached or outlying bodies of troops etc.; short argument. 2 v.i. engage in skirmish.

**skirt** 1 n. woman's outer garment hanging from waist, or this part of complete dress; part of coat etc. that hangs below waist; hanging part round base of hovercraft; border or outlying part; flank of beef etc. 2 v. go or be along or round edge or border of. 3 **skirting-board** narrow board round bottom of room-wall.

**skit** n. light piece of satire, burlesque.

**skite** Aus. colloq. 1 v.i. boast, brag. 2 n. boaster; boasting.

**skittish** /ˈskɪtɪʃ/ a. lively; playful, (of horse etc.) nervous, inclined to shy.

**skittle** /ˈskɪt(ə)l/ n. pin used in game of **skittles**, in which number of wooden pins are set up to be bowled or knocked down.

**skive** v. sl. evade (a duty). **skive off** depart evasively.

**skivvy** /ˈskɪvi/ n. colloq. derog. female domestic servant.

**skua** /ˈskjuːə/ n. large predatory sea-bird.

**skulduggery** /skʌlˈdʌgəri/ n. trickery, unscrupulous behaviour.

**skulk** v.i. lurk or conceal oneself or move stealthily, esp. in cowardly or sinister way, or to shirk duty.

**skull** n. bony case of brain; bony framework of head; representation of this; head as site of intelligence. **skull-cap** close-fitting brimless cap.

**skunk** n. black white-striped bushy-tailed Amer. animal, emitting powerful stench when attacked; sl. contemptible person.

**sky** /skaɪ/ 1 n. region of the atmosphere and outer space seen from the earth. 2 v.t. (past & p.p. **skied** /skaɪd/) hit (cricket-ball etc.) high into air. 3 **sky-blue** bright clear blue; **sky-diving** parachuting in which parachute is opened only at last safe moment; **skyjack** sl. hijack (aircraft); **skylark** lark that soars while singing, (v.i.) play tricks and practical jokes; **skylight** window in roof; **skyline** outline of hills or buildings etc. defined against sky; **sky-rocket** rocket exploding high in air, (v.i.) rise steeply; **skyscraper** very tall building.

# Skye

**Skye** /skaɪ/ *n.* short-legged long-haired Scotch terrier.

**slab** *n.* flat broad thickish piece of solid material.

**slack**[1] *a.* lacking firmness or tautness; lacking energy or activity; sluggish; negligent; (of tide etc.) neither ebbing nor flowing. 2 *n.* slack period; slack part of rope etc.; *colloq.* spell of inactivity; in *pl.* trousers for casual wear. 3 *v.* slacken; *colloq.* take a rest, be lazy. 4 **slack off** loosen, (cause to) lose vigour; **slack up** reduce speed.

**slack**[2] *n.* coal-dust.

**slacken** /ˈslækən/ *v.* make or become slack, slack *off*.

**slacker** /ˈslækə(r)/ *n.* shirker; idler.

**slag** *n.* refuse left after ore has been smelted etc. **slag-heap** hill of refuse from mine etc.

**slain** *p.p.* of **slay**.

**slake** *v.t.* assuage or satisfy (thirst etc.); cause (lime) to heat and crumble by action of water.

**slalom** /ˈslɑːləm/ *n.* downhill ski-race on zigzag course between artificial obstacles.

**slam**[1] 1 *v.* shut or throw or put down violently, with bang; *sl.* criticize severely. 2 *n.* sound or action of slamming.

**slam**[2] *n.* winning of all tricks at cards. **grand slam** winning of all 13 tricks in bridge, winning of all of group of championships in a sport.

**slander** /ˈslɑːndə(r)/ or /ˈslæ-/ 1 *n.* false report maliciously uttered to person's injury. 2 *v.t.* utter slander about. 3 **slanderous** *a.*

**slang** 1 *n.* language in common informal use but not regarded as standard in a language; words or uses of them peculiar to profession or class etc. 2 *v.* use abusive language (to). 3 **slanging-match** prolonged exchange of abuse. 4 **slangy** /ˈslæŋɪ/ *a.*

**slant** 1 *v.* slope; be or put in oblique position; present (news etc.) in biased or unfair way. 2 *n.* slope, oblique position; point of view, esp. biased one. 3 *a.* sloping, oblique.

**slantwise** /ˈslɑːntwaɪz/ *adv.* aslant.

**slap** 1 *v.* strike (as) with palm of hand; lay forcibly; put hastily or carelessly. 2 *n.* slapping stroke or sound. 3 **slapdash** hasty, careless; **slap-happy** *colloq.* cheerfully casual; **slapstick** boisterous knockabout comedy; **slap-up** *sl.* done regardless of expense.

**slash** 1 *v.* cut (at) with sweep of sharp weapon or implement; make gashes in, slit; lash with whip; reduce (prices etc.) drastically; criticize harshly. 2 *n.* slashing cut.

**slat** *n.* long narrow strip of wood or plastic etc., used in sets in Venetian blind or fence or bedstead etc.

**slate** 1 *n.* fine-grained grey rock easily split into thin smooth plates; trimmed plate of this used esp. in roofing or for writing on. 2 *v.t.* cover with slates; *colloq.* criticize severely; *US* make arrangements for (event etc.), nominate for office. 3 **slaty** *a.*

**slater** /ˈsleɪtə(r)/ *n. Aus.* woodlouse.

**slather** /ˈslæðə(r)/ *n. Aus. colloq.* lavish quantity. **open slather** free-for-all.

**slattern** /ˈslætən/ *n.* slovenly woman. **slatternly** *a.*

**slaughter** /ˈslɔːtə(r)/ 1 *n.* killing of animals for food; killing of many persons or animals at once. 2 *v.t.* kill thus. 3 **slaughterhouse** place for slaughter of animals for food.

**Slav** /slɑːv/ 1 *n.* member of group of peoples of East & Central Europe speaking Slavonic languages.

**slave** 1 *n.* person who is owned by another and has to work for him; drudge, person working very hard; helpless influence *of* or *to* some dominating influence. 2 *v.i.* work very hard. 3 **slave-driver** overseer of slaves at work, hard taskmaster; **slave-trade** procuring, transporting, and selling slaves, esp. African Blacks.

**slaver**[1] /ˈsleɪvə(r)/ *n.* ship or person engaged in slave-trade.

**slaver**[2] /ˈslævə(r)/ 1 *n.* saliva running from mouth. 2 *v.* let saliva run from mouth; drool.

**slavery** /ˈsleɪvərɪ/ *n.* condition or work of slave; drudgery; custom of having slaves.

**slavish** /ˈsleɪvɪʃ/ *a.* of or like slaves; without originality.

**Slavonic** /sləˈvɒnɪk/ 1 *a.* of group of languages including Russian and Polish etc. 2 *n.* Slavonic group of languages.

**slay** *v.t.* (*past* **slew**; *p.p.* **slain**) kill.

**sleazy** /ˈsliːzɪ/ a. squalid; tawdry; slatternly.

**sled** n. & v.t. US sledge.

**sledge** 1 n. vehicle on runners instead of wheels for conveying loads or passengers esp. over snow. 2 v. travel or convey in sledge.

**sledge-hammer** n. large heavy hammer.

**sleek** 1 a. (of hair, skin, etc.) smooth and glossy; of well-fed comfortable appearance. 2 v.t. make sleek.

**sleep** 1 n. condition in which eyes are closed, muscles and nerves relaxed, and consciousness suspended; spell of this; inert condition of some hibernating animals. 2 v. (past & p.p. slept) be or fall asleep; spend the night at or in; provide sleeping accommodation for; have sexual intercourse with or together; be inactive or dead. 3 **sleeping-bag** lined or padded bag to sleep in esp. when camping etc.; **sleeping-car, -carriage**, railway coach with beds or berths; **sleeping partner** partner not sharing in actual work of a firm; **sleeping-pill** pill to induce sleep; **sleepwalker** person who walks during sleep; **sleep-walking** n.

**sleeper** /ˈsliːpə(r)/ n. sleeping person; one of beams on which rails of railway etc. rest; sleeping car; ring worn in pierced ear to keep hole from closing.

**sleepy** /ˈsliːpɪ/ a. feeling need of sleep; lacking activity or bustle. **sleepy lizard** Aus. blue-tongued lizard.

**sleet** 1 n. snow and rain together; snow or hail falling in half-melted state. 2 v.i. fall as sleet. 3 **it sleets** sleet falls. 4 **sleety** a.

**sleeve** n. part of garment covering arm; cover for gramophone record; tube enclosing rod or smaller tube etc. **up one's sleeve** concealed but ready for use.

**sleigh** /sleɪ/ 1 n. sledge, esp. as passenger-vehicle drawn by horses. 2 v.i. travel in sleigh.

**sleight** /slaɪt/ n. **sleight-of-hand** conjuring, dexterity.

**slender** /ˈslendə(r)/ a. of small girth or breadth; slim; scanty, slight, meagre.

**slept** past & p.p. of **sleep**.

**sleuth** /sluːθ/ n. detective. **sleuthhound** bloodhound.

**slew**[1] 1 v. turn or swing round to new position. 2 n. such turn.

**slew**[2] past of **slay**.

**slice** 1 n. thin broad piece or wedge cut from something; cooking- or serving-implement with thin broad blade; Golf slicing stroke. 2 v. cut into slices, cut off; cut cleanly or easily; strike ball so that it deviates away from one.

**slick** 1 a. colloq. skilful or efficient; shrewd, wily; sleek, smooth. 2 n. patch or film of oil on water. 3 v.t. colloq. make smooth or sleek.

**slide** 1 v. (past & p.p. slid) (cause to) move along smooth surface touching it always with same part; move or go smoothly or quietly; pass gradually (into state or condition); glide over ice on foot without skates. 2 n. act of sliding; smooth slope down which persons or things can slide; track for sliding esp. on ice; part of machine or instrument that slides; mounted transparency viewed by means of projector etc.; piece of glass holding object for microscope. 3 **let things slide** be negligent, allow deterioration; **slide-rule** ruler with sliding central piece, graduated logarithmically to allow ease in calculations; **sliding scale** scale of fees or taxes or wages etc. that varies as a whole according to changes in some standard.

**slight** /slaɪt/ 1 a. small, inconsiderable; not serious or important; inadequate; slender, slim. 2 v.t. treat with indifference or disrespect, disdain, ignore. 3 n. instance of slighting or being slighted.

**slim** 1 a. slender; not fat or overweight; clever, artful. 2 v. make or become slim, esp. by dieting etc.

**slime** n. oozy or sticky substance.

**slimy** /ˈslaɪmɪ/ a. of or like or covered or smeared with slime; disgustingly obsequious.

**sling**[1] 1 n. strap etc. used to support or raise thing; bandage supporting injured arm; strap or string used to throw small missile; Aus. sl. bribe. 2 v.t. (past & p.p. slung) hurl, throw; suspend with sling; arrange so as to be held or moved from above; Aus. sl. bribe. 3 **sling-back** shoe held in place by strap round back of heel; **sling off at** Aus. colloq. ridicule. **sling one's hook** sl. make off.

**sling**² *n.* sweetened drink of spirit, esp. gin, with water.

**slink** *v.i.* (*past* & *p.p.* **slunk**) go in stealthy, guilty, or sneaking manner.

**slinky** /'slɪŋki/ *a.* slinking; (of garment) close-fitting and sinuous.

**slip**¹ **1** *v.* slide momentarily by accident; lose footing or balance thus; go with sliding motion; get away by being hard to grasp; make one's way quietly or unobserved; make casual mistake; fall below normal standard; place stealthily or casually; release from restraint or connection; put *on*, *off*, get *into*, etc. easily or casually. **2** *n.* act of slipping; accidental or slight error; loose covering or garment, petticoat; slope on which boats are landed or ships are built or repaired etc.; *Crick.* fielder behind wicket on off side, in *pl.* this part of field; finely ground clay mixed with water for coating or decorating earthenware. **3 give person the slip** evade or escape from him; **slip into** *Aus. sl.* attack; **slip-knot** knot that can be undone by pull, knot of running noose; **slip-on** (of shoes or clothes) that can be easily slipped on or off; **slip-over** (esp. sleeveless) pullover; **slipped disc** displaced vertebra; **slip-rail** *Aus.* movable rail in a fence for closing gateway; **slip-road** road for entering or leaving motorway etc.; **slip-stream** current of air or water driven backwards by propeller; **slipway** shipbuilding or landing slip.

**slip**² *n.* small piece of paper for making notes etc.; cutting from plant for grafting or planting.

**slipper** /'slɪpə(r)/ *n.* light loose indoor shoe.

**slippery** /'slɪpərɪ/ *a.* with smooth or polished or oily etc. surface making foothold etc. insecure or object etc. difficult to grasp or hold; elusive, unreliable, shifty. **slippery dip** *Aus.* slide in children's playground.

**slippy** /'slɪpɪ/ *a. colloq.* slippery.

**slipshod** /'slɪpʃɒd/ *a.* slovenly, careless; having shoes down at heel.

**slit 1** *n.* long narrow incision or opening. **2** *v.* (*past* & *p.p.* **slit**) make slit in; cut in strips.

**slither** /'slɪðə(r)/ **1** *v.i.* slide or slip unsteadily. **2** *n.* act of slithering. **3 slithery** *a.*

**sliver** /'slɪvə(r)/ **1** *n.* splinter; small narrow slice or piece. **2** *v.* cut or split into slivers.

**slob** *n. colloq.* large and coarse or stupid person.

**slobber** /'slɒbə(r)/ **1** *v.* slaver, show excessive sentiment (*over*). **2** *n.* slaver. **3 slobbery** *a.*

**sloe** *n.* blackthorn; its small bluish-black fruit.

**slog 1** *v.* hit hard and usu. unskilfully; work or walk doggedly. **2** *n.* heavy random hit; hard steady work; spell of this.

**slogan** /'sləʊgən/ *n.* short catchy phrase used in advertising etc.; party cry, watchword.

**sloop** /slu:p/ *n.* small one-masted fore-and-aft rigged vessel.

**slop 1** *v.* spill or flow over edge of vessel; allow to do this; spill or splash liquid on. **2** *n.* liquid spilled or splashed; in *pl.* dirty water or liquid, waste contents of kitchen vessels or chamber-pot etc.; in *sing.* or *pl.* unappetizing liquid food. **3 slop-basin** basin for receiving dregs of tea-cups.

**slope 1** *n.* inclined position or direction or state; piece of rising or falling ground; difference in level between two ends or sides of a thing; place for skiing. **2** *v.* have or show slope; slant; cause to slope. **3 slope off** *sl.* go away, esp. to evade work etc.

**sloppy** /'slɒpɪ:/ *a.* wet, watery, too liquid; unsystematic, careless, untidy, ill-fitting; weakly emotional.

**slosh 1** *v.* splash or flounder (*about* etc.); *sl.* hit esp. heavily; *colloq.* pour (liquid) clumsily; in *p.p. colloq.* drunk. **2** *n.* slush; sound or act of splashing; *sl.* heavy blow.

**slot 1** *n.* slit or other aperture in machine etc. for something (esp. coin) to be inserted; allotted place in arrangement. **2** *v.t.* put or be placed (as if) into slot; provide with slot(s). **3 slot-machine** machine worked by insertion of coin, esp. delivering small purchased articles or providing amusement.

**sloth** /sləʊθ/ *n.* laziness, indolence; slow-moving arboreal mammal of tropical America.

**slothful** /'sləʊθfəl/ *a.* indolent, lazy.

**slouch** /slaʊtʃ/ **1** *v.* stand or move or sit etc. in drooping or ungainly fashion.

**slough** 526 **small**

2 *n.* slouching posture or movement; downward droop of hat-brim; *sl.* incompetent or slovenly worker. 3 **slouch hat** soft hat with wide flexible brim.

**slough**[1] /slaʊ/ *n.* swamp, miry place. **Slough of Despond** state of hopeless depression.

**slough**[2] /slʌf/ 1 *n.* dead skin or other part of animal (esp. snake) cast off. 2 *v.* cast or drop off or *off* as slough.

**sloven** /'slʌv(ə)n/ *n.* person of careless or untidy or dirty habits.

**slovenly** /'slʌvənlɪ/ *a.* careless and untidy; unmethodical.

**slow** /sləʊ/ 1 *a.* taking relatively long time to do thing(s); acting or moving or done without speed; (of clock etc.) showing earlier than correct time; dull-witted, stupid; tedious; (of fire, oven, etc.) not very hot; reluctant *to* do. 2 *adv.* slowly. 3 *v.* (with *down*, *up*) (cause to) move or act or work less quickly or energetically. 4 **slowcoach** slow or indolent person; **slow motion** speed of film in which actions appear much slower than usual, simulation of this in real action.

**slow-worm** /'sləʊwɜːm/ *n.* small Eur. legless lizard.

**sludge** *n.* thick greasy mud; sewage; muddy or slushy sediment or deposit. **sludgy** *a.*

**slue** var. of **slew**[1].

**slug**[1] *n.* slimy shell-less gastropod; irregularly shaped bullet etc.; missile for airgun; line of type in Linotype printing; *US* tot of liquor.

**slug**[2] 1 *n. Aus.* exorbitant tax or charge. 2 *v. US* hit hard; *Aus.* tax or charge exorbitantly.

**sluggard** /'slʌɡəd/ *n.* lazy person.

**sluggish** /'slʌɡɪʃ/ *a.* inert, slow-moving.

**sluice** /sluːs/ 1 *n.* (also **sluice-gate**) sliding gate or other contrivance for regulating flow or level of water; water regulated by this; (also **sluice-way**) artificial water-channel; place for rinsing. 2 *v.* provide or wash with sluice(s); rinse; pour water freely upon.

**slum** 1 *n.* dirty squalid overcrowded street or district etc. 2 *v.i.* live in slum-like conditions; visit slums esp. in search of amusement. 3 **slummy** *a.*

**slumber** /'slʌmbə(r)/ *n.* & *v.i.* sleep. **slumb(e)rous** *a.*

**slump** 1 *n.* sudden severe or continued fall in prices and demand etc. 2 *v.i.* undergo slump; sit or fall down limply.

**slung** past & p.p. of **sling**.

**slunk** past & p.p. of **slink**.

**slur** 1 *v.* sound or write (words, musical notes, etc.) so that they run into one another; put slur upon (person, character); pass lightly or deceptively *over*. 2 *n.* imputation of wrongdoing, reproach; action of slurring; *Mus.* curved line over or under notes to be slurred.

**slurp** *colloq.* 1 *v.t.* eat or drink noisily. 2 *n.* sound of slurping.

**slurry** /'slʌrɪ/ *n.* thin sloppy cement or mud etc.

**slush** *n.* thawing snow; watery mud; silly sentiment. **slush fund** fund for illegal purposes, esp. bribery.

**slushy** /'slʌʃɪ/ 1 *a.* of or abounding in slush. 2 *n. Aus. colloq.* cook's assistant.

**slut** *n.* slovenly woman, hussy. **sluttish** *a.*

**sly** *a.* crafty, wily; secretive; underhand; knowing, mischievous. **on the sly** secretly; **sly grog** *Aus. colloq.* illegally sold liquor.

**smack**[1] *n.* sharp slap or blow; hard hit; sharp sound of surface struck with palm of hand; loud kiss. 2 *v.* slap; move with smack. 3 *adv. colloq.* with a smack, suddenly, violently.

**smack**[2] 1 *v.i.* taste *of*, suggest presence *of*. 2 *n.* flavour or suggestion *of*.

**smack**[3] *n.* single-masted sailing-boat.

**smacker** /'smækə(r)/ *n. sl.* loud kiss; *sl.* £1, *US* & *Aus.* $1.

**small** /smɔːl/ 1 *a.* not large or big; comparatively little in size or importance or number etc.; doing thing on small scale; petty, mean, paltry. 2 *n. the* slenderest part (esp. *of* back); in *pl. colloq.* small articles of laundry, esp. underwear. 3 *adv.* into small pieces, on small scale, etc. 4 **small arms** portable firearms; **small change** coins as opp. notes; **smallholding** piece of agricultural land smaller than farm; **small hours** night-time after midnight; **smallpox** acute contagious disease with fever and pustules usu. leaving permanent marks; **small print** matter printed small, esp. limitations in contract; **small talk** trivial social conversation; **small-time** unimportant, petty.

**smarmy** /'smɑːmi/ *a. colloq.* ingratiating.

**smart 1** *a.* clever, ingenious, quick-witted; bright and fresh in appearance, neat; fashionable; stylish, conspicuous in society; quick, brisk; painfully severe, sharp, vigorous. **2** *v.i.* feel or give acute pain or distress; rankle. **3** *n.* bodily or mental sharp pain, stinging sensation. **4 smartarse** *Aus. colloq.* know-all.

**smarten** /'smɑːt(ə)n/ *v.* make or become smart (usu. with *up*).

**smash 1** *v.* break to pieces; bring or come to disaster; utterly defeat; bring or drive violently *down*, *into*, etc.; *Tennis* hit (ball) hard downwards over net. **2** *n.* act or sound of smashing; very successful play or song etc. **3** *adv.* with smash. **4 smash-and-grab** *colloq.* (of robbery) with goods snatched from broken shop-window etc.

**smashing** /'smæʃɪŋ/ *a. sl.* very fine, wonderful.

**smattering** /'smætərɪŋ/ *n.* slight knowledge (*of*).

**smear** /smɪə(r)/ **1** *v.* daub with greasy or sticky substance; smudge; (seek to) discredit or defame. **2** *n.* action or result of smearing; material smeared on microscope slide etc. for examination; specimen of this; discrediting or defaming; attempt at this. **3 smeary** *a.*

**smell 1** *n.* sense by which odours are perceived, property perceived by this; unpleasant odour; act of inhaling to ascertain smell. **2** *v.* (*past* & *p.p.* **smelt** or **smelled**) perceive or detect by smell; emit smell; be redolent *of*; stink; have or use sense of smell. **3 smelling-salts** sharp-smelling substances to be sniffed to relieve faintness.

**smelly** /'smeli/ *a.* evil-smelling, stinking.

**smelt**[1] *v.t.* fuse or melt (ore) to extract metal; obtain (metal) thus.

**smelt**[2] *n.* small edible fish with tender oily flesh.

**smelt**[3] *past* & *p.p.* of **smell**.

**smilax** /'smaɪlæks/ *n.* a climbing plant.

**smile 1** *v.* make or have facial expression of amusement or pleasure, usu. with parting of lips and upward turning of their ends; express by smiling; give (smile); be propitious. **2** *n.* act of smiling; smiling expression or aspect.

**smirch** /smɜːtʃ/ *v.t.* & *n.* stain, smear.

**smirk 1** *n.* silly or conceited smile. **2** *v.i.* give smirk.

**smite** *v.* (*past* **smote**; *p.p.* **smitten**) *arch.* strike, hit, chastise; defeat; seize *with* disease or emotion etc.

**smith** /smɪθ/ *n.* worker in metal; blacksmith; *fig.* person who creates specified thing.

**smithereens** /smɪðə'riːnz/ *n.pl. colloq.* small fragments.

**smithy** /'smɪði/ *n.* blacksmith's workshop, forge.

**smitten** *p.p.* of **smite**.

**smock 1** *n.* loose-fitting short shirtlike outer garment, freq. with bands or smocking at yoke. **2** *v.t.* adorn with smocking.

**smocking** /'smɒkɪŋ/ *n.* ornamentation on cloth made by gathering it tightly with stitches.

**smog** *n.* dense smoky fog. **smoggy** *a.*

**smoke 1** *n.* visible vapour from burning substance; *colloq.* spell of smoking tobacco etc.; *sl.* cigar, cigarette; *Aus. colloq.* hiding, concealment. **2** *v.* emit smoke or visible vapour; inhale and exhale smoke of (tobacco etc.); do this habitually; darken or preserve by action of smoke. **3 big smoke** *Aus. sl.* city; **smoke-bomb** bomb emitting dense smoke on bursting; **smoke off** *Aus. colloq.* disappear, depart; **smoke out** drive out by means of smoke, drive out of hiding etc.; **smokescreen** cloud of smoke to conceal military or naval operations etc., device for disguising activities; **smoke-stack** funnel of locomotive or steamship.

**smoker** /'sməʊkə(r)/ *n.* person who smokes tobacco habitually; part of railway coach where smoking is permitted.

**smoko** /'sməʊkəʊ/ *n. Aus. colloq.* stoppage of work for rest and smoke; informal concert or social gathering.

**smoky** /'sməʊki/ *a.* producing or emitting smoke; covered or filled with smoke; obscured (as) with smoke; suggestive of or having the colour of smoke.

**smoodge** /smuːdʒ/ *v.i. Aus.* curry favour; exchange caresses.

**smooth** /smuːð/ **1** *a.* having even surface; free from projections and rough-

**smorgasbord**      528      **sneak**

ness; (of progress, passage, etc.) not interrupted or disturbed by obstacles or storms etc.; conciliatory or plausible or flattering. **2** *v.* make or become smooth; get rid of impediments etc. from. **3** *n.* smoothing touch or stroke. **4 smooth-tongued** insincerely flattering.

**smorgasbord** /'smɔːgəsbɔːd/ *n.* Swedish hors-d'œuvres; buffet meal with variety of dishes.

**smote** past of **smite**.

**smother** /'smʌðə(r)/ **1** *v.t.* suffocate, stifle; overwhelm *with* kisses or gifts etc.; cover entirely with or *with*; extinguish (fire) by heaping with ashes etc.; have difficulty in breathing; suppress or conceal. **2** *n.* cloud of smoke or dust etc.; obscurity caused by this.

**smoulder** /'sməʊldə(r)/ **1** *v.i.* burn and smoke without flame (freq. *fig.*). **2** *n.* such burning.

**smudge 1** *n.* dirty mark or blur or smear. **2** *v.* make smudge on or with; become blurred or smeared. **3 smudgy** *a.*

**smug** *a.* complacent, self-satisfied; consciously respectable.

**smuggle** /'smʌg(ə)l/ *v.* import or export (goods) illegally, esp. without paying customs duties; convey secretly *in* or *out* etc.

**smut 1** *n.* small piece of soot; spot or smudge made by this; obscene talk or pictures or stories; cereal-disease turning parts of plant to black powder. **2** *v.* mark or infect with smut(s); contract smut disease. **3 smutty** *a.*

**snack** *n.* slight or casual or hasty meal; *Aus.* an easy task. **snack-bar** place where snacks are sold.

**snaffle** /'snæf(ə)l/ **1** *n.* simple bridle-bit without curb. **2** *v.t.* put snaffle on; *sl.* take, steal.

**snag 1** *n.* hidden or unexpected obstacle or drawback; jagged projecting stump or point; tear in material caused by snag. **2** *v.t.* catch or tear on snag.

**snags** *n. pl. Aus. sl.* sausages.

**snail** *n.* slow-moving mollusc with spiral shell.

**snake 1** *n.* long limbless reptile; treacherous or ungrateful person. **2** *v.* move or twist etc. like a snake. **3 snake in the grass** secret enemy; **snakes and ladders** game with counters moved along board, with sudden advances and reverses.

**snaky** /'sneɪkɪ/ *a.* of or like a snake; sinuous; treacherous; *Aus. colloq.* angry, irritable.

**snap 1** *v.* break sharply; (cause to) emit sudden sharp sound; open or close with snapping sound; speak with sudden irritation; make sudden audible bite; move quickly; take snapshot of. **2** *n.* act or sound of snapping; catch that fastens with a snap; small crisp biscuit; snapshot; sudden brief spell of cold weather; card-game in which players call 'snap' when two cards of equal rank are exposed. **3** *adv.* with snapping sound. **4** *a.* taken or made suddenly or without notice or warning or preparation etc. **5 snapdragon** plant with flowers that can be made to gape; **snap fastener** press-stud; **snap one's fingers at** defy; **snap out of** *sl.* get out of (mood) by sudden effort; **snapshot** photograph taken informally or casually; **snap up** buy hastily or eagerly.

**snapper** /'snæpə(r)/ *n.* kind of foodfish.

**snappish** /'snæpɪʃ/ *a.* peevish, irritable, petulant.

**snappy** /'snæpɪ/ *a. colloq.* brisk; full of zest; neat and elegant.

**snare** /sneə(r)/ **1** *n.* trap, esp. with noose, for catching birds or animals; thing that tempts one to risk capture or defeat etc.; arrangement of twisted gut or wire etc. stretched across lower head of side-drum to produce buzzing sound. **2** *v.t.* catch in snare, ensnare. **3 snare-drum** side-drum with snare.

**snarl**[1] **1** *v.* make angry growl with bared teeth; speak irritably or cynically. **2** *n.* act or sound of snarling.

**snarl**[2] **1** *v.* (often with *up*) tangle, confuse and hamper movement of (traffic etc.). **2** *n.* tangle.

**snatch 1** *v.* seize quickly or eagerly or unexpectedly; take suddenly *away, from,* etc. **2** *n.* act of snatching; fragment of song or talk etc.; short spell of activity etc. **3 snatch it** or **one's time** *Aus. colloq.* collect due wages and leave job.

**snazzy** /'snæzɪ/ *a. sl.* smart, attractive, excellent.

**sneak 1** *v.* go or take furtively; *sl.* carry off unobserved; *sl.* tell tales. **2** *n.* mean-

**sneakers** / **snow**

**sneakers** /'sni:kəz/ *n.pl. sl.* soft-soled shoes.

**sneaking** /'sni:kɪŋ/ *a.* (of feeling, suspicion, etc.) unavowed, persistent and puzzling.

**sneer 1** *n.* derisive smile or remark. **2** *v.* make sneer (*at*); utter sneeringly.

**sneeze 1** *n.* sudden involuntary explosive expulsion of air from irritated nostrils. **2** *v.i.* make sneeze. **3 not to be sneezed at** not contemptible, worth having.

**snick 1** *v.t.* make slight notch or cut in; *Crick.* deflect (ball) slightly with bat. **2** *n.* such notch or deflection.

**snicker** *v.i.* & *n.* snigger.

**snide** *a. colloq.* sneering, slyly derogatory; counterfeit.

**sniff 1** *v.* draw up air audibly through nose; smell scent of, draw (*up*), take (*in*), etc., by sniffing. **2** *n.* act or sound of sniffing. **3 sniff at** show contempt for or disapproval of.

**sniffle** /'snɪf(ə)l/ **1** *v.i.* sniff repeatedly or slightly. **2** *n.* act of sniffling; in *pl.* cold in the head causing sniffling.

**snifter** /'snɪftə(r)/ *n. sl.* small drink of alcoholic liquor.

**snig** *v.t. Aus.* drag (log) by one end with rope or chain.

**snigger** /'snɪgə(r)/ **1** *n.* half-suppressed laugh. **2** *v.i.* utter snigger.

**snip 1** *v.* cut with scissors etc., esp. in small quick strokes. **2** *n.* act of snipping; piece snipped off; *sl.* something cheaply acquired or easily done.

**snipe 1** *n.* wading bird with long straight bill. **2** *v.* fire shots from hiding usu. at long range; *fig.* make sly critical attack *at*.

**sniper** /'snaɪpə(r)/ *n.* person who snipes; *Aus. sl.* non-union worker on wharf.

**snippet** /'snɪpɪt/ *n.* small piece cut off; (usu. in *pl.*) scrap or fragment of information or knowledge etc.

**snitch** *v. sl.* steal.

**snivel** /'snɪv(ə)l/ *v.i.* (*past* & *p.p.* **snivelled**) sniffle; be tearful; show maudlin emotion. **2** *n.* act of snivelling.

**snob** *n.* person with exaggerated respect for social position or wealth or who despises people with inferior rank or tastes etc. **snobbery** *n.*; **snobbish** *a.*

**snood** /snu:d/ *n.* loose net worn by woman to keep hair in place.

**snook** /snu:k/ *n. colloq.* contemptuous gesture with thumb to nose and fingers spread. **cock a snook at** make this gesture at, show contempt for.

**snooker** /'snu:kə(r)/ **1** *n.* game played with 15 red and 6 other coloured balls on billiard-table; position in this game where direct shot would lose points. **2** *v.t.* subject (player) to snooker; *sl.* (esp. in *p.p.*) thwart, defeat.

**snoop** /snu:p/ *colloq.* **1** *v.i.* pry into another's private affairs; sneak *about* or *around* looking for infringements of rules etc. **2** *n.* act of snooping.

**snooty** /'snu:ti:/ *a. sl.* supercilious, snobbish.

**snooze** /snu:z/ **1** *n.* short sleep, esp. in daytime. **2** *v.i.* take snooze.

**snore 1** *n.* snorting or grunting sound in breathing during sleep. **2** *v.i.* make such sounds.

**snorkel** /'snɔ:k(ə)l/ **1** *n.* device for supplying air to underwater swimmer or submerged submarine. **2** *v.i.* (*past* & *p.p.* **snorkelled**) swim with snorkel.

**snort 1** *n.* loud or harsh sound made by driving breath violently through nose, usu. expr. indignation or incredulity etc.; noise resembling this; *colloq.* small drink of liquor. **2** *v.* make snorting sound; express or utter with snorts.

**snorter** /'snɔ:tə(r)/ *n. sl.* something notably vigorous or difficult etc.

**snot** *n. vulg.* nasal mucus.

**snotty** /'snɒti:/ *a. sl.* running or foul with nasal mucus; *colloq.* contemptible, bad-tempered; supercilious.

**snout** /snaʊt/ *n.* projecting nose (and mouth) of animal; *derog.* person's nose; pointed front of thing.

**snow** /snəʊ/ **1** *n.* frozen vapour falling to earth in light white flakes; fall of this, layer of this on ground; anything resembling this in whiteness or texture etc.; *sl.* cocaine. **2** *v.i.* fall as or like snow; come in large numbers or quantities. **3 it snows** snow falls; **snowball** snow pressed or rolled into ball, esp. for use as missile, (*v.*) pelt with or throw snowballs, increase rapidly;

**Snr.** *abbr.* Senior.

**snow-blind** temporarily blinded by glare of sun on snow; **snow-bound** prevented by snow from going out; **snowdrift** bank of snow piled up by wind; **snowdrop** spring-flowering plant with white drooping flowers; **snowed in** snow-bound; **snowed under** covered (as) with snow, overwhelmed with numbers etc.; **snowed up** snow-bound; **snowflake** each of the small collections of crystals in which snow falls; **snow goose** arctic white goose; **snow-line** level above which snow never melts entirely; **snowman** figure made of snow; **snow-plough** device for clearing road or railway of snow; **snow-shoe** one of pair of light racket-shaped strung frames enabling wearer to walk on surface of snow; **snow-storm** heavy fall of snow esp. with wind; **snow-white** pure white. 4 **snowy** *a.*

**Snr.** *abbr.* Senior.

**snub** 1 *v.t.* rebuff, humiliate, in sharp or cutting manner. 2 *n.* snubbing, rebuff. 3 *a.* (of nose) short and turned up.

**snuff**[1] 1 *v.* remove snuff from (candle). 2 *n.* charred part of candle-wick. **snuff it** *sl.* die; **snuff out** extinguish (candle) by covering or pinching flame, kill or put an end to (hopes etc.), *sl.* die.

**snuff**[2] 1 *n.* powdered tobacco or medicine taken by sniffing it up nostrils. 2 *v.* take snuff; sniff.

**snuffle** /'snʌf(ə)l/ *v.* sniff, esp. audibly or noisily; speak like person with a cold. 2 *n.* snuffling sound or speech.

**snug** 1 *a.* sheltered, well enclosed; closely fitting; comfortable; (of income etc.) sufficing for comfort. 2 *n.* bar-parlour of inn.

**snuggle** /'snʌg(ə)l/ *v.* move or lie close *up to* for warmth etc.

**so**[1] /səʊ/ *adv. & conj.* in this or that way, in the manner or position or state described or implied; to that extent; to a great or notable degree; consequently, therefore; in fact, indeed; also.

**so-and-so** particular person or thing not needing to be specified, *colloq.* unpleasant or contemptible person; **so-called** called or named thus (but perhaps wrongly or inaccurately); **so long** *colloq.* goodbye; **so long as** provided that; **so-so** *colloq.* only moderately well or good.

**so**[2] var. of **soh**.

**soak** 1 *v.* make or become thoroughly wet through saturation with or in liquid; (of rain etc.) drench; take (liquid) *in* or *up*; drink heavily; *sl.* extort money from. 2 *n.* soaking, *colloq.* hard drinker; *Aus.* depression holding water after rain, shallow well. 3 **soak-away** arrangement for disposal of waste water by percolation through soil.

**soap** 1 *n.* cleansing substance yielding lather when rubbed in water. 2 *v.t.* apply soap to; rub with soap. 3 **soap-box** makeshift stand for street orator; **soap opera** sentimental domestic broadcast serial; **soap powder** preparation of soap usu. with additives, for washing clothes etc.; **soapstone** steatite; **soapsuds** froth of soap in water.

**soapy** /'səʊpɪ/ *a.* of or like soap; containing or smeared with soap; unctuous, flattering.

**soar** /sɔː(r)/ *v.i.* fly or rise high; reach high level or standard; fly without flapping of wings or use of motor power.

**sob** 1 *v.* draw breath in convulsive gasps usu. with weeping; utter with sobs. 2 *n.* act or sound of sobbing. 3 **sob-story** *colloq.* narrative meant to evoke sympathy; **sob-stuff** *colloq.* pathos, sentimental writing or behaviour.

**sober** /'səʊbə(r)/ 1 *a.* not drunk; not given to drink; moderate, sane, tranquil; (of colour) quiet. 2 *v.* (often with *down* or *up*) make or become sober.

**sobriety** /sə'braɪətɪ/ *n.* soberness.

**sobriquet** /'səʊbrɪkeɪ/ *n.* nickname.

**Soc.** *abbr.* Socialist; Society.

**soccer** /'sɒkə(r)/ *n. colloq.* Association football.

**sociable** /'səʊʃəb(ə)l/ *a.* fitted for or liking society of other people; friendly. **sociability** *n.*

**social** /'səʊʃ(ə)l/ 1 *a.* of society or its organization; concerned with mutual relations (of classes of) human beings; living in communities; gregarious; unfitted for solitary life. 2 *n.* social gathering. 3 **social science** scientific study of human society and social relationships; **social security** State assistance to those lacking adequate money or welfare; **social services** welfare services such as education, health, housing, pensions, etc., provided by the State;

**social worker** person working, esp. for local authority, to alleviate social problems.

**socialism** /'səʊʃəlɪz(ə)m/ n. political and economic principle that community as whole should have ownership and control of all means of production and distribution; policy or practice based on this theory. **socialist** n.; **socialistic** a.

**socialite** /'səʊʃəlaɪt/ n. person prominent in fashionable society.

**socialize** /'səʊʃəlaɪz/ v. behave sociably; make social; organize in socialistic manner.

**society** /sə'saɪətɪ:/ n. organized and interdependent community, the system and organization of living in this; distinguished or fashionable members of a community, the upper classes; mixing with other people, companionship, company; association of persons sharing common aim or interest etc.

**sociology** /səʊsɪ'ɒlədʒi:/ n. study of society and social problems. **sociological** a.; **sociologist** n.

**sock**[1] n. short stocking usu. not reaching knee; insole.

**sock**[2] sl. 1 v.t. hit hard. 2 n. hard blow. 3 **sock it to** attack or address vigorously.

**socket** /'sɒkət/ n. natural or artificial hollow for thing to fit into etc.; hollow or cavity holding eye or tooth etc.; device receiving electrical plug or lightbulb etc., to make connection.

**Socratic** /sə'krætɪk/ a. of the ancient-Gk philosopher Socrates or his philosophy.

**sod**[1] n. turf, piece of turf; surface of ground.

**sod**[2] vulg. 1 n. unpleasant or despised person. 2 v. damn.

**soda** /'səʊdə/ n. compound of sodium in common use; soda-water; Aus. sl. something easy, a pushover. **sodafountain** device supplying soda-water, shop serving ice-cream and soft drinks etc.; **soda-water** water made effervescent with carbon dioxide and used as drink alone or with spirits etc.

**sodden** /'sɒd(ə)n/ a. saturated with liquid; soaked through; rendered stupid or dull etc. with drunkenness.

**sodium** /'səʊdɪəm/ n. soft silver-white metallic element. **sodium lamp** lamp giving yellow light from electrical discharge in sodium vapour.

**sodomite** /'sɒdəmaɪt/ n. person practising sodomy.

**sodomy** /'sɒdəmi:/ n. unnatural sexual act, esp. between males.

**sofa** /'səʊfə/ n. long seat with raised ends and back.

**soffit** /'sɒfɪt/ n. under-surface of arch or lintel etc.

**soft** 1 a. not hard; yielding to pressure; malleable, plastic, easily cut; smooth or fine textured; mild; (of water) not containing mineral salts which prevent lathering; not loud or strident; not sharply defined; gentle, conciliatory; compassionate, sympathetic; feeble, effeminate; silly; easy; (of drug) not likely to cause addiction. 2 adv. softly. 3 **soft drink** non-alcoholic drink; **soft fruit** highly perishable fruit, esp. small berries etc.; **soft furnishings** curtains and rugs etc.; **soft-hearted** easily affected by others' pain or grief etc.; **soft option** easier alternative; **soft palate** back part of palate; **soft pedal** pedal on piano making tone softer; **soft-pedal** refrain from emphasizing; **soft sell** restrained salesmanship; **soft soap** liquid soap, fig. flattery; **soft spot** sentimental affection for; **soft touch** sl. person readily parting with money; **software** programs etc. for computer; **softwood** wood of coniferous tree.

**soften** /'sɒf(ə)n/ v. make or become soft(er). **soften up** reduce strength or resistance etc. of.

**softie** /'sɒfti:/ n. colloq. weak or silly person.

**soggy** /'sɒgi:/ a. sodden, waterlogged.

**soh** n. Mus. fifth note of scale in tonic sol-fa.

**soil**[1] n. upper layer of earth, in which plants grow; the ground.

**soil**[2] 1 v. smear or stain with dirt etc.; defile; bring discredit to. 2 n. dirty mark; filth, refuse matter. 3 **soil-pipe** discharge-pipe of water-closet.

**soirée** /'swɑ:reɪ/ n. evening party.

**sojourn** /'sɒdʒɜ:n/ 1 n. temporary stay. 2 v.i. make sojourn.

**sola** n. pithy-stemmed E. Ind. swamp plant. **sola topi** sun-helmet made from pith of this.

**solace** /'sɒləs/ 1 n. comfort in distress or disappointment. 2 v.t. give solace to.

**solan** /'səʊlən/ n. large gooselike gannet.

**solar** /'səʊlə(r)/ a. of or reckoned by sun. **solar battery, cell,** device converting solar radiation into electricity; **solar plexus** complex of radiating nerves at pit of stomach; **solar system** sun and the heavenly bodies whose motion is governed by it.

**solarium** /sə'leərɪəm/ n. (pl. -ria) place for enjoyment or medical use of sunshine.

**sold** past & p.p. of **sell**.

**solder** /'səʊldə(r)/ 1 n. fusible alloy used for joining fusible metals or wires etc. 2 v.t. join with solder. 3 **soldering-iron** tool for melting and applying solder.

**soldier** /'səʊldʒə(r)/ 1 n. member of army, esp. private or NCO; man of military skill and experience. 2 v.i. serve as soldier. 3 **soldier on** colloq. persevere doggedly. 4 **soldierly** a.

**soldiery** /'səʊldʒərɪ/ n. soldiers collectively.

**sole**[1] 1 n. under-surface of foot; part of shoe or stocking below foot, esp. part other than heel; lower surface or base of plough or golf-club head etc. 2 v.t. provide with sole.

**sole**[2] n. flat-fish used as food.

**sole**[3] a. one and only; single; exclusive.

**solecism** /'sɒlɪsɪz(ə)m/ n. offence against grammar or idiom or etiquette etc.

**solemn** /'sɒləm/ a. serious and dignified; formal; accompanied by ceremony; impressive; pompous. **solemnity** /-'lem-/ n.

**solemnize** /'sɒləmnaɪz/ v.t. duly perform (esp. marriage ceremony); make solemn. **solemnization** n.

**solenoid** /'səʊlənɔɪd/ n. Electr. cylindrical coil of wire acting as magnet when carrying electric current.

**sol-fa** /sɒl'fɑː/ n. Mus. system of syllables representing musical notes.

**solicit** /sə'lɪsɪt/ v.t. ask repeatedly or earnestly for or seek or invite; (of prostitute) accost (man) for immoral purpose. **solicitation** n.

**solicitor** /sə'lɪsɪtə(r)/ n. member of legal profession qualified to advise clients and instruct barristers.

**solicitous** /sə'lɪsɪtəs/ a. troubled, concerned; anxious, eager (to do).

**solicitude** /sə'lɪsɪtjuːd/ n. being solicitous, anxiety, concern.

**solid** /'sɒlɪd/ 1 a. of stable shape, not liquid or fluid; of solid substance throughout, not hollow etc.; alike all through; rigid, hard and compact; of three dimensions; concerned with solids; Aus. colloq. unreasonable, excessive; sound and reliable; unanimous. 2 n. solid substance or body; in pl. solid food. 3 **solid-state** using electronic properties of solids to replace those of valves. 4 **solidity** n.

**solidarity** /sɒlɪ'dærətɪ/ n. unity, agreement of feelings and action, community of interests, mutual dependence.

**solidify** /sə'lɪdɪfaɪ/ v. make or become solid.

**soliloquy** /sə'lɪləkwɪ/ n. talking to oneself or without addressing any person; period of this. **soliloquize** v.i.

**solipsism** /'sɒlɪpsɪz(ə)m/ n. view that self is all that exists or can be known.

**solitaire** /sɒlɪ'teə(r)/ n. jewel set by itself; game played on special board by one person who removes objects one at a time by jumping others over them; card-game for one person.

**solitary** /'sɒlɪtərɪ/ a. alone, living alone; without companions; single; secluded, lonely. 2 n. recluse; sl. solitary confinement. 3 **solitary confinement** isolation of prisoner in separate cell.

**solitude** /'sɒlɪtjuːd/ n. being solitary; solitary place.

**sollicker** /'sɒlɪkə(r)/ n. Aus. sl. something big, a whopper.

**solo** /'səʊləʊ/ 1 n. (pl. -los) piece of music performed by one person with or without subordinate accompaniment; performance by one person; flight by unaccompanied pilot in aircraft; solo whist. 2 a. & adv. performed as solo, unaccompanied, alone. 3 **solo whist** card-game like whist in which one player may oppose the others.

**soloist** /'səʊləʊɪst/ n. performer of solo.

**solstice** /'sɒlstəs/ n. either of two times (**summer, winter, solstice**) when sun is farthest from equator.

**soluble** /'sɒljəb(ə)l/ a. that can be dissolved or solved. **solubility** n.

**solution** /sə'luːʃ(ə)n/ n. solving or means of solving a problem or difficulty; conversion of solid or gas into liquid form by mixture with liquid; state or substance resulting from this; dissolving or being dissolved.

**solve** *v.t.* explain, resolve; find answer to.

**solvency** /'sɒlvənsi/ *n.* being financially solvent.

**solvent** /'sɒlv(ə)nt/ **1** *a.* that dissolves or can dissolve; able to pay all debts or liabilities. **2** *n.* liquid capable of or used for dissolving something.

**somatic** /sə'mætɪk/ *a.* of the body, not of the mind.

**sombre** /'sɒmbə(r)/ *a.* dark, gloomy, dismal.

**sombrero** /sɒm'breərəʊ/ *n.* (-ros) broad-brimmed hat worn esp. in Latin American countries.

**some** /sʌm/ **1** *a.* an unspecified amount or number of; an unknown or unnamed; approximately so many or so much of; a considerable amount or number of; at least a small amount of; such to a certain extent; *sl.* notably such; **2** *pron.* some people or things; some number or amount. **3** *adv. colloq.* to some extent. **4 somebody** some person, important person; **somehow** in some indefinite or unspecified way, by some means or other; **someone** somebody; **something** some thing esp. unspecified or unknown or unimportant or forgotten, a quantity or quality expressed or understood, important or notable person or thing; **sometime** formerly; **sometimes** at some times; **somewhat** to some extent; **somewhere** in or to some place.

**somersault** /'sʌməsɔːlt/ **1** *n.* leap or roll in which one turns head over heels. **2** *v.i.* perform somersault.

**somnambulism** /sɒm'næmbjəlɪz(ə)m/ *n.* sleep-walking. **somnambulant** *a.*; **somnambulist** *n.*

**somnolent** /'sɒmnələnt/ *a.* sleepy, drowsy; inducing drowsiness. **somnolence** *n.*

**son** /sʌn/ *n.* male child in relation to his parents; male descendant; male member *of* family etc.; product, native, follower. **son-in-law** daughter's husband.

**sonar** /'səʊnɑː(r)/ *n.* system of detecting objects under water by reflection of sonic and ultrasonic waves; apparatus for this.

**sonata** /sə'nɑːtə/ *n.* musical composition for one or two instruments in several related movements.

**song** *n.* singing, vocal music; piece of music or set of words for singing; poem. **for a song** very cheaply; **songbird** bird with musical song; **song thrush** common thrush.

**songster** /'sɒŋstə(r)/ *n.* singer; songbird. **songstress** *n.*

**sonic** /'sɒnɪk/ *a.* of or involving sound or sound-waves. **sonic bang, boom,** noise made when aircraft passes speed of sound.

**sonnet** /'sɒnɪt/ *n.* poem of 14 lines arranged in one of certain definite rhyme-schemes.

**sonny** /'sʌnɪ/ *n.* familiar form of address to young boy.

**sonorous** /'sɒnərəs/ *a.* having a loud or full or deep sound; (of speech etc.) imposing. **sonority** /-'nɒr-/ *n.*

**sook** /sʊk/ *n. Aus. colloq.* timid young person, cry-baby.

**sool** /suːl/ *v.t. Aus.* set a dog on to attack; (of dog) worry; urge person to course of action.

**soon** /suːn/ *adv.* not long after present or time in question; early; readily, willingly. **sooner or later** at some future time.

**sooner** /'suːnə(r)/ *n. Aus. sl.* lazy dog or man.

**soot** /sʊt/ **1** *n.* black powdery substance rising in smoke and deposited by it on surfaces. **2** *v.t.* cover with soot.

**soothe** /suːð/ *v.t.* calm, tranquillize; reduce force or intensity of.

**soothsayer** /'suːθseɪə(r)/ *n.* person who foretells future events.

**sooty** /'sʊtɪ/ *a.* of or like or as black as or black with soot.

**sop 1** *n.* piece of bread etc. dipped in liquid before eating or cooking; something given to pacify or bribe. **2** *v.* soak (*up*).

**sophism** /'sɒfɪz(ə)m/ *n.* false argument, esp. one meant to deceive.

**sophist** /'sɒfəst/ *n.* captious or fallacious reasoner. **sophistic(al)** *a.*

**sophisticate 1** /sə'fɪstɪkeɪt/ *v.t.* (esp. in *p.p.*) make (person etc.) worldly-wise or cultured or refined; make (equipment, technique) highly developed or complex. **2** /sə'fɪstɪkət/ *n.* sophisticated person. **3 sophistication** *n.*

**sophistry** /ˈsɒfəstri/ n. use of sophisms; a sophism.

**sophomore** /ˈsɒfəmɔː(r)/ n. US second-year university or high-school student.

**soporific** /sɒpəˈrɪfɪk/ 1 a. tending to produce sleep. 2 n. soporific drug or influence. 3 **soporifically** adv.

**sopping** /ˈsɒpɪŋ/ a. drenched.

**soppy** /ˈsɒpɪ/ a. soaked, wet; colloq. mawkish, foolishly sentimental.

**soprano** /səˈprɑːnəʊ/ n. (pl. -nos) highest singing voice of women or boys; singer with soprano voice; music for soprano voice.

**sorbet** /ˈsɔːbeɪ/ n. water-ice; sherbet.

**sorcerer** /ˈsɔːsərə(r)/ n. magician, wizard. **sorceress** n.; **sorcery** n.

**sordid** /ˈsɔːdɪd/ a. dirty, squalid; ignoble, mercenary.

**sore** 1 a. painful from injury or disease; suffering pain, aggrieved, vexed (at); arousing painful feelings, irritating. 2 n. sore place or subject etc. 3 adv. arch. grievously, severely.

**sorely** /ˈsɔːlɪ/ adv. very much, severely.

**sorghum** /ˈsɔːgəm/ n. tropical cereal grass.

**sorority** /səˈrɒrətɪ/ n. devotional sisterhood; US women's college or university society.

**sorrel**[1] /ˈsɒr(ə)l/ n. sour-leaved herb.

**sorrel**[2] /ˈsɒr(ə)l/ 1 a. of light reddish-brown colour. 2 n. this colour; sorrel animal, esp. horse.

**sorrow** /ˈsɒrəʊ/ 1 n. mental distress caused by loss or disappointment etc.; thing causing sorrow. 2 v.i. feel sorrow; mourn. 3 **sorrowful** a.

**sorry** /ˈsɒrɪ/ a. pained at or regretful over something; feeling pity (for); wretched, paltry, of poor quality.

**sort** 1 n. kind, variety; colloq. person of specified sort. 2 v.t. arrange according to sort. 3 **of sorts** colloq. of not very satisfactory kind; **out of sorts** slightly unwell, in low spirits; **sort out** separate into sorts, select from miscellaneous group, disentangle, put into order, solve, sl. deal with or punish.

**sortie** /ˈsɔːtɪ/ n. sally, esp. from besieged garrison; operational flight by military aircraft.

**SOS** n. international code-signal of extreme distress; colloq. urgent appeal for help.

**sot** n. habitual drunkard. **sottish** a.

**sotto voce** /ˌsɒtəʊ ˈvəʊtʃeɪ/ in an undertone. [It.]

**sou** /suː/ n. former French coin of low value; colloq. very small amount of money.

**soubrette** /suːˈbret/ n. pert maidservant etc. in comedy; actress taking such part.

**soubriquet** var. of **sobriquet**.

**soufflé** /ˈsuːfleɪ/ n. light spongy dish made with stiffly-beaten egg-white.

**sough** /sʌf or saʊ/ 1 n. moaning or whispering sound, as of wind in trees. 2 v.i. make this sound.

**sought** /sɔːt/ past & p.p. of **seek**. **sought-after** much in demand.

**souk** /suːk/ n. market-place in Muslim countries.

**soul** /səʊl/ n. spiritual or immaterial part of man; moral or emotional or intellectual nature of person or animal; personification or pattern of; an individual; animating or essential part; emotional or intellectual energy or intensity; Black American culture or music etc. **soul-destroying** exceedingly monotonous etc.; **soul mate** person ideally suited to another; **soul-searching** examining one's conscience.

**soulful** /ˈsəʊlfəl/ a. having or expressing or evoking deep feeling.

**soulless** /ˈsəʊlləs/ a. lacking sensitivity or noble qualities; undistinguished, uninteresting.

**sound**[1] /saʊnd/ 1 n. sensation produced in organs of hearing when surrounding air etc. vibrates; vibrations causing this; what is or may be heard. 2 v. (cause to) emit sound; utter, pronounce; convey specified impression; give audible signal for; test condition of by noting sound produced. 3 **sound-barrier** high resistance of air to objects moving at speeds near that of sound; **sound-effect** sound other than speech or music produced artificially for film or broadcast etc.; **sounding-board** canopy projecting sound towards audience; **sound off** colloq. talk loudly, express one's opinions forcefully; **soundproof** impervious to sound, (v.t.) make soundproof; **soundtrack** strip on side of cinema film or videotape for recording sound, the sound itself; **sound wave** wave of condensation and rarefaction by which sound is transmitted in air etc.

**sound²** /saʊnd/ *a.* healthy, free from disease or defects or corruption; correct, orthodox, valid; financially secure; (of sleep) unbroken; thorough. 2 *adv.* soundly, fast *asleep*.

**sound³** /saʊnd/ *v.t.* test depth or quality of bottom of water, esp. with line and lead etc.; (also with *out*) inquire into views etc. of (person) esp. in cautious or indirect manner.

**sound⁴** /saʊnd/ *n.* strait (of water).

**sounding** *n.* measurement of depth of water; in *pl.* region near enough to shore to allow sounding.

**soup** /su:p/ 1 *n.* liquid food made by stewing bones and vegetables etc. 2 *v.t.* (usu. with *up*) *colloq.* increase power of (engine, car, etc.). **3 in the soup** *sl.* in difficulties, in trouble; **soup-kitchen** establishment supplying free soup etc. to the poor in times of distress. **4 soupy** *a.*

**soupçon** /'su:psɔ̃/ *n.* dash or trace (*of*).

**sour** /saʊə(r)/ 1 *a.* having acid taste or smell (as) from unripeness or fermentation; peevish, morose; (of soil) cold and wet. 2 *v.* make or become sour. **3 sour grapes** said when person disparages what he desires but cannot attain; **sourpuss** *sl.* bad-tempered person; **soursob** *Aus.* yellow-flowered garden weed.

**source** /sɔ:s/ *n.* place from which thing comes or is got; person or book etc. providing information; place from which river or stream issues. **at source** at point of origin or issue.

**souse** /saʊs/ 1 *v.* immerse in pickle or other liquid; soak (thing in liquid); in *p.p. sl.* drunk. 2 *n.* pickle made with salt; *US* food in pickle.

**soutane** /su:'ta:n/ *n.* cassock of RC priest.

**south** /saʊθ/ 1 *n.* point of horizon opposite north; southern part of country etc. 2 *a.* situated etc. in or towards south; facing south; (of wind) coming from south. 3 *adv.* towards or in south. **4 south-east, south-west,** (compasspoint) half-way between south and east, west; **southpaw** *colloq.* left-handed person esp. boxer. **5 southward** *a., adv., & n.;* **southwards** *adv.*

**southerly** /'sʌðəli/ *a. & adv.* in southern position or direction; (of wind) blowing from south. **southerly buster** *Aus.* cool southerly gale.

**southern** /'sʌð(ə)n/ *a.* of or in the south. **Southern Cross** constellation with stars forming cross; **southern lights** aurora australis.

**southerner** /'sʌðənə(r)/ *n.* native or inhabitant of south.

**souvenir** /su:və'nɪə(r)/ 1 *n.* thing kept as reminder of person or place or event etc. 2 *v.t. Aus. sl.* pilfer, appropriate without leave.

**sou'wester** /saʊ'westə(r)/ *n.* waterproof hat with broad flap at back; wind from SW.

**sovereign** /'sɒvrɪn/ 1 *n.* supreme ruler, esp. monarch; *hist.* British gold coin worth nominally £1. 2 *a.* supreme; independent; (of remedy etc.) very good. **3 sovereignty** *n.*

**soviet** /'səʊvɪət/ 1 *n.* council elected in district of USSR. 2 *a.* Soviet of the Soviet Union. **3 Soviet Union** USSR.

**sow¹** /səʊ/ *v.t.* (*p.p.* sowed *or* sown) scatter (seed) on or in earth, plant *with* seed; initiate, arouse.

**sow²** /saʊ/ *n.* adult female pig.

**soy** *n.* sauce made from pickled soya beans.

**soya** /'sɔɪə/ *n.* leguminous plant yielding edible oil and flour. **soya bean** seed of this plant.

**sozzled** /'sɒz(ə)ld/ *a. sl.* very drunk.

**spa** /spa:/ *n.* curative mineral spring; place with this.

**space** 1 *n.* continuous expanse in which things exist and move; amount of this taken by particular thing or available for purpose; interval between points or objects; interval of time; expanse of paper used in writing or printing etc.; universe beyond earth's atmosphere; *Print.* piece of metal separating words etc. 2 *attrib. a.* of or used for travelling outside earth's atmosphere. 3 *v.* set or arrange at intervals, put spaces between; spread *out*. **4 space age** era of space travel; **space-bar** bar on typewriter for making spaces between words etc.; **spacecraft** craft for travelling in outer space; **space-heater** self-contained device for heating room; **spaceman** traveller in outer space; **spaceship** spacecraft; **space shuttle** spacecraft for repeated use; **space sta-**

**spacious** /'speɪʃəs/ a. having ample space, roomy.

**spade**[1] n. tool for digging etc., usu. with flattish rectangular blade on long handle; anything resembling this in form or use. **spadework** hard preparatory work.

**spade**[2] n. playing card of suit marked with black figures resembling inverted heart with short stem.

**spaghetti** /spə'geti/ n. pasta in long thin strings.

**span** 1 n. full extent from end to end; maximum lateral extent of aeroplane or its wing; each part of bridge between supports; maximum distance between tips of thumb and little finger, esp. as measure, = 9 in. (23 cm). 2 v.t. extend from side to side or end to end of; bridge (river etc.).

**spandrel** /'spændr(ə)l/ n. space between curve of arch and surrounding rectangular framework, or between curves of adjoining arches and moulding above.

**spangle** /'spæŋg(ə)l/ 1 n. small piece of glittering material esp. one of many as ornament of dress etc. 2 v.t. cover (as) with spangles.

**Spaniard** /'spænjəd/ n. native of Spain.

**spaniel** /'spænjəl/ n. dog with long silky coat and drooping ears.

**Spanish** /'spænɪʃ/ 1 a. of Spain. 2 n. language of Spain.

**spank** 1 v.t. slap on buttocks. 2 n. slap given in spanking.

**spanker** /'spæŋkə(r)/ n. Naut. fore-and-aft sail on mizen-mast.

**spanking** /'spæŋkɪŋ/ colloq. 1 a. striking, excellent; brisk. 2 adv. strikingly; excellently.

**spanner** /'spænə(r)/ n. tool for turning nut on bolt etc. **spanner in the works** upsetting element or influence.

**spar**[1] n. stout pole esp. of kind used for ship's mast etc.

**spar**[2] 1 v.i. use fists (as) in boxing, make motions of boxing, dispute, engage in argument. 2 n. sparring; boxing-match. 3 **sparring-partner** boxer employed to practise with another in training for a fight, person with whom one enjoys arguing.

**spar**[3] n. easily split crystalline mineral.

**spare** /speə(r)/ 1 v. refrain from hurting or destroying or using or bringing into operation; dispense with; afford to give; let (person) have (thing etc. esp. that one does not need); be parsimonious or grudging (with). 2 a. superfluous, not required for ordinary or present use; reserved for emergency or occasional use; (of person) lean, thin, frugal. 3 n. spare part. 4 **spare part** duplicate to replace lost or damaged part; **spare-rib** closely trimmed rib of meat, esp. pork; **spare time** leisure; **spare tyre** colloq. circle of fatness round or above waist.

**sparing** /'speərɪŋ/ a. economical, frugal, grudging.

**spark** 1 n. fiery particle of burning substance; flash of light accompanying electrical discharge; electric spark for firing explosive mixture in internal-combustion engine; flash of wit etc.; minute amount of a quality etc.; lively person. 2 v. emit spark(s); (also with off) stir into activity, initiate. 3 **sparkplug, sparking-plug**, device for making spark in internal-combustion engine.

**sparkle** /'spa:k(ə)l/ v.i. emit or seem to emit sparks; glitter, flash, scintillate; (of wine etc.) effervesce. 2 n. sparkling; glitter.

**sparkler** /'spa:klə(r)/ n. sparkling firework; sl. diamond.

**sparrow** /'spærəʊ/ n. small brownish-grey bird. **sparrow-hawk** a small hawk.

**sparse** /spa:s/ a. thinly scattered. **sparsity** n.

**Spartan** /'spa:t(ə)n/ 1 a. of ancient Sparta; **spartan** austere, hardy, rigorous. 2 n. native of Sparta; **spartan** person of courage and endurance.

**spasm** /'spæz(ə)m/ n. sudden involuntary muscular contraction; sudden convulsive movement or emotion etc.

**spasmodic** /spæz'mɒdɪk/ a. of or occurring in spasms; intermittent.

**spastic** /'spæstɪk/ 1 a. suffering from cerebral palsy with spasm of muscles. 2 n. spastic person.

**spat**[1] *n.* (usu. in *pl.*) short gaiter covering instep and ankle.

**spat**[2] past & *p.p.* of **spit**[1].

**spate** *n.* river-flood; large or excessive amount.

**spathe** /speɪð/ *n. Bot.* large bract(s) enveloping flower-cluster.

**spatial** /ˈspeɪʃ(ə)l/ *a.* of space.

**spatter** /ˈspætə(r)/ 1 *v.* splash or scatter in drips. 2 *n.* spattering; pattering.

**spatula** /ˈspætjələ/ *n.* broad-bladed implement used esp. by artists and in cookery.

**spawn** 1 *v.* (of fish or frog etc.) produce (eggs), be produced as eggs or young; *fig.* produce or generate in large numbers. 2 *n.* eggs of fish or frogs etc.; *derog.* human or other offspring; white fibrous matter from which fungi grow.

**spay** *v.t.* sterilize (female animal) by removing ovaries.

**speak** *v.* (*past* **spoke**; *p.p.* **spoken**) utter words in ordinary way; say something; hold conversation; deliver speech; utter or pronounce; use (specified language) in speaking; reveal, indicate. **speak for** express views or sentiments of; **speak out**, **up**, speak freely, speak loud(er).

**speaker** /ˈspiːkə(r)/ *n.* person who speaks esp. in public; person of specified skill in speech-making; person who speaks specified language; loudspeaker; **Speaker** presiding officer of legislative assembly.

**spear** 1 *n.* thrusting or hurling weapon with long shaft and sharp-pointed head. 2 *v.t.* pierce or strike (as) with spear. 3 **spearhead** *fig.* person(s) leading an attack or challenge, (*v.t.*) act as spearhead of (attack); **spearmint** common garden mint.

**spec** *n. colloq.* speculation; specification. **on spec** experimentally, as a gamble.

**special** /ˈspeʃ(ə)l/ 1 *a.* of particular or peculiar kind; not general; for particular purpose; exceptional. 2 *n.* special constable or edition of newspaper or dish on menu etc. 3 **Special Branch** police department dealing with political security; **special constable** person assisting police in routine duties or in emergencies; **special licence** licence allowing marriage to take place without publication of banns; **special pleading** biased reasoning.

**specialist** /ˈspeʃəlɪst/ *n.* person who specializes in particular branch of profession etc., esp. medicine.

**speciality** /speʃɪˈælɪtɪ/ *n.* special feature; special thing or activity; special product; thing in which a person or place specializes.

**specialize** /ˈspeʃəlaɪz/ *v.* devote oneself to particular branch of profession etc. (with *in*); become or make special. **specialization** *n.*

**specialty** /ˈspeʃəltɪ/ *n.* speciality.

**specie** /ˈspiːʃiː/ *n.* coin as opp. to paper money.

**species** /ˈspiːʃiːz/ *n.* (*pl.* same) class of things having common characteristics; group of animals or plants within genus; kind, sort.

**specific** /spəˈsɪfɪk/ 1 *a.* particular or clearly defined; exact, giving full details; particular, relating to particular thing; (of medicine etc.) for particular disease or condition etc. 2 *n.* specific medicine or aspect. 3 **specific gravity** ratio between weight of substance and that of same volume of water or air. 4 **specifically** *adv.*; **specificity** /-ˈfɪs-/ *n.*

**specification** /spesɪfɪˈkeɪʃ(ə)n/ *n.* (usu. in *pl.*) detailed description of work (to be) undertaken or invention or patent etc.

**specify** /ˈspesɪfaɪ/ *v.* name expressly, mention definitely; include in specifications.

**specimen** /ˈspesɪmən/ *n.* individual or part taken as example of class or whole, esp. serving for investigation etc.; *colloq.* person etc. of specified sort.

**specious** /ˈspiːʃəs/ *a.* seeming good or correct but not being really so; plausible.

**speck** 1 *n.* small spot or stain; particle. 2 *v.t.* (esp. in *p.p.*) mark with specks.

**speckle** /ˈspek(ə)l/ 1 *n.* speck, esp. one of many markings on skin etc. 2 *v.t.* (esp. in *p.p.*) mark with speckles.

**specs** *n.pl. colloq.* (pair of) spectacles.

**spectacle** /ˈspektək(ə)l/ *n.* object of sight, esp. of public attention; impressive or ridiculous sight; public show; in *pl.* pair of lenses set in frame supported on nose, to correct or assist defective eyesight or to protect eyes.

**spectacled** *a.* wearing spectacles.

**spectacular** /spek'tækjələ(r)/ 1 *a.* of or like a public show; striking, lavish. 2 *n.* spectacular performance.

**spectator** /spek'teɪtə(r)/ *n.* person who watches a show or game or incident etc. **spectator sport** sport which attracts many spectators.

**spectra** *pl.* of **spectrum**.

**spectral** /'spektr(ə)l/ *a.* of spectres or spectra; ghostly.

**spectre** /'spektə(r)/ *n.* ghost; haunting presentiment.

**spectroscope** /'spektrəskəʊp/ *n.* instrument for producing and examining spectra. **spectroscopic** /-'skɒp-/ *a.*; **spectroscopy** /-'trɒs-/ *n.*

**spectrum** /'spektrəm/ *n.* (*pl.* -tra) band of colours as seen in rainbow etc.; entire or wide range of anything arranged by degree or quality etc.

**speculate** /'spekjəleɪt/ *v.i.* engage in conjectural thought or writing; buy or sell commodities etc. in expectation of rise or fall in market value; engage in risky financial transactions. **speculation** *n.*; **speculative** /'spek-/ *a.*; **speculator** *n.*

**sped** *past* & *p.p.* of **speed**.

**speech** *n.* act or faculty or manner of speaking; thing said; public address; language, dialect. **freedom of speech** right to express one's views freely; **speech-day** annual prize-giving day in school; **speech therapy** remedial treatment of defective speech.

**speechify** /'spi:tʃɪfaɪ/ *v.i. colloq.* make speeches.

**speechless** /'spi:tʃləs/ *a.* temporarily deprived of speech by emotion etc.

**speed** 1 *n.* rapidity, quickness; rate of progress or motion etc.; gear on bicycle; relative sensitivity of photographic film to light. 2 *v.* (*past* & *p.p.* **sped**) go or send quickly; travel at excessive or illegal speed; *arch.* be or make prosperous or successful. 3 **speedboat** fast motor boat; **speed limit** maximum permitted speed of vehicle on road etc.; **speedway** motor-cycle racing, arena for this, *US* road intended for fast motor vehicles.

**speedo** /'spi:dəʊ/ *n.* (*pl.* -dos) *sl.* speedometer.

**speedometer** /spi:'dɒmɪtə(r)/ *n.* device indicating speed of vehicle.

**speedwell** /'spi:dwel/ *n.* small blue-flowered herbaceous plant.

**speedy** /'spi:dɪ/ *a.* rapid, swift; prompt.

**speleology** /speli:'ɒlədʒi:/ *n.* scientific study of caves etc. **speleologist** *n.*

**spell**[1] *n.* words used as charm; fascination, attraction. **spellbound** held as if by spell, fascinated.

**spell**[2] *v.* (*past* & *p.p.* **spelt** *or* **spelled**) name or write correctly the letters of (word); form (word); imply, involve, mean. **spell out** make out laboriously, spell aloud, explain in detail.

**spell**[3] 1 *n.* period of time or work; period of some activity; *Aus.* period of rest from work etc. 2 *v.t.* relieve or take turns with (person etc.).

**spelt**[1] *n.* kind of wheat giving very fine flour.

**spelt**[2] *past* & *p.p.* of **spell**[2].

**spend** *v.* (*past* & *p.p.* **spent**) pay out (money); use up, consume; pass or occupy (time); in *p.p.* having lost force or strength. **spendthrift** extravagant person.

**sperm** *n.* semen; spermatozoon. **sperm-whale** large whale yielding spermaceti.

**spermaceti** /spɜ:mə'seti:/ *n.* white waxy substance used for ointments etc.

**spermatozoon** /spɜ:mətə'zəʊən/ *n.* (*pl.* -zoa) fertilizing cell of male organism.

**spermicide** /'spɜ:mɪsaɪd/ *n.* substance that kills spermatozoa. **spermicidal** *a.*

**spew** *v.* vomit.

**sphagnum** /'sfægnəm/ *n.* moss growing in swampy places, used as packing etc.

**sphere** /sfɪə(r)/ *n.* figure or body having all points of its surface equidistant from point within it; ball, globe; field of action or influence etc.; place in society; each of several hollow globes in which heavenly bodies were formerly thought to be set.

**spherical** /'sferɪk(ə)l/ *a.* shaped like sphere; of spheres.

**spheroid** /'sfɪərɔɪd/ *n.* spherelike but not perfectly spherical body. **spheroidal** *a.*

**sphincter** /'sfɪŋktə(r)/ *n.* ring of muscle closing and opening orifice.

**sphinx** /sfɪŋks/ *n.* (in Egyptian antiquity) figure of recumbent lion with head of man or animal; *Gk myth* winged

**spice** 1 *n.* aromatic or pungent vegetable substance used as flavouring; spices collectively; *fig.* thing that adds zest or excitement etc. 2 *v.t.* flavour with spice; enhance.

**spick and span** smart, trim, new-looking.

**spicy** /'spaɪsɪ/ *a.* of or flavoured with spice; piquant; improper.

**spider** /'spaɪdə(r)/ *n.* eight-legged arthropod, many species of which spin webs esp. to capture insects as food; thing resembling spider; *Aus.* drink of brandy with lemonade or ginger beer, fizzy soft drink with ice cream added.

**spidery** /'spaɪdərɪ/ *a.* of or like spider; very thin or long.

**spiel** /spiːl/ *sl.* 1 *n.* speech or story, esp. glib or persuasive one. 2 *v.i.* talk lengthily or glibly.

**spieler** /'spiːlə(r)/ *n. Aus. sl.* gambler; card-sharp, swindler.

**spigot** /'spɪgət/ *n.* small peg or plug; device for controlling flow of liquor from cask etc.

**spike**[1] 1 *n.* sharp point; pointed piece of metal, e.g. one of set forming top of iron fence or worn on bottom of running-shoe to prevent slipping; in *pl.* running-shoes fitted with spikes; large nail. 2 *v.t.* put spikes on or into; fix on spike; *colloq.* add alcohol to (drink). 3 **spike person's guns** defeat his plans.

**spike**[2] *n.* long cluster of flowers on short stalks on central stem.

**spikenard** /'spaɪknɑːd/ *n.* tall sweet-smelling plant; aromatic ointment formerly made from this.

**spiky** /'spaɪkɪ/ *a.* like a spike; having spikes; *colloq.* dogmatic, bad-tempered.

**spill**[1] 1 *v.* (*past & p.p.* **spilt** or **spilled**) allow (liquid etc.) to fall or run out from vessel, esp. accidentally or wastefully; (of liquid etc.) run out thus; shed (others' blood); cause to fall from horse or vehicle. 2 *n.* spilling or being spilt; throw or fall, esp. from horse or vehicle; tumble; *Aus.* rearrangement of offices in political party, esp. in Cabinet. **spill the beans** *sl.* divulge secret etc.

**spill**[2] *n.* strip of wood or paper etc. for lighting candle etc.

**spilt** *past & p.p.* of **spill**[1].

**spin** 1 *v.* (*past & p.p.* **spun**) turn rapidly on its own axis, cause to do this; make (yarn) by drawing out and twisting together fibres of wool etc.; make (web etc.) by extrusion of fine viscous thread; (of person's head) be in a whirl; toss (coin); tell or compose (story etc.). 2 *n.* revolving motion, whirl; secondary revolving or twisting motion e.g. of cricket or tennis ball; short or brisk excursion, esp. in motor vehicle; *Aus.* period of particular kind of fortune. 3 **spin bowler** *Crick.* one who imparts spin to ball; **spin-drier** machine for drying clothes etc. by spinning them in rotating drum; **spin-dry** *v.*; **spinning-wheel** household implement for spinning yarn, with spindle driven by wheel with crank or treadle; **spin-off** incidental result, esp. as benefit from industrial or technological development; **spin out** prolong (discussion etc.).

**spina bifida** /ˌspaɪnə 'bɪfɪdə/ congenital defect of spine, with protruding membranes.

**spinach** /'spɪnɪdʒ/ *n.* plant with succulent leaves used as vegetable. **spinach beet** kind of beet with leaves used like spinach.

**spinal** *a.* of spine. **spinal column** spine; **spinal cord** cylindrical nervous structure within spine.

**spindle** /'spɪnd(ə)l/ *n.* slender rod used to twist or wind thread in spinning; pin or axis on which something revolves.

**spindly** /'spɪndlɪ/ *a.* long or tall and thin.

**spindrift** /'spɪndrɪft/ *n.* spray blown along surface of sea.

**spine** *n.* articulated series of vertebrae extending from skull, backbone; sharp needle-like outgrowth of animal or plant; part of book visible when it is one of row on shelf; ridge, sharp projection.

**spine-bashing** *Aus. sl.* resting, idling; **spine-chilling** causing thrill of terror.

**spineless** /'spaɪnləs/ *a.* lacking backbone or resoluteness, timid, weak.

**spinet** /spɪ'net/ *n. hist.* small keyboard instrument of harpsichord kind.

**spinifex** /'spɪnɪfeks/ *n.* coarse grass with spiny leaves that grows in Aus. interior.

**spinnaker** /'spɪnəkə(r)/ *n.* large three-cornered extra sail of racing-yacht.

**spinner** /'spɪnə(r)/ *n.* person or thing that spins; manufacturer engaged in

**spinneret** /'spɪnərɛt/ n. spinning-organ in spider or silkworm etc.

**spinney** /'spɪni/ n. small wood, thicket.

**spinster** /'spɪnstə(r)/ n. unmarried woman.

**spiny** /'spaɪni/ a. having (many) spines. **spiny anteater** echidna; **spiny emex** *Aus.* introduced weed with spiny seeds.

**spiraea** /spaɪ'riːə/ n. garden plant related to meadowsweet.

**spiral** /'spaɪr(ə)l/ 1 a. coiled in a plane or as round a cylinder or cone; having this shape. 2 n. spiral curve; progressive rise or fall. 3 v.i. move in spiral course. 4 **spiral staircase** staircase rising round central axis.

**spirant** /'spaɪrənt/ 1 a. uttered with continuous expulsion of breath. 2 n. spirant consonant.

**spire** /spaɪə(r)/ n. tapering structure in form of tall cone or pyramid rising above tower.

**spirit** /'spɪrɪt/ 1 n. animating or vital principle; person's soul; person from intellectual or moral view; disembodied person or incorporeal being; mental or moral nature or qualities; attitude, mood; vigour, courage, vivacity; general meaning or feeling (*of*); distilled extract, alcoholic solution *of*; (usu. in *pl.*) distilled alcoholic liquor. 2 v.t. convey mysteriously *away* etc. 3 **in high, low, spirits** cheerful, depressed; **spirit gum** quick-drying gum for attaching false hair; **spirit-lamp** lamp burning methylated or other volatile spirit; **spirit-level** device used to test levelness.

**spirited** /'spɪrɪtɪd/ a. full of spirit, lively; courageous; having specified spirit(s).

**spiritual** /'spɪrɪtjʊəl/ 1 a. of or concerned with spirit; religious, divine, inspired. 2 n. religious song, esp. of Amer. Blacks. 3 **spirituality** n.

**spiritualism** /'spɪrɪtjəlɪz(ə)m/ n. belief that spirits of dead can communicate with living, esp. through mediums. **spiritualist** a. & n.; **spiritualistic** a.

**spirituous** /'spɪrɪtjʊəs/ a. alcoholic, distilled as well as fermented.

**spit**[1] 1 v. (*past* & *p.p.* **spat**) eject from mouth; eject saliva from mouth; do this as gesture of contempt; utter vehemently; make spitting sound as sign of anger or hostility; (of rain etc.) fall lightly. 2 n. spittle; spitting. 3 **the (very) spit** spitting image *of*; **spitfire** fiery-tempered person; **spitting image** exact counterpart or likeness (*of*).

**spit**[2] 1 n. rod on which meat is fixed for roasting over fire etc.; small point of land projecting into sea; spade-depth of earth. 2 v.t. pierce (as) with spit.

**spite** 1 n. ill will, malice. 2 v.t. thwart, annoy. 3 **in spite of** notwithstanding, regardless of.

**spiteful** /'spaɪtfəl/ a. full of spite, malicious.

**spittle** /'spɪt(ə)l/ n. saliva, esp. as ejected from mouth.

**spittoon** /spɪ'tuːn/ n. vessel to spit into.

**spiv** n. *sl.* man, esp. flashily-dressed one, living from shady dealings rather than regular work.

**splash** 1 v. agitate (liquid) so that drops of it fly about; wet or stain by splashing; (of liquid) fly about in drops; step or fall etc. *into* etc. with splashing; mark or mottle with irregular patches of colour etc.; *colloq.* display conspicuously esp. in print; spend (money) recklessly or ostentatiously. 2 n. splashing, sound or mark made by it; quantity splashed; large irregular patch of colour etc.; striking or ostentatious display or effect; *colloq.* small quantity of soda-water etc. (in drink). 3 **splashback** panel behind sink etc. to protect wall from splashes; **splash-down** alighting of spacecraft on sea; **splash out** spend money freely.

**splatter** /'splætə(r)/ v. & n. splash, esp. with continuous or noisy action, spatter.

**splay** 1 v. spread apart; (of opening) have sides diverging; make (opening) have divergent sides. 2 n. surface at oblique angle to another. 3 a. splayed.

**spleen** n. abdominal organ maintaining proper condition of blood; moroseness, irritability, spite.

**splendid** /'splɛndəd/ a. magnificent, admirable, glorious, excellent.

## splendiferous / spontaneous

**splendiferous** /splen'dɪfərəs/ *a. colloq.* splendid.

**splendour** /'splendə(r)/ *n.* great brightness; magnificence.

**splenetic** /splə'netɪk/ *a.* bad-tempered; peevish.

**splenic** /'spli:nɪk/ *a.* of or in spleen.

**splice** 1 *v.t.* join pieces of (rope) by interweaving strands; join (pieces of wood or tape etc.) in overlapping position; *colloq.* join in marriage. 2 *n.* junction made by splicing.

**splint** 1 *n.* strip of more or less rigid material holding broken bone in right position while it heals. 2 *v.t.* secure with splint.

**splinter** /'splɪntə(r)/ 1 *n.* rough or sharp-edged or thin fragment broken or split off from some hard material. 2 *v.* split into splinters; come off as or like splinter. 3 **splinter group** small esp. political group that has split off from larger one. 4 **splintery** *a.*

**split** 1 *v.* (*past* & *p.p.* **split**) break, esp. lengthwise or with grain or plane of cleavage; break forcibly; divide into parts or thicknesses; divide into disagreeing or hostile parties; cause fission of (atom); *sl.* reveal secret, inform *on*. 2 *n.* splitting; fissure; disagreement, schism; something formed by splitting; in *pl.* feat of sitting down or leaping with legs widely spread out at right angles to body. 3 **split hairs** make over-subtle distinctions; **split infinitive** one with adverb etc. inserted between *to* and verb; **split-level** built or having components at more than one level; **split personality** change of personality as in schizophrenia; **split pin** pin or bolt etc. held in place by splaying of its split end; **split ring** metal ring, with usu. two spiral turns, for holding keys etc.; **split second** very short period of time; **split up** separate, esp. (of married couple etc.) cease living together.

**splotch** 1 *n.* large irregular spot or patch of colour etc., blotch. 2 *v.t.* mark with splotches. 3 **splotchy** *a.*

**splurge** 1 *n.* noisy or ostentatious display or effort. 2 *v.i.* make splurge.

**splutter** /'splʌtə(r)/ 1 *v.* speak or emit with spitting sound; emit spitting sounds; speak rapidly or incoherently. 2 *n.* spluttering speech or sound.

**spoil** 1 *v.* (*past* & *p.p.* **spoilt** or **spoiled**) make or become useless or unsatisfactory; ruin character of by indulgence; decay, go bad. 2 *n.* in *sing.* or *pl.* plunder, stolen goods; *fig.* profits, advantages accruing from success or public office etc. 3 **spoil-sport** person who spoils others' enjoyment.

**spoiler** /'spɔɪlə(r)/ *n.* device on aircraft to retard it by interrupting air flow; device on vehicle to increase contact with ground at speed.

**spoke**[1] *n.* any of bars running from hub to rim of wheel; rung of ladder. **put a spoke in person's wheel** hinder or thwart his purpose.

**spoke**[2] *past* of **speak**.

**spoken** *p.p.* of **speak**.

**spokesman** /'spəʊksmən/ *n.* (*pl.* -men) person who speaks for others, representative. **spokeswoman** *n.*

**spoliation** /spəʊlɪ'eɪʃ(ə)n/ *n.* plundering, pillage.

**sponge** /spʌndʒ/ 1 *n.* sea animal with porous body-wall and tough elastic skeleton; this skeleton or piece of porous rubber etc. used as absorbent in bathing or cleansing surfaces etc.; thing of spongelike absorbency or consistency; sponge-cake; act of sponging. 2 *v.* wipe or cleanse with sponge; wipe *out* or efface (as) with sponge; take *up* (water etc.) (as) with sponge; live parasitically off others. 3 **sponge-bag** waterproof bag for holding toilet articles; **sponge-cake**, **pudding**, one of light spongelike consistency; **sponge rubber** rubber made porous like sponge.

**sponger** /'spʌndʒə(r)/ *n.* person who habitually sponges on others.

**spongy** /'spʌndʒɪ/ *a.* like a sponge; porous, elastic, absorbent.

**sponsor** /'spɒnsə(r)/ 1 *n.* person who makes himself responsible for another or presents candidate for baptism or introduces legislation or contributes to charity in return for specified activity by another; advertiser who pays for broadcast or sporting event etc., to advertise his wares. 2 *v.t.* be sponsor for. 3 **sponsorship** *n.*

**spontaneous** /spɒn'teɪnɪəs/ *a.* acting or done or occurring without external cause; automatic; instinctive, natural,

# spoof

unconstrained. **spontaneity** /-'ni:əti:/ n.

**spoof** /spu:f/ n. & v.t. colloq. parody; hoax, swindle.

**spook** /spu:k/ n. colloq. ghost. **spooky** a.

**spool** /spu:l/ 1 n. reel on which something is wound; revolving cylinder of angler's reel. 2 v.t. wind on spool.

**spoon** /spu:n/ 1 n. utensil with oval or round bowl and handle for conveying food to mouth or stirring etc.; spoon-shaped thing; spoon-bait. 2 v. take liquid (up, out) with spoon; hit (ball) feebly upwards; colloq. behave in amorous way, esp. foolishly. 3 **spoon-bait** revolving spoon-shaped metal fish-lure; **spoonbill** wading-bird with broad flat tip of bill; **spoon drain** Aus. shallow drain across a street; **spoon-feed** feed (baby etc.) with spoon, give help etc. to (person) without demanding any effort from recipient. 4 **spoonful** n.

**spoonerism** /'spu:nərɪz(ə)m/ n. transposition, usu. accidental, of initial sounds of two or more words.

**spoor** /spʊə(r)/ n. animal's track or scent.

**sporadic** /spə'rædɪk/ a. occurring in isolated instances or very small numbers; scattered, occasional.

**spore** /spɔ:(r)/ n. minute reproductive cell of ferns, fungi, protozoa, etc.

**sporran** /'spɒrən/ n. pouch worn in front of kilt.

**sport** 1 n. game or competitive activity usu. involving physical exertion; these collectively; in pl. meeting for competition in athletics; amusement, fun; colloq. sportsman, good fellow; animal or plant that deviates from type. 2 v. engage in sport; wear or exhibit esp. ostentatiously. 3 **sports car** low-built fast car; **sports coat** men's jacket for informal wear; **sportsman, sportswoman**, person fond of sport, person who behaves fairly and generously; **sportsmanlike** a.

**sporting** /'spɔ:tɪŋ/ a. interested in sport; sportsmanlike. **sporting chance** some possibility of success.

**sportive** /'spɔ:tɪv/ a. playful.

**sporty** /'spɔ:tɪ/ a. colloq. fond of sport; colloq. rakish, showy.

**spot** 1 n. small mark differing in colour etc. from surface it is on; blemish, pimple; particular place, definite locality; particular part of one's body or character; colloq. one's (regular) position in organization or programme etc.; colloq. small quantity of something; spotlight. 2 v. mark or become marked with spot(s); make spots, rain slightly; colloq. pick out, recognize, catch sight of; watch for and take note of (trains, talent, etc.). 3 **in a spot** colloq. in difficulties; **on the spot** at scene of action or event, in position such that response or action is required; **spot cash** money paid immediately after sale; **spot check** sudden or random check; **spotlight** beam of light directed on small area, full attention or publicity, (v.t.) illuminate with spotlight; **spot-on** colloq. precise(ly).

**spotless** /'spɒtləs/ a. absolutely clean, unblemished.

**spotted** a. marked with spots. **spotted dick** sl. suet pudding containing currants.

**spotty** /'spɒtɪ/ a. marked with spots, patchy, irregular.

**spouse** /spaʊs/ n. husband or wife.

**spout** /spaʊt/ 1 n. projecting tube or lip through which liquid is poured or issues from teapot or jug or roof-gutter or fountain etc.; jet of liquid. 2 v. discharge or issue forcibly in jet; utter in declamatory manner. 3 **up the spout** sl. in a bad way or hopeless position, in pawn.

**sprain** 1 v.t. wrench (ankle, wrist, etc.) so as to cause pain and swelling. 2 n. such injury.

**sprang** past of **spring**.

**sprat** n. small sea-fish.

**sprawl** 1 v. fall or lie etc. with limbs spread out in careless or ungainly way; straggle, spread untidily. 2 n. sprawling movement or attitude; straggling group or mass.

**spray**¹ 1 n. water or other liquid flying in small drops; preparation intended for spraying; instrument or apparatus for spraying. 2 v. scatter or diffuse as spray; sprinkle (as) with spray. 3 **spray-gun** apparatus for spraying paint etc.

**spray**² n. slender shoot or twig, graceful branch with flowers etc.; jewel or other ornament in form of spray.

# spread

**spread** /spred/ 1 v. (*past & p.p.* **spread**) extend surface of or cause to cover larger surface; have wide or specified or increasing extent; (cause to) become widely known; cover surface of. 2 n. action or capability or extent of spreading; breadth, diffusion; range; elaborate meal; paste for spreading on bread etc.; printed matter spread across more than one column. 3 **spread eagle** figure of eagle with legs and wings extended as emblem; **spread-eagle** place (person) in position with arms and legs spread out, defeat utterly.

**spree** n. lively outing, bout of drinking etc. **shopping**, **spending**, etc. **spree** occasion of lavish spending.

**sprig** n. small branch, twig, spray; ornament resembling this, esp. on fabric.

**sprigged** /sprɪgd/ a. ornamented with sprigs.

**sprightly** /ˈspraɪtli/ a. vivacious, lively.

**spring** 1 v. (*past* **sprang**; *p.p.* **sprung**) rise rapidly or suddenly, leap; move rapidly (as) by action of a spring; originate or arise (*from*); (cause to) act or appear unexpectedly; contrive escape of (person *from* prison etc.); develop (leak); (usu. in *p.p.*) provide with springs. 2 n. jump, leap; recoil, elasticity; elastic device usu. of bent or coiled metal used esp. to drive clockwork or for cushioning furniture or in vehicles; season of year between winter and summer; early stage of life etc.; place where water or oil etc. wells up from earth; basin or flow so formed; motive for or origin of action or custom etc. 3 **spring balance** device measuring weight by tension of spring; **springboard** springy board giving impetus in leaping or diving etc., *fig.* source of impetus; **spring-clean** thorough cleaning of house or room esp. in spring, (*v.t.*) clean thus; **spring onion** young onion eaten raw; **spring tide** tide of maximum height; **springtime** season of spring.

**springbok** /ˈsprɪŋbɒk/ n. S. Afr. gazelle.

**springer** /ˈsprɪŋə(r)/ n. small spaniel.

**springy** /ˈsprɪŋi/ a. elastic.

**sprinkle** /ˈsprɪŋk(ə)l/ 1 v. scatter in small drops or particles; subject (ground, object) to sprinkling (*with*); (of liquid etc.) fall thus on. 2 n. light shower (*of* rain etc.).

**sprinkler** /ˈsprɪŋklə(r)/ n. contrivance for sprinkling water on lawn or to extinguish fires.

**sprinkling** /ˈsprɪŋklɪŋ/ n. a few or a little here and there.

**sprint** 1 v.i. run etc. at top speed, esp. for short distance. 2 n. such run; similar short effort in cycling or swimming etc.

**sprit** n. small diagonal spar reaching from mast to upper outer corner of sail.

**spritsail** sail extended by sprit.

**sprite** n. elf or fairy.

**sprocket** /ˈsprɒkɪt/ n. projection on rim of wheel engaging with links of chain etc.

**sprout** /spraʊt/ 1 v. put forth (shoots), begin to grow. 2 n. shoot, new growth; in *pl. colloq.* Brussels sprouts.

**spruce**[1] 1 a. of trim smart appearance. 2 v. smarten (*up*), make spruce.

**spruce**[2] n. conifer with dense conical foliage; its wood.

**spruik** /spruːk/ v. Aus. speak in public, used esp. of showman; advertise, sell.

**sprung** *p.p.* of **spring**.

**spry** /spraɪ/ a. active, nimble, lively.

**spud** 1 n. small narrow spade for digging up weeds etc.; *sl.* potato. 2 v.t. dig (*out*, *up*) with spud.

**spume** /spjuːm/ n. & v.i. froth, foam. **spumy** a.

**spun** *past* & *p.p.* of **spin**. **spun silk** cheap material of short-fibred and waste silk, often mixed with cotton.

**spunk** n. *colloq.* mettle, spirit; *sl.* semen. **spunky** a.

**spur** 1 n. device with small spike or spiked wheel, attached to rider's heel for urging horse forward; stimulus, incentive; spur-shaped thing, esp. hard projection on cock's leg; projection from mountain (range); branch road or railway. 2 v. prick (horse) with spur; incite, stimulate; ride hard; (esp. in *p.p.*) provide with spurs. 3 **on the spur of the moment** on a momentary impulse.

**spurge** n. plant with acrid milky juice.

**spurious** /ˈspjʊərɪəs/ a. not genuine or authentic; not what it purports to be.

**spurn** v.t. reject with contempt or disdain; repel with foot.

**spurt** 1 v. (cause to) gush out in jet or stream; make spurt. 2 n. sudden

**sputnik** /ˈspʊtnɪk/ n. Russian artificial earth satellite.

**sputter** /ˈspʌtə(r)/ v. & n. splutter.

**sputum** /ˈspjuːtəm/ n. (pl. -ta) saliva; expectorated matter esp. used to diagnose disease.

**spy** 1 n. person secretly collecting and reporting information esp. relating to another country or rival firm etc.; person keeping secret watch on others. 2 v. discern, make out; act as spy (on). 3 **spyglass** small telescope; **spyhole** peep-hole; **spy out** explore or discover, esp. secretly.

**sq.** abbr. square.

**Sqn. Ldr.** abbr. Squadron Leader.

**squab** /skwɒb/ n. young esp. unfledged pigeon; thickly stuffed loose cushion, esp. as part of seat in motor car; sofa.

**squabble** /ˈskwɒb(ə)l/ 1 n. petty or noisy quarrel. 2 v.i. engage in squabble.

**squad** /skwɒd/ n. small group of people sharing task etc., esp. small number of soldiers. **squad car** US police car having radio link with headquarters.

**squaddie** /ˈskwɒdi/ n. sl. private soldier.

**squadron** /ˈskwɒdrən/ n. organized body of persons etc., esp. cavalry division of 2 troops; detachment of warships employed on particular service; unit of air force with 10 to 18 aircraft. **squadron leader** air force officer commanding squadron, next below wing commander.

**squalid** /ˈskwɒlɪd/ a. dirty, filthy, mean in appearance; wretched, sordid.

**squall** /skwɔːl/ 1 n. sudden violent gust or storm; discordant cry; scream. 2 v. scream loudly or discordantly. 3 **squally** a.

**squalor** /ˈskwɒlə(r)/ n. filthy or squalid state.

**squander** /ˈskwɒndə(r)/ v.t. spend wastefully.

**square** /skweə(r)/ 1 n. rectangle with 4 equal sides; object or area of (roughly) this shape; open space, esp. enclosed by houses etc.; product of number multiplied by itself; L- or T-shaped instrument for measuring or testing right angles. 2 a. having shape of square; having or in form of a right angle; designating unit of measure equal in area to square whose side is one of the unit specified; level or parallel; balanced, equal; solid, sturdy; fair, honest; sl. conventional, old-fashioned. 3 adv. squarely. 4 v. make square; multiply (number) by itself; make or be consistent (with); reconcile; mark out in squares; settle (up) account etc.; place (shoulders etc.) squarely facing forwards; pay or bribe; make scores etc. equal or level. 5 **square dance** one in which 4 couples face inwards from 4 sides; **square deal** fair bargain or treatment; **square leg** Crick. position of fielder on batsman's leg-side nearly in line with stumps; **square meal** substantial one; **square-rigged** having principal sails at right angles to length of ship; **square root** number that when multiplied by itself gives specified number.

**squash**¹ /skwɒʃ/ 1 v. crush or be squeezed flat or into pulp; force into small space; crowd; snub, suppress. 2 n. crowded state; crowd; drink made of crushed fruit; (in full **squash rackets**) game played with rackets and fairly soft ball in closed court. 3 **squashy** a.

**squash**² /skwɒʃ/ n. trailing annual plant; gourd of this.

**squat** /skwɒt/ 1 v. sit on one's heels, or on ground with knees drawn up, or in hunched posture; put into squatting position; colloq. sit down; act as squatter. 2 a. squatting; short and thick, dumpy. 3 n. squatting posture; place occupied by squatter(s); being squatter.

**squatter** /ˈskwɒtə(r)/ n. person who takes unauthorized possession of unoccupied premises etc.; Aus. hist. settler having no formal right to land occupied by him; Aus. sheep-farmer.

**squattocracy** /skwɒˈtɒkrəsi/ n. Aus. rich and powerful people in rural areas.

**squaw** n. N. Amer. Indian woman or wife.

**squawk** 1 n. harsh cry; complaint. 2 v.i. make squawk.

**squeak** 1 n. short high-pitched cry or sound; (also **narrow squeak**) narrow escape. 2 v. emit squeak, utter in squeaking voice; sl. turn informer. 3 **squeaky** a.

**squeal** 1 n. prolonged shrill sound or cry. 2 v. make a squeal; utter (words)

**squeamish** /'skwi:mɪʃ/ a. easily nauseated; fastidious, over-scrupulous.

**squeegee** /'skwi:dʒi:/ 1 n. implement with rubber blade or roller used to remove liquid from surfaces. 2 v.t. clean etc. with squeegee.

**squeeze** 1 v. exert pressure on from opposite or all sides, esp. to extract moisture; reduce size of or alter shape of by squeezing; force or make one's way into or through small or narrow space; harass; bring pressure to bear on; get by entreaty or extortion. 2 n. action or result of squeezing; crowd, crowded state; small quantity produced by squeezing; restriction on borrowing and investment.

**squelch** /skweltʃ/ 1 v. tread or walk heavily in water or wet ground, make sound (as) of this; disconcert, silence. 2 n. act or sound of squelching.

**squib** n. small hissing firework thrown by hand; short satirical composition.

**squid** n. 10-armed marine cephalopod.

**squiffy** /'skwɪfi/ a. sl. slightly drunk.

**squiggle** /'skwɪg(ə)l/ n. short curling line, esp. in handwriting. **squiggly** a.

**squint** 1 v.i. have eyes turned in different directions; look sidelong. 2 n. squinting condition of eyes; colloq. look, glance; oblique opening through wall of church etc.

**squire** /skwaɪə(r)/ 1 n. country gentleman, esp. chief landed proprietor in district; man escorting or attending on woman; hist. attendant on knight. 2 v.t. (of man) escort (woman).

**squirearchy** /'skwaɪərɑːki/ n. landowners collectively.

**squirm** 1 v.i. writhe, wriggle; fig. show or feel embarrassment. 2 n. squirming movement.

**squirrel** /'skwɪr(ə)l/ 1 n. bushy-tailed usu. arboreal rodent. 2 v.t. hoard (*away*).

**squirt** 1 v. eject (liquid etc.) in a jet; be ejected thus. 2 n. jet of water etc.; device for ejecting this; colloq. insignificant person.

**squish** 1 n. slight squelching sound. 2 v.i. move with squish. 3 **squishy** a.

**squiz** n. Aus. sl. look, glance.

**Sr.** abbr. Senior.

**SS** abbr. Saints; steamship; hist. Nazi special police force.

**SSE** abbr. south-south-east.

**SSW** abbr. south-south-west.

**St** abbr. Saint.

**St.** abbr. Street.

**st.** abbr. stone.

**stab** 1 v. pierce or wound with pointed tool or weapon; aim blow with such weapon (*at*); cause sharp pain to. 2 n. act or result of stabbing; colloq. attempt. 3 **stab in the back** treacherous attack.

**stability** /stə'bɪlɪti/ n. being stable.

**stabilize** /'steɪbəlaɪz/ v.t. make or become stable. **stabilization** n.

**stabilizer** /'steɪbəlaɪzə(r)/ n. device to keep aircraft or ship or child's bicycle steady.

**stable** /'steɪb(ə)l/ 1 a. firmly fixed or established, not fluctuating or changing, not easily shaken or decomposed or destroyed etc. 2 n. building in which horses are kept; establishment for training racehorses; racehorses of particular stable; persons or products etc. having common origin or affiliation; such origin or affiliation. 3 v.t. put or keep (horse) in stable.

**stabling** /'steɪblɪŋ/ n. accommodation for horses etc.

**staccato** /stə'kɑːtəʊ/ a. & adv. esp. Mus. with each sound or spoken phrase sharply distinct from the others.

**stack** 1 n. pile or heap, esp. in orderly arrangement; colloq. large quantity; number of chimneys standing together; smoke-stack; tall factory chimney; part of library where books are compactly stored. 2 v.t. pile in stack(s); arrange (cards, or fig. circumstances etc.) secretly for cheating; cause (aircraft) to fly round at different levels while waiting to land.

**stadium** /'steɪdɪəm/ n. (pl. **-diums**) athletic or sports ground with tiers of seats for spectators.

**staff** /stɑːf/ 1 n. stick or pole as weapon or support or as symbol of office; group of persons carrying on work under manager etc.; those in authority in a school etc.; body of officers in army etc. assisting officer in high command; Mus. (pl. **staves**) set of usu. 5 parallel lines to indicate pitch of notes by position. 2 v.t. provide (institution etc.) with staff.

**3 staff officer** *Mil.* officer serving on staff.

**stag** *n.* male deer; *St. Exch.* person who seeks to buy new shares and sell at once for profit. **stag-beetle** large beetle with antler-like mandibles; **stag-party** party for men only.

**stage** 1 *n.* point or period of development or progress; platform, esp. raised one on which plays etc. are performed; *the* theatre or acting profession; scene of action; regular stopping-place on route; interval between stopping-places; section of space-rocket with separate means of propulsion. 2 *v.* put (play etc.) on stage, organize and carry out. 3 **stage-coach** *hist.* coach running regularly between two places; **stage direction** instruction in text of play about actor's movement or sounds heard etc.; **stage door** entrance from street to backstage part of theatre; **stage fright** nervousness at appearing before audience; **stage-manage** arrange or control etc. as or like stage-manager; **stage-manager** person responsible for lighting and mechanical arrangements etc. of play; **stage-struck** strongly wishing to be actor or actress; **stage whisper** loud whisper meant to be heard by others than person addressed.

**stager** *n.* **old stager** experienced person.

**stagger** /'stægə(r)/ 1 *v.* walk or move unsteadily; cause shock or confusion to; arrange (events, hours of work, etc.), so that they do not coincide; arrange (objects) so that they are not in line. 2 *n.* staggering movement; in *pl.* disease, esp. of horses and cattle, causing staggering.

**staggering** /'stægərɪŋ/ *a.* bewildering, astonishing.

**staging** /'steɪdʒɪŋ/ *n.* presentation of play etc.; (temporary) platform; shelving, esp. for plants in greenhouse etc. **staging post** regular stopping-place, esp. on air route.

**stagnant** /'stægnənt/ *a.* not flowing or running, without motion or current; inert, sluggish, without activity. **stagnancy** *n.*

**stagnate** /stæg'neɪt/ *v.i.* be or become stagnant. **stagnation** *n.*

**stagy** /'steɪdʒɪ/ *a.* theatrical, artificial, or exaggerated.

**staid** *a.* sober, steady, sedate.

**stain** 1 *v.* discolour or be discoloured by action of liquid sinking in; spoil or damage; colour (wood or glass) with substance that penetrates the material; treat with colouring agent. 2 *n.* discoloration or mark, esp. one not easily removable; dye etc. for staining; blot, blemish.

**stainless** /'steɪnləs/ *a.* without stains; not liable to stain. **stainless steel** chrome steel that resists rust and corrosion.

**stair** *n.* each of a set of fixed indoor steps; in *pl.* set or flight of these. **below stairs** in or to basement, esp. as servants' part of house; **staircase** flight or series of flights of stairs, part of building containing staircase; **stair-rod** rod for securing carpet in angle between 2 steps; **stairway** staircase.

**stake** 1 *n.* stick or post pointed for driving into ground; *hist.* post to which person was tied for burning alive; money etc. wagered on event; interest or concern, esp. financial; in *pl.* money offered as prize in horse-race; such race. 2 *v.t.* secure or support with stake(s); mark (area) *off* or *out* with stakes; wager (money etc. *on* event); *US colloq.* give financial or other support to. 3 **at stake** wagered, risked, to be won or lost; **stake out** place under surveillance; **stake-out** *n.*

**stalactite** /'stæləktaɪt/ *n.* deposit of calcium carbonate hanging like icicle from roof of cave etc.

**stalagmite** /'stæləgmaɪt/ *n.* deposit of calcium carbonate rising like spike from floor of cave etc.

**stale** 1 *a.* not fresh; the worse for age or use; lacking novelty, trite; (of athlete, musician, etc.) having ability impaired by excessive exertion or practice etc. 2 *v.* become or make stale.

**stalemate** /'steɪlmeɪt/ 1 *n.* state of chess-game in which one player cannot move without going into check; deadlock in proceedings. 2 *v.t.* bring (player) to stalemate; bring to standstill.

**stalk**[1] /stɔːk/ 1 *n.* stem, esp. main stem of herbaceous plant; attachment or support of leaf or flower or animal organ etc.

**stalk²** /stɔːk/ 1 v. pursue or approach (wild animal, enemy) stealthily; stride, walk in stately or haughty manner. 2 n. stalking of game; imposing gait. 3 **stalking-horse** screen etc. behind which hunter hides, pretext concealing one's real intentions or actions.

**stall¹** /stɔːl/ n. stable or cowhouse; compartment for one animal in this; trader's booth in market etc.; fixed seat in choir or chancel, (partly) enclosed at back and sides; any of seats on ground floor of theatre; stalling of engine or aircraft. 2 v. (of motor vehicle or its engine) stop because of inadequate fuel-supply or overloading of engine etc.; (of aircraft) get out of control because speed is insufficient; cause (engine) to stall; put or keep in stalls.

**stall²** /stɔːl/ v. play for time when being questioned etc.; delay or obstruct (person etc.).

**stallion** /ˈstæljən/ n. uncastrated male horse.

**stalwart** /ˈstɔːlwət/ 1 a. sturdy, strong; courageous, resolute. 2 n. stalwart person, esp. loyal uncompromising partisan.

**stamen** /ˈsteɪmən/ n. male fertilizing organ of flowering plant.

**stamina** /ˈstæmənə/ n. ability to endure prolonged physical or mental strain.

**stammer** /ˈstæmə(r)/ 1 v. speak with halting articulation, esp. with pauses or rapid repetitions of same syllable; (often with *out*) utter (words) thus. 2 n. act or habit of stammering.

**stamp** 1 v. bring down (one's foot) heavily on ground etc., crush or flatten thus; impress (pattern or mark) on; impress with pattern or mark etc.; affix postage or other stamp to; *fig.* assign specific character to, mark out. 2 n. instrument for stamping; mark or design made by this; postage stamp; mark impressed on or label etc. fixed to commodity as evidence of quality etc.; act or sound of stamping of foot; characteristic mark of quality. 3 **stamp-duty** duty imposed on certain kinds of legal document; **stamping-ground** favourite place of resort or action; **stamp out** produce by cutting out with die etc., put an end to.

**stampede** /stæmˈpiːd/ 1 n. sudden rush of (usu. frightened) cattle or people etc.; uncontrolled or unreasoning action by large number of people. 2 v. (cause to) take part in stampede.

**stance** /stɑːns or stæns/ n. player's position for making stroke; pose, attitude, standpoint.

**stanch** /stɑːntʃ/ v.t. stop flow of (esp. blood); stop flow from (esp. wound).

**stanchion** /ˈstænʃ(ə)n/ n. upright post or support; device for confining cattle in stall etc.

**stand** 1 v. (*past* & *p.p.* **stood** /stʊd/) have or take or maintain stationary upright position; be situated; be of specified height; be in specified condition; set upright or in specified position; move to and remain in specified condition; remain valid; *Naut.* hold specified course; endure, tolerate; provide at one's expense; offer oneself for election etc. 2 n. act or condition of standing; resistance to attack or compulsion; position adopted; rack or pedestal etc. on or in which things may be placed; stall in market etc.; *Aus.* individual shearing rig; standing-place for vehicles; raised structure with seats at sports ground etc.; *US* witness-box; halt made by touring-company etc. to give performance(s); group *of* growing trees etc. 3 **stand by** stand ready for action, look on without interfering, uphold or support (person); adhere to (terms, beliefs, etc.); **stand-by** thing or person ready if needed in emergency; **stand down** withdraw from position or candidacy, *Aus.* lay off (workers) temporarily during strike by others; **stand for** represent, signify, imply, be candidate for (esp. public office), *colloq.* endure, tolerate; **stand in** deputize *for*; **stand-in** deputy, substitute, esp. for actor or actress; **stand off** move or keep away, temporarily dispense with services of (employee); **stand-off half** *Rugby footb.* half-back who forms link between scrum-half and three-quarters; **stand-offish** cold or distant in manner; **stand on** insist on, observe scrupulously; **stand out** be prominent or conspicuous, persist in resistance *against* or support *for*; **stand over** *Aus.* extort money or compliance from by intimidation; **stand-over** *Aus.* threatening; **standpipe** vertical pipe, esp.

with spout or nozzle, for attachment to water-main; **standpoint** point of view; **standstill** stoppage, inability to proceed; **stand to** abide by, be likely or certain to; **stand to reason** be obvious or logical; **stand up** get on one's feet, maintain upright position, be valid, *colloq.* fail to keep appointment with; **stand-up** (of meal) eaten standing, (of fight) violent, thorough, (of collar) upright; **stand up for** support, side with; **stand up to** face courageously, be resistant to.

**standard** /'stændəd/ 1 *n.* object or quality or measure to which others (should) conform or against which others are judged; required degree of excellence etc.; ordinary procedure etc.; distinctive flag; upright support or pipe; treelike shrub with or grafted on upright stem. 2 *a.* serving or used as standard; of normal or prescribed quality or size etc. 3 **standard-bearer** person who carries distinctive flag, prominent leader in cause; **standard lamp** lamp set on tall holder standing on floor etc.; **standard of living** degree of material comfort enjoyed by person or group; **standard time** time established legally or by custom in region etc.

**standardize** /'stændədaɪz/ *v.t.* (cause to) conform to standard. **standardization** *n.*

**standing** /'stændɪŋ/ 1 *n.* established repute or position; duration. 2 *a.* of permanent kind; constantly ready for use; (of jump) made without run. 3 **standing order** instruction to banker to make regular payments; **standing orders** rules governing procedure in Parliament or council etc.; **standing room** space to stand in.

**stank** *past* of **stink**.

**stanza** /'stænzə/ *n.* group of lines forming division of song or poem.

**staphylococcus** /ˌstæfələ'kɒkəs/ *n.* (*pl.* **-ci** /-kaɪ/) form of pus-producing bacterium. **staphylococcal** *a.*

**staple**[1] /'steɪp(ə)l/ 1 *n.* piece of wire or metal bent into U-shape for driving into wood etc.; various similar contrivances, esp. bent wire for fastening sheets of paper together. 2 *v.t.* furnish or fasten with staple(s).

**staple**[2] /'steɪp(ə)l/ 1 *a.* principal, important as product or export. 2 *n.* important or principal product or article of commerce; chief element or material; textile fibre with respect to its quality or length.

**star** 1 *n.* celestial body appearing as point of light; celestial body considered as influencing human affairs or person's fate; rayed figure or object representing star as ornament etc.; asterisk; brilliant or prominent person, esp. chief actor or actress. 2 *v.* mark or adorn (as) with star(s); present or perform as star actor etc. 3 **starfish** star-shaped sea creature; **star-gazer** *colloq.* astronomer or astrologer; **starlight** light of stars; **Stars and Stripes** US national flag; **star turn** principal item or attraction.

**starboard** /'stɑːbəd/ 1 *n.* right-hand side of ship or aircraft etc. looking forward. 2 *v.t.* turn (helm) to starboard.

**starch** 1 *n.* white carbohydrate forming important constituent of human food; preparation of this for stiffening linen etc.; *fig.* stiffness of manner or conduct. 2 *v.t.* stiffen with starch. 3 **starchy** *a.*

**stardom** /'stɑːdəm/ *n.* being star, status of star.

**stare** /steə(r)/ 1 *v.* look fixedly with eyes wide open, esp. with curiosity or surprise or horror. 2 *n.* staring gaze. 3 **stare person in the face** be clearly evident or imminent.

**stark** 1 *a.* desolate, bare; sharply evident; downright, sheer; completely naked; *arch.* stiff, rigid. 2 *adv.* completely, wholly.

**starlet** /'stɑːlət/ *n.* young film actress likely to become star.

**starling** /'stɑːlɪŋ/ *n.* small gregarious chattering lustrous-plumaged bird.

**starry** /'stɑːrɪ/ *a.* set with stars; bright as star; starlike. **starry-eyed** *colloq.* romantic but unpractical.

**start** 1 *v.* set in motion or action; cause beginning of; set oneself in motion or action; begin journey; cause (machine etc.) to begin operating; (of engine) begin running; found or establish; give signal to (persons) to start in race; make sudden movement from surprise or pain etc.; rouse (game) from lair. 2 *n.* beginning; starting-place of race; advantage granted in beginning a race; advantageous initial position in life or business etc.; sudden movement of surprise or pain etc. **3 starting-block** shaped block against which runner braces feet at start of race; **starting-gate** mechanically operated barrier used to start horse-races; **starting-price** final odds before start of horse-race etc.

**starter** /'stɑːtə(r)/ n. apparatus for starting engine of motor vehicle etc.; person giving signal to start race; competitor starting in race; first course of meal.

**startle** /'stɑːt(ə)l/ v.t. give shock or surprise to.

**starve** v. (cause to) die or suffer acutely from lack of food etc.; colloq. feel hungry; (cause to) be deprived of; force into or out etc. by starvation. **starvation** n.

**starveling** /'stɑːvlɪŋ/ n. starving person or animal.

**stash** sl. **1** v.t. conceal, put away in safe place. **2** n. hiding-place.

**state 1** n. existing position or condition; colloq. excited or agitated condition of mind or feeling; (often **State**), organized political community under one government; civil government; pomp. **2** a. of or concerned with the State or its ceremonial occasions. **3** v.t. express, esp. fully or clearly, in speech or writing; specify; put into form of statement. **4 lie in state** be laid in public place of honour before burial; **State Department** US Department of Foreign Affairs; **state of affairs** existing conditions. **stateroom** state apartment, private compartment in passenger ship; **the States** the USA.

**stately** /'steɪtlɪ/ a. dignified, imposing. **stately home** large magnificent house, esp. one open to visits by the public.

**statement** /'steɪtmənt/ n. stating or being stated; thing stated; formal account of facts, esp. of transactions in bank account or of amount due to tradesman etc.

**statesman** /'steɪtsmən/ n. (pl. **-men**) person skilled in affairs of State; sagacious far-sighted politician. **statesmanlike** a.; **statesmanship** n.

**static** /'stætɪk/ **1** a. stationary, not active or changing; concerned with forces in equilibrium or bodies at rest. **2** n. static electricity; atmospherics. **3 static electricity** electricity produced by friction, not flowing as current.

**statics** n.pl. (usu. treated as sing.) science of static bodies or forces; atmospherics.

**station** /'steɪʃ(ə)n/ **1** n. place or building etc. where person or thing stands or is placed or where particular activity, esp. public service, is based or organized; regular stopping-place on railway line, buildings of this; establishment engaged in broadcasting; military or naval base; position in life, rank, status; Aus. sheep- or other farm. **2** v.t. assign station to; put in position. **stationmaster** official in charge of railway-station; **Stations of the Cross** series of scenes from the Passion successively venerated in some churches; **station-wagon** car with extended compartment at the back for carrying luggage.

**stationary** /'steɪʃənərɪ/ a. not moving or movable; not changing in amount or quantity.

**stationer** /'steɪʃənə(r)/ n. dealer in stationery.

**stationery** /'steɪʃənərɪ/ n. writing materials, office supplies, etc.

**statistic** /stə'tɪstɪk/ n. statistical fact or item.

**statistics** n.pl. numerical facts systematically collected; (usu. treated as sing.) science of collecting or using statistics. **statistician** /stætɪs'tɪʃ(ə)n/ a.

**statistical** /stə'tɪstɪk(ə)l/ a. of or concerned with statistics.

**statuary** /'stætjʊərɪ/ **1** a. of or for statues. **2** n. sculpture, statues.

**statue** /'stætjuː/ n. sculptured or cast or moulded figure of person or animal etc., usu. of or above life size.

**statuesque** /stætjuː'esk/ a. like statue, esp. in beauty or dignity.

**statuette** /stætjuː'et/ n. small statue.

**stature** /'stætjʊə(r)/ n. bodily height; eminence, mental or moral quality.

**status** /'steɪtəs/ n. social or legal position or condition; rank, prestige; superior social etc. position. **status quo** /kwəʊ/ existing or unchanged position; **status symbol** possession considered to show person's high social status.

**statute** /'stætjuːt/ n. law passed by legislative body; permanent rule of corporation etc.

**statutory** /'stætjʊtərɪ/ enacted or required by statute.

**staunch** /stɔːntʃ/ *a.* trustworthy, loyal.

**stave 1** *n.* each of narrow shaped vertical strips forming sides of cask; stanza of song etc.; *Mus.* staff. **2** *v.t.* (*past & p.p.* **stove** *or* **staved**) break hole in, knock out of shape. **3 stave in** crush by forcing inwards; **stave off** avert or defer (danger, misfortune, etc.).

**staves** see **staff**.

**stay**[1] **1** *v.* continue to be in same place or condition, not depart or change; dwell temporarily; (cause to) stop or pause; postpone (judgement etc.); assuage (hunger etc.) esp. for short time; show endurance. **2** *n.* action or period of staying; suspension or postponement of execution of sentence etc. **3 stay-at-home** person remaining habitually at home; **staying-power** endurance; **stay put** *colloq.* remain where it is put or where one is.

**stay**[2] *n.* prop, support; rope etc. supporting mast or flagstaff etc.; tie-piece in aircraft; in *pl.* corset, esp. stiffened with whalebone etc. **staysail** sail extended on stay.

**stayer** /ˈsteɪə(r)/ *n.* person or animal etc. of great endurance.

**STD** *abbr.* subscriber trunk dialling.

**stead** /sted/ *n.* **in person's** *or* **thing's stead** as substitute for him or it; **stand in good stead** be of advantage or service to (person).

**steadfast** /ˈstedfɑːst/ *a.* constant, firm, unwavering.

**steady** /ˈstedɪ/ *a.* firm, stable, not faltering or shaking or rocking or wavering etc.; settled; regular, maintained at even rate of action or change etc.; serious and dependable. **2** *v.* make or become steady. **3** *adv.* steadily. **4** *n. colloq.* regular boy-friend or girl-friend. **5 steady state** unvarying condition, esp. in physical process.

**steak** /steɪk/ *n.* thick slice of meat (esp. beef) or fish, usu. grilled or fried. **steakhouse** restaurant specializing in beef steaks.

**steal 1** *v.* (*past* **stole**; *p.p.* **stolen**) take dishonestly and esp. secretly what is another's; obtain surreptitiously or by surprise, etc.; move secretly or silently. **2** *n. colloq.* stealing, theft; bargain, easy task. **3 steal a march on** gain advantage over by acting surreptitiously; **steal the show** outshine other performers.

**stealth** /stelθ/ *n.* secret or surreptitious behaviour.

**stealthy** /ˈstelθɪ/ *a.* practising or done by stealth.

**steam 1** *n.* gas into which water is changed by boiling; condensed vapour formed from this; power obtained from steam; *colloq.* power, energy. **2** *v.* give out steam; cook or soften etc. with steam; move by power of steam. **3 let off steam** *fig.* relieve pent-up energy or feelings; **steamboat** one propelled by steam; **steam-engine** one worked or propelled by steam; **steam iron** electric iron emitting steam from its flat surface; **steamroller** heavy slow-moving locomotive with roller used in road-making, *fig.* a crushing power or force, (*v.t.*) crush or move along (as) with steam-roller; **steamship** one propelled by steam; **steam train** train pulled by steam-engine; **steam up** cover or become covered with condensed steam, *sl.* (esp. in *p.p.*) make (person) excited or angry; **under one's own steam** *fig.* without help from others. **4 steamy** *a.*

**steamer** /ˈstiːmə(r)/ *n.* steamboat; utensil for steaming food etc.

**steatite** /ˈstiːətaɪt/ *n.* kind of usu. grey talc with greasy feel.

**steed** *n. poet.* horse.

**steel 1** *n.* malleable alloy of iron and carbon, used for tools and weapons and machines etc.; steel rod for sharpening knives. **2** *v.t.* harden, make resolute. **3 steel band** musical band of orig. W. Ind. kind, with instruments made from oil-drums; **steel wool** fine steel shavings used as abrasive; **steelyard** weighing-apparatus with graduated arm along which weight slides.

**steely** /ˈstiːlɪ/ *a.* of or like steel; inflexible, obdurate.

**steep**[1] **1** *a.* sloping sharply; (of rise or fall) rapid; *colloq.* (of price etc.) exorbitant; incredible. **2** *n.* steep hill, precipice.

**steep**[2] **1** *v.* soak or be soaked in liquid. **2** *n.* action of or liquid for steeping. **3 steep in** *fig.* pervade or imbue with, make deeply acquainted with (subject etc.).

**steepen** /'sti:pən/ v. make or become steep(er).

**steeple** /'sti:p(ə)l/ n. tall tower, esp. with spire, above roof of church. **steeplechase** horse-race with obstacles such as fences to jump, cross-country foot-race; **steeplejack** man who repairs steeples and tall chimneys etc.

**steer**[1] v. guide (vehicle or ship etc.) by wheel or rudder etc.; direct or guide in specified direction. **steer clear of** take care to avoid; **steering column** column on which steering-wheel is mounted; **steering committee** one deciding order of business or general course of operations etc.; **steering-wheel** wheel by which vehicle or vessel etc. is steered; **steersman** person who steers ship.

**steer**[2] n. young male ox, esp. bullock.

**steerage** /'stɪərɪdʒ/ n. steering; part of ship allotted to passengers travelling at cheapest rate.

**stein** /staɪn/ n. large earthenware mug for beer etc.

**stela** /'sti:lə/ n. (pl. **-lae** /-li:/) (also **stele** /'sti:li:/) Archaeol. upright slab or pillar, usu. inscribed and sculptured, esp. as gravestone.

**stellar** /'stelə(r)/ a. of stars; star-shaped.

**stem**[1] 1 n. main body or stalk of plant; stalk supporting fruit or flower or leaf; stem-shaped part, e.g. slender part of wineglass between body and foot; Gram. root or main part of noun or verb etc. to which case-endings etc. are added; main upright timber at bow of ship. 2 v.i. spring or originate from.

**stem**[2] v. check, stop, make headway against, (stream etc.).

**Sten** n. (in full **Sten gun**) lightweight machine-gun.

**stench** n. foul or offensive smell.

**stencil** /'stens(ə)l/ 1 n. thin sheet in which pattern is cut, used to produce corresponding pattern on surface beneath it by applying ink or paint etc.; pattern so produced. 2 v.t. produce (pattern) with stencil; mark (surface) thus.

**stenography** /ste'nɒgrəfɪ/ n. shorthand. **stenographer** n.

**stentorian** /sten'tɔ:rɪən/ a. (of voice) extremely loud.

**step** 1 n. complete action of moving and placing one leg in walking or running; distance covered by this; measure or (in pl.) course of action taken; flat-topped structure, esp. one of series, to facilitate movement from one level to another, stair, tread; in pl. step-ladder; short distance; mark or sound made by setting foot down; degree in scale, advance from one degree to another. 2 v. lift and set down foot or alternate feet in walking etc.; go or come in specified direction by stepping; make progress; measure (distance) by stepping; perform (dance). 3 **in step** stepping in time *with* other person(s) or music, moving or acting etc. in conformity or harmony or agreement (*with*); **mind, watch, one's step** take care; **out of step** not in step; **step down** resign; **step in** enter, intervene; **step-ladder** short self-supporting ladder with flat steps; **step on it** *colloq.* hurry; **step out** take long steps, *colloq.* go out for entertainment etc.; **stepping-stone**, raised stone, usu. as one of set in stream etc. to help in crossing, *fig.* means of progress; **step up** come up or forward, increase rate or volume etc. of.

**step-** in comb. related by remarriage of parent. **stepchild, stepdaughter, stepson**, spouse's child by previous marriage; **stepfather, stepmother, step-parent**, mother's or father's later spouse; **stepbrother, stepsister**, child of previous marriage of one's step-parent.

**stephanotis** /stefə'nəʊtɪs/ n. fragrant tropical climbing plant.

**steppe** /step/ n. level treeless plain.

**stereo** /'steri:əʊ/ n. (pl. **-os**) stereophonic record-player etc.; stereophony; stereoscope; stereotype. 2 a. stereophonic; stereoscopic.

**stereo-** in comb. solid; three-dimensional.

**stereophonic** /steri:ə'fɒnɪk/ a. using two or more transmission channels to give effect of naturally-distributed sound. **stereophony** /steri:'ɒf-/ n.

**stereoscope** /'steri:əskəʊp/ n. instrument for combining two pictures of object etc. from slightly different points of view, to give effect of three dimensions. **stereoscopic** /-'skɒp-/ a.

**stereotype** /'steri:ətaɪp/ 1 n. unduly

**sterile** 552 **stifle**

fixed mental impression; conventional idea; printing-plate cast from mould of composed type. **2** *v.t.* formalize, make typical or conventional (usu. in *p.p.*); print from stereotype; make stereotype of.

**sterile** /'steraɪl/ *a.* not able to produce seed or offspring, barren; free from living germs; lacking originality or emotive power etc. **sterility** /-'rɪl-/ *n.*

**sterilize** /'sterəlaɪz/ *v.t.* make sterile; deprive of power of reproduction. **sterilization** *n.*

**sterling** /'stɜːlɪŋ/ **1** *a.* of or in British money; genuine, of standard value or purity; of solid worth, reliable. **2** *n.* British money. **3 sterling silver** silver of 92½% purity.

**stern**[1] *a.* severe, strict; enforcing discipline or submission.

**stern**[2] *n.* rear part of ship or aircraft etc.; any rear part. **stern-post** central upright timber etc. of stern, usu. bearing rudder.

**sternum** /'stɜːnəm/ *n.* (*pl.* **-nums** or **-na**) breastbone. **sternal** *a.*

**steroid** /'stɪərɔɪd/ *n.* any of various organic compounds incl. some hormones and vitamins.

**sterol** /'stɪərɒl/ *n.* one of class of complex solid alcohols.

**stertorous** /'stɜːtərəs/ *a.* (of breathing etc.) producing snoring or rasping sound.

**stet** *v.* (usu. as instruction written on proof-sheet etc.) ignore or cancel correction or alteration, let original form stand.

**stethoscope** /'steθəskəʊp/ *n.* instrument used for listening to heart and lungs etc. **stethoscopic** /-'skɒp-/ *a.*

**stetson** /'stets(ə)n/ *n.* slouch hat with wide brim and high crown.

**stevedore** /'stiːvədɔː(r)/ *n.* man employed in loading and unloading ships.

**stew 1** *v.* cook by long simmering in closed vessel with liquid; make (tea) bitter or strong with too long standing; *colloq.* swelter. **2** *n.* dish of stewed meat etc.; *colloq.* state of great alarm or excitement.

**steward** /'stjuːəd/ **1** *n.* person employed to manage another's property or to arrange supplies of food for college or club or ship etc.; passengers' attendant on ship or aircraft or train; official managing race-meeting or show etc. **stewardship** *n.*

**stewardess** /'stjuːədes/ *n.* female steward, esp. in ship or aircraft.

**stick**[1] *n.* thin branch or piece of wood, esp. trimmed for use as support or as weapon; thin rod of wood etc. for particular purpose; more or less cylindrical piece of something; *UK* punishment, criticism; *colloq.* person, esp. one who is dull or unsociable. **the sticks** *colloq.* rural area, the backwoods; **stick-insect** insect with twiglike body.

**stick**[2] *v.* (*past & p.p.* **stuck**) thrust (point or pointed thing) *in(to)* or *through*; stab; fix or be fixed (as) by point *in(to)* or *on*; fix or become or remain fixed by adhesive etc.; lose or deprive of power of motion or action through friction or jamming etc.; include; put or remain in specified place; *sl.* endure, tolerate. **stick around** *sl.* remain in same place; **stick at** *colloq.* work persistently at; **sticking-plaster** adhesive plaster for wounds etc.; **stick-in-the-mud** unprogressive or old-fashioned person; **stick out** (cause to) protrude, hold out persistently *for*; **stick up** (cause to) protrude, be or make erect, *sl.* rob or threaten (person etc.) with gun; **stick up for** support or defend.

**sticker** /'stɪkə(r)/ *n.* adhesive label.

**stickleback** /'stɪk(ə)lbæk/ *n.* small spiny-finned fish.

**stickler** /'stɪklə(r)/ *n.* person who insists on something.

**sticky** /'stɪkɪ/ *a.* tending or intended to stick or adhere, glutinous, viscous; (of weather) humid; *colloq.* making or likely to make objections; *sl.* very unpleasant or painful. **stickybeak** *Aus. sl.* inquisitive person; **sticky wicket** difficult situation.

**stiff 1** *a.* rigid, not flexible; not working freely, sticking, not supple; aching from exertion; thick and viscous, not fluid; hard to cope with, trying; unbending, unyielding; severe or strong; formal, constrained, haughty; (of alcoholic drink) strong. **2** *n. sl.* corpse. **3 stiff-necked** obstinate or haughty; **stiff upper lip** firmness, fortitude.

**stiffen** /'stɪf(ə)n/ *v.* make or become stiff.

**stifle** /'staɪf(ə)l/ *v.* smother; cause or

experience constraint of breathing or suppression of utterance etc.

**stigma** /'stɪgmə/ n. mark or sign of disgrace or discredit; *Bot.* part of pistil which receives pollen in pollination; (usu. in *pl.*, **stigmata**) marks corresponding to those left on Christ's body by the Crucifixion.

**stigmatize** /'stɪgmətaɪz/ v.t. characterize; describe opprobriously.

**stile** n. set of steps etc. to enable people to pass over fence or wall etc.

**stiletto** /stɪ'letəʊ/ n. (pl. **-tos**) short dagger; small pointed implement for making eyelet-holes etc. **stiletto heel** high narrow heel on shoe.

**still**[1] 1 a. without motion or sound, silent, quiet, calm; (of wine etc.) not effervescent. 2 n. silence; ordinary photograph, esp. illustration from cinema film. 3 adv. without motion or change; now, then, as before; even then, even now; nevertheless; even, yet; always. 4 v. make or become still, quieten. 5 **still birth** birth of dead child; **stillborn** born dead, *fig.* abortive; **still life**, painting of inanimate objects.

**still**[2] n. apparatus for distilling. **still-room** housekeeper's store-room in large house.

**stilt** n. each of pair of poles with supports for feet enabling user to walk at a distance above the ground; each of set of piles or posts supporting building etc.

**stilted** /'stɪltɪd/ a. highflown; stiff and unnatural.

**Stilton** /'stɪlt(ə)n/ n. rich blue-veined cheese.

**stimulant** /'stɪmjələnt/ 1 a. that stimulates, esp. that increases bodily or mental activity. 2 n. stimulant substance or influence.

**stimulate** /'stɪmjəleɪt/ v.t. animate, excite, rouse. **stimulation** n.; **stimulative** a.; **stimulator** n.

**stimulus** /'stɪmjələs/ n. (pl. **-li** /-laɪ/) stimulating thing or effect.

**sting** 1 n. sharp wounding organ of insect or snake or nettle etc.; inflicting of wound with this, the wound or the pain caused by it; wounding or painful quality or effect; keenness, vigour. 2 v. (past & p.p. **stung**) wound with sting; be able to do this; feel or cause tingling physical pain or sharp mental pain; incite by such mental effect; *sl.* charge heavily, swindle. 3 **stinging-nettle** nettle that stings; **sting-ray** broad flat-fish with stinging tail.

**stingy** /'stɪndʒɪ/ a. niggardly, mean.

**stink** 1 v. (*past* **stank** or **stunk**; *p.p.* **stunk**) have strong offensive smell; *colloq.* be or seem very unpleasant. 2 n. strong offensive smell; *colloq.* loud complaint or fuss. 3 **stink-bomb** device emitting stink when exploded; **stink out** drive out by stink, fill (place) with stink.

**stinker** /'stɪŋkə(r)/ n. *sl.* particularly annoying or unpleasant person; very difficult problem etc.; letter etc. conveying strong disapproval.

**stinking** /'stɪŋkɪŋ/ 1 a. that stinks; *sl.* obnoxious, objectionable. 2 adv. *sl.* extremely and usu. objectionably.

**stint** 1 v.t. supply or give in niggardly or grudging way; keep on short allowance. 2 n. limitation of supply or effort; fixed or allotted amount of work etc.

**stipend** /'staɪpend/ n. salary, esp. of clergyman.

**stipendiary** /staɪ'pendɪərɪ/ 1 a. receiving stipend. 2 n. person receiving stipend. 3 **stipendiary magistrate** paid magistrate.

**stipple** /'stɪp(ə)l/ 1 v. draw or paint with dots instead of lines; roughen surface of (paint or cement etc.). 2 n. stippling, effect of stippling.

**stipulate** /'stɪpjəleɪt/ v. demand or specify as part or bargain or agreement. **stipulation** n.

**stir** 1 v. move spoon etc. round and round in (liquid etc.) to mix ingredients; move esp. slightly; be or begin to be in motion; arouse, inspire, excite; *Aus.* seek reforms; make trouble. 2 n. act of stirring; commotion, excitement, sensation. 3 **stir up** mix thoroughly by stirring, stimulate, incite.

**stirrup** /'stɪrəp/ n. support for rider's foot, suspended by strap from saddle. **stirrup-cup** drink offered to person about to depart, orig. on horseback; **stirrup-pump** small portable water-pump with stirrup-shaped foot-rest.

**stitch** 1 n. single pass of needle, or result of this, in sewing or knitting or crochet etc.; thread between two needle-holes; particular method of sewing or knitting etc.; least bit of clothing;

**stoat** 554 **stone**

acute pain in side induced by running etc. **2** v. sew, make stitches (in). **3 in stitches** colloq. laughing uncontrollably.

**stoat** n. ermine, esp. in its brown summer coat.

**stobie** /'stəʊbi/ n. S Aus. (in full **stobie pole**) concrete and metal pole carrying electricity lines.

**stock 1** n. store of goods etc. ready for sale or distribution; supply of things for use; equipment or raw material for trade; farm animals or implements; capital of business company; shares in this; money lent to government at fixed interest; one's reputation or popularity; line of ancestry; liquid made by stewing bones and vegetables etc., as basis for soup etc.; base or support or handle for implement or machine; plant into which graft is inserted; fragrant garden plant; in pl. timbers on which ship rests while building; in pl. hist. wooden framework with holes for feet, where offenders were confined as public punishment; wide band of material worn round neck. **2** a. kept regularly in stock for sale or use; commonly used, constantly recurring. **3** v.t. keep (goods) in stock; equip with goods or requisites etc. **4 stock and station agent** Aus. & NZ dealer in rural properties and stock, supplier of provisions to rural areas; **stockbroker** person who buys and sells stocks on commission; **stock-car** car used in racing where deliberate bumping is allowed; **stock exchange** place where stocks and shares are publicly bought and sold, dealers working there; **stock-in-trade** all requisites for particular trade or occupation etc.; **stockjobber** member of stock exchange dealing in stocks on his own account; **stockman** man employed to look after livestock; **stock-market** stock exchange, transactions on this; **stockpile** reserve supply of raw materials or commodities etc., (v.) accumulate stockpile (of); **stock-pot** cooking-pot in which stock is made and kept; **stockrider** Aus. man employed to ride after stock; **stock-route** Aus. right of way for travelling stock; **stock-still** motionless; **stock-taking** making inventory of goods in shop etc.; **stock up** provide with or get stocks or supplies; **stock up with** gather stock of (food, fuel, etc.); **stockyard** enclosure for sorting or temporary keeping of cattle etc.; **take stock** make inventory of merchandise etc. in hand, make review or estimate (of).

**stockade** /stɒ'keɪd/ **1** n. line of upright stakes as a defence etc. **2** v.t. fortify with stockade.

**stockinet** /stɒkə'net/ (also **-nette**) n. elastic knitted material.

**stocking** /'stɒkɪŋ/ n. covering for foot and all or part of leg, usu. knitted of nylon or silk or wool etc. **stocking mask** nylon stocking worn over head as criminal's disguise; **stocking-stitch** knitting-stitch of alternate rows of plain and purl.

**stockist** /'stɒkɪst/ n. person who stocks specified goods for sale.

**stocky** /'stɒkɪ/ a. short and strongly built.

**stodge** n. food esp. of thick heavy kind; unimaginative person or work.

**stodgy** /'stɒdʒɪ/ a. (of food) heavy, filling; dull, heavy, uninteresting.

**stoic** /'stəʊɪk/ n. person having great self-control in adversity. **stoical** a.; **stoicism** n.

**stoke** v. (often with up) feed and tend (furnace, fire, etc.); colloq. consume food esp. steadily and in large quantities. **stokehold** place where steamer's fires are tended; **stokehole** space for stokers in front of furnace.

**stoker** /'stəʊkə(r)/ n. person who stokes furnace esp. of ship or locomotive.

**stole**[1] n. woman's long garment like scarf worn over shoulders; strip of silk etc. worn as vestment by priest.

**stole**[2] past of **steal**.

**stolen** p.p. of **steal**.

**stolid** /'stɒlɪd/ a. slow to feel or show feeling; not easily excited or moved. **stolidity** n.

**stomach** /'stʌmək/ **1** n. internal organ in which food is digested; lower front of body; appetite or inclination etc. for. **2** v.t. endure, tolerate. **3 stomach-pump** syringe for emptying stomach or forcing liquid into it.

**stomp** n. lively jazz dance usu. with heavy stamping. **2** v. tread heavily (on); dance stomp.

**stone 1** n. solid non-metallic mineral matter of which rock is made; small

**stonker** piece of this; piece of stone of definite shape or purpose; hard morbid concretion in kidney etc.; hard case of kernel in some fruits; precious stone; (*pl.* same) unit of weight (14 lb.). **2** *a.* made of stone. **3** *v.t.* pelt with stones; rid (fruit) of stone(s). **4 Stone Age** stage of civilization marked by use of stone implements and weapons; **stone-cold** completely cold; **stonecrop** creeping plant; **stone-dead** completely dead; **stone-deaf** completely deaf; **stonefruit** fruit with flesh or pulp enclosing stone; **stone's throw** short distance; **stonewall** obstruct by evasive answers, *Crick.* bat with excessive caution; **stoneware** hard dense pottery of flinty clay; **stonework** masonry.

**stonker** /'stɒŋkə(r)/ *v.t. Aus. sl.* baffle; make useless; beat; tire or wear out.

**stony** /'stəʊnɪ/ *a.* full of stones; hard or unfeeling; unresponsive. **stony-broke** *sl.* entirely without money.

**stood** *past* & *p.p.* of **stand**.

**stooge** /stuːdʒ/ **1** *n.* person acting as foil for comedian etc.; subordinate, puppet. **2** *v.i.* move *about* or *around* esp. in aimless way; act as stooge.

**stool** /stuːl/ *n.* seat without arms or back; footstool; faeces; root or stump of felled tree. **stool-pigeon** decoy, police informer.

**stoop**[1] /stuːp/ **1** *v.* bend down; carry head and shoulders bowed forward; deign or condescend (*to*). **2** *n.* stooping posture.

**stoop**[2] /stuːp/ *n. US* porch or small veranda or steps in front of house.

**stop 1** *v.* put an end to progress or motion or operation etc. (of); effectively hinder or prevent; discontinue; come to an end; (cause to) cease action; defeat; *colloq.* remain or stay for short time; block or close up (hole, leak, etc., often with *up*); not permit or supply as usual; put filling in (tooth); *Mus.* obtain desired pitch from (string of violin etc.) by pressing at appropriate point with finger. **2** *n.* stopping or being stopped; place where bus or train etc., regularly stops; sign to show pause in written matter; device for stopping motion at particular point; *Mus.* change of pitch effected by stopping string; (in organ) set of pipes of one character, knob etc. operating these; *Photog.* etc. diaphragm, effective diameter of lens, device reducing this; plosive sound. **3 pull out all the stops** make extreme effort; **stopbank** *Aus.* embankment to prevent overflow of a river; **stopcock** externally operated valve to regulate flow in pipe etc.; **stop dead** stop abruptly; **stopgap** temporary substitute; **stop off, over,** break one's journey; **stop-press** late news inserted in newspaper after printing has begun; **stop short** stop abruptly; **stop-watch** watch with mechanism for instantly starting and stopping it, used in timing of races etc.

**stoppage** /'stɒpɪdʒ/ *n.* condition of being blocked or stopped.

**stopper** /'stɒpə(r)/ *n.* plug for closing bottle etc.

**stopping** /'stɒpɪŋ/ *n.* filling for tooth.

**storage** /'stɔːrɪdʒ/ *n.* storing of goods or data etc.; method of or space for or cost of storing. **storage battery** accumulator; **storage heater** electric heater accumulating heat outside peak hours for later release.

**store 1** *n.* quantity of something ready to be drawn on; in *pl.* articles of particular kind or for special purpose; in *pl.* supply of things needed, stocks, reserves; storehouse; large shop selling goods of many different kinds; *US* shop; device in computer for storing retrievable data etc. **2** *v.t.* put in store; lay up for future use; stock or provide with something useful. **3 in store** in reserve, to come, waiting, *for*; **storehouse** place where things are stored; **storekeeper** person in charge of stores; *US* shopkeeper; **store-room** place where household or other supplies are kept.

**storey** /'stɔːrɪ/ *n.* each stage or portion into which building is divided horizontally.

**stork** *n.* large long-legged wading bird.

**storm 1** *n.* violent disturbance of atmosphere, with high winds and freq. rain and thunder etc.; violent disturbance or tumult in human affairs; heavy discharge or shower (*of* blows, abuse, etc.); assault on (and capture of) fortified place. **2** *v.* rage, be violent; bluster; rush violently; take by storm. **3 storm-centre** comparatively calm central area of cyclonic storm, centre round which storm of controversy etc.

**stormy** rages; **storm-cloud** heavy rain-cloud; **storm troops** shock troops, Nazi political militia; **take by storm** take by assault, quickly captivate.

**stormy** /'stɔːmi/ *a.* of or affected by storm(s); violent, full of outbursts.

**story** /'stɔːri/ *n.* account of real or fictitious events; narrative, tale, anecdote; course of life of person or institution etc.; plot of novel or play etc.; article in newspaper, material for this; *colloq.* lie. **story-teller** person who tells or writes stories, *colloq.* liar.

**stoup** /stuːp/ *n.* holy-water basin; *arch.* flagon, beaker.

**stoush** /staʊʃ/ *Aus. sl.* **1** *v.t.* fight, thrash. **2** *n.* a fight; fighting.

**stout** /staʊt/ **1** *a.* rather fat, corpulent, of considerable thickness or strength; undaunted, resolute. **2** *n.* strong dark type of beer.

**stove**[1] *n.* enclosed apparatus to contain burning fuel or consume electricity etc. for heating or cooking etc. **stove-enamel** heat-proof enamel; **stove-pipe** pipe carrying off smoke etc. from stove.

**stove**[2] *past* & *p.p.* of **stave**.

**stow** /stəʊ/ *v.t.* pack (away) esp. closely or compactly; *sl.* desist from. **stow away** conceal oneself on ship etc., esp. to avoid paying fare; **stowaway** person who stows away.

**stowage** /'stəʊɪdʒ/ *n.* stowing; place for this.

**straddle** /'stræd(ə)l/ **1** *v.* stand or sit across with legs wide apart; spread legs wide apart; drop shots or bombs short of and beyond (target). **2** *n.* act of straddling.

**strafe** /strɑːf/ **1** *v.t.* bombard; harass with gunfire. **2** *n.* act of strafing.

**straggle** /'stræg(ə)l/ **1** *v.i.* lack or lose compactness or tidiness; stray from main body, be dispersed or scattered. **2** *n.* straggling group. **3 straggly** *a.*

**straight** /streɪt/ **1** *a.* without curve or bend or flare, not crooked or curly; direct, successive; level, tidy, in proper order or place or condition; honest, candid; unmodified; undiluted; *sl.* conventional, respectable, heterosexual. **2** *n.* straight part of something, esp. concluding stretch of racecourse; straight condition; *sl.* straight person. **3** *adv.* in a straight line, direct; in right direction,

correctly. **4 go straight** live honestly after being criminal; **straight away** immediately; **straight face** serious expression, esp. avoiding smile though amused; **straight fight** contest between two candidates only; **straightforward** honest, open, presenting no complications; **straight man** performer who says things for comedian to make jokes about; **straight off** *colloq.* immediately, without hesitation etc.; **straight out** frankly, outspokenly.

**straighten** /'streɪt(ə)n/ *v.* make or become straight. **straighten up** stand erect after bending.

**strain**[1] **1** *v.* stretch tightly; make or become taut or tense; exercise (*oneself*, senses, powers, etc.) intensely or excessively; press to extremes, make intense effort; distort from true intention or meaning; overtask or injure by overuse or excessive demands; clear (liquid) of solid matter by passing it through sieve etc.; in *p.p.* constrained, artificial. **2** *n.* act of straining; force exerted in straining; injury caused by straining muscle etc.; severe demand on resources, exertion needed to meet this; snatch or spell of music or poetry; tone or tendency in speech or writing.

**strain**[2] *n.* breed or stock of animals or plants etc.; moral tendency as part of character.

**strainer** /'streɪnə(r)/ *n.* utensil for straining liquids.

**strait 1** *n.* narrow water-passage connecting two large bodies of water; in *pl.* difficult position, need. **2** *a. arch.* narrow, strict. **3 strait-jacket** strong garment put on violent person to confine arms, *fig.* restrictive measures; **strait-laced** severely virtuous, puritanical.

**straiten** /'streɪt(ə)n/ *v.t.* restrict; in *p.p.* of or marked by poverty.

**strand**[1] **1** *v.* run aground; (in *p.p.*) in difficulties, without money or means of transport. **2** *n.* margin of sea or river etc., esp. foreshore.

**strand**[2] *n.* any of strings or wires twisted together to form rope etc.; constituent filament of necklace or hair etc.; *fig.* element in character, theme in story, etc.

**strange** /streɪndʒ/ *a.* unusual, peculiar, surprising, eccentric; unfamiliar, alien, foreign; unaccustomed *to*, not at ease.

**stranger** /ˈstreɪndʒə(r)/ *n.* person in place or company etc. that he does not know or belong to; person one does not know.

**strangle** /ˈstræŋg(ə)l/ *v.t.* kill by external compression of throat; hinder growth of by overcrowding; suppress. **stranglehold** deadly grip (usu. *fig.*).

**strangulate** /ˈstræŋgjəleɪt/ *v.t.* constrict so as to prevent circulation or passage of fluid.

**strangulation** /ˌstræŋgjəˈleɪʃ(ə)n/ *n.* strangling; strangulating.

**strap** 1 *n.* flat strip of leather etc., esp. with buckle etc., for holding things together; loop for grasping to steady oneself in moving vehicle. 2 *v.t.* secure or bind (*up*) with strap; thrash with strap.

**strapping** /ˈstræpɪŋ/ 1 *a.* stalwart; tall and strong. 2 *n.* strip(s) of adhesive plaster.

**strata** *pl.* of **stratum**.

**stratagem** /ˈstrætədʒəm/ *n.* cunning plan or scheme; trick.

**strategic** /strəˈtiːdʒɪk/ *a.* of or serving the ends of strategy; (of materials) essential in war; (of bombing) designed to disorganize or demoralize the enemy; (of nuclear weapons etc.) able to reach the enemy's home territory rather than for use at close quarters.

**strategy** /ˈstrætədʒiː/ *n.* art of war; art of planning and directing larger movements and operations of campaign or war; plan of action or policy in business or politics etc. **strategist** *n.*

**strathspey** /stræθˈspeɪ/ *n.* slow Sc. country dance; music for this.

**stratify** /ˈstrætɪfaɪ/ *v.* arrange in strata or layers etc. **stratification** *n.*

**stratosphere** /ˈstætəsfɪə(r)/ *n.* region of atmosphere above troposphere.

**stratum** /ˈstrɑːtəm/ *n.* (*pl.* **-ta**) layer of rock; layer of deposits in excavation etc.; social grade or class etc.

**straw** *n.* dry cut stalks of various cereals; single stalk or piece of straw; hollow tube for sucking drink through; insignificant thing; pale yellow colour. **straw vote** unofficial ballot as test of opinion.

**strawberry** /ˈstrɔːbəriː/ *n.* pulpy red fruit having surface studded with yellow seeds; plant bearing this. **strawberry-mark** reddish birthmark.

**stray** 1 *v.i.* wander from the right place, become separated from one's companions etc.; go astray; deviate. 2 *n.* strayed domestic animal; homeless friendless person. 3 *a.* strayed; isolated, occasional.

**streak** 1 *n.* thin irregular line or band of different colour or substance from surface etc. in which it appears; flash of lightning; strain, element, trait. 2 *v.* mark with streaks; go at full speed; *colloq.* run naked through public place.

**streaky** /ˈstriːkiː/ *a.* marked with streaks; (of bacon) with fat and lean in layers or streaks.

**stream** 1 *n.* body of running water, esp. small river; current or flow; group of schoolchildren selected as being of similar ability. 2 *v.* flow or move as or in stream; run with liquid; emit stream of; float or wave in wind; arrange (schoolchildren) in streams. 3 **on stream** in active operation or production.

**streamer** /ˈstriːmə(r)/ *n.* long narrow flag; long narrow ribbon of paper.

**streamline** /ˈstriːmlaɪn/ *v.t.* give form which presents least resistance to motion; make simple or more efficient or better organized.

**street** *n.* road in town or village with houses on each side. **man in the street** ordinary person; **on the streets** living as prostitute; **streetcar** *US* tram; **street-walker** prostitute seeking customers in street.

**strength** *n.* quality or extent or manner of being strong; what makes one strong; *Aus.* essence, significance; number of persons present or available. **on the strength of** relying on, arguing from.

**strengthen** /ˈstreŋθ(ə)n/ *v.* make or become stronger.

**strenuous** /ˈstrenjuːəs/ *a.* making or requiring great exertions, energetic.

**streptococcus** /streptəˈkɒkəs/ *n.* (*pl.* **-cocci** /-ˈkɒkaɪ/) bacterium causing serious infections. **streptococcal** *a.*

**streptomycin** /streptəˈmaɪsən/ *n.* an antibiotic drug.

**stress** 1 *n.* pressure, tension; quantity measuring this; demand on physical or mental energy; emphasis. 2 *v.t.* lay

**stress** on, accent, emphasize; subject to stress.

**stressful** /'stresfəl/ *a.* causing stress.

**stretch** 1 *v.* draw or be drawn or admit of being drawn out into greater length or size; make or become taut; place or lie at full length or spread out; extend limbs to tighten muscles; have specified length or extension; extend; strain or exert to utmost or beyond legitimate extent; exaggerate. 2 *n.* stretching or being stretched; continuous expanse or tract or period; *sl.* term of imprisonment. 3 **at a stretch** without intermission, continuously; **stretch one's legs** exercise oneself by walking; **stretch out** extend (hand, foot, etc.), prolong, last for longer period; **stretch a point** agree to something not normally allowed.

**stretcher** /'stretʃə(r)/ *n.* oblong frame with handles at each end for carrying sick or injured etc. person; any of various devices for stretching; brick etc. laid with length in direction of wall.

**stretchy** /'stretʃɪ/ *a. colloq.* able or tending to stretch.

**strew** *v.t.* (*p.p.* **strewn** or **strewed**) scatter over surface; cover (surface etc.) *with* small objects scattered.

**striated** /straɪ'eɪtəd/ *a.* marked with slight ridges or furrows etc. **striation** *n.*

**stricken** 1 *arch. p.p.* of **strike**. 2 *a.* afflicted with disease or grief etc.

**strict** *a.* precisely limited or defined; without exception or deviation; requiring complete obedience or exact performance.

**stricture** /'strɪktʃə(r)/ *n.* (usu. in *pl.*) adverse criticism, critical remark.

**stride** 1 *v.* (*past* **strode**; *p.p.* **stridden**) walk with long steps; pass over with one step; bestride. 2 *n.* single walking or running step; distance covered by long step; (usu. in *pl.*) progress; in *pl. Aus. colloq.* trousers. 3 **take in one's stride** manage without difficulty.

**strident** /'straɪd(ə)nt/ *a.* loud and harsh. **stridency** *n.*

**strife** *n.* conflict, struggle, dispute; *Aus.* trouble of any kind.

**strike** 1 *v.* (*past* **struck**; *p.p.* **struck** or *arch.* exc. in *comb.* **stricken**) subject to impact, deliver (blow) or inflict blow on; come or bring sharply into contact with, propel or divert with blow; (cause to) penetrate; ignite (match) or produce (sparks) by rubbing; make (coin) by stamping; produce (musical note) by striking; (of clock) indicate (time) by sounding of bell etc.; (of time) be indicated thus; afflict; cause to become suddenly; reach or achieve; agree on (bargain); put oneself theatrically into (attitude); discover or come across; find (oil) by drilling; come to attention of or appear to; (of employees) engage in strike, cease work as protest; lower or take down (flag, tent, etc.); take specified direction. 2 *n.* act of striking; employees' concerted refusal to work until some grievance is remedied; similar refusal to participate in other expected activity; sudden find or success; attack, esp. from the air. 3 **on strike** taking part in industrial strike; **strikebreaker** person working or engaged in place of striker; **strike home** deal effective blow; **strike off** remove with stroke, delete; **strike out** hit out, act vigorously, delete; **strike pay** allowance paid to strikers by trade unions; **strike up** start (acquaintance, conversation) casually, begin playing (tune etc.).

**striker** /'straɪkə(r)/ *n.* person or thing that strikes; employee on strike.

**striking** /'straɪkɪŋ/ *a.* noticeable, impressive.

**Strine** 1 *n.* comic transliterations of Aus. speech; *loosely* Aus. English. 2 *a.* Australian.

**string** 1 *n.* twine or fine cord; length of this or some other material serving to tie or attach or lace or activate puppet etc.; piece of catgut or wire etc. on musical instrument, producing note by vibration; in *pl.* stringed instruments in orchestra etc.; in *pl.* awkward condition attached to offer etc.; set of things strung together; group of racehorses trained at particular stable; tough fibre etc. 2 *v.* (*past & p.p.* **strung**) supply with string(s); thread on string; connect or put together or arrange in series or row(s) etc.; remove strings from (beanpod etc.). 3 **string along** *colloq.* deceive; **string-course** raised horizontal band of bricks etc. on building; **string up** hang up on strings, kill by hanging.

**stringed** /strɪŋd/ a. (of musical instrument) having strings.

**stringent** /'strɪndʒ(ə)nt/ a. strict, binding, requiring exact performance. **stringency** n.

**stringer** /'strɪŋə(r)/ n. longitudinal structural member in framework esp. of ship or aircraft; newspaper correspondent not on regular staff.

**stringy** /-ɪ/ a. fibrous; like string. **stringybark** any of a number of Aus. eucalypts with tough fibrous bark.

**strip**[1] v. remove clothes or covering from, undress; deprive (person) of property or titles; leave bare of accessories etc.; remove old paint etc. from; damage thread of (screw). 2 n. act of stripping, esp. of undressing in striptease; *colloq.* clothes worn by member of sports team etc. 3 **strip club** club where strip-tease is performed; **strip-tease** entertainment in which performer gradually undresses before audience.

**strip**[2] n. long narrow piece. **strip cartoon** comic strip; **strip light** tubular fluorescent light; **tear a strip off** (a person) *Aus. sl.* rebuke him.

**stripe** n. long narrow band differing in colour or texture from surface on either side; *Mil.* chevron etc. indicating rank; *arch.* (usu. in *pl.*) blow with scourge or lash. **stripy** a.

**striped** /straɪpt/ a. having stripes.

**stripling** /'strɪplɪŋ/ n. youth not fully grown.

**stripper** /'strɪpə(r)/ n. device or solvent for removing paint etc.; performer of strip-tease.

**strive** v.i. (*past* **strove**; *p.p.* **striven** /'strɪv(ə)n/) try hard; struggle or contend *against*.

**strobe** n. *colloq.* stroboscope.

**stroboscope** /'strəʊbəskəʊp/ n. lamp producing regular intermittent flashes. **stroboscopic** /-'skɒp-/ a.

**strode** *past* of **stride**.

**stroke** 1 n. act of striking; sudden disabling attack esp. of apoplexy; action or movement esp. as one of series or in game etc.; slightest such action; effort or action of specified kind; sound made by striking clock etc.; movement in one direction of pen or paintbrush etc.; detail contributing to general effect; mode or action of moving oar; mode of moving limbs in swimming; oarsman nearest stern, who sets time of stroke; act or spell of stroking. 2 v.t. pass hand gently along surface of; act as stroke of (boat, crew).

**stroll** /strəʊl/ 1 v.i. walk in leisurely fashion. 2 n. leisurely walk. 3 **strolling players** actors etc. going from place to place performing.

**strong** 1 a. physically or morally or mentally powerful or vigorous or robust; powerful in numbers or equipment etc.; performed with muscular strength; difficult to capture or break into or escape from etc.; energetic, effective, decided; powerfully affecting senses or mind etc.; (of drink) with large proportion of alcohol or flavouring ingredient etc.; (of verb) forming inflexions by vowel change in root syllable. 2 *adv.* strongly, vigorously. 3 **going strong** thriving; **strong-arm** use of force; **strong-box** strongly made box for valuables; **stronghold** fortress, citadel, centre of support for a cause etc.; **strong language** swearing; **strong-minded** with vigorous or determined mind; **strong point** fortified position, *fig.* thing at which one excels; **strong-room** strongly-built room for valuables; **strong suit** suit at cards in which one can take tricks, *fig.* thing in which one excels.

**strontium** /'strɒntɪəm/ n. soft silver-white metallic element. **strontium 90** radioactive isotope of this.

**strop** 1 n. device, esp. strip of leather, for sharpening razors. 2 v.t. sharpen on or with strop.

**stroppy** /'strɒpɪ/ a. *sl.* bad-tempered, awkward to deal with.

**strove** *past* of **strive**.

**struck** *past* & *p.p.* of **strike**.

**structuralism** /'strʌktʃərəlɪz(ə)m/ n. doctrine that structure rather than function is important. **structuralist** a. & n.

**structure** /'strʌktʃə(r)/ 1 n. way in which thing is constructed; supporting framework or essential parts; thing constructed; complex whole. 2 v.t. give structure to, organize. 3 **structural** a.

**strudel** /'struːd(ə)l/ n. confection of thin pastry filled esp. with apple.

**struggle** /'strʌg(ə)l/ 1 v.i. throw one's limbs or body about in violent effort

**strum** to get free; make great efforts under difficulties; contend *with* or *against* etc.; make one's way with difficulty. **2** *n.* act or period of struggling; hard or confused contest.

**strum 1** *v.* play on (stringed or keyboard instrument) esp. carelessly or unskilfully. **2** *n.* strumming sound.

**strumpet** /'strʌmpət/ *n. arch.* prostitute.

**strung** *past* & *p.p.* of **string**.

**strut 1** *n.* bar inserted in framework to resist pressure; strutting gait. **2** *v.* walk in stiff pompous way; brace with strut(s).

**'struth** /struːθ/ *int. colloq.* exclamation of surprise.

**strychnine** /'strɪkniːn/ *n.* highly poisonous vegetable alkaloid.

**stub 1** *n.* remnant of pencil or cigarette etc., after use; counterfoil of cheque or receipt etc.; stump, stunted tail, etc. **2** *v.t.* strike (one's toe) against something; (usu. with *out*) extinguish (cigarette etc.) by pressing lighted end against something.

**stubble** /'stʌb(ə)l/ *n.* cut stalks of cereals left sticking up after harvest; short stubble-like growth of hair, esp. on unshaven face. **stubbly** *a.*

**stubborn** /'stʌbən/ *a.* obstinate, inflexible; intractable.

**stubby** /'stʌbɪ/ **1** *a.* short and thick. **2** *n. Aus.* small squat beer bottle.

**stucco** /'stʌkəʊ/ **1** *n.* (*pl.* **-oes**) plaster or cement for coating walls or moulding into architectural decorations. **2** *v.t.* coat with stucco.

**stuck** *past* & *p.p.* of **stick**. **get stuck into** *sl.* start in earnest; **stuck for** at a loss for, needing; **stuck-up** *colloq.* conceited, snobbish; **stuck with** *colloq.* unable to get rid of.

**stud**[1] **1** *n.* projecting nail-head or similar knob on surface; device for fixing separate collar to shirt. **2** *v.t.* set with studs; in *p.p.* thickly set or strewn *with* (jewels, stars, etc.).

**stud**[2] *n.* number of horses kept for breeding etc.; place where these are kept; stallion; stud poker. **stud-book** book giving pedigrees of thoroughbred horses; **stud-farm** place where horses are bred; **stud poker** poker with betting after dealing of successive cards face up.

**student** /'stjuːd(ə)nt/ *n.* person who is studying, esp. at university or other place of higher education; *attrib.* studying in order to become (nurse, teacher, etc.).

**studied** /'stʌdɪd/ *a.* deliberate, intentional, artificial.

**studio** /'stjuːdɪəʊ/ *n.* (*pl.* **-dios**) workroom of sculptor or painter or photographer etc.; room or premises used for transmission of broadcasts etc. or making films or recordings etc. **studio couch** couch that can be converted into a bed.

**studious** /'stjuːdɪəs/ *a.* assiduous in study or reading; painstaking, deliberate.

**study** /'stʌdɪ/ **1** *n.* giving one's attention to acquiring information esp. from books; in *pl.* pursuit of knowledge; piece of work, esp. in painting, done as exercise or preliminary experiment; careful examination or observation *of*; *Mus.* composition designed to develop player's skill; room used for reading or writing etc.; thing that is or deserves to be investigated. **2** *v.* make object of study; apply oneself to study; scrutinize; devote time and thought to understanding subject etc. or assuring desired result.

**stuff 1** *n.* material that thing is made of; substance or things of uncertain kind or quality or not needing to be specified; particular knowledge or activity; woollen fabric; trash, nonsense. **2** *v.* pack, cram; fill out skin to restore original shape of (bird, animal, etc.); fill (receptacle, cushion-cover, etc.) *with*; fill (inside of bird, piece of meat, etc.) with minced seasoning etc. before cooking; eat greedily, overeat *oneself*; push, esp. hastily or clumsily; block *up*.

**stuffing** /'stʌfɪŋ/ *n.* padding used for stuffing cushions; savoury mixture used to stuff fowls etc.

**stuffy** /'stʌfɪ/ *a.* lacking ventilation; close, oppressive; old-fashioned or narrow-minded.

**stultify** /'stʌltɪfaɪ/ *v.t.* make ineffective or useless; reduce to foolishness or absurdity. **stultification** *n.*

**stumble** /'stʌmb(ə)l/ **1** *v.i.* lurch forward or have partial fall from catching or striking foot etc.; make blunder(s) in speaking etc.; come accidentally *across* or (*up*)*on*. **2** *n.* act of stumbling. **3 stumbling-block** obstacle, circumstance causing difficulty or hesitation.

**stumer** /'stu:mə(r)/ *n. Aus. sl.* **come a stumer** be disappointed in the outcome of a race or project.

**stump 1** *n.* projecting remnant of felled or fallen tree; part remaining of broken branch or tooth or amputated limb etc.; stub; *Crick.* one of 3 uprights of wicket. **2** *v.* be too difficult for, cause to be at a loss; *Crick.* put batsman out by touching stumps with ball while he is out of his crease; walk stiffly or clumsily or noisily; traverse (district) making political speeches. **3 stump-jump plough** *Aus.* special plough used in land not cleared of stumps; **stump up** *sl.* produce or pay over money required.

**stumpy** /'stʌmpi/ *a.* stocky, short and thick.

**stun** *v.t.* knock senseless; stupefy, bewilder, shock.

**stung** *past* & *p.p.* of **sting**.

**stunk** *past* & *p.p.* of **stink**.

**stunner** /'stʌnə(r)/ *n. colloq.* stunning person or thing.

**stunning** /'stʌnɪŋ/ *a. colloq.* extremely good or attractive.

**stunt**[1] *v.t.* retard growth or development of, dwarf, cramp.

**stunt**[2] *colloq.* **1** *n.* something unusual done to attract attention; trick or daring manœuvre. **2** *v.i.* perform stunts. **3 stunt man** man employed to take actor's place in performing dangerous stunts.

**stupefy** /'stju:pəfaɪ/ *v.t.* make stupid or insensible; astonish. **stupefaction** *n.*

**stupendous** /stju:'pendəs/ *a.* amazing, of vast size or importance.

**stupid** /'stju:pɪd/ *a.* unintelligent; slow-witted; uninteresting; in state of stupor. **stupidity** *n.*

**stupor** /'stju:pə(r)/ *n.* dazed or torpid state; utter amazement.

**sturdy** /'stɜ:di/ *a.* robust, hardy, strongly built.

**sturgeon** /'stɜ:dʒ(ə)n/ *n.* large edible fish yielding caviare.

**stutter** /'stʌtə(r)/ *v.* & *n.* stammer.

**sty**[1] /staɪ/ *n.* enclosure for pigs; filthy room or dwelling.

**sty**[2] /staɪ/ *n.* inflamed swelling on edge of eyelid.

**Stygian** /'stɪdʒɪən/ *a.* of or like Styx or Hades; murky, gloomy.

**style** /staɪl/ **1** *n.* kind, sort; manner of writing or speaking or doing; distinctive manner of person or school or period; correct way of designating person or thing; superior quality or manner; fashion in dress etc.; implement for scratching or engraving; *Bot.* narrow extension of ovary supporting stigma. **2** *v.t.* design or make etc. in particular style; designate in specified way.

**stylish** /'staɪlɪʃ/ *a.* fashionable, elegant.

**stylist** /'staɪlɪst/ *n.* person having or aiming at good style in writing etc.; person who styles hair.

**stylistic** /staɪ'lɪstɪk/ *a.* of literary or artistic style.

**stylize** /'staɪlaɪz/ *v.t.* (usu. in *p.p.*) make conform to rules of conventional style, conventionalize. **stylization** *n.*

**stylus** /'staɪləs/ *n.* (*pl.* **-li** /laɪ/) needle-like point for producing or following groove in gramophone record; ancient pointed writing-implement.

**stymie** /'staɪmi/ *v.t.* obstruct, thwart.

**styptic** /'stɪptɪk/ **1** *a.* serving to check bleeding. **2** *n.* styptic substance.

**suave** /swɑ:v/ *a.* urbane, gracious, refined. **suavity** *n.*

**sub** *colloq.* **1** *n.* submarine; subscription; substitute; sub-editor. **2** *v.* act as substitute; sub-edit.

**sub-** *in comb.* under, below; more or less, roughly, not quite, on the borders of; subordinate(ly), secondary, further.

**subaltern** /'sʌbəlt(ə)n/ *n. Mil.* officer of rank next below captain.

**subaqua** /sʌb'ækwə/ *a.* (of sport etc.) taking place under water.

**subatomic** /sʌbə'tɒmɪk/ *a.* occurring in or smaller than an atom.

**subcommittee** /'sʌbkəmɪti:/ *n.* committee formed from main committee for special purpose.

**subconscious** /sʌb'kɒnʃəs/ **1** *n.* part of mind that is not fully conscious but is able to influence actions etc. **2** *a.* of the subconscious.

**subcontinent** /sʌb'kɒntɪnənt/ *n.* land-mass of great extent not classed as continent.

**subcontract 1** /'sʌbkɒntrækt/ *n.* arrangement by which person who has contracted to do work arranges for it to be done by others. **2** /sʌbkən'trækt/

**subculture** /ˈsʌbkʌltʃə(r)/ n. social group or its culture within a larger culture.

**subcutaneous** /ˌsʌbkjuːˈteɪnɪəs/ a. under the skin.

**subdivide** /ˌsʌbdəˈvaɪd/ v. divide again after first division.

**subdivision** /ˌsʌbdəˈvɪʒ(ə)n/ n. sub-dividing; subordinate division.

**subdue** /səbˈdjuː/ v.t. conquer, suppress; tame; soften, tone down.

**sub-edit** /sʌbˈedɪt/ v.t. act as sub-editor of.

**sub-editor** /sʌbˈedɪtə(r)/ n. assistant editor; person who prepares material for printing in newspaper or book etc. **sub-editorial** a.

**sub-heading** /sʌbˈhedɪŋ/ n. subordinate division of subject etc.; subordinate heading or title.

**subhuman** /sʌbˈhjuːmən/ a. less than human; not fully human.

**subject 1** /ˈsʌbdʒɪkt/ n. theme of discussion or description or representation or music, matter (to be) studied or thought about; person under political rule; member of State or of subject State; circumstance or person or thing that gives occasion *for* specified feeling or action; branch of study; *Gram.* etc. thing about which something is predicated; thinking or feeling entity, conscious self; person with specified usu. undesirable bodily or mental tendency. **2** /ˈsʌbdʒɪkt/ a. under government; (with *to*) conditional upon; owing obedience *to*; liable or exposed or prone *to*. **3** /ˈsʌbdʒɪkt/ adv. (with *to*) conditionally upon, on the assumption of. **4** /səbˈdʒekt/ v.t. expose or make liable *to*; subdue (nation etc.). **5 subject-matter** matter dealt with in book or lawsuit etc. **6 subjection** n.

**subjective** /səbˈdʒektɪv/ a. of or due to the consciousness or thinking or percipient subject as opp. real or external things, not objective, imaginary; *Gram.* of the subject. **subjectivity** n.

**subjoin** /səbˈdʒɔɪn/ v.t. add at the end.

**sub judice** /sʌb ˈdʒuːdəsɪ/ under judicial consideration, not yet decided. [L]

**subjugate** /ˈsʌbdʒəgeɪt/ v.t. conquer, bring into subjection. **subjugation** n.

**subjunctive** /səbˈdʒʌŋktɪv/ *Gram.* **1** a. (of mood) expressing wish or supposition or possibility. **2** n. subjunctive mood or form.

**sublease 1** /ˈsʌbliːs/ n. lease granted to subtenant. **2** /sʌbˈliːs/ v.t. lease by sublease.

**sublet** /sʌbˈlet/ v.t. (*past* & *p.p.* **-let**) lease to subtenant.

**sublimate 1** /ˈsʌblɪmeɪt/ v.t. divert energy of (primitive impulse etc.) into culturally higher activity; sublime (substance); refine, purify. **2** /ˈsʌblɪmət/ n. sublimated substance. **3 sublimation** n.

**sublime** /səˈblaɪm/ **1** a. of most exalted kind; inspiring awe. **2** v.t. convert (substance) from solid into vapour by heat (and usu. allow to solidify again); (of substance) undergo this process; make sublime. **3 sublimity** /-ˈlɪm-/ n.

**subliminal** /səbˈlɪmən(ə)l/ a. *Psych.* below threshold of consciousness; too faint or rapid to be consciously perceived.

**sub-machine-gun** /sʌbməˈʃiːngʌn/ n. lightweight machine-gun held by hand.

**submarine** /ˌsʌbməˈriːn/ **1** a. existing or occurring or done below surface of sea. **2** n. vessel which can be submerged and navigated under water.

**submerge** /səbˈmɜːdʒ/ v. place or go beneath water. **submergence** n.; **submersion** n.

**submersible** /səbˈmɜːsəb(ə)l/ **1** a. capable of submerging. **2** n. submersible vehicle.

**submicroscopic** /ˌsʌbmaɪkrəˈskɒpɪk/ a. too small to be seen by microscope.

**submission** /səbˈmɪʃ(ə)n/ n. submitting or being submitted; thing submitted; submissive attitude etc.

**submissive** /səbˈmɪsɪv/ a. willing to submit; unresisting, meek.

**submit** /səbˈmɪt/ v. surrender (*oneself*) to the control or authority of another, cease to resist or oppose; present for consideration or decision; subject *to* a process or treatment.

**subnormal** /sʌbˈnɔːm(ə)l/ a. less than normal; below normal.

**subordinate 1** /səˈbɔːdənət/ a. of inferior importance or rank, secondary, subservient. **2** /səˈbɔːdɪnət/ n. subordinate person. **3** /səˈbɔːdɪmeɪt/ v.t. make subordinate; treat or regard as of minor importance. **4 subordinate clause**

**suborn** /sə'bɔːn/ v.t. induce esp. by bribery to commit perjury or other crime.

**subpoena** /səb'piːnə/ 1 n. writ commanding person's attendance in law-court. 2 v.t. (past & p.p. **-poenaed** /-'piːnəd/) serve subpoena on.

**sub rosa** /sʌb 'rəʊzə/ (done) in confidence or in secret. [L]

**subscribe** /səb'skraɪb/ v. pay (specified sum) esp. regularly for membership of an organization or receipt of a publication etc.; agree to pay (such sum); contribute *to* a fund or *for* a purpose; write (esp. one's name) at foot of document etc., sign (document) thus. **subscribe to** arrange to receive (periodical etc.) regularly, agree with (opinion or resolution).

**subscriber** /səb'skraɪbə(r)/ n. person who subscribes, esp. person paying regular sum for hire of telephone. **subscriber trunk dialling** making of trunk-calls by subscriber without assistance of operator.

**subscript** /'sʌbskrɪpt/ 1 a. written or printed below. 2 n. subscript number or symbol.

**subscription** /səb'skrɪpʃ(ə)n/ n. amount subscribed, act of subscribing.

**subsequent** /'sʌbsəkwənt/ a. following a specified or implied event. **subsequent to** later than, after.

**subservient** /səb'sɜːvɪənt/ a. subordinate *to*; obsequious; of use in minor role. **subservience** n.

**subside** /səb'saɪd/ v.i. sink or settle to lower level; cave in, sink; become less active or intense or prominent; (of person) sink into a chair etc. **subsidence** n.

**subsidiary** /səb'sɪdɪərɪ/ 1 a. serving to help or supplement, subordinate, secondary; (of company) controlled by another. 2 n. subsidiary company or person or thing.

**subsidize** /'sʌbsɪdaɪz/ v.t. pay subsidy to; support by subsidies.

**subsidy** /'sʌbsədɪ/ n. money contributed by State or public body etc., to keep prices at desired level or to assist in meeting expenses etc.

**subsist** /səb'sɪst/ v.i. exist, continue to exist; maintain or support oneself.

**subsistence** n. subsisting; means of supporting life. **subsistence farming** farming in which almost all crops are consumed by farmer's household; **subsistence level, wage**, merely enough to provide bare necessities of life.

**subsoil** /'sʌbsɔɪl/ n. soil just below surface soil.

**subsonic** /sʌb'sɒnɪk/ a. relating to speeds less than that of sound.

**subspecies** /'sʌbspiːʃiːz/ n. *Biol.* grouping within a species.

**substance** /'sʌbst(ə)ns/ n. particular kind of material; essence of what is spoken or written; reality, solidity; wealth and possessions.

**substandard** /sʌb'stændəd/ a. inferior; of lower than desired standard.

**substantial** /səb'stænʃ(ə)l/ a. of real importance or value, of considerable amount; of solid structure; having substance, not illusory; well-to-do; in essentials, virtual. **substantiality** n.

**substantiate** /səb'stænʃɪeɪt/ v.t. support or prove truth of. **substantiation** n.

**substantive** /'sʌbstəntɪv/ 1 a. having separate existence; not subordinate; actual, real, permanent. 2 n. noun. 3 **substantival** a.

**substitute** /'sʌbstɪtjuːt/ 1 n. person or thing acting or serving in place of another. 2 v. put in place of another; act as substitute (*for*). 3 a. acting as substitute. 4 **substitution** n.

**substratum** /'sʌbstrɑːtəm/ n. (pl. **-ta**) underlying layer; basis.

**subsume** /sʌb'sjuːm/ v.t. include under particular rule or class etc.

**subtenant** /'sʌbtenənt/ person renting room or house etc. from one who is a tenant. **subtenancy** n.

**subtend** /sʌb'tend/ v.t. (of line) be opposite (angle, line).

**subterfuge** /'sʌbtəfjuːdʒ/ n. evasion, esp. in argument or excuse.

**subterranean** /sʌbtə'reɪnɪən/ a. underground.

**subtitle** /'sʌbtaɪt(ə)l/ 1 n. subordinate or additional title of book etc.; caption of cinema film, esp. translating dialogue in foreign film. 2 v.t. provide with subtitle(s).

**subtle** /'sʌt(ə)l/ a. hard to detect or

**subtract** /səb'trækt/ v.t. deduct (number etc. *from* greater number). **subtraction** n.

**subtropical** /sʌb'trɒpɪk(ə)l/ a. bordering on the tropics; characteristic of such regions.

**suburb** /'sʌbɜ:b/ n. outlying district of city.

**suburban** /sə'bɜ:bən/ a. of or characteristic of suburbs; *derog.* provincial in outlook. **suburbanite** n.

**Suburbia** /sə'bɜ:bɪə/ n. usu. *derog.* suburbs and their inhabitants etc.

**subvention** /səb'venʃ(ə)n/ n. subsidy.

**subversion** /səb'vɜ:ʃ(ə)n/ n. weakening or overthrow, esp. of government; attempt at this.

**subversive** /səb'vɜ:sɪv/ 1 a. attempting subversion. 2 n. subversive person.

**subvert** /səb'vɜ:t/ v.t. effect or attempt subversion of.

**subway** /'sʌbweɪ/ n. underground passage, esp. for pedestrians; *US* underground railway.

**succeed** /sək'si:d/ v. have success (*in*); prosper; follow in order, be subsequent (*to* or *to*); come by inheritance or in due order (*to* title, office, etc.).

**success** /sək'ses/ n. favourable outcome; attainment of object or wealth or fame etc.; person or thing that succeeds or is successful.

**successful** /sək'sesfəl/ a. having success, prosperous.

**succession** /sək'seʃ(ə)n/ n. following in order; series of things in succession; succeeding to inheritance or office or esp. throne, right of this; set of persons with such right. **in succession** one after another.

**successive** /sək'sesɪv/ a. following in succession, consecutive.

**successor** /sək'sesə(r)/ n. person or thing that succeeds (*to*) another.

**succinct** /sək'sɪŋkt/ a. brief, concise.

**succour** /'sʌkə(r)/ 1 n. aid given in time of need. 2 v.t. come to assistance of.

**succulent** /'sʌkjʊlənt/ 1 a. juicy; (of plant) thick and fleshy. 2 n. succulent plant. 3 **succulence** n.

**succumb** /sə'kʌm/ v.i. give way *to*; be overcome; die.

**such** /sʌtʃ/ 1 a. of kind or degree or extent indicated or suggested; of the same kind; so great or extreme. 2 *pron.* such person(s) or thing(s). 3 **as such** as being what has been specified; **such-and-such** particular but unspecified; **suchlike** *colloq.* of such a kind.

**suck** 1 v. draw (liquid) into mouth using lip-muscles etc.; draw liquid or sustenance or advantage from; *fig.* imbibe or gain (knowledge, advantage, etc.); roll tongue round and squeeze (sweet etc.) in mouth; use sucking action or make sucking sound. 2 n. act or period of sucking. 3 **suck up** absorb; **suck up to** *sl.* seek favour of, flatter.

**sucker** /'sʌkə(r)/ n. shoot springing from plant's root beside stem; organ in animal, or part of apparatus, adapted for adhering by suction to surfaces; *sl.* gullible person, simpleton.

**sucking** /'sʌkɪŋ/ a. not yet weaned.

**suckle** /'sʌk(ə)l/ v. feed (young) at breast or udder.

**suckling** /'sʌklɪŋ/ n. unweaned child or animal.

**sucrose** /'su:krəʊz/ n. kind of sugar obtained from cane or beet etc.

**suction** /'sʌkʃ(ə)n/ n. sucking; production of partial vacuum so that external atmospheric pressure forces fluid into vacant space or causes adhesion of surfaces.

**sudden** /'sʌd(ə)n/ a. coming or happening or performed etc. unexpectedly or without warning, abrupt. **all of a sudden** suddenly.

**sudorific** /su:də'rɪfɪk/ 1 a. causing sweating. 2 n. sudorific drug.

**suds** *n.pl.* froth of soap and water. **sudsy** a.

**sue** v. begin lawsuit against (person); plead, appeal (*for*).

**suede** /sweɪd/ n. leather with flesh side rubbed into nap.

**suet** /'su:ɪt/ n. hard fat surrounding kidneys of cattle and sheep, used in cooking etc. **suety** a.

**suffer** /'sʌfə(r)/ v. undergo pain or grief etc.; undergo or be subjected to (pain, loss, punishment, grief, etc.); tolerate; *arch.* permit.

**sufferance** /'sʌfərəns/ n. tacit permission or toleration. **on sufferance** tolerated but not supported.

**suffering** /'sʌfərɪŋ/ n. pain etc. suffered.

**suffice** /sə'faɪs/ v. be enough; meet needs of.

**sufficiency** /sə'fɪʃənsi/ n. a sufficient amount.

**sufficient** /sə'fɪʃ(ə)nt/ a. sufficing; adequate.

**suffix** /'sʌfɪks/ 1 n. verbal element attached to end of word in inflexion or word-formation etc. 2 v.t. add as suffix.

**suffocate** /'sʌfəkeɪt/ v. kill or stifle or choke by stopping respiration; be or feel suffocated. **suffocation** n.

**suffragan** /'sʌfrəgən/ n. bishop assisting diocesan bishop in particular part of diocese.

**suffrage** /'sʌfrɪdʒ/ n. right of voting in political elections.

**suffragette** /sʌfrə'dʒet/ n. hist. woman who agitated for women's suffrage.

**suffuse** /sə'fjuːz/ v.t. (of colour or moisture etc.) spread throughout or over. **suffusion** n.

**sugar** /'ʃʊɡə(r)/ n. sweet crystalline substance obtained from juices esp. of sugar-cane and sugar-beet and used in cookery and confectionery etc.; *Chem.* any of a group of soluble sweet carbohydrates; *fig.* flattery etc. 2 v.t. sweeten or coat with sugar; make sweet or agreeable. 3 **sugar-bag** *Aus.* nest of wild honey; **sugar-beet** kind of white beet from which sugar is manufactured; **sugar-cane** tall stout perennial tropical grass cultivated as source of sugar; **sugar-daddy** *sl.* elderly man who lavishes gifts on young woman; **sugar-grass** *Aus.* a sweetish fodder-grass; **sugar-gum** *Aus.* a eucalypt with sweetish foliage; **sugar-loaf** conical moulded mass of hard refined sugar; **sugar-squirrel** *Aus.* a gliding possum that lives partly on honey.

**sugary** /'ʃʊɡəri/ a. containing or resembling sugar; cloying, sentimental.

**suggest** /sə'dʒest/ v.t. propose for consideration or as a possibility; cause (idea) to present itself, bring (idea) into the mind.

**suggestible** /sə'dʒestəb(ə)l/ a. capable of being influenced by suggestion. **suggestibility** n.

**suggestion** /sə'dʒestʃ(ə)n/ n. suggesting; thing suggested; insinuation of belief or impulse into the mind; hint or slight trace *of*.

**suggestive** /sə'dʒestɪv/ a. conveying a suggestion (*of*); suggesting something indecent.

**suicidal** /suːɪ'saɪd(ə)l/ a. of or tending to suicide; (of person) liable to commit suicide; destructive to one's own interests.

**suicide** /'suːɪsaɪd/ n. intentional self-killing; person who intentionally kills himself; action destructive to one's own interests etc.

***sui generis*** /suːiː 'dʒenərəs/ of its own kind, unique. [L]

**suit** /suːt/ 1 n. set of clothes for wearing together, esp. of same cloth and consisting usu. of jacket and trousers or skirt; clothing for particular purpose; set of pyjamas or armour etc.; any of the 4 sets into which pack of cards is divided; lawsuit; *arch.* suing, seeking of woman's hand in marriage. 2 v. meet requirements of; agree with; be in harmony with; adapt or make appropriate *to*; be agreeable or convenient; in *p.p.* well adapted or fitted etc. to. 3 **suitcase** flat case for carrying clothes, usu. with hinged lid.

**suitable** /'suːtəb(ə)l/ a. suited *to* or *for*; well fitted for purpose; appropriate to occasion. **suitability** n.

**suite** /swiːt/ n. set of rooms or furniture etc.; group of attendants; *Mus.* set of instrumental pieces.

**suitor** /'suːtə(r)/ n. man who woos woman; plaintiff or petitioner in lawsuit.

**sulk** 1 v.i. be sulky. 2 n. (usu. in *pl.*) sulky fit.

**sulky** /'sʌlki/ a. sullen and unsociable from resentment or ill temper.

**sullen** /'sʌlən/ a. ill-humoured, moody, morose, gloomy.

**sully** /'sʌli/ v.t. spoil purity or splendour of (reputation etc.).

**sulphate** /'sʌlfeɪt/ n. salt of sulphuric acid.

**sulphide** /'sʌlfaɪd/ n. compound of sulphur with element or radical.

**sulphite** /'sʌlfaɪt/ n. salt of sulphurous acid.

**sulphonamide** /sʌl'fɒnəmaɪd/ n. kind of antibiotic drug.

**sulphur** /'sʌlfə(r)/ n. pale-yellow non-metallic element burning with blue flame and stifling smell; yellow butterfly.

**sulphureous** /sʌl'fjuːriːəs/ *a.* of or like sulphur.

**sulphuric** /sʌl'fjuːrɪk/ *a.* of or containing sulphur in a higher valency. **sulphuric acid** dense highly corrosive oily acid.

**sulphurous** /'sʌlfərəs/ *a.* of or like sulphur; (also /sʌl'fjuːrəs/) containing sulphur in a lower valency. **sulphurous acid** unstable weak acid used e.g. as bleaching agent.

**sultan** /'sʌlt(ə)n/ *n.* Muslim sovereign.

**sultana** /sʌl'tɑːnə/ *n.* kind of seedless raisin; sultan's wife or mother or concubine or daughter.

**sultanate** /'sʌltənət/ *n.* position of or territory ruled by sultan.

**sultry** /'sʌltri/ *a.* (of weather) oppressively hot; (of person) passionate, sensual.

**sum** 1 *n.* number resulting from addition of items; amount of money; arithmetical problem; working out of this; sum total; summary. 2 *v.* find sum of. 3 **in sum** briefly, to sum up; **sum total** total resulting from addition of items, summary; **sum up** find or give total of, express briefly or summarize, form or express judgement or opinion of, (esp. of judge) recapitulate evidence or argument.

**sumac** /'suːmæk/ *n.* shrub yielding leaves which are dried and ground for use in tanning and dyeing; these leaves.

**summarize** /'sʌməraɪz/ *v.t.* make or be summary of.

**summary** /'sʌməri/ 1 *n.* brief account giving chief points. 2 *a.* brief, without details or formalities.

**summation** /sʌ'meɪʃ(ə)n/ *n.* finding of total or sum; summarizing.

**summer** /'sʌmə(r)/ *n.* warmest season of year; year of life or age. **summerhouse** light building in garden etc. for use in summer; **summer school** course of lectures etc. held during summer vacation; **summer time** time shown by clocks advanced in summer for daylight saving; **summer-time** season or weather of summer. **summery** *a.*

**summit** /'sʌmɪt/ *n.* highest point, top; highest level of achievement or status; (in full **summit conference, meeting**) discussion between heads of governments.

**summon** /'sʌmən/ *v.t.* require presence or attendance of; call together; call upon (to do, appear, etc.); muster up (courage etc.).

**summons** /'sʌmənz/ 1 *n.* authoritative call to attend or do something, esp. to appear in court. 2 *v.t.* serve with summons.

**sump** *n.* casing holding oil in internal-combustion engine; pit or well for collecting water etc.

**sumptuary** /'sʌmptjuːəri/ *a.* regulating (esp. private) expenditure.

**sumptuous** /'sʌmptjuːəs/ *a.* costly, splendid, magnificent.

**sun** 1 *n.* the star round which the earth travels and from which it receives light and warmth; this light or warmth; any fixed star. 2 *v.* expose (oneself) to the sun. 3 **sunbathe** expose one's body to the sun; **sun-beam** ray of sun, *Aus. sl.* unused table utensil not needing to be washed up; **sunburn** inflammation of skin from exposure to sun; **sunburnt** affected by sunburn; **sundial** instrument showing time by shadow of pointer in sunlight; **sundown** sunset; **sundowner** *Aus. hist.* tramp, esp. one arriving at a station asking for a meal but too late to work; **sunflower** tall garden-plant with large golden-rayed flowers; **sun-glasses** tinted spectacles to protect eyes from glare; **sun-lamp** lamp giving ultra-violet rays for therapy or artificial sun-tan; **sun lounge** room designed to receive much sunlight; **sunrise** (time of) sun's rising; **sunset** (time of) sun's setting; **sunshade** light umbrella used to give shade from sun; **sunshine** sunlight, area illuminated by it, cheerfulness or bright influence; **sunspot** dark patch on sun's surface; **sunstroke** acute prostration from excessive heat of sun; **sun-tan** tanning of skin by exposure to sun; **sun-trap** sunny place, esp. sheltered from wind.

**Sun.** *abbr.* Sunday.

**sundae** /'sʌndeɪ/ *n.* confection of ice cream with fruit, nuts, syrup, etc.

**Sunday** /'sʌndeɪ or -diː/ *n.* day of week following Saturday; newspaper published on Sundays. **month of Sundays** very long period; **Sunday school** school held on Sundays for religious instruction of children.

**sunder** /'sʌndə(r)/ *v.t. literary* sever, keep apart.

**sundry** /'sʌndrɪ/ 1 *a.* various, several. 2 *n. Aus.* extra in cricket; in *pl.* oddments, accessories; items not needing to be specified. 3 **all and sundry** everyone.

**sung** *p.p.* of **sing**.

**sunk** *p.p.* of **sink**.

**sunken** /'sʌŋkən/ *a.* that has sunk; lying below general surface; (of eyes, cheeks, etc.) shrunken, hollow.

**Sunni** /'sʌnɪ/ *n.* member of Muslim sect opposed to Shi'ites.

**sunny** /'sʌnɪ/ *a.* bright with or as sunlight; exposed to or warm with sun; cheerful.

**sup** 1 *v.* drink by sips or spoonfuls; take supper. 2 *n.* mouthful of liquid.

**super** /'su:pə(r)/ 1 *a. sl.* excellent, unusually good. 2 *n. colloq.* supernumerary; superintendent, esp. *Aus.* on a sheep-farm; *Aus.* superphosphate.

**super-** *in comb.* on top, over, beyond, besides, exceeding, transcending, of higher kind, more than usually.

**superannuate** /su:pər'ænju:eɪt/ *v.t.* dismiss or discard as too old; discharge with pension; in *p.p.* too old for work.

**superannuation** /su:pərænju:'eɪʃ(ə)n/ *n.* pension; payment made to obtain pension.

**superb** /su:'pɜ:b/ *a.* magnificent, splendid; *colloq.* excellent.

**supercargo** /'su:pəkɑ:gəʊ/ *n.* (*pl.* **-goes**) person in merchant ship managing sales etc. of cargo.

**supercharge** /'su:pətʃɑ:dʒ/ *v.t.* charge to extreme or excess; use supercharger on.

**supercharger** /'su:pətʃɑ:dʒə/ *n.* device forcing extra air or fuel into internal-combustion engine.

**supercilious** /su:pə'sɪlɪəs/ *a.* haughtily contemptuous.

**supererogation** /su:pərerə'geɪʃ(ə)n/ *n.* doing of more than duty requires.

**superficial** /su:pə'fɪʃ(ə)l/ *a.* of or on the surface; without depth of knowledge or feeling etc.; (of measure) square. **superficiality** /-'æl-/ *n.*

**superfluity** /su:pə'flu:ɪtɪ/ *n.* superfluous amount or thing; being superfluous.

**superfluous** /su:'pɜ:flʊəs/ *a.* more than is needed or wanted, useless.

**supergrass** /'su:pəgrɑ:s/ *n. sl.* large-scale police informer.

**superhuman** /su:pə'hju:mən/ *a.* exceeding (normal) human capacity or power.

**superimpose** /su:pərɪm'pəʊz/ *v.t.* place (thing) on or (*up*)on or above something else. **superimposition** *n.*

**superintend** /su:pərɪn'tend/ *v.* manage, watch over (work etc.). **superintendence** *n.*

**superintendent** /su:pərɪn'tend(ə)nt/ *n.* person who superintends; director of institution etc.; police officer above rank of inspector.

**superior** /su:'pɪərɪə(r)/ 1 *a.* higher in rank or quality etc., (*to*); better or greater in some respect; high-quality; priggish; unlikely to yield or not resorting *to*; situated above; written or printed above the line. 2 *n.* person superior to another esp. in rank; head of monastery. 3 **superiority** /-'ɒr-/ *n.*

**superlative** /su:'pɜ:lətɪv/ 1 *a.* of highest degree; excellent; *Gram.* (of degree, inflexional form, adjective or adverb) expressing highest or very high degree of quality etc. denoted by simple word. 2 *n.* superlative degree or (form of) word.

**superman** /'su:pəmæn/ *n.* (*pl.* **-men**) man of superhuman powers or achievement.

**supermarket** /'su:pəmɑ:kɪt/ *n.* large self-service store usu. selling food and some household goods.

**supernatural** /su:pə'nætʃər(ə)l/ *a.* of or manifesting phenomena not explicable by natural or physical laws.

**supernova** /su:pə'nəʊvə/ *n.* (*pl.* **-vae** /-vi:-/ or **vas**) *Astron.* star that suddenly increases very greatly in brightness.

**supernumerary** /su:pə'nju:mərərɪ/ 1 *a.* in excess of normal number; engaged for extra work; (of actor) with non-speaking part. 2 *n.* supernumerary person or thing.

**superphosphate** /su:pə'fɒsfeɪt/ *n.* fertilizer made from phosphate rock.

**superpower** /'su:pəpaʊə(r)/ *n.* extremely powerful nation.

**superscribe** /'su:pəskraɪb/ *v.t.* write (inscription) at top of or outside document etc.

**superscript** /'su:pəskrɪpt/ 1 *a.* written

**superscription** /su:pəˈskrɪpʃ(ə)n/ n. superscribed words.

**supersede** /su:pəˈsi:d/ v.t. take place of; put or use another in place of. **supersession** n.

**supersonic** /su:pəˈsɒnɪk/ a. of or having speed greater than that of sound.

**superstition** /su:pəˈstɪʃ(ə)n/ n. belief in the existence or power of the supernatural; irrational fear of unknown or mysterious; a religion or practice or opinion based on such tendencies; widely held but wrong idea. **superstitious** a.

**superstructure** /ˈsu:pəstrʌktʃə(r)/ n. structure built on top of something else; upper part of building or ship etc.

**supertanker** /ˈsu:pətæŋkə(r)/ n. very large tanker.

**supertax** /ˈsu:pətæks/ n. & v.t. surtax.

**supervene** /su:pəˈvi:n/ v.i. occur as interruption in or change from some state. **supervention** n.

**supervise** /ˈsu:pəvaɪz/ v.t. oversee, superintend. **supervision** n.; **supervisor** n.; **supervisory** a.

**supine** /ˈsu:paɪn/ 1 a. lying face upwards; inactive, indolent. 2 n. type of Latin verbal noun.

**supper** /ˈsʌpə(r)/ n. meal taken late in day, esp. evening meal less formal and substantial than dinner.

**supplant** /səˈplɑ:nt/ v.t. take the place of, esp. by underhand means.

**supple** /ˈsʌp(ə)l/ a. easily bent, pliant, flexible.

**supplement** 1 /ˈsʌpləmənt/ n. thing or part added to remedy deficiencies or amplify information; separate addition to newspaper etc. 2 /ˈsʌpləment/ v.t. make supplement to. 3 **supplemental** a.; **supplementation** n.

**supplementary** /sʌpləˈmentəri/ a. supplemental. **supplementary benefit** payment made by State in cases of hardship.

**suppliant** /ˈsʌplɪənt/ 1 n. humble petitioner. 2 a. supplicating; expressing supplication.

**supplicate** /ˈsʌplɪkeɪt/ v. make humble petition to or for. **supplication** n.; **supplicatory** a.

**supply** /səˈplaɪ/ 1 v.t. furnish or provide (with) thing needed; make up for (deficiency etc.). 2 n. provision of what is needed; stock, store; in pl. necessaries for army or expedition etc.; person, esp. teacher or minister, supplying vacancy or acting as substitute. 3 **supply and demand** quantities available and required, as factors regulating price of commodities.

**support** /səˈpɔ:t/ 1 v.t. carry all or part of weight of; keep from falling or sinking or failing; provide for; strengthen, encourage, give help or corroboration to; speak in favour of; take secondary part to (actor etc.); endure, tolerate. 2 n. supporting or being supported; person or thing that supports. 3 **supportive** a.

**supporter** /səˈpɔ:tə(r)/ n. person or thing that supports; person who is interested in a particular team or sport.

**suppose** /səˈpəʊz/ v.t. assume, be inclined to think; take as possibility or hypothesis; require as condition; in p.p. generally accepted as being so. **be supposed to** be expected or required to, (with neg., colloq.) not be allowed to.

**supposedly** /səˈpəʊzədli/ adv. as is generally supposed.

**supposition** /sʌpəˈzɪʃ(ə)n/ n. what is supposed or assumed.

**suppositious** /sʌpəˈzɪʃəs/ a. hypothetical.

**supposititious** /səpɒzɪˈtɪʃəs/ a. spurious.

**suppository** /səˈpɒzətəri/ n. medical preparation inserted into rectum or vagina to melt.

**suppress** /səˈpres/ v.t. put an end to existence or activity of; withhold or withdraw from publication; keep secret or unexpressed; Electr. partially or wholly eliminate (interference etc.), equip (device) to reduce interference due to it. **suppression** n.; **suppressor** n.

**suppurate** /ˈsʌpjʊəreɪt/ v.i. form or secrete pus; fester. **suppuration** n.

**supra-** in comb. above.

**supranational** /su:prəˈnæʃən(ə)l/ a. transcending national limits.

**supremacy** /su:ˈpreməsi:/ n. being supreme, supreme authority.

**supreme** /su:ˈpri:m/ a. highest in authority or rank; greatest, of highest quality or degree or amount.

**supremo** /suːˈpriːməʊ/ n. (pl. **-mos**) supreme leader.

**surcease** /sɜːˈsiːs/ arch. 1 n. cessation. 2 v.i. cease.

**surcharge** /ˈsɜːtʃɑːdʒ/ 1 n. additional charge or payment; excessive or additional load. 2 v.t. exact surcharge from; exact (sum) as surcharge; overload.

**surd** 1 a. (of number) irrational; (of sound) uttered with breath and not voice. 2 n. surd number or sound.

**sure** /ʃʊə(r) or ʃɔː(r)/ 1 a. having or seeming to have adequate reason for belief, convinced (*of*, *that*); having certain prospect or confident anticipation or satisfactory knowledge *of*; reliable or unfailing; certain (*to do*); undoubtedly true or truthful. 2 *adv. colloq.* certainly. 3 **make sure** make or become certain, ensure; **sure-fire** *colloq.* certain (to succeed); **sure-footed** never stumbling; **to be sure** it is undeniable or admitted.

**surely** /ˈʃʊəli/ *adv.* with certainty or safety; as appeal to likelihood or reason.

**surety** /ˈʃʊərəti/ n. person undertaking to be liable for another's default or non-appearance etc.

**surf** 1 n. swell and white foamy water of sea breaking on rock or (esp. shallow) shore. 2 *v.i.* engage in surf-riding. 3 **surf-board** long narrow board for riding over heavy surf to shore; **surf-riding** sport of riding on surf-board.

**surface** /ˈsɜːfəs/ 1 n. the outside of a thing; any of the limits terminating a solid; the top of a liquid or of soil etc.; outward aspect, what is apprehended of something on casual view or consideration; *Geom.* that which has length or breadth but no thickness. 2 *attrib.a.* of the surface (only), superficial. 3 *v.* give (special) surface to; come to the surface; become visible or known or *colloq.* conscious; bring (submarine) to the surface. 4 **surface mail** mail not carried by air; **surface tension** tension of surface of liquid, tending to minimize its surface area.

**surfeit** /ˈsɜːfɪt/ 1 n. excess, esp. in eating or drinking; satiety. 2 *v.t.* overfeed; satiate *with*, cloy.

**surfie** /ˈsɜːfi/ n. *Aus. colloq.* devotee of surfing.

**surge** 1 *v.i.* move to and fro (as) in waves; move suddenly and powerfully. 2 n. wave(s), surging motion; impetuous onset.

**surgeon** /ˈsɜːdʒ(ə)n/ n. person skilled in surgery; medical practitioner qualified to practise surgery.

**surgery** /ˈsɜːdʒəri/ n. manual or instrumental treatment of injuries or disorders of body; place where or time when doctor or dentist etc. gives advice and treatment, or *colloq.* MP or lawyer etc. is available for consultation.

**surgical** /ˈsɜːdʒɪk(ə)l/ a. of or by surgery or surgeons; (of appliance) used for surgery or in conditions suitable for surgery. **surgical spirit** methylated spirits used for cleansing etc.

**surly** /ˈsɜːli/ a. bad-tempered, unfriendly.

**surmise** /səˈmaɪz/ 1 n. conjecture. 2 *v.* infer doubtfully or conjecturally; guess.

**surmount** /səˈmaʊnt/ *v.t.* overcome, prevail over, get over; in *p.p.* capped or crowned (*by*, *with*).

**surname** /ˈsɜːneɪm/ 1 n. name common to all members of family. 2 *v.t.* give surname to.

**surpass** /səˈpɑːs/ *v.t.* outdo, be better than.

**surpassing** /səˈpɑːsɪŋ/ a. greatly exceeding or excelling others.

**surplice** /ˈsɜːpləs/ n. loose full-sleeved white vestment worn by clergy etc.

**surplus** /ˈsɜːpləs/ 1 n. amount left over when requirements have been met. 2 a. in excess of what is needed or used.

**surprise** /səˈpraɪz/ 1 n. unexpected or astonishing thing; catching of person(s) unprepared; emotion excited by the unexpected. 2 *v.t.* affect with surprise; shock, scandalize; capture by surprise; attack or come upon unawares; lead unawares or betray *into doing* etc.

**surrealism** /səˈriːəlɪz(ə)m/ n. 20th-c. movement in art and literature aiming to express subconscious mind. **surrealist** a. & n.; **surrealistic** a.

**surrender** /səˈrendə(r)/ 1 *v.* hand over, relinquish possession of; accept enemy's demand for submission; submit (*to*); give *oneself* over *to* habit or emotion etc.; give up rights under (insurance policy) in return for smaller sum received immediately. 2 n. surrendering.

**surreptitious** /ˌsʌrəpˈtɪʃəs/ *a.* done by stealth; underhand.

**surrogate** /ˈsʌrəgət/ *n.* deputy esp. of bishop; substitute. **surrogate mother** woman who conceives and gives birth to child on behalf of woman unable to do so.

**surround** /səˈraʊnd/ 1 *v.t.* come or be all round. 2 *n.* border or edging esp. area between walls and carpet.

**surroundings** /səˈraʊndɪŋz/ *n.pl.* things in neighbourhood of, or conditions affecting, a person or thing.

**surtax** /ˈsɜːtæks/ 1 *n.* additional tax, esp. on incomes above a certain amount. 2 *v.t.* impose surtax on.

**surveillance** /səˈveɪləns/ *n.* supervision; close watch esp. on suspected person.

**survey** 1 /səˈveɪ/ *v.t.* take or present general view of; examine condition of (building etc.); determine boundaries and extent and ownership etc. of (district etc.). 2 /ˈsɜːveɪ/ *n.* act or result of surveying; inspection or investigation; map or plan made by surveying.

**surveyor** /səˈveɪə(r)/ *n.* person who surveys land and buildings, esp. professionally.

**survival** /səˈvaɪv(ə)l/ *n.* surviving; relic of earlier time.

**survive** /səˈvaɪv/ *v.* continue to live or exist; live or exist longer than; come alive through or continue to exist in spite of (danger, accident, etc.). **survivor** *n.*

**sus** /sʌs/ *sl.* 1 *n.* suspicion, suspect. 2 *v.t.* (*past* & *p.p.* **sussed**) investigate, inspect, understand (often with *out*).

**susceptible** /səˈsɛptəb(ə)l/ *a.* impressionable, sensitive; readily touched with emotion; accessible or sensitive *to*; admitting *of*. **susceptibility** *n.*

**suspect** 1 /səˈspɛkt/ *v.t.* have an impression of the existence or presence of; half believe *to be*; be inclined to think (*that*); mentally accuse *of*; doubt the innocence or genuineness or truth of. 2 /ˈsʌspɛkt/ *n.* suspected person. 3 /ˈsʌspɛkt/ *a.* subject to suspicion or distrust.

**suspend** /səˈspɛnd/ *v.t.* hang up; keep inoperative or undecided for a time; debar temporarily from function or office etc.; in *p.p.* (of solid in fluid) sustained or floating between top and bottom. **suspended sentence** judicial sentence remaining unenforced on condition of good behaviour.

**suspender** *n.* attachment to hold up stocking or sock by its top; in *pl.* US pair of braces. **suspender belt** woman's undergarment with suspenders.

**suspense** /səˈspɛns/ *n.* state of anxious uncertainty or expectation.

**suspension** /səˈspɛnʃ(ə)n/ *n.* suspending or being suspended; means by which vehicle is supported on its axles; substance consisting of particles suspended in fluid. **suspension bridge** bridge with roadway suspended from cables supported by towers.

**suspicion** /səˈspɪʃ(ə)n/ *n.* feeling or state of mind of one who suspects; suspecting or being suspected; slight trace (*of*).

**suspicious** /səˈspɪʃəs/ *a.* prone to or feeling suspicion; indicating or justifying suspicion.

**sustain** /səˈsteɪn/ *v.t.* bear weight of or support, esp. for long period; endure, stand; undergo or suffer (defeat, injury, loss, etc.); (of court etc.) decide in favour of, uphold; substantiate or corroborate; keep up (effort etc.).

**sustenance** /ˈsʌstənəns/ *n.* nourishment, food, means of support.

**suture** /ˈsuːtʃə(r)/ 1 *n. Surg.* joining of edges of wound by stitching; stitch or thread etc. used for this. 2 *v.t.* stitch (wound).

**suzerain** /ˈsuːzəreɪn/ *n.* feudal overlord; sovereign or State having some control over another State that is internally autonomous. **suzerainty** *n.*

**svelte** /svɛlt/ *a.* slim, slender, graceful.

**SW** *abbr.* South-West(ern).

**swab** /swɒb/ 1 *n.* mop or absorbent pad or cloth for cleansing or mopping up etc.; absorbent pad used in surgery; specimen of secretion etc. taken for examination. 2 *v.t.* clean or wipe (as) with swab.

**swaddle** /ˈswɒd(ə)l/ *v.t.* swathe in bandages or wrappings etc. **swaddling-clothes** narrow bandages wrapped round new-born child to restrain its movements.

**swag** *n.* ornamental festoon of flowers etc.; representation of this; *sl.* thief's booty; *Aus.* traveller's bundle; *Aus. sl.*

# swagger          sweep

large quantity. **swagman** *Aus.* person who carries a swag, a tramp.

**swagger** /ˈswægə(r)/ 1 *v.i.* walk or behave arrogantly or self-importantly; talk boastfully. 2 *n.* swaggering gait or manner.

**swain** *n. arch.* a country youth; *poet.* young lover or suitor.

**swallow**¹ /ˈswɒləʊ/ 1 *v.* make or let pass down one's throat; perform muscular action (as) of swallowing something; accept meekly or credulously; repress (emotion); engulf. 2 *n.* act of swallowing; amount swallowed.

**swallow**² /ˈswɒləʊ/ *n.* migratory insect-eating bird with forked tail. **swallow-dive** dive with arms spread sideways; **swallow-tail** deeply forked tail, butterfly etc. with this.

**swam** *past of* **swim**.

**swamp** /swɒmp/ 1 *n.* piece of wet spongy ground. 2 *v.t.* submerge, inundate; cause to fill with water and sink; overwhelm with numbers or quantity. 3 **swampy** *a.*

**swan** /swɒn/ *n.* large web-footed usu. white water-bird with long flexible neck. **swansdown** down of swan used in trimmings etc.; thick cotton cloth with soft nap on one side; **swan-song** person's final composition or performance etc.; **swan-upping** annual taking up and marking of Thames swans.

**swank** 1 *colloq. n.* ostentation, swagger. 2 *v.i.* behave with swank. 3 **swanky** *a.*

**swannery** /ˈswɒnərɪ/ *n.* place where swans are kept.

**swap** /swɒp/ *colloq.* 1 *v.* exchange by barter. 2 *n.* act of swapping; thing suitable for swapping.

**sward** /swɔːd/ *n. literary* expanse of short grass.

**swarm**¹ /swɔːm/ 1 *n.* large or dense body or multitude of persons or insects etc., esp. moving about; cluster of bees leaving hive etc. with queen bee to establish new hive. 2 *v.i.* move in or form swarm; be overrun or crowded *with*.

**swarm**² /swɔːm/ *v.* climb (*up*) clasping or clinging with arms and legs.

**swarthy** /ˈswɔːðɪ/ *a.* dark-complexioned, dark in colour.

**swashbuckler** /ˈswɒʃbʌklə(r)/ *n.* swaggering bully or ruffian. **swashbuckling** *a. & n.*

**swastika** /ˈswɒstɪkə/ *n.* cross with equal arms, each arm with limb of same length at right angles to its end.

**swat** /swɒt/ 1 *v.t.* hit hard, crush (fly etc.) with blow. 2 *n.* act of swatting.

**swatch** /swɒtʃ/ *n.* sample, esp. of cloth; collection of samples.

**swath** /swɔːθ/ *n.* (*pl.* /swɔːθs, swɔːðz/) row or line of grass or corn etc. as it falls when cut; space covered or width of grass etc. cut by sweep of scythe.

**swathe**¹ /sweɪð/ *v.t.* bind or enclose in bandages or garments etc.

**swathe**² *var. of* **swath**.

**sway** 1 *v.* (cause to) move in different directions alternately; oscillate irregularly; waver; have influence over; rule over. 2 *n.* swaying motion; rule, government.

**swear** /sweə(r)/ *v.* (*past* **swore**; *p.p.* **sworn**) take oath; take oath or promise on oath; cause to take oath; use profane oaths. **swear by** appeal to as witness or guarantee of oath, *colloq.* have great confidence in; **swear in** admit to office etc. by administering oath; **swear off** renounce; **swear to** *colloq.* say that one is certain of; **swear-word** profane or obscene word.

**sweat** /swet/ 1 *n.* moisture exuded from skin esp. when one is hot or nervous; state or period of sweating; *colloq.* state of anxiety; *colloq.* drudgery, effort, laborious task or undertaking; condensed moisture on a surface. 2 *v.* exude sweat; *fig.* be terrified, suffer, etc.; emit like sweat; make (horse, athlete, etc.) sweat by exercise; (cause to) toil or drudge. 3 **sweat-band** band of absorbent material inside hat or round wrist etc. to soak up sweat; **sweated labour** workers employed for long hours at low wages; **sweat-shirt** sleeved cotton sweater; **sweat-shop** workshop where sweated labour is employed. 4 **sweaty** *a.*

**sweater** /ˈswetə(r)/ *n.* woollen etc. pullover.

**Swede** *n.* native of Sweden; **swede** large yellow variety of turnip.

**Swedish** /ˈswiːdɪʃ/ 1 *a.* of Sweden. 2 *n.* language of Sweden.

**sweep** 1 *v.* (*past & p.p.* **swept**) clean or clear with or as with a broom; clean

**sweeping**

room etc. thus; collect or remove (dirt etc.) by sweeping; clear *off* or *away* etc. forcefully; traverse swiftly or lightly; impart sweeping motion to; glide swiftly; go majestically; have continuous extent. 2 *n.* act or motion of sweeping; moving in continuous curve; curve in road etc.; range or scope; chimney-sweep; sortie by aircraft; *colloq.* sweepstake; long oar. 3 **sweep the board** win all the money in gambling-game, win all possible prizes etc.; **sweepstake** form of gambling on horse-races etc., in which money staked is divided among those who have drawn numbered tickets for winners.

**sweeping** *a.* of wide range, regardless of limitations or exceptions.

**sweet** 1 *a.* tasting like sugar or honey etc.; pleasing to sense of smell, fragrant; *Aus. sl.* all right, satisfactory; melodious; fresh; not sour or bitter; gratifying; dear, beloved; amiable, gentle; *colloq.* pretty. 2 *n.* small shaped piece of sugar or chocolate confectionery; sweet dish forming course of meal; in *pl.* delights, gratifications; darling. 3 **sweetbread** pancreas or thymus gland of animal, as food; **sweet-brier** kind of single-flowered fragrant-leaved rose; **sweet chestnut** edible chestnut; **sweet corn** sweet-flavoured maize; **sweetheart** either of pair of lovers; **sweetheart agreement** *Aus.* industrial agreement negotiated without reference to arbitration authority; **sweetmeat** a sweet; **sweet pea** climbing garden annual with showy scented flowers; **sweet pepper** mild-flavoured kind of capsicum; **sweet potato** tropical plant with tuberous roots used for food; **sweet tooth** liking for sweet-tasting things; **sweet-william** garden plant with close clusters of sweet-smelling flowers.

**sweeten** /ˈswiːt(ə)n/ *v.* make or become sweet(er).

**sweetener** /ˈswiːtənə(r)/ *n.* thing that sweetens; *colloq.* bribe.

**sweetie** /ˈswiːtɪ/ *n. colloq.* a sweet; sweetheart.

**swell** 1 *v.* (*p.p.* **swollen** /ˈswəʊlən/ or **swelled**) (cause to) grow bigger or louder or more intense; rise or raise up; bulge *out*. 2 *n.* act or state of swelling; heaving of sea etc. with long rolling waves that do not break; *Mus.* crescendo; mechanism in organ etc. for gradually varying volume; *colloq.* fashionable or stylish person, person of distinction or ability. 3 *a. colloq.* smart, finely dressed, distinguished, first-rate.

**swelling** /ˈswelɪŋ/ *n.* abnormally swollen place esp. on body.

**swelter** /ˈsweltə(r)/ 1 *v.i.* be uncomfortably hot. 2 *n.* sweltering condition.

**swept** *past* & *p.p.* of **sweep**. **swept-wing** (of aircraft) having wings placed at acute angle to axis.

**swerve** 1 *v.* (cause to) change direction, esp. suddenly. 2 *n.* swerving motion.

**swift** 1 *a.* rapid, speedy, quick, prompt. 2 *n.* swift-flying long-winged insectivorous bird.

**swig** *colloq.* 1 *v.* drink in large draughts. 2 *n.* swallow of liquid, esp. of large amount.

**swill** 1 *v.* rinse (*out*), pour water over or through; drink greedily. 2 *n.* swilling; mainly liquid refuse as pig-food; inferior liquor.

**swim** 1 *v.* (*past* **swam**; *p.p.* **swum**) progress in water by working limbs or body; float on or at surface of liquid; appear to undulate or reel or whirl, have dizzy effect or sensation; be flooded *with* moisture. 2 *n.* spell or act of swimming; main current of affairs. 3 **swimming-bath**, **-pool**, pool constructed for swimming; **swimming-costume**, **swim-suit**, bathing-suit.

**swimmingly** /ˈswɪmɪŋlɪ/ *adv.* with easy unobstructed progress.

**swindle** /ˈswɪnd(ə)l/ 1 *v.* cheat; defraud. 2 *n.* act of swindling; person or thing represented as what it is not.

**swine** *n.* (*pl.* same) pig; *colloq.* disgusting or unpleasant person or thing.

**swing** 1 *v.* (*past* & *p.p.* **swung**) (cause to) move with to-and-fro or curving motion; sway or hang like pendulum or door etc.; oscillate; move by gripping something and leaping etc.; go with swinging gait; attempt to hit or punch (*at* person etc.); play (music) with swing rhythm; *sl.* be lively or up-to-date etc.; have decisive influence on (voting etc.). 2 *n.* act or motion or extent of swinging; swinging or smooth gait or rhythm or action; seat slung by ropes or chains etc. for swinging on or in, spell of

**swingeing** ... **syllable**

swinging thus; smooth rhythmic jazz or jazzy dance music; amount by which votes etc. change from one side to another. **3 swing-boat** boat-shaped swing at fairs etc.; **swing bridge** bridge that can be swung aside to let ships etc. pass; **swing-door** door that swings in either direction and closes by itself when released; **swing gate** *Aus.* gate closing one passage while opening another; **swinging voter** *Aus.* voter who is not committed to any party; **swing-wing** (of aircraft) having wings that can be moved backwards and forwards.

**swingeing** /'swɪndʒɪŋ/ *a.* forcible; daunting, huge.

**swinish** /'swaɪnɪʃ/ *a.* bestial, filthy.

**swipe 1** *v. colloq.* hit hard and recklessly; *sl.* steal. **2** *n. colloq.* reckless hard hit or attempt to hit.

**swirl 1** *v.* move or flow or carry along with whirling motion. **2** *n.* swirling motion; twist, curl.

**swish 1** *v.* swing (cane, scythe, etc.) audibly through air or grass etc.; cut (flower etc.) *off* thus; move with or make swishing sound. **2** *n.* swishing action or sound. **3** *a. colloq.* smart, fashionable.

**Swiss 1** *a.* of Switzerland. **2** *n.* (*pl.* same) native of Switzerland. **3 Swiss roll** thin flat sponge-cake spread with jam etc. and rolled up.

**switch 1** *n.* device for making and breaking connection in electric circuit; transfer, change-over, deviation; flexible shoot cut from tree, light tapering rod; railway points. **2** *v.t.* turn *on* or *off* etc. with switch; change or transfer (position or subject etc.); reverse positions of; swing or snatch (thing) suddenly; whip or flick with switch. **3 switchback** railway at fair etc. in which train's ascents are achieved by momentum of previous descents, railway or road with alternate sharp ascents and descents; **switchboard** apparatus for varying connections between electric circuits, esp. in telephony.

**swivel** /'swɪv(ə)l/ **1** *n.* coupling between two parts etc. so that one can turn freely without the other. **2** *v.* turn (as) on swivel, swing round. **3 swivel chair** chair with seat turning horizontally on pivot.

**swizz** *n. sl.* swindle, disappointment.

**swizzle** /'swɪz(ə)l/ *n. colloq.* compounded intoxicating drink esp. of rum or gin and bitters made frothy; *sl.* swizz. **swizzle-stick** stick used for frothing or flattening drinks.

**swollen** *p.p.* of **swell**.

**swoon** /swuːn/ *v.i.* & *n. literary* faint.

**swoop** /swuːp/ **1** *v.i.* come down with rush like bird of prey; make sudden attack (*on*). **2** *n.* act of swooping, sudden pounce. **3 at one fell swoop** at a single blow or stroke.

**swop** var. of **swap**.

**sword** /sɔːd/ *n.* weapon with long blade for cutting or thrusting. **cross swords** have fight or dispute (*with*); **put to the sword** kill; **sword-dance** dance in which performer brandishes swords or steps about swords laid on ground; **swordfish** large sea-fish with sword-like upper jaw; **sword-play** fencing, repartee or lively arguing; **swordsman** person of (usu. specified) skill with sword; **sword-stick** hollow walking-stick containing sword-blade.

**swore** *past* of **swear**.

**sworn 1** *p.p.* of **swear**. **2** *a.* bound (as) by oath.

**swot** *sl.* **1** *v.* work hard, esp. at books. **2** *n.* person who works hard, esp. at learning; hard work or study. **3 swot up** study hurriedly or for particular occasion.

**swum** *p.p.* of **swim**.

**swung** *past* & *p.p.* of **swing**.

**swy** *n. Aus.* two-up.

**sybarite** /'sɪbəraɪt/ *n.* self-indulgent or luxury-loving person. **sybaritic** /-'rɪt-/ *a.*

**sycamore** /'sɪkəmɔː(r)/ *n.* large species of maple.

**sycophant** /'sɪkəfænt/ *n.* flatterer, toady. **sycophancy** *n.*; **sycophantic** /-'fæn-/ *a.*

**Sydney** /'sɪdnɪ/ *n.* **Sydney or the bush** *Aus. sl.* all or nothing; **Sydney red-gum** smooth-barked *Aus.* tree with reddish wood; **Sydney silky** *Aus.* dog with grey-blue and tan long silky coat; **Sydneysider** native or resident of Sydney.

**syllabary** /'sɪləbərɪ/ *n.* set of written characters representing syllables.

**syllabic** /sə'læbɪk/ *a.* of or in syllables.

**syllable** /'sɪləb(ə)l/ *n.* unit of pronunci-

# syllabub     574     syndicate

ation forming whole or part of word and usu. having one vowel-sound often with consonant(s) before or after; character(s) representing syllable; least amount of speech or writing.

**syllabub** /ˈsɪləbʌb/ *n.* dish of cream or milk curdled or whipped with wine etc.

**syllabus** /ˈsɪləbəs/ *n.* (*pl.* **-buses**) programme or conspectus of a course of study or teaching etc.

**syllogism** /ˈsɪlədʒɪz(ə)m/ *n.* form of reasoning in which from two propositions a third is deduced. **syllogistic** *a.*

**sylph** /sɪlf/ *n.* elemental spirit of air; slender graceful woman.

**sylvan** var. of **silvan**.

**symbiosis** /sɪmbaɪˈəʊsɪs/ *n.* (*pl.* **-oses** /-ˈəʊsiːz/) (usu. mutually advantageous) association of two different organisms living attached to one another etc. **symbiotic** /-ˈɒt-/ *a.*

**symbol** /ˈsɪmb(ə)l/ *n.* thing generally regarded as typifying or representing or recalling something; mark or character taken as conventional sign of some object or idea or process etc. **symbolic** *a.*; **symbolically** *adv.*

**symbolism** /ˈsɪmbəlɪz(ə)m/ *n.* symbols; use of symbols; artistic movement or style using symbols to express ideas or emotions etc. **symbolist** *n.*

**symbolize** /ˈsɪmbəlaɪz/ *v.t.* be symbol of; represent by symbol.

**symmetry** /ˈsɪmɪtrɪ/ *n.* correct proportion; beauty resulting from this; structure that allows an object to be divided into parts of equal shape and size; possession of such structure; repetition of exactly similar parts facing each other or a centre. **symmetric(al)** *a.*

**sympathetic** /sɪmpəˈθetɪk/ *a.* of or showing or expressing or due to sympathy; likeable, not antagonistic. **sympathetic magic** magic seeking to affect person through associated object. **sympathetically** *adv.*

**sympathize** /ˈsɪmpəθaɪz/ *v.i.* feel or express sympathy (*with*).

**sympathy** /ˈsɪmpəθɪ/ *n.* state of sharing or tendency to share emotion or sensation or condition etc. of another person or thing; mental participation in another's trouble, compassion; disposition to agree (with) or approve, favourable attitude of mind. **in sympathy** having or showing or resulting from sympathy (*with* another).

**symphony** /ˈsɪmfənɪ/ *n.* musical composition in several movements for full orchestra. **symphony orchestra** large orchestra playing symphonies etc. **symphonic** /-ˈfɒn-/ *a.*

**symposium** /sɪmˈpəʊzɪəm/ *n.* (*pl.* **-sia**) meeting or conference for discussion of subject; collection of opinions delivered or articles contributed by number of persons on special topic.

**symptom** /ˈsɪmptəm/ *n.* aspect of physical or mental condition as sign of disease or injury; sign of the existence of something. **symptomatic** /-ˈmæt-/ *a.*

**synagogue** /ˈsɪnəgɒg/ *n.* (building for) regular assembly of Jews for religious instruction and worship.

**sync** /sɪŋk/ *colloq.* (also **synch**) 1 *n.* synchronization. 2 *v.t.* synchronize.

**synchromesh** /ˈsɪŋkrəmeʃ/ 1 *n.* system of gear-changing, esp. in motor vehicles, in which gear-wheels revolve at same speed during engagement. 2 *a.* of this system.

**synchronize** /ˈsɪŋkrənaɪz/ *v.* make or be synchronous with. **synchronization** *n.*

**synchronous** /ˈsɪŋkrənəs/ *a.* existing or occurring at same time (*with*); operating at same rate and simultaneously.

**syncopate** /ˈsɪŋkəpeɪt/ *v.* displace beats or accents in (music); shorten (word) by omitting syllable or letter(s) in middle. **syncopation** *n.*

**syncope** /ˈsɪŋkəpɪ/ *n.* syncopation; *Med.* unconsciousness through fall of blood-pressure.

**syncretic** /sɪnˈkriːtɪk/ *a.* attempting, esp. inconsistently, to unify or reconcile differing schools of thought. **syncretism** *n.*; **syncretize** *v.*

**syndicalism** /ˈsɪndɪkəlɪz(ə)m/ *n.* movement for transfer of control and ownership of means of production and distribution to workers' unions. **syndicalist** *n.*

**syndicate** 1 /ˈsɪndɪkət/ *n.* combination of persons or commercial firms etc. to promote some common interest; association supplying material simultaneously to a number of periodicals. 2 *v.* /ˈsɪndɪkeɪt/ form into syndicate;

**syndrome**

publish (material) through a syndicate. **3 syndication** n.
**syndrome** /ˈsɪndrəʊm/ n. group of concurrent symptoms of disease; characteristic combination of opinions or emotions etc.
**synecdoche** /səˈnɛkdəki:/ n. figure of speech in which part or individual is put for whole or class.
**synod** /ˈsɪnəd/ n. church council of senior clergy and officials.
**synonym** /ˈsɪnənɪm/ n. word or phrase that means exactly or nearly the same as another in same language. **synonymous** /-ˈnɒn-/ a.
**synopsis** /səˈnɒpsəs/ n. (pl. **-ses** /-siːz/) summary; outline.
**synoptic** /səˈnɒptɪk/ a. of or giving synopsis. **Synoptic Gospels** those of Matthew, Mark, and Luke.
**syntax** /ˈsɪntæks/ n. grammatical arrangement of words; rules or analysis of this. **syntactic** a.
**synthesis** /ˈsɪnθəsəs/ n. (pl. **-ses** /-siːz/) putting together of parts or elements to make up complex whole; artificial production of (esp. organic) substances from simpler ones.
**synthesize** /ˈsɪnθəsaɪz/ v.t. make synthesis of.
**synthesizer** /ˈsɪnθəsaɪzə(r)/ n. electronic musical instrument producing a great variety of sounds.
**synthetic** /sɪnˈθɛtɪk/ **1** a. produced by synthesis; artificial. **2** n. synthetic substance.

**syphilis** /ˈsɪfələs/ n. a contagious venereal disease. **syphilitic** a. & n.
**syringa** /səˈrɪŋɡə/ n. shrub with white scented flowers.
**syringe** /ˈsɪrɪndʒ/ **1** n. device for drawing in quantity of liquid and ejecting it in fine stream. **2** v.t. sluice or spray with syringe.
**syrup** /ˈsɪrəp/ n. water (nearly) saturated with sugar, often flavoured or medicated; condensed sugar-cane juice, molasses, treacle; excessive sweetness of manner. **syrupy** a.
**system** /ˈsɪstəm/ n. complex whole; set of connected things or parts; organized body of things; the animal body as organized whole; method, considered principles of procedure or classification; orderliness; major group of geological strata. **systems analysis** analysis of an operation to decide how a computer may best be used to perform it.
**systematic** /sɪstəˈmætɪk/ a. methodical; according to system; deliberate.
**systematize** /ˈsɪstəmətaɪz/ v.t. make systematic. **systematization** n.
**systemic** /səsˈtɛmɪk/ a. of the bodily system as a whole; (of insecticide etc.) entering plant tissues via roots and shoots. **systemically** adv.
**systole** /ˈsɪstəli:/ n. contraction of heart rhythmically alternating with diastole.

# T

**T, t,** *n.* **cross the t's** be minutely accurate; **to a T** exactly, to a nicety; **T-junction** junction, esp. of two roads, in shape of T; **T-shirt** usu. buttonless casual shirt of knitted cotton etc.; **T-square** T-shaped instrument for measuring or obtaining right angles.

**t.** *abbr.* ton(s); tonne(s).

**ta** /tɑː/ *int. colloq.* thank you.

**TAB** *abbr.* Aus. & NZ Totalizator Agency Board.

**tab** *n.* short broad strap or flat loop or tag etc., by which thing can be taken hold of or fastened or identified etc.; *colloq.* account. **keep tabs on** have under observation or in check.

**tabard** /'tæbɑːd/ *n.* herald's short official coat emblazoned with arms of sovereign; woman's or child's garment of similar shape; *hist.* knight's short emblazoned garment worn over armour.

**tabby** /'tæbɪ/ *n.* grey or brownish cat with dark stripes.

**tabernacle** /'tæbənæk(ə)l/ *n. Jewish hist.* tent used as sanctuary by Israelites in the wilderness; canopied niche or receptacle; Nonconformist meetinghouse.

**tabla** /'tæblə/ *n.* pair of small Indian drums played with hands.

**table** /'teɪb(ə)l/ **1** *n.* piece of furniture with flat top on which things may be placed for use or display; food provided at table; set of facts or figures systematically arranged esp. in columns; flat surface; slab of wood or stone etc., matter inscribed on it. **2** *v.t.* bring forward for discussion or consideration. **3 at table** while taking meal; **tableland** plateau of land; **tablespoon** large spoon for serving etc. and used as measure; **table tennis** indoor game based on lawn tennis, played with small bats and celluloid ball bouncing on table divided by net; **turn the tables** cause complete reversal of state of affairs.

**tableau** /'tæbləʊ/ *n.* (*pl.* **-leaux** /-ləʊz/) picturesque presentation, esp. of group of persons etc.; dramatic or effective situation suddenly brought about.

**table d'hôte** /tɑːbl 'dəʊt/ meal in restaurant etc. served at fixed price and at stated hour(s).

**tablet** /'tæblət/ *n.* fixed amount of drug compressed into small convenient shape; small flat piece of prepared substance, e.g. soap; small slab esp. for display of inscription.

**tabloid** /'tæblɔɪd/ *n.* newspaper, usu. popular in style, printed on sheets of half size of usual newspaper.

**taboo** /tə'buː/ **1** *n.* act or system of setting apart person or thing as sacred or accursed; ban, prohibition. **2** *a.* avoided or prohibited, esp. by social custom. **3** *v.t.* put under taboo; exclude or prohibit by authority or social influence.

**tabor** /'teɪbə(r)/ *n.* small drum.

**tabu** var. of **taboo**.

**tabular** /'tæbjʊlə(r)/ *a.* of or arranged in tables.

**tabulate** /'tæbjʊleɪt/ *v.t.* arrange (figures, facts) in tabular form. **tabulation** *n.*

**tabulator** /'tæbjʊleɪtə(r)/ *n.* attachment to typewriter for advancing to sequence of set positions in tabular work.

**tachograph** /'tækəɡrɑːf, -ɡræf/ *n.* device in motor vehicle to record speed and travel-time.

**tacit** /'tæsɪt/ *a.* implied or understood without being stated.

**taciturn** /'tæsɪtɜːn/ *a.* saying little, uncommunicative. **taciturnity** *n.*

**tack**[1] **1** *n.* small sharp usu. broadheaded nail; long stitch used in fastening materials lightly or temporarily together; direction in which vessel moves as determined by position of sails, one of consecutive series of changes of direction; course of action or policy. **2** *v.* fasten (*down* etc.) with tacks; stitch lightly together; annex, append; change ship's course by turning head to wind, make series of such tacks; change one's conduct or policy etc.

**tack**[2] *n.* riding-harness and saddles etc.

**tackle** /'tæk(ə)l/ **1** *n.* gear or appliances esp. for fishing or other sport; rope(s) and pulley(s) etc. used in working sails or hoisting weights etc.; *Footb.* etc. tackling. **2** *v.t.* grapple with; grasp with endeavour to hold or manage or over-

**tacky** /'tækɪ/ a. (of glue, varnish, etc.) in the sticky stage before complete dryness.

**tact** n. adroitness in dealing with persons or circumstances; intuitive perception of right thing to do or say. **tactful** a.

**tactic** /'tæktɪk/ n. piece of tactics.

**tactical** /'tæktɪk(ə)l/ a. of tactics; (of bombing etc.) done in immediate support of military or naval operation; adroitly planning or planned.

**tactics** /'tæktɪks/ n.pl. also treated as sing. art of disposing armed forces esp. in contact with enemy; procedure calculated to gain some end, skilful device(s). **tactician** n.

**tactile** /'tæktaɪl/ a. of or connected with sense of touch; perceived by touch. **tactility** /-'tɪl-/ n.

**tadpole** /'tædpəʊl/ n. larva of frog or toad etc. at stage of living in water and having gills and tail.

**taffeta** /'tæfətə/ n. fine plain-woven lustrous silk or silklike fabric.

**taffrail** /'tæfreɪl/ n. rail round ship's stern.

**tag** 1 n. metal point of shoelace etc.; loop or flap or label for handling or hanging or marking thing; loose or ragged end; trite quotation, stock phrase. 2 v. furnish with tag(s); tack or fasten *on* etc.; *colloq.* follow, trail behind; go along (*with*).

**tail**¹ 1 n. hindmost part of animal esp. when prolonged beyond body; thing like tail in form or position, esp. part of shirt below waist, hanging part of back of coat, end of procession etc.; inferior or weaker part of anything; in *pl. colloq.* tailcoat, evening dress with this; (usu. in *pl.*) reverse of coin turning up in toss. 2 v. remove stalks of (fruit etc.); follow (inconspicuously) and keep watch on; *Aus.* follow or drive (sheep or cattle in a mob). 3 **tail away**, **off**, fall away in straggling line, diminish and cease; **tail-back** long queue of traffic extending back from an obstruction; **tail-board** hinged or removable back of lorry etc.; **tailcoat** man's coat divided at back into tails and cut away in front; **tail-gate** tail-board, hinged rear door of estate car; **tail-light** light carried at back of train or car etc.; **tailpiece** final part of thing, decoration at end of chapter or book etc.; **tailplane** horizontal stabilizing surface of tail of aircraft; **tail-spin** aircraft's spinning dive, *fig.* state of panic; **tail wind** one blowing in direction of one's travel.

**tail**² *Law* 1 n. limitation of ownership, esp. of estate limited to person and his heirs. 2 a. so limited.

**tailor** /'teɪlə(r)/ 1 n. maker of (esp. men's) outer garments, esp. to order. 2 v. be or work as tailor; make by tailor's methods; (esp. in *p.p.*) furnish with clothes; adapt or fit *to* requirements etc. 3 **tailor-made** made by tailor, *fig.* entirely appropriate to purpose.

**taint** 1 n. spot or trace of decay or corruption or disease; corrupt condition, infection. 2 v. introduce corruption or disease into; infect, be infected.

**taipan** /'taɪpæn/ n. largest venomous snake in Australia.

**take** 1 v. (*past* **took** /tʊk/; *p.p.* **taken**) lay hold of, grasp, seize; capture; obtain, get possession of, acquire, use; be successful or effective; consume, use up; have as necessary accompaniment or requirement or part; cause to come or go with one; remove, dispossess person of; catch, be infected with; ascertain and record; grasp mentally, understand; accept, submit to; deal with; teach, be taught or examined in; make (photograph). 2 n. amount taken or caught; *Cinemat.* scene or sequence photographed at one time without stopping camera. 3 **take after** resemble (parent etc.); **take against** begin to dislike; **take away** remove or carry elsewhere, subtract; **take-away** (cooked meal) bought at restaurant for eating elsewhere, restaurant selling this; **take back** retract, convey to original position; **take care** be careful; **take care of** look after, deal with; **take down** write down (spoken words), dismantle (structure); **take-home** (of pay etc.) given to employee after deduction of tax etc.; **take in** include, make (garment etc.) smaller, understand, cheat; **take in hand** start doing or dealing with, undertake control or reform of; **take it out of** exhaust strength of; **take it out on** relieve frustration by attacking; **take off** remove (clothing) from body, deduct, mimic, jump from ground, become airborne; **take-off** act of mimicking or becoming airborne, place from which one jumps; **take on** undertake, acquire, engage, agree to oppose at game, *colloq*. show violent emotion; **take out** remove, escort on outing, procure (patent, summons, etc.); **take over** succeed to management or ownership of, assume control; **take-over** *n*.; **take place** happen; **take to** begin, have recourse to, form liking for; **take up** absorb, consume, adopt as protégé or pursuit, begin to consort *with*, interrupt or correct (speaker).

**taker** /'teɪkə(r)/ *n*. person who takes esp. a bet etc.

**taking** /'teɪkɪŋ/ **1** *a*. attractive, captivating. **2** *n*. in *pl*. money taken in business.

**talc** *n*. translucent mineral often found in thin glasslike plates; talcum powder.

**talcum** /'tælkəm/ *n*. talc. **talcum powder** (usu. perfumed) powdered talc, for toilet use.

**tale** *n*. narrative or story, esp. fictitious; idle or mischievous gossip, malicious report.

**talent** /'tælənt/ *n*. special aptitude or gift (*for*); high mental or artistic ability; *colloq*. persons of talent; ancient weight and money unit. **talent scout** person engaged in searching for talented people, esp. theatrical etc. performers.

**talented** /'tæləntɪd/ *a*. having high ability.

**talisman** /'tælɪsmən/ *n*. thing believed to bring good luck or protect from harm. **talismanic** /-'mæn-/ *a*.

**talk** /tɔːk/ **1** *v*. convey or exchange ideas or information etc. by speech, have or exercise faculty of speech, utter words; express or utter or discuss in words; gossip; use (language). **2** *n*. conversation; mode of speech; short address or lecture; rumour or gossip, its theme; discussion. **3 talk down** silence by louder or more effective talking, speak patronizingly *to*, bring (aircraft) in to land by verbal instruction to pilot from ground; **talk into** persuade by talking; **talk over** discuss; **talk round** persuade to change opinion etc.; **talk to** speak to, *colloq*. reprove.

**talkative** /'tɔːkətɪv/ *a*. fond of talking.

**tall** /tɔːl/ *a*. of more than average height, or of specified height; higher than surroundings; *sl*. extravagant, excessive. **tallboy** tall chest of drawers; **tall order** exorbitant or unreasonable demand.

**tallow** /'tæləʊ/ *n*. harder kinds of (esp. animal) fat melted down for use in making candles or soap etc. **tallowy** *a*.

**tally 1** *v.i.* agree or correspond (*with*). **2** *n*. reckoning of debt or score; mark registering fixed number of objects delivered or received; *hist*. piece of wood scored with notches for items of account; distinguishing mark or ticket or label; counterpart, duplicate.

**tally-ho** /tælɪ'həʊ/ *int*. huntsman's cry as signal on seeing fox.

**Talmud** /'tælmʊd/ *n*. body of Jewish civil and ceremonial law. **Talmudic** *a*.

**talon** /'tælən/ *n*. claw esp. of bird of prey.

**tamarind** /'tæmərɪnd/ *n*. tropical tree with fruit whose acid pulp is used for medicinal or cooling drinks; this fruit.

**tamarisk** /'tæmərɪsk/ *n*. featheryleaved evergreen shrub growing in sandy places.

**tambour** /'tæmbʊə(r)/ *n*. drum; circular frame for stretching embroiderywork on.

**tambourine** /tæmbə'riːn/ *n*. musical instrument of hoop with parchment stretched over one side and pairs of loose jingling discs in slots round circumference.

**tame 1** *a*. (of animal) domesticated, not wild or shy; lacking spirit; uninteresting, insipid. **2** *v.t*. make tame, domesticate; break in; humble, subdue.

**Tamil** /'tæmɪl/ **1** *n*. member of a people inhabiting S. India and Sri Lanka; their language. **2** *a*. of this people or their language.

**tam-o'-shanter** /tæmə'ʃæntə/ *n*. round woollen Scottish etc. cap.

**tamp** *v.t*. pack or ram down tightly.

**tamper** /'tæmpə(r)/ *v.t*. meddle or interfere *with*.

**tampon** /'tæmpɒn/ **1** *n*. plug of cottonwool etc. used to absorb secretions or stop haemorrhage. **2** *v.t*. plug with tampon.

**tan 1** *n*. bronzed colour of skin exposed to sun etc. or weather; yellowish-brown colour; crushed or bruised bark of oak

etc. used for tanning. 2 *a.* yellowish-brown. 3 *v.* make or become brown by exposure to sun or weather; convert (hide) into leather by steeping in liquid containing tannic acid or by use of mineral salts etc.; *sl.* thrash.
**tandem** 1 *n.* bicycle etc. with 2 or more seats behind each other; vehicle driven tandem. 2 *adv.* with two or more horses etc. harnessed one behind another. 3 **in tandem** one behind the other.
**tang** *n.* strong or penetrating taste or smell; characteristic property; part of tool by which blade is held firm in handle.
**tangent** /'tændʒ(ə)nt/ *n.* straight line touching but not intersecting curve; *Math.* ratio of sides opposite and adjacent to angle in right-angled triangle **at a tangent** diverging from previous course of action or thought etc. **tangential** /-'dʒen-/ *a.*
**tangerine** /tændʒə'riːn/ *n.* kind of small flat sweet-scented orange.
**tangible** /'tændʒəb(ə)l/ *a.* perceptible by touch; definite, clearly intelligible, not elusive or visionary. **tangibility** *n.*
**tangle** 1 *v.* intertwine or become twisted or involved in confused mass; entangle; complicate. 2 *n.* tangled condition or mass. 3 **tangly** *a.*
**tango** /'tæŋgəʊ/ 1 *n.* (*pl.* -gos) S. Amer. slow ballroom dance; music for this. 2 *v.i.* dance tango.
**tank** *n.* large receptacle for liquid or gas etc.; receptacle for fuel in motor vehicle; *Aus.* reservoir formed by excavation and damming; *Mil.* armoured motor vehicle carrying guns and mounted on Caterpillar tracks.
**tankard** /'tæŋkəd/ *n.* tall mug of pewter etc. for beer.
**tanker** /'tæŋkə(r)/ *n.* ship or aircraft or road vehicle for carrying liquids (esp. mineral oils) in bulk.
**tannery** /'tænəri/ *n.* place where hides are tanned.
**tannic** /'tænɪk/ *a.* of tan. **tannic acid** tannin.
**tannin** /'tænɪn/ *n.* any of several substances extracted from tree-barks etc. and used in tanning etc.
**tansy** /'tænzɪ/ *n.* aromatic herb with yellow flowers.
**tantalize** /'tæntəlaɪz/ *v.t.* torment with disappointment, raise and then dash the hopes of. **tantalization** *n.*
**tantalus** /'tæntələs/ *n.* stand in which spirit-decanters are locked up but visible.
**tantamount** /'tæntəmaʊnt/ *pred.a.* equivalent *to.*
**tantra** /'tæntrə/ *n.* any of a class of Hindu or Buddhist mystical or magical writings.
**tantrum** /'tæntrəm/ *n.* outburst of bad temper or petulance.
**tap**¹ 1 *n.* device by which flow of liquid or gas from pipe or vessel can be controlled; act of tapping telephone. 2 *v.t.* provide (cask) with tap, let out (liquid) thus; draw sap from (tree) by cutting into it; draw supplies or information from; divert part of current from (telegraph or telephone wires etc.) to detect message; make screw-thread in. 3 **on tap** ready to be drawn off, ready for immediate use; **taproom** room where liquor on tap is sold and drunk; **tap-root** tapering root growing vertically downwards.
**tap**² 1 *v.* strike (with) light or gentle blow; knock gently; cause to strike lightly *against* etc. 2 *n.* light blow or sound; *Aus. colloq.* a minimum quantity of work. 3 **tap-dancing** stage dancing with rhythmical tapping of feet.
**tape** 1 *n.* narrow woven strip of cotton etc. used as string; piece of tape stretched across race-course at winning-post; strip of paper or transparent film etc. coated with adhesive for fastening packages etc.; magnetic tape; tape-recording; continuous strip of paper on which messages are printed; tape-measure. 2 *v.t.* tie up or join with tape; record on magnetic tape; measure with tape. 3 **have person, thing, taped** *sl.* have summed him up, fully understand it; **tape-machine** device for receiving and recording telegraph messages; **tape-measure** strip of tape or thin flexible metal marked for measuring length; **tape-recorder** apparatus for recording sounds etc. on magnetic tape and afterwards reproducing them; **tape-recording** *n.*; **tapeworm** tape-like worm parasitic in alimentary canal.
**taper** 1 *n.* wick coated with wax etc. for conveying flame. 2 *v.* diminish in width

**tapestry** /'tæpɪstrɪ/ *n.* thick textile fabric in which coloured weft threads are woven (orig. by hand) to form pictures or designs; embroidery usu. in wools on canvas imitating this; piece of such embroidery.

**tapioca** /tæpɪ'əʊkə/ *n.* starchy granular foodstuff prepared from cassava.

**tapir** /'teɪpə(r)/ *n.* small piglike mammal with short flexible snout.

**tappet** /'tæpɪt/ *n.* arm or cam etc. used in machinery to impart intermittent motion.

**tar**[1] 1 *n.* dark thick inflammable liquid distilled from wood or coal etc.; similar substance formed in combustion of tobacco. 2 *v.t.* cover with tar. 3 **tar macadam** road-making material of crushed stone etc. bound with tar.

**tar**[2] *colloq.* sailor.

**taradiddle** /'tærədɪd(ə)l/ *n. colloq.* fib; nonsense.

**tarantella** /tærən'telə/ *n.* rapid whirling S. Italian dance; music for this.

**tarantula** /tə'ræntjʊlə/ *n.* large black spider of S. Europe; large hairy tropical spider; *Aus.* huntsman spider.

**tarboosh** /tɑː'buːʃ/ *n.* cap like fez.

**tardy** /'tɑːdɪ/ *a.* slow to act or come or happen; behind time.

**tare**[1] /teə(r)/ *n.* vetch, esp. as corn-weed or fodder; in *pl.* injurious corn-weed.

**tare**[2] /teə(r)/ *n.* allowance made for weight of box etc. in which goods are packed; weight of motor vehicle without fuel or load.

**target** /'tɑːgɪt/ *n.* mark for shooting at, esp. with concentric circles round central ring or spot; anything aimed at.

**tariff** /'tærɪf/ *n.* table of fixed charges; duty on particular class of goods; list of duties or customs to be paid.

**tarlatan** /'tɑːlət(ə)n/ *n.* thin stiff muslin.

**Tarmac** /'tɑːmæk/ 1 *n.* (**P**) tar macadam; area surfaced with Tarmac. 2 *v.t.* **tarmac** (*past* & *p.p.* **tarmacked**) apply Tarmac to.

**tarn** *n.* small mountain lake.

**tarnish** /'tɑːnɪʃ/ 1 *v.* lessen or destroy lustre of; impair (reputation etc.); lose lustre. 2 *n.* tarnished state; stain, blemish.

**taro** /'tɑːrəʊ/ *n.* (*pl.* **-ros**) tropical plant of arum family with tuberous root used as food.

**tarot** /'tærəʊ/ *n.* pack of 78 playing-cards used in fortune-telling.

**tarp** *n. Aus. sl.* tarpaulin.

**tarpaulin** /tɑː'pɔːlɪn/ *n.* waterproof cloth esp. of tarred canvas; sheet or covering of this.

**tarpy** /'tɑːpɪ/ *n. Aus. sl.* tarpaulin.

**tarragon** /'tærəgən/ *n.* aromatic herb.

**tarry**[1] /'tɑːrɪ/ *a.* of or smeared with tar.

**tarry**[2] /'tærɪ/ *v.i.* delay, be late; linger.

**tarsus** /'tɑːsəs/ *n.* (*pl.* **-si** /-saɪ/) collection of small bones forming ankle. **tarsal** *a.*

**tart**[1] *n.* pastry case containing fruit or jam etc.

**tart**[2] 1 *n. sl.* prostitute, immoral woman. 2 *v. colloq.* dress *up* gaudily, smarten *up*.

**tart**[3] *a.* sharp-tasting, acid; cutting, biting.

**tartan** /'tɑːt(ə)n/ *n.* pattern of coloured stripes crossing at right angles, worn orig. by Scottish Highlanders in distinctive patterns denoting their clans; cloth woven in such pattern.

**tartar**[1] /'tɑːtə(r)/ *n.* hard deposit that forms on teeth; substance deposited in cask by fermentation of wine. **cream of tartar** preparation of tartaric acid used in cookery.

**Tartar**[2] /'tɑːtə(r)/ *n.* native of Tartary; intractable or violent-tempered person.

**tartar sauce** mayonnaise with chopped gherkins etc.

**tartaric** /tɑː'tærɪk/ *a.* of tartar. **tartaric acid** organic acid present in many plants.

**tartlet** /'tɑːtlɪt/ *n.* small tart.

**tarwhine** /'tɑːwaɪn/ *n. Aus.* edible marine fish, sea-bream.

**task** /tɑːsk/ 1 *n.* piece of work to be done. 2 *v.t.* make great demands on. 3 **take to task** accuse of fault, rebuke. **task force** specially organized unit for task; **taskmaster** person who imposes task or burden.

**Tasmanian** /tæz'meɪnɪən/ 1 *a.* of Tasmania. 2 *n.* native or inhabitant of Tasmania. 3 **Tasmanian devil** black bear-like carnivorous marsupial; **Tasmanian tiger** or **wolf** striped wolf-like carnivorous marsupial.

**tassel** /'tæs(ə)l/ *n.* tuft of hanging

**tassie** /'tæzi/ n. Aus. sl. (also **Tassy**) Tasmanian.

**taste** /teɪst/ 1 n. sensation caused in tongue etc. by contact with some substances, flavour; sense by which this is perceived; small portion of food etc. taken as sample; liking, predilection, (*for*); aesthetic discernment in art or literature or conduct, conformity to its dictates. 2 v. perceive or learn flavour of; have specified flavour; eat small portion of, sample; have experience of. **taste-bud** organ of taste in mouth, esp. on tongue.

**tasteful** /'teɪstfəl/ a. done in or having good taste.

**tasteless** /'teɪstləs/ a. flavourless; having or done in bad taste.

**taster** /'teɪstə(r)/ n. person employed to judge teas or wines etc. by taste; *colloq.* small sample of food etc.

**tasty** /'teɪstɪ/ a. *colloq.* of pleasing flavour, appetizing.

**Taswegian** /tæz'wiːdʒ(ə)n/ n. Aus. sl. Tasmanian.

**tat**[1] n. *colloq.* tatty thing(s) or person; tattiness.

**tat**[2] v. do or make by tatting.

**tatter** /'tætə(r)/ n. (usu. in pl.) rag, irregularly torn piece, esp. hanging loose; *fig.* useless remains.

**tattered** /'tætəd/ a. in tatters.

**tatting** /'tætɪŋ/ n. kind of knotted lace made by hand with small shuttle.

**tattle** /'tæt(ə)l/ 1 v.i. gossip idly; repeat or discuss scandal. 2 n. gossip, idle talk.

**tattoo**[1] /tə'tuː/ n. evening signal recalling soldiers to quarters; elaboration of this with music and marching etc. as entertainment; drumming, rapping; drumbeat.

**tattoo**[2] /tə'tuː/ 1 v.t. mark (skin) by puncturing and inserting pigment; make (design) thus. 2 n. such design.

**tatty** /'tætɪ/ a. *colloq.* tattered, shabby, inferior, tawdry.

**taught** *past* & *p.p.* of **teach**.

**taunt** 1 n. insulting or provoking gibe. 2 v.t. reproach or mock at insultingly or contemptuously.

**Taurus** /'tɔːrəs/ n. second sign of zodiac.

**taut** a. drawn tight; stiff, tense; (of ship etc.) in good condition.

**tauten** /'tɔːt(ə)n/ v. make or become taut.

**tautology** /tɔː'tɒlədʒɪ/ n. saying of same thing twice over in different words. **tautological** a.; **tautologous** a.

**tavern** /'tæv(ə)n/ n. inn, public-house.

**tawdry** /'tɔːdrɪ/ a. showy or gaudy without real value.

**tawny** /'tɔːnɪ/ a. of orange-brown colour.

**tax** 1 n. contribution to State revenue legally levied on person or property or business etc.; strain or heavy demand (*up*)on. 2 v.t. impose tax on; pay tax on; make demands on; charge (*with*), call to account. 3 **tax-deductible** (of expenses) that may be paid out of income before deduction of income tax; **tax return** declaration of income etc. for taxation purposes.

**taxation** /tæk'seɪʃ(ə)n/ n. imposition or payment of tax(es).

**taxi** /'tæksɪ/ 1 n. (in full **taxi-cab**) motor car plying for hire and usu. fitted with taximeter. 2 v. (of aircraft) go along ground or surface of water under machine's own power before or after flying; go or convey in taxi.

**taxidermy** /'tæksɪdɜːmɪ/ a. art of preparing, stuffing, and mounting skins of animals with lifelike effect. **taxidermist** n.

**taximeter** /'tæksɪmiːtə(r)/ n. automatic device indicating fare due fitted to taxi.

**taxonomy** /tæk'sɒnəmɪ/ n. classification, esp. in biology; principles of this. **taxonomical** a.; **taxonomist** n.

**TB** *abbr.* tubercle bacillus; *colloq.* tuberculosis.

**te** /tiː/ n. *Mus.* seventh note of scale in tonic sol-fa.

**tea** n. evergreen shrub or small tree grown in China and India etc.; its dried leaves; infusion made from leaves etc. of other plants or beef extract etc.; meal at which tea is served, esp. light meal in afternoon or evening. **tea-bag** small permeable bag holding tea-leaves for infusion; **tea-break** interruption of work allowed for drinking tea; **teacake** light flat usu. sweet bun; **tea-chest** light metal-lined wooden box in which tea is exported; **tea-cloth** cloth for teatable, tea-towel; **tea-leaf** leaf of tea, esp. in *pl.* after infusion; **teapot** vessel with handle and spout, in which tea is made; **tea-rose** rose with scent like tea; **teaspoon** small spoon for stirring tea etc. or used as measure; **tea-towel** cloth for drying washed crockery etc.; **tea-tree** *Aus.* any of various shrubs or trees of the myrtle family.

**teach** *v.* (*past* & *p.p.* **taught** /tɔːt/) give systematic information to (person) or about (subject or skill); enable (person) to do something by instruction; advocate as moral etc. principle. **teach-in** series of lectures and discussions on subject of public interest.

**teachable** /ˈtiːtʃəb(ə)l/ *a.* apt at learning; that can be taught.

**teacher** /ˈtiːtʃə(r)/ *n.* person who teaches esp. in school.

**teaching** /ˈtiːtʃɪŋ/ *n.* what is taught; doctrine; teachers' profession. **teaching hospital** one where medical students are taught.

**teak** *n.* heavy durable timber; Asian tree yielding this.

**teal** *n.* (*pl.* same) small freshwater duck.

**team** *n.* 1 set of players etc. in game or sport; set of persons working together; set of draught animals. 2 *v.* join (*up*) as team or in common action (*with*). 3 **team-work** combined effort, co-operation.

**teamster** /ˈtiːmstə(r)/ *n.* driver of team; *US* lorry-driver.

**tear**[1] /teə(r)/ 1 *v.* (*past* **tore**; *p.p.* **torn**) pull (apart) with some force; make (hole, rent) thus; move violently or impetuously; undergo tearing. 2 *n.* hole made or damage caused by tearing; torn part of cloth etc. 3 **tearaway** hooligan, ruffian.

**tear**[2] /tɪə(r)/ *n.* drop of clear salty liquid appearing in or flowing from eye as result of emotion, esp. grief, or physical irritation etc. **in tears** weeping; **tear-gas** gas that disables by causing severe irritation to the eyes.

**tearful** /ˈtɪəfəl/ *a.* in or given to weeping; accompanied with tears.

**tearing** /ˈtɛərɪŋ/ *a.* extreme, overwhelming.

**TEAS** *abbr. Aus.* Tertiary Education Assistance Scheme.

**tease** /tiːz/ 1 *v.* irritate playfully or maliciously with jests or petty annoyances etc.; pick (wool etc.) into separate fibres; dress (cloth) with teasels etc. 2 *n. colloq.* person fond of teasing others.

**teasel** /ˈtiːz(ə)l/ *n.* plant with prickly flower-heads; such head dried and used for raising nap on cloth.

**teaser** /ˈtiːzə(r)/ *n. colloq.* difficult question or problem.

**teat** *n.* mammary nipple of animal; device of rubber etc. for sucking milk from bottle.

**tec** *n. sl.* detective.

**Tech** /tek/ *n. colloq.* Technical college or school.

**technical** /ˈteknɪk(ə)l/ *a.* of or involving the mechanical arts and applied sciences; of or relating to a particular subject or craft etc.; requiring special knowledge to be understood; in strict legal sense.

**technicality** /teknəˈkælətɪ/ *n.* being technical; technical expression; technical point or detail.

**technician** /tekˈnɪʃ(ə)n/ *n.* expert in practical application of science; person skilled in technique of art or subject.

**technique** /tekˈniːk/ *n.* mechanical skill in art or craft etc.; method of achieving purpose; manner of execution or performance in music or painting etc.

**technocracy** /tekˈnɒkrəsɪ/ *n.* government or control by technical experts.

**technocrat** ˈteknəkræt/ *n.* advocate of technocracy.

**technology** /tekˈnɒlədʒɪ/ *n.* study of use of the mechanical arts and applied sciences; these subjects collectively. **technological** *a.*; **technologist** *n.*

**teddy bear** /ˈtedɪ/ child's toy bear.

**tedious** /ˈtiːdɪəs/ *a.* tiresomely long, wearisome.

**tedium** /ˈtiːdɪəm/ *n.* tediousness.

**tee**[1] *n.* letter T.

**tee**[2] *Golf* 1 *n.* cleared space from which ball is struck at beginning of play for each hole, small pile of sand or small appliance of wood or rubber etc., on which ball is placed before being thus struck. 2 *v.* place (ball) on tee. 3 **tee off** make first stroke in golf, start, begin.

**teem**[1] *v.i.* swarm *with*; be abundant.

**teem**[2] *v.i.* pour (esp. of rain).

**teenage** /ˈtiːneɪdʒ/ *a.* of or characteristic of teenagers.

**teenager** /'ti:neɪdʒə(r)/ n. person in teens.

**teens** n.pl. years of one's age from 13 to 19.

**teeny** /'ti:nɪ/ a. colloq. tiny.

**teeter** /'ti:tə(r)/ v. totter, stand or move unsteadily.

**teeth** pl. of tooth.

**teethe** /ti:ð/ v.i. grow or cut teeth, esp. milk-teeth. **teething troubles** initial troubles in an enterprise etc.

**teetotal** /ti:'təʊt(ə)l/ a. advocating or practising total abstinence from intoxicants. **teetotalism** n.; **teetotaller** n.

**tele-** /telɪ/ in comb. far; at a distance; television.

**telecommunication** /telɪkəmju:nɪ-'keɪʃ(ə)n/ n. communication over long distances by cable or telegraph or telephone or radio; in pl. this branch of technology.

**telegram** /'telɪgræm/ n. message sent by telegraph.

**telegraph** /'telɪgrɑ:f or -græf/ 1 n. transmission of messages to a distance by making and breaking electrical connection; apparatus for this. 2 v. send message by telegraph; send (message) thus.

**telegraphist** /tə'legrəfɪst/ n. person skilled or employed in telegraphy.

**telegraphic** /telɪ'græfɪk/ a. of telegraphs or telegrams; (of style) economically worded. **telegraphically** adv.

**telegraphy** /tə'legrəfɪ/ n. use or construction of telegraph.

**telemeter** /'telɪmi:tə(r)/ n. apparatus for recording readings of instrument at distance, usu. by radio. **telemetry** /tə'lemətri:/ n.

**teleology** /telɪ'ɒlədʒɪ:/ n. view that events etc. are due to purpose or design that is served by them; study of final causes. **teleological** a.

**telepathy** /tə'lepəθɪ/ n. communication between minds other than by known senses. **telepathic** /-'pæθ-/ a.

**telephone** /'telɪfəʊn/ 1 n. apparatus for transmitting speech and other signals to a distance; transmitting and receiving instrument used in this; system of communication by network of telephones. 2 v. send message or speak to by telephone; make telephone call. 3 **telephone directory** book listing names and numbers of telephone subscribers; **telephone booth, box**, kiosk containing telephone for public use; **telephone number** number assigned to particular subscriber and used in making connections to his telephone. 4

**telephonic** /-'fɒn-/ a.; **telephonically** adv.

**telephonist** /tə'lefənɪst/ n. operator in telephone exchange or a switchboard.

**telephony** /tə'lefənɪ/ n. use or system of telephones.

**telephotography** /telɪfə'tɒgrəfɪ/ n. photographing distant object with combined lenses giving large image. **telephoto** a.; **telephotographic** a.

**teleprinter** /'telɪprɪntə(r)/ n. telegraph instrument for sending messages by typing.

**telescope** /'telɪskəʊp/ 1 n. optical instrument using lenses or mirrors to make distant objects appear nearer and larger; (in full **radio telescope**) apparatus for collecting radio waves from celestial objects. 2 v. press or drive (sections of tube etc.) one into another like sections of telescope; close or be driven or be capable of closing thus; compress.

**telescopic** /telɪ'skɒpɪk/ a. of or made with telescope; consisting of sections that telescope. **telescopic sight** small telescope used as sight for firearm etc.

**televise** /'telɪvaɪz/ v.t. transmit by television.

**television** /'telɪvɪʒ(ə)n/ n. system for reproducing on a screen visual images transmitted (with sound) by radio signals; (in full **television set**) apparatus for displaying pictures transmitted by television.

**televisual** /telɪ'vɪzju:əl/ a. of television.

**telex** /'teleks/ 1 n. system of telegraphy using teleprinters and public telecommunication network. 2 v.t. send or communicate with by telex.

**tell** v. (past & p.p. **told** /təʊld/) relate or narrate; utter or express in words; inform or give information of etc.; divulge, reveal; betray secret; ascertain, decide about, distinguish; instruct or order (to do etc.); be of account or weight, produce marked effect (on). **tell off** colloq. scold, reprimand; **tell-tale** person who tells tales, automatic registering device, attrib. serving to reveal

**teller** /'telə(r)/ n. person employed to receive and pay out money in bank etc.; person appointed to count votes.

**telling** /'telɪŋ/ a. having marked effect, striking.

**telly** /'telɪ/ n. colloq. television.

**temerity** /tə'merɪtɪ/ n. rashness, audacity.

**temp** n. colloq. temporary employee, esp. secretary.

**temper** /'tempə(r)/ 1 n. habitual or temporary disposition of mind esp. as regards composure; irritation, anger; condition of metal as regards hardness and elasticity. 2 v.t. bring (clay, metal) to proper consistency or hardness; moderate or mitigate by blending *with* another quality. 3 **lose one's temper** become angry.

**tempera** /'tempərə/ n. method of painting using emulsion e.g. of pigment with egg.

**temperament** /'tempərəmənt/ n. person's distinct nature and character, which permanently affects behaviour.

**temperamental** /tempərə'ment(ə)l/ a. liable to erratic or peculiar moods.

**temperance** /'tempərəns/ n. moderation and self-restraint, esp. in eating and drinking; total or partial abstinence from alcoholic drink.

**temperate** /'tempərət/ a. avoiding excess, moderate; (of climate) not exhibiting extremes of heat or cold.

**temperature** /'tempərətʃə(r)/ n. degree or intensity of heat of body or atmosphere, esp. as shown by thermometer; colloq. body temperature above normal.

**tempest** /'tempəst/ n. violent storm.

**tempestuous** /tem'pestjʊəs/ a. stormy, turbulent.

**template** /'templeɪt/ n. thin board or plate used as guide in cutting or drilling.

**temple**¹ /'temp(ə)l/ n. building treated as the dwelling-place, or devoted to worship, of god(s). **Inner, Middle, Temple** two Inns of Court in London.

**temple**² /'temp(ə)l/ n. flat part of side of head between forehead and ear.

**tempo** /'tempəʊ/ n. (pl. **-pos** or **-pi** /-piː/) speed at which music is (to be) played; rate of motion or activity.

**temporal** /'tempər(ə)l/ a. of worldly as opposed to spiritual affairs, secular; of or denoting time; of the temples of the head.

**temporary** /'tempərərɪ/ 1 a. lasting or meant to last only for a time. 2 n. person employed temporarily. 3 **temporarily** adv.

**temporize** /'tempəraɪz/ v.i. avoid committing oneself, act so as to gain time comply temporarily with requirements of occasion. **temporization** n.

**tempt** v.t. entice, incite; allure, attract risk provoking.

**temptation** /temp'teɪʃ(ə)n/ n. tempting or being tempted; incitement esp to sin; attractive thing or course of action.

**ten** a. & n. one more than nine. **tenfold** a. & adv.; **tenth** a. & n.

**tenable** /'tenəb(ə)l/ a. that can be maintained against attack or objection; that can be held *for* period or *by* person etc

**tenacious** /tə'neɪʃəs/ a. keeping firm hold (*of*); retentive; holding tightly, not easily separable, tough. **tenacity** /-næs-/ n.

**tenancy** /'tenənsɪ/ n. tenant's position

**tenant** /'tenənt/ n. person who rents land or (part of) house from landlord occupant of place.

**tenantry** /'tenəntrɪ/ n. tenants.

**tench** n. (pl. same) freshwater fish of carp family.

**tend**¹ v.i. be apt or inclined, conduce (*to*); be moving or directed in certain direction.

**tend**² v.t. take care of, look after.

**tendency** /'tendənsɪ/ n. tending, leaning, inclination.

**tendentious** /ten'denʃəs/ a. derog. designed to advance a cause.

**tender**¹ /'tendə(r)/ a. not tough or hard easily touched or wounded; delicate fragile; loving, affectionate **tenderfoot** novice, newcomer **tenderloin** middle part of loin of pork

**tender**² /'tendə(r)/ 1 v. offer, hand in present; offer as payment; make tende (*for*). 2 n. offer, esp. to execute work o supply goods at fixed price. 3 **legal tender** currency that cannot legally b refused in payment of debt.

**tender**³ /'tendə(r)/ n. vessel attendin larger one to supply stores etc.; truc

**tenderize** /ˈtendəraɪz/ v.t. render (meat) tender by beating etc.

**tendon** /ˈtend(ə)n/ n. tough fibrous tissue connecting muscle to bone etc.

**tendril** /ˈtendrəl/ n. one of the slender leafless shoots by which some climbing plants cling.

**tenement** /ˈtenəmənt/ n. dwelling-house; portion of house occupied separately; house divided into and let in tenements.

**tenet** /ˈtenət/ n. doctrine held by group or person etc.

**tennis** /ˈtenɪs/ n. (in full **lawn tennis**) ball game played with rackets on court divided by net.

**tenon** /ˈten(ə)n/ n. projection shaped to fit into mortise.

**tenor** /ˈtenə(r)/ n. adult male voice between male alto and baritone; singer with tenor voice; music for tenor voice; general purport; prevailing course of one's life or habits.

**tense**[1] 1 a. stretched tight; strained or highly strung. 2 v. make or become tense.

**tense**[2] n. form taken by verb to indicate time of action etc.; set of such forms for various persons and numbers.

**tensile** /ˈtensaɪl/ a. of tension; capable of being stretched. **tensility** /-ˈsɪl-/ n.

**tension** /ˈtenʃ(ə)n/ n. stretching or being stretched; mental strain or excitement; strained state; effect produced by forces pulling against each other; electromotive force.

**tent** n. portable shelter or dwelling of canvas etc. **born in a tent** Aus. colloq. tending to leave doors open.

**tentacle** /ˈtentək(ə)l/ n. slender flexible appendage of animal, used for feeling, grasping, or moving.

**tentative** /ˈtentətɪv/ a. done by way of trial, experimental; hesitant, not definite.

**tenterhooks** /ˈtentəhʊks/ n.pl. **on tenterhooks** in suspense, distracted by uncertainty.

**tenuous** /ˈtenjʊəs/ a. slight, of little substance; subtle; thin, slender. **tenuity** n.

**tenure** /ˈtenjʊə(r)/ n. holding of property or office; conditions or period of this.

**tepee** /ˈtiːpiː/ n. N. Amer. Indian's conical tent.

**tepid** /ˈtepɪd/ a. slightly warm, lukewarm. **tepidity** n.

**tequila** /teˈkiːlə/ n. Mexican liquor made from agave.

**tercentenary** /tɜːsenˈtiːnərɪ/ n. 300th anniversary; celebration of this.

**terebinth** /ˈterəbɪnθ/ n. S. Eur. tree yielding turpentine.

**tergiversation** /tɜːdʒɪvəˈseɪʃ(ə)n/ n. desertion of party or principles; making of conflicting statements.

**term** 1 n. word used to express definite concept esp. in branch of study etc.; in pl. language used, mode of expression; in pl. relation, footing; in pl. conditions, stipulations, charge, price; limited period; period of action or of contemplated results; period during which instruction is given in school or university or during which lawcourt holds sessions; Math. each quantity in ratio or series, item of compound algebraic expression. 2 v.t. denominate, call. 3 **come to terms with** reconcile oneself to; **terms of reference** points referred to an individual or body of persons for decision or report, scope of inquiry etc., definition of this.

**termagant** /ˈtɜːməgənt/ n. overbearing woman, virago.

**terminable** /ˈtɜːmənəb(ə)l/ a. that may be terminated.

**terminal** /ˈtɜːmən(ə)l/ 1 a. of or forming the last part or terminus; Med. forming or undergoing last stage of fatal disease; of or done etc. each term. 2 n. terminating thing, extremity; terminus; point of connection for closing electric circuit; air terminal; apparatus for transmission of messages to and from computer or communications system etc.

**terminate** /ˈtɜːmənɛɪt/ v. bring or come to an end; end in etc.

**termination** /tɜːməˈneɪʃ(ə)n/ n. ending, way something ends; word's final syllable or letter(s).

**terminology** /tɜːməˈnɒlədʒɪ/ n. system of terms used in particular subject. **terminological** a.

**terminus** /ˈtɜːmənəs/ n. (pl. **-nuses** or **-ni** /-naɪ/) point at end of railway or bus route or of pipeline etc.

**termite** /'tɜːmaɪt/ n. antlike insect destructive to timber.

**tern** n. sea-bird with long pointed wings and forked tail.

**ternary** /'tɜːnərɪ/ a. composed of 3 parts.

**terrace** /'terəs/ n. raised level space, natural or artificial, esp. for walking or standing; row of houses built in one block of uniform style; (usu. in pl.) flight of wide shallow steps as for spectators at sports ground.

**terracotta** /terə'kɒtə/ n. unglazed usu. brownish-red fine pottery; its colour.

**terra firma** /terə 'fɜːmə/ dry land, firm ground.

**terrain** /tə'reɪn/ n. tract of country as regards its natural features.

**terrapin** /'terəpɪn/ n. N. Amer. edible freshwater tortoise.

**terrarium** /te'reərɪəm/ n. (pl. **-riums**) place for keeping small land animals; ornamental transparent structure containing growing plants.

**terrestrial** /te'restrɪəl/ a. of or on the earth; of or on dry land.

**terrible** /'terəb(ə)l/ a. causing or fit to cause terror; dreadful; *colloq.* very great or bad, incompetent.

**terribly** /'terəblɪ/ adv. in a terrible manner; *colloq.* very, extremely.

**terrier** /'terɪə(r)/ n. small active hardy dog.

**terrific** /tə'rɪfɪk/ a. causing terror; *colloq.* of great size or intensity; *colloq.* excellent.

**terrify** /'terɪfaɪ/ v.t. fill with terror, frighten.

**terrine** /tə'riːn/ n. pâté or similar food; earthenware vessel for holding this.

**territorial** /terə'tɔːrɪəl/ **1** a. of territory or territories. **2** n. **Territorial** member of Territorial Army. **3 Territorial Army** volunteer reserve force organized by localities; **territorial waters** waters under State's jurisdiction, esp. part of sea within stated distance of shore.

**Territorian** /terə'tɔːrɪən/ n. Aus. native or inhabitant of the Northern Territory.

**territory** /'terətərɪ/ n. extent of land under jurisdiction of sovereign or State etc.; **Territory**, organized division of a country esp. if not yet admitted to full rights of a State; sphere of action or thought, province; area over which commercial traveller etc. operates; area defended by animal against others of same species or by team etc. in game.

**terror** /'terə(r)/ n. extreme fear; terrifying person or thing; *colloq.* troublesome or tiresome person, esp. child.

**terrorism** /'terərɪz(ə)m/ n. practice of using violent and intimidating methods, esp. to secure political ends. **terrorist** n.

**terrorize** /'terəraɪz/ v. fill with terror; coerce by terrorism. **terrorization** n.

**terry** /'terɪ/ n. pile fabric with loops left uncut.

**terse** /tɜːs/ a. concise, brief and forcible in style; curt.

**tertiary** /'tɜːʃərɪ/ a. of third order or rank etc.

**Terylene** /'terəliːn/ n. (P) synthetic polyester used as textile fabric.

**tessellated** /'tesəleɪtɪd/ a. of or resembling mosaic; having finely chequered surface. **tessellation** n.

**test 1** n. critical examination or trial of qualities or nature of person or thing; means or standard or circumstances suitable for or serving such examination; *colloq.* test match. **2** v.t. subject to test, make trial of; try severely, tax. **3 test bed** equipment for testing aircraft engines etc. before general use; **test case** *Law* case whose decision is taken as settling other similar cases; **test match** one of series of (esp. cricket) matches between different countries; **test-tube** thin glass tube closed at one end used to hold substance undergoing chemical test etc.; **test-tube baby** *colloq.* baby conceived by artificial insemination or developed elsewhere than in a mother's body.

**testaceous** /tes'teɪʃəs/ a. having hard continuous shell.

**testacy** /'testəsɪ/ n. being testate.

**testament** /'testəmənt/ n. a will; *colloq.* written statement of one's beliefs etc. **Old, New, Testament** main divisions of Bible.

**testamentary** /testə'mentərɪ/ a. of or by or in a will.

**testate** /'testeɪt/ **1** a. having left valid will at death. **2** n. testate person.

**testator** /tes'teɪtə(r)/ n. person who has made a will, esp. one who dies testate.

**testatrix** /'testeɪtrɪks/ n. female testator.

**testes** pl. of **testis**.

**testicle** /'testɪk(ə)l/ n. male organ that secretes spermatozoa, esp. one of pair in scrotum behind penis of man and most male mammals.

**testify** /'testɪfaɪ/ v. bear witness; give evidence; affirm, declare, be evidence of.

**testimonial** /testɪ'məʊnɪəl/ n. certificate of character or conduct or qualifications; gift presented as mark of esteem.

**testimony** /'testɪmənɪ/ n. Law oral or written statement made under oath or affirmation; evidence.

**testis** /'testəs/ n. (pl. **-tes** /-tiːz/) testicle.

**testosterone** /tes'tɒstərəʊn/ n. male sex hormone.

**testy** /'testɪ/ a. irascible, short-tempered.

**tetanus** /'tetənəs/ n. bacterial disease with continuous painful contraction of voluntary muscles.

**tetchy** /'tetʃɪ/ a. peevish, irritable.

**tête-à-tête** /teɪtɑː'teɪt/ 1 n. private conversation or interview between two persons. 2 adv. together in private.

**tether** /'teðə(r)/ 1 n. rope etc. by which grazing animal is confined. 2 v.t. fasten with tether. 3 **end of one's tether** extreme limit of one's strength or patience etc.

**tetra-** in comb. four.

**tetrad** /'tetræd/ n. group of 4.

**tetragon** /'tetrəgən/ n. plane figure with 4 sides and angles. **tetragonal** /-'træg-/ a.

**tetrahedron** /tetrə'hiːdrən/ n. (pl. **-drons**) 4-sided triangular pyramid. **tetrahedral** a.

**tetralogy** /te'trælədʒɪ/ n. group of 4 related literary or dramatic works.

**Teutonic** /tjuː'tɒnɪk/ a. of Germanic peoples or languages.

**text** n. main body of book; wording of anything written or printed, esp. opp. to translation or commentary etc.; passage of Scripture quoted or chosen as subject of sermon etc.; subject, theme; in pl. books prescribed for study. **textbook** manual of instruction, standard book in any branch of study.

**textile** /'tekstaɪl/ 1 n. woven material. 2 a. of weaving; woven.

**textual** /'tekstjʊəl/ a. of or in or concerning a text.

**texture** /'tekstʃə(r)/ 1 n. quality of a surface or substance when felt or looked at; arrangement of threads in textile fabric. 2 v.t. give particular esp. rough texture to. 3 **textural** a.

**thalidomide** /θə'lɪdəmaɪd/ n. sedative drug found in 1961 to cause malformation of limbs of embryo when taken by mother early in pregnancy.

**than** /ðæn/ conj. introducing second element in comparison or statement of difference.

**thane** /θeɪn/ n. hist. holder of land from Engl. king by military service, or from Sc. king and ranking below earl; clan-chief.

**thank** /θæŋk/ 1 v.t. express gratitude to. 2 n. in pl. gratitude, expression of gratitude. 3 **thank-offering** gift made in gratitude; **thanksgiving** expression of gratitude esp. to God; **Thanksgiving (Day)** US annual holiday on fourth Thurs. in Nov.; **thanks to** as good or bad result of; **thank you** polite formula acknowledging gift or service or accepted offer, etc.; **no thank you** polite refusal of offer.

**thankful** /'θæŋkfəl/ a. grateful, pleased, expressive of thanks.

**thankless** /'θæŋkləs/ a. not feeling or expressing gratitude; (of task etc.) unprofitable.

**that** /ðæt/ 1 pron. (pl. **those** /ðəʊz/) the person or thing indicated or named or understood; coupled or contrasted with **this**; the one, the person, etc.; used to introduce defining clause. 2 a. (pl. **those**) designating the person or thing indicated etc. 3 adv. to such a degree, so. 4 conj. introducing subordinate clause indicating esp. statement or hypothesis or purpose or result. 5 **at that** too, besides; **that is** in other words, more correctly or intelligibly.

**thatch** /θætʃ/ 1 n. roofing of straw or reeds etc. 2 v.t. roof with thatch.

**thaw** /θɔː/ 1 v. release or escape from frozen state; warm into liquid state or into life or animation or cordiality. 2 n. thawing; warmth of weather that thaws.

**the** (before vowel /ðiː/, before conson-

**theatre** /ˈθɪətə(r)/ n. building or outdoor area for dramatic performances; plays and acting; room or hall for lectures etc. with seats in tiers; scene or field of operation; operating theatre.

**theatrical** /θɪˈætrɪk(ə)l/ 1 a. of or for theatre or acting; calculated for effect, showy. 2 n. in pl. dramatic performances. 3 **theatricality** n.

**thee** /ðiː/ pron. obj. case of **thou**.

**theft** /θeft/ n. stealing.

**their** /ðeər/ pron., poss. case of **they** with absol. form **theirs**.

**theism** /ˈθiːɪz(ə)m/ n. belief in divine creation and conduct of the universe. **theist** n.; **theistic** a.

**them** /ðem/ pron. obj. case of **they**.

**theme** /θiːm/ n. subject or topic (of talk etc.); US school exercise on given subject; Mus. leading melody in a composition. **theme song**, **tune**, signature tune. **thematic** /-ˈmæt-/ a.

**themselves** /ðəmˈselvz/ pron., emphat. and refl. form of **they**.

**then** /ðen/ 1 adv. at that time; after that, next; in that case, accordingly. 2 a. existing etc. at that time. 3 n. that time. 4 **then and there** immediately and on the spot.

**thence** /ðens/ adv. from that place, for that reason. **thenceforth**, **thenceforward**, from that time on.

**theo-** /θiːəʊ/ in comb. God or god.

**theocracy** /θiːˈɒkrəsɪ/ n. form of government by God or god directly or through a priestly order etc. **theocratic** a.; **theocratically** adv.

**theodolite** /θiːˈɒdəlaɪt/ n. surveying-instrument for measuring angles.

**theology** /θiːˈɒlədʒɪ/ n. study or system of (esp. Christian) religion. **theologian** /-ˈləʊdʒ-/ n.; **theological** a.

**theorem** /ˈθɪərəm/ n. general proposition not self-evident but demonstrable by argument.

**theoretical** /θɪəˈretɪk(ə)l/ a. concerned with knowledge but not with its practical application; based on theory rather than experience.

**theoretician** /θɪərəˈtɪʃ(ə)n/ n. person concerned with theoretical part of a subject.

**theorist** /ˈθɪərəst/ n. holder or inventor of a theory.

**theorize** /ˈθɪəraɪz/ v.i. evolve or indulge in theories.

**theory** /ˈθɪərɪ/ n. supposition or system of ideas explaining something, esp. one based on general principles; speculative view; sphere of abstract knowledge or speculative thought; exposition of principles of a science etc.; Math. collection of propositions to illustrate principles of a subject.

**theosophy** /θiːˈɒsəfɪ/ n. philosophy professing to achieve knowledge of God by direct intuition or spiritual ecstasy etc. **theosophical** a.

**therapeutic** /θerəˈpjuːtɪk/ a. of or for or tending to the cure of diseases.

**therapeutics** n.pl. (usu. treated as sing.) branch of medicine concerned with remedial treatment of ill health.

**therapy** /ˈθerəpɪ/ n. curative medical etc. treatment. **therapist** n.

**there** /ðeə(r)/ 1 adv. in or at that place; to that place or point; at that point; in that respect. 2 n. that place or point. 3 int. drawing attention to anything. 4 **thereabout(s)** near that place or amount or time; **thereafter** formal after that; **thereby** by that means or agency; **therefore** for that reason, accordingly, consequently; **therein** in that place or respect; **thereof** formal of that, of it; **thereto** to that or it, in addition; **thereupon** in consequence of that, directly after that.

**therm** /θɜːm/ n. unit of heat, esp. statutory unit of calorific value in gas-supply (100,000 British thermal units).

**thermal** /ˈθɜːm(ə)l/ 1 a. of or for or producing heat. 2 n. rising current of heated air. 3 **British thermal unit** amount of heat required to raise 1 lb. of water 1° F.

**thermionic valve** /θɜːmiˈɒnɪk/ device giving flow of electrons in one direction from heated substance, used esp. in rectification of current and in radio reception.

**thermo-** in comb. heat.

**thermodynamics** /θɜːməʊdaɪˈnæ-

**thermometer** ... mıks/ *n.pl.* usu. treated as *sing.* science of relationship between heat and other forms of energy.

**thermometer** /θə'mɒmətə(r)/ *n.* instrument for measuring temperature, esp. graduated glass tube containing mercury or alcohol. **thermometric** /-'met-/ *a.*; **thermometry** *n.*

**thermonuclear** /θɜːməʊ'njuːklɪə(r)/ *a.* relating to nuclear reactions that occur only at very high temperatures; (of bomb etc.) using such reactions.

**thermoplastic** /θɜːməʊ'plæstɪk/ 1 *a.* becoming soft and plastic on heating and hardening on cooling. 2 *n.* thermoplastic substance.

**Thermos** /'θɜːmɒs/ *n.* (**P**) vacuum flask.

**thermosetting** /θɜːməʊ'setɪŋ/ *a.* (of plastics) setting permanently when heated.

**thermostat** /'θɜːməstæt/ *n.* device for automatic regulation of temperature. **thermostatic** *a.*

**thesaurus** /θə'sɔːrəs/ *n.* (*pl.* **-ri** /-raɪ/) dictionary of synonyms etc.

**these** *pl.* of **this**.

**thesis** /'θiːsɪs/ *n.* (*pl.* **-ses** /-siːz/) proposition to be maintained or proved; dissertation esp. by candidate for university degree.

**Thespian** /'θespɪən/ 1 *a.* of tragedy or dramatic art. 2 *n.* actor or actress.

**thews** /θjuːz/ *n.pl. literary* person's muscular strength.

**they** /ðeɪ/ *pron.* (*obj.* **them** *poss.* **their** /ðeɪ(r)/) *pl.* of **he**, **she**, and **it**.

**thick** /θɪk/ 1 *a.* of great or specified depth between opposite surfaces; (of line etc.) broad, not fine; closely set; numerous; crowded; abounding or packed *with*; firm in consistency; made of thick material; muddy, not clear; *colloq.* dull, stupid; (of voice) indistinct; *colloq.* intimate. 2 *n.* thick part of anything. 3 *adv.* thickly. 4 **a bit thick** *sl.* unreasonable, too much to tolerate; **in the thick of it** in the busiest part of an activity etc.; **thick-headed** stupid; **thickset** set or growing close together, heavily or solidly built; **thick-skinned** not sensitive to criticism or rebuff; **through thick and thin** under all conditions, in spite of all difficulties.

**thicken** /'θɪkən/ *v.* make or become thick(er).

**thicket** /'θɪkət/ *n.* dense growth of small trees or shrubs etc.

**thief** /θiːf/ *n.* (*pl.* **thieves**) one who steals, esp. secretly and without violence.

**thieve** /θiːv/ *v.* be a thief; steal. **thievery** *n.*

**thievish** /'θiːvɪʃ/ *a.* given to stealing.

**thigh** /θaɪ/ *n.* part of leg between hip and knee.

**thimble** /'θɪmb(ə)l/ *n.* metal or plastic cap worn to protect finger and push needle in sewing.

**thimbleful** *n.* small quantity esp. of liquid to drink.

**thin** /θɪn/ 1 *a.* having opposite surfaces close together, of small thickness or diameter; (of line etc.) narrow, fine; made of thin material; lean, not plump; not dense or copious; of slight consistency; weak, lacking an important ingredient; (of excuse etc.) transparent, flimsy; *sl.* wretched and uncomfortable. 2 *v.* make or become thin(ner). 3 *adv.* thinly. 4 **thin out** reduce number of; **thin-skinned** sensitive to criticism.

**thine** /ðaɪn/ *poss. a.* belonging to thee; what is thine.

**thing** /θɪŋ/ *n.* any possible object of thought including persons, material objects, events, qualities, ideas, utterances, and acts; *colloq.* one's special interest or concern; in *pl.* personal belongings or (esp. outer) clothing or equipment; in *pl.* the world in general. **the thing** what is conventionally proper or fashionable, what is needed or required or most important; **have a thing about** be obsessed or prejudiced about.

**thingummy** /'θɪŋəmɪ/ *n. colloq.* (also **thingamajig** etc.) person or thing whose name one forgets or does not know.

**think** /θɪŋk/ 1 *v.* (*past & p.p.* **thought** /θɔːt/) be of opinion; consider; exercise mind; form connected ideas; conceive notion *of* doing; form conception of; contemplate. 2 *n. colloq.* act of thinking. **think about** consider; **think of** consider, imagine, intend, contemplate, entertain ideas of, hit upon; **think out** consider carefully, devise; **think over** reflect upon; **think-tank** body of experts providing advice and ideas on national and commercial problems;

**think twice** avoid hasty action etc.; **think up** *colloq.* devise, produce by thought.

**thinker** /ˈθɪŋkə(r)/ *n.* person who thinks in specified way; person with skilled or powerful mind.

**thinking** /ˈθɪŋkɪŋ/ 1 *a.* thoughtful; intellectual. 2 *n.* opinion, judgement.

**third** /θɜːd/ 1 *a.* next after second. 2 *n.* third person or class etc.; one of 3 equal divisions of whole. 3 **third class** class next after second in accommodation or examination-list etc.; **third degree** severe and protracted interrogation by police etc.; **third man** *Crick.* fieldsman near boundary behind slips; **third party** another party besides the two principals, bystander etc.; **third-party insurance** insurance against damage or injury suffered by person other than the insured; **third-rate** inferior, very poor; **Third World** developing countries of Africa, Asia, and Latin America.

**thirst** /θɜːst/ 1 *n.* desire for a drink; suffering caused by lack of drink; ardent desire, craving. 2 *v.i.* feel thirst.

**thirsty** /ˈθɜːstɪ/ *a.* feeling thirst; (of country or season) dry, parched; *fig.* eager (*for, after*); *colloq.* causing thirst.

**thirteen** /θɜːˈtiːn/ *a.* & *n.* one more than twelve. **thirteenth** *a.* & *n.*

**thirty** /ˈθɜːtɪ/ *a.* & *n.* three times ten. **thirtieth** *a.* & *n.*

**this** /ðɪs/ 1 *pron.* (*pl.* **these** /ðiːz/) the person or thing near or present or just mentioned or understood; contrasted with *that*. 2 *a.* (*pl.* **these**) designating the person or thing close at hand etc.; the present or current. 3 *adv.* to this degree or extent.

**thistle** /ˈθɪs(ə)l/ *n.* prickly herbaceous plant usu. with globular heads of purple flowers; this as Scottish national emblem. **thistledown** down containing thistle-seeds. **thistly** *a.*

**thither** /ˈðɪðə(r)/ *adv.* *arch.* to that place.

**thole** /θəʊl/ *n.* pin in gunwale of boat as fulcrum for oar; each of two such pins between which oar works.

**thong** /θɒŋ/ *n.* narrow strip of hide or leather.

**thorax** /ˈθɔːræks/ *n.* (*pl.* **-races** /-rəsiːz/) part of the body between neck and abdomen. **thoracic** /-ˈræs-/ *a.*

**thorn** /θɔːn/ *n.* stiff sharp-pointed projection on plant; thorn-bearing shrub or tree.

**thorny** /ˈθɔːnɪ/ *a.* having many thorns; *fig.* (of subject) hard to handle without offence.

**thorough** /ˈθʌrə/ *a.* complete, unqualified, not superficial; acting or done with great care etc. **thoroughbred** of pure breed, high-spirited, (*n.*) such animal, esp. horse; **thoroughfare** public way open at both ends, esp. main road; **thoroughgoing** uncompromising, extreme.

**those** *pl.* of *that*.

**thou** /ðaʊ/ *pron.* (*obj.* **thee** *poss.* **thine** and **thy**) of 2nd pers. *sing.*, now *arch.* or *poet.*

**though** /ðəʊ/ 1 *conj.* in spite of the fact that; even if, granting that; **as though** as if. 2 *adv. colloq.* however, all the same.

**thought**¹ /θɔːt/ *n.* process or power or faculty etc. of thinking; sober reflection, consideration; idea, notion; way of thinking; intention, purpose; (usu. in *pl.*) one's opinion. **thought-reader** person able to perceive another's thoughts.

**thoughtful** /ˈθɔːtfəl/ *a.* engaged in or given to meditation; considerate.

**thoughtless** /ˈθɔːtləs/ *a.* careless of consequences or of others' feelings; caused by lack of thought.

**thousand** /ˈθaʊz(ə)nd/ *a.* & *n.* ten hundred. **thousandth** *a.* & *n.*

**thrall** /θrɔːl/ *n.* slave; slavery. **thraldom** *n.*

**thrash** /θræʃ/ *v.t.* beat, esp. with stick or whip; conquer, surpass; thresh; move violently *about* etc. **thrash out** discuss to conclusion.

**thread** /θred/ 1 *n.* spun-out cotton or silk or glass etc.; length of this; thin cord of twisted yarns used esp. in sewing and weaving; anything regarded as threadlike with ref. to its continuity or connectedness; spiral ridge of screw. 2 *v.t.* pass thread through (needle's eye, beads); arrange (material in strip form, e.g. film) in proper position on equipment; pick one's way through (maze, crowded place, etc.). 3 **threadbare** (of cloth) so worn that nap is lost and threads showing, (of person) shabby, (of idea etc.) commonplace, hackneyed.

**threat** /θret/ *n.* declaration of intention to punish or hurt; indication of proximity of something undesirable; person or thing regarded as dangerous.

**threaten** /ˈθret(ə)n/ *v.t.* use threats towards; be sign or indication of (something undesirable); announce one's intention (*to* do); give warning of infliction of (harm etc.).

**three** /θriː/ *a.* & *n.* one more than two. **three-cornered** triangular, (of contest etc.) between 3 persons; **three-cornered jack** *Aus.* spiny emex; **three-decker** ship with 3 decks, sandwich with 3 slices of bread, 3-volume novel; **three-dimensional** having or appearing to have length, breadth, and depth; **three-legged race** race between pairs with right leg of one tied to other's left leg; **three-ply** (wool etc.) having 3 strands, (plywood) having 3 layers; **three-point turn** method of turning vehicle round in narrow space; **three-quarter** *Rugby footb.* any of 4 players just behind half-backs; **threescore** *arch.* 60. **threefold** *adv.*

**threesome** /ˈθriːsəm/ *n.* group of 3 persons.

**threnody** /ˈθrenədi/ *n.* song of lamentation.

**thresh** *v.* beat out or separate grain from husks of corn etc.

**threshold** /ˈθreʃhəʊld/ *n.* plank or stone forming bottom of doorway; point of entry; limit below which stimulus causes no reaction.

**threw** *past* of **throw**.

**thrice** *adv.* three times.

**thrift** *n.* frugality, economical management. **thrifty** *a.*

**thrill** 1 *n.* wave or nervous tremor of emotion or sensation; throb, pulsation. 2 *v.* (cause to) experience thrill; quiver or throb (*as*) with emotion.

**thriller** /ˈθrɪlə(r)/ *n.* sensational or exciting play or story etc.

**thrive** *v.i.* (*past* **throve** or **thrived**; *p.p.* **thriven** /ˈθrɪv(ə)n/ or **thrived**) prosper; grow vigorously.

**throat** *n.* gullet or windpipe; front of neck; narrow passage or entrance.

**throaty** /ˈθrəʊti/ *a.* (of voice) deficient in clarity, hoarsely resonant.

**throb** 1 *v.i.* palpitate, pulsate; (of heart etc.) beat strongly; quiver, vibrate. 2 *n.* throbbing, violent beat or pulsation.

**throe** *n.* (usu. in *pl.*) violent pang. **in the throes of** *colloq.* struggling with the task of.

**thrombosis** /θrɒmˈbəʊsəs/ *n.* (*pl.* **-ses** /-siːz/) coagulation of blood in blood-vessel or organ during life.

**throne** 1 *n.* chair of state for sovereign or bishop etc.; sovereign power. 2 *v.t.* enthrone.

**throng** 1 *n.* crowd, multitude, esp. in small space. 2 *v.* come or go or press in multitudes; fill (as) with crowd.

**throstle** /ˈθrɒs(ə)l/ *n.* song thrush.

**throttle** /ˈθrɒt(ə)l/ 1 *n.* valve controlling flow of steam or fuel in engine; throat. 2 *v.* choke, strangle; control (engine etc.) with throttle. 3 **throttle back**, **down**, reduce speed of (engine etc.) by throttling.

**through** /θruː/ 1 *prep.* from end to end or side to side of; between or among; from beginning to end of; by agency or means or fault of; by reason of; *US* up to and including. 2 *adv.* through something; from end to end; to the end. 3 *a.* (concerned with) going through; going all the way without change of line or vehicle etc.; (of traffic) going through a place to its destination. 4 **be through** have finished (*with*), cease to have dealings (*with*); **through and through** thoroughly, completely; **throughput** amount of material put through a manufacturing etc. process or a computer.

**throughout** /θruːˈaʊt/ 1 *prep.* from end to end of; in every part of. 2 *adv.* in every part or respect.

**throve** *past* of **thrive**.

**throw** /θrəʊ/ 1 *v.* (*past* **threw**; *p.p.* **thrown**) release (thing) after imparting motion, propel through space, send forth or dismiss esp. with some violence; compel to be in specified condition; project (rays, light, etc.); cast (shadow); bring to the ground; *colloq.* disconcert; put (clothes etc.) carelessly or hastily *on* or *off* etc.; cause (dice) to fall on table etc., obtain (specified number) thus; cause to pass or extend suddenly to another state or position; move (switch or lever) to on position; shape (pottery) on wheel; have (fit, tantrum, etc.); *colloq.* give (a party). 2 *n.* act of throwing; distance a missile is or may be thrown; being thrown in

**thrum** 1 v. play monotonously or unskilfully on or *on*; drum or tap idly on or *on*. 2 n. such playing; resultant sound.

**thrush**[1] n. kind of small bird.

**thrush**[2] n. fungoid infection of throat esp. in children, or of vagina.

**thrust** 1 v. (past & p.p. **thrust**) push with sudden impulse or with force; impose (thing) forcibly on; make lunge or stab *with* weapon; force oneself *through* or *past* etc. 2 n. sudden or forcible push or lunge; forward force exerted by propeller or jet etc.; strong attempt to penetrate enemy's line or territory; remark aimed at person; stress between parts of arch etc. 3 **thrust oneself in** obtrude, interfere.

**thud** /θʌd/ 1 n. low dull sound as of blow on non-resonant thing. 2 v.i. make thud; fall with thud.

**thug** /θʌg/ n. vicious or brutal ruffian. **thuggery** n.

**thumb** /θʌm/ 1 n. short thick digit, set apart from the fingers on hand; part of glove for thumb. 2 v.t. soil or wear with thumb; turn over pages (as) with thumb; make request for (lift) by sticking out thumb. 3 **thumb-index** set of lettered grooves cut in fore-edge of dictionary etc. to assist use; **thumbnail sketch** brief verbal description; **thumb-screw** instrument of torture for squeezing thumbs; **under person's thumb** dominated by him.

**thump** /θʌmp/ 1 n. heavy blow, sound of this. 2 v. beat heavily, esp. with fist; deliver heavy blows.

**thumping** /'θʌmpɪŋ/ a. colloq. big.

**thunder** /'θʌndə(r)/ 1 n. loud noise accompanying lightning; any loud deep rumbling or resounding noise; authoritative censure or threats. 2 v. sound with or like thunder; utter or emit in loud or impressive manner; move with loud noise; make violent threats. 3 **thunderbolt** flash of lightning with crash of thunder, imaginary bolt or shaft as destructive agent; **thunderclap** crash of thunder; **thunderstorm** storm with thunder and lightning; **thunderstruck** amazed. 4 **thundery** a.

**thundering** /'θʌndərɪŋ/ a. colloq. very big or great.

**thunderous** /'θʌndərəs/ a. as loud as thunder.

**thurible** /'θjʊərəb(ə)l/ n. censer.

**Thurs.** abbr. Thursday.

**Thursday** /'θɜːzdeɪ or -dɪ/ n. fifth day of week.

**thus** /ðʌs/ adv. in this way, like this; accordingly, and so; to this extent, number, or degree.

**thwack** n. & v.t. hit esp. with stick.

**thwart** /θwɔːt/ 1 v.t. frustrate, foil. 2 n. seat across boat for rower etc.

**thy** /ðaɪ/ pron. poss. case of **thou**.

**thyme** /taɪm/ n. shrubby herb with fragrant aromatic leaves.

**thymol** /'θaɪmɒl/ n. antiseptic made from oil of thyme.

**thymus** /'θaɪməs/ n. ductless gland near base of neck.

**thyroid** /'θaɪrɔɪd/ n. thyroid gland. **thyroid cartilage** large cartilage of larynx, projection of which in man forms Adam's apple; **thyroid gland** large ductless gland near larynx secreting a hormone which regulates growth and development, extract of this.

**thyself** /ðaɪ'self/ pron. emphat. and refl. form of **thou**.

**ti** var. of **te**.

**tiara** /tɪ'ɑːrə/ n. jewelled ornamental band worn on front of woman's hair; Pope's 3-crowned diadem.

**tibia** /'tɪbɪə/ n. (pl. **-biae** /-biː/) shinbone.

**tic** n. habitual spasmodic contraction of muscles, esp. of face.

**tick**[1] 1 n. slight recurring click, esp. that of watch or clock; colloq. moment, instant; small mark set against items

# tick        593        tight

in list etc. in checking. **2** *v.* make sound of tick; mark (*off*) with tick. **3 tick off** *sl.* reprimand; **tick over** (of engine or *fig.*) idle; **tick-tack** kind of manual semaphore signalling by racecourse bookmakers.

**tick**[2] *n.* parasitic arachnid or insect on animals.

**tick**[3] *n. colloq.* credit.

**tick**[4] *n.* case of mattress or bolster; ticking.

**ticker** /'tɪkə(r)/ *n. colloq.* heart; watch, tape-machine. **ticker-tape** *US* paper strip from tape-machine, esp. as thrown from windows to greet a celebrity.

**ticket** /'tɪkɪt/ **1** *n.* piece of paper or card entitling holder to enter place or participate in event or travel by public transport etc.; certificate of discharge from army or of qualification as ship's master or pilot etc.; label attached to thing and giving price etc.; notification of traffic offence etc.; list of candidates put forward by group, esp. political party, principles of party. **2** *v.t.* attach ticket to. **3 the ticket** *sl.* the correct or desirable thing; **have tickets on oneself** *Aus. colloq.* be conceited.

**ticking** /'tɪkɪŋ/ *n.* strong usu. striped linen or cotton material to cover mattress etc.

**tickle** /'tɪk(ə)l/ **1** *v.* touch or stroke lightly so as to excite nerves and usu. produce laughter; feel this sensation; excite agreeably, amuse. **2** *n.* act or sensation of tickling.

**ticklish** /'tɪklɪʃ/ *a.* sensitive to tickling; difficult, requiring careful handling.

**tidal** /'taɪd(ə)l/ *a.* of or due to or affected by or resembling tides. **tidal wave** exceptionally large ocean wave (fig. one attributed to earthquake etc.), widespread manifestation of feeling etc.

**tiddler** /'tɪdlə(r)/ *n. colloq.* small fish, esp. stickleback or minnow; unusually small thing.

**tiddly** /'tɪdlɪ/ *a. sl.* slightly drunk.

**tiddly-winks** /'tɪdlɪwɪŋks/ *n.* game of flipping small counters into receptacle.

**tide 1** *n.* regular rise and fall of sea due to attraction of moon and sun; water as moved by this; trend of opinion or fortune or events; *arch.* time, season. **2** *v.* be carried by the tide. **3 tide-mark** mark made by tide at high water, *colloq.* line of dirt round bath, or on body of person showing extent of washing; **tide person over** help him through temporary need; **tideway** tidal part of river.

**tidings** /'taɪdɪŋz/ *n.* as *sing.* or *pl.* news.

**tidy** /'taɪdɪ/ **1** *a.* neat, orderly; neatly arranged; *colloq.* considerable. **2** *n.* receptacle for odds and ends. **3** *v.t.* make tidy; put in order.

**tie 1** *v.* (*partic.* tying) attach or fasten with cord etc.; form into knot or bow; tie strings etc. of; restrict, bind; make same score as another competitor; bind (rafters etc.) by crosspiece etc.; *Mus.* unite notes by tie; in *p.p.* (of dwelling-house) occupied subject to tenant's working for house's owner, (of public house etc.) bound to supply only particular brewer's liquor. **2** *n.* cord or chain etc. used for fastening; necktie; thing that unites or restricts persons; equality of score or draw or dead heat among competitors; match between any pair of players or teams; rod or beam holding parts of structure together; *Mus.* curved line above or below two notes of same pitch that are to be joined as one. **3 tie-break** means of deciding winner when competitors have tied; **tie-clip, -pin**, ornamental clip, pin, to hold necktie in place; **tie up** fasten with cord etc., invest (money etc.) so that it is not immediately available for use, obstruct.

**tier** /tɪə(r)/ **1** *n.* row or rank or unit of structure, as one of several placed one above another; (in Tasmania) mountain range. **2** *v.t.* arrange in tiers.

**tiff** *n.* slight or petty quarrel.

**tiffin** /'tɪfən/ *n. Anglo-Ind.* lunch.

**tiger** /'taɪgə(r)/ *n.* (*fem.* **tigress**) large Asian animal of cat family, with yellowish and black stripes; fierce or energetic person; *colloq.* formidable opponent in game. **tiger-cat** any moderate-sized feline resembling tiger; **tiger-lily** tall garden lily with dark-spotted orange flowers.

**tight** /taɪt/ **1** *a.* closely held or drawn or fastened or fitting or constructed; impermeable, impervious; tense, stretched; *colloq.* drunk; (of money or materials) not easily obtainable; produced by or requiring great exertion or pressure; stringent, demanding; *colloq.*

**tighten** 1 *a.* presenting difficulties; *colloq.* tight-fisted. 2 *adv.* tightly. 3 *n.* in *pl.* thin close-fitting elastic garment covering legs and lower half of body. 4 **tight-fisted** stingy; **tight-lipped** restraining emotion; **tightrope** tightly stretched rope or wire on which acrobats etc. perform.

**tighten** /'taɪt(ə)n/ *v.* make or become tight(er).

**tilde** /'tɪldə/ *n.* mark (˜) placed over letter, e.g. Spanish *n* in *señor*.

**tile** 1 *n.* thin slab of baked clay or other material for covering roof or floor etc. 2 *v.t.* cover with tiles.

**till**[1] 1 *prep.* up to, as late as. 2 *conj.* up to time when; to degree that.

**till**[2] *n.* money-drawer in counter of bank or shop etc., esp. with device recording amount of each purchase.

**till**[3] *v.t.* cultivate (land).

**tillage** /'tɪlɪdʒ/ *n.* preparation of land for crop-bearing; tilled land.

**tiller** /'tɪlə(r)/ *n.* bar by which rudder is turned.

**tilt** 1 *v.* (cause to) assume sloping position or heel over; thrust or run at with lance etc.; engage in contest *with*. 2 *n.* tilting; sloping position; (of medieval knights etc.) charging with lance against opponent or mark. 3 **at full tilt** at full speed, with full force.

**tilth** /tɪlθ/ *n.* tillage, cultivation; cultivated soil.

**timber** /'tɪmbə(r)/ *n.* wood for building or carpentry etc.; piece of wood, beam, esp. as rib of vessel; large standing trees.

**timbered** /'tɪmbəd/ *a.* made (partly) of timber; wooded.

**timbre** /'tæbr/ *n.* distinctive character of musical sound or voice apart from its pitch and intensity.

**timbrel** /'tɪmbr(ə)l/ *n. arch.* tambourine.

**time** 1 *n.* indefinite continuous duration regarded as dimension; finite duration as distinct from eternity; more or less definite portion of this, historical or other period; allotted or available portion of time; definite or fixed point or portion of time; season; occasion; in *pl.* (preceded by numeral etc.) expressing multiplication; lifetime; in *pl.* prevailing circumstances of period; prison sentence; apprenticeship; measured amount of time worked; rhythm or measure of musical composition. 2 *v.t.* choose time for, do at chosen or appropriate time; ascertain time taken by. 3 **at the same time** simultaneously, nevertheless; **at times** now and then; **behind the times** old-fashioned; **from time to time** occasionally; **in no time** rapidly, in a moment; **in time** not late, early enough, sooner or later, following time of music etc.; **on time** punctually; **time-and-motion** concerned with measuring efficiency of industrial etc. operations; **time bomb** one designed to explode at pre-set time; **time-honoured** respected on account of antiquity, traditional; **timekeeper** person who takes or records time, watch or clock esp. in respect of accuracy; **time-lag** interval between cause etc. and effect; **time off, out,** time used for rest or different activity; **timepiece** clock or watch; **time-server** person who adapts himself to opinions of the times or of persons in power; **time-sharing** use of computer by several persons for different operations at the same time, use of holiday home by several joint owners at different times of year; **time-signal** audible indication of exact time of day; **time-signature** *Mus.* indication of tempo; **time-switch** one operating automatically at set time; **timetable** table showing times of public transport services, scheme of school work etc.; **time zone** range of longitudes where a common standard time is used.

**timeless** /'taɪmləs/ *a.* not affected by passage of time.

**timely** /'taɪmlɪ/ *a.* opportune, coming at right time.

**timer** /'taɪmə(r)/ *n.* person or device that measures time taken.

**timid** /'tɪmɪd/ *a.* easily alarmed; shy. **timidity** *n.*

**timing** /'taɪmɪŋ/ *n.* way thing is timed.

**timorous** /'tɪmərəs/ *a.* timid, frightened.

**timpani** /'tɪmpənɪ/ *n.pl.* kettledrums. **timpanist** *n.*

**tin** 1 *n.* white metal used esp. in alloys and in making tin plate; vessel of tin or tin plate esp. for preserving food; tin plate. 2 *v.t.* pack (food) in tin for preservation; cover or coat with tin. 3 **tin foil**

**tincture** thin sheet of tin or aluminium or tin alloy, used to wrap food for cooking or keeping fresh etc.; **tin hat** *sl.* modern soldier's steel helmet; **tinned dog** *Aus. sl.* canned meat; **tin-pan alley** world of composers and publishers of popular music; **tin plate** sheet iron or steel coated with tin; **tinpot** cheap, inferior; **tin-tack** small round iron tack.

**tincture** /'tɪŋktʃə(r)/ 1 *n.* slight flavour or tinge (*of*); medicinal solution *of* drug in alcohol. 2 *v.t.* colour slightly, tinge, flavour; affect slightly (*with* quality).

**tinder** /'tɪndə(r)/ *n.* dry substance readily taking fire from spark. **tindery** *a.*

**tine** *n.* prong or tooth or point of fork or comb or antler etc.

**tinge** /tɪndʒ/ 1 *v.t.* colour slightly (*with*). 2 *n.* tendency to or trace of some colour; slight admixture of a feeling or quality.

**tingle** /'tɪŋg(ə)l/ 1 *v.i.* feel or cause slight pricking or stinging sensation. 2 *n.* tingling sensation.

**tinker** /'tɪŋkə(r)/ 1 *n.* itinerant mender of kettles and pans etc.; *Sc. & Ir.* gipsy; *colloq.* mischievous person or animal. 2 *v.i.* work in amateurish or clumsy fashion *at* or *with* (thing) by way of repair or alteration; work as tinker.

**tinkle** /'tɪŋk(ə)l/ 1 *n.* sound (as) of small bell. 2 *v.* (cause to) make tinkle.

**tinny** 1 *a.* like tin; flimsy; sounding like struck tin; *Aus. sl.* lucky. 2 *n. Aus. colloq.* can of beer.

**tinsel** /'tɪns(ə)l/ *n.* glittering decorative metallic strips or threads etc.; superficial brilliance or splendour.

**tint** 1 *n.* a variety of a colour; tendency towards or admixture of a different colour; faint colour spread over surface. 2 *v.t.* apply tint to, colour.

**tintinnabulation** /tɪntɪnæbjə'leɪʃ(ə)n/ *n.* ringing of bells.

**tiny** /'taɪnɪ/ *a.* very small.

**tip**[1] 1 *n.* extremity, esp. of small or tapering thing; small piece or part attached to tip, esp. mouthpiece of cigarette. 2 *v.t.* provide with tip. 3 **tiptop** first-rate, of highest excellence.

**tip**[2] 1 *v.* (cause to) lean or slant; overturn, cause to overbalance; discharge contents of (jug, wagon, etc.) thus; give usu. small present of money to, esp. for service; name as likely winner of race or contest; strike or touch lightly. 2 *n.* small present of money esp. for service; piece of useful private or special information, or prediction, given by expert; piece of advice; slight push or tilt; place where refuse etc. is tipped; light touch or blow. 3 **tip-off** a hint; **tip person off** give him warning or hint or inside information; **tip-up** able to be tipped, e.g. of seat as used in theatre to allow passage past.

**tippet** /'tɪpɪt/ *n.* small cape or collar of fur etc.

**tipple** /'tɪp(ə)l/ 1 *v.* drink intoxicating liquor habitually or repeatedly in small quantities. 2 *n. colloq.* alcoholic drink.

**tipster** /'tɪpstə(r)/ *n.* person who gives tips about horse-racing etc.

**tipsy** /'tɪpsɪ/ *a.* slightly intoxicated; caused by or showing intoxication.

**tiptoe** /'tɪptəʊ/ 1 *n.* the tips of the toes. 2 *v.i.* walk on tiptoe or stealthily. 3 *adv.* on tiptoe, with heels off the ground.

**tirade** /taɪ'reɪd/ *n.* long vehement denunciation or declamation.

**tire**[1] /taɪə(r)/ *v.* make or grow weary; exhaust patience or interest in; in *p.p.* having had enough *of.*

**tire**[2] *US* var. of **tyre**.

**tireless** /'taɪələs/ *a.* of inexhaustible energy.

**tiresome** /'taɪəsəm/ *a.* tedious; *colloq.* annoying.

**tiro** /'taɪrəʊ/ *n.* (*pl.* -**ros**) beginner, novice.

**tissue** /'tɪʃuː/ *n.* any of the coherent substances of which animal or plant bodies are made; tissue-paper; disposable piece of thin absorbent paper for wiping or drying etc.; *Aus.* cigarette paper; fine woven esp. gauzy fabric; connected series (*of* lies etc.). **tissue-paper** thin soft unsized paper for wrapping etc.

**tit**[1] *n.* any of various small birds.

**tit**[2] *n.* **tit for tat** blow for blow, retaliation.

**tit**[3] *n. vulg.* woman's breast, nipple.

**Titan** /'taɪt(ə)n/ *n.* person of superhuman size or intellect or strength etc.

**titanic** /taɪ'tænɪk/ *a.* gigantic, colossal.

**titanium** /taɪ'teɪnɪəm/ *n.* dark-grey metallic element.

**titbit** /'tɪtbɪt/ *n.* choice or delicate morsel or item.

**tithe** /taɪð/ *hist.* 1 *n.* tenth part of an-

**Titian** nual produce of land or labour taken as tax for support of clergy and church. **2** *v.t.* subject to tithes.

**Titian** /ˈtɪʃ(ə)n/ *a.* (of hair) bright golden auburn.

**titillate** /ˈtɪtɪleɪt/ *v.t.* excite pleasantly, tickle. **titillation** *n.*

**titivate** /ˈtɪtɪveɪt/ *v.t. colloq.* adorn or smarten (*oneself*); put finishing touches to.

**title** /ˈtaɪt(ə)l/ *n.* name of book or work of art; heading of chapter etc.; title-page; caption or credit title of film; form of nomenclature denoting person's status or used in addressing or referring to person; championship in sport; legal right to possession of (esp. real) property; just or recognized claim (*to*); **title-deed** document constituting evidence of ownership; **title-page** page at beginning of book bearing title and particulars of authorship etc.; **title-role** part in play etc. from which title is taken.

**titled** /ˈtaɪt(ə)ld/ *a.* having title of nobility or rank.

**titmouse** /ˈtɪtmaʊs/ *n.* (*pl.* -**mice**) = **tit**¹.

**titrate** /taɪˈtreɪt/ *v.t.* ascertain quantity of constituent in (solution) by adding measured amounts of reagent. **titration** *n.*

**titter** /ˈtɪtə(r)/ **1** *v.i.* laugh covertly, giggle. **2** *n.* such laugh.

**tittle** /ˈtɪt(ə)l/ *n.* particle, whit.

**tittle-tattle** *n.* & *v.i.* gossip, chatter.

**tittup** /ˈtɪtəp/ **1** *v.i.* go friskily or jerkily, bob up and down, canter. **2** *n.* such gait or movement.

**titular** /ˈtɪtjʊlə(r)/ *a.* held by virtue of title; existing or being such only in name.

**tizzy** /ˈtɪzɪ/ *n. sl.* state of nervous agitation.

**TNT** *abbr.* trinitrotoluene.

**to** /tuː/ **1** *prep.* in direction of; as far as, not short of; used to introduce indirect obj. of verb etc., to introduce infinitive, to express purpose or consequence etc., and to limit meaning or application of adj. **2** *adv.* to or in normal or required position or condition, esp. to a standstill. **3 to and fro** backwards and forwards, from place to place; **to-do** *colloq.* bustle, fuss.

**toad** *n.* froglike amphibian breeding in water but living chiefly on land; repulsive person. **toadflax** a yellow-flowered plant; **toad-in-the-hole** sausages or other meat baked in batter.

**toadstool** /ˈtəʊdstuːl/ *n.* fungus (usu. poisonous) with round top and slender stalk.

**toady** /ˈtəʊdɪ/ **1** *n.* sycophant; obsequious hanger-on. **2** *v.* fawn, behave servilely (*to*); fawn upon. **3 toadyism** *n.*

**toast 1** *n.* bread in slices browned on both sides by heat; person or thing in whose honour company is requested to drink; call to drink or instance of drinking thus. **2** *v.* brown by heat, warm at fire etc.; drink to the health or in honour of. **3 toasting-fork** long-handled fork for toasting bread etc.; **toast-master** person announcing toasts at public dinner; **toast-rack** rack for holding slices of toast at table.

**toaster** /ˈtəʊstə(r)/ *n.* electrical device for making toast.

**tobacco** /təˈbækəʊ/ *n.* (*pl.* -**os**) plant of Amer. origin with leaves used for smoking, chewing, or snuff; its leaves esp. as prepared for smoking etc.

**tobacconist** /təˈbækənɪst/ *n.* dealer in tobacco.

**toboggan** /təˈbɒɡən/ **1** *n.* long light narrow sledge for going downhill esp. over snow. **2** *v.i.* ride on toboggan.

**toby jug** /ˈtəʊbɪ/ mug or small jug in shape of seated man in 3-cornered hat.

**toccata** /təˈkɑːtə/ *n. Mus.* composition for keyboard instrument designed to exhibit performer's touch and technique.

**tocsin** /ˈtɒksɪn/ *n.* alarm-signal; bell used to sound alarm.

**today** /təˈdeɪ/ **1** *adv.* on this present day; nowadays, in modern times. **2** *n.* this present day; modern times.

**toddle** /ˈtɒd(ə)l/ *v.i.* walk with young child's short unsteady steps; *colloq.* take casual or leisurely walk. **2** *n.* toddling walk.

**toddler** /ˈtɒdlə(r)/ *n. colloq.* child just learning to walk.

**toddy** /ˈtɒdɪ/ *n.* sweetened drink of spirits and hot water.

**toe 1** *n.* any of terminal members of foot; part of footwear that covers toes; lower end or tip of implement etc. **2** *v.t.* touch with toe(s). **3 on one's toes** alert, eager; **toe-cap** reinforced part of shoe

# toey        tonality

covering toes; **toe-hold** slight foothold, small beginning or advantage; **toe the line** *fig.* conform esp. under pressure.

**toey** /'təʊi/ *a. Aus. sl.* restless, anxious.

**toff** *n. sl.* distinguished or well-dressed person.

**toffee** /'tɒfi/ *n.* a kind of firm or hard sweet made of boiled butter and sugar etc. **toffee-apple** toffee-coated apple on stick; **toffee-nosed** snobbish or pretentious.

**tog** 1 *n. sl.* in *pl.* clothes; *Aus.* swimming-costume. 2 *v.t. sl.* dress (*out*, *up*).

**toga** /'təʊgə/ *n.* ancient Roman citizen's loose flowing outer garment.

**together** /tə'geðə(r)/ 1 *adv.* in(to) company or conjunction; simultaneously; one with another; in unbroken succession. 2 *a. colloq.* well organized or controlled.

**toggle** /'tɒg(ə)l/ *n.* device for fastening with cross-piece which can pass through hole in one position but not in other; *Computers* command which alternatively activates and switches off a function etc.

**toil** 1 *v.i.* work long or laboriously (*at*); make slow painful progress. 2 *n.* labour; drudgery. 3 **toilsome** *a.*

**toilet** /'tɔɪlɪt/ *n.* lavatory; process of washing oneself and dressing etc. (**make one's toilet** do this). **toilet-paper** soft paper for cleaning oneself after using lavatory; **toilet-roll** roll of toilet-paper; **toilet water** scented liquid used after washing.

**toiletries** /'tɔɪlɪtrɪːz/ *n.pl.* articles used in making one's toilet.

**toils** /tɔɪlz/ *n.pl.* net, snare.

**token** /'təʊkən/ 1 *n.* sign or symbol (of); reminder; keepsake; voucher exchangeable for goods; anything used to represent something else, esp. money. 2 *a.* perfunctory. 3 **token payment** payment of small proportion of sum due as indication that debt is not repudiated; **token strike** brief strike to demonstrate strength of feeling only.

**tokenism** /'təʊkənɪz(ə)m/ *n.* granting minimum concessions.

**told** *past* & *p.p.* of **tell**.

**tolerable** /'tɒlərəb(ə)l/ *a.* endurable; fairly good.

**tolerance** /'tɒlərəns/ *n.* willingness or ability to tolerate; permitted variation in dimension or weight etc.

**tolerant** /'tɒlərənt/ *a.* disposed or accustomed to tolerate others; enduring or patient *of*.

**tolerate** /'tɒləreɪt/ *v.t.* allow the existence or occurrence of without authoritative interference; leave unmolested, not be harmed by; find or treat as endurable. **toleration** *n.*

**toll**[1] /təʊl/ *n.* charge payable for permission to pass barrier or use bridge or road etc.; *fig.* cost or damage caused by disaster or incurred in achievement. **toll-gate** barrier preventing passage until toll is paid.

**toll**[2] /təʊl/ 1 *v.* (of bell) ring with slow succession of strokes, cause (bell) to strike thus, esp. for death or funeral; announce or give out thus. 2 *n.* tolling or stroke of bell.

**toluene** /'tɒljuːiːn/ *n.* colourless liquid hydrocarbon used in manufacture of explosives etc.

**tom** *n.* (in full **tom cat**) male cat.

**tomboy** /'tɒmbɔɪ/ *n.* girl who enjoys rough noisy recreations.

**tomfool** /tɒm'fuːl/ 1 *n.* fool. 2 *a.* extremely foolish. 3 **tomfoolery** *n.*

**tomtit** /'tɒmtɪt/ *n.* tit, esp. blue tit.

**tomahawk** /'tɒməhɔːk/ *n.* war-axe of N. Amer. Indians; *Aus.* hatchet.

**tomato** /tə'mɑːtəʊ/ *n.* (*pl.* **-toes**) glossy red or yellow fleshy edible fruit; plant bearing this.

**tomb** /tuːm/ *n.* grave; burial-vault; sepulchral monument. **tombstone** memorial stone over grave.

**tombola** /tɒm'bəʊlə/ *n.* kind of lottery.

**tome** *n.* large book or volume.

**Tommy** /'tɒmi/ *n.* British private soldier.

**tommy-gun** /'tɒmɪgʌn/ *n.* kind of submachine-gun.

**tomorrow** /tə'mɒrəʊ/ 1 *adv.* on day after today; in future. 2 *n.* the day after today; the near future.

**tom-tom** /'tɒmtɒm/ *n.* kind of drum usu. beaten with hands.

**ton** /tʌn/ *n.* measure of weight, 2,240 lb. (**long ton**) or 2,000 lb. (**short ton**) or 1,000 kg. (**metric ton**); unit of measurement for ship's tonnage; *colloq.* large number or amount.

**tonal** /'təʊn(ə)l/ *a.* of or relating to tone or tonality.

**tonality** /tə'nælɪtɪ/ *n.* relationship between tones of a musical scale or of colour-scheme of a picture; observance of single tonic key as basis of musical composition.

**tone** 1 *n.* sound, esp. with reference to pitch, quality, and strength; modulation of voice to express emotion etc., corresponding style in writing; musical note, sound of definite pitch and character; tint or shade of colour; prevailing character of morals and sentiments etc.; proper firmness of bodily organs, state of (good) health. 2 *v.* give tone or quality to; harmonize; alter tone or colour of. 3 **tone-deaf** unable to perceive differences in musical pitch; **tone down** lessen emphasis or vigour of, undergo such lessening; **tone up** provide with or receive higher tone or greater vigour.

**toneless** /'təʊnləs/ *a.* dull, lifeless; unexpressive.

**tongs** *n.pl.* implement consisting of two limbs connected by hinge or pivot etc. for grasping and lifting things.

**tongue** /tʌŋ/ *n.* muscular organ in mouth used in tasting, speaking, swallowing, etc.; tongue of ox etc. as food; faculty or manner of speaking; words, language; thing like tongue in shape. **tongue-tied** too shy to speak; **tongue-twister** sequence of words difficult to pronounce quickly and correctly.

**tonic** /'tɒnɪk/ 1 *n.* invigorating medicine; anything serving to invigorate; tonic water; *Mus.* keynote. 2 *a.* serving as a tonic, invigorating; of tones in music, esp. of the keynote. 3 **tonic sol-fa** musical notation used esp. in teaching singing; **tonic water** carbonated drink with quinine.

**tonight** /tə'naɪt/ 1 *adv.* on present evening or night; on evening or night of today. 2 *n.* the present evening or night, the evening or night of today.

**tonnage** /'tʌnɪdʒ/ *n.* ship's internal cubic capacity or freight-carrying capacity; charge per ton on cargo or freight.

**tonne** /tʌn/ *n.* metric ton (1,000 kg.).

**tonsil** /'tɒnsɪl/ *n.* either of two small organs on each side of root of tongue.

**tonsillectomy** /tɒnsɪ'lektəmɪ/ *n.* surgical removal of tonsils.

**tonsillitis** /tɒnsɪ'laɪtɪs/ *n.* inflammation of tonsils.

**tonsorial** /tɒn'sɔːrɪəl/ *a.* of barber or his work.

**tonsure** /'tɒnʃə(r)/ 1 *n.* shaving of head or of patch on crown as clerical or monastic symbol; bare patch so made. 2 *v.t.* give tonsure to.

**too** *adv.* to a greater extent than is desirable or permissible; in addition, moreover; *colloq.* extremely.

**took** *past* of **take**.

**tool** /tuːl/ 1 *n.* implement for working upon something, usu. one held in hand; simple machine e.g. lathe; thing used in activity; person used by another merely for his own purposes. 2 *v.* dress (stone) with chisel; impress design on (leather book-cover); *sl.* drive or ride (**along**, **around**) esp. in casual or leisurely manner.

**toot** /tuːt/ 1 *n.* sound (as) of horn etc. 2 *v.* sound (horn etc.); give out such sound.

**tooth** /tuːθ/ *n.* (*pl.* **teeth**) each of a set of hard structures in jaws of most vertebrates, used for biting and chewing things; toothlike projection or thing, e.g. cog of gear-wheel, point of saw or comb etc.; sense of taste; in *pl.* force or effectiveness. **fight tooth and nail** fight fiercely; **get one's teeth into** devote oneself seriously to; **in the teeth of** in spite of, in opposition to, directly against (wind etc.); **show one's teeth** adopt threatening manner. **toothache** pain in teeth; **toothbrush** small brush with long handle, for cleaning teeth; **toothpaste** preparation for cleaning teeth; **toothpick** small sharp instrument for removing food etc. lodged between teeth.

**toothsome** /'tuːθsəm/ *a.* (of food) delicious.

**toothy** /'tuːθɪ/ *a.* having large or numerous or prominent teeth.

**tootle** /'tuːt(ə)l/ *v.* toot gently or continuously.

**top**[1] 1 *n.* highest point or part; upper surface, upper part; cover or cap of container etc.; highest rank, foremost place, person holding this; garment for upper part of body; (usu. in *pl.*) leaves etc. of plant grown chiefly for its root; utmost degree, height; *Naut.* platform round head of lower mast. 2 *a.* highest in position or degree or importance. 3 *v.t.* furnish with top or cap; be higher

**top**        599        **tortoise**

than or superior to; surpass; reach or be at top of; remove top of; hit golfball above centre. **4 on top** above, in superior position; **on top of** *fig.* fully in command of, in addition to; **top brass** *colloq.* high-ranking officers; **topcoat** overcoat, final coat of paint etc.; **top dog** *sl.* victor, master; **top drawer** high social position or origin; **top-dress** apply manure or fertilizer on top of (earth) without ploughing it in; **top-flight** in highest rank of achievement; **top hat** tall silk hat; **top-heavy** overweighted at top; **topknot** bow or tuft or crest etc. worn or growing on top of head; **topmast** smaller mast on top of lower mast; **top-notch** *colloq.* first-rate, excellent; **top secret** most secret, extremely secret; **topside** outer side of round of beef, side of ship above water-line; **topsoil** top layer of soil; **top up** fill up (partly empty container).

**top²** *n.* toy with sharp point at bottom on which it rotates when set in motion.

**topaz** /ˈtəʊpæz/ *n.* semi-precious stone of various colours, esp. yellow.

**toper** /ˈtəʊpə(r)/ *n. arch.* person who drinks to excess, esp. habitually.

**topi** /ˈtəʊpiː/ *n.* (also **topee**) sun hat or helmet.

**topiary** /ˈtəʊpɪərɪ/ **1** *n.* art of clipping trees etc. into ornamental shapes. **2** *a.* of this art.

**topic** /ˈtɒpɪk/ *n.* subject of discourse or argument or discussion etc.

**topical** /ˈtɒpɪk(ə)l/ *a.* dealing with esp. current or local topics. **topicality** /-ˈkæl-/ *n.*

**topless** /ˈtɒpləs/ *a.* without a top; (of woman's garment) leaving breasts bare; (of woman) so clothed.

**topmost** /ˈtɒpməʊst/ *a.* uppermost, highest.

**topography** /təˈpɒɡrəfɪ/ *n.* natural and artificial features of a district; knowledge or description of these. **topographer** *n.*; **topographical** *a.*

**topology** /təˈpɒlədʒɪ/ *n.* study of geometrical properties unaffected by changes of shape and size. **topological** *a.*; **topologist** *n.*

**topper** /ˈtɒpə(r)/ *n. colloq.* top hat.

**topple** /ˈtɒp(ə)l/ *v.* (cause to) fall from vertical to horizontal position.

**topsy-turvy** /ˌtɒpsɪˈtɜːvɪ/ *adv. & a.* upside down; in utter confusion.

**toque** /təʊk/ *n.* woman's close-fitting brimless hat.

**tor** *n.* rocky hill-top.

**torch** *n.* small portable electric lamp; piece of resinous wood or twisted flax etc. soaked in tallow for carrying lighted in hand; source of inspiration etc. **carry a torch for** have (esp. unreturned) love for.

**tore** *past of* **tear¹**.

**toreador** /ˈtɒrɪədɔː(r)/ *n.* bullfighter, esp. on horseback.

**torment 1** /ˈtɔːment/ *n.* (cause of) severe bodily or mental suffering. **2** /-ˈment/ *v.t.* subject to torment, tease or worry excessively. **3 tormentor** *n.*

**tornado** /tɔːˈneɪdəʊ/ *n.* (*pl.* **-does**) violent storm over small area, esp. rotatory one advancing in narrow path.

**torpedo** /tɔːˈpiːdəʊ/ **1** *n.* (*pl.* **-does**) cigar-shaped self-propelled underwater or aerial missile that can be aimed at ship. **2** *v.t.* destroy or attack with torpedo(es); *fig.* make ineffective. **3 torpedo-boat** small fast warship armed with torpedoes.

**torpid** /ˈtɔːpɪd/ *a.* sluggish; dull; dormant; numb. **torpidity** *n.*

**torpor** /ˈtɔːpə(r)/ *n.* apathy; being dormant.

**torque** /tɔːk/ *n.* twisting or rotary force in mechanism etc.; twisted metal necklace worn by ancient Britons and Gauls etc.

**torrent** /ˈtɒrənt/ *n.* rushing stream of water etc.; downpour of rain; violent flow (*of* words etc.). **torrential** /-ˈren-/ *a.*

**torrid** /ˈtɒrɪd/ *a.* scorched, parched; intensely hot.

**torsion** /ˈtɔːʃ(ə)n/ *n.* twisting, twist.

**torso** /ˈtɔːsəʊ/ *n.* (*pl.* **-sos**) trunk of human body; statue lacking head and limbs; mutilated or unfinished work.

**tort** *n.* breach of legal duty (other than under contract) with liability for damages. **tortious** *a.*

**tortilla** /tɔːˈtɪlə/ *n.* Latin Amer. thin flat maize cake eaten hot.

**tortoise** /ˈtɔːtəs/ *n.* land or freshwater slow-moving reptile with body enclosed in horny shell. **tortoiseshell** mottled yellowish-brown turtle-shell, cat or butterfly with markings suggesting tortoiseshell.

**tortuous** /'tɔːtjuːəs/ *a.* winding, indirect, involved. **tortuosity** *n.*

**torture** /'tɔːtʃə(r)/ 1 *n.* infliction of severe bodily pain e.g. as punishment or means of persuasion; severe physical or mental pain. 2 *v.t.* subject to torture; distort, strain, wrench.

**Tory** 1 *n.* member of Conservative party. 2 *a.* Conservative. 3 **Toryism** *n.*

**tosh** *n. sl.* rubbish, nonsense.

**toss** 1 *v.* throw or roll about from side to side, restlessly or with fitful to-and-fro motion; throw, esp. lightly or carelessly or easily; (of bull etc.) fling up with horns; throw back (head), esp. in contempt or impatience; throw (coin) into air to decide choice etc. by way it falls, settle question or dispute with thus. 2 *n.* tossing; sudden jerk, esp. of head; throw from horseback etc. 3 **argue the toss** dispute choice already made; **toss off** dispatch (work) rapidly or easily, drink (liquor) off at a draught; **toss up** toss coin; **toss-up** tossing of coin, doubtful matter.

**tot**[1] *n. colloq.* small child; small quantity of liquor.

**tot**[2] *v.* add (*up*), mount *up* (*to*).

**total** /'təʊt(ə)l/ 1 *a.* complete; comprising the whole; absolute, unqualified. 2 *n.* sum of all items; total amount. 3 *v.* reckon total of; amount to or *to*. 4 **totality** /-'tæl-/ *n.*

**totalitarian** /təʊtælɪ'teərɪən/ *a.* of regime permitting no rival loyalties or parties. **totalitarianism** *n.*

**totalizator** /'təʊtəlaɪzeɪtə(r)/ *n.* device showing number and amount of bets staked on race when total will be divided among those betting on winner; this betting system.

**totalize** /'təʊtəlaɪz/ *v.t.* combine into a total.

**tote**[1] *n. sl.* totalizator.

**tote**[2] *v.t. colloq.* convey, carry. **tote bag** large and capacious bag.

**totem** /'təʊtəm/ *n.* natural object (esp. animal) adopted among N. Amer. Indians as emblem of family or clan; image of this. **totem-pole** post with carved and painted totem(s).

**totter** /'tɒtə(r)/ 1 *v.i.* stand or walk unsteadily or feebly; be shaken, be on the point of falling. 2 *n.* unsteady or shaky movement or gait. 3 **tottery** *a.*

**toucan** /'tuːkən/ *n.* tropical Amer. bird with large bill.

**touch** /tʌtʃ/ 1 *v.* be placed or move so as to meet at one or more points; put one's hand etc. so as to meet thus, cause (two things) to meet thus; strike lightly; reach as far as; approach in excellence; affect slightly, produce slightest effect on; have to do with in slightest degree; affect with tender or painful feelings; (in *p.p.*) slightly crazy. 2 *n.* act or fact of touching; sense of feeling; sensation conveyed by touching; light stroke with pencil etc.; small amount, tinge or trace; manner of touching keys or strings of esp. keyboard musical instrument, instrument's response to this; artistic skill or style; communication, agreement, sympathy; *Footb.* part of ground outside touch-lines; *sl.* act of getting money from person. 3 **touch-and-go** of uncertain result, risky; **touch at** *Naut.* call at (port etc.); **touch down** touch ground behind goal with football, (of aircraft) alight; **touch-down** *n.*; **touch-line** side limit of football field; **touch off** explode by touching with match etc., initiate (process) suddenly; **touch on** refer to or mention briefly or casually, verge on; **touch-paper** paper impregnated with nitre to burn slowly and ignite firework; **touchstone** dark schist or jasper for testing alloys by marks they make on it, criterion; **touch-type** use typewriter without looking at keys; **touch up** correct, give finishing touches to; **touch wood** put hand on something wooden to avert ill-luck; **touchwood** readily inflammable rotten wood.

**touché** /'tuːʃeɪ/ *int.* acknowledging hit by fencing-opponent or justified accusation by another in discussion.

**touching** /'tʌtʃɪŋ/ 1 *a.* arousing tender feelings. 2 *prep.* concerning.

**touchy** /'tʌtʃiː/ *a.* apt to take offence, over-sensitive.

**tough** /tʌf/ *a.* hard to break or cut or tear or chew; able to endure hardship, hardy, stubborn, difficult; *colloq.* acting sternly or vigorously; *colloq.* (of luck etc.) hard; *US sl.* vicious, ruffianly; (of clay etc.) stiff, tenacious. 2 *n.* tough person, esp. ruffian.

**toughen** /ˈtʌf(ə)n/ v. make or become tough(er).

**toupee** /ˈtuːpeɪ/ n. false hair to cover bald part of head.

**tour** /tʊə(r) or tɔː(r)/ 1 n. expedition or pleasure journey including stops at various places; spell of military or diplomatic service; travel through (country etc.). 3 **on tour** going from place to place to give performances etc.

***tour de force*** /tʊə də ˈfɔːs/ feat of strength or skill. [F]

**tourism** /ˈtʊərɪz(ə)m or ˈtɔː-/ n. organized touring or service for tourists, esp. on commercial basis.

**tourist** /ˈtʊərəst or ˈtɔː-/ n. holiday traveller. **tourist class** a cheap class of passenger accommodation in ship or aeroplane etc.

**tourmaline** /ˈtɔːməliːn/ n. mineral with unusual electric properties and used as gem.

**tournament** /ˈtʊənəmənt or ˈtɔː-/ n. medieval sport of mounted combat with blunted weapons; any contest of skill between number of competitors.

**tournedos** /ˈtʊənədəʊ/ n. (pl. same) small piece of fillet of beef.

**tourney** /ˈtʊəni or ˈtɔː-/ hist. 1 n. tournament. 2 v.i. take part in tournament.

**tourniquet** /ˈtʊənɪkeɪ/ n. bandage etc. round limb for stopping flow of blood through artery by compression.

**tousle** /ˈtaʊz(ə)l/ v.t. pull about; make (hair, person) untidy.

**tout** /taʊt/ 1 v. pester possible customers with requests (for orders); solicit custom of or for; spy on horses in training. 2 n. one who touts.

**tow**[1] /təʊ/ 1 v.t. pull along behind, esp. with rope etc. 2 n. towing or being towed. 3 **in tow** being towed, accompanying or in the charge of a person; **on tow** being towed; **tow-path** path beside canal or river orig. for towing.

**tow**[2] /təʊ/ n. fibres of flax etc. ready for spinning. **tow-headed** having head of very light-coloured or tousled hair.

**towards** /təˈwɔːdz/ prep. (also **toward**) in direction of; as regards; in relation to; for the purpose of; near.

**towel** /ˈtaʊəl/ 1 n. absorbent cloth or paper etc. for drying after washing etc. 2 v.t. (past & p.p. **towelled**) rub or dry with towel.

**towelling** /ˈtaʊəlɪŋ/ n. material for towels.

**tower** /ˈtaʊə(r)/ 1 n. tall structure often forming part of castle or church or other large building; similar structure housing machinery etc.; fortress etc. having tower. 2 v.i. reach high (above); soar, be poised, aloft. 3 **tower block** tall modern building; **tower of strength** fig. person who gives strong and reliable support.

**towering** /ˈtaʊərɪŋ/ a. high, lofty; (of rage etc.) violent.

**town** /taʊn/ n. considerable collection of dwellings, densely populated settlement; central business area of one's neighbourhood. **go to town** act or work with energy and enthusiasm; **on the town** in carefree pursuit of urban pleasure; **town clerk** officer of town corporation, in charge of records etc.; **town gas** manufactured inflammable gas for domestic etc. use; **town hall** building for town's official business and public entertainments etc.; **town house** house in town, esp. one of terrace; **town planning** planning for regulated growth of towns; **township** US & Canad. administrative division of county, or district 6 miles square, Aus. & NZ small town or settlement; **townspeople** inhabitants of town.

**townee** /taʊˈniː/ n. (also **townie**) derog. inhabitant of town.

**toxaemia** /tɒkˈsiːmɪə/ n. blood-poisoning; condition of abnormally high blood-pressure in pregnancy.

**toxic** /ˈtɒksɪk/ a. of or caused by or acting as poison.

**toxicology** /tɒksəˈkɒlədʒɪ/ n. study of poisons. **toxicological** a.; **toxicologist** n.

**toxin** /ˈtɒksən/ n. poison esp. of animal or vegetable origin; poison secreted by micro-organism and causing particular disease.

**toy** 1 n. thing to play with; trinket or curiosity. 2 v.i. play or fiddle or dally with. 3 **toy dog** dog of diminutive breed.

**trace**[1] 1 n. mark left behind; indication of existence or occurrence of something; slight amount (of). 2 v.t. follow track or path of; follow course or line

## trace

or history etc. of; observe or find traces of; copy (drawing etc.) by marking its lines on superimposed sheet, esp. of tracing-paper etc.; delineate, mark out, write esp. laboriously. **3 trace element** one occurring or required, esp. in soil, only in minute amounts.

**trace**² *n.* each of two side-straps or chains or ropes by which horse draws vehicle. **kick over the traces** *fig.* become insubordinate or reckless.

**tracer** /'treɪsə(r)/ *n. Mil.* projectile whose course is made visible by flame etc. emitted; *Med.* artificial radio-isotope whose course in human body etc. can be followed by radiation it produces.

**tracery** /'treɪsərɪ/ *n.* decorative stone open-work esp. in head of Gothic window; lacelike pattern resembling this.

**trachea** /trə'kiːə/ *n. Anat.* windpipe.

**tracing** /'treɪsɪŋ/ *n.* traced copy of map or drawing etc.; process of making this.

**tracing-paper** semi-transparent paper placed over drawing etc. to be traced.

**track 1** *n.* mark or series of marks left by person or animal or vehicle etc. in passing along; in *pl.* such marks esp. footprints; path, esp. one beaten by use; course taken; prepared racing-path; continuous railway-line; band round wheels of tank or tractor etc.; particular recorded section on gramophone record or magnetic tape. **2** *v.t.* follow track of; trace (course, development, etc.) from vestiges. **3 in one's tracks** *sl.* where one stands, there and then; **make tracks** *sl.* go or run away; **make tracks for** *sl.* go in pursuit of or towards; **track down** reach or capture by tracking; **track events** running-races; **track record** person's past achievements; **track suit** warm outfit worn by athlete etc. when training.

**tract**¹ *n.* region or area of indefinite extent; *Anat.* bodily organ or system.

**tract**² *n.* essay or pamphlet esp. on religious subject.

**tractable** /'træktəb(ə)l/ *a.* easily managed; docile. **tractability** *n.*

**traction** /'trækʃ(ə)n/ *n.* pulling; hauling; *Med.* therapeutic sustained pull on limb etc. **traction-engine** steam or diesel engine for drawing heavy load.

**tractor** /'træktə(r)/ *n.* motor vehicle for hauling other vehicles or farm machinery etc.; traction-engine.

**trad** *colloq.* **1** *a.* traditional. **2** *n.* traditional jazz.

**trade 1** *n.* exchange of goods for money or other goods; business carried on as means of livelihood or profit; skilled handicraft; *the* persons engaged in one branch of trade. **2** *v.* buy and sell, engage in trade; have a transaction *with*, exchange (goods) in commerce. **3 trade in** give (used article) in part payment for another; **trade mark** device or word(s) legally registered to distinguish goods of a particular manufacturer etc.; **trade name** name by which a thing is known in the trade, or given by manufacturer to proprietary article, or under which business is carried on; **trade off** exchange as compromise; **trade on** take (esp. unscrupulous) advantage of; **tradesman** person engaged in trade, esp. shop-keeper; **trade(s) union** organized association of workpeople of a trade or group of allied trades formed to further their common interests; **trade-unionist** member of trade-union; **trade wind** constant wind-blowing towards equator from NE or SE.

**tradescantia** /trædəs'kænʃə/ *n.* perennial herb with large blue, white, or pink flowers.

**tradition** /trə'dɪʃ(ə)n/ *n.* opinion or belief or custom handed down from one generation to another esp. orally; handing down of these.

**traditional** /trə'dɪʃən(ə)l/ *a.* of or based on or obtained by tradition; (of jazz) based on early style.

**traditionalism** /trə'dɪʃənəlɪz(ə)m/ *n.* great or excessive respect for tradition. **traditionalist** *n.*

**traduce** /trə'djuːs/ *v.t.* slander. **traducement** *n.*

**traffic** /'træfɪk/ **1** *n.* coming and going of persons and vehicles and goods by road, rail, air, sea, etc.; trade, esp. in illicit goods; number or amount of persons or goods conveyed; use of a service. **2** *v.* (*past* & *p.p.* **trafficked**) trade; engage in traffic (in); deal in. **3 traffic island** paved etc. area in road to direct traffic and provide refuge for pedestrians; **traffic lights** automatic signals for controlling road traffic by coloured

**tragacanth** 603 **transatlantic**

**lights; traffic warden** person employed to control movement and parking of road vehicles.

**tragacanth** /ˈtrægəkænθ/ n. vegetable gum used in pharmacy etc.

**tragedian** /trəˈdʒiːdɪən/ n. author of or actor in tragedies.

**tragedienne** /trədʒiːdɪˈen/ n. actress in tragedies.

**tragedy** /ˈtrædʒədɪ/ n. drama of elevated theme and diction and with unhappy ending; sad event, serious accident.

**tragic** /ˈtrædʒɪk/ a. of or like tragedy; sad, calamitous, distressing. **tragically** adv.

**tragicomedy** /trædʒɪˈkɒmədɪ/ n. drama of mixed tragic and comic events.

**trail 1** v. draw or be drawn along behind; drag along, walk wearily; be losing in contest; hang loosely; (of plant) grow or hang downwards, esp. so as to touch or rest on ground; follow trail of, shadow. **2** n. track or scent or other sign of passage left by moving object; beaten path esp. through wild region; thing that trails or is trailed; long line of people or things following behind something. **3 trailing edge** rear edge of aircraft's wing.

**trailer** /ˈtreɪlə(r)/ n. cart etc. drawn by vehicle and used to carry load; set of extracts from film etc. shown in advance to advertise it.

**train 1** n. series of railway carriages or trucks drawn by a locomotive; succession or series of persons or things; body of followers, retinue; thing drawn along behind or forming hinder part, esp. elongated part of woman's skirt or of official robe. **2** v. bring to desired standard of efficiency or obedience etc. by instruction and practice; undergo this process; teach and accustom (to do etc.); bring or come to physical efficiency by exercise and diet; cause (plant) to grow in desired shape; point, aim. **3 in train** arranged, in preparation; **train-bearer** person holding up train of another's robe.

**trainee** /treɪˈniː/ n. person being trained esp. for occupation.

**trainer** /ˈtreɪnə(r)/ n. person who trains horses or athletes etc.; soft shoe worn esp. by athletes in training.

**training** /ˈtreɪnɪŋ/ n. process of training for sport or contest or occupation.

**traipse** v.i. colloq. tramp or trudge wearily; go about on errands.

**trait** /treɪ/ n. feature, distinguishing quality.

**traitor** /ˈtreɪtə(r)/ n. person guilty of betrayal, one who acts disloyally. **traitorous** a.

**trajectory** /trəˈdʒektərɪ/ n. path of body (e.g. comet or bullet) moving under given forces.

**tram** n. (also **tramcar**) passenger vehicle running on rails in public road.

**tramlines** rails for tram, colloq. either pair of parallel lines at edge of tennis etc. court.

**trammel** /ˈtræm(ə)l/ **1** n. kind of fishing-net; (usu. in pl.) impediment, restraint. **2** v.t. hamper.

**tramp 1** v. walk with firm heavy tread; walk laboriously across or along; go on walking expedition; live as tramp. **2** n. person who tramps roads esp. as vagrant; sound (as) of person walking or marching; sl. dissolute woman; freight-vessel, esp. steamer, on no regular line.

**trample** /ˈtræmp(ə)l/ v. tread heavily on or on.

**trampoline** /ˈtræmpəlɪːn/ **1** n. canvas sheet connected by springs to horizontal frame, used for acrobatic exercises etc. **2** v.i. use trampoline.

**trance** /trɑːns/ n. sleeplike state; hypnotic or cataleptic condition; mental abstraction from external things, absorption, ecstasy.

**tranny** /ˈtrænɪ/ n. sl. transistor radio.

**tranquil** /ˈtræŋkwəl/ a. serene, calm, undisturbed. **tranquillity** n.

**tranquillize** /ˈtræŋkwəlaɪz/ v.t. make tranquil esp. by drug etc.

**tranquillizer** n. drug used to diminish anxiety.

**trans-** in comb. across, beyond, over, to or on farther side of.

**transact** /trænˈzækt/ v.t. do, carry on, (action, business, etc.).

**transaction** /trænˈzækʃ(ə)n/ n. transacting of business; piece of commercial or other dealing; in pl. reports of discussions and lectures at meetings of learned society.

**transatlantic** /trænzətˈlæntɪk/ a.

crossing or beyond the Atlantic; American; *US* European.

**transceiver** /træn'si:və(r)/ *n.* combined radio transmitter and receiver.

**transcend** /træn'send/ *v.t.* go beyond or exceed limits of; rise above, surpass, excel.

**transcendent** /træn'send(ə)nt/ *a.* of supreme merit or quality; (of God) existing apart from, or not subject to limitations of, material universe. **transcendence** *n.*; **transcendency** *n.*

**transcendental** /trænsən'dent(ə)l/ *a.* a priori, not based on experience; consisting of or dealing in or inspired by abstraction. **Transcendental Meditation** meditation seeking to induce detachment from problems and relief from anxiety.

**transcontinental** /trænzkɒntə'nent(ə)l/ *a.* extending across a continent.

**transcribe** /træn'skraɪb/ *v.t.* copy out; reproduce in ordinary writing; *Mus.* adapt for other than original instrument or voice. **transcription** *n.*

**transcript** /'trænskrɪpt/ *n.* written copy.

**transducer** /trænz'dju:sə(r)/ *n.* device for changing the variations of a quantity (e.g. pressure) to those of another (e.g. voltage).

**transept** /'trænsept/ *n.* part of cruciform church at right angles to nave; either arm of this.

**transfer** 1 /træns'fɜː(r)/ *v.* (*past & p.p.* **transferred**) convey or transmit or hand over etc. from one person or place etc. *to* another; *Law* convey by legal process; convey (design etc.) from one surface to another; move (person) to, or change or be moved to, another group; change from one station or line etc. to another to continue journey. 2 /'trænsfɜː(r)/ *n.* transferring or being transferred; conveyance of property or right, document effecting this; design etc. that is or can be conveyed from one surface to another. 3 **transferable** *a.*; **transference** /'træns-/ *n.*

**transfigure** /træns'fɪgə(r)/ *v.t.* change appearance of, make more spiritual or elevated. **transfiguration** *n.*

**transfix** /træns'fɪks/ *v.t.* pierce with lance etc.; (of horror etc.) paralyse faculties of (person).

**transform** /trɒns'fɔːm/ *v.t.* change form or appearance or condition or function etc. of, esp. considerably; *Electr.* change voltage of (current). **transformation** *n.*

**transformer** *n. Electr.* apparatus for reducing or increasing voltage of alternating current.

**transfuse** /træns'fjuːz/ *v.t.* cause (fluid, colour, etc.) to permeate *into*; imbue *with*; transfer (blood or other liquid) into blood-vessel to replace that lost. **transfusion** *n.*

**transgress** /trænz'gres/ *v.* infringe (law etc.); overstep (limit laid down); sin. **transgression** *n.*; **transgressor** *n.*

**transient** /'trænzɪənt/ *a.* quickly passing away; fleeting. **transience** *n.*

**transistor** /træn'sɪstə(r)/ *n.* small semi-conductor device capable of replacing thermionic valve; radio set using transistors.

**transistorize** /træn'sɪstəraɪz/ *v.t.* equip with transistors rather than valves.

**transit** /'trænsɪt/ *n.* going or conveying or being conveyed across or over or through; passage, route; apparent passage of heavenly body across disc of another or meridian of place.

**transition** /træn'sɪʃ(ə)n/ *n.* passage or change from one state or subject or set of circumstances etc. to another; period of this. **transitional** *a.*

**transitive** /'trænzətɪv/ *a. Gram.* (of verb) requiring direct object expressed or understood.

**transitory** /'trænzətərɪ/ *a.* not lasting, momentary; brief, fleeting.

**translate** /trænz'leɪt/ *v.t.* express sense of in another language or in other words or another form of representation; infer or declare or convey significance of; remove (bishop) to another see. **translation** *n.*; **translator** *n.*

**transliterate** /trænz'lɪtəreɪt/ *v.t.* represent (word etc.) in more or less corresponding characters of another alphabet or language. **transliteration** *n.*

**translucent** /trænz'luːs(ə)nt/ *a.* allowing light to pass through (esp. without being transparent). **translucence** *n.*

**transmigrate** /trænzmaɪ'greɪt/ *v.* (of soul) pass into different body.

**transmissible** /trænz'mɪsəb(ə)l/ *a.* that may be transmitted. **transmissibility** *n.*

**transmission** /trænz'mɪʃ(ə)n/ *n.* transmitting or being transmitted; broadcast programme; gear transmitting power from engine to axle in motor vehicle etc.

**transmit** /trænz'mɪt/ *v.t.* send or convey etc. to another person or place or thing; allow to pass through, be medium for, serve to communicate (heat, electricity, emotion, message, etc.).

**transmitter** *n.* equipment used to transmit message, (esp. broadcast) signal, etc.

**transmogrify** /trænz'mɒgrəfaɪ/ *v.t. joc.* transform esp. in magical or surprising manner.

**transmutation** /trænzmju:'teɪʃ(ə)n/ *n.* transmuting or being transmuted. **transmutation of metals** turning of other metals into gold as alchemists' aim.

**transmute** /trænz'mju:t/ *v.t.* change form or nature or substance of; convert into different thing. **transmutative** *a.*

**transom** /'trænsəm/ *n.* cross-beam, esp. horizontal bar above door or in window; window above this.

**transparency** /træns'pærənsi/ *n.* being transparent; picture (esp. photograph) to be viewed by light passing through it.

**transparent** /træns'pærənt/ *a.* that can be clearly seen through because allowing light to pass through without diffusion; (of disguise, pretext, etc.) easily seen through, obvious; easily understood.

**transpire** /træns'paɪə(r)/ *v.* (of secret, fact, etc.) come to be known; emit (vapour, moisture) or pass off through pores of skin etc. **transpiration** *n.*

**transplant** 1 /træns'plɑ:nt or -'plænt/ *v.t.* remove and replant or establish elsewhere; transfer (living tissue or organ) from one part of body or one person or animal to another. 2 /'trænsplɑ:nt or -plænt/ *n.* transplanting of tissue or organ; thing transplanted. 3 **transplantation** *n.*

**transport** 1 /træns'pɔ:t/ *v.t.* take from one place to another; *hist.* deport (criminal) to penal colony; (esp. in *p.p.*) affect with strong emotion. 2 /'trænspɔ:t/ *n.* transporting, means of conveyance; ship or aircraft etc. used in transporting troops or military stores; vehement emotion.

**transportation** /trænspɔ:'teɪʃ(ə)n/ *n.* transporting; *hist.* deporting of criminals; *US* transport.

**transporter** /træns'pɔ:tə(r)/ *n.* vehicle used to transport other vehicles or heavy machinery etc. **transporter bridge** bridge carrying vehicles across water on suspended platform.

**transpose** /træns'pəʊz/ *v.t.* cause (two or more things) to change places; change position of (thing) in series; *Mus.* write or play in different key. **transposition** *n.*

**transsexual** /trænz'seksjʊəl/ 1 *a.* having physical characteristics of one sex and psychological characteristics of the other. 2 *n.* transsexual person. 3 **transsexualism** *n.*

**trans-ship** /træn'ʃɪp/ *v.* transfer from one ship or conveyance to another. **trans-shipment** *n.*

**transubstantiation** /trænsəbstænʃɪ'eɪʃ(ə)n/ *n.* conversion of Eucharistic elements wholly into body and blood of Christ.

**transuranic** /trænzjʊ'rænɪk/ *a. Chem.* (of element) having higher atomic number than uranium.

**transverse** /trænz'vɜ:s/ *a.* situated or arranged or acting in crosswise direction.

**transvestism** /trænz'vestɪz(ə)m/ *n.* dressing in garments of opposite sex.

**transvestite** /trænz'vestaɪt/ *n.* person given to transvestism.

**trap** 1 *n.* device, often baited, for catching animals; arrangement to catch out unsuspecting person; device for releasing clay pigeon to be shot at or greyhound at start of race etc.; curve in drain-pipe etc. serving when filled with liquid to seal it against return of gas; two-wheeled carriage; trapdoor; *sl.* mouth. 2 *v.t.* catch (as) in trap; set traps for game etc.; furnish with traps. 3 **trapdoor** door flush with surface of floor or roof etc.

**trapeze** /trə'pi:z/ *n.* horizontal crossbar suspended by ropes as swing for acrobatics etc.

**trapezium** /trə'pi:zɪəm/ *n.* (*pl.* **-zia** or

**trapezoid**

-ziums) quadrilateral with only one pair of sides parallel; *US* trapezoid.

**trapezoid** /'træpəzɔɪd/ *n.* quadrilateral with no sides parallel; *US* trapezium.

**trapper** /'træpə(r)/ *n.* person who traps wild animals for their fur etc.

**trappings** /'træpɪŋz/ *n.pl.* ornamental accessories; ornamental cloth covering for horse.

**traps** *n. pl. colloq.* portable belongings, baggage.

**trash** *n.* waste or worthless stuff; rubbish; worthless or disreputable person(s). **trashy** *a.*

**trauma** /'trɔːmə/ *n.* (*pl.* **-mas**) emotional shock; wound, injury. **traumatic** *a.*

**travail** /'træveɪl/ 1 *n. literary* laborious effort; *arch.* pangs of childbirth. 2 *v.i. literary* make laborious effort; *arch.* suffer pangs of childbirth.

**travel** /'træv(ə)l/ 1 *v.* go from one place to another; make journey(s) esp. of some length or abroad; journey through or pass over, traverse; *colloq.* withstand long journey; act as commercial traveller; move or proceed in specified manner etc.; *colloq.* move quickly; pass from point to point; (of machine or part) move or operate in specified way. 2 *n.* travelling; range or rate or mode of motion of part in machinery. 3 **travel agency** agency making arrangements for travellers; **travelling crane** crane moving on esp. overhead support.

**travelled** /'træv(ə)ld/ *a.* experienced in travelling.

**traveller** /'trævələ(r)/ *n.* person who travels or is travelling; commercial traveller. **traveller's cheque** cheque for fixed amount, encashable on signature for equivalent in most currencies; **traveller's joy** wild clematis.

**travelogue** /'trævəlɒg/ *n.* film or illustrated lecture with narrative of travel.

**traverse** 1 /trə'vɜːs/ *v.* travel or lie across; consider or discuss whole extent of; turn (large gun) horizontally. 2 /'trævəs/ *n.* sideways movement, traversing; thing that crosses another. 3 **traversal** *a.*

**travesty** /'trævəstɪ/ 1 *n.* gross parody, ridiculous imitation. 2 *v.t.* make or be travesty of.

**trawl** 1 *n.* large wide-mouthed fishing-net dragged by boat along bottom of sea etc. 2 *v.* fish with trawl or in trawler; catch with trawl.

**trawler** /'trɔːlə(r)/ *n.* boat used in fishing with trawl-net.

**tray** *n.* flat shallow vessel used for carrying or containing small articles etc.; shallow lidless box or drawer forming compartment of trunk etc.

**treacherous** /'tretʃərəs/ *a.* violating faith or betraying trust; perfidious; not to be relied on, deceptive. **treachery** *n.*

**treacle** /'triːk(ə)l/ *n.* syrup produced in refining sugar; molasses. **treacly** *a.*

**tread** /tred/ 1 *v.* (*past* **trod**; *p.p.* **trodden**) set one's foot down; walk on, press or crush with feet; (of male bird) copulate (with). 2 *n.* manner or sound of walking; top surface of step or stair; part of wheel that touches ground, thick moulded part of vehicle tyre for gripping road, part of sole of boot etc. similarly moulded. 3 **treadmill** device for producing motion by treading on steps on revolving cylinder, formerly used as prison punishment, *fig.* monotonous routine; **tread water** maintain upright position in water by moving feet and hands.

**treadle** /'tred(ə)l/ *n.* lever moved by foot and imparting motion to machine.

**treason** /'triːz(ə)n/ *n.* violation by subject of allegiance to sovereign or State; breach of faith, disloyalty.

**treasonable** /'triːzənəb(ə)l/ *a.* involving or guilty of treason.

**treasonous** /'triːzənəs/ *a.* treasonable.

**treasure** /'treʒə(r)/ 1 *n.* precious metals or gems etc.; hoard of them; thing valued for rarity or associations etc.; accumulated wealth; *colloq.* beloved or highly valued person. 2 *v.t.* store (*up*) as valuable; receive or regard as valuable. 3 **treasure-hunt** search for treasure, game in which players seek hidden object; **treasure trove** treasure of unknown ownership found hidden.

**treasurer** /'treʒərə(r)/ *n.* person in charge of funds of society or municipality etc.

**treasury** /'treʒərɪ/ *n.* place where treasure is kept; funds or revenue of State or institution or society etc.; department managing public revenue of a country. **Treasury bench** government front bench in parliament; **treasury bill** bill of exchange issued by government to raise money for temporary needs.

**treat** 1 *v.* act or behave towards in specified way; deal with or apply process to etc.; deal with disease etc. in order to relieve or cure; provide with food or drink or entertainment at one's own expense; negotiate (*with*); give exposition *of*. 2 *n.* thing that gives great pleasure; entertainment designed to do this; treating of others to food etc.

**treatise** /'tri:təs/ *n.* literary composition dealing esp. formally with subject.

**treatment** /'tri:tmənt/ *n.* process or manner of dealing with or behaving towards person or thing; medical care or attention.

**treaty** /'tri:ti:/ *n.* formally concluded and ratified agreement between States; agreement between persons esp. for purchase of property.

**treble** /'treb(ə)l/ 1 *a.* threefold, triple; 3 times as much or many; (of voice) high-pitched; *Mus.* soprano (esp. of boy's voice or of instrument). 2 *n.* treble quantity or thing; soprano; high-pitched voice. 3 *v.* multiply or be multiplied by 3.

**tree** 1 *n.* perennial plant with single woody self-supporting stem, usu. developing woody branches at some distance from ground; shaped piece of wood for various purposes; chart or diagram like branching tree. 2 *v.t.* cause to take refuge in tree. 3 **tree-creeper** small creeping bird feeding on insects in tree-bark; **tree-fern** kind of large fern with upright woody stem; **tree surgeon** person who treats decayed trees in order to preserve them.

**trefoil** /'trefɔɪl/ *n.* kind of plant with leaves of 3 leaflets; 3-lobed thing esp. ornamentation in tracery etc.

**trek** 1 *v.i.* (*past* & *p.p.* **trekked**) make arduous journey; travel or migrate, esp. by ox-wagon. 2 *n.* such journey; each stage of it.

**trellis** /'treləs/ *n.* lattice or grating of light wooden or metal bars, used as support for climbing plants or as screen etc.

**tremble** /'tremb(ə)l/ 1 *v.i.* shake involuntarily with fear or cold or excitement etc.; be affected with fear or suspense etc.; move in quivering manner. 2 *n.* trembling, quiver, tremor. 3 **trembly** *a.*

**tremendous** /trə'mendəs/ *a.* awe-inspiring, overpowering; *colloq.* remarkable or considerable or excellent.

**tremolo** /'tremələʊ/ *n.* (pl. **-los**) *Mus.* tremulous effect in playing music or singing.

**tremor** /'tremə(r)/ *n.* shaking; quiver; thrill of fear or other emotion; slight earthquake.

**tremulous** /'tremjələs/ *a.* trembling, quivering.

**trench** 1 *n.* deep ditch, esp. one dug by troops as shelter from enemy's fire. 2 *v.* make trench(es) or ditch(es) in, dig trench(es); make series of trenches so as to bring lower soil to surface. 3 **trench coat** lined or padded waterproof coat, loose belted raincoat.

**trenchant** /'trentʃ(ə)nt/ *a.* sharp, keen; incisive, decisive. **trenchancy** *n.*

**trencher** /'trentʃə(r)/ *n.* wooden platter for serving food.

**trencherman** *n.* (pl. **-men**) feeder, eater.

**trend** 1 *v.i.* have specified direction or course or general tendency. 2 *n.* general direction or course or tendency. 3 **trend-setter** person who leads the way in fashion etc.

**trendy** /'trendi/ *colloq.* usu. *derog.* 1 *a.* fashionable. 2 *n.* fashionable person.

**trepan** /trɪ'pæn/ 1 *n.* surgeon's cylindrical saw for making opening in skull. 2 *v.t.* perforate (skull) with trepan.

**trepidation** /trepɪ'deɪʃ(ə)n/ *n.* agitation, alarm, anxiety.

**trespass** /'trespəs/ 1 *v.i.* enter unlawfully on another's land or property etc.; encroach *on*. 2 *n.* act of trespassing; *arch.* sin, offence.

**tress** *n.* lock of hair; in *pl.* hair.

**trestle** /'tres(ə)l/ *n.* supporting structure for table etc. consisting of bar supported by two divergent pairs of legs or of two frames fixed at an angle or hinged; trestle-work. 2 **trestle-table** table of board(s) laid on trestles; **trestle-work** open braced framework to support bridge etc.

**trevally** /trə'vælɪ/ *n. Aus.* any of several edible fishes.

**trews** *n.pl.* close-fitting usu. tartan trousers.

**TRH** *abbr.* Their Royal Highnesses.

**tri-** *in comb.* three (times).

**triad** /ˈtraɪæd/ *n.* group of 3 (esp. notes in chord). **triadic** *a.*

**trial** /ˈtraɪəl/ *n.* judicial examination and determination of issues between parties by judge with or without jury; process or mode of testing qualities; experimental treatment, test; trying thing or experience or person.

**triamble** /ˈtraɪæmb(ə)l/ *n. Aus.* three-lobed pumpkin.

**triangle** /ˈtraɪæŋg(ə)l/ *n.* figure of 3 straight lines each meeting the others at different points; any 3 things not in a straight line, with the imaginary lines joining them; implement etc. of this shape; *Mus.* instrument of steel rod bent into triangle sounded by striking with small steel rod.

**triangular** /traɪˈæŋgjələ(r)/ *a.* triangle-shaped; (of contest, treaty, etc.) between 3 persons or parties; (of pyramid) having 3-sided base.

**triangulate** /traɪˈæŋgjəleɪt/ *v.t.* divide (area) into triangles for surveying purposes. **triangulation** *n.*

**triantelope** /traɪˈætələʊp/ *n. Aus.* tarantula.

**tribe** *n.* (in some societies) group of families under recognized chief and usu. claiming common ancestor; any similar natural or political division; (usu. *derog.*) set or number of persons esp. of one profession etc. or family. **tribesman** member of tribe. **tribal** *a.*

**tribulation** /trɪbjəˈleɪʃ(ə)n/ *n.* great affliction.

**tribunal** /traɪˈbjuːn(ə)l/ *n.* board appointed to adjudicate on particular question; court of justice, judicial assembly.

**tribune**[1] /ˈtrɪbjuːn/ *n.* popular leader, demagogue; *Rom. hist.* officer chosen by the people to protect their liberties.

**tribune**[2] /ˈtrɪbjuːn/ *n.* platform, rostrum.

**tributary** /ˈtrɪbjətərɪ/ **1** *n.* stream etc. that flows into larger stream or lake; person or State paying or subject to tribute. **2** *a.* that is a tributary.

**tribute** /ˈtrɪbjuːt/ *n.* thing done or said or given as mark of respect or affection etc.; periodical payment exacted by one sovereign or State from another; obligation to pay this.

**trice** *n.* instant, moment.

**triceps** /ˈtraɪseps/ *n.* muscle (esp. in upper arm) with 3 points of attachment.

**trichinosis** /trɪkəˈnəʊsɪs/ *n.* disease caused by hairlike worms in muscles.

**trichology** /trɪˈkɒlədʒɪ/ *n.* study of hair. **trichologist** *n.*

**trichromatic** /traɪkrəˈmætɪk/ *a.* 3-coloured.

**trick 1** *n.* thing done to fool or outwit or deceive; optical or other illusion; knack or way of doing something; feat of skill or dexterity; malicious or foolish or stupid act; hoax, joke; characteristic habit; cards played in one round, winning of round. **2** *v.t.* deceive by trick, cheat; take by surprise.

**trickery** /ˈtrɪkərɪ/ *n.* deception, use of tricks.

**trickle** /ˈtrɪk(ə)l/ **1** *v.* (cause to) flow drop by drop; come or go slowly or gradually. **2** *n.* trickling flow. **3 trickle charger** *Electr.* device for slow continuous charging of accumulator.

**trickster** /ˈtrɪkstə(r)/ *n.* deceiver, rogue.

**tricky** /ˈtrɪkɪ/ *a.* requiring care and adroitness; crafty, deceitful.

**tricolour** /ˈtrɪkələ(r)/ *n.* flag of 3 colours, esp. French national flag.

**tricot** /ˈtrɪkəʊ/ *n.* knitted fabric.

**tricycle** /ˈtraɪsɪk(ə)l/ *n.* 3-wheeled pedal-driven vehicle; 3-wheeled motor vehicle for disabled driver. **tricyclist** *n.*

**trident** /ˈtraɪd(ə)nt/ *n.* 3-pronged spear.

**Tridentine** /trəˈdentaɪn/ *a.* of traditional RC orthodoxy.

**triennial** /traɪˈenɪəl/ *a.* lasting 3 years; recurring every 3 years.

**trifle** /ˈtraɪf(ə)l/ **1** *n.* thing of slight value or importance; small amount or article; sweet dish of sponge-cakes with custard and cream etc. **2** *v.i.* talk or act frivolously.

**trifling** *a.* trivial.

**trigger** /ˈtrɪgə(r)/ *n.* lever or catch pulled or pressed to release spring or otherwise set mechanism in motion, esp. catch for releasing hammer of firearm. **2** *v.* set *off* reaction or process etc. by comparatively small action etc. **3 trigger-happy** apt to shoot on slight provocation.

**trigonometry** /trɪgə'nɒmətri/ n. branch of mathematics dealing with measurement of sides and angles of triangles, and with certain functions of angles. **trigonometrical** /-'met-/ a.

**trike** n. colloq. tricycle.

**trilateral** /traɪ'læt(ə)r(ə)l/ a. having 3 sides; existing etc. between 3 parties.

**trilby** /'trɪlbi/ n. soft felt hat with narrow brim and indented crown.

**trilingual** /traɪ'lɪŋgw(ə)l/ a. of or in or speaking 3 languages.

**trill** n. quavering or vibratory sound (e.g. quick alternation of notes in singing, bird's warbling, the letter r). 2 v. produce trill; warble (song); pronounce (r etc.) with trill.

**trillion** /'trɪljən/ n. million million millions; US etc. million millions. **trillionth** a. & n.

**trilobite** /'traɪləbaɪt/ n. kind of fossil crustacean.

**trilogy** /'trɪlədʒi:/ n. set of 3 related dramatic or other literary works.

**trim** 1 v. make neat or tidy; remove irregular or unsightly etc. parts by planing or clipping etc.; ornament; adjust balance of (ship, aircraft) by distribution of weight; arrange (sails etc.) to suit wind. 2 n. state or degree of readiness or fitness or adjustment etc.; good order; ornament or decorative material; trimming of hair etc. 3 a. in good order, neat; not loose or untidy. 4 **trim one's sails** fig. adjust one's policy etc. to changing circumstances.

**trimaran** /'traɪməræn/ n. vessel like catamaran, with 3 hulls side by side.

**trimming** /'trɪmɪŋ/ n. ornamental addition to dress or hat etc.; in pl. colloq. accessories, usual accompaniments.

**trinitrotoluene** /traɪnaɪtrəʊ'tɒlju:i:n/ n. a high explosive.

**trinity** /'trɪnəti:/ n. being 3; group of 3. **the Trinity** Theol. the 3 persons of the Godhead as conceived in orthodox Christian belief; **Trinity Sunday** Sunday after Whit Sunday.

**trinket** /'trɪŋkət/ n. small or trifling ornament; esp. piece of jewellery.

**trio** /'tri:əʊ/ n. (pl. -os) musical composition for 3 performers; the performers; any group of 3.

**trip** 1 v. go lightly and quickly along; catch one's foot and stumble; commit blunder or fault; cause (person) to stumble by entangling his feet; release (part of machine) suddenly by knocking aside catch etc. 2 n. journey or excursion esp. for pleasure; stumble, tripping or being tripped up; colloq. visionary experience caused by drug; contrivance for tripping mechanism etc. 3 **trip up** (cause to) stumble, detect in error or inconsistency etc.; **tripwire** wire stretched close to ground to operate warning device etc. if disturbed.

**tripartite** /traɪ'pɑ:taɪt/ a. consisting of 3 parts; shared by or involving 3 parties.

**tripe** n. first or second stomach of ox or other ruminant prepared as food; sl. worthless or trashy thing, rubbish.

**triple** /'trɪp(ə)l/ 1 a. threefold; of 3 parts or involving 3 parties; 3 times as much or as many. 2 n. number or thing 3 times another; set of 3. 3 v. multiply by 3. 4 **triple crown** pope's tiara, winning of 3 important sporting events; **triple time** Mus. tempo of 3 beats to a bar.

**triplet** /'trɪplət/ n. one of 3 children born at one birth; set of 3 things, esp. of notes played in time of two or verses rhyming together.

**triplex** /'trɪpleks/ a. triple, threefold.

**triplicate** 1 /'trɪpləkət/ a. existing in 3 examples; having 3 corresponding parts; tripled. 2 /'trɪpləkət/ n. state of being triplicate. 3 /'trɪpləkeɪt/ v.t. make in triplicate; multiply by 3. 4 **triplication** n.

**tripod** /'traɪpɒd/ n. 3-legged or 3-footed stand or support or seat etc.

**tripper** /'trɪpə(r)/ n. person who goes on pleasure trip.

**triptych** /'trɪptɪk/ n. picture etc. with 3 panels hinged vertically together.

**trireme** /'traɪəri:m/ n. ancient warship, prob. with 3 men at each oar.

**trisect** /traɪ'sekt/ v.t. divide into 3 (usu. equal) parts. **trisection** n.

**trite** a. well-worn, hackneyed, commonplace.

**tritium** /'trɪtɪəm/ n. Chem. radioactive isotope of hydrogen with mass about 3 times that of ordinary hydrogen.

**triumph** /'traɪəmf/ 1 n. state of being victorious; great success or achievement; joy at success; supreme example of; Rom. hist. processional entry of victorious general into Rome. 2 v.i. gain

**triumphal** /traɪˈʌmf(ə)l/ *a.* of or celebrating or used in a triumph or victory.

**triumphant** /traɪˈʌmf(ə)nt/ *a.* victorious, successful, exultant.

**triumvir** /traɪˈʌmvə(r)/ *n.* (*pl.* **-viri** /-vɪriː/ or **-virs**) member of a triumvirate.

**triumvirate** /traɪˈʌmvərət/ *n.* government or board of 3 men.

**trivet** /ˈtrɪvɪt/ *n.* iron tripod or bracket for cooking-pot or kettle to stand on.

**trivia** /ˈtrɪviːə/ *n.pl.* trifles, trivialities.

**trivial** /ˈtrɪviːəl/ *a.* of small value or importance; concerned only with trivial things. **triviality** *n.*

**trod** *past* of **tread**.

**trodden** *p.p.* of **tread**.

**troglodyte** /ˈtrɒglədaɪt/ *n.* cave-dweller.

**troika** /ˈtrɔɪkə/ *n.* Russian vehicle drawn by 3 horses abreast.

**Trojan** /ˈtrəʊdʒ(ə)n/ **1** *a.* of ancient Troy. **2** *n.* inhabitant of ancient Troy. **3 Trojan Horse** *fig.* person or device insinuated to bring about enemy's downfall.

**troll**[1] /trəʊl/ *n.* supernatural being, giant or dwarf, in Scandinavian mythology.

**troll**[2] /trəʊl/ *v.* sing out in carefree manner; fish by drawing bait along in water.

**trolley** /ˈtrɒliː/ *n.* small table on wheels or castors; small handcart for carrying luggage etc. or for use in supermarket etc.; low truck, esp. running along rails; wheel attached to pole etc. for collecting current from overhead electric wire to drive vehicle. **trolley bus** electric bus using trolley.

**trollop** /ˈtrɒləp/ *n.* disreputable girl or woman.

**trombone** /trɒmˈbəʊn/ *n.* large brass wind-instrument with sliding tube; *Aus.* green or yellow pumpkin bulbous at one end. **trombonist** *n.*

**troop** /truːp/ **1** *n.* assembled company, assemblage of persons or animals; in *pl.* soldiers, armed forces; cavalry unit commanded by captain; artillery unit; group of 3 or more Scout patrols. **2** *v.* come together or move in a troop. **3 troop the colour** transfer flag ceremonially at public mounting of garrison guards; **troop-ship** ship for transporting troops.

**trooper** /ˈtruːpə(r)/ *n.* private soldier in cavalry or armoured unit; *US & Aus.* mounted or motor-borne policeman; troop-ship.

**trope** *n.* figure of speech.

**trophy** /ˈtrəʊfiː/ *n.* thing kept as prize or memento of any contest or success; group of things arranged for ornamental display.

**tropic** /ˈtrɒpɪk/ *n.* parallel of latitude 23° 27′ N. or S. of equator. **the tropics** region lying between these.

**tropical** /ˈtrɒpɪk(ə)l/ *a.* of or peculiar to or suggestive of the tropics.

**troposphere** /ˈtrɒpəsfɪə(r)/ *n.* layer of atmosphere extending from earth's surface to stratosphere.

**trot** **1** *v.* (of person) run at moderate pace esp. with short strides; (of horse etc.) proceed at steady pace faster than walk; traverse (distance) thus. **2** *n.* action or exercise of trotting; *Aus.* run of specified kind of luck; in *pl. Aus.* trotting races. **3 on the trot** *colloq.* continually busy, in succession; **trot out** *fig.* produce or introduce (as if) for inspection or approval.

**troth** /trəʊθ/ *n. arch.* faith, fidelity.

**trotter** /ˈtrɒtə(r)/ *n.* horse bred or trained for trotting; animal's foot esp. as food.

**troubadour** /ˈtruːbədɔː(r)/ *n.* medieval romantic or amatory poet.

**trouble** /ˈtrʌb(ə)l/ **1** *n.* vexation, affliction; inconvenience, unpleasant exertion; cause of annoyance; faulty condition or operation; in *pl.* public disturbances. **2** *v.* cause distress to; agitate, disturb; afflict, cause pain etc. to; subject or be subjected to inconvenience or unpleasant exertion. **3 in trouble** subject to censure or punishment etc.; **trouble-maker** person who habitually causes trouble; **trouble-shooter** person who traces and corrects faults in machinery etc., mediator in dispute.

**troublesome** /ˈtrʌbəlsəm/ *a.* causing trouble, annoying.

**troublous** /ˈtrʌbləs/ *a. arch.* full of troubles, disturbed.

**trough** /trɒf/ *n.* long narrow open receptacle for water or animal feed etc. to stand in; channel or hollow comparable

**trounce** /traʊns/ v.t. inflict severe punishment or defeat on.

**troupe** /truːp/ n. company of actors or acrobats etc.

**trouper** /ˈtruːpə(r)/ n. member of obsequitrical troupe; staunch colleague.

**trousers** /ˈtraʊzəz/ n.pl. two-legged outer garment from waist usu. to ankles. **trouser-suit** woman's suit of trousers and jacket.

**trousseau** /ˈtruːsəʊ/ n. (pl. -eaus) bride's collection of clothes etc.

**trout** /traʊt/ n. (pl. same) kind of fish related to salmon.

**trove** n. treasure-trove.

**trow** /traʊ/ v.t. arch. think, believe.

**trowel** /ˈtraʊəl/ n. flat-bladed tool for spreading mortar etc.; scoop for lifting small plants or earth.

**troy** n. system of weights used for precious metals etc.

**truant** /ˈtruːənt/ n. child who absents himself from school; person missing from work etc. **play truant** stay away thus. **truancy** n.

**truce** n. temporary cessation of hostilities; respite; agreement for this.

**truck**[1] n. strong vehicle for heavy goods; open railway wagon; handcart, barrow for moving luggage etc.

**truck**[2] n. **have no truck** avoid dealing with.

**truckie** /ˈtrʌki/ n. colloq. lorry-driver.

**truckle** /ˈtrʌk(ə)l/ v.i. submit obsequiously (to). **truckle-bed** low bed on wheels that may be pushed under another.

**truculent** /ˈtrʌkjʊlənt/ a. aggressive, fierce. **truculence** n.

**trudge** /trʌdʒ/ v.i. walk laboriously or without spirit. 2 n. trudging walk.

**true** 1 a. in accordance with fact or reality; genuine, real, correct, proper; accurately placed or fitted or shaped; (of ground etc.) level, smooth, even; loyal, faithful, constant (to). 2 adv. truly, accurately; without variation.

**truffle** /ˈtrʌf(ə)l/ n. underground fungus with rich flavour; sweet made of soft chocolate mixture.

**trug** n. shallow oblong garden-basket.

**truism** /ˈtruːɪz(ə)m/ n. self-evident or hackneyed truth.

**truly** /ˈtruːli/ adv. with truth; sincerely; loyally; accurately. **yours truly** formula preceding signature of letter, *joc.* I, me.

**trump**[1] 1 n. playing-card of suit temporarily ranking above others; advantage, esp. involving surprise; *colloq.* helpful or excellent person. 2 v. defeat with trump; play trump. 3 **trump card** card turned up to determine trump suit, *fig.* valuable resource; **trump up** fabricate or invent (story, accusation, etc.); **turn up trumps** *colloq.* turn out well or successfully, prove extremely kind or generous etc.

**trump**[2] n. *arch.* (sound of) trumpet.

**trumpery** /ˈtrʌmpəri/ 1 a. showy but worthless, delusive, shallow. 2 n. worthless finery.

**trumpet** /ˈtrʌmpɪt/ 1 n. metal tubular or conical wind instrument with flared mouth and bright penetrating tone; trumpet-shaped thing; sound (as) of trumpet, esp. elephant's loud cry. 2 v. blow trumpet; (of elephant) make trumpet; proclaim loudly.

**trumpeter** n. player of trumpet.

**truncate** /trʌŋˈkeɪt/ v.t. cut off top or end of; cut short. **truncation** n.

**truncheon** /ˈtrʌntʃ(ə)n/ n. short club carried by policeman; staff or baton as sign of authority.

**trundle** /ˈtrʌnd(ə)l/ v. roll or move on wheels; move heavily or noisily.

**trunk** n. main stem of tree; person's or animal's body apart from head and limbs; large luggage-box with hinged lid; *US* boot of car; elephant's elongated prehensile nose; in *pl.* men's close-fitting shorts worn for swimming or boxing etc. **trunk-call** telephone call on trunk-line with charges according to distance; **trunk-line** main line of railway or telephone system etc.; **trunk-road** important main road.

**truss** 1 n. supporting framework of roof or bridge etc.; surgical appliance for support in cases of hernia etc.; bundle of hay or straw. 2 v.t. tie up (fowl) compactly for cooking; tie person (*up*) with arms to sides; support with truss(es).

**trust** 1 n. firm belief that a person or thing may be relied upon; state of being relied upon; confident expectation; thing or person committed to one's care, resulting obligation; *Law* trust-

**trustee**    612    **tucker**

eeship, board of trustees, property committed to trustee(s); association of several companies for purpose of united action to prevent competition. **2** *v.* place trust in, believe in, rely on; consign *to*; allow credit to; hope earnestly. **3 trustworthy** deserving of trust, reliable. **4 trustful** *a.*

**trustee** /trʌsˈtiː/ *n.* person or member of board given possession of property with legal obligation to administer it solely for purposes specified; State made responsible for government of an area. **trusteeship** *n.*

**trusting** /ˈtrʌstɪŋ/ *a.* not given to suspicion or apprehension.

**trusty** /ˈtrʌsti/ **1** *a. arch.* trustworthy. **2** *n.* prisoner who is given special privileges for good behaviour.

**truth** /truːθ/ *n.* quality or state of being true or truthful; what is true.

**truthful** /ˈtruːθfəl/ *a.* habitually speaking the truth, true.

**try 1** *v.* attempt, endeavour; test (quality), test qualities of (person, thing) by experiment, ascertain by experiment; make severe demands on; examine effectiveness or usefulness of for purpose; investigate and decide (case, issue) judicially, subject (person) to trial (*for* crime). **2** *n.* attempt; *Rugby footb.* touching-down of ball by player behind goal-line, entitling his side to a kick at goal. **try one's hand** have attempt *at*; **try on** put (clothes etc.) on to test fit etc., begin experimentally to see how much will be tolerated; **try-on** *colloq.* act of trying something on, attempt to deceive; **try out** put to the test, test thoroughly; **try-out** experimental test.

**trying** *a.* difficult to bear; exhausting; exasperating.

**tryst** /trɪst/ *n. arch.* time and place for meeting esp. of lovers.

**tsar** *n.* title of former emperor of Russia.

**tsetse** /ˈtsetsi/ *n.* Afr. fly carrying disease to men and animals by biting.

**T-shirt, T-square**: see **T**.

**tub 1** *n.* open flat-bottomed usu. round vessel; *colloq.* bath; *derog.* or *joc.* clumsy slow boat. **2** *v.* plant or bathe or wash in tub. **3 tub-thumper** ranting preacher or orator.

**tuba** /ˈtjuːbə/ *n.* low-pitched brass wind instrument.

**tubby** /ˈtʌbi/ *a.* tub-shaped; short and fat.

**tube 1** *n.* long hollow cylinder, natural or artificial structure having approximately this shape with open or closed ends and serving for passage of fluid etc. or as receptacle; *colloq.* underground electric railway; inner tube containing air in pneumatic tyre; cathode-ray tube, esp. in television; *US* thermionic valve; *Aus. sl.* can of beer. **2** *v.t.* equip with tubes; enclose in tube. **3 the tube** *US* television.

**tuber** /ˈtjuːbə(r)/ *n.* short thick rounded root or underground stem of plant.

**tubercle** /ˈtjuːbək(ə)l/ *n.* small rounded swelling in part or organ of body, esp. as characteristic of tuberculosis in lungs.

**tubercular** /tjuːˈbɜːkjələ(r)/ *a.* of or affected with tuberculosis.

**tuberculin** /tjuːˈbɜːkjələn/ *n.* preparation from cultures of tubercle bacillus used for treatment and diagnosis of tuberculosis. **tuberculin-tested** (of milk) from cows shown by tuberculin test to be free of tuberculosis.

**tuberculosis** /tjuːbɜːkjəˈləʊsəs/ *n.* infectious bacterial disease marked by tubercles, esp. in lungs.

**tuberculous** /tjuːˈbɜːkjələs/ *a.* of or having or caused by tubercles or tuberculosis.

**tuberose** /ˈtjuːbərəʊz/ *n.* plant with creamy-white fragrant flowers.

**tuberous** /ˈtjuːbərəs/ *a.* having tubers; of or like a tuber.

**tubing** /ˈtjuːbɪŋ/ *n.* length of tube or quantity of tubes; material for tubes.

**tubular** /ˈtjuːbjələ(r)/ *a.* tube-shaped; having or consisting of tubes.

**tuck 1** *v.* draw or fold or turn outer or end parts of (cloth or clothes etc.) close together or so as to be held; draw together into small compass; cover snugly and comfortably *in* or *up*; stow (thing) away in specified way; make stitched fold in (material or garment). **2** *n.* flattened fold sewn in garment etc.; *sl.* eatables, esp. cakes and sweets. **3 tuck in** *sl.* eat heartily; **tuck-shop** shop selling sweets etc. to schoolchildren.

**tucker** /ˈtʌkə(r)/ **1** *v.t. US colloq.* tire (*out*), exhaust. **2** *n. Aus. sl.* food. **3 tucker-bag, -box**, *Aus. sl.* receptacle for food.

# Tudor

**Tudor** /'tju:də(r)/ *a.* of royal family of England from Henry VII to Elizabeth I; of the architectural style of this period.

**Tues.** *abbr.* Tuesday.

**Tuesday** /'tju:zdeɪ or -di:/ *n.* day of week following Monday.

**tufa** /'tju:fə/ *n.* porous rock formed round springs of mineral water; tuff.

**tuff** *n.* rock formed from volcanic ashes.

**tuft** *n.* number of feathers or threads or hairs or grass-blades etc. growing or joined together in cluster or knot.

**tug 1** *v.* pull hard, pull violently *at*; tow (vessel) by means of tugboat. **2** *n.* hard or violent or jerky pull; tugboat. **3 tugboat** small powerful boat for towing others; **tug of war** trial of strength between two sides pulling opposite ways on a rope.

**tuition** /tju:'ɪʃ(ə)n/ *n.* teaching, instruction.

**tulip** /'tju:lɪp/ *n.* bulbous spring-flowering plant with showy cup-shaped flowers; its flower. **tulip-tree** tree with tulip-like flowers.

**tulle** /tju:l/ *n.* thin soft fine silk net for veils and dresses.

**tumble** /'tʌmb(ə)l/ **1** *v.* fall suddenly or headlong; fall rapidly in amount etc.; roll, toss; move or rush in headlong or blundering fashion; fling or push roughly or carelessly; perform acrobatic feats esp. somersaults; disarrange, rumple. **2** *n.* fall; somersault or other acrobatic feat. **3 tumbledown** falling or fallen into ruin, dilapidated; **tumble-drier** machine for drying washed clothes etc. in heated rotating drum; **tumble to** *colloq.* grasp meaning of (idea etc.).

**tumbler** *n.* drinking-glass without handle or foot; acrobat; part of mechanism of lock.

**tumbrel** /'tʌmbr(ə)l/ *n.* (also **tumbril**) open cart in which condemned persons were carried to guillotine during French Revolution.

**tumescent** /tju:'mes(ə)nt/ *a.* swelling.

**tumid** /'tju:mɪd/ *a.* swollen, inflated, pompous. **tumidity** *n.*

**tummy** /'tʌmi:/ *n. colloq.* stomach.

**tumour** /'tju:mə(r)/ *n.* abnormal or morbid swelling in the body.

**tumult** /'tju:mʌlt/ *n.* riot, angry demonstration of a mob; uproar or din; conflict of emotions etc. **tumultuous** *a.*

# turbo-

**tumulus** /'tju:mjələs/ *n.* (*pl.* **-li** /-laɪ/) ancient burial mound.

**tun** *n.* large cask or barrel; brewer's fermenting-vat.

**tuna** /'tju:nə/ *n.* tunny; (also **tuna-fish**) its flesh as food.

**tundra** /'tʌndrə/ *n.* vast level treeless Arctic region where subsoil is frozen.

**tune 1** *n.* melody with or without harmony; correct pitch or intonation in singing or playing, adjustment of instrument to obtain this. **2** *v.* put (instrument) in tune; adjust (radio receiver) to desired wavelength etc.; adjust (engine etc.) to run smoothly; adjust or adapt (*to* purpose etc.). **3 change one's tune** change one's manner esp. from insolent to respectful; **in, out of, tune**, in, out of, proper pitch or intonation, or *fig.* proper condition or harmony (*with*); **tune in** set radio receiver to right wavelength to receive signal; **tune up** bring (instrument) up to proper pitch, adjust instruments for playing together; **tuning-fork** two-pronged steel instrument giving particular note when struck.

**tuneful** /'tju:nfəl/ *a.* melodious, musical.

**tuner** /'tju:nə(r)/ *n.* person who tunes pianos etc.

**tungsten** /'tʌŋst(ə)n/ *n.* heavy steel-grey metallic element.

**tunic** /'tju:nɪk/ *n.* close-fitting short coat of police or military uniform; loose often sleeveless garment.

**tunnel** /'tʌn(ə)l/ **1** *n.* artificial underground passage under hill or river or roadway etc.; underground passage dug by burrowing animal. **2** *v.* make tunnel through (hill etc.); make one's way so.

**tunny** /'tʌni:/ *n.* large edible sea-fish.

**tuppence, tuppenny,** = *twopence, twopenny.*

**turban** /'tɜ:bən/ *n.* man's head-dress of linen or silk etc. wound round cap, worn esp. by Muslims and Sikhs; woman's hat or head-dress resembling this.

**turbid** /'tɜ:bɪd/ *a.* muddy, thick, not clear; confused, disordered. **turbidity** *n.*

**turbine** /'tɜ:baɪn/ *n.* rotary motor driven by flow of water or gas.

**turbo-** in comb. turbine.

**turbo-jet** /'tɜːbəʊdʒet/ n. jet engine in which jet also operates turbine-driven air-compressor; aircraft with this.

**turbo-prop** /'tɜːbəʊprɒp/ n. jet engine in which turbine is used as in turbo-jet and also to drive propeller; aircraft with this.

**turbot** /'tɜːbət/ n. large flat-fish valued as food.

**turbulent** /'tɜːbjələnt/ a. disturbed, in commotion; (of flow of air) varying irregularly; insubordinate, riotous. **turbulence** n.

**turd** n. vulg. ball or lump of excrement.

**tureen** /tʊˈriːn/ n. deep covered dish for serving soup.

**turf** 1 n. (pl. **turves** or **turfs**) short grass with surface earth bound together by its roots; piece of this cut from ground; slab of peat for fuel. 2 v.t. lay (ground) with turf; sl. throw out. 3 **the turf** racecourse, horse-racing; **turf accountant** bookmaker. 4 **turfy** a.

**turgid** /'tɜːdʒɪd/ a. swollen, inflated; (of language) pompous, bombastic. **turgidity** n.

**Turk** n. native of Turkey.

**turkey** /'tɜːkɪ/ n. large orig. Amer. bird bred for food; its flesh. **turkey-cock** male turkey.

**Turkey carpet** /'tɜːkɪ/ thick-piled woollen carpet with bold design.

**Turkish** /'tɜːkɪʃ/ 1 a. of Turkey. 2 n. language of Turkey. 3 **Turkish bath** hot-air or steam bath followed by massage etc.; **Turkish delight** kind of gelatinous sweet; **Turkish towel** one made of cotton terry.

**turmeric** /'tɜːmərɪk/ n. E. Ind. plant of ginger family; its aromatic root powdered as flavouring or dye.

**turmoil** /'tɜːmɔɪl/ n. din and bustle and confusion.

**turn** 1 v. move round so as to keep at same distance from a centre; (cause to) receive such motion; change from one side to another, invert, reverse; give new direction to, take new direction, adapt, have recourse to; move to other side of, go round; pass age or time of; cause to go, send, put; change in nature, form, condition, etc., (cause to) become; shape (object) in lathe; give (esp. elegant) form to. 2 n. act or fact or process of turning; turning of road; point of turning or change; change of tide from ebb to flow or flow to ebb; tendency, formation; short performance on stage, in circus, etc.; opportunity, occasion, privilege, or obligation, that comes successively to each of several persons etc.; service of specified kind; one round in coil of rope etc.; colloq. momentary nervous shock; Mus. ornament of principal note with those above and below it. 3 **do a hand's turn** make slightest effort; **in turn** in succession; **on the turn** just changing; **take turns** work etc. alternately; **turn against** make or become hostile to; **turncoat** person who changes sides; **turn down** fold down, place face downwards, reduce (volume of sound, heat, etc.) by turning knob, reduce flame etc. of by turning tap, reject; **turn in** fold or incline inwards, hand in, colloq. go to bed; **turnkey** gaoler; **turn off** enter side-road, stop flow or working of by means of tap, knob, etc., colloq. cause to lose interest; **turn on** start flow or working of by means of tap or knob etc., colloq. arouse interest or emotions of, depend on, face hostilely; **turn out** expel, extinguish (light etc.), fold or incline outwards, equip, dress, produce (manufactured goods etc.), empty of contents or expose thus, colloq. get out of bed, colloq. go out of doors, (cause to) assemble for duty, be found, prove to be the case, result; **turn-out** turning out esp. for duty, number of persons who go to vote etc., equipage; **turn over** (cause to) fall over, expose or bring uppermost the other side of, cause (engine etc.) to revolve, consider thoroughly, transfer conduct of (thing to person); **turnover** turning over, pie or tart made by turning half of pastry over filling, amount of money taken in business, number of persons entering or leaving employment etc.; **turnpike** US road on which toll is collected at gates; **turnstile** admission-gate with arms revolving on post; **turntable** circular revolving platform; **turn to** begin work, apply oneself to, go on to consider next; **turn turtle** capsize; **turn up** unearth, make one's appearance, increase (volume of sound, heat, etc.) by turning knob, increase flame etc. of by turning tap, place face up, colloq. cause to vomit; **turn-up** thing turned up,

**turner** /'tɜːnə(r)/ n. lathe-worker.

**turnery** /'tɜːnərɪ/ n. objects made on lathe; work with lathe.

**turning** /'tɜːnɪŋ/ n. place where roads meet, road meeting another; use of lathe; in *pl.* chips or shavings from this. **turning-circle** smallest circle in which vehicle can turn; **turning-point** point at which decisive change occurs.

**turnip** /'tɜːnɪp/ n. plant with globular root used as vegetable and fodder; its root.

**turpentine** /'tɜːpəntaɪn/ n. resin got from terebinth and other trees; (in full **oil of turpentine**) volatile inflammable oil distilled from turpentines and used in mixing paints etc.

**turpitude** /'tɜːpɪtjuːd/ n. baseness, wickedness.

**turps** n. *colloq.* oil of turpentine.

**turquoise** /'tɜːkwɔɪz/ n. opaque precious stone, usu. greenish-blue; this colour.

**turret** /'tʌrət/ n. small tower, esp. decorative addition to building; usu. revolving armoured structure in which guns are mounted or housed; rotating holder for tools in lathe etc.

**turtle** n. sea reptile with horny shell and flippers. **turtle-neck** high closefitting neck or collar.

**turtle dove** /'tɜːt(ə)l/ wild dove noted for soft cooing and affection for its mate.

**tusk** n. long pointed tooth esp. projecting beyond mouth as in elephant or walrus or boar.

**tussle** /'tʌs(ə)l/ n. & v.i. struggle, scuffle.

**tussock** /'tʌsək/ n. clump of grass etc.

**tut** *int.*, n., & v. = tut-tut.

**tutelage** /'tjuːtəlɪdʒ/ n. guardianship; being under this; instruction, tuition.

**tutelary** /'tjuːtələrɪ/ a. serving as protector or patron.

**tutor** /'tjuːtə(r)/ n. 1 private teacher; university teacher supervising studies and welfare of assigned undergraduates; instruction book. 2 v. act as tutor (to); restrain; discipline. 3 **tutorship** n.

**tutorial** /tjuːˈtɔːrɪəl/ 1 a. of tutor. 2 n. period of instruction given to single student or small group.

**tut-tut** 1 *int.* expr. rebuke or impatience or contempt. 2 n. such exclamation. 3 v.i. exclaim thus.

**tutu** /'tuːtuː/ n. dancer's short skirt of layers of stiffened frills.

**tuxedo** /tʌkˈsiːdəʊ/ n. (*pl.* **-dos**) *US* dinner-jacket.

**TV** *abbr.* television.

**twaddle** /'twɒd(ə)l/ 1 n. useless or dull writing or talk. 2 v.i. indulge in this.

**twain** n. & a. *arch.* two.

**twang** 1 n. sound made by plucked string of musical instrument or bow etc.; quality of voice compared to this, esp. nasal intonation. 2 v. emit twang, cause to twang.

**tweak** 1 v.t. pinch and twist or jerk. 2 n. such action.

**twee** a. affectedly dainty or quaint.

**tweed** n. rough-surfaced woollen cloth freq. of mixed colours; in *pl.* suit of tweed. **tweedy** a.

**tweet** 1 n. chirp of small bird. 2 v.i. make chirping noise.

**tweeter** n. loudspeaker for high frequencies.

**tweezers** /'twiːzəz/ *n.pl.* small pair of pincers for picking up small objects or plucking out hairs etc.

**twelfth** /twelfθ/ 1 a. next after eleventh. 2 n. one of twelve equal parts. 3 **Twelfth night** eve of Epiphany.

**twelve** /twelv/ a. & n. one more than eleven. **twelvemonth** year.

**twenty** /'twentɪ/ a. & n. twice ten. **twentieth** a. & n.

**twerp** n. *sl.* stupid or objectionable person.

**twice** *adv.* two times; on two occasions; doubly.

**twiddle** /'twɪd(ə)l/ 1 v.t. twist idly about. 2 n. act of twiddling. 3 **twiddle one's thumbs** twirl them idly esp. for lack of anything to do.

**twig**[1] n. small shoot or branch of tree or plant.

**twig**[2] v. *colloq.* understand, catch meaning (of); observe, notice.

**twilight** /'twaɪlaɪt/ n. light from sky when sun is below horizon, esp. in evening; period of this; state of imperfect understanding; period of decline. **twilight zone** area between others in position and character.

**twilit** /'twaɪlɪt/ a. dimly illuminated (as) by twilight.

**twill** *n.* textile fabric with surface of parallel diagonal ribs.

**twilled** /twɪld/ *a.* woven as twill.

**twin 1** *n.* each of two children or animals born at a birth; each of closely related pair; counterpart. **2** *a.* born as (one of) twins; forming one of a pair. **3** *v.* join or match closely, pair; bear twins. **4 twin bed** either of pair of single beds; **twin set** woman's matching jumper and cardigan.

**twine 1** *n.* thread or string of thickness used for tying small parcels or sewing coarse materials etc.; coil, twist. **2** *v.* twist strands together to form cord; wreathe, clasp; twist, coil, wind.

**twinge** /twɪndʒ/ **1** *n.* sharp momentary local pain. **2** *v.i.* suffer twinge.

**twinkle** /'twɪŋk(ə)l/ **1** *v.i.* shine with rapidly intermittent light, sparkle; move rapidly; emit (light) in quick gleams. **2** *n.* sparkle or gleam of eyes; slight flash of light; short rapid movement.

**twirl 1** *v.t.* spin or swing or twist quickly and lightly round. **2** *n.* twirling, whirling; thing that twirls.

**twist 1** *v.* change the form of by rotating one end and not the other or the two ends opposite ways; undergo such change; make or become spiral, distort, wrench; wind strands etc. about each other to form rope etc.; take curved course; *colloq.* cheat. **2** *n.* twisting, being twisted; thing made by twisting; peculiar tendency of mind or character etc.; distortion; unexpected development etc.

**twister** /'twɪstə(r)/ *n. colloq.* swindler.

**twit**[1] *n. sl.* foolish person.

**twit**[2] *v.t.* reproach, taunt, (*with*).

**twitch 1** *v.* quiver or jerk spasmodically; pull with light jerk, pull at. **2** *n.* twitching. **3 twitchy** *a.*

**twitter** /'twɪtə(r)/ **1** *v.* (of bird, or *fig.* of person) utter succession of light tremulous sounds; utter or express thus. **2** *n.* twittering; *colloq.* tremulously excited state.

**two** /tu:/ *a. & n.* one more than one. **two-dimensional** having or appearing to have length and breadth but no depth; *fig.* ambiguous; **two-edged** having 2 cutting edges, *fig.* ambiguous; **two-faced** insincere; **two-handed** used with both hands or by 2 persons; **twopence** /'tʌpəns/ sum of 2 pence, thing of little value; **twopenny** /'tʌpnɪ/ worth twopence, *fig.* cheap, worthless; **twopenny-halfpenny** /tʌpnɪ:'heɪpnɪ/ *fig.* contemptible, insignificant; **two-piece** suit of clothes or woman's bathing-suit comprising 2 separate parts; **two-ply** (wool etc.) having 2 strands, (plywood) having 2 layers; **two-step** ballroom dance in march or polka time; **two-stroke** (of internal-combustion engine) having power cycle completed in one up-and-down movement of piston; **two-time** *sl.* deceive (esp. by infidelity); **two-up** *Aus. & NZ* gambling-game played by tossing two coins; **two-way** operating in two directions. **twofold** *a.*

**twosome** /'tu:səm/ *n.* pair or couple of persons.

**tycoon** /taɪ'ku:n/ *n. colloq.* business magnate.

**tying** *partic.* of **tie**.

**tyke** *n.* cur; low or objectionable fellow.

**tympanum** /'tɪmpənəm/ *n.* (*pl.* -na) ear-drum, middle ear; space between lintel and arch above door etc.

**type 1** *n.* class of things having common characteristics; person or thing or event or model serving as illustration or symbol or characteristic specimen etc.; small block with raised letter or figure etc. on upper surface for use in printing; set or supply or kind of these; *colloq.* person, esp. one of specified character. **2** *v.* write with typewriter; typify; determine type of, classify according to type. **3 type-cast** cast (performer) in role appropriate to his nature or previous successful roles; **typeface** set of types in one design, inked surface of types; **type-script** typewritten document; **typesetter** compositor; **typewriter** machine with keys enabling user to produce printlike characters; **typewritten** produced thus.

**typhoid** /'taɪfɔɪd/ *n.* (in full **typhoid fever**) infectious bacterial fever attacking intestines.

**typhoon** /taɪ'fu:n/ *n.* violent hurricane in E. Asian seas.

**typhus** /'taɪfəs/ *n.* an acute contagious fever.

**typical** /'tɪpɪk(ə)l/ *a.* serving as characteristic example, distinctive.

**typify** /'tɪpɪfaɪ/ *v.t.* be representative

example of; represent by type. **typification** *n*.

**typist** /ˈtaɪpɪst/ *n*. (esp. professional) user of typewriter.

**typography** /taɪˈpɒgrəfɪ/ *n*. printing as an art; style or appearance of printed matter. **typographer** *n*.; **typographical** *a*.

**tyrannical** /tɪˈrænɪk(ə)l/ *a*. acting like or characteristic of tyrant.

**tyrannize** /ˈtɪrənaɪz/ *v.i.* exercise tyranny (*over*); rule despotically.

**tyrannous** /ˈtɪrənəs/ *a*. tyrannical.

**tyranny** /ˈtɪrənɪ/ *n*. cruel and arbitrary use of authority; rule by tyrant; period of this; State thus ruled.

**tyrant** /ˈtaɪrənt/ *n*. oppressive or cruel ruler; person exercising power or authority arbitrarily or cruelly.

**tyre** *n*. rubber covering, usu. inflated, placed round wheel to prevent jarring.

**tyro** var. of **tiro**.

# U

**ubiquitous** /juːˈbɪkwətəs/ a. present everywhere or in several places simultaneously; often encountered. **ubiquity** n.

**udder** /ˈʌdə(r)/ n. pendulous baggy milk-secreting organ of cow etc.

**UDI** abbr. unilateral declaration of independence.

**UFO** abbr. unidentified flying object.

**ugh** /ʌh or ʊh/ int. expr. disgust etc.

**ugli** /ˈʌɡliː/ n. mottled green and yellow citrus fruit.

**ugly** /ˈʌɡli/ a. unpleasing or repulsive to sight or hearing; unpleasant, threatening, abusive; morally repulsive, vile. **ugly duckling** person who turns out to be more beautiful or talented etc. than was at first expected.

**UHF** abbr. ultra-high frequency.

**UK** abbr. United Kingdom.

**ukulele** /juːkəˈleɪliː/ n. small 4-stringed guitar.

**ulcer** /ˈʌlsə(r)/ n. open sore on external or internal surface of body; corroding or corrupting influence. **ulcerous** a.

**ulcerate** /ˈʌlsəreɪt/ v. form ulcer (in or on). **ulceration** n.

**ulna** /ˈʌlnə/ n. (pl. **-nae** /-niː/) bone of forearm on opp. side to thumb; corresponding bone in animal's foreleg or bird's wing. **ulnar** a.

**ulster** /ˈʌlstə(r)/ n. long loose overcoat of rough cloth.

**ult.** abbr. ultimo.

**ulterior** /ʌlˈtɪərɪə(r)/ a. beyond what is obvious or admitted.

**ultimate** /ˈʌltəmeɪt/ a. last, final; fundamental, unanalysable.

**ultimatum** /ʌltəˈmeɪtəm/ n. (pl. **-tums**) final statement of terms, rejection of which by opposite party may lead to war or end of co-operation etc.

**ultimo** /ˈʌltəməʊ/ adv. of last month.

**ultra-** in comb. extremely, excessively; beyond.

**ultra-high** /ˈʌltrəhaɪ/ a. (of frequency) between 300 and 3000 megahertz.

**ultramarine** /ʌltrəməˈriːn/ 1 n. brilliant deep-blue pigment. 2 a. of this colour.

**ultrasonic** /ʌltrəˈsɒnɪk/ a. pitched above upper limit of human hearing.

**ultrasound** /ˈʌltrəsaʊnd/ n. ultrasonic waves.

**ultraviolet** /ʌltrəˈvaɪələt/ a. of or using invisible rays just beyond violet end of spectrum.

**ululate** /ˈjuːljəleɪt/ v.i. howl, wail. **ululation** n.

**umbel** /ˈʌmb(ə)l/ n. flower-cluster in which stalks of nearly equal length spring from common centre. **umbellate** a.

**umbelliferous** /ʌmbəˈlɪfərəs/ a. (of plant) belonging to the family including carrots and celery etc.

**umber** /ˈʌmbə(r)/ 1 n. dark brown earth used as pigment. 2 a. umber-coloured.

**umbilical** /ʌmˈbɪlɪk(ə)l/ a. of navel. **umbilical cord** flexible cord-like structure attaching foetus to placenta.

**umbra** /ˈʌmbrə/ n. (pl. **-brae** /-briː/ or **-bras**) shadow cast by moon or earth in eclipse. **umbral** a.

**umbrage** /ˈʌmbrɪdʒ/ n. offence; sense of slight or injury.

**umbrella** /ʌmˈbrelə/ n. light portable device for protection against weather, consisting of collapsible usu. circular canopy of cloth mounted on central stick; protection, means of this; co-ordinating agency.

**umpire** /ˈʌmpaɪə(r)/ 1 n. person chosen to decide between disputants etc. and enforce rules of game or contest etc. 2 v. act as umpire (in).

**umpteen** /ˈʌmptiːn/ a. sl. many; an indefinite number of. **umpteenth** a.

**un-** pref. freely used in comb. with adjs. and nouns to express negation, not, in-, non-; in comb. with verbs, verbal derivatives, etc. to express contrary or reverse action, deprivation or removal of quality or property, etc. The number of words with this prefix being practically unlimited, many of those whose meaning is obvious are not listed here.

**UN** abbr. United Nations.

**unaccountable** /ʌnəˈkaʊntəb(ə)l/ a. that cannot be explained, strange; (of person) not responsible.

**unaffected** /ʌnəˈfektəd/ a. free from affectation; sincere; not affected (by).

**unalloyed** /ʌnəˈlɔɪd/ a. unmixed, pure.

**unanimous** /juːˈnænɪməs/ a. all of one mind; agreeing in opinion; held or given etc. with general agreement or consent. **unanimity** /-ˈnɪm-/ n.

# unanswerable

**unanswerable** /ˌʌnˈɑːnsərəb(ə)l/ or -ˈæns-/ *a.* that cannot be answered or refuted.

**unassailable** /ˌʌnəˈseɪləb(ə)l/ *a.* that cannot be attacked or questioned.

**unassuming** /ˌʌnəˈsjuːmɪŋ/ *a.* making little of one's own merits or status.

**unawares** /ˌʌnəˈweəz/ *adv.* unexpectedly; unconsciously; by surprise.

**unbacked** /ʌnˈbækt/ *a.* not supported, having no backers (esp. in betting); having no back or backing.

**unbalanced** /ʌnˈbælənst/ *a.* not balanced; mentally unstable or deranged.

**unbeknown** /ˌʌnbəˈnəʊn/ *a.* (also **unbeknownst**) not known. **unbeknown to** without the knowledge of.

**unbend** /ʌnˈbend/ *v.* (*past & p.p.* -**bent**) change from bent position, straighten, relax from strain or exertion or severity; become affable.

**unbidden** /ʌnˈbɪd(ə)n/ *a.* unasked, uninvited.

**unblock** /ʌnˈblɒk/ *v.t.* remove obstruction from.

**unblushing** /ʌnˈblʌʃɪŋ/ *a.* shameless.

**unbosom** /ʌnˈbʊz(ə)m/ *v.t.* disclose; **unbosom oneself** disclose one's thoughts or feelings etc.

**unbridled** /ʌnˈbraɪd(ə)ld/ *a.* unrestrained, uncontrolled.

**uncalled-for** /ʌnˈkɔːldfɔː(r)/ *a.* impertinently offered or intruded.

**uncanny** /ʌnˈkæni/ *a.* mysterious, uncomfortably strange or unfamiliar.

**unceremonious** /ˌʌnserəˈməʊnɪəs/ *a.* informal; abrupt in manner, lacking courtesy.

**uncertain** /ʌnˈsɜːt(ə)n/ *a.* not certain; not to be depended on; changeable. **uncertainty** *n.*

**uncle** /ˈʌŋk(ə)l/ *n.* parent's brother or brother-in-law; *sl.* pawnbroker. **Uncle Sam** *colloq.* US government.

**unclean** /ʌnˈkliːn/ *a.* not clean, foul; ceremonially impure.

**uncommon** /ʌnˈkɒmən/ *a.* unusual, remarkable.

**uncompromising** /ʌnˈkɒmprəmaɪzɪŋ/ *a.* refusing compromise; unyielding, inflexible.

**unconcern** /ˌʌnkənˈsɜːn/ *n.* freedom from anxiety; indifference, apathy.

**unconscionable** /ʌnˈkɒnʃənəb(ə)l/ *a.* having no conscience; not right or reasonable, excessive.

# underclothes

**unconscious** /ʌnˈkɒnʃəs/ **1** *a.* not aware (*of*); not conscious; done etc. without conscious intention. **2** *n.* the part of the mind not normally accessible to consciousness.

**unconsidered** /ˌʌnkənˈsɪdəd/ *a.* disregarded; not based on consideration.

**uncork** /ʌnˈkɔːk/ *v.t.* draw cork from (bottle); *colloq.* give vent to (feelings).

**uncouple** /ʌnˈkʌp(ə)l/ *v.t.* release from couples or coupling.

**uncouth** /ʌnˈkuːθ/ *a.* awkward, clumsy, boorish.

**uncover** /ʌnˈkʌvə(r)/ *v.* remove cover or covering from; lay bare, disclose; take off one's hat or cap.

**unction** /ˈʌŋkʃ(ə)n/ *n.* anointing with oil as religious rite or symbol; thing used in anointing; fervent or sympathetic quality in words or tone caused by or causing deep emotion; pretence of this.

**unctuous** /ˈʌŋktjʊəs/ *a.* full of (esp. simulated) unction; greasy.

**uncut** /ʌnˈkʌt/ *a.* not cut; (of book) with leaves not cut open or margins not trimmed; (of film) not censored; (of diamond) not shaped; (of fabric) with loops of pile not cut.

**undeceive** /ˌʌndəˈsiːv/ *v.t.* free from deception or mistake.

**undeniable** /ˌʌndəˈnaɪəb(ə)l/ *a.* that cannot be denied or disputed.

**under** /ˈʌndə(r)/ **1** *prep.* in or to position lower than, below; inferior to, less than; subjected to, undergoing, liable to; governed, controlled, or bound by; in accordance with; in the time of. **2** *adv.* in or to lower place or subordinate position. **3** *a.* lower. **4 undermost** *a.*

**underarm** /ˈʌndərɑːm/ *a.* *Crick.* etc. (of bowling) with arm below shoulder-level.

**underbelly** /ˈʌndəbeli/ *n.* under surface of animal etc. esp. as vulnerable to attack.

**underbid** /ˌʌndəˈbɪd/ *v.* make lower bid than; bid too little (on).

**undercarriage** /ˈʌndəkærɪdʒ/ *n.* landing-gear of aircraft; supporting framework of vehicle etc.

**undercliff** /ˈʌndəklɪf/ *n.* terrace or lower cliff formed by landslip.

**underclothes** /ˈʌndəkləʊðz/ *n.pl.* (also **underclothing**) clothes worn under others, esp. next to skin.

**undercoat** /'ʌndəkəʊt/ n. layer of paint under another; (in animals) coat of hair under another.

**undercover** /ʌndə'kʌvə(r)/ a. surreptitious, spying esp. by working among those observed.

**undercroft** /'ʌndəkrɒft/ n. crypt.

**undercurrent** /'ʌndəkʌrənt/ n. current flowing below surface; suppressed or underlying activity or force etc.

**undercut** /ʌndə'kʌt/ 1 v.t. (past & p.p. -cut) sell or work at lower price than; strike (golf etc. ball) to make it rise high. 2 n. under-side of sirloin.

**underdog** /'ʌndədɒg/ n. loser in fight etc.; person in state of subjection or inferiority.

**underdone** /ʌndə'dʌn/ a. lightly or insufficiently cooked.

**underemployed** /ʌndərəm'plɔɪd/ a. not fully occupied.

**underestimate** 1 /ʌndə'restəmeɪt/ v.t. form too low an estimate of. 2 /ʌndə'restəmət/ n. estimate that is too low.

**underfelt** /'ʌndəfelt/ n. felt for laying under carpet.

**underfoot** /ʌndə'fʊt/ adv. under one's feet; into state of subjection or inferiority.

**undergarment** /'ʌndəgɑːmənt/ n. piece of underclothing.

**undergo** /ʌndə'gəʊ/ v.t. (past -went; p.p. -gone /-'gɒn/) be subjected to, endure.

**undergraduate** /ʌndə'grædjuːət/ n. member of university who has not taken first degree.

**underground** 1 /ʌndə'graʊnd/ adv. below surface of ground; in(to) secrecy or hiding. 2 /'ʌndəgraʊnd/ a. situated underground; secret or hidden. 3 /'ʌndəgraʊnd/ n. underground railway; secret group or activity esp. aiming at subversion.

**undergrowth** /'ʌndəgrəʊθ/ n. shrubs or small trees growing under large ones.

**underhand** /ʌndə'hænd/ a. secret, deceptive; *Crick*. etc. underarm.

**underlay** 1 /ʌndə'leɪ/ v.t. (past & p.p. -laid) lay thing under (another) to support or raise. 2 /'ʌndəleɪ/ n. thing laid under another, esp. carpet.

**underlie** /ʌndə'laɪ/ v.t. (past -lay; p.p. -lain) lie under (stratum etc.); *fig.* be basis of, exist beneath superficial aspect of.

**underline** 1 /ʌndə'laɪn/ v.t. draw line under (words etc.); emphasize. 2 /'ʌndəlaɪn/ n. line placed under word or illustration.

**underling** /'ʌndəlɪŋ/ n. (usu. *derog.*) subordinate.

**undermanned** /ʌndə'mænd/ a. having too few people as crew or staff.

**undermine** /ʌndə'maɪn/ v.t. make excavation under; wear away base of; injure or wear out etc. insidiously or secretly or imperceptibly.

**underneath** /ʌndə'niːθ/ 1 *prep.* at or to lower place than, below. 2 *adv.* at or to lower place; inside. 3 *n.* lower surface or part.

**underpants** /'ʌndəpænts/ *n.pl.* undergarment for lower body and part of legs.

**underpass** /'ʌndəpɑːs/ n. road etc. passing under another.

**underpin** /ʌndə'pɪn/ v.t. place masonry etc. support under; support, strengthen.

**underprivileged** /ʌndə'prɪvəlɪdʒd/ a. less privileged than others; not enjoying normal living standard or rights.

**underrate** /ʌndə'reɪt/ v.t. have too low an opinion of.

**underseal** /ʌndəsiːl/ v.t. seal underpart of (esp. motor vehicle against rust etc.).

**under-secretary** /ʌndə'sekrətəri:/ n. subordinate official, esp. junior minister or senior civil servant.

**undersell** /ʌndə'sel/ v.t. (past & p.p. -sold) sell at lower price than.

**undershoot** /ʌndə'ʃuːt/ v.i. (past & p.p. -shot) (of aircraft) land short of (runway etc.).

**undershot** /ʌndəʃɒt/ a. (of wheel) turned by water flowing under it.

**undersigned** /ʌndə'saɪnd/ a. whose signature is appended.

**undersized** /ʌndəsaɪzd/ a. of less than usual size.

**understaffed** /ʌndə'stɑːft/ a. having too few staff.

**understand** /ʌndə'stænd/ v. (past & p.p. -stood /-'stʊd/) comprehend, perceive meaning of; know how to deal with; infer, esp. from information received; take for granted.

**understanding** 1 n. intelligence;

ability to understand; agreement, thing agreed upon. 2 *a.* having understanding or insight; sympathetic.

**understate** /ʌndəˈsteɪt/ *v.t.* express in restrained terms; represent as being less than it really is. **understatement** *n.*

**understudy** /ˈʌndəstʌdi/ 1 *n.* person who studies another's role or duties so as to act in his absence. 2 *v.t.* study (role etc.) thus; act as understudy to.

**undertake** /ʌndəˈteɪk/ *v.t.* (*past* -**took** /-ˈtʊk/; *p.p.* -**taken**) agree to perform; make oneself responsible for; engage in; accept obligation (*to* do); guarantee, affirm *that*.

**undertaker** /ˈʌndəteɪkə(r)/ *n.* person who professionally makes arrangements for funerals.

**undertaking** /ʌndəˈteɪkɪŋ/ *n.* work etc. undertaken; enterprise; promise; /ˈʌn-/ management of funerals.

**undertone** /ˈʌndətəʊn/ *n.* subdued tone, underlying quality or feeling.

**undertow** /ˈʌndətəʊ/ *n.* current below sea surface in opposite direction to surface current.

**undervalue** /ʌndəˈvæljuː/ *v.t.* value insufficiently.

**underwater** /ˈʌndəˈwɔːtə(r)/ 1 *a.* situated or done under water. 2 *adv.* under water.

**underwear** /ˈʌndəweə(r)/ *n.* underclothes.

**underweight** /ʌndəˈweɪt/ *a.* below normal or suitable weight.

**underworld** /ˈʌndəwɜːld/ *n.* those who live by organized crime and immorality; *Myth.* abode of the dead.

**underwrite** /ʌndəˈraɪt/ *v.t.* (*past* -**wrote**; *p.p.* -**written**) sign and accept liability under (insurance policy); accept (liability) thus; undertake to finance or support.

**underwriter** /ˈʌndəraɪtə(r)/ *n.* insurer, esp. of shipping.

**undesirable** /ʌndəˈzaɪərəb(ə)l/ 1 *a.* unpleasant, objectionable. 2 *n.* undesirable person.

**undies** /ˈʌndiːz/ *n.pl. colloq.* (esp. women's) underclothes.

**undo** /ʌnˈduː/ *v.t.* (*past* -**did**; *p.p.* -**done** /-ˈdʌn/) unfasten and open; annul; ruin prospects or reputation or morals of.

**undone** 1 *p.p.* of **undo**. 2 *a.* not done.

**undoubted** /ʌnˈdaʊtɪd/ *a.* certain, not questioned.

**undress** 1 /ʌnˈdres/ *v.* take off one's clothes; take off clothes of. 2 /ˈʌndres/ *n.* ordinary dress opposed to full dress or uniform; casual or informal dress.

**undue** /ʌnˈdjuː/ *a.* excessive, disproportionate; improper. **unduly** *adv.*

**undulate** /ˈʌndjʊleɪt/ *v.i.* have wavy motion or look. **undulation** *n.*; **undulatory** *a.*

**unduly**: see **undue**.

**undying** /ʌnˈdaɪɪŋ/ *a.* immortal.

**unearth** /ʌnˈɜːθ/ *v.t.* discover by search or in course of digging or rummaging.

**unearthly** /ʌnˈɜːθlɪ/ *a.* supernatural, mysterious; *colloq.* absurdly early.

**uneasy** /ʌnˈiːzɪ/ *a.* disturbed or uncomfortable in body or mind.

**unemployable** /ʌnəmˈplɔɪəb(ə)l/ *a.* unfitted by character etc. for paid employment.

**unemployed** /ʌnəmˈplɔɪd/ *a.* temporarily out of work; lacking employment; not used.

**unemployment** /ʌnəmˈplɔɪmənt/ *n.* lack of employment. **unemployment benefit** payment made by State to unemployed worker.

**unequivocal** /ʌnəˈkwɪvəkl(ə)l/ *a.* not ambiguous, plain, unmistakable.

**UNESCO** /juːˈneskəʊ/ *abbr.* United Nations Educational, Scientific, and Cultural Organization.

**unexampled** /ʌnəgˈzɑːmp(ə)ld or -ˈzæmp-/ *a.* without precedent.

**unexceptionable** /ʌnəkˈsepʃənəb(ə)l/ *a.* with which no fault can be found.

**unexceptional** /ʌnəkˈsepʃən(ə)l/ *a.* not out of the ordinary.

**unfaithful** /ʌnˈfeɪθfəl/ *a.* not faithful, esp. adulterous.

**unfeeling** /ʌnˈfiːlɪŋ/ *a.* lacking sensitivity, unsympathetic, cruel.

**unfit** /ʌnˈfɪt/ 1 *a.* not fit, unsuitable; in poor health. 2 *v.t.* make unsuitable (*for*).

**unflappable** /ʌnˈflæpəb(ə)l/ *a. colloq.* imperturbable.

**unfledged** /ʌnˈfledʒd/ *a.* inexperienced; not fledged.

**unfold** /ʌnˈfəʊld/ *v.* open out; reveal; become opened out; develop.

**unfortunate** /ʌnˈfɔːtjənət/ 1 *a.* unlucky; unhappy; ill-advised. 2 *n.* unfortunate person.

**unfrock** /ʌnˈfrɒk/ *v.t.* deprive of ecclesiastical status.

**unfurl** /ʌnˈfɜːl/ *v.* unroll, spread out.

**ungainly** /ʌnˈgeɪnlɪ/ *a.* awkward, clumsy, ungraceful.

**unget-at-able** /ʌngetˈætəb(ə)l/ *a. colloq.* inaccessible.

**ungodly** /ʌnˈgɒdlɪ/ *a.* impious, wicked; *colloq.* outrageous, dreadful.

**ungovernable** /ʌnˈgʌvənəb(ə)l/ *a.* uncontrollable, unruly.

**ungracious** /ʌnˈgreɪʃəs/ *a.* not kindly or courteous.

**unguarded** /ʌnˈgɑːdəd/ *a.* incautious, thoughtless; not guarded.

**unguent** /ˈʌŋgjʊənt/ *n.* ointment.

**ungulate** /ˈʌŋgjʊlət/ 1 *a.* hoofed. 2 *n.* hoofed mammal.

**unhallowed** /ʌnˈhæləʊd/ *a.* unconsecrated; not sacred; wicked.

**unhand** /ʌnˈhænd/ *v.t.* take one's hands off.

**unhappy** /ʌnˈhæpɪ/ *n.* not happy; unfortunate; unsuccessful.

**unhealthy** /ʌnˈhelθɪ/ *a.* not in good health; harmful to health; unwholesome; *sl.* dangerous to life.

**unheard-of** /ʌnˈhɜːdɒv/ *a.* unprecedented.

**unhinge** /ʌnˈhɪndʒ/ *v.t.* derange, disorder (mind).

**unholy** /ʌnˈhəʊlɪ/ *a.* profane, wicked; *colloq.* awful, dreadful.

**uni** /ˈjuːnɪ/ *n. Aus. colloq.* university.

**uni-** *in comb.* having or composed of one.

**unicameral** /juːnɪˈkæmər(ə)l/ *a.* having one legislative chamber.

**UNICEF** /ˈjuːnɪsef/ *abbr.* United Nations Children's Fund.

**unicellular** /juːnəˈseljələ(r)/ *a.* consisting of a single cell.

**unicorn** /ˈjuːnəkɔːn/ *n.* mythical animal resembling horse, with single horn projecting from its forehead.

**unicycle** /ˈjuːnɪsaɪk(ə)l/ *n.* one-wheeled pedal-propelled vehicle.

**unification** /juːnəfəˈkeɪʃ(ə)n/ *n.* unifying or being unified.

**uniform** /ˈjuːnəfɔːm/ 1 *a.* unvarying, plain, unbroken; conforming to same standard or rule. 2 *n.* distinctive clothing worn by members of same school or organization etc. 2 **uniformity** *n.*

**unify** /ˈjuːnəfaɪ/ *v.t.* reduce to unity or uniformity.

**unilateral** /juːnɪˈlætər(ə)l/ *a.* done by or affecting one side only.

**unimpeachable** /ʌnɪmˈpiːtʃəb(ə)l/ *a.* giving no opportunity for censure.

**uninviting** /ʌnɪnˈvaɪtɪŋ/ *a.* unattractive, repellent.

**union** /ˈjuːnɪən/ *n.* uniting, being united; whole resulting from combination of parts or members; trade union; marriage; concord, agreement; **Union** general social club and debating society at some universities. **Union Jack** national flag of UK with combined crosses of 3 patron saints.

**unionist** /ˈjuːnɪənəst/ *n.* member of trade union, advocate of trade unions or of union, esp. supporter of maintenance of union between Britain and Northern Ireland. **unionism** *n.*

**unionize** /ˈjuːnɪənaɪz/ *v.t.* bring under trade-union organization or rules.

**unique** /juːˈniːk/ *a.* being the only one of its kind; having no like or equal or parallel.

**unisex** /ˈjuːnɪseks/ *a.* designed in a style suitable for either sex.

**unison** /ˈjuːnəs(ə)n/ *n.* coincidence in pitch; combination of voices or instruments at same pitch. **in unison** at same pitch, *fig.* in agreement or harmony.

**unit** /ˈjuːnət/ *n.* individual thing or person or group regarded as complete; quantity chosen as standard for expressing other quantities; smallest share in unit trust; device with specified function in complex mechanism; piece of furniture for fitting with others like it or made of complementary parts; group with special function in an organization. **unit trust** company investing in varied stocks the combined contributions from many persons.

**Unitarian** /juːnəˈteərɪən/ *n.* member of religious body maintaining that God is one person not Trinity. **Unitarianism** *n.*

**unitary** /ˈjuːnətərɪ/ *a.* of unit(s); marked by unity or uniformity.

**unite** /juːˈnaɪt/ *v.* join together; make or become one, combine; consolidate; agree, co-operate (in). **United Kingdom** Great Britain and Northern Ireland; **United Nations** international peace-seeking organization; **United States (of America)** republic in N. America.

**unity** /'ju:nəti:/ *n.* oneness, being one or single or individual; due interconnection of parts; harmony between persons etc.; thing forming complex whole; *Math.* the number one.

**universal** /ju:nə'vɜ:s(ə)l/ *a.* of or belonging to or used or done by etc. all persons or things in world or in class concerned; applicable to all cases. **universal coupling, joint,** one transmitting power by a shaft at any selected angle. **universality** /-'sæl-/ *n.*

**universe** /'ju:nəvɜ:s/ *n.* all existing things; all creation; all mankind.

**university** /ju:nə'vɜ:səti:/ *n.* educational institution instructing or examining students in many branches of advanced learning, and conferring degrees; members of this collectively.

**unkempt** /ʌn'kempt/ *a.* dishevelled, untidy, neglected-looking.

**unleash** /ʌn'li:ʃ/ *v.t.* free from leash or restraint; set free in order to pursue or attack etc.

**unless** /ʌn'les/ *conj.* if not; except when.

**unlettered** /ʌn'letəd/ *a.* illiterate.

**unlike** /ʌn'laɪk/ *a. & adv.* not like, different(ly).

**unlikely** /ʌn'laɪkli:/ *a.* improbable; unpromising.

**unlisted** /ʌn'lɪstəd/ *a.* not included in list, esp. of Stock Exchange prices or of telephone numbers.

**unload** /ʌn'ləʊd/ *v.t.* remove cargo or anything carried or conveyed from; remove (cargo); remove charge from (gun); relieve of burden; *fig.* get rid of.

**unlock** /ʌn'lɒk/ *v.t.* release lock of; *fig.* disclose (secret etc.).

**unlooked-for** /ʌn'lʊktfɔ:(r)/ *a.* unexpected.

**unlucky** /ʌn'lʌki:/ *a.* not lucky or fortunate or successful; wretched; bringing bad luck; ill-judged.

**unman** /ʌn'mæn/ *v.t.* deprive of courage or self-control etc.

**unmannerly** /ʌn'mænəli:/ *a.* rude; without good manners.

**unmask** /ʌn'mɑ:sk/ *v.* remove mask from; expose true character of; take off one's mask.

**unmentionable** /ʌn'menʃənəb(ə)l/ *a.* not fit to be mentioned; unspeakable.

**unmistakable** /ʌnmɪ'steɪkəb(ə)l/ *a.* that cannot be mistaken or doubted.

**unmitigated** /ʌn'mɪtəgeɪtəd/ *a.* not modified; absolute.

**unnatural** /ʌn'nætʃər(ə)l/ *a.* contrary or doing violence to nature; lacking natural feelings; artificial, forced.

**unnecessary** /ʌn'nesəseri:/ *a.* not necessary; more than necessary.

**unnerve** /ʌn'nɜ:v/ *v.t.* deprive of strength or resolution etc.

**UNO** *abbr.* United Nations Organization.

**unofficial** /ʌnə'fɪʃ(ə)l/ *a.* not officially authorized or confirmed; (of strike) not formally approved by strikers' trade union.

**unparalleled** /ʌn'pærəleld/ *a.* having no parallel or equal.

**unparliamentary** /ʌnpɑ:lə'mentəri:/ *a.* contrary to parliamentary usage. **unparliamentary language** oaths, abuse.

**unpick** /ʌn'pɪk/ *v.t.* undo stitching of.

**unplaced** /ʌn'pleɪst/ *a.* not placed as one of the first three in race etc.

**unpleasant** /ʌn'plez(ə)nt/ *a.* disagreeable.

**unpopular** /ʌn'pɒpjələ(r)/ *a.* not in popular favour, disliked.

**unpractised** /ʌn'præktəst/ *a.* not experienced or skilled, not put into practice.

**unprecedented** /ʌn'presədentəd/ *a.* for which there is no precedent, unparalleled, novel.

**unprincipled** /ʌn'prɪnsəp(ə)ld/ *a.* not having or based on sound or honest principles of conduct.

**unprintable** /ʌn'prɪntəb(ə)l/ *a.* too indecent or libellous etc. to be printed.

**unprofessional** /ʌnprə'feʃən(ə)l/ *a.* not professional; not worthy of member of profession.

**unprofitable** /ʌn'prɒfətəb(ə)l/ *a.* without profit; serving no purpose.

**unqualified** /ʌn'kwɒləfaɪd/ *a.* not qualified or competent; not modified or limited.

**unquestionable** /ʌn'kwestʃənəb(ə)l/ *a.* that cannot be questioned or doubted.

**unquote** /ʌn'kwəʊt/ *v.i.* terminate passage that is within quotation-marks.

**unravel** /ʌn'ræv(ə)l/ *v.* separate threads of, disentangle; undo, esp. by pulling single thread(s); become or be unravelled.

**unreasonable** /ʌnˈriːzənəb(ə)l/ *a.* exceeding the bounds of reason; not guided by or listening to reason.

**unrelieved** /ʌnrəˈliːvd/ *a.* lacking the relief given by contrast or variation.

**unremitting** /ʌnrəˈmɪtɪŋ/ *a.* incessant.

**unreservedly** /ʌnrəˈzɜːvədli/ *adv.* without reservation.

**unrest** /ʌnˈrest/ *n.* disturbance, turmoil, trouble.

**unrivalled** /ʌnˈraɪv(ə)ld/ *a.* having no equal, peerless.

**unroll** /ʌnˈrəʊl/ *v.* open out from rolled-up state; display, be displayed.

**unruly** /ʌnˈruːli/ *a.* not amenable to rule or discipline; turbulent.

**unsaturated** /ʌnˈsætʃəreɪtəd/ *a.* not saturated; *Chem.* able to combine with hydrogen to form a third substance by joining of molecules.

**unsavoury** /ʌnˈseɪvəri/ *a.* uninviting; disgusting.

**unscathed** /ʌnˈskeɪðd/ *a.* uninjured, unharmed.

**unscientific** /ʌnsaɪənˈtɪfɪk/ *a.* not in accordance with scientific principles.

**unscrew** /ʌnˈskruː/ *v.t.* unfasten by removing screws, loosen (screw).

**unscripted** /ʌnˈskrɪptəd/ *a.* made or delivered etc. without prepared script.

**unscrupulous** /ʌnˈskruːpjələs/ *a.* without scruples; unprincipled.

**unseat** /ʌnˈsiːt/ *v.t.* remove from seat; dislodge from horseback; depose (MP etc.) from seat.

**unseen** /ʌnˈsiːn/ 1 *a.* not seen; invisible; (of translation) to be done without preparation. 2 *n.* unseen translation.

**unselfish** /ʌnˈselfɪʃ/ *a.* not selfish or self-regarding; generous.

**unsettled** /ʌnˈset(ə)ld/ *a.* not settled; open to further discussion; liable to change; not paid.

**unsex** /ʌnˈseks/ *v.t.* deprive of qualities of one's (esp. female) sex.

**unsighted** /ʌnˈsaɪtəd/ *a.* not yet in sight; prevented from seeing.

**unsightly** /ʌnˈsaɪtli/ *a.* unpleasing to look at; ugly.

**unsocial** /ʌnˈsəʊʃ(ə)l/ *a.* not social; not suitable for or seeking society.

**unsophisticated** /ʌnsəˈfɪstɪkeɪtəd/ *a.* artless, simple, natural.

**unsound** /ʌnˈsaʊnd/ *a.* not sound; unhealthy; rotten; erroneous; unreliable.

**unsparing** /ʌnˈspeərɪŋ/ *a.* lavish.

**unspeakable** /ʌnˈspiːkəb(ə)l/ *a.* that words cannot express; good or bad beyond description.

**unstick** /ʌnˈstɪk/ *v.t.* (*past* & *p.p.* **-stuck**) separate (thing stuck to another). **come unstuck** *colloq.* fail.

**unstressed** /ʌnˈstrest/ *a.* not subjected to or pronounced with stress.

**unstring** /ʌnˈstrɪŋ/ *v.t.* (*past* & *p.p.* **-strung**) remove string(s) of; loosen string(s) of (bow, harp); take (beads etc.) off string.

**unstructured** /ʌnˈstrʌktʃəd/ *a.* without structure; informal.

**unstudied** /ʌnˈstʌdid/ *a.* easy, natural, spontaneous.

**unswerving** /ʌnˈswɜːvɪŋ/ *a.* steady, constant.

**unthinkable** /ʌnˈθɪŋkəb(ə)l/ *a.* that cannot be imagined or grasped by the mind; *colloq.* highly unlikely or undesirable.

**untidy** /ʌnˈtaɪdi/ *a.* not tidy, not neat in appearance or habits. **untidiness** *n.*

**until** /ʌnˈtɪl/ *prep.* & *conj.* = **till**[1].

**untimely** /ʌnˈtaɪmli/ *a.* inopportune; premature.

**unto** /ˈʌntʊ/ *prep. arch.* to.

**untold** /ʌnˈtəʊld/ *a.* not told; not counted; beyond count.

**untouchable** /ʌnˈtʌtʃəb(ə)l/ *n.* Hindu of group held to defile higher castes on contact.

**untoward** /ʌntəˈwɔːd/ *a.* perverse; awkward; unlucky.

**untruth** /ʌnˈtruːθ/ *n.* being untrue; falsehood, lie.

**unusual** /ʌnˈjuːʒʊəl/ *a.* not usual; remarkable.

**unutterable** /ʌnˈʌtərəb(ə)l/ *a.* above or beyond description.

**unvarnished** /ʌnˈvɑːnɪʃt/ *a.* not varnished; plain, direct, simple.

**unveil** /ʌnˈveɪl/ *v.t.* withdraw drapery from (new statue etc.) with ceremonies; reveal (secrets etc.).

**unwarrantable** /ʌnˈwɒrəntəb(ə)l/ *a.* (also **unwarranted**) unauthorized, unjustified.

**unwell** /ʌnˈwel/ *a.* not in good health; indisposed.

**unwieldy** /ʌnˈwiːldi/ *a.* slow or clumsy of movement; awkward to handle etc. by reason of size or shape or weight.

**unwitting** /ʌn'wɪtɪŋ/ a. not knowing, unaware; unintentional.

**unworkmanlike** /ʌn'wɜːkmənlaɪk/ a. amateurish.

**unworthy** /ʌn'wɜːðɪ/ a. not worthy of or befitting the character (*of*); discreditable; contemptible, base.

**unwritten** /ʌn'rɪt(ə)n/ a. not written (down); oral; traditional.

**unzip** /ʌn'zɪp/ v. undo zip-fastener of; admit of being unzipped.

**up 1** *adv.* towards or in higher place or state or number; to or in capital or university or place further north or in question etc.; to or in erect or vertical position, out of bed, out of lying or sitting or kneeling posture, in(to) condition of efficiency or activity; (with vbs., usu.) expressing complete or effectual result etc.; *colloq.* amiss, wrong. **2** *prep.* upwards along or through or into; at higher part of. **3** *a.* directed upwards. **4** *v. colloq.* start (abruptly or unexpectedly) to say or do something; raise, esp. abruptly. **5 on the up-and-up** *colloq.* steadily improving, honest(ly); **up against** close to, in(to) contact with, *colloq.* confronted with; **up against it** *colloq.* in great difficulties; **up-and-coming** *colloq.* (of person) making good progress and likely to succeed; **uphill** sloping up, ascending; arduous; **upstairs** up the stairs, to or on or of upper floor of house etc.; **upstream** against flow of stream etc., moving upstream; **up to** until, not more than, equal to, incumbent on, capable of, occupied or busy with; **uptown** *US* residential part of town or city; **up with us** *int.* expr. wish for success of. **6 upward** *a.* & *adv.*; **upwards** *adv.*

**upbeat** /'ʌpbiːt/ **1** *n. Mus.* unaccented beat. **2** *a.* optimistic, cheerful.

**upbraid** /ʌp'breɪd/ v.t. chide, reproach.

**upbringing** /'ʌpbrɪŋɪŋ/ n. bringing up (of child), education.

**up-country** /ʌp'kʌntrɪ/ a. & adv. inland.

**update** /ʌp'deɪt/ v.t. bring up to date.

**up-end** /ʌp'end/ v. set or rise up on end.

**upgrade** /ʌp'greɪd/ v.t. raise in rank etc.

**upheaval** /ʌp'hiːv(ə)l/ n. sudden esp. violent change or disturbance.

**uphold** /ʌp'həʊld/ v.t. (*past* & *p.p.* -held) give support to; maintain, confirm.

**upholster** /ʌp'həʊlstə(r)/ v.t. provide (chair etc.) with textile covering or padding etc. **upholstery** n.

**upkeep** /'ʌpkiːp/ n. maintenance in good condition; cost or means of this.

**upland** /'ʌplənd/ **1** n. higher part of country. **2** a. of this part.

**uplift 1** /ʌp'lɪft/ v.t. raise. **2** /'ʌplɪft/ n. *colloq.* elevating influence.

**upon** /ə'pɒn/ *prep.* on.

**upper** /'ʌpə(r)/ **1** a. higher in place; situated above; superior in rank or dignity etc. **2** n. upper part of shoe or boot. **3 on one's uppers** extremely short of money; **upper case** capital letters; **upper crust** *colloq.* the aristocracy; **upper-cut** hit upwards with arm bent; **the upper hand** mastery, control, advantage; **Upper House** House of Lords or other higher legislative assembly.

**uppermost** /'ʌpəməʊst/ **1** a. highest in rank or place. **2** adv. on or to the top.

**uppish** /'ʌpɪʃ/ a. *colloq.* (also **uppity**) self-assertive, arrogant.

**upright** /'ʌpraɪt/ **1** a. erect, vertical; (of piano) with vertical frame; strictly honourable or honest. **2** n. post or rod fixed upright, esp. as support to some structure; upright piano.

**uprising** /'ʌpraɪzɪŋ/ n. insurrection.

**uproar** /'ʌprɔː(r)/ n. tumult, violent disturbance, clamour.

**uproarious** /ʌp'rɔːrɪəs/ a. very noisy, with loud laughter.

**uproot** /ʌp'ruːt/ v.t. pull (plant etc.) up from ground together with its roots; displace (person) from accustomed location, eradicate.

**upset 1** /ʌp'set/ v. (*past* & *p.p.* -set) overturn; disturb temper or digestion or composure of. **2** /'ʌpset/ n. disturbance, surprising result.

**upshot** /'ʌpʃɒt/ n. outcome, conclusion.

**upside-down** /ʌpsaɪd'daʊn/ adv. & a. with upper part where lower part should be, inverted; in(to) total disorder.

**upstage** /ʌp'steɪdʒ/ **1** a. & adv. nearer back of theatre stage. **2** v.t. move upstage from (actor) to make him face away from audience; *fig.* divert attention from (person) to oneself.

**upstanding** /ʌp'stændɪŋ/ a. standing up; strong and healthy; honest.

**upstart** /'ʌpstɑːt/ 1 *n.* person who has risen suddenly to prominence or who behaves arrogantly. 2 *a.* that is an upstart; of upstarts.

**upswept** /'ʌpswept/ *a.* (of hair) combed to top of head.

**upswing** /'ʌpswɪŋ/ *n.* upward movement or trend.

**uptake** /'ʌpteɪk/ *n. colloq.* understanding.

**uptight** /ʌp'taɪt/ *a. colloq.* nervously tense, angry; rigidly conventional.

**upturn** 1 /ʌp'tɜːn/ *v.t.* turn up or upside-down. 2 /'ʌptɜːn/ *n.* upward trend, improvement.

**uranium** /juː'reɪnɪəm/ *n.* radioactive heavy grey metallic element capable of nuclear fission and used as source of nuclear energy.

**urban** /'ɜːbən/ *a.* of or living or situated in city or town. **urban guerrilla** terrorist operating in cities etc. by kidnapping etc.

**urbane** /ɜː'beɪn/ *a.* courteous; suave. **urbanity** /-'bæn-/ *n.*

**urbanize** /'ɜːbənaɪz/ *v.t.* render urban; remove rural quality of (district). **urbanization** *n.*

**urchin** /'ɜːtʃɪn/ *n.* mischievous child, esp. boy; sea-urchin.

**ureter** /juː'riːtə(r)/ *n.* either of two ducts conveying urine into bladder.

**urethra** /juː'riːθrə/ *n.* (*pl.* **-ras**) duct through which urine is discharged from bladder.

**urge** /ɜːdʒ/ 1 *v.t.* drive forcibly, impel; entreat or exhort earnestly or persistently; advocate pressingly. 2 *n.* urging impulse or tendency; strong desire.

**urgent** /'ɜːdʒ(ə)nt/ *a.* requiring immediate action or attention; importunate. **urgency** *n.*

**uric** /'juːrɪk/ *a.* of urine.

**urinal** /juː'raɪn(ə)l/ *n.* place or receptacle for urinating.

**urinary** /'juːrənərɪ/ *a.* of or relating to urine.

**urinate** /'juːrəneɪt/ *v.i.* discharge urine. **urination** *n.*

**urine** /'juːrɪn/ *n.* fluid secreted by kidneys and discharged from bladder.

**urn** *n.* vase with foot, esp. as used for storing ashes of the dead; large vessel with tap in which water is kept hot or tea etc. made.

**ursine** /'ɜːsaɪn/ *a.* of or like a bear.

**us** *pron. obj.* case of **we**.

**US** *abbr.* United States (of America).

**USA** *abbr.* United States of America.

**usage** /'juːsɪdʒ/ *n.* manner of using or treating; customary practice, established use (esp. of word).

**use** 1 /juːz/ *v.* cause to act or serve for purpose or as instrument or material; put into operation, avail oneself of; treat in specified manner; in *p.p.* second-hand; in *past* (usu. /juːst/) had as one's or its constant or frequent practice or state (*to* do, be, etc.); in *p.p.* (/juːst/) familiar by habit, accustomed, *to*. 2 /juːs/ *n.* using, employment; right or power of using; serviceability, utility, purpose for which thing can be used; custom, usage; ritual and liturgy of church or diocese etc. 3 **make use** of use, benefit from; **no use** of no value or utility; **use up** consume, find use for (remainder).

**useful** /'juːsfəl/ *a.* of use, serviceable; producing or able to produce good results; *colloq.* creditable, efficient.

**useless** /'juːslɪs/ *a.* serving no purpose, unavailing.

**user-friendly** /juːzə'frendlɪ/ *a.* (of computer or program etc.) easy for user to understand and operate.

**usher** /'ʌʃə(r)/ 1 *n.* person who shows people to their seats in hall or theatre etc.; door-keeper of court etc.; officer walking before person of rank. 2 *v.t.* act as usher to; announce or show *in* etc.

**usherette** /ʌʃə'ret/ *n.* female usher, esp. in cinema.

**USSR** *abbr.* Union of Soviet Socialist Republics.

**usual** /'juːʒʊəl/ *a.* such as commonly occurs, customary; habitual. **as usual** as commonly occurs.

**usurer** /'juːʒərə(r)/ *n.* person who practises usury.

**usurp** /juː'zɜːp/ *v.* seize or assume power or right etc. wrongfully. **usurpation** *n.*

**usury** /'juːʒərɪ/ *n.* lending of money at interest, esp. at exorbitant or illegal rate. **usurious** /juː'zjʊərɪəs/ *a.*

**ute** /juːt/ *n. Aus. colloq.* utility truck.

**utensil** /juː'tens(ə)l/ *n.* implement or vessel, esp. in domestic use.

**uterus** /'juːtərəs/ *n.* (*pl.* **-ri** /-raɪ/) womb. **uterine** /-raɪn/ *a.*

## utilitarian

**utilitarian** /juːtɪləˈteərɪən/ 1 *a.* designed to be useful rather than attractive; of utilitarianism. 2 *n.* adherent of utilitarianism.

**utilitarianism** *n.* doctrine that actions are justified if they are useful or for benefit of majority.

**utility** /juːˈtɪlətɪ/ 1 *n.* usefulness, profitableness; useful thing. 2 *a.* severely practical and standardized; made or serving for utility. 3 **utility room** room containing large fixed domestic appliances; **utility truck** *Aus.* truck with carrying compartment unroofed.

**utilize** /ˈjuːtəlaɪz/ *v.t.* make use of, turn to account, use. **utilization** *n.*

**utmost** /ˈʌtməʊst/ 1 *a.* farthest, extreme; that is such in highest degree. 2 *n.* the utmost point or degree etc. 3 **do one's utmost** do all that one can.

## uxorious

**Utopia** /juːˈtəʊpɪə/ *n.* imaginary perfect social and political system. **Utopian** *a.*

**utter**[1] /ˈʌtə(r)/ *a.* complete, total, unqualified. **uttermost** *a.*

**utter**[2] /ˈʌtə(r)/ *v.t.* express in words; emit audibly; put (esp. forged money) into circulation.

**utterance** /ˈʌtərəns/ *n.* uttering; power or manner of speaking; thing spoken.

**U-turn** /ˈjuːtɜːn/ *n.* turning a vehicle to face in opposite direction without reversing; reversal of policy.

**UV** *abbr.* ultraviolet.

**uvula** /ˈjuːvjələ/ *n.* (*pl.* **-lae** /-liː/) fleshy part of soft palate hanging above throat. **uvular** *a.*

**uxorious** /ʌkˈsɔːrɪəs/ *a.* excessively fond of one's wife.

# V

**V, v,** Roman numeral 5.

**V** *abbr.* volt(s).

**v.** *abbr.* verse; versus; very; *vide*.

**vac** *n. colloq.* vacation.

**vacancy** /'veɪkənsɪ/ *n.* being vacant; unoccupied post or place etc.

**vacant** /'veɪkənt/ *a.* not filled or occupied; not mentally active, showing no interest. **vacant possession** ownership of unoccupied house etc.

**vacate** /vəˈkeɪt/ *v.t.* leave vacant; cease to occupy.

**vacation** /vəˈkeɪʃ(ə)n/ *n.* fixed period of cessation from work esp. in lawcourts and universities; *US* holiday; vacating or being vacated.

**vaccinate** /'væksɪneɪt/ *v.t.* inoculate with vaccine. **vaccination** *n.*

**vaccine** /'væksiːn/ *n.* preparation used for inoculation, esp. one of cowpox virus giving immunity to smallpox.

**vacillate** /'væsɪleɪt/ *v.i.* fluctuate in opinion or resolution. **vacillation** *n.*; **vacillator** *n.*

**vacuity** /vəˈkjuːɪtɪ/ *n.* vacuousness.

**vacuous** /'vækjʊəs/ *a.* vacant, unintelligent.

**vacuum** /'vækjuːm/ **1** *n.* (*pl.* **-cua** or **-cuums**) space entirely devoid of matter; space or vessel from which air has been completely or partly removed by pump etc.; absence of normal or previous content; *colloq.* (*pl.* **-cuums**) vacuum cleaner. **2** *v. colloq.* use vacuum cleaner (on). **3 vacuum brake** brake worked by exhaustion of air; **vacuum cleaner** apparatus for removing dust etc. by suction; **vacuum flask** vessel with double wall enclosing vacuum so that liquid in inner receptacle retains its temperature; **vacuum-packed** sealed after partial removal of air; **vacuum tube** tube containing near-vacuum for free passage of electric current.

**vag** *Aus. sl.* **1** *n.* vagrant. **2** *v.t.* arrest under provisions of vagrancy Act. **3 on the vag** according to the provisions of the Vagrancy Act.

**vagabond** /'vægəbɒnd/ **1** *n.* wanderer, esp. idle one. **2** *a.* wandering, having no settled habitation or home.

**vagary** /'veɪɡərɪ/ *n.* caprice, eccentric act or idea.

**vagina** /vəˈdʒaɪnə/ *n.* (*pl.* **-nae** /-niː/ or **-nas**) canal joining womb and vulva of female mammal. **vaginal** *a.*

**vagrant** /'veɪɡrənt/ **1** *n.* person without settled home or regular work. **2** *a.* wandering, roving. **3 vagrancy** *n.*

**vague** /veɪɡ/ *a.* not clearly expressed or perceived, uncertain, ill-defined; not clear-thinking; inexact, indefinite.

**vain** *a.* conceited, proud (*of*); empty, of no effect, unavailing. **in vain** without result or success.

**vainglory** /veɪnˈɡlɔːrɪ/ *n.* extreme vanity; boastfulness. **vainglorious** *a.*

**valance** /'veɪləns/ *n.* short curtain round frame or canopy of bedstead or over window etc.

**vale** *n.* valley.

**valediction** /vælɪˈdɪkʃ(ə)n/ *n.* bidding farewell; words used in this. **valedictory** *a.*

**valence**[1] /'veɪləns/ *n.* valency.

**valence**[2] var. of **valance**.

**valency** /'veɪlənsɪ/ *n. Chem.* unit of combining-power of an atom; this power.

**valentine** /'væləntaɪn/ *n.* (usu. anonymous) letter or card sent to person of opposite sex on St. Valentine's day (14 Feb.); sweetheart chosen on that day.

**valerian** /vəˈlɪərɪən/ *n.* any of various kinds of flowering herb.

**valet** /'væleɪ/ **1** *n.* man's personal servant. **2** *v.* act as valet (to).

**valetudinarian** /vælɪtjuːdɪˈneərɪən/ **1** *n.* person who is of poor health or unduly anxious about his health. **2** *a.* that is a valetudinarian.

**valiant** /'vælɪənt/ *a.* brave, courageous.

**valid** /'vælɪd/ *a.* sound, defensible; having legal force. **validity** *n.*

**validate** /'vælɪdeɪt/ *v.t.* make valid, ratify. **validation** *n.*

**valise** /vəˈliːz/ *n.* travelling-bag, suitcase.

**valley** /'vælɪ/ *n.* long depression or hollow between hills; any valley-like hollow.

**valour** /'vælə(r)/ *n.* courage, esp. in battle. **valorous** *a.*

**valuable** /'væljʊəb(ə)l/ **1** *a.* of great value or price or worth. **2** *n.* (usu. in *pl.*) valuable thing.

**valuation** /vælju:'eɪʃ(ə)n/ n. estimation (esp. by professional valuer) of thing's worth; estimated value.

**value** /'vælju:/ 1 n. worth, desirability; qualities on which these depend; worth as estimated; amount of money or goods for which thing can be exchanged in open market; equivalent of a thing; what represents or is represented by or may be substituted for a thing; something well worth the money spent; ability of a thing to serve a purpose or cause an effect; in pl. one's principles or standards, one's judgement of what is valuable or important in life; Mus. duration of sound signified by note; Math. amount denoted by algebraical term or expression. 2 v.t. estimate value of, appraise; have high or specified opinion of, attach importance to. 3 **value added tax** tax on amount by which value of an article has been increased at each stage of its production; **value judgement** subjective estimate of quality etc.

**valuer** n. person who estimates or assesses values professionally.

**valve** n. automatic or other device for controlling passage of fluid through pipe etc., usu. to allow movement in one direction only; membranous part of organ etc. allowing flow of blood etc. in one direction only; thermionic valve; device to vary length of tube in trumpet etc.; each of two shells of oyster or mussel etc.

**valvular** /'vælvjələ(r)/ a. having valve(s); having form or function of valve.

**vamoose** /və'mu:s/ v.i. US sl. depart hurriedly.

**vamp**[1] 1 n. upper front part of boot or shoe. 2 v. repair or make *up* or produce (as) by patching or piecing together; improvise musical accompaniment (to).

**vamp**[2] colloq. 1 n. unscrupulous flirt; woman who exploits men. 2 v. allure or exploit (man); act as vamp.

**vampire** /'væmpaɪə(r)/ n. ghost or reanimated corpse supposed to suck blood of sleeping persons; person who preys on others; blood-sucking bat.

**van**[1] n. covered vehicle or closed railway-truck for conveyance of goods etc.

**van**[2] n. vanguard, forefront.

**vanadium** /və'neɪdɪəm/ n. hard grey metallic element used to strengthen steel.

**vandal** /'vænd(ə)l/ n. wilful or ignorant destroyer or damager of works of art or other property. **vandalism** n.

**vandalize** /'vændəlaɪz/ v.t. destroy or damage wilfully.

**Vandyke** /væn'daɪk/ n. **Vandyke beard** small neat pointed beard; **Vandyke brown** deep rich brown.

**vane** n. weathercock; blade of windmill or propeller etc.

**vanguard** /'vænɡɑːd/ n. foremost part of army or fleet etc. moving forward or onward; leaders of movement or of opinion etc.

**vanilla** /və'nɪlə/ n. extract obtained from vanilla-pod or synthetically and used to flavour ices and chocolate etc.; tropical climbing orchid with fragrant flowers; fruit of this. **vanilla-pod** fruit of vanilla.

**vanish** /'vænɪʃ/ v.i. disappear; cease to exist. **vanishing-point** point at which receding parallel lines viewed in perspective appear to meet.

**vanity** /'vænɪtɪ/ n. desire for admiration because of one's personal attainments or attractions; futility, unreal thing; ostentatious display. **vanity bag, case,** bag containing small mirror and make-up etc.

**vanquish** /'væŋkwɪʃ/ v.t. literary conquer, overcome.

**vantage** /'vɑːntɪdʒ/ or /'væn-/ n. advantage, esp. in tennis. **vantage-point** place affording good view.

**vapid** /'væpɪd/ a. insipid, flat. **vapidity** n.

**vaporize** /'veɪpəraɪz/ v. convert or be converted into vapour. **vaporization** n.

**vaporous** /'veɪpərəs/ a. in the form of or consisting of vapour.

**vapour** /'veɪpə(r)/ n. moisture or other substance diffused or suspended in air; Phys. gaseous form of a normally liquid or solid substance. **vapour trail** trail of condensed water from aircraft etc. **vapoury** a.

**variable** /'veərɪəb(ə)l/ 1 a. that can be varied or adapted; apt to vary, not constant, unsteady; Math. (of quantity) indeterminate, able to assume different

**variance** /ˈveərɪəns/ *n.* difference of opinion; dispute; discrepancy.

**variant** /ˈveərɪənt/ **1** *a.* differing in form or details from that named or considered; differing thus among themselves. **2** *n.* variant form or spelling or type etc.

**variation** /veərɪˈeɪʃ(ə)n/ *n.* varying; departure from former or normal condition etc. or from standard or type; extent of this; thing that varies from a type; *Mus.* tune or theme repeated in changed or elaborated form.

**varicose** /ˈværɪkəʊs/ *a.* (of vein etc.) permanently and abnormally dilated.

**variegated** /ˈveərɪəgeɪtɪd/ *a.* marked with irregular patches of different colours. **variegation** *n.*

**variety** /vəˈraɪətɪ/ *n.* diversity; absence of monotony or uniformity; collection of different things; class of things differing in some common qualities from the rest of a larger class to which they belong; specimen or member of such class; different form or kind or sort (*of*); *Biol.* grouping within subspecies. **variety entertainment, show**, mixed series of dances and songs and comedy acts etc.

**various** /ˈveərɪəs/ *a.* of several kinds; diverse; several.

**varlet** /ˈvɑːlət/ *n. arch.* menial, rascal.

**varnish** /ˈvɑːnɪʃ/ **1** *n.* resinous solution or other preparation applied to surface to produce hard shiny transparent coating. **2** *v.t.* coat with varnish; gloss (over), disguise.

**varsity** /ˈvɑːsətɪ/ *n. colloq.* university.

**vary** /ˈveərɪ/ *v.* change, make or become different, modify, diversify; be different or of different kinds.

**vas deferens** /væs ˈdefərenz/ (*pl.* **vasa deferentia** /ˈveɪsə defəˈrenʃɪə/) sperm duct of testicle.

**vascular** /ˈvæskjʊlə(r)/ *a.* of or containing vessels for conveying blood or sap etc.

**vase** /vɑːz/ *n.* vessel, usu. tall and circular, used as ornament or container for flowers etc.

**vasectomy** /vəˈsektəmɪ/ *n.* removal of part of each vas deferens esp. for sterilization of patient.

**Vaseline** /ˈvæsəliːn/ *n.* (**P**) type of petroleum jelly used in ointments etc.

**vassal** /ˈvæs(ə)l/ *n.* humble dependant; *hist.* holder of land by feudal tenure.

**vast** /vɑːst/ *a.* immense, huge, very great.

**vat** *n.* large tank or other vessel, esp. for holding liquids or something in liquid in process of brewing or tanning or dyeing etc.

**vaudeville** /ˈvɔːdəvɪl/ *n.* variety entertainment.

**vault** **1** *n.* arched roof; vaultlike covering; underground room as place of storage; underground burial-chamber; act of vaulting. **2** *v.* leap or spring, esp. while resting on hand(s) or with help of pole; spring over thus; make in form of vault; furnish with vaults.

**vaunt** *n.* & *v. arch.* boast.

**VC** *abbr.* Victoria Cross.

**VD** *abbr.* venereal disease.

**VDT** *abbr.* visual display terminal.

**VDU** *abbr.* visual display unit.

**veal** *n.* calf's flesh as food.

**vector** /ˈvektə(r)/ *n. Math.* quantity having both magnitude and direction; carrier of disease. **vectorial** /-ˈtɔːr-/ *a.*

**veer** *v.* change direction, esp. (of wind) in direction of sun's course; change in opinion or course.

**vegan** /ˈviːgən/ **1** *a.* eating no animals or animal products. **2** *n.* vegan person.

**vegetable** /ˈvedʒətəb(ə)l/ **1** *n.* esp. herbaceous plant or part of one used for food; person living uneventful and monotonous life; person incapable of normal intellectual activity through injury etc. **2** *a.* of or of the nature of or derived from or concerned with or comprising plants.

**vegetarian** /vedʒəˈteərɪən/ **1** *n.* person who eats no animal products or none obtained by destruction of animal life. **2** *a.* of vegetarian(s); living on or consisting of vegetables. **3 vegetarianism** *n.*

**vegetate** /ˈvedʒəteɪt/ *v.i.* lead dull monotonous life; grow as plants do.

**vegetation** /vedʒəˈteɪʃ(ə)n/ *n.* plants collectively; plant life.

**vegetative** /ˈvedʒətətɪv/ *a.* concerned with growth and development rather than sexual reproduction; of vegetation.

**vehement** /ˈviːəmənt/ *a.* showing or

**vehicle** 631 **ventilator**

caused by strong feeling, ardent. **vehemence** n.

**vehicle** /'viːək(ə)l/ n. carriage or conveyance used on land or in space; thing or person used as medium for thought or feeling or action; liquid etc. as medium for suspending pigments or drugs etc. **vehicular** /və'hɪkjələ(r)/ a.

**veil** /veɪl/ 1 n. piece of usu. more or less transparent material attached to woman's hat or otherwise forming part of head-dress, esp. to conceal face or protect against sun or dust etc.; piece of linen etc. as part of nun's head-dress; curtain, esp. that separating sanctuary in Jewish Temple; disguise, pretext. 2 v.t. cover (as) with veil; partially conceal. 3 **beyond the veil** in the unknown state of after death; **draw a veil over** avoid discussing or drawing attention to; **take the veil** become nun.

**vein** /veɪn/ n. any of the tubes carrying blood from all parts of body back to heart; pop. any blood-vessel; rib of leaf or insect's wing; streak or stripe of different colour in wood or marble or cheese etc.; fissure in rock filled with ore; distinctive character or tendency, mood. **veined** a.; **veiny** a.

**Velcro** /'velkrəʊ/ n. (**P**) fastener for clothes etc. consisting of 2 strips of nylon fabric which adhere when pressed together.

**veld** /velt/ n. (also **veldt**) S. Afr. open country.

**vellum** /'veləm/ n. fine parchment orig. from calf's skin; manuscript on this; smooth writing-paper imitating vellum.

**velocity** /və'lɒsɪti/ n. speed esp. of motion in particular direction.

**velour** /və'lʊə(r)/ n. (also **velours**) woven fabric with plushlike pile.

**velvet** /'velvɪt/ 1 n. closely woven fabric with thick short pile on one side; furry skin growing on antler. 2 a. of or like or soft as velvet. 3 **on velvet** in advantageous or prosperous position; **velvet glove** outward gentleness cloaking inflexibility. 4 **velvety** a.

**velveteen** /velvə'tiːn/ n. cotton fabric with pile like velvet.

**Ven.** abbr. Venerable.

**venal** /'viːn(ə)l/ a. that may be bribed; (of action etc.) characteristic of venal person. **venality** n.

**vend** v. sell; offer (esp. small articles) for sale. **vending-machine** machine for automatic retail of small articles. **vendor** n.

**vendetta** /ven'detə/ n. blood feud; prolonged bitter hostility.

**veneer** /və'nɪə(r)/ 1 v.t. cover (wood) with thin layer of finer wood. 2 n. thin coating; superficial disguise.

**venerable** /'venərəb(ə)l/ a. entitled to veneration on account of age or character etc.; title of archdeacon. **venerability** n.

**venerate** /'venəreɪt/ v.t. regard with deep respect. **veneration** n.

**venereal** /və'nɪərɪəl/ a. of sexual desire or intercourse; (of disease) communicated by sexual intercourse with infected person.

**Venetian** /və'niːʃ(ə)n/ 1 a. of Venice. 2 n. native or dialect of Venice. 3 **Venetian blind** window-blind of horizontal slats that may be turned to admit or exclude light.

**vengeance** /'vendʒ(ə)ns/ n. retribution exacted for wrong to oneself or to person etc. whose cause one supports. **with a vengeance** in extreme degree, thoroughly, violently.

**vengeful** /'vendʒfəl/ a. seeking vengeance, vindictive.

**venial** /'viːnɪəl/ a. (of sin or fault) pardonable, not mortal. **veniality** n.

**venison** /'venəs(ə)n/ n. deer's flesh as food.

**Venn diagram** Math. diagram using overlapping and intersecting circles etc. to show relationships between sets.

**venom** /'venəm/ n. poisonous fluid of snakes or scorpions etc.; malignity, virulence of feeling or language or conduct. **venomous** a.

**venous** /'viːnəs/ a. of or full of or contained in veins.

**vent**[1] n. small outlet or inlet for air or smoke etc.; anus esp. of lower animals; outlet, free passage, free play. 2 v.t. give vent or free expression to.

**vent**[2] n. slit in garment, esp. in back of coat.

**ventilate** /'ventɪleɪt/ v.t. cause air to circulate in (room etc.); make public, discuss freely. **ventilation** n.

**ventilator** /'ventɪleɪtə(r)/ n. appliance or aperture for ventilating room etc.

**ventral** /'ventr(ə)l/ *a.* of or on abdomen.

**ventricle** /'ventrɪk(ə)l/ *n.* cavity of body; hollow part of organ, esp. brain or heart.

**ventricular** /ven'trɪkjələ(r)/ *a.* of or shaped like ventricle.

**ventriloquism** /ven'trɪləkwɪz(ə)m/ *n.* act or art of producing vocal sounds without visible movement of lips. **ventriloquist** *n.*; **ventriloquize** *v.i.*

**venture** /'ventʃə(r)/ 1 *n.* undertaking of risk, commercial speculation; 2 *v.* dare, not be afraid; dare to go; take risks, expose to risk, stake. 3 **at a venture** at random, without previous consideration; **Venture Scout** senior Scout.

**venturesome** /'ventʃəsəm/ *a.* disposed to take risks.

**venue** /'venju:/ *n.* appointed meeting-place, esp. for match; *Law* district in which case is to be tried.

**veracious** /və'reɪʃəs/ *a.* truthful, true. **veracity** /-'ræs-/ *n.*

**veranda** /və'rændə/ *n.* open roofed platform along side of house.

**verb** *n.* part of speech which expresses action or occurrence or being.

**verbal** /'vɜ:b(ə)l/ *a.* of or concerned with words; oral, not written; *Gram.* of (the nature of) a verb; (of translation) literal.

**verbalism** /'vɜ:bəlɪz(ə)m/ *n.* minute attention to words.

**verbalize** /'vɜ:bəlaɪz/ *v.* express in words; be verbose. **verbalization** *n.*

**verbatim** /vɜ:'beɪtɪm/ *adv.* & *a.* in exactly the same words.

**verbena** /vɜ:'bi:nə/ *n.* plant of a genus of herbs and small shrubs.

**verbiage** /'vɜ:bi:ədʒ/ *n.* needless accumulation of words.

**verbose** /vɜ:'bəʊs/ *a.* using or expressed in more words than are needed. **verbosity** /-'bɒs-/ *n.*

**verdant** /'vɜ:d(ə)nt/ *a.* abounding in green foliage; green. **verdancy** *n.*

**verdict** /'vɜ:dɪkt/ *n.* decision of jury; decision, judgement.

**verdigris** /'vɜ:dəgrɪs/ *n.* green deposit forming on copper or brass.

**verdure** /'vɜ:dʒə(r)/ *n.* green vegetation; greenness of this.

**verge¹** *n.* brink, border; grass edging of path etc.

**verge²** *v.i.* incline downwards or in specified direction. **verge on** border on, approach closely.

**verger** /'vɜ:dʒə(r)/ *n.* caretaker and attendant in church; official carrying rod etc. before dignitaries of cathedral or university etc.

**verify** /'verəfaɪ/ *v.t.* establish truth or correctness of by examination or demonstration; fulfil, bear out. **verification** *n.*

**verily** /'verəlɪ/ *adv. arch.* in truth, really.

**verisimilitude** /verəsɪ'mɪlɪtju:d/ *n.* appearance of truth or reality.

**veritable** /'verətəb(ə)l/ *a.* real, properly or correctly so called.

**verity** /'verətɪ/ *n.* true statement; truth.

**vermicelli** /vɜ:mɪ'tʃelɪ/ *n.* pasta made in long slender threads.

**vermicide** /'vɜ:məsaɪd/ *n.* substance used to kill worms.

**vermiform** /'vɜ:mɪfɔ:m/ *a.* worm-shaped. **vermiform appendix** small blind tube extending from caecum in man and some other mammals.

**vermilion** /və'mɪljən/ 1 *n.* brilliant scarlet pigment made esp. from cinnabar; colour of this. 2 *a.* of this colour.

**vermin** /'vɜ:mɪn/ *n.* (usu. treated as *pl.*) mammals and birds injurious to game or crops etc.; noxious or parasitic worms or insects; vile persons.

**verminous** /'vɜ:mənəs/ *a.* of the nature of or infested with vermin.

**vermouth** /'vɜ:məθ/ *n.* wine flavoured with aromatic herbs.

**vernacular** /və'nækjələ(r)/ 1 *n.* language or dialect of the country; language of a particular class or group; homely speech. 2 *a.* (of language) of one's own country, not learned or foreign.

**vernal** /'vɜ:n(ə)l/ *a.* of or in or appropriate to season of spring.

**vernier** /'vɜ:nɪə(r)/ *n.* small movable graduated scale for obtaining fractional parts of subdivisions on fixed scale of barometer etc.

**veronica** /və'rɒnɪkə/ *n.* kind of flowering herb or shrub.

**verruca** /və'ru:kə/ *n.* (*pl.* **-cae** /-si:/ or **-cas**) wart or similar protuberance, esp. on foot.

**versatile** /'vɜ:sətaɪl/ *a.* turning easily

or readily from one subject or occupation etc. to another, showing facility in varied subjects, many-sided. **versatility** /-'tɪl-/ *n.*

**verse** *n.* metrical composition, poetry; stanza of metrical lines; metrical line; numbered subdivision of Bible chapter.

**versed** /vɜːst/ *a.* experienced or skilled *in.*

**versicle** /'vɜːsɪk(ə)l/ *n.* short sentence, esp. each of series in liturgy said or sung by minister or priest alternately with response of congregation.

**versify** /'vɜːsɪfaɪ/ *v.* turn into or express in verse; compose verses. **versification** *n.*

**version** /'vɜːʃ(ə)n/ *n.* particular form of statement or account etc.; particular rendering of work etc. in another language.

**verso** /'vɜːsəʊ/ *n.* (*pl.* **-sos**) left-hand page of open book, back of leaf.

**versus** /'vɜːsəs/ *prep.* against.

**vertebra** /'vɜːtəbrə/ *n.* (*pl.* **-brae** /-briː/) each segment of backbone. **vertebral** *a.*

**vertebrate** /'vɜːtəbrət/ 1 *a.* having spinal column. 2 *n.* vertebrate animal.

**vertex** /'vɜːteks/ *n.* (*pl.* **-tices** /-tɪsiːz/ or **-texes**) highest point, top, apex; meeting-point of lines that form an angle.

**vertical** /'vɜːtɪk(ə)l/ 1 *a.* at right angles to plane of horizon; in direction from top to bottom of picture etc.; of or at vertex. 2 *n.* vertical line or plane. 3 **vertical take-off** taking off without needing a long runway.

**vertiginous** /vɜː'tɪdʒɪnəs/ *a.* of or causing vertigo.

**vertigo** /'vɜːtɪɡəʊ/ *n.* dizziness.

**vervain** /'vɜːveɪn/ *n.* herbaceous plant of verbena genus, esp. one with small blue or white or purple flowers.

**verve** *n.* enthusiasm, energy, vigour.

**very** /'veri/ 1 *adv.* in high degree, to great extent, extremely. 2 *a.* real, true, properly so called etc. 3 **very high frequency** in range 30–300 megahertz; **very well** formula of consent or approval.

**vesicle** /'vesɪk(ə)l/ *n.* small bladder or blister or bubble.

**vespers** /'vespəz/ *n.pl.* evening service.

**vessel** /'ves(ə)l/ *n.* hollow receptacle esp. for liquid; ship or boat, esp. large one; duct or canal etc. holding or conveying blood or sap etc.

**vest** 1 *n.* singlet; *US & Commerc.* waistcoat. 2 *v.t.* furnish (person *with* powers, property, etc.). 3 **vested interests** or **rights**, etc. interests or rights the possession of which is established by right or by long association; **vest in** (of property, rights, etc.) come into possession of (person); **vest** (property, powers) **in person** confer formally on him an immediate fixed right of present or future possession of; **vest-pocket** of size suitable for the (waistcoat-)pocket.

**vestal virgin** /'vest(ə)l/ virgin consecrated to Vesta, Roman goddess of hearth and home, and vowed to chastity.

**vestibule** /'vestɪbjuːl/ *n.* antechamber, lobby; entrance-hall.

**vestige** /'vestɪdʒ/ *n.* trace, evidence; slight amount, particle; *Biol.* part or organ now degenerate but well developed in ancestors. **vestigial** *a.*

**vestment** /'vestmənt/ *n.* any of official garments worn by priest etc. during divine service etc.; (esp. ceremonial) garment.

**vestry** /'vestri/ *n.* room or part of church for keeping of vestments etc.; *hist.* meeting of parishioners usu. in vestry for parochial business, body of parishioners meeting thus.

**vet** *colloq.* 1 *n.* veterinary surgeon. 2 *v.t.* submit to careful and critical examination; examine or treat (animal).

**vetch** *n.* plant of pea family largely used for fodder.

**veteran** /'vetərən/ *n.* person who has grown old in service or occupation, esp. in armed forces; *US* ex-serviceman. **veteran car** one made before 1916, or before 1905.

**veterinarian** /vetərə'neəriːən/ *n.* veterinary surgeon.

**veterinary** /'vetərənəri/ 1 *a.* of or for diseases and injuries of domestic and other animals, or their treatment. 2 *n.* veterinary surgeon. 3 **veterinary surgeon** person skilled in veterinary treatment.

**veto** /'viːtəʊ/ 1 *n.* (*pl.* **-toes**) constitutional right to prohibit passing or putting in force of enactment or resolution etc.; exercise of this; prohibition. 2 *v.t.* exercise veto against; forbid.

**vex** *v.t.* anger by slight or petty annoyance, irritate; *arch.* grieve, afflict. **vexed question** question much discussed.

**vexation** /vekˈseɪʃ(ə)n/ *n.* vexing or being vexed; annoying or distressing thing.

**vexatious** /vekˈseɪʃəs/ *a.* such as to cause vexation; *Law* not having sufficient grounds for action and seeking only to annoy defendant.

**VFL** *abbr. Aus.* Victorian Football League.

**VHF** *abbr.* very high frequency.

**via** /ˈvaɪə/ *prep.* by way of, through.

**viable** /ˈvaɪəb(ə)l/ *a.* capable of living or surviving; (of plan etc.) feasible, esp. from economic standpoint.

**viaduct** /ˈvaɪədʌkt/ *n.* bridgelike structure carrying railway or road over valley or river etc.

**vial** /ˈvaɪəl/ *n.* small glass bottle.

**viands** /ˈvaɪəndz/ *n.pl.* articles of food.

**viaticum** /vaɪˈætɪkəm/ *n.* Eucharist given to person dying or in danger of dying.

**vibes** /vaɪbz/ *n.pl. colloq.* vibraphone, vibrations.

**vibrant** /ˈvaɪbrənt/ *a.* vibrating, thrilling *with*, resonant. **vibrancy** *n.*

**vibraphone** /ˈvaɪbrəfəʊn/ *n.* percussion instrument of metal bars with motor-driven resonators and metal tubes giving vibrato effect.

**vibrate** /vaɪˈbreɪt/ *v.* move unceasingly to and fro, esp. rapidly; (of sound) have quivering or pulsating effect; quiver; (cause to) swing to and fro periodically, oscillate. **vibratory** /ˈvaɪ-/ *a.*

**vibration** /vaɪˈbreɪʃ(ə)n/ *n.* vibrating; in *pl.* mental (esp. occult) influence.

**vibrato** /vəˈbrɑːtəʊ/ *n.* (*pl.* **-tos**) *Mus.* tremulous effect in pitch of singing or of playing stringed or wind instrument.

**vibrator** /vaɪˈbreɪtə(r)/ *n.* thing that vibrates, esp. *Med.* electric or other instrument used in massage.

**vicar** /ˈvɪkə(r)/ *n.* incumbent of C. of E. parish where tithes formerly belonged to chapter or religious house or layman. **Vicar of Christ** the Pope.

**vicarage** /ˈvɪkərɪdʒ/ *n.* vicar's house.

**vicarial** /vɪˈkeərɪəl/ *a.* of or serving as vicar.

**vicarious** /vɪˈkeərɪəs/ *a.* experienced imaginatively through another person; acting or done etc. for another; deputed, delegated.

**vice**[1] *n.* evil, esp. grossly immoral, habit or conduct; bad habit; particular form of depravity; defect, blemish. **vice squad** police department enforcing laws against prostitution etc.

**vice**[2] *n.* instrument with two jaws in which things may be gripped and held steady.

**vice**[3] /ˈvaɪsɪ/ *prep.* in place of, in succession to.

**vice-** *in comb.* person acting in place of, assistant, person next in rank to.

**vice-chancellor** /vaɪsˈtʃɑːnsələ(r) or -ˈtʃæns-/ *n.* deputy chancellor (esp. of university, discharging most administrative duties).

**vicegerent** /vaɪsˈdʒerənt/ **1** *a.* exercising delegated power, deputy. **2** *n.* deputy.

**viceregal** /vaɪsˈriːg(ə)l/ *a.* of viceroy.

**vicereine** /ˈvaɪsreɪn/ *n.* viceroy's wife; woman viceroy.

**viceroy** /ˈvaɪsrɔɪ/ *n.* ruler on behalf of sovereign in colony or province etc.

**vice versa** /vaɪsə ˈvɜːsə/ with order of terms changed, the other way round.

**Vichy water** /ˈviːʃɪ/ effervescent mineral water from Vichy in France.

**vicinage** /ˈvɪsɪnɪdʒ/ *n.* neighbourhood, surrounding district; relation of neighbours.

**vicinity** /vəˈsɪnɪtɪ/ *n.* surrounding district; nearness in place. **in the vicinity (of)** near.

**vicious** /ˈvɪʃəs/ *a.* of the nature of or addicted to vice; bad-tempered, spiteful. **vicious circle** unbroken sequence of reciprocal cause and effect or action and reaction, fallacious reasoning by which proposition is proved by conclusion drawn from it.

**vicissitude** /vəˈsɪsɪtjuːd/ *n.* change of circumstances, esp. of condition or fortune.

**victim** /ˈvɪktɪm/ *n.* person killed or made to suffer by cruelty or oppression; one who suffers injury or hardship etc.; living creature sacrificed to deity etc.

**victimize** /ˈvɪktɪmaɪz/ *v.t.* single out (person) for punishment or unfair treatment; make (person etc.) a victim. **victimization** *n.*

**victor** /ˈvɪktə(r)/ *n.* conqueror; winner of contest.

**Victoria Cross** /vɪk'tɔːrɪə/ decoration awarded for conspicuous bravery in armed services.

**Victorian** /vɪk'tɔːrɪən/ 1 *a.* of time of Queen Victoria; of State of Victoria. 2 *n.* person of this time or of State of Victoria.

**victorious** /vɪk'tɔːrɪəs/ *a.* conquering, triumphant; marked by victory.

**victory** /'vɪktərɪ/ *n.* winning of battle or war or contest.

**victual** /'vɪt(ə)l/ 1 *n.* (usu. in *pl.*) food, provisions. 2 *v.* supply with victuals, lay in supply of victuals; eat victuals.

**victualler** /'vɪtələ(r)/ *n.* person who furnishes victuals. **licensed victualler** innkeeper licensed to sell alcoholic liquor etc.

**vicuña** /vɪ'kjuːnə/ *n.* S. Amer. mammal with fine silky wool; cloth made from its wool; imitation of this.

*vide* /'vɪdeɪ/ *v.t.* in *imper.* refer to, consult. [L]

**videlicet** /vɪ'deləset/ *adv.* that is to say; namely.

**video** /'vɪdɪəʊ/ 1 *a.* relating to recording of images on videotape or playing or broadcasting of these. 2 *n.* (*pl.* -**os**) such recording or broadcasting; apparatus for recording or playing videotapes; a videotape.

**videotape** /'vɪdɪəʊteɪp/ 1 *n.* magnetic tape suitable for recording television pictures and sound. 2 *v.t.* make recording of (broadcast material) with this.

**vie** *v.i.* (*partic.* **vying**) contend or compete (*with*) for superiority.

**view** /vjuː/ 1 *n.* inspection by eye or mind; what is seen, scene, prospect; picture etc. of view; range of vision; mental survey, mental attitude; opinion. 2 *v.* survey with eyes or mind; form mental impression or judgement of; watch television. 3 **in view of** having regard to, considering; **on view** open to inspection; **viewdata** news and information service from computer source to which TV screen is connected by telephone link; **viewfinder** part of camera showing extent of picture; **viewpoint** point of view, standpoint; **with a view to** with the hope or intention of.

**viewer** /'vjuːə(r)/ *n.* television-watcher; device for looking at film transparencies etc.

**vigil** /'vɪdʒɪl/ *n.* keeping awake during time usually given to sleep, watchfulness; eve of festival, esp. eve that is a fast.

**vigilance** /'vɪdʒələns/ *n.* watchfulness; caution. **vigilance committee** *US* self-appointed committee for maintenance of order. **vigilant** *a.*

**vigilante** /vɪdʒə'læntɪ/ *n.* member of vigilance committee or similar body.

**vignette** /viː'njet/ *n.* illustration not in definite border; photograph etc. with background gradually shaded off; short description, character sketch.

**vigour** /'vɪgə(r)/ *n.* activity and strength of body or mind; healthy growth, animation. **vigorous** *a.*

**Viking** /'vaɪkɪŋ/ *n.* Scandinavian trader and pirate of 8th-10th cc.

**vile** *a.* disgusting; morally base, depraved; *colloq.* abominably bad.

**vilify** /'vɪlɪfaɪ/ *v.t.* speak ill of, defame. **vilification** *n.*

**villa** /'vɪlə/ *n.* detached or semi-detached small house in residential district; country residence; house for holiday-makers at seaside etc.

**village** /'vɪlɪdʒ/ *n.* group of houses etc. in country district, larger than hamlet and smaller than town.

**villager** /'vɪlədʒə(r)/ *n.* inhabitant of village.

**villain** /'vɪlən/ *n.* person guilty or capable of great wickedness; *colloq.* criminal.

**villainous** /'vɪlənəs/ *a.* worthy of a villain; *colloq.* abominably bad.

**villainy** /'vɪlənɪ/ *n.* villainous behaviour.

**villein** /'vɪlən/ *n. hist.* feudal tenant entirely subject to lord or attached to manor. **villeinage** *n.*

**vim** *n. colloq.* vigour, energy.

**vinaigrette** /vɪnə'gret/ *n.* salad dressing of oil and wine vinegar.

**vindicate** /'vɪndɪkeɪt/ *v.t.* clear of suspicion; establish existence or merits or justice etc. of. **vindication** *n.*; **vindicator** *n.*; **vindicatory** *a.*

**vindictive** /vɪn'dɪktɪv/ *a.* tending to seek revenge; punitive.

**vine** *n.* trailing or climbing woody-stemmed plant bearing grapes; any trailing or climbing plant.

**vinegar** /'vɪnɪgə(r)/ *n.* sour liquid produced by fermentation of wine or malt

**vinery** /'vaɪnərɪ/ *n.* vine greenhouse.

**vineyard** /'vɪnjəd/ *n.* plantation of grape-vines, esp. for wine-making.

***vingt-et-un*** /væter'ɜː/ *n.* pontoon¹. [F]

**vinous** /'vaɪnəs/ *a.* of or like or due to or addicted to wine.

**vintage** /'vɪntɪdʒ/ 1 *n.* grape-harvest; season of this; season's produce of grapes; wine made from this; wine of high quality kept separate from others; year etc. when thing was made; thing made etc. in particular year etc. 2 *a.* of high quality (of a past season. 3 **vintage car** car made between 1917 and 1930.

**vintner** /'vɪntnə(r)/ *n.* wine-merchant.

**vinyl** /'vaɪnl/ *n.* any of a group of plastics made by polymerization.

**viol** /'vaɪəl/ *n.* medieval stringed musical instrument similar in shape to violin.

**viola**¹ /viːˈəʊlə/ *n.* kind of large violin.

**viola**² /'vaɪələ/ *n.* any of group of plants including violet and pansy, esp. a cultivated hybrid.

**violate** /'vaɪəleɪt/ *v.t.* disregard, fail to comply with; transgress; infringe; break in upon; rape. **violation** *n.*; **violator** *n.*

**violence** /'vaɪələns/ *n.* being violent; violent conduct or treatment; unlawful exercise of physical force. **do violence to** act contrary to, outrage.

**violent** /'vaɪələnt/ *a.* involving great physical force; intense, vehement; (of death) resulting from external force or from poison.

**violet** /'vaɪələt/ 1 *n.* plant with usu. blue, purple, or white flowers; colour at opposite end of spectrum from red, blue with slight admixture of red; violet colour or paint or clothes etc. 2 *a.* of this colour.

**violin** /vaɪəˈlɪn/ *n.* musical instrument with 4 strings of treble pitch played with bow; player of this. **violinist** *n.*

**violist**¹ /'vaɪəlɪst/ *n.* viol-player.

**violist**² /viːˈəʊləst/ *n.* viola-player.

**violoncello** /vaɪələnˈtʃeləʊ/ *n.* (*pl.* **-os**) cello.

**VIP** *abbr.* very important person.

**viper** /'vaɪpə(r)/ *n.* small venomous snake; malignant or treacherous person.

**virago** /vəˈrɑːgəʊ/ *n.* (*pl.* **-gos**) fierce or abusive woman.

**viral** /'vaɪər(ə)l/ *a.* of or caused by a virus.

**virgin** /'vɜːdʒɪn/ 1 *n.* person, esp. woman, who has had no sexual intercourse. 2 *a.* of or befitting or being a virgin; not previously used etc. 3 **the Virgin** Christ's mother, the Blessed Virgin Mary. 4 **virginity** *n.*

**virginal** /'vɜːdʒɪn(ə)l/ 1 *a.* that is or befits a virgin. 2 *n.* (usu. in *pl.*) legless spinet in box.

**Virginia creeper** /vəˈdʒɪmɪə/ vine cultivated for ornament.

**Virgo** /'vɜːgəʊ/ *n.* sixth sign of zodiac.

**virile** /'vɪraɪl/ *a.* having masculine vigour or strength; of or having procreative power; of man as opp. woman or child. **virility** /-'rɪl-/ *n.*

**virtual** /'vɜːtjʊəl/ *a.* that is such for practical purposes though not in name or according to strict definition.

**virtue** /'vɜːtjuː/ *n.* moral goodness; particular moral excellence; chastity, esp. of woman; good quality or influence, efficacy. **by, in, virtue of** on strength or ground of.

**virtuoso** /vɜːtjʊˈəʊsəʊ/ *n.* (*pl.* **-si** /-siː/ or **-sos**) person skilled in technique of an art, esp. music. **virtuosity** /-'ɒs-/ *n.*

**virtuous** /'vɜːtjuːəs/ *a.* possessing or showing moral rectitude, chaste.

**virulent** /'vɪrələnt/ *a.* poisonous; malignant, (of disease) extremely violent; bitter. **virulence** *n.*

**virus** /'vaɪrəs/ *n.* any of numerous kinds of very simple organisms smaller than bacteria, able to cause diseases; *fig.* poison, source of disease.

**visa** /'viːzə/ *n.* (*pl.* **-sas**) endorsement on passport etc. permitting holder to enter or leave a country. **visaed** /-zəd/ *a.*

**visage** /'vɪzɪdʒ/ *n.* literary face.

***vis-à-vis*** /viːzɑːˈviː/ 1 *prep.* in relation to, opposite to. 2 *adv.* facing one another. 3 *n.* person or thing facing another. [F]

**viscera** /'vɪsərə/ *n.pl.* internal organs of the body. **visceral** *a.*

**viscid** /'vɪsɪd/ *a.* glutinous, sticky. **viscidity** *n.*

**viscose** /'vɪskəʊz/ *n.* viscous solution of cellulose used in making rayon etc.

**viscosity** /vɪˈskɒsətɪ/ n. quality or degree of being viscous.

**viscount** /ˈvaɪkaʊnt/ n. British nobleman ranking between earl and baron. **viscountcy** n.

**viscountess** /ˈvaɪkaʊntəs/ n. viscount's wife or widow; woman with own rank of viscount.

**viscous** /ˈvɪskəs/ a. glutinous, sticky; semifluid, not flowing freely.

**visibility** /vɪzəˈbɪlətɪ/ n. being visible; range or possibility of vision as determined by conditions of light and atmosphere.

**visible** /ˈvɪzəb(ə)l/ a. capable of being seen, that can be seen; in sight; apparent, open, obvious.

**vision** /ˈvɪʒ(ə)n/ n. act or faculty of seeing; sight; thing or person etc. seen in dream or trance; thing seen vividly in imagination; imaginative insight; foresight, sagacity in planning; person etc. of unusual beauty; what is seen on TV screen.

**visionary** /ˈvɪʒənərɪ/ 1 a. given to seeing visions or to indulging in fanciful theories; existing only in vision or in imagination, unpractical. 2 n. visionary person.

**visit** /ˈvɪzɪt/ 1 v. go or come to see (person, place, etc., or absol.) socially or on business etc.; reside temporarily with or at; (of disease, calamity, etc.) come upon, attack; *Bibl.* punish, inflict punishment for (sin) *upon* person. 2 n. act of visiting, temporary residence with person or at place; occasion of going *to* doctor etc., formal or official call.

**visitant** /ˈvɪzɪt(ə)nt/ n. (supernatural) visitor.

**visitation** /vɪzəˈteɪʃ(ə)n/ n. official visit of inspection etc.; divine dispensation of punishment or reward.

**visitor** /ˈvɪzɪtə(r)/ n. person etc. who visits person or place; migratory bird.

**visor** /ˈvaɪzə(r)/ n. movable part of helmet covering face; shield at top of vehicle windscreen to protect eyes from bright sunshine; *hist.* mask.

**vista** /ˈvɪstə/ n. view or prospect, esp. through avenue of trees or other long narrow opening; mental view of long succession of events etc.

**visual** /ˈvɪzjuːəl/ a. of or concerned with or used in seeing; received through sight. **visual display terminal, unit**, device displaying output or input of computer on screen.

**visualize** /ˈvɪzjuːəlaɪz/ v.t. make visible esp. to one's mind (thing not visible to the eye). **visualization** n.

**vital** /ˈvaɪt(ə)l/ 1 a. of or concerned with or essential to organic life; essential to existence or success etc.; full of life or activity; fatal. 2 n. in *pl.* vital parts, e.g. lungs and heart. 3 **vital statistics** those relating to births and deaths and health etc., *colloq.* measurements of woman's bust, waist, and hips.

**vitality** /vaɪˈtælətɪ/ n. animation, liveliness; ability to sustain life.

**vitalize** /ˈvaɪtəlaɪz/ v.t. endow with life, infuse with vigour. **vitalization** n.

**vitamin** /ˈvɪtəmɪn/ n. any of a number of substances occurring in certain foodstuffs and essential to health and normal growth etc.

**vitaminize** /ˈvɪtəmənaɪz/ v.t. introduce vitamins into (food).

**vitiate** /ˈvɪʃɪeɪt/ v.t. impair quality or efficiency of, debase; make invalid or ineffectual. **vitiation** n.

**viticulture** /ˈvɪtɪkʌltʃə(r)/ n. vine-growing.

**vitreous** /ˈvɪtrɪəs/ a. of or of the nature of glass.

**vitrify** /ˈvɪtrɪfaɪ/ v. change into glass or glassy substance, esp. by heat. **vitrification** n.

**vitriol** /ˈvɪtrɪəl/ n. sulphuric acid or a sulphate; caustic speech or criticism. **vitriolic** /-ˈɒl-/ a.

**vituperate** /vəˈtjuːpəreɪt/ v.t. revile, abuse. **vituperation** n.; **vituperative** a.

**viva**[1] /ˈviːvə/ 1 *int.* 'long live'. 2 n. cry of this as salute. [It.]

**viva**[2] /ˈvaɪvə/ n. & v.t. (*past* & *p.p.* **vivaed** /-vəd/) *colloq.* viva(-)voce.

**vivacious** /vəˈveɪʃəs/ a. lively, animated. **vivacity** /vəˈvæsətɪ/ n.

**vivarium** /vəˈveərɪəm/ n. (*pl.* **-ria**) place for keeping living animals etc. in natural conditions.

**viva voce** /vaɪvə ˈvəʊtʃɪ/ oral(ly); oral examination.

**viva-voce** v.t. examine viva voce.

**vivid** /ˈvɪvɪd/ a. bright; intense; lively; incisive; graphic.

**vivify** /ˈvɪvɪfaɪ/ v.t. give life to, animate.

**viviparous** /vəˈvɪpərəs/ *a.* bringing forth young alive, not egg-laying.

**vivisect** /ˈvɪvəsekt/ *v.t.* perform vivisection on.

**vivisection** /vɪvəˈsekʃ(ə)n/ *n.* dissection or other painful treatment of living animals for scientific research. **vivisectionist** *n.*

**vixen** /ˈvɪks(ə)n/ *n.* she-fox; spiteful woman.

**viz.** *abbr.* videlicet.

**vizier** /vɪˈzɪə(r)/ *n.* high administrative official in some Muslim countries.

**vocable** /ˈvəʊkəb(ə)l/ *n.* word, esp. with ref. to form not meaning.

**vocabulary** /vəˈkæbjələri/ *n.* words used by a language or book or branch of science, or author; list of these; person's range of language.

**vocal** /ˈvəʊk(ə)l/ *a.* of or concerned with or uttered by the voice; expressing one's feelings freely in speech. **vocal cords** voice-producing part of larynx; **vocal music** music written for or produced by the voice.

**vocalic** /vəˈkælɪk/ *a.* of or consisting of vowel(s).

**vocalist** /ˈvəʊkəlɪst/ *n.* singer.

**vocalize** /ˈvəʊkəlaɪz/ *v.* form (sound) or utter (word) with voice. **vocalization** *n.*

**vocation** /vəˈkeɪʃ(ə)n/ *n.* divine call to, or sense of fitness for, career or occupation; employment, trade, profession. **vocational** *a.*

**vocative** /ˈvɒkətɪv/ **1** *n.* case of noun used in addressing or invoking. **2** *a.* of or in the vocative.

**vociferate** /vəˈsɪfəreɪt/ *v.* utter noisily; shout, bawl. **vociferation** *n.*

**vociferous** /vəˈsɪfərəs/ *a.* noisy, clamorous; loud and insistent in speech.

**vodka** /ˈvɒdkə/ *n.* alcoholic spirit distilled esp. in Russia from rye etc.

**vogue** /vəʊɡ/ *n.* prevailing fashion; popular favour. **in vogue** in fashion, generally current; **vogue-word** word currently fashionable.

**voice 1** *n.* sound formed in larynx etc. and uttered by mouth, esp. human utterance in speaking or singing etc.; ability to produce this; use of voice, utterance esp. in spoken words, opinion so expressed; right to express opinion; *Gram.* set of verbal forms showing whether verb is active or passive. **2** *v.t.* give utterance to, express; utter with vibration of vocal cords. **3 voice-over** narration in film not accompanied by picture of speaker.

**void 1** *a.* empty, vacant; not valid or binding. **2** *n.* empty space; sense of loss. **3** *v.t.* invalidate; excrete.

**voile** /vɔɪl/ *n.* thin semi-transparent dress-material.

**vol.** *abbr.* volume.

**volatile** /ˈvɒlətaɪl/ *a.* readily evaporating at ordinary temperature; changeable, flighty, lively; transient. **volatility** /-ˈtɪl-/ *n.*

**volatilize** /vəˈlætəlaɪz/ *v.* turn into vapour. **volatilization** *n.*

**vol-au-vent** /ˈvɒləʊvɑ̃/ *n.* (usu. small) round case of puff pastry filled with savoury mixture.

**volcanic** /vɒlˈkænɪk/ *a.* of or like or produced by volcano.

**volcano** /vɒlˈkeɪnəʊ/ *n.* (*pl.* **-noes**) mountain or hill with opening(s) through which ashes and gases and (molten) rocks etc. are or have been periodically ejected.

**vole** *n.* small herbivorous rodent.

**volition** /vəˈlɪʃ(ə)n/ *n.* act or faculty of willing. **volitional** *a.*

**volley** /ˈvɒlɪ/ **1** *n.* simultaneous discharge of a number of weapons; bullets etc. thus discharged at once; noisy emission (*of* oaths etc.) in quick succession; *Tennis, Footb.*, etc. playing of ball before it touches ground. **2** *v.t.* return or send by volley. **3 volley-ball** game for two teams of 6 sending large ball by hand over net.

**volt** /vəʊlt/ *n.* unit of electromotive force, difference of potential capable of sending current of one ampere through conductor with resistance of one ohm.

**voltmeter** instrument measuring electric potential in volts.

**voltage** /ˈvəʊltɪdʒ/ *n.* electromotive force expressed in volts.

**volte-face** /vəʊltˈfɑːs/ *n.* complete change of position in argument or opinion.

**voluble** /ˈvɒljəb(ə)l/ *a.* with vehement or incessant flow of words. **volubility** *n.*

**volume** /ˈvɒljuːm/ *n.* set of usu. printed sheets bound together usu. within cover and containing part of a book or one or more books; solid content, bulk;

**volumetric** /ˌvɒljəˈmetrɪk/ a. of measurement by volume.

**voluminous** /vəˈljuːmənəs/ a. (of book or writer) running to many volumes or great length; (of drapery etc.) loose or ample.

**voluntary** /ˈvɒləntəri/ 1 a. done or acting or able to act of one's own free will; unpaid; (of institution) supported by voluntary contributions; brought about by voluntary action; controlled by the will. 2 n. organ solo played before, during, or after church service.

**volunteer** /vɒlənˈtɪə(r)/ 1 n. person who voluntarily offers services or enrols himself for enterprise, esp. for service in any of armed services. 2 v. undertake or offer voluntarily; make voluntary offer of one's services.

**voluptuary** /vəˈlʌptjuəri/ n. person given up to luxury and gratification of senses.

**voluptuous** /vəˈlʌptjuəs/ a. of or tending to or occupied with or derived from sensuous or sensual pleasure.

**volute** /vəˈljuːt/ n. spiral scroll in stonework as ornament of capital.

**vomit** /ˈvɒmɪt/ 1 v. eject contents of stomach through mouth; be sick; eject violently; belch forth, spew out. 2 n. matter vomited from stomach.

**voodoo** /ˈvuːduː/ 1 n. use of or belief in religious witchcraft as practised among W. Ind. etc. Blacks. 2 v.t. affect by voodoo, bewitch.

**voracious** /vəˈreɪʃəs/ a. greedy in eating, ravenous. **voracity** /-ˈræs-/ n.

**vortex** /ˈvɔːteks/ n. (pl. **-tices** /-tsiːz/ or **-texes**) whirlpool, whirlwind, whirling motion or mass; thing viewed as swallowing those who approach it. **vortical** a.

**votary** /ˈvəʊtəri/ n. person bound by vow(s), esp. to religious life; devotee, ardent follower (of). **votaress** n.

**vote** 1 n. formal expression of will or opinion in regard to election or passing of law or resolution etc., signified by ballot or show of hands etc.; *the* right to vote; opinion expressed by majority of votes; *the* collective votes given by party etc. 2 v. give vote; enact etc. by majority of votes; *colloq.* pronounce by general consent, announce one's proposal (*that*) by voting; **vote in** elect by votes.

**voter** n. person entitled to vote.

**votive** /ˈvəʊtɪv/ a. given or consecrated in fulfilment of vow.

**vouch** /vaʊtʃ/ v.i. answer or be surety *for*.

**voucher** /ˈvaʊtʃə(r)/ n. document exchangeable for goods or services as token of payment made or promised; document establishing payment of money or truth of accounts.

**vouchsafe** /vaʊtʃˈseɪf/ v.t. condescend to grant or *to* do.

**vow** /vaʊ/ 1 n. solemn promise or engagement, esp. to deity or saint. 2 v.t. promise solemnly; *arch.* declare, esp. solemnly.

**vowel** /ˈvaʊəl/ n. speech-sound produced by vibrations of vocal cords, but without audible friction; letter representing this.

**vox populi** /vɒks ˈpɒpjəliː/ public opinion, general verdict, popular belief. [L]

**voyage** /ˈvɔɪɪdʒ/ 1 n. expedition to a distance by water or air or in space. 2 v.i. make voyage.

**voyeur** /vwaːˈjɜː(r)/ n. person who derives sexual gratification from looking at sexual organs or acts of others. **voyeurism** n.

**vs.** *abbr.* versus.

**VTO(L)** *abbr.* vertical take-off (and landing).

**vulcanite** /ˈvʌlkənaɪt/ n. hard black vulcanized rubber.

**vulcanize** /ˈvʌlkənaɪz/ v.t. make (rubber etc.) stronger and more elastic by treating with sulphur at high temperature. **vulcanization** n.

**vulgar** /ˈvʌlɡə(r)/ a. of or characteristic of the common people; coarse; in common use, generally prevalent. **vulgar fraction** fraction expressed by numerator and denominator, not decimally; **the vulgar tongue** native or vernacular language. **vulgarity** /-ˈɡær-/ n.

**vulgarian** /vʌlˈɡeərɪən/ n. vulgar (esp. rich) person.

**vulgarism** /ˈvʌlɡərɪz(ə)m/ n. word or expression in coarse or uneducated use, instance of coarse or uneducated behaviour.

**vulgarize** /'vʌlgəraɪz/ v.t. affect with vulgarity, spoil by making too common or frequented or well known. **vulgarization** n.

**Vulgate** /'vʌlgeɪt/ n. 4th-c. Latin version of Bible.

**vulnerable** /'vʌlnərəb(ə)l/ a. that may be wounded, open to or not proof against attack or injury or criticism etc. **vulnerability** n.

**vulpine** /'vʌlpaɪn/ a. of or like fox; crafty, cunning.

**vulture** /'vʌltʃə(r)/ n. large bird of prey feeding chiefly on carrion; rapacious person.

**vulva** /'vʌlvə/ n. external female genitals.

**vv.** abbr. verses.

**vying** partic. of vie.

# W

**W** *abbr.* watt(s); west(ern).

**w.** *abbr.* wicket(s); wide(s); with.

**WA** *abbr.* Western Australia.

**wacky** /'wæki/ *a. sl.* crazy.

**wad** /wɒd/ 1 *n.* lump of soft material to keep things apart or in place or to block hole; roll of bank-notes. 2 *v.t.* fix or stuff with wad; stuff or line with wadding.

**wadding** /'wɒdɪŋ/ *n.* soft material usu. of cotton or wool for stuffing quilts or packing fragile articles in etc.

**waddle** /'wɒd(ə)l/ 1 *v.i.* walk with short steps and swaying motion. 2 *n.* such walk.

**waddy** /'wɒdɪ/ *n. Aus.* club or bludgeon.

**wade** 1 *v.* walk through water or other impeding medium; progress slowly or with difficulty (*through* etc.). 2 *n.* spell of wading.

**wader** /'weɪdə(r)/ *n.* long-legged waterbird; in *pl.* high waterproof boots.

**wadi** /'wɒdɪ/ *n.* rocky watercourse in N. Africa etc., dry except in rainy season.

**wafer** /'weɪfə(r)/ 1 *n.* very thin light crisp biscuit; disc of unleavened bread used in Eucharist; disc of red paper stuck on law papers instead of seal. 2 *v.t.* seal with wafer. 3 **wafer-thin** very thin. 4 **wafery** *a.*

**waffle**[1] /'wɒf(ə)l/ 1 *n.* aimless verbose talk or writing. 2 *v.i.* indulge in waffle.

**waffle**[2] /'wɒf(ə)l/ *n.* small crisp battercake. **waffle-iron** utensil for cooking waffles.

**waft** /wɒft/ 1 *v.* convey or be conveyed smoothly (as) through air or over water. 2 *n.* whiff of perfume etc.

**wag** 1 *v.* shake or move to and fro. 2 *n.* single wagging motion; facetious person. 3 **wagtail** kind of long-tailed small bird.

**wage** 1 *n.* in *sing.* or *pl.* employee's regular pay, esp. paid weekly. 2 *v.t.* carry on (war). 3 **wage freeze** ban on wage-increases; **wage-plug** *Aus.* worker for wages.

**wager** /'weɪdʒə(r)/ *n. & v.* bet.

**Wagga** /'wɒgə/ *n. Aus.* (in full **Wagga blanket** or **rug**) covering made from two sacks cut open and sewn together.

**waggish** /'wægɪʃ/ *a.* playful, facetious.

**waggle** /'wæg(ə)l/ *v. colloq.* wag.

**wagon** /'wægən/ *n.* (also **waggon**) 4-wheeled vehicle for heavy loads; open railway truck. **on the wagon** *sl.* abstaining from alcohol.

**wagoner** /'wægənə(r)/ *n.* (also **waggoner**) driver of wagon.

**waif** *n.* homeless and helpless person, esp. abandoned child; *Law* object or animal found ownerless.

**wail** 1 *n.* prolonged plaintive inarticulate cry of pain or grief etc.; sound resembling this. 2 *v.i.* utter wail or persistent lamentations or complaints.

**wain** *n. poet.* etc. wagon.

**wainscot** /'weɪnskət/ *n.* wooden panelling or boarding on room-wall.

**waist** *n.* part of human body between ribs and hips; narrowness marking this; circumference of waist; middle narrower part of anything; part of garment corresponding to waist; bodice, blouse; *Naut.* middle part of (upper deck of) ship. **waistcoat** usu. sleeveless and collarless garment covering upper part of body down to waist and worn under jacket etc.; **waistline** outline or size of waist.

**wait** 1 *v.* defer action until expected event occurs; pause; await, bide; defer (meal) until someone arrives; act as waiter or attendant. 2 *n.* act or time of waiting; watching for enemy; in *pl.* street singers of Christmas carols. 3 **waiting-list** list of applicants etc. for thing not immediately available; **waiting-room** room for persons to wait in esp. at railway station or surgery; **wait (up)on** await convenience of, be attendant or respectful visitor to.

**waiter** /'weɪtə(r)/ *n.* man who takes orders and brings food etc. at hotel or restaurant tables. **waitress** *n.*

**waive** *v.t.* refrain from insisting on or using.

**waiver** /'weɪvə(r)/ *n. Law* waiving.

**wake**[1] 1 *v.* (*past* **woke** or **waked**; *p.p.* **woken** or **waked**) cease to sleep, rouse from sleep; *arch.* be awake; disturb with noise; evoke. 2 *n.* (chiefly in Ireland) vigil beside corpse before burial, attendant lamentations and merrymaking.

**wake**[2] *n.* track left by moving ship etc.

**wakeful** /'weɪkfəl/ a. unable to sleep, sleepless, vigilant.

**waken** /'weɪkən/ v. make or become awake.

**wale** n. weal, ridge on corduroy etc.; *Naut.* broad thick timber along ship's side.

**walk** /wɔːk/ **1** v. move by lifting and setting down each foot in turn with one foot always on the ground at any time; travel or go on foot, take exercise thus; traverse (distance) in walking; tread floor or surface of; cause to walk with one. **2** n. act of walking; ordinary human gait; slowest gait of animal; person's action in walking; spell or distance of walking; excursion on foot; place or track meant or fit for walking. **3 walkabout** informal stroll by royal person etc., Aus. Aboriginal's period of wandering; **walking-stick** stick carried or used as support when walking; **walk off with** *colloq.* steal, win easily; **walk of life** one's occupation; **walk out** depart esp. suddenly or angrily; **walk-out** n.; **walk out on** desert; **walk-over** easy victory; **walk the streets** be prostitute; **walkway** passage or path for walking along.

**walker** n. person etc. who walks esp. as recreation; framework for person unable to walk unaided.

**walkie-talkie** /wɔːkiːˈtɔːkiː/ n. small portable radio transmitting and receiving set.

**wall** /wɔːl/ **1** n. continuous narrow upright structure of stone or brick etc., enclosing or protecting or separating a house or town or room or field etc.; thing like wall in appearance or effect; outermost layer of animal or plant organ or cell etc. **2** v.t. block *up* with wall; (esp. in *p.p.*) provide or protect with wall, shut *in* or *off* thus. **3 go to the wall** fare badly in competition; **wallflower** fragrant garden plant with deep-coloured flowers, *colloq.* partnerless woman at dance; **wallpaper** paper for covering interior walls of rooms.

**wallaby** /'wɒləbɪ/ n. small species of kangaroo. **on the wallaby (track)** *Aus.* wandering or tramping about; **wallaby bush** *Aus.* pinkwood; **wallaby-grass** *Aus.* kind of danthonia.

**wallah** /'wɒlə/ n. *Anglo-Ind.* person connected with a specified occupation or task; *colloq.* man, person.

**wallaroo** /wɒləˈruː/ n. *Aus.* large brownish-black kangaroo found in rocky areas.

**wallet** /'wɒlɪt/ n. flat case for holding paper money and documents etc.

**wall-eye** /'wɔːlaɪ/ n. eye with iris whitish or streaked etc. or with outward squint. **wall-eyed** a.

**wallop** /'wɒləp/ *sl.* **1** v.t. thrash, beat. **2** n. whack; beer.

**walloper** n. *Aus. sl.* policeman.

**wallow** /'wɒləʊ/ **1** v.i. roll about in mud or sand or water etc.; take gross delight *in*. **2** n. act of wallowing; place where animals wallow.

**walnut** /'wɔːlnʌt/ n. nut with kernel in pair of boat-shaped shells; tree bearing this; its timber used in cabinet-making.

**walrus** /'wɔːlrəs/ n. long-tusked amphibious arctic mammal. **walrus moustache** long thick drooping moustache.

**waltz** /wɔːls/ **1** n. dance in triple time performed by couples progressing with smooth sliding steps; music for this. **2** v.i. dance waltz; dance *in* or *out* etc. in joy etc.; move easily or casually.

**wampum** /'wɒmpəm/ n. strings of shell-beads formerly used by N. Amer. Indians for money and ornament etc.

**wan** /wɒn/ a. pale, colourless, weary-looking.

**wand** /wɒnd/ n. magician's or music conductor's baton; slender rod or staff carried as sign of office etc.

**wander** /'wɒndə(r)/ v.i. go from place to place without settled route or aim; go aimlessly *in* or *off* etc.; diverge from right way; be unsettled or incoherent in mind or talk etc., be inattentive or delirious, rave. **wanderlust** strong or irresistible desire to travel or wander.

**wandoo** /'wɒnduː/ n. a white-barked eucalypt of WA.

**wane** **1** v.i. (of moon) decrease in apparent size; decrease in size or splendour, lose power or importance. **2** n. process of waning. **3 on the wane** declining.

**wangle** /'wæŋg(ə)l/ *sl.* **1** v.t. obtain or bring about etc. by scheming or contrivance. **2** n. act of wangling.

**want** /wɒnt/ **1** n. desire for something,

**wanting** thing desired; lack or deficiency of; poverty. 2 v. have desire for, wish for possession or presence of; require, need; be without or insufficiently supplied with; be in want (for); in p.p. suspected of being criminal etc.

**vanting** /'wɒntɪŋ/ a. lacking quality or quantity; unequal to requirements, absent.

**vanton** /'wɒnt(ə)n/ 1 a. licentious, unchaste; unprovoked, reckless, arbitrary; sportive, capricious; luxuriant, wild. 2 n. licentious person. 3 v.i. be sportive or capricious.

**vapiti** /'wɒpɪtiː/ n. large N. Amer. deer.

**var** /wɔː(r)/ 1 n. strife usu. between nations conducted by armed force; hostility between persons; efforts against crime or disease etc. 2 v.i. make war, be at war. 3 **at war** engaged in war; **go to war** begin hostile operations; **warcry** phrase or name shouted in battle, party catchword; **war-dance** dance performed by primitive peoples before war or after victory; **warhead** explosive head of missile; **war-horse** trooper's horse, fig. veteran soldier; **war memorial** monument to those killed in a war; **warmonger** /-mʌŋgə(r)/ person who seeks to cause war; **ar-paint** paint put on body esp. by N. Amer. Indians before battle; **warpath** march of N. Amer. Indians to make war (**on the war-path** engaged in conflict, taking hostile attitude); **warship** ship for use in war; **warwidow** woman whose husband has been killed in war.

**varatah** /'wɒrətɑː/ n. Aus. a shrub with crimson or scarlet flowers; floral emblem of NSW.

**varble** /'wɔːb(ə)l/ 1 v. sing in sweet gentle continuous trilling manner. 2 n. warbling sound.

**varbler** n. any of various kinds of small bird.

**vard** /wɔːd/ 1 n. separate room or division of hospital etc.; administrative division esp. for elections; minor etc. under care of guardian or court; guarding, guardianship; in pl. notches and projections in key and lock to prevent opening by wrong key. 2 v.t. (usu. with off) parry (blow), avert (danger etc.). **wardroom** officers' quarters in warship.

**warden** /'wɔːd(ə)n/ n. president or governor of institution; official with supervisory duties; traffic warden.

**warder** /'wɔːdə(r)/ n. official in charge of prisoners in jail. **wardress** n.

**wardrobe** /'wɔːdrəʊb/ n. place, esp. large cupboard, where clothes are kept; room where theatrical costumes and properties are kept; stock of clothes.

**wardrobe master, mistress**, person in charge of theatrical wardrobe or costumes.

**wardship** /'wɔːdʃɪp/ n. tutelage.

**ware** n. articles made for sale, goods, esp. vessels etc. of pottery; in pl. things person has for sale.

**warehouse** /'weəhaʊs/ 1 n. building in which goods are stored or shown for sale. 2 v.t. store in warehouse.

**warfare** /'wɔːfeə(r)/ n. state of war; campaigning.

**warlike** /'wɔːlaɪk/ a. fond of or skilful in war; military.

**warlock** /'wɔːlɒk/ n. arch. sorcerer.

**warm** /wɔːm/ 1 a. of or at fairly high temperature; (of person) at natural temperature or with skin temperature raised by exercise or external heat; (of clothes) serving to keep one warm; hearty, animated, affectionate, passionate; (of reception, welcome, etc.) heartily friendly or vigorously hostile; (of colour) suggesting warmth esp. by presence of red or yellow; (of scent in hunting) fresh and strong. 2 v. make or become warm. 3 **getting warm** near what is sought; **warm-blooded** (of animals) having blood temperature well above that of environment; **warmhearted** affectionate, sympathetic; **warming-pan** flat closed vessel holding live coals, formerly used for warming beds; **warm up** make or become warm, reach temperature of efficient working, prepare for performance by exercise or practice.

**warmth** /wɔːmθ/ n. being warm.

**warn** /wɔːn/ v.t. put on guard, caution against; give timely notice of impending danger or misfortune; give cautionary notice or advice. **warn off** give notice to keep away (from).

**warning** n. what is said or done or occurs to warn person.

**warp** /wɔːp/ 1 v. make or become crooked or twisted esp. by uneven

## warrant

shrinkage or expansion; distort or pervert (person's mind); suffer such distortion; move (ship etc.) by hauling on rope attached to fixed point. **2** *n.* threads stretched lengthwise in loom to be crossed by weft; contorted state of warped wood etc.; mental perversion or bias; rope used in warping a ship.

**warrant** /'wɒrənt/ **1** *n.* thing that authorizes an action; written authorization to receive or supply money or goods or services or to carry out arrest or search; certificate of service rank held by warrant-officer. **2** *v.t.* serve as warrant for, justify; guarantee. **warrant-officer** officer of rank between commissioned and non-commissioned officers.

**warranty** /'wɒrəntɪ/ *n.* authority or justification; seller's undertaking that thing sold is his and fit for use etc., often accepting responsibility for repairs needed over a period.

**warren** /'wɒrən/ *n.* piece of land where rabbits breed or abound; densely populated or labyrinthine building or district.

**warrigal** /'wɒrɪg(ə)l/ *Aus.* **1** *n.* dingo; untamed horse or person. **2** *a.* wild, untamed.

**warrior** /'wɒrɪə(r)/ *n.* person famous or skilled in war; fighting man (esp. of primitive peoples); *attrib.* martial.

**wart** /wɔːt/ *n.* small round dry growth on skin; protuberance on skin of animal or surface of plant etc. **wart-hog** Afr. wild pig. **warty** *a.*

**wary** /'weərɪ/ *a.* on one's guard; cautious, circumspect.

**was**: see **be**.

**wash** /wɒʃ/ **1** *v.* cleanse with liquid; take *away* or *off* or *out* by washing; wash oneself or esp. one's hands (and face); wash clothes; (of fabric or dye) bear washing without damage; *colloq.* bear scrutiny or investigation; moisten, (of water) flow past, beat upon, sweep *over*, surge *against*, carry *along* or *away* etc.; sift (ore) by action of water; brush watery colour over. **2** *n.* washing, being washed; treatment at laundry; quantity of clothes for washing; motion of agitated water or air esp. due to passage of vessel or aircraft; kitchen slops given to pigs; thin or weak or inferior or animals' liquid food; liquid to spread over surface to cleanse or heal or colour. **3 wash-basin** basin for washing one's hands etc.; **wash down** accompany or follow (food) *with* drink; **washed out** faded by washing, *fig.* limp, enfeebled; **washed up** *sl.* defeated, having failed; **wash one's hands** decline responsibility *of*; **wash out** clean inside of by washing, *colloq.* cancel; **wash-out** breach in railway or road caused by flood, *sl.* complete failure; **wash-stand** piece of furniture for holding wash-basin and soap-dish etc.; **wash up** wash (table utensils etc. or usu. abs.) after use, (of sea) carry on to shore.

**washable** /'wɒʃəb(ə)l/ *a.* that may be washed without damage.

**washer** /'wɒʃə(r)/ *n.* flattened ring of metal or leather or rubber etc. placed between two surfaces or under plunger of tap or nut etc. to tighten joint; *Aus.* face-cloth; washing machine.

**washerwoman** /'wɒʃəwʊmən/ *n.* (*pl.* -women /-wɪmɪn/) laundress.

**washing** /'wɒʃɪŋ/ *n.* clothes to be washed or that have been washed. **washing-machine** machine for washing clothes; **washing-powder** powder of soap or detergent for washing clothes; **washing-up** washing of table utensils after use, dishes etc. for washing.

**washy** /'wɒʃɪ/ *a.* too watery or weak, lacking vigour.

**wasp** /wɒsp/ *n.* stinging insect with black and yellow stripes. **wasp-waist** very slender waist.

**WASP** /wɒsp/ *abbr.* US (usu. *derog.*) White Anglo-Saxon Protestant.

**waspish** /'wɒspɪʃ/ *a.* irritable, snappish.

**wassail** /'wɒseɪl/ **1** *n.* festive drinking. **2** *v.i.* make merry.

**wastage** /'weɪstɪdʒ/ *n.* amount wasted, loss by use or wear or decay etc.; loss of employees other than by redundancy.

**waste** /weɪst/ **1** *a.* superfluous, no longer serving a purpose; not inhabited or cultivated. **2** *v.* use to no purpose or for inadequate result or extravagantly; fail to use; wear away; become or become weak; lay waste. **3** *n.* act of wasting; waste material; waste region; diminution from use or wear; waste-pipe. **4 lay waste** devastate, ravage; **run to**

**waste** be wasted; **waste land** land not utilized for cultivation or building; **waste paper** paper thrown away as spoiled or useless etc.; **waste-pipe** pipe carrying off superfluous or used water or steam; **waste product** useless by-product of manufacture or bodily process etc.

**wasteful** /ˈweɪstfəl/ *a.* extravagant, causing or showing waste.

**waster** /ˈweɪstə(r)/ *n.* wasteful person; *sl.* wastrel.

**wastrel** /ˈweɪstr(ə)l/ *n.* good-for-nothing person.

**watch** /wɒtʃ/ 1 *n.* small portable timepiece for carrying on person; state of being on the look-out, constant attention; *Naut.* 4-hour spell of duty, part of crew taking it; *hist.* watchman or -men. 2 *v.* be on the watch, be vigilant, be *for* opportunity etc.; exercise protecting care *over*; keep eyes fixed on, keep under observation; follow observantly; look out for, await (opportunity etc.). 3 **on the watch** waiting for expected or feared occurrence; **watch-dog** dog kept to guard property, person etc. charged with protecting rights etc.; **watching brief** brief of barrister who follows case for client not directly concerned; **watchman** man employed to look after empty building etc. at night; **watch-night service** religious service on last night of year; **watch out** be on one's guard; **watchtower** tower for observation of approaching danger; **watchword** phrase summarizing some party principle.

**watchful** /ˈwɒtʃfəl/ *a.* accustomed to watching, on the watch.

**water** /ˈwɔːtə(r)/ 1 *n.* transparent colourless tasteless odourless liquid forming seas and rivers etc., and falling as rain etc.; this as supplied for domestic use; tears, saliva, urine, etc.; sheet or body of water; in *pl.* part of sea or river, mineral water at spa, etc.; state of tide; solution of specified substance in water; transparency and lustre of diamond or pearl. 2 *v.* supply (plant or animal) with water; dilute with water; (of mouth, eyes) secrete or run with water; in *p.p.* (of silk fabric etc.) having irregular wavy finish. 3 **make water** urinate; **of the first water** of finest or extreme quality; **water-bag** *Aus.* canvas bag for carrying water; **water-bed** rubber mattress filled with water; **water-biscuit** thin unsweetened biscuit; **water-cannon** device giving powerful water-jet to disperse crowd etc.; **water-closet** lavatory with means of flushing pan with water; **water-colour** pigment diluted with water and not oil, picture painted or art or method of painting with this; **watercourse** stream of water, bed of this; **watercress** kind of cress with pungent leaves growing in springs and clear running streams; **water-diviner** dowser; **water down** dilute, make less forceful or horrifying; **waterfall** stream or river falling over precipice or down steep hill; **waterfowl** bird(s) frequenting water; **waterfront** part of town adjoining river etc.; **water-hole** shallow depression in which water collects; **water hyacinth** introduced floating weed in NSW; **water-ice** frozen confection of flavoured water and sugar; **watering-can** portable vessel for watering plants; **watering-place** pool where animals drink, spa or seaside resort; **water-jump** place where horses in steeplechase or show-jumping must jump over water; **water-level** surface of water, height of this, water-table; **water-lily** aquatic plant with broad floating leaves and showy flowers; **water-line** line along which surface of water touches ship's side; **waterlogged** filled or saturated with water so as to be unbuoyant, (of ground etc.) made useless by saturation with water; **waterman** boatman plying for hire; **watermark** distinguishing mark or design in paper visible when it is held up to the light; **water-meadow** meadow periodically flooded by stream; **water-melon** elliptical smooth kind with red pulp and watery juice; **water-mill** mill worked by water-wheel; **water-mole** *Aus.* platypus; **water-pistol** toy pistol shooting jet of water etc.; **water polo** game played by teams of swimmers with ball like football; **water-power** mechanical force from weight or motion of water; **waterproof** impervious to water, (*n.*) such garment or material, (*v.t.*) make waterproof; **water-rate** charge for use of public water-supply; **watershed** line

**watery**

between waters flowing to different river basins, turning-point in events; **waterside** margin of sea or lake or river; **watersider** *Aus.* wharf-labourer; **water-ski** one of pair of skis on which person towed by motor boat can skim water-surface; **waterspout** gyrating column of water and spray produced by action of whirlwind on sea and clouds above it; **water-table** plane below which ground is saturated with water; **watertight** so closely constructed or fitted that water cannot leak through, (of argument etc.) unassailable; **water-tower** tower with elevated tank to give pressure for distributing water; **waterway** navigable channel; **water-wheel** wheel rotated by action of water and used for driving machinery or used to raise water; **water-wings** inflated floats used to support person learning to swim; **waterworks** establishment for managing water-supply, *sl.* shedding of tears, *sl.* urinary system.

**watery** /'wɔːtəriː/ *a.* of or consisting of water; containing too much water; *fig.* vapid, uninteresting, (of colour) pale.

**watt** /wɒt/ *n.* unit of electrical power.

**wattage** /'wɒtɪdʒ/ *n.* amount of electrical power expressed in watts.

**wattle**¹ /'wɒt(ə)l/ *n. Aus.* acacia with fragrant golden-yellow flowers; interlaced rods and twigs or branches used for fences etc. **wattle and daub** wickerwork plastered with mud or clay as building-material.

**wattle**² /'wɒt(ə)l/ *n.* fleshy appendage hanging from head or neck of turkey etc.

**wave** 1 *v.* move (hand etc.) to and fro in greeting or as signal; show sinuous or sweeping motion; give such motion to; wave hand or held thing *to* person as signal or greeting; tell or direct thus, express thus; give undulating form to, have such form. 2 *n.* ridge of water between two depressions; long body of water curling into arched form and breaking on shore; thing compared to this; gesture of waving; waving of hair; temporary heightening of influence or condition; disturbance of particles in fluid medium to form ridges and troughs for propagation of motion or heat or light or sound etc.; single curve in this. 3 **wave aside** dismiss as intrusive or irrelevant; **wave down** wave to (vehicle or driver) as signal to stop; **wavelength** distance between crests of successive waves, this as distinctive feature of radio waves from a transmitter, *fig.* person's way of thinking.

**wavelet** /'weɪvlət/ *n.* small wave.

**waver** /'weɪvə(r)/ *v.i.* become unsteady or irresolute; begin to give way.

**wavy** /'weɪviː/ *a.* having waves or alternate contrary curves.

**wax**¹ 1 *n.* sticky plastic yellowish substance secreted by bees as material of honeycomb; this bleached and purified for candles or modelling or as basis of polishes etc.; any similar substance. 2 *v.t.* cover or treat with wax. 3 **wax-eye** *Aus.* silver-eye; **waxwork** object esp. lifelike dummy modelled in wax, making of these, in *pl.* exhibition of wax dummies.

**wax**² *v.i.* (of moon) increase in apparent size; grow larger; *arch.* become.

**waxen** /'wæks(ə)n/ *a.* smooth and pale and translucent like wax; made of wax.

**way** 1 *n.* road, track, path, street course, route; method, means; distance (to be) travelled; unimpeded opportunity for passage or advance or progress etc.; (direction of) travel or motion; habitual course or manner of action; normal course of events; state condition; in *pl.* structure of timber etc. down which new ship is launched. 2 *adv. colloq.* far. 3 **by the way** *fig.* incidentally, in passing; **by way of** by means of, as a form or method of passing through; **give way** retreat, fail to resist, make concessions, break down, collapse; **give way to** yield to, be superseded by; **lead the way** act as guide or leader; **make one's way** go, prosper; **make way** allow to pass, be superseded by; **out of the way** unusual, not obstructing, remote, disposed of; **pay one's way** pay expenses as they arise, contrive to avoid debt; **under way** in motion or progress; **way back** *colloq.* long ago; **way-bill** list of passengers or goods conveyed; **wayfarer** traveller, esp. on foot; **wayfaring** *n.*; **waylay** lie in wait for, stop to rob or accost; **way-leave** right of way rented to another; **way of life** principles or habits governing one's ac-

# wayward

tions; **way-out** *colloq.* unusual, progressive, excellent; **wayside** side of road, land at side of road.

**wayward** /'weɪwəd/ *a.* childishly self-willed; capricious.

**WC** *abbr.* water-closet; West Central.

**W/Cdr.** *abbr.* Wing Commander.

**we** *pron.* (*obj.* **us**, *poss.* **our** /aʊə/) *pl.* of I² (used also for *I* in royal proclamations etc. and by editorial writer in newspaper).

**weak** *a.* lacking in strength or power or number; fragile; feeble; unsound. **weak-kneed** lacking resolution; **weak-minded** mentally deficient, lacking resolution; **weak verb** one forming inflexions by suffix, not by vowel-change only.

**weaken** /'wiːkən/ *v.* make or become weak(er).

**weakling** /'wiːklɪŋ/ *n.* feeble person or animal.

**weakly** /'wiːklɪ/ *a.* sickly, not robust.

**weakness** /'wiːknəs/ *n.* being weak; weak point; self-indulgent liking *for*.

**weal**¹ 1 *n.* ridge raised on flesh by stroke of lash etc. 2 *v.t.* raise weals on.

**weal**² *n. arch.* welfare, well-being.

**wealth** /welθ/ *n.* riches; being rich; abundance or *a* profusion *of*.

**wealthy** /'welθɪ/ *a.* having abundance of money.

**wean** *v.t.* accustom (infant or other young mammal) to food other than mother's milk; detach, alienate *from*, reconcile gradually to being deprived of something.

**weaner** *n.* calf, pig, or lamb weaned during current year.

**weapon** /'wepən/ *n.* thing designed or used or usable for inflicting bodily harm; means employed for getting the better in a conflict.

**wear** /weə(r)/ 1 *v.* (*past* **wore**; *p.p.* **worn**) be dressed in, have on or as part of one's person; waste or damage or deteriorate gradually by use or attrition; make (hole etc.) by attrition; exhaust, tire or be tired out; endure continued use (*well* etc.), last; (of time) pass esp. tediously. 2 *n.* wearing or being worn; things worn; fashionable or suitable apparel; (also **wear and tear**) damage from ordinary use. 3 **wear out** use or be used until no longer usable, tire or be tired out.

# Wed.

**wearisome** /'wɪərɪsəm/ *a.* causing weariness, monotonous, fatiguing.

**weary** /'wɪərɪ/ 1 *a.* tired, worn out, intensely fatigued; sick *of*; tiring, tedious. 2 *v.* make or become weary.

**weasel** /'wiːz(ə)l/ *n.* small ferocious reddish-brown carnivorous animal.

**weather** /'weðə(r)/ 1 *n.* atmospheric conditions prevailing at specified time or place with respect to heat or cold and sunshine or fog and strength of wind etc.; *attrib.* windward. 2 *v.* expose to or affect by atmospheric changes; wear away or discolour etc. by exposure to weather; come safely through (storm etc.); get to windward of. 3 **keep a weather eye open** be watchful; **make heavy weather of** find trying or difficult; **under the weather** *colloq.* indisposed; **weather-beaten** affected by exposure to weather; **weatherboard** sloping board attached at bottom of door to keep out rain, one of series of horizontal boards with overlapping edges covering walls etc.; **weathercock** revolving pointer on church spire etc. to show direction of wind, inconstant person; **weather forecast** prediction of weather for next few hours or longer; **weather-vane** weathercock.

**weave**¹ 1 *v.* (*past* **wove**; *p.p.* **woven**) form (fabric) by interlacing threads, form fabric out of (threads), esp. in loom; intermingle, form or introduce *into* whole; make (story etc.) thus. 2 *n.* style of weaving.

**weave**² *v.i.* move repeatedly or deviously from side to side.

**weaver** /'wiːvə(r)/ *n.* person whose occupation is weaving; kind of tropical bird building elaborately interwoven nest.

**web** *n.* woven fabric; amount woven in one piece; complex series; cobweb or similar tissue; membrane connecting toes of aquatic bird or animal; large roll of paper for printing. **web-footed** having toes connected by web.

**webbed** /webd/ *a.* (of bird's or animal's foot) having toes connected by web.

**webbing** /'webɪŋ/ *n.* strong narrow closely-woven fabric for belts etc.

**wed** *v.* (*past* **wedded**; *p.p.* **wedded** or **wed**) marry; unite or join *to* or *with*.

**Wed.** *abbr.* Wednesday.

**wedded** /ˈwedəd/ *a.* of marriage; obstinately attached *to* pursuit etc.

**wedding** /ˈwedɪŋ/ *n.* marriage ceremony with its attendant festivities. **wedding breakfast** meal between wedding and departure for honeymoon; **wedding-cake** rich decorated cake distributed to guests at wedding and to absent friends; **wedding-ring** ring used at wedding and worn on finger of married person.

**wedge 1** *n.* piece of wood or metal etc. with sharp edge at one end, used for splitting stone etc. or forcing things apart or fixing them immovably etc.; wedge-shaped thing. **2** *v.t.* force open or *apart* or fix firmly with wedge; drive or push (object) into position where it is held fast; pack or crowd (*together*) in limited space. **3 thin end of the wedge** small beginning that may lead to something greater; **wedge-tailed eagle** large brown Aus. eagle with wedge-shaped tail.

**wedlock** /ˈwedlɒk/ *n.* married state. **born in, out of, wedlock** born of married, unmarried, parents.

**Wednesday** /ˈwenzdeɪ or -dɪ/ *n.* day of week following Tuesday.

**wee** *a.* tiny, very small.

**weed 1** *n.* wild plant growing where it is not wanted; lanky and weakly horse or person; *colloq.* tobacco. **2** *v.* rid of weeds; remove or destroy weeds; eradicate or remove or clear *out* (faults, inferior individuals, etc.).

**weeds** *n.pl.* deep mourning worn by widow.

**weedy** /ˈwiːdɪ/ *a.* full of weeds; growing freely like a weed; lanky and weak.

**week** *n.* 7-day period reckoned usu. from Saturday midnight; any 7-day period; the 6 days between Sundays; the 5 days Monday to Friday, period of work then done. **weekday** day other than (Saturday or) Sunday; **weekend** Saturday and Sunday; **weekender** *Aus.* weekend cottage.

**weekly** /ˈwiːklɪ/ **1** *a.* done or produced or occurring once every week. **2** *adv.* every week. **3** *n.* weekly newspaper or periodical.

**weeny** /ˈwiːnɪ/ *a. colloq.* tiny.

**weep 1** *v.* (*past* & *p.p.* **wept**) shed tears (*over*); lament for; shed moisture in drops, exude. **2** *n.* fit or spell of weeping.

**weeping** /ˈwiːpɪŋ/ *a.* (of tree) having drooping branches.

**weepy** /ˈwiːpɪ/ *a. colloq.* inclined to weep, tearful.

**weevil** /ˈwiːv(ə)l/ *n.* destructive granary-beetle.

**weft** *n.* threads crossing from side to side of web and interwoven with warp.

**weigh** /weɪ/ *v.* find weight of; balance in hand (as if) to guess weight of; estimate relative value or importance of, consider, ponder; be of specified weight or importance; have influence (*with*); heave up (anchor) before sailing. **weighbridge** weighing-machine for vehicles on road; **weigh down** bring down by weight, depress, oppress; **weigh in** be weighed (of boxer before contest, or jockey after race); **weigh in with** *colloq.* advance (argument etc.) confidently; **weigh one's words** choose those words which precisely express one's meaning; **weigh up** *colloq.* form estimate of.

**weight** /weɪt/ **1** *n.* tendency of bodies to fall to earth; quantitative expression of a body's weight, a scale of such weights; body of known weight for use in weighing; heavy body esp. used in mechanism etc.; load or burden; influence, importance; preponderance (*of* evidence etc.); = **shot**² (in athletics). **2** *v.t.* attach a weight to, hold down with a weight; impede or burden *with*. **3 weight-lifting** sport or exercise of lifting heavy objects.

**weighting** /ˈweɪtɪŋ/ *n.* extra pay in special cases.

**weighty** /ˈweɪtɪ/ *a.* heavy, momentous; deserving attention or carrying weight; influential, authoritative.

**weir** /wɪə(r)/ *n.* dam or barrier across river etc. to retain water and regulate its flow.

**weird** /wɪəd/ *a.* uncanny, supernatural; *colloq.* queer, incomprehensible.

**welcome** /ˈwelkəm/ **1** *int.* of greeting. **2** *n.* kind or glad reception or entertainment. **3** *v.t.* give welcome to, receive gladly; greet. **4** *a.* gladly received; acceptable as visitor; ungrudgingly permitted or given right *to*. **5 make welcome** receive hospitably; **welcome swallow** *Aus.* a swallow with a swift swooping flight.

**weld** 1 *v.t.* unite (pieces of esp. heated metal etc.) into solid mass by hammering or pressure; form by welding into some article, *fig.* fashion effectually *into* a whole. 2 *n.* welded joint.

**welfare** /'welfeə(r)/ *n.* good fortune, happiness, or well-being; maintenance of persons in such condition, money given for this purpose. **Welfare State** State with highly-developed social services controlled or financed by government; **welfare work** organized effort for welfare of class or group.

**welkin** /'welkɪn/ *n. literary* sky.

**well**¹ 1 *adv.* in right or satisfactory way; in kind way; thoroughly, carefully; with heartiness or approval; probably, reasonably; to considerable extent. 2 *a.* in good health; in satisfactory state or position; advisable. 3 *int.* introducing remark or statement; expr. astonishment or resignation etc. 4 **as well** with equal reason, preferably, in addition, also; **as well as** to the same extent as, in the same degree as, in addition to; **well-advised** prudent; **well and truly** decisively; **well-appointed** properly equipped or fitted out; **well away** having made considerable progress; **well-balanced** sensible, sane, equally matched; **well-being** happy or healthy or prosperous condition, moral or physical welfare; **well-born** of noble family; **well-bred** having or showing good breeding or manners; **well-connected** related to good families; **well-groomed** with carefully tended hair and clothes etc.; **well-heeled** *colloq.* wealthy; **well in** *Aus. sl.* prosperous; **well-informed** having much knowledge or information about subject; **well-intentioned** having or showing good intentions; **well-judged** opportunely or skilfully done; **well-knit** compact; **well-known** known to many; **well-meaning** well-intentioned; **well off** fortunately situated, fairly rich; **well-read** having read (and learnt) much; **well-spoken** ready or refined in speech; **well-to-do** prosperous; **well-tried** often tried or tested with good result; **well-wisher** person who wishes well to another or to a cause etc.; **well-worn** trite, hackneyed.

**well**² 1 *n.* shaft sunk in ground to obtain water or oil etc.; enclosed space resembling well-shaft, esp. central open space of staircase, lift-shaft, or deep narrow space between surrounding walls of building(s); receptacle for liquid, esp. ink. 2 *v.i.* spring *up* or *out* etc. (as) from fountain. 3 **well-head, -spring**, original or chief source.

**wellington** /'welɪŋt(ə)n/ *n.* waterproof rubber boot usu. reaching knee.

**Welsh**¹ 1 *a.* of Wales. 2 *n.* language of Wales; *the* Welsh people. 3 **Welshman, Welshwoman**, native of Wales; **Welsh rabbit** (or **rarebit**) dish of melted cheese on toast.

**welsh**² *v.i.* (of loser of bet, esp. bookmaker) decamp without paying; break an agreement, esp. avoid paying debts.

**welt** 1 *n.* leather rim sewn to shoe-upper for sole to be attached to; mark of heavy blow, weal; ribbed or reinforced border of garment. 2 *v.t.* provide with welt; raise weals on, thrash.

**welter** /'weltə(r)/ 1 *v.i.* roll or lie prostrate, be soaked *in*. 2 *n.* state of turmoil or upheaval; surging or confused mass.

**welterweight** /'weltəweɪt/ *n.* boxing-weight (up to 67 kg.).

**wen** *n.* benign tumour on skin.

**wench** *n. joc.* girl or young woman.

**wend** *v. arch.* wend one's way go.

**went** past of **go**¹.

**wept** past & p.p. of **weep**.

**were** see **be**.

**werewolf** /'wɪəwʊlf/ *n.* (pl. **-wolves**) *Myth.* human being who changes into wolf.

**Wesleyan** /'wezlɪən/ *hist.* 1 *a.* of Protestant denomination founded by John Wesley. 2 *n.* member of this denomination.

**west** 1 *n.* point of horizon where sun sets; western part of world or country or town etc. 2 *a.* towards or at or near or facing west; coming from west. 3 *adv.* towards or at or near west. 4 **go west** *sl.* be killed or wrecked etc.; **West End** fashionable part of London. 5 **westward** *adv.*, *a.*, & *n.*; **westwards** *adv.*

**westering** /'westərɪŋ/ *a.* (of sun) nearing the west.

**westerly** /'westəlɪ/ *a.* from or to west.

**western** /'west(ə)n/ 1 *a.* of or in west. 2 *n.* film or novel about cowboys in western N. Amer. 3 **westernize** *v.*

**westerner** /'westənə(r)/ *n.* inhabitant of west.

**wet 1** *a.* soaked or covered with water or other liquid; (of weather) rainy; (of paint) not yet dried; used with water; *sl.* mistaken, feeble. **2** *v.t.* make wet. **3** *n.* liquid that wets something; *Aus.* rainy season; rainy weather; *sl.* feeble or spiritless person; *sl.* drink. **4 wet blanket** person or thing damping or discouraging enthusiasm or cheerfulness etc.; **wet-nurse** woman employed to suckle another's child, (*v.t.*) act as wet-nurse to, *fig.* treat as if helpless.

**wether** /'weðə(r)/ *n.* castrated ram.

**Wg. Cdr.** *abbr.* Wing Commander.

**whack** *v.t. colloq.* hit, esp. with stick; in *p.p.* tired out. **2** *n.* sharp or resounding blow; *sl.* share.

**whacking** /'wækɪŋ/ *colloq.* **1** *a.* large. **2** *adv.* very.

**whale 1** *n.* large fishlike marine mammal. **2** *v.i.* hunt whales. **3 whalebone** elastic horny substance in upper jaw of some whales; **whale-oil** oil obtained from blubber of some whales.

**whaler** /'weɪlə(r)/ *n.* whaling ship or seaman.

**wham** *int.* expr. forcible impact.

**wharf** /wɔːf/ **1** *n.* (*pl.* **wharfs**) structure at water's edge for loading or unloading of vessels lying alongside. **2** *v.t.* moor (ship) at wharf; store (goods) on wharf.

**wharfie** /'wɔːfiː/ *n. Aus. colloq.* watersider.

**what** /wɒt/ **1** *interrog. a.* asking for selection from indefinite number or for specification of amount or number or kind etc. **2** *excl. a.* how great, how strange, how remarkable! etc. **3** *rel. a.* the or any...that. **4** *interrog. pron.* what thing(s)?; what did you say? **5** *excl. pron.* what thing(s), how much! **6** *rel. pron.* that or those which; thing(s) that, anything that. **7** *adv.* to what extent. **8 know what's what** have good judgement or comprehension, know the matter in hand etc.; **whatever** = *what* (in relative uses) with emphasis or indefiniteness, though any(thing), with *neg.* or *interrog.*) at all, of any kind; **what for?** for what reason?; **what have you** anything else similar; **what not** other similar things; **whatsoever** = *whatever*; **what with** because of.

**wheat** *n.* a cereal bearing dense 4-sided seed-spikes, from which bread is usu. made; its grain. **wheat-meal** wholemeal.

**wheaten** /'wiːt(ə)n/ *a.* made of wheat.

**wheedle** /'wiːd(ə)l/ *v.t.* coax by flattery or endearments; get *out of* by wheedling.

**wheel 1** *n.* circular frame or disc arranged to revolve on axle and used to facilitate motion of vehicle or for various mechanical purposes; steering-wheel; wheel-like thing; motion as of wheel; movement of line of men etc. with one end as pivot. **2** *v.* turn on axis or pivot; swing round in line with one end as pivot; (cause to) change direction or face another way; push or pull (wheeled thing); go in circles or curves. **3 wheel and deal** *US* engage in political and commercial scheming; **wheelbarrow** shallow open box with shafts and one wheel for carrying small loads on; **wheelbase** distance between axles of vehicle; **wheelchair** invalid's chair on wheels; **wheel-spin** rotation of vehicle's wheels without traction; **wheels within wheels** intricate machinery, *fig.* indirect or secret agencies; **wheelwright** maker of wheels.

**wheelie** /'wiːlɪ/ *n.* manœuvre on two-wheeled vehicle etc. in which front wheel is held off the ground; violent noisy skid while accelerating round corner or from standing start.

**wheeze 1** *v.i.* breathe hard with audible whistling sound. **2** *n.* sound of wheezing; *sl.* trick, dodge.

**wheezy** /'wiːzɪ/ *a.* wheezing or sounding like a wheeze.

**whelk** *n.* spiral-shelled marine mollusc.

**whelp 1** *n.* young dog, puppy; *arch.* cub; ill-mannered child or youth. **2** *v.i.* bring forth whelp(s).

**when 1** *adv.* at what time?; on what occasion?, how soon?; (time etc.) at or on which. **2** *conj.* at the or any time that, as soon as; although; after which, and just then. **3** *pron.* what time?; which time. **4** *n.* time, occasion. **5 whenever**, **whensoever**, at whatever time, on whatever occasion, every time that.

**whence 1** *adv.* from where, from what place or source; (place etc.) from which. **2** *conj.* to the place from which; and thence.

**where** /weə(r)/ **1** *adv.* in or to what place or position?; in what respect, from what source, etc.; in or to which. **2** *conj.* in or to the or any place or direction or respect in which; and there. **3** *pron.* what place? **4** *n.* place, locality. **5 whereabouts** in or near what place?; (*n.*) person's or thing's location roughly defined; **whereas** in contrast or comparison with the fact that, taking into consideration the fact that; **whereby** by which, by what; **wherefore** for what reason?; **wherein**, **whereof**, **whereon**, **wherewith**, in, of, on, with, what or which; **whereupon** immediately after which; **wherever** in or to whatever place etc.; **wherewithal** /-wɪðɔːl/ *colloq.* money etc. needed for a purpose.

**wherry** /ˈwerɪ/ *n.* light rowing-boat, usu. for carrying passengers; large light barge.

**whet** *v.t.* sharpen; make (more) acute. **whetstone** stone for sharpening cutting-tools.

**whether** /ˈweðə(r)/ *conj.* introducing dependent question etc. and expressing doubt or choice etc. between alternatives.

**whew** /hjuː/ *int.* expr. astonishment or consternation or relief.

**whey** *n.* watery liquid left after separation of curd from milk.

**which 1** *interrog. a.* asking for choice from definite set of alternatives. **2** *rel. a.* being the one just referred to, and this or these. **3** *interrog. pron.* which person(s) or thing(s)? **4** *rel. pron.* which person(s) or thing(s). **5 whichever** any which.

**whiff** *n.* puff of air or smoke or odour etc.; small cigar.

**Whig** *n. hist.* member of British political party succeeded by Liberals. **Whiggery** *n.*; **Whiggism** *n.*; **Whiggish** *a.*

**while 1** *n.* space of time, esp. time spent in doing something. **2** *rel. adv.* (with *time* etc.) during which. **3** *conj.* during the time that; for as long as; although; and at the same time, besides that. **4** *v.t.* pass (time etc.) *away* in leisurely manner or without wearisomeness. **5 for a while** for some time; **in a while** soon; **once in a while** occasionally.

**whilst** /waɪlst/ *adv. & conj.* while.

**whim** *n.* sudden fancy, caprice.

**whimper** /ˈwɪmpə(r)/ **1** *v.i.* cry querulously; whine softly. **2** *n.* feeble whining sound.

**whimsical** /ˈwɪmzɪk(ə)l/ *a.* capricious; fantastic. **whimsicality** *n.*

**whimsy** /ˈwɪmzɪ/ *n.* whim.

**whine 1** *n.* long-drawn complaining cry (as) of dog or child; querulous tone; feeble complaint. **2** *v.* utter whine(s); utter whiningly, complain.

**whinge** /wɪndʒ/ *Aus.* **1** *v.i.* complain, be querulous. **2** *n.* complaint.

**whinny** /ˈwɪnɪ/ **1** *n.* gentle or joyful neigh. **2** *v.i.* emit whinny.

**whip 1** *n.* stick with lash attached, for urging on or for flogging or beating; person appointed to maintain discipline of political party in House of Parliament; whip's written notice requesting member's attendance; in *pl. Aus. colloq.* an abundance; food made with whipped cream etc. **2** *v.* apply whip to; urge *on* thus; whip (eggs, cream, etc.) light and frothy by stirring or beating; move suddenly or briskly; snatch; make *up* quickly or hastily; *sl.* steal, excel, defeat; bind round closely with twine or thread etc.; sew with overcast stitches. **3 whip-bird** *Aus.* either of two birds with cry like crack of whip; **whipcord** tightly twisted cord; **whip hand** upper hand, control (of), advantage; **whiplash** lash of whip, similar sudden jerk; **whipping-boy** scapegoat, *hist.* boy educated with young prince and chastised in his stead; **whipping-top** top kept spinning by strokes of lash; **whip-round** appeal for contributions from group of people; **whipstock** handle of whip; **whiptail** *Aus.* light-coloured wallaby with slender tail, deep-sea fish.

**whipper-snapper** /ˈwɪpəsnæpə(r)/ *n.* young and insignificant but impertinent person.

**whippet** /ˈwɪpɪt/ *n.* small dog of greyhound type, used for racing.

**whippoorwill** /ˈwɪppʊəwɪl/ *n.* N. Amer. nightjar.

**whippy** /ˈwɪpɪ/ *a.* flexible, springy.

**whirl 1** *v.* swing round and round, revolve rapidly; send or travel swiftly in orbit or curve; convey or go rapidly in car etc.; be giddy, seem to spin round. **2** *n.* whirling movement; state of in-

## whirligig

tense activity or confusion. **3 whirlpool** circular eddy in sea or river etc.; **whirlwind** whirling mass or column of air moving over land or water.

**whirligig** /'wɜːlɪgɪg/ *n.* spinning or whirling toy; merry-go-round; revolving motion.

**whirr 1** *n.* continuous buzzing or softly clicking sound. **2** *v.i.* make this sound.

**whisk 1** *v.* brush or sweep lightly and rapidly from surface; beat esp. with whisk; convey or go or move with light rapid sweeping motion. **2** *n.* instrument for whipping eggs or cream etc.; bunch of twigs or bristles etc. for brushing or dusting; whisking movement.

**whisker** /'wɪskə(r)/ *n.* hair on cheeks or sides of face of adult man; projecting hair or bristle on upper lip or near mouth of cat etc.; *colloq.* small distance. **whiskery** *a.*

**whiskey** /'wɪskɪ/ *n.* Irish whisky.

**whisky** /'wɪskɪ/ *n.* spirit distilled esp. from malted barley.

**whisper** /'wɪspə(r)/ **1** *v.* use breath instead of vocal cords; talk or say in barely audible tone or confidential way; rustle, murmur. **2** *n.* whispering speech or sound; thing whispered.

**whist** *n.* card game, usu. for two pairs of opponents. **whist drive** whist-party with players moving on from table to table.

**whistle** /'wɪs(ə)l/ **1** *n.* clear shrill sound made by forcing breath through lips contracted to narrow opening; similar sound made by bird or wind or missile, or produced by pipe etc.; instrument used to produce it, e.g. as signal. **2** *v.* emit whistle; summon or give signal thus; produce or utter or call or send (*away, up,* etc.), by whistling. **3 whistle for** *colloq.* seek or expect in vain; **whistle-stop** *US* small unimportant town on railway, politician's brief pause for electioneering speech on tour.

**whit¹** *n.* smallest particle, least possible amount.

**Whit²** *a.* connected with or belonging to or following **Whit Sunday** 7th Sunday after Easter, commemorating Pentecost.

**white 1** *a.* of colour produced by reflection or transmission of all light; of colour of snow or milk; pale; **White** of the human racial group having light-coloured skin; *fig.* innocent, unstained. **2** *n.* white colour or paint or clothes etc.; (player using) lighter-coloured pieces in chess etc.; translucent or white part round yolk of egg; visible part of eyeball round iris; **White** White person. **3 white ant** termite; **whitebait** small silvery-white food-fish; **white bread** bread made from fine bolted flour; **white cell** leucocyte; **white Christmas** one with snow; **white coffee** coffee with milk or cream; **white-collar** (of worker) not engaged in manual labour; **white corpuscle** leucocyte; **white elephant** burdensome or useless possession; **white-eye** *Aus.* silver-eye; **white feather** symbol of cowardice; **white flag** plain white flag of truce or surrender; **white heat** degree of heat making metal etc. glow white, *fig.* state of intense anger or passion; **white hope** person expected to achieve much; **white horses** white-crested waves; **white-hot** at white heat; **white lead** lead carbonate as white pigment; **white lie** harmless or trivial untruth; **White Paper** Government report giving information; **white pepper** pepper made by grinding husked berry; **white sale** sale of household linen; **white sauce** sauce of flour and melted butter and milk etc.; **white slave** woman entrapped for prostitution; **white spirit** light petroleum as solvent; **white sugar** purified sugar; **white tie** man's white bow-tie worn with full evening dress; **whitewash** liquid composition of lime or whiting and water etc. for whitening walls etc., *fig.* glossing over of faults, (*v.*) apply whitewash (to), *fig.* gloss over, clear of blame etc.; **whitewood** light-coloured wood esp. prepared for staining etc. **4 whitish** *a.*

**whiten** /'waɪt(ə)n/ *v.* make or become white.

**whither** /'wɪðə(r)/ *arch.* **1** *interrog. adv.* to what place or state? **2** *rel. adv.* (with *place* etc.) to which. **3** *conj.* to the or any place to which; and thither.

**whiting¹** /'waɪtɪŋ/ *n.* edible sea-fish.

**whiting²** /'waɪtɪŋ/ *n.* chalk prepared for use in whitewashing or plate-cleaning.

**whitlow** /'wɪtləʊ/ *n.* small abscess esp. under or near nail.

# Whitsun

**Whitsun** /'wɪts(ə)n/ **1** *n.* weekend or week including Whit Sunday. **2** *a.* Whit². **3 Whitsuntide** Whitsun.

**whittle** /'wɪt(ə)l/ *v.* pare or shape wood by cutting thin slices or shavings from surface; reduce by repeated subtractions.

**whizz** (also **whiz**) **1** *n.* sound made by body moving through air at great speed. **2** *v.i.* move with or make a whiz. **3 whizz-kid** *colloq.* brilliant or highly successful young person.

**who** /hu:/ *pron.* (*obj.* **whom**, *poss.* **whose** /hu:z/) what or which person(s), what sort of person(s); (person or persons) that; and or but he or they etc. **whoever, whosoever,** whatever person(s), any (one) who, no matter who.

**WHO** *abbr.* World Health Organization.

**whoa** /wəʊ/ *int.* command to horse etc. to stop or stand still.

**whodunit** /hu:'dʌnɪt/ *n. colloq.* murder or detective story.

**whole** /həʊl/ **1** *a.* in uninjured or unbroken or intact or undiminished or undivided etc. state; all, all of. **2** *n.* full or complete or total amount (*of*); complete thing; organic unity, total made up of parts. **3 on the whole** all things considered, in general, for the most part; **whole foods** foods not artificially processed or refined; **wholehearted** given or done or acting etc. with all one's heart, sincere; **wholemeal** meal or flour or bread made from whole grain of wheat, not bolted.

**wholesale** /'həʊlseɪl/ **1** *n.* selling in large quantities, esp. for retail by others. **2** *a.* & *adv.* by wholesale; on a large scale. **3** *v.t.* sell wholesale.

**wholesome** /'həʊlsəm/ *a.* promoting physical or mental or moral health.

**wholly** /'həʊllɪ/ *adv.* entirely, without limitation, purely.

**whom** /hu:m/ *pron.*, obj. case of **who**. **whomsoever** obj. case of **whosoever**.

**whoop** /hu:p or wu:p/ **1** *n.* cry expressing excitement etc.; characteristic drawing-in of breath after cough in whooping-cough. **2** *v.i.* utter whoop. **3 whooping-cough** /'hu:pɪŋ/ infectious disease esp. of children, with violent convulsive cough.

**whoopee** /'wʊpi:/ *int.* expr. wild joy or excitement etc. **make whoopee** *colloq.* rejoice noisily or hilariously.

**whoops** /wʊps/ *int. colloq.* apology for obvious mistake.

**whop** *v.t. sl.* thrash, defeat.

**whopper** /'wɒpə(r)/ *n. sl.* big specimen; great lie.

**whopping** /'wɒpɪŋ/ *a. sl.* very big.

**whore** /hɔː(r)/ *n.* prostitute; sexually immoral woman. **whore-house** brothel.

**whorl** /wɜːl/ *n.* ring of leaves round stem; one turn of spiral; circle formed by ridges in finger-print.

**whortleberry** /'wɜːtəlberɪ/ *n.* bilberry.

**whose** /hu:z/ *pron.* poss. case of **who** and occas. of **which**.

**why** /waɪ/ **1** *interrog. adv.* on what ground?; for what reason or purpose? **2** *rel. adv.* on account of which. **3** *int.* expressing esp. mild or slight surprise or slight protest etc. **4** *n.* reason, explanation.

**WI** *abbr.* West Indies; Women's Institute.

**wick** *n.* strip or thread feeding flame with fuel.

**wicked** /'wɪkɪd/ *a.* sinful, vicious, morally depraved; *colloq.* very bad, malicious, mischievous.

**wicker** /'wɪkə(r)/ *n.* plaited osiers etc. as material of baskets or chairs etc. **wickerwork** wicker, things made of wicker.

**wicket** /'wɪkɪt/ *n.* small gate or door, esp. beside or in larger one; *Crick.* set of 3 upright stumps with bails in position defended by batsman, ground between the two wickets, state of this, batsman's avoidance of being out. **wicket-keeper** fielder stationed close behind batsman's wicket.

# wide

**wide 1** *a.* having sides far apart, broad, not narrow; extending far, not restricted; open to full extent; far from, or not within reasonable distance of, point or mark; (appended to measurement) in width. **2** *adv.* at or to many points; with wide interval or opening; so as to miss mark or way. **3** *n.* wide ball. **4 far and wide** over or through large space or region; **wide awake** fully awake, *colloq.* fully aware of what is going on, alert; **wide ball** *Crick.* ball judged by umpire to be beyond batsman's reach;

**wide-eyed** surprised, naïve; **widespread** widely distributed.

**widen** /'waɪd(ə)n/ v. make or become wide or wider.

**widgeon** /'wɪdʒ(ə)n/ n. kind of wild duck.

**widow** /'wɪdəʊ/ 1 n. woman who has lost her husband by death and not married again. 2 v.t. make into widow or widower.

**widower** /'wɪdəʊə(r)/ n. man who has lost his wife by death and not married again.

**widowhood** /'wɪdəʊhʊd/ n. being a widow or widower.

**width** n. measurement from side to side; piece of material of full width; large extent. **widthways** adv.

**wield** /wi:ld/ v.t. hold and use, control, manage.

**wife** n. (pl. **wives**) married woman esp. in relation to her husband.

**wifely** /'waɪflɪ/ a. befitting a wife.

**wig**[1] n. artificial head of hair.

**wig**[2] v.t. colloq. rebuke sharply.

**wiggle** /'wɪg(ə)l/ colloq. 1 v. (cause to) move from side to side. 2 n. wiggling movement.

**wight** /waɪt/ n. arch. person.

**wigwam** /'wɪgwɒm/ n. N. Amer. Indian's hut or tent.

**wilco** /'wɪlkəʊ/ int. expr. compliance or agreement.

**wild** /waɪld/ 1 a. in original natural state; not domesticated or tamed or cultivated; uncivilized; tempestuous; lawless; out of control; violently excited or agitated; passionately desirous (to do); elated, enthusiastic; rash, ill-aimed, random. 2 adv. in wild manner. 3 n. wild or waste place, desert. 4 **run wild** grow or stray unchecked or undisciplined; **wildcat** fig. hot-tempered or violent person, (a.) reckless, financially unsound, (of strike) unofficial; **wildfire** highly inflammable composition used in warfare etc. (**like wildfire** with extraordinary speed); **wild-goose chase** foolish or hopeless quest; **wildlife** wild animals collectively; **wild oat** tall grass resembling oats (**sow one's wild oats** indulge in youthful follies before becoming steady); **Wild West** western US in time of lawlessness.

**wildebeest** /'wɪldəbi:st/ n. gnu.

**wilderness** /'wɪldənəs/ n. desert, uncultivated and uninhabited land or tract; confused mixture of. **in the wilderness** (of political party) out of office, (of person) in exile or disgrace, out of favour.

**wile** 1 n. trick, cunning procedure. 2 v.t. lure away, into, etc.

**wilful** /'wɪlfəl/ a. deliberate, intentional; obstinately self-willed; wayward.

**will** 1 v.aux. (pres. **will**, past **would** /wʊd/) expr. future or conditional statement or order or question. 2 v.t. desire or choose to or consent or be persuaded or have constant tendency to be accustomed or likely to; (with regular inflexional forms) intend unconditionally, impel by will-power, bequeath by will. 3 n. faculty by which one decides what to do; will-power; fixed desire or intention; arbitrary discretion; disposition towards others; usu. written directions in legal form for disposition of one's property after death. 4 **against one's will** under compulsion; **at will** whenever one wishes; **will-power** control by deliberate purpose over impulse; **with a will** vigorously.

**willing** /'wɪlɪŋ/ 1 n. cheerful intention. 2 a. ready to consent or undertake; given etc. by willing person.

**will-o'-the-wisp** /wɪləðə'wɪsp/ n. phosphorescent light seen on marshy ground; elusive or delusive thing or person.

**willow** /'wɪləʊ/ n. waterside tree or shrub with pliant branches; **willow-pattern** conventional Chinese design of blue on white china etc.

**willowy** /'wɪləʊɪ/ a. having willows; lithe and slender.

**willy-nilly** /wɪlɪ'nɪlɪ/ adv. whether one likes it or not.

**willy wagtail** Aus. black and white fantail.

**willy-willy** /'wɪlɪwɪlɪ/ n. Aus. upward-spiralling dust-storm; whirlwind.

**wilt** 1 v. (cause to) fade, droop, become limp. 2 n. plant-disease causing wilting.

**wily** /'waɪlɪ/ a. crafty, cunning.

**wimple** /'wɪmp(ə)l/ n. head-dress covering neck and sides of face, worn by nuns etc.

**win** v. (past & p.p. **won** /wʌn/) get or gain as result of fight or contest or bet

## wince

etc.; be victorious in (game, battle, race, etc.), gain victory; make one's way *to* or *through* etc. **2** *n.* victory in game or contest. **3 win the day** be victorious in battle.

**wince** **1** *n.* start or involuntary shrinking movement of pain etc. **2** *v.i.* give wince.

**winceyette** /wɪnsɪˈet/ *n.* kind of lightweight napped flannelette used for night-clothes etc.

**winch** **1** *n.* crank of wheel or axle; windlass. **2** *v.t.* lift with winch.

**wind**[1] /wɪnd/ **1** *n.* air in natural motion; smell carried by this as indicating presence; artificially-produced air-current esp. for sounding a wind instrument, air (to be) so used; wind instruments in orchestra etc.; breath as needed in exertion or speech, power of breathing without difficulty; point below centre of chest where blow temporarily paralyses breathing; gas generated in bowels; empty talk. **2** *v.* exhaust wind of by exertion or blow; make breath quick and deep by exercise; detect presence of by scent. **3 get wind of** begin to suspect; **get, have, the wind up** *sl.* become, be, frightened; **in the wind** *fig.* about to happen; **put the wind up** *sl.* frighten; **take the wind out of person's sails** frustrate him by anticipation; **windbag** wordy orator; **windbreak** thing, esp. row of trees etc., used to break force of wind; **wind-cheater** windproof jacket; **windfall** fruit blown down by wind, piece of unexpected good fortune, esp. receipt of money; **wind instrument** musical instrument in which sound is produced by current of air; **wind-jammer** merchant sailing-ship; **windmill** mill worked by action of wind on sails; **wind-pipe** air-passage between throat and lungs; **windscreen** screen of glass in front of driver of car etc.; **wind-sock** canvas cylinder or cone on mast to show direction of wind; **wind-swept** exposed to high winds; **wind-tunnel** enclosed chamber for testing (models or parts of) aircraft in winds of known velocities.

**wind**[2] /waɪnd/ **1** *v.* (*past* & *p.p.* **wound** /waʊnd/) go in spiral or crooked or curved course; make one's way thus;

## wing

coil, wrap closely around something or upon itself, enclose or encircle thus; tighten *up* coiled spring of (clock etc.). **2** *n.* bend or turn in course. **3 wind down** unwind, lower by winding; **winding-sheet** linen in which corpse is wrapped for burial; **wind up** coil whole of, tighten coiling or coiled spring of or *fig.* tension or intensity of, bring to a conclusion, end, arrange affairs of and dissolve (company), *colloq.* arrive finally.

**windlass** /ˈwɪndləs/ *n.* mechanical device with horizontal axle for hauling or hoisting.

**window** /ˈwɪndəʊ/ *n.* opening, usu. with glass, in wall etc. to admit light and air; the glass itself; space behind window of shop for display of goods etc.; opening resembling window in shape or function. **window-box** box placed outside window for cultivating plants; **window-dressing** art of arranging display in shop-window etc., adroit presentation of facts etc. to give falsely favourable impression; **window-seat** seat below window; **window-shopping** looking at displays in shop-windows without buying anything.

**windsurfing** /ˈwɪndsɜːfɪŋ/ *n.* sport of riding on board similar to surf-board with sail.

**windward** /ˈwɪndwəd/ **1** *a.* & *adv.* in the direction from which wind is blowing. **2** *n.* this direction.

**windy** /ˈwɪndɪ/ *a.* exposed to or stormy with wind; generating or characterized by flatulence; wordy; *sl.* frightened, apprehensive.

**wine** **1** *n.* fermented grape-juice as alcoholic drink; fermented drink resembling it made from other fruits etc.; colour of red wine. **2** *v.* drink wine, entertain to wine. **3 wine-bibber** tippler; **wine-cellar** cellar used for storing wine, its contents; **wineglass** small glass for wine, usu. with stem and foot; **winepress** press in which grape-juice is extracted for wine.

**wing** **1** *n.* one of the limbs or organs by which flying is effected; winglike supporting part of aircraft; projecting part of building or organ or structure or battle array; in *pl.* sides of theatre

**winger** /'wɪŋə(r)/ n. Footb. etc. wing player; Footb. etc. player at either end of line, side part of playing-area; extreme section of political party; mudguard of motor vehicle; air-force unit of several squadrons. 2 v. traverse or travel on wings; equip with wings, enable to fly; send in flight; wound in wing or arm. 3 **on the wing** flying; **take wing** fly away; **take under one's wing** treat as protégé; **wing-case** horny covering of insect's wing; **wing-chair** chair with projecting side-pieces at top of high back; **wing-collar** man's high stiff collar with turned-down corners; **wing commander** officer of air force next below group captain; **wing-nut** nut with projections to turn it by; **wing-span, -spread**, measurement right across wings.

**winger** /'wɪŋə(r)/ n. Footb. etc. wing player.

**wink** 1 v. blink; close eye(s) for a moment; close one eye momentarily; (cause to) flicker like eyelid, twinkle; convey signal or hint etc. by winking or flashing lights etc. 2 n. act of winking; short sleep (**not a wink** no sleep at all). **wink at** purposely avoid seeing, pretend not to notice.

**winkle** /'wɪŋk(ə)l/ 1 n. edible sea snail. 2 v.t. (with *out*) extract, prise out. 3 **winkle-picker** sl. long pointed shoe.

**winning** /'wɪnɪŋ/ 1 a. bringing victory; attractive. 2 n. in pl. money won. 3 **winning-post** post marking end of race.

**winnow** /'wɪnəʊ/ v.t. blow (grain) free of chaff etc.; blow (chaff etc.) *away* or *from*; sift, separate (*out*) from worthless or inferior elements.

**winsome** /'wɪnsəm/ a. winning, engaging; twee.

**winter** /'wɪntə(r)/ 1 n. coldest season of year. 2 a. characteristic of or fit for winter. 3 v. spend the winter *at* or *in* etc. 4 **winter garden** garden of plants flourishing in winter; **winter-green** kind of plant remaining green all winter; **winter sports** skiing, skating, and other open-air sports practised on snow or ice.

**wintry** /'wɪntrɪ/ a. characteristic of winter; lacking warmth.

**winy** /'waɪnɪ/ a. wine-flavoured.

**wipe** 1 v. clean or dry surface of by rubbing with something soft; get rid of (tears), or clean (vessel) *out* or make clean etc. by wiping. 2 n. act of wiping. 3 **wipe out** avenge (insult etc.), utterly destroy or defeat.

**wiper** /'waɪpə(r)/ n. device for keeping windscreen clear of rain etc.

**wire** 1 n. metal drawn out into slender flexible rod or thread; piece of this; length or line of this used for fencing or as conductor of electric current etc.; colloq. telegram. 2 v. provide or support or stiffen or secure with wires; colloq. telegraph. 3 **get one's wires crossed** fig. become confused; **wire-haired** (of dog) having rough hard wiry coat; **wire netting** netting made of wire twisted into meshes; **wire-tapping** tapping of telephone wires; **wire wool** mass of fine wire for cleaning; **wire-worm** destructive larva of a kind of beetle.

**wireless** /'waɪələs/ n. radio, radio receiving set.

**wiring** /'waɪərɪŋ/ n. electrical circuits in a building.

**wiry** /'waɪərɪ/ a. tough and flexible as wire; sinewy; untiring.

**wisdom** /'wɪzdəm/ n. being wise; soundness of judgement in matters relating to life and conduct; knowledge, experience, learning. **wisdom tooth** hindmost molar tooth on each side of upper and lower jaws, usu. cut at age of about 20.

**wise**[1] /waɪz/ a. having or showing or dictated by wisdom; having knowledge; suggestive of wisdom; sl. alert, crafty. **wisecrack** colloq. smart remark, witticism; **wise man** wizard, esp. one of the Magi; **wise to** sl. aware or informed of.

**wise**[2] /waɪz/ n. arch. way, manner, degree.

**wiseacre** /'waɪzeɪkə(r)/ n. person who affects to be wise.

**wish** 1 v. have or express desire or aspiration *for*; want or want (person) *to* do; request; desire esp. something good for (person etc.). 2 n. desire or request, expression of this; thing desired. 3 **wishbone** forked bone between neck and breast of cooked bird; **wish-fulfilment** tendency of esp. unconscious wishes to be satisfied in fantasy.

**wishful** /'wɪʃfəl/ a. desiring (*to* do). **wishful thinking** belief founded on wishes rather than facts.

**wishy-washy** /ˈwɪʃiwɒʃi/ a. feeble or poor in quality or character.

**wisp** n. small bundle or twist of straw etc.; small separate quantity *of* smoke or hair etc. **wispy** a.

**wistaria** /wɪˈstɛəriə/ n. (also **wisteria**) climbing shrub with blue or purple or white hanging flowers.

**wistful** /ˈwɪstfəl/ a. yearningly or mournfully expectant or wishful.

**wit** n. intelligence, understanding; in *sing.* imaginative and inventive faculty; amusing ingenuity of speech or ideas; person noted for this. **at one's wits' end** utterly at a loss or in despair; **have one's wits about one** be mentally alert; **out of one's wits** mad, distracted; **to wit** that is to say, namely.

**witch** n. woman supposed to have dealings with devil or evil spirits; old hag; fascinating or bewitching woman. **witchcraft** use of magic, sorcery; **witch-doctor** sorcerer of primitive people; **witch-hunt** searching out and persecution of supposed witches or persons suspected of unpopular or unorthodox political etc. views.

**witchery** /ˈwɪtʃəri/ n. witchcraft; fascination exercised by beauty or eloquence or the like.

**witchetty grub** /ˈwɪtʃəti/ *Aus.* edible larva of various moths and beetles.

**with** /wɪð/ *prep.* expr. instrumentality or means, cause, possession, circumstances, manner, material, agreement and disagreement, company and parting of company, and antagonism. **with it** *colloq.* up to date, (capable of) understanding new ideas etc.; **with that** thereupon.

**withal** /wɪˈðɔːl/ *adv. arch.* moreover; as well.

**withdraw** /wɪðˈdrɔː/ v. (*past* -**drew**; *p.p.* -**drawn**) pull aside or back; take away, remove; cancel (statement, promise, etc.); retire or go apart; in *p.p.* unsociable. **withdrawal** n.

**withe** /wɪð/ n. tough flexible branch or shoot, esp. of willow.

**wither** /ˈwɪðə(r)/ v. make or become dry or shrivelled; deprive of or lose vigour or freshness etc.; blight with scorn etc.

**withers** *n.pl.* ridge between shoulder-blades of horse etc.

**withhold** /wɪðˈhəʊld/ v.t. (*past* & *p.p.* -**held**) refuse to give or grant or allow; hold back, restrain.

**within** /wɪˈðɪn/ 1 *adv.* inside; indoors. 2 *prep.* inside; not out of or beyond; not transgressing or exceeding; not further off than.

**without** /wɪˈðaʊt/ 1 *prep.* not having or feeling or showing; in want of; free from; in absence of; *arch.* outside. 2 *adv. arch.* outside, out-of-doors.

**withstand** /wɪðˈstænd/ v.t. (*past* & *p.p.* -**stood** /-stʊd/) hold out against, oppose.

**withy** /ˈwɪði/ n. withe.

**witless** /ˈwɪtləs/ a. foolish; crazy.

**witness** /ˈwɪtnəs/ 1 n. person giving sworn testimony; person attesting another's signature to document; person present, spectator; testimony, evidence, confirmation; person or thing whose existence or position etc. is testimony *to* or proof *of*. 2 v. sign (document) as witness; see, be spectator of; serve as evidence or indication of; bear witness. 3 **bear witness (to)** give or be evidence (of), be confirmation (of); **witness-box** (*US* -**stand**) enclosed space in lawcourt from which witness gives evidence.

**witticism** /ˈwɪtɪsɪz(ə)m/ n. witty remark.

**wittingly** /ˈwɪtɪŋli/ *adv.* knowingly, intentionally.

**witty** /ˈwɪti/ a. showing verbal wit.

**wives** *pl.* of **wife**.

**wizard** /ˈwɪzəd/ 1 n. person of extraordinary powers; magician, conjuror. 2 a. *colloq.* wonderful. 3 **wizardry** n.

**wizened** /ˈwɪz(ə)nd/ a. of shrivelled or dried-up appearance.

**WO** *abbr.* Warrant Officer.

**woad** n. plant yielding a blue dye; the dye.

**wobbegong** /ˈwɒbɪgɒŋ/ n. *Aus.* any of various sharks with richly-patterned brown and white skin.

**wobble** /ˈwɒb(ə)l/ 1 *v.i.* move unsteadily or uncertainly from side to side or backwards and forwards; rock, quiver, shake; hesitate, waver. 2 n. wobbling motion. 3 **wobbly** a.

**woe** n. affliction, bitter grief; in *pl.* calamities, troubles. **woebegone** dismal-looking.

**woeful** /ˈwəʊfəl/ a. feeling affliction; afflicting; very bad.

**wok** *n.* bowl-shaped frying-pan used esp. in Chinese cookery.

**woke, woken,** *past* & *p.p.* of **wake**[1].

**wold** /wəʊld/ *n. UK* high open uncultivated or moorland tract.

**wolf** /wʊlf/ **1** *n.* (*pl.* **wolves**) wild animal related to dog; *sl.* man who pursues women. **2** *v.t.* devour greedily. **3 cry wolf** raise false alarm; **keep the wolf from the door** avert starvation; **wolfhound** dog of kind used orig. to hunt wolves; **wolfsbane** aconite; **wolfwhistle** whistle expressing man's admiration of woman's appearance.

**wolfram** /'wʊlfrəm/ *n.* tungsten; tungsten ore.

**wolverine** /'wʊlvəri:n/ *n.* N. Amer. animal of weasel family.

**woman** /'wʊmən/ *n.* (*pl.* **women** /wɪmən/) adult human female; the female sex; *attrib.* female.

**womanhood** /'wʊmənhʊd/ *n.* state of being a woman; womanliness; womankind.

**womanish** /'wʊmənɪʃ/ *a.* effeminate, unmanly.

**womanize** /'wʊmənaɪz/ *v.i.* (of man) be promiscuous.

**womankind** /'wʊmənkaɪnd/ *n.* women in general.

**womanly** /'wʊmənlɪ/ *a.* having or showing qualities befitting a woman.

**womb** /wu:m/ *n.* organ in female mammals in which child or young is conceived and nourished till birth; place where anything is generated or produced.

**wombat** /'wɒmbæt/ *n.* burrowing herbivorous Aus. marsupial.

**women** /'wɪmən/ *pl.* of **woman**. **Women's Lib, Liberation,** movement for release of women from subservient status; **women's rights** position of legal and social equality with men.

**womenfolk** /'wɪmənfəʊk/ *n.* women in general; women in family.

**won** *past* & *p.p.* of **win**.

**wonder** /'wʌndə(r)/ **1** *n.* strange or remarkable thing or specimen or event etc.; emotion excited by what is unexpected or unfamiliar or inexplicable. **2** *v.* marvel, be affected with wonder; feel doubt or curiosity, be desirous to know or learn. **3 no wonder** this event is quite natural; **wonderland** fairyland, place of surprises or marvels.

**wonderful** /'wʌndəfəl/ *a.* very remarkable or admirable.

**wonderment** /'wʌndəmənt/ *n.* surprise.

**wondrous** /'wʌndrəs/ *poet.* **1** *a.* wonderful. **2** *adv.* wonderfully.

**wonga-wonga**[1] /'wɒŋgəwɒŋgə/ *n.* large Aus. pigeon with white or grey breast and brown wings.

**wonga-wonga**[2] /'wɒŋgəwɒŋgə/ *n. Aus.* (also **wonga-vine**) an evergreen climbing plant.

**wonky** /'wɒŋkɪ/ *a. sl.* shaky, unsteady; unreliable.

**wont** /wəʊnt/ *arch.* **1** *a.* accustomed, used (*to do*). **2** *n.* custom; habit.

**won't** /wəʊnt/ will not.

**wonted** /'wəʊntɪd/ *a.* habitual, usual.

**woo** *v.* court, seek love of; seek to win, invite.

**wood** /wʊd/ *n.* hard compact fibrous substance of tree, whether growing or cut for timber or fuel; growing trees occupying piece of ground; wooden cask used for storing wine etc.; bowl in game of bowls, wooden-headed golf-club. **out of the wood** clear of danger or difficulty etc.; **woodbine** honeysuckle; **wood chip** industrially useful finely chopped wood; **woodchuck** N. Amer. marmot; **woodcock** game-bird related to snipe; **woodcut** design cut in relief on wood block, print made from this; **woodland** wooded country; **wood-louse** small land crustacean with many legs; **woodman** forester; **woodpecker** kind of bird pecking holes in tree-trunks etc. to find insects etc.; **wood-pigeon** ring-dove; **woodpulp** wood-fibre prepared as material for paper etc.; **woodwind** wind instruments of orchestra made (orig.) of wood; **woodwork** work done in wood, wooden part (*of*), esp. wooden interior parts of building; **woodworm** beetle larva that bores in wood.

**wooded** /'wʊdɪd/ *a.* having woods.

**wooden** /'wʊd(ə)n/ *a.* made of wood; like wood; stiff or clumsy.

**woody** /'wʊdɪ/ *a.* wooded; of or like wood.

**woof**[1] /wʊf/ **1** *n.* gruff bark of dog. **2** *v.i.* give woof.

**woof**[2] /wu:f/ *n. arch.* weft.

**woofer** /'wʊfə(r)/ *n.* loudspeaker for low frequencies.

**wool** /wʊl/ n. fine soft wavy hair forming fleece of sheep etc.; woollen yarn or cloth or garments; wool-like substance. **wool-classer** person who grades shorn wool; **wool-clip** annual yield of wool; **woolgathering** absentmindedness; **Woolsack** Lord Chancellor's seat in House of Lords; **woolshed** shearing and wool-packing shed.

**woollen** /'wʊlən/ **1** a. made (partly) of wool. **2** n. woollen fabric; in pl. woollen garments.

**woolly** /'wʊli/ **1** a. bearing or like wool; indistinct; confused. **2** n. colloq. woollen (esp. knitted) garment.

**woomera** /'wʊmərə/ n. Aus. Abor. throwing-stick used to launch dart or spear; short club used as missile.

**woop-woop** /'wʊpwʊp/ n. Aus. sl. remote outback district or settlement.

**word** /wɜːd/ **1** n. meaningful element of speech usu. shown with space on either side of it when written or printed; speech as opp. action; one's promise or assurance; in sing. or pl. thing said, remark, conversation; in pl. text of song or actor's part; in pl. angry talk; news, message; command, password, motto; unit of expression in computer. **2** v.t put into words, select words to express. **3 word-blindness** dyslexia; **word for word** in exactly the same words, literally; **the Word of God** the Bible; **word of honour** assurance given on one's honour; **word of mouth** speech (only); **word-perfect** having memorized one's part etc. perfectly; **word-processor** computer programmed for storing text entered from keyboard, incorporating corrections, and producing printout.

**wording** /'wɜːdɪŋ/ n. form of words used, phrasing.

**wordy** /'wɜːdi/ a. using (too) many words; consisting of words.

**wore** past of **wear**.

**work** /wɜːk/ **1** n. application of effort to a purpose, use of energy; task to be undertaken, materials to be used in task; thing done or made by work, result of action; employment esp. as means of earning money; literary or musical composition; in pl. all such pieces by an author or composer etc.; doings or experiences of specified kind; things made of specified material or with specified tools etc.; in pl. operative part of clock etc.; sl. in pl. all that is available; in pl. operations of building or repair; in pl. (often treated as sing.) place of manufacture; (usu. in pl.) defensive structure. **2** v. make efforts, engage in work; be in action, do appointed work; be craftsman in material; operate or function, esp. effectively; carry on, manage, control; put or keep in operation or at work; cause to toil; produce as result; knead, hammer, bring to desired shape or consistency; do or make by needlework etc.; (cause to) make way or make (way) slowly or with difficulty; gradually become by motion; excite artificially into mood etc.; solve (sum) by mathematics; purchase with labour instead of money; be in motion or agitated, ferment; have influence (on, upon). **3 workaday** ordinary, everyday, practical; **workbasket** basket etc. for holding sewing materials; **workday** day on which work is usu. done. **work-force** workers engaged or available, number of these; **workhouse** hist. public institution for maintenance of paupers; **work in** find place for in composition or structure; **work-load** amount of work to be done; **workman** man hired to do manual labour, craftsman, person who works in specified manner; **workmanlike** showing practised skill; **workmanship** degree of skill in workman or of finish in his product; **workmate** person engaged in same work as another; **work off** get rid of by work or activity; **work out** solve (sum) or find (amount) by calculation, be calculated at, have result, provide for all details of; **work-out** practice or test or performance of exercises; **work over** examine thoroughly, colloq. treat with violence; **workpeople** persons engaged in labour for wages; **workshop** room or building in which manufacture is carried on, place for concerted activity, such activity; **work-shy** disinclined for work, lazy; **work to rule** follow rules of one's occupation with pedantic precision to reduce efficiency as form of protest; **work up** bring gradually to efficient state, advance gradually to, elaborate or excite by degrees, learn (subject) by study.

**workable** /'wɜːkəb(ə)l/ a. that can be

worked or will work or is worth working. **workability** *n*.

**worker** /'wɜːkə(r)/ *n*. manual or industrial etc. employee; neuter bee or ant.

**working** /'wɜːkɪŋ/ 1 *a*. engaged in work, esp. in manual or industrial work; functioning, able to function. 2 *n*. activity of work; functioning; mine or quarry. 3 **working capital** capital used in conduct of business, not invested in buildings etc.; **working class** class of those employed for wages, esp. in manual or industrial work; **working day** workday, part of day devoted to work; **working knowledge** knowledge adequate to work with; **working order** condition in which machine works; **working party** committee appointed to advise on some question.

**world** /wɜːld/ *n*. the earth or a heavenly body like it; the universe, all that exists; time or state or scene of human existence; secular interests and affairs; human affairs, active life; average or respectable people or their customs or opinions; all that concerns or all who belong to specified class or sphere of activity; vast amount *of*. **out of this world** *colloq*. incredibly good etc.; **think the world of** have the highest possible regard for; **world-famous** known throughout the world; **world war** one involving many important nations; **world-wide** covering or known in all parts of the world.

**worldly** /'wɜːldlɪ/ *a*. temporal, earthly; engrossed in temporal affairs, esp. pursuit of wealth and pleasure. **worldly-wise** prudent as regards one's own interests.

**worm** /wɜːm/ 1 *n*. any of several types of creeping invertebrate animal with long slender body and no limbs; larva of insect; in *pl*. internal parasites; abject or contemptible person; spiral of screw. 2 *v*. move with crawling or wriggling motion; insinuate *oneself* into favour etc.; draw *out* (secret etc.) by craft. 3 **worm-cast** convoluted mass of earth voided by earthworm and left on surface of ground; **worm-eaten** full of holes made by burrowing insect larva.

**wormwood** /'wɜːmwʊd/ *n*. woody herb with bitter aromatic taste; bitter humiliation; source of this.

**wormy** /'wɜːmɪ/ *a*. full of worms; worm-eaten.

**worn** 1 *p.p.* of **wear**. 2 *a*. impaired by use or exposure or wear; looking tired and exhausted.

**worry** /'wʌrɪ/ 1 *v*. make or be anxious and ill at ease; harass, importune; be trouble or anxiety to; shake or pull about with teeth, kill or injure thus. 2 *n*. thing that causes anxiety or disturbs tranquillity; disturbed state of mind, anxiety. 3 **worry beads** string of beads manipulated with fingers to occupy or calm oneself.

**worse** /wɜːs/ 1 *a*. (*compar*. of **bad**) more bad; in or into worse health; in worse condition. 2 *adv*. (*compar*. of **badly**) more badly or ill. 3 *n*. worse thing(s).

**worsen** /'wɜːs(ə)n/ *v*. make or become worse.

**worship** /'wɜːʃɪp/ 1 *n*. homage or service paid to deity; acts or rites or ceremonies displaying this; adoration, devotion. 2 *v*. adore as divine; honour with religious rites; idolize; attend public worship. 3 **your, his, Worship** title of respect for magistrate or mayor etc.

**worshipful** /'wɜːʃɪpfəl/ *a*. honourable or distinguished (esp. in old titles of companies or officers).

**worst** /wɜːst/ 1 *a*. (*superl*. of **bad**) most bad. 2 *adv*. (*superl*. of **badly**) in worst manner; to worst degree. 3 *n*. that which is worst. 4 *v.t*. get the better of, defeat. 5 **at (the) worst** in the worst possible case; **do one's worst** do the utmost harm possible; **get the worst of** be defeated in; **if the worst comes to the worst** if things fall out as badly as possible or conceivable.

**worsted** /'wʊstəd/ *n*. fine woollen yarn; fabric made from this.

**wort** /wɜːt/ *n*. infusion of malt or other grain before it is fermented into beer.

**worth** /wɜːθ/ 1 *a*. of value of (specified amount, sum, etc.), equivalent to or good return for; deserving or worthy of; possessed of. 2 *n*. value; equivalent (*of*). 3 **worth it** *colloq*. worth while; **worth (one's) while** worth the time or effort spent; **worthwhile** that is worth while.

**worthless** /'wɜːθləs/ *a*. without value or merit.

**worthy** /'wɜːðɪ/ 1 *a*. estimable, deserving respect; deserving *of*; of sufficient

**worth** or desert or merit etc. (*to do*). 2 *n.* worthy person; person of some distinction in his country or time etc.

**would**: see **will**. **would-be** vainly aspiring to be.

**wound**[1] /wu:nd/ 1 *n.* injury done by cut or blow to living tissues; injury to reputation, pain inflicted on feelings. 2 *v.* inflict wound (on).

**wound**[2] *past* & *p.p.* of **wind**[2].

**wove, woven**, *past* & *p.p.* of **weave**[1].

**wow** /waʊ/ 1 *int.* expr. astonishment or admiration. 2 *n. sl.* sensational success. 3 *v.t. sl.* have immense success with.

**wowser** /'waʊzə(r)/ *n. Aus.* fanatical puritan; killjoy; teetotaller.

**w.p.b.** *abbr.* waste-paper basket.

**w.p.m.** *abbr.* words per minute.

**WRAAC** *abbr.* Women's Royal Australian Army Corps.

**WRAAF** *abbr.* Women's Royal Australian Air Force.

**WRAC** *abbr.* Women's Royal Army Corps.

**wrack** *n.* seaweed cast up or growing on seashore.

**WRAF** *abbr.* Women's Royal Air Force.

**wraith** /reɪθ/ *n.* ghost; spectral appearance of living person supposed to portend his death.

**wrangle** /'ræŋg(ə)l/ 1 *n.* noisy argument or dispute. 2 *v.i.* engage in wrangle.

**WRANS** *abbr.* Women's Royal Australian Naval Service.

**wrap** 1 *v.* envelop in folded or soft encircling material; arrange or draw (pliant covering) *round* or *about* etc. 2 *n.* shawl or scarf or other such addition to clothing. 3 **under wraps** *fig.* in secrecy; **wrap up** finish off (matter), protect oneself from cold with wraps, in *p.p.* engrossed or absorbed *in*.

**wrapper** /'ræpə(r)/ *n.* paper cover for sweet or book or posted newspaper etc.; loose enveloping robe or gown.

**wrapping** /'ræpɪŋ/ *n.* (esp. in *pl.*) wraps, wrappers, enveloping garments. **wrapping paper** strong or decorative paper for wrapping parcels.

**wrasse** /ræs/ *n.* brilliant-coloured edible sea-fish.

**wrath** /rɒθ/ *n.* anger, indignation. **wrathful** *a.*

**wreak** *v.t.* give play to (vengeance etc.) (*up*)*on*; cause (damage etc.).

**wreath** /ri:θ/ *n.* (*pl. pr.* /ri:ðz/) flowers or leaves wound together into ring esp. as ornament for head or building or for laying on grave etc.; curl or ring *of* smoke or cloud etc.

**wreathe** /ri:ð/ *v.* encircle as or (as) with wreath; wind (flexible object) round or over something; move in wreathlike shape.

**wreck** 1 *n.* destruction or disablement, esp. of ship; ship that has suffered wreck; greatly damaged or disabled building or thing or person. 2 *v.* cause wreck of (ship, hopes, etc.); suffer wreck; in *p.p.* involved in wreck.

**wreckage** /'rekɪdʒ/ *n.* wrecked material; remnants of wreck.

**wrecker** /'rekə(r)/ *n.* person who demolishes old buildings to clear sites or dismantles old cars for parts.

**wren**[1] *n.* small short-winged usu. brown song-bird.

**Wren**[2] *n.* member of WRNS.

**wrench** 1 *n.* violent twist or pull or turn; tool for gripping and turning nuts etc.; *fig.* pain caused by parting etc. 2 *v.t.* twist, turn; pull (*away, off,* etc.) violently or with effort; injure or pain by straining or stretching.

**wrest** *v.t.* twist, distort, pervert; force or wrench away *from* person's grasp.

**wrestle** /'res(ə)l/ 1 *n.* contest in which two opponents grapple and try to throw each other to ground; tussle, hard struggle. 2 *v.* have wrestling-match (*with*); struggle *with* or *against*; do one's utmost to deal *with*.

**wretched** /'retʃəd/ *a.* unhappy or miserable; of bad quality or no merit; contemptible, unsatisfactory or displeasing.

**wriggle** /'rɪg(ə)l/ 1 *v.* twist or turn body about with short writhing movements; move or make way etc. with wriggling motion; be slippery, practise evasion. 2 *n.* wriggling movement.

**wring** 1 *v.t.* (*past* & *p.p.* **wrung**), press, squeeze or twist, esp. so as to drain or make dry; distress, rack; extort, get (money, concession) *out of* or *from* by exaction or importunity; clasp (person's *hand*) forcibly or with emotion. 2 *n.* act of wringing. 3 **wringing wet** so wet that water can be wrung out; **wring**

**wringer** /ˈrɪŋə(r)/ n. device for wringing water from washed clothes etc.

**wrinkle** /ˈrɪŋk(ə)l/ 1 n. crease or furrow of skin or other flexible surface; *colloq.* useful hint, clever expedient. 2 v. make wrinkles in; form wrinkles. 3 **wrinkly** a.

**wrist** n. joint connecting hand and forearm; part of garment covering wrist. **wrist-watch** small watch worn on strap etc. round wrist.

**wristlet** /ˈrɪstlət/ n. band or ring worn on wrist to strengthen it or as ornament or to hold watch etc.

**writ** n. formal written court order to do or refrain from doing specified act.

**write** v. (*past* **wrote**; *p.p.* **written**) mark paper or other surface with symbols, letters, or words; form or mark (such symbols etc.); form or mark symbols of (word or document etc.); fill or complete with writing; put (data) into computer store; engage in writing or authorship; produce writing; convey (message etc.) by letter. **write down** set down in writing, write in disparagement or depreciation of, reduce to lower amount; **write off** cancel (debt etc.), reckon as lost; **write-off** vehicle etc. so damaged as not to be worth repair; **write up** write full account of, praise in writing; **write-up** laudatory description in newspaper etc.

**writer** /ˈraɪtə(r)/ n. person who writes, esp. author. **writer's cramp** muscular spasm due to excessive writing.

**writhe** /raɪð/ v. twist or roll oneself about (as) in acute pain; suffer mental torture.

**writing** /ˈraɪtɪŋ/ n. handwriting; written document; in *pl.* writer's works. **in writing** in written form.

**written** *p.p.* of **write**.

**WRNS** *abbr.* Women's Royal Naval Service.

**wrong** 1 a. mistaken; not true; in error; unsuitable, less or least desirable; contrary to law or morality; amiss, out of order. 2 adv. in wrong direction or manner, with incorrect result. 3 n. what is morally wrong; wrong or unjust action. 4 v.t. treat unjustly; mistakenly attribute bad motives to. 5 **go wrong** take wrong path, get out of working order, cease virtuous behaviour; **in the wrong** responsible for quarrel or mistake or offence; **wrongdoer** person guilty of breach of law or morality; **wrong-doing** n.; **wrong-headed** perverse and obstinate; **wrong side** worse or undesirable or unusable side; **wrong way round,** in opposite of normal orientation.

**wrongful** /ˈrɒŋfəl/ a. unwarranted, unjustified.

**wrote** *past* of **write**.

**wroth** /rəʊθ/ a. *arch.* angry.

**wrought** /rɔːt/ *arch. past* & *p.p.* of **work**. **wrought iron** tough malleable form of iron suitable for forging or rolling, not cast.

**wrung** *past* & *p.p.* of **wring**.

**WRVS** *abbr.* Women's Royal Voluntary Service.

**wry** /raɪ/ a. distorted, turned to one side; contorted in disgust or disappointment or mockery; (of humour) dry and mocking. **wryneck** small bird able to turn head over shoulder.

**wt.** *abbr.* weight.

**wurley** /ˈwɜːlɪ/ n. *Aus.* (also **wurlie**) Abor. hut or shelter.

**wych-** /wɪtʃ/ *pref.* in names of trees etc. with pliant branches. **wych-hazel** N. Amer. shrub, astringent extract of its bark.

# X

**X, x,** *n.* Roman numeral 10; first unknown quantity in algebra; cross-shaped symbol esp. used to indicate position or incorrectness, or to symbolize kiss or vote, or as signature of person who cannot write.

**xenophobia** /zenə'fəʊbɪə/ *n.* morbid dislike of foreigners.

**Xerox** /'zɪərɒks/ 1 *n.* (**P**) a dry copying process; copy so made. 2 *v.t.* **xerox** reproduce by this process.

**Xmas** *abbr.* Christmas.

**X-ray** /'eksreɪ/ 1 *n.* in *pl.* electromagnetic radiation of short wavelength, able to pass through opaque bodies; in *sing.* photograph made by X-rays. 2 *v.t.* photograph or examine or treat with X-rays.

**xylophone** /'zaɪləfəʊn/ *n.* musical instrument of graduated wooden bars struck with hammer(s).

# Y

**Y, y,** *n.* second unknown quantity in algebra; Y-shaped thing.

**yabber** /'jæbə(r)/ *v.i.* & *n. Aus. sl.* talk.

**yabbie** /'jæbɪ/ *Aus.* (also **yabby**) 1 *n.* small freshwater crayfish; salt-water prawn used as bait. 2 *v.i.* go out to catch yabbies.

**yacht** /jɒt/ 1 *n.* light sailing-vessel; larger usu. power-driven vessel used for private pleasure excursions and cruising etc. 2 *v.i.* race or cruise in yacht. 3 **yacht-club** club for yacht-racing; **yachtsman** person who yachts.

**yacker** var. of **yakka.**

**yah** *int.* of derision, defiance, etc.

**yahoo** /jə'huː/ *n.* bestial person.

**yak** *n.* long-haired Tibetan ox.

**yakka** /'jækə/ *n. Aus. colloq.* (also **yakker**) work.

**yam** *n.* tropical or subtropical climbing plant; edible starchy tuberous root of this; sweet potato. **yam-stick** *Aus.* long sharpened stick used by Aboriginals for digging yams.

**yandy** /'jændɪ/ *Aus.* 1 *n.* long shallow dish used by Aboriginals for separating grass-seed from husks; similar iron dish for separating minerals from rubbish. 2 *v.t.* winnow; separate minerals from rubbish.

**yank**[1] *n.* & *v.* pull with a jerk.

**Yank**[2] *n. colloq.* (also **Yankee**) inhabitant of US, American; *US* inhabitant of New England or of northern States of USA.

**yap** 1 *v.i.* bark shrilly or fussily; *colloq.* talk noisily or foolishly. 2 *n.* sound of yapping.

**yapp** *n.* limp-leather book-binding with overlapping edges or flaps.

**yard**[1] *n.* linear measure of 3 ft. (0.9144 m.); this length of material; square or cubic yard; spar slung across mast for sail to hang from. **yard-arm** either end of ship's yard; **yardstick** rod a yard long usu. divided into inches etc., standard of comparison.

**yard**[2] *n.* piece of enclosed ground, esp. surrounded by or attached to building(s) or used for particular purpose; garden of house.

**yardage** /'jɑːdɪdʒ/ *n.* number of yards of material etc.

**yarmulka** /'jɑːmʊlkə/ *n.* skull-cap worn by Jewish man.

**yarn** 1 *n.* fibre spun and prepared for weaving or knitting etc.; *colloq.* story, tale. 2 *v.i. colloq.* tell yarns.

**yarraman** /'jærəmən/ *n. Aus.* Abor. term for horse.

**yarran** /ˈjærən/ n. Aus. any of several acacias.

**yarrow** /ˈjærəʊ/ n. kind of perennial herb, esp. milfoil.

**yashmak** /ˈjæʃmæk/ n. veil concealing face except eyes, worn by some Muslim women.

**yate** n. a south-western Aus. eucalypt yielding tough timber; this timber.

**yaw** 1 v.i. (of ship, aircraft, spacecraft) fail to hold straight course, go unsteadily. 2 n. yawing of ship etc. from course.

**yawl** n. kind of ship's boat or sailing- or fishing-boat.

**yawn** 1 v.i. open the mouth wide and inhale esp. in sleepiness or boredom; (of chasm etc.) gape, be wide open. 2 n. act of yawning.

**yaws** n.pl. (usu. treated as sing.) contagious tropical skin-disease.

**yd(s).** abbr. yard(s).

**ye** pron. arch. pl. of thou.

**yea** /jeɪ/ adv. & n. arch. yes.

**yeah** /jeə/ adv. colloq. yes.

**year** n. time occupied by one revolution of earth round sun (about 365¼ days); period from 1 Jan. to 31 Dec. inclusive, any period of 12 calendar months; in pl. age, old age; (usu. in pl.) period, times, a very long time. **year-book** annual publication bringing information on subject up to date.

**yearling** /ˈjɪəlɪŋ/ n. animal between 1 and 2 years old.

**yearly** /ˈjɪəlɪ/ 1 a. done or produced or occurring once every year; of or for or lasting a year. 2 adv. once every year.

**yearn** /jɜːn/ v.i. be filled with longing or compassion or tenderness.

**yeast** n. greyish-yellow fungous substance, got esp. from fermenting malt liquors and used as fermenting agent and in raising bread etc.

**yeasty** /ˈjiːstɪ/ a. frothy; in a ferment; working like yeast.

**yell** 1 n. sharp loud outcry of strong and sudden emotion; shout of pain or anger or laughter etc.; Aus. colloq. call. 2 v. make or utter with yell.

**yellow** /ˈjeləʊ/ 1 a. of the colour of gold or lemons or buttercups etc.; having yellow skin or complexion; colloq. cowardly. 2 n. yellow colour or paint or clothes etc. 3 v. turn yellow. 4 **yellow-belly** any of various Aus. fish with yellow underparts, golden perch; **yellow fever** tropical fever with jaundice etc.; **yellow-jacket** Aus. eucalypt with yellowish bark; **yellow pages** section of telephone directory on yellow paper and listing business subscribers according to goods or services they offer; **yellow streak** trace of cowardice; **yellow-tail** Aus. any of several yellowish-green fish, kingfish.

**yelp** 1 n. sharp shrill bark or cry (as) of dog in excitement or pain etc. 2 v.i. utter yelp.

**yen¹** n. (pl. same) Japanese monetary unit.

**yen²** 1 n. intense desire or longing. 2 v.i. feel longing.

**yeoman** /ˈjəʊmən/ n. (pl. -men) man owning and farming small estate; member of yeomanry force. **yeoman service** efficient or useful help in need.

**yeomanry** /ˈjəʊmənrɪ/ n. body of yeomen; hist. volunteer cavalry force in British army.

**yes** /jes/ adv. expr. affirmative reply to question or command etc. 2 n. the word yes. **yes-man** colloq. person who endorses or supports all opinions or proposals of a superior.

**yesterday** /ˈjestədeɪ or -dɪ/ 1 adv. on the day before today. 2 n. the day before today.

**yet** 1 adv. up to this or that time; (with neg. or interrog.) as soon as or by now or then; again, in addition; in the time that remains before the matter ends; (with compar.) even; nevertheless, and or but in spite of that. 2 conj. but nevertheless. 3 **as yet** hitherto; **not yet** still not, not by this or that time.

**yeti** /ˈjetɪ/ n. unidentified anthropoid or ursine animal in Himalayas.

**yew** n. dark-leaved evergreen coniferous tree; its wood.

**Yiddish** /ˈjɪdɪʃ/ 1 n. language used by Jews in or from Europe. 2 a. of this language.

**yield** /jiːld/ 1 v. produce or return as fruit or profit or result; surrender or make submission (to); concede; give way to persuasion or entreaty etc., give consent; give right of way (to). 2 n. amount yielded or produced.

**yippee** /ˈjɪpiː/ int. expr. delight or excitement.

**YMCA** abbr. Young Men's Christian Association.

**yob** *n.* (also **yobbo**, *pl.* **-os**) *sl.* lout, hooligan.

**yodel** /'jəʊd(ə)l/ 1 *v.* sing with melodious inarticulate sounds and frequent changes between falsetto and normal voice, in manner of Swiss mountain-dwellers. 2 *n.* yodelling cry.

**yoga** /'jəʊgə/ *n.* Hindu system of meditation and asceticism etc.; system of physical exercises and breathing control used in yoga.

**yoghurt** /'jɒgət/ *n.* semi-solid sourish food made from milk fermented by added bacteria.

**yogi** /'jəʊgiː/ *n.* devotee of yoga.

**yoicks** *int.* used in foxhunting to urge on hounds.

**yoke** 1 *n.* wooden cross-piece fastened over necks of two oxen etc. and attached to plough or wagon to be drawn; pair *of* oxen etc.; object like yoke in form or function, e.g. wooden shoulder-piece for carrying pair of pails; top part of dress or skirt etc., from which the rest hangs; sway or dominion or servitude; bond of union esp. of marriage. 2 *v.* put yoke on; couple or unite (pair); link (one *to* another); match or work together.

**yokel** /'jəʊk(ə)l/ *n.* country bumpkin.

**yolk** /jəʊk/ *n.* yellow internal part of egg.

**yon** *arch.* 1 *a.* & *adv.* yonder. 2 *pron.* yonder person or thing.

**yonder** /'jɒndə(r)/ 1 *adv.* over there; at some distance (but within sight). 2 *a.* situated yonder.

**yore** *n. literary* **of yore** in or of time long past.

**york** *v.t. Crick.* bowl out with yorker.

**yorker** /'jɔːkə(r)/ *n. Crick.* ball that pitches immediately under the bat.

**Yorkshire** /'jɔːkʃə(r)/ *n.* **Yorkshire pudding** light baked batter pudding usu. eaten with or before roast meat; **Yorkshire terrier** small long-haired terrier.

**you** *pron.* (*obj.* same, *poss.* **your**) 2nd pers. sing. and pl. pronoun; the person(s) or thing(s) addressed; (in general statements) one, a person.

**young** /jʌŋ/ 1 *a.* not far advanced in life or development or existence; not yet old; immature, inexperienced; characteristic of youth. 2 *n. collect.* offspring esp. of animals before or soon after birth.

**youngster** /'jʌŋstə(r)/ *n.* child, young person.

**your** /jɔː(r)/ *pron. poss.* case of **you**, with abs. form **yours**.

**yourself** /jɔː'self/ *pron.* (*pl.* **-selves**) *emphat.* & *refl.* form of **you**.

**youth** /juːθ/ *n.* (*pl. pr.* /juːðz/) being young; early part of life, esp. adolescence; the young; young man; quality or condition characteristic of the young. **youth club** place for young people's leisure activities; **youth hostel** place where (esp. young) holidaymakers etc. can put up cheaply for the night.

**youthful** /'juːθfəl/ *a.* young or having characteristics of youth.

**yowl** /jaʊl/ 1 *n.* loud wailing cry (as) of cat or dog in distress. 2 *v.i.* utter yowl.

**Yo-yo** /'jəʊjəʊ/ *n.* (P) (*pl.* **-yos**) toy consisting of pair of discs with deep groove between them in which string is attached and wound, and which can be made to fall and rise.

**yr.** *abbr.* year(s); younger; your.

**yrs.** *abbr.* years; yours.

**yucca** /'jʌkə/ *n.* white-flowered garden plant.

**Yugoslav** /'juːgəslɑːv/ 1 *a.* of Yugoslavia. 2 *n.* native or inhabitant of Yugoslavia.

**yule** *n.* festival of Christmas. **yule-log** large log burnt at Christmas; **yule-tide** period of yule.

**yummy** /'jʌmi/ *a. colloq.* tasty, delicious.

**YWCA** *abbr.* Young Women's Christian Association.

# Z

**zabaglione** /zɑ:bɑ:li:'əʊni:/ *n.* Italian sweet of whipped and heated egg yolks and sugar and wine.

**zack** *n. Aus. hist.* sixpence.

**zambuk** /'zæmbʌk/ *n. Aus. hist.* first-aid man at public gathering.

**zany** /'zeɪnɪ/ 1 *a.* comically idiotic; crazily ridiculous. 2 *n.* buffoon, simpleton.

**zap** *v.t. sl.* hit, attack, kill.

**zeal** *n.* ardour or eagerness in pursuit of end or in favour of person or cause.

**zealous** /'zeləs/ *a.*

**zealot** /'zelət/ *n.* extreme partisan, fanatic.

**zebra** /'zebrə or 'zi:-/ *n.* African striped horselike animal. **zebra crossing** striped street-crossing where pedestrians have precedence.

**zebu** /'zi:bu:/ *n.* humped ox domesticated in India etc.

**Zen** *n.* form of Buddhism emphasizing value of meditation and intuition.

**zenana** /zə'nɑ:nə/ *n.* part of house for seclusion of women of high-caste families in India and Iran.

**zenith** /'zenəθ/ *n.* point of heavens directly overhead; highest point or state, culmination.

**zephyr** /'zefə(r)/ *n.* soft mild gentle wind or breeze.

**zero** /'zɪərəʊ/ 1 *n.* (pl. **-os**) figure 0, nought, nil; point marked 0 on graduated scale, esp. in thermometer etc.; lowest point, bottom of scale; (in full **zero-hour**) hour at which planned (esp. military) operation is timed to begin, crucial or decisive moment. 2 *v.i.* **zero in on** take aim at, focus attention on.

**zest** *n.* piquancy; keen interest or enjoyment, relish, gusto; orange or lemon peel.

**ziff** *n. Aus. colloq.* beard.

**zigzag** /'zɪgzæg/ 1 *n.* succession of straight lines with abrupt alternate right and left turns. 2 *a.* with abrupt alternate right and left turns. 3 *adv.* in zigzag manner or course. 4 *v.i.* move in zigzag course.

**zillion** /'zɪljən/ *n. colloq.* indefinite large number.

**zinc** *n.* hard bluish-white metallic element.

**zing** *colloq.* 1 *n.* vigour, energy. 2 *v.i.* move swiftly or shrilly.

**zinnia** /'zɪnɪə/ *n.* garden plant with showy flowers.

**zip** 1 *n. colloq.* light sharp sound; energy, force, impetus; zip-fastener. 2 *v.* close or fasten (*up*) with zip-fastener; move or go with sound of zip or with great rapidity or force. 3 **zip-fastener** fastening device of two flexible strips with interlocking projections closed and opened by sliding clip pulled along them.

**zipper** /'zɪpə(r)/ *n.* zip-fastener.

**zircon** /'zɜ:kən/ *n.* translucent crystalline native silicate of zirconium used as gem.

**zirconium** /zɜ:'kəʊnɪəm/ *n.* grey metallic element.

**zither** /'zɪðə(r)/ *n.* musical instrument with flat sound-box and many strings, held horizontally and played by plucking.

**zodiac** /'zəʊdɪæk/ *n.* belt of the heavens including all apparent positions of sun and planets as known to ancient astronomers, and divided into 12 equal parts called **signs of the zodiac**. **zodiacal** /zəʊ'daɪək(ə)l/ *a.*

**zombie** /'zɒmbɪ/ *n.* corpse said to be revived by witchcraft; *colloq.* dull or apathetic person.

**zone** 1 *n.* area having particular features or properties or purpose or use; any well-defined region of more or less beltlike form; area between two concentric circles; encircling band of colour etc.; *arch.* girdle or belt. 2 *v.t.* encircle as or with zone; arrange or distribute by zones; assign to specific area. 3 **zonal** *a.*

**zoo** *n.* zoological garden.

**zoological** /zəʊə'lɒdʒɪk(ə)l or zu:-/ *a.* of zoology. **zoological garden(s)** public garden or park with collection of animals for exhibition and study.

**zoology** /zəʊ'ɒlədʒɪ or zu:-/ *n.* scientific study of animals. **zoologist** *n.*

**zoom** /zu:m/ 1 *v.i.* move quickly, esp. with buzzing sound; cause aeroplane to mount at high speed and steep angle; (of camera) change (esp. quickly) from long shot to close-up. 2 *n.* aeroplane's steep climb. **3 zoom lens** lens allowing camera to zoom by varying focus.

**zoophyte** /'zəʊəfaɪt/ n. animal resembling plant or flower in form.

**zucchini** /zuːˈkiːniː/ n. (pl. same or **-nis**) courgette.

**zygote** /'zaɪgəʊt/ n. cell formed by union of two gametes.

# APPENDIX I
# Countries of the world and related adjectives

**Afghanistan** /æfˈgænəstɑːn/, Afghan /ˈæfgæn/
**Albania** /ælˈbeɪniːə/, Albanian
**Algeria** /ælˈdʒɪəriːə/, Algerian
**American**: see United States of America
**Andorra** /ænˈdɔːrə/, Andorran
**Angola** /æŋˈgəʊlə/, Angolan
**Antigua and Barbuda** /ænˈtiːgə, bɑːˈbuːdə/, Antiguan /ænˈtiːgən/, Barbudan
**Argentina** /ɑːdʒənˈtiːnə/, Argentine /ˈɑːdʒəntaɪn/ or Argentinian /ɑːdʒənˈtɪniːən/
**Australia** /ɔːˈstreɪljə/, Australian
**Austria** /ˈɔːstriːə/, Austrian
**Bahamas, the** /bəˈhɑːməz/, Bahamian /bəˈheɪmiːən/
**Bahrein** /bɑːˈreɪn/, Bahreini
**Bangladesh** /bæŋgləˈdeʃ/, Bangladeshi
**Barbados** /bɑːˈbeɪdəs/, Barbadian
**Belgium** /ˈbeldʒ(ə)m/, Belgian
**Belize** /beˈliːz/, Belizean
**Benin** /beˈniːn/, Beninese /benɪˈniːz/
**Bhutan** /buːˈtɑːn/, Bhutanese /buːtəˈniːz/
**Bolivia** /bəˈlɪviːə/, Bolivian
**Botswana** /bɒtˈswɑːnə/
**Brazil** /brəˈzɪl/, Brazilian
**British**: see United Kingdom
**Brunei** /ˈbruːnaɪ/, Bruneian /bruːˈnaɪən/
**Bulgaria** /bʌlˈgeəriːə/, Bulgarian
**Burkina** /bɜːˈkiːnə/, Burkinan
**Burma** /ˈbɜːmə/, Burmese /bɜːˈmiːz/
**Burundi** /bʊˈrʌndiː/, Burundian
**Cambodia** /kæmˈbəʊdiːə/, Cambodian
**Cameroon** /kæməˈruːn/, Cameroonian
**Canada** /ˈkænədə/, Canadian /kəˈneɪdiːən/
**Cape Verde** /keɪp vɜːd/, Cape Verdean
**Central African Republic**

**Chad** /tʃæd/, Chadian /tʃædi:ən/
**Chile** /ˈtʃɪli:/, Chilean
**China** /ˈtʃaɪnə/, Chinese /tʃaɪˈni:z/
**Colombia** /kəˈlʌmbi:ə/, Colombian
**Comoros** /kəˈmɔ:rəʊz/, Comoran
**Congo** /ˈkɒŋgəʊ/, Congolese /kɒŋgəˈli:z/
**Costa Rica** /ˈkɒstə ˈri:kə/, Costa Rican
**Cuba** /ˈkju:bə/, Cuban
**Cyprus** /ˈsaɪprəs/, Cypriot /ˈsɪpri:ət/
**Czechoslovakia** /tʃekəʊsləˈvæki:ə/, Czech /tʃek/ or Czechoslovak /tʃekəˈsləʊvæk/ or Czechoslovakian
**Denmark** /ˈdenmɑ:k/, Danish /ˈdeɪnɪʃ/
**Djibouti** /dʒəˈbu:ti:/
**Dominica** /dɒməˈni:kə/, Dominican /dɒməˈni:kən/
**Dominican Republic** /dəˈmɪnəkən/, Dominican /dəˈmɪnəkən/
**Dutch**: see Netherlands, the
**Ecuador** /ˈekwədɔ:(r)/, Ecuadorean /ekwəˈdɔ:ri:ən/
**Egypt** /ˈi:dʒəpt/, Egyptian /ɪˈdʒɪpʃ(ə)n/
**El Salvador** /el ˈsælvədɔ:(r)/, Salvadorean /sælvəˈdɔ:ri:ən/
**England** /ˈɪŋglənd/, English /ˈɪŋglɪʃ/
**Equatorial Guinea** /ˈgmi:/
**Ethiopia** /i:θɪˈəʊpi:ə/, Ethiopian
**Fiji** /ˈfi:dʒi:/, Fijian
**Filipino**: see Philippines, the
**Finland** /ˈfɪnlənd/, Finnish /ˈfɪnɪʃ/
**France** /frɑ:ns or fræns/, French /frentʃ/
**Gabon** /gæˈbɒn/, Gabonese /gæbəˈni:z/
**Gambia** /ˈgæmbi:ə/, Gambian
**German Democratic Republic** /ˈdʒɜ:mən/, East German
**Germany, Federal Republic of** /ˈdʒɜ:məni:/, West German
**Ghana** /ˈgɑ:nə/, Ghanaian /gɑ:ˈneɪən/
**Greece** /gri:s/, Greek
**Grenada** /grəˈneɪdə/, Grenadian
**Guatemala** /gwætəˈmɑ:lə/, Guatemalan
**Guinea** /ˈgmi:/, Guinean /ˈgmi:ən/
**Guinea-Bissau** /gmi:ˈbɪsaʊ/
**Guyana** /gaɪˈɑ:nə/, Guyanese /gaɪəˈni:z/
**Haiti** /ˈhaɪti:/, Haitian /ˈhaɪʃ(ə)n/
**Honduras** /hɒnˈdjʊərəs/, Honduran
**Hungary** /ˈhʌŋgəri:/, Hungarian /hʌŋˈgeəri:ən/

**Iceland** /ˈaɪslənd/, Icelandic /aɪsˈlændɪk/
**India** /ˈɪndiːə/, Indian
**Indonesia** /ɪndəˈniːʒə/, Indonesian
**Iran** /ɪˈrɑːn/, Iranian /ɪˈreɪmiːən/
**Iraq** /ɪˈrɑːk/, Iraqi /ɪˈrɑːkiː/
**Irish Republic** /ˈaɪərɪʃ/, Irish
**Israel** /ˈɪzreɪl/, Israeli /ɪzˈreɪliː/
**Italy** /ˈɪtəliː/, Italian /ɪˈtæljən/
**Ivory Coast** /ˈaɪvəriː kəʊst/
**Jamaica** /dʒəˈmeɪkə/, Jamaican
**Japan** /dʒəˈpæn/, Japanese /dʒæpəˈniːz/
**Jordan** /ˈdʒɔːd(ə)n/, Jordanian /dʒɔːˈdeɪniːən/
**Kenya** /ˈkenjə/, Kenyan
**Kiribati** /ˈkɪrəbæs/, i-Kiribati
**Korea** /kəˈriːə/, Korean
**Kuwait** /kʊˈweɪt/, Kuweiti
**Laos** /ˈlɑːɒs/, Laotian /lɑːˈəʊʃ(ə)n/
**Lebanon** /ˈlebənən/, Lebanese /lebəˈniːz/
**Lesotho** /ləˈsəʊtəʊ/
**Liberia** /laɪˈbɪəriːə/, Liberian
**Libya** /ˈlɪbjə/, Libyan
**Liechtenstein** /ˈlɪktənstaɪn/
**Luxembourg** /ˈlʌksəmbɜːg/
**Madagascar** /mædəˈgæskə(r)/, Malagasy /mæləˈgæsiː/
**Malawi** /məˈlɑːwiː/, Malawian
**Malaysia** /məˈleɪziːə/, Malaysian
**Maldives, the** /ˈmɔːldɪvz/, Maldivian
**Mali** /ˈmɑːliː/, Malian
**Malta** /ˈmɔːltə/, Maltese /mɔːlˈtiːz/
**Mauritania** /mɒrəˈteɪniːə/, Mauritanian
**Mauritius** /məˈrɪʃəs/, Mauritian
**Mexico** /ˈmeksəkəʊ/, Mexican
**Monaco** /ˈmɒnəkəʊ/, Monegasque /mɒnɪˈgæsk/
**Mongolia** /mɒŋˈgəʊliːə/, Mongolian
**Morocco** /məˈrɒkəʊ/, Moroccan
**Mozambique** /məʊzæmˈbiːk/, Mozambican /məʊzəmˈbiːkən/
**Nauru** /nɑːˈʊruː/, Nauruan
**Nepal** /nəˈpɔːl/, Nepalese /nepəˈliːz/
**Netherlands, the** /ˈneðələndz/, Dutch
**New Zealand** /ˈziːlənd/

**Nicaragua** /nɪkə'rægju:ə/, Nicaraguan
**Niger** /ni:'ʒeə(r)/
**Nigeria** /naɪ'dʒɪəri:ə/, Nigerian
**Northern Ireland** /'aɪələnd/, Northern Irish
**Norway** /'nɔ:weɪ/, Norwegian /nɔ:'wi:dʒ(ə)n/
**Oman** /əʊ'mɑ:n/, Omani
**Pakistan** /pɑ:kə'stɑ:n/, Pakistani
**Panama** /'pænəmɑ:/, Panamanian /pænə'meɪni:ən/
**Papua New Guinea** /'pæpu:ə nju:'gɪni:/
**Paraguay** /'pærə'gwaɪ/, Paraguayan
**Peru** /pə'ru:/, Peruvian /pə'ru:vi:ən/
**Philippines, the** /'fɪləpi:nz/, Filipino /fɪlə'pi:nəʊ/ or Philippine
**Poland** /'pəʊlənd/, Polish /'pəʊlɪʃ/
**Portugal** /'pɔ:tjəgəl/, Portuguese /pɔ:tjə'gi:z/
**Qatar** /'kætɑ:(r)/, Qatari
**Romania** /ru:'meɪni:ə/, Romanian
**Russia**: see Union of Soviet Socialist Republics
**Rwanda** /ru:'ændə/, Rwandan
**Saint Kitts-Nevis** /kɪts'ni:vəs/, Kittitian /kə'tɪʃ(ə)n/, Nevisian /nə'vɪʃ(ə)n/
**Saint Lucia** /'lu:ʃə/, Saint Lucian
**Saint Vincent** /'vɪns(ə)nt/, Vincentian /vɪn'senʃ(ə)n/
**Salvadorean**: see El Salvador
**San Marino** /sæn mə'ri:nəʊ/
**São Tomé and Principe** /saʊ 'tʊmeɪ, 'prɪnsəpi:/
**Saudi Arabia** /saʊdi: ə'reɪbi:ə/, Saudi Arabian
**Scotland** /'skɒtlənd/, Scotch, Scots, or Scottish
**Senegal** /senə'gɔ:l/, Senegalese /senəgə'li:z/
**Seychelles** /seɪ'ʃelz/
**Sierra Leone** /si:erə li:'əʊn/, Sierra Leonean /li:'əʊni:ən/
**Singapore** /sɪŋgə'pɔ:(r)/, Singaporean /sɪŋgə'pɔ:ri:ən/
**Solomon Islands** /'sɒləmən/
**Somalia** /sə'mɑ:li:ə/, Somalian
**South Africa** /'æfrɪkə/, South African
**Soviet**: see Union of Soviet Socialist Republics
**Spain** /speɪn/, Spanish /'spænɪʃ/
**Sri Lanka** /ʃrɪ 'læŋkə/, Sri Lankan
**Sudan** /su:'dɑ:n/, Sudanese /su:də'ni:z/
**Surinam** /sʊərə'næm/, Surinamese /sʊərənæ'mi:z/
**Swaziland** /'swɑ:zi:lænd/, Swazi

**Sweden** /ˈswiːdən/, Swedish /ˈswiːdɪʃ/
**Switzerland** /ˈswɪtsələnd/, Swiss
**Syria** /ˈsɪriːə/, Syrian
**Tanzania** /tænzəˈniːə/, Tanzanian
**Thailand** /ˈtaɪlənd/, Thai
**Togo** /ˈtəʊgəʊ/, Togolese /təʊgəʊˈliːz/
**Tonga** /ˈtɒŋgə/, Tongan
**Trinidad and Tobago** /ˈtrɪnədæd, təˈbeɪgəʊ/, Trinidadian /trɪnəˈdeɪdiːən/, Tobagan /təˈbeɪgən/
**Tunisia** /tjuːˈnɪziːə/, Tunisian
**Turkey** /ˈtɜːkiː/, Turkish /ˈtɜːkɪʃ/
**Tuvalu** /tuːˈvɑːluː/, Tuvaluan
**Uganda** /juːˈgændə/, Ugandan
**Union of Soviet Socialist Republics,** Russian /ˈrʌʃ(ə)n/ or Soviet /ˈsəʊviːət/
**United Arab Emirates**
**United Kingdom**
**United States of America** /əˈmerɪkə/, American
**Uruguay** /ˈjʊərəgwaɪ/, Uruguayan
**Vanuatu** /vænwɑːˈtuː/, ni-Vanuatu
**Vatican City** /ˈvætɪkən/
**Venezuela** /venəzˈweɪlə/, Venezuelan
**Vietnam** /vjetˈnɑːm/, Vietnamese /vjetnəˈmiːz/
**Wales** /weɪlz/, Welsh /welʃ/
**Western Samoa** /səˈməʊə/, Western Samoan
**Yemen** /ˈjemən/, Yemeni
**Yugoslavia** /juːgəʊˈslɑːviːə/, Yugoslav /ˈjuːgəʊslɑːv/ or Yugoslavian
**Zaire** /zɑːˈɪə(r)/, Zairean
**Zambia** /ˈzæmbiːə/, Zambian
**Zimbabwe** /zɪmˈbɑːbwiː/, Zimbabwean

# APPENDIX II

# The metric system of weights and measures

*Linear Measure*
| | |
|---|---|
| 1 millimetre | = 0.039 inch |
| 1 centimetre = 10 mm | = 0.394 inch |
| 1 decimetre = 10 cm | = 3.94 inches |
| 1 metre = 10 dm | = 1.094 yards |
| 1 decametre = 10 m | = 10.94 yards |
| 1 hectometre = 100 m | = 109.4 yards |
| 1 kilometre = 1,000 m | = 0.6214 mile |

*Square Measure*
| | |
|---|---|
| 1 square centimetre | = 0.155 sq. inch |
| 1 square metre | = 1.196 sq. yards |
| 1 are /ɑː(r)/ = 100 sq. metres | = 119.6 sq. yards |
| 1 hectare /ˈhekteə(r)/ = 100 ares | = 2.471 acres |
| 1 square kilometre | = 0.386 sq. mile |

*Cubic Measure*
| | |
|---|---|
| 1 cubic centimetre | = 0.061 cu. inch |
| 1 cubic metre | = 1.308 cu. yards |

*Capacity Measure*
| | |
|---|---|
| 1 millilitre | = 0.002 pint (British) |
| 1 centilitre = 10 ml | = 0.018 pint |
| 1 decilitre = 10 cl | = 0.176 pint |
| 1 litre = 10 dl | = 1.76 pints |
| 1 decalitre = 10 litres | = 2.20 gallons |

*Note* 1 litre is exactly equivalent to 1,000 cubic centimetres

*Weight*
| | |
|---|---|
| 1 milligram | = 0.015 grain |
| 1 centigram = 10 mg | = 0.154 grain |
| 1 decigram = 10 cg | = 1.543 grains |
| 1 gram = 10 dg | = 15.43 grains |

## APPENDIX II

1 decagram = 10 g = 5.64 drams
1 hectogram = 100 g = 3.527 ounces
1 kilogram = 1,000 g = 2.205 pounds
1 tonne (metric ton) = 1,000 kg = 0.984 (long) ton